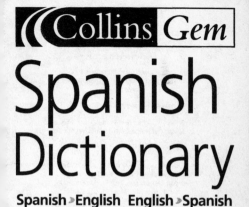

Collins Gem

Spanish Dictionary

Spanish › English   English › Spanish

grijalbo

Collins Gem

An Imprint of HarperCollinsPublishers

first published in this edition 1982
fifth edition 2001

© William Collins Sons & Co. Ltd. 1982, 1989
© HarperCollins Publishers 1993, 1998, 2001

latest reprint 2003

HarperCollins Publishers
Westerhill Road, Bishopbriggs, Glasgow G64 2QT
Great Britain

www.collinsdictionaries.com

Collins Gem® and Bank of English® are registered
trademarks of HarperCollins Publishers Limited

ISBN 0-00-472414-3

based on previous editions by/basada en las ediciones anteriores de
Mike Gonzalez, Alicia de Benito de Harland,
Soledad Pérez-López, José Ramón Parrondo,
Bob Grossmith, Teresa Álvarez García

contributors/colaboradores
Joyce Littlejohn, Claire Evans, Sharon Hunter,
Val McNulty, Jeremy Butterfield

Grupo Editorial Random House Mondadori, S.L.
Travessera de Gràcia 47-49, 08021 Barcelona

www.diccionarioscollins.com

ISBN 84-253-3513-2

A catalogue record for this book is available from the British Library

Typeset by Morton Word Processing Ltd, Scarborough

Printed by Legoprint S.P.A.

ÍNDICE

CONTENTS

INTRODUCCIÓN

Estamos muy satisfechos de que hayas decidido comprar (
Diccionario de Inglés Collins Gem y esperamos que lo disfrutes
que te sirva de gran ayuda ya sea en el colegio, en el trabajo, en tu
vacaciones o en casa.

Esta introducción pretende darte algunas indicaciones par
ayudarte a sacar el mayor provecho de este diccionario; no sólo d
su extenso vocabulario, sino de toda la información que
proporciona cada entrada. Esta te ayudará a leer y comprender —
también a comunicarte y a expresarte — en inglés moderno.

El Diccionario de Inglés Collins Gem comienza con una lista d
abreviaturas utilizadas en el texto y con una ilustración de la
sonidos representados por los símbolos fonéticos. Al final d
diccionario encontrarás una tabla de los verbos irregulares de
inglés, y para terminar, una sección sobre el uso de los números
de las expresiones de tiempo.

EL MANEJO DE TU DICCIONARIO COLLINS GEM

La amplia información que te ofrece este diccionario aparec
presentada en distintas tipografías, con caracteres de divers
tamaños y con distintos símbolos, abreviaturas y paréntesis. L
apartados siguientes explican las reglas y símbolos utilizados.

Entradas

Las palabras que consultas en el diccionario — las "entradas" -
aparecen ordenadas alfabéticamente y en **caracteres gruesos** par
una identificación más rápida. Las dos palabras que ocupan
margen superior de cada página indican la primera y la últim
entrada de la página en cuestión.

La información sobre el uso o la forma de determinadas entrad
aparece entre paréntesis, detrás de la transcripción fonética,
generalmente en forma abreviada y en cursiva (p.ej.: (fam), (COM)

En algunos casos se ha considerado oportuno agrupar palabras (

una misma familia (**nación, nacionalismo; accept, acceptance**) bajo una misma entrada, en caracteres gruesos de tamaño algo más pequeño que los de la entrada principal.

Las expresiones de uso corriente en las que aparece una entrada se dan en negrita (p.ej.: **to be in a hurry**).

Símbolos fonéticos

La transcripción fonética de cada entrada (que indica su pronunciación) aparece entre corchetes, inmediatamente después de la entrada (p.ej.: **knead** [ni:d]). En la página x encontrarás una lista de los símbolos fonéticos utilizados en este diccionario.

Traducciones

Las traducciones de las entradas aparecen en caracteres normales, y en los casos en los que existen significados o usos diferentes, éstos aparecen separados mediante un punto y coma. A menudo encontrarás también otras palabras en cursiva y entre paréntesis antes de las traducciones. Estas sugieren contextos en los que la entrada podría aparecer (p.ej.: **rough** (*voice*) o (*weather*)) o proporcionan sinónimos (p.ej.: **rough** (*violent*)).

Palabras clave

Particular relevancia reciben ciertas palabras inglesas y españolas que han sido consideradas palabras ''clave'' en cada lengua. Estas pueden, por ejemplo, ser de utilización muy corriente o tener distintos usos (**de, haber; get, that**). La combinación de rombos ♦ y números te permitirá distinguir las diferentes categorías gramaticales y los diferentes significados. Las indicaciones en cursiva y entre paréntesis proporcionan además importante información adicional.

Información gramatical

Las categorías gramaticales aparecen en forma abreviada y en cursiva después de la transcripción fonética de cada entrada (*vt, adv, conj*).

También se indican la forma femenina y los plurales irregulares de los sustantivos del inglés (**child, ~ren**).

v

INTRODUCTION

We are delighted you have decided to buy the Collins Gem Spanish Dictionary and hope you will enjoy and benefit from using it at school, at home, on holiday or at work.

This introduction gives you a few tips on how to get the most out of your dictionary — not simply from its comprehensive wordlist but also from the information provided in each entry. This will help you to read and understand modern Spanish, as well as communicate and express yourself in the language.

The Collins Gem Spanish Dictionary begins by listing the abbreviations used in the text and illustrating the sounds shown by the phonetic symbols. You will find Spanish verb tables at the back, followed by a final section on numbers and time expressions.

USING YOUR COLLINS GEM DICTIONARY

A wealth of information is presented in the dictionary, using various typefaces, sizes of type, symbols, abbreviations and brackets. The conventions and symbols used are explained in the following sections.

Headwords

The words you look up in a dictionary — "headwords" — are listed alphabetically. They are printed in **bold type** for rapid identification. The two headwords appearing at the top of each page indicate the first and last word dealt with on the page in question.

Information about the usage or form of certain headwords is given in brackets after the phonetic spelling. This usually appears in abbreviated form and in italics (e.g. (*fam*), (*COMM*)).

Where appropriate, words related to headwords are grouped in the same entry (**nación, nacionalismo; accept, acceptance**) in a slightly smaller bold type than the headword.

Common expressions in which the headword appears are shown in a different bold roman type (e.g. **hacer calor**).

Phonetic spellings

The phonetic spelling of each headword (indicating its pronunciation) is given in square brackets immediately after the headword (e.g. **dónde** ['donde]). A list of these symbols is given on page x.

Translations

Headword translations are given in ordinary type and, where more than one meaning or usage exists, these are separated by a semi-colon. You will often find other words in italics in brackets before the translations. These offer suggested contexts in which the headword might appear (e.g. **grande** (*de tamaño*)) or provide synonyms (e.g. **grande** (*alto*) *o* (*distinguido*)).

The gender of the translation also appears in *italics* immediately following the key element of the translation, except where this is a regular masculine singular noun ending in "o", or a regular singular feminine noun ending in "a".

"Key" words

Special status is given to certain Spanish and English words which are considered as "key" words in each language. They may, for example, occur very frequently or have several types of usage (e.g. **de, haber**). A combination of lozenges ♦ and numbers helps you to distinguish different parts of speech and different meanings. Further helpful information is provided in brackets and in italics.

Grammatical information

Parts of speech are given in abbreviated form in italics after the phonetic spellings of headwords (e.g. *vt, adv, conj*).

Genders of Spanish nouns are indicated as follows: *nm* for a masculine and *nf* for a feminine noun. Feminine and irregular plural forms of nouns are also shown (**irlandés, esa; luz,** (*pl* **luces**)).

ABREVIATURAS

ABBREVIATIONS

abreviatura	ab(b)r	abbreviation
adjetivo, locución adjetiva	adj	adjective, adjectival phrase
administración	ADMIN	administration
adverbio, locución adverbial	adv	adverb, adverbial phrase
agricultura	AGR	agriculture
América Latina	AM	Latin America
anatomía	ANAT	anatomy
arquitectura	ARQ, ARCH	architecture
el automóvil	AUT(O)	the motor car and motoring
aviación, viajes aéreos	AVIAT	flying, air travel
biología	BIO(L)	biology
botánica, flores	BOT	botany
inglés británico	BRIT	British English
química	CHEM	chemistry
comercio, finanzas, banca	COM(M)	commerce, finance, banking
informática	COMPUT	computers
conjunción	conj	conjunction
construcción	CONSTR	building
compuesto	cpd	compound element
cocina	CULIN	cookery
economía	ECON	economics
electricidad, electrónica	ELEC	electricity, electronics
enseñanza, sistema escolar y universitario	ESCOL	schooling, schools and universities
España	Esp	Spain
especialmente	esp	especially
exclamación, interjección	excl	exclamation, interjection
femenino	f	feminine
lengua familiar (! vulgar)	fam (!)	colloquial usage (! particularly offensive)
ferrocarril	FERRO	railways
uso figurado	fig	figurative use
fotografía	FOTO	photography
(verbo inglés) del cual la partícula es inseparable	fus	(phrasal verb) where the particle is inseparable
generalmente	gen	generally
geografía, geología	GEO	geography, geology
geometría	GEOM	geometry
uso familiar (! vulgar)	inf (!)	colloquial usage (! particularly offensive)
infinitivo	infin	infinitive
informática	INFORM	computers
invariable	inv	invariable
irregular	irreg	irregular
lo jurídico	JUR	law
América Latina	LAM	Latin America
gramática, lingüística	LING	grammar, linguistics

ABREVIATURAS

ABBREVIATIONS

masculino	**m**	masculine
matemáticas	**MATH**	mathematics
masculino/femenino	**m/f**	masculine/feminine
medicina	**MED**	medicine
lo militar, ejército	**MIL**	military matters
música	**MUS**	music
sustantivo, nombre	**n**	noun
navegación, náutica	**NAUT**	sailing, navigation
sustantivo numérico	**num**	numeral noun
complemento	**obj**	(grammatical) object
	o.s.	oneself
peyorativo	**pey, pej**	derogatory, pejorative
fotografía	**PHOT**	photography
fisiología	**PHYSIOL**	physiology
plural	**pl**	plural
política	**POL**	politics
participio de pasado	**pp**	past participle
preposición	**prep**	preposition
pronombre	**pron**	pronoun
psicología, psiquiatría	**PSICO, PSYCH**	psychology, psychiatry
tiempo pasado	**pt**	past tense
química	**QUÍM**	chemistry
ferrocarril	**RAIL**	railways
religión	**REL**	religion
	sb	somebody
enseñanza, sistema escolar y universitario	**SCH**	schooling, schools and universities
singular	**sg**	singular
España	**SP**	Spain
	sth	something
sujeto	**su(b)j**	(grammatical) subject
subjuntivo	**subjun**	subjunctive
tauromaquia	**TAUR**	bullfighting
también	**tb**	also
técnica, tecnología	**TEC(H)**	technical term, technology
telecomunicaciones	**TELEC, TEL**	telecommunications
imprenta, tipografía	**TIP, TYP**	typography, printing
televisión	**TV**	television
universidad	**UNIV**	university
inglés norteamericano	**US**	American English
verbo	**vb**	verb
verbo intransitivo	**vi**	intransitive verb
verbo pronominal	**vr**	reflexive verb
verbo transitivo	**vt**	transitive verb
zoología	**ZOOL**	zoology
marca registrada	**®**	registered trademark
indica un equivalente cultural	**≈**	introduces a cultural equivalent

ix

SPANISH PRONUNCIATION

Consonants

c	[k]	caja	c before a, o or u is pronounced as in cat
ce, ci	[θe, θi]	cero cielo	c before e or i is pronounced as in thin
ch	[tʃ]	chiste	ch is pronounced as ch in chair
d	[d, ð]	danés ciudad	at the beginning of a phrase or after l or n, d is pronounced as in English. In any other position it is pronounced like th in the
g	[g, ɣ]	gafas paga	g before a, o or u is pronounced as in gap, if at the beginning of a phrase or after n. In other positions the sound is softened
ge, gi	[xe, xi]	gente girar	g before e or i is pronounced similar to ch in Scottish loch
h		haber	h is always silent in Spanish
j	[x]	jugar	j is pronounced similar to ch in Scottish loch
ll	[ʎ]	talle	ll is pronounced like the lli in million
ñ	[ɲ]	niño	ñ is pronounced like the ni in onion
q	[k]	que	q is pronounced as k in king
r, rr	[r, rr]	quitar garra	r is always pronounced in Spanish, unlike the silent r in dancer. rr is trilled, like a Scottish r
s	[s]	quizás isla	s is usually pronounced as in pass, but before b, d, g, l, m or n it is pronounced as in rose
v	[b, ß]	vía dividir	v is pronounced something like b. At the beginning of a phrase or after m or n it is pronounced as b in boy. In any other position the sound is softened
z	[θ]	tenaz	z is pronounced as th in thin

b, f, k, l, m, n, p, t and x are pronounced as in English.

Vowels

a	[a]	p*a*ta	not as long as *a* in f*a*r. When followed by a consonant in the same syllable (i.e. in a closed syllable), as in amante, the *a* is short, as in b*a*t
e	[e]	m*e*	like *e* in th*e*y. In a closed syllable, as in gente, the *e* is short as in p*e*t
i	[i]	p*i*no	as in m*ea*n or mach*i*ne
o	[o]	l*o*	as in l*o*cal. In a closed syllable, as in control, the *o* is short as in c*o*t
u	[u]	lun*e*s	as in r*u*le. It is silent after *q*, and in *gue*, *gui*, unless marked *güe*, *güi* e.g. antigüedad

Diphthongs

ai, ay	[ai]	b*ai*le	as *i* in r*i*de
au	[au]	*au*to	as *ou* in sh*ou*t
ei, ey	[ei]	buey	as *ey* in gr*ey*
eu	[eu]	d*eu*da	both elements pronounced independently [e]+[u]
oi, oy	[oi]	h*oy*	as *oy* in t*oy*

Stress

The rules of stress in Spanish are as follows:
(a) when a word ends in a vowel or in *n* or *s*, the second last syllable is stressed: pat*a*ta, pat*a*tas, c*o*me, c*o*men
(b) when a word ends in a consonant other than *n* or *s*, the stress falls on the last syllable: par*e*d, habl*a*r
(c) when the rules set out in a and b are not applied, an acute accent appears over the stressed vowel: com*ú*n, geograf*í*a, ingl*é*s

In the phonetic transcription, the symbol ['] precedes the syllable on which the stress falls.

PRONUNCIACIÓN INGLESA

Vocales y diptongos

	Ejemplo inglés	Ejemplo español/explicación
ɑ:	father	Entre *a* de *padre* y *o* de *noche*
ʌ	but, come	*a* muy breve
æ	man, cat	Se mantienen los labios en la posición de *e* en *pena* y luego se pronuncia el sonido *a*
ə	father, ago	Sonido indistinto parecido a una *e* u *o* casi mudas
ə:	bird, heard	Entre *e* abierta, y *o* cerrada, sonido alargado
ɛ	get, bed	como en *perro*
ɪ	it, big	Más breve que en *si*
i:	tea, see	Como en *fino*
ɔ	hot, wash	Como en *torre*
ɔ:	saw, all	Como en *por*
u	put, book	Sonido breve, más cerrado que *burro*
u:	too, you	Sonido largo, como en *uno*
aɪ	fly, high	Como en *fraile*
au	how, house	Como en *pausa*
ɛə	there, bear	Casi como en *vea*, pero el sonido *a* se mezcla con el indistinto [ə]
eɪ	day, obey	*e* cerrada seguida por una *i* débil
ɪə	here, hear	Como en *manía*, mezclándose el sonido *a* con el indistinto [ə]
əu	go, note	[ə] seguido por una breve *u*
ɔɪ	boy, oil	Como en *voy*
uə	poor, sure	*u* bastante larga más el sonido indistinto [ə]

Consonantes

	Ejemplo inglés	Ejemplo español/explicación
d	men**d**ed	Como en con**d**e, an**d**ar
g	**g**o, **g**et, bi**g**	Como en **g**rande, **g**ol
dʒ	**g**in, **j**udge	Como en la **ll** andaluza y en **G**eneralitat (catalán)
ŋ	si**ng**	Como en ví**n**culo
h	**h**ouse, **h**e	Como la **j**ota hispanoamericana
j	**y**oung, **y**es	Como en **y**a
k	**c**ome, mo**ck**	Como en **c**aña, Es**c**ocia
r	**r**ed, t**r**ead	Se pronuncia con la punta de la lengua hacia atrás y sin hacerla vibrar
s	**s**and, ye**s**	Como en **c**asa, se**s**ión
z	ro**s**e, **z**ebra	Como en de**s**de, mi**s**mo
ʃ	**sh**e, ma**ch**ine	Como en **ch**ambre (francés), ro**x**o (portugués)
tʃ	**ch**in, ri**ch**	Como en **ch**ocolate
v	**v**alley	Como en f, pero se retiran los dientes superiores vibrándolos contra el labio inferior
w	**w**ater, **wh**ich	Como en la **u** de h**u**evo, p**u**ede
ʒ	vi**s**ion	Como en **j**ournal (francés)
θ	**th**ink, my**th**	Como en re**c**eta, **z**apato
ð	**th**is, **th**e	Como en la **d** de habla**d**o, verda**d**

b, p, f, m, n, l, t iguales que en español

El signo * indica que la r final escrita apenas se pronuncia en inglés británico cuando la palabra siguiente empieza con vocal.

El signo ['] indica la sílaba acentuada.

ESPAÑOL • INGLÉS
SPANISH • ENGLISH

ESPAÑOL - INGLÉS
SPANISH - ENGLISH

A, a

a [a] (**a**+ **el** = **al**) prep **1** (*dirección*) to; **fueron ~ Madrid/Grecia** they went to Madrid/Greece; **me voy ~ casa** I'm going home

2 (*distancia*): **está ~ 15 km de aquí** it's 15 kms from here

3 (*posición*): **estar ~ la mesa** to be at table; **al lado de** next to, beside; *ver tb* **puerta**

4 (*tiempo*): **~ las 10/~ medianoche** at 10/midnight; **~ la mañana siguiente** the following morning; **~ los pocos días** after a few days; **estamos ~ 9 de julio** it's the ninth of July; **~ los 24 años** at the age of 24; **al año/~ la semana** (*AM*) a year/week later

5 (*manera*): **~ la francesa** the French way; **~ caballo** on horseback; **~ oscuras** in the dark

6 (*medio, instrumento*): **~ lápiz** in pencil; **~ mano** by hand; **cocina ~ gas** gas stove

7 (*razón*): **~ 30 ptas el kilo** at 30 pesetas a kilo; **~ más de 50 km/h** at more than 50 kms per hour

8 (*dativo*): **se lo di ~ él** I gave it to him; **vi al policía** I saw the policeman; **se lo compré ~ él** I bought it from him

9 (*tras ciertos verbos*): **voy ~ verle** I'm going to see him; **empezó ~ trabajar** he started working o to work

10 (+ *infin*): **al verle, le reconocí inmediatamente** when I saw him I recognized him at once; **el camino ~ recorrer** the distance we (*etc*) have to travel; **¡~ callar!** keep quiet!; **¡~ comer!** let's eat!

abad, esa [a'βaδ, 'δesa] *nm/f* abbot/abbess; **~ía** *nf* abbey

abajo [a'βaxo] *adv* (*situación*) (down) below, underneath; (*en edificio*) downstairs; (*dirección*) down, downwards; **el piso de ~** the downstairs flat; **la parte de ~** the lower part; **¡~ el gobierno!** down with the government!; **cuesta/río ~** downhill/downstream; **de arriba ~** from top to bottom; **de ~** the undersigned; **más ~** lower o further down

abalanzarse [aβalan'θarse] *vr*: **~ sobre** o **contra** to throw o.s. at

abandonado, a [aβando'naδo, a] *adj* derelict; (*desatendido*) abandoned; (*desierto*) deserted; (*descuidado*) neglected

abandonar [aβando'nar] *vt* to leave; (*persona*) to abandon, desert; (*cosa*) to abandon, leave behind; (*descuidar*) to neglect; (*renunciar a*) to give up; (*INFORM*) to quit; **~se** *vr* **~se a** to abandon o.s. to; **abandono** *nm* (*acto*) desertion, abandonment; (*estado*) abandon, neglect; (*renuncia*) withdrawal, retirement; **ganar por abandono** to win by default

abanicar [aβani'kar] *vt* to fan; **abanico** *nm* fan; (*NAUT*) derrick

abaratar [aβara'tar] *vt* to lower the price of; **~se** *vr* to go o come down in price

abarcar [aβar'kar] *vt* to include, embrace; (AM) to monopolize

abarrotado, a [aβarro'taðo, a] *adj* packed

abarrotar [aβarro'tar] *vt* (local, estadio, teatro) to fill, pack

abarrotero, a [aβarro'tero, a] (AM) *nm/f* grocer; **abarrotes** *nmpl* (AM) groceries, provisions

abastecer [aβaste'θer] *vt*: **~ (de)** to supply (with); **abastecimiento** *nm* supply

abasto [a'βasto] *nm* supply; **no dar ~ a** to be unable to cope with

abatido, a [aβa'tiðo, a] *adj* dejected, downcast

abatimiento [aβati'mjento] *nm* (depresión) dejection, depression

abatir [aβa'tir] *vt* (muro) to demolish; (pájaro) to shoot o bring down; (fig) to depress; **~se** *vr* to get depressed; **~se sobre** to swoop o pounce on

abdicación [aβðika'θjon] *nf* abdication

abdicar [aβði'kar] *vi* to abdicate

abdomen [aβ'ðomen] *nm* abdomen; **abdominales** *nmpl* (tb: ejercicios abdominales) sit-ups

abecedario [aβeθe'ðarjo] *nm* alphabet

abedul [aβe'ðul] *nm* birch

abeja [a'βexa] *nf* bee

abejorro [aβe'xorro] *nm* bumblebee

abertura [aβer'tura] *nf* = **apertura**

abeto [a'βeto] *nm* fir

abierto, a [a'βjerto, a] *pp de* **abrir** ♦ *adj* open; (AM) generous

abigarrado, a [aβiɣa'rraðo, a] *adj* multi-coloured

abismal [aβis'mal] *adj* (fig) vast, enormous

abismar [aβis'mar] *vt* to humble, cast down; **~se** *vr* to sink; **~se en** (fig) to be plunged into

abismo [a'βismo] *nm* abyss

abjurar [aβxu'rar] *vi*: **~ de** to abjure, forswear

ablandar [aβlan'dar] *vt* to soften; **~se**

vr to get softer

abnegación [aβneɣa'θjon] *nf* self-denial

abnegado, a [aβne'ɣaðo, a] *adj* self-sacrificing

abocado, a [aβo'kaðo, a] *adj*: **~verse ~ al desastre** to be heading for disaster

abochornar [aβotʃor'nar] *vt* to embarrass

abofetear [aβofete'ar] *vt* to slap (in the face)

abogado, a [aβo'ɣaðo, a] *nm/f* lawyer; (notario) solicitor; (en tribunal) barrister (BRIT), attorney (US); **~ defensor** defence lawyer o attorney (US)

abogar [aβo'ɣar] *vi*: **~ por** to plead for; (fig) to advocate

abolengo [aβo'lenɣo] *nm* ancestry, lineage

abolición [aβoli'θjon] *nf* abolition

abolir [aβo'lir] *vt* to abolish; (cancelar) to cancel

abolladura [aβoʎa'ðura] *nf* dent

abollar [aβo'ʎar] *vt* to dent

abominable [aβomi'naβle] *adj* abominable

abonado, a [aβo'naðo, a] *adj* (deuda) paid(-up) ♦ *nm/f* subscriber

abonar [aβo'nar] *vt* (deuda) to settle; (terreno) to fertilize; (idea) to endorse; **~se** *vr* to subscribe; **abono** *nm* payment; fertilizer; subscription

abordar [aβor'ðar] *vt* (barco) to board; (asunto) to broach

aborigen [aβo'rixen] *nm/f* aborigine

aborrecer [aβorre'θer] *vt* to hate, loathe

abortar [aβor'tar] *vi* (malparir) to have a miscarriage; (deliberadamente) to have an abortion; **aborto** *nm* miscarriage; abortion

abotonar [aβoto'nar] *vt* to button (up), do up

abovedado, a [aβoβe'ðaðo, a] *adj* vaulted, domed

abrasar [aβra'sar] *vt* to burn (up);

(AGR) to dry up, parch

abrazar [aβra'θar] vt to embrace, hug

abrazo [a'βraθo] nm embrace, hug; **un ~** (en carta) with best wishes

abrebotellas [aβreβo'teλas] nm inv bottle opener

abrecartas [aβre'kartas] nm inv letter opener

abrelatas [aβre'latas] nm inv tin (BRIT) o can opener

abreviar [aβre'βjar] vt to abbreviate; (texto) to abridge; (plazo) to reduce; **abreviatura** nf abbreviation

abridor [aβri'ðor] nm bottle opener; (de latas) tin (BRIT) o can opener

abrigar [aβri'ɣar] vt (proteger) to shelter; (suj: ropa) to keep warm; (fig) to cherish

abrigo [a'βriɣo] nm (prenda) coat, overcoat; (lugar protegido) shelter

abril [a'βril] nm April

abrillantar [aβriλan'tar] vt to polish

abrir [a'βrir] vt to open (up) ♦ vi to open; **~se** vr to open (up); (extenderse) to open out; (cielo) to clear; **~se paso** to find o force a way through

abrochar [aβro'tʃar] vt (con botones) to button (up); (zapato, con broche) to do up

abrumar [aβru'mar] vt to overwhelm; (sobrecargar) to weigh down

abrupto, a [a'βrupto, a] adj abrupt; (empinado) steep

absceso [aβs'θeso] nm abscess

absentismo [aβsen'tismo] nm absenteeism

absolución [aβsolu'θjon] nf (REL) absolution; (JUR) acquittal

absoluto, a [aβso'luto, a] adj absolute; **en ~** adv not at all

absolver [aβsol'βer] vt to absolve; (JUR) to pardon; (: acusado) to acquit

absorbente [aβsor'βente] adj absorbent; (interesante) absorbing

absorber [aβsor'βer] vt to absorb; (embeber) to soak up

absorción [aβsor'θjon] nf absorption;

(COM) takeover

absorto, a [aβ'sorto, a] pp de **absorber** ♦ adj absorbed, engrossed

abstemio, a [aβs'temjo, a] adj teetotal

abstención [aβsten'θjon] nf abstention

abstenerse [aβste'nerse] vr: **~ (de)** to abstain o refrain (from)

abstinencia [aβsti'nenθja] nf abstinence; (ayuno) fasting

abstracción [aβstrak'θjon] nf abstraction

abstracto, a [aβs'strakto, a] adj abstract

abstraer [aβstra'er] vt to abstract; **~se** vr to be o become absorbed

abstraído, a [aβstra'iðo, a] adj absent-minded

absuelto [aβ'swelto] pp de **absolver**

absurdo, a [aβ'surðo, a] adj absurd

abuchear [aβutʃe'ar] vt to boo

abuelo, a [a'βwelo, a] nm/f grandfather/mother; **~s** nmpl grandparents

abulia [a'βulja] nf apathy

abultado, a [aβul'taðo, a] adj bulky

abultar [aβul'tar] vi to be bulky

abundancia [aβun'danθja] nf: **una ~ de** plenty of; **abundante** adj abundant, plentiful

abundar [aβun'dar] vi to abound, be plentiful

aburguesarse [aβurɣe'sarse] vr to become middle-class

aburrido, a [aβu'rriðo, a] adj (hastiado) bored; (que aburre) boring; **aburrimiento** nm boredom, tedium

aburrir [aβu'rrir] vt to bore; **~se** vr to be bored, get bored

abusar [aβu'sar] vi to go too far; **~ de** to abuse

abusivo, a [aβu'siβo, a] adj (precio) exorbitant

abuso [a'βuso] nm abuse

abyecto, a [aβ'jekto, a] adj wretched, abject

acá [a'ka] adv (lugar) here; **¿de cuándo ~?** since when?

acabado, a [aka'βaðo, a] adj finished, complete; (perfecto) perfect; (agotado) worn out; (fig) masterly ♦ nm finish

acabar [aka'βar] vt (llevar a su fin) to finish, complete; (consumir) to use up; (rematar) to finish off ♦ vi to finish, end; **~se** vr to finish, stop; (terminarse) to be over; (agotarse) to run out; **~ con** to put an end to; **~ de llegar** to have just arrived; **~ por hacer** to end (up) by doing; **~se** vr: **¡se acabó!** it's all over!; **¡basta!** that's enough!

acabóse [aka'βose] nm: **esto es el ~** this is the last straw

academia [aka'ðemja] nf academy; **académico, a** adj academic

acaecer [akae'θer] vi to happen, occur

acallar [aka'ʎar] vt (a persona) to silence; (protestas, rumores) to suppress

acalorado, a [akalo'raðo, a] adj (discusión) heated

acalorarse [akalo'rarse] vr (fig) to get heated

acampar [akam'par] vi to camp

acantilado [akanti'laðo] nm cliff

acaparar [akapa'rar] vt to monopolize; (acumular) to hoard

acariciar [akari'θjar] vt to caress; (esperanza) to cherish

acarrear [akarre'ar] vt to transport; (fig) to cause, result in

acaso [a'kaso] adv perhaps, maybe; **(por) si ~** (just) in case

acatamiento [akata'mjento] nm respect; (ley) observance

acatar [aka'tar] vt to respect; (ley) obey

acatarrarse [akata'rrarse] vr to catch a cold

acaudalado, a [akauða'laðo, a] adj well-off

acaudillar [akauði'ʎar] vt to lead, command

acceder [akθe'ðer] vi: **~ a** (petición etc) to agree to; (tener acceso a) to have access to; (INFORM) to access

accesible [akθe'sißle] adj accessible

acceso [ak'θeso] nm access, entry; (camino) access, approach; (MED) attack, fit

accesorio, a [akθe'sorjo, a] adj, nm accessory

accidentado, a [akθiðen'taðo, a] adj uneven; (montañoso) hilly; (azaroso) eventful ♦ nm/f accident victim

accidental [akθiðen'tal] adj accidental; **accidentarse** vr to have an accident

accidente [akθi'ðente] nm accident; **~s** nmpl (de terreno) unevenness sg

acción [ak'θjon] nf action, act; (acto) action, act; (COM) share; (JUR) action, lawsuit; **accionar** vt to work, operate; (INFORM) to drive

accionista [akθjo'nista] nm/f shareholder, stockholder

acebo [a'θeßo] nm holly; (árbol) holly tree

acechar [aθe'tʃar] vt to spy on; (aguardar) to lie in wait for; **acecho** nm: **estar al acecho (de)** to lie in wait (for)

aceitar [aθei'tar] vt to oil, lubricate

aceite [a'θeite] nm oil; (de oliva) olive oil; **~ra** nf oilcan; **aceitoso, a** adj oily

aceituna [aθei'tuna] nf olive

acelerador [aθelera'ðor] nm accelerator

acelerar [aθele'rar] vt to accelerate

acelga [a'θelɣa] nf chard, beet

acento [a'θento] nm accent; (acentuación) stress

acentuar [aθen'twar] vt to accent; to stress; (fig) to accentuate

acepción [aθep'θjon] nf meaning

aceptable [aθep'taßle] adj acceptable

aceptación [aθepta'θjon] nf acceptance; (aprobación) approval

aceptar [aθep'tar] vt to accept; (aprobar) to approve

acequia [a'θekja] nf irrigation ditch

acera [a'θera] nf pavement (BRIT), sidewalk (US)

acerca [a'θerka]: **~ de** prep about, concerning

acercar [aθer'kar] vt to bring o move nearer; **~se** vr to approach, come near

acerico [aθe'riko] nm pincushion

acero [a'θero] nm steel

acérrimo, a [a'θerrimo, a] adj (partidario) staunch; (enemigo) bitter

acertado, a [aθer'taðo, a] adj correct; (apropiado) apt; (sensato) sensible

acertar [aθer'tar] vt (blanco) to hit; (solución) to get right; (adivinar) to guess ♦ vi to get it right, be right; **~ a** to manage to; **~ con** to happen o hit on

acertijo [aθer'tixo] nm riddle, puzzle

achacar [atʃa'kar] vt to attribute

achacoso, a [atʃa'koso, a] adj sickly

achantar [atʃan'tar] (fam) vt to scare, frighten; **~se** vr to back down

achaque etc [a'tʃake] vb ver **achacar** ♦ nm ailment

achicar [atʃi'kar] vt to reduce; (NAUT) to bale out

achicharrar [atʃitʃa'rrar] vt to scorch, burn

achicoria [atʃi'korja] nf chicory

aciago, a [a'θjaɣo, a] adj ill-fated, fateful

acicalar [aθika'lar] vt to polish; (persona) to dress up; **~se** vr to get dressed up

acicate [aθi'kate] nm spur

acidez [aθi'ðeθ] nf acidity

ácido, a ['aθiðo, a] adj sour, acid ♦ nm acid

acierto etc [a'θjerto] vb ver **acertar** ♦ nm success; (buen paso) wise move; (solución) solution; (habilidad) skill, ability

aclamación [aklama'θjon] nf acclamation; (aplausos) applause

aclamar [akla'mar] vt to acclaim; (aplaudir) to applaud

aclaración [aklara'θjon] nf clarification, explanation

aclarar [akla'rar] vt to clarify, explain;

(ropa) to rinse ♦ vi to clear up; **~se** vr (explicarse) to understand; **~se la garganta** to clear one's throat

aclaratorio, a [aklara'torjo, a] adj explanatory

aclimatación [aklimata'θjon] nf acclimatization

aclimatar [aklima'tar] vt to acclimatize; **~se** vr to become acclimatized

acné [ak'ne] nm acne

acobardar [akoβar'ðar] vt to intimidate

acodarse [ako'ðarse] vr: **~ en** to lean on

acogedor, a [akoxe'ðor, a] adj welcoming; (hospitalario) hospitable

acoger [ako'xer] vt to welcome; (abrigar) to shelter; **~se** vr to take refuge

acogida [ako'xiða] nf reception; refuge

acometer [akome'ter] vt to attack; (emprender) to undertake; **acometida** nf attack, assault

acomodado, a [akomo'ðaðo, a] adj (persona) well-to-do

acomodador, a [akomoða'ðor, a] nm/f usher(ette)

acomodar [akomo'ðar] vt to adjust; (alojar) to accommodate; **~se** vr to conform; (instalarse) to install o.s.; (adaptarse) to adapt (to)

acompañar [akompa'ɲar] vt to accompany; (documentos) to enclose

acondicionar [akondiθjo'nar] vt to arrange, prepare; (pelo) to condition

acongojar [akongo'xar] vt to distress, grieve

aconsejar [akonse'xar] vt to advise, counsel; **~se** vr: **~se con** to consult

acontecer [akonte'θer] vi to happen, occur; **acontecimiento** nm event

acopio [a'kopjo] nm store, stock

acoplamiento [akopla'mjento] nm coupling, joint; **acoplar** vt to fit; (ELEC) to connect; (vagones) to couple

acorazado, a [akora'θaðo, a] adj

armour-plated, armoured ♦ nm
battleship

acordar [akorˈðar] vt (resolver) to
agree, resolve; (recordar) to remind;
~se vr to agree; ~se (de algo) to
remember (sth); **acorde** adj (MUS)
harmonious; **acorde con** (medidas etc)
in keeping with ♦ nm chord

acordeón [akorðeˈon] nm accordion

acordonado, a [akorðoˈnaðo, a] adj
(calle) cordoned-off

acorralar [akorraˈlar] vt to round up,
corral

acortar [akorˈtar] vt to shorten;
(duración) to cut short; (cantidad) to
reduce; ~se vr to become shorter

acosar [akoˈsar] vt to pursue
relentlessly; (fig) to hound, pester;
acoso nm harassment; **acoso sexual**
sexual harassment

acostar [akosˈtar] vt (en cama) to put
to bed; (en suelo) to lay down; ~se vr
to go to bed; to lie down; ~se con
uno to sleep with sb

acostumbrado, a [akostumˈbraðo, a]
adj usual; ~ a used to

acostumbrar [akostumˈbrar] vt: ~ a
uno a algo to get sb used to sth ♦ vi:
~ (a) hacer to be in the habit of
doing; ~se vr: ~se a to get used to

acotación [akotaˈθjon] nf marginal
note; (GEO) elevation mark; (de límite)
boundary mark; (TEATRO) stage
direction

ácrata [ˈakrata] adj, nm/f anarchist

acre [ˈakre] adj (olor) acrid; (fig) biting
♦ nm acre

acrecentar [akreθenˈtar] vt to
increase, augment

acreditar [akreðiˈtar] vt (garantizar) to
vouch for, guarantee; (autorizar) to
authorize; (dar prueba de) to prove;
(COM: abonar) to credit; (embajador) to
accredit; ~se vr to become famous

acreedor, a [akreeˈðor, a] adj: ~ de
worthy of ♦ nm/f creditor

acribillar [akriβiˈʎar] vt: ~ a balazos

to riddle with bullets

acróbata [aˈkroβata] nm/f acrobat

acta [ˈakta] nf certificate; (de comisión)
minutes pl, record; ~ de
nacimiento/de matrimonio birth/
marriage certificate; ~ **notarial**
affidavit

actitud [aktiˈtuð] nf attitude; (postura)
posture

activar [aktiˈβar] vt to activate;
(acelerar) to speed up

actividad [aktiβiˈðað] nf activity

activo, a [akˈtiβo, a] adj active; (vivo)
lively ♦ nm (COM) assets pl

acto [ˈakto] nm act, action; (ceremonia)
ceremony; (TEATRO) act; **en el** ~
immediately

actor [akˈtor] nm actor; (JUR) plaintiff
♦ adj: **parte ~a** prosecution

actriz [akˈtriθ] nf actress

actuación [aktwaˈθjon] nf action;
(comportamiento) conduct, behaviour;
(JUR) proceedings pl; (desempeño)
performance

actual [akˈtwal] adj present(-day),
current; ~**idad** nf present; ~**idades**
nfpl (noticias) news sg; **en la ~idad** at
present; (hoy día) nowadays

actualizar [aktwaliˈθar] vt to update,
modernize

actualmente [aktwalˈmente] adv at
present; (hoy día) nowadays

actuar [akˈtwar] vi (obrar) to work,
operate; (actor) to act, perform ♦ vt to
work, operate; ~ **de** to act as

acuarela [akwaˈrela] nf watercolour

acuario [aˈkwarjo] nm aquarium;
(ASTROLOGÍA): **A~** Aquarius

acuartelar [akwarteˈlar] vt (MIL) to
confine to barracks

acuático, a [aˈkwatiko, a] adj aquatic

acuchillar [akutʃiˈʎar] vt (TEC) to plane
(down), smooth

acuciante [akuˈθjante] adj urgent

acuciar [akuˈθjar] vt to urge on

acudir [akuˈðir] vi (asistir) to attend;
(ir) to go; ~ **a** (fig) to turn to; ~ **en**

ayuda de to go to the aid of
acuerdo *etc* |a'kwerðo| *vb ver* **acordar**
♦ *nm* agreement; **¡de ~!** agreed!; **de ~ con** (*persona*) in agreement with; (*acción, documento*) in accordance with; **estar de ~ to** be agreed, agree

acumular |akumu'lar| *vt* to accumulate, collect

acuñar |aku'ɲar| *vt* (*moneda*) to mint; (*frase*) to coin

acupuntura |akupun'tura| *nf* acupuncture

acurrucarse |akurru'karse| *vr* to crouch; (*ovillarse*) to curl up

acusación |akusa'θjon| *nf* accusation

acusar |aku'sar| *vt* to accuse; (*revelar*) to reveal; (*denunciar*) to denounce

acuse |a'kuse| *nm*: **~ de recibo** acknowledgement of receipt

acústica |a'kustika| *nf* acoustics *pl*

acústico, a |a'kustiko, a| *adj* acoustic

adaptación |aðapta'θjon| *nf* adaptation

adaptador |aðapta'ðor| *nm* (ELEC.) adapter

adaptar |aðap'tar| *vt* to adapt; (*acomodar*) to fit

adecuado, a |aðe'kwaðo, a| *adj* (*apto*) suitable; (*oportuno*) appropriate

adecuar |aðe'kwar| *vt* to adapt; to make suitable

a. de J.C. *abr* (= *antes de Jesucristo*) B.C.

adelantado, a |aðelan'taðo, a| *adj* advanced; (*reloj*) fast; **pagar por ~ to** pay in advance

adelantamiento |aðelanta'mjento| *nm* (AUTO.) overtaking

adelantar |aðelan'tar| *vt* to move forward; (*avanzar*) to advance; (*acelerar*) to speed up; (AUTO.) to overtake ♦ *vi* to go forward, advance; **~se** *vr* to go forward, advance

adelante |aðe'lante| *adv* forward(s), ahead ♦ *excl* come in!; **de hoy en ~** from now on; **más ~** later on; (*más allá*) further on

adelanto |aðe'lanto| *nm* advance; (*mejora*) improvement; (*progreso*) progress

adelgazar |aðelɣa'θar| *vt* to thin (down) ♦ *vi* to get thin; (*con régimen*) to slim down, lose weight

ademán |aðe'man| *nm* gesture; **ademanes** *nmpl* manners; **en ~ de** as if to

además |aðe'mas| *adv* besides; (*por otra parte*) moreover; (*también*) also; **~ de** besides, in addition to

adentrarse |aðen'trarse| *vr*: **~ en** to go into, get inside; (*penetrar*) to penetrate (into)

adentro |a'ðentro| *adv* inside, in; **mar ~** out at sea; **tierra ~** inland

adepto, a |a'ðepto, a| *nm/f* supporter

aderezar |aðere'θar| *vt* (*ensalada*) to dress; (*comida*) to season; **aderezo** *nm* dressing; seasoning

adeudar |aðeu'ðar| *vt* to owe; **~se** *vr* to run into debt

adherirse |aðe'rirse| *vr*: **~ a** to adhere to; (*partido*) to join

adhesión |aðe'sjon| *nf* adhesion; (*fig*) adherence

adicción |aðik'θjon| *nf* addiction

adición |aði'θjon| *nf* addition

adicto, a |a'ðikto, a| *adj*: **~ a** addicted to; (*dedicado*) devoted to ♦ *nm/f* supporter, follower; (*toxicómano etc*) addict

adiestrar |aðjes'trar| *vt* to train, teach; (*conducir*) to guide, lead; **~se** *vr* to practise; (*enseñarse*) to learn to o.s.

adinerado, a |aðine'raðo, a| *adj* wealthy

adiós |a'ðjos| *excl* (*para despedirse*) goodbye!, cheerio!; (*al pasar*) hello!

aditivo |aði'tiβo| *nm* additive

adivinanza |aðiβi'nanθa| *nf* riddle

adivinar |aðiβi'nar| *vt* to prophesy; (*conjeturar*) to guess; **adivino, a** *nm/f* fortune-teller

adj *abr* (= *adjunto*) encl.

adjetivo |aðxe'tiβo| *nm* adjective

adjudicación [aðxuðika'θjon] nf award; adjudication

adjudicar [aðxuði'kar] vt to award; **~se vr: ~se algo** to appropriate sth

adjuntar [aðxun'tar] vt to attach, enclose; **adjunto, a** adj attached, enclosed ♦ nm/f assistant

administración [aðministra'θjon] nf administration; (dirección) management; **administrador, a** nm/f administrator; manager(ess)

administrar [aðminis'trar] vt to administer; **administrativo, a** adj administrative

admirable [aðmi'raßle] adj admirable

admiración [aðmira'θjon] nf admiration; (asombro) wonder; (LING) exclamation mark

admirar [aðmi'rar] vt to admire; (extrañar) to surprise; **~se vr** to be surprised

admisible [aðmi'sißle] adj admissible

admisión [aðmi'sjon] nf admission; (reconocimiento) acceptance

admitir [aðmi'tir] vt to admit; (aceptar) to accept

admonición [aðmoni'θjon] nf warning

adobar [aðo'ßar] vt (CULIN) to season

adobe [a'ðoße] nm adobe, sun-dried brick

adoctrinar [aðoktri'nar] vt: **~ en** to indoctrinate with

adolecer [aðole'θer] vi: **~ de** to suffer from

adolescente [aðoles'θente] nm/f adolescent, teenager

adonde [a'ðonðe] conj (to) where

adónde [a'ðonðe] adv = dónde

adopción [aðop'θjon] nf adoption

adoptar [aðop'tar] vt to adopt

adoptivo, a [aðop'tißo, a] adj (padres) adoptive; (hijo) adopted

adoquín [aðo'kin] nm paving stone

adorar [aðo'rar] vt to adore

adormecer [aðorme'θer] vt to put to sleep; **~se vr** to become sleepy;

(dormirse) to fall asleep

adornar [aðor'nar] vt to adorn

adorno [a'ðorno] nm ornament; (decoración) decoration

adosado, a [aðo'saðo, a] adj: **casa adosada** semi-detached house

adquiero etc vb ver **adquirir**

adquirir [aðki'rir] vt to acquire, obtain

adquisición [aðkisi'θjon] nf acquisition

adrede [a'ðreðe] adv on purpose

adscribir [aðskri'ßir] vt to appoint

adscrito pp de **adscribir**

aduana [a'ðwana] nf customs pl

aduanero, a [a'ðwa'nero, a] adj customs cpd ♦ nm/f customs officer

aducir [aðu'θir] vt to adduce; (dar como prueba) to offer as proof

adueñarse [aðwe'narse] vr: **~ de** to take possession of

adulación [aðula'θjon] nf flattery

adular [aðu'lar] vt to flatter

adulterar [aðulte'rar] vt to adulterate

adulterio [aðul'terjo] nm adultery

adúltero, a [a'ðultero, a] adj adulterous ♦ nm/f adulterer/adulteress

adulto, a [a'ðulto, a] adj, nm/f adult

adusto, a [a'ðusto, a] adj stern; (austero) austere

advenedizo, a [aðßene'ðiθo, a] adj upstart

advenimiento [aðßeni'mjento] nm arrival; (al trono) accession

adverbio [að'ßerßjo] nm adverb

adversario, a [að'ßer'sarjo, a] nm/f adversary

adversidad [aðßersi'ðað] nf adversity; (contratiempo) setback

adverso, a [að'ßerso, a] adj adverse

advertencia [aðßer'tenθja] nf warning; (prefacio) preface, foreword

advertir [aðßer'tir] vt to notice; (avisar): **~ a uno de** to warn sb about o of

Adviento [að'ßjento] nm Advent

advierto etc vb ver **advertir**

adyacente [aðja'θente] adj adjacent

aéreo, a [a'ereo, a] *adj* aerial

aerobic [ae'roßik] *nm* aerobics *sg*

aerodeslizador [aeroðesliθa'ðor] *nm* hovercraft

aeromozo, a [aero'moθo, a] (AM) *nm/f* air steward(ess)

aeronáutica [aero'nautika] *nf* aeronautics *sg*

aeronave [aero'naße] *nm* spaceship

aeroplano [aero'plano] *nm* aeroplane

aeropuerto [aero'pwerto] *nm* airport

aerosol [aero'sol] *nm* aerosol

afabilidad [afaßili'ðað] *nf* friendliness; **afable** *adj* affable

afamado, a [afa'maðo, a] *adj* famous

afán [a'fan] *nm* hard work; (deseo) desire

afanar [afa'nar] *vt* to harass; (fam) to pinch; **~se** *vr*: **~se por hacer** to strive to do

afear [afe'ar] *vt* to disfigure

afección [afek'θjon] *nf* (MED) disease

afectación [afekta'θjon] *nf* affectation; **afectado, a** *adj* affected

afectar [afek'tar] *vt* to affect

afectísimo, a [afek'tisimo, a] *adj* affectionate; **suyo ~** yours truly

afectivo, a [afek'tißo, a] *adj* (problema etc) emotional

afecto [a'fekto] *nm* affection; **tenerle ~ a uno** to be fond of sb

afectuoso, a [afek'twoso, a] *adj* affectionate

afeitar [afei'tar] *vt* to shave; **~se** *vr* to shave

afeminado, a [afemi'naðo, a] *adj* effeminate

Afganistán [afɣanis'tan] *nm* Afghanistan

afianzamiento [afjanθa'mjento] *nm* strengthening; security

afianzar [afjan'θar] *vt* to strengthen; to secure; **~se** *vr* to become established

afiche [a'fitʃe] (AM) *nm* poster

afición [afi'θjon] *nf* fondness, liking; **la ~ the fans** *pl*; **pinto por ~** I paint as a

hobby; **aficionado, a** *adj* keen, enthusiastic; (no profesional) amateur ♦ *nm/f* enthusiast, fan; amateur; **ser aficionado a algo** to be very keen on o fond of sth

aficionar [afiθjo'nar] *vt*: **~ a uno a algo** to make sb like sth; **~se** *vr*: **~se a algo** to grow fond of sth

afilado, a [afi'laðo, a] *adj* sharp

afilar [afi'lar] *vt* to sharpen

afiliarse [afi'ljarse] *vr* to affiliate

afín [a'fin] *adj* (parecido) similar; (conexo) related

afinar [afi'nar] *vt* (TEC) to refine; (MUS) to tune ♦ *vi* (tocar) to play in tune; (cantar) to sing in tune

afincarse [afin'karse] *vr* to settle

afinidad [afini'ðað] *nf* affinity; (parentesco) relationship; **por ~** by marriage

afirmación [afirma'θjon] *nf* affirmation

afirmar [afir'mar] *vt* to affirm, state; **afirmativo, a** *adj* affirmative

aflicción [aflik'θjon] *nf* affliction; (dolor) grief

afligir [afli'xir] *vt* to afflict; (apenar) to distress; **~se** *vr* to grieve

aflojar [aflo'xar] *vt* to slacken; (desatar) to loosen, undo; (relajar) to relax ♦ *vi* to drop; (bajar) to go down; **~se** *vr* to relax

aflorar [aflo'rar] *vi* to come to the surface, emerge

afluente [aflu'ente] *adj* flowing ♦ *nm* tributary

afluir [aflu'ir] *vi* to flow

afmo, a *abr* (= afectísimo(a) suyo(a)) Yours

afónico, a [a'foniko, a] *adj*: **estar ~** to have a sore throat; **to have lost one's voice**

aforo [a'foro] *nm* (de teatro etc) capacity

afortunado, a [afortu'naðo, a] *adj* fortunate, lucky

afrancesado, a [afranθe'saðo, a] *adj*

francophile; (pey) Frenchified

afrenta [a'frenta] nf affront, insult; (deshonra) dishonour, shame

África ['afrika] nf Africa; **africano, a** adj, nm/f African

afrontar [afron'tar] vt to confront; (poner cara a cara) to bring face to face

afuera [a'fwera] adv out, outside; **~s** nfpl outskirts

agachar [aɣa'tʃar] vt to bend, bow; **~se** vr to stoop, bend

agalla [a'ɣaʎa] nf (ZOOL) gill; **tener ~s** (fam) to have guts

agarradera [aɣarra'ðera] (esp AM) nf handle

agarrado, a [aɣa'rraðo, a] adj mean, stingy

agarrar [aɣa'rrar] vt to grasp, grab; (AM) to take, catch; (recoger) to pick up ♦ vi (planta) to take root; **~se** vr to hold on (tightly)

agarrotar [aɣarro'tar] vt (persona) to squeeze tightly; (reo) to garrotte; (MED) to stiffen

agasajar [aɣasa'xar] vt to treat well, fête

agazaparse [aɣaθa'parse] vr to crouch down

agencia [a'xenθja] nf agency; **~ inmobiliaria** (BRIT) o real estate (US) agent's (office); **~ de viajes** travel agency

agenciarse [axen'θjarse] vr to obtain, procure

agenda [a'xenda] nf diary

agente [a'xente] nm/f agent; (de policía) policeman/woman; **~ inmobiliario** estate agent (BRIT), realtor (US); **~ de seguros** insurance agent

ágil [a'xil] adj agile, nimble; **agilidad** nf agility, nimbleness

agilizar [axili'θar] vt (trámites) to speed up

agitación [axita'θjon] nf (de mano etc) shaking, waving; (de líquido etc) stirring; (fig) agitation

agitado, a [axi'taðo, a] adj hectic; (viaje) bumpy

agitar [axi'tar] vt to wave, shake; (líquido) to stir; (fig) to stir up, excite; **~se** vr to get excited; (inquietarse) to get worried o upset

aglomeración [aɣlomera'θjon] nf: **~ de tráfico/gente** traffic jam/mass of people

aglomerar [aɣlome'rar] vt to crowd together; **~se** vr to crowd together

agnóstico, a [aɣ'nostiko, a] adj, nm/f agnostic

agobiar [aɣo'βjar] vt to weigh down; (oprimir) to oppress; (cargar) to burden

agolparse [aɣol'parse] vr to crowd together

agonía [aɣo'nia] nf death throes pl; (fig) agony, anguish

agonizante [aɣoni'θante] adj dying

agonizar [aɣoni'θar] vi to be dying

agosto [a'ɣosto] nm August

agotado, a [aɣo'taðo, a] adj (persona) exhausted; (libros) out of print; (acabado) finished; (COM) sold out

agotador, a [aɣota'ðor, a] adj exhausting

agotamiento [aɣota'mjento] nm exhaustion

agotar [aɣo'tar] vt to exhaust; (consumir) to drain; (recursos) to use up, deplete; **~se** vr to be exhausted; (acabarse) to run out; (libro) to go out of print

agraciado, a [aɣra'θjaðo, a] adj (atractivo) attractive; (en sorteo etc) lucky

agradable [aɣra'ðaβle] adj pleasant, nice

agradar [aɣra'ðar] vt: **él me agrada** I like him

agradecer [aɣraðe'θer] vt to thank; (favor etc) to be grateful for; **agradecido, a** adj grateful; **¡muy agradecido!** thanks a lot!; **agradecimiento** nm thanks pl;

gratitude

agradezco etc vb ver **agradecer**

agrado |a'vraðo| nm: **ser de tu** etc ~ to be to your etc liking

agrandar |avran'dar| vt to enlarge; (fig) to exaggerate; **~se** vr to get bigger

agrario, a |a'vrarjo, a| adj agrarian, land cpd; (política) agricultural, farming

agravante |avra'ßante| adj aggravating ♦ nm: **con el ~ de que** ... with the further difficulty that ....

agravar |avra'ßar| vt (pesar sobre) to make heavier; (irritar) to aggravate; **~se** vr to worsen, get worse

agraviar |avra'ßjar| vt to offend; (ser injusto con) to wrong; **~se** vr to take offence; **agravio** nm offence; wrong; (JUR) grievance

agredir |avre'ðir| vt to attack

agregado, a |avre'vaðo, a| nm/f: **A-** ≈ teacher (who is not head of department) ♦ nm aggregate; (persona) attaché

agregar |avre'var| vt to gather; (añadir) to add; (persona) to appoint

agresión |avre'sjon| nf aggression

agresivo, a |avre'sißo, a| adj aggressive

agriar |a'vrjar| vt (to turn) sour; **~se** vr to turn sour

agrícola |a'vrikola| adj farming cpd, agricultural

agricultor, a |avrikul'tor, a| nm/f farmer

agricultura |avrikul'tura| nf agriculture, farming

agridulce |avri'ðulθe| adj bittersweet; (CULIN) sweet and sour

agrietarse |avrje'tarse| vr to crack; (piel) to chap

agrimensor, a |avrimen'sor, a| nm/f surveyor

agrio, a |'avrjo, a| adj bitter

agrupación |avrupa'θjon| nf group; (acto) grouping

agrupar |avru'par| vt to group

agua |'avwa| nf water; (NAUT) wake; (ARQ) slope of a roof; **~s** nfpl (de piedra) water sg, sparkle sg; (MED) water sg, urine sg; (NAUT) waters; **~s abajo/arriba** downstream/upstream; **~ bendita/destilada/potable** holy/ distilled/drinking water; **~ caliente** hot water; **~ corriente** running water; **~ de colonia** eau de cologne; **~ mineral (con/sin gas)** (carbonated/uncarbonated) mineral water; **~ oxigenada** hydrogen peroxide; **~s jurisdiccionales** territorial waters

aguacate |avwa'kate| nm avocado (pear)

aguacero |avwa'θero| nm (heavy) shower, downpour

aguado, a |a'vwaðo, a| adj watery, watered down

aguafiestas |avwa'fjestas| nm/f inv spoilsport, killjoy

aguanieve |avwa'njeße| nf sleet

aguantar |avwan'tar| vt to bear, put up with; (sostener) to hold up ♦ vi to last; **~se** vr to restrain o.s.; **aguante** nm (paciencia) patience; (resistencia) endurance

aguar |a'vwar| vt to water down

aguardar |avwar'ðar| vt to wait for

aguardiente |avwar'ðjente| nm brandy, liquor

aguarrás |avwa'rras| nm turpentine

agudeza |avu'ðeθa| nf sharpness; (ingenio) wit

agudizar |avuði'θar| vt (crisis) to make worse; **~se** vr to get worse

agudo, a |a'vuðo, a| adj sharp; (voz) high-pitched, piercing; (dolor, enfermedad) acute

agüero |a'vwero| nm: **buen/mal ~** good/bad omen

aguijón |avi'xon| nm sting; (fig) spur

águila |'avila| nf eagle; (fig) genius

aguileño, a |avi'leno, a| adj (nariz) aquiline; (rostro) sharp-featured

aguinaldo |avi'naldo| nm Christmas

box

aguja [a'vuxa] nf needle; (de reloj) hand; (ARQ) spire; (TEC) firing-pin; **~s** nfpl (ZOOL) ribs; (FERRO) points

agujerear [axuxere'ar] vt to make holes in

agujero [axu'xero] nm hole

agujetas [axu'xetas] nfpl stitch sg; (rigidez) stiffness sg

aguzar [axu'θar] vt to sharpen; (fig) to incite

ahí [a'i] adv there; **de ~ que** so that, with the result that; **~ llega** here he comes; **por ~** that way; (allá) over there; **por ~ 200 o** so **200 or so**

ahijado, a [ai'xaðo, a] nm/f godson/daughter

ahínco [a'inko] nm earnestness

ahogar [ao'xar] vt to drown; (asfixiar) to suffocate, smother; (fuego) to put out; **~se** vr (en el agua) to drown; (por asfixia) to suffocate

ahogo [a'oxo] nm breathlessness; (fig) financial difficulty

ahondar [aon'dar] vt to deepen, make deeper; (fig) to study thoroughly ♦ vi: **~ en** to study thoroughly

ahora [a'ora] adv now; (hace poco) a moment ago, just now; (dentro de poco) in a moment; **~ voy** I'm coming; **~ mismo** right now; **~ bien** now then; **por ~** for the present

ahorcar [aor'kar] vt to hang

ahorita [ao'rita] (fam: esp AM) adv right now

ahorrar [ao'rrar] vt (dinero) to save; (esfuerzos) to save, avoid; **ahorro** nm (acto) saving; **ahorros** nmpl (dinero) savings

ahuecar [awe'kar] vt to hollow (out); (voz) to deepen; **~se** vr to give o.s. airs

ahumar [au'mar] vt to smoke, cure; (llenar de humo) to fill with smoke ♦ vi to smoke; **~se** vr to fill with smoke

ahuyentar [aujen'tar] vt to drive off, frighten off; (fig) to dispel

airado, a [ai'raðo, a] adj angry

airar [ai'rar] vt to anger; **~se** vr to get angry

aire ['aire] nm air; (viento) wind; (corriente) draught; (MUS) tune; **~s** nmpl: **darse ~s** to give o.s. airs; **al ~ libre** in the open air; **~ acondicionado** air conditioning; **airearse** vr (persona) to go out for a breath of fresh air; **airoso, a** adj windy; draughty; (fig) graceful

aislado, a [ais'laðo, a] adj isolated; (incomunicado) cut-off; (ELEC) insulated

aislar [ais'lar] vt to isolate; (ELEC) to insulate

ajardinado, a [axarði'naðo, a] adj landscaped

ajedrez [axe'ðreθ] nm chess

ajeno, a [a'xeno, a] adj (que pertenece a otro) somebody else's; **~ a** foreign to

ajetreado, a [axetre'aðo, a] adj busy

ajetreo [axe'treo] nm bustle

ají [a'xi] (AM) nm chil(l)i, red pepper; (salsa) chil(l)i sauce

ajillo [a'xiλo] nm: **gambas al ~** garlic prawns

ajo ['axo] nm garlic

ajuar [a'xwar] nm household furnishings pl; (de novia) trousseau; (de niño) layette

ajustado, a [axus'taðo, a] adj (tornillo) tight; (cálculo) right; (ropa) tight(-fitting); (resultado) close

ajustar [axus'tar] vt (adaptar) to adjust; (encajar) to fit; (TEC) to engage; (IMPRENTA) to make up; (apretar) to tighten; (concertar) to agree (on); (reconciliar) to reconcile; (cuentas, deudas) to settle ♦ vi to fit; **~se** vr: **~se a** (precio etc) to be in keeping with, fit in with; **~ las cuentas a uno** to get even with sb

ajuste [a'xuste] nm adjustment; (COSTURA) fitting; (acuerdo) compromise; (de cuenta) settlement

al [al] (= **a + el**) ver **a**

ala ['ala] nf wing; (de sombrero) brim; (futbolista) winger; **~ delta** hang-glider

alabanza [ala'ßanθa] nf praise

alabar [ala'ßar] vt to praise

alacena [ala'θena] nf kitchen cupboard (BRIT), kitchen closet (US)

alacrán [ala'kran] nm scorpion

alambique [alam'bike] nm still

alambrada [alam'braða] nf wire fence; (red) wire netting

alambrado [alam'braðo] nm = **alambrada**

alambre [a'lambre] nm wire; ~ **de púas** barbed wire

alameda [ala'meða] nf (plantío) poplar grove; (lugar de paseo) avenue, boulevard

álamo ['alamo] nm poplar; ~ **temblón** aspen

alarde [a'larðe] nm show, display; **hacer ~ de** to boast of

alargador [alarɣa'ðor] nm (ELEC.) extension lead

alargar [alar'ɣar] vt to lengthen, extend; (paso) to hasten; (brazo) to stretch out; (cuerda) to pay out; (conversación) to spin out; ~**se** vr to get longer

alarido [ala'riðo] nm shriek

alarma [a'larma] nf alarm

alarmar vt to alarm; ~**se** to get alarmed; **alarmante** [alar'mante] adj alarming

alba ['alßa] nf dawn

albacea [alßa'θea] nm/f executor/executrix

albahaca [al'ßaka] nf basil

Albania [al'ßanja] nf Albania

albañil [alßa'ɲil] nm bricklayer; (cantero) mason

albarán [alßa'ran] nm (COM) delivery note, invoice

albaricoque [alßari'koke] nm apricot

albedrío [alße'ðrio] nm: **libre ~** free will

alberca [al'ßerka] nf reservoir; (AM) swimming pool

albergar [alßer'ßar] vt to shelter

albergue etc [al'ßerɣe] vb ver **albergar** ♦ nm shelter, refuge; **~ juvenil** youth hostel

albóndiga [al'ßondiɣa] nf meatball

albornoz [alßor'noθ] nm (de los árabes) burnous; (para el baño) bathrobe

alborotar [alßoro'tar] vi to make a row ♦ vt to agitate, stir up; ~**se** vr to get excited; (mar) to get rough; **alboroto** nm row, uproar

alborozar [alßoro'θar] vt to gladden; ~**se** vr to rejoice

alborozo [alßo'roθo] nm joy

álbum ['alßum] (pl ~**s**, ~**es**) nm album; **~ de recortes** scrapbook

alcachofa [alka'tʃofa] nf artichoke

alcalde, esa [al'kalde, esa] nm/f mayor(ess)

alcaldía [alkal'dia] nf mayoralty; (lugar) mayor's office

alcance etc [al'kanθe] vb ver **alcanzar** ♦ nm reach; (COM) adverse balance

alcantarilla [alkanta'riʎa] nf (de aguas cloacales) sewer; (en la calle) gutter

alcanzar [alkan'θar] vt (algo: con la mano, el pie) to reach; (alguien: en el camino etc) to catch up (with); (autobús) to catch; (suj: bala) to strike ♦ vi (ser suficiente) to be enough; **~ a hacer** to manage to do

alcaparra [alka'parra] nf caper

alcayata [alka'jata] nf hook

alcázar [al'kaθar] nm fortress; (NAUT) quarter-deck

alcoba [al'koßa] nf bedroom

alcohol [al'kol] nm alcohol; **~ metílico** methylated spirits pl (BRIT), wood alcohol (US); **alcohólico, a** adj, nm/f alcoholic

alcoholímetro [alko'limetro] nm Breathalyser ® (BRIT), drunkometer (US)

alcoholismo [alko'lismo] nm alcoholism

alcornoque [alkor'noke] nm cork tree; (fam) idiot

alcurnia [al'kurnja] *nf* lineage
aldaba [al'daβa] *nf* (door) knocker
aldea [al'dea] *nf* village; **~no, a** *adj* village *cpd* ♦ *nm/f* villager
aleación [alea'θjon] *nf* alloy
aleatorio, a [alea'torjo, a] *adj* random
aleccionar [alekθjo'nar] *vt* to instruct; (*adiestrar*) to train
alegación [aleɣa'θjon] *nf* allegation
alegar [ale'ɣar] *vt* to claim; (*JUR*) to plead ♦ *vi* (*AM*) to argue
alegato [ale'ɣato] *nm* (*JUR*) allegation; (*AM*) argument
alegoría [aleɣo'ria] *nf* allegory
alegrar [ale'ɣrar] *vt* (*causar alegría*) to cheer (up); (*fuego*) to poke; (*fiesta*) to liven up; **~se** *vr* (*fam*) to get merry o tight; **~se de** to be glad about
alegre [a'leɣre] *adj* happy, cheerful; (*fam*) merry, tight; (*chiste*) risqué, blue; **alegría** *nf* happiness; merriment
alejamiento [alexa'mjento] *nm* removal; (*distancia*) remoteness
alejar [ale'xar] *vt* to remove; (*fig*) to estrange; **~se** *vr* to move away
alemán, ana [ale'man, ana] *adj*, *nm/f* German ♦ *nm* (*LING*) German
Alemania [ale'manja] *nf*:
~ Occidental West Germany
alentador, a [alenta'ðor, a] *adj* encouraging
alentar [alen'tar] *vt* to encourage
alergia [a'lerxja] *nf* allergy
alero [a'lero] *nm* (*de tejado*) eaves *pl*; (*de carruaje*) mudguard
alerta [a'lerta] *adj*, *nm* alert
aleta [a'leta] *nf* (*de pez*) fin; (*de ave*) wing; (*de foca*, *DEPORTE*) flipper; (*AUTO*) mudguard
aletargar [aletar'ɣar] *vt* to make drowsy; (*entumecer*) to make numb; **~se** *vr* to grow drowsy; to become numb
aletear [alete'ar] *vi* to flutter
alevín [ale'βin] *nm* fry, young fish
alevosía [aleβo'sia] *nf* treachery
alfabeto [alfa'βeto] *nm* alphabet

alfalfa [al'falfa] *nf* alfalfa, lucerne
alfarería [alfare'ria] *nf* pottery; (*tienda*) pottery shop; **alfarero, a** *nm/f* potter
alféizar [al'feiθar] *nm* window-sill
alférez [al'fereθ] *nm* (*MIL*) second lieutenant; (*NAUT*) ensign
alfil [al'fil] *nm* (*AJEDREZ*) bishop
alfiler [alfi'ler] *nm* pin; (*broche*) clip
alfiletero [alfile'tero] *nm* needlecase
alfombra [al'fombra] *nf* carpet; (*más pequeña*) rug; **alfombrar** *vt* to carpet; **alfombrilla** *nf* rug, mat; (*INFORM*) mouse mat o pad
alforja [al'forxa] *nf* saddlebag
algarabía [alɣara'βia] (*fam*) *nf* gibberish; (*griterío*) hullabaloo
algas [alɣas] *nfpl* seaweed
álgebra [al'xeβra] *nf* algebra
álgido, a [al'xiðo, a] *adj* (*momento etc*) crucial, decisive
algo [al'ɣo] *pron* something; anything ♦ *adv* somewhat, rather; **¿~ más?** anything else?; (*en tienda*) is that all?; **por ~ será** there must be some reason for it
algodón [alɣo'ðon] *nm* cotton; (*planta*) cotton plant; **~ de azúcar** candy floss (*BRIT*), cotton candy (*US*); **~ hidrófilo** cotton wool (*BRIT*), absorbent cotton (*US*)
algodonero, a [alɣoðo'nero, a] *adj* cotton *cpd* ♦ *nm/f* cotton grower ♦ *nm* cotton plant
alguacil [alɣwa'θil] *nm* bailiff; (*TAUR*) mounted official
alguien [al'ɣjen] *pron* someone, somebody; (*en frases interrogativas*) anyone, anybody
alguno, a [al'ɣuno, a] *adj* (*delante de nm*: **algún**) some; (*después de n*): **no tiene talento ~** he has no talent, he doesn't have any talent ♦ *pron* (*alguien*) someone, somebody; **algún que otro libro** some book or other; **algún día iré** I'll go one o some day; **sin interés ~** without the slightest interest; **~ que otro** an occasional

one; **~s piensan** some (people) think

alhaja [a'laxa] nf jewel; (tesoro) precious object, treasure

alhelí [ale'li] nm wallflower, stock

aliado, a [a'ljaðo, a] adj allied

alianza [a'ljanθa] nf alliance; (anillo) wedding ring

aliar [a'ljar] vt to ally; **~se** vr to form an alliance

alias ['aljas] adv alias

alicates [ali'kates] nmpl pliers; **~ de uñas** nail clippers

aliciente [ali'θjente] nm incentive; (atracción) attraction

alienación [aljena'θjon] nf alienation

aliento [a'ljento] nm breath; (respiración) breathing; **sin ~** breathless

aligerar [alixe'rar] vt to lighten; (reducir) to shorten; (aliviar) to alleviate; (mitigar) to ease; (paso) to quicken

alijo [a'lixo] nm consignment

alimaña [ali'maɲa] nf pest

alimentación [alimenta'θjon] nf (comida) food; (acción) feeding; (tienda) grocer's (shop); **alimentador** nm: **alimentador de papel** sheet-feeder

alimentar [alimen'tar] vt to feed; (nutrir) to nourish; **~se** vr to feed

alimenticio, a [alimen'tiθjo, a] adj food cpd; (nutritivo) nourishing, nutritious

alimento [ali'mento] nm food; (nutrición) nourishment

alineación [alinea'θjon] nf alignment; (DEPORTE) line-up

alinear [aline'ar] vt to align; **~se** vr (DEPORTE) to line up; **~se en** to fall in with

aliñar [ali'ɲar] vt (CULIN) to season; **aliño** nm dressing

alioli [ali'oli] nm garlic mayonnaise

alisar [ali'sar] vt to smooth

aliso [a'liso] nm alder

alistarse [alis'tarse] vr to enlist; (inscribirse) to enrol

aliviar [ali'βjar] vt (carga) to lighten; (persona) to relieve; (dolor) to relieve, alleviate

alivio [a'liβjo] nm alleviation, relief

aljibe [al'xiβe] nm cistern

allá [a'ʎa] adv (lugar) there; (por ahí) over there; (tiempo) then; **~ abajo** down there; **más ~** further on; **más ~ de** beyond; **¡~ tú!** that's your problem!

allanamiento [aʎana'mjento] nm: **~ de morada** burglary

allanar [aʎa'nar] vt to flatten, level (out); (igualar) to smooth (out); (fig) to subdue; (JUR) to burgle, break into

allegado, a [aʎe'ɣaðo, a] adj near, close ♦ nm/f relation

allí [a'ʎi] adv there; **~ mismo** right there; **por ~** over there; (por ese camino) that way

alma ['alma] nf soul; (persona) person

almacén [alma'θen] nm (depósito) warehouse, store; (MIL) magazine; (AM) shop; **(grandes) almacenes** nmpl department store sg; **almacenaje** nm storage

almacenar [almaθe'nar] vt to store, put in storage; (proveerse) to stock up with; **almacenero** nm (AM) shopkeeper

almanaque [alma'nake] nm almanac

almeja [al'mexa] nf clam

almendra [al'mendra] nf almond; **almendro** nm almond tree

almíbar [al'miβar] nm syrup

almidón [almi'ðon] nm starch; **almidonar** vt to starch

almirante [almi'rante] nm admiral

almirez [almi'reθ] nm mortar

almizcle [al'miθkle] nm musk

almohada [almo'aða] nf pillow; (funda) pillowcase; **almohadilla** nf cushion; (TEC) pad; (AM) pincushion

almohadón [almoa'ðon] nm large pillow; bolster

almorranas [almo'rranas] nfpl piles, haemorrhoids

almorzar [almor'θar] vt: ~ **una tortilla** to have an omelette for lunch ♦ vi to (have) lunch

almuerzo etc [al'mwerθo] vb ver **almorzar** ♦ nm lunch

alocado, a [alo'kaðo, a] adj crazy

alojamiento [aloxa'mjento] nm lodging(s) (pl); (viviendas) housing

alojar [alo'xar] vt to lodge; ~**se** vr to lodge, stay

alondra [a'londra] nf lark, skylark

alpargata [alpar'γata] nf rope-soled sandal, espadrille

Alpes ['alpes] nmpl: **los** ~ the Alps

alpinismo [alpi'nismo] nm mountaineering, climbing; **alpinista** nm/f mountaineer, climber

alpiste [al'piste] nm birdseed

alquilar [alki'lar] vt (suj: propietario: inmuebles) to let, rent (out); (: coche) to hire out; (: TV) to rent (out); (suj: alquilador: inmuebles, TV) to rent; (: coche) to hire; "**se alquila casa**" "house to let (BRIT) o for rent (US)"

alquiler [alki'ler] nm renting; letting; hiring; (arriendo) rent; hire charge; ~ **de automóviles** car hire; **de** ~ for hire

alquimia [al'kimja] nf alchemy

alquitrán [alki'tran] nm tar

alrededor [alreðe'ðor] adv around, about; ~ **de** around; about; **mirar a su** ~ to look (round) about one; ~**es** nmpl surroundings

alta ['alta] nf (certificate of) discharge; **dar de** ~ to discharge

altanería [altane'ria] nf haughtiness, arrogance; **altanero, a** adj arrogant, haughty

altar [al'tar] nm altar

altavoz [alta'βoθ] nm loudspeaker; (amplificador) amplifier

alteración [altera'θjon] nf alteration; (alboroto) disturbance

alterar [alte'rar] vt to alter; to disturb; ~**se** vr (persona) to get upset

altercado [alter'kaðo] nm argument

alternar [alter'nar] vt to alternate ♦ vi to alternate; (turnar) to take turns; ~**se** vr to alternate; to take turns; ~ **con** to mix with; **alternativa** nf alternative; (elección) choice; **alternativo, a** adj alternative; (alterno) alternating; **alterno, a** adj alternate; (ELEC) alternating

Alteza [al'teθa] nf (tratamiento) Highness

altibajos [alti'βaxos] nmpl ups and downs

altiplanicie [altipla'niθje] nf high plateau

altiplano [alti'plano] nm = **altiplanicie**

altisonante [altiso'nante] adj high-flown, high-sounding

altitud [alti'tuð] nf height; (AVIAT, GEO) altitude

altivez [alti'βeθ] nf haughtiness, arrogance; **altivo, a** adj haughty, arrogant

alto, a ['alto, a] adj high; (persona) tall; (sonido) high, sharp; (noble) high, lofty ♦ nm halt; (MUS) alto; (GEO) hill; (AM) pile ♦ adv (de sitio) high; (de sonido) loud, loudly ♦ excl halt!; **la pared tiene 2 metros de** ~ the wall is 2 metres high; **en alta mar** on the high seas; **en voz alta** in a loud voice; **las altas horas de la noche** the small o wee hours; **en lo** ~ **de** at the top of; **pasar por** ~ to overlook

altoparlante [altopar'lante] (AM) nm loudspeaker

altruismo [altru'ismo] nm altruism

altura [al'tura] nf height; (NAUT) depth; (GEO) latitude; **la pared tiene 1.80 de** ~ the wall is 1 metre 80cm high; **a estas** ~**s** at this point; **a estas** ~**s del año** at this time of the year

alubia [a'luβja] nf bean

alucinación [aluθina'θjon] nf hallucination

alucinar [aluθi'nar] vi to hallucinate ♦ vt to deceive; (fascinar) to fascinate

alud [a'luð] nm avalanche; (fig) flood

aludir [alu'ðir] vi: ~ a to allude to; **darse por aludido** to take the hint

alumbrado [alum'braðo] nm lighting; **alumbramiento** nm lighting; (MED) childbirth, delivery

alumbrar [alum'brar] vt to light (up) ♦ vi (MED) to give birth

aluminio [alu'minjo] nm aluminium (BRIT), aluminum (US)

alumno, a [a'lumno, a] nm/f pupil, student

alunizar [aluni'θar] vi to land on the moon

alusión [alu'sjon] nf allusion

alusivo, a [alu'siβo, a] adj allusive

aluvión [aluβ'jon] nm alluvium; (fig) flood

alverja [al'βerxa] (AM) nf pea

alza [al'θa] nf rise; (MIL) sight

alzada [al'θaða] nf (de caballos) height; (JUR) appeal

alzamiento [alθa'mjento] nm (rebelión) rising

alzar [al'θar] vt to lift (up); (precio, muro) to raise; (cuello de abrigo) to turn up; (AGR) to gather in; (IMPRENTA) to gather; ~se vr to get up, rise; (rebelarse) to revolt; (COM) to go fraudulently bankrupt; (JUR) to appeal

ama ['ama] nf lady of the house; (dueña) owner; (institutriz) governess; (madre adoptiva) foster mother; ~ de casa housewife; ~ de llaves housekeeper

amabilidad [amaβili'ðað] nf kindness; (simpatía) niceness; **amable** adj kind; nice; **es usted muy amable** that's very kind of you

amaestrado, a [amaes'traðo, a] adj (animal: en circo etc) performing

amaestrar [amaes'trar] vt to train

amago [a'maɣo] nm threat; (gesto) threatening gesture; (MED) symptom

amainar [amai'nar] vi (viento) to die down

amalgama [amal'ɣama] nf amalgam;

amalgamar vt to amalgamate; (combinar) to combine, mix

amamantar [amaman'tar] vt to suckle, nurse

amanecer [amane'θer] vi to dawn ♦ nm dawn; ~ afiebrado to wake up with a fever

amanerado, a [amane'raðo, a] adj affected

amansar [aman'sar] vt to tame; (persona) to subdue; ~se vr (persona) to calm down

amante [a'mante] adj: ~ de fond of ♦ nm/f lover

amapola [ama'pola] nf poppy

amar [a'mar] vt to love

amargado, a [amar'ɣaðo, a] adj bitter

amargar [amar'ɣar] vt to make bitter; (fig) to embitter; ~se vr to become embittered

amargo, a [a'marɣo, a] adj bitter; **amargura** nf bitterness

amarillento, a [amari'ʎento, a] adj yellowish; (tez) sallow; **amarillo, a** adj, nm yellow

amarrar [ama'rrar] vt to moor; (sujetar) to tie up

amarras [a'marras] nfpl: **soltar ~** to set sail

amasar [ama'sar] vt (masa) to knead; (mezclar) to mix, prepare; (confeccionar) to concoct; **amasijo** nm kneading; mixing; (fig) hotchpotch

amateur ['amatur] nm/f amateur

amazona [ama'θona] nf horsewoman; **A~s** nm: **el A~s** the Amazon

ambages [am'baxes] nmpl: **sin ~** in plain language

ámbar ['ambar] nm amber

ambición [ambi'θjon] nf ambition; **ambicionar** vt to aspire to; **ambicioso, a** adj ambitious

ambidextro, a [ambi'ðekstro, a] adj ambidextrous

ambientación [ambjenta'θjon] nf (CINE, TEATRO etc) setting; (RADIO) sound effects

ambiente [am'bjente] nm (tb fig) atmosphere; (medio) environment

ambigüedad [ambiγwe'ðað] nf ambiguity; **ambiguo, a** adj ambiguous

ámbito ['ambito] nm (campo) field; (fig) scope

ambos, as ['ambos, as] adj pl, pron pl both

ambulancia [ambu'lanθja] nf ambulance

ambulante [ambu'lante] adj travelling cpd, itinerant

ambulatorio [ambula'torjo] nm state health-service clinic

amedrentar [ameðren'tar] vt to scare

amén [a'men] excl amen; **~ de** besides

amenaza [ame'naθa] nf threat

amenazar [amena'θar] vt to threaten
♦ vi: **~ con hacer** to threaten to do

amenidad [ameni'ðað] nf pleasantness

ameno, a [a'meno, a] adj pleasant

América [a'merika] nf America; **~ del Norte/del Sur** North/South America; **~ Central/Latina** Central/Latin America; **americana** nf coat, jacket; ver tb **americano; americano, a** adj, nm/f American

amerizar [ameri'θar] vi (avión) to land (on the sea)

ametralladora [ametraʎa'ðora] nf machine gun

amianto [a'mjanto] nm asbestos

amigable [ami'γaβle] adj friendly

amígdala [a'miγðala] nf tonsil; **amigdalitis** nf tonsillitis

amigo, a [a'miγo, a] adj friendly
♦ nm/f friend; (amante) lover; **ser ~ de algo** to be fond of sth; **ser muy ~s** to be close friends

amilanar [amila'nar] vt to scare; **~se** vr to get scared

aminorar [amino'rar] vt to diminish; (reducir) to reduce; **~ la marcha** to slow down

amistad [amis'tað] nf friendship; **~es** nfpl (amigos) friends; **amistoso, a** adj friendly

amnesia [am'nesja] nf amnesia

amnistía [amnis'tia] nf amnesty

amo [a'mo] nm owner; (jefe) boss

amodorrarse [amoðo'rrarse] vr to get sleepy

amoldar [amol'dar] vt to mould; (adaptar) to adapt

amonestación [amonesta'θjon] nf warning; **amonestaciones** nfpl (REL) marriage banns

amonestar [amones'tar] vt to warn; (REL) to publish the banns of

amontonar [amonto'nar] vt to collect, pile up; **~se** vr to crowd together; (acumularse) to pile up

amor [a'mor] nm love; (amante) lover; **hacer el ~** to make love; **~ propio** self-respect

amoratado, a [amora'taðo, a] adj purple

amordazar [amorða'θar] vt to muzzle; (fig) to gag

amorfo, a [a'morfo, a] adj amorphous, shapeless

amoroso, a [amo'roso, a] adj affectionate, loving

amortajar [amorta'xar] vt to shroud

amortiguador [amortiγwa'ðor] nm shock absorber; (parachoques) bumper; **~es** nmpl (AUTO) suspension sg

amortiguar [amorti'γwar] vt to deaden; (ruido) to muffle; (color) to soften

amortización [amortiθa'θjon] nf (de deuda) repayment; (de bono) redemption

amotinar [amoti'nar] vt to stir up, incite (to riot); **~se** vr to mutiny

amparar [ampa'rar] vt to protect; **~se** vr to seek protection; (de la lluvia etc) to shelter; **amparo** nm help, protection; **al amparo de** under the protection of

amperio [am'perjo] nm ampère, amp

ampliación [amplja'θjon] nf enlargement; (extensión) extension

ampliar [am'pljar] vt to enlarge; to extend

amplificación [amplifika'θjon] nf enlargement; **amplificador** nm amplifier

amplificar [amplifi'kar] vt to amplify

amplio, a ['ampljo, a] adj spacious; (de falda etc) full; (extenso) extensive; (ancho) wide; **amplitud** nf spaciousness; extent; (fig) amplitude

ampolla [am'poʎa] nf blister; (MED) ampoule

ampuloso, a [ampu'loso, a] adj bombastic, pompous

amputar [ampu'tar] vt to cut off, amputate

amueblar [amwe'βlar] vt to furnish

amurallar [amura'ʎar] vt to wall up o in

anacronismo [anakro'nismo] nm anachronism

anales [a'nales] nmpl annals

analfabetismo [analfaβe'tismo] nm illiteracy; **analfabeto, a** adj, nm/f illiterate

analgésico [anal'xesiko] nm painkiller, analgesic

análisis [a'nalisis] nm inv analysis

analista [ana'lista] nm/f (gen) analyst

analizar [anali'θar] vt to analyse

analogía [analo'xia] nf analogy

analógico, a [ana'loxiko, a] adj (INFORM) analog; (reloj) analogue (BRIT), analog (US)

análogo, a [a'naloɣo, a] adj analogous, similar

ananá(s) [ana'na(s)] (AM) nm pineapple

anaquel [ana'kel] nm shelf

anarquía [anar'kia] nf anarchy; **anarquismo** nm anarchism; **anarquista** nm/f anarchist

anatomía [anato'mia] nf anatomy

anca ['aŋka] nf rump, haunch; **~s** nfpl (fam) behind sg

ancho, a ['antʃo, a] adj wide; (falda) full; (fig) liberal ♦ nm width; (FERRO)

gauge; **ponerse ~** to get conceited; **estar a sus anchas** to be at one's ease

anchoa [an'tʃoa] nf anchovy

anchura [an'tʃura] nf width; (extensión) wideness

anciano, a [an'θjano, a] adj old, aged ♦ nm/f old man/woman; elder

ancla ['aŋkla] nf anchor; **~dero** nm anchorage; **anclar** vi to (drop) anchor

andadura [anda'ðura] nf gait; (de caballo) pace

Andalucía [andalu'θia] nf Andalusia; **andaluz, a** adj, nm/f Andalusian

andamiaje [anda'mjaxe] nm = andamio

andamio [an'damjo] nm scaffold(ing)

andar [an'dar] vt to go, cover, travel ♦ vi to go, walk, travel; (funcionar) to go, work; (estar) to be ♦ nm walk, gait, pace; **~se** vr to go away; **~ a pie/a caballo/en bicicleta** to go on foot/ on horseback/by bicycle; **~ haciendo algo** to be doing sth; **¡anda!** (sorpresa) go on!; **anda por o en los 40** he's about 40

andén [an'den] nm (FERRO) platform; (NAUT) quayside; (AM: de la calle) pavement (BRIT), sidewalk (US)

Andes ['andes] nmpl: **los ~** the Andes

Andorra [an'dorra] nf Andorra

andrajo [an'draxo] nm rag; **~so, a** adj ragged

anduve etc [an'duβe] vb ver **andar**

anécdota [a'nekðota] nf anecdote, story

anegar [ane'ɣar] vt to flood; (ahogar) to drown; **~se** vr to drown; (hundirse) to sink

anejo, a [a'nexo, a] adj, nm = anexo

anemia [a'nemja] nf anaemia

anestesia [anes'tesja] nf (sustancia) anaesthetic; (proceso) anaesthesia

anexar [anek'sar] vt to annex; (documento) to attach; **anexión** nf annexation; **anexionamiento** nm annexation; **anexo, a** adj attached

♦ *nm* annexe

anfibio, a [an'fiβjo, a] *adj* amphibious
♦ *nm* amphibian

anfiteatro [anfite'atro] *nm*
amphitheatre; (TEATRO) dress circle

anfitrión, ona [anfi'trjon, ona] *nm/f*
host(ess)

ángel ['anxel] *nm* angel; ~ **de
la guarda** guardian angel; **tener** ~ to be
charming; **angelical** *adj*, **angélico, a**
adj angelic(al)

angina [an'xina] *nf* (MED)
inflammation of the throat; ~ **de
pecho** angina; **tener** ~**s** to have
tonsillitis

anglicano, a [angli'kano, a] *adj, nm/f*
Anglican

anglosajón, ona [anglosa'xon, ona]
adj Anglo-Saxon

angosto, a [an'gosto, a] *adj* narrow

anguila [an'gila] *nf* eel

angula [an'gula] *nf* elver, baby eel

ángulo ['angulo] *nm* angle; (esquina)
corner; (curva) bend

angustia [an'gustja] *nf* anguish;
angustiar *vt* to distress, grieve

anhelar [ane'lar] *vt* to be eager for;
(desear) to long for, desire ♦ *vi* to pant,
gasp; **anhelo** *nm* eagerness; desire

anidar [ani'ðar] *vi* to nest

anillo [a'niʎo] *nm* ring; ~ **de boda**
wedding ring

animación [anima'θjon] *nf* liveliness;
(vitalidad) life; (actividad) activity;
bustle

animado, a [ani'maðo, a] *adj* lively;
(vivaz) animated; **animador, a** *nm/f*
(TV) host(ess), compère; (DEPORTE)
cheerleader

animadversión [animaðßer'sjon] *nf*
ill-will, antagonism

animal [ani'mal] *adj* animal; (fig)
stupid ♦ *nm* animal; (fig) fool; (bestia)
brute

animar [ani'mar] *vt* to animate,
give life to; (fig) to liven up, brighten
up, cheer up; (estimular) to stimulate;

~**se** *vr* to cheer up; to feel encouraged;
(decidirse) to make up one's mind

ánimo ['animo] *nm* (alma) soul;
(mente) mind; (valentía) courage ♦ *excl*
cheer up!

animoso, a [ani'moso, a] *adj* brave;
(vivo) lively

aniquilar [aniki'lar] *vt* to annihilate,
destroy

anís [a'nis] *nm* aniseed; (licor) anisette

aniversario [anißer'sarjo] *nm*
anniversary

anoche [a'notʃe] *adv* last night; **antes
de** ~ the night before last

anochecer [anotʃe'θer] *vi* to get dark
♦ *nm* nightfall, dark; **al** ~ at nightfall

anodino, a [ano'ðino, a] *adj* dull,
anodyne

anomalía [anoma'lia] *nf* anomaly

anonadado, a [anona'ðaðo, a] *adj*:
estar/quedar/sentirse ~ to be
overwhelmed o amazed

anonimato [anoni'mato] *nm*
anonymity

anónimo, a [a'nonimo, a] *adj*
anonymous; (COM) limited ♦ *nm* (carta)
anonymous letter; (: maliciosa) poison-
pen letter

anormal [anor'mal] *adj* abnormal

anotación [anota'θjon] *nf* note;
annotation

anotar [ano'tar] *vt* to note down;
(comentar) to annotate

anquilosamiento [ankilosa'mjento]
nm (fig) paralysis; stagnation

anquilosarse [ankilo'sarse] *vr* (fig:
persona) to get out of touch; (método,
costumbres) to go out of date

ansia ['ansja] *nf* anxiety; (añoranza)
yearning; **ansiar** *vt* to long for

ansiedad [ansje'ðað] *nf* anxiety

ansioso, a [an'sjoso, a] *adj* anxious;
(anhelante) eager; **de** o **por algo**
greedy for sth

antagónico, a [anta'yoniko, a] *adj*
antagonistic; (opuesto) contrasting;
antagonista *nm/f* antagonist

antaño [an'taɲo] *adv* long ago, formerly

Antártico [an'tartiko] *nm*: **el ~** the Antarctic

ante ['ante] *prep* before, in the presence of; (*problema etc*) faced with ♦ *nm* (*piel*) suede; **~ todo** above all

anteanoche [antea'notʃe] *adv* the night before last

anteayer [antea'jer] *adv* the day before yesterday

antebrazo [ante'ßraθo] *nm* forearm

antecedente [anteθe'ðente] *adj* previous ♦ *nm* antecedent; **~s** *nmpl* (*JUR*): **~s penales** criminal record; (*procedencia*) background

anteceder [anteθe'ðer] *vt* to precede, go before

antecesor, a [anteθe'sor, a] *nm/f* predecessor

antedicho, a [ante'ðitʃo, a] *adj* aforementioned

antelación [antela'θjon] *nf*: **con ~** in advance

antemano [ante'mano]: **de ~** *adv* beforehand, in advance

antena [an'tena] *nf* antenna; (*de televisión etc*) aerial; **~ parabólica** satellite dish

anteojo [ante'oxo] *nm* eyeglass; **~s** *nmpl* (*AM*) glasses, spectacles

antepasados [antepa'saðos] *nmpl* ancestors

anteponer [antepo'ner] *vt* to place in front; (*fig*) to prefer

anteproyecto [antepro'jekto] *nm* preliminary sketch; (*fig*) blueprint

anterior [ante'rjor] *adj* preceding, previous; **~idad** *nf*: **con ~idad a** prior to, before

antes ['antes] *adv* (*con prioridad*) before ♦ *prep*: **~ de** before ♦ *conj*: **~ de ir/de que te vayas** before going/before you go; **~ bien** (but) rather; **dos días ~** two days before o previously; **no quiso venir ~** she didn't want to come any earlier; **tomo**

el avión ~ que el barco I take the plane rather than the boat; **~ que yo** before me; **lo ~ posible** as soon as possible; **cuanto ~ mejor** the sooner the better

antiaéreo, a [antia'ereo, a] *adj* anti-aircraft

antibalas [anti'ßalas] *adj inv*: **chaleco ~** bullet-proof jacket

antibiótico [anti'ßjotiko] *nm* antibiotic

anticipación [antiθipa'θjon] *nf* anticipation; **con 10 minutos de ~** 10 minutes early

anticipado, a [antiθi'paðo, a] *adj* (*pago*) advance; **por ~** in advance

anticipar [antiθi'par] *vt* to anticipate; (*adelantar*) to bring forward; (*COM*) to advance; **~se** *vr*: **~se a su época** to be ahead of one's time

anticipo [anti'θipo] *nm* (*COM*) advance

anticonceptivo, a [antikonθep'tißo, a] *adj, nm* contraceptive

anticongelante [antikonxe'lante] *nm* antifreeze

anticuado, a [anti'kwaðo, a] *adj* out-of-date, old-fashioned; (*desusado*) obsolete

anticuario [anti'kwarjo] *nm* antique dealer

anticuerpo [anti'kwerpo] *nm* (*MED*) antibody

antidepresivo [antiðepre'sißo] *nm* antidepressant

antídoto [an'tiðoto] *nm* antidote

antiestético, a [anties'tetiko, a] *adj* unsightly

antifaz [anti'faθ] *nm* mask; (*velo*) veil

antigualla [anti'ɣwaʎa] *nf* antique; (*reliquia*) relic

antiguamente [antiɣwa'mente] *adv* formerly; (*hace mucho tiempo*) long ago

antigüedad [antiɣwe'ðað] *nf* antiquity; (*artículo*) antique; (*rango*) seniority

antiguo, a [an'tiɣwo, a] *adj* old,

ancient; (que fue) former

Antillas [an'tiʎas] nfpl: **las ~** the West Indies

antílope [an'tilope] nm antelope

antinatural [antinatu'ral] adj unnatural

antipatía [antipa'tia] nf antipathy, dislike; **antipático, a** adj disagreeable, unpleasant

antirrobo [anti'rroβo] adj inv (alarma etc) anti-theft

antisemita [antise'mita] adj anti-Semitic ♦ nm/f anti-Semite

antiséptico, a [anti'septiko, a] adj antiseptic ♦ nm antiseptic

antítesis [an'titesis] nf inv antithesis

antojadizo, a [antoxa'ðiθo, a] adj capricious

antojarse [anto'xarse] vr (desear): **se me antoja comprarlo** I have a mind to buy it; (pensar): **se me antoja que** I have a feeling that

antojo [an'toxo] nm caprice, whim; (rosa) birthmark; (lunar) mole

antología [antolo'xia] nf anthology

antorcha [an'tortʃa] nf torch

antro ['antro] nm cavern

antropófago, a [antro'pofaɣo, a] adj, nm/f cannibal

antropología [antropolo'xia] nf anthropology

anual [a'nwal] adj annual

anuario [a'nwarjo] nm yearbook

anudar [anu'ðar] vt to knot, tie; (unir) to join; **~se** vr to get tied up

anulación [anula'θjon] nf annulment; (cancelación) cancellation

anular [anu'lar] vt (contrato) to annul, cancel; (ley) to revoke, repeal; (suscripción) to cancel ♦ nm ring finger

Anunciación [anunθja'θjon] nf (REL) Annunciation

anunciante [anun'θjante] nm/f (COM) advertiser

anunciar [anun'θjar] vt to announce; (proclamar) to proclaim; (COM) to advertise

anuncio [a'nunθjo] nm announcement; (señal) sign; (COM) advertisement; (cartel) poster

anzuelo [an'θwelo] nm hook; (para pescar) fish hook

añadidura [aɲaði'ðura] nf addition, extra; **por ~** besides, in addition

añadir [aɲa'ðir] vt to add

añejo, a [a'ɲexo, a] adj old; (vino) mellow

añicos [a'ɲikos] nmpl: **hacer ~** to smash, shatter

añil [a'ɲil] nm (BOT, color) indigo

año ['aɲo] nm year; **¡Feliz A~ Nuevo!** Happy New Year; **tener 15 ~s** to be 15 (years old); **los ~s 90** the nineties; **~ bisiesto/escolar** leap/school year; **el ~ que viene** next year

añoranza [aɲo'ranθa] nf nostalgia; (anhelo) longing

apabullar [apaβu'ʎar] vt (tb fig) to crush, squash

apacentar [apaθen'tar] vt to pasture, graze

apacible [apa'θiβle] adj gentle, mild

apaciguar [apaθi'ɣwar] vt to pacify, calm (down)

apadrinar [apaðri'nar] vt to sponsor, support; (REL) to be godfather to

apagado, a [apa'ɣaðo, a] adj (volcán) extinct; (color) dull; (voz) quiet; (sonido) muted, muffled; (persona: apático) listless; **estar ~** (fuego, luz) to be out; (RADIO, TV etc) to be off

apagar [apa'ɣar] vt to put out; (ELEC, RADIO, TV) to turn off; (sonido) to silence, muffle; (sed) to quench

apagón [apa'ɣon] nm blackout; power cut

apalabrar [apala'βrar] vt to agree to; (contratar) to engage

apalear [apale'ar] vt to beat, thrash

apañar [apa'ɲar] vt to pick up; (asir) to take hold of, grasp; (reparar) to mend, patch up; **~se** vr to manage, get along

aparador [apara'ðor] nm sideboard; (AM: escaparate) shop window

aparato [apaˈrato] nm apparatus; (máquina) machine; (doméstico) appliance; (boato) ostentation; **de facsímil** facsimile (machine), fax; **~ digestivo** (ANAT) digestive system; **~so, a** adj showy, ostentatious

aparcamiento [aparkaˈmjento] nm car park (BRIT), parking lot (US)

aparcar [aparˈkar] vt, vi to park

aparear [apareˈar] vt (objetos) to pair, match; (animales) to mate; **~se** vr to make a pair; to mate

aparecer [apareˈθer] vi to appear; **~se** vr to appear

aparejado, a [apareˈxaðo, a] adj fit, suitable; **llevar o traer ~** to involve; **aparejador, a** nm/f (ARQ) master builder

aparejo [apaˈrexo] nm harness; rigging; (de poleas) block and tackle

aparentar [aparenˈtar] vt (edad) to look; (fingir): **~ tristeza** to pretend to be sad

aparente [apaˈrente] adj apparent; (adecuado) suitable

aparezco etc vb ver **aparecer**

aparición [apariˈθjon] nf appearance; (de libro) publication; (espectro) apparition

apariencia [apaˈrjenθja] nf (outward) appearance; **en ~** outwardly, seemingly

apartado, a [aparˈtaðo, a] adj separate; (lejano) remote ♦ nm (tipográfico) paragraph; **~ (de correos)** post office box

apartamento [apartaˈmento] nm apartment, flat (BRIT)

apartamiento [apartaˈmjento] nm separation; (aislamiento) remoteness, isolation; (AM) apartment, flat (BRIT)

apartar [aparˈtar] vt to separate; (quitar) to remove; **~se** vr to separate, part; (irse) to move away; to keep away

aparte [aˈparte] adv (separadamente) separately; (además) besides ♦ nm

aside; (tipográfico) new paragraph

aparthotel [apartoˈtel] nm serviced apartments

apasionado, a [apasjoˈnaðo, a] adj passionate

apasionar [apasjoˈnar] vt to excite; **le apasiona el fútbol** she's crazy about football; **~se** vr to get excited

apatía [apaˈtia] nf apathy

apático, a [aˈpatiko, a] adj apathetic

Apdo abr (= Apartado de Correos) PO Box

apeadero [apeaˈðero] nm halt, stop, stopping place

apearse [apeˈarse] vr (jinete) to dismount; (bajarse) to get down o out; (AUTO, FERRO) to get off o out

apechugar [apetʃuˈɣar] vr: **~ con algo** to face up to sth

apedrear [apeðreˈar] vt to stone

apegarse [apeˈɣarse] vr: **~ a** to become attached to sth; **apego** [aˈpeɣo] nm attachment, devotion

apelación [apelaˈθjon] nf appeal

apelar [apeˈlar] vi to appeal; **~ a** (fig) to resort to

apellidar [apeʎiˈðar] vt to call, name; **~se** vr: **se apellida Pérez** her (sur)name's Pérez

apellido [apeˈʎiðo] nm surname

apelmazarse [apelmaˈθarse] vr (masa, arroz) to go hard; (prenda de lana) to shrink

apenar [apeˈnar] vt to grieve, trouble; (AM: avergonzar) to embarrass; **~se** vr to grieve; (AM) to be embarrassed

apenas [aˈpenas] adv scarcely, hardly ♦ conj as soon as, no sooner

apéndice [aˈpendiθe] nm appendix; **apendicitis** nf appendicitis

aperitivo [aperiˈtiβo] nm (bebida) aperitif; (comida) appetizer

apero [aˈpero] nm (AGR) implement; **~s** nmpl farm equipment sg

apertura [aperˈtura] nf opening; (POL) liberalization

apesadumbrar [apesaðumˈbrar] vt to

grieve, sadden; **~se** to distress o.s.

apestar |apes'tar| vt to infect ♦ vi:
~ (a) to stink (of)

apetecer |apete'θer| vt: **¿te apetece
un café?** do you fancy a (cup of)
coffee?; **apetecible** adj desirable;
(comida) appetizing

apetito |ape'tito| nm appetite; **~so, a**
adj appetizing; (fig) tempting

apiadarse |apja'ðarse| vr: **~ de** to take
pity on

ápice |'apiθe| nm whit, iota

apilar |api'lar| vt to pile o heap up;
~se vr to pile up

apiñarse |api'narse| vr to crowd o
press together

apio |'apjo| nm celery

apisonadora |apisona'ðora| nf
steamroller

aplacar |apla'kar| vt to placate; **~se** vr
to calm down

aplanar |apla'nar| vt to smooth, level;
(allanar) to roll flat, flatten

aplastante |aplas'tante| adj
overwhelming; (lógica) compelling

aplastar |aplas'tar| vt to squash (flat);
(fig) to crush

aplatanarse |aplata'narse| vr to get
lethargic

aplaudir |aplau'ðir| vt to applaud

aplauso |a'plauso| nm applause; (fig)
approval, acclaim

aplazamiento |aplaθa'mjento| nm
postponement

aplazar |apla'θar| vt to postpone,
defer

aplicación |aplika'θjon| nf
application; (esfuerzo) effort

aplicado, a |apli'kaðo, a| adj diligent,
hard-working

aplicar |apli'kar| vt (ejecutar) to apply;
~se vr to apply o.s.

aplique etc |a'plike| vb ver **aplicar**
♦ nm wall light

aplomo |a'plomo| nm aplomb, self-
assurance

apocado, a |apo'kaðo, a| adj timid

apodar |apo'ðar| vt to nickname

apoderado |apoðe'raðo| nm agent,
representative

apoderarse |apoðe'rarse| vr: **~ de** to
take possession of

apodo |a'poðo| nm nickname

apogeo |apo'xeo| nm peak, summit

apolillarse |apoli'ʎarse| vr to get
moth-eaten

apología |apolo'xia| nf eulogy;
(defensa) defence

apoltronarse |apoltro'narse| vr to get
lazy

apoplejía |apople'xia| nf apoplexy,
stroke

apoquinar |apoki'nar| (fam) vt to fork
out, cough up

aporrear |aporre'ar| vt to beat (up)

aportar |apor'tar| vt to contribute ♦ vi
to reach port; **~se** vr (AM: llegar) to
arrive, come

aposento |apo'sento| nm lodging;
(habitación) room

aposta |a'posta| adv deliberately, on
purpose

apostar |apos'tar| vt to bet, stake;
(tropas etc) to station, post ♦ vi to bet

apóstol |a'postol| nm apostle

apóstrofo |a'postrofo| nm apostrophe

apoyar |apo'jar| vt to lean, rest; (fig) to
support, back; **~se** vr: **~se en** to lean
on; **apoyo** |a'pojo| nm (gen) support; backing,
help

apreciable |apre'θjaßle| adj
considerable; (fig) esteemed

apreciar |apre'θjar| vt to evaluate,
assess; (COM) to appreciate, value;
(persona) to respect; (tamaño) to
gauge, assess; (detalles) to notice

aprecio |a'preθjo| nm valuation,
estimate; (fig) appreciation

aprehender |apreen'der| vt to
apprehend, detain

apremiante |apre'mjante| adj urgent,
pressing

apremiar |apre'mjar| vt to compel,
force ♦ vi to be urgent, press;

apremio *nm* urgency

aprender [apren'der] *vt, vi* to learn

aprendiz, a [apren'diθ, a] *nm/f* apprentice; (*principiante*) learner; **~ de conductor** learner driver; **~aje** *nm* apprenticeship

aprensión [apren'sjon] *nm* apprehension, fear; **aprensivo, a** *adj* apprehensive

apresar [apre'sar] *vt* to seize; (*capturar*) to capture

aprestar [apres'tar] *vt* to prepare, get ready; (*TEC*) to prime, size; **~se** *vr* to get ready

apresurado, a [apresu'raðo, a] *adj* hurried, hasty; **apresuramiento** *nm* hurry, haste

apresurar [apresu'rar] *vt* to hurry, accelerate; **~se** *vr* to hurry, make haste

apretado, a [apre'taðo, a] *adj* tight; (*escritura*) cramped

apretar [apre'tar] *vt* to squeeze; (*TEC*) to tighten; (*presionar*) to press together, pack ♦ *vi* to be too tight

apretón [apre'ton] *nm* squeeze; **~ de manos** handshake

aprieto [a'prjeto] *nm* squeeze; (*dificultad*) difficulty; **estar en un ~** to be in a fix

aprisa [a'prisa] *adv* quickly, hurriedly

aprisionar [aprisjo'nar] *vt* to imprison

aprobación [aproβa'θjon] *nf* approval

aprobar [apro'βar] *vt* to approve (of); (*examen, materia*) to pass ♦ *vi* to pass

apropiación [apropja'θjon] *nf* appropriation

apropiado, a [apro'pjaðo, a] *adj* suitable

apropiarse [apro'pjarse] *vr*: **~ de** to appropriate

aprovechado, a [aproβe'tʃaðo, a] *adj* industrious, hard-working; (*económico*) thrifty; (*pey*) unscrupulous

aprovechamiento *nm* use; exploitation

aprovechar [aproβe'tʃar] *vt* to use; (*explotar*) to exploit; (*experiencia*) to

profit from; (*oferta, oportunidad*) to take advantage of ♦ *vi* to progress, improve; **~se** *vr*: **~se de** to make use of; to take advantage of; **¡que aproveche!** enjoy your meal!

aproximación [aproksima'θjon] *nf* approximation; (*de lotería*) consolation prize; **aproximado, a** *adj* approximate

aproximar [aproksi'mar] *vt* to bring nearer; **~se** *vr* to come near, approach

apruebo *etc vb ver* **aprobar**

aptitud [apti'tuð] *nf* aptitude

apto, a [a'pto, a] *adj* suitable

apuesta [a'pwesta] *nf* bet, wager

apuesto, a [a'pwesto, a] *adj* neat, elegant

apuntador [apunta'ðor] *nm* prompter

apuntalar [apunta'lar] *vt* to prop up

apuntar [apun'tar] *vt* (*con arma*) to aim at; (*con dedo*) to point at o to; (*anotar*) to note (down); (*TEATRO*) to prompt; **~se** *vr* (*DEPORTE*: *tanto, victoria*) to score; (*ESCOL*) to enrol

apunte [a'punte] *nm* note

apuñalar [apuɲa'lar] *vt* to stab

apurado, a [apu'raðo, a] *adj* needy; (*difícil*) difficult; (*peligroso*) dangerous; (*AM*) hurried, rushed

apurar [apu'rar] *vt* (*agotar*) to drain; (*recursos*) to use up; (*molestar*) to annoy; **~se** *vr* (*preocuparse*) to worry; (*darse prisa*) to hurry

apuro [a'puro] *nm* (*aprieto*) fix, jam; (*escasez*) want, hardship; (*vergüenza*) embarrassment; (*AM*) haste, urgency

aquejado, a [ake'xaðo, a] *adj*: **~ de** (*MED*) afflicted by

aquél, aquélla [a'kel, a'keʎa] (*pl* **aquéllos, as**) *pron* that (one); (*pl*) those (ones)

aquel, aquella [a'kel, a'keʎa] (*pl* **aquellos, as**) *adj* that; (*pl*) those

aquello [a'keʎo] *pron* that, that business

aquí [a'ki] *adv* (*lugar*) here; (*tiempo*) now; **~ arriba** up here; **~ mismo**

right here; **~ yace** here lies; **de ~ a
siete días** a week from now

aquietar [akje'tar] *vt* to quieten
(down), calm (down)

ara ['ara] *nf*: **en ~s de** for the sake of

árabe ['araβe] *adj, nm/f* Arab ♦ *nm*
(LING) Arabic

Arabia [a'raβja] *nf*: **~ Saudí** o
Saudita Saudi Arabia

arado [a'raðo] *nm* plough

Aragón [ara'ɣon] *nm* Aragon;
aragonés, esa *adj, nm/f* Aragonese

arancel [aran'θel] *nm* tariff, duty; **~ de
aduanas** customs (duty)

arandela [aran'dela] *nf* (TEC) washer

araña [a'raɲa] *nf* (ZOOL) spider;
(*lámpara*) chandelier

arañar [ara'ɲar] *vt* to scratch

arañazo [ara'naθo] *nm* scratch

arar [a'rar] *vt* to plough, till

arbitraje [arβi'traxe] *nm* arbitration

arbitrar [arβi'trar] *vt* to arbitrate in;
(DEPORTE) to referee ♦ *vi* to arbitrate

arbitrariedad [arβitrarje'ðað] *nf*
arbitrariness; (*acto*) arbitrary act;
arbitrario, a *adj* arbitrary

arbitrio [ar'βitrjo] *nm* free will; (JUR)
adjudication, decision

árbitro ['arβitro] *nm* arbitrator;
(DEPORTE) referee; (TENIS) umpire

árbol ['arβol] *nm* (BOT) tree; (NAUT)
mast; (TEC) axle, shaft; **arbolado, a**
adj wooded; (*camino etc*) tree-lined
♦ *nm* woodland

arboleda [arβo'leða] *nf* grove,
plantation

arbusto [ar'βusto] *nm* bush, shrub

arca ['arka] *nf* chest, box

arcada [ar'kaða] *nf* arcade; (*de puente*)
arch, span; **~s** *nfpl* (*náuseas*) retching
sg

arcaico, a [ar'kaiko, a] *adj* archaic

arce ['arθe] *nm* maple tree

arcén [ar'θen] *nm* (*de autopista*) hard
shoulder; (*de carretera*) verge

archipiélago [artʃi'pjelaɣo] *nm*
archipelago

archivador [artʃiβa'ðor] *nm* filing
cabinet

archivar [artʃi'βar] *vt* to file (away);
archivo *nm* file, archive(s) (*pl*)

arcilla [ar'θiʎa] *nf* clay

arco ['arko] *nm* arch; (MAT) arc; (MIL,
MUS) bow; **~ iris** rainbow

arder [ar'ðer] *vi* to burn; **estar que
arde** (*persona*) to fume

ardid [ar'ðið] *nm* ploy, trick

ardiente [ar'ðjente] *adj* burning,
ardent

ardilla [ar'ðiʎa] *nf* squirrel

ardor [ar'ðor] *nm* (*calor*) heat; (*fig*)
ardour; **~ de estómago** heartburn

arduo, a ['arðwo, a] *adj* arduous

área ['area] *nf* area; (DEPORTE) penalty
area

arena [a'rena] *nf* sand; (*de una lucha*)
arena; **~ movedizas** quicksand *sg*

arenal [are'nal] *nm* (*arena movediza*)
quicksand

arengar [aren'gar] *vt* to harangue

arenisca [are'niska] *nf* sandstone;
(*cascajo*) grit

arenoso, a [are'noso, a] *adj* sandy

arenque [a'renke] *nm* herring

argamasa [arɣa'masa] *nf* mortar,
plaster

Argel [ar'xel] *n* Algiers; **Argelia** *nf*
Algeria; **argelino, a** *adj, nm/f* Algerian

Argentina [arxen'tina] *nf*: **(la) ~**
Argentina

argentino, a [arxen'tino, a] *adj*
Argentinian; (*de plata*) silvery ♦ *nm/f*
Argentinian

argolla [ar'ɣoʎa] *nf* (*large*) ring

argot [ar'ɣo] *(pl* **~s**) *nm* slang

argucia [ar'ɣuθja] *nf* subtlety, sophistry

argüir [ar'ɣwir] *vt* to deduce; (*discutir*)
to argue; (*indicar*) to indicate, imply;
(*censurar*) to reproach ♦ *vi* to argue

argumentación [arɣumenta'θjon] *nf*
(line of) argument

argumentar [arɣumen'tar] *vt, vi* to
argue

argumento [arɣu'mento] *nm*

argument; (*razonamiento*) reasoning; (*de novela etc*) plot; (*CINE, TV*) storyline

aria ['arja] *nf* aria

aridez [ari'ðeθ] *nf* aridity, dryness

árido, a ['ariðo, a] *adj* arid, dry; **~s** *nmpl* (COM) dry goods

Aries ['arjes] *nm* Aries

ario, a ['arjo, a] *adj* Aryan

arisco, a [a'risko, a] *adj* surly; (*insociable*) unsociable

aristócrata [aris'tokrata] *nm/f* aristocrat

aritmética [arit'metika] *nf* arithmetic

arma ['arma] *nf* arm; **~s** *nfpl* arms; **~ blanca** blade, knife; (*espada*) sword; **~ de fuego** firearm; **~s cortas** small arms

armada [ar'maða] *nf* armada; (*flota*) fleet

armadillo [arma'ðiλo] *nm* armadillo

armado, a [ar'maðo, a] *adj* armed; (TEC) reinforced

armador [arma'ðor] *nm* (NAUT) shipowner

armadura [arma'ðura] *nf* (MIL) armour; (TEC) framework; (ZOOL) skeleton; (FÍSICA) armature

armamento [arma'mento] *nm* armament; (NAUT) fitting-out

armar [ar'mar] *vt* (*soldado*) to arm; (*máquina*) to assemble; (*navío*) to fit out; **~la, ~ un lío** to start a row, kick up a fuss

armario [ar'marjo] *nm* wardrobe; (*de cocina, baño*) cupboard

armatoste [arma'toste] *nm* (*mueble*) monstrosity; (*máquina*) contraption

armazón [arma'θon] *nm o nf* body, chassis; (*de mueble etc*) frame; (ARQ) skeleton

armería [arme'ria] *nf* gunsmith's

armiño [ar'miɲo] *nm* stoat; (*piel*) ermine

armisticio [armis'tiθjo] *nm* armistice

armonía [armo'nia] *nf* harmony

armónica [ar'monika] *nf* harmonica

armonioso, a [armo'njoso, a] *adj* harmonious

armonizar [armoni'θar] *vt* to harmonize; (*diferencias*) to reconcile ♦ *vi*: **~ con** to be in keeping with; (*colores*) to tone in with, blend

arnés [ar'nes] *nm* armour; **arneses** *nmpl* (*de caballo etc*) harness *sg*

aro ['aro] *nm* ring; (*tejo*) quoit; (AM: *pendiente*) earring

aroma [a'roma] *nm* aroma, scent

aromático, a [aro'matiko, a] *adj* aromatic

arpa ['arpa] *nf* harp

arpía [ar'pia] *nf* shrew

arpillera [arpi'λera] *nf* sacking, sackcloth

arpón [ar'pon] *nm* harpoon

arquear [arke'ar] *vt* to arch, bend; **~se** *vr* to arch, bend

arqueología [arkeolo'xia] *nf* archaeology; **arqueólogo, a** *nm/f* archaeologist

arquero [ar'kero] *nm* archer, bowman

arquetipo [arke'tipo] *nm* archetype

arquitecto [arki'tekto] *nm* architect; **arquitectura** *nf* architecture

arrabal [arra'ßal] *nm* suburb; (AM) slum; **~es** *nmpl* (*afueras*) outskirts

arraigado, a [arrai'ɣaðo, a] *adj* deep-rooted; (*fig*) established

arraigar [arrai'ɣar] *vt* to establish ♦ *vi* to take root; **~se** *vr* to take root; (*persona*) to settle

arrancar [arran'kar] *vt* (*sacar*) to extract, pull out; (*arrebatar*) to snatch (away); (INFORM) to boot; (*fig*) to extract ♦ *vi* (AUTO, *máquina*) to start; (*ponerse en marcha*) to get going; **~ de** to stem from

arranque *etc* [a'rranke] *vb ver* **arrancar** ♦ *nm* sudden start; (AUTO) start; (*fig*) fit, outburst

arrasar [arra'sar] *vt* (*aplanar*) to level, flatten; (*destruir*) to demolish

arrastrado, a [arras'traðo, a] *adj* poor, wretched; (AM) servile

arrastrar [arras'trar] *vt* to drag

(along); (fig) to drag down, degrade; (suj: agua, viento) to carry away ♦ vi to drag, trail on the ground; **~se** vr to crawl; (fig) to grovel; **llevar algo arrastrado** to drag sth along

arrastre [a'rrastre] nm drag, dragging

arre [arre] excl gee up!

arrear [arre'ar] vt to drive on, urge on ♦ vi to hurry along

arrebatado, a [arreβa'taðo, a] adj rash, impetuous; (repentino) sudden, hasty

arrebatar [arreβa'tar] vt to snatch (away), seize; (fig) to captivate; **~se** to get carried away, get excited

arrebato [arre'βato] nm fit of rage, fury; (éxtasis) rapture

arrecife [arre'θife] nm (tb: ~ de coral) reef

arredrarse [arre'ðrarse] vr: ~ (ante algo) to be intimidated (by sth)

arreglado, a [arre'ɣlaðo, a] adj (ordenado) neat, orderly; (moderado) moderate, reasonable

arreglar [arre'ɣlar] vt (poner orden) to tidy up; (algo roto) to fix, repair; (problema) to solve; **~se** vr to reach an understanding; **arreglárselas** (fam) to get by, manage

arreglo [a'rreɣlo] nm settlement; (orden) order; (acuerdo) agreement; (MUS) arrangement, setting

arrellanarse [arreʎa'narse] vr: ~ en to sit back/in/on

arremangar [arreman'gar] vt to roll up, turn up; **~se** vr to roll up one's sleeves

arremeter [arreme'ter] vi: ~ contra to attack, rush at

arrendamiento [arrenda'mjento] nm letting; (alquilar) hiring; (contrato) lease; (alquiler) rent; **arrendar** vt to let, lease; to rent; **arrendatario, a** nm/f tenant

arreos [a'rreos] nmpl (de caballo) harness sg, trappings

arrepentimiento [arrepenti'mjento]

nm regret, repentance

arrepentirse [arrepen'tirse] vr to repent; ~ **de** to regret

arrestar [arres'tar] vt to arrest; (encarcelar) to imprison; **arresto** nm arrest; (MIL) detention; (audacia) boldness, daring; **arresto domiciliario** house arrest

arriar [a'rrjar] vt (velas) to haul down; (bandera) to lower, strike; (cable) to pay out

arriba [a'rriβa] adv 1 (posición) above; desde ~ from above; ~ **de todo** at the very top, right on top; **Juan está ~** Juan is upstairs; **lo ~ mencionado** the aforementioned

2 (dirección): **calle ~** up the street

3: **de ~ abajo** from top to bottom; **mirar a uno de ~ abajo** to look sb up and down

4: **para ~**: **de 5000 pesetas para ~** from 5000 pesetas up(wards)

♦ adj: **de ~**: **el piso de ~** the upstairs flat (BRIT) o apartment; **la parte de ~** the top o upper part

♦ prep: ~ **de** (AM) above; ~ **de 200 dólares** more than 200 dollars

♦ excl: **¡~!** up!; **¡manos ~!** hands up!; **¡~ España!** long live Spain!

arribar [arri'βar] vi to put into port; (llegar) to arrive

arribista [arri'βista] nm/f parvenu(e), upstart

arriendo etc [a'rrjendo] vb ver **arrendar** ♦ nm = **arrendamiento**

arriero [a'rrjero] nm muleteer

arriesgado, a [arrjes'xaðo, a] adj (peligroso) risky; (audaz) bold, daring

arriesgar [arrjes'xar] vt to risk; (poner en peligro) to endanger; **~se** vr to take a risk

arrimar [arri'mar] vt (acercar) to bring close; (poner de lado) to set aside; **~se** vr to come close o closer; **~se a** to lean on

arrinconar [arrinko'nar] vt (colocar) to put in a corner; (enemigo) to corner; (fig) to put on one side; (abandonar) to push aside

arrodillarse [arroði'ʎarse] vr to kneel (down)

arrogancia [arro'ɣanθja] nf arrogance; **arrogante** adj arrogant

arrojar [arro'xar] vt to throw, hurl; (humo) to emit, give out; (COM) to yield, produce; ~se vr to throw o hurl o.s.

arrojo [a'rroxo] nm daring

arrollador, a [arroʎa'ðor, a] adj overwhelming

arrollar [arro'ʎar] vt (AUTO etc) to run over, knock down; (DEPORTE) to crush

arropar [arro'par] vt to cover, wrap up; ~se vr to wrap o.s. up

arroyo [a'rrojo] nm stream; (de la calle) gutter

arroz [a'rroθ] nm rice; ~ con leche rice pudding

arruga [a'rruɣa] nf (de cara) wrinkle; (de vestido) crease

arrugar [arru'ɣar] vt to wrinkle; to crease; ~se vr to get creased

arruinar [arrwi'nar] vt to ruin, wreck; ~se vr to be ruined, go bankrupt

arrullar [arru'ʎar] vi to coo ♦ vt to lull to sleep

arsenal [arse'nal] nm naval dockyard; (MIL) arsenal

arsénico [ar'seniko] nm arsenic

arte ['arte] (gen m en sg y siempre f en pl) nm sg; (maña) skill, guile; ~s nfpl (bellas ~s) arts

artefacto [arte'fakto] nm appliance

arteria [ar'terja] nf artery

artesanía [artesa'nia] nf craftsmanship; (artículos) handicrafts pl; **artesano, a** nm/f artisan, craftsman/woman

ártico, a ['artiko, a] adj Arctic ♦ nm: **el Á~** the Arctic

articulación [artikula'θjon] nf

articulation; (MED, TEC) joint;

articulado, a adj articulate; jointed

articular [artiku'lar] vt to articulate; to join together

artículo [ar'tikulo] nm article; (cosa) thing, article; ~s nmpl (COM) goods

artífice [ar'tifiθe] nm/f (fig) architect

artificial [artifi'θjal] adj artificial

artificio [arti'fiθjo] nm art, skill; (astucia) cunning

artillería [artiʎe'ria] nf artillery

artillero [arti'ʎero] nm artilleryman, gunner

artilugio [arti'luxjo] nm gadget

artimaña [arti'maɲa] nf trap, snare; (astucia) cunning

artista [ar'tista] nm/f (pintor) artist, painter; (TEATRO) artist, artiste; ~ de cine film actor/actress; **artístico, a** adj artistic

artritis [ar'tritis] nf arthritis

arveja [ar'βexa] (AM) nf pea

arzobispo [arθo'βispo] nm archbishop

as [as] nm ace

asa ['asa] nf handle; (fig) lever

asado [a'saðo] nm roast (meat); (AM: barbacoa) barbecue

asador [asa'ðor] nm spit

asadura [asa'ðura] nf entrails pl, offal

asalariado, a [asala'rjaðo, a] adj paid, salaried ♦ nm/f wage earner

asaltante [asal'tante] nm/f attacker

asaltar [asal'tar] vt to attack, assault; (fig) to assail; **asalto** nm attack, assault; (DEPORTE) round

asamblea [asam'blea] nf assembly; (reunión) meeting

asar [a'sar] vt to roast

asbesto [as'βesto] nm asbestos

ascendencia [asθen'denθja] nf ancestry; (AM) ascendancy; **de ~ francesa** of French origin

ascender [asθen'der] vi (subir) to ascend, rise; (ser promovido) to gain promotion ♦ vt to promote; ~ a to amount to; **ascendiente** nm influence ♦ nm/f ancestor

ascensión [asθen'sjon] nf ascent; (REL): **la A~** the Ascension

ascenso [as'θenso] nm ascent; (promoción) promotion

ascensor [asθen'sor] nm lift (BRIT), elevator (US)

ascético, a [as'θetiko, a] adj ascetic

asco ['asko] nm: **¡qué ~!** how revolting o disgusting; **el ajo me da ~** I hate o loathe garlic; **estar hecho un ~** to be filthy

ascua ['askwa] nf ember; **estar en ~s** to be on tenterhooks

aseado, a [ase'aðo, a] adj clean; (arreglado) tidy; (pulcro) smart

asear [ase'ar] vt to clean, wash; to tidy (up)

asediar [ase'ðjar] vt (MIL) to besiege, lay siege to; (fig) to chase, pester; **asedio** nm siege; (COM) run

asegurado, a [aseɣu'raðo, a] adj insured

asegurador, a nm/f insurer

asegurar [aseɣu'rar] vt (consolidar) to secure, fasten; (dar garantía de) to guarantee; (preservar) to safeguard; (afirmar, dar por cierto) to assert, affirm; (tranquilizar) to reassure; (tomar un seguro) to insure; **~se** vr to assure o.s., make sure

asemejarse [aseme'xarse] vr to be alike; **~ a** to be like, resemble

asentado, a [asen'taðo, a] adj established, settled

asentar [asen'tar] vt (sentar) to seat, sit down; (poner) to place, establish; (alisar) to level, smooth down o out; (anotar) to note down ♦ vi to be suitable, suit

asentir [asen'tir] vi to assent, agree; **~ con la cabeza** to nod (one's head)

aseo [a'seo] nm cleanliness; **~s** nmpl (servicios) toilet sg (BRIT), cloakroom sg (BRIT), restroom sg (US)

aséptico, a [a'septiko, a] adj germ-free, free from infection

asequible [ase'kiβle] adj (precio)

reasonable; (meta) attainable; (persona) approachable

aserradero [aserra'ðero] nm sawmill; **aserrar** vt to saw

asesinar [asesi'nar] vt to murder; (POL) to assassinate; **asesinato** nm murder; assassination

asesino, a [ase'sino, a] nm/f murderer, killer; (POL) assassin

asesor, a [ase'sor, a] nm/f adviser, consultant

asesorar [aseso'rar] vt (JUR) to advise, give legal advice to; (COM) to act as consultant to; **~se** vr: **~se con o de** to take advice from, consult; **asesoría** nf (cargo) consultancy; (oficina) consultant's office

asestar [ases'tar] vt (golpe) to deal, strike

asfalto [as'falto] nm asphalt

asfixia [as'fiksja] nf asphyxia, suffocation

asfixiar [asfik'sjar] vt to asphyxiate, suffocate; **~se** vr to be asphyxiated, suffocate

asgo etc vb ver **asir**

así [a'si] adv (de esta manera) in this way, like this, thus; (aunque) although; (tan pronto como) as soon as; **~ que** so; **~ como** as well as; **~ y todo** even so; **¿no es ~?** isn't it?, didn't you? etc; **~ de grande** this big

Asia ['asja] nf Asia; **asiático, a** adj, nm/f Asian, Asiatic

asidero [asi'ðero] nm handle

asiduidad [asiðwi'ðað] nf assiduousness; **asiduo, a** adj assiduous; (frecuente) frequent ♦ nm/f regular (customer)

asiento [a'sjento] nm (mueble) seat, chair; (de coche, en tribunal etc) seat; (localidad) seat, place; (fundamento) site; **~ delantero/trasero** front/back seat

asignación [asiɣna'θjon] nf (atribución) assignment; (reparto) allocation; (sueldo) salary; **~ (semanal)**

pocket money

asignar [asiɣ'nar] vt to assign, allocate

asignatura [asiɣna'tura] nf subject; course

asilado, a [asi'laðo, a] nm/f inmate; (POL) refugee

asilo [a'silo] nm (refugio) asylum, refuge; (establecimiento) home, institution; ~ **político** political asylum

asimilación [asimila'θjon] nf assimilation

asimilar [asimi'lar] vt to assimilate

asimismo [asi'mismo] adv in the same way, likewise

asir [a'sir] vt to seize, grasp

asistencia [asis'tenθja] nf audience; (MED) attendance; (ayuda) assistance; **asistente** nm/f assistant; **los asistentes** those present; **asistente social** social worker

asistido, a [asis'tiðo, a] adj: ~ **por ordenador** computer-assisted

asistir [asis'tir] vt to assist, help ♦ vi: ~ **a** to attend, be present at

asma ['asma] nf asthma

asno ['asno] nm donkey; (fig) ass

asociación [asoθja'θjon] nf association; (COM) partnership; **asociado, a** adj associate ♦ nm/f associate; (COM) partner

asociar [aso'θjar] vt to associate

asolar [aso'lar] vt to destroy

asomar [aso'mar] vt to show, stick out ♦ vi to appear; ~**se** vr to appear, show up; ~ **la cabeza por la ventana** to put one's head out of the window

asombrar [asom'brar] vt to amaze, astonish; ~**se** vr (sorprenderse) to be amazed; (asustarse) to get a fright; **asombro** nm amazement, astonishment; (susto) fright; **asombroso, a** adj astonishing, amazing

asomo [a'somo] nm hint, sign

aspa ['aspa] nf (cruz) cross; (de molino) sail; **en** ~ X-shaped

aspaviento [aspa'βjento] nm

exaggerated display of feeling; (fam) fuss

aspecto [as'pekto] nm (apariencia) look, appearance; (fig) aspect

aspereza [aspe'reθa] nf roughness; (agrura) sourness; (de carácter) surliness; **áspero, a** adj rough; bitter, sour; harsh

aspersión [asper'sjon] nf sprinkling

aspiración [aspira'θjon] nf breath, inhalation; (MUS) short pause; **aspiraciones** nfpl (ambiciones) aspirations

aspirador [aspira'ðor] nm = **aspiradora**

aspiradora [aspira'ðora] nf vacuum cleaner, Hoover ®

aspirante [aspi'rante] nm/f (candidato) candidate; (DEPORTE) contender

aspirar [aspi'rar] vt to breathe in ♦ vi: ~ **a** to aspire to

aspirina [aspi'rina] nf aspirin

asquear [aske'ar] vt to sicken ♦ vi to be sickening; ~**se** vr to feel disgusted; **asqueroso, a** adj disgusting, sickening

asta ['asta] nf lance; (arpón) spear; (mango) shaft, handle; (ZOOL) horn; **a media** ~ at half mast

asterisco [aste'risko] nm asterisk

astilla [as'tiʎa] nf splinter; (pedacito) chip; ~**s** nfpl (leña) firewood sg

astillero [asti'ʎero] nm shipyard

astringente [astrin'xente] adj, nm astringent

astro ['astro] nm star

astrología [astrolo'xia] nf astrology; **astrólogo, a** nm/f astrologer

astronauta [astro'nauta] nm/f astronaut

astronave [astro'naβe] nm spaceship

astronomía [astrono'mia] nf astronomy; **astrónomo, a** nm/f astronomer

astucia [as'tuθja] nf astuteness; (ardid) clever trick

asturiano, a [astu'rjano, a] adj, nm/f

Asturian

astuto, a [as'tuto, a] *adj* astute; *(taimado)* cunning

asumir [asu'mir] *vt* to assume

asunción [asun'θjon] *nf* assumption; *(REL)*: **A~** Assumption

asunto [a'sunto] *nm (tema)* matter, subject; *(negocio)* business

asustar [asus'tar] *vt* to frighten; **~se** *vr* to be (o become) frightened

atacar [ata'kar] *vt* to attack

atadura [ata'ðura] *nf* bond, tie

atajar [ata'xar] *vt (enfermedad, mal)* to stop ♦ *vi (persona)* to take a short cut

atajo [a'taxo] *nm* short cut

atañer [ata'ɲer] *vi*: **~ a** to concern

ataque *etc* [a'take] *vb ver* **atacar** ♦ *nm* attack; **~ cardiaco** heart attack

atar [a'tar] *vt* to tie, tie up

atardecer [ataɾðe'θer] *vi* to get dark ♦ *nm* evening; *(crepúsculo)* dusk

atareado, a [atare'aðo, a] *adj* busy

atascar [atas'kar] *vt* to clog up; *(obstruir)* to jam; *(fig)* to hinder; **~se** *vr* to stall; *(cañería)* to get blocked up; **atasco** *nm* obstruction; *(AUTO)* traffic jam

ataúd [ata'uð] *nm* coffin

ataviar [ata'βjar] *vt* to deck, array; **~se** *vr* to dress up

atavío [ata'βio] *nm* attire, dress; **~s** *nmpl* finery sg

atemorizar [atemori'θar] *vt* to frighten, scare; **~se** *vr* to get scared

Atenas [a'tenas] *n* Athens

atención [aten'θjon] *nf* attention; *(bondad)* kindness ♦ *excl* (be) careful!, look out!

atender [aten'der] *vt* to attend to, look after ♦ *vi* to pay attention

atenerse [ate'nerse] *vr*: **~ a** to abide by, adhere to

atentado [aten'taðo] *nm* crime, illegal act; *(asalto)* assault; **~ contra la vida de uno** attempt on sb's life

atentamente [atenta'mente] *adv*: **Le saluda ~** Yours faithfully

atentar [aten'tar] *vi*: **~ a** o **contra** to commit an outrage against

atento, a [a'tento, a] *adj* attentive, observant; *(cortés)* polite, thoughtful

atenuante [ate'nwante] *adj* extenuating

atenuar [ate'nwar] *vt (disminuir)* to lessen, minimize

ateo, a [a'teo, a] *adj* atheistic ♦ *nm/f* atheist

aterciopelado, a [aterθjope'laðo, a] *adj* velvety

aterido, a [ate'riðo, a] *adj*: **~ de frío** frozen stiff

aterrador, a [aterra'ðor, a] *adj* frightening

aterrar [ate'rrar] *vt* to frighten; to terrify

aterrizaje [aterri'θaxe] *nm* landing

aterrizar [aterri'θar] *vi* to land

aterrorizar [aterrori'θar] *vt* to terrify

atesorar [ateso'rar] *vt* to hoard

atestado, a [ates'taðo, a] *adj* packed ♦ *nm (JUR)* affidavit

atestar [ates'tar] *vt* to pack, stuff; *(JUR)* to attest, testify to

atestiguar [atesti'ɣwar] *vt* to testify to, bear witness to

atiborrar [atiβo'rrar] *vt* to fill, stuff; **~se** *vr* to stuff o.s.

ático [a'tiko] *nm* attic; **~ de lujo** penthouse (flat *(BRIT)* o apartment)

atinado, a [ati'naðo, a] *adj (sensato)* wise; *(correcto)* right, correct

atinar [ati'nar] *vi (al disparar)*: **~ al blanco** to hit the target; *(fig)* to be right

atisbar [atis'βar] *vt* to spy on; *(echar una ojeada)* to peep at

atizar [ati'θar] *vt* to poke; *(horno etc)* to stoke; *(fig)* to stir up, rouse

atlántico, a [a'tlantiko, a] *adj* Atlantic ♦ *nm*: **el (o océano) A~** the Atlantic (Ocean)

atlas [a'tlas] *nm* atlas

atleta [a'tleta] *nm* athlete; **atlético, a** *adj* athletic; **atletismo** *nm* athletics *sg*

atmósfera [at'mosfera] nf atmosphere

atolladero [atoʎa'ðero] nm (fig) jam, fix

atolondramiento [atolondra'mjento] nm bewilderment; (insensatez) silliness

atómico, a [a'tomiko, a] adj atomic

atomizador [atomiθa'ðor] nm atomizer; (de perfume) spray

átomo ['atomo] nm atom

atónito, a [a'tonito, a] adj astonished, amazed

atontado, a [aton'taðo, a] adj stunned; (bobo) silly, daft

atontar [aton'tar] vt to stun; ~se vr to become confused

atormentar [atormen'tar] vt to torture; (molestar) to torment; (acosar) to plague, harass

atornillar [atorni'ʎar] vt to screw on o down

atosigar [atosi'ɣar] vt to harass, pester

atracador, a [atraka'ðor, a] nm/f robber

atracar [atra'kar] vt (NAUT) to moor; (robar) to hold up, rob ♦ vi to moor; ~se vr: ~se (de) to stuff o.s. (with)

atracción [atrak'θjon] nf attraction

atraco [a'trako] nm holdup, robbery

atracón [atra'kon] nm: **darse o pegarse un ~ (de)** (fam) to stuff o.s. (with)

atractivo, a [atrak'tiβo, a] adj attractive ♦ nm appeal

atraer [atra'er] vt to attract

atragantarse [atraɣan'tarse] vr: ~ **(con)** to choke (on); **se me ha atragantado el chico** I can't stand the boy

atrancar [atran'kar] vt (puerta) to bar, bolt

atrapar [atra'par] vt to trap; (resfriado etc) to catch

atrás [a'tras] adv (movimiento) back (-wards); (lugar) behind; (tiempo) previously; **ir hacia ~** to go back(wards); to go to the rear; **estar ~** to be behind o at the back

atrasado, a [atra'saðo, a] adj slow; (pago) overdue; late; (país) backward

atrasar [atra'sar] vi to be slow; ~se vr to remain behind; (tren) to be o run late; **atraso** nm slowness; lateness, delay; (de país) backwardness; **atrasos** nmpl (COM) arrears

atravesar [atraβe'sar] vt (cruzar) to cross (over); (traspasar) to pierce; to go through; (poner al través) to lay o put across; ~se vr to come in between; (intervenir) to interfere

atraviesa etc vb ver **atravesar**

atrayente [atra'jente] adj attractive

atreverse [atre'βerse] vr to dare; (insolentarse) to be insolent; **atrevido, a** adj daring; insolent; **atrevimiento** nm daring; insolence

atribución [atriβu'θjon] nf: **atribuciones** (POL) powers; (ADMIN) responsibilities

atribuir [atriβu'ir] vt to attribute; (funciones) to confer

atribular [atriβu'lar] vt to afflict, distress

atributo [atri'βuto] nm attribute

atril [a'tril] nm (para libro) lectern; (MUS) music stand

atrocidad [atroθi'ðað] nf atrocity, outrage

atropellar [atrope'ʎar] vt (derribar) to knock over o down; (empujar) to push (aside); (AUTO) to run over, run down; (agraviar) to insult; ~se vr to act hastily; **atropello** nm (AUTO) accident; (empujón) push; (agravio) wrong; (atrocidad) outrage

atroz [a'troθ] adj atrocious, awful

ATS nmf abr (= Ayudante Técnico Sanitario) nurse

atto, a abr = **atento**

atuendo [a'twendo] nm attire

atún [a'tun] nm tuna

aturdir [atur'ðir] vt to stun; (de ruido) to deafen; (fig) to dumbfound, bewilder

atusar [atu'sar] vt to smooth (down)

audacia [au'ðaθja] nf boldness, audacity; **audaz** adj bold, audacious

audible [au'ðiβle] adj audible

audición [auði'θjon] nf hearing; (TEATRO) audition

audiencia [au'ðjenθja] nf audience; A~ (JUR) High Court

audífono [au'ðifono] nm (para sordos) hearing aid

auditor [auði'tor] nm (JUR) judge advocate; (COM) auditor

auditorio [auði'torjo] nm audience; (sala) auditorium

auge ['auxe] nm boom; (clímax) climax

augurar [auɣu'rar] vt to predict; (presagiar) to portend

augurio [au'ɣurjo] nm omen

aula ['aula] nf classroom; (en universidad etc) lecture room

aullar [au'ʎar] vi to howl, yell

aullido [au'ʎiðo] nm howl, yell

aumentar [aumen'tar] vt to increase; (precios) to put up; (producción) to step up; (con microscopio, anteojos) to magnify ♦ vi to increase, be on the increase; **~se** vr to increase, be on the increase; **aumento** nm increase; rise

aun [a'un] adv even; **~ así** even so; **~ más** even o yet more

aún [a'un] adv: **~ está aquí** he's still here; **~ no lo sabemos** we don't know yet; **¿no ha venido ~?** hasn't she come yet?

aunque [a'unke] conj though, although, even though

aúpa [a'upa] excl come on!

aureola [aure'ola] nf halo

auricular [auriku'lar] nm (TEL) receiver; **~es** nmpl (cascos) headphones

aurora [au'rora] nf dawn

auscultar [auskul'tar] vt (MED: pecho) to listen to, sound

ausencia [au'senθja] nf absence

ausentarse [ausen'tarse] vr to go away; (por poco tiempo) to go out

ausente [au'sente] adj absent

auspicios [aus'piθjos] nmpl auspices

austero, a [aus'tero, a] adj austere

austral [aus'tral] adj southern ♦ nm monetary unit of Argentina

Australia [aus'tralja] nf Australia; **australiano, a** adj, nm/f Australian

Austria ['austrja] nf Austria; **austríaco, a** adj, nm/f Austrian

auténtico, a [au'tentiko, a] adj authentic

auto ['auto] nm (JUR) edict, decree; (: orden) writ; (AUTO) car; **~s** nmpl (JUR) proceedings; (: acta) court record sg

autoadhesivo [autoaðe'siβo] adj self-adhesive; (sobre) self-sealing

autobiografía [autoβjoɣra'fia] nf autobiography

autobronceador [autoβronθea'ðor] adj self-tanning

autobús [auto'βus] nm bus

autocar [auto'kar] nm coach (BRIT), (passenger) bus (US)

autóctono, a [au'toktono, a] adj native, indigenous

autodefensa [autoðe'fensa] nf self-defence

autodeterminación [autoðetermina'θjon] nf self-determination

autodidacta [autoði'ðakta] adj self-taught

autoescuela [autoes'kwela] nf driving school

autógrafo [au'toɣrafo] nm autograph

autómata [au'tomata] nm automaton

automático, a [auto'matiko, a] adj automatic ♦ nm press stud

automotor, triz [automo'tor, 'triθ] adj self-propelled ♦ nm diesel train

automóvil [auto'moβil] nm (motor) car (BRIT), automobile (US)

automovilismo [automoβi'lizmo] nm (actividad) motoring; (DEPORTE) motor racing;

automovilista nm/f motorist, driver; **automovilístico, a** adj (industria) motor cpd

autonomía [autono'mia] nf autonomy; **autónomo, a** (ESP),

autonómico, a (ESP) adj (POL) autonomous

autopista |auto'pista| nf motorway (BRIT), freeway (US); ~ **de peaje** toll road (BRIT), turnpike road (US)

autopsia |au'topsja| nf autopsy, postmortem

autor, a |au'tor, a| nm/f author

autoridad |autori'ðað| nf authority; **autoritario, a** adj authoritarian

autorización |autoriθa'θjon| nf authorization; **autorizado, a** adj authorized; (aprobado) approved

autorizar |autori'θar| vt to authorize; (aprobar) to approve

autorretrato |autorre'trato| nm self-portrait

autoservicio |autoser'ßiθjo| nm (tienda) self-service shop (BRIT) o store (US); (restaurante) self-service restaurant

autostop |auto'stop| nm hitch-hiking; **hacer** ~ to hitch-hike; **~ista** nm/f hitch-hiker

autosuficiencia |autosufi'θjenθja| nf self-sufficiency

autovía |auto'ßia| nf ≈ A-road (BRIT), dual carriageway (BRIT); ≈ state highway (US)

auxiliar |auksi'ljar| vt to help ♦ nm/f assistant; **auxilio** nm assistance, help; **primeros auxilios** first aid sg

Av abr (= Avenida) Av(e).

aval |a'ßal| nm guarantee; (persona) guarantor

avalancha |aßa'lantʃa| nf avalanche

avance |a'ßanθe| nm advance; (pago) advance payment; (CINE) trailer

avanzar |aßan'θar| vt, vi to advance

avaricia |aßa'riθja| nf avarice, greed; **avaricioso, a** adj avaricious, greedy

avaro, a |a'ßaro, a| adj miserly, mean ♦ nm/f miser

avasallar |aßasa'ʎar| vt to subdue, subjugate

Avda abr (= Avenida) Av(e).

AVE |'aße| nm abr (= Alta Velocidad Española) ≈ bullet train

ave |'aße| nf bird; ~ **de rapiña** bird of prey

avecinarse |aßeθi'narse| vr (tormenta, fig) to be on the way

avellana |aße'ʎana| nf hazelnut; **avellano** nm hazel tree

avemaría |aßema'ria| nm Hail Mary, Ave Maria

avena |a'ßena| nf oats pl

avenida |aße'niða| nf (calle) avenue

avenir |aße'nir| vt to reconcile; **~se** vr to come to an agreement, reach a compromise

aventajado, a |aßenta'xaðo, a| adj outstanding

aventajar |aßenta'xar| vt (sobrepasar) to surpass, outstrip

aventura |aßen'tura| nf adventure; **aventurado, a** adj risky; **aventurero, a** adj adventurous

avergonzar |aßerɣon'θar| vt to shame; (desconcertar) to embarrass; **~se** vr to be ashamed; to be embarrassed

avería |aße'ria| nf (TEC) breakdown, fault

averiado, a |aße'rjaðo, a| adj broken down; "~~" "out of order"

averiguación |aßeriɣwa'θjon| nf investigation; (descubrimiento) ascertainment

averiguar |aßeri'ɣwar| vt to investigate; (descubrir) to find out, ascertain

aversión |aßer'sjon| nf aversion, dislike

avestruz |aßes'truθ| nm ostrich

aviación |aßja'θjon| nf aviation; (fuerzas aéreas) air force

aviador, a |aßja'ðor, a| nm/f aviator, airman/woman

avicultura |aßikul'tura| nf poultry farming

avidez |aßi'ðeθ| nf avidity, eagerness; **ávido, a** adj avid, eager

avinagrado, a |aßina'ɣraðo, a| adj sour, acid

avión |a'ßjon| nm aeroplane; (ave)

martin; **~ de reacción** jet (plane)

avioneta [aβjo'neta] nf light aircraft

avisar [aβi'sar] vt (*advertir*) to warn, notify; (*informar*) to tell; (*aconsejar*) to advise, counsel; **aviso** nm warning; (*noticia*) notice

avispa [a'βispa] nf wasp

avispado, a [aβis'paðo, a] adj sharp, clever

avispero [aβis'pero] nm wasp's nest

avispón [aβis'pon] nm hornet

avistar [aβis'tar] vt to sight, spot

avituallar [aβitwa'ʎar] vt to supply with food

avivar [aβi'βar] vt to strengthen, intensify; **~se** vr to revive, acquire new life

axila [ak'sila] nf armpit

axioma [ak'sjoma] nm axiom

ay [ai] excl (*dolor*) owl!, ouch!; **¡~ de mí!** poor me!

aya ['aja] nf governess; (*niñera*) nanny

ayer [a'jer] adv, nm yesterday; **antes de ~** the day before yesterday

ayote [a'jote] nm (AM) pumpkin

ayuda [a'juða] nf help, assistance ♦ nm page; **ayudante, a** nm/f assistant, helper; (ESCOL) assistant; (MIL) adjutant

ayudar [aju'ðar] vt to help, assist

ayunar [aju'nar] vi to fast; **ayunas** nfpl: **estar en ayunas** to be fasting; **ayuno** nm fast; fasting

ayuntamiento [ajunta'mjento] nm (*consejo*) town o (city) council; (*edificio*) town o (city) hall

azabache [aθa'βatʃe] nm jet

azada [a'θaða] nf hoe

azafata [aθa'fata] nf air stewardess

azafrán [aθa'fran] nm saffron

azahar [aθa'ar] nm orange/lemon blossom

azar [a'θar] nm (*casualidad*) chance, fate; (*desgracia*) misfortune, accident; **por ~** by chance; **al ~** at random

azoramiento [aθora'mjento] nm alarm; (*confusión*) confusion

azorar [aθo'rar] vt to alarm; **~se** vr to

get alarmed

Azores [a'θores] nfpl: **las ~** the Azores

azotar [aθo'tar] vt to whip, beat; (*pegar*) to spank; **azote** nm (*látigo*) whip; (*latigazo*) lash, stroke; (*en las nalgas*) spank; (*calamidad*) calamity

azotea [aθo'tea] nf (flat) roof

azteca [aθ'teka] adj, nm/f Aztec

azúcar [a'θukar] nm sugar;
azucarado, a [aθuka'raðo, a] adj sugary, sweet

azucarero, a [aθuka'rero, a] adj sugar cpd ♦ nm sugar bowl

azucena [aθu'θena] nf white lily

azufre [a'θufre] nm sulphur

azul [a'θul] adj, nm blue; **~ marino** navy blue

azulejo [aθu'lexo] nm tile

azuzar [aθu'θar] vt to incite, egg on

B, b

B.A. abr (= Buenos Aires) B.A.

baba ['baβa] nf spittle, saliva; **babear** vi to drool, slaver

babero [ba'βero] nm bib

babor [ba'βor] nm port (side)

baboso, a [ba'βoso, a] adj (AM: fam) silly

baca ['baka] nf (AUTO) luggage o roof rack

bacalao [baka'lao] nm cod(fish)

bache ['batʃe] nm pothole, rut; (fig) bad patch

bachillerato [batʃiʎe'rato] nm higher secondary school course

bacteria [bak'terja] nf bacterium, germ

báculo ['bakulo] nm stick, staff

bagaje [ba'vaxe] nm baggage, luggage

Bahama [ba'ama]: **las (Islas) ~** nfpl the Bahamas

bahía [ba'ia] nf bay

bailar [bai'lar] vt, vi to dance; **~ín, ína** nm/f (ballet) dancer; **baile** nm dance; (*formal*) ball

baja ['baxa] nf drop, fall; (MIL) casualty; **dar de ~** (*soldado*) to discharge;

(empleado) to dismiss

bajada [ba'xaða] nf descent; (camino) slope; (de aguas) ebb

bajar [ba'xar] vi to go down, come down; (temperatura, precios) to drop, fall ♦ vt (cabeza) to bow; (escalera) to go down, come down; (precio, voz) to lower; (llevar abajo) to take down; **~se** vr (de coche) to get out; (de autobús, tren) to get off; **~ de** (coche) to get out of; (autobús, tren) to get off

bajeza [ba'xeθa] nf baseness no pl; (una ~) vile deed

bajío [ba'xio] nm (AM) lowlands pl

bajo, a ['baxo, a] adj (mueble, número, precio) low; (piso) ground; (de estatura) small, short; (color) pale; (sonido) faint, soft, low; (voz: en tono) deep; (metal) base; (humilde) low, humble ♦ adv (hablar) softly, quietly; (volar) low ♦ prep under, below, underneath ♦ nm (MUS) bass; ~ **la lluvia** in the rain

bajón [ba'xon] nm fall, drop

bakalao [baka'lao] (fam) nm rave (music)

bala ['bala] nf bullet

balance [ba'lanθe] nm (COM) balance; (: libro) balance sheet; (: cuenta general) stocktaking

balancear [balanθe'ar] vt to balance ♦ vi to swing (to and fro); (vacilar) to hesitate; **~se** vr to swing (to and fro); to hesitate; **balanceo** nm swinging

balanza [ba'lanθa] nf scales pl, balance; (ASTROLOGÍA) **B~** Libra; ~ **comercial** balance of trade; ~ **de pagos** balance of payments

balar [ba'lar] vi to bleat

balaustrada [balaus'traða] nf balustrade; (pasamanos) banisters pl

balazo [ba'laθo] nm (golpe) shot; (herida) bullet wound

balbucear [balβuθe'ar] vi, vt to stammer, stutter; **balbuceo** nm stammering, stuttering

balbucir [balβu'θir] vi, vt to stammer, stutter

balcón [bal'kon] nm balcony

balde ['balde] nm bucket, pail; **de ~** (for) free, for nothing; **en ~** in vain

baldío, a [bal'dio, a] adj uncultivated; (terreno) waste ♦ nm waste land

baldosa [bal'dosa] nf (azulejo) floor tile; (grande) flagstone; **baldosín** (small) tile

Baleares [bale'ares] nfpl: **las (Islas) ~** the Balearic Islands

balido [ba'liðo] nm bleat, bleating

baliza [ba'liθa] nf (AVIAT) beacon; (NAUT) buoy

ballena [ba'ʎena] nf whale

ballesta [ba'ʎesta] nf crossbow; (AUTO) spring

ballet [ba'le] (pl ~s) nm ballet

balneario, a [balne'arjo, a] adj: **estación balnearia** (AM) (bathing) resort ♦ nm spa, health resort

balón [ba'lon] nm ball

baloncesto [balon'θesto] nm basketball

balonmano [balon'mano] nm handball

balonvolea [balombo'lea] nm volleyball

balsa ['balsa] nf raft; (BOT) balsa wood

bálsamo ['balsamo] nm balsam, balm

baluarte [ba'lwarte] nm bastion, bulwark

bambolear [bambole'ar] vi to swing, sway; (silla) to wobble; **~se** vr to swing, sway; to wobble; **bamboleo** nm swinging, swaying; wobbling

bambú [bam'bu] nm bamboo

banana [ba'nana] (AM) nf banana; **banano** (AM) nm banana tree

banca ['banka] nf (COM) banking

bancario, a [ban'karjo, a] adj banking cpd, bank cpd

bancarrota [banka'rrota] nf bankruptcy; **hacer ~** to go bankrupt

banco ['banko] nm bench; (ESCOL) desk; (COM) bank; (GEO) stratum; ~ **de crédito/de ahorros** credit/savings bank; ~ **de arena** sandbank; ~ **de**

datos databank

banda [ˈbanda] nf band; (pandilla) gang; (NAUT) side, edge; **la B~ Oriental** Uruguay; **~ sonora** soundtrack

bandada [banˈdaða] nf (de pájaros) flock; (de peces) shoal

bandazo [banˈdaθo] nm: **dar ~s** to sway from side to side

bandeja [banˈdexa] nf tray

bandera [banˈdera] nf flag

banderilla [bandeˈriʎa] nf banderilla

banderín [bandeˈrin] nm pennant, small flag

bandido [banˈdiðo] nm bandit

bando [ˈbando] nm (edicto) edict, proclamation; (facción) faction; **los ~s** (REL) the banns

bandolera [bandoˈlera] nf: **llevar en ~** to wear across one's chest

bandolero [bandoˈlero] nm bandit, brigand

banquero [banˈkero] nm banker

banqueta [banˈketa] nf stool; (AM: en la calle) pavement (BRIT), sidewalk (US)

banquete [banˈkete] nm banquet; (para convidados) formal dinner

banquillo [banˈkiʎo] nm (JUR) dock, prisoner's bench; (banco) bench; (para los pies) footstool

bañador [baɲaˈðor] nm swimming costume (BRIT), bathing suit (US)

bañar [baˈɲar] vt to bath, bathe; (objeto) to dip; (de barniz) to coat; **~se** vr (en el mar) to bathe, swim; (en la bañera) to have a bath

bañera [baˈɲera] nf bath(tub)

bañero, a [baˈɲero, a] (AM) nm/f lifeguard

bañista [baˈɲista] nm/f bather

baño [ˈbaɲo] nm (en bañera) bath; (en río) dip, swim; (cuarto) bathroom; (bañera) bath(tub); (capa) coating

baqueta [baˈketa] nf (MUS) drumstick

bar [bar] nm bar

barahúnda [baraˈunda] nf uproar, hubbub

baraja [baˈraxa] nf pack (of cards);

barajar vt (naipes) to shuffle; (fig) to jumble up

baranda [baˈranda] nf = **barandilla**

barandilla [baranˈdiʎa] nf rail, railing

baratija [baraˈtixa] nf trinket

baratillo [baraˈtiʎo] nm (tienda) junkshop; (subasta) bargain sale; (conjunto de cosas) secondhand goods pl

barato, a [baˈrato, a] adj cheap ♦ adv cheap, cheaply

baraúnda [baraˈunda] nf = **barahúnda**

barba [ˈbarβa] nf (mentón) chin; (pelo) beard

barbacoa [barβaˈkoa] nf (parrilla) barbecue; (carne) barbecued meat

barbaridad [barβariˈðað] nf (acto) barbarism; (atrocidad) outrage; **una ~** (fam) loads; **¡qué ~!** (fam) how awful!

barbarie [barˈβarje] nf barbarism, savagery; (crueldad) barbarity

barbarismo [barβaˈrismo] nm = **barbarie**

bárbaro, a [ˈbarβaro, a] adj barbarous, cruel; (grosero) rough, uncouth ♦ nm/f barbarian ♦ adv: **lo pasamos ~** (fam) we had a great time; **¡qué ~!** (fam) how marvellous!; **un éxito ~** (fam) a terrific success; **es un tipo ~** (fam) he's a great bloke

barbecho [barˈβetʃo] nm fallow land

barbero [barˈβero] nm barber, hairdresser

barbilla [barˈβiʎa] nf chin, tip of the chin

barbo [ˈbarβo] nm barbel; **~ de mar** red mullet

barbotear [barβoteˈar] vt, vi to mutter, mumble

barbudo, a [barˈβuðo, a] adj bearded

barca [ˈbarka] nf (small) boat; **~ pesquera** fishing boat; **~ de pasaje** ferry; **~za** nf barge; **~za de desembarco** landing craft

Barcelona [barθe'lona] n Barcelona

barcelonés, esa [barθelo'nes, esa] adj of o from Barcelona

barco ['barko] nm boat; (grande) ship; ~ **de carga** cargo boat; ~ **de vela** sailing ship

baremo [ba'remo] nm (MAT, fig) scale

barítono [ba'ritono] nm baritone

barman ['barman] nm barman

Barna n = Barcelona

barniz [bar'niθ] nm varnish; (en la loza) glaze; (fig) veneer; **~ar** vt to varnish; (loza) to glaze

barómetro [ba'rometro] nm barometer

barquero [bar'kero] nm boatman

barquillo [bar'kiʎo] nm cone, cornet

barra ['barra] nf bar, rod; (de un bar, café) bar; (de pan) French stick; (palanca) lever; ~ **de carmín** o **de labios** lipstick; ~ **libre** free bar

barraca [ba'rraka] nf hut, cabin

barranco [ba'rranko] nm ravine; (fig) difficulty

barrena [ba'rrena] nf drill; **barrenar** vt to drill (through), bore; **barreno** nm large drill

barrer [ba'rrer] vt to sweep; (quitar) to sweep away

barrera [ba'rrera] nf barrier

barriada [ba'rrjaða] nf quarter, district

barricada [barri'kaða] nf barricade

barrida [ba'rriða] nf sweep, sweeping

barrido [ba'rriðo] nm = **barrida**

barriga [ba'rriɣa] nf belly; (panza) paunch; **barrigón, ona** adj potbellied; **barrigudo, a** adj potbellied

barril [ba'rril] nm barrel, cask

barrio ['barrjo] nm (vecindad) area, neighborhood (US); (en las afueras) suburb; ~ **chino** red-light district

barro ['barro] nm (lodo) mud; (objetos) earthenware; (MED) pimple

barroco, a [ba'rroko, a] adj, nm baroque

barrote [ba'rrote] nm (de ventana) bar

barruntar [barrun'tar] vt (conjeturar)

to guess; (presentir) to suspect; **barrunto** nm guess; suspicion

bartola [bar'tola]: **a la ~** adv: **tirarse a la ~** to take it easy, be lazy

bártulos ['bartulos] nmpl things, belongings

barullo [ba'ruʎo] nm row, uproar

basar [ba'sar] vt to base; **~se** vr: **~se en** to be based on

báscula ['baskula] nf (platform) scales

base ['base] nf base; **a ~ de** on the basis of; (mediante) by means of; **~ de datos** (INFORM) database

básico, a ['basiko, a] adj basic

basílica [ba'silika] nf basilica

PALABRA CLAVE

bastante [bas'tante] adj **1** (suficiente) enough; ~ **dinero** enough o sufficient money; **~s libros** enough books **2** (valor intensivo): ~ **gente** quite a lot of people; **tener ~ calor** to be rather hot

♦ adv: **~ bueno/malo** quite good/ rather bad; ~ **rico** pretty rich; **(lo) ~ inteligente (como) para hacer algo** clever enough o sufficiently clever to do sth

---

bastar [bas'tar] vi to be enough o sufficient; **~se** vr to be self-sufficient; ~ **para** to be enough to; **¡basta!** (that's) enough!

bastardilla [bastar'ðiʎa] nf italics

bastardo, a [bas'tarðo, a] adj, nm/f bastard

bastidor [basti'ðor] nm frame; (de coche) chassis; (TEATRO) wing; **entre ~es** (fig) behind the scenes

basto, a ['basto, a] adj coarse, rough; **~s** nmpl (NAIPES) ≈ clubs

bastón [bas'ton] nm stick, staff; (para pasear) walking stick

bastoncillo [baston'θiʎo] nm cotton bud

basura [ba'sura] nf rubbish (BRIT), garbage (US)

basurero [basu'rero] nm (hombre) dustman (BRIT), garbage man (US); (lugar) dump; (cubo) (rubbish) bin (BRIT), trash can (US)

bata ['bata] nf (gen) dressing gown; (cubretodo) smock, overall; (MED, TEC etc) lab(oratory) coat

batalla [ba'taʎa] nf battle; **de ~** (fig) for everyday use

batallar [bata'ʎar] vi to fight

batallón [bata'ʎon] nm battalion

batata [ba'tata] nf sweet potato

batería [bate'ria] nf battery; (MUS) drums; **~ de cocina** kitchen utensils

batido, a [ba'tiðo, a] adj (camino) beaten, well-trodden ♦ nm (CULIN): **~ (de leche)** milk shake

batidora [bati'ðora] nf beater, mixer; **~ eléctrica** food mixer, blender

batir [ba'tir] vt to beat, strike; (vencer) to beat, defeat; (revolver) to beat, mix; **~se** vr to fight; **~ palmas** to applaud

batuta [ba'tuta] nf baton; **llevar la ~** (fig) to be the boss, be in charge

baúl [ba'ul] nm trunk; (AUTO) boot (BRIT), trunk (US)

bautismo [bau'tismo] nm baptism, christening

bautizar [bauti'θar] vt to baptize, christen; (fam: diluir) to water down; **bautizo** nm baptism, christening

baya ['baja] nf berry

bayeta [ba'jeta] nf floorcloth

baza ['baθa] nf trick; **meter ~** to butt in

bazar [ba'θar] nm bazaar

bazofia [ba'θofja] nf trash

BCE nm abr (= Banco Central Europeo) ECB

beato, a [be'ato, a] adj blessed; (piadoso) pious

bebé [be'ße] (pl **~s**) nm baby

bebedor, a [beße'ðor, a] adj hard-drinking

beber [be'ßer] vt, vi to drink

bebida [be'ßiða] nf drink; **bebido, a** adj drunk

beca ['beka] nf grant, scholarship

becario, a [be'karjo, a] nm/f scholarship holder, grant holder

bedel [be'ðel] nm (ESCOL) janitor; (UNIV) porter

béisbol ['beisßol] nm (DEPORTE) baseball

belén [be'len] nm (de navidad) nativity scene, crib; **B~** Bethlehem

belga ['belxa] adj, nm/f Belgian

Bélgica ['belxika] nf Belgium

bélico, a ['beliko, a] adj (actitud) warlike; **belicoso, a** adj (guerrero) warlike; (agresivo) aggressive, bellicose

beligerante [belixe'rante] adj belligerent

belleza [be'ʎeθa] nf beauty

bello, a ['beʎo, a] adj beautiful, lovely; **Bellas Artes** Fine Art

bellota [be'ʎota] nf acorn

bemol [be'mol] nm (MUS) flat; **esto tiene ~es** (fam) this is a tough one

bencina [ben'θina] nf (AM: gasolina) petrol (BRIT), gasoline (US)

bendecir [bende'θir] vt to bless

bendición [bendi'θjon] nf blessing

bendito, a [ben'dito, a] pp de **bendecir** ♦ adj holy; (afortunado) lucky; (feliz) happy; (sencillo) simple ♦ nm/f simple soul

beneficencia [benefi'θenθja] nf charity

beneficiar [benefi'θjar] vt to benefit, be of benefit to; **~se** vr to benefit, profit; **~io, a** nm/f beneficiary

beneficio [benefi'θjo] nm (bien) benefit, advantage; (ganancia) profit, gain; **~so, a** adj beneficial

benéfico, a [be'nefiko, a] adj charitable

beneplácito [bene'plaθito] nm approval, consent

benevolencia [beneßo'lenθja] nf benevolence, kindness; **benévolo, a** adj benevolent, kind

benigno, a [be'niɣno, a] adj kind; (suave) mild; (MED: tumor) benign, non-malignant

berberecho [berβe'retʃo] nm (ZOOL, CULIN) cockle

berenjena [beren'xena] nf aubergine (BRIT), eggplant (US)

Berlín [ber'lin] n Berlin; **berlinés, esa** adj o from Berlin ♦ nm/f Berliner

bermudas [ber'muðas] nfpl Bermuda shorts

berrear [berre'ar] vi to bellow, low

berrido [be'rriðo] nm bellow(ing)

berrinche [be'rrintʃe] (fam) nm temper, tantrum

berro ['berro] nm watercress

berza ['berθa] nf cabbage

besamel [besa'mel] nf (CULIN) white sauce, bechamel sauce

besar [be'sar] vt to kiss; (fig: tocar) to graze; **~se** vr to kiss (one another); **beso** nm kiss

bestia ['bestja] nf beast, animal; (fig) idiot; **~ de carga** beast of burden

bestial [bes'tjal] adj bestial; (fam) terrific; **~idad** nf bestiality; (fam) stupidity

besugo [be'suɣo] nm sea bream; (fam) idiot

besuquear [besuke'ar] vt to cover with kisses; **~se** vr to kiss and cuddle

betún [be'tun] nm shoe polish; (QUÍM) bitumen

biberón [biße'ron] nm feeding bottle

Biblia ['biβlja] nf Bible

bibliografía [biβljoɣra'fia] nf bibliography

biblioteca [biβljo'teka] nf library; (mueble) bookshelves; **~ de consulta** reference library; **~rio, a** nm/f librarian

bicarbonato [bikarßo'nato] nm bicarbonate

bicho ['bitʃo] nm (animal) small animal; (sabandija) bug, insect; (TAUR) bull

bici ['biθi] (fam) nf bike

bicicleta [biθi'kleta] nf bicycle, cycle; **ir en ~** to cycle

bidé [bi'ðe] (pl **~s**) nm bidet

bidón [bi'ðon] nm (de aceite) drum;

(de gasolina) can

PALABRA CLAVE

bien [bjen] nm 1 (bienestar) good; **te lo digo por tu ~** I'm telling you for your own good; **el ~ y el mal** good and evil

2 (posesión): **~es** goods; **~es de consumo** consumer goods; **~es inmuebles** o **raíces/~es muebles** real estate sg/personal property sg

♦ adv 1 (de manera satisfactoria, correcta etc) well; **trabaja/come ~** she works/eats well; **contestó ~** he answered correctly; **me siento ~** I feel fine; **no me siento ~** I don't feel very well; **se está ~ aquí** it's nice here

2 (frases): **hiciste ~ en llamarme** you were right to call me

3 (valor intensivo) very; **un cuarto ~ caliente** a nice warm room; **~ se ve que ...** it's quite clear that ...

4: **estar ~**: **estoy muy ~ aquí** I feel very happy here; **está ~ que vengan** it's all right for them to come; **¡está ~! lo haré** oh all right, I'll do it

5 (de acuerdo): **yo ~ que iría pero ...** I'd gladly go but ...

♦ excl **¡~!** (aprobación) O.K.!; **¡muy ~!** well done!

♦ adj inv (matiz despectivo): **niño ~** rich kid; **gente ~** posh people

♦ conj 1: **~ ... ~ ...**: o **en coche** o **en tren** either by car or by train

2: **no ~** (esp AM): **no ~ llegue te llamaré** as soon as I arrive I'll call you

3: **si ~** even though; ver tb **más**

bienal [bje'nal] adj biennial

bienaventurado, a [bjenaβentu'raðo, a] adj (feliz) happy, fortunate

bienestar [bjenes'tar] nm well-being, welfare

bienhechor, a [bjene'tʃor, a] adj beneficent ♦ nm/f benefactor/benefactress

bienvenida [bjembe'niða] nf welcome; **dar la ~ a uno** to welcome sb

bienvenida [bjembe'niða] excl welcome!

bife ['bife] (AM) nm steak

bifurcación [bifurka'θjon] nf fork

bifurcarse [bifur'karse] vr (camino, carretera, río) to fork

bigamia [bi'ɣamja] nf bigamy; **bígamo, a** adj bigamous ♦ nm/f bigamist

bigote [bi'ɣote] nm moustache; **bigotudo, a** adj with a big moustache

bikini [bi'kini] nm bikini; (CULIN) toasted ham and cheese sandwich

bilbaíno, a [bilβa'ino, a] adj from o of Bilbao

bilingüe [bi'lingwe] adj bilingual

billar [bi'ʎar] nm billiards sg; (lugar) billiard hall; (mini-casino) amusement arcade; **~ americano** pool

billete [bi'ʎete] nm ticket; (de banco) (bank)note (BRIT), bill (US); (carta) note; **~ sencillo, ~ de ida solamente** single (BRIT) o one-way (US) ticket; **~ de ida y vuelta** return (BRIT) o round-trip (US) ticket; **~ de 20 libras** £20 note

billetera [biʎe'tera] nf wallet

billetero [biʎe'tero] nm = **billetera**

billón [bi'ʎon] nm billion

bimensual [bimen'swal] adj twice monthly

bimotor [bimo'tor] adj twin-engined ♦ nm twin-engined plane

bingo ['bingo] nm bingo

biodegradable [bioðeɣra'ðaβle] adj biodegradable

biografía [bjoɣra'fia] nf biography; **biógrafo, a** nm/f biographer

biología [bjolo'xia] nf biology; **biológico, a** adj (cultivo, producto) organic; **biólogo, a** nm/f biologist

biombo ['bjombo] nm (folding) screen

biquini [bi'kini] nm bikini

birlar [bir'lar] (fam) vt to pinch

Birmania [bir'manja] nf Burma

birria ['birrja] nf: **ser una ~** (película, libro) to be rubbish

bis [bis] excl encore! ♦ adv: **viven en el 27 ~** they live at 27a

bisabuelo, a [bisa'βwelo, a] nm/f great-grandfather/mother

bisagra [bi'saɣra] nf hinge

bisiesto [bi'sjesto] adj: **año ~** leap year

bisnieto, a [bis'njeto, a] nm/f great-grandson/daughter

bisonte [bi'sonte] nm bison

bisté [bis'te] nm = **bistec**

bistec [bis'tek] nm steak

bisturí [bistu'ri] nm scalpel

bisutería [bisute'ria] nf imitation o costume jewellery

bit [bit] nm (INFORM) bit

bizco, a ['biθko, a] adj cross-eyed

bizcocho [biθ'kotʃo] nm (CULIN) sponge cake

bizquear [biθke'ar] vi to squint

blanca ['blanka] nf (MUS) minim; **estar sin ~** to be broke; ver tb **blanco**

blanco, a ['blanko, a] adj white ♦ nm/f white man/woman, white ♦ nm (color) white; (en texto) blank; (MIL, fig) target; **en ~** blank; **noche en ~** sleepless night

blancura [blan'kura] nf whiteness

blandir [blan'dir] vt to brandish

blando, a ['blando, a] adj soft; (tierno) tender, gentle; (carácter) mild; (fam) cowardly; **blandura** nf softness; tenderness; mildness

blanquear [blanke'ar] vt to whiten; (fachada) to whitewash; (paño) to bleach ♦ vi to turn white; **blanquecino, a** adj whitish

blasfemar [blasfe'mar] vi to blaspheme, curse; **blasfemia** nf blasphemy

blasón [bla'son] nm coat of arms

bledo ['bleðo] nm: **me importa un ~** I couldn't care less

blindado, a |blin'daðo, a| adj (MIL) armour-plated; (antibala) bullet-proof; **coche** (ESP) **o carro** (AM) ~ armoured car

blindaje |blin'daxe| nm armour, armour-plating

bloc |blok| (pl ~s) nm writing pad

bloque |'bloke| nm block; (POL) bloc; ~ **de cilindros** cylinder block

bloquear |bloke'ar| vt to blockade; **bloqueo** |blo'keo| nm blockade; (COM) freezing, blocking

blusa |'blusa| nf blouse

boato |bo'ato| nm show, ostentation

bobada |bo'βaða| nf foolish action; foolish statement; **decir ~s** to talk nonsense

bobería |boβe'ria| nf = **bobada**

bobina |bo'βina| nf (TEC) bobbin; (FOTO) spool; (ELEC) coil

bobo, a |'boβo, a| adj (tonto) daft, silly; (cándido) naïve ♦ nm/f (payaso) fool, idiot ♦ nm (TEATRO) clown, funny man

boca |'boka| nf mouth; (de crustáceo) pincer; (de cañón) muzzle; (entrada) mouth, entrance; ~ **abajo/arriba** face down/up; **se me hace agua la** ~ my mouth is watering

bocacalle |boka'kaʎe| nf (entrance to a) street; **la primera** ~ **the first turning o street**

bocadillo |boka'ðiʎo| nm sandwich

bocado |bo'kaðo| nm mouthful, bite; (de caballo) bridle; ~ **de Adán** Adam's apple

bocajarro |boka'xarro|: **a** ~ adv (disparar, preguntar) point-blank

bocanada |boka'naða| nf (de vino) mouthful, swallow; (de aire) gust, puff

bocata |bo'kata| (fam) nm sandwich

bocazas |bo'kaθas| (fam) nm inv bigmouth

boceto |bo'θeto| nm sketch, outline

bochorno |bo'tʃorno| nm (vergüenza) embarrassment; (calor): **hace** ~ it's very muggy; **~so, a** adj muggy;

embarrassing

bocina |bo'θina| nf (MUS) trumpet; (AUTO) horn; (para hablar) megaphone

boda |'boða| nf (tb: ~s) wedding, marriage; (fiesta) wedding reception; **~s de plata/de oro** silver/golden wedding

bodega |bo'ðexa| nf (de vino) (wine) cellar; (depósito) storeroom; (de barco) hold

bodegón |boðe'xon| nm (ARTE) still life

bofe |'bofe| nm (tb: ~s: de res) lights

bofetada |bofe'taða| nf slap (in the face)

bofetón |bofe'ton| nm = **bofetada**

boga |'boxa| nf: **en** ~ (fig) in vogue

bogar |bo'xar| vi (remar) to row; (navegar) to sail

bogavante |boxa'βante| nm lobster

Bogotá |boxo'ta| n Bogotá

bohemio, a |bo'emjo, a| adj, nm/f Bohemian

boicot |boi'kot| (pl ~s) nm boycott; **~ear** vt to boycott; **~eo** nm boycott

boina |'boina| nf beret

bola |'bola| nf ball; (canica) marble; (NAIPES) (grand) slam; (betún) shoe polish; (mentira) tale, story; **~s** (AM) nfpl bolas sg; ~ **de billar** billiard ball; ~ **de nieve** snowball

bolchevique |boltʃe'βike| adj, nm/f Bolshevik

boleadoras |bolea'ðoras| (AM) nfpl bolas sg

bolera |bo'lera| nf skittle o bowling alley

boleta |bo'leta| (AM) nf (billete) ticket; (permiso) pass, permit

boletería |bolete'ria| (AM) nf ticket office

boletín |bole'tin| nm bulletin; (periódico) journal, review; ~ **de noticias** news bulletin

boleto |bo'leto| nm ticket

boli |'boli| (fam) nm Biro ®, pen

bolígrafo |bo'lixrafo| nm ball-point

bolívar

pen, Biro ®

bolívar [bo'lißar] nm monetary unit of Venezuela

Bolivia [bo'lißja] nf Bolivia; **boliviano, a** adj, nm/f Bolivian

bollería [boʎe'ria] nf cakes pl and pastries pl

bollo ['boʎo] nm (pan) roll; (bulto) bump, lump; (abolladura) dent

bolo ['bolo] nm skittle; (píldora) (large) pill; (**juego de**) **~s** nmpl skittles sg

bolsa ['bolsa] nf bag; (AM) pocket; (ANAT) cavity, sac; (COM) stock exchange; (MINERÍA) pocket; **de ~** pocket cpd; **~ de agua caliente** hot water bottle; **~ de aire** air pocket; **~ de papel** paper bag; **~ de plástico** plastic bag

bolsillo [bol'siʎo] nm pocket; (cartera) purse; **de ~** pocket(-size)

bolsista [bol'sista] nm/f stockbroker

bolso ['bolso] nm (bolsa) bag; (de mujer) handbag

bomba ['bomba] nf (MIL) bomb; (TEC) pump ♦ (fam) adj: **noticia ~** bombshell ♦ (fam) adv: **pasarlo ~** to have a great time; **~ atómica/de humo/de efecto retardado** atomic/smoke/time bomb

bombardear [bombarðe'ar] vt to bombard; (MIL) to bomb; **bombardeo** nm bombardment; bombing

bombardero [bombar'ðero] nm bomber

bombear [bombe'ar] vt (agua) to pump (out o up); **~se** vr to warp

bombero [bom'bero] nm fireman

bombilla [bom'biʎa] (ESP) nf (light) bulb

bombín [bom'bin] nm bowler hat

bombo ['bombo] nm (MUS) bass drum; (TEC) drum

bombón [bom'bon] nm chocolate

bombona [bom'bona] nf (de butano, oxígeno) cylinder

bonachón, ona [bona'tʃon, ona] adj good-natured, easy-going

bonanza [bo'nanθa] nf (NAUT) fair weather; (fig) bonanza; (MINERÍA) rich pocket o vein

bondad [bon'dað] nf goodness, kindness; **tenga la ~ de** (please) be good enough to; **~oso, a** adj good, kind

bonificación [bonifika'θjon] nf bonus

bonito, a [bo'nito, a] adj pretty; (agradable) nice ♦ nm (atún) tuna (fish)

bono ['bono] nm voucher; (FIN) bond

bonobús [bono'ßus] (ESP) nm bus pass

bonoloto [bono'loto] nm state-run weekly lottery

boquerón [boke'ron] nm (pez) (kind of) anchovy; (agujero) large hole

boquete [bo'kete] nm gap, hole

boquiabierto, a [bokia'ßjerto, a] adj: **quedar ~** to be amazed o flabbergasted

boquilla [bo'kiʎa] nf (para riego) nozzle; (para cigarro) cigarette holder; (MUS) mouthpiece

borbotón [borßo'ton] nm: **salir a borbotones** to gush out

borda ['borða] nf (NAUT) (ship's) rail; **tirar algo/caerse por la ~** to throw sth/fall overboard

bordado [bor'ðaðo] nm embroidery

bordar [bor'ðar] vt to embroider

borde ['borðe] nm edge, border; (de camino etc) side; (en la costura) hem; **al ~ de** (fig) on the verge o brink of; **ser ~** (ESP: fam) to be rude; **~ar** vt to border

bordillo [bor'ðiʎo] nm kerb (BRIT), curb (US)

bordo ['borðo] nm (NAUT) side; **a ~** on board

borinqueño, a [borin'kenjo, a] adj, nm/f Puerto Rican

borla ['borla] nf (adorno) tassel

borrachera [borra'tʃera] nf (ebriedad) drunkenness; (orgía) spree, binge

borracho, a [bo'rratʃo, a] adj drunk ♦ nm/f (habitual) drunkard, drunk; (temporal) drunk, drunk man/woman

borrador [borra'ðor] nm (escritura) first draft, rough sketch; (goma) rubber (BRIT), eraser

borrar [bo'rrar] vt to erase, rub out

borrasca [bo'rraska] nf storm

borrico, a [bo'rriko, a] nm/f donkey/ she-donkey; (fig) stupid man/woman

borrón [bo'rron] nm (mancha) stain

borroso, a [bo'rroso, a] adj vague, unclear; (escritura) illegible

bosque ['boske] nm wood; (grande) forest

bosquejar [boske'xar] vt to sketch; **bosquejo** nm sketch

bostezar [boste'θar] vi to yawn; **bostezo** nm yawn

bota ['bota] nf (calzado) boot; (para vino) leather wine bottle; **~s de agua**, **~s de goma** Wellingtons

botánica [bo'tanika] nf (ciencia) botany; ver tb **botánico**

botánico, a [bo'taniko, a] adj botanical ♦ nm/f botanist

botar [bo'tar] vt to throw, hurl; (NAUT) to launch; (AM) to throw out ♦ vi to bounce

bote ['bote] nm (salto) bounce; (golpe) thrust; (vasija) tin, can; (embarcación) boat; **de ~ en ~** packed, jammed full; **~ de la basura** (AM) dustbin (BRIT); **~ salvavidas** lifeboat

botella [bo'teʎa] nf bottle; **botellín** nm small bottle

botica [bo'tika] nf chemist's (shop) (BRIT), pharmacy; **~rio, a** nm/f chemist (BRIT), pharmacist

botijo [bo'tixo] nm (earthenware) jug

botín [bo'tin] nm (calzado) half boot; (polaina) spat; (MIL) booty

botiquín [boti'kin] nm (armario) medicine cabinet; (portátil) first-aid kit

botón [bo'ton] nm button; (BOT) bud; **~ de oro** buttercup

botones [bo'tones] nm inv bellboy (BRIT), bellhop (US)

bóveda ['boβeða] nf (ARQ) vault

boxeador [boksea'ðor] nm boxer

boxear [bokse'ar] vi to box

boxeo [bok'seo] nm boxing

boya ['boja] nf (NAUT) buoy; (de caña) float

boyante [bo'jante] adj prosperous

bozal [bo'θal] nm (de caballo) halter; (de perro) muzzle

bracear [braθe'ar] vi (agitar los brazos) to wave one's arms

bracero [bra'θero] nm labourer; (en el campo) farmhand

bragas ['braxas] nfpl (de mujer) panties, knickers (BRIT)

bragueta [bra'βeta] nf fly, flies pl

braille [breil] nm braille

bramar [bra'mar] vi to bellow, roar; **bramido** nm bellow, roar

brasa ['brasa] nf live o hot coal

brasero [bra'sero] nm brazier

Brasil [bra'sil] nm: **(el) ~** Brazil; **brasileño, a** adj, nm/f Brazilian

bravata [bra'βata] nf boast

braveza [bra'βeθa] nf (valor) bravery; (ferocidad) ferocity

bravío, a [bra'βio, a] adj wild; (feroz) fierce

bravo, a ['braβo, a] adj (valiente) brave; (feroz) ferocious; (salvaje) wild; (mar etc) rough, stormy ♦ excl bravo!; **bravura** nf bravery; ferocity

braza ['braθa] nf fathom; **nadar a la ~** to swim (the) breast-stroke

brazada [bra'θaða] nf stroke

brazado [bra'θaðo] nm armful

brazalete [braθa'lete] nm (pulsera) bracelet; (banda) armband

brazo ['braθo] nm arm; (ZOOL) foreleg; (BOT) limb, branch; **luchar a ~ partido** to fight hand-to-hand; **ir cogidos del ~** to walk arm in arm

brea ['brea] nf pitch, tar

brebaje [bre'βaxe] nm potion

brecha ['bretʃa] nf (hoyo, vacío) gap, opening; (MIL, fig) breach

brega ['breβa] nf (lucha) struggle; (trabajo) hard work

breva ['breβa] nf early fig

breve ['breβe] adj short, brief ♦ nm (MUS) breve; **~dad** nf brevity, shortness

brezo ['breθo] nm heather

bribón, ona [bri'βon, ona] adj idle, lazy ♦ nm/f (pícaro) rascal, rogue

bricolaje [briko'laxe] nm do-it-yourself, DIY

brida ['briða] nf bridle, rein; (TEC) clamp; **a toda ~** at top speed

bridge [britʃ] nm bridge

brigada [bri'γaða] nf (unidad) brigade; (trabajadores) squad, gang ♦ nm ≈ staff-sergeant, sergeant-major

brillante [bri'ʎante] adj brilliant ♦ nm diamond

brillar [bri'ʎar] vi (tb fig) to shine; (joyas) to sparkle

brillo ['briʎo] nm shine; (brillantez) brilliance; (fig) splendour; **sacar ~ a** to polish

brincar [brin'kar] vi to skip about, hop about; jump about; **está que brinca** he's hopping mad

brinco ['brinko] nm jump, leap

brindar [brin'dar] vi: **~ a o por** to drink (a toast) to ♦ vt to offer, present

brindis ['brindis] nm inv toast

brío ['brio] nm spirit, dash; **brioso, a** adj spirited, dashing

brisa ['brisa] nf breeze

británico, a [bri'taniko, a] adj British ♦ nm/f Briton, British person

brizna ['briθna] nf (de hierba, paja) blade; (de tabaco) leaf

broca ['broka] nf (TEC) drill, bit

brocal [bro'kal] nm rim

brocha ['brotʃa] nf (large) paintbrush; **~ de afeitar** shaving brush

broche ['brotʃe] nm brooch

broma ['broma] nf joke; **en ~** in fun, as a joke; **~ pesada** practical joke; **bromear** vi to joke

bromista [bro'mista] adj fond of joking ♦ nm/f joker, wag

bronca ['bronka] nf row; **echar una ~ a uno** to tick sb off

bronce ['bronθe] nm bronze; **~ado, a**

adj bronze; (por el sol) tanned ♦ nm (sun)tan; (TEC) bronzing

bronceador [bronθea'ðor] nm suntan lotion

broncearse [bronθe'arse] vr to get a suntan

bronco, a ['bronko, a] adj (manera) rude, surly; (voz) harsh

bronquio ['bronkjo] nm (ANAT) bronchial tube

bronquitis [bron'kitis] nf inv bronchitis

brotar [bro'tar] vi (BOT) to sprout; (aguas) to gush (forth); (MED) to break out

brote ['brote] nm (BOT) shoot; (MED, fig) outbreak

bruces ['bruθes]: **de ~** adv: **caer o dar de ~** to fall headlong, fall flat

bruja ['bruxa] nf witch; **brujería** nf witchcraft

brujo ['bruxo] nm wizard, magician

brújula ['bruxula] nf compass

bruma ['bruma] nf mist; **brumoso, a** adj misty

bruñir [bru'ɲir] vt to polish

brusco, a ['brusko, a] adj (súbito) sudden; (áspero) brusque

Bruselas [bru'selas] n Brussels

brutal [bru'tal] adj brutal

brutalidad [brutali'ðað] nf brutality

bruto, a ['bruto, a] adj (idiota) stupid; (bestial) brutish; (peso) gross; **en ~** raw, unworked

Bs.As. abr (= Buenos Aires) B.A.

bucal [bu'kal] adj oral; **por vía ~** orally

bucear [buθe'ar] vi to dive ♦ vt to explore; **buceo** nm diving

bucle ['bukle] nm curl

budismo [bu'ðismo] nm Buddhism

buen [bwen] adj ver **bueno**

buenamente [bwena'mente] adv (fácilmente) easily; (voluntariamente) willingly

buenaventura [bwenaβen'tura] nf (suerte) good luck; (adivinación) fortune

bueno, a |'bweno, a| *adj (antes de nmsg:* **buen**) **1** *(excelente etc)* good; **es un libro ~, es un buen libro** it's a good book; **hace ~, hace buen tiempo** the weather is fine, it is fine; **el ~ de Paco** good old Paco; **fue muy ~ conmigo** he was very nice o kind to me

2 *(apropiado):* **ser ~ para** to be good for; **creo que vamos por buen camino** I think we're on the right track

3 *(irónico):* **le di un buen rapapolvo** I gave him a good o real ticking off; **¡buen conductor estás hecho!** some o a fine driver you are!; **¡estaría ~ que ...!** a fine thing it would be if ...!

4 *(atractivo, sabroso):* **está ~ este bizcocho** this sponge is delicious; **Carmen está muy buena** Carmen is gorgeous

5 *(saludos):* **¡buen día!, ¡~s días!** (good) morning!; **¡buenas tardes!** (good) afternoon!; *(más tarde)* (good) evening!; **¡buenas noches!** good night!

6 *(otras locuciones):* **estar de buenas** to be in a good mood; **por las buenas o por las malas** by hook or by crook; **de buenas a primeras** all of a sudden

♦ *excl:* **¡~!** all right!; **~, ¿y qué?** well, so what?

Buenos Aires *nm* Buenos Aires
buey |bwei| *nm* ox
búfalo |'bufalo| *nm* buffalo
bufanda |bu'fanda| *nf* scarf
bufar |bu'far| *vi* to snort
bufete |bu'fete| *nm (despacho de abogado)* lawyer's office
buffer |'bufer| *nm (INFORM)* buffer
bufón |bu'fon| *nm* clown
buhardilla |buar'ðiʎa| *nf* attic

búho |'buo| *nm* owl; *(fig)* hermit, recluse
buhonero |buo'nero| *nm* pedlar
buitre |'bwitre| *nm* vulture
bujía |bu'xia| *nf (vela)* candle; *(ELEC)* candle (power); *(AUTO)* spark plug
bula |'bula| *nf (papal)* bull
bulbo |'bulβo| *nm* bulb
bulevar |bule'βar| *nm* boulevard
Bulgaria |bul'varja| *nf* Bulgaria; **búlgaro, a** *adj, nm/f* Bulgarian
bulla |'buʎa| *nf (ruido)* uproar; *(de gente)* crowd
bullicio |bu'ʎiθjo| *nm (ruido)* uproar; *(movimiento)* bustle
bullir |bu'ʎir| *vi (hervir)* to boil; *(burbujear)* to bubble
bulto |'bulto| *nm (paquete)* package; *(fardo)* bundle; *(tamaño)* size, bulkiness; *(MED)* swelling, lump; *(silueta)* vague shape
buñuelo |bu'ɲwelo| *nm* ≈ doughnut *(BRIT)*, ≈ donut *(US)*; *(fruta de sartén)* fritter
BUP |bup| *nm abr (ESP:* = *Bachillerato Unificado Polivalente) secondary education and leaving certificate for 14-17 age group*
buque |'buke| *nm* ship, vessel
burbuja |bur'βuxa| *nf* bubble; **burbujear** *vi* to bubble
burdel |bur'ðel| *nm* brothel
burdo, a |'burðo, a| *adj* coarse, rough
burgués, esa |bur'ɣes, esa| *adj* middle-class, bourgeois; **burguesía** *nf* middle class, bourgeoisie
burla |'burla| *nf (mofa)* gibe; *(broma)* joke; *(engaño)* trick
burladero |burla'ðero| *nm (bullfighter's)* refuge
burlar |bur'lar| *vt (engañar)* to deceive
♦ *vi* to joke; **~se** *vr* to joke; **~se de** to make fun of
burlesco, a |bur'lesko, a| *adj* burlesque
burlón, ona |bur'lon, ona| *adj* mocking

burocracia [buro'kraθja] *nf* civil service

burócrata [bu'rokrata] *nm/f* civil servant

burrada [bu'rraða] *nf:* **decir/soltar ~s** to talk nonsense; **hacer ~s** to act stupid; **una ~** (*mucho*) a (hell of a) lot

burro, a ['burro, a] *nm/f* donkey/she-donkey; (*fig*) ass, idiot

bursátil [bur'satil] *adj* stock-exchange *cpd*

bus [bus] *nm* bus

busca ['buska] *nf* search, hunt ♦ *nm* (*TEL*) bleeper; **en ~ de** in search of

buscar [bus'kar] *vt* to look for, search for, seek ♦ *vi* to look, search, seek; **se busca secretaria** secretary wanted

busque *etc vb ver* **buscar**

búsqueda ['buskeða] *nf* = **busca** *nf*

busto ['busto] *nm* (*ANAT, ARTE*) bust

butaca [bu'taka] *nf* armchair; (*de cine, teatro*) stall, seat

butano [bu'tano] *nm* butane (gas)

buzo ['buθo] *nm* diver

buzón [bu'θon] *nm* (*en puerta*) letter box; (*en la calle*) pillar box

C, c

C. *abr* (= *centígrado*) C; (= *compañía*) Co.

c. *abr* (= *capítulo*) ch.

C/ *abr* (= *calle*) St

c.a. *abr* (= *corriente alterna*) AC

cabal [ka'βal] *adj* (*exacto*) exact; (*correcto*) right, proper; (*acabado*) finished, complete; **~es** *nmpl:* **estar en sus ~es** to be in one's right mind

cábalas ['kaβalas] *nfpl:* **hacer ~** to guess

cabalgar [kaβal'γar] *vt, vi* to ride

cabalgata [kaβal'γata] *nf* procession

caballa [ka'βaʎa] *nf* mackerel

caballeresco, a [kaβaʎe'resko, a] *adj* noble, chivalrous

caballería [kaβaʎe'ria] *nf* mount; (*MIL*) cavalry

caballeriza [kaβaʎe'riθa] *nf* stable; **caballerizo** *nm* groom, stableman

caballero [kaβa'ʎero] *nm* gentleman; (*de la orden de caballería*) knight; (*trato directo*) sir

caballerosidad [kaβaʎerosi'ðað] *nf* chivalry

caballete [kaβa'ʎete] *nm* (*ARTE*) easel; (*TEC*) trestle

caballito [kaβa'ʎito] *nm* (*caballo pequeño*) small horse, pony; **~s** *nmpl* (*en verbena*) roundabout, merry-go-round

caballo [ka'βaʎo] *nm* horse; (*AJEDREZ*) knight; (*NAIPES*) queen; **ir en ~** to ride; **~ de vapor** o **de fuerza** horsepower; **~ de carreras** racehorse

cabaña [ka'βaɲa] *nf* (*casita*) hut, cabin

cabaré [kaβa're] (*pl* **~s**) *nm* cabaret

cabaret [kaβa're] (*pl* **~s**) *nm* cabaret

cabecear [kaβeθe'ar] *vt, vi* to nod

cabecera [kaβe'θera] *nf* head; (*IMPRENTA*) headline

cabecilla [kaβe'θiʎa] *nm* ringleader

cabellera [kaβe'ʎera] *nf* (head of) hair; (*de cometa*) tail

cabello [ka'βeʎo] *nm* (*tb:* **~s**) hair

caber [ka'βer] *vi* (*entrar*) to fit, go; **caben 3 más** there's room for 3 more

cabestrillo [kaβes'triʎo] *nm* sling

cabestro [ka'βestro] *nm* halter

cabeza [ka'βeθa] *nf* head; (*POL*) chief, leader; **~ rapada** skinhead; **~da** *nf* (*golpe*) butt; **dar ~das** to nod off; **cabezón, ona** *adj* (*vino*) heady; (*fam: persona*) pig-headed

cabida [ka'βiða] *nf* space

cabildo [ka'βildo] *nm* (*de iglesia*) chapter; (*POL*) town council

cabina [ka'βina] *nf* cabin; (*de camión*) cab; **~ telefónica** telephone box (*BRIT*) o booth

cabizbajo, a [kaβiθ'βaxo, a] *adj* crestfallen, dejected

cable ['kaβle] *nm* cable

cabo ['kaβo] *nm* (*de objeto*) end,

extremity; (MIL) corporal; (NAUT) rope, cable; (GEO) cape; **al ~ de 3 días** after 3 days

cabra ['kaβra] nf goat

cabré etc vb ver **caber**

cabrear [kaβre'ar] (fam) vt to bug; **~se** vr (enfadarse) to fly off the handle

cabrío, a [ka'βrio, a] adj goatish; **macho ~** (he-)goat, billy goat

cabriola [ka'βrjola] nf caper

cabritilla [kaβri'tiʎa] nf kid, kidskin

cabrito [ka'βrito] nm kid

cabrón [ka'βron] nm cuckold; (fam!) bastard (!)

caca ['kaka] (fam) nf pooh

cacahuete [kaka'wete] (ESP) nm peanut

cacao [ka'kao] nm cocoa; (BOT) cacao

cacarear [kakare'ar] vi (persona) to boast; (gallina) to crow

cacería [kaθe'ria] nf hunt

cacerola [kaθe'rola] nf pan, saucepan

cachalote [katʃa'lote] nm (ZOOL) sperm whale

cacharro [ka'tʃarro] nm earthenware pot; **~s** nmpl pots and pans

cachear [katʃe'ar] vt to search, frisk

cachemir [katʃe'mir] nm cashmere

cacheo [ka'tʃeo] nm searching, frisking

cachete [ka'tʃete] nm (ANAT) cheek; (bofetada) slap (in the face)

cachiporra [katʃi'porra] nf truncheon

cachivache [katʃi'βatʃe] nm (trasto) piece of junk; **~s** nmpl junk sg

cacho ['katʃo] nm (small) bit; (AM: cuerno) horn

cachondeo [katʃon'deo] (fam) nm farce, joke

cachondo, a [ka'tʃondo, a] adj (ZOOL) on heat; (fam: sexualmente) randy; (: gracioso) funny

cachorro, a [ka'tʃorro, a] nm/f (perro!) pup, puppy; (león) cub

cacique [ka'θike] nm chief, local ruler; (POL) local party boss; **caciquismo** nm system of control by the local boss

caco ['kako] nm pickpocket

cacto ['kakto] nm cactus

cactus ['kaktus] nm inv cactus

cada ['kaða] adj inv each; (antes de número) every; **~ día** each day, every day; **~ dos días** every other day; **~ uno/a** each one, every one; **~ vez más/menos** more and more/less and less; **uno de ~ diez** one out of every ten

cadalso [ka'ðalso] nm scaffold

cadáver [ka'ðaβer] nm (dead) body, corpse

cadena [ka'ðena] nf chain; (TV) channel; **trabajo en ~** assembly line work; **~ perpetua** (JUR) life imprisonment

cadencia [ka'ðenθja] nf rhythm

cadera [ka'ðera] nf hip

cadete [ka'ðete] nm cadet

caducar [kaðu'kar] vi to expire; **caduco, a** adj expired; (persona) very old

caer [ka'er] vi to fall (down); **~se** vr to fall (down); **me cae bien/mal** I get on well with him/I can't stand him; **~ en la cuenta** to realize; **su cumpleaños cae en viernes** her birthday falls on a Friday

café [ka'fe] (pl **~s**) nm (bebida, planta) coffee; (lugar) café ♦ adj (color) brown; **~ con leche** white coffee; **~ solo** black coffee

cafetera [kafe'tera] nf coffee pot

cafetería [kafete'ria] nf (gen) café

cafetero, a [kafe'tero, a] adj coffee cpd; **ser muy ~** to be a coffee addict

cagar [ka'yar] (fam!) vt to bungle, mess up ♦ vi to have a shit (!)

caída [ka'iða] nf fall; (declive) slope; (disminución) fall, drop

caído, a [ka'iðo, a] adj drooping

caiga etc vb ver **caer**

caimán [kai'man] nm alligator

caja ['kaxa] nf box; (para reloj) case; (de ascensor) shaft; (COM) cashbox; (donde se hacen los pagos) cashdesk; (: en supermercado) checkout, till; **~ de**

ahorros savings bank; ~ **de cambios** gearbox; ~ **fuerte**, ~ **de caudales** safe, strongbox

cajero, a [ka'xero, a] nm/f cashier; ~ **automático** cash dispenser

cajetilla [kaxe'tiʎa] nf (de cigarrillos) packet

cajón [ka'xon] nm big box; (de mueble) drawer

cal [kal] nf lime

cala ['kala] nf (GEO) cove, inlet; (de barco) hold

calabacín [kalaβa'θin] nm (BOT) baby marrow; (: más pequeño) courgette (BRIT), zucchini (US)

calabaza [kala'βaθa] nf (BOT) pumpkin

calabozo [kala'βoθo] nm (cárcel) prison; (celda) cell

calada [ka'laða] nf (de cigarrillo) puff

calado, a [ka'laðo, a] adj (prenda) lace cpd ♦ nm (NAUT) draught

calamar [kala'mar] nm squid

calambre [ka'lambre] nm (tb: ~s) cramp

calamidad [kalami'ðað] nf calamity, disaster

calar [ka'lar] vt to soak, drench; (penetrar) to pierce, penetrate; (comprender) to see through; (vela) to lower; ~**se** vr (AUTO) to stall; ~**las gafas** to stick one's glasses on

calavera [kala'βera] nf skull

calcar [kal'kar] vt (reproducir) to trace; (imitar) to copy

calcetín [kalθe'tin] nm sock

calcinar [kalθi'nar] vt to burn, blacken

calcio ['kalθjo] nm calcium

calcomanía [kalkoma'nia] nf transfer

calculador, a [kalkula'ðor, a] adj (persona) calculating

calculadora [kalkula'ðora] nf calculator

calcular [kalku'lar] vt (MAT) to calculate, compute; ~ **que** ... to reckon that ...; **cálculo** nm calculation

caldear [kalde'ar] vt to warm (up), heat (up)

caldera [kal'dera] nf boiler

calderilla [kalde'riʎa] nf (moneda) small change

caldero [kal'dero] nm small boiler

caldo ['kaldo] nm stock; (consomé) consommé

calefacción [kalefak'θjon] nf heating; ~ **central** central heating

calendario [kalen'darjo] nm calendar

calentador [kalenta'ðor] nm heater

calentamiento [kalenta'mjento] nm (DEPORTE) warm-up

calentar [kalen'tar] vt to heat (up); ~**se** vr to heat up, warm up; (fig: discusión etc) to get heated

calentura [kalen'tura] nf (MED) fever, (high) temperature

calibrar [kali'βrar] vt to gauge, measure; **calibre** nm (de cañón) calibre, bore; (diámetro) diameter; (fig) calibre

calidad [kali'ðað] nf quality; **de ~** quality cpd; **en ~ de** in the capacity of, as

cálido, a ['kaliðo, a] adj hot; (fig) warm

caliente etc [ka'ljente] vb ver **calentar** ♦ adj hot; (fig) fiery; (disputa) heated; (fam: cachondo) randy

calificación [kalifika'θjon] nf qualification; (de alumno) grade, mark

calificar [kalifi'kar] vt to qualify; (alumno) to grade, mark; ~ **de** to describe as

calima [ka'lima] nf (cerca del mar) mist

cáliz [ka'liθ] nm chalice

caliza [ka'liθa] nf limestone

calizo, a [ka'liθo, a] adj lime cpd

callado, a [ka'ʎaðo, a] adj quiet

callar [ka'ʎar] vt (asunto delicado) to keep quiet about, say nothing about; (persona, opinión) to silence ♦ vi to keep quiet, be silent; ~**se** vr to keep quiet, be silent; ¡**cállate**! be quiet!, shut up!

calle ['kaʎe] nf street; (DEPORTE) lane; ~ **arriba/abajo** up/down the street;

~ de un solo sentido one-way street

calleja [ka'ʎexa] nf alley, narrow street;

callejear vi to wander (about) the streets; **callejero, a** adj street cpd ♦ nm street map; **callejón** nm alley, passage; **callejón sin salida** cul-de-sac; **callejuela** nf side-street, alley

callista [ka'ʎista] nm/f chiropodist

callo ['kaʎo] nm callus; (en el pie) corn; **~s** nmpl (CULIN) tripe sg

calma ['kalma] nf calm

calmante [kal'mante] nm sedative, tranquilizer

calmar [kal'mar] vt to calm, calm down ♦ vi (tempestad) to abate; (mente etc) to become calm

calmoso, a [kal'moso, a] adj calm, quiet

calor [ka'lor] nm heat; (agradable) warmth; **hace ~** it's hot; **tener ~** to be hot

caloría [kalo'ria] nf calorie

calumnia [ka'lumnja] nf calumny, slander; **calumnioso, a** adj slanderous

caluroso, a [kalu'roso, a] adj hot; (sin exceso) warm; (fig) enthusiastic

calva ['kalβa] nf bald patch; (en bosque) clearing

calvario [kal'βarjo] nm stations pl of the cross

calvicie [kal'βiθje] nf baldness

calvo, a ['kalβo, a] adj bald; (terreno) bare, barren; (tejido) threadbare

calza ['kalθa] nf wedge, chock

calzada [kal'θaða] nf roadway, highway

calzado, a [kal'θaðo, a] adj shod ♦ nm footwear

calzador [kalθa'ðor] nm shoehorn

calzar [kal'θar] vt (zapatos etc) to wear; (un mueble) to put a wedge under; **~se** vr: **~se los zapatos** to put on one's shoes; **¿qué (número) calza?** what size do you take?

calzón [kal'θon] nm (tb: **calzones** nmpl) shorts; (AM: de hombre) (under)pants; (: de mujer) panties

calzoncillos [kalθon'θiʎos] nmpl underpants

cama ['kama] nf bed; **~ individual/de matrimonio** single/double bed

camafeo [kama'feo] nm cameo

camaleón [kamale'on] nm chameleon

cámara ['kamara] nf chamber; (habitación) room; (sala) hall; (CINE) cine camera; (fotográfica) camera; **~ de aire** inner tube; **~ de comercio** chamber of commerce; **~ frigorífica** cold-storage room

camarada [kama'raða] nm comrade, companion

camarera [kama'rera] nf (en restaurante) waitress; (en casa, hotel) maid

camarero [kama'rero] nm waiter

camarilla [kama'riʎa] nf clique

camarón [kama'ron] nm shrimp

camarote [kama'rote] nm cabin

cambiable [kam'bjaβle] adj (variable) changeable, variable; (intercambiable) interchangeable

cambiante [kam'bjante] adj variable

cambiar [kam'bjar] vt to change; (dinero) to exchange ♦ vi to change; **~se** vr (mudarse) to move; (de ropa) to change; **~ de idea** to change one's mind; **~ de ropa** to change (one's clothes)

cambio ['kambjo] nm change; (trueque) exchange; (COM) rate of exchange; (oficina) bureau de change; (dinero menudo) small change; **en ~** on the other hand; (en lugar de) instead; **~ de divisas** foreign exchange; **~ de velocidades** gear lever

camelar [kame'lar] vt to sweet-talk

camello [ka'meʎo] nm camel; (fam: traficante) pusher

camerino [kame'rino] nm dressing room

camilla [ka'miʎa] nf (MED) stretcher

caminante [kami'nante] nm/f traveller

caminar [kami'nar] vi (marchar) to walk, go ♦ vt (recorrer) to cover, travel

caminata [kami'nata] nf long walk; (por el campo) hike

camino [ka'mino] nm way, road; (sendero) track; **a medio ~** halfway (there); **en el ~** on the way, en route; **~ de** on the way to; **~ particular** private road

---

Camino de Santiago

The **Camino de Santiago** is a medieval pilgrim route stretching from the Pyrenees to Santiago de Compostela in north-west Spain, where tradition has it the body of the Apostle James is buried. Nowadays it is a popular tourist route as well as a religious one.

---

camión [ka'mjon] nm lorry (BRIT), truck (US); **~ de la basura** dustcart (BRIT), garbage truck (US); **camionero, a** nm/f lorry o truck driver

camioneta [kamjo'neta] nf van, light truck

camisa [ka'misa] nf shirt; (BOT) skin; **~ de fuerza** straitjacket; **camisería** nf outfitter's (shop)

camiseta [kami'seta] nf (prenda) tee-shirt; (: ropa interior) vest; (de deportista) top

camisón [kami'son] nm nightdress, nightgown

camorra [ka'morra] nf: **buscar ~** to look for trouble

campamento [kampa'mento] nm camp

campana [kam'pana] nf bell; **~ de cristal** bell jar; **~da** nf peal; **~rio** nm belfry

campanilla [kampa'niλa] nf small bell

campaña [kam'paɲa] nf (MIL, POL) campaign

campechano, a [kampe'tʃano, a] adj (franco) open

campeón, ona [kampe'on, ona] nm/f champion; **campeonato** nm championship

campesino, a [kampe'sino, a] adj country cpd, rural; (gente) peasant cpd ♦ nm/f countryman/woman; (agricultor) farmer

campestre [kam'pestre] adj country cpd, rural

camping ['kampin] (pl **~s**) nm camping; (lugar) campsite; **ir de o hacer ~** to go camping

campo ['kampo] nm (fuera de la ciudad) country, countryside; (AGR, ELEC) field; (de fútbol) pitch; (de golf) course; (MIL) camp; **~ de batalla** battlefield; **~ de deportes** sports ground, playing field

camposanto [kampo'santo] nm cemetery

camuflaje [kamu'flaxe] nm camouflage

cana ['kana] nf white o grey hair; **tener ~s** to be going grey

Canadá [kana'ða] nm Canada; **canadiense** adj, nm/f Canadian ♦ nf fur-lined jacket

canal [ka'nal] nm canal; (GEO) channel, strait; (de televisión) channel; (de tejado) gutter; **~ de Panamá** Panama Canal; **~izar** vt to channel

canalla [ka'naλa] nf rabble, mob ♦ nm swine

canalón [kana'lon] nm (conducto vertical) drainpipe; (del tejado) gutter

canapé [kana'pe] (pl **~s**) nm sofa, settee; (CULIN) canapé

Canarias [ka'narjas] nfpl: **(las Islas) ~** the Canary Islands, the Canaries

canario, a [ka'narjo, a] adj, nm/f (native) of the Canary Isles ♦ nm (ZOOL) canary

canasta [ka'nasta] nf (round) basket; **canastilla** nf small basket; (de niño) layette

canasto [ka'nasto] nm large basket

cancela [kan'θela] nf gate

cancelación [kanθela'θjon] nf cancellation

cancelar [kanθe'lar] vt to cancel; (una

deuda) to write off

cáncer ['kanθer] nm (MED) cancer; (ASTROLOGÍA): **C~** Cancer

cancha ['kantʃa] nf (de baloncesto, tenis etc) court; (AM: de fútbol) pitch

canciller [kanθi'λer] nm chancellor

canción [kan'θjon] nf song; **~ de cuna** lullaby; **cancionero** nm song book

candado [kan'daðo] nm padlock

candente [kan'dente] adj red-hot; (fig: tema) burning

candidato, a [kandi'ðato, a] nm/f candidate

candidez [kandi'ðeθ] nf (sencillez) simplicity; (simpleza) naiveté; **cándido, a** adj simple; naive

candil [kan'dil] nm oil lamp; **~ejas** nfpl (TEATRO) footlights

candor [kan'dor] nm (sinceridad) frankness; (inocencia) innocence

canela [ka'nela] nf cinnamon

canelones [kane'lones] nmpl cannelloni

cangrejo [kan'grexo] nm crab

canguro [kan'guro] nm kangaroo; **hacer de ~** to babysit

caníbal [ka'niβal] adj, nm/f cannibal

canica [ka'nika] nf marble

canijo, a [ka'nixo, a] adj frail, sickly

canino, a [ka'nino, a] adj canine ♦ nm canine (tooth)

canjear [kanxe'ar] vt to exchange

cano, a ['kano, a] adj grey-haired, white-haired

canoa [ka'noa] nf canoe

canon ['kanon] nm canon; (pensión) rent; (COM) tax

canónigo [ka'noniɣo] nm canon

canonizar [kanoni'θar] vt to canonize

canoso, a [ka'noso, a] adj grey-haired

cansado, a [kan'saðo, a] adj tired, weary; (tedioso) tedious, boring

cansancio [kan'sanθjo] nm tiredness, fatigue

cansar [kan'sar] vt (fatigar) to tire, tire out; (aburrir) to bore; (fastidiar) to

bother; **~se** vr to tire, get tired; (aburrirse) to get bored

cantábrico, a [kan'taβriko, a] adj Cantabrian; **mar C~** Bay of Biscay

cantante [kan'tante] adj singing ♦ nm/f singer

cantar [kan'tar] vt to sing ♦ vi to sing; (insecto) to chirp ♦ nm (acción) singing; (canción) song; (poema) poem

cántara ['kantara] nf large pitcher

cántaro ['kantaro] nm pitcher, jug; **llover a ~s** to rain cats and dogs

cante ['kante] nm: **~ jondo** flamenco singing

cantera [kan'tera] nf quarry

cantidad [kanti'ðað] nf quantity, amount

cantimplora [kantim'plora] nf (frasco) water bottle, canteen

cantina [kan'tina] nf canteen; (de estación) buffet

canto ['kanto] nm singing; (canción) song; (borde) edge, rim; (de un cuchillo) back; **~ rodado** boulder

cantor, a [kan'tor, a] nm/f singer

canturrear [kanturre'ar] vi to sing softly

canuto [ka'nuto] nm (tubo) small tube; (fam: droga) joint

caña ['kaɲa] nf (BOT: tallo) stem, stalk; (carrizo) reed; (vaso) tumbler; (de cerveza) glass of beer; (ANAT) shinbone; **~ de azúcar** sugar cane; **~ de pescar** fishing rod

cañada [ka'ɲaða] nf (entre dos montañas) gully, ravine; (camino) cattle track

cáñamo ['kaɲamo] nm hemp

cañería [kaɲe'ria] nf (tubo) pipe

caño ['kaɲo] nm (tubo) tube, pipe; (de albañal) sewer; (MUS) pipe; (de fuente) jet

cañón [ka'ɲon] nm (MIL) cannon; (de fusil) barrel; (GEO) canyon, gorge

caoba [ka'oβa] nf mahogany

caos ['kaos] nm chaos

cap. abr (= capítulo) ch.

capa ['kapa] nf cloak, cape; (GEO) layer, stratum; **so ~ de** under the pretext of; **~ de ozono** ozone layer

capacidad [kapaθi'ðað] nf (medida) capacity; (aptitud) capacity, ability

capacitar [kapaθi'tar] vt: **~ a algn para (hacer)** to enable sb to (do)

capar [ka'par] vt to castrate, geld

caparazón [kapara'θon] nm shell

capataz [kapa'taθ] nm foreman

capaz [ka'paθ] adj able, capable; (amplio) capacious, roomy

capcioso, a [kap'θjoso, a] adj wily, deceitful

capellán [kape'ʎan] nm chaplain; (sacerdote) priest

caperuza [kape'ruθa] nf hood

capicúa [kapi'kua] adj inv (número, fecha) reversible

capilla [ka'piʎa] nf chapel

capital [kapi'tal] adj capital ♦ nm (COM) capital ♦ nf (de ciudad) capital; **~ social** share o authorized capital

capitalismo [kapita'lismo] nm capitalism; **capitalista** adj, nm/f capitalist

capitán [kapi'tan] nm captain

capitanear [kapitane'ar] vt to captain

capitulación [kapitula'θjon] nf (rendición) capitulation, surrender; (acuerdo) agreement, pact; **capitulaciones (matrimoniales)** nfpl marriage contract sg

capitular [kapitu'lar] vi to make an agreement

capítulo [ka'pitulo] nm chapter

capó [ka'po] nm (AUTO) bonnet

capón [ka'pon] nm (gallo) capon

capota [ka'pota] nf (de mujer) bonnet; (AUTO) hood (BRIT), top (US)

capote [ka'pote] nm (abrigo: de militar) greatcoat; (: de torero) cloak

capricho [ka'pritʃo] nm whim, caprice; **~so, a** adj capricious

Capricornio [kapri'kornjo] nm Capricorn

cápsula ['kapsula] nf capsule

captar [kap'tar] vt (comprender) to understand; (RADIO) to pick up; (atención, apoyo) to attract

captura [kap'tura] nf capture; (JUR) arrest; **capturar** vt to capture; to arrest

capucha [ka'putʃa] nf hood, cowl

capullo [ka'puʎo] nm (BOT) bud; (ZOOL) cocoon; (fam) idiot

caqui ['kaki] nm khaki

cara ['kara] nf (ANAT, de moneda) face; (de disco) side; (descaro) boldness; **~ a** facing; **de ~** opposite, facing; **dar la ~** to face the consequences; **¿~ o cruz?** heads or tails?; **¡qué ~ (más dura)!** what a nerve!

carabina [kara'βina] nf carbine, rifle; (persona) chaperone

Caracas [ka'rakas] n Caracas

caracol [kara'kol] nm (ZOOL) snail; (concha) (sea) shell

carácter [ka'rakter] (pl **caracteres**) nm character; **tener buen/mal ~** to be good natured/bad tempered

característica [karakte'ristika] nf characteristic

característico, a [karakte'ristiko, a] adj characteristic

caracterizar [karakteri'θar] vt to characterize, typify

caradura [kara'ðura] nm/f: **es un ~** he's got a nerve

carajillo [kara'xiʎo] nm coffee with a dash of brandy

carajo [ka'raxo] (fam!) nm: **¡~!** shit! (!)

caramba [ka'ramba] excl good gracious!

carámbano [ka'rambano] nm icicle

caramelo [kara'melo] nm (dulce) sweet; (azúcar fundida) caramel

caravana [kara'βana] nf caravan; (fig) group; (AUTO) tailback

carbón [kar'βon] nm coal; **papel ~** carbon paper; **carboncillo** nm (ARTE) charcoal; **carbonero, a** nm/f coal merchant; **carbonilla** [-'niʎa] nf coal dust

carbonizar [karβoni'θar] *vt* to carbonize; (*quemar*) to char

carbono [kar'βono] *nm* carbon

carburador [kaißura'ðor] *nm* carburettor

carburante [karßu'rante] *nm* (*para motor*) fuel

carcajada [karka'xaða] *nf* (loud) laugh, guffaw

cárcel [ˈkarθel] *nf* prison, jail; (*TEC*) clamp; **carcelero, a** *adj* prison ♦ *nm/f* warder

carcoma [kar'koma] *nf* woodworm

carcomer [karko'mer] *vt* to bore into, eat into; (*fig*) to undermine; **~se** *vr* to become worm-eaten; (*fig*) to decay

cardar [kar'ðar] *vt* (*pelo*) to backcomb

cardenal [karðe'nal] *nm* (*REL*) cardinal; (*MED*) bruise

cardiaco, a [kar'ðiako, a] *adj* cardiac, heart *cpd*

cardinal [karði'nal] *adj* cardinal

cardo [ˈkarðo] *nm* thistle

carearse [kare'arse] *vr* to come face to face

carecer [kare'θer] *vi*: **~ de** to lack, be in need of

carencia [ka'renθja] *nf* lack; (*escasez*) shortage; (*MED*) deficiency

carente [ka'rente] *adj*: **~ de** lacking in, devoid of

carestía [kares'tia] *nf* (*escasez*) scarcity, shortage; (*COM*) high cost

careta [ka'reta] *nf* mask

carga [ˈkarγa] *nf* (*peso, ELEC*) load; (*de barco*) cargo, freight; (*MIL*) charge; (*responsabilidad*) duty, obligation

cargado, a [karˈγaðo, a] *adj* loaded; (*ELEC*) live; (*café, té*) strong; (*cielo*) overcast

cargamento [karγa'mento] *nm* (*acción*) loading; (*mercancías*) load, cargo

cargar [kar'γar] *vt* (*barco, arma*) to load; (*ELEC*) to charge; (*COM: algo en cuenta*) to charge; (*INFORM*) to load ♦ *vi* (*MIL*) to charge; (*AUTO*) to load (up);

~ con to pick up, carry away; (*peso, fig*) to shoulder, bear; **~se** *vr* (*estropear*) to break; (*matar*) to bump off

cargo [ˈkarγo] *nm* (*puesto*) post, office; (*responsabilidad*) duty, obligation; (*JUR*) charge; **hacerse ~ de** to take charge of *o* responsibility for

carguero [kar'γero] *nm* freighter, cargo boat; (*avión*) freight plane

Caribe [ka'riße] *nm*: **el ~ the** Caribbean; **del ~** Caribbean

caribeño, a [kari'βeɲo, a] *adj* Caribbean

caricatura [karika'tura] *nf* caricature

caricia [ka'riθja] *nf* caress

caridad [kari'ðað] *nf* charity

caries [ˈkarjes] *nf inv* tooth decay

cariño [ka'riɲo] *nm* affection, love; (*caricia*) caress; (*en carta*) love ...; **tener ~ a** to be fond of; **~so, a** *adj* affectionate

carisma [ka'risma] *nm* charisma

caritativo, a [karita'tißo, a] *adj* charitable

cariz [ka'riθ] *nm*: **tener o tomar buen/mal ~** to look good/bad

carmesí [karme'si] *adj, nm* crimson

carmín [kar'min] *nm* lipstick

carnal [kar'nal] *adj* carnal; **primo ~** first cousin

carnaval [karna'ßal] *nm* carnival

---

carnaval

Carnaval is a traditional period of fun, feasting and partying which takes place in the three days before the start of Lent ("Cuaresma"). Although in decline during the Franco years the carnival has grown in popularity recently in Spain. Cádiz and Tenerife are particularly well-known for their flamboyant celebrations with fancy-dress parties, parades and firework displays being the order of the day.

carne ['karne] nf flesh; (CULIN) meat; ~ **de cerdo/cordero/ternera/vaca** pork/lamb/veal/beef; ~ **de gallina** (fig): **se me pone la ~ de gallina sólo verlo** I get the creeps just seeing it

carné [kar'ne] (pl ~s) nm: ~ **de conducir** driving licence (BRIT), driver's license (US); ~ **de identidad** identity card

carnero [kar'nero] nm sheep, ram; (carne) mutton

carnet [kar'ne] (pl ~s) nm = **carné**

carnicería [karniθe'ria] nf butcher's (shop); (fig: matanza) carnage, slaughter

carnicero, a [karni'θero, a] adj carnivorous ♦ nm/f (tb fig) butcher; (carnívoro) carnivore

carnívoro, a [kar'niβoro, a] adj carnivorous

carnoso, a [kar'noso, a] adj beefy, fat

caro, a ['karo, a] adj dear; (COM) dear, expensive ♦ adv dear, dearly

carpa ['karpa] nf (pez) carp; (de circo) big top; (AM: de camping) tent

carpeta [kar'peta] nf folder, file

carpintería [karpinte'ria] nf carpentry, joinery; **carpintero** nm carpenter

carraspear [karraspe'ar] vi to clear one's throat

carraspera [karras'pera] nf hoarseness

carrera [ka'rrera] nf (acción) run(ning); (espacio recorrido) run; (competición) race; (trayecto) course; (profesión) career; (ESCOL) course

carreta [ka'rreta] nf wagon, cart

carrete [ka'rrete] nm reel, spool; (TEC) coil

carretera [karre'tera] nf (main) road, highway; ~ **de circunvalación** ring road; ~ **nacional** ≈ A road (BRIT), ≈ state highway (US)

carretilla [karre'tiʎa] nf trolley; (AGR) (wheel)barrow

carril [ka'rril] nm furrow; (de autopista) lane; (FERRO) rail

carrillo [ka'rriʎo] nm (ANAT) cheek; (TEC) pulley

carrito [ka'rrito] nm trolley

carro ['karro] nm cart, wagon; (MIL) tank; (AM: coche) car

carrocería [karroθe'ria] nf bodywork, coachwork

carroña [ka'rroɲa] nf carrion no pl

carroza [ka'rroθa] nf (carruaje) coach

carrusel [karru'sel] nm merry-go-round, roundabout

carta ['karta] nf letter; (CULIN) menu; (naipe) card; (mapa) map; (JUR) document; (TV) test card; ~ **de crédito** credit card; ~ **certificada** registered letter; ~ **marítima** chart; ~ **verde** (AUTO) green card

cartabón [karta'βon] nm set square

cartel [kar'tel] nm (anuncio) poster, placard; (ESCOL) wall chart; (COM) cartel; ~**era** nf hoarding, billboard; (en periódico etc) entertainments guide; **"en ~era"** "showing"

cartera [kar'tera] nf (de bolsillo) wallet; (de colegial, cobrador) satchel; (de señora) handbag; (para documentos) briefcase; (COM) portfolio; **ocupa la ~ de Agricultura** she is Minister of Agriculture

carterista [karte'rista] nm/f pickpocket

cartero [kar'tero] nm postman

cartilla [kar'tiʎa] nf primer, first reading book; ~ **de ahorros** savings book

cartón [kar'ton] nm cardboard; ~ **piedra** papier-mâché

cartulina [kartu'lina] nf card

casa ['kasa] nf house; (hogar) home; (COM) firm, company; **en ~** at home; ~ **consistorial** town hall; ~ **de huéspedes** boarding house; ~ **de socorro** first aid post

casado, a [ka'saðo, a] adj married ♦ nm/f married man/woman

casamiento [kasa'mjento] *nm* marriage, wedding

casar [ka'sar] *vt* to marry; *(JUR)* to quash, annul; **~se** *vr* to marry, get married

cascabel [kaska'βel] *nm* (small) bell

cascada [kas'kaða] *nf* waterfall

cascanueces [kaska'nweθes] *nm inv* nutcrackers *pl*

cascar [kas'kar] *vt* to crack, split, break (open); **~se** *vr* to crack, split, break (open)

cáscara ['kaskara] *nf* (de huevo, fruta seca) shell; (de fruta) skin; (de limón) peel

casco ['kasko] *nm* (de bombero, soldado) helmet; *(NAUT: de barco)* hull; *(ZOOL: de caballo)* hoof; (botella) empty bottle; (de ciudad): **el ~ antiguo** the old part; **el ~ urbano** the town centre; **los ~s azules** the UN peace-keeping force, the blue berets

cascote [kas'kote] *nm* rubble

caserío [kase'rio] *nm* hamlet; (casa) country house

casero, a [ka'sero, a] *adj* (pan etc) home-made ♦ *nm/f* (propietario) landlord/lady; **ser muy ~** to be home-loving; **"comida casera"** "home cooking"

caseta [ka'seta] *nf* hut; (para bañista) cubicle; (de feria) stall

casete [ka'sete] *nm o f* = **cassette**

casi ['kasi] *adv* almost, nearly; **~ nada** hardly anything; **~ nunca** hardly ever, almost never; **~ te caes** you almost fell

casilla [ka'siʎa] *nf* (casita) hut, cabin; *(AJEDREZ)* square; (para cartas) pigeonhole; **casillero** *nm* (para cartas) pigeonholes *pl*

casino [ka'sino] *nm* club; (de juego) casino

caso ['kaso] *nm* case; **en ~ de ...** in case of ...; **en ~ de que ...** in case ...; **el ~ es que** the fact is that; **en ese ~** in that case; **hacer ~ a** to pay

attention to; **hacer o venir al ~** to be relevant

caspa ['kaspa] *nf* dandruff

cassette [ka'sete] *nm o f* = **casete**

casta ['kasta] *nf* caste; (raza) breed; (linaje) lineage

castaña [kas'taɲa] *nf* chestnut

castañetear [kastaɲete'ar] *vi* (dientes) to chatter

castaño, a [kas'taɲo, a] *adj* chestnut (-coloured), brown ♦ *nm* chestnut tree

castañuelas [kasta'ɲwelas] *nfpl* castanets

castellano, a [kaste'ʎano, a] *adj, nm/f* Castilian ♦ *nm (LING)* Castilian, Spanish

castidad [kasti'ðað] *nf* chastity, purity

castigar [kasti'var] *vt* to punish; *(DEPORTE)* to penalize; **castigo** *nm* punishment; *(DEPORTE)* penalty

Castilla [kas'tiʎa] *nf* Castille

castillo [kas'tiʎo] *nm* castle

castizo, a [kas'tiθo, a] *adj (LING)* pure

casto, a ['kasto, a] *adj* chaste, pure

castor [kas'tor] *nm* beaver

castrar [kas'trar] *vt* to castrate

castrense [kas'trense] *adj* (disciplina, vida) military

casual [ka'swal] *adj* chance, accidental; **~idad** *nf* chance, accident; (combinación de circunstancias) coincidence; **¡qué ~idad!** what a coincidence!

cataclismo [kata'klismo] *nm* cataclysm

catador, a [kata'ðor, a] *nm/f* wine taster

catalán, ana [kata'lan, ana] *adj, nm/f* Catalan ♦ *nm (LING)* Catalan

catalizador [kataliβa'ðor] *nm* catalyst; *(AUT)* catalytic convertor

catalogar [katalo'var] *vt* to catalogue; **~ a algn (de)** (fig) to categorize sb (as)

catálogo [ka'taloxo] *nm* catalogue

Cataluña [kata'luɲa] *nf* Catalonia

catar [ka'tar] *vt* to taste, sample

catarata [kata'rata] *nf (GEO)* waterfall;

(MED) cataract

catarro [ka'tarro] nm catarrh;
(constipado) cold

catástrofe [ka'tastrofe] nf catastrophe

catear [kate'ar] (fam) vt (examen,
alumno) to fail

cátedra ['kateðra] nf (UNIV) chair,
professorship

catedral [kate'ðral] nf cathedral

catedrático, a [kate'ðratiko, a] nm/f
professor

categoría [katevo'ria] nf category;
(rango) rank, standing; (calidad)
quality; **de ~** (hotel) top-class

categórico, a [kate'voriko, a] adj
categorical

cateto, a ['kateto, a] (pey) nm/f
peasant

catolicismo [katoli'θismo] nm
Catholicism

católico, a [ka'toliko, a] adj, nm/f
Catholic

catorce [ka'torθe] num fourteen

cauce ['kauθe] nm (de río) riverbed;
(fig) channel

caucho ['kautʃo] nm rubber; (AM:
llanta) tyre

caución [kau'θjon] nf bail; **caucionar**
vt (JUR) to bail, go bail for

caudal [kau'ðal] nm (de río) volume,
flow; (fortuna) wealth; (abundancia)
abundance; **~oso, a** adj (río) large

caudillo [kau'ðiʎo] nm leader, chief

causa ['kausa] nf cause; (razón) reason;
(JUR) lawsuit, case; **a ~ de** because of

causar [kau'sar] vt to cause

cautela [kau'tela] nf caution,
cautiousness; **cauteloso, a** adj
cautious, wary

cautivar [kauti'ßar] vt to capture;
(atraer) to captivate

cautiverio [kauti'ßerjo] nm captivity

cautividad [kautißi'ðað] nf =
cautiverio

cautivo, a [kau'tißo, a] adj, nm/f
captive

cauto, a ['kauto, a] adj cautious,
careful

cava ['kaßa] nm champagne-type wine

cavar [ka'ßar] vt to dig

caverna [ka'ßerna] nf cave, cavern

cavidad [kaßi'ðað] nf cavity

cavilar [kaßi'lar] vt to ponder

cayado [ka'jaðo] nm (de pastor) crook;
(de obispo) crozier

cayendo etc vb ver **caer**

caza ['kaθa] nf (acción: gen) hunting;
(: con fusil) shooting; (una ~) hunt,
chase; (animales) game ♦ nm (AVIAT)
fighter

cazador, a [kaθa'ðor, a] nm/f hunter;
cazadora nf jacket

cazar [ka'θar] vt to hunt; (perseguir) to
chase; (prender) to catch

cazo ['kaθo] nm saucepan

cazuela [ka'θwela] nf (vasija)
pan; (guisado) casserole

CD abbr (= compact disc) CD

CD-ROM abbr nm CD-ROM

CE nf abr (= Comunidad Europea) EC

cebada [θe'ßaða] nf barley

cebar [θe'ßar] vt (animal) to fatten
(up); (anzuelo) to bait; (MIL, TEC) to
prime

cebo ['θeßo] nm (para animales) feed,
food; (para peces, fig) bait; (de arma)
charge

cebolla [θe'ßoʎa] nf onion; **cebolleta**
nf spring onion; **cebollín** nm spring
onion

cebra ['θeßra] nf zebra

cecear [θeθe'ar] vi to lisp; **ceceo** nm
lisp

ceder [θe'ðer] vt to hand over, give up,
part with ♦ vi (renunciar) to give in,
yield; (disminuir) to diminish, decline;
(romperse) to give way

cedro ['θeðro] nm cedar

cédula ['θeðula] nf certificate,
document

cegar [θe'var] vt to blind; (tubería etc)
to block up, stop up ♦ vi to go blind;
~se vr: **~se (de)** to be blinded (by)

ceguera [θe'vera] nf blindness

CEI *abbr* (= *Confederación de Estados Independientes*) CIS

ceja ['θexa] *nf* eyebrow

cejar [θe'xar] *vi* (*fig*) to back down

celador, a [θela'ðor, a] *nm/f* (*de edificio*) watchman; (*de museo etc*) attendant

celda ['θelda] *nf* cell

celebración [θeleβra'θjon] *nf* celebration

celebrar [θele'βrar] *vt* to celebrate; (*alabar*) to praise ♦ *vi* to be glad; **~se** *vr* to occur, take place

célebre ['θelebre] *adj* famous

celebridad [θeleβri'ðað] *nf* fame; (*persona*) celebrity

celeste [θe'leste] *adj* (*azul*) sky-blue

celestial [θeles'tjal] *adj* celestial, heavenly

celibato [θeli'βato] *nm* celibacy

célibe ['θeliβe] *adj, nm/f* celibate

celo¹ ['θelo] *nm* zeal; (*REL*) fervour; (*ZOOL*): **en ~** on heat; **~s** *nmpl* jealousy *sg*; **tener ~s** to be jealous

celo² ® ['θelo] *nm* Sellotape ®

celofán [θelo'fan] *nm* cellophane

celoso, a [θe'loso, a] *adj* jealous; (*trabajador*) zealous

celta ['θelta] *adj* Celtic ♦ *nm/f* Celt

célula ['θelula] *nf* cell; **~ solar** solar cell

celulitis [θelu'litis] *nf* cellulite

cementerio [θemen'terjo] *nm* cemetery, graveyard

cemento [θe'mento] *nm* cement; (*hormigón*) concrete; (*AM*: *cola*) glue

cena ['θena] *nf* evening meal, dinner

cenagal [θena'val] *nm* bog, quagmire

cenar [θe'nar] *vt* to have for dinner ♦ *vi* to have dinner

cenicero [θeni'θero] *nm* ashtray

cenit [θe'nit] *nm* zenith

ceniza [θe'niθa] *nf* ash, ashes *pl*

censo ['θenso] *nm* census; **~ electoral** electoral roll

censura [θen'sura] *nf* (*POL*) censorship

censurar [θensu'rar] *vt* (*idea*) to

censure; (*cortar: película*) to censor

centella [θen'teʎa] *nf* spark

centellear [θenteʎe'ar] *vi* (*metal*) to gleam; (*estrella*) to twinkle; (*fig*) to sparkle

centenar [θente'nar] *nm* hundred

centenario, a [θente'narjo, a] *adj* centenary; hundred-year-old ♦ *nm* centenary

centeno [θen'teno] *nm* (*BOT*) rye

centésimo, a [θen'tesimo, a] *adj* hundredth

centígrado [θen'tivraðo] *adj* centigrade

centímetro [θen'timetro] *nm* centimetre (*BRIT*), centimeter (*US*)

céntimo ['θentimo] *nm* cent

centinela [θenti'nela] *nm* sentry, guard

centollo [θen'toʎo] *nm* spider crab

central [θen'tral] *adj* central ♦ *nf* head office; (*TEC*) plant; (*TEL*) exchange; **~ eléctrica** power station; **~ nuclear** nuclear power station; **~ telefónica** telephone exchange

centralita [θentra'lita] *nf* switchboard

centralizar [θentrali'θar] *vt* to centralize

centrar [θen'trar] *vt* to centre

céntrico, a ['θentriko, a] *adj* central

centrifugar [θentrifu'var] *vt* to spin-dry

centrista [θen'trista] *adj* centre *cpd*

centro ['θentro] *nm* centre; **~ comercial** shopping centre; **~ juvenil** youth club; **~ de atención al cliente** call centre

centroamericano, a [θentroameri'kano, a] *adj, nm/f* Central American

ceñido, a [θe'niðo, a] *adj* (*chaqueta, pantalón*) tight(-fitting)

ceñir [θe'nir] *vt* (*rodear*) to encircle, surround; (*ajustar*) to fit (tightly)

ceño ['θeno] *nm* frown, scowl; **fruncir el ~** to frown, knit one's brow

CEOE *nf abr* (*ESP*: = *Confederación*

Española de Organizaciones Empresariales ≈ CBI (*BRIT*), employers' organization

cepillar [θepiˈʎar] vt to brush; (*madera*) to plane (down)

cepillo [θeˈpiʎo] nm brush; (*para madera*) plane; ~ **de dientes** toothbrush

cera [ˈθera] nf wax

cerámica [θeˈramika] nf pottery; (*arte*) ceramics

cerca [ˈθerka] nf fence ♦ adv near, nearby, close; ~ **de** near, close to

cercanías [θerkaˈnias] nfpl (*afueras*) outskirts, suburbs

cercano, a [θerˈkano, a] adj close, near

cercar [θerˈkar] vt to fence in; (*rodear*) to surround

cerciorar [θerθjoˈrar] vt (*asegurar*) to assure; ~**se** vr (*asegurarse*) to make sure

cerco [ˈθerko] nm (*AGR*) enclosure; (*AM*) fence; (*MIL*) siege

cerdo, a [ˈθerðo, a] nm/f pig/sow

cereal [θereˈal] nm cereal; ~**es** nmpl cereals, grain sg

cerebro [θeˈreβro] nm brain; (*fig*) brains pl

ceremonia [θereˈmonja] nf ceremony; **ceremonial** adj, nm ceremonial; **ceremonioso, a** adj ceremonious

cereza [θeˈreθa] nf cherry

cerilla [θeˈriʎa] nf (*fósforo*) match

cernerse [θerˈnerse] vr to hover

cero [ˈθero] nm nothing, zero

cerrado, a [θeˈrraðo, a] adj closed, shut; (*con llave*) locked; (*tiempo*) cloudy, overcast; (*curva*) sharp; (*acento*) thick, broad

cerradura [θerraˈðura] nf (*acción*) closing; (*mecanismo*) lock

cerrajero [θerraˈxero] nm locksmith

cerrar [θeˈrrar] vt to close, shut; (*paso, carretera*) to close; (*grifo*) to turn off; (*cuenta, negocio*) to close ♦ vi to close, shut; (*la noche*) to come down; ~**se** vr

to close, shut; ~ **con llave** to lock; ~ **un trato** to strike a bargain

cerro [ˈθerro] nm hill

cerrojo [θeˈrroxo] nm (*herramienta*) bolt; (*de puerta*) latch

certamen [θerˈtamen] nm competition, contest

certero, a [θerˈtero, a] adj (*gen*) accurate

certeza [θerˈteθa] nf certainty

certidumbre [θertiˈðumbre] nf = **certeza**

certificado [θertifiˈkaðo] nm certificate

certificar [θertifiˈkar] vt (*asegurar, atestar*) to certify

cervatillo [θerβaˈtiʎo] nm fawn

cervecería [θerβeθeˈria] nf (*fábrica*) brewery; (*bar*) public house, pub

cerveza [θerˈβeθa] nf beer

cesante [θeˈsante] adj redundant

cesar [θeˈsar] vi to cease, stop ♦ vt (*funcionario*) to remove from office

cesárea [θeˈsarea] nf (*MED*) Caesarean operation o section

cese [ˈθese] nm (*de trabajo*) dismissal; (*de pago*) suspension

césped [ˈθespeð] nm grass, lawn

cesta [ˈθesta] nf basket

cesto [ˈθesto] nm (*large*) basket, hamper

cetro [ˈθetro] nm sceptre

cfr abr (= *confróntese*) cf.

chabacano, a [tʃaβaˈkano, a] adj vulgar, coarse

chabola [tʃaˈβola] nf shack; **barrio de ~s** shanty town sg

chacal [tʃaˈkal] nm jackal

chacha [ˈtʃatʃa] (*fam*) nf maid

cháchara [ˈtʃatʃara] nf chatter; **estar de ~** to chatter away

chacra [ˈtʃakra] (*AM*) nf smallholding

chafar [tʃaˈfar] vt (*aplastar*) to crush; (*plan etc*) to ruin

chal [tʃal] nm shawl

chalado, a [tʃaˈlaðo, a] (*fam*) adj crazy

chalé [tʃaˈle] (*pl* ~**s**) nm villa; ≈

detached house

chaleco |tʃa'leko| nm waistcoat, vest (US); **~ salvavidas** life jacket

chalet |tʃa'le| (pl **~s**) nm = **chalé**

champán |tʃam'pan| nm champagne

champaña |tʃam'paɲa| nm = **champán**

champiñón |tʃampi'ɲon| nm mushroom

champú |tʃam'pu| (pl **champúes**, **champús**) nm shampoo

chamuscar |tʃamus'kar| vt to scorch, sear, singe

chance |'tʃanθe| (AM) nm chance

chancho, a |'tʃantʃo, a| (AM) nm/f pig

chanchullo |tʃan'tʃuʎo| (fam) nm fiddle

chandal |tʃan'dal| nm tracksuit

chantaje |tʃan'taxe| nm blackmail

chapa |'tʃapa| nf (de metal) plate, sheet; (de madera) board, panel; (AM: AUTO) number (plate) o license (US) plate; **~do, a** adj: **~do en oro** gold-plated

chaparrón |tʃapa'rron| nm downpour, cloudburst

chapotear |tʃapote'ar| vi to splash about

chapurrear |tʃapurre'ar| vt (idioma) to speak badly

chapuza |tʃa'puθa| nf botched job

chapuzón |tʃapu'θon| nm: **darse un ~** to go for a dip

chaqueta |tʃa'keta| nf jacket

chaquetón |tʃake'ton| nm long jacket

charca |'tʃarka| nf pond, pool

charco |'tʃarko| nm pool, puddle

charcutería |tʃarkute'ria| nf (tienda) shop selling chiefly pork meat products; (productos) cooked pork meats pl

charla |'tʃarla| nf talk, chat; (conferencia) lecture

charlar |tʃar'lar| vi to talk, chat

charlatán, ana |tʃarla'tan, ana| nm/f (hablador) chatterbox; (estafador) trickster

charol |tʃa'rol| nm varnish; (cuero) patent leather

chascarrillo |tʃaska'rriʎo| (fam) nm funny story

chasco |'tʃasko| nm (desengaño) disappointment

chasis |'tʃasis| nm inv chassis

chasquear |tʃaske'ar| vt (látigo) to crack; (lengua) to click; **chasquido** nm crack; click

chatarra |tʃa'tarra| nf scrap (metal)

chato, a |'tʃato, a| adj flat; (nariz) snub

chaval, a |tʃa'βal, a| nm/f kid, lad/lass

checo, a |'tʃeko, a| adj, nm/f Czech
♦ nm (LING) Czech

checo(e)slovaco, a |'tʃeko(e)slo'βako, a| adj, nm/f Czech, Czechoslovak

Checo(e)slovaquia |tʃeko(e)slo'-βakja| nf Czechoslovakia

cheque |'tʃeke| nm cheque (BRIT), check (US); **~ de viajero** traveller's cheque (BRIT), traveler's check (US)

chequeo |tʃe'keo| nm (MED) check-up; (AUTO) service

chequera |tʃe'kera| (AM) nf chequebook (BRIT), checkbook (US)

chicano, a |tʃi'kano, a| adj, nm/f chicano

chícharo |'tʃitʃaro| (AM) nm pea

chichón |tʃi'tʃon| nm bump, lump

chicle |'tʃikle| nm chewing gum

chico, a |'tʃiko, a| adj small, little ♦ nm/f (niño) child; (muchacho) boy/girl

chiflado, a |tʃi'flaðo, a| adj crazy

chiflar |tʃi'flar| vt to hiss, boo

Chile |'tʃile| nm Chile; **chileno, a** |tʃi'leno, a| adj, nm/f Chilean

chile |'tʃile| nm chilli pepper

chillar |tʃi'ʎar| vi (persona) to yell, scream; (animal salvaje) to howl; (cerdo) to squeal

chillido |tʃi'ʎiðo| nm (de persona) yell, scream; (de animal) howl

chillón, ona |tʃi'ʎon, ona| adj (niño) noisy; (color) loud, gaudy

chimenea |tʃime'nea| nf chimney; (hogar) fireplace

China ['tʃina] nf: **(la)** ~ China

chinche ['tʃintʃe] nf (insecto) (bed)bug; (TEC) drawing pin (BRIT), thumbtack (US) ♦ nm/f nuisance, pest

chincheta [tʃin'tʃeta] nf drawing pin (BRIT), thumbtack (US)

chino, -a ['tʃino, a] adj, nm/f Chinese ♦ nm (LING) Chinese

chipirón [tʃipi'ron] nm (ZOOL, CULIN) squid

Chipre ['tʃipre] nf Cyprus; **chipriota** adj, nm/f Cypriot

chiquillo, -a [tʃi'kiʎo, a] nm/f (fam) kid

chirimoya [tʃiri'moja] nf custard apple

chiringuito [tʃirin'gwito] nm small open-air bar

chiripa [tʃi'ripa] nf fluke

chirriar [tʃi'rrjar] vi to creak, squeak

chirrido [tʃi'rrido] nm creak(ing), squeak(ing)

chis [tʃis] excl sh!

chisme ['tʃisme] nm (habladurías) piece of gossip; (fam: objeto) thingummyjig

chismoso, -a [tʃis'moso, a] adj gossiping ♦ nm/f gossip

chispa ['tʃispa] nf spark; (fig) sparkle; (ingenio) wit; (fam) drunkenness

chispear [tʃispe'ar] vi (lloviznar) to drizzle

chisporrotear [tʃisporrote'ar] vi (fuego) to throw out sparks; (leña) to crackle; (aceite) to hiss, splutter

chiste ['tʃiste] nm joke, funny story

chistoso, -a [tʃis'toso, a] adj funny, amusing

chivo, -a ['tʃiβo, a] nm/f (billy-/nanny-) goat; ~ **expiatorio** scapegoat

chocante [tʃo'kante] adj startling; (extraño) odd; (ofensivo) shocking

chocar [tʃo'kar] vi (coches etc) to collide, crash ♦ vt to startle; (sorprender) to startle; ~ **con** to collide with; (fig) to run into, run up against; **¡chócala!** (fam) put it there!

chochear [tʃotʃe'ar] vi to be senile

chocho, -a ['tʃotʃo, a] adj doddering, senile; (fig) soft, doting

chocolate [tʃoko'late] adj, nm chocolate; **chocolatina** nf chocolate

chófer [tʃo'fer] nm = **chófer**

chófer ['tʃofer] nm driver

chollo ['tʃoʎo] nm (fam) bargain, snip

choque ['tʃoke] vb ver **chocar** ♦ nm (impacto) impact; (golpe) jolt; (AUTO) crash; (fig) conflict; ~ **frontal** head-on collision

chorizo [tʃo'riθo] nm hard pork sausage, (type of) salami

chorrada [tʃo'rraða] (fam) nf: **¡es una ~!** that's crap! (!); **decir ~s** to talk crap (!)

chorrear [tʃorre'ar] vi to gush (out), spout (out); (gotear) to drip, trickle

chorro ['tʃorro] nm jet; (fig) stream

choza ['tʃoθa] nf hut, shack

chubasco [tʃu'βasko] nm squall

chubasquero [tʃuβas'kero] nm lightweight raincoat

chuchería [tʃutʃe'ria] nf trinket

chuleta [tʃu'leta] nf chop, cutlet

chulo ['tʃulo] nm (de prostituta) pimp

chupar [tʃu'par] vt to suck; (absorber) to absorb; ~**se** vr to grow thin

chupete [tʃu'pete] nm dummy (BRIT), pacifier (US)

chupito [tʃu'pito] (fam) nm shot

churro ['tʃurro] nm (type of) fritter

chusma ['tʃusma] nf rabble, mob

chutar [tʃu'tar] vi to shoot (at goal)

Cía abr (= **compañía**) Co.

cianuro [θja'nuro] nm cyanide

cibercafé [θiβerka'fe] nm cybercafé

cicatriz [θika'triθ] nf scar; ~**arse** vr to heal (up), form a scar

ciclismo [θi'klismo] nm cycling

ciclista [θi'klista] adj cycle cycle ♦ nm/f cyclist

ciclo ['θiklo] nm cycle; ~**turismo** nm: **hacer ~turismo** to go on a cycling holiday

ciclón [θi'klon] nm cyclone

ciego, a ['θjeɣo, a] adj blind ♦ nm/f blind man/woman

cielo ['θjelo] nm sky; (REL) heaven; ¡~s! good heavens!

ciempiés [θjem'pjes] nm inv centipede

cien [θjen] num ver **ciento**

ciénaga ['θjenaɣa] nf marsh, swamp

ciencia ['θjenθja] nf science; ~s nfpl (ESCOL) science sg; ~-ficción nf science fiction

cieno ['θjeno] nm mud, mire

científico, a [θjen'tifiko, a] adj scientific ♦ nm/f scientist

ciento ['θjento] (tb: **cien**) num hundred; **pagar al 10 por** ~ to pay at 10 per cent

cierre etc ['θjerre] vb ver **cerrar** ♦ nm closing, shutting; (con llave) locking; ~ **de cremallera** zip (fastener)

cierro etc vb ver **cerrar**

cierto, a ['θjerto, a] adj sure, certain; (un tal) a certain; (correcto) right, correct; ~ **hombre** a certain man; **ciertas personas** certain o some people; **sí, es** ~ yes, that's correct

ciervo ['θjerβo] nm deer; (macho) stag

cierzo ['θjerθo] nm north wind

cifra ['θifra] nf number; (secreta) code

cifrar [θi'frar] vt to code, write in code

cigala [θi'ɣala] nf Norway lobster

cigarra [θi'ɣarra] nf cicada

cigarrillo [θiɣa'rriʎo] nm cigarette

cigarro [θi'ɣarro] nm cigarette; (puro) cigar

cigüeña [θi'ɣweɲa] nf stork

cilíndrico, a [θi'lindriko, a] adj cylindrical

cilindro [θi'lindro] nm cylinder

cima ['θima] nf (de montaña) top, peak; (de árbol) top; (fig) height

cimbrearse [θimbre'arse] vr to sway

cimentar [θimen'tar] vt to lay the foundations of; (fig: fundar) to found

cimiento [θi'mjento] nm foundation

cinc [θink] nm zinc

cincel [θin'θel] nm chisel; ~**ar** vt to chisel

cinco ['θinko] num five

cincuenta [θin'kwenta] num fifty

cine ['θine] nm cinema

cineasta [θine'asta] nm/f film director

cinematográfico, a [θinemato'ɣrafiko, a] adj cine-, film cpd

cínico, a ['θiniko, a] adj cynical ♦ nm/f cynic

cinismo [θi'nismo] nm cynicism

cinta ['θinta] nf band, strip; (de tela) ribbon; (película) reel; (de máquina de escribir) ribbon; ~ **adhesiva** sticky tape; ~ **de vídeo** videotape; ~ **magnetofónica** tape; ~ **métrica** tape measure

cintura [θin'tura] nf waist

cinturón [θintu'ron] nm belt; ~ **de seguridad** safety belt

ciprés [θi'pres] nm cypress (tree)

circo ['θirko] nm circus

circuito [θir'kwito] nm circuit

circulación [θirkula'θjon] nf circulation; (AUTO) traffic

circular [θirku'lar] adj, nf circular ♦ vi, vt to circulate ♦ vi (AUTO) to drive; **"circule por la derecha"** "keep (to the) right"

círculo ['θirkulo] nm circle; ~ **vicioso** vicious circle

circuncidar [θirkunθi'dar] vt to circumcise

circundar [θirkun'dar] vt to surround

circunferencia [θirkunfe'renθja] nf circumference

circunscribir [θirkunskri'βir] vt to circumscribe; ~**se** vr to be limited

circunscripción [θirkunskrip'θjon] nf (POL) constituency

circunspecto, a [θirkuns'pekto, a] adj circumspect, cautious

circunstancia [θirkuns'tanθja] nf circumstance

cirio ['θirjo] nm (wax) candle

ciruela [θi'rwela] nf plum; ~ **pasa** prune

cirugía

64

cloaca

cirugía |θiru'xia| nf surgery;
~ estética o plástica plastic surgery

cirujano |θiru'xano| nm surgeon

cisne |'θisne| nm swan

cisterna |θis'terna| nf cistern, tank

cita |'θita| nf appointment, meeting;
(de novios) date; (referencia) quotation

citación |θita'θjon| nf (JUR) summons
sg

citar |θi'tar| vt (gen) to make an
appointment with; (JUR) to summons;
(un autor, texto) to quote; **~se** vr: **se
citaron en el cine** they arranged to
meet at the cinema

cítricos |'θitrikos| nmpl citrus fruit(s)

ciudad |θju'ðað| nf town; (más grande)
city; **~anía** nf citizenship; **~ano, a**
nm/f citizen

cívico, a |'θiβiko, a| adj civic

civil |θi'βil| adj civil ♦ nm (guardia)
policeman

civilización |θiβiliθa'θjon| nf
civilization

civilizar |θiβili'θar| vt to civilize

civismo |θi'βismo| nm public spirit

cizaña |θi'θaɲa| nf (fig) discord

cl. abr (= centilitro) cl.

clamar |kla'mar| vt to clamour for, cry
out for ♦ vi to cry out, clamour

clamor |kla'mor| nm clamour, protest

clandestino, a |klandes'tino, a| adj
clandestine; (POL) underground

clara |'klara| nf (de huevo) egg white

claraboya |klara'βoja| nf skylight

clarear |klare'ar| vi (el día) to dawn; (el
cielo) to clear up, brighten up; **~se** vr
to be transparent

clarete |kla'rete| nm rosé (wine)

claridad |klari'ðað| nf (del día)
brightness; (de estilo) clarity

clarificar |klarifi'kar| vt to clarify

clarinete |klari'nete| nm clarinet

clarividencia |klariβi'ðenθja| nf
clairvoyance; (fig) far-sightedness

claro, a |'klaro, a| adj clear; (luminoso)
bright; (color) light; (evidente) clear,
evident; (poco espeso) thin ♦ nm (en

bosque) clearing ♦ adv clearly ♦ excl
(tb: **~ que sí**) of course!

clase |'klase| nf class; **~ alta/media/
obrera** upper/middle/working class;
~s particulares private lessons,
private tuition sg

clásico, a |'klasiko, a| adj classical

clasificación |klasifika'θjon| nf
classification; (DEPORTE) league (table)

clasificar |klasifi'kar| vt to classify

claudicar |klauði'kar| vi to give in

claustro |'klaustro| nm cloister

cláusula |'klausula| nf clause

clausura |klau'sura| nf closing, closure;
clausurar vt (congreso etc) to bring to
a close

clavar |kla'βar| vt (clavo) to hammer
in; (cuchillo) to stick, thrust

clave |'klaβe| nf key; (MUS) clef

clavel |kla'βel| nm carnation

clavícula |kla'βikula| nf collar bone

clavija |kla'βixa| nf peg, dowel, pin;
(ELEC) plug

clavo |'klaβo| nm (de metal) nail; (BOT)
clove

claxon |'klakson| (pl **~s**) nm horn

clemencia |kle'menθja| nf mercy,
clemency

cleptómano, a |klep'tomano, a| nm/f
kleptomaniac

clérigo |'klerixo| nm priest

clero |'klero| nm clergy

cliché |kli'tʃe| nm cliché; (FOTO)
negative

cliente, a |'kljente, a| nm/f client,
customer

clientela |kljen'tela| nf clientele,
customers pl

clima |'klima| nm climate

climatizado, a |klimati'θaðo, a| adj
air-conditioned

clímax |'klimaks| nm inv climax

clínica |'klinika| nf clinic; (particular)
private hospital

clip |klip| (pl **~s**) nm paper clip

clítoris |'klitoris| nm inv (ANAT) clitoris

cloaca |klo'aka| nf sewer

cloro |'kloro| nm chlorine

club |klub| (pl ~s o ~es) nm club; ~ **de jóvenes** youth club

cm abr (= centímetro, centímetros) cm

C.N.T. (ESP) abr = Confederación Nacional de Trabajo

coacción |koak'θjon| nf coercion, compulsion; **coaccionar** vt to coerce

coagular |koaɣu'lar| vt (leche, sangre) to clot; ~**se** vr to clot; **coágulo** nm clot

coalición |koali'θjon| nf coalition

coartada |koar'taða| nf alibi

coartar |koar'tar| vt to limit, restrict

coba |'koβa| nf: **dar ~ a uno** to soft-soap sb

cobarde |ko'βarðe| adj cowardly ♦ nm coward; **cobardía** nf cowardice

cobaya |ko'βaja| nf guinea pig

cobertizo |koβer'tiθo| nm shelter

cobertura |koβer'tura| nf cover

cobija |ko'βixa| nf (AM) blanket

cobijar |koβi'xar| vt (cubrir) to cover; (proteger) to shelter; **cobijo** nm shelter

cobra |'koβra| nf cobra

cobrador, a |koβra'ðor, a| nm/f (de autobús) conductor/conductress; (de impuestos, gas) collector

cobrar |ko'βrar| vt (cheque) to cash; (sueldo) to collect, draw; (objeto) to recover; (precio) to charge; (deuda) to collect ♦ vi to be paid; **cóbrese al entregar** cash on delivery

cobre |'koβre| nm copper; ~**s** nmpl (MUS) brass instruments

cobro |'koβro| nm (de cheque) cashing; **presentar al ~** to cash

cocaína |koka'ina| nf cocaine

cocción |kok'θjon| nf (CULIN) cooking; (en agua) boiling

cocear |koθe'ar| vi to kick

cocer |ko'θer| vt, vi to cook; (en agua) to boil; (en horno) to bake

coche |'kotʃe| nm (AUTO) car (BRIT), automobile (US); (de tren, de caballos) coach, carriage; (para niños) pram (BRIT), baby carriage (US); **ir en ~** to

drive; ~ **celular** Black Maria, prison van; ~ **de bomberos** fire engine; ~ **fúnebre** hearse; **coche-cama** (pl **coches-cama**) nm (FERRO) sleeping car, sleeper

cochera |ko'tʃera| nf garage; (de autobuses, trenes) depot

coche restaurante (pl **coches restaurante**) nm (FERRO) dining car, diner

cochinillo |kotʃi'niʎo| nm (CULIN) suckling pig, sucking pig

cochino, a |ko'tʃino, a| adj filthy, dirty ♦ nm/f pig

cocido |ko'θiðo| nm stew

cocina |ko'θina| nf kitchen; (aparato) cooker, stove; (acto) cookery; ~ **eléctrica/de gas** electric/gas cooker; ~ **francesa** French cuisine; **cocinar** vt, vi to cook

cocinero, a |koθi'nero, a| nm/f cook

coco |'koko| nm coconut

cocodrilo |koko'ðrilo| nm crocodile

cocotero |koko'tero| nm coconut palm

cóctel |'koktel| nm cocktail

codazo |ko'ðaθo| nm: **dar un ~ a uno** to nudge sb

codicia |ko'ðiθja| nf greed; **codiciar** vt to covet; **codicioso, a** adj covetous

código |'koðiɣo| nm code; ~ **de barras** bar code; ~ **civil** common law; ~ **de (la) circulación** highway code; ~ **postal** postcode

codillo |ko'ðiʎo| nm (ZOOL) knee; (TEC) elbow (joint)

codo |'koðo| nm (ANAT, de tubo) elbow; (ZOOL) knee

codorniz |koðor'niθ| nf quail

coerción |koer'θjon| nf coercion

coetáneo, a |koe'taneo, a| adj, nm/f contemporary

coexistir |koe(k)sis'tir| vi to coexist

cofradía |kofra'ðia| nf brotherhood, fraternity

cofre |'kofre| nm (de joyas) case; (de dinero) chest

coger |ko'xer| (ESP) vt to take (hold of); (objeto caído) to pick up; (frutas) to pick, harvest; (resfriado, ladrón, pelota) to catch ♦ vi: ~ por el buen camino to take the right road; **~se** vr (el dedo) to catch; **~se a algo** to get hold of sth

cogollo |ko'ɣoʎo| nm (de lechuga) heart

cogote |ko'ɣote| nm back o nape of the neck

cohabitar |koaβi'tar| vi to live together, cohabit

cohecho |ko'etʃo| nm (acción) bribery; (soborno) bribe

coherente |koe'rente| adj coherent

cohesión |koe'sjon| nm cohesion

cohete |ko'ete| nm rocket

cohibido, a |koi'βiðo, a| adj (PSICO) inhibited; (tímido) shy

cohibir |koi'βir| vt to restrain, restrict

coincidencia |koinθi'ðenθja| nf coincidence

coincidir |koinθi'ðir| vi (en idea) to coincide, agree; (en lugar) to coincide

coito |'koito| nm intercourse, coitus

coja etc vb ver coger

cojear |koxe'ar| vi (persona) to limp, hobble; (mueble) to wobble, rock

cojera |ko'xera| nf lameness

cojín |ko'xin| nm cushion; **cojinete** nm (TEC) ball bearing

cojo, a etc |'koxo, a| vb ver coger ♦ adj (que no puede andar) lame, crippled; (mueble) wobbly ♦ nm/f lame person, cripple

cojón |ko'xon| (fam) nm: **¡cojones!** shit! (!); **cojonudo, a** (fam) adj great, fantastic

col |kol| nf cabbage; **~es de Bruselas** Brussels sprouts

cola |'kola| nf tail; (de gente) queue; (lugar) end, last place; (para pegar) glue, gum; **hacer ~** to queue (up)

colaborador, a |kolaβora'ðor, a| nm/f collaborator

colaborar |kolaβo'rar| vi to collaborate

colada |ko'laða| nf: **hacer la ~** to do the washing

colador |kola'ðor| nm (de líquidos) strainer; (para verduras etc) colander

colapso |ko'lapso| nm collapse; **~ nervioso** nervous breakdown

colar |ko'lar| vt (líquido) to strain off; (metal) to cast ♦ vi to ooze, seep (through); **~se** vr to jump the queue; **~se en** to get into without paying; (fiesta) to gatecrash

colcha |'koltʃa| nf bedspread

colchón |kol'tʃon| nm mattress; **~ inflable** o **neumático** air bed, air mattress

colchoneta |koltʃo'neta| nf (en gimnasio) mat; (de playa) air bed

colección |kolek'θjon| nf collection; **coleccionar** vt to collect; **coleccionista** nm/f collector

colecta |ko'lekta| nf collection

colectivo, a |kolek'tiβo, a| adj collective, joint ♦ nm (AM) (small) bus

colega |ko'leɣa| nm/f colleague

colegial, a |kole'xjal, a| nm/f schoolboy/girl

colegio |ko'lexjo| nm college; (escuela) school; (de abogados etc) association; **~ electoral** polling station; **~ mayor** hall of residence

<hr>

colegio

A **colegio** is normally a private primary or secondary school. In the state system it means a primary school although these are also called **escuelas**. State secondary schools are called **institutos**.

<hr>

colegir |kole'xir| vt to infer, conclude

cólera |'kolera| nf (ira) anger; (MED) cholera; **colérico, a** |ko'leriko, a| adj irascible, bad-tempered

colesterol |koleste'rol| nm cholesterol

coleta |ko'leta| nf pigtail

colgante |kol'ɣante| adj hanging ♦ nm (joya) pendant

colgar |kol'ɣar| vt to hang (up); (ropa) to hang out ♦ vi to hang; (TELEC) to hang up

cólico ['koliko] nm colic

coliflor |koli'flor| nf cauliflower

colilla |ko'liʎa| nf cigarette end, butt

colina |ko'lina| nf hill

colisión |koli'sjon| nf collision; ~ **de frente** head-on crash

collar |ko'ʎar| nm necklace; (de perro) collar

colmar |kol'mar| vt to fill to the brim; (fig) to fulfil, realize

colmena |kol'mena| nf beehive

colmillo |kol'miʎo| nm (diente) eye tooth; (de elefante) tusk; (de perro) fang

colmo |'kolmo| nm: ¡es el ~! it's the limit!

colocación |koloka'θjon| nf (acto) placing; (empleo) job, position

colocar |kolo'kar| vt to place, put, position; (dinero) to invest; (poner en empleo) to find a job for; ~**se** vr to get a job

Colombia |ko'lombja| nf Colombia; **colombiano, a** adj, nm/f Colombian

colonia |ko'lonja| nf colony; (de casas) housing estate; (agua de ~) cologne

colonización |koloniθa'θjon| nf colonization; **colonizador, a** |koloniθa'ðor, a| adj colonizing ♦ nm/f colonist, settler

colonizar |koloni'θar| vt to colonize

coloquio |ko'lokjo| nm conversation; (congreso) conference

color |ko'lor| nm colour

colorado, a |kolo'raðo, a| adj (rojo) red; (LAM: chiste) rude

colorante |kolo'rante| nm colouring

colorear |kolore'ar| vt to colour

colorete |kolo'rete| nm blusher

colorido |kolo'riðo| nm colouring

columna |ko'lumna| nf column; (pilar) pillar; (apoyo) support

columpiar |kolum'pjar| vt to swing; ~**se** vr to swing; **columpio** nm swing

coma |'koma| nf comma ♦ nm (MED)

coma

comadre |ko'maðre| nf (madrina) godmother; (chismosa) gossip; **comadrona** ♦ nm midwife

comandancia |koman'danθja| nf command

comandante |koman'dante| nm commandant

comarca |ko'marka| nf region

comba |'komba| nf (curva) curve; (cuerda) skipping rope; **saltar a la ~** to skip

combar |kom'bar| vt to bend, curve

combate |kom'bate| nm fight; **combatiente** nm combatant

combatir |komba'tir| vt to fight, combat

combinación |kombina'θjon| nf combination; (QUÍM) compound; (prenda) slip

combinar |kombi'nar| vt to combine

combustible |kombus'tiβle| nm fuel

combustión |kombus'tjon| nf combustion

comedia |ko'meðja| nf comedy; (TEATRO) play, drama

comediante |kome'ðjante| nm/f (comic) actor/actress

comedido, a |kome'ðiðo, a| adj moderate

comedor |kome'ðor, a| nm (habitación) dining room; (cantina) canteen

comensal |komen'sal| nm/f fellow guest (o diner)

comentar |komen'tar| vt to comment on

comentario |komen'tarjo| nm comment, remark; (literario) commentary; ~**s** nmpl (chismes) gossip sg

comentarista |komenta'rista| nm/f commentator

comenzar |komen'θar| vt, vi to begin, start; ~ **a hacer algo** to begin o start doing sth

comer |ko'mer| vt to eat; (DAMAS,

AJEDREZ) to take, capture ♦ vi to eat; (almorzar) to have lunch; ~se vr to eat up

comercial [komer'θjal] adj commercial; (relativo al negocio) business cpd; **comercializar** vt (producto) to market; (pey) to commercialize

comerciante [komer'θjante] nm/f trader, merchant.

comerciar [komer'θjar] vi to trade, do business

comercio [ko'merθjo] nm commerce, trade; (negocio) business; (fig) dealings pl; ~ **electrónico** e-commerce

comestible [komes'tiβle] adj eatable, edible; ~s nmpl food sg, foodstuffs

cometa [ko'meta] nm comet ♦ nf kite

cometer [kome'ter] vt to commit

cometido [kome'tiðo] nm task, assignment

comezón [kome'θon] nf itch, itching

cómic ['komik] nm comic

comicios [ko'miθjos] nmpl elections

cómico, a ['komiko, a] adj comic(al) ♦ nm/f comedian

comida [ko'miða] nf (alimento) food; (almuerzo, cena) meal; (de mediodía) lunch

comidilla [komi'ðiʎa] nf: **ser la ~ de la ciudad** to be the talk of the town

comienzo etc [ko'mjenθo] vb ver **comenzar** ♦ nm beginning, start

comillas [ko'miʎas] nfpl quotation marks

comilona [komi'lona] (fam) nf blow-out

comino [ko'mino] nm: **(no) me importa un ~** I don't give a damn

comisaría [komisa'ria] nf (de policía) police station; (MIL) commissariat

comisario [komi'sarjo] nm (MIL etc) commissary; (POL) commissar

comisión [komi'sjon] nf commission

comité [komi'te] (pl ~s) nm committee

comitiva [komi'tiβa] nf retinue

como ['komo] adv as; (tal ~) like; (aproximadamente) about, approximately ♦ conj (ya que, puesto que) as, since; **¡~ no!** of course!; **no lo haga hoy** unless he does it today; **~ si** as if; **es tan alto ~ ancho** it is as high as it is wide

cómo ['komo] adv how?, why? ♦ excl what?, I beg your pardon? ♦ nm: **el ~ y el porqué** the whys and wherefores

cómoda ['komoða] nf chest of drawers

comodidad [komoði'ðað] nf comfort; **venga a su ~** come at your convenience

comodín [komo'ðin] nm joker

cómodo, a ['komoðo, a] adj comfortable; (práctico, de fácil uso) convenient

compact disc nm compact disk player

compacto, a [kom'pakto, a] adj compact

compadecer [kompaðe'θer] vt to pity, be sorry for; ~se vr: **~se de** to pity, be o feel sorry for

compadre [kom'paðre] nm (padrino) godfather; (amigo) friend, pal

compañero, a [kompa'nero, a] nm/f companion; (novio) boy/girlfriend; **~ de clase** classmate

compañía [kompa'nia] nf company

comparación [kompara'θjon] nf comparison; **en ~ con** in comparison with

comparar [kompa'rar] vt to compare

comparecer [kompare'θer] vi to appear (in court)

comparsa [kom'parsa] nm/f (TEATRO) extra

compartimento [komparti'mjento] nm (FERRO) compartment

compartir [kompar'tir] vt to share; (dinero, comida etc) to divide (up), share (out)

compás [kom'pas] nm (MUS) beat, rhythm; (MAT) compasses pl; (NAUT etc) compass

compasión [kompa'sjon] nf
compassion, pity

compasivo, a [kompa'siβo, a] adj
compassionate

compatibilidad [kompatiβili'ðað] nf
compatibility

compatible [kompa'tiβle] adj
compatible

compatriota [kompa'trjota] nm/f
compatriot, fellow countryman/woman

compendiar [kompen'djar] vt to
summarize; **compendio** nm
summary

compenetrarse [kompene'trarse] vr
to be in tune

compensación [kompensa'θjon] nf
compensation

compensar [kompen'sar] vt to
compensate

competencia [kompe'tenθja] nf
(incumbencia) domain, field; (JUR,
habilidad) competence; (rivalidad)
competition

competente [kompe'tente] adj
competent

competición [kompeti'θjon] nf
competition

competir [kompe'tir] vi to compete

compilar [kompi'lar] vt to compile

complacencia [kompla'θenθja] nf
(placer) pleasure; (tolerancia excesiva)
complacency

complacer [kompla'θer] vt to please;
~se vr to be pleased

complaciente [kompla'θjente] adj
kind, obliging, helpful

complejo, a [kom'plexo, a] adj, nm
complex

complementario, a
[komplemen'tarjo, a] adj
complementary

completar [komple'tar] vt to
complete

completo, a [kom'pleto, a] adj
complete; (perfecto) perfect; (lleno) full
♦ nm full complement

complicado, a [kompli'kaðo, a] adj

complicated; **estar ~ en** to be mixed
up in

cómplice ['kompliθe] nm/f accomplice

complot [kom'plo(t)] (pl ~s) nm plot

componer [kompo'ner] vt (MUS,
LITERATURA, IMPRENTA) to compose;
(algo roto) to mend, repair; (arreglar)
to arrange; **~se** vr: **~se de** to consist
of; **componérselas para hacer algo**
to manage to do sth

comportamiento [komporta'mjento]
nm behaviour, conduct

comportarse [kompor'tarse] vr to
behave

composición [komposi'θjon] nf
composition

compositor, a [komposi'tor, a] nm/f
composer

compostura [kompos'tura] nf
(actitud) composure

compra ['kompra] nf purchase; **ir de
~s** to go shopping; **comprador, a**
nm/f buyer, purchaser

comprar [kom'prar] vt to buy,
purchase

comprender [kompren'der] vt to
understand; (incluir) to comprise,
include

comprensión [kompren'sjon] nf
understanding; **comprensivo, a** adj
(actitud) understanding

compresa [kom'presa] nf:
~ higiénica sanitary towel (BRIT) o
napkin (US)

comprimido, a [kompri'miðo, a] adj
compressed ♦ nm (MED) pill, tablet

comprimir [kompri'mir] vt to
compress

comprobante [kompro'βante] nm
proof; (COM) voucher; **~ de recibo**
receipt

comprobar [kompro'βar] vt to check;
(probar) to prove; (TEC) to check, test

comprometer [komprome'ter] vt to
compromise; (poner en peligro) to
endanger; **~se** vr (involucrarse) to get
involved

compromiso |kompro'miso| nm
(*obligación*) obligation; (*cometido*)
commitment; (*convenio*) agreement;
(*apuro*) awkward situation

compuesto, a |kom'pwesto, a| adj:
~ **de** composed of, made up of ♦ nm
compound

computador |komputa'ðor| nm
computer; ~ **central** mainframe
computer; ~ **personal** personal
computer

computadora |komputa'ðora| nf =
computador

cómputo |'komputo| nm calculation

comulgar |komul'ɣar| vi to receive
communion

común |ko'mun| adj common ♦ nm:
el ~ the community

comunicación |komunika'θjon| nf
communication; (*informe*) report

comunicado |komuni'kaðo| nm
announcement; ~ **de prensa** press
release

comunicar |komuni'kar| vt to
communicate; ~**se** vr to communicate;
está comunicando (*TEL*) the line's
engaged (*BRIT*); a busy (*US*);
comunicativo, a adj communicative

comunidad |komuni'ðað| nf
community; ~ **autónoma** (*POL*)
autonomous region; **C~ Económica
Europea** European Economic
Community

comunión |komu'njon| nf
communion

comunismo |komu'nismo| nm
communism; **comunista** adj, nm/f
communist

PALABRA CLAVE

---

con |kon| prep **1** (*medio, compañía*)
with; **comer ~ cuchara** to eat with a
spoon; **pasear ~ uno** to go for a walk
with sb

2 (*a pesar de*): ~ **todo, merece
nuestros respetos** all the same, he
deserves our respect

3 (*para ~*): **es muy bueno para
~ los niños** he's very good with (the)
children

4 (+ *infin*): ~ **llegar tan tarde se
quedó sin comer** by arriving so late
he missed out on eating

♦ *conj*: ~ **que: será suficiente ~ que
le escribas** it will be sufficient if you
write to her

---

conato |ko'nato| nm attempt; ~ **de
robo** attempted robbery

concebir |konθe'βir| vt, vi to conceive

conceder |konθe'ðer| vt to concede

concejal, a |konθe'xal, a| nm/f town
councillor

concentración |konθentra'θjon| nf
concentration

concentrar |konθen'trar| vt to
concentrate; ~**se** vr to concentrate

concepción |konθep'θjon| nf
conception

concepto |kon'θepto| nm concept

concernir |konθer'nir| vi to concern;
en lo que concierne a ... as far as ...
is concerned; **en lo que a mí
concierne** as far as I'm concerned

concertar |konθer'tar| vt (*MUS*) to
harmonize; (*acordar: precio*) to agree;
(: *tratado*) to conclude; (*trato*) to
arrange, fix up; (*combinar: esfuerzos*) to
coordinate ♦ vi to harmonize, be in
tune

concesión |konθe'sjon| nf concession

concesionario |konθesjo'narjo| nm
(licensed) dealer, agent

concha |'kontʃa| nf shell

conciencia |konθjen'θja| nf
conscience; **tener/tomar ~ de** to be/
become aware of; **tener la ~ limpia/
tranquila** to have a clear conscience

concienciar |konθjen'θjar| vt to make
aware; ~**se** vr to become aware

concienzudo, a |konθjen'θuðo, a|
adj conscientious

concierto etc |kon'θjerto| vb ver
concertar ♦ nm concert; (*obra*)

concerto
conciliar [konθi'ljar] *vt* to reconcile
concilio [kon'θiljo] *nm* council
conciso, a [kon'θiso, a] *adj* concise
concluir [konklu'ir] *vt*, *vi* to conclude;
~se *vr* to conclude
conclusión [konklu'sjon] *nf*
conclusion
concluyente [konklu'jente] *adj*
(*prueba, información*) conclusive
concordar [konkor'ðar] *vt* to reconcile
♦ *vi* to agree, tally
concordia [kon'korðja] *nf* harmony
concretar [konkre'tar] *vt* to make
concrete, make more specific; **~se** *vr*
to become more definite
concreto, a [kon'kreto, a] *adj* (*AM*) concrete; **en ~** (*en resumen*) to
sum up; (*específicamente*) specifically;
no hay nada en ~ there's nothing
definite
concurrencia [konku'rrenθja] *nf*
turnout
concurrido, a [konku'rriðo, a] *adj*
(*calle*) busy; (*local, reunión*) crowded
concurrir [konku'rrir] *vi* (*juntarse: ríos*)
to meet, come together; (: *personas*) to
gather, meet
concursante [konkur'sante] *nm/f*
competitor
concurso [kon'kurso] *nm* (*de público*)
crowd; (*ESCOL, DEPORTE, competencia*)
competition; (*ayuda*) help, cooperation
condal [kon'dal] *adj*: **la Ciudad C~**
Barcelona
conde ['konde] *nm* count
condecoración [kondekora'θjon] *nf*
(*MIL*) medal
condecorar [kondeko'rar] *vt* (*MIL*) to
decorate
condena [kon'dena] *nf* sentence
condenación [kondena'θjon] *nf*
condemnation; (*REL*) damnation
condenar [konde'nar] *vt* to condemn;
(*JUR*) to convict; **~se** *vr* (*REL*) to be
damned
condensar [konden'sar] *vt* to

condense
condesa [kon'desa] *nf* countess
condición [kondi'θjon] *nf* condition;
condicional *adj* conditional
condicionar [kondiθjo'nar] *vt*
(*acondicionar*) to condition; **~ algo a**
to make sth conditional on
condimento [kondi'mento] *nm*
seasoning
condolerse [kondo'lerse] *vr* to
sympathize
condón [kon'don] *nm* condom
conducir [kondu'θir] *vt* to take,
convey; (*AUTO*) to drive ♦ *vi* to drive;
(*fig*) to lead; **~se** *vr* to behave
conducta [kon'dukta] *nf* conduct,
behaviour
conducto [kon'dukto] *nm* pipe, tube;
(*fig*) channel
conductor, a [konduk'tor, a] *adj*
leading, guiding ♦ *nm* (*FÍSICA*)
conductor; (*de vehículo*) driver
conduje *etc vb ver* **conducir**
conduzco *etc vb ver* **conducir**
conectado, a [konek'taðo, a] *adj*
(*INFORM*) on-line
conectar [konek'tar] *vt* to connect;
(*enchufar*) to plug in
conejillo [kone'xiλo] *nm*: **~ de Indias**
(*ZOOL*) guinea pig
conejo [ko'nexo] *nm* rabbit
conexión [konek'sjon] *nf* connection
confección [konfek'θjon] *nf*
preparation; (*industria*) clothing
industry
confeccionar [konfekθjo'nar] *vt* to
make (up)
confederación [konfeðera'θjon] *nf*
confederation
conferencia [konfe'renθja] *nf*
conference; (*lección*) lecture; (*TEL*) call
conferir [konfe'rir] *vt* to award
confesar [konfe'sar] *vt* to confess,
admit
confesión [konfe'sjon] *nf* confession
confesionario [konfesjo'narjo] *nm*
confessional

confeti [kon'feti] *nm* confetti

confiado, a [kon'fjaðo, a] *adj* (*crédulo*) trusting; (*seguro*) confident

confianza [kon'fjanθa] *nf* trust; (*seguridad*) confidence; (*familiaridad*) intimacy, familiarity

confiar [kon'fjar] *vt* to entrust ♦ *vi* to trust

confidencia [konfi'ðenθja] *nf* confidence

confidencial [konfiðen'θjal] *adj* confidential

confidente [konfi'ðente] *nm/f* confidant/e; (*policial*) informer

configurar [konfiɣu'rar] *vt* to shape, form

confín [kon'fin] *nm* limit; **confines** *nmpl* confines, limits

confinar [konfi'nar] *vi* to confine; (*desterrar*) to banish

confirmar [konfir'mar] *vt* to confirm

confiscar [konfis'kar] *vt* to confiscate

confite [kon'fite] *nm* sweet (*BRIT*), candy (*US*)

confitería [konfite'ria] *nf* (*tienda*) confectioner's (shop)

confitura [konfi'tura] *nf* jam

conflictivo, a [konflik'tiβo, a] *adj* (*asunto, propuesta*) controversial; (*país, situación*) troubled

conflicto [kon'flikto] *nm* conflict; (*fig*) clash

confluir [kon'flwir] *vi* (*ríos*) to meet; (*gente*) to gather

conformar [konfor'mar] *vt* to shape, fashion ♦ *vi* to agree; **~se** *vr* to conform; (*resignarse*) to resign o.s.

conforme [kon'forme] *adj* (*correspondiente*): **~ con** in line with; (*de acuerdo*): **estar ~s (con algo)** to be in agreement (with sth) ♦ *adv* as ♦ *excl* agreed! ♦ *prep*: **~ a** in accordance with; **quedarse ~ (con algo)** to be satisfied (with sth)

conformidad [konformi'ðað] *nf* (*semejanza*) similarity; (*acuerdo*) agreement; **conformista** *adj, nm/f*

conformist

confortable [konfor'taβle] *adj* comfortable

confortar [konfor'tar] *vt* to comfort

confrontar [konfron'tar] *vt* to confront; (*dos personas*) to bring face to face; (*cotejar*) to compare

confundir [konfun'dir] *vt* (*equivocar*) to mistake, confuse; (*turbar*) to confuse; **~se** *vr* (*turbarse*) to get confused; (*equivocarse*) to make a mistake; (*mezclarse*) to mix

confusión [konfu'sjon] *nf* confusion

confuso, a [kon'fuso, a] *adj* confused

congelado, a [konxe'laðo, a] *adj* frozen; **~s** *nmpl* frozen food(s)

congelador [konxela'ðor] *nm* (*aparato*) freezer, deep freeze

congelar [konxe'lar] *vt* to freeze; **~se** *vr* (*sangre, grasa*) to congeal

congeniar [konxe'njar] *vi* to get on (*BRIT*) o along (*US*) well

congestión [konxes'tjon] *nf* congestion

congestionar [konxestjo'nar] *vt* to congest

congoja [kon'goxa] *nf* distress, grief

congraciarse [kongra'θjarse] *vr* to ingratiate o.s.

congratular [kongratu'lar] *vt* to congratulate

congregación [kongreɣa'θjon] *nf* congregation

congregar [kongre'ɣar] *vt* to gather together; **~se** *vr* to gather together

congresista [kongre'sista] *nm/f* delegate, congressman/woman

congreso [kon'greso] *nm* congress

congrio ['kongrjo] *nm* conger eel

conjetura [konxe'tura] *nf* guess; **conjeturar** *vt* to guess

conjugar [konxu'ɣar] *vt* to combine, fit together; (*LING*) to conjugate

conjunción [konxun'θjon] *nf* conjunction

conjunto, a [kon'xunto, a] *adj* joint, united ♦ *nm* whole; (*MUS*) band; **en ~**

as a whole
conjurar [konxu'rar] vt (REL) to
exorcise; (fig) to ward off ♦ vi to plot
conmemoración [konmemora'θjon]
nf commemoration
conmemorar [konmemo'rar] vt to
commemorate
conmigo [kon'miɣo] pron with me
conmoción [konmo'θjon] nf shock;
(fig) upheaval; ~ **cerebral** (MED)
concussion
conmovedor, a [konmoße'ðor, a] adj
touching, moving; (emocionante)
exciting
conmover [konmo'ßer] vt to shake,
disturb; (fig) to move
conmutador [konmuta'ðor] nm
switch; (AM: TEL: centralita)
switchboard; (: central) telephone
exchange
cono ['kono] nm cone
conocedor, a [konoθe'ðor, a] adj
expert, knowledgeable ♦ nm/f expert
conocer [kono'θer] vt to know; (por
primera vez) to meet, get to know;
(entender) to know about; (reconocer)
to recognize; ~**se** vr (una persona) to
know o.s.; (dos personas) to (get to)
know each other
conocido, a [kono'θiðo, a] adj (well-)
known ♦ nm/f acquaintance
conocimiento [konoθi'mjento] nm
knowledge; (MED) consciousness; ~**s**
nmpl (saber) knowledge sg
conozco etc vb ver **conocer**
conque ['konke] conj and so, so then
conquista [kon'kista] nf conquest;
conquistador, a adj conquering
♦ nm conqueror
conquistar [konkis'tar] vt to conquer
consagrar [konsa'ɣrar] vt (REL) to
consecrate; (fig) to devote
consciente [kons'θjente] adj
conscious
consecución [konseku'θjon] nf
acquisition; (de fin) attainment
consecuencia [konse'kwenθja] nf

consequence, outcome; (coherencia)
consistency
consecuente [konse'kwente] adj
consistent
consecutivo, a [konseku'tißo, a] adj
consecutive
conseguir [konse'ɣir] vt to get,
obtain; (objetivo) to attain
consejero, a [konse'xero, a] nm/f
adviser, consultant; (POL) councillor
consejo [kon'sexo] nm advice; (POL)
council; ~ **de administración** (COM)
board of directors; ~ **de guerra** court
martial; ~ **de ministros** cabinet
meeting
consenso [kon'senso] nm consensus
consentimiento [konsenti'mjento]
nm consent
consentir [konsen'tir] vt (permitir,
tolerar) to consent to; (mimar) to
pamper, spoil; (aguantar) to put up
with ♦ vi to agree, consent; ~ **que
uno haga algo** to allow sb to do sth
conserje [kon'serxe] nm caretaker;
(portero) porter
conservación [konserßa'θjon] nf
conservation; (de alimentos, vida)
preservation
conservador, a [konserßa'ðor, a] adj
(POL) conservative ♦ nm/f conservative
conservante [konser'ßante] nm
preservative
conservar [konser'ßar] vt to conserve,
keep; (alimentos, vida) to preserve; ~**se**
vr to survive
conservas [kon'serßas] nfpl canned
food(s) (pl)
conservatorio [konserßa'torjo] nm
(MUS) conservatoire, conservatory
considerable [konsiðe'raßle] adj
considerable
consideración [konsiðera'θjon] nf
consideration; (estimación) respect
considerado, a [konsiðe'raðo, a] adj
(atento) considerate; (respetado)
respected
considerar [konsiðe'rar] vt to consider

consigna [kon'siɣna] nf (orden) order, instruction; (para equipajes) left-luggage office

consigo etc [kon'siɣo] vb ver **conseguir** ♦ pron (m) with him; (f) with her; (Vd) with you; (reflexivo) with o.s.

consiguiendo etc vb ver **conseguir**

consiguiente [konsi'ɣjente] adj consequent; **por ~** and so, therefore, consequently

consistente [konsis'tente] adj consistent; (sólido) solid, firm; (válido) sound

consistir [konsis'tir] vi: **~ en** (componerse de) to consist of

consola [kon'sola] nf (mueble) console table; (de videojuegos) console

consolación [konsola'θjon] nf consolation

consolar [konso'lar] vt to console

consolidar [konsoli'ðar] vt to consolidate

consomé [konso'me] (pl **~s**) nm consommé, clear soup

consonante [konso'nante] adj consonant, harmonious ♦ nf consonant

consorcio [kon'sorθjo] nm consortium

conspiración [konspira'θjon] nf conspiracy

conspirador, a [konspira'ðor, a] nm/f conspirator

conspirar [konspi'rar] vi to conspire

constancia [kons'tanθja] nf constancy; **dejar ~ de** to put on record

constante [kons'tante] adj, nf constant

constar [kons'tar] vi (evidenciarse) to be clear o evident; **~ de** to consist of

constatar [konsta'tar] vt to verify

consternación [konsterna'θjon] nf consternation

constipado, a [konsti'paðo, a] adj: **estar ~** to have a cold ♦ nm cold

constitución [konstitu'θjon] nf constitution; **constitucional** adj constitutional

constituir [konstitu'ir] vt (formar, componer) to constitute, make up; (fundar, erigir, ordenar) to constitute, establish

constituyente [konstitu'jente] adj constituent

constreñir [konstre'nir] vt (restringir) to restrict

construcción [konstruk'θjon] nf construction, building

constructor, a [konstruk'tor, a] nm/f builder

construir [konstru'ir] vt to build, construct

construyendo etc vb ver **construir**

consuelo [kon'swelo] nm consolation, solace

cónsul [ˈkonsul] nm consul; **consulado** nm consulate

consulta [kon'sulta] nf consultation; (MED): **horas de ~** surgery hours

consultar [konsul'tar] vt to consult

consultorio [konsul'torjo] nm (MED) surgery

consumar [konsu'mar] vt to complete, carry out; (crimen) to commit; (sentencia) to carry out

consumición [konsumi'θjon] nf consumption; (bebida) drink; (comida) food; **~ mínima** cover charge

consumidor, a [konsumi'ðor, a] nm/f consumer

consumir [konsu'mir] vt to consume; **~se** vr to be consumed; (persona) to waste away

consumismo [konsu'mismo] nm consumerism

consumo [kon'sumo] nm consumption

contabilidad [kontaβili'ðað] nf accounting, book-keeping; (profesión) accountancy; **contable** nm/f accountant

contacto [kon'takto] nm contact; (AUTO) ignition

contado, a [kon'taðo, a] adj: **~s**

(escasos) numbered, scarce, few ♦ *nm*:
pagar al ~ to pay (in) cash
contador [konta'ðor] *nm (aparato)*
meter; *(AM: contante)* accountant
contagiar [konta'xjar] *vt (enfermedad)*
to pass on, transmit; *(persona)* to
infect; **~se** *vr* to become infected
contagio [kon'taxjo] *nm* infection;
contagioso, a *adj* infectious; *(fig)*
catching
contaminación [kontamina'θjon] *nf*
contamination; *(polución)* pollution
contaminar [kontami'nar] *vt (aire, agua)* to
contaminate; *(aire, agua)* to pollute
contante [kon'tante] *adj*: **dinero ~ (y
sonante)** cash
contar [kon'tar] *vt (páginas, dinero)* to
count; *(anécdota, chiste etc)* to tell ♦ *vi*
to count; **~ con** to rely on, count on
contemplación [kontempla'θjon] *nf*
contemplation
contemplar [kontem'plar] *vt* to
contemplate; *(mirar)* to look at
contemporáneo, a
[kontempo'raneo, a] *adj, nm/f*
contemporary
contendiente [konten'djente] *nm/f*
contestant
contenedor [kontene'ðor] *nm*
container
contener [konte'ner] *vt* to contain,
hold; *(retener)* to hold back, contain;
~se *vr* to control o restrain o.s.
contenido, a [konte'niðo, a] *adj*
(moderado) restrained; *(risa etc)*
suppressed ♦ *nm* contents *pl*, content
contentar [konten'tar] *vt (satisfacer)*
to satisfy; *(complacer)* to please; **~se** *vr*
to be satisfied
contento, a [kon'tento, a] *adj (alegre)*
pleased; *(feliz)* happy
contestación [kontesta'θjon] *nf*
answer, reply
contestador [kontesta'ðor] *nm*:
~ automático answering machine
contestar [kontes'tar] *vt* to answer,
reply; *(JUR)* to corroborate, confirm

contexto [kon'te(k)sto] *nm* context
contienda [kon'tjenda] *nf* contest
contigo [kon'tixo] *pron* with you
contiguo, a [kon'tiwo, a] *adj*
adjacent, adjoining
continente [konti'nente] *adj, nm*
continent
contingencia [kontin'xenθja] *nf*
contingency; *(riesgo)* risk;
contingente *adj, nm* contingent
continuación [kontinwa'θjon] *nf*
continuation; **a ~** then, next
continuar [konti'nwar] *vt* to continue,
go on with ♦ *vi* to continue, go on;
~ hablando to continue talking o to
talk
continuidad [kontinwi'ðað] *nf*
continuity
continuo, a [kon'tinwo, a] *adj (sin
interrupción)* continuous; *(acción
perseverante)* continual
contorno [kon'torno] *nm* outline;
(GEO) contour; **~s** *nmpl* neighbourhood
sg, surrounding area *sg*
contorsión [kontor'sjon] *nf*
contortion
contra ['kontra] *prep, ad* against ♦ *nm
inv* con ♦ *nf*: **la C~** *(de Nicaragua)* the
Contras *pl*
contraataque [kontraa'take] *nm*
counter-attack
contrabajo [kontra'ßaxo] *nm* double
bass
contrabandista [kontraßan'dista]
nm/f smuggler
contrabando [kontra'ßando] *nm*
(acción) smuggling; *(mercancías)*
contraband
contracción [kontrak'θjon] *nf*
contraction
contracorriente [kontrako'rrjente]:
(a) ~ *adv* against the current
contradecir [kontraðe'θir] *vt* to
contradict
contradicción [kontraðik'θjon] *nf*
contradiction
contradictorio, a [kontraðik'torjo, a]

adj contradictory
contraer [kontra'er] *vt* to contract;
(*limitar*) to restrict; **~se** *vr* to contract;
(*limitarse*) to limit o.s.
contraluz [kontra'luθ] *nf*: **a ~** against
the light
contrapartida [kontrapar'tiða] *nf*:
como ~ (de) in return (for)
contrapelo [kontra'pelo]: **a ~** *adv* the
wrong way
contrapesar [kontrape'sar] *vt* to
counterbalance; (*fig*) to offset;
contrapeso *nm* counterweight
contraportada [kontrapor'taða] *nf*
(*de revista*) back cover
contraproducente
[kontraproðu'θente] *adj*
counterproductive
contrariar [kontra'rjar] *vt* (*oponerse*)
to oppose; (*poner obstáculo*) to
impede; (*enfadar*) to vex
contrariedad [kontrarje'ðað] *nf*
(*obstáculo*) obstacle, setback; (*disgusto*)
vexation, annoyance
contrario, a [kon'trarjo, a] *adj*
contrary; (*persona*) opposed; (*sentido,
lado*) opposite ♦ *nm/f* enemy,
adversary; (*DEPORTE*) opponent; **al/por
el ~** on the contrary; **de lo ~**
otherwise
contrarreloj [kontrarre'lo] *nf* (*tb:
prueba ~*) time trial
contrarrestar [kontrarres'tar] *vt* to
counteract
contrasentido [kontrasen'tiðo] *nm*:
es un ~ que él ... it doesn't make
sense for him to ...
contraseña [kontra'seɲa] *nf* (*INFORM*)
password
contrastar [kontras'tar] *vt, vi* to
contrast
contraste [kon'traste] *nm* contrast
contratar [kontra'tar] *vt* (*firmar un
acuerdo para*) to contract for;
(*empleados, obreros*) to hire, engage;
~se *vr* to sign on
contratiempo [kontra'tjempo] *nm*

setback
contratista [kontra'tista] *nm/f*
contractor
contrato [kon'trato] *nm* contract
contravenir [kontraβe'nir] *vi*: **~ a** to
contravene, violate
contraventana [kontraβen'tana] *nf*
shutter
contribución [kontriβu'θjon] *nf*
(*municipal etc*) tax; (*ayuda*)
contribution
contribuir [kontriβu'ir] *vt, vi* to
contribute; (*COM*) to pay (in taxes)
contribuyente [kontriβu'jente] *nm/f*
(*COM*) taxpayer; (*que ayuda*)
contributor
contrincante [kontrin'kante] *nm*
opponent
control [kon'trol] *nm* control;
(*inspección*) inspection, check; **~ador,
a** *nm/f* controller; **~ador aéreo** air-
traffic controller
controlar [kontro'lar] *vt* to control;
(*inspeccionar*) to inspect, check
controversia [kontro'βersja] *nf*
controversy
contundente [kontun'dente] *adj*
(*instrumento*) blunt; (*argumento,
derrota*) overwhelming
contusión [kontu'sjon] *nf* bruise
convalecencia [kombale'θenθja] *nf*
convalescence
convalecer [kombale'θer] *vi* to
convalesce, get better
convaleciente [kombale'θjente] *adj,
nm/f* convalescent
convalidar [kombali'ðar] *vt* (*título*) to
recognize
convencer [komben'θer] *vt* to
convince
convencimiento [kombenθi'mjento]
nm (*certidumbre*) conviction
convención [komben'θjon] *nf*
convention
conveniencia [kombe'njenθja] *nf*
suitability; (*conformidad*) agreement;
(*utilidad, provecho*) usefulness; **~s** *nfpl*

(*convenciones*) conventions; (*COM*) property *sg*

conveniente [kombe'njente] *adj* suitable; (*útil*) useful

convenio [kom'benjo] *nm* agreement, treaty

convenir [kombe'nir] *vi* (*estar de acuerdo*) to agree; (*venir bien*) to suit, be suitable

convento [kom'bento] *nm* convent

convenza *etc vb ver* **convencer**

converger [komber'xer] *vi* to converge

convergir [komber'xir] *vi* = **converger**

conversación [kombersa'θjon] *nf* conversation

conversar [komber'sar] *vi* to talk, converse

conversión [komber'sjon] *nf* conversion

convertir [komber'tir] *vt* to convert

convicción [kombik'θjon] *nf* conviction

convicto, a [kom'bikto, a] *adj* convicted

convidado, a [kombi'ðaðo, a] *nm/f* guest

convidar [kombi'ðar] *vt* to invite

convincente [kombin'θente] *adj* convincing

convite [kom'bite] *nm* invitation; (*banquete*) banquet

convivencia [kombi'βenθja] *nf* coexistence, living together

convivir [kombi'βir] *vi* to live together

convocar [kombo'kar] *vt* to summon, call (together)

convocatoria [komboka'torja] *nf* (*de oposiciones, elecciones*) notice; (*de huelga*) call

convulsión [kombul'sjon] *nf* convulsion

conyugal [konju'xal] *adj* conjugal; **cónyuge** ['konjuxe] *nm/f* spouse

coñac [ko'ɲa(k)] (*pl* **~s**) *nm* cognac, brandy

coño ['koɲo] (*fam!*) *excl* (*enfado*) shit! (*!*); (*sorpresa*) bloody hell! (*!*)

cooperación [koopera'θjon] *nf* cooperation

cooperar [koope'rar] *vi* to cooperate

cooperativa [koopera'tiβa] *nf* cooperative

coordinadora [koorðina'ðora] *nf* (*comité*) coordinating committee

coordinar [koorði'nar] *vt* to coordinate

copa ['kopa] *nf* cup; (*vaso*) glass; (*bebida*): (**tomar una**) ~ (to have a) drink; (*de árbol*) top; (*de sombrero*) crown; **~s** *nfpl* (*NAIPES*) ≈ hearts

copia ['kopja] *nf* copy; **~ de respaldo** o **seguridad** (*INFORM*) back-up copy; **copiar** *vt* to copy

copioso, a [ko'pjoso, a] *adj* copious, plentiful

copla ['kopla] *nf* verse; (*canción*) (popular) song

copo ['kopo] *nm*: **~ de nieve** snowflake; **~s de maíz** cornflakes

coqueta [ko'keta] *adj* flirtatious, coquettish; **coquetear** *vi* to flirt

coraje [ko'raxe] *nm* courage; (*ira*) anger

coral [ko'ral] *adj* choral ♦ *nf* (*MUS*) choir ♦ *nm* (*ZOOL*) coral

coraza [ko'raθa] *nf* (*armadura*) armour; (*blindaje*) armour-plating

corazón [kora'θon] *nm* heart

corazonada [koraθo'naða] *nf* impulse; (*presentimiento*) hunch

corbata [kor'βata] *nf* tie

corchete [kor'tʃete] *nm* catch, clasp

corcho ['kortʃo] *nm* cork; (*PESCA*) float

cordel [kor'ðel] *nm* cord, line

cordero [kor'ðero] *nm* lamb

cordial [kor'ðjal] *adj* cordial; **~idad** *nf* warmth, cordiality

cordillera [korði'ʎera] *nf* range (of mountains)

Córdoba ['korðoβa] *n* Cordova

cordón [kor'ðon] *nm* (*cuerda*) cord, string; (*de zapatos*) lace; (*MIL etc*) cordon

cordura [kor'ðura] nf: **con ~** (obrar, hablar) sensibly

corneta [kor'neta] nf bugle

cornisa [kor'nisa] nf (ARQ) cornice

coro ['koro] nm chorus; (conjunto de cantores) choir

corona [ko'rona] nf crown; (de flores) garland; **coronación** nf coronation; **coronar** vt to crown

coronel [koro'nel] nm colonel

coronilla [koro'niʎa] nf (ANAT) crown (of the head)

corporación [korpora'θjon] nf corporation

corporal [korpo'ral] adj corporal, bodily

corpulento, a [korpu'lento a] adj (persona) heavily-built

corral [ko'rral] nm farmyard

correa [ko'rrea] nf strap; (cinturón) belt; (de perro) lead, leash

corrección [korrek'θjon] nf correction; (reprensión) rebuke; **correccional** nm reformatory

correcto, a [ko'rrekto, a] adj correct; (persona) well-mannered

corredizo, a [korre'ðiθo, a] adj (puerta etc) sliding

corredor, a [korre'ðor, a] nm (pasillo) corridor; (balcón corrido) gallery; (COM) agent, broker ♦ nm/f (DEPORTE) runner

corregir [korre'xir] vt (error) to correct; **~se** vr to reform

correo [ko'rreo] nm post, mail; (persona) courier; **C~s** nmpl Post Office sg; **~ aéreo** airmail; **~ electrónico** electronic mail, e-mail

correr [ko'rrer] vt to run; (cortinas) to draw; (cerrojo) to shoot ♦ vi to run; (líquido) to run, flow; **~se** vr to slide, move; (colores) to run

correspondencia [korrespon'denθja] nf correspondence; (FERRO) connection

corresponder [korrespon'der] vi to correspond; (convenir) to be suitable; (pertenecer) to belong; (concernir) to concern; **~se** vr (por escrito) to correspond; (amarse) to love one another

correspondiente [korrespon'djente] adj corresponding

corresponsal [korrespon'sal] nm/f correspondent

corrida [ko'rriða] nf (de toros) bullfight

corrido, a [ko'rriðo, a] adj (avergonzado) abashed; **3 noches corridas** 3 nights running; **un kilo ~** a good kilo

corriente [ko'rrjente] adj (agua) running; (dinero etc) current; (común) ordinary, normal ♦ nf current ♦ nm current month; **~ eléctrica** electric current

corrija etc vb ver **corregir**

corrillo [ko'rriʎo] nm ring, circle of people); (fig) clique

corro [ko'rro] nm ring, circle (of people)

corroborar [korroßo'rar] vt to corroborate

corroer [korro'er] vt to corrode; (GEO) to erode

corromper [korrom'per] vt (madera) to rot; (fig) to corrupt

corrosivo, a [korro'sißo, a] adj corrosive

corrupción [korrup'θjon] nf rot, decay; (fig) corruption

corsé [kor'se] nm corset

cortacésped [korta'θespeð] nm lawn mower

cortado, a [kor'taðo, a] adj (gen) cut; (leche) sour; (tímido) shy; (avergonzado) embarrassed ♦ nm coffee (with a little milk)

cortar [kor'tar] vt to cut; (suministro) to cut off; (un pasaje) to cut out ♦ vi to cut; **~se** vr (avergonzarse) to become embarrassed; (leche) to turn, curdle; **~se el pelo** to have one's hair cut

cortaúñas [korta'uɲas] nm inv nail clippers pl

corte ['korte] nm cut, cutting; (de tela)

piece, length ♦ nf: **las C~s** the Spanish Parliament; **~ y confección** dressmaking; **~ de luz** power cut

cortejar |korte'xar| vt to court

cortejo |kor'texo| nm entourage; **~ fúnebre** funeral procession

cortés |kor'tes| adj courteous, polite

cortesía |korte'sia| nf courtesy

corteza |kor'teθa| nf (de árbol) bark; (de pan) crust

cortijo |kor'tixo| nm farm, farmhouse

cortina |kor'tina| nf curtain

corto, a |'korto, a| adj (breve) short; (tímido) bashful; **~ de luces** not very bright; **~ de vista** short-sighted; **estar ~ de fondos** to be short of funds; **~circuito** nm short circuit; **~metraje** nm (CINE) short

cosa |'kosa| nf thing; **~ de** about; **eso es ~ mía** that's my business

coscorrón |kosko'rron| nm bump on the head

cosecha |ko'setʃa| nf (AGR) harvest; (de vino) vintage

cosechar |kose'tʃar| vt to harvest, gather (in)

coser |ko'ser| vt to sew

cosmético, a |kos'metiko, a| adj, nm cosmetic

cosquillas |kos'kiλas| nfpl: **hacer ~ to** tickle; **tener ~** to be ticklish

costa |'kosta| nf (GEO) coast; **C~ Brava** Costa Brava; **C~ Cantábrica** Cantabrian Coast; **C~ del Sol** Costa del Sol; **a toda ~** at all costs

costado |kos'taðo| nm side

costar |kos'tar| vt (valer) to cost; **me cuesta hablarle** I find it hard to talk to him

Costa Rica nf Costa Rica; **costarricense** adj, nm/f Costa Rican; **costarriqueño, a** adj, nm/f Costa Rican

coste |'koste| nm = **costo**

costear |koste'ar| vt to pay for

costero, a |kos'tero, a| adj (pueblecito, camino) coastal

costilla |kos'tiλa| nf rib; (CULIN) cutlet

costo |'kosto| nm cost, price; **~ de la vida** cost of living; **~so, a** adj costly, expensive

costra |'kostra| nf (corteza) crust; (MED) scab

costumbre |kos'tumbre| nf custom, habit

costura |kos'tura| nf sewing, needlework; (zurcido) seam

costurera |kostu'rera| nf dressmaker

costurero |kostu'rero| nm sewing box o case

cotejar |kote'xar| vt to compare

cotidiano, a |koti'ðjano, a| adj daily, day to day

cotilla |ko'tiλa| nm/f (fam) gossip; **cotillear** vi to gossip; **cotilleo** nm gossip(ing)

cotización |kotiθa'θjon| nf (COM) quotation, price; (de club) dues pl

cotizar |koti'θar| vt (COM) to quote, price; **~se** vr: **~se a** to sell at; fetch; (BOLSA) to stand at, be quoted at

coto |'koto| nm (terreno cercado) enclosure; (de caza) reserve

cotorra |ko'torra| nf parrot

COU |kou| (ESP) nm abr (= Curso de Orientación Universitaria) 1 year course leading to final school-leaving certificate and university entrance examinations

coyote |ko'jote| nm coyote, prairie wolf

coyuntura |kojun'tura| nf juncture, occasion

coz |koθ| nf kick

crack nm (droga) crack

cráneo |'kraneo| nm skull, cranium

cráter |'krater| nm crater

creación |krea'θjon| nf creation

creador, a |krea'ðor, a| adj creative ♦ nm/f creator

crear |kre'ar| vt to create, make

crecer |kre'θer| vi to grow; (precio) to rise

creces |'kreθes| : **con ~** adv amply, fully

crecido, a [kre'θiðo, a] *adj* (*persona, planta*) full-grown; (*cantidad*) large

creciente [kre'θjente] *adj* growing; (*cantidad*) increasing; (*luna*) crescent ♦ *nm* crescent

crecimiento [kreθi'mjento] *nm* growth; (*aumento*) increase

credenciales [kreðen'θjales] *nfpl* credentials

crédito ['kreðito] *nm* credit

credo ['kreðo] *nm* creed

crédulo, a ['kreðulo, a] *adj* credulous

creencia [kre'enθja] *nf* belief

creer [kre'er] *vt, vi* to think, believe; **~se** *vr* to believe o.s. (to be); **~ en** to believe in; **¡ya lo creo!** I should think so!

creíble [kre'iβle] *adj* credible, believable

creído, a [kre'iðo, a] *adj* (*engreído*) conceited

crema ['krema] *nf* cream; **~ pastelera** (*confectioner's*) custard

cremallera [krema'ʎera] *nf* zip (fastener)

crematorio [krema'torjo] *nm* (*tb: horno ~*) crematorium

crepitar [krepi'tar] *vi* to crackle

crepúsculo [kre'puskulo] *nm* twilight, dusk

cresta ['kresta] *nf* (GEO, ZOOL) crest

creyendo *vb ver* **creer**

creyente [kre'jente] *nm/f* believer

creyó *etc vb ver* **creer**

crezco *etc vb ver* **crecer**

cría *etc* ['kria] *vb ver* **criar** ♦ *nf* (*de animales*) rearing, breeding; (*animal*) young; *ver tb* **crio**

criadero [kria'ðero] *nm* (ZOOL) breeding place

criado, a [kri'aðo, a] *nm* servant ♦ *nf* servant, maid

criador [kria'ðor] *nm* breeder

crianza [kri'anθa] *nf* rearing, breeding; (*fig*) breeding

criar [kri'ar] *vt* (*educar*) to bring up; (*producir*) to grow, produce; (*animales*)

to breed

criatura [kria'tura] *nf* creature; (*niño*) baby, (small) child

criba ['kriβa] *nf* sieve; **cribar** *vt* to sieve

crimen ['krimen] *nm* crime

criminal [krimi'nal] *adj, nm/f* criminal

crin [krin] *nf* (*tb: ~es*) mane

crio, a ['krio, a] (*fam*) *nm/f* (*niño*) kid

crisis ['krisis] *nf inv* crisis; **~ nerviosa** nervous breakdown

crispar [kris'par] *vt* (*nervios*) to set on edge

cristal [kris'tal] *nm* crystal; (*de ventana*) glass, pane; (*lente*) lens; **~ino, a** *adj* crystalline; (*fig*) clear ♦ *nm* lens (of the eye); **~izar** *vt, vi* to crystallize

cristiandad [kristjan'daθ] *nf* Christendom

cristianismo [kristja'nismo] *nm* Christianity

cristiano, a [kris'tjano, a] *adj, nm/f* Christian

Cristo ['kristo] *nm* Christ; (*crucifijo*) crucifix

criterio [kri'terjo] *nm* criterion; (*juicio*) judgement

crítica ['kritika] *nf* criticism; *ver tb* **crítico**

criticar [kriti'kar] *vt* to criticize

crítico, a ['kritiko, a] *adj* critical ♦ *nm/f* critic

Croacia *nf* Croatia

croar [kro'ar] *vi* to croak

cromo ['kromo] *nm* chrome

crónica ['kronika] *nf* chronicle, account

crónico, a ['kroniko, a] *adj* chronic

cronómetro [kro'nometro] *nm* stopwatch

croqueta [kro'keta] *nf* croquette

cruce *etc* ['kruθe] *vb ver* **cruzar** ♦ *nm* crossing; (*de carreteras*) crossroads

crucificar [kruθifi'kar] *vt* to crucify

crucifijo [kruθi'fixo] *nm* crucifix

crucigrama [kruθi'γrama] *nm* crossword (puzzle)

crudo, a ['kruðo, a] *adj* raw; *(no maduro)* unripe; *(petróleo)* crude; *(rudo, cruel)* cruel ♦ *nm* crude (oil)

cruel [krwel] *adj* cruel; **~dad** *nf* cruelty

crujido [kru'xiðo] *nm (de madera etc)* creak

crujiente [kru'xjente] *adj (galleta etc)* crunchy

crujir [kru'xir] *vi (madera etc)* to creak; *(dedos)* to crack; *(dientes)* to grind; *(nieve, arena)* to crunch

cruz [kruθ] *nf* cross; *(de moneda)* tails *sg;* **~ gamada** swastika

cruzada [kru'θaða] *nf* crusade

cruzado, a [kru'θaðo, a] *adj* crossed ♦ *nm* crusader

cruzar [kru'θar] *vt* to cross; **~se** *vr (líneas etc)* to cross; *(personas)* to pass each other

Cruz Roja *nf* Red Cross

cuaderno [kwa'ðerno] *nm* notebook; *(de escuela)* exercise book; *(NAUT)* logbook

cuadra ['kwaðra] *nf (caballeriza)* stable; *(AM)* block

cuadrado, a [kwa'ðraðo, a] *adj* square ♦ *nm (MAT)* square

cuadrar [kwa'ðrar] *vt* to square ♦ *vi:* **~ con** to square with, tally with; **~se** *vr (soldado)* to stand to attention

cuadrilátero [kwaðri'latero] *nm (DEPORTE)* boxing ring; *(GEOM)* quadrilateral

cuadrilla [kwa'ðriʎa] *nf* party, group

cuadro ['kwaðro] *nm* square; *(ARTE)* painting; *(TEATRO)* scene; *(diagrama)* chart; *(DEPORTE, MED)* team; **tela a ~s** checked *(BRIT)* o chequered *(US)* material

cuádruple ['kwaðruple] *adj* quadruple

cuajar [kwa'xar] *vt (leche)* to curdle; *(sangre)* to congeal; *(CULIN)* to set; **~se** *vr* to curdle; to congeal; to set; *(llenarse)* to fill up

cuajo ['kwaxo] *nm:* **de ~** *(arrancar)* by the roots; *(cortar)* completely

cual [kwal] *adv* like, as ♦ *pron:* **el ~** *etc*

which; *(persona: sujeto)* who; *(: objeto)* whom ♦ *adj* such as; **cada ~** each one; **déjalo tal ~** leave it just as it is

cuál [kwal] *pron interr* which (one)

cualesquier(a) [kwales'kjer(a)] *pl de* **cualquier(a)**

cualidad [kwali'ðað] *nf* quality

cualquier [kwal'kjer] *adj ver* **cualquiera**

cualquiera [kwal'kjera] *(pl* **cualesquiera**) *adj (delante de nm y f:* **cualquier**) any ♦ *pron* anybody; **un coche ~ servirá** any car will do; **no es un hombre ~** he isn't just anybody; **cualquier día/libro** any day/book; **eso ~ lo sabe hacer** anybody can do that; **es un ~** he's a nobody

cuando ['kwando] *adv* when; *(aún si)* if, even if ♦ *conj (puesto que)* since ♦ *prep:* **yo, ~ niño ...** when I was a child ...; **~ no sea así** even if it is not so; **~ más** at (the) most; **~ menos** at least; **~ no** if not, otherwise; **de ~ en ~** from time to time

cuándo ['kwando] *adv* when; **¿desde ~?, ¿de ~ acá?** since when?

cuantía [kwan'tia] *nf (importe: de pérdidas, deuda, daños)* extent

cuantioso, a [kwan'tjoso, a] *adj* substantial

PALABRA CLAVE

---

cuanto, a ['kwanto, a] *adj* **1** *(todo):* **tiene todo ~ desea** he's got everything he wants; **le daremos ~s ejemplares necesite** we'll give him as many copies as o all the copies he needs; **~s hombres la ven** all the men who see her

2: unos ~s: había unos ~s periodistas there were a few journalists

3 (+ *más*): **~ más vino bebes peor te sentirás** the more wine you drink the worse you'll feel

♦ *pron:* **tiene ~ desea** he has

everything he wants; **tome ~/~s quiera** take as much/many as you want

♦ *adv*: **en ~**: **en ~ profesor** as a teacher; **en ~ a mí** as for me; *ver tb* **antes**

♦ *conj* **1**: **~ más gana menos gasta** the more he earns the less he spends; **~ más joven más confiado** the younger you are the more trusting you are

2: **en ~**: **en ~ llegue/llegué** as soon as I arrive/arrived

cuánto, a ['kwanto, a] *adj (exclamación)* what a lot of; *(interr: sg)* how much?; (: *pl*) how many? ♦ *pron, adv* how; *(interr: sg)* how much?; (: *pl*) how many?; **¡cuánta gente!** what a lot of people!; **¿~ cuesta?** how much does it cost?; **¿a ~s estamos?** what's the date?; **Señor no sé ~** Mr. So-and-So

cuarenta [kwa'renta] *num* forty

cuarentena [kwaren'tena] *nf* quarantine

cuaresma [kwa'resma] *nf* Lent

cuarta ['kwarta] *nf* (MAT) quarter, fourth; *(palmo)* span

cuartel [kwar'tel] *nm* (MIL) barracks *pl*; **~ general** headquarters *pl*

cuarteto [kwar'teto] *nm* quartet

cuarto, a ['kwarto, a] *adj* fourth ♦ *nm* (MAT) quarter, fourth; *(habitación)* room; **~ de baño** bathroom; **~ de estar** living room; **~ de hora** quarter (of an) hour; **~ de kilo** quarter kilo

cuatro ['kwatro] *num* four

Cuba ['kuβa] *nf* Cuba; **cubano, a** *adj, nm/f* Cuban

cuba ['kuβa] *nf* cask, barrel

cubata [ku'βata] *nm (fam)* large drink *(of rum and coke etc)*

cúbico, a ['kuβiko, a] *adj* cubic

cubierta [ku'βjerta] *nf* cover, covering; *(neumático)* tyre; (NAUT) deck

cubierto, a [ku'βjerto, a] *pp de* **cubrir**

♦ *adj* covered ♦ *nm* cover; *(lugar en la mesa)* place; **~s** *nmpl* cutlery *sg*; **a ~** under cover

cubil [ku'βil] *nm* den; **~ete** *nm (en juegos)* cup

cubito [ku'βito] *nm*: **~ de hielo** ice-cube

cubo ['kuβo] *nm* (MATH) cube; *(balde)* bucket, tub; (TEC) drum

cubrecama [kuβre'kama] *nm* bedspread

cubrir [ku'βrir] *vt* to cover; **~se** *vr (cielo)* to become overcast

cucaracha [kuka'ratʃa] *nf* cockroach

cuchara [ku'tʃara] *nf* spoon; (TEC) scoop; **~da** *nf* spoonful; **~dita** *nf* teaspoonful

cucharilla [kutʃa'riʎa] *nf* teaspoon

cucharón [kutʃa'ron] *nm* ladle

cuchichear [kutʃitʃe'ar] *vi* to whisper

cuchilla [ku'tʃiʎa] *nf* (large) knife; *(de arma blanca)* blade; **~ de afeitar** razor blade

cuchillo [ku'tʃiʎo] *nm* knife

cuchitril [kutʃi'tril] *nm* hovel

cuclillas [ku'kliʎas] *nfpl*: **en ~** squatting

cuco, a ['kuko, a] *adj* pretty; *(astuto)* sharp ♦ *nm* cuckoo

cucurucho [kuku'rutʃo] *nm* cornet

cuello ['kweʎo] *nm* (ANAT) neck; *(de vestido, camisa)* collar

cuenca ['kwenka] *nf* (ANAT) eye socket; (GEO) bowl, deep valley

cuenco ['kwenko] *nm* bowl

cuenta *etc* ['kwenta] *vb ver* **contar**

♦ *nf (cálculo)* count, counting; *(en café, restaurante)* bill (BRIT), check (US); (COM) account; *(de collar)* bead; **a fin de ~s** in the end; **caer en la ~** to catch on; **darse ~ de** to realize; **tener en ~** to bear in mind; **echar ~s** to take stock; **~ corriente/de ahorros** current/savings account; **~ atrás** countdown; **~-kilómetros** *nm inv* = milometer; *(de velocidad)* speedometer

cuento *etc* ['kwento] *vb ver* **contar**

♦ *nm* story

cuerda ['kwerða] *nf* rope; (*fina*) string; (*de reloj*) spring; **dar ~ a un reloj** to wind up a clock; **~ floja** tightrope

cuerdo, a ['kwerðo, a] *adj* sane; (*prudente*) wise, sensible

cuerno ['kwerno] *nm* horn

cuero ['kwero] *nm* leather; **en ~s** stark naked; **~ cabelludo** scalp

cuerpo ['kwerpo] *nm* body

cuervo ['kwerβo] *nm* crow

cuesta *etc* ['kwesta] *vb ver* **costar** ♦ *nf* slope; (*en camino etc*) hill; **~ arriba/abajo** uphill/downhill; **a ~s** on one's back

cueste *etc vb ver* **costar**

cuestión [kwes'tjon] *nf* matter, question, issue

cueva ['kweβa] *nf* cave

cuidado [kwi'ðaðo] *nm* care, carefulness; (*preocupación*) care, worry ♦ *excl* careful!, look out!

cuidadoso, a [kwiða'ðoso, a] *adj* careful; (*preocupado*) anxious

cuidar [kwi'ðar] *vt* (MED) to care for; (*ocuparse de*) to take care of, look after ♦ *vi*: **~ de** to take care of, look after; **~se** *vr* to look after o.s.; **~se de hacer algo** to take care to do sth

culata [ku'lata] *nf* (*de fusil*) butt

culebra [ku'leβra] *nf* snake

culebrón [kule'βron] (*fam*) *nm* (TV) soap(-opera)

culinario, a [kuli'narjo, a] *adj* culinary, cooking *cpd*

culminación [kulmina'θjon] *nf* culmination

culo ['kulo] *nm* bottom, backside; (*de vaso, botella*) bottom

culpa ['kulpa] *nf* fault; (JUR) guilt; **por ~** because of; **tener la ~ (de)** to be to blame (for); **~bilidad** *nf* guilt; **~ble** *adj* guilty ♦ *nm/f* culprit

culpar [kul'par] *vt* to blame; (*acusar*) to accuse

cultivar [kulti'βar] *vt* to cultivate

cultivo [kul'tiβo] *nm* (*acto*) cultivation;

(*plantas*) crop

culto, a ['kulto, a] *adj* (*que tiene cultura*) cultured, educated ♦ *nm* (*homenaje*) worship; (*religión*) cult

cultura [kul'tura] *nf* culture

culturismo [kultu'rismo] *nm* body-building

cumbre ['kumbre] *nf* summit, top

cumpleaños [kumple'aɲos] *nm inv* birthday

cumplido, a [kum'pliðo, a] *adj* (*abundante*) plentiful; (*cortés*) courteous ♦ *nm* compliment; **visita de ~** courtesy call

cumplidor, a [kumpli'ðor, a] *adj* reliable

cumplimentar [kumplimen'tar] *vt* to congratulate

cumplimiento [kumpli'mjento] *nm* (*de un deber*) fulfilment; (*acabamiento*) completion

cumplir [kum'plir] *vt* (*orden*) to carry out, obey; (*promesa*) to carry out, fulfil; (*condena*) to serve ♦ *vi*: **~ con** (*deberes*) to carry out, fulfil; **~se** *vr* (*plazo*) to expire; **hoy cumple dieciocho años** he is eighteen today

cúmulo ['kumulo] *nm* heap

cuna ['kuna] *nf* cradle, cot

cundir [kun'dir] *vi* (*noticia, rumor, pánico*) to spread; (*rendir*) to go a long way

cuneta [ku'neta] *nf* ditch

cuña ['kuɲa] *nf* wedge

cuñado, a [ku'ɲaðo, a] *nm/f* brother-/sister-in-law

cuota ['kwota] *nf* (*parte proporcional*) share; (*cotización*) fee, dues *pl*

cupe *etc vb ver* **caber**

cupiera *etc vb ver* **caber**

cupo ['kupo] *vb ver* **caber** ♦ *nm* quota

cupón [ku'pon] *nm* coupon

cúpula ['kupula] *nf* dome

cura ['kura] *nf* (*curación*) cure; (*método curativo*) treatment ♦ *nm* priest

curación [kura'θjon] *nf* (*acción*) curing

curandero, a |kuran'dero, a| nm/f
quack

curar |ku'rar| vt (MED: herida) to treat,
dress; (: enfermo) to cure; (CULIN) to
cure, salt; (cuero) to tan; **~se** vr to get
well, recover

curiosear |kurjose'ar| vt to glance at,
look over ♦ vi to look round, wander
round; (explorar) to poke about

curiosidad |kurjosi'ðað| nf curiosity

curioso, a |ku'rjoso, a| adj curious
♦ nm/f bystander, onlooker

currante |ku'rrante| (fam) nm/f worker

currar |ku'rrar| (fam) vi to work

currículo |ku'rrikulo| = **curriculum**

curriculum |ku'rrikulum| nm
curriculum vitae

cursi |'kursi| (fam) adj affected

cursillo |kur'siλo| nm short course

cursiva |kur'siβa| nf italics pl

curso |'kurso| nm course; **en ~** (año)
current; (proceso) going on, under way

cursor |kur'sor| nm (INFORM) cursor

curtido, a |kur'tiðo, a| adj (cara etc)
weather-beaten; (fig: persona)
experienced

curtir |kur'tir| vt (cuero etc) to tan

curva |'kurβa| nf curve, bend

cúspide |'kuspiðe| nf (GEO) peak; (fig)
top

custodia |kus'toðja| nf safekeeping;
custody; **custodiar** vt (conservar) to
take care of; (vigilar) to guard

cutis |'kutis| nm inv skin, complexion

cutre |'kutre| (fam) adj (lugar) grotty

cuyo, a |'kujo, a| pron (de algún)
whose; (de que) whose, of which; **en
~ caso** in which case

C.V. abr (= caballos de vapor) H.P.

D, d

D. abr (= Don) Esq.

Da. abr = **Doña**

dádiva |'daðiβa| nf (donación)
donation; (regalo) gift; **dadivoso, a**

adj generous

dado, a |'daðo, a| pp de **dar** ♦ nm die;
~s nmpl dice; **~ que** given that

daltónico, a |dal'toniko, a| adj
colour-blind

dama |'dama| nf (gen) lady; (AJEDREZ)
queen; **~s** nfpl (juego) draughts sg

damnificar |damnifi'kar| vt to harm;
(persona) to injure

danés, esa |da'nes, esa| adj Danish
♦ nm/f Dane

danzar |dan'θar| vt, vi to dance

dañar |da'ɲar| vt (objeto) to damage;
(persona) to hurt; **~se** vr (objeto) to get
damaged

dañino, a |da'ɲino, a| adj harmful

daño |'daɲo| nm (a un objeto) damage;
(a una persona) harm, injury; **~s y
perjuicios** (JUR) damages; **hacer ~ a**
to damage; (persona) to hurt, injure;
hacerse ~ to hurt o.s.

PALABRA CLAVE

---

dar |dar| vt 1 (gen) to give; (obra de
teatro) to put on; (film) to show;
(fiesta) to hold; **~ algo a uno** to give
sth to o to give sb sth; **~ de beber a uno**
to give sb a drink

2 (producir: intereses) to yield; (fruta) to
produce

3 (locuciones + n): **da gusto
escucharle** it's a pleasure to listen to
him; ver tb **paseo** y otros sustantivos

4 (+ n: = perífrasis de verbo): **me da
asco** it sickens me

5 (considerar): **~ algo por
descontado/entendido** to take sth
for granted/as read; **~ algo por
concluido** to consider sth finished

6 (hora): **el reloj dio las 6** the clock
struck 6 (o'clock)

7: **me da lo mismo** it's all the same
to me; ver tb **igual, más**

♦ vi 1: **~ con**: **dimos con él dos
horas más tarde** we came across him
two hours later; **al final di con la
solución** I eventually came up with

the answer
2: ~ **en** (blanco, suelo) to hit; **el sol me da en la cara** the sun is shining (right) on my face
3: ~ **de sí** (zapatos etc) to stretch, give ♦ ~**se** vr **1:** ~**se por vencido** to give up
2 (ocurrir): **se han dado muchos casos** there have been a lot of cases
3: ~**se a: se ha dado a la bebida** he's taken to drinking
4: se me dan bien/mal las ciencias I'm good/bad at science
5: dárselas de: se las da de experto he fancies himself o poses as an expert

---

dardo ['darðo] nm dart
datar [da'tar] vi: ~ **de** to date from
dátil ['datil] nm date
dato ['dato] nm fact, piece of information; ~**s personales** personal details

DC abbr m (= disco compacto) CD
dcha. abr (= derecha) r.h.
d. de J.C. abr (= después de Jesucristo) A.D.

PALABRA CLAVE

de [de] prep (de+ el = del) **1** (posesión) of; **la casa** ~ **Isabel/mis padres** Isabel's/my parents' house; **es** ~ **ellos** it's theirs
2 (origen, distancia, con números) from; **soy** ~ **Gijón** I'm from Gijón; ~ **8 a 20** from 8 to 20; **salir del cine** to go out o leave the cinema; ~ **2 en 2 2** by 2, 2 at a time
3 (valor descriptivo): **una copa** ~ **vino** a glass of wine; **la mesa** ~ **la cocina** the kitchen table; **un billete** ~ **1000 pesetas** a 1000 peseta note; **un niño** ~ **tres años** a three-year-old (child); **una máquina** ~ **coser** a sewing machine; **ir vestido** ~ **gris** to be dressed in grey; **la niña del vestido azul** the girl in the blue dress; **trabaja**

~ **profesora** she works as a teacher; ~ **lado** sideways; ~ **atrás/delante** rear/front
4 (hora, tiempo): **a las 8** ~ **la mañana** at 8 o'clock in the morning; ~ **día/noche** by day/night; ~ **hoy en ocho días** a week from now; ~ **niño era gordo** as a child he was fat
5 (comparaciones): **más/menos** ~ **cien personas** more/less than a hundred people; **el más caro** ~ **la tienda** the most expensive in the shop; **menos/más** ~ **lo pensado** less/more than expected
6 (causa): **del calor** from the heat; ~ **puro tonto** out of sheer stupidity
7 (tema) about; **clases** ~ **inglés** English classes; **¿sabes algo** ~ **él?** do you know anything about him?; **un libro** ~ **física** a physics book
8 (adj + de + infin): **fácil** ~ **entender** easy to understand
9 (oraciones pasivas): **fue respetado** ~ **todos** he was loved by all
10 (condicional + infin) if; ~ **ser posible** if possible; ~ **no terminarlo hoy** if I etc don't finish it today

dé vb ver **dar**
deambular [deambu'lar] vi to wander
debajo [de'βaxo] adv underneath; ~ **de** below, under; **por** ~ **de** beneath
debate [de'βate] nm debate; **debatir** vt to debate
deber [de'βer] nm duty ♦ vt to owe ♦ vi: **debe** (it must, it should); ~**es** nmpl (ESCOL) homework; **debo hacerlo** I must do it; **debe ir** he should go; ~**se** vr: ~**se a** to be owing o due to
debido, a [de'βiðo, a] adj proper, just; ~ **a** due to, because of
débil ['deβil] adj (persona, carácter) weak; (luz) dim; **debilidad** nf weakness; dimness
debilitar [deβili'tar] vt to weaken; ~**se** vr to grow weak

debutar [deβu'tar] vi to make one's debut

década ['dekaða] nf decade

decadencia [deka'ðenθja] nf (estado) decadence; (proceso) decline, decay

decaer [deka'er] vi (declinar) to decline; (debilitarse) to weaken

decaído, a [deka'iðo, a] adj: **estar ~** (abatido) to be down

decaimiento [dekai'mjento] nm (declinación) decline; (desaliento) discouragement; (MED: estado débil) weakness

decano, a [de'kano, a] nm/f (de universidad etc) dean

decapitar [dekapi'tar] vt to behead

decena [de'θena] nf: **una ~** ten (or so)

decencia [de'θenθja] nf decency

decente [de'θente] adj decent

decepción [deθep'θjon] nf disappointment

decepcionar [deθepθjo'nar] vt to disappoint

decidir [deθi'ðir] vt, vi to decide; **~se** vr: **~se a** to make up one's mind to

décimo, a ['deθimo, a] adj tenth ♦ nm tenth

decir [de'θir] vt to say; (contar) to tell; (hablar) to speak ♦ nm saying; **~se** vr: **se dice que** it is said that; **~ para o entre sí** to say to o.s.; **querer ~** to mean; **¡dígame!** (TEL) hello!; (en tienda) can I help you?

decisión [deθi'sjon] nf (resolución) decision; (firmeza) decisiveness

decisivo, a [deθi'siβo, a] adj decisive

declaración [deklara'θjon] nf (manifestación) statement; (de amor) declaration; **~ de ingresos** o **de la renta** o **fiscal** income-tax return

declarar [dekla'rar] vt to declare ♦ vi to declare; (JUR) to testify; **~se** vr to propose

declinar [dekli'nar] vt (gen) to decline; (JUR) to reject ♦ vi (el día) to draw to a close

declive [de'kliβe] nm (cuesta) slope;

(fig) decline

decodificador [dekoðifika'ðor] nm decoder

decolorarse [dekolo'rarse] vr to become discoloured

decoración [dekora'θjon] nf decoration

decorado [deko'raðo] nm (CINE, TEATRO) scenery, set

decorar [deko'rar] vt to decorate; **decorativo, a** adj ornamental, decorative

decoro [de'koro] nm (respeto) respect; (dignidad) decency; (recato) propriety; **~so, a** adj (decente) decent; (modesto) modest; (digno) proper

decrecer [dekre'θer] vi to decrease, diminish

decrépito, a [de'krepito, a] adj decrepit

decretar [dekre'tar] vt to decree; **decreto** nm decree

dedal [de'ðal] nm thimble

dedicación [deðika'θjon] nf dedication

dedicar [deði'kar] vt (libro) to dedicate; (tiempo, dinero) to devote; (palabras: decir, consagrar) to dedicate, devote; **dedicatoria** nf (de libro) dedication

dedo ['deðo] nm finger; **~ (del pie)** toe; **~ pulgar** thumb; **~ índice** index finger; **~ corazón** middle finger; **~ anular** ring finger; **~ meñique** little finger; **hacer ~** (fam) to hitch (a lift)

deducción [deðuk'θjon] nf deduction

deducir [deðu'θir] vt (concluir) to deduce, infer; (COM) to deduct

defecto [de'fekto] nm defect, flaw; **defectuoso, a** adj defective, faulty

defender [defen'der] vt to defend

defensa [de'fensa] nf defence ♦ nm (DEPORTE) defender, back; **defensivo, a** adj defensive; **a la defensiva** on the defensive

defensor, a [defen'sor, a] adj defending ♦ nm/f (abogado ~)

defending counsel; (*protector*) protector

deficiencia |defi'θjenθja| nf deficiency

deficiente |defi'θjente| adj (*defectuoso*) defective; ~ **en** lacking o deficient in; **ser un ~ mental** to be mentally handicapped

déficit |'defiθit| (pl ~s) nm deficit

definición |defini'θjon| nf definition

definir |defi'nir| vt (*determinar*) to determine, establish; (*decidir*) to define; (*aclarar*) to clarify; **definitivo, a** adj definitive; **en definitiva** definitively; (*en resumen*) in short

deformación |deforma'θjon| nf (*alteración*) deformation; (*RADIO etc*) distortion

deformar |defor'mar| vt (*gen*) to deform; **~se** vr to become deformed; **deforme** adj (*informe*) deformed; (*feo*) ugly; (*malhecho*) misshapen

defraudar |defrau'ðar| vt (*decepcionar*) to disappoint; (*estafar*) to defraud

defunción |defun'θjon| nf death, demise

degeneración |dexenera'θjon| nf (*de las células*) degeneration; (*moral*) degeneracy

degenerar |dexene'rar| vi to degenerate

degollar |dexo'ʎar| vt to behead; (*fig*) to slaughter

degradar |devra'ðar| vt to debase, degrade; **~se** vr to demean o.s.

degustación |devusta'θjon| nf sampling, tasting

deificar |deifi'kar| vt to deify

dejadez |dexa'ðeθ| nf (*negligencia*) neglect; (*descuido*) untidiness, carelessness

dejar |de'xar| vt to leave; (*permitir*) to allow, let; (*abandonar*) to abandon, forsake; (*beneficios*) to produce, yield ♦ vi: ~ **de** (*parar*) to stop; (*no hacer*) to fail to; **no dejes de comprar un billete** make sure you buy a ticket; ~ **a un lado** to leave o set aside

dejo |'dexo| nm (*LING*) accent

del |del| (= **de+ el**) ver **de**

delantal |delan'tal| nm apron

delante |de'lante| adv in front, (*enfrente*) opposite; (*adelante*) ahead; ~ **de** in front of, before

delantera |delan'tera| nf (*de vestido, casa etc*) front part; (*DEPORTE*) forward line; **llevar la ~ (a uno)** to be ahead (of sb)

delantero, a |delan'tero, a| adj front ♦ nm (*DEPORTE*) forward, striker.

delatar |dela'tar| vt to inform on o against, betray; **delator, a** nm/f informer

delegación |deleva'θjon| nf (*acción, delegados*) delegation; (*COM: oficina*) office, branch; ~ **de policía** police station

delegado, a |dele'vaðo, a| nm/f delegate; (*COM*) agent

delegar |dele'var| vt to delegate

deletrear |deletre'ar| vt to spell (out)

deleznable |deleθ'naβle| adj brittle; (*excusa, idea*) feeble

delfín |del'fin| nm dolphin

delgadez |delva'ðeθ| nf thinness, slimness

delgado, a |del'vaðo, a| adj thin; (*persona*) slim, thin; (*tela etc*) light, delicate

deliberación |deliβera'θjon| nf deliberation

deliberar |deliβe'rar| vt to debate, discuss

delicadeza |delika'ðeθa| nf (*gen*) delicacy; (*refinamiento, sutileza*) refinement

delicado, a |deli'kaðo, a| adj (*gen*) delicate; (*sensible*) sensitive; (*quisquilloso*) touchy

delicia |de'liθja| nf delight

delicioso, a |deli'θjoso, a| adj (*gracioso*) delightful; (*exquisito*) delicious

delimitar |delimi'tar| vt (*funciones, responsabilidades*) to define

delincuencia |delin'kwenθja| nf
delinquency; **delincuente** nm/f
delinquent; (*criminal*) criminal

delineante |deline'ante| nm/f
draughtsman/woman

delinear |deline'ar| vt (*dibujo*) to draw;
(*fig, contornos*) to outline

delinquir |delin'kir| vi to commit an
offence

delirante |deli'rante| adj delirious

delirar |deli'rar| vi to be delirious, rave

delirio |de'lirjo| nm (MED) delirium;
(*palabras insensatas*) ravings pl

delito |de'lito| nm (gen) crime;
(*infracción*) offence

delta |'delta| nm delta

demacrado, a |dema'krado, a| adj:
estar ~ to look pale and drawn, be
wasted away

demagogo, a |dema'vovo, a| nm/f
demagogue

demanda |de'manda| nf (*pedido*, COM)
demand; (*petición*) request; (JUR)
action, lawsuit

demandante |deman'dante| nm/f
claimant

demandar |deman'dar| vt (gen) to
demand; (JUR) to sue, file a lawsuit
against

demarcación |demarka'θjon| nf (*de
terreno*) demarcation

demás |de'mas| adj: **los ~ niños** the
other children, the remaining children
♦ pron: **los/las ~** the others, the rest
(of them); **lo ~** the rest (of it)

demasía |dema'sia| nf (*exceso*) excess,
surplus; **comer en ~** to eat to excess

demasiado, a |dema'sjaðo, a| adj:
~ vino too much wine ♦ adv (*antes de
adj, adv*) too; **~s libros** too many
books; **¡esto es ~!** that's the limit!;
hace ~ calor it's too hot; **~ despacio**
too slowly; **~s** too many

demencia |de'menθja| nf (*locura*)
madness; **demente** nm/f lunatic ♦ adj
mad, insane

democracia |demo'kraθja| nf

democracy

demócrata |de'mokrata| nm/f
democrat; **democrático, a** adj
democratic

demoler |demo'ler| vt to demolish;
demolición nf demolition

demonio |de'monjo| nm devil,
demon; **¡~s!** hell!, damn!; **¿cómo ~s?**
how the hell?

demora |de'mora| nf delay; **demorar**
vt (*retardar*) to delay, hold back;
(*detener*) to hold up ♦ vi to linger, stay
on; **~se** vr to be delayed

demos vb ver **dar**

demostración |demostra'θjon| nf
(MAT) proof; (*de afecto*) show, display

demostrar |demos'trar| vt (*probar*) to
prove; (*mostrar*) to show; (*manifestar*)
to demonstrate

demudado, a |demu'ðaðo, a| adj
(*rostro*) pale

den vb ver **dar**

denegar |dene'var| vt (*rechazar*) to
refuse; (JUR) to reject

denigrar |deni'xrar| vt (*desacreditar,
infamar*) to denigrate; (*injuriar*) to insult

┌─────────────────────────────┐
│ **Denominación de Origen** │
└─────────────────────────────┘

*The Denominación de Origen,
abbreviated to D.O., is a prestigious
classification awarded to food
products such as wines, cheeses,
sausages and hams which meet the
stringent quality and production
standards of the designated region.
D.O. labels serve as a guarantee of
quality.*

denotar |deno'tar| vt to denote

densidad |densi'ðað| nf density; (*fig*)
thickness

denso, a |'denso, a| adj dense;
(*espeso, pastoso*) thick; (*fig*) heavy

dentadura |denta'ðura| nf (*set of*)
teeth pl; **~ postiza** false teeth pl

dentera |den'tera| nf (*sensación
desagradable*) shivers pl

dentífrico, a |den'tifriko, a| adj dental
♦ nm toothpaste

dentista |den'tista| nm/f dentist

dentro ['dentro| adv inside ♦ prep:
~ **de** in, inside, within; **por** ~ (on the)
inside; **mirar por** ~ to look inside;
~ **de tres meses** within three months

denuncia |de'nunθja| nf (delación)
denunciation; (acusación) accusation;
(de accidente) report; **denunciar** |denun'θjar| vt to
report; (delatar) to inform on o against

departamento |departa'mento| nm
(sección administrativa) department,
section; (AM: apartamento) flat (BRIT),
apartment

dependencia |depen'denθja| nf
dependence; (POL) dependency; (COM)
office, section

depender |depen'der| vi: ~ **de** to
depend on

dependienta |depen'djenta| nf
saleswoman, shop assistant

dependiente |depen'djente| adj
dependent ♦ nm salesman, shop
assistant

depilar |depi'lar| vt (con cera) to wax;
(cejas) to pluck; **depilatorio** nm hair
remover

deplorable |deplo'raβle| adj
deplorable

deplorar |deplo'rar| vt to deplore

deponer |depo'ner| vt to lay down
♦ vi (JUR) to give evidence; (declarar) to
make a statement

deportar |depor'tar| vt to deport

deporte |de'porte| nm sport; **hacer** ~
to play sports; **deportista** adj sports
cpd ♦ nm/f sportsman/woman;
deportivo, a adj (club, periódico)
sports cpd ♦ nm sports car

depositar |deposi'tar| vt (dinero) to
deposit; (mercancías) to put away,
store; ~**se** vr to settle; ~**io, a** nm/f
trustee

depósito |de'posito| nm (gen) deposit;
(almacén) warehouse, store; (de agua,
gasolina etc) tank; ~ **de cadáveres**

mortuary

depreciar |depre'θjar| vt to
depreciate, reduce the value of; ~**se** vr
to depreciate, lose value

depredador, a |depreða'ðor, a| adj
predatory ♦ nm predator

depresión |depre'sjon| nf depression

deprimido, a |depri'miðo, a| adj
depressed

deprimir |depri'mir| vt to depress;
~**se** vr (persona) to become depressed

deprisa |de'prisa| adv quickly,
hurriedly

depuración |depura'θjon| nf
purification; (POL) purge

depurar |depu'rar| vt to purify;
(purgar) to purge

derecha |de'retʃa| nf right(-hand) side;
(POL) right; **a la** ~ (estar) on the right;
(torcer etc) (to the) right

derecho, a |de'retʃo, a| adj right,
right-hand ♦ nm (privilegio) right;
(lado) right(-hand) side; (leyes) law
♦ adv straight, directly; ~**s** nmpl (de
aduana) duty sg; (de autor) royalties;
tener ~ **a** to have a right to

deriva |de'riβa| nf: **ir** o **estar a la** ~ to
drift, be adrift

derivado |deri'βaðo| nm (COM) by-
product

derivar |deri'βar| vt to derive; (desviar)
to direct ♦ vi to derive, be derived;
(NAUT) to drift; ~**se** vr to derive, be
derived; to drift

derramamiento |derrama'mjento|
nm (dispersión) spilling; ~ **de sangre**
bloodshed

derramar |derra'mar| vt to spill;
(verter) to pour out; (esparcir) to
scatter; ~**se** vr to pour out;
~ **lágrimas** to weep

derrame |de'rrame| nm (de líquido)
spilling; (de sangre) shedding; (de tubo
etc) overflow; (pérdida) leakage; (MED)
discharge

derredor |derre'ðor| adv: **al** o **en** ~ de
around, about

derretido, a [derre'tiðo, a] adj melted; (metal) molten

derretir [derre'tir] vt (gen) to melt; (nieve) to thaw; **~se** vr to melt

derribar [derri'ßar] vt to knock down; (construcción) to demolish; (persona, gobierno, político) to bring down

derrocar [derro'kar] vt (gobierno) to bring down, overthrow

derrochar [derro'tʃar] vt to squander; **derroche** nm (despilfarro) waste, squandering

derrota [de'rrota] nf (NAUT) course; (MIL, DEPORTE etc) defeat, rout; **derrotar** vt (gen) to defeat; **derrotero** nm (rumbo) course

derruir [derru'ir] vt (edificio) to demolish

derrumbar [derrum'bar] vt (edificio) to knock down; **~se** vr (edificio) to collapse

derruyendo etc vb ver **derruir**

des vb ver **dar**

desabotonar [desaßoto'nar] vt to unbutton, undo; **~se** vr to come undone

desabrido, a [desa'ßriðo, a] adj (comida) insipid, tasteless; (persona) rude, surly; (respuesta) sharp; (tiempo) unpleasant

desabrochar [desaßro'tʃar] vt (botones, broches) to undo, unfasten; **~se** vr (ropa etc) to come undone

desacato [desa'kato] nm (falta de respeto) disrespect; (JUR) contempt

desacertado, a [desaθer'taðo, a] adj (equivocado) mistaken; (inoportuno) unwise

desacierto [desa'θjerto] nm mistake, error

desaconsejado, a [desakonse'xaðo, a] adj ill-advised

desaconsejar [desakonse'xar] vt to advise against

desacreditar [desakreði'tar] vt (desprestigiar) to discredit, bring into disrepute; (denigrar) to run down

desacuerdo [desa'kwerðo] nm disagreement, discord

desafiar [desa'fjar] vt (retar) to challenge; (enfrentarse a) to defy

desafilado, a [desafi'laðo, a] adj blunt

desafinado, a [desafi'naðo, a] adj: **estar ~** to be out of tune

desafinar [desafi'nar] vi (al cantar) to be o go out of tune

desafío etc [desa'fio] vb ver **desafiar**
♦ nm (reto) challenge; (combate) duel; (resistencia) defiance

desaforado, a [desafo'raðo, a] adj (grito) ear-splitting; (comportamiento) outrageous

desafortunadamente [desafortunaða'mente] adv unfortunately

desafortunado, a [desafortu'naðo, a] adj (desgraciado) unfortunate, unlucky

desagradable [desaɣra'ðaßle] adj (fastidioso, enojoso) unpleasant; (irritante) disagreeable

desagradar [desaɣra'ðar] vi (disgustar) to displease; (molestar) to bother

desagradecido, a [desaɣraðe'θiðo, a] adj ungrateful

desagrado [desa'ɣraðo] nm (disgusto) displeasure; (contrariedad) dissatisfaction

desagraviar [desaɣra'ßjar] vt to make amends to

desagüe [des'aɣwe] nm (de un líquido) drainage; (cañería) drainpipe; (salida) outlet, drain

desaguisado, a [desaɣi'saðo] nm outrage

desahogado, a [desao'ɣaðo, a] adj (holgado) comfortable; (espacioso) roomy, large

desahogar [desao'ɣar] vt (aliviar) to ease, relieve; (ira) to vent; **~se** vr (relajarse) to relax; (desfogarse) to let off steam

desahogo [desa'oɣo] nm (alivio) relief; (comodidad) comfort, ease

desahuciar [desau'θjar] vt (enfermo) to give up hope for; (inquilino) to evict;

desahucio nm eviction
desairar [desai'rar] vt (menospreciar) to slight, snub
desaire [des'aire] nm (menosprecio) slight; (falta de garbo) unattractiveness
desajustar [desaxus'tar] vt (desarreglar) to disarrange; (desconcertar) to throw off balance; **~se** vr to get out of order; (aflojarse) to loosen
desajuste [desa'xuste] nm (de máquina) disorder; (situación) imbalance
desalentador, a [desalenta'ðor, a] adj discouraging
desalentar [desalen'tar] vt (desanimar) to discourage
desaliento etc [desa'ljento] vb ver **desalentar ♦** nm discouragement
desaliño [desa'liɲo] nm slovenliness
desalmado, a [desal'maðo, a] adj (cruel) cruel, heartless
desalojar [desalo'xar] vt (expulsar, echar) to eject; (abandonar) to move out ♦ vi to move out
desamor [desa'mor] nm (frialdad) indifference; (odio) dislike
desamparado, a [desampa'raðo, a] adj (persona) helpless; (lugar: expuesto) exposed; (desierto) deserted
desamparar [desampa'rar] vt (abandonar) to desert, abandon; (JUR) to leave defenceless; (barco) to abandon
desandar [desan'dar] vt: **~ lo andado** o **el camino** to retrace one's steps
desangrar [desan'grar] vt to bleed; (fig: persona) to bleed dry; **~se** vr to lose a lot of blood
desanimado, a [desani'maðo, a] adj (persona) downhearted; (espectáculo, fiesta) dull
desanimar [desani'mar] vt (desalentar) to discourage; (deprimir) to depress; **~se** vr to lose heart
desapacible [desapa'θißle] adj (gen) unpleasant

desaparecer [desapare'θer] vi (gen) to disappear; (el sol, la luz) to vanish; **desaparecido, a** adj missing; **desaparición** nf disappearance
desapasionado, a [desapasjo'naðo, a] adj dispassionate, impartial
desapego [desa'pexo] nm (frialdad) coolness; (distancia) detachment
desapercibido, a [desaperθi'ßiðo, a] adj (desprevenido) unprepared; **pasar ~** to go unnoticed
desaprensivo, a [desapren'sißo, a] adj unscrupulous
desaprobar [desapro'ßar] vt (reprobar) to disapprove of; (condenar) to condemn; (no consentir) to reject
desaprovechado, a [desaproße'tʃaðo, a] adj (oportunidad, tiempo) wasted; (estudiante) slack
desaprovechar [desaproße'tʃar] vt to waste
desarmar [desar'mar] vt (MIL, fig) to disarm; (TEC) to take apart, dismantle; **desarme** nm disarmament
desarraigar [desarrai'xar] vt to uproot; **desarraigo** nm uprooting
desarreglar [desarre'xlar] vt (desordenar) to disarrange; (trastocar) to upset, disturb
desarreglo [desa'rrexlo] nm (de casa, persona) untidiness; (desorden) disorder
desarrollar [desarro'ʎar] vt (gen) to develop; **~se** vr to develop; (ocurrir) to take place; (FOTO) to develop; **desarrollo** nm development
desarticular [desartiku'lar] vt (hueso) to dislocate; (objeto) to take apart; (fig) to break up
desasir [desa'sir] vt to loosen
desasosegar [desasose'xar] vt (inquietar) to disturb, make uneasy; **~se** vr to become uneasy
desasosiego etc [desaso'sjexo] vb ver **desasosegar**
desasosiego ♦ nm (intranquilidad) uneasiness, restlessness; (ansiedad) anxiety
desastrado, a [desas'traðo, a] adj

(*desaliñado*) shabby; (*sucio*) dirty

desastre [de'sastre] *nm* disaster;
desastroso, a *adj* disastrous

desatado, a [desa'taðo, a] *adj*
(*desligado*) untied; (*violento*) violent,
wild

desatar [desa'tar] *vt* (*nudo*) to untie;
(*paquete*) to undo; (*separar*) to detach;
~**se** *vr* (*zapatos*) to come untied;
(*tormenta*) to break

desatascar [desatas'kar] *vt* (*cañería*) to
unblock, clear

desatender [desaten'der] *vt* (*no
prestar atención a*) to disregard;
(*abandonar*) to neglect

desatento, a [desa'tento, a] *adj*
(*distraído*) inattentive; (*descortés*)
discourteous

desatinado, a [desati'naðo, a] *adj*
foolish, silly; **desatino** *nm* (*idiotez*)
foolishness, folly; (*error*) blunder

desatornillar [desatorni'ʎar] *vt* to
unscrew

desatrancar [desatran'kar] *vt* (*puerta*)
to unbolt; (*cañería*) to clear, unblock

desautorizado, a [desautori'θaðo, a]
adj unauthorized

desautorizar [desautori'θar] *vt*
(*oficial*) to deprive of authority;
(*informe*) to deny

desavenencia [desaβe'nenθja] *nf*
(*desacuerdo*) disagreement;
(*discrepancia*) quarrel

desayunar [desaju'nar] *vi* to have
breakfast ♦ *vt* to have for breakfast;
desayuno *nm* breakfast

desazón [desa'θon] *nf* anxiety

desazonarse [desaθo'narse] *vr* to
worry, be anxious

desbandarse [desβan'darse] *vr* (*MIL*)
to disband; (*fig*) to flee in disorder

desbarajuste [desβara'xuste] *nm*
confusion, disorder

desbaratar [desβara'tar] *vt* (*deshacer,
destruir*) to ruin

desbloquear [desβloke'ar] *vt*
(*negociaciones, tráfico*) to get going

again; (*COM: cuenta*) to unfreeze

desbocado, a [desβo'kaðo, a] *adj*
(*caballo*) runaway

desbordar [desβor'ðar] *vt* (*sobrepasar*)
to go beyond; (*exceder*) to exceed; ~**se**
vr (*río*) to overflow; (*entusiasmo*) to
erupt

descabalgar [deskaβal'var] *vi* to
dismount

descabellado, a [deskaβe'ʎaðo, a]
adj (*disparatado*) wild, crazy

descafeinado, a [deskafei'naðo, a]
adj decaffeinated ♦ *nm* decaffeinated
coffee

descalabro [deska'laβro] *nm* blow;
(*desgracia*) misfortune

descalificar [deskalifi'kar] *vt* to
disqualify; (*desacreditar*) to discredit

descalzar [deskal'θar] *vt* (*zapato*) to
take off; **descalzo, a** *adj* barefoot(ed)

descambiar [deskam'bjar] *vt* to
exchange

descaminado, a [deskami'naðo, a]
adj (*equivocado*) on the wrong road;
(*fig*) misguided

descampado [deskam'paðo] *nm* open
space

descansado, a [deskan'saðo, a] *adj*
(*gen*) rested; (*que tranquiliza*) restful

descansar [deskan'sar] *vt* (*gen*) to rest
♦ *vi* to rest, have a rest; (*echarse*) to lie
down

descansillo [deskan'siʎo] *nm* (*de
escalera*) landing

descanso [des'kanso] *nm* (*reposo*) rest;
(*alivio*) relief; (*pausa*) break; (*DEPORTE*)
interval, half time

descapotable [deskapo'taβle] *nm* (tb:
coche ~) convertible

descarado, a [deska'raðo, a] *adj*
shameless; (*insolente*) cheeky

descarga [des'karva] *nf* (*ARQ, ELEC,
MIL*) discharge; (*NAUT*) unloading

descargar [deskar'var] *vt* to unload;
(*golpe*) to let fly; ~**se** *vr* to unburden
o.s.; **descargo** *nm* (*COM*) receipt; (*JUR*)
evidence

descaro [des'karo] *nm* nerve

descarriar [deska'rrjar] *vt* (*descaminar*) to misdirect; (*fig*) to lead astray; **~se** *vr* (*perderse*) to lose one's way; (*separarse*) to stray; (*pervertirse*) to err, go astray

descarrilamiento [deskarrila'mjento] *nm* (*de tren*) derailment

descarrilar [deskarri'lar] *vi* to be derailed

descartar [deskar'tar] *vt* (*rechazar*) to reject; (*eliminar*) to rule out; **~se de** (*NAIPES*) to discard; **~se de** to shirk

descascarillado, a [deskaskari'ʎaðo, a] *adj* (*paredes*) peeling

descendencia [desθen'denθja] *nf* (*origen*) origin, descent; (*hijos*) offspring

descender [desθen'der] *vt* (*bajar: escalera*) to go down ♦ *vi* to descend; (*temperatura, nivel*) to fall, drop; **~ de** to be descended from

descendiente [desθen'djente] *nm/f* descendant

descenso [des'θenso] *nm* descent; (*de temperatura*) drop

descifrar [desθi'frar] *vt* to decipher; (*mensaje*) to decode

descolgar [deskol'ɣar] *vt* (*bajar*) to take down; (*teléfono*) to pick up; **~se** *vr* to let o.s. down

descolorido, a [deskolo'riðo, a] *adj* faded; (*pálido*) pale

descompasado, a [deskompa'saðo, a] *adj* (*sin proporción*) out of all proportion; (*excesivo*) excessive

descomponer [deskompo'ner] *vt* (*desordenar*) to disarrange, disturb; (*TEC*) to put out of order; (*dividir*) to break down (into parts); (*fig*) to provoke; **~se** *vr* (*corromperse*) to rot, decompose; (*TEC*) to break down

descomposición [deskomposi'θjon] *nf* (*de un objeto*) breakdown; (*de fruta etc*) decomposition; **~ de vientre** stomach upset, diarrhoea

descompuesto, a [deskom'pwesto, a] *adj* (*corrompido*) decomposed; (*roto*)

broken

descomunal [deskomu'nal] *adj* (*enorme*) huge

desconcertar [deskonθer'taðo, a] *adj* disconcerted, bewildered

desconcertar [deskonθer'tar] *vt* (*confundir*) to baffle; (*incomodar*) to upset, put out; **~se** *vr* (*turbarse*) to be upset

desconcierto *etc* [deskon'θjerto] *vb* ver **desconcertar** ♦ *nm* (*gen*) disorder; (*desorientación*) uncertainty; (*inquietud*) uneasiness

desconectar [deskonek'tar] *vt* to disconnect

desconfianza [deskon'fjanθa] *nf* distrust

desconfiar [deskon'fjar] *vi* to be distrustful; **~ de** to distrust, suspect

descongelar [deskonxe'lar] *vt* to defrost; (*COM, POL*) to unfreeze

descongestionar [deskonxestjo'nar] *vt* (*cabeza, tráfico*) to clear

desconocer [deskono'θer] *vt* (*ignorar*) not to know, be ignorant of

desconocido, a [deskono'θiðo, a] *adj* unknown ♦ *nm/f* stranger

desconocimiento [deskonoθi'mjento] *nm* (*falta de conocimientos*) ignorance

desconsiderado, a [deskonsiðe'raðo, a] *adj* inconsiderate; (*insensible*) thoughtless

desconsolar [deskonso'lar] *vt* to distress; **~se** *vr* to despair

desconsuelo *etc* [deskon'swelo] *vb* ver **desconsolar** ♦ *nm* (*tristeza*) distress; (*desesperación*) despair

descontado, a [deskon'taðo, a] *adj*: **dar por ~ (que)** to take (it) for granted (that)

descontar [deskon'tar] *vt* (*deducir*) to take away, deduct; (*rebajar*) to discount

descontento, a [deskon'tento, a] *adj*

descorazonar 94 desecar

dissatisfied ♦ nm dissatisfaction, discontent

descorazonar [deskoraθo'nar] vt to discourage, dishearten

descorchar [deskor'tʃar] vt to uncork

descorrer [desko'rrer] vt (cortinas, cerrojo) to draw back

descortés [deskor'tes] adj (mal educado) discourteous; (grosero) rude

descoser [desko'ser] vt to unstitch; **~se** vr to come apart (at the seams)

descosido, a [desko'siðo, a] adj (COSTURA) unstitched

descrédito [des'kreðito] nm discredit

descreído, a [deskre'iðo, a] adj (incrédulo) incredulous; (falto de fe) unbelieving

descremado, a [deskre'maðo, a] adj skimmed

describir [deskri'βir] vt to describe; **descripción** [deskrip'θjon] nf description

descrito [des'krito] pp de **describir**

descuartizar [deskwarti'θar] vt (animal) to cut up

descubierto, a [desku'βjerto, a] pp de **descubrir** ♦ adj uncovered, bare; (persona) bareheaded ♦ nm (bancario) overdraft; **al ~** in the open

descubrimiento [deskuβri'mjento] nm (hallazgo) discovery; (revelación) revelation

descubrir [desku'βrir] vt to discover, find; (inaugurar) to unveil; (vislumbrar) to detect; (revelar) to reveal, show; (destapar) to uncover; **~se** vr to reveal o.s.; (quitarse sombrero) to take off one's hat; (confesar) to confess

descuento etc [des'kwento] vb ver **descontar** ♦ nm discount

descuidado, a [deskwi'ðaðo, a] adj (sin cuidado) careless; (desordenado) untidy; (olvidadizo) forgetful; (dejado) neglected; (desprevenido) unprepared

descuidar [deskwi'ðar] vt (dejar) to neglect; (olvidar) to overlook; **~se** vr (distraerse) to be careless;

(abandonarse) to let o.s. go; (desprevenirse) to drop one's guard; **¡descuida!** don't worry!; **descuido** nm (dejadez) carelessness; (olvido) negligence

---

PALABRA CLAVE

---

desde [ˈdesðe] prep 1 (lugar) from; **~ Burgos hasta mi casa hay 30 km** it's 30 kms from Burgos to my house 2 (posición): **hablaba ~ el balcón** she was speaking from the balcony 3 (tiempo: + ad, n): **~ ahora** from now on; **~ la boda** since the wedding; **~ niño** since I etc was a child; **~ 3 años atrás** since 3 years ago 4 (tiempo: + vb, fecha) since; for; **nos conocemos ~ 1992/ ~ hace 20 años** we've known each other since 1992/for 20 years; **no le veo ~ 1997/~ hace 5 años** I haven't seen him since 1997/for 5 years 5 (gama): **~ los más lujosos hasta los más económicos** from the most luxurious to the most reasonably priced 6: **~ luego (que no)** of course (not) ♦ conj: **~ que**: **~ que recuerdo** for as long as I can remember; **~ que llegó no ha salido** he hasn't been out since he arrived

---

desdecirse [desðe'θirse] vr to retract; **~ de** to go back on

desdén [des'ðen] nm scorn

desdeñar [desðe'ɲar] vt (despreciar) to scorn

desdicha [des'ðitʃa] nf (desgracia) misfortune; (infelicidad) unhappiness; **desdichado, a** adj (sin suerte) unlucky; (infeliz) unhappy

desdoblar [desðo'βlar] vt (extender) to spread out; (desplegar) to unfold

desear [dese'ar] vt to want, desire, wish for

desecar [dese'kar] vt to dry up; **~se** vr to dry up

desechar [dese'tʃar] vt (basura) to throw out o away; (ideas) to reject, discard; **desechos** nmpl rubbish sg, waste sg

desembalar [desemba'lar] vt to unpack

desembarazar [desembara'θar] vt (desocupar) to clear; **~se** vr: **~se de** (deshacerse) to free o.s. of, get rid of

desembarcar [desembar'kar] vt (mercancías etc) to unload ♦ vi to disembark; **~se** vr to disembark

desembocadura [desemboka'ðura] nf (de río) mouth; (de calle) opening

desembocar [desembo'kar] vi (río) to flow into; (fig) to result in

desembolso [desem'bolso] nm payment

desembragar [desembra'var] vi to declutch

desembrollar [desembro'ʎar] vt (madeja) to unravel; (asunto, malentendido) to sort out

desemejanza [deseme'xanθa] nf dissimilarity

desempaquetar [desempake'tar] vt (regalo) to unwrap; (mercancía) to unpack

desempatar [desempa'tar] vi to replay, play a play-off; **desempate** nm (FÚTBOL) replay, play-off; (TENIS) tie-break(er)

desempeñar [desempe'ɲar] vt (cargo) to hold; (papel) to perform; (lo empeñado) to redeem; **~ un papel** (fig) to play a role

desempeño [desem'peɲo] nm redeeming; (de cargo) occupation

desempleado, a [desemple'aðo, a] nm/f unemployed person; **desempleo** nm unemployment

desempolvar [desempol'ßar] vt (muebles etc) to dust; (lo olvidado) to revive

desencadenar [desenkaðe'nar] vt to unchain; (ira) to unleash; **~se** vr to

break loose; (tormenta) to burst; (guerra) to break out

desencajar [desenka'xar] vt (hueso) to dislocate; (mecanismo, pieza) to disconnect, disengage

desencanto [desen'kanto] nm disillusionment

desenchufar [desentʃu'far] vt to unplug

desenfadado, a [desenfa'ðaðo, a] adj (desenvuelto) uninhibited; (descarado) forward; **desenfado** nm (libertad) freedom; (comportamiento) free and easy manner; (descaro) forwardness

desenfocado, a [desenfo'kaðo, a] adj (FOTO) out of focus

desenfrenado, a [desenfre'naðo, a] adj (descontrolado) uncontrolled; (inmoderado) unbridled; **desenfreno** nm wildness; (de las pasiones) lack of self-control

desenganchar [desengan'tʃar] vt (gen) to unhook; (FERRO) to uncouple

desengañar [desenga'ɲar] vt to disillusion; **~se** vr to become disillusioned; **desengaño** nm disillusionment; (decepción) disappointment

desenlace [desen'laθe] nm outcome

desenmarañar [desenmara'ɲar] vt (fig) to unravel

desenmascarar [desenmaska'rar] vt to unmask

desenredar [desenre'ðar] vt (pelo) to untangle; (problema) to sort out

desenroscar [desenros'kar] vt to unscrew

desentenderse [desenten'derse] vr: **~ de** to pretend not to know about; (apartarse) to have nothing to do with

desenterrar [desente'rrar] vt to exhume; (tesoro, fig) to unearth, dig up

desentonar [desento'nar] vi (MUS) to sing (o play) out of tune; (color) to clash

desentrañar [desentra'ɲar] vt (misterio) to unravel

desentumecer |desentume'θer| vt (*pierna etc*) to stretch

desenvoltura |desenβol'tura| nf ease

desenvolver |desenβol'βer| vt (*paquete*) to unwrap; (*fig*) to develop; **~se** (*desarrollarse*) to unfold, develop; (*arreglárselas*) to cope

deseo |de'seo| nm desire, wish; **~so, a** adj: **estar ~so de** to be anxious to

desequilibrado, a |desekili'βraðo, a| adj unbalanced

desertar |deser'tar| vi to desert

desértico, a |de'sertiko, a| adj desert cpd

desesperación |desespera'θjon| nf (*impaciencia*) desperation, despair; (*irritación*) fury

desesperar |desespe'rar| vt to drive to despair; (*exasperar*) to drive to distraction ♦ vi: **~ de** to despair of; **~se** vr to despair, lose hope

desestabilizar |desestaβili'θar| vt to destabilize

desestimar |desesti'mar| vt (*menospreciar*) to have a low opinion of; (*rechazar*) to reject

desfachatez |desfatʃa'teθ| nf (*insolencia*) impudence; (*descaro*) rudeness

desfalco |des'falko| nm embezzlement

desfallecer |desfaʎe'θer| vi (*perder las fuerzas*) to become weak; (*desvanecerse*) to faint

desfasado, a |desfa'saðo, a| adj (*anticuado*) old-fashioned; **desfase** nm (*diferencia*) gap

desfavorable |desfaβo'raβle| adj unfavourable

desfigurar |desfiɣu'rar| vt (*cara*) to disfigure; (*cuerpo*) to deform

desfiladero |desfila'ðero| nm gorge

desfilar |desfi'lar| vi to parade; **desfile** nm procession

desfogarse |desfo'ɣarse| vr (*fig*) to let off steam

desgajar |desɣa'xar| vt (*arrancar*) to tear off; (*romper*) to break off; **~se** vr

to come off

desgana |des'ɣana| nf (*falta de apetito*) loss of appetite; (*apatía*) unwillingness; **~do, a** adj: **estar ~do** (*sin apetito*) to have no appetite; (*sin entusiasmo*) to have lost interest

desgarrador, a |desɣarra'ðor, a| adj (*fig*) heartrending

desgarrar |desɣa'rrar| vt to tear (up); (*fig*) to shatter; **desgarro** nm (*en tela*) tear; (*aflicción*) grief

desgastar |desɣas'tar| vt (*deteriorar*) to wear away o down; (*estropear*) to spoil; **~se** vr to get worn out; **desgaste** nm wear (and tear)

desglosar |desɣlo'sar| vt (*factura*) to break down

desgracia |des'ɣraθja| nf misfortune; (*accidente*) accident; (*vergüenza*) disgrace; (*contratiempo*) setback; **por ~** unfortunately

desgraciado, a |desɣra'θjaðo, a| adj (*sin suerte*) unlucky, unfortunate; (*miserable*) wretched; (*infeliz*) miserable

desgravación |desɣraβa'θjon| nf (COM): **~ fiscal** tax relief

desgravar |desɣra'βar| vt (*impuestos*) to reduce the tax o duty on

deshabitado, a |desaβi'taðo, a| adj uninhabited

deshacer |desa'θer| vt (*casa*) to break up; (TEC) to take apart; (*enemigo*) to defeat; (*diluir*) to melt; (*contrato*) to break; (*intriga*) to solve; **~se** vr (*disolverse*) to melt; (*despedazarse*) to come apart o undone; **~se de** to get rid of; **~se en lágrimas** to burst into tears

desharrapado, a |desarra'paðo, a| adj (*persona*) shabby

deshecho, a |des'etʃo, a| adj undone; (*roto*) smashed; (*persona*): **estar ~** to be shattered

desheredar |desere'ðar| vt to disinherit

deshidratar |desiðra'tar| vt to dehydrate

deshielo |des'jelo| nm thaw

deshonesto, a |deso'nesto, a| adj indecent

deshonra |des'onra| nf (deshonor) dishonour; (vergüenza) shame

deshora |des'ora|: **a ~** adv at the wrong time

deshuesar |deswe'sar| vt (carne) to bone; (fruta) to stone

desierto, a |de'sjerto, a| adj (casa, calle, negocio) deserted ♦ nm desert

designar |desix'nar| vt (nombrar) to designate; (indicar) to fix

designio |de'sixnjo| nm plan

desigual |desi'ɣwal| adj (terreno) uneven; (lucha etc) unequal

desilusión |desilu'sjon| nf (decepción) disillusionment; (desengaño) disappointment; **desilusionar** vt to disillusion; to disappoint; **desilusionarse** vr to become disillusioned

desinfectar |desinfek'tar| vt to disinfect

desinflar |desin'flar| vt to deflate

desintegración |desinteɣra'θjon| nf disintegration

desinterés |desinte'res| nm (desgana) lack of interest; (altruismo) unselfishness

desintoxicarse |desintoksi'karse| vr (drogadicto) to undergo detoxification

desistir |desis'tir| vi (renunciar) to stop, desist

desleal |desle'al| adj (infiel) disloyal; (COM: competencia) unfair; **~tad** nf disloyalty

desleír |desle'ir| vt (líquido) to dilute; (sólido) to dissolve

deslenguado, a |deslen'gwaðo, a| adj (grosero) foul-mouthed

desligar |desli'ɣar| vt (desatar) to untie, undo; (separar) to separate; **~se** vr (de un compromiso) to extricate o.s.

desliz |des'liθ| nm (fig) lapse; **~ar** vt to slip, slide

deslucido, a |deslu'θiðo, a| adj dull;

(torpe) awkward, graceless; (deslustrado) tarnished

deslumbrar |deslum'brar| vt to dazzle

desmadrarse |desma'ðrarse| (fam) vr (descontrolarse) to run wild; (divertirse) to let one's hair down; **desmadre** (fam) nm (desorganización) chaos; (jaleo) commotion

desmán |des'man| nm (exceso) outrage; (abuso de poder) abuse

desmandarse |desman'darse| vr (portarse mal) to behave badly; (excederse) to get out of hand; (caballo) to bolt

desmantelar |desmante'lar| vt (deshacer) to dismantle; (casa) to strip

desmaquillador |desmakiʎa'ðor| nm make-up remover

desmayar |desma'jar| vi to lose heart; **~se** vr (MED) to faint; **desmayo** nm (MED: acto) faint; (: estado) unconsciousness

desmedido, a |desme'ðiðo, a| adj excessive

desmejorar |desmexo'rar| vt (dañar) to impair, spoil; (MED) to weaken

desmembrar |desmem'brar| vt (MED) to dismember; (fig) to separate

desmemoriado, a |desmemo'rjaðo, a| adj forgetful

desmentir |desmen'tir| vt (contradecir) to contradict; (refutar) to deny

desmenuzar |desmenu'θar| vt (deshacer) to crumble; (carne) to chop; (examinar) to examine closely

desmerecer |desmere'θer| vt to be unworthy of ♦ vi (deteriorarse) to deteriorate

desmesurado, a |desmesu'raðo, a| adj disproportionate

desmontable |desmon'taßle| adj (que se quita: pieza) detachable; (que se puede plegar etc) collapsible, folding

desmontar |desmon'tar| vt (deshacer) to dismantle; (tierra) to level ♦ vi to dismount

desmoralizar |desmorali'θar| vt to

demoralize

desmoronar [desmoro'nar] vt to wear away, erode; **~se** vr (edificio, dique) to collapse; (economía) to decline

desnatado, a [desna'taðo, a] adj skimmed

desnivel [desni'ßel] nm (de terreno) unevenness

desnudar [desnu'ðar] vt (desvestir) to undress; (despojar) to strip; **~se** vr (desvestirse) to get undressed;

desnudo, a adj naked ♦ nm/f nude; **desnudo de** devoid or bereft of

desnutrición [desnutri'θjon] nf malnutrition; **desnutrido, a** adj undernourished

desobedecer [desoßeðe'θer] vt, vi to disobey; **desobediencia** nf disobedience

desocupado, a [desoku'paðo, a] adj at leisure; (desempleado) unemployed; (deshabitado) empty, vacant

desocupar [desoku'par] vt to vacate

desodorante [desoðo'rante] nm deodorant

desolación [desola'θjon] nf (de lugar) desolation; (fig) grief

desolar [deso'lar] vt to ruin, lay waste

desorbitado, a [desorßi'taðo, a] adj (excesiva: ambición) boundless; (deseos) excessive; (: precio) exorbitant

desorden [des'orðen] nm confusion; (político) disorder, unrest

desorganizar [desorxani'θar] vt (desordenar) to disorganize; **desorganización** nf (de persona) disorganization; (en empresa, oficina) disorder, chaos

desorientar [desorjen'tar] vt (extraviar) to mislead; (confundir, desconcertar) to confuse; **~se** vr (perderse) to lose one's way

despabilado, a [despaßi'laðo, a] adj (despierto) wide-awake; (fig) alert, sharp

despabilar [despaßi'lar] vt (el ingenio) to sharpen ♦ vi to wake up; (fig) to get

a move on; **~se** vr to wake up; to get a move on

despachar [despa'tʃar] vt (negocio) to do, complete; (enviar) to send, dispatch; (vender) to sell, deal in; (billete) to issue; (mandar ir) to send away

despacho [des'patʃo] nm (oficina) office; (de paquetes) dispatch; (venta) sale; (comunicación) message

despacio [des'paθjo] adv slowly

desparpajo [despar'paxo] nm self-confidence; (pey) nerve

desparramar [desparra'mar] vt (esparcir) to scatter; (líquido) to spill

despavorido, a [despaßo'riðo, a] adj terrified

despecho [des'petʃo] nm spite; **a ~ de** in spite of

despectivo, a [despek'tißo, a] adj (despreciativo) derogatory; (LING) pejorative

despedazar [despeða'θar] vt to tear to pieces

despedida [despe'ðiða] nf (adiós) farewell; (de obrero) sacking

despedir [despe'ðir] vt (visita) to see off, show out; (empleado) to dismiss; (inquilino) to evict; (objeto) to hurl; (olor etc) to give out o off; **~se** vr: **~se de** to say goodbye to

despegar [despe'xar] vt to unstick ♦ vi (avión) to take off; **~se** vr to come loose, come unstuck; **despego** nm detachment

despegue etc [des'peve] vb ver **despegar** ♦ nm takeoff

despeinado, a [despei'naðo, a] adj dishevelled, unkempt

despejado, a [despe'xaðo, a] adj (lugar) clear, free; (cielo) clear; (persona) wide-awake, bright

despejar [despe'xar] vt (gen) to clear; (misterio) to clear up ♦ vi (el tiempo) to clear; **~se** vr (tiempo, cielo) to clear (up); (misterio) to become clearer; (cabeza) to clear

despellejar [despeλe'xar] vt (animal) to skin

despensa [des'pensa] nf larder

despeñadero [despeɲa'ðero] nm (GEO) cliff, precipice

despeñarse [despe'ɲarse] vr to hurl o.s. down; (coche) to tumble over

desperdicio [desper'ðiθjo] nm (despilfarro) squandering; ~s nmpl (basura) rubbish sg (BRIT), garbage sg (US); (residuos) waste sg

desperdigarse [desperði'γarse] vr (rebaño, familia) to scatter, spread out; (granos de arroz, semillas) to scatter

desperezarse [despere'θarse] vr to stretch

desperfecto [desper'fekto] nm (deterioro) slight damage; (defecto) flaw, imperfection

despertador [desperta'ðor] nm alarm clock

despertar [desper'tar] nm awakening ♦ vt (persona) to wake up; (recuerdos) to revive; (sentimiento) to arouse ♦ vi to awaken, wake up; ~se vr to awaken, wake up

despiadado, a [despja'ðaðo, a] adj (ataque) merciless; (persona) heartless

despido etc [des'piðo] vb ver **despedir** ♦ nm dismissal, sacking

despierto, a etc [des'pjerto, a] vb ver **despertar** ♦ adj awake; (fig) sharp, alert

despilfarro [despil'farro] nm (derroche) squandering; (lujo desmedido) extravagance

despistar [despis'tar] vt to throw off the track o scent; (confundir) to mislead, confuse; ~se vr to take the wrong road; (confundirse) to become confused

despiste [des'piste] nm absent-mindedness; **un ~** a mistake, slip

desplazamiento [desplaθa'mjento] nm displacement

desplazar [despla'θar] vt to move;

(NAUT) to displace; (INFORM) to scroll; (fig) to oust; ~se vr (persona) to travel

desplegar [desple'γar] vt (tela, papel) to unfold, open out; (bandera) to unfurl; **despliegue** etc [des'pleγe] vb ver **desplegar** ♦ nm display

desplomarse [desplo'marse] vr (edificio, gobierno, persona) to collapse

desplumar [desplu'mar] vt (ave) to pluck; (fam: estafar) to fleece

despoblado, a [despo'βlaðo, a] adj (sin habitantes) uninhabited

despojar [despo'xar] vt (alguien: de sus bienes) to divest of, deprive of; (casa) to strip, leave bare; (alguien: de su cargo) to strip of

despojo [des'poxo] nm (acto) plundering; (objetos) plunder, loot; ~s nmpl (de ave, res) offal sg

desposado, a [despo'saðo, a] adj, nm/f newly-wed

desposar [despo'sar] vt to marry; ~se vr to get married

desposeer [despose'er] vt: ~ **a uno de** (puesto, autoridad) to strip sb of

déspota ['despota] nm/f despot

despreciar [despre'θjar] vt (desdeñar) to despise, scorn; (afrentar) to slight

desprecio nm scorn, contempt; slight

desprender [despren'der] vt (broche) to unfasten; (olor) to give off; ~se vr (botón: caerse) to fall off; (broche) to come unfastened; (olor, perfume) to be given off; ~se de algo que ... to draw from sth that ...

desprendimiento [desprendi'mjento] nm (gen) loosening; (generosidad) disinterestedness; (de tierra, rocas) landslide

despreocupado, a [despreoku'paðo, a] adj (sin preocupación) unworried, nonchalant; (negligente) careless

despreocuparse [despreoku'parse] vr not to worry; ~ **de** to have no interest in

desprestigiar [despresti'xjar] vt (criticar) to run down; (desacreditar) to discredit

desprevenido, a |despre'βe'nido, a| adj (no preparado) unprepared, unready

desproporcionado, a |desproporθjo'nado, a| adj disproportionate, out of proportion

desprovisto, a |despro'βisto, a| adj: ~ de devoid of

después |des'pwes| adv afterwards, later; (próximo paso) next; ~ de comer after lunch; un año ~ a year later; ~ se debatió el tema next the matter was discussed; ~ de corregido el texto after the text had been corrected; ~ de todo after all

desquiciado, a |deski'θjaðo, a| adj deranged

desquite |des'kite| nm (satisfacción) satisfaction; (venganza) revenge

destacar |desta'kar| vt to emphasize, point up; (MIL) to detach, detail ♦ vi (resaltarse) to stand out; (persona) to be outstanding o exceptional; ~se vr to stand out; to be outstanding o exceptional

destajo |des'taxo| nm: trabajar a ~ to do piecework

destapar |desta'par| vt (botella) to open; (cacerola) to take the lid off; (descubrir) to uncover; ~se vr (revelarse) to reveal one's true character

destartalado, a |destarta'laðo, a| adj (desordenado) untidy; (ruinoso) tumbledown

destello |des'teʎo| nm (de estrella) twinkle; (de faro) signal light

destemplado, a |destem'plaðo, a| adj (MUS) out of tune; (voz) harsh; (MED) out of sorts; (tiempo) unpleasant, nasty

desteñir |deste'nir| vt to fade ♦ vi to fade; ~se vr to fade; esta tela no destiñe this fabric will not run

desternillarse |desterni'ʎarse| vr: ~ de risa to split one's sides laughing

desterrar |deste'rrar| vt (exilar) to

exile; (fig) to banish, dismiss

destiempo |des'tjempo|: a ~ adv out of turn

destierro etc |des'tjerro| vb ver **desterrar** ♦ nm exile

destilar |desti'lar| vt to distil; **destilería** nf distillery

destinar |desti'nar| vt (funcionario) to appoint, assign; (fondos): ~ (a) to set aside (for)

destinatario, a |destina'tarjo, a| nm/f addressee

destino |des'tino| nm (suerte) destiny; (de avión, viajero) destination

destituir |destitu'ir| vt to dismiss

destornillador |destorniʎa'ðor| nm screwdriver

destornillar |destorni'ʎar| vt (tornillo) to unscrew; ~se vr to unscrew

destreza |des'treθa| nf (habilidad) skill; (maña) dexterity

destrozar |destro'θar| vt (romper) to smash, break (up); (estropear) to ruin; (nervios) to shatter

destrozo |des'troθo| nm (acción) destruction; (desastre) smashing; ~s nmpl (pedazos) pieces; (daños) havoc sg

destrucción |destruk'θjon| nf destruction

destruir |destru'ir| vt to destroy

desuso |des'uso| nm disuse; caer en ~ to become obsolete

desvalido, a |desβa'liðo, a| adj (desprotegido) destitute; (sin fuerzas) helpless

desvalijar |desβali'xar| vt (persona) to rob; (casa, tienda) to burgle; (coche) to break into

desván |des'βan| nm attic

desvanecer |desβane'θer| vt (disipar) to dispel; (borrar) to blur; ~se vr (humo etc) to vanish, disappear; (color) to fade; (recuerdo, sonido) to fade away; (MED) to pass out; (duda) to be dispelled

desvanecimiento |desβaneθi'mjento| *nm* (*desaparición*) disappearance; (*de colores*) fading; (*evaporación*) evaporation; (*MED*) fainting fit

desvariar |desβa'rjar| *vt* (*enfermo*) to be delirious; **desvarío** *nm* delirium

desvelar |desβe'lar| *vt* to stay awake; **~se** *vr* (*no poder dormir*) to stay awake; (*preocuparse*) to be vigilant o watchful

desvelos |des'βelos| *nmpl* worrying *sg*

desvencijado, a |desβenθi'xaðo, a| *adj* (*silla*) rickety; (*máquina*) broken-down

desventaja |desβen'taxa| *nf* disadvantage

desventura |desβen'tura| *nf* misfortune

desvergonzado, a |desβervon'θaðo, a| *adj* shameless

desvergüenza |desβer'ɣwenθa| *nf* (*descaro*) shamelessness; (*insolencia*) impudence; (*mala conducta*) effrontery

desvestir |desβes'tir| *vt* to undress; **~se** *vr* to undress

desviación |desβja'θjon| *nf* deviation; (*AUTO*) diversion, detour

desviar |des'βjar| *vt* to turn aside; (*río*) to alter the course of; (*navío*) to divert, re-route; (*conversación*) to sidetrack; **~se** *vr* (*apartarse del camino*) to turn aside; (: *barco*) to go off course

desvío *etc* |des'βio| *vb ver* **desviar** ♦ *nm* (*desviación*) detour, diversion; (*fig*) indifference

desvirtuar |desβir'twar| *vt* to distort

desvivirse |desβi'βirse| *vr*: **~ por** (*anhelar*) to long for, crave for; (*hacer lo posible por*) to do one's utmost for

detallar |deta'ʎar| *vt* to detail

detalle |de'taʎe| *nm* detail; (*gesto*) gesture, token; **al ~** in detail; (*COM*) retail

detallista |deta'ʎista| *nm/f* (*COM*) retailer

detective |detek'tiβe| *nm/f* detective

detener |dete'ner| *vt* (*gen*) to stop; (*JUR*) to arrest; (*objeto*) to keep; **~se** *vr*

to stop; (*demorarse*): **~se en** to delay over, linger over

detenidamente |deteniða'mente| *adv* (*minuciosamente*) carefully; (*extensamente*) at great length

detenido, a |dete'niðo, a| *adj* (*arrestado*) under arrest ♦ *nm/f* person under arrest, prisoner

detenimiento |deteni'mjento| *nm*: **con ~** thoroughly; (*observar, considerar*) carefully

detergente |deter'xente| *nm* detergent

deteriorar |deterjo'rar| *vt* to spoil, damage; **~se** *vr* to deteriorate; **deterioro** *nm* deterioration

determinación |determina'θjon| *nf* (*empeño*) determination; (*decisión*) decision; **determinado, a** *adj* specific

determinar |determi'nar| *vt* (*plazo*) to fix; (*precio*) to settle; **~se** *vr* to decide

detestar |detes'tar| *vt* to detest

detractor, a |detrak'tor, a| *nm/f* slanderer, libeller

detrás |de'tras| *adv* behind; (*atrás*) at the back; **~ de** behind

detrimento |detri'mento| *nm*: **en ~ de** to the detriment of

deuda |'deuða| *nf* debt

devaluación |deβalwa'θjon| *nf* devaluation

devastar |deβas'tar| *vt* (*destruir*) to devastate

devoción |deβo'θjon| *nf* devotion

devolución |deβolu'θjon| *nf* (*reenvío*) return, sending back; (*reembolso*) repayment; (*JUR*) devolution

devolver |deβol'βer| *vt* to return; (*lo extraviado, lo prestado*) to give back; (*carta al correo*) to send back; (*COM*) to repay, refund ♦ *vi* (*vomitar*) to be sick

devorar |deβo'rar| *vt* to devour

devoto, a |de'βoto, a| *adj* devout ♦ *nm/f* admirer

devuelve *pp de* **devolver**

devuelva *etc vb ver* **devolver**

di *vb ver* **dar**; **decir**

día ['dia] nm day; **¿qué ~ es?** what's the date?; **estar/poner al ~** to be/ keep up to date; **el ~ de hoy/de mañana** today/tomorrow; **al ~ siguiente** (on) the following day; **vivir al ~** to live from hand to mouth; **de ~** by day, in daylight; **en pleno ~** in full daylight; **D~ de Reyes** Epiphany; **~ festivo** (ESP) o **feriado** (AM) holiday; **~ libre** day off

diabetes [dja'βetes] nf diabetes

diablo ['djaβlo] nm devil; **diablura** nf prank

diadema [dja'ðema] nf tiara

diafragma [dja'fraɣma] nm diaphragm

diagnosis [djaɣ'nosis] nf inv diagnosis

diagnóstico [djaɣ'nostiko] nm = diagnosis

diagonal [djaɣo'nal] adj diagonal

diagrama [dja'ɣrama] nm diagram; **~ de flujo** flowchart

dial [djal] nm dial

dialecto [dja'lekto] nm dialect

dialogar [djalo'ɣar] vi: **~ con** (POL) to hold talks with

diálogo ['djaloɣo] nm dialogue

diamante [dja'mante] nm diamond

diana ['djana] nf (MIL) reveille; (de blanco) centre, bull's-eye

diapositiva [djaposi'tiβa] nf (FOTO) slide, transparency

diario, a ['djarjo, a] adj daily ♦ nm newspaper; **a ~** daily; **de ~** everyday

diarrea [dja'rrea] nf diarrhoea

dibujar [dißu'xar] vt to draw, sketch; **dibujo** nm drawing; **dibujos animados** cartoons

diccionario [dikθjo'narjo] nm dictionary

dice etc vb ver **decir**

dicho, a ['ditʃo, a] pp de **decir** ♦ adj: **en ~s países** in the aforementioned countries ♦ nm saying

dichoso, a [di'tʃoso, a] adj happy

diciembre [di'θjembre] nm December

dictado [dik'taðo] nm dictation

dictador [dikta'ðor] nm dictator;

dictadura nf dictatorship

dictamen [dik'tamen] nm (opinión) opinion; (juicio) judgment; (informe) report

dictar [dik'tar] vt (carta) to dictate; (JUR: sentencia) to pronounce; (decreto) to issue; (AM: clase) to give

didáctico, a [di'ðaktiko, a] adj educational

diecinueve [djeθi'nweße] num nineteen

dieciocho [djeθi'otʃo] num eighteen

dieciséis [djeθi'seis] num sixteen

diecisiete [djeθi'sjete] num seventeen

diente ['djente] nm (ANAT, TEC) tooth; (ZOOL) fang; (: de elefante) tusk; (de ajo) clove; **hablar entre ~s** to mutter, mumble

diera etc vb ver **dar**

diesel ['disel] adj: **motor ~** diesel engine

diestro, a ['djestro, a] adj (derecho) right; (hábil) skilful

dieta ['djeta] nf diet; **dietética** nf: **tienda de dietética** health food shop; **dietético, a** adj diet (atr), dietary

diez [djeθ] num ten

diezmar [djeθ'mar] vt (población) to decimate

difamar [difa'mar] vt (JUR: hablando) to slander; (: por escrito) to libel

diferencia [dife'renθja] nf difference; **diferenciar** vt to differentiate between ♦ vi to differ; **diferenciarse** vr to differ, be different; (distinguirse) to distinguish o.s.

diferente [dife'rente] adj different

diferido [dife'riðo] nm: **en ~** (TV etc) recorded

difícil [di'fiθil] adj difficult

dificultad [difikul'taθ] nf difficulty; (problema) trouble

dificultar [difikul'tar] vt (complicar) to complicate, make difficult; (estorbar) to obstruct

difteria [dif'terja] nf diphtheria

difundir |difun'dir| vt (calor, luz) to diffuse; (RADIO, TV) to broadcast; **~ una noticia** to spread a piece of news; **~se** vr to spread (out)

difunto, a |di'funto, a| adj dead, deceased ♦ nm/f deceased (person)

difusión |difu'sjon| nf (RADIO, TV) broadcasting

diga etc vb ver **decir**

digerir |dixe'rir| vt to digest; (fig) to absorb; **digestión** nf digestion;

digestivo, a adj digestive

digital |dixi'tal| adj digital

dignarse |diɣ'narse| vr to deign to

dignatario, a |diɣna'tarjo, a| nm/f dignitary

dignidad |diɣni'ðað| nf dignity

digno, a |'diɣno, a| adj worthy

digo etc vb ver **decir**

dije etc vb ver **decir**

dilapidar |dilapi'ðar| vt (dinero, herencia) to squander, waste

dilatar |dila'tar| vt (cuerpo) to dilate; (prolongar) to prolong

dilema |di'lema| nm dilemma

diligencia |dili'xenθja| nf diligence; (ocupación) errand, job; **~s** nfpl (JUR) formalities; **diligente** adj diligent

diluir |dilu'ir| vt to dilute

diluvio |di'lußjo| nm deluge, flood

dimensión |dimen'sjon| nf dimension

diminuto, a |dimi'nuto, a| adj tiny, diminutive

dimitir |dimi'tir| vi to resign

dimos vb ver **dar**

Dinamarca |dina'marka| nf Denmark

dinámico, a |di'namiko, a| adj dynamic

dinamita |dina'mita| nf dynamite

dinamo |'dinamo| nf dynamo

dineral |dine'ral| nm large sum of money, fortune

dinero |di'nero| nm money; **~ contante, ~ efectivo** (ready) cash; **~ suelto** (loose) change

dio vb ver **dar**

dios |djos| nm god; **¡D~ mío!** (oh,

my God!

diosa |'djosa| nf goddess

diploma |di'ploma| nm diploma

diplomacia |diplo'maθja| nf diplomacy; (fig) tact

diplomado, a |diplo'maðo, a| adj qualified

diplomático, a |diplo'matiko, a| adj diplomatic ♦ nm/f diplomat

diputación |diputa'θjon| nf (tb: ~ provincial) ≈ county council

diputado, a |dipu'taðo, a| nm/f delegate; (POL) ≈ member of parliament (BRIT), ≈ representative (US)

dique |'dike| nm dyke

diré etc vb ver **decir**

dirección |direk'θjon| nf direction; (señas) address; (AUTO) steering; (gerencia) management; (POL) leadership; **~ única/prohibida** one-way street/no entry

directa |di'rekta| nf (AUT) direct

directiva |direk'tißa| nf (DEP, tb: junta ~) board of directors

directo, a |di'rekto, a| adj direct; (RADIO, TV) live; **transmitir en ~ to** broadcast live

director, a |direk'tor, a| adj leading ♦ nm/f director; (ESCOL) head(teacher) (BRIT), principal (US); (gerente) manager(ess); (PRENSA) editor; **~ de cine** film director; **~ general** managing director

dirigente |diri'xente| nm/f (POL) leader

dirigir |diri'xir| vt to direct; (carta) to address; (obra de teatro, film) to direct; (MUS) to conduct; (negocio) to manage; **~se** vr: **~se a** to go towards, make one's way towards; (hablar con) to speak to

dirija etc vb ver **dirigir**

discernir |disθer'nir| vt to discern

disciplina |disθi'plina| nf discipline

discípulo, a |dis'θipulo, a| nm/f disciple

disco |'disko| nm disc; (DEPORTE)

discus; (TEL) dial; (AUTO: semáforo) light; (MUS) record; (INFORM): ~ **flexible/rígido** floppy/hard disk; ~ **compacto/de larga duración** compact disc/long-playing record; ~ **de freno** brake disc

disconforme [diskon'forme] adj differing; **estar** ~ **(con)** to be in disagreement (with)

discordia [dis'korðja] nf discord

discoteca [disko'teka] nf disco(theque)

discreción [diskre'θjon] nf discretion; (reserva) prudence; **comer a** ~ to eat as much as one wishes; **discrecional** adj (facultativo) discretionary

discrepancia [diskre'panθja] nf (diferencia) discrepancy; (desacuerdo) disagreement

discreto, a [dis'kreto, a] adj discreet

discriminación [diskrimina'θjon] nf discrimination

disculpa [dis'kulpa] nf excuse; (pedir perdón) apology; **pedir** ~**s a/por** to apologize to/for; **disculpar** vt to excuse, pardon; **disculparse** vr to excuse o.s.; to apologize

discurrir [disku'rrir] vi (pensar, reflexionar) to think, meditate; (el tiempo) to pass, go by

discurso [dis'kurso] nm speech

discusión [disku'sjon] nf (diálogo) discussion; (riña) argument

discutir [disku'tir] vt (debatir) to discuss; (pelear) to argue about; (contradecir) to argue against ♦ vi (debatir) to discuss; (pelearse) to argue

disecar [dise'kar] vt (conservar: animal) to stuff; (: planta) to dry

diseminar [disemi'nar] vt to disseminate, spread

diseñar [dise'nar] vt, vi to design

diseño [di'seno] nm design

disfraz [dis'fraθ] nm (máscara) disguise; (excusa) pretext; ~**ar** vt to disguise; ~**arse** vr: ~**arse de** to disguise o.s. as

disfrutar [disfru'tar] vt to enjoy ♦ vi to enjoy o.s.; ~ **de** to enjoy, possess

disgregarse [disre'ɣarse] vr (muchedumbre) to disperse

disgustar [disɣus'tar] vt (no gustar) to displease; (contrariar, enojar) to annoy, upset; ~**se** (enfadarse) to get upset; (dos personas) to fall out

disgusto [dis'ɣusto] nm (contrariedad) annoyance; (tristeza) grief; (riña) quarrel

disidente [disi'ðente] nm dissident

disimular [disimu'lar] vt (ocultar) to hide, conceal ♦ vi to dissemble

disipar [disi'par] vt to dispel; (fortuna) to squander; ~**se** vr (nubes) to vanish; (indisciplinarse) to dissipate

dislocarse [dislo'karse] vr (articulación) to sprain, dislocate

disminución [disminu'θjon] nf decrease, reduction

disminuido, a [disminu'iðo, a] nm/f: ~ **mental/físico** mentally/physically handicapped person

disminuir [disminu'ir] vt to decrease, diminish

disociarse [diso'θjarse] vr: ~ **(de)** to dissociate o.s. (from)

disolver [disol'ßer] vt (gen) to dissolve; ~**se** vr to dissolve; (COM) to go into liquidation

dispar [dis'par] adj different

disparar [dispa'rar] vt, vi to shoot, fire

disparate [dispa'rate] nm (tontería) foolish remark; (error) blunder; **decir** ~**s** to talk nonsense

disparo [dis'paro] nm shot

dispensar [dispen'sar] vt to dispense; (disculpar) to excuse

dispersar [disper'sar] vt to disperse; ~**se** vr to scatter

disponer [dispo'ner] vt (arreglar) to arrange; (ordenar) to put in order; (preparar) to prepare, get ready ♦ vr: ~ **de** to have, own; ~**se** vr: ~**se a** o **para hacer** to prepare to do

disponible [dispo'nißle] adj available

disposición [disposi'θjon] nf
arrangement, disposition; (INFORM)
layout; **a la ~ de** at the disposal of;
~ de animo state of mind

dispositivo [disposi'tiβo] nm device,
mechanism

dispuesto, a [dis'pwesto, a] pp de
disponer ♦ adj (arreglado) arranged;
(preparado) disposed

disputar [dispu'tar] vt (carrera) to
compete in

disquete [dis'kete] nm floppy disk,
diskette

distancia [dis'tanθja] nf distance

distanciar [distan'θjar] vt to space
out; **~se** vr to become estranged

distante [dis'tante] adj distant

distar [dis'tar] vi: **dista 5km de aquí**
it is 5km from here

diste vb ver **dar**

disteis ['disteis] vb ver **dar**

distension [disten'sjon] nf (en las
relaciones) relaxation; (POL) détente;
(muscular) strain

distinción [distin'θjon] nf distinction;
(elegancia) elegance; (honor) honour

distinguido, a [distin'ɡiðo, a] adj
distinguished

distinguir [distin'ɡir] vt to distinguish;
(escoger) to single out; **~se** vr to be
distinguished

distintivo [distin'tiβo] nm badge; (fig)
characteristic

distinto, a [dis'tinto, a] adj different;
(claro) clear

distracción [distrak'θjon] nf
distraction; (pasatiempo) hobby,
pastime; (olvido) absent-mindedness,
distraction

distraer [distra'er] vt (atención) to
distract; (divertir) to amuse; (fondos) to
embezzle; **~se** vr (entretenerse) to
amuse o.s.; (perder la concentración) to
allow one's attention to wander

distraído, a [distra'iðo, a] adj (gen)
absent-minded; (entretenido) amusing

distribuidor, a [distriβui'ðor, a] nm/f

distributor; **distribuidora** nf (COM)
dealer, agent; (CINE) distributor

distribuir [distriβu'ir] vt to distribute

distrito [dis'trito] nm (sector, territorio)
region; (barrio) district

disturbio [dis'turβjo] nm disturbance;
(desorden) riot

disuadir [diswa'ðir] vt to dissuade

disuelto [di'swelto] pp de **disolver**

disyuntiva [disjun'tiβa] nf dilemma

DIU nm abr (= dispositivo intrauterino)
IUD

diurno, a ['djurno, a] adj day cpd

divagar [diβa'ɣar] vi (desviarse) to
digress

diván [di'βan] nm divan

divergencia [diβer'xenθja] nf
divergence

diversidad [diβersi'ðað] nf diversity,
variety

diversificar [diβersifi'kar] vt to
diversify

diversión [diβer'sjon] nf (gen)
entertainment; (actividad) hobby,
pastime

diverso, a [di'βerso, a] adj diverse; **~s
libros** several books; **~s** nmpl sundries

divertido, a [diβer'tiðo, a] adj (chiste)
amusing; (fiesta etc) enjoyable

divertir [diβer'tir] vt (entretener,
recrear) to amuse; **~se** vr (pasarlo bien)
to have a good time; (distraerse) to
amuse o.s.

dividendos [diβi'ðendos] nmpl (COM)
dividends

dividir [diβi'ðir] vt (gen) to divide;
(distribuir) to distribute, share out

divierta etc vb ver **divertir**

divino, a [di'βino, a] adj divine

divirtiendo etc vb ver **divertir**

divisa [di'βisa] nf (emblema) emblem,
badge; **~s** nfpl foreign exchange sg

divisar [diβi'sar] vt to make out,
distinguish

división [diβi'sjon] nf (gen) division;
(de partido) split; (de país) partition

divorciar [diβor'θjar] vt to divorce;

~se vr to get divorced; **divorcio** nm divorce

divulgar |diβul'ɣar| vt (ideas) to spread; (secreto) to divulge

DNI (ESP) nm abr (= Documento Nacional de Identidad) national identity card

---

DNI

The Documento Nacional de Identidad is a Spanish ID card which must be carried at all times and produced on request from the police. It contains the holder's photo, fingerprints and personal details. It is also known as the DNI or "carnet de identidad".

Dña. abr (= doña) Mrs

do |do| nm (MUS) do, C

dobladillo |doβla'ðiλo| nm (de vestido) hem; (de pantalón: vuelta) turn-up (BRIT), cuff (US)

doblar |do'βlar| vt (papel) to fold; (caño) to bend; (la esquina) to turn, go round; (film) to dub ♦ vi to turn; (campana) to toll; **~se** vr (plegarse) to fold (up), crease; (encorvarse) to bend

doble ['doβle] adj double; (de dos aspectos) dual; (fig) two-faced ♦ nm double ♦ nm/f (TEATRO) double, stand-in; **~s** nmpl (DEPORTE) doubles sg; **con ~ sentido** ~ with a double meaning

doblegar |doβle'ɣar| vt to fold, crease; **~se** vr to yield

doblez |do'βleθ| nm fold, hem ♦ nf insincerity, duplicity

doce ['doθe] adj twelve; **~na** nf dozen

docente |do'θente| adj: **centro/personal ~** teaching establishment/staff

dócil |'doθil| adj (pasivo) docile; (obediente) obedient

docto, a ['dokto, a] adj: **~ en** instructed in

doctor, a |dok'tor, a| nm/f doctor

doctorado |dokto'raðo| nm doctorate

doctrina |dok'trina| nf doctrine, teaching

documentación |dokumenta'θjon| nf documentation, papers pl

documental |dokumen'tal| adj, nm documentary

documento |doku'mento| nm (certificado) document; **~ nacional de identidad** identity card

dólar |'dolar| nm dollar

doler |do'ler| vt, vi to hurt; (fig) to grieve; **~se** vr (de su situación) to grieve, feel sorry; (de las desgracias ajenas) to sympathize; **me duele el brazo** my arm hurts

dolor |do'lor| nm pain; (fig) grief, sorrow; **~ de cabeza** headache; **~ de estómago** stomachache

domar |do'mar| vt = **domesticar**

domesticar |domesti'kar| vt = **domar**

doméstico, a |do'mestiko, a| adj (vida, servicio) home; (tareas) household; (animal) tame, pet

domiciliación |domiθilia'θjon| nf: **~ de pagos** (COM) standing order

domicilio |domi'θiljo| nm home; **~ particular** private residence; **~ social** (COM) head office; **sin ~ fijo** of no fixed abode

dominante |domi'nante| adj dominant; (persona) domineering

dominar |domi'nar| vt (gen) to dominate; (idiomas) to be fluent in ♦ vi to dominate, prevail; **~se** vr to control o.s.

domingo |do'mingo| nm Sunday

dominio |do'minjo| nm (tierras) domain; (autoridad) power, authority; (de las pasiones) grip, hold; (de idiomas) command

don |don| nm (talento) gift; **~ Juan Gómez** Mr Juan Gómez, Juan Gómez Esq (BRIT)

donaire |do'naire| nm charm

Don/Doña

The term **don/doña** often abbreviated to D./Dña is placed before the first name as a mark of respect to an older or more senior person - eg Don Diego, Doña Inés. Although becoming rarer in Spain it is still used with names and surnames on official documents and formal correspondence - eg "Sr. D. Pedro Rodríguez Hernández", "Sra. Dña. Inés Rodríguez Hernández".

donar |do'nar| vt to donate

donativo |dona'tiβo| nm donation

doncella |don'θeʎa| nf (criada) maid

donde |'donde| adv where ♦ prep: **el coche está allí ~ el farol** the car is over there by the lamppost o where the lamppost is; **en ~** where, in which

dónde |'donde| adv interrogativo where?; **¿a ~ vas?** where are you going (to)?; **¿de ~ vienes?** where have you been?; **¿por ~?** where?, whereabouts?

dondequiera |donde'kjera| adv anywhere; **por ~** everywhere, all over the place ♦ conj: **~ que** wherever

doña |'doɲa| nf: **~ Alicia** Alicia; **~ Victoria Benito** Mrs Victoria Benito

dorado, a |do'raðo, a| adj (color) golden; (TEC) gilt

dormir |dor'mir| vt: **~ la siesta** to have an afternoon nap ♦ vi to sleep; **~se** vr to fall asleep

dormitar |dormi'tar| vi to doze

dormitorio |dormi'torjo| nm bedroom; **~ común** dormitory

dorsal |dor'sal| nm (DEPORTE) number

dorso |'dorso| nm (de mano) back; (de hoja) other side

dos |dos| num two

dosis |'dosis| nf inv dose, dosage

dotado, a |do'taðo, a| adj gifted; **~ de** endowed with

dotar |do'tar| vt to endow; **dote** nf dowry; **dotes** nfpl (talentos) gifts

doy vb ver **dar**

dragar |dra'ɣar| vt (río) to dredge; (minas) to sweep

drama |'drama| nm drama

dramaturgo |drama'turɣo| nm dramatist, playwright

drástico, a |'drastiko, a| adj drastic

drenaje |dre'naxe| nm drainage

droga |'droɣa| nf drug

drogadicto, a |droɣa'ðikto, a| nm/f drug addict

droguería |droɣe'ria| nf hardware shop (BRIT) o store (US)

ducha |'dutʃa| nf (baño) shower; (MED) douche; **ducharse** vr to take a shower

duda |'duða| nf doubt; **dudar** vt, vi to doubt; **dudoso, a** |du'ðoso, a| adj (incierto) hesitant; (sospechoso) doubtful

duela etc vb ver **doler**

duelo |'dwelo| vb ver **doler** ♦ nm (combate) duel; (luto) mourning

duende |'dwende| nm imp, goblin

dueño, a |'dweɲo, a| nm/f (propietario) owner; (de pensión, taberna) landlord/lady; (empresario) employer

duermo etc vb ver **dormir**

dulce |'dulθe| adj sweet ♦ adv gently, softly ♦ nm sweet

dulzura |dul'θura| nf sweetness; (ternura) gentleness

duna |'duna| nf (GEO) dune

dúo |'duo| nm duet

duplicar |dupli'kar| vt (hacer el doble de) to duplicate; **~se** vr to double

duque |'duke| nm duke; **~sa** nf duchess

duración |dura'θjon| nf (de película, disco etc) length; (de pila etc) life; (curso: de acontecimientos etc) duration

duradero, a |dura'ðero, a| adj (tela etc) hard-wearing; (fe, paz) lasting

durante |du'rante| prep during

durar |du'rar| vi to last; (recuerdo) to remain

durazno [du'raθno] (AM) nm (fruta)
peach; (árbol) peach tree

durex ['dureks] (AM) nm (tira adhesiva)
Sellotape ® (BRIT), Scotch tape ® (US)

dureza [du'reθa] nf (calidad) hardness

duro, a ['duro, a] adj hard; (carácter)
tough ♦ adv hard ♦ nm (moneda) five
peseta coin o piece

DVD nm abr (= disco de vídeo digital)
DVD

E, e

E abr (= este) E

e [e] conj and

ebanista [eßa'nista] nm/f
cabinetmaker

ébano ['eßano] nm ebony

ebrio, a ['eßrjo, a] adj drunk

ebullición [eßuʎi'θjon] nf boiling

eccema [ek'θema] nf (MED) eczema

echar [e'tʃar] vt to throw; (agua, vino)
to pour (out); (empleado: despedir) to
fire, sack; (hojas) to sprout; (cartas) to
post; (humo) to emit, give out ♦ vi: ~ a
correr/llorar to run off/burst into
tears; **~se** vr to lie down; **~ llave** a to
lock (up); **~ abajo** (gobierno) to
overthrow; (edificio) to demolish;
~ mano a uno to lay hands on; **~ una
mano a uno** (ayudar) to give sb a
hand; **~ de menos** to miss

eclesiástico, a [ekle'sjastiko, a] adj
ecclesiastical

eco ['eko] nm echo; **tener ~** to catch
on

ecología [ekolo'xia] nf ecology;
ecológico, a adj (producto, método)
environmentally-friendly; (agricultura)
organic; **ecologista** adj ecological,
environmental ♦ nm/f environmentalist

economato [ekono'mato] nm
cooperative store

economía [ekono'mia] nf (sistema)
economy; (carrera) economics

económico, a [eko'nomiko, a] adj

(barato) cheap, economical;
(ahorrativo) thrifty; (COM: año etc)
financial; (: situación) economic

economista [ekono'mista] nm/f
economist

ECU [eku] nm ECU

ecuador [ekwa'ðor] nm equator; **(el)
E~** Ecuador

ecuánime [e'kwanime] adj (carácter)
level-headed; (estado) calm

ecuatoriano, a [ekwato'rjano, a] adj,
nm/f Ecuadorian

ecuestre [e'kwestre] adj equestrian

eczema [ek'θema] nm = **eccema**

edad [e'ðað] nf age; **¿qué ~ tienes?**
how old are you?; **tiene ocho años
de ~** he is eight (years old); **de
~ mediana/avanzada** middle-aged/
advanced in years; **la E~ Media** the
Middle Ages

edición [eði'θjon] nf (acto)
publication; (ejemplar) edition

edificar [eðifi'kar] vt, vi to build

edificio [eði'fiθjo] nm building; (fig)
edifice, structure

Edimburgo [eðim'burxo] nm
Edinburgh

editar [eði'tar] vt (publicar) to publish;
(preparar textos) to edit

editor, a [eði'tor, a] nm/f (que publica)
publisher; (redactor) editor ♦ adj: **casa
~a** publishing house, publisher; **~ial**
adj editorial ♦ nm leading article,
editorial; **casa ~ial** publisher

edredón [eðre'ðon] nm duvet

educación [eðuka'θjon] nf education;
(crianza) upbringing; (modales) (good)
manners pl

educado, a [eðu'kaðo, a] adj: **bien/
mal ~** well/badly behaved

educar [eðu'kar] vt to educate; (criar)
to bring up; (voz) to train

EE. UU. nmpl abr (= Estados Unidos)
USA(s)

efectista [efek'tista] adj sensationalist

efectivamente [efektißa'mente] adv
(como respuesta) exactly, precisely;

(*verdaderamente*) really; (*de hecho*) in fact

efectivo, a [efek'tiβo, a] *adj* effective; (*real*) actual, real ♦ *nm*: **pagar en ~** to pay (in) cash; **hacer ~ un cheque** to cash a cheque

efecto [e'fekto] *nm* effect, result; **~s** *nmpl* (~**s** *personales*) effects; (*bienes*) goods; (COM) assets; **en ~** in fact; (*respuesta*) exactly, indeed; **~ 2000** millennium bug; **~ invernadero** greenhouse effect

efectuar [efek'twar] *vt* to carry out; (*viaje*) to make

eficacia [efi'kaθja] *nf* (*de persona*) efficiency; (*de medicamento etc*) effectiveness

eficaz [efi'kaθ] *adj* (*persona*) efficient; (*acción*) effective

eficiente [efi'θjente] *adj* efficient

efusivo, a [efu'siβo, a] *adj* effusive; **mis más efusivas gracias** my warmest thanks

EGB (ESP) *nf abr* (ESCOL) = Educación General Básica

egipcio, a [e'xipθjo, a] *adj, nm/f* Egyptian

Egipto [e'xipto] *nm* Egypt

egoísmo [exo'ismo] *nm* egoism

egoísta [exo'ista] *adj* egoistical, selfish ♦ *nm/f* egoist

egregio, a [e'vrexjo, a] *adj* eminent, distinguished

Eire ['eire] *nm* Eire

ej. *abr* (= *ejemplo*) eg

eje ['exe] *nm* (GEO, MAT) axis; (*de rueda*) axle; (*de máquina*) shaft, spindle

ejecución [exeku'θjon] *nf* execution; (*cumplimiento*) fulfilment; (MUS) performance; (JUR: *embargo de deudor*) attachment

ejecutar [exeku'tar] *vt* to execute, carry out; (*matar*) to execute; (*cumplir*) to fulfil; (MUS) to perform; (JUR: *embargar*) to attach, distrain (on)

ejecutivo, a [exeku'tiβo, a] *adj* executive; **el (poder) ~** the executive

(power)

ejemplar [exem'plar] *adj* exemplary ♦ *nm* example; (ZOOL) specimen; (*de libro*) copy; (*de periódico*) number, issue

ejemplo [e'xemplo] *nm* example; **por ~** for example

ejercer [exer'θer] *vt* to exercise; (*influencia*) to exert; (*un oficio*) to practise ♦ *vi* (*practicar*) to practise (as)

ejercicio [exer'θiθjo] *nm* exercise; (*período*) tenure; **~ comercial** financial year

ejército [e'xerθito] *nm* army; **entrar en el ~** to join the army, join up

ejote [e'xote] (AM) *nm* green bean

PALABRA CLAVE

el [el] (*f* **la**, *pl* **los, las**, *neutro* **lo**) *art def* **1** the; **el libro/la mesa/los estudiantes** the book/table/students
2 (*con* *abstracto: no se traduce*): **el amor/la juventud** love/youth
3 (*posesión: se traduce a menudo por adj posesivo*): **romperse el brazo** to break one's arm; **levantó la mano** he put his hand up; **se puso el sombrero** he put her hat on
4 (*valor descriptivo*): **tener la boca grande/los ojos azules** to have a big mouth/blue eyes
5 (*con días*) on; **me iré el viernes** I'll leave on Friday; **los domingos suelo ir a nadar** on Sundays I generally go swimming
6 (*lo + adj*): **lo difícil/caro** what is difficult/expensive; (= *cuán*): **no se da cuenta de lo pesado que es** he doesn't realise how boring he is
♦ *pron demos* **1**: **mi libro y el de usted** my book and yours; **las de Pepe son mejores** Pepe's are better; **no la(s) blanca(s) sino la(s) gris(es)** not the white one(s) but the grey one(s)
2: **lo de:** **lo de ayer** what happened yesterday; **lo de las facturas** that business about the invoices

♦ *pron relativo*: **el que** *etc* **1** (*indef*): **el (los) que quiera(n) se vaya(n)** anyone who wants to can leave; **llévese el que más le guste** take the one you like best

2 (*def*): **el que compré ayer** the one I bought yesterday; **los que se van** those who leave

3: lo que: lo que pienso yo/más me gusta what I think/like most

♦ *conj*: **el que** or **lo que lo diga** the fact that he says so; **el que sea tan vago me molesta** his being so lazy bothers me

♦ *excl*: **¡el susto que me diste!** what a fright you gave me!

♦ *pron personal* **1** (*persona: m*) him; (*: f*) her; (*: pl*) them; **lo/las veo** I can see him/them

2 (*animal, cosa: sg*) it; (*: pl*) them; **lo** (o **la**) **veo** I can see it; **los** (o **las**) **veo** I can see them

3: lo (*como sustituto de frase*): **no lo sabía** I didn't know; **ya lo entiendo** I understand now

---

él [el] *pron* (*persona*) he; (*cosa*) it; (*después de prep: persona*) him; (*: cosa*) it; **de ~ his**

elaborar [elaβo'rar] *vt* (*producto*) to make, manufacture; (*preparar*) to prepare; (*madera, metal etc*) to work; (*proyecto etc*) to work on o out

elasticidad [elastiθi'ðað] *nf* elasticity

elástico, a [e'lastiko, a] *adj* elastic; (*flexible*) flexible ♦ *nm* elastic; (*un ~*) elastic band

elección [elek'θjon] *nf* election; (*selección*) choice, selection

electorado [elekto'raðo] *nm* electorate, voters *pl*

electricidad [elektriθi'ðað] *nf* electricity

electricista [elektri'θista] *nm/f* electrician

eléctrico, a [e'lektriko, a] *adj* electric

electro... [elektro] *prefijo* electro...;

~cardiograma *nm* electrocardiogram; **~cutar** *vt* to electrocute; **~do** *nm* electrode; **~domésticos** *nmpl* (electrical) household appliances; **~magnético, a** *adj* electromagnetic

electrónica [elek'tronika] *nf* electronics *sg*

electrónico, a [elek'troniko, a] *adj* electronic

elefante [ele'fante] *nm* elephant

elegancia [ele'vanθja] *nf* elegance, grace; (*estilo*) stylishness

elegante [ele'vante] *adj* elegant, graceful; (*estiloso*) stylish, fashionable

elegir [ele'xir] *vt* (*escoger*) to choose, select; (*optar*) to opt for; (*presidente*) to elect

elemental [elemen'tal] *adj* (*claro, obvio*) elementary; (*fundamental*) elemental, fundamental

elemento [ele'mento] *nm* element; (*fig*) ingredient; **~s** *nmpl* elements, rudiments

elepé [ele'pe] (*pl*: **elepés**) *nm* L.P.

elevación [eleβa'θjon] *nf* elevation; (*acto*) raising, lifting; (*de precios*) rise; (*GEO etc*) height, altitude

elevar [ele'βar] *vt* to raise, lift (up); (*precio*) to put up; **~se** *vr* (*edificio*) to rise; (*precios*) to go up

eligiendo *etc vb ver* **elegir**

elija *etc vb ver* **elegir**

eliminar [elimi'nar] *vt* to eliminate, remove

eliminatoria [elimina'torja] *nf* heat, preliminary (round)

elite [e'lite] *nf* elite

ella ['eʎa] *pron* (*persona*) she; (*cosa*) it; (*después de prep: persona*) her; (*: cosa*) it; **de ~ hers**

ellas ['eʎas] *pron* (*personas y cosas*) they; (*después de prep*) them; **de ~ theirs**

ello ['eʎo] *pron* it

ellos ['eʎos] *pron* they; (*después de prep*) them; **de ~ theirs**

elocuencia [elo'kwenθja] *nf*

eloquence

elogiar [elo'xjar] vt to praise; **elogio** nm praise

elote [e'lote] (AM) nm corn on the cob

eludir [elu'ðir] vt to avoid

emanar [ema'nar] vi: ~ **de** to emanate from, come from; (derivar de) to originate in

emancipar [emanθi'par] vt to emancipate; ~**se** vr to become emancipated, free o.s.

embadurnar [embaður'nar] vt to smear

embajada [emba'xaða] nf embassy

embajador, a [embaxa'ðor, a] nm/f ambassador/ambassadress

embalaje [emba'laxe] nm packing

embalar [emba'lar] vt to parcel, wrap (up); ~**se** vr to go fast

embalsamar [embalsa'mar] vt to embalm

embalse [em'balse] nm (presa) dam; (lago) reservoir

embarazada [embara'θaða] adj pregnant ♦ nf pregnant woman

embarazo [emba'raθo] nm (de mujer) pregnancy; (impedimento) obstacle, obstruction; (timidez) embarrassment; **embarazoso, a** adj awkward, embarrassing

embarcación [embarka'θjon] nf (barco) boat, craft; (acto) embarkation, boarding

embarcadero [embarka'ðero] nm pier, landing stage

embarcar [embar'kar] vt (cargamento) to ship, stow; (persona) to embark, put on board; ~**se** vr to embark, go on board

embargar [embar'var] vt (JUR) to seize, impound

embargo [em'barvo] nm (JUR) seizure; (COM, POL) embargo

embargue [em'barve] etc vb ver **embargar**

embarque etc [em'barke] vb ver **embarcar** ♦ nm shipment, loading

embaucar [embau'kar] vt to trick, fool

embeber [embe'ßer] vt (absorber) to absorb, soak up; (empapar) to saturate ♦ vi to shrink; ~**se** vr: to be engrossed o absorbed in a book

embellecer [embeλe'θer] vt to embellish, beautify

embestida [embes'tiða] nf attack, onslaught; (carga) charge

embestir [embes'tir] vt to attack, assault; to charge, attack ♦ vi to attack

emblema [em'blema] nm emblem

embobado, a [embo'ßaðo, a] adj (atontado) stunned, bewildered

embolia [em'bolja] nf (MED) clot

émbolo [em'bolo] nm (AUTO) piston

embolsar [embol'sar] vt to pocket, put in one's pocket

emborrachar [emborra'tʃar] vt to make drunk, intoxicate; ~**se** vr to get drunk

emboscada [embos'kaða] nf ambush

embotar [embo'tar] vt to blunt, dull; ~**se** vr (adormecerse) to go numb

embotellamiento [emboteλa'-mjento] nm (AUTO) traffic jam

embotellar [embote'λar] vt to bottle

embrague [em'braxe] nm (tb: pedal de ~) clutch

embriagar [embrja'var] vt (emborrachar) to make drunk; ~**se** vr (emborracharse) to get drunk

embrión [em'brjon] nm embryo

embrollar [embro'λar] vt (el asunto) to confuse, complicate; (implicar) to involve, embroil; ~**se** vr (confundirse) to get into a muddle o mess

embrollo [em'broλo] nm (enredo) muddle, confusion; (aprieto) fix, jam

embrujado, a [embru'xado, a] adj bewitched; **casa embrujada** haunted house

embrutecer [embrute'θer] vt (atontar) to stupefy; ~**se** vr to be stupefied

embudo [em'buðo] nm funnel

embuste [em'buste] nm (mentira) lie;

~ro, a adj lying, deceitful ♦ nm/f (mentiroso) liar

embutido [embu'tiðo] nm (CULIN) sausage; (TEC) inlay

emergencia [emer'xenθja] nf emergency; (surgimiento) emergence

emerger [emer'ver] vi to emerge, appear

emigración [emivra'θjon] nf emigration; (de pájaros) migration

emigrar [emi'vrar] vi (personas) to emigrate; (pájaros) to migrate

eminencia [emi'nenθja] nf eminence; **eminente** adj eminent, distinguished; (elevado) high

emisario [emi'sarjo] nm emissary

emisión [emi'sjon] nf (acto) emission; (COM etc) issue; (RADIO, TV: acto) broadcasting; (: programa) broadcast, programme (BRIT), program (US)

emisora [emi'sora] nf radio o broadcasting station

emitir [emi'tir] vt (olor etc) to emit, give off; (moneda etc) to issue; (opinión) to express; (RADIO) to broadcast

emoción [emo'θjon] nf emotion; (excitación) excitement; (sentimiento) feeling

emocionante [emoθjo'nante] adj (excitante) exciting, thrilling

emocionar [emoθjo'nar] vt (excitar) to excite, thrill; (conmover) to move, touch; (impresionar) to impress

emotivo, a [emo'tiβo, a] adj emotional

empacar [empa'kar] vt (gen) to pack; (en caja) to bale, crate

empacho [em'patʃo] nm (MED) indigestion; (fig) embarrassment

empadronarse [empaðro'narse] vr (POL: como elector) to register

empalagoso, a [empala'voso, a] adj cloying; (fig) tiresome

empalmar [empal'mar] vt to join, connect ♦ vi (dos caminos) to meet, join; **empalme** nm joint, connection;

junction; (de trenes) connection

empanada [empa'naða] nf pie, pasty

empantanarse [empanta'narse] vr to get swamped; (fig) to get bogged down

empañarse [empa'narse] vr (cristales etc) to steam up

empapar [empa'par] vt (mojar) to soak, saturate; (absorber) to soak up, absorb; **~se vr: ~se de** to soak up

empapelar [empape'lar] vt (paredes) to paper

empaquetar [empake'tar] vt to pack, parcel up

empastar [empas'tar] vt (embadurnar) to paste; (diente) to fill

empaste [em'paste] nm (de diente) filling

empatar [empa'tar] vi to draw, tie; **empate** nm draw, tie

empecé etc vb ver **empezar**

empedernido, a [empeðer'niðo, a] adj hard, heartless; (fumador) inveterate

empedrado, a [empe'ðraðo, a] adj paved ♦ nm paving

empeine [em'peine] nm (de pie, zapato) instep

empellón [empe'ʎon] nm push, shove

empeñado, a [empe'paðo, a] adj (persona) determined; (objeto) pawned

empeñar [empe'par] vt (objeto) to pawn, pledge; (persona) to compel; **~se** vr (endeudarse) to get into debt; **~se en** to be set on, be determined to

empeño [em'peno] nm (determinación, insistencia) determination, insistence; **casa de ~s** pawnshop

empeorar [empeo'rar] vt to make worse, worsen ♦ vi to get worse, deteriorate

empequeñecer [empekepe'θer] vt to dwarf; (minusvalorar) to belittle

emperador [empera'ðor] nm emperor; **emperatriz** nf empress

empezar [empe'θar] vt, vi to begin, start

empiece etc vb ver **empezar**

empiezo etc vb ver **empezar**

empinar [empi'nar] vt to raise; **~se** vr (persona) to stand on tiptoe; (animal) to rear up; (camino) to climb steeply

empírico, a [em'piriko, a] adj empirical

emplasto [em'plasto] nm (MED) plaster

emplazamiento [emplaθa'mjento] nm site, location; (JUR) summons sg

emplazar [empla'θar] vt (ubicar) to site, place, locate; (JUR) to summons; (convocar) to summon

empleado, a [emple'aðo, a] nm/f (gen) employee; (de banco etc) clerk

emplear [emple'ar] vt (usar) to use, employ; (dar trabajo a) to employ; **~se** vr (conseguir trabajo) to be employed; (ocuparse) to occupy o.s.

empleo [em'pleo] nm (puesto) job; (puestos: colectivamente) employment; (uso) use, employment

empobrecer [empobre'θer] vt to impoverish; **~se** vr to become poor o impoverished

empollar [empo'ʎar] (fam) vt, vi to swot (up); **empollón, ona** (fam) nm/f swot

emporio [em'porjo] nm (AM: gran almacén) department store

empotrado, a [empo'traðo, a] adj (armario etc) built-in

emprender [empren'der] vt (empezar) to begin, embark on; (acometer) to tackle, take on

empresa [em'presa] nf (de espíritu etc) enterprise; (COM) company, firm; **~rio, a** nm/f (COM) businessman/woman

empréstito [em'prestito] nm (public) loan

empujar [empu'xar] vt to push, shove

empujón [empu'xon] nm push, shove

empuñar [empu'ɲar] vt (asir) to grasp, take (firm) hold of

emular [emu'lar] vt to emulate; (rivalizar) to rival

---

en [en] prep 1 (posición) in; (: sobre) on; **está ~ el cajón** it's in the drawer; **~ Argentina/La Paz** in Argentina/La Paz; **~ la oficina/el colegio** at the office/school; **está ~ el suelo/quinto piso** it's on the floor/the fifth floor 2 (dirección) into; **entró ~ el aula** she went into the classroom; **meter algo ~ el bolso** to put sth into one's bag 3 (tiempo) in; on; **~ 1605/3 semanas/invierno** in 1605/3 weeks/ winter; **~ (el mes de) enero** in (the month of) January; **~ aquella ocasión/época** on that occasion/at that time 4 (precio) for; **lo vendió ~ 20 dólares** he sold it for 20 dollars 5 (diferencia) by; **reducir/aumentar ~ una tercera parte/un 20 por ciento** to reduce/increase by a third/ 20 per cent 6 (manera): **avión/autobús** by plane/bus; **escrito ~ inglés** written in English 7 (después de vb que indica gastar etc) on; **han cobrado demasiado ~ dietas** they've charged too much to expenses; **se le va la mitad del sueldo ~ comida** he spends half his salary on food 8 (tema, ocupación): **experto ~ la materia** expert on the subject; **trabaja ~ la construcción** he works in the building industry 9 (adj + ~ + infin): **lento ~ reaccionar** slow to react

---

enaguas [e'naγwas] nfpl petticoat sg, underskirt sg

enajenación [enaxena'θjon] nf: **~ mental** mental derangement

enajenar [enaxe'nar] vt (volver loco) to drive mad

enamorado, a [enamo'raðo, a] adj in love ♦ nm/f lover

enamorar |enamo'rar| vt to win the love of; **~se** vr: **~se de alguien** to fall in love with sb

enano, a |e'nano, a| adj tiny ♦ nm/f dwarf

enardecer |enarðe'θer| vt (pasiones) to fire, inflame; (persona) to fill with enthusiasm; (persona) to urge, encourage; **~se** vr: **~se por** to get excited about; (entusiasmarse) to get enthusiastic about

encabezamiento |enkaβeθa'mjento| nm (de carta) heading; (de periódico) headline

encabezar |enkaβe'θar| vt (movimiento, revolución) to lead, head; (lista) to head, be at the top of; (carta) to put a heading to

encadenar |enkaðe'nar| vt to chain (together); (poner grilletes a) to shackle

encajar |enka'xar| vt (ajustar): ~ (en) to fit (into); (fam: golpe) to take ♦ vi to fit (well); (fig: corresponder a) to match; **~se** vr: **~se en un sillón** to squeeze into a chair

encaje |en'kaxe| nm (labor) lace

encalar |enka'lar| vt (pared) to whitewash

encallar |enka'ʎar| vi (NAUT) to run aground

encaminar |enkami'nar| vt to direct, send; **~se** vr: to set out for

encantado, a |enkan'taðo, a| adj (hechizado) bewitched; (muy contento) delighted; **¡~!** how do you do, pleased to meet you

encantador, a |enkanta'ðor, a| adj charming, lovely ♦ nm/f magician, enchanter/enchantress

encantar |enkan'tar| vt (agradar) to charm, delight; (hechizar) to bewitch, cast a spell on; **me encanta eso** I love that; **encanto** nm (hechizo) spell, charm; (fig) charm, delight

encarcelar |enkarθe'lar| vt to imprison, jail

encarecer |enkare'θer| vt to put up the price of; **~se** vr to get dearer

encarecimiento |enkareθi'mjento| nm price increase

encargado, a |enkar'ɣaðo, a| adj in charge ♦ nm/f agent, representative; (responsable) person in charge

encargar |enkar'ɣar| vt to entrust; (recomendar) to urge, recommend; **~se** vr: **~se de** to look after, take charge of

encargo |en'karɣo| nm (tarea) assignment, job; (responsabilidad) responsibility; (COM) order

encariñarse |enkari'ɲarse| vr: ~ **con** to grow fond of, get attached to

encarnación |enkarna'θjon| nf incarnation, embodiment

encarnizado, a |enkarni'θaðo, a| adj (lucha) bloody, fierce

encarrilar |enkarri'lar| vt (tren) to put back on the rails; (fig) to correct, put on the right track

encasillar |enkasi'ʎar| vt (tb fig) to pigeonhole; (actor) to typecast

encauzar |enkau'θar| vt to channel

encendedor |enθende'ðor| nm lighter

encender |enθen'der| vt (con fuego) to light; (luz, radio) to put on, switch on; (avivar: pasiones) to inflame; **~se** vr to catch fire; (excitarse) to get excited; (de cólera) to flare up; (el rostro) to blush

encendido |enθen'diðo| nm (AUTO) ignition

encerado |enθe'raðo| nm (ESCOL) blackboard

encerrar |enθe'rrar| vt (suelo) to wax, polish

encerrar |enθe'rrar| vt (confinar) to shut in, shut up; (comprender, incluir) to include, contain

encharcado, a |entʃar'kaðo, a| adj (terreno) flooded

encharcarse |entʃar'karse| vr to get flooded

enchufado, a |entʃu'faðo, a| nm/f (fam) well-connected person

enchufar |entʃu'far| vt (ELEC) to plug in; (TEC) to connect, fit together; **enchufe** nm (ELEC: clavija) plug;

(: *toma*) socket; (*de dos tubos*) joint, connection; (*fam: influencia*) contact, connection; (: *puesto*) cushy job

encía |en'θia| *nf* gum

encienda *etc vb ver* **encender**

encierro *etc* |en'θjerro| *vb ver* **encerrar** ♦ *nm* shutting in, shutting up; (*calabozo*) prison

encima |en'θima| *adv* (*sobre*) above, over; (*además*) besides; **~ de** (*en*) on, on top of; (*sobre*) above, over; (*además de*) besides, on top of; **por ~ de** over; **¿llevas dinero ~?** have you (got) any money on you?; **se me vino ~** it took me by surprise

encina |en'θina| *nf* holm oak

encinta |en'θinta| *adj* pregnant

enclenque |en'klenke| *adj* weak, sickly

encoger |enko'xer| *vt* to shrink, contract; **~se** *vr* to shrink, contract; (*fig*) to cringe; **~se de hombros** to shrug one's shoulders

encolar |enko'lar| *vt* (*engomar*) to glue, paste; (*pegar*) to stick down

encolerizar |enkoleri'θar| *vt* to anger, provoke; **~se** *vr* to get angry

encomendar |enkomen'dar| *vt* to entrust, commend; **~se** *vr*: **~se a** to put one's trust in

encomiar |enko'mjar| *vt* to praise, pay tribute to

encomienda *etc* |enko'mjenda| *vb ver* **encomendar** ♦ *nf* (*encargo*) charge, commission; (*elogio*) tribute; **~ postal** (*AM*) parcel post

encontrado, a |enkon'traðo, a| *adj* (*contrario*) contrary, conflicting

encontrar |enkon'trar| *vt* (*hallar*) to find; (*inesperadamente*) to meet, run into; **~se** *vr* to meet (each other); (*situarse*) to be (situated); **~se con** to meet; **~se bien (de salud)** to feel well

encrespar |enkres'par| *vt* (*cabellos*) to curl; (*fig*) to anger, irritate; **~se** *vr* (*el mar*) to get rough; (*fig*) to get cross, get irritated

encrucijada |enkruθi'xaða| *nf* crossroads *sg*

encuadernación |enkwaðerna'θjon| *nf* binding

encuadernador, a |enkwaðerna'ðor, a| *nm/f* bookbinder

encuadrar |enkwa'ðrar| *vt* (*retrato*) to frame; (*ajustar*) to fit, insert; (*contener*) to contain

encubrir |enku'ßrir| *vt* (*ocultar*) to hide, conceal; (*criminal*) to harbour, shelter

encuentro *etc* |en'kwentro| *vb ver* **encontrar** ♦ *nm* (*de personas*) meeting; (*AUTO etc*) collision, crash; (*DEPORTE*) match, game; (*MIL*) encounter

encuesta |en'kwesta| *nf* inquiry, investigation; (*sondeo*) (public) opinion poll; **~ judicial** post mortem

encumbrar |enkum'brar| *vt* (*persona*) to exalt

endeble |en'deßle| *adj* (*argumento, excusa, persona*) weak

endémico, a |en'demiko, a| *adj* (*MED*) endemic; (*fig*) rife, chronic

endemoniado, a |en'demo'njaðo, a| *adj* possessed (of the devil); (*travieso*) devilish

enderezar |endere'θar| *vt* (*poner derecho*) to straighten (out); (: *verticalmente*) to set upright; (*situación*) to straighten o sort out; (*dirigir*) to direct; **~se** *vr* (*persona sentada*) to straighten up

endeudarse |endeu'ðarse| *vr* to get into debt

endiablado, a |endja'ßlaðo, a| *adj* devilish, diabolical; (*travieso*) mischievous

endilgar |endil'var| (*fam*) *vt*: **~le algo a uno** to lumber sb with sth; **~le un sermón a uno** to lecture sb

endiñar |endi'ɲar| (*fam*) *vt* (*bofetón*) to land, belt

endosar |endo'sar| *vt* (*cheque etc*) to endorse

endulzar |endul'θar| vt to sweeten; (suavizar) to soften

endurecer |endure'θer| vt to harden; **~se** vr to harden, grow hard

enema |e'nema| nm (MED) enema

enemigo, a |ene'miɣo, a| adj enemy, hostile ♦ nm/f enemy

enemistad |enemis'tað| nf enmity

enemistar |enemis'tar| vt to make enemies of, cause a rift between; **~se** vr to become enemies; (amigos) to fall out

energía |ener'xia| nf (vigor) energy, drive; (empuje) push; (TEC, ELEC) energy, power; **~ eólica** wind power; **~ solar** solar energy/power

enérgico, a |e'nerxiko, a| adj (gen) energetic; (voz, modales) forceful

energúmeno, a |ener'ɣumeno, a| (fam) nm/f (fig) madman/woman

enero |e'nero| nm January

enfadado, a |enfa'ðaðo, a| adj angry, annoyed

enfadar |enfa'ðar| vt to anger, annoy; **~se** vr to get angry o annoyed

enfado |en'faðo| nm (enojo) anger, annoyance; (disgusto) trouble, bother

énfasis |'enfasis| nm emphasis, stress

enfático, a |en'fatiko, a| adj emphatic

enfermar |enfer'mar| vt to make ill ♦ vi to fall ill, be taken ill

enfermedad |enferme'ðað| nf illness; **~ venérea** venereal disease

enfermera |enfer'mera| nf nurse

enfermería |enferme'ria| nf infirmary; (de colegio etc) sick bay

enfermero |enfer'mero| nm (male) nurse

enfermizo, a |enfer'miθo, a| adj (persona) sickly, unhealthy; (fig) unhealthy

enfermo, a |en'fermo, a| adj ill, sick ♦ nm/f invalid, sick person; (en hospital) patient

enflaquecer |enflake'θer| vt (adelgazar) to make thin; (debilitar) to weaken

enfocar |enfo'kar| vt (foto etc) to focus; (problema etc) to approach

enfoque etc |en'foke| vb ver **enfocar** ♦ nm focus.

enfrascarse |enfras'karse| vr: **~ en algo** to bury o.s. in sth

enfrentar |enfren'tar| vt (peligro) to face (up to), confront; (oponer) to bring face to face; **~se** vr (dos personas) to face o confront each other; (DEPORTE: dos equipos) to meet; **~se a** o **con** to face up to, confront

enfrente |en'frente| adv opposite; **la casa de ~** the house opposite, the house across the street; **~ de** opposite, facing

enfriamiento |enfria'mjento| nm chilling, refrigeration; (MED) cold, chill

enfriar |enfri'ar| vt (alimentos) to cool, chill; (algo caliente) to cool down; **~se** vr to cool down; (MED) to catch a chill; (amistad) to cool

enfurecer |enfure'θer| vt to enrage, madden; **~se** vr to become furious, fly into a rage; (mar) to get rough

engalanar |engala'nar| vt (adornar) to adorn; (ciudad) to decorate; **~se** vr to get dressed up

enganchar |engan'tʃar| vt to hook; (dos vagones) to hitch up; (TEC) to couple, connect; (MIL) to recruit; **~se** vr (MIL) to enlist, join up

enganche |en'gantʃe| nm hook; (TEC) coupling, connection; (acto) hooking (up); (MIL) recruitment, enlistment; (AM: depósito) deposit

engañar |enga'ɲar| vt to deceive; (estafar) to cheat, swindle; **~se** vr (equivocarse) to be wrong; (disimular la verdad) to deceive o.s.

engaño |en'gaɲo| nm deceit; (estafa) trick, swindle; (error) mistake, misunderstanding; (ilusión) delusion; **~so, a** adj (tramposo) crooked; (mentiroso) dishonest, deceitful; (aspecto) deceptive; (consejo) misleading

engarzar [engar'θar] vt (joya) to set, mount; (fig) to link, connect

engatusar [engatu'sar] (fam) vt to coax

engendrar [enxen'drar] vt to breed; (procrear) to beget; (causar) to cause, produce; **engendro** nm (BIO) foetus; (fig) monstrosity

englobar [englo'βar] vt to include, comprise

engordar [engor'ðar] vt to fatten ♦ vi to get fat, put on weight

engorroso, a [engo'rroso, a] adj bothersome, trying

engranaje [engra'naxe] nm (AUTO) gear

engrandecer [engrande'θer] vt to enlarge, magnify; (alabar) to praise, speak highly of; (exagerar) to exaggerate

engrasar [engra'sar] vt (TEC: poner grasa) to grease; (: lubricar) to lubricate, oil; (manchar) to make greasy

engreído, a [engre'iðo, a] adj vain, conceited

engrosar [engro'sar] vt (ensanchar) to enlarge; (aumentar) to increase; (hinchar) to swell

enhebrar [ene'βrar] vt to thread

enhorabuena [enora'βwena] excl: ¡~! congratulations! ♦ nf: **dar la ~ a** to congratulate

enigma [e'niɣma] nm enigma; (problema) puzzle; (misterio) mystery

enjabonar [enxaβo'nar] vt to soap; (fam: adular) to soft-soap

enjambre [en'xambre] nm swarm

enjaular [enxau'lar] vt (a: (put in a) cage; (fam) to jail, lock up

enjuagar [enxwa'ɣar] vt (ropa) to rinse (out)

enjuague etc [en'xwaxe] vb ver **enjuagar** ♦ nm (MED) mouthwash; (de ropa) rinse, rinsing

enjugar [enxu'ɣar] vt to wipe (off); (lágrimas) to dry; (déficit) to wipe out

enjuiciar [enxwi'θjar] vt (JUR: procesar) to prosecute, try; (fig) to judge

enlace [en'laθe] nm link, connection; (relación) relationship; (tb: ~ matrimonial) marriage; (de carretera, trenes) connection; **~ sindical** shop steward

enlatado, a [enla'taðo, a] adj (comida, productos) tinned, canned

enlazar [enla'θar] vt (unir con lazos) to bind together; (atar) to tie; (conectar) to link, connect; (AM) to lasso

enlodar [enlo'ðar] vt to cover in mud; (fig: manchar) to stain; (: rebajar) to debase

enloquecer [enloke'θer] vt to drive mad ♦ vi to go mad; **~se** vr to go mad

enlutado, a [enlu'taðo, a] adj (persona) in mourning

enmarañar [enmara'ɲar] vt (enredar) to tangle (up), entangle; (complicar) to complicate; (confundir) to confuse; **~se** vr (enredarse) to become entangled; (confundirse) to get confused

enmarcar [enmar'kar] vt (cuadro) to frame

enmascarar [enmaska'rar] vt to mask; **~se** vr to put on a mask

enmendar [enmen'dar] vt to emend, correct; (constitución etc) to amend; (comportamiento) to reform; **~se** vr to reform, mend one's ways; **enmienda** nf correction; amendment; reform

enmohecerse [enmoe'θerse] vr (metal) to rust, go rusty; (muro, plantas) to get mouldy

enmudecer [enmuðe'θer] vi (perder el habla) to fall silent; (guardar silencio) to remain silent

ennegrecer [ennevre'θer] vt (poner negro) to blacken; (oscurecer) to darken; **~se** vr to turn black; (oscurecerse) to get dark, darken

ennoblecer [ennoβle'θer] vt to ennoble

enojar [eno'xar] vt (encolerizar) to

anger; (*disgustar*) to annoy, upset; **~se**
vr to get angry; to get annoyed

enojo |e'noxo| *nm* (*cólera*) anger;
(*irritación*) annoyance; **~so, a** *adj*
annoying

enorgullecerse |enorɣuʎe'θerse| *vr*
to be proud; **~ de** to pride o.s. on, be
proud of

enorme |e'norme| *adj* enormous,
huge; (*fig*) monstrous; **enormidad** *nf*
hugeness, immensity

enrarecido, a |enrare'θiðo, a| *adj*
(*atmósfera, aire*) rarefied

enredadera |enreða'ðera| *nf* (*BOT*)
creeper, climbing plant

enredar |enre'ðar| *vt* (*cables, hilos etc*)
to tangle (up), entangle; (*situación*)
to complicate, confuse; (*meter cizaña*)
to sow discord among o between;
(*implicar*) to embroil, implicate; **~se** *vr*
to get entangled, get tangled (up);
(*situación*) to get complicated;
(*persona*) to get embroiled; (*AM: fam*)
to meddle

enredo |en'reðo| *nm* (*maraña*)
tangle; (*confusión*) mix-up, confusion;
(*intriga*) intrigue

enrejado |enre'xaðo| *nm* fence,
railings *pl*

enrevesado, a |enreβe'saðo, a| *adj*
(*asunto*) complicated, involved

enriquecer |enrike'θer| *vt* to make
rich, enrich; **~se** *vr* to get rich

enrojecer |enroxe'θer| *vt* to redden
♦ *vi* (*persona*) to blush; **~se** *vr* to blush

enrolar |enro'lar| *vt* (*MIL*) to enlist;
(*reclutar*) to recruit; **~se** *vr* (*MIL*) to join
up; (*afiliarse*) to enrol

enrollar |enro'ʎar| *vt* to roll (up), wind
(up)

enroscar |enros'kar| *vt* (*torcer, doblar*)
to coil (round), wind; (*tornillo, rosca*) to
screw in; **~se** *vr* to coil, wind

ensalada |ensa'laða| *nf* salad

ensaladilla (rusa) *nf* Russian salad

ensalzar |ensal'θar| *vt* (*alabar*) to
praise, extol; (*exaltar*) to exalt

ensamblaje |ensam'blaxe| *nm*
assembly; (*TEC*) joint

ensanchar |ensan'tʃar| *vt* (*hacer más
ancho*) to widen; (*agrandar*) to enlarge,
expand; (*COSTURA*) to let out; **~se** *vr* to
get wider, expand; **ensanche** *nm* (*de
calle*) widening

ensangrentar |ensangren'tar| *vt* to
stain with blood

ensañar |ensa'ɲar| *vt* to enrage; **~se**
vr: **~se con** to treat brutally

ensartar |ensar'tar| *vt* (*cuentas, perlas
etc*) to string (together)

ensayar |ensa'jar| *vt* to test, try (out);
(*TEATRO*) to rehearse

ensayo |en'sajo| *nm* test, trial; (*QUÍM*)
experiment; (*TEATRO*) rehearsal;
(*DEPORTE*) try; (*ESCOL, LITERATURA*) essay

enseguida |ense'ɣiða| *adv* at once,
right away

ensenada |ense'naða| *nf* inlet, cove

enseñanza |ense'ɲanθa| *nf*
(*educación*) education; (*acción*)
teaching; (*doctrina*) teaching, doctrine

enseñar |ense'ɲar| *vt* (*educar*) to
teach; (*mostrar, señalar*) to show

enseres |en'seres| *nmpl* belongings

ensillar |ensi'ʎar| *vt* to saddle (up)

ensimismarse |ensimis'marse| *vr*
(*abstraerse*) to become lost in thought;
(*AM*) to become conceited

ensombrecer |ensombre'θer| *vt* to
darken, cast a shadow over; (*fig*) to
overshadow, put in the shade

ensordecer |ensorðe'θer| *vt* to deafen
♦ *vi* to go deaf

ensortijado, a |ensorti'xaðo, a| *adj*
(*pelo*) curly

ensuciar |ensu'θjar| *vt* (*manchar*) to
dirty, soil; (*fig*) to defile; **~se** *vr* to get
dirty; (*niño*) to wet o.s.

ensueño |en'sweɲo| *nm* (*sueño*)
dream, fantasy; (*ilusión*) illusion;
(*soñando despierto*) daydream

entablar |enta'βlar| *vt* (*recubrir*) to
board (up); (*AJEDREZ, DAMAS*) to set up;
(*conversación*) to strike up; (*JUR*) to

♦ vi to draw

entablillar [entaβli'ʎar] vt (MED) to (put in a) splint

entallar [enta'ʎar] vt (traje) to tailor ♦ vi: **el traje entalla bien** the suit fits well

ente ['ente] nm (organización) body, organization; (fam: persona) odd character

entender [enten'der] vt (comprender) to understand; (darse cuenta) to realize ♦ vi to understand; (creer) to think, believe; **~se** vr (comprenderse) to be understood; (2 personas) to get on together; (ponerse de acuerdo) to agree, reach an agreement; **~ de** to know all about; **~ algo de** to know a little about; **~ en** to deal with, have to do with; **~se mal** (2 personas) to get on badly

entendido, a [enten'diðo, a] adj (comprendido) understood; (hábil) skilled; (inteligente) knowledgeable ♦ nm/f (experto) expert ♦ excl agreed!; **entendimiento** nm (comprensión) understanding; (inteligencia) mind, intellect; (juicio) judgement

enterado, a [ente'raðo, a] adj well-informed; **estar ~ de** to know about, be aware of

enteramente [entera'mente] adv entirely, completely

enterar [ente'rar] vt (informar) to inform, tell; **~se** vr to find out, get to know

entereza [ente'reθa] nf (totalidad) entirety; (fig: carácter) strength of mind; (: honradez) integrity

enternecer [enterne'θer] vt (ablandar) to soften; (apiadar) to touch, move; **~se** vr to be touched, be moved

entero, a [en'tero, a] adj (total) whole, entire; (fig: honesto) honest; (: firme) firm, resolute ♦ nm (COM: punto) point; (AM: pago) payment

enterrador [enterra'ðor] nm gravedigger

enterrar [ente'rrar] vt to bury

entibiar [enti'βjar] vt (enfriar) to cool; (calentar) to warm; **~se** vr (fig) to cool

entidad [enti'ðað] nf (empresa) firm, company; (organismo) body; (sociedad) society; (FILOSOFÍA) entity

entiendo etc vb ver **entender**

entierro [en'tjerro] nm (acción) burial; (funeral) funeral

entonación [entona'θjon] nf (LING) intonation

entonar [ento'nar] vt (canción) to intone; (colores) to tone; (MED) to tone up ♦ vi to be in tune

entonces [en'tonθes] adv then, at that time; **desde ~** since then; **en aquel ~** at that time; **(pues) ~** and so

entornar [entor'nar] vt (puerta, ventana) to half close, leave ajar; (los ojos) to screw up

entorpecer [entorpe'θer] vt (entendimiento) to dull; (impedir) to obstruct, hinder; (: tránsito) to slow down, delay

entrada [en'traða] nf (acción) entry, access; (sitio) entrance, way in; (INFORM) input; (COM) receipts pl, takings pl; (CULIN) starter; (DEPORTE) innings sg; (TEATRO) house, audience; (billete) ticket; (COM): **~s y salidas** income and expenditure; (TEC:): **~ de aire** air intake o inlet; **de ~** from the outset

entrado, a [en'traðo, a] adj: **~ en años** elderly; **una vez ~ el verano** in the summer(time), when summer comes

entramparse [entram'parse] vr to get into debt

entrante [en'trante] adj next, coming; **mes/año ~** next month/year; **~s** nmpl starters

entraña [en'traɲa] nf (fig: centro) heart, core; (raíz) root; **~s** nfpl (ANAT) entrails; (fig) heart sg; **sin ~s** heartless; **entrañable** adj close, intimate; **entrañar** vt to entail

entrar [en'trar] vt (*introducir*) to bring in; (*INFORM*) to input ♦ vi (*meterse*) to go in, come in, enter; (*comenzar*): ~ **diciendo** to begin by saying; **hacer** ~ to show in; **no me entra** I can't get the hang of it

entre ['entre] prep (*dos*) between; (*más de dos*) among(st)

entreabrir [entrea'βrir] vt to half-open, open halfway

entrecejo [entre'θexo] nm: **fruncir el** ~ to frown

entrecortado, a [entrekor'taðo, a] adj (*respiración*) difficult; (*habla*) faltering

entredicho [entre'ðitʃo] nm (*JUR*) injunction; **poner en** ~ to cast doubt on; **estar en** ~ to be in doubt

entrega [en'treɣa] nf (*de mercancías*) delivery; (*de novela etc*) instalment

entregar [entre'ɣar] vt (*dar*) to hand (over), deliver; ~**se** vr (*rendirse*) to surrender, give in, submit; (*dedicarse*) to devote o.s.

entrelazar [entrela'θar] vt to entwine

entremeses [entre'meses] nmpl hors d'œuvres

entremeter [entreme'ter] vt to insert, put in; ~**se** vr to meddle, interfere; **entremetido, a** adj meddling, interfering

entremezclar [entremeθ'klar] vt to intermingle; ~**se** vr to intermingle

entrenador, a [entrena'ðor, a] nm/f trainer, coach

entrenarse [entre'narse] vr to train

entrepierna [entre'pjerna] nf crotch

entresacar [entresa'kar] vt to pick out, select

entresuelo [entre'swelo] nm mezzanine

entretanto [entre'tanto] adv meanwhile, meantime

entretejer [entrete'xer] vt to interweave

entretener [entrete'ner] vt (*divertir*) to entertain, amuse; (*detener*) to hold up,

delay; ~**se** vr (*divertirse*) to amuse o.s.; (*retrasarse*) to delay, linger;

entretenido, a adj entertaining, amusing; **entretenimiento** nm entertainment, amusement

entrever [entre'βer] vt to glimpse, catch a glimpse of

entrevista [entre'βista] nf interview; **entrevistar** vt to interview; **entrevistarse** vr to have an interview

entristecer [entriste'θer] vt to sadden, grieve; ~**se** vr to grow sad

entrometerse [entrome'terse] vr: ~ **(en)** to interfere (in o with)

entroncar [entron'kar] vi to be connected o related

entumecer [entume'θer] vt to numb, benumb; ~**se** vr (*por el frío*) to go o become numb; **entumecido, a** adj numb, stiff

enturbiar [entur'βjar] vt (*el agua*) to make cloudy; (*fig*) to confuse; ~**se** vr (*oscurecerse*) to become cloudy; (*fig*) to get confused, become obscure

entusiasmar [entusjas'mar] vt to excite, fill with enthusiasm; (*gustar mucho*) to delight; ~**se** vr: ~**se con** o **por** to get enthusiastic o excited about

entusiasmo [entu'sjasmo] nm enthusiasm; (*excitación*) excitement

entusiasta [entu'sjasta] adj enthusiastic ♦ nm/f enthusiast

enumerar [enume'rar] vt to enumerate

enunciación [enunθja'θjon] nf enunciation

enunciado [enun'θjaðo] nm enunciation

envainar [embai'nar] vt to sheathe

envalentonar [embalento'nar] vt to give courage to; ~**se** vr (*pey: jactarse*) to boast, brag

envanecer [embane'θer] vt to make conceited; ~**se** vr to grow conceited

envasar [emba'sar] vt (*empaquetar*) to pack, wrap; (*enfrascar*) to bottle; (*enlatar*) to can; (*embolsar*) to pocket

envase [em'base] nm (en paquete) packing, wrapping; (en botella) bottling; (en lata) canning; (recipiente) container; (paquete) package; (botella) bottle; (lata) tin (BRIT), can

envejecer [embexe'θer] vt to make old, age ♦ vi (volverse viejo) to grow old; (parecer viejo) to age; ~se vr to grow old; to age

envenenar [embene'nar] vt to poison; (fig) to embitter

envergadura [emberγa'ðura] nf (fig) scope, compass

envés [em'bes] nm (de tela) back, wrong side

enviar [em'bjar] vt to send

enviciarse [embi'θjarse] vr: ~ (con) to get addicted (to)

envidia [em'biðja] nf envy; **tener** ~ **a** to envy, be jealous of; **envidiar** vt to envy

envío [em'bio] nm (acción) sending; (de mercancías) consignment; (de dinero) remittance

enviudar [embju'ðar] vi to be widowed

envoltura [embol'tura] nf (cobertura) cover; (embalaje) wrapper, wrapping; **envoltorio** nm package

envolver [embol'βer] vt to wrap (up); (cubrir) to cover; (enemigo) to surround; (implicar) to involve, implicate

envuelto [em'bwelto] pp de **envolver**

enyesar [enje'sar] vt (pared) to plaster; (MED) to put in plaster

enzarzarse [enθar'θarse] vr: ~ **en** (pelea) to get mixed up in; (disputa) to get involved in

épica ['epika] nf epic

épico, a ['epiko, a] adj epic

epidemia [epi'ðemja] nf epidemic

epilepsia [epi'lepsja] nf epilepsy

epílogo [e'piloγo] nm epilogue

episodio [epi'soðjo] nm episode

epístola [e'pistola] nf epistle

época ['epoka] nf period, time;

(HISTORIA) age, epoch; **hacer** ~ to be epoch-making

equilibrar [ekili'βrar] vt to balance; **equilibrio** nm balance, equilibrium; **equilibrista** nm/f (funámbulo) tightrope walker; (acróbata) acrobat

equipaje [eki'paxe] nm luggage; (avíos): ~ **de mano** hand luggage

equipar [eki'par] vt (proveer) to equip

equipararse [ekipa'rarse] vr: ~ **con** to be on a level with

equipo [e'kipo] nm (conjunto de cosas) equipment; (DEPORTE) team; (de obreros) shift

equis ['ekis] nf inv (the letter) X

equitación [ekita'θjon] nf horse riding

equitativo, a [ekita'tiβo, a] adj equitable, fair

equivalente [ekiβa'lente] adj, nm equivalent

equivaler [ekiβa'ler] vi to be equivalent o equal

equivocación [ekiβoka'θjon] nf mistake, error

equivocado, a [ekiβo'kaðo, a] adj wrong, mistaken

equivocarse [ekiβo'karse] vr to be wrong, make a mistake; ~ **de camino** to take the wrong road

equívoco, a [e'kiβoko, a] adj (dudoso) suspect; (ambiguo) ambiguous ♦ nm (malentendido) misunderstanding

era ['era] vb ver **ser** ♦ nf era, age

erais vb ver **ser**

éramos vb ver **ser**

eran vb ver **ser**

erario [e'rarjo] nm exchequer (BRIT), treasury

eras vb ver **ser**

erección [erek'θjon] nf erection

eres vb ver **ser**

erguir [er'xir] vt to raise, lift; (poner derecho) to straighten; ~se vr to straighten up

erigir [eri'xir] vt to erect, build; ~se vr: ~se to set o.s. up as

erizarse [eri'θarse] vr (pelo: de perro) to bristle; (: de persona) to stand on end

erizo [e'riθo] nm (ZOOL) hedgehog; ~ **de mar** sea-urchin

ermita [er'mita] nf hermitage

ermitaño, a [ermi'taɲo, a] nm/f hermit

erosión [ero'sjon] nf erosion

erosionar [erosjo'nar] vt to erode

erótico, a [e'rotiko, a] adj erotic; **erotismo** nm eroticism

erradicar [erraði'kar] vt to eradicate

errante [e'rrante] adj wandering, errant

errar [e'rrar] vi (vagar) to wander, roam; (equivocarse) to be mistaken
♦ vt: **el camino** to take the wrong road; **~ el tiro** to miss

erróneo, a [e'rroneo, a] adj (equivocado) wrong, mistaken

error [e'rror] nm error, mistake; (INFORM) bug; **~ de imprenta** misprint

eructar [eruk'tar] vt to belch, burp

erudito, a [eru'ðito, a] adj erudite, learned

erupción [erup'θjon] nf eruption; (MED) rash

es vb ver **ser**

esa ['esa] (pl **esas**) adj demos ver **ese**

ésa ['esa] (pl **esas**) pron ver **ése**

esbelto, a [es'βelto, a] adj slim, slender

esbozo [es'βoθo] nm sketch, outline

escabeche [eska'βetʃe] nm brine; (de aceitunas etc) pickle; **en ~** pickled

escabroso, a [eska'βroso, a] adj (accidentado) rough, uneven; (fig) tough, difficult; (: atrevido) risqué

escabullirse [eskaβu'ʎirse] vr to slip away, to clear out

escafandra [eska'fandra] nf (buzo) diving suit; (~ espacial) space suit

escala [es'kala] nf (proporción, MUS) scale; (de mano) ladder; (AVIAT) stopover; **hacer ~ en** to stop o call in at

escalafón [eskala'fon] nm (escala de salarios) salary scale, wage scale

escalar [eska'lar] vt to climb, scale

escalera [eska'lera] nf stairs pl, staircase; (escala) ladder; (NAIPES) run; **~ mecánica** escalator; **~ de caracol** spiral staircase

escalfar [eskal'far] vt (huevos) to poach

escalinata [eskali'nata] nf staircase

escalofriante [eskalo'frjante] adj chilling

escalofrío [eskalo'frio] nm (MED) chill; **~s** nmpl (fig) shivers

escalón [eska'lon] nm step, stair; (de escalera) rung

escalope [eska'lope] nm (CULIN) escalope

escama [es'kama] nf (de pez, serpiente) scale; (de jabón) flake; (fig) resentment

escamar [eska'mar] vt (fig) to make wary o suspicious

escamotear [eskamote'ar] vt (robar) to lift, swipe; (hacer desaparecer) to make disappear

escampar [eskam'par] vb impers to stop raining

escandalizar [eskandali'θar] vt to scandalize, shock; **~se** vr to be shocked; (ofenderse) to be offended

escándalo [es'kandalo] nm scandal; (alboroto, tumulto) row, uproar; **escandaloso, a** adj scandalous, shocking

escandinavo, a [eskandi'naβo, a] adj, nm/f Scandinavian

escaño [es'kaɲo] nm bench; (POL) seat

escapar [eska'par] vi (gen) to escape, run away; (DEPORTE) to break away; **~se** vr to escape, get away; (agua, gas) to leak (out)

escaparate [eskapa'rate] nm shop window

escape [es'kape] nm (de agua, gas) leak; (de motor) exhaust

escarabajo [eskara'βaxo] nm beetle

escaramuza [eskara'muθa] nf skirmish

escarbar [eskar'ßar] vt (tierra) to scratch

escarceos [eskar'θeos] nmpl (fig): **en mis ~ con la política ...** in my dealings with politics ...; **~ amorosos** love affairs

escarcha [es'kartʃa] nf frost

escarchado, a [eskar'tʃaðo, a] adj (CULIN: fruta) crystallized

escarlata [eskar'lata] adj inv scarlet; **escarlatina** nf scarlet fever

escarmentar [eskarmen'tar] vt to punish severely ♦ vi to learn one's lesson

escarmiento etc [eskar'mjento] vb ver **escarmentar** ♦ nm (ejemplo) lesson; (castigo) punishment

escarnio [es'karnjo] nm mockery; (injuria) insult

escarola [es'karola] nf endive

escarpado, a [eskar'paðo, a] adj (pendiente) sheer, steep; (rocas) craggy

escasear [eskase'ar] vi to be scarce

escasez [eska'seθ] nf (falta) shortage, scarcity; (pobreza) poverty

escaso, a [es'kaso, a] adj (poco) scarce; (raro) rare; (ralo) thin, sparse; (limitado) limited

escatimar [eskati'mar] vt to skimp (on), be sparing with

escayola [eska'jola] nf plaster

escena [es'θena] nf scene

escenario [esθe'narjo] nm (TEATRO) stage; (CINE) set; (fig) scene; **escenografía** nf set design

escepticismo [esθepti'θismo] nm scepticism; **escéptico, a** adj sceptical ♦ nm/f sceptic

escisión [esθi'sjon] nf (de partido, secta) split

esclarecer [esklare'θer] vt (misterio, problema) to shed light on

esclavitud [esklaßi'tuð] nf slavery

esclavizar [esklaßi'θar] vt to enslave

esclavo, a [es'klaßo, a] nm/f slave

esclusa [es'klusa] nf (de canal) lock; (compuerta) floodgate

escoba [es'koßa] nf broom; **escobilla** nf brush

escocer [esko'θer] vi to burn, sting; **~se** vr to chafe, get chafed

escocés, esa [esko'θes, esa] adj Scottish ♦ nm/f Scotsman/woman, Scot

Escocia [es'koθja] nf Scotland

escoger [esko'xer] vt to choose, pick, select; **escogido, a** adj chosen, selected

escolar [esko'lar] adj school cpd ♦ nm/f schoolboy/girl, pupil

escollo [es'koʎo] nm (obstáculo) pitfall

escolta [es'kolta] nf escort; **escoltar** vt to escort

escombros [es'kombros] nmpl (basura) rubbish sg; (restos) debris sg

esconder [eskon'der] vt to hide, conceal; **~se** vr to hide; **escondidas** (AM) nfpl: **a escondidas** secretly; **escondite** nm hiding place; (juego) hide-and-seek; **escondrijo** nm hiding place, hideout

escopeta [esko'peta] nf shotgun

escoria [es'korja] nf (de alto horno) slag; (fig) scum, dregs pl

Escorpio [es'korpjo] nm Scorpio

escorpión [eskor'pjon] nm scorpion

escotado, a [esko'taðo, a] adj low-cut

escote [es'kote] nm (de vestido) low neck; **pagar a ~** to share the expenses

escotilla [esko'tiʎa] nf (NAUT) hatch(way)

escozor [esko'θor] nm (dolor) sting(ing)

escribir [eskri'ßir] vt, vi to write; **~ a máquina** to type; **¿cómo se escribe?** how do you spell it?

escrito, a [es'krito, a] pp de **escribir** ♦ nm (documento) document; (manuscrito) text, manuscript; **por ~** in writing

escritor, a [eskri'tor, a] nm/f writer

escritorio [eskri'torjo] nm desk

escritura [eskri'tura] nf (acción) writing; (caligrafía) (hand)writing; (JUR: documento) deed

escrúpulo [es'krupulo] *nm* scruple; (*minuciosidad*) scrupulousness; **escrupuloso, a** *adj* scrupulous

escrutar [eskru'tar] *vt* to scrutinize, examine; (*votos*) to count

escrutinio [eskru'tinjo] *nm* (*examen atento*) scrutiny; (POL: *recuento de votos*) count(ing)

escuadra [es'kwaðra] *nf* (MIL etc) squad; (NAUT) squadron; (*de coches etc*) fleet; **escuadrilla** *nf* (*de aviones*) squadron; (AM: *de obreros*) gang

escuadrón [eskwa'ðron] *nm* squadron

escuálido, a [es'kwaliðo, a] *adj* skinny, scraggy; (*sucio*) squalid

escuchar [esku'tʃar] *vt* to listen to ♦ *vi* to listen

escudilla [esku'ðiʎa] *nf* bowl, basin

escudo [es'kuðo] *nm* shield

escudriñar [eskuðri'ɲar] *vt* (*examinar*) to investigate, scrutinize; (*mirar de lejos*) to scan

escuela [es'kwela] *nf* school; ~ **de artes y oficios** (ESP) ≈ technical college; ~ **normal** teacher training college

escueto, a [es'kweto, a] *adj* plain; (*estilo*) simple

escuincle [es'kwinkle] (AM: *fam*) *nm/f* kid

esculpir [eskul'pir] *vt* to sculpt; (*grabar*) to engrave; (*tallar*) to carve; **escultor, a** *nm/f* sculptor/tress; **escultura** *nf* sculpture

escupidera [eskupi'ðera] *nf* spittoon

escupir [esku'pir] *vt, vi* to spit (out)

escurreplatos [eskurre'platos] *nm inv* plate rack

escurridizo, a [eskurri'ðiθo, a] *adj* slippery

escurridor [eskurri'ðor] *nm* colander

escurrir [esku'rrir] *vt* (*ropa*) to wring out; (*verduras, platos*) to drain ♦ *vi* (*líquidos*) to drip; ~**se** *vr* (*secarse*) to drain; (*resbalarse*) to slip, slide; (*escaparse*) to slip away

ese [ese] (*f* **esa**, *pl* **esos, esas**) *adj*

demos (*sg*) that; (*pl*) those

ése [ese] (*f* **ésa**, *pl* **ésos, ésas**) *pron* (*sg*) that (one); (*pl*) those (ones); ~ ... **éste** ... the former ... the latter ...; **no me vengas con ésas** don't give me any more of that nonsense

esencia [e'senθja] *nf* essence; **esencial** *adj* essential

esfera [es'fera] *nf* sphere; (*de reloj*) face; **esférico, a** *adj* spherical

esforzarse [esfor'θarse] *vr* to exert o.s., make an effort

esfuerzo *etc* [es'fwerθo] *vb ver* **esforzar** ♦ *nm* effort

esfumarse [esfu'marse] *vr* (*apoyo, esperanzas*) to fade away

esgrima [es'rima] *nf* fencing

esgrimir [esri'mir] *vt* (*arma*) to brandish; (*argumento*) to use

esguince [es'inθe] *nm* (MED) sprain

eslabón [esla'ßon] *nm* link

eslip [ez'lip] *nm* pants *pl* (BRIT), briefs *pl*

eslovaco, a [eslo'ßako, a] *adj, nm/f* Slovak, Slovakian ♦ *nm* (LING) Slovak, Slovakian

Eslovaquia [eslo'ßakja] *nf* Slovakia

esmaltar [esmal'tar] *vt* to enamel; **esmalte** *nm* enamel; **esmalte de uñas** nail varnish o polish

esmerado, a [esme'raðo, a] *adj* careful, neat

esmeralda [esme'ralda] *nf* emerald

esmerarse [esme'rarse] *vr* (*aplicarse*) to take great pains, exercise great care; (*afanarse*) to work hard

esmero [es'mero] *nm* (great) care

esnob [es'noß] (*pl* ~s) *adj* (*persona*) snobbish ♦ *nm/f* snob; ~**ismo** *nm* snobbery

eso [eso] *pron* that, that thing o matter; ~ **de su coche** that business about his car; ~ **de ir al cine** all that about going to the cinema; **a ~ de las cinco** at about five o'clock; **en ~** thereupon, at that point; ~ **es** that's it; **¡~ sí que es vida!** now that's really living!; **por ~ te lo dije** that's why I

told you; **y ~ que llovía** in spite of
the fact it was raining

esos ['esos] *adj demos ver* **ese**

ésos ['esos] *pron ver* **ése**

espabilar *etc* [espaßi'lar] =
despabilar *etc*

espacial [espa'θjal] *adj (del espacio)*
space *cpd*

espaciar [espa'θjar] *vt* to space (out)

espacio [es'paθjo] *nm (gen)* space; *(MUS)*
interval; *(RADIO, TV)* programme *(BRIT)*,
program *(US)*; **el ~** space; **~so, a** *adj*
spacious, roomy

espada [es'paða] *nf* sword; **~s** *nfpl*
(NAIPES) spades

espaguetis [espa'γetis] *nmpl* spaghetti
sg

espalda [es'palda] *nf (gen)* back; **~s**
nfpl (hombros) shoulders; **a ~s de** one
behind sb's back; **tenderse de ~s** to
lie (down) on one's back; **volver la
~ a alguien** to cold-shoulder sb

espantajo [espan'taxo] *nm* =
espantapájaros

espantapájaros [espanta'paxaros]
nm inv scarecrow

espantar [espan'tar] *vt (asustar)* to
frighten, scare; *(ahuyentar)* to frighten
off; *(asombrar)* to horrify, appal; **~se**
vr to get frightened o scared; to be
appalled

espanto [es'panto] *nm (susto)* fright;
(terror) terror; *(asombro)* astonishment;
~so, a *adj* frightening; terrifying;
astonishing

España [es'paɲa] *nf* Spain; **español, a**
adj Spanish ♦ *nm/f* Spaniard ♦ *nm*
(LING) Spanish

esparadrapo [espara'ðrapo] *nm*
(sticking) plaster *(BRIT)*, adhesive tape
(US)

esparcimiento [esparθi'mjento] *nm*
(dispersión) spreading; *(diseminación)*
scattering; *(fig)* cheerfulness

esparcir [espar'θir] *vt* to spread;
(diseminar) to scatter; **~se** *vr* to spread
(out); to scatter; *(divertirse)* to enjoy

o.s.

espárrago [es'parraγo] *nm* asparagus

esparto [es'parto] *nm* esparto (grass)

espasmo [es'pasmo] *nm* spasm

espátula [es'patula] *nf* spatula

especia [es'peθja] *nf* spice

especial [espe'θjal] *adj* special; **~idad**
nf speciality *(BRIT)*, specialty *(US)*

especie [es'peθje] *nf (BIO)* species;
(clase) kind, sort; **en ~** in kind

especificar [espeθifi'kar] *vt* to specify;
específico, a *adj* specific

espécimen [es'peθimen] *(pl*
especímenes) *nm* specimen

espectáculo [espek'takulo] *nm (gen)*
spectacle; *(TEATRO etc)* show

espectador, a [espekta'ðor, a] *nm/f*
spectator

espectro [es'pektro] *nm* ghost; *(fig)*
spectre

especular [espeku'lar] *vt, vi* to
speculate

espejismo [espe'xismo] *nm* mirage

espejo [es'pexo] *nm* mirror;
~ retrovisor rear-view mirror

espeluznante [espeluθ'nante] *adj*
horrifying, hair-raising

espera [es'pera] *nf (pausa, intervalo)*
wait; *(JUR: plazo)* respite; **en ~ de**
waiting for; *(con expectativa)* expecting

esperanza [espe'ranθa] *nf (confianza)*
hope; *(expectativa)* expectation; **hay
pocas ~s de que venga** there is little
prospect of his coming

esperar [espe'rar] *vt (aguardar)* to wait
for; *(tener expectativa de)* to expect;
(desear) to hope for ♦ *vi* to wait; to
expect; to hope

esperma [es'perma] *nf* sperm

espesar [espe'sar] *vt* to thicken; **~se** *vr*
to thicken, get thicker

espeso, a [es'peso, a] *adj* thick;
espesor *nm* thickness

espía [es'pia] *nm/f* spy; **espiar** *vt*
(observar) to spy on

espiga [es'piγa] *nf (BOT: de trigo etc)*
ear

espigón [espi'yon] *nm* (*BOT*) ear; (*NAUT*) breakwater

espina [es'pina] *nf* thorn; (*de pez*) bone; **~ dorsal** (*ANAT*) spine

espinaca [espi'naka] *nf* spinach

espinazo [espi'naθo] *nm* spine, backbone

espinilla [espi'niʎa] *nf* (*ANAT: tibia*) shin(bone); (*grano*) blackhead

espinoso, a [espi'noso, a] *adj* (*planta*) thorny, prickly; (*asunto*) difficult

espionaje [espjo'naxe] *nm* spying, espionage

espiral [espi'ral] *adj, nf* spiral

espirar [espi'rar] *vt* to breathe out, exhale

espiritista [espiri'tista] *adj, nm/f* spiritualist

espíritu [es'piritu] *nm* spirit; **espiritual** *adj* spiritual

espita [es'pita] *nf* tap

espléndido, a [es'plendiðo, a] *adj* (*magnífico*) magnificent, splendid; (*generoso*) generous

esplendor [esplen'dor] *nm* splendour

espolear [espole'ar] *vt* to spur on

espoleta [espo'leta] *nf* (*de bomba*) fuse

espolón [espo'lon] *nm* sea wall

espolvorear [espolβore'ar] *vt* to dust, sprinkle

esponja [es'ponxa] *nf* sponge; (*fig*) sponger; **esponjoso, a** *adj* spongy

espontaneidad [espontanei'ðað] *nf* spontaneity; **espontáneo, a** *adj* spontaneous

esposa [es'posa] *nf* wife; **~s** *nfpl* handcuffs; **esposar** *vt* to handcuff

esposo [es'poso] *nm* husband

espray [es'prai] *nm* spray

espuela [es'pwela] *nf* spur

espuma [es'puma] *nf* foam; (*de cerveza*) froth, head; (*de jabón*) lather; **espumadera** *nf* (*utensilio*) skimmer; **espumoso, a** *adj* frothy, foamy; (*vino*) sparkling

esqueleto [eske'leto] *nm* skeleton

esquema [es'kema] *nm* (*diagrama*) diagram; (*dibujo*) plan; (*FILOSOFÍA*) schema

esquí [es'ki] (*pl* **~s**) *nm* (*objeto*) ski; (*DEPORTE*) skiing; **~ acuático** water-skiing; **esquiar** *vi* to ski

esquilar [eski'lar] *vt* to shear

esquimal [eski'mal] *adj, nm/f* Eskimo

esquina [es'kina] *nf* corner

esquinazo [eski'naθo] *nm*: **dar ~ a algn** to give sb the slip

esquirol [eski'rol] *nm* blackleg

esquivar [eski'βar] *vt* to avoid

esquivo, a [es'kiβo, a] *adj* evasive; (*tímido*) reserved; (*huraño*) unsociable

esta [esta] *adj* demos ver **este²**

está *vb ver* **estar**

ésta [esta] *pron ver* **éste**

estabilidad [estaβili'ðað] *nf* stability; **estable** *adj* stable

establecer [estaβle'θer] *vt* to establish; **~se** *vr* to establish o.s.; (*echar raíces*) to settle (down); **establecimiento** *nm* establishment

establo [es'taβlo] *nm* (*AGR*) stable

estaca [es'taka] *nf* stake, post; (*de tienda de campaña*) peg

estacada [esta'kaða] *nf* (*cerca*) fence, fencing; (*palenque*) stockade

estación [esta'θjon] *nf* station; (*del año*) season; **~ de autobuses** bus station; **~ balnearia** seaside resort; **~ de servicio** service station

estacionamiento [estaθjona'mjento] *nm* (*AUTO*) parking; (*MIL*) stationing

estacionar [estaθjo'nar] *vt* (*AUTO*) to park; (*MIL*) to station; **~io, a** *adj* stationary; (*COM: mercado*) slack

estadio [es'taðjo] *nm* (*fase*) stage, phase; (*DEPORTE*) stadium

estadista [esta'ðista] *nm* (*POL*) statesman; (*ESTADÍSTICA*) statistician

estadística [esta'ðistika] *nf* figure, statistic; (*ciencia*) statistics *sg*

estado [es'taðo] *nm* (*POL: condición*) state; **~ de ánimo** state of mind; **~ de cuenta** bank statement; **~ de sitio** state of siege; **~ civil** marital status;

~ mayor staff; **estar en ~** to be pregnant; **(los) E~s Unidos** nmpl the United States (of America) sg

estadounidense [estaðouni'ðense] adj United States cpd, American ♦ nm/f American

estafa [es'tafa] nf swindle, trick;

estafar vt to swindle, defraud

estafeta [esta'feta] nf (oficina de correos) post office; **~ diplomática** diplomatic bag

estáis vb ver **estar**

estallar [esta'ʎar] vi to burst; (bomba) to explode, go off; (epidemia, guerra, rebelión) to break out; **~ en llanto** to burst into tears; **estallido** nm explosion; (fig) outbreak

estampa [es'tampa] nf print, engraving

estampado, a [estam'paðo, a] adj printed ♦ nm (impresión: acción) printing; (: efecto) print; (marca) stamping

estampar [estam'par] vt (imprimir) to print; (marcar) to stamp; (metal) to engrave; (poner sello en) to stamp; (fig) to stamp, imprint

estampida [estam'piða] nf stampede

estampido [estam'piðo] nm bang, report

están vb ver **estar**

estancado, a [estan'kaðo, a] adj stagnant

estancar [estan'kar] vt (aguas) to hold up, hold back; (COM) to monopolize; (fig) to block, hold up; **~se** vr to stagnate

estancia [es'tanθja] nf (permanencia) stay; (sala) room; (AM) farm, ranch; **estanciero** (AM) nm farmer, rancher

estanco, a [es'tanko, a] adj watertight ♦ nm tobacconist's (shop), cigar store (US)

Estanco

Cigarettes, tobacco, postage stamps and official forms are all sold under

state monopoly in shops called an estanco. Although tobacco products can also be bought in bars and quioscos they are generally more expensive.

estándar [es'tandar] adj, nm standard;

estandarizar vt to standardize

estandarte [estan'darte] nm banner, standard

estanque [es'tanke] nm (lago) pool, pond; (AGR) reservoir

estanquero, a [estan'kero, a] nm/f tobacconist

estante [es'tante] nm (armario) rack, stand; (biblioteca) bookcase; (anaquel) shelf; (AM) prop; **estantería** nf shelving, shelves pl

estaño [es'taɲo] nm tin

PALABRA CLAVE

estar [es'tar] vi **1** (posición) to be; **está en la plaza** it's in the square; **¿está Juan?** is Juan in?; **estamos a 30 km de Junín** we're 30 kms from Junín
2 (+ adj: estado) to be; **~ enfermo** to be ill; **está muy elegante** he's looking very smart; **¿cómo estás?** how are you keeping?
3 (+ gerundio) to be; **estoy leyendo** I'm reading
4 (uso pasivo): **está condenado a muerte** he's been condemned to death; **está envasado en ...** it's packed in ...
5 (con fechas): **¿a cuántos estamos?** what's the date today?; **estamos a 5 de mayo** it's the 5th of May
6 (locuciones): **¿estamos?** (¿de acuerdo?) okay?; (¿listo?) ready?; **¡ya está bien!** that's enough!
7: **~ de**: **~ de vacaciones/viaje** to be on holiday/away on a trip; **está de camarero** he's working as a waiter
8: **~ para**: **está para salir** he's about to leave; **no estoy para bromas** I'm not in the mood for jokes

9: ~ por (*propuesta etc*) to be in favour of; (*persona etc*) to support, side with; **está por limpiar** it still has to be cleaned

10: ~ sin: ~ sin dinero to have no money; **está sin terminar** it isn't finished yet

♦ **~se** *vr*: **se estuvo en la cama toda la tarde** he stayed in bed all afternoon

estas ['estas] *adj demos ver* **este²**

éstas ['estas] *pron ver* **éste**

estatal [esta'tal] *adj* state *cpd*

estático, a [es'tatiko, a] *adj* static

estatua [es'tatwa] *nf* statue

estatura [esta'tura] *nf* stature, height

estatuto [esta'tuto] *nm* (*JUR*) statute; (*de ciudad*) bye-law; (*de comité*) rule

este¹ ['este] *nm* east

este² ['este] (*f* **esta**, *pl* **estos, estas**) *adj demos* (*sg*) this; (*pl*) these

esté *etc vb ver* **estar**

éste ['este] (*f* **ésta**, *pl* **éstos, éstas**) *pron* (*sg*) this (one); (*pl*) these (ones); **ése ... ~ ...** the former ... the latter ....

estelar [este'lar] *adj* (*ASTRO*) stellar; (*actuación, reparto*) star (*atr*)

estén *etc vb ver* **estar**

estepa [es'tepa] *nf* (*GEO*) steppe

estera [es'tera] *nf* mat(ting)

estéreo [es'tereo] *adj inv, nm* stereo; **estereotipo** *nm* stereotype

estéril [es'teril] *adj* sterile, barren; (*fig*) vain, futile; **esterilizar** *vt* to sterilize

esterlina [ester'lina] *adj*: **libra ~** pound sterling

estés *etc vb ver* **estar**

estética [es'tetika] *nf* aesthetics *sg*

estético, a [es'tetiko, a] *adj* aesthetic

estibador [estiβa'ðor] *nm* stevedore, docker

estiércol [es'tjerkol] *nm* dung, manure

estigma [es'tiɣma] *nm* stigma

estilarse [esti'larse] *vr* to be in fashion

estilo [es'tilo] *nm* style; (*TEC*) stylus; (*NATACIÓN*) stroke; **algo por el ~**

something along those lines

estima [es'tima] *nf* esteem, respect

estimación [estima'θjon] *nf* (*evaluación*) estimation; (*aprecio, afecto*) esteem, regard

estimar [esti'mar] *vt* (*evaluar*) to estimate; (*valorar*) to value; (*apreciar*) to esteem, respect; (*pensar, considerar*) to think, reckon

estimulante [estimu'lante] *adj* stimulating ♦ *nm* stimulant

estimular [estimu'lar] *vt* to stimulate; (*excitar*) to excite

estímulo [es'timulo] *nm* stimulus; (*ánimo*) encouragement

estipulación [estipula'θjon] *nf* stipulation, condition

estipular [estipu'lar] *vt* to stipulate

estirado, a [esti'raðo, a] *adj* (*tenso*) (stretched *o* drawn) tight; (*fig*: *persona*) stiff, pompous

estirar [esti'rar] *vt* to stretch; (*dinero, suma etc*) to stretch out; **~se** *vr* to stretch

estirón [esti'ron] *nm* pull, tug; (*crecimiento*) spurt, sudden growth; **dar un ~** (*niño*) to shoot up

estirpe [es'tirpe] *nf* stock, lineage

estival [esti'βal] *adj* summer *cpd*

esto ['esto] *pron* this, this thing *o* matter; **~ de la boda** this business about the wedding

Estocolmo [esto'kolmo] *nm* Stockholm

estofado [esto'faðo] *nm* stew

estofar [esto'far] *vt* to stew

estómago [es'tomaɣo] *nm* stomach; **tener ~** to be thick-skinned

estorbar [estor'βar] *vt* to hinder, obstruct; (*molestar*) to bother, disturb ♦ *vi* to be in the way; **estorbo** *nm* (*molestia*) bother, nuisance; (*obstáculo*) hindrance, obstacle

estornudar [estornu'ðar] *vi* to sneeze

estos ['estos] *adj demos ver* **este²**

éstos ['estos] *pron ver* **éste**

estoy *vb ver* **estar**

estrado [es'traðo] nm platform

estrafalario, a [estrafa'larjo, a] adj odd, eccentric

estrago [es'travo] nm ruin, destruction; **hacer ~s en** to wreak havoc among

estragón [estra'von] nm tarragon

estrambótico, a [estram'botiko, a] adj (persona) eccentric; (peinado, ropa) outlandish

estrangulador, a [estrangula'ðor, a] nm/f strangler ♦ nm (TEC) throttle; (AUTO) choke

estrangular [estrangu'lar] vt (persona) to strangle; (MED) to strangulate

estratagema [estrata'xema] nf (MIL) stratagem; (astucia) cunning

estrategia [estra'texja] nf strategy; **estratégico, a** adj strategic

estrato [es'trato] nm stratum, layer

estrechamente [es'tretʃamente] adv (íntimamente) closely, intimately; (pobremente: vivir) poorly

estrechar [estre'tʃar] vt (reducir) to narrow; (COSTURA) to take in; (abrazar) to hug, embrace; **~se** vr (reducirse) to narrow, grow narrow; (abrazarse) to embrace; **~ la mano** to shake hands

estrechez [estre'tʃeθ] nf narrowness; (de ropa) tightness; **estrecheces** nfpl (dificultades económicas) financial difficulties

estrecho, a [es'tretʃo, a] adj narrow; (apretado) tight; (íntimo) close, intimate; (miserable) mean ♦ nm strait; **~ de miras** narrow-minded

estrella [es'treʎa] nf star; **~ de mar** (ZOOL) starfish; **~ fugaz** shooting star; **estrellado, a** adj (forma) star-shaped; (cielo) starry

estrellar [estre'ʎar] vt (hacer añicos) to smash (to pieces); (huevos) to fry; **~se** vr to smash; (chocarse) to crash; (fracasar) to fail

estremecer [estreme'θer] vt to shake; **~se** vr to shake, tremble; **estremecimiento** nm (temblor)

trembling, shaking

estrenar [estre'nar] vt (vestido) to wear for the first time; (casa) to move into; (película, obra de teatro) to première; **~se** vr (persona) to make one's début; **estreno** nm (CINE etc) première

estreñido, a [estre'ɲiðo, a] adj constipated

estreñimiento [estreɲi'mjento] nm constipation

estrépito [es'trepito] nm noise, racket; (fig) fuss; **estrepitoso, a** adj noisy; (fiesta) rowdy

estría [es'tria] nf groove

estribación [estriβa'θjon] nf (GEO) spur, foothill

estribar [estri'ßar] vi: **~ en** to lie on

estribillo [estri'ßiʎo] nm (LITERATURA) refrain; (MUS) chorus

estribo [es'trißo] nm (de jinete) stirrup; (de coche, tren) step; (de puente) support; (GEO) spur; **perder los ~s** to fly off the handle

estribor [estri'ßor] nm (NAUT) starboard

estricto, a [es'trikto, a] adj (riguroso) strict; (severo) severe

estridente [estri'ðente] adj (color) loud; (voz) raucous

estropajo [estro'paxo] nm scourer

estropear [estrope'ar] vt to spoil; (dañar) to damage; **~se** vr (objeto) to get damaged; (persona: la piel etc) to be ruined

estructura [estruk'tura] nf structure

estruendo [es'trwendo] nm (ruido) racket, din; (fig: alboroto) uproar, turmoil

estrujar [estru'xar] vt (apretar) to squeeze; (aplastar) to crush; (fig) to drain, bleed

estuario [es'twarjo] nm estuary

estuche [es'tutʃe] nm box, case

estudiante [estu'ðjante] nm/f student; **estudiantil** adj student cpd

estudiar [estu'ðjar] vt to study

estudio [es'tuðjo] nm study; (CINE,

ARTE, RADIO) studio; **~s** *nmpl* studies; (*erudición*) learning *sg*; **~so, a** *adj* studious

estufa [es'tufa] *nf* heater, fire

estupefaciente [estupefa'θjente] *nm* drug, narcotic

estupefacto, a [estupe'fakto, a] *adj* speechless, thunderstruck

estupendo, a [estu'pendo, a] *adj* wonderful, terrific; (*fam*) great; **¡~!** that's great!, fantastic!

estupidez [estupi'ðeθ] *nf* (*torpeza*) stupidity; (*acto*) stupid thing (to do)

estúpido, a [es'tupiðo, a] *adj* stupid, silly

estupor [estu'por] *nm* stupor; (*fig*) astonishment, amazement

estuve *etc vb ver* **estar**

esvástica [es'βastika] *nf* swastika

ETA ['eta] (*ESP*) *nf abr* (= Euskadi ta Askatasuna) ETA

etapa [e'tapa] *nf* (*de viaje*) stage; (*DEPORTE*) leg; (*parada*) stopping place; (*fase*) stage, phase

etarra [e'tarra] *nm/f* member of ETA

etc. *abr* (= etcétera) etc

etcétera [et'θetera] *adv* etcetera

eternidad [eterni'ðað] *nf* eternity; **eterno, a** *adj* eternal, everlasting

ética ['etika] *nf* ethics *pl*

ético, a ['etiko, a] *adj* ethical

etiqueta [eti'keta] *nf* (*modales*) etiquette; (*rótulo*) label, tag

Eucaristía [eukaris'tia] *nf* Eucharist

eufemismo [eufe'mismo] *nm* euphemism

euforia [eu'forja] *nf* euphoria

euro ['euro] *sm* (*moneda*) euro

eurodiputado, a [euroðipu'taðo, a] *nm/f* Euro MP, MEP

Europa [eu'ropa] *nf* Europe; **europeo, a** *adj, nm/f* European

Euskadi [eus'kaði] *nm* the Basque Country *o* Provinces *pl*

euskera [eus'kera] *nm* (*LING*) Basque

evacuación [eβakwa'θjon] *nf* evacuation

evacuar [eβa'kwar] *vt* to evacuate

evadir [eβa'ðir] *vt* to evade, avoid; **~se** *vr* to escape

evaluar [eβa'lwar] *vt* to evaluate

evangelio [eβan'xeljo] *nm* gospel

evaporar [eβapo'rar] *vt* to evaporate; **~se** *vr* to vanish

evasión [eβa'sjon] *nf* escape, flight; (*fig*) evasion; **~ de capitales** flight of capital

evasiva [eβa'siβa] *nf* (*pretexto*) excuse

evasivo, a [eβa'siβo, a] *adj* evasive, non-committal

evento [e'βento] *nm* event

eventual [eβen'twal] *adj* possible, conditional (upon circumstances); (*trabajador*) casual, temporary

evidencia [eβi'ðenθja] *nf* evidence, proof; **evidenciar** *vt* (*hacer patente*) to make evident; (*probar*) to prove, show; **evidenciarse** *vr* to be evident

evidente [eβi'ðente] *adj* obvious, clear, evident

evitar [eβi'tar] *vt* (*evadir*) to avoid; (*impedir*) to prevent

evocar [eβo'kar] *vt* to evoke, call forth

evolución [eβolu'θjon] *nf* (*desarrollo*) evolution, development; (*cambio*) change; (*MIL*) manoeuvre; **evolucionar** *vi* to evolve; to manoeuvre

ex [eks] *adj* ex-; **el ~ ministro** the former minister, the ex-minister

exacerbar [eksaθer'βar] *vt* to irritate, annoy

exactamente [eksakta'mente] *adv* exactly

exactitud [eksakti'tuð] *nf* exactness; (*precisión*) accuracy; (*puntualidad*) punctuality; **exacto, a** *adj* exact; accurate; punctual; **¡exacto!** exactly!

exageración [eksaxera'θjon] *nf* exaggeration

exagerar [eksaxe'rar] *vt, vi* to exaggerate

exaltado, a [eksal'taðo, a] *adj* (*apasionado*) over-excited, worked-up; (*POL*) extreme

exaltar [eksal'tar] vt to exalt, glorify; **~se** vr (excitarse) to get excited o worked-up

examen [ek'samen] nm examination

examinar [eksami'nar] vt to examine; **~se** vr to be examined, take an examination

exasperar [eksaspe'rar] vt to exasperate; **~se** vr to get exasperated, lose patience

Exca. abr = **Excelencia**

excavadora [ekskaßa'ðora] nf excavator

excavar [ekska'ßar] vt to excavate

excedencia [eksθe'ðenθja] nf: **estar en ~** to be on leave; **pedir** o **solicitar la ~** to ask for leave

excedente [eksθe'ðente] adj, nm excess, surplus

exceder [eksθe'ðer] vt to exceed, surpass; **~se** vr (extralimitarse) to go too far

excelencia [eksθe'lenθja] nf excellence; **E~** Excellency; **excelente** adj excellent

excentricidad [eksθentriθi'ðað] nf eccentricity; **excéntrico, a** adj, nm/f eccentric

excepción [eksθep'θjon] nf exception; **excepcional** adj exceptional

excepto [eks'θepto] adv excepting, except (for)

exceptuar [eksθep'twar] vt to except, exclude

excesivo, a [eksθe'sißo, a] adj excessive

exceso [eks'θeso] nm (gen) excess; (COM) surplus; **~ de equipaje/peso** excess luggage/weight

excitación [eksθita'θjon] nf (sensación) excitement; (acción) excitation

excitado, a [eksθi'taðo, a] adj excited; (emociones) aroused

excitar [eksθi'tar] vt to excite; (incitar) to urge; **~se** vr to get excited

exclamación [eksklama'θjon] nf exclamation

exclamar [ekskla'mar] vi to exclaim

excluir [eksklu'ir] vt to exclude; (dejar fuera) to shut out; (descartar) to reject; **exclusión** nf exclusion

exclusiva [eksklu'sißa] nf (PRENSA) exclusive, scoop; (COM) sole right

exclusivo, a [eksklu'sißo, a] adj exclusive; **derecho ~** sole o exclusive right

Excmo. abr = **excelentísimo**

excomulgar [ekskomul'ʊar] vt (REL) to excommunicate

excomunión [ekskomu'njon] nf excommunication

excursión [ekskur'sjon] nf excursion, outing; **excursionista** nm/f (turista) sightseer

excusa [eks'kusa] nf excuse; (disculpa) apology

excusar [eksku'sar] vt to excuse; **~se** vr (disculparse) to apologize

exhalar [eksa'lar] vt to exhale, breathe out; (olor etc) to give off; (suspiro) to breathe, heave

exhaustivo, a [eksaus'tißo, a] adj (análisis) thorough; (estudio) exhaustive

exhausto, a [ek'sausto, a] adj exhausted

exhibición [eksißi'θjon] nf exhibition, display, show

exhibir [eksi'ßir] vt to exhibit, display, show

exhortar [eksor'tar] vt: **~ a** to exhort to

exigencia [eksi'xenθja] nf demand, requirement; **exigente** adj demanding

exigir [eksi'xir] vt (gen) to demand, require; **~ el pago** to demand payment

exiliado, a [eksi'ljaðo, a] adj exiled ♦ nm/f exile

exilio [ek'siljo] nm exile

eximir [eksi'mir] vt to exempt

existencia [eksis'tenθja] nf existence; **~s** nfpl stock(s) (pl)

existir [eksis'tir] vi to exist, be

éxito ['eksito] nm (triunfo) success; (MUS etc) hit; **tener ~** to be successful

exonerar [eksone'rar] vt to exonerate; **~ de una obligación** to free from an obligation

exorbitante [eksorßi'tante] adj (precio) exorbitant; (cantidad) excessive

exorcizar [eksorθi'θar] vt to exorcize

exótico, a [ek'sotiko, a] adj exotic

expandir [ekspan'dir] vt to expand

expansión [ekspan'sjon] nf expansion

expansivo, a [ekspan'sißo, a] adj: **onda ~a** shock wave

expatriarse [ekspa'trjarse] vr to emigrate; (POL) to go into exile

expectativa [ekspekta'tißa] nf (espera) expectation; (perspectiva) prospect

expedición [ekspeði'θjon] nf (excursión) expedition

expediente [ekspe'ðjente] nm expedient; (JUR: procedimiento) action, proceedings pl; (: papeles) dossier, file, record

expedir [ekspe'ðir] vt (despachar) to send, forward; (pasaporte) to issue

expendedor, a [ekspende'ðor, a] nm/f (vendedor) dealer

expensas [eks'pensas] nfpl: **a ~ de** at the expense of

experiencia [ekspe'rjenθja] nf experience

experimentado, a [eksperimen'taðo, a] adj experienced

experimentar [eksperimen'tar] vt (en laboratorio) to experiment with; (probar) to test, try out; (notar, observar) to experience; (deterioro, pérdida) to suffer; **experimento** nm experiment

experto, a [eks'perto, a] adj expert, skilled ♦ nm/f expert

expiar [ekspi'ar] vt to atone for

expirar [ekspi'rar] vi to expire

explanada [ekspla'naða] nf (llano) plain

explayarse [ekspla'jarse] vr (en discurso) to speak at length; **~ con**

uno to confide in sb

explicación [eksplika'θjon] nf explanation

explicar [ekspli'kar] vt to explain; **~se** vr to explain (o.s.)

explícito, a [eks'pliθito, a] adj explicit

explique etc vb ver **explicar**

explorador, a [eksplora'ðor, a] nm/f (pionero) explorer; (MIL) scout ♦ nm (MED) probe; (TEC) (radar) scanner

explorar [eksplo'rar] vt to explore; (MED) to probe; (radar) to scan

explosión [eksplo'sjon] nf explosion; **explosivo, a** adj explosive

explotación [eksplota'θjon] nf exploitation; (de planta etc) running

explotar [eksplo'tar] vt to exploit; to run, operate ♦ vi to explode

exponer [ekspo'ner] vt to expose; (cuadro) to display; (vida) to risk, (idea) to explain; **~se** vr: **~se a (hacer) algo** to run the risk of (doing) sth

exportación [eksporta'θjon] nf (acción) export; (mercancías) exports pl

exportar [ekspor'tar] vt to export

exposición [eksposi'θjon] nf (gen) exposure; (de arte) show, exhibition; (explicación) explanation; (declaración) account, statement

expresamente [ekspresa'mente] adv (decir) clearly; (a propósito) expressly

expresar [ekspre'sar] vt to express; **expresión** nf expression

expresivo, a [ekspre'sißo, a] adj (persona, gesto, palabras) expressive; (cariñoso) affectionate

expreso, a [eks'preso, a] pp de **expresar** ♦ adj (explícito) express; (claro) specific, clear; (tren) fast ♦ adv: **mandar ~** to send by express (delivery)

express [eks'pres] (AM) adv: **enviar algo ~** to send sth special delivery

exprimidor [eksprimi'ðor] nm squeezer

exprimir [ekspri'mir] vt (fruta) to squeeze; (zumo) to squeeze out

expropiar |ekspro'pjar| *vt* to expropriate

expuesto, a |eks'pwesto, a| *pp de* **exponer ♦** *adj* exposed; (*cuadro etc*) on show, on display

expulsar |ekspul'sar| *vt* (*echar*) to eject, throw out; (*alumno*) to expel; (*despedir*) to sack, fire; (*DEPORTE*) to send off; **expulsión** *nf* expulsion; sending-off

exquisito, a |ekski'sito, a| *adj* exquisite; (*comida*) delicious

éxtasis |'ekstasis| *nm* ecstasy

extender |eksten'der| *vt* to extend; (*los brazos*) to stretch out, hold out; (*mapa, tela*) to spread (out), open (out); (*mantequilla*) to spread; (*certificado*) to issue; (*cheque, recibo*) to make out; (*documento*) to draw up; **~se** *vr* (*gen*) to extend; (*persona: en el suelo*) to stretch out; (*epidemia*) to spread; **extendido, a** *adj* (*abierto*) spread out, open; (*brazos*) outstretched; (*costumbre*) widespread

extensión |eksten'sjon| *nf* (*de terreno, mar*) expanse, stretch; (*de tiempo*) length, duration; (*TEL*) extension; **en toda la ~ de la palabra** in every sense of the word

extenso, a |eks'tenso, a| *adj* extensive

extenuar |ekste'nwar| *vt* (*debilitar*) to weaken

exterior |ekste'rjor| *adj* (*de fuera*) external; (*afuera*) outside, exterior; (*apariencia*) outward; (*deuda, relaciones*) foreign ♦ *nm* (*gen*) exterior, outside; (*aspecto*) outward appearance; (*DEPORTE*) wing(er); (*países extranjeros*) abroad; **en el ~** abroad; **al ~** outwardly, on the surface

exterminar |ekstermi'nar| *vt* to exterminate; **exterminio** *nm* extermination

externo, a |eks'terno, a| *adj* (*exterior*) external, outside; (*superficial*) outward ♦ *nm/f* day pupil

extinguir |ekstin'gir| *vt* (*fuego*) to

extinguish, put out; (*raza, población*) to wipe out; **~se** *vr* (*fuego*) to go out; (*BIO*) to die out, become extinct

extinto, a |eks'tinto, a| *adj* extinct

extintor |ekstin'tor| *nm* (*fire*) extinguisher

extirpar |ekstir'par| *vt* (*MED*) to remove (surgically)

extorsión |ekstor'sjon| *nf* extortion

extra |'ekstra| *adj inv* (*tiempo*) extra; (*chocolate, vino*) good-quality ♦ *nm/f* extra ♦ *nm* (*bono*) bonus

extracción |ekstrak'θjon| *nf* extraction; (*en lotería*) draw

extracto |eks'trakto| *nm* extract

extradición |ekstraði'θjon| *nf* extradition

extraer |ekstra'er| *vt* to extract, take out

extraescolar |ekstraesko'lar| *adj*: **actividad ~** extracurricular activity

extralimitarse |ekstralimi'tarse| *vr* to go too far

extranjero, a |ekstran'xero, a| *adj* foreign ♦ *nm/f* foreigner ♦ *nm* foreign countries *pl*; **en el ~** abroad

extrañar |ekstra'ɲar| *vt* (*sorprender*) to find strange o odd; (*echar de menos*) to miss; **~se** *vr* (*sorprenderse*) to be amazed, be surprised

extrañeza |ekstra'ɲeθa| *nf* (*rareza*) strangeness, oddness; (*asombro*) amazement, surprise

extraño, a |eks'traɲo, a| *adj* (*extranjero*) foreign; (*raro, sorprendente*) strange, odd

extraordinario, a |ekstraorði'narjo, a| *adj* extraordinary; (*edición, número*) special ♦ *nm* (*de periódico*) special edition; **horas extraordinarias** overtime *sg*

extrarradio |ekstra'rraðjo| *nm* suburbs

extravagancia |ekstraβa'xanθja| *nf* oddness; outlandishness;

extravagante *adj* (*excéntrico*) eccentric; (*estrafalario*) outlandish

extraviado, a |ekstra'βjaðo, a| *adj*

lost, missing

extraviar [ekstra'βjar] vt (persona: desorientar) to mislead, misdirect; (perder) to lose, misplace; **~se** vr to lose one's way, get lost; **extravío** nm loss; (fig) deviation

extremar [ekstre'mar] vt to carry to extremes; **~se** vr to do one's utmost, make every effort

extremaunción [ekstremaun'θjon] nf extreme unction

extremidad [ekstremi'ðað] nf (punta) extremity; **~es** nfpl (ANAT) extremities

extremo, a [eks'tremo, a] adj extreme; (último) last ♦ nm end; (límite, grado sumo) extreme; **en último ~** as a last resort

extrovertido, a [ekstroßer'tiðo, a] adj, nm/f extrovert

exuberancia [eksuße'ranθja] nf exuberance; **exuberante** adj exuberant; (fig) luxuriant, lush

eyacular [ejaku'lar] vt, vi to ejaculate

F, f

f.a.b. abr (= franco a bordo) f.o.b.

fabada [fa'βaða] nf bean and sausage stew

fábrica [fa'βrika] nf factory; **marca de ~** trademark; **precio de ~** factory price

fabricación [faβrika'θjon] nf (manufactura) manufacture; (producción) production; **de ~ casera** home-made; **~ en serie** mass production

fabricante [faβri'kante] nm/f manufacturer

fabricar [faβri'kar] vt (manufacturar) to manufacture, make; (construir) to build; (cuento) to fabricate, devise

fábula ['faβula] nf (cuento) fable; (chisme) rumour; (mentira) fib

fabuloso, a [faβu'loso, a] adj (oportunidad, tiempo) fabulous, great

facción [fak'θjon] nf (POL) faction;

facciones nfpl (del rostro) features

faceta [fa'θeta] nf facet

facha ['fatʃa] (fam) nf (aspecto) look; (cara) face

fachada [fa'tʃaða] nf (ARQ) façade, front

fácil ['faθil] adj (simple) easy; (probable) likely

facilidad [faθili'ðað] nf (capacidad) ease; (sencillez) simplicity; (de palabra) fluency; **~es** nfpl facilities

facilitar [faθili'tar] vt (hacer fácil) to make easy; (proporcionar) to provide

fácilmente [faθil'mente] adv easily

facsímil [fak'simil] nm facsimile, fax

factible [fak'tiβle] adj feasible

factor [fak'tor] nm factor

factura [fak'tura] nf (cuenta) bill; **facturación** nf (de equipaje) check-in; (COM) invoicing

facturar vt (COM) to invoice, charge for; (equipaje) to check in

facultad [fakul'tað] nf (aptitud, ESCOL etc) faculty; (poder) power

faena [fa'ena] nf (trabajo) work; (quehacer) task, job

faisán [fai'san] nm pheasant

faja ['faxa] nf (para la cintura) sash; (de mujer) corset; (de tierra) strip

fajo ['faxo] nm (de papeles) bundle; (de billetes) wad

falacia [fa'laθja] nf fallacy

falda ['falda] nf (prenda de vestir) skirt

falla ['faʎa] nf (defecto) fault, flaw

fallar [fa'ʎar] vt (JUR) to pronounce sentence on ♦ vi (memoria) to fail; (motor) to miss

---

Fallas

In the week of 19 March (the feast of San José), Valencia honours its patron saint with a spectacular fiesta called **Las Fallas.** *The* **Fallas** *are huge papier-mâché, cardboard and wooden sculptures which are built by competing teams throughout the year. They depict politicians and well-known public figures and are thrown*

onto bonfires and set alight once a
jury has judged them - only the best
sculpture escapes the flames.

fallecer [faʎe'θer] vi to pass away, die;
fallecimiento nm decease, demise
fallido, a [fa'ʎiðo, a] adj (gen)
frustrated, unsuccessful
fallo ['faʎo] nm (JUR) verdict, ruling;
(fracaso) failure; ~ **cardíaco** heart
failure
falsedad [false'ðað] nf falseness;
(hipocresía) hypocrisy; (mentira)
falsehood
falsificar [falsifi'kar] vt (firma etc) to
forge; (moneda) to counterfeit
falso, a ['falso, a] adj false;
(documento, moneda etc) fake; **en ~**
falsely
falta ['falta] nf (defecto) fault, flaw;
(privación) lack, want; (ausencia)
absence; (carencia) shortage;
(equivocación) mistake; (DEPORTE) foul;
echar en ~ to miss; **hacer ~ hacer**
algo to be necessary to do sth; **me**
hace ~ una pluma I need a pen;
~ de educación bad manners pl
faltar [fal'tar] vi (escasear) to be
lacking, be wanting; (ausentarse) to be
absent, be missing; **faltan 2 horas**
para llegar there are 2 hours to go till
arrival; **~ al respeto a uno** to be
disrespectful to sb; **¡no faltaba más!**
(no hay de qué) don't mention it!
fama ['fama] nf (renombre) fame;
(reputación) reputation
famélico, a [fa'meliko, a] adj starving
familia [fa'milja] nf family; **~ política**
in-laws pl
familiar [fami'ljar] adj (relativo a la
familia) family cpd; (conocido, informal)
familiar ♦ nm relative, relation; **~idad**
nf (gen) familiarity; (informalidad)
homeliness; **~izarse** vr: **~izarse con**
to familiarize o.s. with
famoso, a [fa'moso, a] adj
(renombrado) famous

fanático, a [fa'natiko, a] adj fanatical
♦ nm/f fanatic; (CINE, DEPORTE) fan;
fanatismo nm fanaticism
fanfarrón, ona [fanfa'rron, ona] adj
boastful
fango ['fango] nm mud; **~so, a** adj
muddy
fantasía [fanta'sia] nf fantasy,
imagination; **joyas de ~** imitation
jewellery sg
fantasma [fan'tasma] nm (espectro)
ghost, apparition; (fanfarrón) show-off
fantástico, a [fan'tastiko, a] adj
fantastic
farmacéutico, a [farma'θeutiko, a]
adj pharmaceutical ♦ nm/f chemist
(BRIT), pharmacist
farmacia [far'maθja] nf chemist's
(shop) (BRIT), pharmacy; **~ de turno**
duty chemist; **~ de guardia** all-night
chemist
fármaco [farmako] nm drug
faro ['faro] nm (NAUT: torre) lighthouse;
(AUTO) headlamp; **~s antiniebla** fog
lamps; **~s delanteros/traseros**
headlights/rear lights
farol [fa'rol] nm lantern, lamp
farola [fa'rola] nf street lamp (BRIT) o
light (US)
farsa ['farsa] nf (gen) farce
farsante [far'sante] nm/f fraud, fake
fascículo [fas'θikulo] nm (de revista)
part, instalment
fascinar [fasθi'nar] vt (gen) to
fascinate
fascismo [fas'θismo] nm fascism;
fascista adj, nm/f fascist
fase ['fase] nf phase
fastidiar [fasti'ðjar] vt (molestar) to
annoy, bother; (estropear) to spoil; **~se**
vr: **¡que se fastidie!** (fam) he'll just
have to put up with it!
fastidio [fas'tiðjo] nm (molestia)
annoyance; **~so, a** adj (molesto)
annoying
fastuoso, a [fas'twoso, a] adj
(banquete, boda) lavish; (acto)

pompous

fatal [fa'tal] *adj* (*gen*) fatal;
(*desgraciado*) ill-fated; (*fam: malo,
pésimo*) awful; **~idad** *nf* (*destino*) fate;
(*mala suerte*) misfortune

fatiga [fa'tiɣa] *nf* (*cansancio*) fatigue,
weariness

fatigar [fati'ɣar] *vt* to tire, weary; **~se**
vr to get tired

fatigoso, a [fati'ɣoso, a] *adj* (*cansador*)
tiring

fatuo, a ['fatwo, a] *adj* (*vano*) fatuous;
(*presuntuoso*) conceited

favor [fa'ßor] *nm* favour; **estar a ~ de**
to be in favour of; **haga el ~ de...**
would you be so good as to...,
kindly...; **por ~** please; **~able** *adj*
favourable

favorecer [faßore'θer] *vt* to favour;
(*vestido etc*) to become, flatter; **este
peinado le favorece** this hairstyle
suits him

favorito, a [faßo'rito, a] *adj, nm/f*
favourite

fax [faks] *nm inv* fax; **mandar por ~** to
fax

faz [faθ] *nf* face; **la ~ de la tierra** the
face of the earth

fe [fe] *nf* (*REL*) faith; (*documento*)
certificate; **prestar ~ a** to believe,
credit; **actuar con buena/mala ~** to
act in good/bad faith; **dar ~ de** to
bear witness to

fealdad [feal'dad] *nf* ugliness

febrero [fe'ßrero] *nm* February

febril [fe'ßril] *adj* (*fig: actividad*) hectic;
(*mente, mirada*) feverish

fecha ['fetʃa] *nf* date; **~ de caducidad**
(*de producto alimenticio*) sell-by date;
(*de contrato etc*) expiry date; **con
~ adelantada** postdated; **en
~ próxima** soon; **hasta la ~** to date,
so far; **poner ~** to date; **fechar** *vt* to
date

fecundar [fekun'dar] *vt* (*generar*) to
fertilize, make fertile; **fecundo, a** *adj*
(*fértil*) fertile; (*fig*) prolific; (*productivo*)

productive

federación [feðera'θjon] *nf* federation

felicidad [feliθi'dad] *nf* happiness; **~es**
nfpl (*felicitaciones*) best wishes,
congratulations

felicitación [feliθita'θjon] *nf*:
¡felicitaciones! congratulations!

felicitar [feliθi'tar] *vt* to congratulate

feligrés, esa [feli'ɣres, esa] *nm/f*
parishioner

feliz [fe'liθ] *adj* happy

felpudo [fel'puðo] *nm* doormat

femenino, a [feme'nino, a] *adj, nm*
feminine

feminista [femi'nista] *adj, nm/f*
feminist

fenómeno [fe'nomeno] *nm*
phenomenon; (*fig*) freak, accident
♦ *adj* great ♦ *excl* great!, marvellous!;
fenomenal *adj* = **fenómeno**

feo, a ['feo, a] *adj* (*gen*) ugly;
(*desagradable*) bad, nasty

féretro ['feretro] *nm* (*ataúd*) coffin;
(*sarcófago*) bier

feria ['ferja] *nf* (*gen*) fair; (*descanso*)
holiday, rest day; (*AM: mercado*) village
market; (: *cambio*) loose o small
change

fermentar [fermen'tar] *vi* to ferment

ferocidad [feroθi'dad] *nf* fierceness,
ferocity

feroz [fe'roθ] *adj* (*cruel*) cruel; (*salvaje*)
fierce

férreo, a ['ferreo, a] *adj* iron

ferretería [ferrete'ria] *nf* (*tienda*)
ironmonger's (shop) (*BRIT*), hardware
store

ferrocarril [ferroka'rril] *nm* railway

ferroviario, a [ferro'ßjarjo, a] *adj* rail
cpd

fértil ['fertil] *adj* (*productivo*) fertile;
(*rico*) rich; **fertilidad** *nf* (*gen*) fertility;
(*productividad*) fruitfulness

ferviente [fer'ßjente] *adj* fervent

fervor [fer'ßor] *nm* fervour; **~oso, a**
adj fervent

festejar [feste'xar] *vt* (*celebrar*) to

celebrate

festejo [fes'texo] nm celebration; **festejos** nmpl (fiestas) festivals

festín [fes'tin] nm feast, banquet

festival [festi'βal] nm festival

festividad [festiβi'ðað] nf festivity

festivo, a [fes'tiβo, a] adj (de fiesta) festive; (CINE, LITERATURA) humorous; **día ~** holiday

fétido, a ['fetiðo, a] adj foul-smelling

feto ['feto] nm foetus

fiable ['fjaβle] adj (persona) trustworthy; (máquina) reliable

fiador, a [fja'ðor, a] nm/f (JUR) surety, guarantor; (COM) backer; **salir ~ por uno** to stand bail for sb

fiambre ['fjambre] nm cold meat

fianza ['fjanθa] nf surety; (JUR): **libertad bajo ~** release on bail

fiar [fi'ar] vt (salir garante de) to guarantee; (vender a crédito) to sell on credit; (secreto): **~ a** to confide to ♦ vi to trust; **~se** vr to trust (in), rely on; **~se de uno** to rely on sb

fibra ['fiβra] nf fibre; **~ óptica** optical fibre

ficción [fik'θjon] nf fiction

ficha ['fitʃa] nf (TEL) token; (en juegos) counter, marker; (tarjeta) (index) card; **fichar** vt (archivar) to file, index; (DEPORTE) to sign; **estar fichado** to have a record; **fichero** nm box file; (INFORM) file

ficticio, a [fik'tiθjo, a] adj (imaginario) fictitious; (falso) fabricated

fidelidad [fiðeli'ðað] nf (lealtad) fidelity, loyalty; **alta ~** high fidelity, hi-fi

fideos [fi'ðeos] nmpl noodles

fiebre ['fjeβre] nf (MED) fever; (fig) fever, excitement; **~ amarilla/del heno** yellow/hay fever; **~ palúdica** malaria; **tener ~** to have a temperature

fiel [fjel] adj (leal) faithful, loyal; (fiable) reliable; (exacto) accurate, faithful ♦ nm: **los ~es** the faithful

fieltro ['fjeltro] nm felt

fiera ['fjera] nf (animal feroz) wild animal o beast; (fig) dragon; ver tb **fiero**

fiero, a ['fjero, a] adj (cruel) cruel; (feroz) fierce; (duro) harsh

fiesta ['fjesta] nf party; (de pueblo) festival; (vacaciones, tb: **~s**) holiday sg; (REL): **~ de guardar** day of obligation

Fiestas

Fiestas can be official public holidays or holidays set by each autonomous region, many of which coincide with religious festivals. There are also many **fiestas** *all over Spain for a local patron saint or the Virgin Mary. These often last several days and can include religious processions, carnival parades, bullfights and dancing.*

figura [fi'ɣura] nf (gen) figure; (forma, imagen) shape, form; (NAIPES) face card

figurar [fiɣu'rar] vt (representar) to represent; (fingir) to figure ♦ vi to figure; **~se** vr (imaginarse) to imagine; (suponer) to suppose

fijador [fixa'ðor] nm (FOTO etc) fixative; (de pelo) gel

fijar [fi'xar] vt (gen) to fix; (estampilla) to affix, stick (on); **~se** vr: **~se en** to notice

fijo, a ['fixo, a] adj (gen) fixed; (firme) firm; (permanente) permanent ♦ adv: **mirar ~** to stare

fila ['fila] nf row; (MIL) rank; **ponerse en ~** to line up, get into line

filántropo, a [fi'lantropo, a] nm/f philanthropist

filatelia [fila'telja] nf philately, stamp collecting

filete [fi'lete] nm (carne) fillet steak; (pescado) fillet

filiación [filja'θjon] nf (POL) affiliation

filial [fi'ljal] adj filial ♦ nf subsidiary

Filipinas [fili'pinas] nfpl: **las ~** the Philippines; **filipino, a** adj, nm/f

filmar [fil'mar] vt to film, shoot

filo ['filo] nm (gen) edge; **sacar ~ a** to sharpen; **al ~ del mediodía** at about midday; **de doble ~** double-edged

filón [fi'lon] nm (MINERÍA) vein, lode; (fig) goldmine

filosofía [filoso'fia] nf philosophy; **filósofo, a** nm/f philosopher

filtrar [fil'trar] vt, vi to filter, strain; **~se** vr to filter; **filtro** nm (TEC, utensilio) filter

fin [fin] nm end; (objetivo) aim, purpose; **al ~ y al cabo** when all's said and done; **a ~ de** in order to; **por ~** finally; **en ~** in short; **de semana** weekend

final [fi'nal] adj final ♦ nm end, conclusion ♦ nf final; **~idad** nf (propósito) purpose, intention; **~ista** nm/f finalist; **~izar** vt to end, finish; (INFORM) to log out o off ♦ vi to end, come to an end

financiar [finan'θjar] vt to finance; **financiero, a** adj financial ♦ nm/f financier

finca ['finka] nf (bien inmueble) property, land; (casa de campo) country house; (AM) farm

fingir [fin'xir] vt (simular) to simulate, feign ♦ vi (aparentar) to pretend

finlandés, esa [finlan'des, esa] adj Finnish ♦ nm/f Finn, nm (LING) Finnish

Finlandia [fin'landja] nf Finland

fino, a ['fino, a] adj fine; (delgado) slender; (de buenas maneras) polite, refined; (jerez) fino, dry

firma ['firma] nf signature; (COM) firm, company

firmamento [firma'mento] nm firmament

firmar [fir'mar] vt to sign

firme ['firme] adj firm; (estable) stable; (sólido) solid; (constante) steady; (decidido) resolute ♦ nm road surface; **~mente** adv firmly; **~za** nf firmness; (constancia) steadiness; (solidez) solidity

fiscal [fis'kal] adj fiscal ♦ nm/f public prosecutor; **año ~** tax o fiscal year

fisco ['fisko] nm (hacienda) treasury, exchequer (BRIT)

fisgar [fis'var] vt to pry into

fisgonear [fisvone'ar] vt to poke one's nose into ♦ vi to pry, spy

física ['fisika] nf physics sg; ver tb **físico**

físico, a ['fisiko, a] adj physical ♦ nm physique ♦ nm/f physicist

fisura [fi'sura] nf crack; (MED) fracture

flác(c)ido, a [fla(k)θiðo, a] adj flabby

flaco, a ['flako, a] adj (muy delgado) skinny, thin; (débil) weak, feeble

flagrante [fla'vrante] adj flagrant

flamante [fla'mante] (fam) adj brilliant; (nuevo) brand-new

flamenco, a [fla'menko, a] adj (de Flandes) Flemish; (baile, música) flamenco ♦ nm (baile, música) flamenco

flan [flan] nm creme caramel

flaqueza [fla'keθa] nf (delgadez) thinness, leanness; (fig) weakness

flash [flaʃ] (pl ~s o ~es) nm (FOTO) flash

flauta ['flauta] nf (MUS) flute

flecha ['fletʃa] nf arrow

flechazo [fle'tʃaθo] nm love at first sight

fleco ['fleko] nm fringe

flema ['flema] nm phlegm

flequillo [fle'kiʎo] nm (pelo) fringe

flexible [flek'sißle] adj flexible

flexión [flek'sjon] nf press-up

flexo ['flekso] nm adjustable table-lamp

flojera [flo'xera] (AM: fam) nf: **me da ~** I can't be bothered

flojo, a ['floxo, a] adj (gen) loose; (sin fuerzas) limp; (débil) weak

flor [flor] nf flower; **a ~ de** on the surface of; **~ecer** (BOT) to flower, bloom; (fig) to flourish; **~eciente** adj (BOT) in flower, flowering; (fig) thriving; **~ero** nm vase; **~istería** nf florist's (shop)

flota ['flota] nf fleet

flotador [flota'ðor] nm (gen) float; (para nadar) rubber ring

flotar [flo'tar] vi (gen) to float; **flote** nm: **a flote** afloat; **salir a flote** (fig) to get back on one's feet

fluctuar [fluk'twar] vi (oscilar) to fluctuate

fluidez [flui'ðeθ] nf fluidity; (fig) fluency

flúido, a ['fluiðo, a] adj, nm fluid

fluir [flu'ir] vi to flow

flujo ['fluxo] nm flow; **~ y reflujo** ebb and flow

flúor ['fluor] nm fluoride

fluvial [flu'βjal] adj (navegación, cuenca) fluvial, river cpd

foca ['foka] nf seal

foco ['foko] nm focus; (ELEC) floodlight; (AM) (light) bulb

fofo, a ['fofo, a] adj soft, spongy; (carnes) flabby

fogata [fo'ɣata] nf bonfire

fogón [fo'ɣon] nm (de cocina) ring, burner

fogoso, a [fo'ɣoso, a] adj spirited

folio ['foljo] nm folio, page

follaje [fo'ʎaxe] nm foliage

folletín [foʎe'tin] nm newspaper serial

folleto [fo'ʎeto] nm (POL) pamphlet

follón [fo'ʎon] (fam) nm (lío) mess; (conmoción) fuss; **armar un ~** to kick up a row

fomentar [fomen'tar] vt (MED) to foment; **fomento** nm (promoción) promotion

fonda ['fonda] nf inn

fondo ['fondo] nm (de mar) bottom; (de coche, sala) back; (ARTE etc) background; (reserva) fund; **~s** nmpl (COM) funds, resources; **una investigación a ~** a thorough investigation; **en el ~** at bottom, deep down

fonobuzón [fonoβu'θon] nm voice mail

fontanería [fontane'ria] nf plumbing; **fontanero, a** nm/f plumber

footing ['futiŋ] nm jogging; **hacer ~**

to jog, go jogging

forastero, a [foras'tero, a] nm/f stranger

forcejear [forθexe'ar] vi (luchar) to struggle

forense [fo'rense] nm/f pathologist

forjar [for'xar] vt to forge

forma ['forma] nf (figura) form, shape; (MED) fitness; (método) way, means; **las ~s** the conventions; **estar en ~** to be fit

formación [forma'θjon] nf (gen) formation; (educación) education; **~ profesional** vocational training

formal [for'mal] adj (gen) formal; (fig: serio) serious; (: de fiar) reliable; **~idad** nf formality; seriousness; **~izar** vt (JUR) to formalize; (situación) to put in order, regularize; **~izarse** vr (situación) to be put in order, be regularized

formar [for'mar] vt (componer) to form, shape; (constituir) to make up, constitute; (ESCOL) to train, educate; **~se** vr (ESCOL) to be trained, educated; (cobrar forma) to form, take form; (desarrollarse) to develop

formatear [formate'ar] vt to format

formativo, a [forma'tiβo, a] adj (lecturas, años) formative

formato [for'mato] nm format

formidable [formi'ðaßle] adj (temible) formidable; (estupendo) tremendous

fórmula ['formula] nf formula

formular [formu'lar] vt (queja) to make, lodge; (petición) to draw up; (pregunta) to pose

formulario [formu'larjo] nm form

fornido, a [for'niðo, a] adj well-built

forrar [fo'rrar] vt (abrigo) to line; (libro) to cover; **forro** nm (de cuaderno) cover; (COSTURA) lining; (de sillón) upholstery

fortalecer [fortale'θer] vt to strengthen

fortaleza [forta'leθa] nf (MIL) fortress, stronghold; (fuerza) strength; (determinación) resolution

fortuito, a [for'twito, a] *adj* accidental

fortuna [for'tuna] *nf* (*suerte*) fortune, (good) luck; (*riqueza*) fortune, wealth

forzar [for'θar] *vt* (*puerta*) to force (open); (*compeler*) to compel

forzoso, a [for'θoso, a] *adj* necessary

fosa ['fosa] *nf* (*sepultura*) grave; (*en tierra*) pit; **~s nasales** nostrils

fósforo ['fosforo] *nm* (QUÍM) phosphorus; (*cerilla*) match

foso ['foso] *nm* ditch; (TEATRO) pit; (AUTO): **~ de reconocimiento** inspection pit

foto ['foto] *nf* photo, snap(shot); **sacar una ~** to take a photo o picture

fotocopia [foto'kopja] *nf* photocopy; **fotocopiadora** *nf* photocopier; **fotocopiar** *vt* to photocopy

fotografía [fotoɣra'fia] *nf* (ARTE) photography; (*una ~*) photograph; **fotografiar** *vt* to photograph

fotógrafo, a [fo'toɣrafo, a] *nm/f* photographer

fracasar [fraka'sar] *vi* (*gen*) to fail

fracaso [fra'kaso] *nm* failure

fracción [frak'θjon] *nf* fraction; **fraccionamiento** (AM) *nm* housing estate

fractura [frak'tura] *nf* fracture, break

fragancia [fra'ɣanθja] *nf* (*olor*) fragrance, perfume

frágil ['fraxil] *adj* (*débil*) fragile; (COM) breakable

fragmento [fraɣ'mento] *nm* (*pedazo*) fragment

fragua ['fraɣwa] *nf* forge; **fraguar** *vt* to forge; (*fig*) to concoct ♦ *vi* to harden

fraile ['fraile] *nm* (REL) friar; (: *monje*) monk

frambuesa [fram'bwesa] *nf* raspberry

francamente *adv* (*hablar, decir*) frankly; (*realmente*) really

francés, esa [fran'θes, esa] *adj* French ♦ *nm/f* Frenchman/woman ♦ *nm* (LING) French

Francia ['franθja] *nf* France

franco, a ['franko, a] *adj* (*cándido*)

---

frank, open; (COM: *exento*) free ♦ *nm* (*moneda*) franc

francotirador, a [frankotira'ðor, a] *nm/f* sniper

franela [fra'nela] *nf* flannel

franja ['franxa] *nf* fringe

franquear [franke'ar] *vt* (*camino*) to clear; (*carta, paquete postal*) to frank, stamp; (*obstáculo*) to overcome

franqueo [fran'keo] *nm* postage

franqueza [fran'keθa] *nf* (*candor*) frankness

frasco ['frasko] *nm* bottle, flask; **~ al vacío** (*vacuum*) flask

frase ['frase] *nf* sentence; **~ hecha** set phrase; (*pey*) stock phrase

fraterno, a [fra'terno, a] *adj* brotherly, fraternal

fraude ['frauðe] *nm* (*cualidad*) dishonesty; (*acto*) fraud; **fraudulento, a** *adj* fraudulent

frazada [fra'saða] (AM) *nf* blanket

frecuencia [fre'kwenθja] *nf* frequency; **con ~** frequently, often

frecuentar [frekwen'tar] *vt* to frequent

fregadero [freɣa'ðero] *nm* (kitchen) sink

fregar [fre'ɣar] *vt* (*frotar*) to scrub; (*platos*) to wash (up); (AM) to annoy

fregona [fre'ɣona] *nf* mop

freír [fre'ir] *vt* to fry

frenar [fre'nar] *vt* to brake; (*fig*) to check

frenazo [fre'naθo] *nm*: **dar un ~** to brake sharply

frenesí [frene'si] *nm* frenzy; **frenético, a** *adj* frantic

freno ['freno] *nm* (TEC, AUTO) brake; (*de cabalgadura*) bit; (*fig*) check

frente ['frente] *nm* (ARQ, POL) front; (*de objeto*) front part ♦ *nf* forehead; brow; **~ a** in front of; (*en situación opuesta de*) opposite; **al ~ de** at the head of; **chocar de ~** to crash head-on; **hacer ~ a** to face up to

fresa ['fresa] (ESP) *nf* strawberry

fresco, a ['fresko, a] *adj* (*nuevo*) fresh;

(*frío*) cool; (*descarado*) cheeky ♦ *nm* (*aire*) fresh air; (ARTE) fresco; (AM: *jugo*) fruit drink ♦ *nm/f* (*fam*): **ser un ~** to have a nerve; **tomar el ~** to get some fresh air; **frescura** *nf* freshness; (*descaro*) cheek, nerve

frialdad [frial'daθ] *nf* (*gen*) coldness; (*indiferencia*) indifference

fricción [frik'θjon] *nf* (*gen*) friction; (*acto*) rub(bing); (MED) massage

frigidez [frixi'δeθ] *nf* frigidity

frigorífico [friγo'rifiko] *nm* refrigerator

frijol [fri'xol] *nm* kidney bean

frío, a *etc* ['frio, a] *vb ver* **freír** ♦ *adj* cold; (*indiferente*) indifferent ♦ *nm* cold; (*indiferencia*) indifference; **hace ~** it's cold; **tener ~** to be cold

frito, a ['frito, a] *adj* fried; **me trae ~ ese hombre** I'm sick and tired of that man; **fritos** *nmpl* fried food

frívolo, a ['friβolo, a] *adj* frivolous

frontal [fron'tal] *adj* frontal; **choque ~** head-on collision

frontera [fron'tera] *nf* frontier

fronterizo, a [fronte'riθo, a] *adj* frontier *cpd*; (*contiguo*) bordering

frontón [fron'ton] *nm* (DEPORTE: *cancha*) pelota court; (: *juego*) pelota

frotar [fro'tar] *vt* to rub; *vr*: **~se las manos** to rub one's hands

fructífero, a [fruk'tifero, a] *adj* fruitful

fruncir [frun'θir] *vt* to pucker; (COSTURA) to pleat; **~ el ceño** to knit one's brow

frustrar [frus'trar] *vt* to frustrate

fruta ['fruta] *nf* fruit; **frutería** *nf* fruit shop; **frutero, a** *adj* fruit *cpd* ♦ *nm/f* fruiterer ♦ *nm* fruit bowl

frutilla [fru'tiλa] (AM) *nf* strawberry

fruto ['fruto] *nm* fruit; (*fig*: *resultado*) result; (: *beneficio*) benefit; **~s secos** nuts; (*pasas etc*) dried fruit *sg*

fue *vb ver* **ser**; **ir**

fuego ['fweγo] *nm* (*gen*) fire; **a ~ lento** on a low heat; **¿tienes ~?** have you (got) a light?; **~s artificiales** *o* **de artificio** fireworks

fuente ['fwente] *nf* fountain; (*manantial*, *fig*) spring; (*origen*) source; (*plato*) large dish

fuera *etc* ['fwera] *vb ver* **ser**, **ir** ♦ *adv* out(side); (*en otra parte*) away; (*excepto*, *salvo*) except, save ♦ *prep*: **~ de** outside; (*fig*) besides; **~ de sí** beside o.s.; *por* **~** (on the) outside

fuera-borda [fwera'βorða] *nm* speedboat

fuerte ['fwerte] *adj* strong; (*golpe*) hard; (*ruido*) loud; (*comida*) rich; (*lluvia*) heavy; (*dolor*) intense ♦ *adv* strongly; hard; loud(ly)

fuerza *etc* ['fwerθa] *vb ver* **forzar** ♦ *nf* (*fortaleza*) strength; (TEC, ELEC) power; (*coacción*) force; (MIL: *tb*: **~s**) forces *pl*; **a ~ de** by dint of; **cobrar ~s** to recover one's strength; **tener ~s para** to have the strength to; **a la ~** forcibly, by force; *por* **~** of necessity; **~ de voluntad** willpower

fuga ['fuγa] *nf* (*huida*) flight, escape; (*de gas etc*) leak

fugarse [fu'γarse] *vr* to flee, escape

fugaz [fu'γaθ] *adj* fleeting

fugitivo, a [fuxi'tiβo, a] *adj*, *nm/f* fugitive

fui *vb ver* **ser**; **ir**

fulano, a [fu'lano, a] *nm/f* so-and-so, what's-his-name/what's-her-name

fulminante [fulmi'nante] *adj* (*fig*: *mirada*) fierce; (MED: *enfermedad*, *ataque*) sudden; (*fam*: *éxito*, *golpe*) sudden

fumador, a [fuma'ðor, a] *nm/f* smoker

fumar [fu'mar] *vt*, *vi* to smoke; **~ en pipa** to smoke a pipe

función [fun'θjon] *nf* function; (*en trabajo*) duties *pl*; (*espectáculo*) show; **entrar en funciones** to take up one's duties

funcionar [funθjo'nar] *vi* (*gen*) to function; (*máquina*) to work; **"no funciona"** "out of order"

funcionario, a [funθjo'narjo, a] *nm/f* civil servant

funda |'funda| nf (gen) cover; (de almohada) pillowcase

fundación |funda'θjon| nf foundation

fundamental |fundamen'tal| adj fundamental, basic

fundamentar |fundamen'tar| vt (poner base) to lay the foundations of; (establecer) to found; (fig) to base; **fundamento** nm (base) foundation

fundar |fun'dar| vt to found; **~se** vr: **~se en** to be founded on

fundición |fundi'θjon| nf fusing; (fábrica) foundry

fundir |fun'dir| vt (gen) to fuse; (metal) to smelt, melt down; (nieve etc) to melt; (COM) to merge; (estatua) to cast; **~se** vr (colores etc) to merge, blend; (unirse) to fuse together; (ELEC: fusible, lámpara etc) to fuse, blow; (nieve etc) to melt

fúnebre |'funeβre| adj funeral cpd, funereal

funeral |fune'ral| nm funeral; **funeraria** nf undertaker's

funesto, a |fu'nesto, a| adj (día) ill-fated; (decisión) fatal

furgón |fur'yon| nm wagon; **furgoneta** nf (AUTO, COM) (transit) van (BRIT), pick-up (truck) (US)

furia |'furja| nf (ira) fury; (violencia) violence; **furibundo, a** adj furious; **furioso, a** adj (iracundo) furious; (violento) violent; **furor** nm (cólera) rage

furtivo, a |fur'tiβo, a| adj furtive ♦ nm poacher

fusible |fu'siβle| nm fuse

fusil |fu'sil| nm rifle; **~ar** vt to shoot

fusión |fu'sjon| nf (gen) melting; (unión) fusion; (COM) merger

fútbol |'futβol| nm football; **futbolín** nm table football; **futbolista** nm footballer

futuro, a |fu'turo, a| adj, nm future

G, g

gabardina |gaβar'ðina| nf raincoat, gabardine

gabinete |gaβi'nete| nm (POL) cabinet; (estudio) study; (de abogados etc) office

gaceta |ga'θeta| nf gazette

gachas |'gatʃas| nfpl porridge sg

gafas |'gafas| nfpl glasses; **~ de sol** sunglasses

gafe |'gafe| nm jinx

gaita |'gaita| nf bagpipes pl

gajes |'gaxes| nmpl: **los ~ del oficio** occupational hazards

gajo |'gaxo| nm (de naranja) segment

gala |'gala| nf (traje de etiqueta) full dress; **~s** nfpl (ropa) finery sg; **estar de ~** to be in one's best clothes; **hacer ~ de** to display

galante |ga'lante| adj gallant; **galantería** nf (caballerosidad) gallantry; (cumplido) politeness; (comentario) compliment

galápago |ga'lapaxo| nm (ZOOL) turtle

galardón |galar'ðon| nm award, prize

galaxia |ga'laksja| nf galaxy

galera |ga'lera| nf (nave) galley; (carro) wagon; (IMPRENTA) galley

galería |gale'ria| nf (gen) gallery; (balcón) veranda(h); (pasillo) corridor

Gales |'gales| nm (tb: País de ~) Wales; **galés, esa** adj Welsh ♦ nm/f Welshman/woman ♦ nm (LING) Welsh

galgo, a |'galvo, a| nm/f greyhound

galimatías |galima'tias| nmpl (lenguaje) gibberish sg, nonsense sg

gallardía nf (valor) bravery

gallego, a |ga'ʎevo, a| adj, nm/f Galician

galleta |ga'ʎeta| nf biscuit (BRIT), cookie (US)

gallina |ga'ʎina| nf hen ♦ nm/f (fam: cobarde) chicken; **gallinero** nm henhouse; (TEATRO) top gallery

gallo |'gaʎo| nm cock, rooster

galón |ga'lon| nm (MIL) stripe;
(COSTURA) braid; (medida) gallon

galopar |galo'par| vi to gallop

gama |'gama| nf (fig) range

gamba |'gamba| nf prawn (BRIT),
shrimp (US)

gamberro, a |gam'berro, a| nm/f
hooligan, lout

gamuza |ga'muθa| nf chamois

gana |'gana| nf (deseo) desire, wish;
(apetito) appetite; (voluntad) will;
(añoranza) longing; **de buena ~**
willingly; **de mala ~** reluctantly; **me
da ~s de** I feel like, I want to; **no me
da la ~** I don't feel like it; **tener ~s de**
to feel like

ganadería |ganaðe'ria| nf (ganado)
livestock; (ganado vacuno) cattle pl;
(cría, comercio) cattle raising

ganado |ga'naðo| nm livestock;
~ lanar sheep pl; **~ mayor** cattle pl;
~ porcino pigs pl

ganador, a |gana'ðor, a| adj winning
♦ nm/f winner

ganancia |ga'nanθja| nf (lo ganado)
gain; (aumento) increase; (beneficio)
profit; **~s** nfpl (ingresos) earnings,
(beneficios) profit sg, winnings

ganar |ga'nar| vt (obtener) to get,
obtain; (sacar ventaja) to gain; (salario
etc) to earn; (DEPORTE, premio) to win;
(derrotar a) to beat; (alcanzar) to reach
♦ vi (DEPORTE) to win; **~se** vr: **~se la
vida** to earn one's living

ganchillo |gan'tʃiʎo| nm crochet

gancho |'gantʃo| nm (gen) hook;
(colgador) hanger

gandul, a |gan'dul, a| adj,
good-for-nothing, layabout

ganga |'ganga| nf bargain

gangrena |gan'grena| nf gangrene

ganso, a |'ganso, a| nm/f (ZOOL)
goose; (fam) idiot

ganzúa |gan'θua| nf skeleton key

garabatear |garaβate'ar| vi, vt (al
escribir) to scribble, scrawl

garabato |gara'βato| nm (escritura)

scrawl, scribble

garaje |ga'raxe| nm garage

garante |ga'rante| adj responsible
♦ nm/f guarantor

garantía |garan'tia| nf guarantee

garantizar |garanti'θar| vt to
guarantee

garbanzo |gar'βanθo| nm chickpea
(BRIT), garbanzo (US)

garbo |'garβo| nm grace, elegance

garfio |'garfjo| nm grappling iron

garganta |gar'ɣanta| nf (ANAT) throat;
(de botella) neck; **gargantilla** nf
necklace

gárgaras |'garɣaras| nfpl: **hacer ~** to
gargle

garita |ga'rita| nf cabin, hut; (MIL)
sentry box

garra |'garra| nf (de gato, TEC) claw;
(de ave) talon; (fam: mano) hand, paw

garrafa |ga'rrafa| nf carafe, decanter

garrapata |garra'pata| nf tick

garrote |ga'rrote| nm (palo) stick;
(porra) cudgel; (suplicio) garrotte

garza |'garθa| nf heron

gas |gas| nm gas

gasa |'gasa| nf gauze

gaseosa |gase'osa| nf lemonade

gaseoso, a |gase'oso, a| adj gassy,
fizzy

gasoil |ga'soil| nm diesel (oil)

gasóleo |ga'soleo| nm = **gasoil**

gasolina |gaso'lina| nf petrol,
gas(oline) (US); **gasolinera** nf petrol
(BRIT) o gas (US) station

gastado, a |gas'taðo, a| adj (dinero)
spent; (ropa) worn out; (usado: frase
etc) trite

gastar |gas'tar| vt (dinero, tiempo) to
spend; (fuerzas) to use up;
(desperdiciar) to waste; (llevar) to wear;
~se vr to wear out; (estropearse) to
waste; **~ en bromas** to crack jokes; **¿qué número gastas?**
what size (shoe) do you take?

gasto |'gasto| nm (desembolso)
expenditure, spending; (consumo, uso)

use; **~s** nmpl (desembolsos) expenses; (cargos) charges, costs

gastronomía [gastrono'mia] nf gastronomy

gatear [gate'ar] vi (andar a gatas) to go on all fours

gatillo [ga'tiʎo] nm (de arma de fuego) trigger; (de dentista) forceps

gato, a ['gato, a] nm/f cat ♦ nm (TEC) jack; **andar a gatas** to go on all fours

gaviota [ga'βjota] nf seagull

gay [ge] adj inv, nm gay, homosexual

gazpacho [gaθ'patʃo] nm gazpacho

gel [xel] nm (tb: **~ de baño/ducha**) gel

gelatina [xela'tina] nf jelly; (polvos etc) gelatine

gema ['xema] nf gem

gemelo, a [xe'melo, a] adj, nm/f twin; **~s** nmpl (de camisa) cufflinks; (prismáticos) field glasses, binoculars

gemido [xe'miðo] nm (quejido) moan, groan; (aullido) howl

Géminis ['xeminis] nm Gemini

gemir [xe'mir] vi (quejarse) to moan, groan; (aullar) to howl

generación [xenera'θjon] nf generation

general [xene'ral] adj general ♦ nm general; **por lo o en ~** in general; **G~itat** nf Catalan parliament; **~izar** vt to generalize; **~izarse** vr to become generalized, spread; **~mente** adv generally

generar [xene'rar] vt to generate

género ['xenero] nm (clase) kind, sort; (tipo) type; (BIO) genus; (LING) gender; (COM) material; **~ humano** human race

generosidad [xenerosi'ðað] nf generosity; **generoso, a** adj generous

genial [xe'njal] adj inspired; (idea) brilliant; (afable) genial

genio ['xenjo] nm (carácter) nature, disposition; (humor) temper; (facultad creadora) genius; **de mal ~** bad-tempered

genital [xeni'tal] adj genital; **genitales** nmpl genitals

gente ['xente] nf (personas) people pl; (parientes) relatives pl

gentil [xen'til] adj (elegante) graceful; (encantador) charming; **~eza** nf grace; charm; (cortesía) courtesy

gentío [xen'tio] nm crowd, throng

genuino, a [xe'nwino, a] adj genuine

geografía [xeoɣra'fia] nf geography

geología [xeolo'xia] nf geology

geometría [xeome'tria] nf geometry

gerencia [xe'renθja] nf management; **gerente** nm/f (supervisor) manager; (jefe) director

geriatría [xeria'tria] nf (MED) geriatrics sg

germen ['xermen] nm germ

germinar [xermi'nar] vi to germinate

gesticular [xestiku'lar] vi to gesticulate; (hacer muecas) to grimace; **gesticulación** nf gesticulation; (mueca) grimace

gestión [xes'tjon] nf management; (diligencia, acción) negotiation; **gestionar** vt (lograr) to try to arrange; (dirigir) to manage

gesto ['xesto] nm (mueca) grimace; (ademán) gesture

Gibraltar [xiβral'tar] nm Gibraltar; **gibraltareño, a** [xiβralta'reɲo, a] adj, nm/f Gibraltarian

gigante [xi'xante] adj, nm/f giant; **gigantesco, a** adj gigantic

gilipollas [xili'poʎas] (fam) adj inv daft ♦ nm/f inv wally

gimnasia [xim'nasja] nf gymnastics pl; **gimnasio** nm gymnasium; **gimnasta** nm/f gymnast

gimotear [ximote'ar] vi to whine, whimper

ginebra [xi'neβra] nf gin

ginecólogo, a [xine'koloɣo, a] nm/f gynaecologist

gira ['xira] nf tour, trip

girar [xi'rar] vt (dar la vuelta) to turn (around); (: rápidamente) to spin; (COM: giro postal) to draw; (: letra de cambio) to issue ♦ *vi* to turn (round); (*rápido*) to spin

girasol [xira'sol] *nm* sunflower

giratorio, a [xira'torjo, a] *adj* revolving

giro ['xiro] *nm* (*movimiento*) turn, revolution; (*LING*) expression; (*COM*) draft; ~ **bancario/postal** bank giro/postal order

gis [xis] (*AM*) *nm* chalk

gitano, a [xi'tano, a] *adj, nm/f* gypsy

glacial [gla'θjal] *adj* icy, freezing

glaciar [gla'θjar] *nm* glacier

glándula ['glandula] *nf* gland

global [glo'βal] *adj* global

globo ['gloβo] *nm* (*esfera*) globe, sphere; (*aerostato, juguete*) balloon

glóbulo ['gloβulo] *nm* globule; (*ANAT*) corpuscle

gloria ['glorja] *nf* glory

glorieta [glo'rjeta] *nf* (*de jardín*) bower, arbour; (*plazoleta*) roundabout (*BRIT*), traffic circle (*US*)

glorificar [glorifi'kar] *vt* (*enaltecer*) to glorify, praise

glorioso, a [glo'rjoso, a] *adj* glorious

glotón, ona [glo'ton, ona] *adj* gluttonous, greedy ♦ *nm/f* glutton

glucosa [glu'kosa] *nf* glucose

gobernador, a [goβerna'ðor, a] *adj* governing ♦ *nm/f* governor; **gobernante** *adj* governing

gobernar [goβer'nar] *vt* (*dirigir*) to guide, direct; (*POL*) to rule, govern ♦ *vi* to govern; (*NAUT*) to steer

gobierno *etc* [go'βjerno] *vb ver* **gobernar** ♦ *nm* (*POL*) government; (*dirección*) guidance, direction; (*NAUT*) steering

goce *etc* ['goθe] *vb ver* **gozar** ♦ *nm* enjoyment

gol [gol] *nm* goal

golf [golf] *nm* golf

golfa ['golfa] (*fam!*) *nf* (*mujer*) slut, whore

golfo, a ['golfo, a] *nm* (*GEO*) gulf ♦ *nm/f* (*fam: niño*) urchin; (*gamberro*) lout

golondrina [golon'drina] *nf* swallow

golosina [golo'sina] *nf* (*dulce*) sweet; **goloso, a** *adj* sweet-toothed

golpe ['golpe] *nm* blow; (*de puño*) punch; (*de mano*) smack; (*de remo*) stroke; (*fig: choque*) clash; **no dar ~** to be bone idle; **de un ~** with one blow; **de ~** suddenly; **~ (de estado)** coup (d'état); **golpear** *vt, vi* to strike, knock; (*asestar*) to beat; (*de puño*) to punch; (*golpetear*) to tap

goma ['goma] *nf* (*caucho*) rubber; (*elástico*) elastic; (*una ~*) elastic band; **~ espuma** foam rubber; **~ de pegar** gum, glue; **~ de borrar** eraser, rubber (*BRIT*)

gomina [go'mina] *nf* hair gel

gordo, a ['gorðo, a] *adj* (*gen*) fat; (*fam*) enormous; **el (premio) ~** (*en lotería*) first prize; **gordura** *nf* fat; (*corpulencia*) fatness, stoutness

gorila [go'rila] *nm* gorilla

gorjear [gorxe'ar] *vi* to twitter, chirp

gorra ['gorra] *nf* cap; (*de niño*) bonnet; (*militar*) bearskin; **entrar de ~** (*fam*) to gatecrash; **ir de ~** to sponge

gorrión [go'rrjon] *nm* sparrow

gorro ['gorro] *nm* (*gen*) cap; (*de niño, mujer*) bonnet

gorrón, ona [go'rron, ona] *nm/f* scrounger; **gorronear** (*fam*) *vi* to scrounge

gota ['gota] *nf* (*gen*) drop; (*de sudor*) bead; (*MED*) gout; **gotear** *vi* to drip; (*lloviznar*) to drizzle; **gotera** *nf* leak

gozar [go'θar] *vt* to enjoy o.s.; **~ de** (*disfrutar*) to enjoy; (*poseer*) to possess

gozne ['goθne] *nm* hinge

gozo ['goθo] *nm* (*alegría*) joy; (*placer*) pleasure

gr. *abr* (= *gramo, gramos*) g

grabación [graβa'θjon] *nf* recording

grabado [gra'βaðo] *nm* print, engraving

grabadora [graβa'ðora] *nf* tape-recorder

grabar [graˈβar] vt to engrave; (discos, cintas) to record

gracia [ˈgraθja] nf (encanto) grace, gracefulness; (humor) humour, wit; **¡(muchas) ~s!** thanks (very much)!; **~s a** thanks to; **tener ~** (chiste etc) to be funny; **no me hace ~** I am not keen; **gracioso, a** adj (divertido) funny, amusing; (cómico) comical
♦ nm/f (TEATRO) comic character

grada [ˈgraða] nf (de escalera) step; (de anfiteatro) tier, row; **~s** nfpl (DEPORTE: de estadio) terraces pl

gradería [graðeˈria] nf (gradas) (flight of) steps pl; (de anfiteatro) tiers pl, rows pl; (DEPORTE: de estadio) terraces pl; **~ cubierta** covered stand

grado [ˈgraðo] nm degree; (de aceite, vino) grade; (grada) step; (MIL) rank; **de buen ~** willingly

graduación [graðwaˈθjon] nf (del alcohol) proof, strength; (ESCOL) graduation; (MIL) rank

gradual [graˈðwal] adj gradual

graduar [graˈðwar] vt (gen) to graduate; (MIL) to commission; **~se** vr to graduate; **~se la vista** to have one's eyes tested

gráfica [ˈgrafika] nf graph

gráfico, a [ˈgrafiko, a] adj graphic
♦ nm diagram; **~s** nmpl (INFORM) graphics

grajo [ˈgraxo] nm rook

Gral abr (= General) Gen.

gramática [graˈmatika] nf grammar

gramo [ˈgramo] nm gramme (BRIT), gram (US)

gran [gran] adj ver **grande**

grana [ˈgrana] nf (color, tela) scarlet

granada [graˈnaða] nf pomegranate; (MIL) grenade

granate [graˈnate] adj deep red

Gran Bretaña [-breˈtaɲa] nf Great Britain

grande [ˈgrande] adj (antes de nmsg: **gran**) adj (de tamaño) big, large; (alto) tall; (distinguido) great; (impresionante)

grand ♦ nm grandee; **grandeza** nf greatness

grandioso, a [granˈdjoso, a] adj magnificent, grand

granel: **a ~** adv (COM) in bulk

granero [graˈnero] nm granary, barn

granito [graˈnito] nm (AGR) small grain; (roca) granite

granizado [graniˈθaðo] nm iced drink

granizar [graniˈθar] vi to hail; **granizo** nm hail

granja [ˈgranxa] nf (gen) farm; **granjear** vt to win, gain; **granjearse** vr to win, gain; **granjero, a** nm/f farmer

grano [ˈgrano] nm grain; (semilla) seed; (de café) bean; (MED) pimple, spot

granuja [graˈnuxa] nm rogue; (golfillo) urchin

grapa [ˈgrapa] nf staple; (TEC) clamp; **grapadora** nf stapler

grasa [ˈgrasa] nf grease; (de cocinar) fat, lard; (sebo) suet; (mugre) filth; **grasiento, a** adj greasy; (de aceite) oily; **graso, a** adj (leche, queso, carne) fatty; (pelo, piel) greasy

gratificación [gratifikaˈθjon] nf (bono) bonus; (recompensa) reward

gratificar [gratifiˈkar] vt to reward

gratinar [gratiˈnar] vt to cook au gratin

gratis [ˈgratis] adv free

gratitud [gratiˈtuð] nf gratitude

grato, a [ˈgrato, a] adj (agradable) pleasant, agreeable

gratuito, a [graˈtwito, a] adj (gratis) free; (sin razón) gratuitous

gravamen [graˈβamen] nm (impuesto) tax

gravar [graˈβar] vt to tax

grave [ˈgraβe] adj heavy; (serio) grave, serious; **~dad** nf gravity

gravilla [graˈβiʎa] nf gravel

gravitar [graβiˈtar] vi to gravitate; **~ sobre** to rest on

graznar [graθˈnar] vi (cuervo) to squawk; (pato) to quack; (hablar ronco) to croak

Grecia ['greθja] nf Greece

gremio ['gremjo] nm trade, industry

greña ['greɲa] nf (cabellos) shock of hair

gresca ['greska] nf uproar

griego, a ['grjeɣo, a] adj, nm/f Greek

grieta ['grjeta] nf crack

grifo ['grifo] nm tap; (AM: AUTO) petrol (BRIT) o gas (US) station

grilletes [gri'ʎetes] nmpl fetters

grillo ['griʎo] nm (ZOOL) cricket

gripe ['gripe] nf flu, influenza

gris [gris] adj (color) grey

gritar [gri'tar] vt, vi to shout, yell; **grito** nm shout, yell; (de horror) scream

grosella [gro'seʎa] nf (red)currant; **~ negra** blackcurrant

grosería [grose'ria] nf (actitud) rudeness; (comentario) vulgar comment; **grosero, a** (poco cortés) rude, bad-mannered; (ordinario) vulgar, crude

grosor [gro'sor] nm thickness

grotesco, a [gro'tesko, a] adj grotesque

grúa ['grua] nf (TEC) crane; (de petróleo) derrick

grueso, a ['grweso, a] adj thick; (persona) stout ♦ nm bulk; **el ~ de** the bulk of

grulla ['gruʎa] nf crane

grumo ['grumo] nm clot, lump

gruñido [gru'ɲiðo] nm grunt; (de persona) grumble

gruñir [gru'ɲir] vi (animal) to growl; (persona) to grumble

grupa ['grupa] nf (ZOOL) rump

grupo ['grupo] nm group; (TEC) unit, set

gruta ['gruta] nf grotto

guadaña [gwa'ðaɲa] nf scythe

guagua [gwa'ɣwa] (AM) nf (niño) baby; (bus) bus

guante ['gwante] nm glove; **~ra** nf glove compartment

guapo, a ['gwapo, a] adj good-looking, attractive; (elegante) smart

guarda ['gwarða] nm/f (persona) guard, keeper ♦ nf (de acto) guarding; (custodia) custody; **~bosques** nm inv gamekeeper; **~costas** nm inv coastguard vessel ♦ nm/f guardian, protector; **~espaldas** nm/f inv bodyguard; **~meta** nm/f goalkeeper; **guardar** vt (gen) to keep; (vigilar) to guard, watch over; (dinero: ahorrar) to save; **guardarse** vr (preservarse) to protect o.s.; (evitar) to avoid; **guardar cama** to stay in bed; **~rropa** nm (armario) wardrobe; (en establecimiento público) cloakroom

guardería [gwarðe'ria] nf nursery

guardia ['gwarðja] nf (MIL) guard; (cuidado) care, custody ♦ nm/f guard; (policía) policeman/woman; **estar de ~** to be on guard; **montar la ~** to mount guard; **G~ Civil** Civil Guard; **G~ Nacional** National Guard

guardián, ana [gwar'ðjan, ana] nm/f (gen) guardian, keeper

guarecer [gware'θer] vt (proteger) to protect; (abrigar) to shelter; **~se** vr to take refuge

guarida [gwa'riða] nf (de animal) den, lair; (refugio) refuge

guarnecer [gwarne'θer] vt (equipar) to provide; (adornar) to adorn; (TEC) to reinforce; **guarnición** nf (de vestimenta) trimming; (de piedra) mount; (CULIN) garnish; (arneses) harness; (MIL) garrison

guarro, a ['gwarro, a] nm/f pig

guasa ['gwasa] nf joke; **guasón, ona** adj (bromista) joking ♦ nm/f wit; joker

Guatemala [gwate'mala] nf Guatemala

guay [gwai] (fam) adj super, great

gubernativo, a [guβerna'tiβo, a] adj governmental

guerra ['gerra] nf war; **~ civil** civil war; **~ fría** cold war; **dar ~** to annoy; **guerrear** vi to wage war; **guerrero, a**

adj fighting; (*carácter*) warlike ♦ *nm/f* warrior

guerrilla [ge'rriʎa] *nf* guerrilla warfare; (*tropas*) guerrilla band o group

guía *etc* ['gia] *vb ver* **guiar** ♦ *nm/f* (*persona*) guide ♦ *nf* (*libro*) guidebook; ~ **de ferrocarriles** railway timetable; ~ **telefónica** telephone directory

guiar [gi'ar] *vt* to guide, direct; (*AUTO*) to steer; ~**se** *vr*: ~**se por** to be guided by

guijarro [gi'xarro] *nm* pebble

guillotina [giʎo'tina] *nf* guillotine

guinda ['ginda] *nf* morello cherry

guindilla [gin'diʎa] *nf* chilli pepper

guiñapo [gi'napo] *nm* (*harapo*) rag; (*persona*) reprobate, rogue

guiñar [gi'nar] *vt* to wink

guión [gi'on] *nm* (*LING*) hyphen, dash; (*CINE*) script; **guionista** *nm/f* scriptwriter

guiri ['giri] (*fam: pey*) *nm/f* foreigner

guirnalda [gir'nalda] *nf* garland

guisado [gi'saðo] *nm* stew

guisante [gi'sante] *nm* pea

guisar [gi'sar] *vt, vi* to cook; **guiso** ['gisou] *nm* cooked dish

guitarra [gi'tarra] *nf* guitar

gula ['gula] *nf* gluttony, greed

gusano [gu'sano] *nm* worm; (*lombriz*) earthworm

gustar [gus'tar] *vt* to taste, sample ♦ *vi* to please, be pleasing; ~ **de algo** to like o enjoy sth; **me gustan las uvas** I like grapes; **le gusta nadar** she likes o enjoys swimming

gusto ['gusto] *nm* (*sentido, sabor*) taste; (*placer*) pleasure; **tiene ~ a menta** it tastes of mint; **tener buen ~** to have good taste; **sentirse a ~** to feel at ease; **mucho ~ (en conocerle)** pleased to meet you; **el ~ es mío** the pleasure is mine; **con ~** willingly, gladly; ~**so, a** *adj* (*sabroso*) tasty; (*agradable*) pleasant

H, h

ha *vb ver* **haber**

haba ['aßa] *nf* bean

Habana [a'ßana] *nf*: **la ~** Havana

habano [a'ßano] *nm* Havana cigar

habéis *vb ver* **haber**

PALABRA CLAVE
---

haber [a'ßer] *vb aux* **1** (*tiempos compuestos*) to have; **había comido** I had eaten; **antes/después de ~lo visto** before seeing/after seeing o having seen it

2: **¡lo dicho antes!** you should have said so before!

3: ~ **de: he de hacerlo** I have to do it; **ha de llegar mañana** it should arrive tomorrow

♦ *vb impers* **1** (*existencia: sg*) there is; (*: pl*) there are; **hay un hermano/dos hermanos** there is one brother/there are two brothers; **¿cuánto hay de aquí a Sucre?** how far is it from here to Sucre?

2 (*obligación*): **hay que hacer algo** something must be done; **hay que apuntarlo para acordarse** you have to write it down to remember

3: **¡hay que ver!** well I never!

4: **¡no hay de o por (AM) qué!** don't mention it!, not at all!

5: **¿qué hay?** (*¿qué pasa?*) what's up?, what's the matter?; (*¿qué tal?*) how's it going?

♦ ~**se** *vr*: **habérselas con uno** to have it out with sb

♦ *vt*: **hay unas sugerencias** here are some suggestions; **no hay cintas blancas pero sí las hay rojas** there aren't any white ribbons but there are some red ones

♦ *nm* (*en cuenta*) credit side; ~**es** *nmpl* assets; **¿cuánto tengo en el ~?** how much do I have in my account?; **tiene**

varias novelas en su ~ he has
several novels to his credit

habichuela [aβitʃwela] nf kidney bean

hábil ['aβil] adj (listo) clever, smart;
(capaz) fit, capable; (experto) expert;
día ~ working day; **habilidad** nf skill,
ability

habilitar [aβili'tar] vt (capacitar) to
enable; (dar instrumentos) to equip;
(financiar) to finance

hábilmente [aβil'mente] adv skilfully,
expertly

habitación [aβita'θjon] nf (cuarto)
room; (BIO: morada) habitat;
~ sencilla o **individual** single room;
~ doble o **de matrimonio** double
room

habitante [aβi'tante] nm/f inhabitant

habitar [aβi'tar] vt (residir en) to
inhabit; (ocupar) to occupy ♦ vi to live

hábito ['aβito] nm habit

habitual [aβi'twal] adj usual

habituar [aβi'twar] vt to accustom;
~se vr: **~se a** to get used to

habla ['aβla] nf (capacidad de hablar)
speech; (idioma) language; (dialecto)
dialect; **perder el ~** to become
speechless; **de ~ francesa** French-
speaking; **estar al ~** to be in contact;
(TEL) to be on the line; **¡González al
~!** (TEL) González speaking

hablador, a [aβla'ðor, a] adj talkative
♦ nm/f chatterbox

habladuría [aβlaðu'ria] nf rumour; **~s**
nfpl gossip sg

hablante [a'βlante] adj speaking
♦ nm/f speaker

hablar [a'βlar] vt to speak, talk ♦ vi to
speak; **~se** vr to speak to each other;
~ con to speak to; **~ de** to speak of o
about; **"se habla inglés"** "English
spoken here"; **¡ni ~!** it's out of the
question!

habré etc vb ver **haber**

hacendoso, a [aθen'doso, a] adj
industrious

hacer [a'θer] vt **1** (fabricar, producir) to
make; (construir) to build; **~ una
película/un ruido** to make a film/
noise; **el guisado lo hice yo** I made
o cooked the stew

2 (ejecutar: trabajo etc) to do; **~ la
colada** to do the washing; **~ la
comida** to do the cooking; **¿qué
haces?** what are you doing?; **~ el
malo** o **el papel del malo** (TEATRO)
to play the villain

3 (estudios, algunos deportes) to do;
~ español/económicas to do o
study Spanish/economics; **~ yoga/
gimnasia** to do yoga/go to gym

4 (transformar, incidir en): **esto lo
hará más difícil** this will make it
more difficult; **salir te hará sentir
mejor** going out will make you feel
better

5 (cálculo): **2 y 2 hacen 4** 2 and 2
make 4; **éste hace 100** this one
makes 100

6 (+ sub): **esto hará que ganemos**
this will make us win; **harás que no
quiera venir** you'll stop him wanting
to come

7 (como sustituto de vb) to do; **él
bebió y yo hice lo mismo** he drank
and I did likewise

8: **no hace más que criticar** all he
does is criticize

♦ vb semi-aux: **hacer + infin 1**
(directo): **les hice venir** I made o had
them come; **~ trabajar a los demás**
to get others to work

2 (por intermedio de otros): **~ reparar
algo** to get sth repaired

♦ vi **1**: **haz como que no lo sabes**
act as if you don't know

2 (ser apropiado): **si os hace** if it's
alright with you

3: **~ de: ~ de madre para uno** to be
like a mother to sb; (TEATRO): **~ de
Otelo** to play Othello

♦ vb impers **1**: **hace calor/frío** it's hot/cold; ver tb **bueno**; **sol**; **tiempo**

2 (tiempo): **hace 3 años** 3 years ago; **hace un mes que voy/no voy** I've been going/I haven't been for a month

3: **¿cómo has hecho para llegar tan rápido?** how did you manage to get here so quickly?

♦ **~se** vr **1** (volverse) to become; **se hicieron amigos** they became friends

2 (acostumbrarse): **~se a** to get used to

3: **se hace con huevos y leche** it's made out of eggs and milk; **eso no se hace** that's not done

4 (obtener): **~se de o con algo** to get hold of sth

5 (fingirse): **~se el sueco** to turn a deaf ear

hacha ['atʃa] nf axe; (antorcha) torch

hachís [a'tʃis] nm hashish

hacia ['aθja] prep (en dirección de) towards; (cerca de) near; (actitud) towards; **~ arriba/abajo** up(wards)/down(wards); **~ mediodía** about noon

hacienda [a'θjenda] nf (propiedad) property; (finca) farm; (AM) ranch; **~ pública** public finance; (Ministerio de) **H~** Exchequer (BRIT), Treasury Department (US)

hada ['aða] nf fairy

hago etc vb ver **hacer**

Haití [ai'ti] nm Haiti

halagar [ala'ɣar] vt to flatter

halago [a'laɣo] nm flattery; **halagüeño, a** adj flattering

halcón [al'kon] nm falcon, hawk

hallar [a'ʎar] vt (gen) to find; (descubrir) to discover; (toparse con) to run into; **~se** vr to be (situated)

hallazgo nm discovery; (cosa) find

halterofilia [altero'filja] nf weightlifting

hamaca [a'maka] nf hammock

hambre ['ambre] nf hunger; (plaga) famine; (deseo) longing; **tener ~** to be

hungry; **hambriento, a** adj hungry, starving

hamburguesa [ambur'ɣesa] nf hamburger; **hamburguesería** nf burger bar

han vb ver **haber**

harapiento, a [ara'pjento, a] adj tattered, in rags

harapos [a'rapos] nmpl rags

haré etc vb ver **hacer**

harina [a'rina] nf flour

hartar [ar'tar] vt to satiate, glut; (fig) to tire, sicken; **~se** vr (de comida) to fill o.s., gorge o.s.; (cansarse) to get fed up (de with); **hartazgo** nm surfeit, glut; **harto, a** adj (lleno) full; (cansado) fed up ♦ adv (bastante) enough; (muy) very; **estar harto de** to be fed up with

has vb ver **haber**

hasta ['asta] adv even ♦ prep (alcanzando a) as far as; up to; down to; (de tiempo: a tal hora) till, until; (antes de) before ♦ conj: **~ que** until; **~ luego/el sábado** see you soon/on Saturday

hastiar [as'tjar] vt (gen) to weary; (aburrir) to bore; **~se** vr: **~se de** to get fed up with; **hastío** nm weariness; boredom

hatillo [a'tiʎo] nm belongings pl, kit; (montón) bundle, heap

hay vb ver **haber**

Haya ['aja] nf: **la ~ The** Hague

haya etc ['aja] vb ver **haber** ♦ nf beech tree

haz [aθ] vb ver **hacer** ♦ nm (de luz) beam

hazaña [a'θaɲa] nf feat, exploit

hazmerreir [aθmerre'ir] nm inv laughing stock

he vb ver **haber**

hebilla [e'βiʎa] nf buckle, clasp

hebra ['eβra] nf thread; (BOT: fibra) fibre, grain

hebreo, a [e'βreo, a] adj, nm/f Hebrew ♦ nm (LING) Hebrew

hechizar [etʃi'θar] vt to cast a spell on, bewitch

hechizo [e'tʃiθo] nm witchcraft, magic; (acto de magia) spell, charm

hecho, a ['etʃo, a] pp de **hacer** ♦ adj (carne) done; (COSTURA) ready-to-wear ♦ nm deed, act; (dato) fact; (cuestión) matter; (suceso) event ♦ excl agreed!, done!; **¡bien ~!** well done!; **de ~** in fact, as a matter of fact

hechura [e'tʃura] nf (forma) form, shape; (de persona) build

hectárea [ek'tarea] nf hectare

heder [e'ðer] vi to stink, smell

hediondo, a [e'ðjondo, a] adj stinking

hedor [e'ðor] nm stench

helada [e'laða] nf frost

heladera [ela'ðera] (AM) nf (refrigerador) refrigerator

helado, a [e'laðo, a] adj frozen; (glacial) icy; (fig) chilly, cold ♦ nm ice cream

helar [e'lar] vt to freeze, ice (up); (dejar atónito) to amaze; (desalentar) to discourage ♦ vi to freeze; **~se** vr to freeze

helecho [e'letʃo] nm fern

hélice ['eliθe] nf (TEC) propeller

helicóptero [eli'koptero] nm helicopter

hembra ['embra] nf (BOT, ZOOL) female; (mujer) woman; (TEC) nut

hemorragia [emo'rraxja] nf haemorrhage

hemorroides [emo'rroiðes] nfpl haemorrhoids, piles

hemos vb ver **haber**

hendidura [endi'ðura] nf crack, split

heno ['eno] nm hay

herbicida [erβi'θiða] nm weedkiller

heredad [ere'ðað] nf landed property; (granja) farm

heredar [ere'ðar] vt to inherit; **heredero, a** nm/f heir(ess)

hereje [e'rexe] nm/f heretic

herencia [e'renθja] nf inheritance

herida [e'riða] nf wound, injury; ver tb

herido

herido, a [e'riðo, a] adj injured, wounded ♦ nm/f casualty

herir [e'rir] vt to wound, injure; (fig) to offend

hermanastro, a [erma'nastro, a] nm/f stepbrother/sister

hermandad [erman'dað] nf brotherhood

hermano, a [er'mano, a] nm/f brother/sister; **~ gemelo** twin brother; **hermana gemela** twin sister; **~ político** brother-in-law; **hermana política** sister-in-law

hermético, a [er'metiko, a] adj hermetic; (fig) watertight

hermoso, a [er'moso, a] adj beautiful, lovely; (estupendo) splendid; (guapo) handsome; **hermosura** nf beauty

hernia ['ernja] nf hernia

héroe ['eroe] nm hero

heroína [ero'ina] nf (mujer) heroine; (droga) heroin

heroísmo [ero'ismo] nm heroism

herradura [erra'ðura] nf horseshoe

herramienta [erra'mjenta] nf tool

herrero [e'rrero] nm blacksmith

herrumbre [e'rrumbre] nf rust

hervidero [erβi'ðero] nm (fig) swarm; (POL etc) hotbed

hervir [er'βir] vi to boil; (burbujear) to bubble; (fig): **~ de** to teem with; **~ a fuego lento** to simmer; **hervor** nm boiling; (fig) ardour, fervour

heterosexual [eterosek'swal] adj heterosexual

hice etc vb ver **hacer**

hidratante [iðra'tante] adj: **crema ~** moisturizing cream, moisturizer; **hidratar** vt (piel) to moisturize; **hidrato** nm: **hidratos de carbono** carbohydrates

hidráulica [i'ðraulika] nf hydraulics sg

hidráulico, a [i'ðrauliko, a] adj hydraulic

hidro... [iðro] prefijo hydro..., water-...; **~eléctrico, a** adj hydroelectric

~fobia nf hydrophobia, rabies;
hidrógeno nm hydrogen
hiedra ['jeðra] nf ivy
hiel [jel] nf gall, bile; (fig) bitterness
hiela etc vb ver **helar**
hielo ['jelo] nm (gen) ice; (escarcha) frost; (fig) coldness, reserve
hiena ['jena] nf hyena
hierba ['jerßa] nf (pasto) grass; (CULIN, MED: planta) herb; **mala** ~ weed; (fig) evil influence; **~buena** nf mint
hierro ['jerro] nm (metal) iron; (objeto) iron object
hígado ['iɣaðo] nm liver
higiene [i'xjene] nf hygiene;
higiénico, a adj hygienic
higo ['iɣo] nm fig; **higuera** nf fig tree
hijastro, a [i'xastro, a] nm/f stepson/ daughter
hijo, a ['ixo, a] nm/f son/daughter, child; **~s** nmpl children, sons and daughters; **~ de papá/mamá** daddy's/mummy's boy; **~ de puta** (fam!) bastard (!), son of a bitch (!)
hilar [i'lar] vt to spin; **~ fino** to split hairs
hilera [i'lera] nf row, file
hilo ['ilo] nm thread; (BOT) fibre; (metal) wire; (de agua) trickle, thin stream
hilvanar [ilßa'nar] vt (COSTURA) to tack (BRIT), baste (US); (fig) to do hurriedly
himno ['imno] nm hymn; ~ **nacional** national anthem
hincapié [inka'pje] nm: **hacer ~ en** to emphasize
hincar [in'kar] vt to drive (in), thrust (in); **~se** vr: **~se de rodillas** to kneel down
hincha ['intʃa] (fam) nm/f fan
hinchado, a [in'tʃaðo, a] adj (gen) swollen; (persona) pompous
hinchar [in'tʃar] vt (gen) to swell; (inflar) to blow up, inflate; (fig) to exaggerate; **~se** vr (inflarse) to swell up; (fam: de comer) to stuff o.s.
hinchazón nf (MED) swelling; (altivez)

arrogance
hinojo [i'noxo] nm fennel
hipermercado [ipermer'kaðo] nm hypermarket, superstore
hípico, a [ipiko, a] adj horse cpd
hipnotismo [ipno'tismo] nm hypnotism; **hipnotizar** vt to hypnotize
hipo ['ipo] nm hiccups pl
hipocresía [ipokre'sia] nf hypocrisy;
hipócrita adj hypocritical ♦ nm/f hypocrite
hipódromo [i'poðromo] nm racetrack
hipopótamo [ipo'potamo] nm hippopotamus
hipoteca [ipo'teka] nf mortgage
hipótesis [i'potesis] nf inv hypothesis
hiriente [i'rjente] adj offensive, wounding
hispánico, a [is'paniko, a] adj Hispanic
hispano, a [is'pano, a] adj Hispanic, Spanish, Hispano- ♦ nm/f Spaniard; **H~américa** nf Latin America; **~americano, a** adj, nm/f Latin American
histeria [is'terja] nf hysteria
historia [is'torja] nf history; (cuento) story, tale; **~s** nfpl (chismes) gossip sg; **dejarse de ~s** to come to the point; **pasar a la ~** to go down in history; **~dor, a** nm/f historian; **historial** nm (profesional) curriculum vitae, C.V.; (MED) case history; **histórico, a** adj historical; (memorable) historic
historieta [isto'rjeta] nf tale, anecdote; (dibujos) comic strip
hito ['ito] nm (fig) landmark
hizo vb ver **hacer**
Hnos abr (= Hermanos) Bros.
hocico [o'θiko] nm snout
hockey ['xoki] nm hockey; **~ sobre hielo** ice hockey
hogar [o'ɣar] nm fireplace, hearth; (casa) home; (vida familiar) home life; **~eño, a** adj home cpd; (persona) home-loving
hoguera [o'ɣera] nf (gen) bonfire

hoja ['oxa] nf (gen) leaf; (de flor) petal; (de papel) sheet; (página) page; **~ de afeitar** razor blade

hojalata [oxa'lata] nf tin(plate)

hojaldre [o'xaldre] nm (CULIN) puff pastry

hojear [oxe'ar] vt to leaf through, turn the pages of

hola ['ola] excl hello!

Holanda [o'landa] nf Holland; **holandés, esa** [olan'des, esa] adj, nm/f Dutchman/woman ♦ nm (LING) Dutch

holgado, a [ol'xaðo, a] adj (ropa) loose, baggy; (rico) comfortable

holgar [ol'xar] vi (descansar) to rest; (sobrar) to be superfluous; **huelga decir que** it goes without saying that

holgazán, ana [olxa'θan, ana] adj idle, lazy ♦ nm/f loafer

holgura [ol'xura] nf looseness, bagginess; (TEC) play, free movement; (vida) comfortable living

hollín [o'ʎin] nm soot

hombre ['ombre] nm (gen) man; (raza humana): **el ~** man(kind) ♦ excl ¡sí ~! (claro) of course!; (para énfasis) man, old boy; **~ de negocios** businessman; **~ de pro** honest man; **~-rana** frogman

hombrera [om'brera] nf shoulder strap

hombro ['ombro] nm shoulder

hombruno, a [om'bruno, a] adj mannish

homenaje [ome'naxe] nm (gen) homage; (tributo) tribute

homicida [omi'θiða] adj homicidal ♦ nm/f murderer; **homicidio** nm murder, homicide

homologar [omolo'xar] vt (COM: productos, tamaños) to standardize; **homólogo, a** nm/f: **su** etc **homólogo** his etc counterpart o opposite number

homosexual [omosek'swal] adj, nm/f homosexual

hondo, a ['ondo, a] adj deep; **lo ~** the depth(s) (pl), the bottom; **~nada** nf

hollow, depression; (cañón) ravine

Honduras [on'duras] nf Honduras

hondureño, a [ondu'reɲo, a] adj, nm/f Honduran

honestidad [onesti'ðað] nf purity, chastity; (decencia) decency; **honesto, a** adj chaste; decent, honest; (justo) just

hongo ['ongo] nm (BOT: gen) fungus; (: comestible) mushroom; (: venenoso) toadstool

honor [o'nor] nm (gen) honour; **en ~ a la verdad** to be fair; **~able** adj honourable

honorario, a [ono'rarjo, a] adj honorary; **~s** nmpl fees

honra ['onra] nf (gen) honour; (renombre) good name; **~dez** nf honesty; (de persona) integrity; **~do, a** adj honest, upright

honrar [on'rar] vt to honour; **~se** vr: **~se con algo/de hacer algo** to be honoured by sth/to do sth

honroso, a [on'roso, a] adj (honrado) honourable; (respetado) respectable

hora ['ora] nf (una ~) hour; (tiempo) time; **¿qué ~ es?** what time is it?; **¿a qué ~?** at what time?; **media ~** half an hour; **a la ~ de recreo** at playtime; **a primera ~** first thing (in the morning); **a última ~** at the last moment; **a altas ~s** at the small hours; **¡a buena ~!** about time, too!; **dar la ~** to strike the hour; **~s de oficina/de trabajo** office/working hours; **~s de visita** visiting times; **~s extras** o **extraordinarias** overtime sg; **~s punta** rush hours

horadar [ora'ðar] vt to drill, bore

horario, a [o'rarjo, a] adj hourly, hour cpd ♦ nm timetable; **~ comercial** business hours pl

horca ['orka] nf gallows sg

horcajadas [orka'xaðas]: **a ~** adv astride

horchata [or'tʃata] nf cold drink made from tiger nuts and water, tiger nut milk

horizontal [oriθon'tal] *adj* horizontal

horizonte [ori'θonte] *nm* horizon

horma ['orma] *nf* mould

hormiga [or'miɣa] *nf* ant; **~s** *nfpl* (MED) pins and needles

hormigón [ormi'ɣon] *nm* concrete; **~ armado/pretensado** reinforced/prestressed concrete

hormigueo [ormi'ɣeo] *nm* (comezón) itch

hormona [or'mona] *nf* hormone

hornada [or'naða] *nf* batch (of loaves etc)

hornillo [or'niʎo] *nm* (cocina) portable stove

horno ['orno] *nm* (CULIN) oven; (TEC) furnace; **alto ~** blast furnace

horóscopo [o'roskopo] *nm* horoscope

horquilla [or'kiʎa] *nf* hairpin; (AGR) pitchfork

horrendo, a [o'rrendo, a] *adj* horrendous, frightful

horrible [o'rriβle] *adj* horrible, dreadful

horripilante [orripi'lante] *adj* hair-raising, horrifying

horror [o'rror] *nm* horror, dread; (atrocidad) atrocity; **¡qué ~!** (fam) how awful!; **~izar** *vt* to horrify, frighten; **~izarse** *vr* to be horrified; **~oso, a** *adj* horrifying, ghastly

hortaliza [orta'liθa] *nf* vegetable

hortelano, a [orte'lano, a] *nm/f* (market) gardener

hortera [or'tera] (fam) *adj* tacky

hosco, a ['osko, a] *adj* sullen, gloomy

hospedar [ospe'ðar] *vt* to put up; **~se** *vr* to stay, lodge

hospital [ospi'tal] *nm* hospital

hospitalario, a [ospita'larjo, a] *adj* (acogedor) hospitable; **hospitalidad** *nf* hospitality

hostal [os'tal] *nm* small hotel

hostelería [ostele'ria] *nf* hotel business o trade

hostia ['ostja] *nf* (REL) host, consecrated wafer; (fam!: golpe) whack, punch ♦ *excl* (fam!): **¡~(s)!** damn!

hostigar [osti'ɣar] *vt* to whip; (fig) to harass, pester

hostil [os'til] *adj* hostile; **~idad** *nf* hostility

hotel [o'tel] *nm* hotel; **~ero, a** *adj* hotel *cpd* ♦ *nm/f* hotelier

---

Hotel

In Spain you can choose from the following categories of accommodation, in descending order of quality and price: **hotel** (from 5 stars to 1), **hostal**, **pensión**, **casa de huéspedes**, **fonda**. The State also runs luxury hotels called **paradores**, which are usually sited in places of particular historical interest and are often historic buildings themselves.

---

hoy [oi] *adv* (este día) today; (la actualidad) now(adays) ♦ *nm* present time; **~ (en) día** now(adays)

hoyo ['ojo] *nm* hole, pit; **hoyuelo** *nm* dimple

hoz [oθ] *nf* sickle

hube etc vb ver **haber**

hucha ['utʃa] *nf* money box

hueco, a ['weko, a] *adj* (vacío) hollow, empty; (resonante) booming ♦ *nm* hollow, cavity

huelga etc vb ver **holgar** ♦ *nf* strike; **declararse en ~** to go on strike, come out on strike; **~ de hambre** hunger strike

huelguista [wel'ɣista] *nm/f* striker

huella ['weʎa] *nf* (pisada) tread; (marca del paso) footprint, footstep; (: de animal, máquina) track; **~ digital** fingerprint

huelo etc vb ver **oler**

huérfano, a ['werfano, a] *adj* orphan(ed) ♦ *nm/f* orphan

huerta ['werta] *nf* market garden; (en Murcia y Valencia) irrigated region

huerto ['werto] *nm* kitchen garden; (de árboles frutales) orchard

hueso ['weso] *nm* (ANAT) bone; (*de fruta*) stone

huésped, a ['wespeð, a] *nm/f* guest

huesudo, a [we'suðo, a] *adj* bony, big-boned

hueva ['weßa] *nf* roe

huevera [we'ßera] *nf* eggcup

huevo ['weßo] *nm* egg; ~ **duro/ escalfado/frito** (ESP) o **estrellado** (AM)/**pasado por agua** hard-boiled/ poached/fried/soft-boiled egg; ~**s revueltos** scrambled eggs

huida [u'iða] *nf* escape, flight

huidizo, a [ui'ðiθo, a] *adj* shy

huir [u'ir] *vi* (*escapar*) to flee, escape; (*evitar*) to avoid; ~**se** *vr* (*escaparse*) to escape

hule ['ule] *nm* oilskin

humanidad [umani'ðað] *nf* (*género humano*) man(kind); (*cualidad*) humanity

humanitario, a [umani'tarjo, a] *adj* humanitarian

humano, a [u'mano, a] *adj* (*gen*) human; (*humanitario*) humane ♦ *nm* human; **ser** ~ human being

humareda [uma'reða] *nf* cloud of smoke

humedad [ume'ðað] *nf* (*del clima*) humidity; (*de pared etc*) dampness; **a prueba de** ~ damp-proof; **humedecer** *vt* to moisten, wet; **humedecerse** *vr* to get wet

húmedo, a ['umeðo, a] *adj* (*mojado*) damp, wet; (*tiempo etc*) humid

humildad [umil'dað] *nf* humility, humbleness; **humilde** *adj* humble, modest

humillación [umiʎa'θjon] *nf* humiliation; **humillante** *adj* humiliating

humillar [umi'ʎar] *vt* to humiliate; ~**se** *vr* to humble o.s., grovel

humo ['umo] *nm* (*de fuego*) smoke; (*gas nocivo*) fumes *pl*; (*vapor*) steam, vapour; ~**s** *nmpl* (*fig*) conceit *sg*

humor [u'mor] *nm* (*disposición*) mood,

temper; (*lo que divierte*) humour; **de buen/mal** ~ in a good/bad mood; ~**ista** *nm/f* comic; ~**ístico, a** *adj* funny, humorous

hundimiento [undi'mjento] *nm* (*gen*) sinking; (*colapso*) collapse

hundir [un'dir] *vt* to sink; (*edificio, plan*) to ruin, destroy; ~**se** *vr* to sink, collapse

húngaro, a ['ungaro, a] *adj, nm/f* Hungarian

Hungría [un'gria] *nf* Hungary

huracán [ura'kan] *nm* hurricane

huraño, a [u'raɲo, a] *adj* (*antisocial*) unsociable

hurgar [ur'xar] *vt* to poke, jab; (*remover*) to stir (up); ~**se** *vr*: ~**se (las narices)** to pick one's nose

hurón, ona [u'ron, ona] *nm* (ZOOL) ferret

hurtadillas [urta'ðiʎas]: **a** ~ *adv* stealthily, on the sly

hurtar [ur'tar] *vt* to steal; **hurto** *nm* theft, stealing

husmear [usme'ar] *vt* (*oler*) to sniff out, scent; (*fam*) to pry into

huyo *etc vb ver* **huir**

I, i

iba *etc vb ver* **ir**

ibérico, a [i'ßeriko, a] *adj* Iberian

iberoamericano, a [ißeroameri'kano, a] *adj, nm/f* Latin American

Ibiza [i'ßiθa] *nf* Ibiza

iceberg [iθe'ßer] *nm* iceberg

icono [i'kono] *nm* ikon, icon

iconoclasta [ikono'klasta] *adj* iconoclastic ♦ *nm/f* iconoclast

ictericia [ikte'riθja] *nf* jaundice

I + D *abr* (= *Investigación y Desarrollo*) R & D

ida [i'ða] *nf* going, departure; ~ **y vuelta** round trip, return

idea [i'ðea] *nf* idea; **no tengo la menor** ~ I haven't a clue

ideal [iðe'al] *adj, nm* ideal; **~ista** *nm/f* idealist; **~izar** *vt* to idealize

idear [iðe'ar] *vt* to think up; *(aparato)* to invent; *(viaje)* to plan

idem ['iðem] *pron* ditto

idéntico, a [i'ðentiko, a] *adj* identical

identidad [iðenti'ðað] *nf* identity

identificación [iðentifika'θjon] *nf* identification

identificar [iðentifi'kar] *vt* to identify; **~se** *vr*: **~se con** to identify with

ideología [iðeolo'xia] *nf* ideology

idilio [i'ðiljo] *nm* love-affair

idioma [i'ðjoma] *nm (gen)* language

idiota [i'ðjota] *adj* idiotic ♦ *nm/f* idiot; **idiotez** *nf* idiocy

ídolo ['iðolo] *nm (tb: fig)* idol

idóneo, a [i'ðoneo, a] *adj* suitable

iglesia [i'ɣlesja] *nf* church

ignorancia [iɣno'ranθja] *nf* ignorance; **ignorante** *adj* ignorant, uninformed ♦ *nm/f* ignoramus

ignorar [iɣno'rar] *vt* not to know, be ignorant of; *(no hacer caso a)* to ignore

igual [i'ɣwal] *adj* equal; *(similar)* like, similar; *(mismo)* (the) same; *(constante, temperatura)* even ♦ *nm/f* equal; **~ que** like, the same as; **me da o es ~** I don't care; **son ~es** they're the same; **al ~ que** *prep, conj* like, just as

igualada [iɣwa'laða] *nf* equaliser

igualar [iɣwa'lar] *vt (gen)* to equalize, make equal; *(allanar, nivelar)* to level (off), even (out); **~se** *vr (platos de balanza)* to balance out

igualdad [iɣwal'dað] *nf* equality; *(similaridad)* sameness; *(uniformidad)* uniformity

igualmente [iɣwal'mente] *adv* equally; *(también)* also, likewise ♦ *excl* the same to you!

ikurriña [iku'rriɲa] *nf* Basque flag

ilegal [ile'ɣal] *adj* illegal

ilegítimo, a [ile'xitimo, a] *adj* illegitimate

ileso, a [i'leso, a] *adj* unhurt

ilícito, a [i'liθito] *adj* illicit

ilimitado, a [ilimi'taðo, a] *adj* unlimited

ilógico, a [i'loxiko, a] *adj* illogical

iluminación [ilumina'θjon] *nf* illumination; *(alumbrado)* lighting

iluminar [ilumi'nar] *vt* to illuminate, light (up); *(fig)* to enlighten

ilusión [ilu'sjon] *nf* illusion; *(quimera)* delusion; *(esperanza)* hope; **hacerse ilusiones** to build up one's hopes; **ilusionado, a** *adj* excited; **ilusionar** *vt*: **le ilusiona ir de vacaciones** he's looking forward to going on holiday; **ilusionarse** *vr*: **ilusionarse (con)** to get excited (about)

ilusionista [ilusjo'nista] *nm/f* conjurer

iluso, a [i'luso, a] *adj* easily deceived ♦ *nm/f* dreamer

ilusorio, a [ilu'sorjo, a] *adj (de ilusión)* illusory, deceptive; *(esperanza)* vain

ilustración [ilustra'θjon] *nf* illustration; *(saber)* learning, erudition; **la I~** the Enlightenment; **ilustrado, a** *adj* illustrated; learned

ilustrar [ilus'trar] *vt* to illustrate; *(instruir)* to instruct; *(explicar)* to explain, make clear; **~se** *vr* to acquire knowledge

ilustre [i'lustre] *adj* famous, illustrious

imagen [i'maxen] *nf (gen)* image; *(dibujo)* picture

imaginación [imaxina'θjon] *nf* imagination

imaginar [imaxi'nar] *vt* to imagine; *(idear)* to think up; *(suponer)* to suppose; **~se** *vr* to imagine; **~io, a** *adj* imaginary; **imaginativo, a** *adj* imaginative

imán [i'man] *nm* magnet

imbécil [im'beθil] *nm/f* imbecile, idiot

imitación [imita'θjon] *nf* imitation

imitar [imi'tar] *vt* to imitate; *(parodiar, remedar)* to mimic, ape

impaciencia [impa'θjenθja] *nf* impatience; **impaciente** *adj* impatient; *(nervioso)* anxious

impacto

imposición

impacto [im'pakto] *nm* impact

impar [im'par] *adj* odd

imparcial [impar'θjal] *adj* impartial, fair

impartir [impar'tir] *vt* to impart, give

impasible [impa'siβle] *adj* impassive

impecable [impe'kaβle] *adj* impeccable

impedimento [impeði'mento] *nm* impediment, obstacle

impedir [impe'ðir] *vt* (*obstruir*) to impede, obstruct; (*estorbar*) to prevent

impenetrable [impene'traβle] *adj* impenetrable; (*fig*) incomprehensible

imperar [impe'rar] *vi* (*reinar*) to rule, reign; (*fig*) to prevail, reign; (*precio*) to be current

imperativo, a [impera'tiβo, a] *adj* (*urgente*, LING) imperative

imperceptible [imperθep'tiβle] *adj* imperceptible

imperdible [imper'ðiβle] *nm* safety pin

imperdonable [imperðo'naβle] *adj* unforgivable, inexcusable

imperfección [imperfek'θjon] *nf* imperfection

imperfecto, a [imper'fekto, a] *adj* imperfect

imperial [impe'rjal] *adj* imperial; **~ismo** *nm* imperialism

imperio [im'perjo] *nm* empire; (*autoridad*) rule, authority; (*fig*) pride, haughtiness; **~so, a** *adj* imperious; (*urgente*) urgent; (*imperativo*) imperative

impermeable [imperme'aβle] *adj* waterproof ♦ *nm* raincoat, mac (BRIT)

impersonal [imperso'nal] *adj* impersonal

impertinencia [imperti'nenθja] *nf* impertinence; **impertinente** *adj* impertinent

imperturbable [impertur'βaβle] *adj* imperturbable

ímpetu ['impetu] *nm* (*impulso*) impetus, impulse; (*impetuosidad*)

impetuosity; (*violencia*) violence

impetuoso, a [impe'twoso, a] *adj* impetuous; (*río*) rushing; (*acto*) hasty

impío, a [im'pio, a] *adj* impious, ungodly

implacable [impla'kaβle] *adj* implacable

implantar [implan'tar] *vt* to introduce

implicar [impli'kar] *vt* to involve; (*entrañar*) to imply

implícito, a [im'pliθito, a] *adj* (*tácito*) implicit; (*sobreentendido*) implied

implorar [implo'rar] *vt* to beg, implore

imponente [impo'nente] *adj* (*impresionante*) impressive, imposing; (*solemne*) grand

imponer [impo'ner] *vt* (*gen*) to impose; (*exigir*) to exact; **~se** *vr* to assert o.s.; (*prevalecer*) to prevail; **imponible** *adj* (COM) taxable

impopular [impopu'lar] *adj* unpopular

importación [importa'θjon] *nf* (*acto*) importing; (*mercancías*) imports *pl*

importancia [impor'tanθja] *nf* importance; (*valor*) value, significance; (*extensión*) size, magnitude; **importante** *adj* important; valuable, significant

importar [impor'tar] *vt* (*del extranjero*) to import; (*costar*) to amount to ♦ *vi* to be important, matter; **me importa un rábano** I couldn't care less; **no importa** it doesn't matter; **¿le importa que fume?** do you mind if I smoke?

importe [im'porte] *nm* (*total*) amount; (*valor*) value

importunar [importu'nar] *vt* to bother, pester

imposibilidad [imposiβili'ðað] *nf* impossibility; **imposibilitar** *vt* to make impossible, prevent

imposible [impo'siβle] *adj* (*gen*) impossible; (*insoportable*) unbearable, intolerable

imposición [imposi'θjon] *nf*

imposition; (COM: *impuesto*) tax;
(: *inversión*) deposit

impostor, a [impos'tor, a] nm/f
impostor

impotencia [impo'tenθja] nf
impotence; **impotente** adj impotent

impracticable [imprakti'kaßle] adj
(*irrealizable*) impracticable;
(*intransitable*) impassable

impreciso, a [impre'θiso, a] adj
imprecise, vague

impregnar [imprex'nar] vt to
impregnate; **~se** vr to become
impregnated

imprenta [im'prenta] nf (*acto*)
printing; (*aparato*) press; (*casa*)
printer's; (*letra*) print

imprescindible [impresθin'dißle] adj
essential, vital

impresión [impre'sjon] nf (*gen*)
impression; (IMPRENTA) printing;
(*edición*) edition; (FOTO) print; (*marca*)
imprint; **~ digital** fingerprint

impresionable [impresjo'naßle] adj
(*sensible*) impressionable

impresionante [impresjo'nante] adj
impressive; (*tremendo*) tremendous;
(*maravilloso*) great, marvellous

impresionar [impresjo'nar] vt
(*conmover*) to move; (*afectar*) to
impress, strike; (*película fotográfica*) to
expose; **~se** vr to be impressed;
(*conmoverse*) to be moved

impreso, a [im'preso, a] pp de
imprimir ♦ adj printed; **~s** nmpl
printed matter; **impresora** nf printer

imprevisto, a [impre'ßisto, a] adj
(*gen*) unforeseen; (*inesperado*)
unexpected

imprimir [impri'mir] vt to imprint,
impress, stamp; (*textos*) to print;
(INFORM) to output, print out

improbable [impro'ßaßle] adj
improbable; (*inverosímil*) unlikely

improcedente [improθe'ðente] adj
inappropriate

improductivo, a [improðuk'tißo, a]
adj unproductive

improperio [impro'perjo] nm insult

impropio, a [im'propjo, a] adj
improper

improvisado, a [improßi'saðo, a] adj
improvised

improvisar [improßi'sar] vt to
improvise

improviso, a [impro'ßiso, a] adj: **de
~** unexpectedly, suddenly

imprudencia [impru'ðenθja] nf
imprudence; (*indiscreción*) indiscretion;
(*descuido*) carelessness; **imprudente**
adj unwise, imprudent; (*indiscreto*)
indiscreet

impúdico, a [im'puðiko, a] adj
shameless; (*lujurioso*) lecherous

impuesto, a [im'pwesto, a] adj
imposed ♦ nm tax; **~ sobre el valor
añadido** value added tax

impugnar [impux'nar] vt to oppose,
contest; (*refutar*) to refute, impugn

impulsar [impul'sar] vt to drive;
(*promover*) to promote, stimulate

impulsivo, a [impul'sißo, a] adj
impulsive; **impulso** nm impulse;
(*fuerza, empuje*) thrust, drive; (*fig:
sentimiento*) urge, impulse

impune [im'pune] adj unpunished

impureza [impu'reθa] nf impurity;
impuro, a adj impure

imputar [impu'tar] vt to attribute

inacabable [inaka'ßaßle] adj (*infinito*)
endless; (*interminable*) interminable

inaccesible [inakθe'sißle] adj
inaccessible

inacción [inak'θjon] nf inactivity

inaceptable [inaθep'taßle] adj
unacceptable

inactividad [inaktißi'ðað] nf inactivity;
(COM) dullness; **inactivo, a** adj
inactive

inadecuado, a [inaðe'kwaðo, a] adj
(*insuficiente*) inadequate; (*inapto*)
unsuitable

inadmisible [inaðmi'sißle] adj
inadmissible

inadvertido, a [inaðβer'tiðo, a] *adj* (*no visto*) unnoticed

inagotable [inaɣo'taβle] *adj* inexhaustible

inaguantable [inaɣwan'taβle] *adj* unbearable

inalterable [inalte'raβle] *adj* immutable, unchangeable

inanición [inani'θjon] *nf* starvation

inanimado, a [inani'maðo, a] *adj* inanimate

inapreciable [inapre'θjaβle] *adj* (*cantidad, diferencia*) imperceptible; (*ayuda, servicio*) invaluable

inaudito, a [inau'ðito, a] *adj* unheard-of

inauguración [inauɣura'θjon] *nf* inauguration; opening

inaugurar [inauɣu'rar] *vt* to inaugurate; (*exposición*) to open

inca ['inka] *nm/f* Inca

incalculable [inkalku'laβle] *adj* incalculable

incandescente [inkandes'θente] *adj* incandescent

incansable [inkan'saβle] *adj* tireless, untiring

incapacidad [inkapaθi'ðað] *nf* incapacity; (*incompetencia*) incompetence; **~ física/mental** physical/mental disability

incapacitar [inkapaθi'tar] *vt* (*inhabilitar*) to incapacitate, render unfit; (*descalificar*) to disqualify

incapaz [inka'paθ] *adj* incapable

incautación [inkauta'θjon] *nf* confiscation

incautarse [inkau'tarse] *vr*: **~ de** to seize, confiscate

incauto, a [in'kauto, a] *adj* (*imprudente*) incautious, unwary

incendiar [inθen'djar] *vt* to set fire to; (*fig*) to inflame; **~se** *vr* to catch fire; **~io, a** *adj* incendiary

incendio [in'θendjo] *nm* fire

incentivo [inθen'tiβo] *nm* incentive

incertidumbre [inθerti'ðumbre] *nf*

(*inseguridad*) uncertainty; (*duda*) doubt

incesante [inθe'sante] *adj* incessant

incesto [in'θesto] *nm* incest

incidencia [inθi'ðenθja] *nf* (MAT) incidence

incidente [inθi'ðente] *nm* incident

incidir [inθi'ðir] *vi* (*influir*) to influence; (*afectar*) to affect; **~ en un error** to fall into error

incienso [in'θjenso] *nm* incense

incierto, a [in'θjerto, a] *adj* uncertain

incineración [inθinera'θjon] *nf* incineration; (*de cadáveres*) cremation

incinerar [inθine'rar] *vt* to burn; (*cadáveres*) to cremate

incipiente [inθi'pjente] *adj* incipient

incisión [inθi'sjon] *nf* incision

incisivo, a [inθi'siβo, a] *adj* sharp, cutting; (*fig*) incisive

incitar [inθi'tar] *vt* to incite, rouse

inclemencia [inkle'menθja] *nf* (*severidad*) harshness, severity; (*del tiempo*) inclemency

inclinación [inklina'θjon] *nf* (*gen*) inclination; (*de tierras*) slope, incline; (*de cabeza*) nod, bow; (*fig*) leaning, bent

inclinar [inkli'nar] *vt* to incline; (*cabeza*) to nod, bow ♦ *vi* to lean, slope; **~se** *vr* to bow; (*encorvarse*) to stoop; **~se a** (*parecerse a*) to take after, resemble; **~se ante** to bow down to; **me inclino a pensar que** I'm inclined to think that

incluir [inklu'ir] *vt* to include; (*incorporar*) to incorporate; (*meter*) to enclose

inclusive [inklu'siβe] *adv* inclusive ♦ *prep* including

incluso [in'kluso] *adv* even

incógnita [in'koɣnita] *nf* (MAT) unknown quantity

incógnito [in'koɣnito] *nm*: **de ~** incognito

incoherente [inkoe'rente] *adj* incoherent

incoloro, a [inko'loro, a] *adj*

colourless

incólume [in'kolume] *adj* unhurt, unharmed

incomodar [inkomo'ðar] *vt* to inconvenience; (*molestar*) to bother, trouble; (*fastidiar*) to annoy; **~se** *vr* to put o.s. out; (*fastidiarse*) to get annoyed

incomodidad [inkomoði'ðað] *nf* inconvenience; (*fastidio, enojo*) annoyance; (*de vivienda*) discomfort

incómodo, a [in'komoðo, a] *adj* (*incofortable*) uncomfortable; (*molesto*) annoying; (*inconveniente*) inconvenient

incomparable [inkompa'raßle] *adj* incomparable

incompatible [inkompa'tißle] *adj* incompatible

incompetencia [inkompe'tenθja] *nf* incompetence; **incompetente** *adj* incompetent

incompleto, a [inkom'pleto, a] *adj* incomplete, unfinished

incomprensible [inkompren'sißle] *adj* incomprehensible

incomunicado, a [inkomuni'kaðo, a] *adj* (*aislado*) cut off, isolated; (*confinado*) in solitary confinement

inconcebible [inkonθe'ßißle] *adj* inconceivable

incondicional [inkondiθjo'nal] *adj* unconditional; (*apoyo*) wholehearted; (*partidario*) staunch

inconexo, a [inko'nekso, a] *adj* (*gen*) unconnected; (*desunido*) disconnected

inconfundible [inkonfun'dißle] *adj* unmistakable

incongruente [inkon'grwente] *adj* incongruous

inconsciencia [inkons'θjenθja] *nf* unconsciousness; (*fig*) thoughtlessness; **inconsciente** *adj* unconscious; thoughtless

inconsecuente [inkonse'kwente] *adj* inconsistent

inconsiderado, a [inkonsiðe'raðo, a] *adj* inconsiderate

inconsistente [inkonsis'tente] *adj* weak; (*tela*) flimsy

inconstancia [inkon'stanθja] *nf* inconstancy; (*inestabilidad*) unsteadiness; **inconstante** *adj* inconstant

incontable [inkon'taßle] *adj* countless, innumerable

incontestable [inkontes'taßle] *adj* unanswerable; (*innegable*) undeniable

incontinencia [inkonti'nenθja] *nf* incontinence

inconveniencia [inkombe'njenθja] *nf* unsuitability, inappropriateness; (*descortesía*) impoliteness; **inconveniente** *adj* unsuitable; impolite ♦ *nm* obstacle; (*desventaja*) disadvantage; **el inconveniente es que ...** the trouble is that ...

incordiar [inkor'ðjar] *vt* (*fam*) to dug, annoy

incorporación [inkorpora'θjon] *nf* incorporation

incorporar [inkorpo'rar] *vt* to incorporate; **~se** *vr* to sit up

incorrección [inkorrek'θjon] *nf* (*gen*) incorrectness, inaccuracy; (*descortesía*) bad-mannered behaviour; **incorrecto, a** *adj* (*gen*) incorrect, wrong; (*comportamiento*) bad-mannered

incorregible [inkorre'xißle] *adj* incorrigible

incredulidad [inkreðuli'ðað] *nf* incredulity; (*escepticismo*) scepticism; **incrédulo, a** *adj* incredulous, unbelieving; sceptical

increíble [inkre'ißle] *adj* incredible

incremento [inkre'mento] *nm* increment; (*aumento*) rise, increase

increpar [inkre'par] *vt* to reprimand

incruento, a [in'krwento, a] *adj* bloodless

incrustar [inkrus'tar] *vt* to incrust; (*piedras: en joya*) to inlay

incubar [inku'ßar] *vt* to incubate

inculcar [inkul'kar] *vt* to inculcate

inculpar [inkul'par] *vt* (*acusar*) to

accuse; (*achacar, atribuir*) to charge, blame

inculto, a [in'kulto, a] *adj* (*persona*) uneducated; (*grosero*) uncouth ♦ *nm/f* ignoramus

incumplimiento [inkumpli'mjento] *nm* non-fulfilment; ~ **de contrato** breach of contract

incurrir [inku'rrir] *vi*: ~ **en** to incur; (*crimen*) to commit; ~ **en un error** to make a mistake

indagación [indaɣa'θjon] *nf* investigation; (*búsqueda*) search; (*JUR*) inquest

indagar [inda'ɣar] *vt* to investigate; to search; (*averiguar*) to ascertain

indecente [inde'θente] *adj* indecent, improper; (*lascivo*) obscene

indecible [inde'θiβle] *adj* unspeakable; (*indescriptible*) indescribable

indeciso, a [inde'θiso, a] *adj* (*por decidir*) undecided; (*vacilante*) hesitant

indefenso, a [inde'fenso, a] *adj* defenceless

indefinido, a [indefi'niðo, a] *adj* indefinite; (*vago*) vague, undefined

indeleble [inde'leβle] *adj* indelible

indemne [in'demne] *adj* (*objeto*) undamaged; (*persona*) unharmed, unhurt

indemnizar [indemni'θar] *vt* to indemnify; (*compensar*) to compensate

independencia [indepen'denθja] *nf* independence

independiente [indepen'djente] *adj* (*libre*) independent; (*autónomo*) self-sufficient

indeterminado, a [indetermi'naðo, a] *adj* indefinite; (*desconocido*) indeterminate

India ['indja] *nf*: **la** ~ India

indicación [indika'θjon] *nf* indication; (*señal*) sign; (*sugerencia*) suggestion, hint

indicado, a [indi'kaðo, a] *adj* (*momento, método*) right; (*tratamiento*) appropriate; (*solución*) likely

indicador [indika'ðor] *nm* indicator; (*TEC*) gauge, meter

indicar [indi'kar] *vt* (*mostrar*) to indicate, show; (*termómetro etc*) to read, register; (*señalar*) to point to

índice ['indiθe] *nm* index; (*catálogo*) catalogue; (*ANAT*) index finger, forefinger

indicio [in'diθjo] *nm* indication, sign; (*en pesquisa etc*) clue

indiferencia [indife'renθja] *nf* indifference; (*apatía*) apathy; **indiferente** *adj* indifferent

indígena [in'dixena] *adj* indigenous, native ♦ *nm/f* native

indigencia [indi'xenθja] *nf* poverty, need

indigestión [indixes'tjon] *nf* indigestion

indigesto, a [indi'xesto, a] *adj* (*alimento*) indigestible; (*fig*) turgid

indignación [indiɣna'θjon] *nf* indignation

indignar [indiɣ'nar] *vt* to anger, make indignant; ~**se** *vr*: ~**se por** to get indignant about

indigno, a [in'diɣno, a] *adj* (*despreciable*) low, contemptible; (*inmerecido*) unworthy

indio, a ['indjo, a] *adj, nm/f* Indian

indirecta [indi'rekta] *nf* insinuation, innuendo; (*sugerencia*) hint

indirecto, a [indi'rekto, a] *adj* indirect

indiscreción [indiskre'θjon] *nf* (*imprudencia*) indiscretion; (*irreflexión*) tactlessness; (*acto*) gaffe, faux pas

indiscreto, a [indis'kreto, a] *adj* indiscreet

indiscriminado, a [indiskrimi'naðo, a] *adj* indiscriminate

indiscutible [indisku'tiβle] *adj* indisputable, unquestionable

indispensable [indispen'saβle] *adj* indispensable, essential

indisponer [indispo'ner] *vt* to spoil, upset; (*salud*) to make ill; ~**se** *vr* to fall ill; ~**se con uno** to fall out with sb

indisposición [indisposi'θjon] nf indisposition

indispuesto, a [indis'pwesto, a] adj (enfermo) unwell, indisposed

indistinto, a [indis'tinto, a] adj indistinct; (vago) vague

individual [indiβi'ðwal] adj individual; (habitación) single ♦ nm (DEPORTE) singles sg

individuo [indi'βiðwo, a] adj, nm individual

índole ['indole] nf (naturaleza) nature; (clase) sort, kind

indómito, a [in'domito, a] adj indomitable

inducir [indu'θir] vt to induce; (inferir) to infer; (persuadir) to persuade

indudable [indu'ðaβle] adj undoubted; (incuestionable) unquestionable

indulgencia [indul'xenθja] nf indulgence

indultar [indul'tar] vt (perdonar) to pardon, reprieve; (librar de pago) to exempt; **indulto** nm pardon; exemption

industria [in'dustrja] nf industry; (habilidad) skill; **industrial** adj industrial ♦ nm industrialist

inédito, a [in'eðito, a] adj (texto) unpublished; (nuevo) new

inefable [ine'faβle] adj ineffable, indescribable

ineficaz [inefi'kaθ] adj (inútil) ineffective; (ineficiente) inefficient

ineludible [inelu'ðiβle] adj inescapable, unavoidable

ineptitud [inepti'tuð] nf ineptitude, incompetence; **inepto, a** adj inept, incompetent

inequívoco, a [ine'kiβoko, a] adj unequivocal; (inconfundible) unmistakable

inercia [in'erθja] nf inertia; (pasividad) passivity

inerme [in'erme] adj (sin armas) unarmed; (indefenso) defenceless

inerte [in'erte] adj inert; (inmóvil) motionless

inesperado, a [inespe'raðo, a] adj unexpected, unforeseen

inestable [ines'taβle] adj unstable

inevitable [ineβi'taβle] adj inevitable

inexactitud [ineksakti'tuð] nf inaccuracy; **inexacto, a** adj inaccurate; (falso) untrue

inexperto, a [inek'sperto, a] adj (novato) inexperienced

infalible [infa'liβle] adj infallible; (plan) foolproof

infame [in'fame] adj infamous; (horrible) dreadful; **infamia** nf infamy; (deshonra) disgrace

infancia [in'fanθja] nf infancy, childhood

infantería [infante'ria] nf infantry

infantil [infan'til] adj (pueril, aniñado) infantile; (cándido) childlike; (literatura, ropa etc) children's

infarto [in'farto] nm (tb: ~ de miocardio) heart attack

infatigable [infati'vaβle] adj tireless, untiring

infección [infek'θjon] nf infection; **infeccioso, a** adj infectious

infectar [infek'tar] vt to infect; **~se** vr to become infected

infeliz [infe'liθ] adj unhappy, wretched ♦ nm/f wretch

inferior [infe'rjor] adj inferior; (situación) lower ♦ nm/f inferior, subordinate

inferir [infe'rir] vt (deducir) to infer, deduce; (causar) to cause

infestar [infes'tar] vt to infest

infidelidad [infiðeli'ðað] nf (gen) infidelity, unfaithfulness

infiel [in'fjel] adj unfaithful, disloyal; (erróneo) inaccurate ♦ nm/f infidel, unbeliever

infierno [in'fjerno] nm hell

infiltrarse [infil'trarse] vr: ~ **en** to infiltrate into(to); (persona) to work one's way in(to)

ínfimo, a [ˈinfimo, a] adj (más bajo) lowest; (despreciable) vile, mean

infinidad [infiniˈðað] nf infinity; (abundancia) great quantity

infinito, a [infiˈnito, a] adj, nm infinite

inflación [inflaˈθjon] nf (hinchazón) swelling; (monetaria) inflation; (fig) conceit; **inflacionario, a** adj inflationary

inflamar [inflaˈmar] vt (MED, fig) to inflame; ~**se** vr to catch fire; to become inflamed

inflar [inˈflar] vt (hinchar) to inflate, blow up; (fig) to exaggerate; ~**se** vr to swell (up); (fig) to get conceited

inflexible [inflekˈsiβle] adj inflexible; (fig) unbending

infligir [infliˈxir] vt to inflict

influencia [influˈenθja] nf influence; **influenciar** vt to influence

influir [influˈir] vt to influence

influjo [inˈfluxo] nm influence

influya etc vb ver **influir**

influyente [influˈjente] adj influential

información [informaˈθjon] nf information; (noticias) news sg; (JUR) inquiry; **I~** (oficina) Information Office; (mostrador) Information Desk; (TEL) Directory Enquiries

informal [inforˈmal] adj (gen) informal

informar [inforˈmar] vt (gen) to inform; (revelar) to reveal, make known ♦ vi (JUR) to plead; (denunciar) to inform; (dar cuenta de) to report on; ~**se** vr to find out; ~**se de** to inquire into

informática [inforˈmatika] nf computer science, information technology

informe [inˈforme] adj shapeless ♦ nm report

infortunio [inforˈtunjo] nm misfortune

infracción [infrakˈθjon] nf infraction, infringement

infranqueable [infrankeˈaβle] adj impassable; (fig) insurmountable

infravalorar [infrabaloˈrar] vt to undervalue, underestimate

infringir [infrinˈxir] vt to infringe, contravene

infructuoso, a [infrukˈtwoso, a] adj fruitless, unsuccessful

infundado, a [infunˈdaðo, a] adj groundless, unfounded

infundir [infunˈdir] vt to infuse, instil

infusión [infuˈsjon] nf infusion; ~ **de manzanilla** camomile tea

ingeniar [inxeˈnjar] vt to think up, devise; ~**se** vr: ~**se para** to manage to

ingeniería [inxenjeˈria] nf engineering; ~ **genética** genetic engineering; **ingeniero, a** nm/f engineer; **ingeniero de caminos/de sonido** civil engineer/sound engineer

ingenio [inˈxenjo] nm (talento) talent; (agudeza) wit; (habilidad) ingenuity, inventiveness; ~ **azucarero** (AM) sugar refinery

ingenioso, a [inxeˈnjoso, a] adj ingenious, clever; (divertido) witty

ingenuidad [inxenwiˈðað] nf ingenuousness; (sencillez) simplicity; **ingenuo, a** adj ingenuous

ingerir [inxeˈrir] vt to ingest; (tragar) to swallow; (consumir) to consume

Inglaterra [inglaˈterra] nf England

ingle [ˈingle] nf groin

inglés, esa [inˈgles, esa] adj English ♦ nm/f Englishman/woman ♦ nm (LING) English

ingratitud [ingratiˈtuð] nf ingratitude; **ingrato, a** adj (gen) ungrateful

ingrediente [ingreˈðjente] nm ingredient

ingresar [ingreˈsar] vt (dinero) to deposit ♦ vi to come in; ~ **en un club** to join a club; ~ **en el hospital** to go into hospital

ingreso [inˈgreso] nm (entrada) entry; (: en hospital etc) admission; ~**s** nmpl (dinero) income sg; (: COM) takings pl

inhabitable [inaβiˈtaβle] adj uninhabitable

inhalar [inaˈlar] vt to inhale

inherente [ine'rente] *adj* inherent

inhibir [ini'βir] *vt* to inhibit

inhóspito, a [i'nospito, a] *adj* (región, paisaje) inhospitable

inhumano, a [inu'mano, a] *adj* inhuman

inicial [ini'θjal] *adj, nf* initial

iniciar [ini'θjar] *vt* (persona) to initiate; (empezar) to begin, commence; (conversación) to start up

iniciativa [iniθja'tiβa] *nf* initiative; **la ~ privada** private enterprise

ininterrumpido, a [ininterrum'piδo, a] *adj* uninterrupted

injerencia [inxe'renθja] *nf* interference

injertar [inxer'tar] *vt* to graft; **injerto** *nm* graft

injuria [in'xurja] *nf* (agravio, ofensa) offence; (insulto) insult; **injuriar** *vt* to insult; **injurioso, a** *adj* offensive; insulting

injusticia [inxus'tiθja] *nf* injustice

injusto, a [in'xusto, a] *adj* unjust, unfair

inmadurez [inmaðu'reθ] *nf* immaturity

inmediaciones [inmeðja'θjones] *nfpl* neighbourhood *sg*, environs

inmediato, a [inme'ðjato, a] *adj* immediate; (contiguo) adjoining; (rápido) prompt; (próximo) neighbouring, next; **de ~** immediately

inmejorable [inmexo'raβle] *adj* unsurpassable; (precio) unbeatable

inmenso, a [in'menso, a] *adj* immense, huge

inmerecido, a [inmere'θiðo, a] *adj* undeserved

inmigración [inmiɣra'θjon] *nf* immigration

inmiscuirse [inmisku'irse] *vr* to interfere, meddle

inmobiliaria [inmoβi'ljarja] *nf* estate agency

inmobiliario, a [inmoβi'ljarjo, a] *adj* real-estate *cpd*, property *cpd*

inmolar [inmo'lar] *vt* to immolate, sacrifice

inmoral [inmo'ral] *adj* immoral

inmortal [inmor'tal] *adj* immortal; **~izar** *vt* to immortalize

inmóvil [in'moβil] *adj* immobile

inmueble [in'mweβle] *adj*: **bienes ~s** real estate, landed property ♦ *nm* property

inmundicia [inmun'diθja] *nf* filth; **inmundo, a** *adj* filthy

inmune [in'mune] *adj*: **~ (a)** (MED) immune (to)

inmunidad [inmuni'ðað] *nf* immunity

inmutarse [inmu'tarse] *vr* to turn pale; **no se inmutó** he didn't turn a hair

innato, a [in'nato, a] *adj* innate

innecesario, a [inneθe'sarjo, a] *adj* unnecessary

innoble [in'noβle] *adj* ignoble

innovación [innoβa'θjon] *nf* innovation

innovar [inno'βar] *vt* to introduce

inocencia [ino'θenθja] *nf* innocence

inocentada [inoθen'taða] *nf* practical joke

inocente [ino'θente] *adj* (ingenuo) naive, innocent; (inculpable) innocent; (sin malicia) harmless ♦ *nm/f* simpleton

Día de los Santos Inocentes

The 28th December, el día de los (Santos) Inocentes, is when the Church commemorates the story of Herod's slaughter of the innocent children of Judaea. On this day Spaniards play inocentadas (practical jokes) on each other, much like our April Fool's Day pranks.

inodoro [ino'ðoro] *nm* toilet, lavatory (BRIT)

inofensivo, a [inofen'siβo, a] *adj* inoffensive, harmless

inolvidable [inolβi'ðaβle] *adj* unforgettable

inopinado, a [inopi'naðo, a] *adj*

unexpected
inoportuno, a [inopor'tuno, a] *adj*
untimely; *(molesto)* inconvenient
inoxidable [inoksi'ðaßle] *adj:* **acero ~**
stainless steel
inquebrantable [inkeßran'taßle] *adj*
unbreakable
inquietar [inkje'tar] *vt* to worry,
trouble; **~se** *vr* to worry, get upset;
inquieto, a *adj* anxious, worried;
inquietud *nf* anxiety, worry
inquilino, a [inki'lino, a] *nm/f* tenant
inquirir [inki'rir] *vt* to enquire into,
investigate
insaciable [insa'θjaßle] *adj* insatiable
insalubre [insa'lußre] *adj* unhealthy
inscribir [inskri'ßir] *vt* to inscribe; (~ a
uno en *(lista)* to put sb on; *(censo)* to
register sb on
inscripción [inskrip'θjon] *nf*
inscription; *(ESCOL etc)* enrolment;
(censo) registration
insecticida [insekti'θiða] *nm*
insecticide
insecto [in'sekto] *nm* insect
inseguridad [insevuri'ðað] *nf*
insecurity
inseguro, a [inse'vuro, a] *adj*
insecure; *(inconstante)* unsteady;
(incierto) uncertain
insensato, a [insen'sato, a] *adj*
foolish, stupid
insensibilidad [insensißili'ðað] *nf*
(gen) insensitivity; *(dureza de corazón)*
callousness
insensible [insen'sißle] *adj (gen)*
insensitive; *(movimiento)* imperceptible;
(sin sentido) numb
insertar [inser'tar] *vt* to insert
inservible [inser'ßißle] *adj* useless
insidioso, a [insi'ðjoso, a] *adj*
insidious
insignia [in'sivnja] *nf (señal distintiva)*
badge; *(estandarte)* flag
insignificante [insivnifi'kante] *adj*
insignificant
insinuar [insi'nwar] *vt* to insinuate,

imply
insípido, a [in'sipiðo, a] *adj* insipid
insistencia [insis'tenθja] *nf* insistence
insistir [insis'tir] *vi* to insist; **~ en algo**
to insist on sth; *(enfatizar)* to stress sth
insolación [insola'θjon] *nf (MED)*
sunstroke
insolencia [inso'lenθja] *nf* insolence;
insolente *adj* insolent
insólito, a [in'solito, a] *adj* unusual
insoluble [inso'lußle] *adj* insoluble
insolvencia [insol'ßenθja] *nf*
insolvency
insomnio [in'somnjo] *nm* insomnia
insondable [inson'daßle] *adj*
bottomless; *(fig)* impenetrable
insonorizado, a [insonori'θaðo, a]
adj (cuarto etc) soundproof
insoportable [insopor'taßle] *adj*
unbearable
insospechado, a [insospe'tʃaðo, a]
adj (inesperado) unexpected
inspección [inspek'θjon] *nf*
inspection, check; **inspeccionar** *vt*
(examinar) to inspect, examine;
(controlar) to check
inspector, a [inspek'tor, a] *nm/f*
inspector
inspiración [inspira'θjon] *nf*
inspiration
inspirar [inspi'rar] *vt* to inspire; *(MED)*
to inhale; **~se** *vr:* **~se en** to be
inspired by
instalación [instala'θjon] *nf (equipo)*
fittings *pl*, equipment; **~ eléctrica**
wiring
instalar [insta'lar] *vt (establecer)* to
instal; *(erguir)* to set up, erect; **~se** *vr*
to establish o.s; *(en una vivienda)* to
move into
instancia [ins'tanθja] *nf (JUR)* petition;
(ruego) request; **en última ~** as a last
resort
instantánea [instan'tanea] *nf*
snap(shot)
instantáneo, a [instan'taneo, a] *adj*
instantaneous; **café ~** instant coffee

instante [ins'tante] *nm* instant, moment

instar [ins'tar] *vt* to press, urge

instaurar [instau'rar] *vt* (*costumbre*) to establish; (*normas, sistema*) to bring in, introduce; (*gobierno*) to instal

instigar [insti'ɣar] *vt* to instigate

instinto [ins'tinto] *nm* instinct; **por ~** instinctively

institución [institu'θjon] *nf* institution, establishment

instituir [institu'ir] *vt* to establish; (*fundar*) to found; **instituto** *nm* (*ESP: ESCOL*) ≈ comprehensive (*BRIT*) o high (*US*) school

institutriz [institu'triθ] *nf* governess

instrucción [instruk'θjon] *nf* instruction

instructivo, a [instruk'tiβo, a] *adj* instructive

instruir [instru'ir] *vt* (*gen*) to instruct; (*enseñar*) to teach, educate

instrumento [instru'mento] *nm* (*gen*) instrument; (*herramienta*) tool, implement

insubordinarse [insuβorðiˈnarse] *vr* to rebel

insuficiencia [insufiˈθjenθja] *nf* (*carencia*) lack; (*inadecuación*) inadequacy; **insuficiente** *adj* (*gen*) insufficient; (*ESCOL: calificación*) unsatisfactory

insufrible [insuˈfriβle] *adj* insufferable

insular [insuˈlar] *adj* insular

insultar [insulˈtar] *vt* to insult; **insulto** *nm* insult

insumiso, a [insuˈmiso, a] *nm/f* (*POL*) person who refuses to do military service or its substitute, community service

insuperable [insupeˈraβle] *adj* (*excelente*) unsurpassable; (*problema etc*) insurmountable

insurgente [insurˈxente] *adj, nm/f* insurgent

insurrección [insurrekˈθjon] *nf* insurrection, rebellion

intachable [intaˈtʃaβle] *adj* irreproachable

intacto, a [inˈtakto, a] *adj* intact

integral [inteˈɣral] *adj* integral; (*completo*) complete; **pan ~** wholemeal (*BRIT*) o wholewheat (*US*) bread

integrar [inteˈɣrar] *vt* to make up, compose; (*MAT, fig*) to integrate

integridad [inteɣriˈðað] *nf* wholeness; (*carácter*) integrity; **íntegro, a** *adj* whole, entire; (*honrado*) honest

intelectual [intelekˈtwal] *adj, nm/f* intellectual

inteligencia [inteliˈxenθja] *nf* intelligence; (*ingenio*) ability; **inteligente** *adj* intelligent

inteligible [inteliˈxiβle] *adj* intelligible

intemperie [intemˈperje] *nf*: **a la ~** out in the open, exposed to the elements

intempestivo, a [intempesˈtiβo, a] *adj* untimely

intención [intenˈθjon] *nf* (*gen*) intention, purpose; **con segundas intenciones** maliciously; **con ~** deliberately

intencionado, a [intenθjoˈnaðo, a] *adj* deliberate; **bien ~** well-meaning; **mal ~** ill-disposed, hostile

intensidad [intensiˈðað] *nf* (*gen*) intensity; (*ELEC, TEC*) strength; **llover con ~** to rain hard

intenso, a [inˈtenso, a] *adj* intense; (*sentimiento*) profound, deep

intentar [intenˈtar] *vt* (*tratar*) to try, attempt; **intento** *nm* attempt

interactivo, a [interakˈtiβo, a] *adj* (*INFORM*) interactive

intercalar [interkaˈlar] *vt* to insert

intercambio [interˈkambjo] *nm* exchange, swap

interceder [interθeˈðer] *vi* to intercede

interceptar [interθepˈtar] *vt* to intercept

intercesión [interθeˈsjon] *nf* intercession

interés [inteˈres] *nm* (*gen*) interest; (*parte*) share, part; (*pey*) self-interest;

intereses creados vested interests
interesado, a [intere'saðo, a] *adj* interested; (*prejuiciado*) prejudiced; (*pey*) mercenary, self-seeking
interesante [intere'sante] *adj* interesting
interesar [intere'sar] *vt, vi* to interest, be of interest to; **~se** *vr*: **~se en** o **por** to take an interest in
interferir [interfe'rir] *vt* to interfere with; (*TEL*) to jam ♦ *vi* to interfere
interfono [inter'fono] *nm* intercom
interino, a [inte'rino, a] *adj* temporary ♦ *nm/f* temporary holder of a post; (*MED*) locum; (*ESCOL*) supply teacher
interior [inte'rjor] *adj* inner, inside; (*COM*) domestic, internal ♦ *nm* interior, inside; (*fig*) soul, mind; **Ministerio del I~** = Home Office (*BRIT*), = Department of the Interior (*US*)
interjección [interxek'θjon] *nf* interjection
interlocutor, a [interloku'tor, a] *nm/f* speaker
intermedio, a [inter'meðjo, a] *adj* intermediate ♦ *nm* interval
interminable [intermi'naßle] *adj* endless
intermitente [intermi'tente] *adj* intermittent ♦ *nm* (*AUTO*) indicator
internacional [internaθjo'nal] *adj* international
internado [inter'naðo] *nm* boarding school
internar [inter'nar] *vt* to intern; (*en un manicomio*) to commit; **~se** *vr* (*penetrar*) to penetrate
Internet [inter'net] *nm* o *nf*: **el** o **la ~** the Internet
interno, a [in'terno, a] *adj* internal, interior; (*POL etc*) domestic ♦ *nm/f* (*alumno*) boarder
interponer [interpo'ner] *vt* to interpose, put in; **~se** *vr* to intervene
interpretación [interpreta'θjon] *nf* interpretation

interpretar [interpre'tar] *vt* to interpret; (*TEATRO, MUS*) to perform, play; **intérprete** *nm/f* (*LING*) interpreter, translator; (*MUS, TEATRO*) performer, artist(e)
interrogación [interroɣa'θjon] *nf* interrogation; (*LING: tb: signo de ~*) question mark
interrogar [interro'ɣar] *vt* to interrogate, question
interrumpir [interrum'pir] *vt* to interrupt
interrupción [interrup'θjon] *nf* interruption
interruptor [interrup'tor] *nm* (*ELEC*) switch
intersección [intersek'θjon] *nf* intersection
interurbano, a [interur'ßano, a] *adj*: **llamada interurbana** long-distance call
intervalo [inter'ßalo] *nm* interval; (*descanso*) break; **a ~s** at intervals, every now and then
intervenir [interße'nir] *vt* (*controlar*) to control, supervise; (*MED*) to operate on ♦ *vi* (*participar*) to take part, participate; (*mediar*) to intervene
interventor, a [interßen'tor, a] *nm/f* inspector; (*COM*) auditor
intestino [intes'tino] *nm* (*MED*) intestine
intimar [inti'mar] *vi* to become friendly
intimidad [intimi'ðað] *nf* intimacy; (*familiaridad*) familiarity; (*vida privada*) private life; (*JUR*) privacy
íntimo, a [i'intimo, a] *adj* intimate
intolerable [intole'raßle] *adj* intolerable, unbearable
intoxicación [intoksika'θjon] *nf* poisoning
intranet [intra'net] *nf* intranet
intranquilizarse [intrankili'θarse] *vr* to get worried o anxious; **intranquilo, a** *adj* worried
intransitable [intransi'taßle] *adj*

impassable

intrépido, a [in'trepiðo, a] adj
intrepid

intriga [in'triɣa] nf intrigue; (plan)
plot; **intrigar** vt, vi to intrigue

intrincado, a [intrin'kaðo, a] adj
intricate

intrínseco, a [in'trinseko, a] adj
intrinsic

introducción [introðuk'θjon] nf
introduction

introducir [introðu'θir] vt (gen) to
introduce; (moneda etc) to insert;
(INFORM) to input, enter

intromisión [intromi'sjon] nf
interference, meddling

introvertido, a [introβer'tiðo, a] adj,
nm/f introvert

intruso, a [in'truso, a] adj intrusive
♦ nm/f intruder

intuición [intwi'θjon] nf intuition

inundación [inunda'θjon] nf
flood(ing); **inundar** vt to flood; (fig) to
swamp, inundate

inusitado, a [inusi'taðo, a] adj
unusual, rare

inútil [in'util] adj useless; (esfuerzo)
vain, fruitless; **inutilidad** nf uselessness

inutilizar [inutili'θar] vt to make o
render useless; **~se** vr to become
useless

invadir [imba'ðir] vt to invade

inválido, a [im'baliðo, a] adj invalid
♦ nm/f invalid

invariable [imba'rjaβle] adj invariable

invasión [imba'sjon] nf invasion

invasor, a [imba'sor, a] adj invading
♦ nm/f invader

invención [imben'θjon] nf invention

inventar [imben'tar] vt to invent

inventario [imben'tarjo] nm inventory

inventiva [imben'tiβa] nf
inventiveness

invento [im'bento] nm invention

inventor, a [imben'tor, a] nm/f
inventor

invernadero [imberna'ðero] nm

greenhouse

inverosímil [imbero'simil] adj
implausible

inversión [imber'sjon] nf (COM)
investment

inverso, a [im'berso, a] adj inverse,
opposite; **en el orden ~** in reverse
order; **a la inversa** inversely, the other
way round

inversor, a [imber'sor, a] nm/f (COM)
investor

invertir [imber'tir] vt (COM) to invest;
(volcar) to turn upside down; (tiempo
etc) to spend

investigación [imbestiɣa'θjon] nf
investigation; (ESCOL) research; **~ de
mercado** market research

investigar [imbesti'ɣar] vt to
investigate; (ESCOL) to do research into

invierno [im'bjerno] nm winter

invisible [imbi'siβle] adj invisible

invitado, a [imbi'taðo, a] nm/f guest

invitar [imbi'tar] vt to invite; (incitar)
to entice; (pagar) to buy, pay for

invocar [imbo'kar] vt to invoke, call on

involucrar [imbolu'krar] vt: **~ en** to
involve in; **~se** vr (persona): **~ en** to
get mixed up in

involuntario, a [imbolun'tarjo, a] adj
(movimiento, gesto) involuntary; (error)
unintentional

inyección [injek'θjon] nf injection

inyectar [injek'tar] vt to inject

PALABRA CLAVE

ir [ir] vi **1** to go; (a pie) to walk; (viajar)
to travel; **~ caminando** to walk; **fui
en tren** I went o travelled by train;
¡(ahora) voy! (I'm just) coming!
2: **~ (a) por: ~ (a) por el médico** to
fetch the doctor
3 (progresar: persona, cosa) to go; **el
trabajo va muy bien** work is going
very well; **¿cómo te va?** how are
things going?; **me va muy bien** I'm
getting on very well; **le fue fatal** it
went awfully badly for him

4 (*funcionar*): **el coche no va muy bien** the car isn't running very well
5: te va estupendamente ese color that colour suits you fantastically well
6 (*locuciones*): **¿vino? – ¡que va!** did he come? – of course not!; **vamos, no llores** come on, don't cry; **¡vaya coche!** what a car!, that's some car!
7: no vaya a ser: tienes que correr, no vaya a ser que pierdas el tren you'll have to run so as not to miss the train
8 (+ *pp*): **iba vestido muy bien** he was very well dressed
9: no me da igual no va ni me viene I *etc* don't care
♦ *vb aux* **1:** ~ **a: voy/iba a hacerlo hoy** I am/was going to do it today
2 (+ *gerundio*): **iba anocheciendo** it was getting dark; **todo se me iba aclarando** everything was gradually becoming clearer to me
3 (+ *pp* = *pasivo*): **van vendidos 300 ejemplares** 300 copies have been sold so far
♦ ~**se** *vr* **1: ¿por dónde se va al zoológico?** which is the way to the zoo?
2 (*marcharse*) to leave; **ya se habrán ido** they must already have left o gone

ira |'ira| *nf* anger, rage
Irak |i'rak| *nm* = **Iraq**
Irán |i'ran| *nm* Iran; **iraní** *adj, nm/f* Iranian
Iraq |i'rak| *nm* Iraq; **iraquí** *adj, nm/f* Iraqi
iris |'iris| *nm inv* (*tb: arco* ~) rainbow; (*ANAT*) iris
Irlanda |ir'landa| *nf* Ireland; **irlandés, esa** *adj* Irish ♦ *nm/f* Irishman/woman; **los irlandeses** the Irish
ironía |iro'nia| *nf* irony; **irónico, a** *adj* ironic(al)
IRPF |i 'erre 'pe 'efe| *nm abr* (= *Impuesto sobre la Renta de las Personas Físicas*) (personal) income tax

irreal |irre'al| *adj* unreal
irrecuperable |irrekupe'raßle| *adj* irrecoverable, irretrievable
irreflexión |irreflek'sjon| *nf* thoughtlessness
irregular |irrexu'lar| *adj* (*gen*) irregular; (*situación*) abnormal
irremediable |irreme'ðjaßle| *adj* irremediable; (*vicio*) incurable
irreparable |irrepa'raßle| *adj* (*daños*) irreparable; (*pérdida*) irrecoverable
irresoluto, a |irreso'luto, a| *adj* irresolute, hesitant
irrespetuoso, a |irrespe'twoso, a| *adj* disrespectful
irresponsable |irrespon'saßle| *adj* irresponsible
irreversible |irreßer'sible| *adj* irreversible
irrigar |irri'var| *vt* to irrigate
irrisorio, a |irri'sorjo, a| *adj* derisory, ridiculous
irritar |irri'tar| *vt* to irritate, annoy
irrupción |irrup'θjon| *nf* irruption; (*invasión*) invasion
isla |'isla| *nf* island
islandés, esa |islan'des, esa| *adj* Icelandic ♦ *nm/f* Icelander
Islandia |is'landja| *nf* Iceland
isleño, a |is'leno, a| *adj* island *cpd* ♦ *nm/f* islander
Israel |isra'el| *nm* Israel; **israelí** *adj, nm/f* Israeli
istmo |'istmo| *nm* isthmus
Italia |i'talja| *nf* Italy; **italiano, a** *adj, nm/f* Italian
itinerario |itine'rarjo| *nm* itinerary, route
IVA |'ißa| *nm abr* (= *impuesto sobre el valor añadido*) VAT
izar |i'θar| *vt* to hoist
izdo, a *abr* (= *izquierdo, a*) l.
izquierda |iθ'kjerda| *nf* left; (*POL*) left (wing); **a la** ~ (*estar*) on the left; (*torcer etc*) to (the) left
izquierdista |iθkjer'ðista| *nm/f* left-winger, leftist

izquierdo, a [iθ'kjerðo, a] adj left

J, j

jabalí [xaßa'li] nm wild boar

jabalina [xaßa'lina] nf javelin

jabón [xa'ßon] nm soap; **jabonar** vt to soap

jaca ['xaka] nf pony

jacinto [xa'θinto] nm hyacinth

jactarse [xak'tarse] vr to boast, brag

jadear [xaðe'ar] vi to pant, gasp for breath; **jadeo** nm panting, gasping

jaguar [xa'ɣwar] nm jaguar

jalea [xa'lea] nf jelly

jaleo [xa'leo] nm racket, uproar; **armar un ~** to kick up a racket

jalón [xa'lon] (AM) nm tug

jamás [xa'mas] adv never

jamón [xa'mon] nm ham; **~ dulce, ~ de York** cooked ham; **~ serrano** cured ham

Japón [xa'pon] nm: **el ~** Japan; **japonés, esa** adj, nm/f Japanese ♦ nm (LING) Japanese

jaque ['xake] nm: **~ mate** checkmate

jaqueca [xa'keka] nf (very bad) headache, migraine

jarabe [xa'raße] nm syrup

jarcia ['xarθja] nf (NAUT) ropes pl, rigging

jardín [xar'ðin] nm garden; **~ de infancia** (ESP) o **de niños** (AM) nursery (school); **jardinería** nf gardening; **jardinero, a** nm/f gardener

jarra ['xarra] nf jar; (jarro) jug

jarro ['xarro] nm jug

jarrón [xa'rron] nm vase

jaula ['xaula] nf cage

jauría [xau'ria] nf pack of hounds

jazmín [xaθ'min] nm jasmine

J. C. abr (= Jesucristo) J.C.

jefa ['xefa] nf ver **jefe**

jefatura [xefa'tura] nf: **~ de policía** police headquarters sg

jefe, a ['xefe, a] nm/f (gen) chief, head; (patrón) boss; **~ de cocina** chef; **~ de estación** stationmaster; **~ de estado** head of state

jengibre [xen'xißre] nm ginger

jeque ['xeke] nm sheik

jerarquía [xerar'kia] nf (orden) hierarchy; (rango) rank; **jerárquico, a** adj hierarchic(al)

jerez [xe'reθ] nm sherry

jerga ['xerɣa] nf jargon

jeringa [xe'ringa] nf syringe; (AM) annoyance, bother; **~ de engrase** grease gun; **jeringar** vt (fam) to annoy, bother; **jeringuilla** nf syringe

jeroglífico [xero'vlifiko] nm hieroglyphic

jersey [xer'sei] (pl **~s**) nm jersey, pullover, jumper

Jerusalén [xerusa'len] n Jerusalem

Jesucristo [xesu'kristo] nm Jesus Christ

jesuita [xe'swita] adj, nm Jesuit

Jesús [xe'sus] nm Jesus; **¡~!** good heavens!; (al estornudar) bless you!

jinete, a [xi'nete, a] nm/f horseman-woman, rider

jipijapa [xipi'xapa] (AM) nm straw hat

jirafa [xi'rafa] nf giraffe

jirón [xi'ron] nm rag, shred

jocoso, a [xo'koso, a] adj humorous, jocular

joder [xo'ðer] (fam!) vt, vi to fuck(!)

jofaina [xo'faina] nf washbasin

jornada [xor'naða] nf (viaje de un día) day's journey; (camino o viaje entero) journey; (día de trabajo) working day

jornal [xor'nal] nm (day's) wage; **~ero** nm (day) labourer

joroba [xo'roßa] nf hump, hunched back; **~do, a** adj hunchbacked ♦ nm/f hunchback

jota ['xota] nf (the letter) J; (danza) Aragonese dance; **no saber ni ~** to have no idea

joven ['xoßen] (pl **jóvenes**) adj young

♦ *nm* young man, youth ♦ *nf* young woman, girl

jovial [xo'ßjal] *adj* cheerful, jolly

joya ['xoja] *nf* jewel, gem; (*fig: persona*) gem; **joyería** *nf* (*joyas*) jewellery; (*tienda*) jeweller's (shop); **joyero, a** *nm* (*persona*) jeweller; (*caja*) jewel case

juanete [xwa'nete] *nm* (*del pie*) bunion

jubilación [xußila'θjon] *nf* (*retiro*) retirement

jubilado, a [xußi'laðo, a] *adj* retired ♦ *nm/f* pensioner (*BRIT*), senior citizen

jubilar [xußi'lar] *vt* to pension off, retire; (*fam*) to discard; **~se** *vr* to retire

júbilo ['xußilo] *nm* joy, rejoicing; **jubiloso, a** *adj* jubilant

judía [xu'ðia] *nf* (*CULIN*) bean; **~ verde** French bean; *ver tb* **judío**

judicial [xuði'θjal] *adj* judicial

judío, a [xu'ðio, a] *adj* Jewish ♦ *nm/f* Jew(ess)

judo ['juðo] *nm* judo

juego *etc* ['xwexo] *vb ver* **jugar** ♦ *nm* (*gen*) play; (*pasatiempo, partido*) game; (*en casino*) gambling; (*conjunto*) set; **fuera de** (*DEPORTE: persona*) offside; (*: pelota*) out of play; **J~s Olímpicos** Olympic Games

juerga ['xwerɣa] *nf* binge; (*fiesta*) party; **ir de ~** to go out on a binge

jueves ['xweßes] *nm inv* Thursday

juez [xweθ] *nm/f* judge; **~ de línea** linesman; **~ de salida** starter

jugada [xu'ɣaða] *nf* play; **buena ~** good move/shot/stroke *etc*

jugador, a [xuɣa'ðor, a] *nm/f* player; (*en casino*) gambler

jugar [xu'ɣar] *vt, vi* to play; (*en casino*) to gamble; (*apostar*) to bet; **~ al fútbol** to play football

juglar [xu'ɣlar] *nm* minstrel

jugo ['xuɣo] *nm* (*BOT*) juice; (*fig*) essence, substance; **~ de fruta** (*AM*) fruit juice; **~so, a** *adj* juicy; (*fig*) substantial, important

juguete [xu'ɣete] *nm* toy; **~ar** *vi* to play; **~ría** *nf* toyshop

juguetón, ona [xuɣe'ton, ona] *adj* playful

juicio ['xwiθjo] *nm* judgement; (*razón*) sanity, reason; (*opinión*) opinion; **~so, a** *adj* wise, sensible

julio ['xuljo] *nm* July

junco ['xunko] *nm* rush, reed

jungla ['xungla] *nf* jungle

junio ['xunjo] *nm* June

junta ['xunta] *nf* (*asamblea*) meeting, assembly; (*comité, consejo*) board, council, committee; (*TEC*) joint

juntar [xun'tar] *vt* to join, unite; (*maquinaria*) to assemble, put together; (*dinero*) to collect; **~se** *vr* to join, meet; (*reunirse: personas*) to meet, assemble; (*arrimarse*) to approach, draw closer; **~se con uno** to join sb

junto, a ['xunto, a] *adj* joined; (*unido*) united; (*anexo*) near, close; (*contiguo, próximo*) next, adjacent ♦ *adv:* **todo ~** all at once; **~s** together; **~ a** near (to), next to

jurado [xu'raðo] *nm* (*JUR: individuo*) juror; (*: grupo*) jury; (*de concurso: grupo*) panel (of judges); (*: individuo*) member of a panel

juramento [xura'mento] *nm* oath; (*maldición*) oath, curse; **prestar ~** to take the oath; **tomar ~ a** to swear in, administer the oath to

jurar [xu'rar] *vt, vi* to swear; **~ en falso** to commit perjury; **jurárselas a uno** to have it in for sb

jurídico, a [xu'riðiko, a] *adj* legal

jurisdicción [xurisðik'θjon] *nf* (*poder, autoridad*) jurisdiction; (*territorio*) district

jurisprudencia [xurispru'ðenθja] *nf* jurisprudence

jurista [xu'rista] *nm/f* jurist

justamente [xusta'mente] *adv* justly, fairly; (*precisamente*) just, exactly

justicia [xus'tiθja] *nf* justice; (*equidad*) fairness, justice; **justiciero, a** *adj* just, righteous

justificación [xustifika'θjon] *nf* justification; **justificar** vt to justify

justo, a ['xusto, a] adj (equitativo) just, fair, right; (preciso) exact, correct; (ajustado) tight ♦ adv (precisamente) exactly, precisely; (AM: apenas a tiempo) just in time

juvenil [xuße'nil] adj youthful

juventud [xußen'tuð] nf (adolescencia) youth; (jóvenes) young people pl

juzgado [xuθ'γaðo] nm tribunal; (JUR) court

juzgar [xuθ'γar] vt to judge; **a ~ por ...** to judge by ..., judging by ...

K, k

kg abr (= kilogramo) kg

kilo ['kilo] nm kilo ♦ pref: **~gramo** nm kilogramme; **~metraje** nm distance in kilometres, ≈ mileage; **kilómetro** nm kilometre; **~vatio** nm kilowatt

kiosco ['kjosko] nm = quiosco

Kosovo [ko'soßo] nm Kosovo

km abr (= kilómetro) km

kv abr (= kilovatio) kw

L, l

l abr (= litro) l

la [la] art def the ♦ pron her; (Ud.) you; (cosa) it ♦ nm (MUS) la; **~ del sombrero rojo** the girl in the red hat; tb ver **el**

laberinto [laße'rinto] nm labyrinth

labia ['laßja] nf fluency; (pey) glib tongue

labio ['laßjo] nm lip

labor [la'ßor] nf labour; (AGR) farm work; (tarea) job, task; (COSTURA) needlework; **~able** adj (AGR) workable; **día ~able** working day; **~al** adj (accidente) at work; (jornada) working

laboratorio [laßora'torjo] nm laboratory

laborioso, a [laßo'rjosa, a] adj

(persona) hard-working; (trabajo) tough

laborista [laßo'rista] adj: **Partido L~** Labour Party

labrado, a [la'ßraðo, a] adj worked; (madera) carved; (metal) wrought

labrador, a [laßra'ðor, a] adj farming cpd ♦ nm/f farmer

labranza [la'ßranθa] nf (AGR) cultivation

labrar [la'ßrar] vt (gen) to work; (madera etc) to carve; (fig) to cause, bring about

labriego, a [la'ßrjevo, a] nm/f peasant

laca ['laka] nf lacquer

lacayo [la'kajo] nm lackey

lacio, a ['laθjo, a] adj (pelo) straight

lacón [la'kon] nm shoulder of pork

lacónico, a [la'koniko, a] adj laconic

lacra ['lakra] nf (fig) blot; **lacrar** vt (cerrar) to seal (with sealing wax); **lacre** nm sealing wax

lactancia [lak'tanθja] nf lactation

lactar [lak'tar] vt, vi to suckle

lácteo, a [la'kteo, a] adj: **productos ~s** dairy products

ladear [laðe'ar] vt to tip, tilt ♦ vi to tilt; **~se** vr to lean

ladera [la'ðera] nf slope

lado ['laðo] nm (gen) side; (fig) protection; (MIL) flank; **al ~ de** beside; **poner de ~** to put on its side; **poner a un ~** to put aside; **por todos ~s** on all sides, all round (BRIT)

ladrar [la'ðrar] vi to bark; **ladrido** nm bark, barking

ladrillo [la'ðriljo] nm (gen) brick; (azulejo) tile

ladrón, ona [la'ðron, ona] nm/f thief

lagartija [lavar'tixa] nf (ZOOL) (small) lizard

lagarto [la'varto] nm (ZOOL) lizard

lago ['lavo] nm lake

lágrima ['lavrima] nf tear

laguna [la'vuna] nf (lago) lagoon; (hueco) gap

laico, a ['laiko, a] adj lay

lamentable [lamen'taßle] adj

lamentable, regrettable; (*miserable*) pitiful

lamentar |lamen'tar| vt (*sentir*) to regret; (*deplorar*) to lament; **lo lamento mucho** I'm very sorry; **~se** vr to lament; **lamento** nm lament

lamer |la'mer| vt to lick

lámina |'lamina| nf (*plancha delgada*) sheet; (*para estampar, estampa*) plate

lámpara |'lampara| nf lamp; **~ de alcohol/gas** spirit/gas lamp; **~ de pie** standard lamp

lamparón |lampa'ron| nm grease spot

lana |'lana| nf wool

lancha |'lantʃa| nf launch; **~ de pesca** fishing boat; **~ salvavidas/torpedera** lifeboat/torpedo boat

langosta |lan'gosta| nf (*crustáceo*) lobster; (: *de río*) crayfish; **langostino** nm Dublin Bay prawn

languidecer |langiðe'θer| vi to languish; **languidez** nf languour; **lánguido, a** adj (*gen*) languid; (*sin energía*) listless

lanilla |la'niʎa| nf nap

lanza |'lanθa| nf (*arma*) lance, spear

lanzamiento |lanθa'mjento| nm (*gen*) throwing; (*NAUT, COM*) launch, launching; **~ de peso** putting the shot

lanzar |lan'θar| vt (*gen*) to throw; (*DEPORTE: pelota*) to bowl; (*NAUT, COM*) to launch; (*JUR*) to evict; **~se** vr to throw o.s.

lapa |'lapa| nf limpet

lapicero |lapi'θero| nm pencil; (*AM: bolígrafo*) Biro ®

lápida |'lapiða| nf stone; **~ mortuoria** headstone; **~ conmemorativa** memorial stone; **lapidario, a** adj, nm lapidary

lápiz |'lapiθ| nm pencil; **~ de color** coloured pencil; **~ de labios** lipstick

lapón, ona |la'pon, ona| nm/f Laplander, Lapp

lapso |'lapso| nm (*de tiempo*) interval; (*error*) error

lapsus |'lapsus| nm inv error, mistake

largar |lar'var| vt (*soltar*) to release; (*aflojar*) to loosen; (*lanzar*) to launch; (*fam*) to let fly; (*velas*) to unfurl; (*AM*) to throw; **~se** vr (*fam*) to beat it; **~se a** (*AM*) to start to

largo, a |'larvo, a| adj (*longitud*) long; (*tiempo*) lengthy; (*fig*) generous ♦ nm length; (*MUS*) largo; **dos años ~s** two long years; **tiene 9 metros de ~** it is 9 metres long; **a lo ~ de** along; (*tiempo*) all through, throughout; **~metraje** nm feature film

laringe |la'rinxe| nf larynx; **laringitis** nf laryngitis

larva |'larßa| nf larva

las |las| art def the ♦ pron them; **~ que cantan** the ones/women/girls who sing; tb ver **el**

lascivo, a |las'θißo, a| adj lewd

láser |'laser| nm laser

lástima |'lastima| nf (*pena*) pity; **dar ~** to be pitiful; **es una ~ que** it's a pity that; **¡qué ~!** what a pity!; **ella está hecha una ~** she looks pitiful

lastimar |lasti'mar| vt (*herir*) to wound; (*ofender*) to offend; **~se** vr to hurt o.s.; **lastimero, a** adj pitiful, pathetic

lastre |'lastre| nm (*TEC, NAUT*) ballast; (*fig*) dead weight

lata |'lata| nf (*metal*) tin; (*caja*) tin (*BRIT*), can; (*fam*) nuisance; **en ~** tinned (*BRIT*), canned; **dar (la) ~** to be a nuisance

latente |la'tente| adj latent

lateral |late'ral| adj side cpd, lateral ♦ nm (*TEATRO*) wings

latido |la'tiðo| nm (*del corazón*) beat

latifundio |lati'fundjo| nm large estate; **latifundista** nm/f owner of a large estate

latigazo |lati'vaθo| nm (*golpe*) lash; (*sonido*) crack

látigo |'lativo| nm whip

latín |la'tin| nm Latin

latino, a |la'tino, a| adj Latin; **~americano, a** adj, nm/f Latin-

American

latir |la'tir| vi (corazón, pulso) to beat

latitud |lati'tuð| nf (GEO) latitude

latón |la'ton| nm brass

latoso, a |la'toso, a| adj (molesto) annoying; (aburrido) boring

laúd |la'uð| nm lute

laurel |lau'rel| nm (BOT) laurel; (CULIN) bay

lava |'laßa| nf lava

lavabo |la'ßaßo| nm (pila) washbasin; (tb: ~s) toilet

lavado |la'ßaðo| nm washing; (de ropa) laundry; (ARTE) wash; ~ **de cerebro** brainwashing; ~ **en seco** dry-cleaning

lavadora |laßa'ðora| nf washing machine

lavanda |la'ßanda| nf lavender

lavandería |laßande'ria| nf laundry; (automática) launderette

lavaplatos |laßa'platos| nm inv dishwasher

lavar |la'ßar| vt to wash; (borrar) to wipe away; ~**se** vr to wash o.s.; ~**se las manos** to wash one's hands; ~**se los dientes** to brush one's teeth; ~ **y marcar** (pelo) to shampoo and set; ~ **en seco** to dry-clean; ~ **los platos** to wash the dishes

lavavajillas |laßaßa'xiʎas| nm inv dishwasher

laxante |lak'sante| nm laxative

lazada |la'θaða| nf bow

lazarillo |laθa'riʎo| nm: **perro** ~ guide dog

lazo |'laθo| nm knot; (lazada) bow; (para animales) lasso; (trampa) snare; (vínculo) tie

le |le| pron (directo) him o (o her); (: usted) you; (indirecto) to him (o her o it); (: usted) to you

leal |le'al| adj loyal; ~**tad** nf loyalty

lección |lek'θjon| nf lesson

leche |'letʃe| nf milk; **tiene mala** ~ (fam!) he's a swine (!); ~ **conden-sada/en polvo** condensed/powdered milk; ~ **desnatada** skimmed milk; ~**ra**

nf (vendedora) milkmaid; (recipiente) (milk) churn; (AM) cow; ~**ro, a** adj dairy

lecho |'letʃo| nm (cama, de río) bed; (GEO) layer

lechón |le'tʃon| nm sucking (BRIT) o suckling (US) pig

lechoso, a |le'tʃoso, a| adj milky

lechuga |le'tʃuɣa| nf lettuce

lechuza |le'tʃuθa| nf owl

lector, a |lek'tor, a| nm/f reader ♦ nm: ~ **de discos compactos** CD player

lectura |lek'tura| nf reading

leer |le'er| vt to read

legado |le'ɣaðo| nm (don) bequest; (herencia) legacy; (enviado) legate

legajo |le'ɣaxo| nm file

legal |le'ɣal| adj (gen) legal; (persona) trustworthy; ~**idad** nf legality

legalizar |leɣali'θar| vt to legalize; (documento) to authenticate

legaña |le'ɣaɲa| nf sleep (in eyes)

legar |le'ɣar| vt to bequeath, leave

legendario, a |lexen'darjo, a| adj legendary

legión |le'xjon| nf legion; **legionario, a** adj legionary ♦ nm legionnaire

legislación |lexisla'θjon| nf legislation

legislar |lexis'lar| vi to legislate

legislatura |lexisla'tura| nf (POL) period of office

legitimar |lexiti'mar| vt to legitimize; **legítimo, a** adj (genuino) authentic; (legal) legitimate

lego, a |'leɣo, a| adj (REL) secular; (ignorante) ignorant ♦ nm layman

legua |'leɣwa| nf league

legumbres |le'ɣumbres| nfpl pulses

leído, a |le'iðo, a| adj well-read

lejanía |lexa'nia| nf distance; **lejano, a** adj far-off; (en el tiempo) distant; (fig) remote

lejía |le'xia| nf bleach

lejos |'lexos| adv far, far away; **a lo** ~ in the distance; **de** o **desde** ~ from afar; ~ **de** far from

lelo, a |'lelo, a| adj silly ♦ nm/f idiot

lema ['lema] nm motto; (POL) slogan

lencería [lenθe'ria] nf linen, drapery

lengua ['lengwa] nf tongue; (LING) language; **morderse la ~** to hold one's tongue

lenguado [len'gwaðo] nm sole

lenguaje [len'gwaxe] nm language

lengüeta [len'gweta] nf (ANAT) epiglottis; (zapatos) tongue; (MUS) reed

lente ['lente] nf lens, (lupa) magnifying glass; **~s** nfpl (gafas) glasses; **~s de contacto** contact lenses

lenteja [len'texa] nf lentil; **lentejuela** nf sequin

lentilla [len'tiʎa] nf contact lens

lentitud [lenti'tuð] nf slowness; **con ~** slowly

lento, a ['lento, a] adj slow

leña ['leɲa] nf firewood; **~dor, a** nm/f woodcutter

leño ['leɲo] nm (trozo de árbol) log; (madera) timber; (fig) blockhead

Leo ['leo] nm Leo

león [le'on] nm lion; **~ marino** sea lion

leopardo [leo'parðo] nm leopard

leotardos [leo'tarðos] nmpl tights

lepra ['lepra] nf leprosy; **leproso, a** nm/f leper

lerdo, a ['lerðo, a] adj (lento) slow; (patoso) clumsy

les [les] pron (directo) them; (: ustedes) you; (indirecto) to them; (: ustedes) to you

lesbiana [les'βjana] adj, nf lesbian

lesión [le'sjon] nf wound, lesion; (DEPORTE) injury; **lesionado, a** adj injured ♦ nm/f injured person

letal [le'tal] adj lethal

letanía [leta'nia] nf litany

letargo [le'tarɣo] nm lethargy

letra ['letra] nf letter; (escritura) handwriting; (MUS) lyrics pl; **~ de cambio** bill of exchange; **~ de imprenta** print; **~do, a** adj learned ♦ nm/f lawyer; **letrero** nm (cartel) sign; (etiqueta) label

letrina [le'trina] nf latrine

leucemia [leu'θemja] nf leukaemia

levadizo [leβa'ðiθo] adj: **puente ~** drawbridge

levadura [leβa'ðura] nf (para el pan) yeast; (de la cerveza) brewer's yeast

levantamiento [leβanta'mjento] nm raising, lifting; (rebelión) revolt, uprising; **~ de pesos** weight-lifting

levantar [leβan'tar] vt (gen) to raise; (del suelo) to pick up; (fig: ánimo arriba) to lift (up); (plan) to make, draw up; (mesa) to clear; (campamento) to strike; (fig) to cheer up, hearten; **~se** vr to get up; (enderezarse) to straighten up; (rebelarse) to rebel; **~ el ánimo** to cheer up

levante [le'βante] nm east coast; **el L~** region of Spain extending from Castellón to Murcia

levar [le'βar] vt to weigh

leve ['leβe] adj light; (fig) trivial; **~dad** nf lightness

levita [le'βita] nf frock coat

léxico ['leksiko] nm (vocabulario) vocabulary

ley [lei] nf (gen) law; (metal) standard

leyenda [le'jenda] nf legend

leyó etc vb ver **leer**

liar [li'ar] vt to tie (up); (unir) to bind; (envolver) to wrap (up); (enredar) to confuse; (cigarillo) to roll; **~se** vr (fam) to get involved; **~se a palos** to get involved in a fight

Líbano ['liβano] nm: **el ~** (the) Lebanon

libelo [li'βelo] nm satire, lampoon

libélula [li'βelula] nf dragonfly

liberación [liβera'θjon] nf liberation; (de la cárcel) release

liberal [liβe'ral] adj, nm/f liberal; **~idad** nf liberality, generosity

liberar [liβe'rar] vt to liberate

libertad [liβer'tað] nf liberty, freedom; **~ de culto/de prensa/de comercio** freedom of worship/of the press/of trade; **~ condicional** probation; **~ bajo palabra** parole; **~ bajo fianza**

bail

libertar [liβer'tar] vt (preso) to set free; (de una obligación) to release; (eximir) to exempt

libertino, a [liβer'tino, a] adj permissive ♦ nm/f licentious person

libra ['liβra] nf pound; (ASTROLOGÍA): L~ Libra; ~ esterlina pound sterling

librar [li'βrar] vt (de peligro) to save; (batalla) to wage, fight; (de impuestos) to exempt; (cheque) to make out; (JUR) to exempt; ~se vr: ~se de to escape from, free o.s. from

libre ['liβre] adj free; (lugar) unoccupied; (asiento) vacant; (de deudas) free of debts; ~ de impuestos free of tax; tiro ~ free kick; los 100 metros ~ the 100 metres free-style (race); al aire ~ in the open air

librería [liβre'ria] nf (tienda) bookshop; **librero, a** nm/f bookseller

libreta [li'βreta] nf notebook; ~ de ahorros savings book

libro ['liβro] nm book; ~ de bolsillo paperback; ~ de caja cashbook; ~ de cheques chequebook (BRIT), checkbook (US); ~ de texto textbook

Lic. abr = licenciado

licencia [li'θenθja] nf (gen) licence; (permiso) permission; ~ por enfermedad sick leave; ~ de caza game licence; ~do, a adj licensed ♦ nm/f graduate; **licenciar** vt (empleado) to dismiss; (permitir) to permit, allow; (soldado) to discharge; (estudiante) to confer a degree upon; **licenciarse** vr: **licenciarse en letras** to graduate in arts

licencioso, a [liθen'θjoso, a] adj licentious

licitar [liθi'tar] vt to bid for; (AM) to sell by auction

lícito, a [li'θito, a] adj (legal) lawful; (justo) fair, just; (permisible) permissible

licor [li'kor] nm spirits pl (BRIT); (US); (de frutas etc) liqueur

licuadora [likwa'ðora] nf blender

licuar [li'kwar] vt to liquidize

líder ['liðer] nm/f leader; **liderato** nm leadership; **liderazgo** nm leadership

lidia ['liðja] nf bullfighting; (una ~) bullfight; **toros de ~** fighting bulls; **lidiar** vt, vi to fight

liebre ['ljeβre] nf hare

lienzo ['ljenθo] nm linen; (ARTE) canvas; (ARQ) wall

liga ['liya] nf (de medias) garter, suspender; (AM: gomita) rubber band; (confederación) league

ligadura [liya'ðura] nf bond, tie; (MED, MUS) ligature

ligamento [liya'mento] nm ligament

ligar [li'yar] vt (atar) to tie; (unir) to join; (MED) to bind up; (MUS) to slur ♦ vi to mix, blend; (fam): **(él) liga mucho** he pulls a lot of women; ~se vr to commit o.s.

ligereza [lixe'reθa] nf lightness; (rapidez) swiftness; (agilidad) agility; (superficialidad) flippancy

ligero, a [li'xero, a] adj (de peso) light; (tela) thin; (rápido) swift, quick; (ágil) agile, nimble; (de importancia) slight; (de carácter) flippant, superficial ♦ adv: **a la ligera** superficially

liguero [li'yero] nm suspender (BRIT) o garter (US) belt

lija ['lixa] nf (ZOOL) dogfish; (tb: papel de ~) sandpaper

lila ['lila] nf lilac

lima ['lima] nf file; (BOT) lime; ~ de uñas nailfile; **limar** vt to file

limitación [limita'θjon] nf limitation, limit; ~ de velocidad speed limit

limitar [limi'tar] vt to limit; (reducir) to reduce, cut down ♦ vi: ~ con to border on; ~se vr: ~se a to limit o.s. to

límite ['limite] nm (gen) limit; (fin) end; (frontera) border; ~ de velocidad speed limit

limítrofe [li'mitrofe] adj neighbouring

limón [li'mon] nm lemon ♦ adj:

amarillo ~ lemon-yellow; **limonada** nf lemonade

limosna [li'mosna] nf alms pl; **vivir de** ~ to live on charity

limpiaparabrisas [limpjapara'ßrisas] nm inv windscreen (BRIT) o windshield (US) wiper

limpiar [lim'pjar] vt to clean; (con trapo) to wipe; (quitar) to wipe away; (zapatos) to shine, polish; (fig) to clean up

limpieza [lim'pjeθa] nf (estado) cleanliness; (acto) cleaning; (: de las calles) cleansing; (: de zapatos) polishing; (habilidad) skill; (fig: POLICÍA) clean-up; (pureza) purity; (MIL): **operación de** ~ mopping-up operation; ~ **en seco** dry cleaning

limpio, a [ˈlimpjo, a] adj clean; (moralmente) pure; (COM) clear, net; (fam) honest ♦ adv: **jugar** ~ to play fair; **pasar a** (ESP) **o en** (AM) ~ to make a clean copy

linaje [liˈnaxe] nm lineage, family

lince [ˈlinθe] nm lynx

linchar [linˈtʃar] vt to lynch

lindar [linˈdar] vi to adjoin; ~ **con** to border on; **linde** nm o f boundary; **lindero, a** adj adjoining ♦ nm boundary

lindo, a [ˈlindo, a] adj pretty, lovely ♦ adv: **nos divertimos de lo** ~ we had a marvellous time; **canta muy** ~ (AM) he sings beautifully

línea [ˈlinea] nf (gen) line; en ~ (INFORM) on line; ~ **aérea** airline; ~ **de meta** goal line; (de carrera) finishing line; ~ **recta** straight line

lingote [linˈgote] nm ingot

lingüista [linˈgwista] nm/f linguist; **lingüística** nf linguistics sg

lino [ˈlino] nm linen; (BOT) flax

linóleo [liˈnoleo] nm lino, linoleum

linterna [linˈterna] nf torch (BRIT), flashlight (US)

lío [ˈlio] nm bundle; (fam) fuss; (desorden) muddle, mess; **armar un** ~

to make a fuss

liquen [ˈliken] nm lichen

liquidación [likiðaˈθjon] nf liquidation; **venta de** ~ clearance sale

liquidar [likiˈðar] vt (mercancías) to liquidate; (deudas) to pay off; (empresa) to wind up

líquido, a [ˈlikiðo, a] adj liquid; (ganancia) net ♦ nm liquid; ~ **imponible** net taxable income

lira [ˈlira] nf (MUS) lyre; (moneda) lira

lírico, a [ˈliriko, a] adj lyrical

lirio [ˈlirjo] nm (BOT) iris

lirón [liˈron] nm (ZOOL) dormouse; (fig) sleepyhead

Lisboa [lisˈßoa] n Lisbon

lisiado, a [liˈsjaðo, a] adj injured ♦ nm/f cripple

lisiar [liˈsjar] vt to maim; ~**se** vr to injure o.s.

liso, a [ˈliso, a] adj (terreno) flat; (cabello) straight; (superficie) even; (tela) plain

lisonja [liˈsonxa] nf flattery

lista [ˈlista] nf list; (de alumnos) school register; (de libros) catalogue; (de platos) menu; (de precios) price list; **pasar** ~ to call the roll; ~ **de correos** poste restante; ~ **de espera** waiting list; **tela de** ~**s** striped material; **listín** nm: ~ **(telefónico)** telephone directory

listo, a [ˈlisto, a] adj (perspicaz) smart, clever; (preparado) ready

listón [lisˈton] nm (de madera, metal) strip

litera [liˈtera] nf (en barco, tren) berth; (en dormitorio) bunk, bunk bed

literal [liteˈral] adj literal

literario, a [liteˈrarjo, a] adj literary

literato, a [liteˈrato, a] adj literary ♦ nm/f writer

literatura [literaˈtura] nf literature

litigar [litiˈɣar] vt to fight ♦ vi (JUR) to go to law; (fig) to dispute, argue

litigio [liˈtixjo] nm (JUR) lawsuit; (fig): **en** ~ **con** in dispute with

litografía [litoɣraˈfia] nf lithography,

(una ~) lithograph

litoral [lito'ral] adj coastal ♦ nm coast, seaboard

litro ['litro] nm litre

liviano, a [li'βjano, a] adj (cosa, objeto) trivial

lívido, a ['liβiðo, a] adj livid

llaga ['ʎaɣa] nf wound

llama ['ʎama] nf flame; (ZOOL) llama

llamada [ʎa'maða] nf call; ~ **al orden** call to order; ~ **a pie de página** reference note

llamamiento [ʎama'mjento] nm call

llamar [ʎa'mar] vt to call; (atención) to attract ♦ vi (por teléfono) to telephone; (a la puerta) to knock o ring; (por señas) to beckon; (MIL) to call up; ~se vr to be called, be named; ¿cómo se llama usted? what's your name?

llamarada [ʎama'raða] nf (llamas) blaze; (rubor) flush

llamativo, a [ʎama'tiβo, a] adj showy; (color) loud

llano, a ['ʎano, a] adj (superficie) flat; (persona) straightforward; (estilo) clear ♦ nm plain, flat ground

llanta ['ʎanta] nf (wheel) rim; (AM): ~ **(de goma)** tyre; (: cámara) inner (tube)

llanto ['ʎanto] nm weeping

llanura [ʎa'nura] nf plain

llave ['ʎaβe] nf key; (del agua) tap; (MECÁNICA) spanner; (de la luz) switch; (MUS) key; ~ **inglesa** monkey wrench; ~ **maestra** master key; ~ **de contacto** (AUTO) ignition key; ~ **de paso** stopcock; **echar la ~ a** to lock up; **~ro** nm keyring

llegada [ʎe'ɣaða] nf arrival

llegar [ʎe'ɣar] vi to arrive; (alcanzar) to reach; (bastar) to be enough; ~se vr: ~se a to approach; ~ a to manage to, succeed in; ~ a saber to find out; ~ a ser to become; ~ a las manos de to come into the hands of

llenar [ʎe'nar] vt to fill; (espacio) to cover; (formulario) to fill in o up; (fig)

to heap

lleno, a ['ʎeno, a] adj full, filled; (repleto) full up ♦ nm (TEATRO) full house; **dar de ~ contra un muro** to hit a wall head-on

llevadero, a [ʎeβa'ðero, a] adj bearable, tolerable

llevar [ʎe'βar] vt to take; (ropa) to wear; (cargar) to carry; (quitar) to take away; (en coche) to drive; (transportar) to transport; (traer: dinero) to carry; (conducir) to lead; (MAT) to carry ♦ vi (suj: camino etc): ~ a to lead to; ~se vr to carry off, take away; **llevamos dos días aquí** we have been here two days; **él me lleva 2 años** he's 2 years older than me; (COM): ~ **los libros** to keep the books; ~se **bien** to get on well (together)

llorar [ʎo'rar] vt, vi to cry, weep; ~ **de risa** to cry with laughter

lloriquear [ʎorike'ar] vi to snivel, whimper

lloro ['ʎoro] nm crying, weeping; **llorón, ona** adj tearful ♦ nm/f cry-baby; ~**so, a** adj (gen) weeping, tearful; (triste) sad, sorrowful

llover [ʎo'βer] vi to rain

llovizna [ʎo'βiθna] nf drizzle; **lloviznar** vi to drizzle

llueve etc vb ver **llover**

lluvia ['ʎuβja] nf rain; ~ **radioactiva** (radioactive) fallout; **lluvioso, a** adj rainy

lo [lo] art def: ~ **bello** the beautiful, what is beautiful, that which is beautiful ♦ pron (persona) him; (cosa) it; tb ver **el**

loable [lo'aβle] adj praiseworthy; **loar** vt to praise

lobo ['loβo] nm wolf; ~ **de mar** (fig) sea dog; ~ **marino** seal

lóbrego, a ['loβreɣo, a] adj dark; (fig) gloomy

lóbulo ['loβulo] nm lobe

local [lo'kal] adj local ♦ nm place, site; (oficinas) premises pl; ~**idad** nf (barrio) locality; (*lugar*) location; (*TEATRO*) seat, ticket; **~izar** vt (*ubicar*) to locate, find; (*restringir*) to localize; (*situar*) to place

loción [lo'θjon] nf lotion

loco, a ['loko, a] adj mad ♦ nm/f lunatic, mad person

locomotora [lokomo'tora] nf engine, locomotive

locuaz [lo'kwaθ] adj loquacious

locución [loku'θjon] nf expression

locura [lo'kura] nf madness; (*acto*) crazy act

locutor, a [loku'tor, a] nm/f (*RADIO*) announcer; (*comentarista*) commentator; (*TV*) newsreader

locutorio [loku'torjo] nm (*en telefónica*) telephone booth

lodo ['loðo] nm mud

lógica ['loxika] nf logic

lógico, a ['loxiko, a] adj logical

logística [lo'xistika] nf logistics sg

logotipo [loðo'tipo] nm logo

logrado, a [lo'ðraðo, a] adj (*interpretación, reproducción*) polished, excellent

lograr [lo'ɣrar] vt to achieve; (*obtener*) to get, obtain; **~ hacer** to manage to do; **~ que uno venga** to manage to get sb to come

logro ['loɣro] nm achievement, success

loma ['loma] nf hillock (*BRIT*), small hill

lombriz [lom'briθ] nf worm

lomo ['lomo] nm (*de animal*) back; (*CULIN: de cerdo*) pork loin; (*: de vaca*) rib steak; (*de libro*) spine

lona ['lona] nf canvas

loncha ['lontʃa] nf = **lonja**

lonche ['lontʃe] (*AM*) nm lunch; **~ría** (*AM*) nf snack bar, diner (*US*)

Londres ['londres] n London

longaniza [longa'niθa] nf pork sausage

longitud [lonxi'tuð] nf length; (*GEO*) longitude; **tener 3 metros de ~** to be 3 metres long; **~ de onda** wavelength

lonja ['lonxa] nf slice; (*de tocino*) rasher; **~ de pescado** fish market

loro ['loro] nm parrot

los [los] art def the ♦ pron them; (*ustedes*) you; **mis libros y ~ tuyos** my books and yours; tb ver **el**

losa ['losa] nf stone; **~ sepulcral** gravestone

lote ['lote] nm portion; (*COM*) lot

lotería [lote'ria] nf lottery; (*juego*) lotto

loza ['loθa] nf crockery

lubina [lu'βina] nf sea bass

lubricante [luβri'kante] nm lubricant

lubricar [luβri'kar] vt to lubricate

lucha ['lutʃa] nf fight, struggle; **~ de clases** class struggle; **~ libre** wrestling; **luchar** vi to fight

lucidez [luθi'ðeθ] nf lucidity

lúcido, a ['luθiðo, a] adj (*persona*) lucid; (*mente*) logical; (*idea*) crystal-clear

luciérnaga [lu'θjernaɣa] nf glow-worm

lucir [lu'θir] vt to illuminate, light (up); (*ostentar*) to show off ♦ vi (*brillar*) to shine; **~se** vr (*irónico*) to make a fool of o.s.

lucro ['lukro] nm profit, gain

lúdico, a ['luðiko, a] adj (*aspecto, actividad*) play cpd

luego ['lweɣo] adv (*después*) next; (*más tarde*) later, afterwards

lugar [lu'ɣar] nm place; (*sitio*) spot; **en ~ de** instead of; **hacer ~** to make room; **fuera de ~** out of place; **tener ~** to take place; **~ común** commonplace

lugareño, a [luɣaˈreɲo, a] *adj* village *cpd* ♦ *nm/f* villager

lugarteniente [luɣarteˈnjente] *nm* deputy

lúgubre [ˈluɣuβre] *adj* mournful

lujo [ˈluxo] *nm* luxury; (*fig*) profusion, abundance; **~so, a** *adj* luxurious

lujuria [luˈxurja] *nf* lust

lumbre [ˈlumbre] *nf* fire; (*para cigarrillo*) light

lumbrera [lumˈbrera] *nf* luminary

luminoso, a [lumiˈnoso, a] *adj* luminous, shining

luna [ˈluna] *nf* moon; (*de un espejo*) glass; (*de gafas*) lens; (*fig*) crescent; **~ llena/nueva** full/new moon; **estar en la ~** to have one's head in the clouds; **~ de miel** honeymoon

lunar [luˈnar] *adj* lunar ♦ *nm* (ANAT) mole; **tela de ~es** spotted material

lunes [ˈlunes] *nm inv* Monday

lupa [ˈlupa] *nf* magnifying glass

lustrar [lusˈtrar] *vt* (*mueble*) to polish; (*zapatos*) to shine; **lustre** *nm* polish; (*fig*) lustre; **dar lustre a** to polish; **lustroso, a** *adj* shining

luto [ˈluto] *nm* mourning; **llevar el o vestirse de ~** to be in mourning

Luxemburgo [luksemˈburɣo] *nm* Luxembourg

luz [luθ] (*pl* **luces**) *nf* light; **dar a ~ un niño** to give birth to a child; **sacar a la ~** to bring to light; **dar o encender** (ESP) *o* **prender** (AM)/**apagar la ~** to switch the light on/off; **a todas luces** by any reckoning; **tener pocas luces** to be dim *o* stupid; **~ roja/verde** red/green light; **~ de freno** brake light; **luces de tráfico** traffic lights; **traje de luces** bullfighter's costume

M, m

m *abr* (= *metro*) m; (= *minuto*) m

macarrones [makaˈrrones] *nmpl* macaroni *sg*

macedonia [maθeˈðonja] *nf*: **~ de frutas** fruit salad

macerar [maθeˈrar] *vt* to macerate

maceta [maˈθeta] *nf* (*de flores*) pot of flowers; (*para plantas*) flowerpot

machacar [matʃaˈkar] *vt* to crush, pound ♦ *vi* (*insistir*) to go on, keep on

machete [maˈtʃete] (AM) *nm* machete, (large) knife

machismo [maˈtʃismo] *nm* male chauvinism; **machista** *adj*, *nm* sexist

macho [ˈmatʃo] *adj* male; (*fig*) virile ♦ *nm* male; (*fig*) he-man

macizo, a [maˈθiθo, a] *adj* (*grande*) massive; (*fuerte, sólido*) solid ♦ *nm* mass, chunk

madeja [maˈðexa] *nf* (*de lana*) skein, hank; (*de pelo*) mass, mop

madera [maˈðera] *nf* wood; (*fig*) nature, character; **una ~** a piece of wood

madero [maˈðero] *nm* beam

madrastra [maˈðrastra] *nf* stepmother

madre [ˈmaðre] *adj* mother *cpd*; (*fig*) tremendous ♦ *nf* mother; (*de vino etc*) dregs *pl*; **~ política/soltera** mother-in-law/unmarried mother

Madrid [maˈðrið] *n* Madrid

madriguera [maðriˈɣera] *nf* burrow

madrileño, a [maðriˈleɲo, a] *adj* of *o* from Madrid ♦ *nm/f* native of Madrid

madrina [maˈðrina] *nf* godmother; (ARQ) prop, shore; (TEC) brace; (*de boda*) bridesmaid

madrugada [maðruˈɣaða] *nf* early morning; (*alba*) dawn, daybreak

madrugador, a [maðruɣaˈðor, a] *adj* early-rising

madrugar [maðruˈɣar] *vi* to get up early; (*fig*) to get ahead

madurar [maðuˈrar] *vt*, *vi* (*fruta*) to ripen; (*fig*) to mature; **madurez** *nf* ripeness; maturity; **maduro, a** *adj* ripe; mature

maestra [maˈestra] *nf ver* **maestro**

maestría [maesˈtria] *nf* mastery; (*habilidad*) skill, expertise

maestro, a [ma'estro, a] adj masterly; (principal) main ♦ nm/f master/mistress; (profesor) teacher ♦ nm (autoridad) authority; (MUS) maestro; (AM) skilled workman; ~ **albañil** master mason

magdalena [mayða'lena] nf fairy cake

magia ['maxja] nf magic; **mágico, a** adj magic(al) ♦ nm/f magician

magisterio [maxis'terjo] nm (enseñanza) teaching; (profesión) teaching profession; (maestros) teachers pl

magistrado [maxis'traðo] nm magistrate

magistral [maxis'tral] adj magisterial; (fig) masterly

magnánimo, a [may'nanimo, a] adj magnanimous

magnate [may'nate] nm magnate, tycoon

magnético, a [may'netiko, a] adj magnetic; **magnetizar** vt to magnetize

magnetofón [maxneto'fon] nm tape recorder; **magnetofónico, a** adj: **cinta magnetofónica** recording tape

magnetófono [mayne'tofono] nm = **magnetofón**

magnífico, a [may'nifiko, a] adj splendid, magnificent

magnitud [mayni'tuð] nf magnitude

mago, a ['mayo, a] nm/f magician; **los Reyes M~s** the Magi, the Three Wise Men

magro, a ['mayro, a] adj (carne) lean

maguey [ma'yei] nm agave

magullar [mayu'ʎar] vt (amoratar) to bruise; (dañar) to damage

mahometano, a [maome'tano, a] adj Mohammedan

mahonesa [mao'nesa] nf mayonnaise

maíz [ma'iθ] nm maize (BRIT), corn (US); sweet corn

majadero, a [maxa'ðero, a] adj silly, stupid

majestad [maxes'taθ] nf majesty; **majestuoso, a** adj majestic

majo, a ['maxo, a] adj nice; (guapo) attractive, good-looking; (elegante) smart

mal [mal] adv badly; (equivocadamente) wrongly ♦ adj = **malo** ♦ nm evil; (desgracia) misfortune; (daño) harm, damage; (MED) illness; **~ que bien** rightly or wrongly; **ir de ~ en peor** to get worse and worse

malabarismo [malaßa'rismo] nm juggling; **malabarista** nm/f juggler

malaria [ma'larja] nf malaria

malcriado, a [mal'krjaðo, a] adj spoiled

maldad [mal'daθ] nf evil, wickedness

maldecir [malde'θir] vt to curse ♦ vi: **~ de** to speak ill of

maldición [maldi'θjon] nf curse

maldito, a [mal'dito, a] adj (condenado) damned; (perverso) wicked; **¡~ sea!** damn it!

maleante [male'ante] nm/f criminal, crook

maledicencia [maleði'θenθja] nf slander, scandal

maleducado, a [maleðu'kaðo, a] adj bad-mannered, rude

malentendido [malenten'diðo] nm misunderstanding

malestar [males'tar] nm (gen) discomfort; (fig: inquietud) uneasiness; (POL) unrest

maleta [ma'leta] nf case, suitcase; (AUTO) boot (BRIT), trunk (US); **hacer las ~s** to pack; **maletera** (AM) nf, **maletero** nm (AUTO) boot (BRIT), trunk (US); **maletín** nm small case, bag

malévolo, a [ma'leßolo, a] adj malicious, spiteful

maleza [ma'leθa] nf (hierbas malas) weeds pl; (arbustos) thicket

malgastar [malyas'tar] vt (tiempo, dinero) to waste; (salud) to ruin

malhechor [male'tʃor, a] nm/f delinquent

malhumorado, a [malumo'raðo, a] adj bad-tempered

malicia [ma'liθja] nf (maldad) wickedness; (astucia) slyness, guile; (mala intención) malice, spite; (carácter travieso) mischievousness; **malicioso, a** adj wicked, evil; sly, crafty; malicious, spiteful; mischievous

maligno, a [ma'liɣno, a] adj evil; (malévolo) malicious; (MED) malignant

malla ['maʎa] nf mesh; (de baño) swimsuit; (de ballet, gimnasia) leotard; ~s nfpl tights; **~ de alambre** wire mesh

Mallorca [ma'ʎorka] nf Majorca

malo, a ['malo, a] adj bad; (falso) false ♦ nm/f villain; **estar ~** to be ill

malograr [malo'ɣrar] vt to spoil; (plan) to upset; (ocasión) to waste; **~se** vr (plan etc) to fail, come to grief; (persona) to die before one's time

malparado, a [malpa'raðo, a] adj: **salir ~** to come off badly

malpensado, a [malpen'saðo, a] adj nasty

malsano, a [mal'sano, a] adj unhealthy

malteada [malte'aða] (AM) nf milk shake

maltratar [maltra'tar] vt to ill-treat, mistreat

maltrecho, a [mal'tretʃo, a] adj battered, damaged

malvado, a [mal'βaðo, a] adj evil, villainous

malversar [malβer'sar] vt to embezzle, misappropriate

Malvinas [mal'βinas]: **Islas ~** nfpl Falkland Islands

malvivir [malβi'βir] vi to live poorly

mama ['mama] nf (de animal) teat; (de mujer) breast

mamá [ma'ma] (pl **~s**) (fam) nf mum, mummy

mamar [ma'mar] vt, vi to suck

mamarracho [mama'rratʃo] nm sight, mess

mamífero [ma'mifero] nm mammal

mampara [mam'para] nf (entre habitaciones) partition; (biombo) screen

mampostería [mamposte'ria] nf masonry

manada [ma'naða] nf (ZOOL) herd; (: de leones) pride; (: de lobos) pack

manantial [manan'tjal] nm spring

manar [ma'nar] vi to run, flow

mancha ['mantʃa] nf stain, mark; (ZOOL) patch; **manchar** vt (gen) to stain, mark; (ensuciar) to soil, dirty

manchego, a [man'tʃevo, a] adj of o from La Mancha

manco, a ['manko, a] adj (de un brazo) one-armed; (de una mano) one-handed; (fig) defective, faulty

mancomunar [mankomu'nar] vt to unite, bring together; (recursos) to pool; (JUR) to make jointly responsible; **mancomunidad** nf union, association; (comunidad) community; (JUR) joint responsibility

mandamiento [manda'mjento] nm (orden) order, command; (REL) commandment; **~ judicial** warrant

mandar [man'dar] vt (ordenar) to order; (dirigir) to lead, command; (enviar) to send; (pedir) to order, ask for ♦ vi to be in charge; (pey) to be bossy; **¿mandé?** (AM) pardon?, excuse me?; **~ hacer un traje** to have a suit made

mandarina [manda'rina] nf tangerine, mandarin (orange)

mandato [man'dato] nm (orden) order; (POL: período) term of office; (: territorio) mandate; **~ judicial** (search) warrant

mandíbula [man'diβula] nf jaw

mandil [man'dil] nm apron

mando ['mando] nm (MIL) command; (de país) rule; (el primer lugar) lead; (POL) term of office; (TEC) control; **~ a la izquierda** left-hand drive

mandón, ona [man'don, ona] adj bossy, domineering

manejable [mane'xaßle] adj manageable

manejar [mane'xar] vt to manage;

(*máquina*) to work, operate; (*caballo etc*) to handle; (*casa*) to run, manage; (*AM: AUTO*) to drive; **~se** *vr* (*comportarse*) to act, behave; (*arreglárselas*) to manage; **manejo** *nm* management; handling; running; driving; (*facilidad de trato*) ease, confidence; **manejos** *nmpl* (*intrigas*) intrigues

manera [ma'nera] *nf* way, manner, fashion; **~s** *nfpl* (*modales*) manners; **su ~ de ser** the way he is; (*aire*) his manner; **de ninguna ~** no way, by no means; **de otra ~** otherwise; **de todas ~s** at any rate; **no hay ~ de persuadirle** there's no way of convincing him

manga ['manga] *nf* (*de camisa*) sleeve; (*de riego*) hose

mangar [man'gar] (*fam*) *vt* to pinch, nick

mango ['mango] *nm* handle; (*BOT*) mango

mangonear [mangone'ar] *vi* (*meterse*) to meddle, interfere; (*ser mandón*) to boss people about

manguera [man'gera] *nf* hose

mania [ma'nia] *nf* (*MED*) mania; (*fig: moda*) rage, craze; (*disgusto*) dislike; (*malicia*) spite; **maníaco, a** *adj* maniac(al) ♦ *nm/f* maniac

maniatar [manja'tar] *vt* to tie the hands of

maniático, a [ma'njatiko, a] *adj* maniac(al) ♦ *nm/f* maniac

manicomio [mani'komjo] *nm* mental hospital (*BRIT*), insane asylum (*US*)

manifestación [manifesta'θjon] *nf* (*declaración*) statement, declaration; (*de emoción*) show, display; (*POL: desfile*) demonstration; (: *concentración*) mass meeting

manifestar [manifes'tar] *vt* to show, manifest; (*declarar*) to state, declare; **manifiesto, a** *adj* clear, manifest ♦ *nm* manifesto

manillar [mani'ʎar] *nm* handlebars *pl*

maniobra [ma'njoβra] *nf* manoeuvre; **~s** *nfpl* (*MIL*) manoeuvres; **maniobrar** *vt* to manoeuvre

manipulación [manipula'θjon] *nf* manipulation

manipular [manipu'lar] *vt* to manipulate; (*manejar*) to handle

maniquí [mani'ki] *nm* dummy ♦ *nm/f* model

manirroto, a [mani'rroto, a] *adj* lavish, extravagant ♦ *nm/f* spendthrift

manivela [mani'ßela] *nf* crank

manjar [man'xar] *nm* (*tasty*) dish

mano ['mano] *nf* hand; (*ZOOL*) foot, paw; (*de pintura*) coat; (*serie*) lot, series; **a ~** by hand; **a ~ derecha/izquierda** on the right(-hand side)/left(-hand side); **de primera ~** (at) first hand; **de segunda ~** (at) second hand; **robo a ~ armada** armed robbery; **~ de obra** labour, manpower; **estrechar la ~ a uno** to shake sb's hand

manojo [ma'noxo] *nm* handful, bunch; **~ de llaves** bunch of keys

manopla [ma'nopla] *nf* mitten

manoseado, a [manose'aðo, a] *adj* well-worn

manosear [manose'ar] *vt* (*tocar*) to handle, touch; (*desordenar*) to mess up, rumple; (*insistir en*) to overwork; (*AM*) to caress, fondle

manotazo [mano'taθo] *nm* slap, smack

mansalva [man'salßa]: **a ~** *adv* indiscriminately

mansedumbre [manse'ðumbre] *nf* gentleness, meekness

mansión [man'sjon] *nf* mansion

manso, a ['manso, a] *adj* gentle, mild; (*animal*) tame

manta ['manta] *nf* blanket; (*AM: poncho*) poncho

manteca [man'teka] *nf* fat; (*AM*) butter; **~ de cacahuete/cacao** peanut/cocoa butter; **~ de cerdo** lard

mantecado [mante'kaðo] (*AM*) *nm* ice

cream

mantel [man'tel] *nm* tablecloth

mantendré *etc vb ver* **mantener**

mantener [mante'ner] *vt* to support, maintain; (*alimentar*) to sustain; (*conservar*) to keep; (*TEC*) to maintain, service; **~se** *vr* (*seguir de pie*) to be still standing; (*no ceder*) to hold one's ground; (*subsistir*) to sustain o.s., keep going; **mantenimiento** *nm* maintenance; sustenance; (*sustento*) support

mantequilla [mante'kiʎa] *nf* butter

mantilla [man'tiʎa] *nf* mantilla; **~s** *nfpl* (*de bebé*) baby clothes

manto ['manto] *nm* (*capa*) cloak; (*de ceremonia*) robe, gown

mantuve *etc vb ver* **mantener**

manual [ma'nwal] *adj* manual ♦ *nm* manual, handbook

manufactura [manufak'tura] *nf* manufacture; (*fábrica*) factory; **manufacturado, a** *adj* (*producto*) manufactured

manuscrito, a [manus'krito, a] *adj* handwritten ♦ *nm* manuscript

manutención [manuten'θjon] *nf* maintenance; (*sustento*) support

manzana [man'θana] *nf* apple; (*ARQ*) block (of houses)

manzanilla [manθa'niʎa] *nf* (*planta*) camomile; (*infusión*) camomile tea

manzano [man'θano] *nm* apple tree

maña ['maɲa] *nf* (*gen*) skill, dexterity; (*pey*) guile; (*destreza*) trick, knack

mañana [ma'ɲana] *adv* tomorrow ♦ *nm* future ♦ *nf* morning; **de o por la ~** in the morning; **¡hasta ~!** see you tomorrow!; **~ por la ~** tomorrow morning

mañoso, a [ma'ɲoso, a] *adj* (*hábil*) skilful; (*astuto*) smart, clever

mapa ['mapa] *nm* map

maqueta [ma'keta] *nf* (scale) model

maquillaje [maki'ʎaxe] *nm* make-up; (*acto*) making up

maquillar [maki'ʎar] *vt* to make up;

~se *vr* to put on (some) make-up

máquina ['makina] *nf* machine; (*de tren*) locomotive, engine; (*FOTO*) camera; (*AM: coche*) car; (*fig*) machinery; **escrito a ~** typewritten; **~ de escribir** typewriter; **~ de coser/lavar** sewing/washing machine

maquinación [makina'θjon] *nf* machination, plot

maquinal [maki'nal] *adj* (*fig*) mechanical, automatic

maquinaria [maki'narja] *nf* (*máquinas*) machinery; (*mecanismo*) mechanism, works *pl*

maquinilla [maki'niʎa] *nf*: **~ de afeitar** razor

maquinista [maki'nista] *nm/f* (*de tren*) engine driver; (*TEC*) operator; (*NAUT*) engineer

mar [mar] *nm o f* sea; **~ adentro** *o* **afuera** out at sea; **en alta ~** on the high seas; **la ~ de** (*fam*) lots of; **el M~ Negro/Báltico** the Black/Baltic Sea

maraña [ma'raɲa] *nf* (*maleza*) thicket; (*confusión*) tangle

maravilla [mara'βiʎa] *nf* marvel, wonder; (*BOT*) marigold; **maravillar** *vt* to astonish, amaze; **maravillarse** *vr* to be astonished, be amazed; **maravilloso, a** *adj* wonderful, marvellous

marca ['marka] *nf* (*gen*) mark; (*sello*) stamp; (*COM*) make, brand; **de ~** excellent, outstanding; **~ de fábrica** trademark; **~ registrada** registered trademark

marcado, a [mar'kaðo, a] *adj* marked, strong

marcador [marka'ðor] *nm* (*DEPORTE*) scoreboard; (: *persona*) scorer

marcapasos [marka'pasos] *nm inv* pacemaker

marcar [mar'kar] *vt* (*gen*) to mark; (*número de teléfono*) to dial; (*gol*) to score; (*números*) to record, keep a tally of; (*pelo*) to set ♦ *vi* (*DEPORTE*) to score;

(TEL) to dial

marcha ['martʃa] nf march; (TEC) running, working; (AUTO) gear; (velocidad) speed; (fig) progress; (dirección) course; **poner en ~** to put into gear; (fig) to set in motion, get going; **dar ~ atrás** to reverse, put into reverse; **estar en ~** to be under way, be in motion

marchar [mar'tʃar] vi (ir) to go; (funcionar) to work, go; **~se** vr to go (away), leave

marchitar [martʃi'tar] vt to wither, dry up; **~se** vr (BOT) to wither; (fig) to fade away; **marchito, a** adj withered, faded; (fig) in decline

marcial [mar'θjal] adj martial, military

marciano, a [mar'θjano, a] adj, nm/f Martian

marco ['marko] nm frame; (moneda) mark; (fig) framework

marea [ma'rea] nf tide

marear [mare'ar] vt (fig) to annoy, upset; (MED): **~ a uno** to make sb feel sick; **~se** vr (tener náuseas) to feel sick; (desvanecerse) to feel faint; (aturdirse) to feel dizzy; (fam: emborracharse) to get tipsy

maremoto [mare'moto] nm tidal wave

mareo [ma'reo] nm (náusea) sick feeling; (en viaje) travel sickness; (aturdimiento) dizziness; (fam: lata) nuisance

marfil [mar'fil] nm ivory

margarina [marva'rina] nf margarine

margarita [marva'rita] nf (BOT) daisy; (rueda) ~ daisywheel

margen ['marxen] nm (borde) edge, border; (fig) margin, space ♦ nf (de río etc) bank; **dar ~ para** to give an opportunity for; **mantenerse al ~** to keep out (of things)

marginar [marxi'nar] vt (socialmente) to marginalize, ostracize

marica [ma'rika] (fam) nm sissy

maricón [mari'kon] (fam) nm queer

marido [ma'riðo] nm husband

marihuana [mari'wana] nf marijuana, cannabis

marina [ma'rina] nf navy; **~ mercante** merchant navy

marinero, a [mari'nero, a] adj sea cpd ♦ nm sailor, seaman

marino, a [ma'rino, a] adj sea cpd, marine ♦ nm sailor

marioneta [marjo'neta] nf puppet

mariposa [mari'posa] nf butterfly

mariquita [mari'kita] nf ladybird (BRIT), ladybug (US)

mariscos [ma'riskos] nmpl shellfish inv, seafood(s)

marítimo, a [ma'ritimo, a] adj sea cpd, maritime

mármol ['marmol] nm marble

marqués, esa [mar'kes, esa] nm/f marquis/marchioness

marrón [ma'rron] adj brown

marroquí [marro'ki] adj, nm/f Moroccan ♦ nm Morocco (leather)

Marruecos [ma'rrwekos] nm Morocco

martes ['martes] nm inv Tuesday

martillo [mar'tiʎo] nm hammer; **~ neumático** pneumatic drill (BRIT), jackhammer

mártir ['martir] nm/f martyr; **martirio** nm martyrdom; (fig) torture, torment

marxismo [mark'sismo] nm Marxism; **marxista** adj, nm/f Marxist

marzo ['marθo] nm March

PALABRA CLAVE

más [mas] adj, adv 1: **~ (que, de)** (comparar) more ... than, ...+ er (than); **~ grande/inteligente** bigger/more intelligent; **trabaja ~ (que yo)** he

works more (than me); *ver tb* **cada**
2 (*superl*): **el ~ the** most, ...+ est; **el**
~ grande/inteligente (de) the
biggest/most intelligent (of)
3 (*negativo*): **no tengo ~ dinero** I
haven't got any more money; **no**
viene ~ por aquí he doesn't come
round here any more
4 (*adicional*): **no le veo ~ solución**
que ... I see no other solution than to
...; **¿quién ~?** anybody else?
5 (+ *adj*: *valor intensivo*). **¡qué perro**
~ sucio! what a filthy dog!; **¡es**
~ tonto! he's so stupid!
6 (*locuciones*): **~ o menos** more or
less; **los ~** most people; **es ~**
furthermore; **bien** rather; **¡qué**
~ da! what does it matter!; *ver tb* **qué**
7: **por ~: por ~ que te esfuerces** no
matter how hard you try; **por ~ que**
quisiera ... much as I should like to ...
8: de ~: veo que aquí estoy de ~ I
can see I'm not needed here;
tenemos uno de ~ we've got one
extra

♦ *prep*: **2 ~ 3 son 4** 2 and plus 2
are 4

♦ *nm inv*: **este trabajo tiene sus ~ y**
sus menos this job's got its good
points and its bad points

mas |mas| *conj* but

masa |'masa| *nf* (*mezcla*) dough;
(*volumen*) volume, mass; (FÍSICA) mass;
en ~ en masse; **las ~s** (POL) the
masses

masacre |ma'sakre| *nf* massacre

masaje |ma'saxe| *nm* massage

máscara |'maskara| *nf* mask;
mascarilla *nf* (*de belleza*, MED) mask

masculino, a |masku'lino, a| *adj*
masculine; (BIO) male

masía |ma'sia| *nf* farmhouse

masificación |masifika'θjon| *nf*
overcrowding

masivo, a |ma'siβo, a| *adj* mass *cpd*

masón |ma'son| *nm* (free)mason

masoquista |maso'kista| *nm/f*
masochist

masticar |masti'kar| *vt* to chew

mástil |'mastil| *nm* (*de navío*) mast; (*de*
guitarra) neck

mastín |mas'tin| *nm* mastiff

masturbación |mastur'βaθjon| *nf*
masturbation

masturbarse |mastur'βarse| *vr* to
masturbate

mata |'mata| *nf* (*arbusto*) bush, shrub;
(*de hierba*) tuft

matadero |mata'ðero| *nm*
slaughterhouse, abattoir

matador, a |mata'ðor, a| *adj* killing
♦ *nm/f* killer ♦ *nm* (TAUR) matador,
bullfighter

matamoscas |mata'moskas| *nm inv*
(*palo*) fly swat

matanza |ma'tanθa| *nf* slaughter

matar |ma'tar| *vt, vi* to kill; **~se** *vr*
(*suicidarse*) to kill o.s., commit suicide;
(*morir*) to be o get killed; **~ el hambre**
to stave off hunger

matasellos |mata'seʎos| *nm inv*
postmark

mate |'mate| *adj* matt ♦ *nm* (*en*
ajedrez) (check)mate; (AM: *hierba*)
maté; (: *vasija*) gourd

matemáticas |mate'matikas| *nfpl*
mathematics; **matemático, a** *adj*
mathematical ♦ *nm/f* mathematician

materia |ma'terja| *nf* (*gen*) matter;
(TEC) material; (ESCOL) subject; **en**
~ de on the subject of; **~ prima** raw
material; **material** *adj* material ♦ *nm*
material; (TEC) equipment;
materialismo *nm* materialism;
materialista *adj* materialist(ic);
materialmente *adv* materially; (*fig*)
absolutely

maternal |mater'nal| *adj* motherly,
maternal

maternidad |materni'ðað| *nf*
motherhood, maternity; **materno, a**
adj maternal; (*lengua*) mother *cpd*

matinal |mati'nal| *adj* morning *cpd*

matiz |ma'tiθ| *nm* shade; **~ar** *vt*
(*variar*) to vary; (*ARTE*) to blend; **~ar**
de to tinge with

matón |ma'ton| *nm* bully

matorral |mato'rral| *nm* thicket

matraca |ma'traka| *nf* rattle

matrícula |ma'trikula| *nf* (*registro*)
register; (*AUTO*) registration number;
(: *placa*) number plate; **matricular** *vt*
to register, enrol

matrimonial |matrimo'njal| *adj*
matrimonial

matrimonio |matri'monjo| *nm*
(*pareja*) (married) couple; (*unión*)
marriage

matriz |ma'triθ| *nf* (*ANAT*) womb;
(*TEC*) mould; (*casa* ~ (*COM*) head office

matrona |ma'trona| *nf* (*persona de
edad*) matron; (*comadrona*) midwife

maullar |mau'ʎar| *vi* to mew, miaow

maxilar |maksi'lar| *nm* jaw(bone)

máxima |'maksima| *nf* maxim

máxime |'maksime| *adv* especially

máximo, a |'maksimo, a| *adj*
maximum; (*más alto*) highest; (*más
grande*) greatest ♦ *nm* maximum

mayo |'majo| *nm* May

mayonesa |majo'nesa| *nf* mayonnaise

mayor |ma'jor| *adj* main, chief;
(*adulto*) adult; *de edad avanzada*)
elderly; (*MUS*) major; (*comparº de
tamaño*) bigger; (: *de edad*) older;
(*super: de tamaño*) biggest; (: *de edad*)
oldest ♦ *nm* (*adulto*) adult; **al por ~**
wholesale; **~ de edad** adult; **~es** *nmpl*
(*antepasados*) ancestors

mayoral |majo'ral| *nm* foreman

mayordomo |major'ðomo| *nm* butler

mayoría |majo'ria| *nf* majority, greater
part

mayorista |majo'rista| *nm/f*
wholesaler

mayoritario, a |majori'tarjo, a| *adj*
majority *cpd*

mayúscula |ma'juskula| *nf* capital
letter

mayúsculo, a |ma'juskulo, a| *adj* (*fig*)

big, tremendous

mazapán |maθa'pan| *nm* marzipan

mazo |'maθo| *nm* (*martillo*) mallet; (*de
flores*) bunch; (*DEPORTE*) bat

me |me| *pron* (*directo*) me; (*indirecto*)
(to) me; (*reflexivo*) (to) myself;
¡dámelo! give it to me!

mear |me'ar| (*fam*) *vi* to pee, piss (!)

mecánica |me'kanika| *nf* (*ESCOL*)
mechanics *sg*; (*mecanismo*) mechanism;
ver tb **mecánico**

mecánico, a |me'kaniko, a| *adj*
mechanical ♦ *nm/f* mechanic

mecanismo |meka'nismo| *nm*
mechanism; (*marcha*) gear

mecanografía |mekanoɣra'fia| *nf*
typewriting; **mecanógrafo, a** *nm/f*
typist

mecate |me'kate| (*AM*) *nm* rope

mecedora |meθe'ðora| *nf* rocking
chair

mecer |me'θer| *vt* (*cuna*) to rock; **~se**
vr to rock; (*ramo*) to sway

mecha |'metʃa| *nf* (*de vela*) wick; (*de
bomba*) fuse

mechero |me'tʃero| *nm* (*cigarette*)
lighter

mechón |me'tʃon| *nm* (*gen*) tuft; (*de
pelo*) lock

medalla |me'ðaʎa| *nf* medal

media |'meðja| *nf* (*ESP*) stocking; (*AM*)
sock; (*promedio*) average

mediado, a |me'ðjaðo, a| *adj* half-full;
(*trabajo*) half-completed; **a ~s de** in
the middle of, halfway through

mediano, a |me'ðjano, a| *adj* (*regular*)
medium, average; (*mediocre*) mediocre

medianoche |meðja'notʃe| *nf*
midnight

mediante |me'ðjante| *adv* by (means
of), through

mediar |me'ðjar| *vi* (*interceder*) to
mediate, intervene

medicación |meðika'θjon| *nf*
medication, treatment

medicamento |meðika'mento| *nm*
medicine, drug

medicina [meði'θina] nf medicine

medición [meði'θjon] nf measurement

médico, a [a l'meðiko, a] adj medical
♦ nm/f doctor

medida [me'ðiða] nf measure; (medición) measurement; (prudencia) moderation, prudence; **en ciertas/gran ~** up to a point/to a great extent; **un traje a la ~** a made-to-measure suit; **~ de cuello** collar size; **~ de** in proportion to; (de acuerdo con) in keeping with; **a ~ que** (conforme) as

medio, a [a l'meðjo, a] adj half (a); (punto) mid, middle; (promedio) average ♦ adv half ♦ nm (centro) middle, center; (promedio) average; (método) means, way; (ambiente) environment; **~s** nmpl means, resources; **~ litro** half a litre; **las tres y media** half past three; **medio ambiente** environment; **M~ Oriente** Middle East; **a ~ terminar** half finished; **pagar a medias** to share the cost; **~ambiental** (política, efectos) environmental

mediocre [me'ðjokre] adj mediocre

mediodía [meðjo'ðia] nm midday, noon

medir [me'ðir] vt, vi (gen) to measure

meditar [meði'tar] vt to ponder, think over, meditate on; (planear) to think out

mediterráneo, a [meðite'rraneo, a] adj Mediterranean ♦ nm: **el M~ the** Mediterranean (Sea)

médula ['meðula] nf (ANAT) marrow; **~ espinal** spinal cord

medusa [me'ðusa] (ESP) nf jellyfish

megafonía [meðafo'nia] nf public address system, PA system; **megáfono** nm megaphone

megalómano, a [meða'lomano, a] nm/f megalomaniac

mejicano, a [mexi'kano, a] adj, nm/f Mexican

Méjico ['mexiko] nm Mexico

mejilla [me'xiáa] nf cheek

mejillón [mexi'áon] nm mussel

mejor [me'xor] adj, adv (comparativo) better; (superl) best; **a lo ~** probably; (quizá) maybe; **~ dicho** rather; **tanto ~** so much the better

mejora [me'xora] nf improvement; **mejorar** vt to improve, make better ♦ vi to improve, get better; **mejorarse** vr to improve, get better

melancólico, a [melan'koliko, a] adj (triste) sad, melancholy; (soñador) dreamy

melena [me'lena] nf (de persona) long hair; (ZOOL) mane

mellizo, a [me'áiθo, a] adj, nm/f twin; **~s** nmpl (AM) cufflinks

melocotón [meloko'ton] (ESP) nm peach

melodía [melo'ðia] nf melody, tune

melodrama [melo'ðrama] nm melodrama; **melodramático, a** adj melodramatic

melón [me'lon] nm melon

membrete [mem'brete] nm letterhead

membrillo [mem'briáo] nm quince; **carne de ~** quince jelly

memorable [memo'raßle] adj memorable

memoria [me'morja] nf (gen) memory; **~s** nfpl (de autor) memoirs; **memorizar** vt to memorize

menaje [me'naxe] nm: **~ de cocina** kitchenware

mencionar [menθjo'nar] vt to mention

mendigar [mendi'var] vt to beg (for)

mendigo, a [men'divo, a] nm/f beggar

mendrugo [men'druvo] nm crust

menear [mene'ar] vt to move; **~se** vr to shake; (balancearse) to sway; (moverse) to move; (fig) to get a move on

menestra [me'nestra] nf: **~ de verduras** vegetable stew

menguante [men'gwante] adj

decreasing, diminishing

menguar [men'gwar] vt to lessen, diminish ♦ vi to diminish, decrease

menopausia [meno'pausja] nf menopause

menor [me'nor] adj (más pequeño: compar) smaller; (: superl) smallest; (más joven: compar) younger; (: superl) youngest; (MUS) minor ♦ nm/f (joven) young person, juvenile; **no tengo la ~ idea** I haven't the faintest idea; **al por ~** retail; **~ de edad** person under age

Menorca [me'norka] nf Minorca

PALABRA CLAVE

menos [menos] ♦ adj **1**: **~ (que, de)** (compar: cantidad) less (than); (: número) fewer (than); **con ~ entusiasmo** with less enthusiasm; **~ gente** fewer people; ver tb **cada**

2 (superl): **es el ~ listo de su clase** he's the least bright in his class; **de todas ellas es la que ~ me agrada** out of all of them she's the one I like least; **(por) lo ~** at (the very) least

3 (locuciones): **no quiero verle y ~ visitarle** I don't want to see him let alone visit him; **tenemos 7 de ~** we're seven short

♦ prep except; (cifras) minus; **todos ~ él** everyone except (for) him; **5 ~ 2** 5 minus 2

♦ conj: **a ~ que**: **a ~ que venga mañana** unless he comes tomorrow

menospreciar [menospre'θjar] vt to underrate, undervalue; (despreciar) to scorn, despise

mensaje [men'saxe] nm message; **~ro, a** nm/f messenger

menstruación [menstrua'θjon] nf menstruation

menstruar [mens'trwar] vi to menstruate

mensual [men'swal] adj monthly; **1000 ptas ~es** 1000 ptas a month; **~idad** nf (salario) monthly salary; (COM) monthly payment, monthly instalment

menta ['menta] nf mint

mental [men'tal] adj mental; **~idad** nf mentality; **~izar** vt (sensibilizar) to make aware; (convencer) to convince; (padres) to prepare (mentally); **~izarse** vr (concienciarse) to become aware; **~izarse (de)** to get used to the idea (of); **~izarse de que ...** (convencerse) to get it into one's head that ...

mentar [men'tar] vt to mention, name

mente ['mente] nf mind

mentir [men'tir] vi to lie

mentira [men'tira] nf (una ~) lie; (acto) lying; (invención) fiction; **parece ~ que ...** it seems incredible that ..., I can't believe that ...

mentiroso, a [menti'roso, a] adj lying ♦ nm/f liar

menú [me'nu] (pl ~s) nm menu; (AM) set meal; **~ del día** set menu

menudo, a [me'nuðo, a] adj (pequeño) small, tiny; (sin importancia) petty, insignificant; **¡~ negocio!** (fam) some deal!; **a ~** often, frequently

meñique [me'ɲike] nm little finger

meollo [me'oʎo] nm (fig) core

mercado [mer'kaðo] nm market

mercancía [merkan'θia] nf commodity; **~s** nfpl goods, merchandise sg

mercantil [merkan'til] adj mercantile, commercial

mercenario, a [merθe'narjo, a] adj, nm mercenary

mercería [merθe'ria] nf haberdashery (BRIT), notions (US); (tienda) haberdasher's (BRIT), notions store (US); (AM) drapery

mercurio [mer'kurjo] nm mercury

merecer |mere'θer| vt to deserve, merit ♦ vi to be deserving, be worthy; **merece la pena** it's worthwhile; **merecido, a** adj (well) deserved; **llevar su merecido** to get one's deserts

merendar |meren'dar| vt to have for tea ♦ vi to have tea; (en el campo) to have a picnic; **merendero** nm open-air cafe

merengue |me'renge| nm meringue

meridiano |meri'ðjano| nm (GEO) meridian

merienda |me'rjenda| nf (light) tea, afternoon snack; (de campo) picnic

mérito |'merito| nm merit; (valor) worth, value

merluza |mer'luθa| nf hake

merma |'merma| nf decrease; (pérdida) wastage; **mermar** vt to reduce, lessen ♦ vi to decrease, dwindle

mermelada |merme'laða| nf jam

mero, a |'mero, a| adj mere; (AM: fam) very

merodear |meroðe'ar| vi: ~ **por** to prowl about

mes |mes| nm month

mesa |'mesa| nf table; (de trabajo) desk; (GEO) plateau; ~ **directiva** board; ~ **redonda** (reunión) round table; **poner/quitar la** ~ to lay/clear the table; **mesero, a** (AM) nm/f waiter/waitress

meseta |me'seta| nf (GEO) meseta, tableland

mesilla |me'siʎa| nf: ~ **(de noche)** bedside table

mesón |me'son| nm inn

mestizo, a |mes'tiθo, a| adj half-caste, of mixed race ♦ nm/f half-caste

mesura |me'sura| nf moderation, restraint

meta |'meta| nf goal; (de carrera) finish

metabolismo |metaβo'lismo| nm metabolism

metáfora |me'tafora| nf metaphor

metal |me'tal| nm (materia) metal;

(MUS) brass; **metálico, a** adj metallic; (de metal) metal ♦ nm (dinero contante) cash

metalurgia |meta'lurxja| nf metallurgy

meteoro |mete'oro| nm meteor; **~logía** nf meteorology

meter |me'ter| vt (colocar) to put, place; (introducir) to put in, insert; (involucrar) to involve; (causar) to make, cause; **~se** vr: **~se en** to go into, enter; (fig) to interfere in, meddle in; **~se a** to start; **~se a escritor** to become a writer; **~se con uno** to provoke sb, pick a quarrel with sb

meticuloso, a |metiku'loso, a| adj meticulous, thorough

metódico, a |me'toðiko, a| adj methodical

método |'metoðo| nm method

metralleta |metra'ʎeta| nf sub-machine-gun

métrico, a |'metriko, a| adj metric

metro |'metro| nm metre; (tren) underground (BRIT), subway (US)

México |'mexiko| nm Mexico; **Ciudad de** ~ Mexico City

mezcla |'meθkla| nf mixture; **mezclar** vt to mix (up); **mezclarse** vr to mix, mingle; **mezclarse** vr to get mixed up in, get involved in

mezquino, a |meθ'kino, a| adj mean

mezquita |meθ'kita| nf mosque

mg. abr (= miligramo) mg

mi |mi| adj pos my ♦ nm (MUS) E

mí |mi| pron me; myself

mía |'mia| pron ver **mío**

miaja |'mjaxa| nf crumb

michelín |mitʃe'lin| (fam) nm (de grasa) spare tyre

micro |'mikro| (AM) nm minibus

microbio |mi'kroβjo| nm microbe

micrófono |mi'krofono| nm microphone

microondas |mikro'ondas| nm inv (tb: horno ~) microwave (oven)

microscopio |mikro'skopjo| nm

microscope

miedo ['mjeðo] *nm* fear; *(nerviosismo)* apprehension, nervousness; **tener ~ to be afraid; de ~ wonderful, marvellous; hace un frío de ~** *(fam)* it's terribly cold; **~so, a** *adj* fearful, timid

miel [mjel] *nf* honey

miembro ['mjembro] *nm* limb; *(socio)* member; **~ viril** penis

mientras ['mjentras] *conj* while; *(duración)* as long as ♦ *adv* meanwhile; **~ tanto** meanwhile; **~ más tiene, más quiere** the more he has, the more he wants

miércoles ['mjerkoles] *nm inv* Wednesday

mierda ['mjerða] *(fam!)* *nf* shit (!)

miga ['miɣa] *nf* crumb; *(fig: meollo)* essence; **hacer buenas ~s** *(fam)* to get on well

mil [mil] *num* thousand; **dos ~ libras** two thousand pounds

milagro [mi'laɣro] *nm* miracle; **~so, a** *adj* miraculous

milésima [mi'lesima] *nf (de segundo)* thousandth

mili ['mili] *(fam)* *nf:* **hacer la ~** to do one's military service

milicia [mi'liθja] *nf* militia; *(servicio militar)* military service

milímetro [mi'limetro] *nm* millimetre

militante [mili'tante] *adj* militant

militar [mili'tar] *adj* military ♦ *nm/f* soldier ♦ *vi (MIL)* to serve; *(en un partido)* to be a member

milla ['miʎa] *nf* mile

millar [mi'ʎar] *nm* thousand

millón [mi'ʎon] *num* million; **millonario, a** *nm/f* millionaire

mimar [mi'mar] *vt* to spoil, pamper

mimbre ['mimbre] *nm* wicker

mímica ['mimika] *nf (para comunicarse)* sign language; *(imitación)* mimicry

mimo ['mimo] *nm (caricia)* caress; *(de niño)* spoiling; *(TEATRO)* mime; *(: actor)* mime artist

mina ['mina] *nf* mine; **minar** *vt* to mine; *(fig)* to undermine

mineral [mine'ral] *adj* mineral ♦ *nm (GEO)* mineral; *(mena)* ore

minero, a [mi'nero, a] *adj* mining *cpd* ♦ *nm/f* miner

miniatura [minja'tura] *adj inv, nf* miniature

minidisco [mini'disko] *nm* MiniDisc®

minifalda [mini'falda] *nf* miniskirt

mínimo, a ['minimo, a] *adj, nm* minimum

minino, a [mi'nino, a] *(fam)* *nm/f* puss, pussy

ministerio [minis'terjo] *nm* Ministry; **M~ de Hacienda/de Asuntos Exteriores** Treasury *(BRIT)*, Treasury Department *(US)*/Foreign Office *(BRIT)*, State Department *(US)*

ministro, a [mi'nistro, a] *nm/f* minister

minoría [mino'ria] *nf* minority

minucioso, a [minu'θjoso, a] *adj* thorough, meticulous; *(prolijo)* very detailed

minúscula [mi'nuskula] *nf* small letter

minúsculo, a [mi'nuskulo, a] *adj* tiny, minute

minusválido, a [minus'βaliðo, a] *adj* (physically) handicapped ♦ *nm/f* (physically) handicapped person

minuta [mi'nuta] *nf (de comida)* menu

minutero [minu'tero] *nm* minute hand

minuto [mi'nuto] *nm* minute

mío, a ['mio, a] *pron:* **el ~/la mía** mine; **un amigo ~** a friend of mine; **lo ~** what is mine

miope [mi'ope] *adj* short-sighted

mira ['mira] *nf (de arma)* sight(s) (pl); *(fig)* aim, intention

mirada [mi'raða] *nf* look, glance; *(expresión)* look, expression; **clavar la ~ en** to stare at; **echar una ~ a** to glance at

mirado, a [mi'raðo, a] *adj (sensato)* sensible; *(considerado)* considerate;

bien/mal ~ well/not well thought of;
bien ~ all things considered
mirador |mira'ðor| nm viewpoint,
vantage point
mirar |mi'rar| vt to look at; (observar)
to watch; (considerar) to consider,
think over; (vigilar, cuidar) to watch,
look after ♦ vi to look; (ARQ) to face;
~**se** vr (dos personas) to look at each
other; ~ **bien/mal** to think highly of/
have a poor opinion of; ~**se al espejo**
to look at o.s. in the mirror
mirilla |mi'riʎa| nf spyhole, peephole
mirlo |'mirlo| nm blackbird
misa |'misa| nf mass
miserable |mise'raßle| adj (avaro)
mean, stingy; (nimio) squalid, paltry;
(lugar) squalid; (fam) vile, despicable
♦ nm/f (malvado) rogue
miseria |mi'serja| nf (pobreza) poverty;
(tacañería) meanness, stinginess;
(condiciones) squalor; **una** ~ a pittance
misericordia |miseri'korðja| nf
(compasión) compassion, pity; (piedad)
mercy
misil |mi'sil| nm missile
misión |mi'sjon| nf mission;
misionero, a nm/f missionary
mismo, a |'mismo, a| adj (semejante)
same; (después de pron) -self; (para
énfasis) very ♦ adv: **aquí/hoy** ~ right
here/this very day; **ahora** ~ right now
♦ conj: **lo** ~ **que** just like, just as; **el**
~ **traje** the same suit; **en ese**
~ **momento** at that very moment;
vino el ~ **Ministro** the minister
himself came; **yo** ~ **lo vi** I saw it
myself; **lo** ~ (the same (thing); **da lo** ~
it's all the same; **quedamos en las
mismas** we're no further forward; **por
lo** ~ for the same reason
misterio |mis'terjo| nm mystery; ~**so,
a** adj mysterious
mitad |mi'tað| nf (medio) half; (centro)
middle; **a** ~ **de precio** (a) half-price;
en o a ~ **del camino** halfway along
the road; **cortar por la** ~ to cut

through the middle
mitigar |miti'ɣar| vt to mitigate;
(dolor) to ease; (sed) to quench
mitin |'mitin| (pl **mítines**) nm
meeting
mito |'mito| nm myth
mixto, a |'miksto, a| adj mixed
ml. abr (= mililitro) ml
mm. abr (= milímetro) mm
mobiliario |moßi'ljarjo| nm furniture
mochila |mo'tʃila| nf rucksack (BRIT),
back-pack
moción |mo'θjon| nf motion
moco |'moko| nm mucus; ~**s** nmpl
(fam) snot; **limpiarse los** ~**s de la
nariz** (fam) to wipe one's nose
moda |'moða| nf fashion; (estilo) style;
a la o de ~ in fashion, fashionable;
pasado de ~ out of fashion
modales |mo'ðales| nmpl manners
modalidad |moðali'ðað| nf kind,
variety
modelar |moðe'lar| vt to model
modelo |mo'ðelo| adj inv, nm/f model
módem |'moðem| nm (INFORM)
modem
moderado, a |moðe'raðo, a| adj
moderate
moderar |moðe'rar| vt to moderate;
(violencia) to restrain, control;
(velocidad) to reduce; ~**se** vr to restrain
o.s., control o.s.
modernizar |moðerni'θar| vt to
modernize
moderno, a |mo'ðerno, a| adj
modern; (actual) present-day
modestia |mo'ðestja| nf modesty;
modesto, a adj modest
módico, a |'moðiko, a| adj moderate,
reasonable
modificar |moðifi'kar| vt to modify
modisto, a |mo'ðisto, a| nm/f
(diseñador) couturier, designer; (que
confecciona) dressmaker
modo |'moðo| nm way, manner; (MUS)
mode; ~**s** nmpl manners; **de ningún** ~
in no way; **de todos** ~**s** at any rate;

~ de empleo directions pl (for use)

modorra [mo'ðorra] nf drowsiness

mofa ['mofa] nf: **hacer ~ de** to mock; **mofarse** vr: **mofarse de** to mock, scoff at

mogollón [moɣo'ʎon] (fam) adv a hell of a lot

moho ['moo] nm mould, mildew; (en metal) rust; **~so, a** adj mouldy; rusty

mojar [mo'xar] vt to wet; (humedecer) to damp(en), moisten; (calar) to soak; **~se** vr to get wet

mojón [mo'xon] nm boundary stone

molde ['molde] nm mould; (COSTURA) pattern; (fig) model; **~ado** nm soft perm; **~ar** vt to mould

mole ['mole] nf mass, bulk; (edificio) pile

moler [mo'ler] vt to grind, crush

molestar [moles'tar] vt to bother; (fastidiar) to annoy; (incomodar) to inconvenience, put out ♦ vi to be a nuisance; **~se** vr to bother; (incomodarse) to go to trouble; (ofenderse) to take offence; **¿(no) te molesta si ...?** do you mind if ...?

molestia [mo'lestja] nf bother, trouble; (incomodidad) inconvenience; (MED) discomfort; **es una ~** it's a nuisance; **molesto, a** adj (que fastidia) annoying; (incómodo) inconvenient; (inquieto) uncomfortable, ill at ease; (enfadado) annoyed

molido, a [mo'liðo, a] adj: **estar ~** (fig) to be exhausted o dead beat

molinillo [moli'niʎo] nm: **~ de carne/café** mincer/coffee grinder

molino [mo'lino] nm (edificio) mill; (máquina) grinder

momentáneo, a [momen'taneo, a] adj momentary

momento [mo'mento] nm moment; **de ~** at the moment, for the moment

momia ['momja] nf mummy

monarca [mo'narka] nm/f monarch, ruler; **monarquía** nf monarchy; **monárquico, a** nm/f royalist,

monarchist

monasterio [monas'terjo] nm monastery

mondar [mon'dar] vt to peel; **~se** vr: **~se de risa** (fam) to split one's sides laughing

moneda [mo'neða] nf (tipo de dinero) currency, money; (pieza) coin; **una ~ de 5 pesetas** a 5 peseta piece; **monedero** nm purse; **monetario, a** adj monetary, financial

monitor, a [moni'tor, a] nm/f instructor, coach ♦ nm (TV) set; (INFORM) monitor

monja ['monxa] nf nun

monje ['monxe] nm monk

mono, a ['mono, a] adj (bonito) lovely, pretty; (gracioso) nice, charming ♦ nm/f monkey, ape ♦ nm dungarees pl; (overoles) overalls pl

monopatín [monopa'tin] nm skateboard

monopolio [mono'poljo] nm monopoly; **monopolizar** vt to monopolize

monotonía [monoto'nia] nf (sonido) monotone; (fig) monotony

monótono, a [mo'notono, a] adj monotonous

monstruo ['monstrwo] nm monster ♦ adj inv fantastic; **~so, a** adj monstrous

montaje [mon'taxe] nm assembly; (TEATRO) décor; (CINE) montage

montaña [mon'taɲa] nf (monte) mountain; (sierra) mountains pl, mountainous area; (AM: selva) forest; **~ rusa** roller coaster; **montañero, a** nm/f mountaineer; **montañés, esa** nm/f highlander; **montañismo** nm mountaineering

montar [mon'tar] vt (subir a) to mount, get on; (TEC) to assemble, put together; (negocio) to set up; (arma) to cock; (colocar) to lift on to; (CULIN) to beat ♦ vi to mount, get on; (sobresalir) to overlap; **~ en cólera** to get angry;

~ a caballo to ride, go horseriding

monte ['monte] nm (montaña) mountain; (bosque) woodland; (área sin cultivar) wild area, wild country; **M~ de Piedad** pawnshop

montón [mon'ton] nm heap, pile; (fig): **un ~** heaps of, lots of

monumento [monu'mento] nm monument

monzón [mon'θon] nm monsoon

moño ['moɲo] nm bun

moqueta [mo'keta] nf fitted carpet

mora ['mora] nf blackberry; ver tb **moro**

morada [mo'raða] nf (casa) dwelling, abode

morado, a [mo'raðo, a] adj purple, violet ♦ nm bruise

moral [mo'ral] adj moral ♦ nf (ética) ethics pl; (moralidad) morals pl, morality; (ánimo) morale

moraleja [mora'lexa] nf moral

moralidad [morali'ðað] nf morals pl, morality

morboso, a [mor'ßoso, a] adj morbid

morcilla [mor'θiʎa] nf blood sausage, ≈ black pudding (BRIT)

mordaz [mor'ðaθ] adj (crítica) biting, scathing

mordaza [mor'ðaθa] nf (para la boca) gag; (TEC) clamp

morder [mor'ðer] vt to bite; (fig: consumir) to eat away, eat into; **mordisco** nm bite

moreno, a [mo'reno, a] adj (color) (dark) brown; (de tez) dark; (de pelo ~) dark-haired; (negro) black

morfina [mor'fina] nf morphine

moribundo, a [mori'ßundo, a] adj dying

morir [mo'rir] vi to die; (fuego) to die down; (luz) to go out; **~se** vr to die; (fig) to be dying; **murió en un accidente** he was killed in an accident; **~se por algo** to be dying for sth

moro, a ['moro, a] adj Moorish ♦ nm/f Moor

moroso, a [mo'roso, a] nm/f bad debtor, defaulter

morral [mo'rral] nm haversack

morro ['morro] nm (ZOOL) snout, nose; (AUTO, AVIAT) nose

morsa ['morsa] nf walrus

mortadela [morta'ðela] nf mortadella

mortaja [mor'taxa] nf shroud

mortal [mor'tal] adj mortal; (golpe) deadly; **~idad** nf mortality

mortero [mor'tero] nm mortar

mortífero, a [mor'tifero, a] adj deadly, lethal

mortificar [mortifi'kar] vt to mortify

mosca ['moska] nf fly

Moscú [mos'ku] n Moscow

mosquearse [moske'arse] (fam) vr (enojarse) to get cross; (ofenderse) to take offence

mosquitero [moski'tero] nm mosquito net

mosquito [mos'kito] nm mosquito

mostaza [mos'taθa] nf mustard

mosto ['mosto] nm (unfermented) grape juice

mostrador [mostra'ðor] nm (de tienda) counter; (de café) bar

mostrar [mos'trar] vt to show; (exhibir) to display, exhibit; (explicar) to explain; **~se** vr: **~se amable** to be kind; to prove to be kind; **no se muestra muy inteligente** he doesn't seem (to be) very intelligent

mota ['mota] nf speck, tiny piece; (en diseño) dot

mote ['mote] nm nickname

motín [mo'tin] nm (del pueblo) revolt, rising; (del ejército) mutiny

motivar [moti'ßar] vt (causar) to cause, motivate; (explicar) to explain, justify; **motivo** nm motive, reason

moto ['moto] (fam) nf = **motocicleta**

motocicleta [motoθi'kleta] nf motorbike (BRIT), motorcycle

motor [mo'tor] nm motor, engine; **~ a chorro o de reacción/de explosión**

jet engine/internal combustion
engine

motora [mo'tora] *nf* motorboat

movedizo, a [moβe'ðiθo, a] *adj* **ver
arena**

mover [mo'βer] *vt* to move; (*cabeza*)
to shake; (*accionar*) to drive; (*fig*) to
cause, provoke; **~se** *vr* to move; (*fig*)
to get a move on

móvil ['moβil] *adj* mobile; (*pieza de
máquina*) moving; (*mueble*) movable
♦ *nm* motive; **movilidad** *nf* mobility;
movilizar *vt* to mobilize

movimiento [moβi'mjento] *nm*
movement; (*TEC*) motion; (*actividad*)
activity

mozo, a ['moθo, a] *adj* (*joven*) young
♦ *nm/f* youth, young man/girl

muchacho, a [mu't∫at∫o, a] *nm/f*
(*niño*) boy/girl; (*criado*) servant; (*criada*)
maid

muchedumbre [mut∫e'ðumbre] *nf*
crowd

PALABRA CLAVE
---

mucho, a ['mut∫o, a] *adj* **1** (*cantidad*)
a lot of, much; (*número*) lots of, a lot
of, many; **~ dinero** a lot of money;
hace ~ calor it's very hot; **muchas
amigas** lots o a lot of friends

2 (*sg: grande*): **ésta es mucha casa
para él** this house is much too big for
him

♦ *pron*: **tengo ~ que hacer** I've got a
lot to do; **~s dicen que ...** a lot of
people say that ...; *ver tb* **tener**

♦ *adv* **1**: **me gusta ~** I like it a lot; **lo
siento ~** I'm very sorry; **come ~** he
eats a lot; **¿te vas a quedar ~?** are
you going to be staying long?

2 (*respuesta*) very; **¿estás cansado? –
¡~!** are you tired? – very!

3 (*locuciones*): **como ~** at (the) most;
con ~: el mejor con ~ by far the
best; **ni ~ menos: no es rico ni ~
menos** he's far from being rich

4: **por ~ que: por ~ que le creas** no

matter how o however much you
believe her

---

muda ['muða] *nf* change of clothes

mudanza [mu'ðanθa] *nf* (*de casa*)
move

mudar [mu'ðar] *vt* to change; (*ZOOL*)
to shed ♦ *vi* to change; **~se** *vr* (*la ropa*)
to change; **~se de casa** to move
house

mudo, a ['muðo, a] *adj* dumb;
(*callado, CINE*) silent

mueble ['mweβle] *nm* piece of
furniture; **~s** *nmpl* furniture *sg*

mueca ['mweka] *nf* face, grimace;
hacer ~s a to make faces at

muela ['mwela] *nf* (*back*) tooth

muelle ['mweʎe] *nm* spring; (*NAUT*)
wharf; (*malecón*) pier

muero *etc vb ver* **morir**

muerte ['mwerte] *nf* death; (*homicidio*)
murder; **dar ~ a** to kill

muerto, a ['mwerto, a] *pp de* **morir**
♦ *adj* dead ♦ *nm/f* dead man/woman;
(*difunto*) deceased; (*cadáver*) corpse;
estar ~ de cansancio to be dead
tired

muestra ['mwestra] *nf* (*señal*)
indication, sign; (*demostración*)
demonstration; (*prueba*) proof;
(*estadística*) sample; (*modelo*) model,
pattern; (*testimonio*) token

muestreo [mwes'treo] *nm* sample,
sampling

muestro *etc vb ver* **mostrar**

muevo *etc vb ver* **mover**

mugir [mu'xir] *vi* (*vaca*) to moo

mugre ['muxre] *nf* dirt, filth;
mugriento, a *adj* dirty, filthy

mujer [mu'xer] *nf* woman; (*esposa*)
wife; **~iego** *nm* womanizer

mula ['mula] *nf* mule

muleta [mu'leta] *nf* (*para andar*)
crutch; (*TAUR*) stick with red cape
attached

mullido, a [mu'ʎiðo, a] *adj* (*cama*)
soft; (*hierba*) soft, springy

multa |'multa| nf fine; **poner una ~ a** to fine; **multar** vt to fine

multicines |multi'θines| nmpl multiscreen cinema

multinacional |multinaθjo'nal| nf multinational

múltiple |'multiple| adj multiple; (pl) many, numerous

multiplicar |multipli'kar| vt (MAT) to multiply; (fig) to increase; **~se** vr (BIO) to multiply; (fig) to be everywhere at once

multitud |multi'tuð| nf (muchedumbre) crowd; **~ de** lots of

mundano, a |mun'dano, a| adj worldly

mundial |mun'djal| adj world-wide, universal; (guerra, récord) world cpd

mundo |'mundo| nm world; **todo el ~** everybody; **tener ~** to be experienced, know one's way around

munición |muni'θjon| nf ammunition

municipal |muniθi'pal| adj municipal, local

municipio |muni'θipjo| nm (ayuntamiento) town council, corporation; (territorio administrativo) town, municipality

muñeca |mu'neka| nf (ANAT) wrist; (juguete) doll

muñeco |mu'neko| nm (figura) figure; (marioneta) puppet; (fig) puppet, pawn

mural |mu'ral| adj mural, wall cpd ♦ nm mural

muralla |mu'raʎa| nf (city) wall(s) (pl)

murciélago |mur'θjelaɣo| nm bat

murmullo |mur'muʎo| nm murmur(ing); (cuchicheo) whispering

murmuración |murmura'θjon| nf gossip; **murmurar** vi to murmur, whisper; (cotillear) to gossip

muro |'muro| nm wall

muscular |musku'lar| adj muscular

músculo |'muskulo| nm muscle

museo |mu'seo| nm museum; **~ de arte** art gallery

musgo |'musɣo| nm moss

música |'musika| nf music; ver tb **músico**

músico, a |'musiko, a| adj musical ♦ nm/f musician

muslo |'muslo| nm thigh

mustio, a |'mustjo, a| adj (persona) depressed, gloomy; (planta) faded, withered

musulmán, ana |musul'man, ana| nm/f Moslem

mutación |muta'θjon| nf (BIO) mutation; (cambio) (sudden) change

mutilar |muti'lar| vt to mutilate; (a una persona) to maim

mutismo |mu'tismo| nm (de persona) uncommunicativeness; (de autoridades) silence

mutuamente |mutwa'mente| adv mutually

mutuo, a |'mutwo, a| adj mutual

muy |mwi| adv very; (demasiado) too; **M~ Señor mío** Dear Sir; **~ de noche** very late at night; **eso es ~ de él** that's just like him

N, n

N abr (= norte) N

nabo |'naβo| nm turnip

nácar |'nakar| nm mother-of-pearl

nacer |na'θer| vi to be born; (de huevo) to hatch; (vegetal) to sprout; (río) to rise; **nací en Barcelona** I was born in Barcelona; **nació una sospecha en su mente** a suspicion formed in her mind; **nacido, a** adj born; **recién nacido** newborn; **naciente** adj new, emerging; (sol) rising; **nacimiento** nm birth; (de Navidad) Nativity; (de río) source

nación |na'θjon| nf nation; **nacional** adj national; **nacionalismo** nm nationalism; **nacionalista** nm/f nationalist; **nacionalizar** vt to nationalize; **nacionalizarse** vr (persona) to become naturalized

nada [ˈnaða] *pron* nothing ♦ *adv* not at all, in no way; **no decir ~** to say nothing, not to say anything; **~ más** nothing else; **de ~** don't mention it

nadador, a [naðaˈðor, a] *nm/f* swimmer

nadar [naˈðar] *vi* to swim

nadie [ˈnaðje] *pron* nobody, no-one; **~ habló** nobody spoke; **no había ~** there was nobody there, there wasn't anybody there

nado [ˈnaðo]: **a ~** *adv*: **pasar a ~** to swim across

nafta [ˈnafta] *(AM) nf* petrol *(BRIT)*, gas *(US)*

naipe [ˈnaipe] *nm* (playing) card; **~s** *nmpl* cards

nalgas [ˈnalɣas] *nfpl* buttocks

nana [ˈnana] *nf* lullaby

naranja [naˈranxa] *adj inv, nf* orange; **media ~** *(fam)* better half; **naranjada** *nf* orangeade; **naranjo** *nm* orange tree

narciso [narˈθiso] *nm* narcissus

narcótico, a [narˈkotiko, a] *adj, nm* narcotic; **narcotizar** *vt* to drug; **narcotráfico** *nm* drug trafficking *o* running

nardo [ˈnarðo] *nm* lily

narigudo, a [nariˈɣuðo, a] *adj* big-nosed

nariz [naˈriθ] *nf* nose

narración [narraˈθjon] *nf* narration; **narrador, a** *nm/f* narrator

narrar [naˈrrar] *vt* to narrate, recount; **narrativa** *nf* narrative

nata [ˈnata] *nf* cream

natación [nataˈθjon] *nf* swimming

natal [naˈtal] *adj*: **ciudad ~** home town; **~idad** *nf* birth rate

natillas [naˈtiʎas] *nfpl* custard *sg*

nativo, a [naˈtiβo, a] *adj, nm/f* native

nato, a [ˈnato, a] *adj* born; **un músico ~** a born musician

natural [natuˈral] *adj* natural; *(fruta etc)* fresh ♦ *nm/f* native ♦ *nm (disposición)* nature

naturaleza [naturaˈleθa] *nf* nature;

(género) nature, kind; **~ muerta** still life

naturalidad [naturaliˈðað] *nf* naturalness

naturalmente [naturalˈmente] *adv (de modo natural)* in a natural way; **¡~!** of course!

naufragar [naufraˈɣar] *vi* to sink; **naufragio** *nm* shipwreck; **náufrago, a** *nm/f* castaway, shipwrecked person

nauseabundo, a [nauseaˈβundo, a] *adj* nauseating, sickening

náuseas [ˈnauseas] *nfpl* nausea *sg*; **me da ~** it makes me feel sick

náutico, a [ˈnautiko, a] *adj* nautical

navaja [naˈβaxa] *nf* knife; *(de barbero, peluquero)* razor

naval [naˈβal] *adj* naval

Navarra [naˈβarra] *n* Navarre

nave [ˈnaβe] *nf (barco)* ship, vessel; *(ARQ)* nave; **~ espacial** spaceship

navegación [naβeɣaˈθjon] *nf* navigation; *(viaje)* sea journey; **~ aérea** air traffic; **~ costera** coastal shipping; **navegador** *nm (INFORM)* browser; **navegante** *nm/f* navigator; **navegar** *vi (barco)* to sail; *(avión)* to fly

navidad [naβiˈðað] *nf* Christmas; **~es** *nfpl* Christmas time; **Feliz N~** Merry Christmas; **navideño, a** *adj* Christmas *cpd*

navío [naˈβio] *nm* ship

nazca *etc vb ver* **nacer**

nazi [ˈnaθi] *adj, nm/f* Nazi

NE *abr (= nor(d)este)* NE

neblina [neˈβlina] *nf* mist

nebulosa [neβuˈlosa] *nf* nebula

necesario, a [neθeˈsarjo, a] *adj* necessary

neceser [neθeˈser] *nm* toilet bag; *(bolsa grande)* holdall

necesidad [neθesiˈðað] *nf* need; *(lo inevitable)* necessity; *(miseria)* poverty; **en caso de ~** in case of need *o* emergency; **hacer sus ~es** to relieve o.s.

necesitado, a [neθesiˈtaðo, a] *adj* needy, poor; **~ de** in need of

necesitar [neθesi'tar] *vt* to need, require

necio, a ['neθjo, a] *adj* foolish

necrópolis [ne'kropolis] *nf inv* cemetery

nectarina [nekta'rina] *nf* nectarine

nefasto, a [ne'fasto, a] *adj* ill-fated, unlucky

negación [neɣa'θjon] *nf* negation; (*rechazo*) refusal, denial

negar [ne'ɣar] *vt* (*renegar, rechazar*) to refuse; (*prohibir*) to refuse, deny; (*desmentir*) to deny; **~se** *vr*: **~se a** to refuse to

negativa [neɣa'tiβa] *nf* negative; (*rechazo*) refusal, denial

negativo, a [neɣa'tiβo, a] *adj, nm* negative

negligencia [neɣli'xenθja] *nf* negligence; **negligente** *adj* negligent

negociado [neɣo'θjaðo] *nm* department, section

negociante [neɣo'θjante] *nm/f* businessman/woman

negociar [neɣo'θjar] *vt, vi* to negotiate; **~ en** to deal in, trade in

negocio [ne'ɣoθjo] *nm* (*COM*) business; (*asunto*) affair, business; (*operación comercial*) deal, transaction; (*AM*) firm; (*lugar*) place of business; **los ~s** business *sg*; **hacer ~** to do business

negra ['neɣra] *nf* (*MUS*) crotchet; *ver tb* **negro**

negro, a ['neɣro, a] *adj* black; (*suerte*) awful ♦ *nm* black ♦ *nm/f* black man/woman

nene, a ['nene, a] *nm/f* baby, small child

nenúfar [ne'nufar] *nm* water lily

neologismo [neolo'xismo] *nm* neologism

neón [ne'on] *nm*: **luces/lámpara de ~** neon lights/lamp

neoyorquino, a [neojor'kino, a] *adj* (of) New York

nervio ['nerβjo] *nm* nerve;

nerviosismo *nm* nervousness, nerves

pl; **~so, a** *adj* nervous

neto, a ['neto, a] *adj* net

neumático, a [neu'matiko, a] *adj* pneumatic ♦ *nm* (*ESP*) tire (*BRIT*), tire (*US*); **~ de recambio** spare tyre

neurasténico, a [neuras'teniko, a] *adj* (*fig*) hysterical

neurólogo, a [neu'roloɣo, a] *nm/f* neurologist

neurona [neu'rona] *nf* nerve cell

neutral [neu'tral] *adj* neutral; **~izar** *vt* to neutralize; (*contrarrestar*) to counteract

neutro, a ['neutro, a] *adj* (*BIO*, *LING*) neuter

neutrón [neu'tron] *nm* neutron

nevada [ne'βaða] *nf* snowstorm; (*caída de nieve*) snowfall

nevar [ne'βar] *vi* to snow

nevera [ne'βera] *nf* (*ESP*) refrigerator (*BRIT*), icebox (*US*)

nevería [neβe'ria] *nf* (*AM*) ice-cream parlour

nexo ['nekso] *nm* link, connection

ni [ni] *conj* nor, neither; (*tb*: **~ siquiera**) not ... even; **~ aunque que** not even if; **~ blanco ~ negro** neither white nor black

Nicaragua [nika'raɣwa] *nf* Nicaragua; **nicaragüense** *adj, nm/f* Nicaraguan

nicotina [niko'tina] *nf* nicotine

nido ['niðo] *nm* nest

niebla ['njeβla] *nf* fog; (*neblina*) mist

niego *etc vb ver* **negar**

nieto, a ['njeto, a] *nm/f* grandson/daughter; **~s** *nmpl* grandchildren

nieve *etc* ['njeβe] *vb ver* **nevar** ♦ *nf* snow; (*AM*) icecream

N.I.F. *nm abr* (= *Número de Identificación Fiscal*) personal identification number used for financial and tax purposes

nimiedad [nimje'ðað] *nf* triviality

nimio, a ['nimjo, a] *adj* trivial, insignificant

ninfa ['ninfa] *nf* nymph

ningún [niŋ'gun] adj ver **ninguno**

ninguno, a [niŋ'guno, a] (delante de nm: **ningún**) adj no ♦ pron (nadie) nobody; (ni uno) none, not one; (ni uno ni otro) neither; **de ninguna manera** by no means, not at all

niña ['niɲa] nf (ANAT) pupil; ver tb **niño**

niñera [ni'ɲera] nf nursemaid, nanny; **niñería** nf childish act

niñez [ni'ɲeθ] nf childhood; (infancia) infancy

niño, a ['niɲo, a] adj (joven) young; (inmaduro) immature ♦ nm/f child, boy/girl

nipón, ona [ni'pon, ona] adj, nm/f Japanese

níquel ['nikel] nm nickel; **niquelar** vt (TEC) to nickel-plate

níspero ['nispero] nm medlar

nitidez [niti'ðeθ] nf (claridad) clarity; (: de imagen) sharpness; **nítido, a** adj clear; sharp

nitrato [ni'trato] nm nitrate

nitrógeno [ni'troxeno] nm nitrogen

nivel [ni'βel] nm (GEO) level; (norma) level, standard; (altura) height; **~ de aceite** oil level; **~ de aire** spirit level; **~ de vida** standard of living; **nivelar** vt to level out; (fig) to even up; (COM) to balance

NN. UU. nfpl abr (= Naciones Unidas) UN sg

no [no] adv no; not; (con verbo) not ♦ excl no!; **~ tengo nada** I don't have anything, I have nothing; **~ es mío** it's not mine; **ahora ~** not now; **¿~ lo sabes?** don't you know?; **~ mucho** not much; **~ bien termine, lo entregaré** as soon as I'll hand it over; **~ más: ayer ~ más** just yesterday; **¡pase ~ más!** come in!; **¡a que ~ lo sabes!** I bet you don't know!; **¡cómo ~!** of course!; **los países ~ alineados** the non-aligned countries; **la ~ intervención** non-intervention

noble ['noβle] adj, nm/f noble; **~za** nf nobility

noche ['notʃe] nf night, night-time; (la tarde) evening; **de ~, por la ~** at night; **es de ~** it's dark

┌─────────────────────────────┐
│ **Noche de San Juan**   │
└─────────────────────────────┘

The **Noche de San Juan** on the 24th June is a fiesta coinciding with the summer solstice and which has taken the place of other ancient pagan festivals. Traditionally fire plays a major part in these festivities with celebrations and dancing taking place around bonfires in towns and villages across the country.

nochebuena [notʃe'βwena] nf Christmas Eve

┌─────────────────────────────┐
│ **Nochebuena**   │
└─────────────────────────────┘

Traditional Christmas celebrations in Spanish-speaking countries mainly take place on the night of **Nochebuena**, Christmas Eve. Families gather together for a large meal and the more religiously inclined attend Midnight Mass. While presents are traditionally given by **los Reyes Magos** on the 6th January, more and more people are exchanging gifts on Christmas Eve.

nochevieja [notʃe'βjexa] nf New Year's Eve

noción [no'θjon] nf notion

nocivo, a [no'θiβo, a] adj harmful

noctámbulo, a [nok'tambulo, a] nm/f sleepwalker

nocturno, a [nok'turno, a] adj (de la noche) nocturnal, night cpd; (de la tarde) evening cpd ♦ nm nocturne

nodriza [no'ðriθa] nf wet nurse; **buque** o **nave** ~ supply ship

nogal [no'val] nm walnut tree

nómada ['nomaða] adj nomadic ♦ nm/f nomad

nombramiento [nombra'mjento] *nm* naming; (*a un empleo*) appointment

nombrar [nom'brar] *vt* (*designar*) to name; (*mencionar*) to mention; (*dar puesto a*) to appoint

nombre ['nombre] *nm* name; (*sustantivo*) noun; **~ y apellidos** name in full; **~ común/propio** common/ proper noun; **~ de pila/de soltera** Christian/maiden name; **poner ~ a** to call, name

nómina ['nomina] *nf* (*lista*) payroll; (*hoja*) payslip

nominal [nomi'nal] *adj* nominal

nominar [nomi'nar] *vt* to nominate

nominativo, a [nomina'tiβo, a] *adj* (*COM*): **cheque ~ a X** cheque made out to X

nono, a ['nono, a] *adj* ninth

nordeste [nor'ðeste] *adj* north-east, north-eastern, north-easterly ♦ *nm* north-east

nórdico, a ['norðiko, a] *adj* Nordic

noreste [no'reste] *adj*, *nm* = **nordeste**

noria ['norja] *nf* (*AGR*) waterwheel; (*de carnaval*) big (*BRIT*) o Ferris (*US*) wheel

norma ['norma] *nf* rule (of thumb)

normal [nor'mal] *adj* (*corriente*) normal; (*habitual*) usual, natural; **~idad** *nf* normality; **restablecer la ~idad** to restore order; **~izar** *vt* (*reglamentar*) to normalize; (*TEC*) to standardize; **~izarse** *vr* to return to normal; **~mente** *adv* normally

normando, a [nor'mando, a] *adj*, *nm/f* Norman

normativa [norma'tiβa] *nf* (*set of*) rules *pl*, regulations *pl*

noroeste [noro'este] *adj* north-west, north-western, north-westerly ♦ *nm* north-west

norte ['norte] *adj* north, northern, northerly ♦ *nm* north; (*fig*) guide

norteamericano, a [norteameri'kano, a] *adj*, *nm/f* (North) American

Noruega [no'rweɣa] *nf* Norway

noruego, a [no'rweɣo, a] *adj*, *nm/f* Norwegian

nos [nos] *pron* (*directo*) us; (*indirecto*) us; to us; for us; from us; (*reflexivo*) (to) ourselves; (*recíproco*) (to) each other; **~ levantamos a las 7** we get up at 7

nosotros, as [no'sotros, as] *pron* (*sujeto*) we; (*después de prep*) us

nostalgia [nos'talxja] *nf* nostalgia

nota ['nota] *nf* note; (*ESCOL*) mark

notable [no'taβle] *adj* notable; (*ESCOL*) outstanding

notar [no'tar] *vt* to notice, note; **~se** *vr* to be obvious; **se nota que ...** one observes that ...

notarial [nota'rjal] *adj*: **acta ~** affidavit

notario [no'tarjo] *nm* notary

noticia [no'tiθja] *nf* (*información*) piece of news; **las ~s** the news *sg*; **tener ~s de alguien** to hear from sb

noticiero [noti'θjero] (*AM*) *nm* news bulletin

notificación [notifika'θjon] *nf* notification; **notificar** *vt* to notify, inform

notoriedad [notorje'ðað] *nf* fame, renown; **notorio, a** *adj* (*público*) well-known; (*evidente*) obvious

novato, a [no'βato, a] *adj* inexperienced ♦ *nm/f* beginner, novice

novecientos, as [noβe'θjentos, as] *num* nine hundred

novedad [noβe'ðað] *nf* (*calidad de nuevo*) newness; (*noticia*) piece of news; (*cambio*) change, (new) development

novel [no'βel] *adj* new; (*inexperto*) inexperienced ♦ *nm/f* beginner

novela [no'βela] *nf* novel

noveno, a [no'βeno, a] *adj* ninth

noventa [no'βenta] *num* ninety

novia ['noβja] *nf ver* **novio**

noviazgo [no'βjaθɣo] *nm* engagement

novicio, a [no'βiðjo, a] *nm/f* novice

noviembre [no'βjembre] *nm* November

novillada [noβi'ʎaða] nf (TAUR) bullfight with young bulls; **novillero** nm novice bullfighter; **novillo** nm young bull, bullock; **hacer novillos** (fam) to play truant

novio, a ['noβjo, a] nm/f boyfriend/girlfriend; (prometido) fiancé/fiancée; (recién casado) bridegroom/bride; **los ~s** the newly-weds

nubarrón [nuβa'rron] nm storm cloud

nube ['nuβe] nf cloud

nublado, a [nu'βlaðo, a] adj cloudy; **nublarse** vr to grow dark

nubosidad [nuβosi'ðað] nf cloudiness; **había mucha ~** it was very cloudy

nuca ['nuka] nf nape of the neck

nuclear [nukle'ar] adj nuclear

núcleo ['nukleo] nm (centro) core; (FÍSICA) nucleus

nudillo [nu'ðiʎo] nm knuckle

nudista [nu'ðista] adj nudist

nudo ['nuðo] nm knot; **~so, a** adj knotty

nuera ['nwera] nf daughter-in-law

nuestro, a ['nwestro, a] adj pos our ♦ pron ours; **~ padre** our father; **un amigo ~** a friend of ours; **es el ~** it's ours

nueva ['nweβa] nf piece of news

nuevamente [nweβa'mente] adv (otra vez) again; (de nuevo) anew

Nueva York [-'jɔrk] n New York

Nueva Zelanda [-θe'landa] nf New Zealand

nueve ['nweβe] num nine

nuevo, a ['nweβo, a] adj (gen) new; **de ~** again

nuez [nweθ] nf walnut; **~ de Adán** Adam's apple; **~ moscada** nutmeg

nulidad [nuli'ðað] nf (incapacidad) incompetence; (abolición) nullity

nulo, a ['nulo, a] adj (inepto, torpe) useless; (inválido) (null and) void; (DEPORTE) drawn, tied

núm. abr (= número) no

numeración [numera'θjon] nf (cifras) numbers pl; (arábiga, romana etc)

numerals pl

numeral [nume'ral] nm numeral

numerar [nume'rar] vt to number

número ['numero] nm (gen) number; (tamaño: de zapato) size; (ejemplar: de diario) number, issue; **sin ~** numberless, unnumbered; **~ de matrícula/de teléfono** registration/telephone number; **~ atrasado** back number

numeroso, a [nume'roso, a] adj numerous

nunca ['nunka] adv (jamás) never; **~ lo pensé** I never thought it; **no viene ~** he never comes; **~ más** never again; **más que ~** more than ever

nupcias ['nupθjas] nfpl wedding sg, nuptials

nutria ['nutrja] nf otter

nutrición [nutri'θjon] nf nutrition

nutrido, a [nu'triðo, a] adj (alimentado) nourished; (fig: grande) large; (abundante) abundant

nutrir [nu'trir] vt (alimentar) to nourish; (dar de comer) to feed; (fig) to strengthen; **nutritivo, a** adj nourishing, nutritious

nylon [ni'lon] nm nylon

Ñ ñ

ñato, a ['ɲato, a] (AM) adj snub-nosed

ñoñería [ɲoɲe'ria] nf insipidness

ñoño, a ['ɲoɲo, a] adj (AM: tonto) silly, stupid; (soso) insipid; (persona) spineless

O, o

O abr (= oeste) W

o [o] conj or

o/ abr (= orden) o.

oasis [o'asis] nm inv oasis

obcecarse [oββe'karse] vr to get o

become stubborn

obedecer [oβeðe'θer] vt to obey;
obediencia nf obedience; **obediente**
adj obedient

obertura [oβer'tura] nf overture

obesidad [oβesi'ðað] nf obesity;
obeso, a adj obese

obispo [o'βispo] nm bishop

objeción [oβxe'θjon] nf objection;
poner objeciones to raise objections

objetar [oβxe'tar] vt, vi to object

objetivo, a [oβxe'tiβo, a] adj, nm
objective

objeto [oβ'xeto] nm (cosa) object; (fin)
aim

objetor, a [oβxe'tor, a] nm/f objector

oblicuo, a [o'βlikwo, a] adj oblique;
(mirada) sidelong

obligación [oβliγa'θjon] nf obligation;
(COM) bond

obligar [oβli'var] vt to force; **~se** vr to
bind o.s.; **obligatorio, a** adj
compulsory, obligatory

oboe [o'βoe] nm oboe

obra ['oβra] nf work; (ARQ)
construction, building; (TEATRO) play;
~ maestra masterpiece; **~s públicas**
public works; **por ~ de** thanks to the
efforts of); **obrar** vt to work; (tener
efecto) to have an effect on ♦ vi to act,
behave; (tener efecto) to have an effect;
la carta obra en su poder the letter
is in his/her possession

obrero, a [o'βrero, a] adj (clase)
working; (movimiento) labour cpd
♦ nm/f (gen) worker; (sin oficio)
labourer

obscenidad [oβsθeni'ðað] nf
obscenity; **obsceno, a** adj obscene

obscu... = oscu...

obsequiar [oβse'kjar] vt (ofrecer) to
present with; (agasajar) to make a fuss
of, lavish attention on; **obsequio** nm
(regalo) gift; (cortesía) courtesy,
attention

observación [oβserβa'θjon] nf
observation; (reflexión) remark

observador, a [oβserβa'ðor, a] nm/f
observer

observar [oβser'βar] vt to observe;
(anotar) to notice; **~se** vr to keep to,
observe

obsesión [oβse'sjon] nf obsession;
obsesivo, a adj obsessive

obsoleto, a [oβso'leto, a] adj obsolete

obstáculo [oβs'takulo] nm obstacle;
(impedimento) hindrance, drawback

obstante [oβs'tante]: **no ~** adv
nevertheless

obstinado, a [oβsti'naðo, a] adj
obstinate, stubborn

obstinarse [oβsti'narse] vr to be
obstinate; **~ en** to persist in

obstrucción [oβstruk'θjon] nf
obstruction; **obstruir** vt to obstruct

obtener [oβte'ner] vt (gen) to obtain;
(premio) to win

obturador [oβtura'ðor] nm (FOTO)
shutter

obvio, a ['oβßjo, a] adj obvious

oca ['oka] nf (animal) goose; (juego)
≈ snakes and ladders

ocasión [oka'sjon] nf (oportunidad)
opportunity, chance; (momento)
occasion, time; (causa) cause; **de ~**
secondhand; **ocasionar** vt to cause

ocaso [o'kaso] nm (fig) decline

occidente [okθi'ðente] nm west

OCDE nf abr (= Organización de
Cooperación y Desarrollo Económico)
OECD

océano [o'θeano] nm ocean; **el
~ Índico** the Indian Ocean

ochenta [o'tʃenta] num eighty

ocho ['otʃo] num eight; **~ días** a week

ocio ['oθjo] nm (tiempo) leisure; (pey)
idleness; **~so, a** adj (inactivo) idle;
(inútil) useless

octavilla [okta'viʎa] nf leaflet,
pamphlet

octavo, a [ok'taβo, a] adj eighth

octubre [ok'tuβre] nm October

ocular [oku'lar] adj ocular, eye cpd;
testigo ~ eyewitness

oculista [oku'lista] nm/f oculist

ocultar [okul'tar] vt (esconder) to hide; (callar) to conceal; **oculto, a** adj hidden; (fig) secret

ocupación [okupa'θjon] nf occupation

ocupado, a [oku'paðo, a] adj (persona) busy; (plaza) occupied, taken; (teléfono) engaged; **ocupar** vt (gen) to occupy; **ocuparse** vr: **ocuparse de o en** (gen) to concern o.s. with; (cuidar) to look after

ocurrencia [oku'rrenθja] nf (idea) bright idea

ocurrir [oku'rrir] vi to happen; ~se vr: **se me ocurrió que ...** it occurred to me that ...

odiar [o'ðjar] vt to hate; **odio** nm hate, hatred; **odioso, a** adj (gen) hateful; (malo) nasty

odontólogo, a [oðon'toloɣo, a] nm/f dentist, dental surgeon

OEA nf abr (= Organización de Estados Americanos) OAS

oeste [o'este] nm west; **una película del ~** a western

ofender [ofen'der] vt (agraviar) to offend; (insultar) to insult; ~se vr to take offence; **ofensa** nf offence; **ofensiva** nf offensive; **ofensivo, a** adj offensive

oferta [o'ferta] nf offer; (propuesta) proposal; **la ~ y la demanda** supply and demand; **artículos en ~** goods on offer

oficial [ofi'θjal] adj official ♦ nm (MIL) officer

oficina [ofi'θina] nf office; **~ de correos** post office; **~ de turismo** tourist office; **oficinista** nm/f clerk

oficio [o'fiθjo] nm (profesión) profession; (puesto) post; (REL) service; **ser del ~** to be an old hand; **tener mucho ~** to have a lot of experience; **~ de difuntos** funeral service

oficioso, a [ofi'θjoso, a] adj (pey) officious; (no oficial) unofficial, informal

ofimática [ofi'matika] nf office

automation

ofrecer [ofre'θer] vt (dar) to offer; (proponer) to propose; ~se vr (persona) to offer o.s., volunteer; (situación) to present itself; **¿qué se le ofrece?, ¿se le ofrece algo?** what can I do for you?, can I get you anything?

ofrecimiento [ofreθi'mjento] nm offer

oftalmólogo, a [oftal'moloɣo, a] nm/f ophthalmologist

ofuscar [ofus'kar] vt (por pasión) to blind; (por luz) to dazzle

oída [o'iða] nf: **de ~s** by hearsay

oído [o'iðo] nm (ANAT) ear; (sentido) hearing

oigo etc vb ver **oír**

oír [o'ir] vt (gen) to hear; (atender a) to listen to; **¡oiga!** listen! ; **~ misa** to attend mass

OIT nf abr (= Organización Internacional del Trabajo) ILO

ojal [o'xal] nm buttonhole

ojalá [oxa'la] excl if only (it were so)!, some hope! ♦ conj if only ...!, would that ...!: **~ (que) venga hoy** I hope he comes today

ojeada [oxe'aða] nf glance

ojera [o'xera] nf: **tener ~s** to have bags under one's eyes

ojeriza [oxe'riθa] nf ill-will

ojeroso, a [oxe'roso, a] adj haggard

ojo [o'xo] nm eye; (de puente) span; (de cerradura) keyhole ♦ excl careful!; **tener ~ para** to have an eye for; **~ de buey** porthole

okupa [o'kupa] (fam) nm/f squatter

ola [o'la] nf wave

olé [o'le] excl bravo!, olé!

oleada [ole'aða] nf big wave, swell; (fig) wave

oleaje [ole'axe] nm swell

óleo [oleo] nm oil; **oleoducto** nm (oil) pipeline

oler [o'ler] vt (gen) to smell; (inquirir) to pry into; (fig: sospechar) to sniff out ♦ vi to smell; **~ a** to smell of

olfatear [olfate'ar] vt to smell; (inquirir)

to pry into; **olfato** *nm* sense of smell

oligarquía [oliɣar'kia] *nf* oligarchy

olimpíada [olim'piaða] *nf*: **las O~s** the Olympics; **olímpico, a** [o'limpiko, a] *adj* Olympic

oliva [o'liβa] *nf* (*aceituna*) olive; **aceite de ~** olive oil; **olivo** [o'liβo] *nm* olive tree

olla ['oʎa] *nf* pan; (*comida*) stew; **~ a presión** o **exprés** pressure cooker; **~ podrida** type of Spanish stew

olmo ['olmo] *nm* elm (tree)

olor [o'lor] *nm* smell; **~oso, a** *adj* scented

olvidar [olβi'ðar] *vt* to forget; (*omitir*) to omit; **~se** *vr* (*fig*) to forget o.s.; **se me olvidó** I forgot

olvido [ol'βiðo] *nm* oblivion; (*despiste*) forgetfulness

ombligo [om'bliɣo] *nm* navel

omisión [omi'sjon] *nf* (*abstención*) omission; (*descuido*) neglect

omiso, a [o'miso, a] *adj*: **hacer caso ~ de** to ignore, pass over

omitir [omi'tir] *vt* to omit

omnipotente [omnipo'tente] *adj* omnipotent

omóplato [o'moplato] *nm* shoulder blade

OMS *nf abr* (= *Organización Mundial de la Salud*) WHO

once ['onθe] *num* eleven; **~s** *nfpl* (*AM*) tea break

onda ['onda] *nf* wave; **~ corta/larga/media** short/long/medium wave; **ondear** *vt*, *vi* to wave; (*tener ondas*) to be wavy; (*agua*) to ripple; **ondearse** *vr* to swing, sway

ondulación [ondula'θjon] *nf* undulation; **ondulado, a** *adj* wavy

ondular [ondu'lar] *vt* (*el pelo*) to wave ♦ *vi* to undulate; **~se** *vr* to undulate

ONG *nf abr* (= *organización no gubernamental*) NGO

ONU ['onu] *nf abr* (= *Organización de las Naciones Unidas*) UNO

opaco, a [o'pako, a] *adj* opaque

opción [op'θjon] *nf* (*gen*) option;

(*derecho*) right, option

OPEP ['opep] *nf abr* (= *Organización de Países Exportadores de Petróleo*) OPEC

ópera ['opera] *nf* opera; **~ bufa** o **cómica** comic opera

operación [opera'θjon] *nf* (*gen*) operation; (*COM*) transaction, deal

operador, a [opera'ðor, a] *nm/f* operator; (*CINE*: *proyección*) projectionist; (: *rodaje*) cameraman

operar [ope'rar] *vt* (*producir*) to produce, bring about; (*MED*) to operate on ♦ *vi* (*COM*) to operate, deal; **~se** *vr* to occur; (*MED*) to have an operation

opereta [ope'reta] *nf* operetta

opinar [opi'nar] *vt* to think ♦ *vi* to give one's opinion; **opinión** (*creencia*) belief; (*criterio*) opinion

opio ['opjo] *nm* opium

oponente [opo'nente] *nm/f* opponent

oponer [opo'ner] *vt* (*resistencia*) to put up, offer; **~se** *vr* (*objetar*) to object; (*estar frente a frente*) to be opposed; (*dos personas*) to oppose each other; **~ A a B** to set A against B; **me opongo a pensar que ...** I refuse to believe o think that ...

oportunidad [oportuni'ðað] *nf* (*ocasión*) opportunity; (*posibilidad*) chance

oportuno, a [opor'tuno, a] *adj* (*en su tiempo*) opportune, timely; (*respuesta*) suitable; **en el momento ~** at the right moment

oposición [oposi'θjon] *nf* opposition; **oposiciones** *nfpl* (*ESCOL*) public examinations

opositor, a [oposi'tor, a] *nm/f* (*adversario*) opponent; (*candidato*): **~ (a)** candidate (for)

opresión [opre'sjon] *nf* oppression; **opresivo, a** *adj* oppressive; **opresor, a** *nm/f* oppressor

oprimir [opri'mir] *vt* to squeeze; (*fig*) to oppress

optar [op'tar] *vi* (*elegir*) to choose; **~**

por a opt for; **optativo, a** *adj* optional

óptico, a |'optiko, a| *adj* optic(al) ♦ *nm/f* optician; **óptica** *nf* optician's (shop); **desde esta óptica** from this point of view

optimismo |opti'mismo| *nm* optimism; **optimista** *nm/f* optimist

óptimo, a |'optimo, a| *adj* (*el mejor*) very best

opuesto, a |o'pwesto, a| *adj* (*contrario*) opposite; (*antagónico*) opposing

opulencia |opu'lenθja| *nf* opulence; **opulento, a** *adj* opulent

oración |ora'θjon| *nf* (REL) prayer; (LING) sentence

orador, a |ora'ðor, a| *nm/f* (*conferenciante*) speaker, orator

oral |o'ral| *adj* oral

orangután |orangu'tan| *nm* orangutan

orar |o'rar| *vi* to pray

oratoria |ora'torja| *nf* oratory

órbita |'orßita| *nf* orbit

orden |'orðen| *nm* (*gen*) order ♦ *nf* (*gen*) command; **~ del día** agenda; **de primer ~** first-rate; **en ~ de prioridad** in order of priority

ordenado, a |orðe'naðo, a| *adj* (*metódico*) methodical; (*arreglado*) orderly

ordenador |orðena'ðor| *nm* computer; **~ central** mainframe computer

ordenanza |orðe'nanθa| *nf* ordinance

ordenar |orðe'nar| *vt* (*mandar*) to order; (*poner orden*) to put in order, arrange; **~se** *vr* (REL) to be ordained

ordeñar |orðe'ɲar| *vt* to milk

ordinario, a |orði'narjo, a| *adj* (*común*) ordinary, usual; (*vulgar*) vulgar, common

orégano |o'reɣano| *nm* oregano

oreja |o'rexa| *nf* ear; (MECÁNICA) lug, flange

orfanato |orfa'nato| *nm* orphanage

orfandad |orfan'daθ| *nf* orphanhood

orfebrería |orfeßre'ria| *nf* gold/silver work

orgánico, a |or'ßaniko, a| *adj* organic

organigrama |orɣani'ɣrama| *nm* flow chart

organismo |orɣa'nismo| *nm* (BIO) organism; (POL) organization

organización |orɣaniθa'θjon| *nf* organization; **organizar** *vt* to organize

órgano |'orɣano| *nm* organ

orgasmo |or'ɣasmo| *nm* orgasm

orgía |or'xia| *nf* orgy

orgullo |or'ɣuʎo| *nm* pride; **orgulloso, a** *adj* (*gen*) proud; (*altanero*) haughty

orientación |orjenta'θjon| *nf* (*posición*) position; (*dirección*) direction

oriental |orjen'tal| *adj* eastern; (*del Lejano Oriente*) oriental

orientar |orjen'tar| *vt* (*situar*) to orientate; (*señalar*) to point; (*dirigir*) to direct; (*guiar*) to guide; **~se** *vr* to get one's bearings

oriente |o'rjente| *nm* east; **Cercano/Medio/Lejano O~** Near/Middle/Far East

origen |o'rixen| *nm* origin

original |orixi'nal| *adj* (*nuevo*) original; (*extraño*) odd, strange; **~idad** *nf* originality

originar |orixi'nar| *vt* to start, cause; **~se** *vr* to originate; **~io, a** *adj* original; **~io de** native of

orilla |o'riʎa| *nf* (*borde*) border; (*de río*) bank; (*de bosque, tela*) edge; (*de mar*) shore

orina |o'rina| *nf* urine; **orinal** *nm* (chamber) pot; **orinar** *vi* to urinate; **orinarse** *vr* to wet o.s.; **orines** *nmpl* urine

oriundo, a |o'rjundo, a| *adj*: **~ de** native of

ornitología |ornitolo'xia| *nf* ornithology, bird-watching

oro |'oro| *nm* gold; **~s** *nmpl* (NAIPES) hearts

oropel [oro'pel] *nm* tinsel

orquesta [or'kesta] *nf* orchestra; **~ de cámara/sinfónica** chamber/symphony orchestra

orquídea [or'kiðea] *nf* orchid

ortiga [or'tiɣa] *nf* nettle

ortodoxo, a [orto'ðokso, a] *adj* orthodox

ortografía [ortoɣra'fia] *nf* spelling

ortopedia [orto'peðja] *nf* orthopaedics *sg*; **ortopédico, a** *adj* orthopaedic

oruga [o'ruɣa] *nf* caterpillar

orzuelo [or'θwelo] *nm* stye

os [os] *pron* (*gen*) you; (*a vosotras*) to you

osa ['osa] *nf* (she-)bear; **O~ Mayor/Menor** Great/Little Bear

osadía [osa'ðia] *nf* daring

osar [o'sar] *vi* to dare

oscilación [osθila'θjon] *nf* (*movimiento*) oscillation; (*fluctuación*) fluctuation

oscilar [osθi'lar] *vi* to oscillate; to fluctuate

oscurecer [oskure'θer] *vt* to darken ♦ *vi* to grow dark; **~se** *vr* to grow o get dark

oscuridad [oskuri'ðað] *nf* obscurity; (*tinieblas*) darkness

oscuro, a [os'kuro, a] *adj* dark; (*fig*) obscure; **a oscuras** in the dark

óseo, a ['oseo, a] *adj* bone *cpd*

oso ['oso] *nm* bear; **~ de peluche** teddy bear; **~ hormiguero** anteater

ostentación [ostenta'θjon] *nf* (*gen*) ostentation; (*acto*) display

ostentar [osten'tar] *vt* (*gen*) to show; (*pey*) to flaunt, show off; (*poseer*) to have, possess

ostra ['ostra] *nf* oyster

OTAN ['otan] *nf abr* (= *Organización del Tratado del Atlántico Norte*) NATO

otear [ote'ar] *vt* to observe; (*fig*) to look into

otitis [o'titis] *nf* earache

otoñal [oto'ɲal] *adj* autumnal

otoño [o'toɲo] *nm* autumn

otorgar [otor'ɣar] *vt* (*conceder*) to concede; (*dar*) to grant

otorrino, a [oto'rrino, a], **otorrinolaringólogo, a** [otorrinolarin'golɣo, a] *nm/f* ear, nose and throat specialist

---

PALABRA CLAVE

---

otro, a ['otro, a] *adj* **1** (*distinto: sg*) another; (: *pl*) other; **con ~s amigos** with other o different friends

2 (*adicional*): **tráigame ~ café** (*más*), **por favor** can I have another coffee please; **~s 10 días más** another ten days

♦ *pron* **1**: **el ~** the other one; (**los**) **~s** (the) others; **de ~** somebody else's; **que lo haga ~** let somebody else do it

2 (*recíproco*): **se odian (la) una a (la) otra** they hate one another o each other

3: **~ tanto: comer ~ tanto** to eat the same o as much again; **recibió una decena de telegramas y otras tantas llamadas** he got about ten telegrams and as many calls

---

ovación [oβa'θjon] *nf* ovation

oval [o'βal] *adj* oval; **~ado, a** *adj* oval; **óvalo** *nm* oval

ovario [o'βarjo] *nm* ovary

oveja [o'βexa] *nf* sheep

overol [oβe'rol] (*AM*) *nm* overalls *pl*

ovillo [o'βiʎo] *nm* (*de lana*) ball of wool; **hacerse un ~** to curl up

OVNI ['oβni] *nm abr* (= *objeto volante no identificado*) UFO

ovulación [oβula'θjon] *nf* ovulation; **óvulo** *nm* ovum

oxidación [oksiða'θjon] *nf* rusting

oxidar [oksi'ðar] *vt* to rust; **~se** *vr* to go rusty

óxido [o'ksiðo] *nm* oxide

oxigenado, a [oksixe'naðo, a] (*QUÍM*) oxygenated; (*pelo*) bleached

oxígeno [o'ksixeno] *nm* oxygen

oyente [o'jente] nm/f listener
oyes etc vb ver **oír**
ozono [o'θono] nm ozone

P, p

P abr (= padre) Fr.
pabellón [paβe'ʎon] nm bell tent; (ARQ) pavilion; (de hospital etc) block, section; (bandera) flag
pacer [pa'θer] vi to graze
paciencia [pa'θjenθja] nf patience
paciente [pa'θjente] adj, nm/f patient
pacificación [paθifika'θjon] nf pacification
pacificar [paθifi'kar] vt to pacify; (tranquilizar) to calm
pacífico, a [pa'θifiko, a] adj (persona) peaceable; (existencia) peaceful; **el (océano) P~** the Pacific (Ocean)
pacifismo [paθi'fismo] nm pacifism; **pacifista** nm/f pacifist
pacotilla [pako'tiʎa] nf: **de ~** (actor, escritor) third-rate; (mueble etc) cheap
pactar [pak'tar] vt to agree to o on ♦ vi to come to an agreement
pacto ['pakto] nm (tratado) pact; (acuerdo) agreement
padecer [paðe'θer] vt (sufrir) to suffer; (soportar) to endure, put up with; **padecimiento** nm suffering
padrastro [pa'ðrastro] nm stepfather
padre ['paðre] nm father ♦ adj (fam): **un éxito ~** a tremendous success; **~s** nmpl parents
padrino [pa'ðrino] nm (REL) godfather; (tb: **~ de boda**) best man; (fig) sponsor, patron; **~s** nmpl godparents
padrón [pa'ðron] nm (censo) census, roll
paella [pa'eʎa] nf paella, dish of rice with meat, shellfish etc
paga ['paxa] nf (pago) payment; (sueldo) pay, wages pl
pagano, a [pa'xano, a] adj, nm/f

pagan, heathen
pagar [pa'xar] vt to pay; (las compras, crimen) to pay for; (fig: favor) to repay ♦ vi to pay; **al contado/a plazos** to pay (in) cash/in instalments
pagaré [paxa're] nm I.O.U.
página ['paxina] nf page; **~ de inicio** (INFORM) home page
pago ['paxo] nm (dinero) payment; **~ anticipado/a cuenta/contra reembolso/en especie** advance payment/payment on account/cash on delivery/payment in kind; **en ~ de** in return for
pág(s). abr (= página(s)) p(p).
pague etc vb ver **pagar**
país [pa'is] nm (gen) country; (región) land; **los P~es Bajos** the Low Countries; **el P~ Vasco** the Basque Country
paisaje [pai'saxe] nm landscape, scenery
paisano, a [pai'sano, a] adj of the same country ♦ nm/f (compatriota) fellow countryman/woman; **vestir de ~** (soldado) to be in civvies; (guardia) to be in plain clothes
paja ['paxa] nf straw; (fig) rubbish (BRIT), trash (US)
pajarita [paxa'rita] nf (corbata) bow tie
pájaro ['paxaro] nm bird; **~ carpintero** woodpecker
pajita [pa'xita] nf (drinking) straw
pala ['pala] nf spade, shovel; (raqueta etc) bat; (: de tenis) racquet; (CULIN) slice; **~ matamoscas** fly swat
palabra [pa'laβra] nf word; (facultad) (power of) speech; (derecho de hablar) right to speak; **tomar la ~** (en mitin) to take the floor
palabrota [pala'βrota] nf swearword
palacio [pa'laθjo] nm palace; (mansión) mansion, large house; **~ de justicia** courthouse; **~ municipal** town/city hall
paladar [pala'ðar] nm palate; **paladear** vt to taste

palanca |paˈlanka| nf lever; (fig) pull, influence

palangana |palanˈgana| nf washbasin

palco |ˈpalko| nm box

Palestina |palesˈtina| nf Palestine; **palestino, a** nm/f Palestinian

paleta |paˈleta| nf (de pintor) palette; (de albañil) trowel; (de ping-pong) bat; (AM) ice lolly

paleto, a |paˈleto, a| (fam, pey) nm/f yokel

paliar |paˈljar| vt (mitigar) to mitigate, alleviate; **paliativo** nm palliative

palidecer |paliðeˈθer| vi to turn pale; **palidez** nf paleness; **pálido, a** adj pale

palillo |paˈliʎo| nm (mondadientes) toothpick; (para comer) chopstick

paliza |paˈliθa| nf beating, thrashing

palma |ˈpalma| nf (ANAT) palm; (árbol) palm tree; **batir** o **dar ~s** to clap, applaud; **~da** nf slap; **~das** nfpl clapping sg, applause sg

palmar |palˈmar| (fam) vi (tb: ~la) to die, kick the bucket

palmear |palmeˈar| vi to clap

palmera |palˈmera| nf (BOT) palm tree

palmo |ˈpalmo| nm (medida) span; (fig) small amount; **~ a ~** inch by inch

palo |ˈpalo| nm stick; (poste) post; (de tienda de campaña) pole; (mango) handle, shaft; (golpe) blow, hit; (de golf) club; (de béisbol) bat; (NAUT) mast; (NAIPES) suit

paloma |paˈloma| nf dove, pigeon

palomitas |paloˈmitas| nfpl popcorn sg

palpar |palˈpar| vt to touch, feel

palpitación |palpitaˈθjon| nf palpitation

palpitante |palpiˈtante| adj palpitating; (fig) burning

palpitar |palpiˈtar| vi to palpitate; (latir) to beat

palta |ˈpalta| (AM) nf avocado (pear)

paludismo |paluˈðismo| nm malaria

pamela |paˈmela| nf picture hat, sun hat

pampa |ˈpampa| (AM) nf pampas, prairie

pan |pan| nm bread; (una barra) loaf; **~ integral** wholemeal (BRIT) o wholewheat (US) bread; **~ rallado** breadcrumbs pl

pana |ˈpana| nf corduroy

panadería |panaðeˈria| nf baker's (shop); **panadero, a** nm/f baker

Panamá |panaˈma| nm Panama; **panameño, a** adj Panamanian

pancarta |panˈkarta| nf placard, banner

panda |ˈpanda| nm (ZOOL) panda

pandereta |pandeˈreta| nf tambourine

pandilla |panˈdiʎa| nf set, group; (de criminales) gang; (pey: camarilla) clique

panecillo |paneˈθiʎo| nm (bread) roll

panel |panel| nm panel; **~ solar** solar panel

panfleto |panˈfleto| nm pamphlet

pánico |ˈpaniko| nm panic

panorama |panoˈrama| nm panorama; (vista) view

pantalla |panˈtaʎa| nf (de cine) screen; (de lámpara) lampshade

pantalón |pantaˈlon| nm trousers; **pantalones** nmpl trousers

pantano |panˈtano| nm (ciénaga) marsh, swamp; (depósito: de agua) reservoir; (fig) jam, difficulty

panteón |panteˈon| nm: **~ familiar** family tomb

pantera |panˈtera| nf panther

panti(es) |ˈpantis| nmpl tights

pantomima |pantoˈmima| nf pantomime

pantorrilla |pantoˈrriʎa| nf calf (of the leg)

pantufla |panˈtufla| nf slipper

panty(s) |ˈpanti(s)| nm(pl) tights

panza |ˈpanθa| nf belly, paunch

pañal |paˈɲal| nm nappy (BRIT), diaper (US); **~es** nmpl (fig) early stages, infancy sg

paño |ˈpaɲo| nm (tela) cloth; (pedazo

de tela) (piece of) cloth; (*trapo*) duster, rag; **~ higiénico** sanitary towel; **~s menores** underclothes

pañuelo |pa'nwelo| *nm* handkerchief, hanky (*fam*); (*para la cabeza*) (head)scarf

papa |'papa| *nm*: **el P~** the Pope ♦ *nf* (*AM*) potato

papá |pa'pa| (*pl* **~s**) (*fam*) *nm* dad(dy), pa (*US*)

papada |pa'paða| *nf* double chin

papagayo |papa'γajo| *nm* parrot

papanatas |papa'natas| (*fam*) *nm inv* simpleton

paparrucha |papa'rrutʃa| *nf* piece of nonsense

papaya |pa'paja| *nf* papaya

papear |pape'ar| (*fam*) *vt, vi* to scoff

papel |pa'pel| *nm* paper; (*hoja de ~*) sheet of paper; (*TEATRO, fig*) role; **~ de calco/carbón/de cartas** tracing paper/carbon paper/stationery; **~ de envolver/pintado** wrapping paper/ wallpaper; **~ de aluminio/higiénico** aluminium (*BRIT*) o aluminum (*US*) foil/ toilet paper; **~ de estaño** o **plata** tinfoil; **~ de lija** sandpaper; **~ moneda** paper money; **~ secante** blotting paper

papeleo |pape'leo| *nm* red tape

papelera |pape'lera| *nf* wastepaper basket; (*en la calle*) litter bin

papelería |papele'ria| *nf* stationer's (shop)

papeleta |pape'leta| *nf* (*POL*) ballot paper; (*ESCOL*) report

paperas |pa'peras| *nfpl* mumps *sg*

papilla |pa'piʎa| *nf* (*para niños*) baby food

paquete |pa'kete| *nm* (*de cigarrillos etc*) packet; (*CORREOS etc*) parcel; (*AM*) package tour; (: *fam*) nuisance

par |par| *adj* (*igual*) like, equal; (*MAT*) even ♦ *nm* equal; (*de guantes*) pair; (*de veces*) couple; (*POL*) peer; (*GOLF, COM*) par; **abrir** o **en** ~ to open wide

para |'para| *prep* for; **no es** ~ **comer**

it's not for eating; **decir** ~ **sí** to say to o.s.; **¿~ qué lo quieres?** what do you want it for?; **se casaron** ~ **separarse otra vez** they married only to separate again; **lo tendré** ~ **mañana** I'll have it (for) tomorrow; **ir** ~ **casa** to go home, head for home; ~ **profesor es muy estúpido** he's very stupid for a teacher; **¿quién es usted** ~ **gritar así?** who are you to shout like that?; **tengo bastante** ~ **vivir** I have enough to live on; *ver tb* **con**

parabién |para'βjen| *nm* congratulations *pl*

parábola |pa'raβola| *nf* parable; (*MAT*) parabola; **parabólica** *nf* (*tb*: **antena** ~) satellite dish

parabrisas |para'βrisas| *nm inv* windscreen (*BRIT*), windshield (*US*)

paracaídas |paraka'iðas| *nm inv* parachute; **paracaidista** *nm/f* parachutist; (*MIL*) paratrooper

parachoques |para'tʃokes| *nm inv* (*AUTO*) bumper; (*MECÁNICA etc*) shock absorber

parada |pa'raða| *nf* stop; (*acto*) stopping; (*de industria*) shutdown, stoppage; (*lugar*) stopping place; ~ **de autobús** bus stop

paradero |para'ðero| *nm* stopping-place; (*situación*) whereabouts

parado, a |pa'raðo, a| *adj* (*persona*) motionless, standing still; (*fábrica*) closed, at a standstill; (*coche*) stopped; (*AM*) standing (up); (*sin empleo*) unemployed, idle

paradoja |para'ðoxa| *nf* paradox

parador |para'ðor| *nm* parador, state-run hotel

paráfrasis |pa'rafrasis| *nf inv* paraphrase

paraguas |pa'raγwas| *nm inv* umbrella

Paraguay |para'ɣwai| *nm*: **el** ~ Paraguay; **paraguayo, a** *adj, nm/f* Paraguayan

paraíso |para'iso| *nm* paradise, heaven

paraje |pa'raxe| *nm* place, spot

paralelo, a [para'lelo, a] *adj* parallel

parálisis [pa'ralisis] *nf inv* paralysis; **paralítico, a** *adj, nm/f* paralytic

paralizar [parali'θar] *vt* to paralyse; **~se** *vr* to become paralysed; *(fig)* to come to a standstill

paramilitar [paramili'tar] *adj* paramilitary

páramo ['paramo] *nm* bleak plateau

parangón [paran'gon] *nm:* **sin ~** incomparable

paranoico, a [para'noiko, a] *nm/f* paranoiac

parapente [para'pente] *nm (deporte)* paragliding; *(aparato)* paraglider

parapléjico, a [para'plexiko, a] *adj, nm/f* paraplegic

parar [pa'rar] *vt* to stop; *(golpe)* to ward off ♦ *vi* to stop; **~se** *vr* to stop; *(AM)* to stand up; **ha parado de llover** it has stopped raining; **van a ir a ~ a comisaria** they're going to end up in the police station; **~se en** to pay attention to

pararrayos [para'rrajos] *nm inv* lightning conductor

parásito, a [pa'rasito, a] *nm/f* parasite

parcela [par'θela] *nf* plot, piece of ground

parche ['partʃe] *nm (gen)* patch

parchís [par'tʃis] *nm* ludo

parcial [par'θjal] *adj (pago)* part-; *(eclipse)* partial; *(JUR)* prejudiced, biased; *(POL)* partisan; **~idad** *nf* prejudice, bias

pardillo, a [par'ðiʎo, a] *(pey) adj* yokel

parecer [pare'θer] *nm (opinión)* opinion, view; *(aspecto)* looks pl ♦ *vi (tener apariencia)* to seem, look; *(asemejarse)* to look o seem like; *(aparecer, llegar)* to appear; **~se** *vr* to look alike, resemble each other; **~se a** to look like, resemble; **según parece** evidently, apparently; **me parece que** I think (that), it seems to me that

parecido, a [pare'θiðo, a] *adj* similar ♦ *nm* similarity, likeness, resemblance;

bien ~ good-looking, nice-looking

pared [pa'reð] *nf* wall

pareja [pa'rexa] *nf (par)* pair; *(dos personas)* couple; *(otro: de un par)* other one (of a pair); *(persona)* partner

parentela [paren'tela] *nf* relations *pl*

parentesco [paren'tesko] *nm* relationship

paréntesis [pa'rentesis] *nm inv* parenthesis; *(en escrito)* bracket

parezco *etc vb ver* **parecer**

pariente, a [pa'rjente, a] *nm/f* relative, relation

parir [pa'rir] *vt* to give birth to ♦ *vi (mujer)* to give birth, have a baby

Paris [pa'ris] *n* Paris

parking ['parkin] *nm* car park *(BRIT)*, parking lot *(US)*

parlamentar [parlamen'tar] *vi* to parley

parlamentario, a [parlamen'tarjo, a] *adj* parliamentary ♦ *nm/f* member of parliament

parlamento [parla'mento] *nm* parliament

parlanchín, ina [parlan'tʃin, ina] *adj* indiscreet ♦ *nm/f* chatterbox

parlar [par'lar] *vi* to chatter (away)

paro ['paro] *nm (huelga)* stoppage (of work), strike; *(desempleo)* unemployment; **subsidio de ~** unemployment benefit

parodia [pa'roðja] *nf* parody; **parodiar** *vt* to parody

parpadear [parpaðe'ar] *vi (ojos)* to blink; *(luz)* to flicker

párpado ['parpaðo] *nm* eyelid

parque ['parke] *nm (lugar verde)* park; **~ de atracciones/infantil/zoológico** fairground/playground/zoo

parqué [par'ke] *nm* parquet *(flooring)*

parquímetro [par'kimetro] *nm* parking meter

parra ['parra] *nf* (grape)vine

párrafo ['parrafo] *nm* paragraph; **echar un ~** *(fam)* to have a chat

parranda [pa'rranda] *(fam) nf* spree,

parrilla |pa'rriʎa| nf (CULIN) grill; (de coche) grille; **(carne a la) ~ barbecue; ~da** nf barbecue

párroco |'parroko| nm parish priest

parroquia |pa'rrokja| nf parish; (iglesia) parish church; (COM) clientele, customers pl; **~no, a** nm/f parishioner; client, customer

parsimonia |parsi'monja| nf calmness, point-headedness

parte |'parte| nm message; (informe) report ♦ nf part; (lado, cara) side; (de reparto) share; (JUR) party; **en alguna ~ de Europa** somewhere in Europe; **en/por todas ~s** everywhere; **en gran ~** to a large extent; **la mayor ~ de los españoles** most Spaniards; **de un tiempo a esta ~** for some time past; **de ~ de alguien** on sb's behalf; **¿de ~ de quién?** (TEL) who is speaking?; **por ~ de** on the part of; **por mí ~** I for my part; **por otra ~** on the other hand; **dar ~ a** to inform; **tomar ~** to take part

partición |parti'θjon| nf division, sharing-out; (POL) partition

participación |partiθipa'θjon| nf (acto) participation, taking part; (parte, COM) share; (de lotería) shared prize; (aviso) notice, notification

participante |partiθi'pante| nm/f participant

participar |partiθi'par| vt to notify, inform ♦ vi to take part, participate

partícipe |par'tiθipe| nm/f participant

particular |partiku'lar| adj (especial) particular, special; (individual, personal) private, personal ♦ nm (punto, asunto) particular, point; (individuo) individual; **tiene coche ~** he has a car of his own

partida |par'tiða| nf (salida) departure; (COM) entry, item; (juego) game; (grupo de personas) band, group; **mala ~** dirty trick; **~ de nacimiento / matrimonio / defunción** birth/marriage/death certificate

partidario, a |parti'ðarjo, a| adj partisan ♦ nm/f supporter, follower

partido |par'tiðo| nm (POL) party; (DEPORTE) game, match; **sacar ~ de** to profit o benefit from; **tomar ~** to take sides

partir |par'tir| vt (dividir) to split, divide; (compartir, distribuir) to share (out), distribute; (romper) to break open, split open; (rebanada) to cut (off) ♦ vi (ponerse en camino) to set off o out; (comenzar) to start (off o out); **~se** vr to crack o split o break (in two etc); **a ~ de** (starting) from

partitura |parti'tura| nf (MUS) score

parto |'parto| nm birth; (fig) product, creation; **estar de ~** to be in labour

pasa |'pasa| nf raisin; **~ de Corinto/de Esmirna** currant/sultana

pasada |pa'saða| nf passing, passage; **de ~** in passing, incidentally; **una mala ~** a dirty trick

pasadizo |pasa'ðiθo| nm (pasillo) passage, corridor; (callejuela) alley

pasado, a |pa'saðo, a| adj past; (malo: comida, fruta) bad; (muy cocido) overdone; (anticuado) out of date ♦ nm past; **~ mañana** the day after tomorrow; **el mes ~** last month

pasador |pasa'ðor| nm (cerrojo) bolt; (de pelo) hair slide; (horquilla) grip

pasaje |pa'saxe| nm (gen) passage; (pago de viaje) fare; (los pasajeros) passengers pl; (pasillo) passageway

pasajero, a |pasa'xero, a| adj passing; (situación, estado) temporary; (amor, enfermedad) brief ♦ nm/f passenger

pasamontañas |pasamon'taɲas| nm inv balaclava helmet

pasaporte |pasa'porte| nm passport

pasar |pa'sar| vt to pass; (tiempo) to spend; (desgracias) to suffer, endure; (noticia) to give, pass on; (río) to cross; (barrera) to pass through; (falta) to overlook, tolerate; (contincante) to surpass, do better than; (coche) to overtake; (CINE) to show; (enfermedad)

to give, infect with ♦ vi (gen)
to pass; (terminarse) to be over; (ocurrir) to
happen; **~se** vr (flores) to fade;
(comida) to go bad o off; (fig) to
overdo it, go too far; **~ de** to go
beyond, exceed; **~ por** (AM) to fetch;
~lo bien/mal to have a good/bad
time; **¡pase!** come in!; **hacer ~** to
show in; **~se al enemigo** to go over
to the enemy; **se me pasó** I forgot;
no se le pasa nada he misses
nothing; **pase lo que pase** come
what may; **¿qué pasa?** what's going
on?, what's up?; **¿qué te pasa?**
what's wrong?

pasarela [pasa'rela] nf footbridge; (en
barco) gangway

pasatiempo [pasa'tjempo] nm
pastime, hobby

Pascua ['paskwa] nf: **~ (de
Resurrección)** Easter; **~ de Navidad**
Christmas; **~s** nfpl Christmas (time);
¡felices ~s! Merry Christmas!

pase ['pase] nm pass; (CINE)
performance, showing

pasear [pase'ar] vt to take for a walk;
(exhibir) to parade, show off ♦ vi to
walk, go for a walk; **~se** vr to walk,
go for a walk; **~ en coche** to go for a
drive; **paseo** nm (avenida) avenue;
(distancia corta) stroll, walk; **dar un o
ir de paseo** to go for a walk

pasillo [pa'siʎo] nm passage, corridor

pasión [pa'sjon] nf passion

pasivo, a [pa'siβo, a] adj passive;
(inactivo) inactive ♦ nm (COM) liabilities
pl, debts pl

pasmar [pas'mar] vt (asombrar) to
amaze, astonish; **pasmo** nm
amazement, astonishment; (resfriado)
chill; (fig) wonder, marvel; **pasmoso,
a** adj amazing, astonishing

paso, a ['paso, a] adj dried ♦ nm step;
(modo de andar) walk; (huella)
footprint; (rapidez) speed, pace, rate;
(camino accesible) way through;
passage; (cruce) crossing; (pasaje)

passing, passage; (GEO) pass; (estrecho)
strait; **~ a nivel** (FERRO) level-crossing;
~ de peatones pedestrian crossing; **a
ese ~** (fig) at that rate; **salir al ~ de**
a to waylay; **estar de ~** to be passing
through; **~ elevado** flyover;
prohibido el ~ no entry; **ceda el ~**
give way

pasota [pa'sota] (fam) adj, nm/f ≈
dropout; **ser un (tipo) ~** to be a bit of
a dropout; (ser indiferente) not to care
about anything

pasta ['pasta] nf paste; (CULIN: masa)
dough; (: de bizcochos etc) pastry;
(fam) dough; **~s** nfpl (bizcochos)
pastries, small cakes; (fideos, espaguetis
etc) pasta; **~ de dientes** o **dentífrica**
toothpaste

pastar [pas'tar] vt, vi to graze

pastel [pas'tel] nm (dulce) cake; (ARTE)
pastel; **~ de carne** meat pie; **~ería** nf
cake shop

pasteurizado, a [pasteuri'θaðo, a] adj
pasteurized

pastilla [pas'tiʎa] nf (de jabón,
chocolate) bar; (píldora) tablet, pill

pasto ['pasto] nm (hierba) grass; (lugar)
pasture, field

pastor, a [pas'tor, a] nm/f shepherd/
ess ♦ nm (REL) clergyman, pastor;
~ alemán Alsatian

pata ['pata] nf (pierna) leg; (pie) foot;
(de muebles) leg; **~s arriba** upside
down; **metedura de ~** (fam) gaffe;
meter la ~ (fam) to put one's foot in
it; (TEC): **~ de cabra** crowbar; **tener
buena/mala ~** to be lucky/unlucky;
~da nf kick; (en el suelo) stamp

patalear [patale'ar] vi (en el suelo) to
stamp one's feet

patata [pa'tata] nf potato; **~s fritas**
chips, French fries; (de bolsa) crisps

paté [pa'te] nm pâté

patear [pate'ar] vt (pisar) to stamp on,
trample (on); (pegar con el pie) to kick
♦ vi to stamp (with rage), stamp one's
feet

patentar [paten'tar] vt to patent

patente [pa'tente] adj obvious, evident; (COM) patente ♦ nf patent

paternal [pater'nal] adj fatherly, paternal; **paterno, a** adj paternal

patético, a [pa'tetiko, a] adj pathetic, moving

patilla [pa'tiʎa] nf (de gafas) side(piece); ~s nfpl sideburns

patín [pa'tin] nm skate; (de trineo) runner; **patinaje** nm skating; **patinar** vi to skate; (resbalarse) to skid, slip; (fam) to slip up, blunder

patio ['patjo] nm (de casa) patio, courtyard; ~ **de recreo** playground

pato ['pato] nm duck; **pagar el ~** (fam) to take the blame, carry the can

patológico, a [pato'loxiko, a] adj pathological

patoso, a [pa'toso, a] (fam) adj clumsy

patraña [pa'traɲa] nf story, fib

patria ['patrja] nf native land, mother country

patrimonio [patri'monjo] nm inheritance; (fig) heritage

patriota [pa'trjota] nm/f patriot; **patriotismo** nm patriotism

patrocinar [patroθi'nar] vt to sponsor; **patrocinio** nm sponsorship

patrón, ona [pa'tron, ona] nm/f (jefe) boss, chief, master/mistress; (propietario) landlord/lady; (REL) patron saint ♦ nm (TEC, COSTURA) pattern

patronal [patro'nal] adj: **la clase ~** management

patronato [patro'nato] nm sponsorship; (acto) patronage; (fundación benéfica) trust, foundation

patrulla [pa'truʎa] nf patrol

pausa ['pausa] nf pause, break

pausado, a [pau'saðo, a] adj slow, deliberate

pauta ['pauta] nf line, guide line

pavimento [paβi'mento] nm (con losas) pavement, paving

pavo ['paβo] nm turkey; ~ **real** peacock

pavor [pa'βor] nm dread, terror

payaso, a [pa'jaso, a] nm/f clown

payo, a ['pajo, a] nm/f non-gipsy

paz [paθ] nf peace; (tranquilidad) peacefulness, tranquility; **hacer las paces** to make peace; (fig) to make up

pazo ['paθo] nm country house

P.D. abr (= posdata) P.S., p.s.

peaje [pe'axe] nm toll

peatón [pea'ton] nm pedestrian

peca ['peka] nf freckle

pecado [pe'kaðo] nm sin; **pecador, a** adj sinful ♦ nm/f sinner

pecaminoso, a [pekami'noso, a] adj sinful

pecar [pe'kar] vi (REL) to sin; **peca de generoso** he is generous to a fault

pecera [pe'θera] nf fish tank; (redondo) goldfish bowl

pecho [pe'tʃo] nm (ANAT) chest; (de mujer) breast; **dar el ~ a** to breast-feed; **tomar algo a ~** to take sth to heart

pechuga [pe'tʃuγa] nf breast

peculiar [peku'ljar] adj special, peculiar; (característico) typical, characteristic; ~**idad** nf peculiarity; special feature, characteristic

pedal [pe'ðal] nm pedal; ~**ear** vi to pedal

pedante [pe'ðante] adj pedantic ♦ nm/f pedant; ~**ría** nf pedantry

pedazo [pe'ðaθo] nm piece, bit; **hacerse ~s** to smash, shatter

pedernal [peðer'nal] nm flint

pediatra [pe'ðjatra] nm/f paediatrician

pedido [pe'ðiðo] nm (COM) order; (petición) request

pedir [pe'ðir] vt to ask for, request; (comida, COM): to order; (necesitar) to need, demand, require ♦ vi to ask; **me pidió que cerrara la puerta** he asked me to shut the door; **¿cuánto piden por el coche?** how much are they asking for the car?

pedo ['peðo] (fam!) nm fart

pega ['peγa] nf snag; **poner ~s (a)** to

complain (about)

pegadizo, a |pexa'ðiθo, a| adj (MUS) catchy

pegajoso, a |pexa'xoso, a| adj sticky, adhesive

pegamento |pexa'mento| nm gum, glue

pegar |pe'xar| vt (papel, sellos) to stick (on); (cartel) to stick up; (coser) to sew (on); (unir: partes) to join, fix together; (MED) to give, infect with; (dar: golpe) to give, deal ♦ vi (adherirse) to stick, adhere; (ir juntos: colores) to match, go together; (golpear) to hit; (quemar: el sol) to strike hot, burn (fig); **~se** vr (dos personas) to hit each other, fight; (fam): **~ un grito** to let out a yell; **~ un salto** to jump (with fright); **~ en** to touch; **~se un tiro** to shoot o.s.

pegatina |pexa'tina| nf sticker

pegote |pe'xote| (fam) nm eyesore, sight

peinado |pei'naðo| nm hairstyle

peinar |pei'nar| vt to comb; (hacer estilo) to style; **~se** vr to comb one's hair

peine |'peine| nm comb; **~ta** nf ornamental comb

p.ej. abr (= por ejemplo) e.g.

Pekín |pe'kin| n Pekín(g)

pelado, a |pe'laðo, a| adj (fruta, patata etc) peeled; (cabeza) shorn; (campo, fig) bare; (fam: sin dinero) broke

pelaje |pe'laxe| nm (ZOOL) fur, coat; (fig) appearance

pelar |pe'lar| vt (fruta, patatas etc) to peel; (cortar el pelo a) to cut the hair of; (quitar la piel: animal) to skin; **~se** vr (la piel) to peel off; **voy a ~me** I'm going to get my hair cut

peldaño |pel'daɲo| nm step

pelea |pe'lea| nf (lucha) fight; (discusión) quarrel, row

peleado, a |pe'leaðo, a| adj: **estar ~ (con uno)** to have fallen out (with sb)

pelear |pele'ar| vi to fight; **~se** vr to fight; (reñirse) to fall out, quarrel

peletería |pelete'ria| nf furrier's, fur shop

pelícano |pe'likano| nm pelican

película |pe'likula| nf film; (cobertura ligera) thin covering; (FOTO: rollo) roll o reel of film

peligro |pe'liɣro| nm danger; (riesgo) risk; **correr ~ de** to run the risk of; **~so, a** adj dangerous; risky

pelirrojo, a |peli'rroxo, a| adj red-haired, red-headed ♦ nm/f redhead

pellejo |pe'ʎexo| nm (de animal) skin, hide

pellizcar |peʎiθ'kar| vt to pinch, nip

pelma |'pelma| (fam) nm/f pain (in the neck)

pelmazo |pel'maθo| (fam) nm = **pelma**

pelo |'pelo| nm (cabellos) hair; (de barba, bigote) whisker; (de animal: pellejo) hair, fur, coat; **al ~** just right; **venir al ~** to be exactly what one needs; **un hombre de ~ en pecho** a brave man; **por los ~s** by the skin of one's teeth; **no tener ~s en la lengua** to be outspoken, not mince words; **tomar el ~ a uno** to pull sb's leg

pelota |pe'lota| nf ball; **en ~s** stark naked; **hacer la ~ (a uno)** (fam) to creep (to sb); **~ vasca** pelota

pelotari |pelo'tari| nm pelota player

pelotón |pelo'ton| nm (MIL) squad, detachment

peluca |pe'luka| nf wig

peluche |pe'lutʃe| nm: **oso/muñeco de ~** teddy bear/soft toy

peludo, a |pe'luðo, a| adj hairy, shaggy

peluquería |peluke'ria| nf hairdresser's; **peluquero, a** nm/f hairdresser

pelusa |pe'lusa| nf (BOT) down; (en tela) fluff

pena |'pena| nf (congoja) grief,

sadness; (*remordimiento*) regret; (*dificultad*) trouble; (*dolor*) pain; (*JUR*) sentence; **merecer** o **valer la ~ to be** worthwhile; **a duras ~s** with great difficulty; **~ de muerte** death penalty; **~ pecuniaria** fine; **¡qué ~!** what a shame!

penal [pe'nal] *adj* penal ♦ *nm* (*cárcel*) prison

penalidad [penali'ðað] *nf* (*problema*, *dificultad*) trouble, hardship; (*JUR*) penalty, punishment; **~es** *nfpl* trouble, hardship

penalti, penalty [pe'nalti] (*pl* **~s** o **~es**) *nm* penalty (kick)

pendiente [pen'djente] *adj* pending, unsettled ♦ *nm* earring ♦ *nf* hill, slope

pene |'pene] *nm* penis

penetración [penetra'θjon] *nf* (*acto*) penetration; (*agudeza*) sharpness, insight

penetrante [pene'trante] *adj* (*herida*) deep; (*persona, arma*) sharp; (*sonido*) penetrating, piercing; (*mirada*) searching; (*viento, ironía*) biting

penetrar [pene'trar] *vt* to penetrate, pierce; (*entender*) to grasp ♦ *vi* to penetrate, go in; (*entrar*) to enter, go in; (*líquido*) to soak in; (*fig*) to pierce

penicilina [peniθi'lina] *nf* penicillin

península [pe'ninsula] *nf* peninsula; **peninsular** *adj* peninsular

penique [pe'nike] *nm* penny

penitencia [peni'tenθja] *nf* penance

penoso, a [pe'noso, a] *adj* (*lamentable*) distressing; (*difícil*) arduous, difficult

pensador, a [pensa'ðor, a] *nm/f* thinker

pensamiento [pensa'mjento] *nm* thought; (*mente*) mind; (*idea*) idea

pensar [pen'sar] *vt* to think over, think out; (*considerar*) to think over, think out; (*proponerse*) to intend, plan; (*imaginarse*) to think up, invent ♦ *vi* to think; **~ en** to aim at, aspire to; **pensativo, a** *adj* thoughtful, pensive

pensión [pen'sjon] *nf* (*casa*) boarding o guest house; (*dinero*) pension; (*cama y comida*) board and lodging; **~ completa** full board; **media ~** half-board; **pensionista** *nm/f* (*jubilado*) (old-age) pensioner; (*huésped*) lodger

penúltimo, a [pe'nultimo, a] *adj* penultimate, last but one

penumbra [pe'numbra] *nf* half-light

penuria [pe'nurja] *nf* shortage, want

peña ['peɲa] *nf* (*roca*) rock; (*cuesta*) cliff, crag; (*grupo*) group, circle; (*AM: club*) club folk club

peñasco [pe'ɲasko] *nm* large rock, boulder

peñón [pe'ɲon] *nm* wall of rock; **el P~** the Rock of Gibraltar

peón [pe'on] *nm* labourer; (*AM*) farm labourer, farmhand; (*AJEDREZ*) pawn

peonza [pe'onθa] *nf* spinning top

peor [pe'or] *adj* (*comparativo*) worse; (*superlativo*) worst ♦ *adv* worse; worst; **de mal en ~** from bad to worse

pepinillo [pepi'niʎo] *nm* gherkin

pepino [pe'pino] *nm* cucumber; **(no) me importa un ~** I don't care one bit

pepita [pe'pita] *nf* (*BOT*) pip; (*MINERÍA*) nugget

pepito [pe'pito] *nm*: **~ (de ternera)** steak sandwich

pequeñez [peke'neθ] *nf* smallness, littleness; (*trivialidad*) trifle, triviality

pequeño, a [pe'keɲo, a] *adj* small, little

pera ['pera] *nf* pear; **peral** *nm* pear tree

percance [per'kanθe] *nm* setback, misfortune

percatarse [perka'tarse] *vr*: **~ de** to notice, take note of

percebe [per'θeβe] *nm* barnacle

percepción [perθep'θjon] *nf* (*vista*) perception; (*idea*) notion, idea

percha ['pertʃa] *nf* (*coat*)hanger; (*ganchos*) coat hooks *pl*; (*de ave*) perch

percibir [perθi'ßir] *vt* to perceive, notice; (*COM*) to earn, get

percusión [perku'sjon] nf percussion

perdedor, a [perðe'ðor, a] adj losing
♦ nm/f loser

perder [per'ðer] vt to lose; (tiempo, palabras) to waste; (oportunidad) to lose, miss; (tren) to miss ♦ vi to lose; **~se** vr (extraviarse) to get lost; (desaparecer) to disappear, be lost to view; (arruinarse) to be ruined; **echar a ~** (comida) to spoil, ruin; (oportunidad) to waste

perdición [perði'θjon] nf perdition, ruin

pérdida ['perðiða] nf loss; (de tiempo) waste; **~s** nfpl (COM) losses

perdido, a [per'ðiðo, a] adj lost

perdiz [per'ðiθ] nf partridge

perdón [per'ðon] nm (disculpa) pardon, forgiveness; (clemencia) mercy; **¡~!** sorry!, I beg your pardon!; **perdonar** vt to pardon, forgive; (la vida) to spare; (excusar) to excuse; **¡perdone (usted)!** sorry!, I beg your pardon!

perdurar [perðu'rar] vi (resistir) to last, endure; (seguir existiendo) to stand, still exist

perecedero, a [pereθe'ðero, a] adj perishable

perecer [pere'θer] vi to perish, die

peregrinación [pereɣrina'θjon] nf (REL) pilgrimage

peregrino, a [pere'ɣrino, a] adj (idea) strange, absurd ♦ nm/f pilgrim

perejil [pere'xil] nm parsley

perenne [pe'renne] adj everlasting, perennial

pereza [pe'reθa] nf laziness, idleness; **perezoso, a** adj lazy, idle

perfección [perfek'θjon] nf perfection; **perfeccionar** vt to perfect; (mejorar) to improve; (acabar) to complete, finish

perfectamente [perfekta'mente] adv perfectly

perfecto, a [per'fekto, a] adj perfect; (total) complete

perfil [per'fil] nm profile; (contorno) silhouette, outline; (ARQ) (cross) section; **~es** nmpl features; **~ar** vt (trazar) to outline; (fig) to shape, give character to

perforación [perfora'θjon] nf perforation; (con taladro) drilling; **perforadora** nf punch

perforar [perfo'rar] vt to perforate; (agujero) to drill, bore; (papel) to punch a hole in ♦ vi to drill, bore

perfume [per'fume] nm perfume, scent

pericia [pe'riθja] nf skill, expertise

periferia [peri'ferja] nf periphery; (de ciudad) outskirts pl

periférico [peri'feriko] (AM) nm ring road (BRIT), beltway (US)

perímetro [pe'rimetro] nm perimeter

periódico, a [pe'rjoðiko, a] adj periodic(al) ♦ nm newspaper

periodismo [perjo'ðismo] nm journalism; **periodista** nm/f journalist

periodo [pe'rjoðo] nm period

período [pe'rjoðo] nm = **periodo**

periquito [peri'kito] nm budgerigar, budgie

perito, a [pe'rito, a] adj (experto) expert; (diestro) skilled, skilful ♦ nm/f expert; skilled worker; (técnico) technician

perjudicar [perxuði'kar] vt (gen) to damage, harm; **perjudicial** adj damaging, harmful; (en detrimento) detrimental; **perjuicio** nm damage, harm

perjurar [perxu'rar] vi to commit perjury

perla ['perla] nf pearl; **me viene de ~s** it suits me fine

permanecer [permane'θer] vi (quedarse) to stay, remain; (seguir) to continue to be

permanencia [perma'nenθja] nf permanence; (estancia) stay

permanente [perma'nente] adj permanent, constant ♦ nf perm

permiso [per'miso] nm permission; (licencia) permit, licence; **con ~** excuse me; **estar de ~** (MIL) to be on leave; **~ de conducir** driving licence (BRIT), driver's license (US)

permitir [permi'tir] vt to permit, allow

pernera [per'nera] nf trouser leg

pernicioso, a [perni'θjoso, a] adj pernicious

pero ['pero] conj but; (aún) yet ♦ nm (defecto) flaw, defect; (reparo) objection

perpendicular [perpendiku'lar] adj perpendicular

perpetrar [perpe'trar] vt to perpetrate

perpetuar [perpe'twar] vt to perpetuate; **perpetuo, a** adj perpetual

perplejo, a [per'plexo, a] adj perplexed, bewildered

perra ['perra] nf (ZOOL) bitch; **estar sin una ~** to be flat broke

perrera [pe'rrera] nf kennel

perrito [pe'rrito] nm: **~ caliente** hot dog

perro ['perro] nm dog

persa ['persa] adj, nm/f Persian

persecución [perseku'θjon] nf pursuit, chase; (REL, POL) persecution

perseguir [perse'vir] vt to pursue, hunt; (cortejar) to chase after; (molestar) to pester, annoy; (REL, POL) to persecute

perseverante [perseβe'rante] adj persevering, persistent

perseverar [perseβe'rar] vi to persevere, persist

persiana [per'sjana] nf (Venetian) blind

persignarse [persiv'narse] vr to cross o.s.

persistente [persis'tente] adj persistent

persistir [persis'tir] vi to persist

persona [per'sona] nf person; **~ mayor** elderly person

personaje [perso'naxe] nm important person, celebrity; (TEATRO etc)

character

personal [perso'nal] adj (particular) personal; (para una persona) single, for one person ♦ nm personnel, staff; **~idad** nf personality

personarse [perso'narse] vr to appear in person

personificar [personifi'kar] vt to personify

perspectiva [perspek'tiβa] nf perspective; (vista, panorama) view, panorama; (posibilidad futura) outlook, prospect

perspicacia [perspi'kaθja] nf discernment, perspicacity

perspicaz [perspi'kaθ] adj shrewd

persuadir [perswa'ðir] vt (gen) to persuade; (convencer) to convince; **~se** vr to become convinced; **persuasión** nf persuasion; **persuasivo, a** adj persuasive; convincing

pertenecer [pertene'θer] vi to belong; (fig) to concern; **perteneciente** adj: **perteneciente a** belonging to; **pertenencia** nf ownership; **pertenencias** nfpl (bienes) possessions, property sg

pertenezca etc vb ver **pertenecer**

pértiga ['pertiva] nf: **salto de ~** pole vault

pertinente [perti'nente] adj relevant, pertinent; (apropiado) appropriate; **~ a** concerning, relevant to

perturbación [perturβa'θjon] nf (POL) disturbance; (MED) upset, disturbance

perturbado, a [pertur'βaðo, a] adj mentally unbalanced

perturbar [pertur'βar] vt (el orden) to disturb; (MED) to upset, disturb; (mentalmente) to perturb

Perú [pe'ru] nm: **el ~** Peru; **peruano, a** adj, nm/f Peruvian

perversión [perβer'sjon] nf perversion; **perverso, a** adj perverse; (depravado) depraved

pervertido, a [perβer'tiðo, a] adj perverted ♦ nm/f pervert

pervertir [perßer'tir] vt to pervert, corrupt

pesa ['pesa] nf weight; (DEPORTE) shot

pesadez [pesa'ðeθ] nf (de peso) heaviness; (lentitud) slowness; (aburrimiento) tediousness

pesadilla [pesa'ðiλa] nf nightmare, bad dream

pesado, a [pe'saðo, a] adj heavy; (lento) slow; (difícil, duro) tough, hard; (aburrido) boring, tedious; (tiempo) sultry

pésame [pesame] nm expression of condolence, message of sympathy; **dar el ~** to express one's condolences

pesar [pe'sar] vt to weigh ♦ vi to weigh; (ser pesado) to weigh a lot, be heavy; (fig: opinión) to carry weight; **no pesa mucho** it is not very heavy ♦ nm (arrepentimiento) regret; (pena) grief, sorrow; **a ~ de o pese a (que)** in spite of, despite

pesca ['peska] nf (acto) fishing; (lo pescado) catch; **ir de ~** to go fishing

pescadería [peskaðe'ria] nf fish shop, fishmonger's (BRIT)

pescadilla [peska'ðiλa] nf whiting

pescado [pes'kaðo] nm fish

pescador, a [peska'ðor, a] nm/f fisherman/woman

pescar [pes'kar] vt (tomar) to catch; (intentar tomar) to fish for; (conseguir: trabajo) to manage to get ♦ vi to fish, go fishing

pescuezo [pes'kweθo] nm neck

pesebre [pe'seßre] nm manger

peseta [pe'seta] nf peseta

pesimista [pesi'mista] adj pessimistic ♦ nm/f pessimist

pésimo, a ['pesimo, a] adj awful, dreadful

peso ['peso] nm weight; (balanza) scales pl; (moneda) peso; **~ bruto/ neto** gross/net weight; **vender al ~** to sell by weight

pesquero, a [pes'kero, a] adj fishing cpd

pesquisa [pes'kisa] nf inquiry, investigation

pestaña [pes'tana] nf (ANAT) eyelash; (borde) rim; **pestañear** vi to blink

peste ['peste] nf plague; (mal olor) stink, stench

pesticida [pesti'θiða] nm pesticide

pestillo [pes'tiλo] nm (cerrojo) bolt; (picaporte) doorhandle

petaca [pe'taka] nf (de cigarros) cigarette case; (de pipa) tobacco pouch; (AM: maleta) suitcase

pétalo ['petalo] nm petal

petardo [pe'tarðo] nm firework, firecracker

petición [peti'θjon] nf (pedido) request, plea; (memorial) petition; (JUR) plea

petrificar [petrifi'kar] vt to petrify

petróleo [pe'troleo] nm oil, petroleum; **petrolero, a** adj petroleum cpd ♦ nm (oil) tanker

peyorativo, a [pejora'tißo, a] adj pejorative

pez [peθ] nm fish

pezón [pe'θon] nm teat, nipple

pezuña [pe'θuna] nf hoof

piadoso, a [pja'ðoso, a] adj (devoto) pious, devout; (misericordioso) kind, merciful

pianista [pja'nista] nm/f pianist

piano ['pjano] nm piano

piar [pjar] vi to cheep

pibe, a ['piße, a] (AM) nm/f boy/girl

picadero [pika'ðero] nm riding school

picadillo [pika'ðiλo] nm mince, minced meat

picado, a [pi'kaðo, a] adj pricked, punctured; (CULIN) minced, chopped; (mar) choppy; (diente) bad; (tabaco) cut; (enfadado) cross

picador [pika'ðor] nm (TAUR) picador; (minero) faceworker

picadura [pika'ðura] nf (pinchazo) puncture; (de abeja) sting; (de mosquito) bite; (tabaco picado) cut tobacco

picante [pi'kante] *adj* hot; *(comentario)* racy, spicy

picaporte [pika'porte] *nm (manija)* doorhandle; *(pestillo)* latch

picar [pi'kar] *vt (agujerear, perforar)* to prick, puncture; *(abeja)* to sting; *(mosquito, serpiente)* to bite; *(CULIN)* to mince, chop; *(incitar)* to incite, goad; *(dañar, irritar)* to annoy, bother; *(quemar: lengua)* to burn, sting ♦ *vi (pez)* to bite, take the bait; *(sol)* to burn, scorch; *(abeja, MED)* to sting; *(mosquito)* to bite; **~se** *vr (agriarse)* to turn sour, go off; *(ofenderse)* to take offence

picardía [pikar'ðia] *nf* villainy; *(astucia)* slyness, craftiness; *(una ~)* dirty trick; *(palabra)* rude/bad word o expression

pícaro, a ['pikaro, a] *adj (malicioso)* villainous; *(travieso)* mischievous ♦ *nm (astuto)* crafty sort; *(sinvergüenza)* rascal, scoundrel

pichón [pi'tʃon] *nm* young pigeon

pico ['piko] *nm (de ave)* beak; *(punta)* sharp point; *(TEC)* pick, pickaxe; *(GEO)* peak, summit; **y ~** and a bit

picor [pi'kor] *nm* itch

picotear [pikote'ar] *vt* to peck ♦ *vi* to nibble, pick

picudo, a [pi'kuðo, a] *adj* pointed, with a point

pidió *etc vb ver* **pedir**

pido *etc vb ver* **pedir**

pie [pje] *(pl* **~s)** *nm* foot; *(fig: motivo)* motive, basis; *(: fundamento)* foothold; **ir a ~** to go on foot, walk; **estar de ~** to be standing (up); **ponerse de ~** to stand up; **de ~s a cabeza** from top to bottom; **al ~ de la letra** *(citar)* literally, verbatim; *(copiar)* exactly, word for word; **en ~ de guerra** on a war footing; **dar ~ a** to give cause for; **hacer ~** *(en el agua)* to touch the bottom

piedad [pje'ðað] *nf (lástima)* pity, compassion; *(clemencia)* mercy; *(devoción)* piety, devotion

piedra ['pjeðra] *nf* stone; *(roca)* rock; *(de mechero)* flint; *(METEOROLOGÍA)* hailstone

piel [pjel] *nf (ANAT)* skin, hide, fur; *(ZOOL)* skin, hide, fur; *(cuero)* leather; *(BOT)* skin, peel

pienso *etc vb ver* **pensar**

pierdo *etc vb ver* **perder**

pierna ['pjerna] *nf* leg

pieza ['pjeθa] *nf* piece; *(habitación)* room; **~ de recambio** o **repuesto** spare (part)

pigmeo, a [pix'meo, a] *adj, nm/f* pigmy

pijama [pi'xama] *nm* pyjamas pl

pila ['pila] *nf (ELEC)* battery; *(montón)* heap, pile; *(lavabo)* sink

píldora ['pildora] *nf* pill; **la ~ (anticonceptiva)** the (contraceptive) pill

pileta [pi'leta] *nf* basin, bowl; *(AM)* swimming pool

pillaje [pi'ʎaxe] *nm* pillage, plunder

pillar [pi'ʎar] *vt (saquear)* to pillage, plunder; *(fam: coger)* to catch; *(: agarrar)* to grasp, seize; *(: entender)* to grasp, catch on to; **~se** *vr:* **~se un dedo con la puerta** to catch one's finger in the door

pillo, a ['piʎo, a] *adj* villainous; *(astuto)* sly, crafty ♦ *nm/f* rascal, rogue, scoundrel

piloto [pi'loto] *nm* pilot; *(de aparato)* (pilot) light; *(AUTO: luz)* tail o rear light; *(: conductor)* driver

pimentón [pimen'ton] *nm* paprika

pimienta [pi'mjenta] *nf* pepper

pimiento [pi'mjento] *nm* pepper, pimiento

pin [pin] *(pl* **pins)** *nm* badge

pinacoteca [pinako'teka] *nf* art gallery

pinar [pi'nar] *nm* pine forest *(BRIT)*, pine grove *(US)*

pincel [pin'θel] *nm* paintbrush

pinchadiscos [pintʃa'ðiskos] *nm/f inv* disc-jockey, DJ

pinchar [pin'tʃar] *vt (perforar)* to prick,

pierce; (neumático) to puncture; (fig) to prod

pinchazo [pin'tʃaθo] nm (perforación) prick; (de neumático) puncture; (fig) prod

pincho ['pintʃo] nm savoury (snack); ~ **moruno** shish kebab; ~ **de tortilla** small slice of omelette

ping-pong [pin'pon] nm table tennis

pingüino [pin'gwino] nm penguin

pino ['pino] nm pine (tree)

pinta ['pinta] nf spot; (de líquidos) spot, drop; (aspecto) appearance, looks (pl); ~**do, a** adj spotted; (de colores) colourful; ~**das** nfpl graffiti sg

pintar [pin'tar] vt to paint ♦ vi to paint; (fam) to count, be important; ~**se** vr to put on make-up

pintor, a [pin'tor, a] nm/f painter

pintoresco, a [pinto'resko, a] adj picturesque

pintura [pin'tura] nf painting; ~ **a la acuarela** watercolour; ~ **al óleo** oil painting

pinza ['pinθa] nf (ZOOL) claw; (para colgar ropa) clothes peg; (TEC) pincers pl; ~**s** nfpl (para depilar etc) tweezers pl

piña ['pina] nf (fruto del pino) pine cone; (fruta) pineapple; (fig) group

piñón [pi'non] nm (fruto) pine nut; (TEC) pinion

pío, a [pi, a] adj (devoto) pious, devout; (misericordioso) merciful

piojo [pi'oxo] nm louse

pionero, a [pjo'nero, a] adj pioneering ♦ nm/f pioneer

pipa ['pipa] nf pipe; ~**s** nfpl (BOT) (edible) sunflower seeds

pipí [pi'pi] (fam) nm: **hacer** ~ to have a wee(-wee) (BRIT), have to go (wee-wee) (US)

pique ['pike] nm (resentimiento) pique, resentment; (rivalidad) rivalry, competition; **irse a** ~ to sink; (esperanza, familia) to be ruined

piqueta [pi'keta] nf pick(axe)

piquete [pi'kete] nm (MIL) squad,

party; (de obreros) picket

pirado, a [pi'raðo, a] (fam) adj round the bend ♦ nm/f nutter

piragua [pi'rawa] nf canoe; **piragüismo** [pira'wismo] nm canoeing

pirámide [pi'ramiðe] nf pyramid

pirata [pi'rata] adj, nm pirate ♦ nm/f: ~ **informático/a** hacker

Pirineo(s) [piri'neo(s)] nm(pl) Pyrenees pl

pirómano, a [pi'romano, a] nm/f (MED, JUR) arsonist

piropo [pi'ropo] nm compliment, (piece of) flattery

pirueta [pi'rweta] nf pirouette

pis [pis] (fam) nm pee, piss; **hacer** ~ to have a pee; (para niños) to wee-wee

pisada [pi'saða] nf (paso) footstep; (huella) footprint

pisar [pi'sar] vt (caminar sobre) to walk on, tread on; (apretar con el pie) to press; (fig) to trample on, walk all over ♦ vi to tread, step, walk

piscina [pis'θina] nf swimming pool

Piscis ['pisθis] nm Pisces

piso ['piso] nm (suelo, planta) floor; (apartamento) flat (BRIT), apartment; **primer** ~ (ESP) first floor; (AM) ground floor

pisotear [pisote'ar] vt to trample (on o underfoot)

pista ['pista] nf track, trail; (indicio) clue; ~ **de aterrizaje** runway; ~ **de baile** dance floor; ~ **de hielo** ice rink; ~ **de tenis** tennis court

pistola [pis'tola] nf pistol; (TEC) spray-gun; **pistolero, a** nm/f gunman/woman, gangster

pistón [pis'ton] nm (TEC) piston; (MUS) key

pitar [pi'tar] vt (silbato) to blow; (rechiflar) to whistle at, boo ♦ vi to whistle; (AUTO) to sound o toot one's horn; (AM) to smoke

pitillo [pi'tiʎo] nm cigarette

pito ['pito] nm whistle; (de coche) horn

pitón [pi'ton] nm (ZOOL) python

pitonisa [pito'nisa] nf fortune-teller

pitorreo [pito'rreo] nm joke; **estar de ~** to be joking

pizarra [pi'θarra] nf (piedra) slate; (encerado) blackboard

pizca ['piθka] nf pinch, spot; (fig) spot, speck; **ni ~** not a bit

placa ['plaka] nf plate; (distintivo) badge, insignia; **~ de matrícula** number plate

placentero, a [plaθen'tero, a] adj pleasant, agreeable

placer [pla'θer] nm pleasure ♦ vt to please

plácido, a ['plaθiðo, a] adj placid

plaga ['plaxa] nf pest; (MED) plague; (abundancia) abundance; **plagar** vt to infest, plague; (llenar) to fill

plagio ['plaxjo] nm plagiarism

plan [plan] nm (esquema, proyecto) plan; (idea, intento) idea, intention; **tener ~** to have a date; **tener un ~** (fam) to have an affair; **en ~ económico** (fam) on the cheap; **vamos en ~ de turismo** we're going as tourists; **si te pones en ese ~ ...** if that's your attitude ...

plana ['plana] nf sheet (of paper), page; (TEC) trowel; **en primera ~** on the front page; **~ mayor** staff

plancha ['plantʃa] nf (para planchar) iron; (rótulo) plate, sheet; (NAUT) gangway; **a la ~** (CULIN) grilled; **~o** nm ironing; **planchar** vt to iron ♦ vi to do the ironing

planeador [planea'ðor] nm glider

planear [plane'ar] vt to plan ♦ vi to glide

planeta [pla'neta] nm planet

planicie [pla'niθje] nf plain

planificación [planifika'θjon] nf planning; **~ familiar** family planning

plano, a ['plano, a] adj flat, level, even ♦ nm (MAT, TEC) plane; (FOTO) shot; (ARQ) plan; (GEO) map; (de ciudad) map, street plan; **primer ~** close-up; **caer de ~** to fall flat

planta ['planta] nf (BOT, TEC) plant; (ANAT) sole of the foot, foot; (piso) floor; (AM: personal) staff; **~ baja** ground floor

plantación [planta'θjon] nf (AGR) plantation; (acto) planting

plantar [plan'tar] vt (BOT) to plant; (levantar) to erect, set up; **~se** vr to stand firm; **~ a uno en la calle** to throw sb out; **dejar plantado a uno** (fam) to stand sb up

plantear [plante'ar] vt (problema) to pose; (dificultad) to raise

plantilla [plan'tiʎa] nf (de zapato) insole; (personal) personnel; **ser de ~** to be on the staff

plantón [plan'ton] nm (MIL) guard, sentry; (fam) long wait; **dar (un) ~ a uno** to stand sb up

plasmar [plas'mar] vt (dar forma) to mould, shape; (representar) to represent; **~se** vr: **~se en** to take the form of

plasta ['plasta] (fam) adj inv boring ♦ nm/f bore

plástico, a ['plastiko, a] adj plastic ♦ nm plastic

Plastilina ® [plasti'lina] nf Plasticine ®

plata ['plata] nf (metal) silver; (cosas hechas de ~) silverware; (AM) cash, dough; **hablar en ~** to speak bluntly o frankly

plataforma [plata'forma] nf platform; **~ de lanzamiento/perforación** launch(ing) pad/drilling rig

plátano ['platano] nm (fruta) banana; (árbol) plane tree; banana tree

platea [pla'tea] nf (TEATRO) pit

plateado, a [plate'aðo, a] adj silver; (TEC) silver-plated

plática ['platika] nf talk, chat; **platicar** vi to talk, chat

platillo [pla'tiʎo] nm saucer; **~s** nmpl (MUS) cymbals; **~ volador** o **volante** flying saucer

platino [pla'tino] nm platinum; **~s**

nmpl (AUTO) contact points

plato |'plato| *nm* plate, dish; (*parte de comida*) course; (*comida*) dish; **~ combinado** set main course (*served on one plate*); **~ fuerte** main course; **primer ~** first course

playa |'plaja| *nf* beach; (*costa*) seaside; **~ de estacionamiento** (AM) car park

playera |pla'jera| *nf* (AM: *camiseta*) T-shirt; **~s** *nfpl* (*zapatos*) canvas shoes

plaza |'plaθa| *nf* square; (*mercado*) market(place); (*sitio*) room, space; (*en vehículo*) seat, place; (*colocación*) post, job; **~ de toros** bullring

plazo |'plaθo| *nm* (*lapso de tiempo*) time, period; (*fecha de vencimiento*) expiry date; (*pago parcial*) instalment; **a corto/largo ~** short-/long-term; **comprar algo a ~s** to buy sth on hire purchase (BRIT) o on time (US)

plazoleta |plaθo'leta| *nf* small square

pleamar |plea'mar| *nf* high tide

plebe |'pleβe| *nf*: **la ~** the common people *pl*, the masses *pl*; (*pey*) the plebs *pl*; **~yo, a** *adj* plebeian; (*pey*) coarse, common

plebiscito |pleβis'θito| *nm* plebiscite

plegable |ple'xaβle| *adj* collapsible; (*silla*) folding

plegar |ple'xar| *vt* (*doblar*) to fold, bend; (COSTURA) to pleat; **~se** *vr* to yield, submit

pleito |'pleito| *nm* (JUR) lawsuit, case; (*fig*) dispute, feud

plenilunio |pleni'lunjo| *nm* full moon

plenitud |pleni'tuð| *nf* plenitude, fullness; (*abundancia*) abundance

pleno, a |'pleno, a| *adj* full; (*completo*) complete ♦ *nm* plenum; **en ~ día** in broad daylight; **en ~ verano** o **en verano** in the height of summer; **en plena cara** full in the face

pliego etc |'pljexo| *vb ver* **plegar** ♦ *nm* (*hoja*) sheet (of paper); (*carta*) sealed letter/document; **~ de condiciones** details *pl*, specifications *pl*

pliegue etc |'pljexe| *vb ver* **plegar**

♦ *nm* fold, crease; (*de vestido*) pleat

plomero |plo'mero| *nm* (AM) plumber

plomo |'plomo| *nm* (*metal*) lead; (ELEC.) fuse; **sin ~** unleaded

pluma |'pluma| *nf* feather; (*para escribir*): **~ (estilográfica)** ink pen; **~ fuente** (AM) fountain pen

plumero |plu'mero| *nm* (*para el polvo*) feather duster

plumón |plu'mon| *nm* (*de ave*) down; (AM: *fino*) felt-tip pen; (: *ancho*) marker

plural |plu'ral| *adj* plural; **~idad** *nf* plurality

pluriempleo |pluriem'pleo| *nm* having more than one job

plus |plus| *nm* bonus; **~valía** *nf* (COM) appreciation

población |poβla'θjon| *nf* population; (*pueblo, ciudad*) town, city

poblado, a |po'βlaðo, a| *adj* inhabited ♦ *nm* (*aldea*) village; (*pueblo*) (small) town; **densamente ~** densely populated

poblador, a |poβla'ðor, a| *nm/f* settler, colonist

poblar |po'βlar| *vt* (*colonizar*) to colonize; (*fundar*) to found; (*habitar*) to inhabit

pobre |'poβre| *adj* poor ♦ *nm/f* poor person; **~za** *nf* poverty

pocilga |po'θilxa| *nf* pigsty

pócima |'poθima| *nf* = **poción**

PALABRA CLAVE

poco, a |'poko, a| *adj* **1** (*sg*) little, not much; **~ tiempo** little o not much time; **de ~ interés** of little interest, not very interesting; **poca cosa** not much

2 (*pl*) few, not many; **unos ~s** a few, some; **~s niños comen lo que les conviene** few children eat what they need

♦ *adv* **1** little, not much; **cuesta ~** it doesn't cost much

2 (+ *adj*: = negativo, *antónimo*): **~ amable/inteligente** not very nice/

intelligent
3: por ~ me caigo I almost fell
4: a ~: a ~ de haberse casado shortly after getting married
5: ~ a ~ little by little
♦ *nm* a little, a bit; **un ~ triste; un dinero** a little sad/money

podar [po'ðar] *vt* to prune

───────────────
PALABRA CLAVE
───────────────

poder [po'ðer] *vi* **1** *(capacidad)* can, be able to; **no puedo hacerlo** I can't do it, I'm unable to do it
2 *(permiso)* can, may, be allowed to; **¿se puede?** may I (o we)?; **puedes irte ahora** you may go now; **no se puede fumar en este hospital** smoking is not allowed in this hospital
3 *(posibilidad)* may, might, could; **puede llegar mañana** he may *o* might arrive tomorrow; **pudiste haberte hecho daño** you might *o* could have hurt yourself; **¡podías habérmelo dicho antes!** you might have told me before!
4: puede ser: perhaps; **puede ser que lo sepa Tomás** Tomás may *o* might know
5: ¡no puedo más! I've had enough!; **no pude menos que dejarlo** I couldn't help but leave it; **es tonto a más no ~** he's as stupid as they come
6: ~ con: no puedo con este crío this kid's too much for me
♦ *nm* power; **~ adquisitivo** purchasing power; **detentar** *o* **ocupar** *o* **estar en el ~** to be in power

poderoso, a [poðe'roso, a] *adj (político, país)* powerful
podio ['poðjo] *nm (DEPORTE)* podium
podium ['poðjum] = **podio**
podrido, a [po'ðriðo, a] *adj* rotten, bad; *(fig)* rotten, corrupt
podrir [po'ðrir] = **pudrir**
poema [po'ema] *nm* poem

poesía [poe'sia] *nf* poetry
poeta [po'eta] *nm/f* poet; **poético, a** *adj* poetic(al)
poetisa [poe'tisa] *nf* (woman) poet
póker ['poker] *nm* poker
polaco, a [po'lako, a] *adj* Polish
♦ *nm/f* Pole
polar [po'lar] *adj* polar; **~idad** *nf* polarity; **~izarse** *vr* to polarize
polea [po'lea] *nf* pulley
polémica [po'lemika] *nf* polemics *sg;* *(una ~)* controversy, polemic
polen ['polen] *nm* pollen
policía [poli'θia] *nm/f* policeman/ woman ♦ *nf* police; **~co, a** *adj* police *cpd;* **novela policíaca** detective story; **policial** *adj* police *cpd*
polideportivo [poliðepor'tiβo] *nm* sports centre *o* complex
poligamia [poli'xamja] *nf* polygamy
polígono [po'lixono] *nm (MAT)* polygon; **~ industrial** industrial estate
polilla [po'liʎa] *nf* moth
polio ['poljo] *nf* polio
política [po'litika] *nf* politics *sg;* *(económica, agraria etc)* policy; *ver tb* **político**
político, a [po'litiko, a] *adj* political; *(discreto)* tactful; *(de familia)* -in-law ♦ *nm/f* politician; **padre ~** father-in-law
póliza ['poliθa] *nf* certificate, voucher; *(impuesto)* tax stamp; **~ de seguros** insurance policy
polizón [poli'θon] *nm* stowaway
pollera [po'ʎera] *(AM) nf* skirt
pollería [poʎe'ria] *nf* poulterer's (shop)
pollo ['poʎo] *nm* chicken
polo ['polo] *nm (GEO, ELEC)* pole; *(helado)* ice lolly; *(DEPORTE)* polo; *(suéter)* polo-neck; **~ Norte/Sur** North/South Pole
Polonia [po'lonja] *nf* Poland
poltrona [pol'trona] *nf* easy chair
polución [polu'θjon] *nf* pollution
polvera [pol'βera] *nf* powder compact
polvo ['polβo] *nm* dust; *(QUÍM, CULIN,*

MED) powder; **~s** nmpl (maquillaje) powder sg; **quitar el ~** to dust; **~ de talco** talcum powder; **estar hecho ~** (fam) to be worn out o exhausted

pólvora ['polβora] nf gunpowder; (fuegos artificiales) fireworks pl

polvoriento, a [polβo'rjento, a] adj (superficie) dusty; (sustancia) powdery

pomada [po'maða] nf cream, ointment

pomelo [po'melo] nm grapefruit

pómez ['pomeθ] nf: **piedra ~** pumice stone

pomo ['pomo] nm doorknob

pompa ['pompa] nf (burbuja) bubble; (bomba) pump; (esplendor) pomp, splendour; **pomposo, a** adj splendid, magnificent; (pey) pompous

pómulo ['pomulo] nm cheekbone

pon [pon] vb ver **poner**

ponche ['pontʃe] nm punch

poncho ['pontʃo] nm poncho

ponderar [ponde'rar] vt (considerar) to weigh up, consider; (elogiar) to praise highly, speak in praise of

pondré etc vb ver **poner**

PALABRA CLAVE

poner [po'ner] vt 1 (colocar) to put; (telegrama) to send; (obra de teatro) to put on; (película) to show; **ponlo más fuerte** turn it up; **¿qué ponen en el Excelsior?** what's on at the Excelsior?
2 (tienda) to open; (instalar: gas etc) to put in; (radio, TV) to switch o turn on
3 (suponer) **pongamos que ...** let's suppose that ...
4 (contribuir): **el gobierno ha puesto otro millón** the government has contributed another million
5 (TELEC): **póngame con el Sr. López** can you put me through to Mr. López?
6: **~ de**: **le han puesto de director general** they've appointed him general manager
7 (+ adj) to make; **me estás**

poniendo nerviosa you're making me nervous
8 (dar nombre): **al hijo le pusieron Diego** they called their son Diego
♦ vi (gallina) to lay
♦ **~se** vr 1 (colocarse): **se puso a mi lado** he came and stood beside me; **tú ponte en esa silla** you go and sit on that chair
2 (vestido, cosméticos) to put on; **¿por qué no te pones el vestido nuevo?** why don't you put on o wear your new dress?
3 (+ adj) to turn; to get, become; **se puso muy serio** he got very serious; **después de lavarla la tela se puso azul** after washing it the material turned blue
4: **~se a**: **se puso a llorar** he started to cry; **tienes que ~te a estudiar** you must get down to studying
5: **~se a bien con uno** to make it up with sb; **~se a mal con uno** to get on the wrong side of sb

pongo etc vb ver **poner**

poniente [po'njente] nm (occidente) west; (viento) west wind

pontífice [pon'tifiθe] nm pope, pontiff

popa ['popa] nf stern

popular [popu'lar] adj popular; (cultura) of the people, folk cpd; **~idad** nf popularity; **~izarse** vr to become popular

PALABRA CLAVE

por [por] prep 1 (objetivo) for; **luchar ~ la patria** to fight for one's country
2 (+ infin): **~ no llegar tarde** so as not to arrive late; **~ citar unos ejemplos** to give a few examples
3 (causa) out of, because of; **~ escasez de fondos** through o for lack of funds
4 (tiempo): **~ la mañana/noche** in the morning/at night; **se queda ~ una semana** she's staying (for) a

week

5 (*lugar*): **pasar ~ Madrid** to pass through Madrid; **ir a Guayaquil ~ Quito** to go to Guayaquil via Quito; **caminar ~ la calle** to walk along the street; *ver tb* **todo**

6 (*cambio, precio*): **te doy uno nuevo ~ el que tienes** I'll give you a new one (in return) for the one you've got

7 (*valor distributivo*): **550 pesetas ~ hora/cabeza** 550 pesetas *o* per hour/a per head

8 (*modo, medio*) by; **~ correo/avión** by post/air; **día ~ día** day by day; **entrar ~ la entrada principal** to go in through the main entrance

9: **10 ~ 10 son 100** 10 times 10 is 100

10 (*en lugar de*): **vino él ~ su jefe** he came instead of his boss

11: **~ mí que revienten** as far as I'm concerned they can drop dead

12: **¿~ qué?** why?; **¿~ qué no?** why not?

---

porcelana [porθe'lana] *nf* porcelain; (*china*) china

porcentaje [porθen'taxe] *nm* percentage

porción [por'θjon] *nf* (*parte*) portion, share; (*cantidad*) quantity, amount

pordiosero, a [porðjo'sero, a] *nm/f* beggar

porfiar [por'fjar] *vi* to persist, insist; (*disputar*) to argue stubbornly

pormenor [porme'nor] *nm* detail, particular

pornografía [pornoɣra'fia] *nf* pornography

poro ['poro] *nm* pore; **~so, a** *adj* porous

porque ['porke] *conj* (*a causa de*) because; (*ya que*) since; (*con el fin de*) so that, in order that

porqué [por'ke] *nm* reason, cause

porquería [porke'ria] *nf* (*suciedad*) filth, dirt; (*acción*) dirty trick; (*objeto*)

small thing, trifle; (*fig*) rubbish

porra ['porra] *nf* (*arma*) stick, club

porrazo [po'rraθo] *nm* blow, bump

porro ['porro] *nm* (*fam*: *droga*) joint (*fam*)

porrón [po'rron] *nm* glass wine jar with a long spout

portaaviones [porta(a)'βjones] *nm inv* aircraft carrier

portada [por'taða] *nf* (*de revista*) cover

portador, a [porta'ðor, a] *nm/f* carrier, bearer; (*COM*) bearer, payee

portaequipajes [portaeki'paxes] *nm inv* (*AUTO*: *maletero*) boot; (: *baca*) luggage rack

portal [por'tal] *nm* (*entrada*) vestibule, hall; (*portada*) porch, doorway; (*puerta de entrada*) main door

portamaletas [portama'letas] *nm inv* (*AUTO*: *maletero*) boot; (: *baca*) roof rack

portarse [por'tarse] *vr* to behave, conduct o.s.

portátil [por'tatil] *adj* portable

portavoz [porta'βoθ] *nm/f* spokesman/woman

portazo [por'taθo] *nm*: **dar un ~** to slam the door

porte ['porte] *nm* (*COM*) transport; (*precio*) transport charges *pl*

portento [por'tento] *nm* marvel, wonder; **~so, a** *adj* marvellous, extraordinary

porteño, a [por'teɲo, a] *adj* of o from Buenos Aires

portería [porte'ria] *nf* (*oficina*) porter's office; (*DEPORTE*) goal

portero, a [por'tero, a] *nm/f* porter; (*conserje*) caretaker; (*ujier*) doorman; (*DEPORTE*) goalkeeper; **~ automático** intercom

pórtico [por'tiko] *nm* (*patio*) portico, porch; (*fig*) gateway; (*arcada*) arcade

portorriqueño, a [portorri'keɲo, a] *adj* Puerto Rican

Portugal [portu'val] *nm* Portugal; **portugués, esa** *adj, nm/f* Portuguese

♦ nm (LING) Portuguese

porvenir |porße'nir| nm future

pos |pos| prep: **en ~ de** after, in pursuit of

posada |po'saða| nf (refugio) shelter, lodging; (mesón) guest house; **dar ~ a** to give shelter to, take in

posaderas |posa'ðeras| nfpl backside sg, buttocks

posar |po'sar| vt (en el suelo) to lay down, put down; (la mano) to place, put gently ♦ vi (modelo) to sit, pose; **~se** vr to settle; (pájaro) to perch; (avión) to land, come down

posavasos |posa'basos| nm inv coaster; (para cerveza) beermat

posdata |pos'ðata| nf postscript

pose |'pose| nf pose

poseedor, a |posee'ðor, a| nm/f owner, possessor; (de récord, puesto) holder

poseer |pose'er| vt to possess, own; (ventaja) to enjoy; (récord, puesto) to hold

posesión |pose'sjon| nf possession; **posesionarse** vr: **posesionarse de** to take possession of, take over

posesivo, a |pose'sißo, a| adj possessive

posgrado |pos'graðo| nm: **curso de ~** postgraduate course

posibilidad |posißili'ðað| nf possibility; (oportunidad) chance; **posibilitar** vt to make possible; (hacer realizable) to make feasible

posible |po'sißle| adj possible; (realizable) feasible; **de ser ~** if possible; **en lo ~** as far as possible

posición |posi'θjon| nf position; (rango social) status

positivo, a |posi'tißo, a| adj positive

poso |'poso| nm sediment; (heces) dregs pl

posponer |pospo'ner| vt (relegar) to put behind/below; (aplazar) to postpone

posta |'posta| nf: **a ~** deliberately, on

purpose

postal |pos'tal| adj postal ♦ nf postcard

poste |'poste| nm (de telégrafos etc) post, pole; (columna) pillar

póster |'poster| (pl **pósteres, pósters**) nm poster

postergar |poster'var| vt to postpone, delay

posteridad |posteri'ðað| nf posterity

posterior |poste'rjor| adj back, rear; (siguiente) following, subsequent; (más tarde) later; **~idad** nf: **con ~idad** later, subsequently

postgrado |post'graðo| nm = posgrado

postizo, a |pos'tiθo, a| adj false, artificial ♦ nm hairpiece

postor |pos'tor, a| nm/f bidder

postre |'postre| nm sweet, dessert

postrero, a |pos'trero, a| adj (delante de nmsg: **postrer**) adj (último) last; (que viene detrás) rear

postulado |postu'laðo| nm postulate

póstumo, a |'postumo, a| adj posthumous

postura |pos'tura| nf (del cuerpo) posture, position; (fig) attitude, position

potable |po'taßle| adj drinkable; **agua ~** drinking water

potaje |po'taxe| nm thick vegetable soup

pote |'pote| nm pot, jar

potencia |po'tenθja| nf power; **~l** |poten'θjal| adj, nm potential; **~r** vt to boost

potente |po'tente| adj powerful

potro, a |'potro, a| nm/f (ZOOL) colt/ filly ♦ nm (de gimnasia) vaulting horse

pozo |'poθo| nm well; (de río) deep pool; (de mina) shaft

P.P. abr (= porte pagado) CP

práctica |'praktika| nf practice; (método) method; (arte, capacidad) skill; **en la ~** in practice

practicable |prakti'kaßle| adj

practicable; (camino) passable

practicante |prakti'kante| nm/f (MED: ayudante de doctor) medical assistant; (: enfermero) nurse; (quien practica algo) practitioner ♦ adj practising

practicar |prakti'kar| vt to practise; (DEPORTE) to play; (realizar) to carry out, perform

práctico, a |'praktiko, a| adj practical; (instruido: persona) skilled, expert

practique etc vb ver practicar

pradera |pra'ðera| nf meadow; (US etc) prairie

prado |'praðo| nm (campo) meadow, field; (pastizal) pasture

Praga |'praxa| n Prague

pragmático, a |prax'matiko, a| adj pragmatic

preámbulo |pre'ambulo| nm preamble, introduction

precario, a |pre'karjo, a| adj precarious

precaución |prekau'θjon| nf (medida preventiva) preventive measure, precaution; (prudencia) caution, wariness

precaver |preka'ßer| vt to guard against; (impedir) to forestall; ~se vr: ~se de o contra algo to (be on one's) guard against sth; **precavido, a** adj cautious, wary

precedente |preθe'ðente| adj preceding; (anterior) former ♦ nm precedent

preceder |preθe'ðer| vt, vi to precede, go before, come before

precepto |pre'θepto| nm precept

preciado, a |pre'θjaðo, a| adj (estimado) esteemed, valuable

preciarse |pre'θjarse| vr to boast; ~se de to pride o.s. on, boast of being

precinto |pre'θinto| nm (tb: ~ de garantía) seal

precio |'preθjo| nm price; (costo) cost; (valor) value, worth; (de viaje) fare; ~ al contado/de coste o de oportunidad cash/cost/bargain price; ~ al detalle o

al por menor retail price; ~ **tope** top price

preciosidad |preθjosi'ðað| nf (valor) (high) value, (great) worth; (encanto) charm; (cosa bonita) beautiful thing; **es una** ~ it's lovely, it's really beautiful

precioso, a |pre'θjoso, a| adj precious; (de mucho valor) valuable; (fam) lovely, beautiful

precipicio |preθi'piθjo| nm cliff, precipice; (fig) abyss

precipitación |preθipita'θjon| nf haste; (lluvia) rainfall

precipitado, a |preθipi'taðo, a| adj (conducta) hasty, rash; (salida) hasty, sudden

precipitar |preθipi'tar| vt (arrojar) to hurl down, throw; (apresurar) to hasten; (acelerar) to speed up, accelerate; ~se vr to throw o.s.; (apresurarse) to rush; (actuar sin pensar) to act rashly

precisamente |preθisa'mente| adv precisely; (exactamente) precisely, exactly

precisar |preθi'sar| vt (necesitar) to need, require; (fijar) to determine exactly, fix; (especificar) to specify

precisión |preθi'sjon| nf (exactitud) precision

preciso, a |pre'θiso, a| adj (exacto) precise; (necesario) necessary, essential

preconcebido, a |prekonθe'ßiðo, a| adj preconceived

precoz |pre'koθ| adj (persona) precocious; (calvicie etc) premature

precursor, a |prekur'sor, a| nm/f predecessor, forerunner

predecir |preðe'θir| vt to predict, forecast

predestinado, a |preðesti'naðo, a| adj predestined

predicar |preði'kar| vt, vi to preach

predicción |preðik'θjon| nf prediction

predilecto, a |preði'lekto, a| adj favourite

predisponer |preðispo'ner| vt to

predispose; (pey) to prejudice;
predisposición nf inclination;
prejudice, bias

predominante [preðoˈminante] adj
predominant

predominar [preðomiˈnar] vt to
dominate ♦ vi to predominate; to
(prevalecer) to prevail; **predominio**
nm predominance; prevalence

preescolar [pre(e)skoˈlar] adj
preschool

prefabricado, a [prefaβriˈkaðo, a] adj
prefabricated

prefacio [preˈfaθjo] nm preface

preferencia [prefeˈrenθja] nf
preference; **de ~** preferably, for
preference

preferible [prefeˈriβle] adj preferable

preferir [prefeˈrir] vt to prefer

prefiero etc vb ver **preferir**

prefijo [preˈfixo] nm (TELEC) (dialling)
code

pregonar [preɣoˈnar] vt to proclaim,
announce

pregunta [preˈɣunta] nf question;
hacer una ~ to ask a question

preguntar [preɣunˈtar] vt to ask;
(cuestionar) to question ♦ vi to ask; **~se**
vr to wonder; **~ por alguien** to ask for
sb

preguntón, ona [preɣunˈton, ona]
adj inquisitive

prehistórico, a [preisˈtoriko, a] adj
prehistoric

prejuicio [preˈxwiθjo] nm (acto)
prejudgement; (idea preconcebida)
preconception; (parcialidad) prejudice,
bias

preliminar [prelimiˈnar] adj
preliminary

preludio [preˈluðjo] nm prelude

prematuro, a [premaˈturo, a] adj
premature

premeditación [premeðitaˈθjon] nf
premeditation

premeditar [premeðiˈtar] vt to
premeditate

premiar [preˈmjar] vt to reward; (en
un concurso) to give a prize to

premio [ˈpremjo] nm reward; prize;
(COM) premium

premonición [premoniˈθjon] nf
premonition

prenatal [prenaˈtal] adj antenatal,
prenatal

prenda [ˈprenda] nf (ropa) garment,
article of clothing; (garantía) pledge;
~s nfpl (talentos) talents, gifts

prendedor [prendeˈðor] nm brooch

prender [prenˈder] vt (captar) to catch,
capture; (detener) to arrest; (COSTURA)
to pin, attach; (sujetar) to fasten ♦ vi to
catch; (arraigar) to take root; **~se** vr
(encenderse) to catch fire

prendido, a [prenˈdiðo, a] (AM) adj
(luz etc) on

prensa [ˈprensa] nf press; **la ~** the
press; **prensar** vt to press

preñado, a [preˈɲaðo, a] adj
pregnant; **~ de** pregnant with, full of

preocupación [preokupaˈθjon] nf
worry, concern; (ansiedad) anxiety

preocupado, a [preokuˈpaðo, a] adj
worried, concerned; (ansioso) anxious

preocupar [preokuˈpar] vt to worry;
~se vr to worry; **~se de algo** (hacerse
cargo) to take care of sth

preparación [preparaˈθjon] nf (acto)
preparation; (estado) readiness;
(entrenamiento) training

preparado, a [prepaˈraðo, a] adj
(dispuesto) prepared; (CULIN) ready (to
serve) ♦ nm preparation

preparar [prepaˈrar] vt (disponer) to
prepare, get ready; (TEC: tratar) to
prepare, process; (entrenar) to teach,
train; **~se** vr: **~se a** o **para** to prepare
to o for, get ready to o for;
preparativo, a adj preparatory,
preliminary; **preparativos** nmpl
preparations; **preparatoria** (AM) nf
sixth-form college (BRIT), senior high
school (US)

prerrogativa [prerroɣaˈtiβa] nf

prerogative, privilege

presa ['presa] nf (cosa apresada) catch; (víctima) victim; (de animal) prey; (de agua) dam

presagiar [presa'xjar] vt to presage, forebode; **presagio** nm omen

prescindir [presθin'dir] vi: ~ **de** (privarse de) to do without, go without; (descartar) to dispense with

prescribir [preskri'βir] vt to prescribe; **prescripción** nf prescription

presencia [pre'senθja] nf presence; **presencial** adj: **testigo presencial** eyewitness; **presenciar** vt to be present at; (asistir a) to attend; (ver) to see, witness

presentación [presenta'θjon] nf presentation; (introducción) introduction

presentador, a [presenta'ðor, a] nm/f presenter, compère

presentar [presen'tar] vt to present; (ofrecer) to offer; (mostrar) to show, display; (a una persona) to introduce; ~**se** vr (llegar inesperadamente) to appear, turn up; (ofrecerse como candidato) to run, stand; (aparecer) to show, appear; (solicitar empleo) to apply

presente [pre'sente] adj present ♦ nm present; **hacer** ~ to state, declare; **tener** ~ to remember, bear in mind

presentimiento [presenti'mjento] nm premonition, presentiment

presentir [presen'tir] vt to have a premonition of

preservación [preserβa'θjon] nf protection, preservation

preservar [preser'βar] vt to protect, preserve; **preservativo** nm sheath, condom

presidencia [presi'ðenθja] nf presidency; (de comité) chairmanship

presidente [presi'ðente] nm/f president; (de comité) chairman/woman

presidiario [presi'ðjarjo] nm convict

presidio [pre'sidjo] nm prison, penitentiary

presidir [presi'ðir] vt (dirigir) to preside at, preside over; (: comité) to take the chair at; (dominar) to dominate, rule ♦ vi to preside; to take the chair

presión [pre'sjon] nf pressure; **presionar** vt to press; (fig) to press, put pressure on ♦ vi: **presionar para** to press for

preso, a ['preso, a] nm/f prisoner; **tomar** o **llevar** ~ **a uno** to arrest sb, take sb prisoner

prestación [presta'θjon] nf service; (subsidio) benefit; **prestaciones** nfpl (TEC, AUT) performance features

prestado, a [pres'taðo, a] adj on loan; **pedir** ~ to borrow

prestamista [presta'mista] nm/f moneylender

préstamo ['prestamo] nm loan; ~ **hipotecario** mortgage

prestar [pres'tar] vt to lend, loan; (atención) to pay; (ayuda) to give

presteza [pres'teθa] nf speed, promptness

prestigio [pres'tixjo] nm prestige; ~**so, a** adj (honorable) prestigious; (famoso, renombrado) renowned, famous

presumido, a [presu'miðo, a] adj (persona) vain

presumir [presu'mir] vt to presume ♦ vi (tener aires) to be conceited; **según cabe** ~ as may be presumed, presumably; **presunción** nf presumption; **presunto, a** adj (supuesto) supposed, presumed; (así llamado) so-called; **presuntuoso, a** adj conceited, presumptuous

presuponer [presupo'ner] vt to presuppose

presupuesto [presu'pwesto] pp de **presuponer** ♦ nm (FINANZAS) budget; (estimación: de costo) estimate

pretencioso, a [preten'θjoso, a] adj pretentious

pretender [preten'der] vt (intentar) to try to, seek to; (reivindicar) to claim; (buscar) to seek, try for; (cortejar) to woo, court; **~ que** to expect that; **pretendiente** nm/f (amante) suitor; (al trono) pretender; **pretensión** nf (aspiración) aspiration; (reivindicación) claim; (orgullo) pretension

pretexto [pre'teksto] nm pretext; (excusa) excuse

prevalecer [preβale'θer] vi to prevail

prevención [preβen'θjon] nf prevention; (precaución) precaution

prevenido, a [preβe'niðo, a] adj prepared, ready; (cauteloso) cautious

prevenir [preβe'nir] vt (impedir) to prevent; (predisponer) to prejudice, bias; (avisar) to warn; (preparar) to prepare, get ready; **~se** vr to get ready, prepare; **~se contra** to take precautions against; **preventivo, a** adj preventive, precautionary

prever [pre'βer] vt to foresee

previo, a ['preβjo, a] adj (anterior) previous; (preliminar) preliminary ♦ prep: **~ acuerdo de los otros** subject to the agreement of the others

previsión [preβi'sjon] nf (perspicacia) foresight; (predicción) forecast; **previsto, a** adj anticipated, forecast

prima ['prima] nf (COM) bonus; **~ de seguro** insurance premium; ver tb **primo**

primacía [prima'θia] nf primacy

primario, a [pri'marjo, a] adj primary

primavera [prima'βera] nf spring(-time)

primera [pri'mera] nf (AUTO) first gear; (FERRO: tb: **~ clase**) first class; **de ~** (fam) first-class, first-rate

primero, a [pri'mero, a] adj (delante de nmsg: **primer**) first; (principal) prime ♦ adv first; (más bien) sooner, rather; **primera plana** front page

primicia [pri'miθja] nf (tb: **~ informativa**) scoop

primitivo, a [primi'tiβo, a] adj

primitive; (original) original

primo, a ['primo, a] adj prime ♦ nm/f cousin; (fam) fool, idiot; **~ hermano** first cousin; **materias primas** raw materials

primogénito, a [primo'xenito, a] adj first-born

primordial [primor'ðjal] adj basic, fundamental

primoroso, a [primo'roso, a] adj exquisite, delicate

princesa [prin'θesa] nf princess

principal [prinθi'pal] adj principal, main ♦ nm (jefe) chief, principal

príncipe [prin'θipe] nm prince

principiante [prinθi'pjante] nm/f beginner

principio [prin'θipjo] nm (comienzo) beginning, start; (origen) origin; (primera etapa) rudiment, basic idea; (moral) principle; **a ~s de** at the beginning of

pringoso, a [prin'xoso, a] adj (grasiento) greasy; (pegajoso) sticky

pringue ['pringe] nm (grasa) grease, fat, dripping

prioridad [priori'ðað] nf priority

prisa ['prisa] nf (apresuramiento) hurry, haste; (rapidez) speed; (urgencia) (sense of) urgency; **a o de ~** quickly; **correr ~** to be urgent; **darse ~** to hurry up; **estar o tener ~** to be in a hurry

prisión [pri'sjon] nf (cárcel) prison; (período de cárcel) imprisonment; **prisionero, a** nm/f prisoner

prismáticos [pris'matikos] nmpl binoculars

privación [priβa'θjon] nf deprivation; (falta) want, privation

privado, a [pri'βaðo, a] adj private

privar [pri'βar] vt to deprive; **privativo, a** adj exclusive

privilegiado, a [priβile'xjaðo, a] adj privileged; (memoria) very good

privilegiar [priβile'xjar] vt to grant a privilege to; (favorecer) to favour

privilegio [priβi'lexjo] nm privilege;

(concesión) concession

pro [pro] *nm* o *f* profit, advantage ♦ *prep:* **asociación ~ ciegos** association for the blind ♦ *prefijo:* **~ soviético/americano** pro-Soviet/ American; **en ~ de** on behalf of, for; **los ~s y los contras** the pros and cons

proa ['proa] *nf* bow, prow; **de ~** bow *cpd*, fore

probabilidad [proßaßili'ðað] *nf* probability, likelihood; *(oportunidad, posibilidad)* chance, prospect; **probable** *adj* probable, likely

probador [proßa'ðor] *nm (en tienda)* fitting room

probar [pro'ßar] *vt (demostrar)* to prove; *(someter a prueba)* to test, try out; *(ropa)* to try on; *(comida)* to taste ♦ *vi* to try; **~se un traje** to try on a suit

probeta [pro'ßeta] *nf* test tube

problema [pro'ßlema] *nm* problem

procedente [proθe'ðente] *adj (razonable)* reasonable; *(conforme a derecho)* proper, fitting; **~ de** coming from, originating in

proceder [proθe'ðer] *vi (avanzar)* to proceed; *(actuar)* to act; *(ser correcto)* to be right (and proper), be fitting ♦ *nm (comportamiento)* behaviour, conduct; **~ de** to come from, originate in; **procedimiento** *nm* procedure; *(proceso)* process; *(método)* means *pl*, method

procesado, a [proθe'saðo, a] *nm/f* accused

procesador [proθesa'ðor] *nm:* **~ de textos** word processor

procesar [proθe'sar] *vt* to try, put on trial

procesión [proθe'sjon] *nf* procession

proceso [pro'θeso] *nm* process; *(JUR)* trial

proclamar [prokla'mar] *vt* to proclaim

procreación [prokrea'θjon] *nf* procreation

procrear [prokre'ar] *vt, vi* to procreate

procurador, a [prokura'ðor, a] *nm/f* attorney

procurar [proku'rar] *vt (intentar)* to try, endeavour; *(conseguir)* to get, obtain; *(asegurar)* to secure; *(producir)* to produce

prodigio [pro'ðixjo] *nm* prodigy; *(milagro)* wonder, marvel; **~so, a** *adj* prodigious, marvellous

pródigo, a ['proðixo, a] *adj:* **hijo ~** prodigal son

producción [proðuk'θjon] *nf (gen)* production; *(producto)* output; **~ en serie** mass production

producir [proðu'θir] *vt* to produce; *(causar)* to cause, bring about; **~se** *vr (cambio)* to come about; *(accidente)* to take place; *(problema etc)* to arise; *(hacerse)* to be produced, be made; *(estallar)* to break out

productividad [proðuktißi'ðað] *nf* productivity; **productivo, a** *adj* productive; *(provechoso)* profitable

producto [pro'ðukto] *nm* product

productor, a [proðuk'tor, a] *adj* productive, producing ♦ *nm/f* producer

proeza [pro'eθa] *nf* exploit, feat

profanar [profa'nar] *vt* to desecrate, profane; **profano, a** *adj* profane ♦ *nm/f* layman/woman

profecía [profe'θia] *nf* prophecy

proferir [profe'rir] *vt (palabra, sonido)* to utter; *(injuria)* to hurl, let fly

profesión [profe'sjon] *nf* profession; **profesional** *adj* professional

profesor, a [profe'sor, a] *nm/f* teacher; **~ado** *nm* teaching profession

profeta [pro'feta] *nm* prophet; **profetizar** *vt, vi* to prophesy

prófugo, a ['profuxo, a] *nm/f* fugitive; *(MIL: desertor)* deserter

profundidad [profundi'ðað] *nf* depth; **profundizar** *vi:* **profundizar en** to go deeply into; **profundo, a** *adj* deep; *(misterio, pensador)* profound

progenitor [proxeni'tor] *nm* ancestor;

~es nmpl (padres) parents

programa [proˈɣrama] nm
programme (BRIT), program (US);
~ción nf programming; **~dor, a** nm/f
programmer; **programar** vt to
program

progresar [proɣreˈsar] vi to progress,
make progress; **progresista** adj, nm/f
progressive; **progresivo, a** adj
progressive; (gradual) gradual;
(continuo) continuous; **progreso** nm
progress

prohibición [proiβiˈθjon] nf
prohibition, ban

prohibir [proiˈβir] vt to prohibit, ban,
forbid; **se prohibe fumar, prohibido
fumar** no smoking; **"prohibido el
paso"** "no entry"

prójimo, a [ˈproximo, a] nm/f fellow
man; (vecino) neighbour

proletariado [proletaˈrjaðo] nm
proletariat

proletario, a [proleˈtarjo, a] adj, nm/f
proletarian

proliferación [proliferaˈθjon] nf
proliferation

proliferar [prolifeˈrar] vi to proliferate;
prolífico, a adj prolific

prólogo [ˈproloxo] nm prologue

prolongación [prolongaˈθjon] nf
extension; **prolongado, a** adj (largo)
long; (alargado) lengthy

prolongar [prolonˈɣar] vt to extend;
(reunión etc) to prolong; (calle, tubo) to
extend

promedio [proˈmeðjo] nm average;
(de distancia) middle, mid-point

promesa [proˈmesa] nf promise

prometer [promeˈter] vt to promise
♦ vi to show promise; **~se** vr (novios)
to get engaged; **prometido, a** adj
promised; engaged ♦ nm/f fiancé/
fiancée

prominente [promiˈnente] adj
prominent

promiscuo, a [proˈmiskwo, a] adj
promiscuous

promoción [promoˈθjon] nf
promotion

promotor [promoˈtor] nm promoter;
(instigador) instigator

promover [promoˈβer] vt to promote;
(causar) to cause; (instigar) to instigate,
stir up

promulgar [promulˈɣar] vt to
promulgate; (anunciar) to proclaim

pronombre [proˈnombre] nm
pronoun

pronosticar [pronostiˈkar] vt to
predict, foretell, forecast; **pronóstico**
nm prediction, forecast; **pronóstico
del tiempo** weather forecast

pronto, a [ˈpronto, a] adj (rápido)
prompt, quick; (preparado) ready ♦ adv
quickly, promptly; (en seguida) at once,
right away; (dentro de poco) soon;
(temprano) early ♦ nm: **tener ~s de
enojo** to be quick-tempered; **de ~**
suddenly; **por lo ~** meanwhile, for the
present

pronunciación [pronunθjaˈθjon] nf
pronunciation

pronunciar [pronunˈθjar] vt to
pronounce; (discurso) to make, deliver;
~se vr to revolt, rebel; (declararse) to
declare o.s.

propagación [propaɣaˈθjon] nf
propagation

propaganda [propaˈɣanda] nf
(política) propaganda; (comercial)
advertising

propagar [propaˈɣar] vt to propagate

propensión [propenˈsjon] nf
inclination, propensity; **propenso, a**
adj inclined to; **ser propenso a** to be
inclined to, have a tendency to

propicio, a [proˈpiθjo, a] adj
favourable, propitious

propiedad [propjeˈðað] nf property;
(posesión) possession, ownership;
~ particular private property

propietario, a [propjeˈtarjo, a] nm/f
owner, proprietor

propina [proˈpina] nf tip

propio, a [ˈpropjo, a] *adj* own, of
one's own; (*característico*)
characteristic, typical; (*debido*) proper;
(*mismo*) selfsame, very; **el ~ ministro**
the minister himself; **¿tienes casa
propia?** have you a house of your
own?

proponer [propoˈner] *vt* to propose,
put forward; (*problema*) to pose; **~se**
vr to propose, intend

proporción [proporˈθjon] *nf*
proportion; (*MAT*) ratio; **proporciones**
nfpl (*dimensiones*) dimensions; (*fig*) size
sg; **proporcionado, a** *adj*
proportionate; (*regular*) medium,
middling; (*justo*) just right;
proporcionar *vt* (*dar*) to give, supply,
provide

proposición [proposiˈθjon] *nf*
proposition; (*propuesta*) proposal

propósito [proˈposito] *nm* purpose;
(*intento*) aim, intention ♦ *adv*: **a ~** by
the way, incidentally; (*a posta*) on
purpose, deliberately; **a ~ de** about,
with regard to

propuesta [proˈpwesta] *vb ver*
proponer ♦ *nf* proposal

propulsar [propulˈsar] *vt* to drive,
propel; (*fig*) to promote, encourage;
propulsión *nf* propulsion;
propulsión a chorro o **por reacción**
jet propulsion

prórroga [ˈprorroxa] *nf* extension;
(*JUR*) stay; (*COM*) deferment; (*DEPORTE*)
extra time; **prorrogar** *vt* (*período*) to
extend; (*decisión*) to defer, postpone

prorrumpir [prorrumˈpir] *vi* to burst
forth, break out

prosa [ˈprosa] *nf* prose

proscrito, a [proˈskrito, a] *adj* banned

proseguir [proseˈxir] *vt* to continue,
carry on ♦ *vi* to continue, go on

prospección [prospekˈθjon] *nf*
exploration; (*del oro*) prospecting

prospecto [prosˈpekto] *nm* prospectus

prosperar [prospeˈrar] *vi* to prosper,
thrive, flourish; **prosperidad** *nf*

prosperity; (*éxito*) success; **próspero,
a** *adj* prosperous, flourishing; (*que tiene
éxito*) successful

prostíbulo [prosˈtiβulo] *nm* brothel
(*BRIT*), house of prostitution (*US*)

prostitución [prostituˈθjon] *nf*
prostitution

prostituir [prostiˈtwir] *vt* to prostitute;
~se *vr* to prostitute o.s., become a
prostitute

prostituta [prostiˈtuta] *nf* prostitute

protagonista [protaxoˈnista] *nm/f*
protagonist

protagonizar [protaxoniˈθar] *vt* to
take the chief rôle in

protección [protekˈθjon] *nf* protection

protector, a [protekˈtor, a] *adj*
protective, protecting ♦ *nm/f* protector

proteger [proteˈxer] *vt* to protect;
protegido, a *nm/f* protégé/protégée

proteína [proteˈina] *nf* protein

protesta [proˈtesta] *nf* protest;
(*declaración*) protestation

protestante [protesˈtante] *adj*
Protestant

protestar [protesˈtar] *vt* to protest,
declare ♦ *vi* to protest

protocolo [protoˈkolo] *nm* protocol

prototipo [protoˈtipo] *nm* prototype

prov. *abr* (= *provincia*) prov

provecho [proˈβetʃo] *nm* advantage,
benefit; (*FINANZAS*) profit; **¡buen ~!**
bon appétit!; **en ~ de** to the benefit
of; **sacar ~ de** to benefit from, profit
by

proveer [proβeˈer] *vt* to provide,
supply ♦ *vi*: **~ a** to provide for

provenir [proβeˈnir] *vi*: **~ de** to come
from, stem from

proverbio [proˈβerβjo] *nm* proverb

providencia [proβiˈðenθja] *nf*
providence

provincia [proˈβinθja] *nf* province;
~no, a *adj* provincial; (*del campo*)
country *cpd*

provisión [proβiˈsjon] *nf* provision;
(*abastecimiento*) provision, supply;

(*medida*) measure, step

provisional [proßisjo'nal] *adj* provisional

provocación [proßoka'θjon] *nf* provocation

provocar [proßo'kar] *vt* to provoke; (*alentar*) to tempt, invite; (*causar*) to bring about, lead to; (*promover*) to promote; (*estimular*) to rouse, stimulate; **¿te provoca un café?** (*AM*) would you like a coffee?;

provocativo, a *adj* provocative

próximamente [proksima'mente] *adv* shortly, soon

proximidad [proksimi'ðað] *nf* closeness, proximity; **próximo, a** *adj* near, close; (*vecino*) neighbouring; (*siguiente*) next

proyectar [projek'tar] *vt* (*objeto*) to hurl, throw; (*luz*) to cast, shed; (*CINE*) to screen, show; (*planear*) to plan

proyectil [projek'til] *nm* projectile, missile

proyecto [pro'jekto] *nm* plan; (*estimación de costo*) detailed estimate

proyector [projek'tor] *nm* (*CINE*) projector

prudencia [pru'ðenθja] *nf* (*sabiduría*) wisdom; (*cuidado*) care; **prudente** *adj* sensible, wise; (*conductor*) careful

prueba *etc* [pru'eßa] *vb ver* **probar** ♦ *nf* proof; (*ensayo*) test, trial; (*degustación*) tasting, sampling; (*de ropa*) fitting; **a ~** on trial; **a ~ de** proof against; **a ~ de agua/fuego** waterproof/fireproof; **someter a ~** to put to the test

prurito [pru'rito] *nm* itch; (*de bebé*) nappy (*BRIT*) o diaper (*US*) rash

psico... [siko] *prefijo* psycho...;
~análisis *nm inv* psychoanalysis;
~logía *nf* psychology; **~lógico, a** *adj* psychological; **psicólogo, a** *nm/f* psychologist; **psicópata** *nm/f* psychopath; **~sis** *nf inv* psychosis

psiquiatra [si'kjatra] *nm/f* psychiatrist; **psiquiátrico, a** *adj* psychiatric

psíquico, a ['sikiko, a] *adj* psychic(al)

PSOE [pe'soe] *nm abr* = **Partido Socialista Obrero Español**

pta(s) *abr* = **peseta(s)**

pts *abr* = **pesetas**

púa ['pua] *nf* (*BOT, ZOOL*) prickle, spine; (*para guitarra*) plectrum (*BRIT*), pick (*US*); **alambre de ~** barbed wire

pubertad [pußer'tað] *nf* puberty

publicación [pußlika'θjon] *nf* publication

publicar [pußli'kar] *vt* (*editar*) to publish; (*hacer público*) to publicize; (*divulgar*) to make public, divulge

publicidad [pußliθi'ðað] *nf* publicity; (*COM: propaganda*) advertising; **publicitario, a** *adj* publicity *cpd*; advertising *cpd*

público, a ['pußliko, a] *adj* public ♦ *nm* public; (*TEATRO etc*) audience

puchero [pu'tʃero] *nm* (*CULIN: guiso*) stew; (: *olla*) cooking pot; **hacer ~s** to pout

pude *etc vb ver* **poder**

púdico, a ['puðiko, a] *adj* modest

pudiente [pu'ðjente] *adj* (*rico*) wealthy, well-to-do

pudiera *etc vb ver* **poder**

pudor [pu'ðor] *nm* modesty

pudrir [pu'ðrir] *vt* to rot; **~se** *vr* to rot, decay

pueblo ['pweßlo] *nm* people; (*nación*) nation; (*aldea*) village

puedo *etc vb ver* **poder**

puente ['pwente] *nm* bridge; **hacer ~** (*inf*) to take extra days off work between 2 public holidays; to take a long weekend; **~ aéreo** shuttle service; **~ colgante** suspension bridge

---

hacer puente

When a public holiday in Spain falls on a Tuesday or Thursday it is common practice for employers to make the Monday or Friday a holiday as well and to give everyone a four-day weekend. This is known as hacer puente. *When a named public holiday such as the* **Día de la Constitución** *falls on a Tuesday or Thursday, people refer to the whole holiday period as e.g. the* **puente de la Constitución.**

puerco, a ['pwerko, a] *nm/f* pig/sow ♦ *adj* (*sucio*) dirty, filthy; (*obsceno*) disgusting; ~ **de mar** porpoise; ~ **marino** dolphin

pueril [pwe'ril] *adj* childish

puerro ['pwerro] *nm* leek

puerta ['pwerta] *nf* door; (*de jardín*) gate; (*portal*) doorway; (*fig*) gateway; (*portería*) goal; **a la ~** at the door; **a ~ cerrada** behind closed doors; ~ **giratoria** revolving door

puerto ['pwerto] *nm* port; (*paso*) pass; (*fig*) haven, refuge

Puerto Rico [pwerto'riko] *nm* Puerto Rico; **puertorriqueño, a** *adj, nm/f* Puerto Rican

pues [pwes] *adv* (*entonces*) then; (*bueno*) well, well then; (*así que*) so ♦ *conj* (*ya que*) since; ¡~! (*sí*) yes!, certainly!

puesta ['pwesta] *nf* (*apuesta*) bet, stake; ~ **en marcha** starting; ~ **del sol** sunset

puesto, a ['pwesto, a] *pp de* **poner** ♦ *adj*: **tener algo ~** to have sth on, be wearing sth ♦ *nm* (*lugar, posición*) place; (*trabajo*) post, job; (*COM*) stall ♦ *conj*: ~ **que** since, as

púgil ['puxil] *nm* boxer

pugna ['puxna] *nf* battle, conflict; **pugnar** *vi* (*luchar*) to struggle, fight; (*pelear*) to fight

pujar [pu'xar] *vi* (*en subasta*) to bid; (*esforzarse*) to struggle, strain

pulcro, a ['pulkro, a] *adj* neat, tidy

pulga ['pulɣa] *nf* flea

pulgada [pul'ɣaða] *nf* inch

pulgar [pul'ɣar] *nm* thumb

pulir [pu'lir] *vt* to polish; (*alisar*) to smooth; (*fig*) to polish up, touch up

pulla ['puʎa] *nf* cutting remark

pulmón [pul'mon] *nm* lung; **pulmonía** *nf* pneumonia

pulpa ['pulpa] *nf* pulp; (*de fruta*) flesh, soft part

pulpería [pulpe'ria] (*AM*) *nf* (*tienda*) small grocery store

púlpito ['pulpito] *nm* pulpit

pulpo ['pulpo] *nm* octopus

pulsación [pulsa'θjon] *nf* beat; **pulsaciones** pulse rate

pulsar [pul'sar] *vt* (*tecla*) to touch, tap; (*MUS*) to play; (*botón*) to press, push ♦ *vi* to pulsate; (*latir*) to beat, throb; (*MED*): ~ **a uno** to take sb's pulse

pulsera [pul'sera] *nf* bracelet

pulso ['pulso] *nm* (*ANAT*) pulse; (*fuerza*) strength; (*firmeza*) steadiness, steady hand

pulverizador [pulβeriθa'ðor] *nm* spray, spray gun

pulverizar [pulβeri'θar] *vt* to pulverize; (*líquido*) to spray

puna ['puna] (*AM*) *nf* mountain sickness

punitivo, a [puni'tiβo, a] *adj* punitive

punta ['punta] *nf* point, tip; (*extremidad*) end; (*fig*) touch, trace; **horas ~s** peak hours, rush hours; **sacar ~ a** to sharpen

puntada [pun'taða] *nf* (*COSTURA*) stitch

puntal [pun'tal] *nm* prop, support

puntapié [punta'pje] *nm* kick

puntear [punte'ar] *vt* to tick, mark

puntería [punte'ria] *nf* (*de arma*) aim, aiming; (*destreza*) marksmanship

puntero, a [pun'tero, a] *adj* leading ♦ *nm* (*palo*) pointer

puntiagudo, a [puntja'ɣuðo, a] *adj* sharp, pointed

puntilla [pun'tiʎa] *nf* (*encaje*) lace edging o trim; (**andar de ~s**) (to walk) on tiptoe

punto ['punto] *nm* (*gen*) point; (*señal diminuta*) spot, dot; (*COSTURA, MED*) stitch; (*lugar*) spot, place; (*momento*) point, moment; **a ~** ready; **estar a ~ de** to be on the point of o about to;

en ~ on the dot; ~ **muerto** dead centre; (AUTO) neutral (gear); ~ **final** full stop (BRIT), period (US); ~ **y coma** semicolon; ~ **de interrogación** question mark; ~ **de vista** point of view, viewpoint; **hacer** ~ (tejer) to knit

puntuación [puntwa'θjon] nf punctuation; (puntos: en examen) mark's (pl); (DEPORTE) score

puntual [pun'twal] adj (a tiempo) punctual; (exacto) exact, accurate; ~**idad** nf punctuality; exactness, accuracy; ~**izar** vt to fix, specify

puntuar [pun'twar] vi (DEPORTE) to score, count

punzada [pun'θaða] nf (de dolor) twinge

punzante [pun'θante] adj (dolor) shooting, sharp; (herramienta) sharp; **punzar** vt to prick, pierce ♦ vi to shoot, stab

puñado [pu'naðo] nm handful

puñal [pu'nal] nm dagger; ~**ada** nf stab

puñetazo [pune'taθo] nm punch

puño ['puno] nm (ANAT) fist; (cantidad) fistful, handful; (COSTURA) cuff; (de herramienta) handle

pupila [pu'pila] nf pupil

pupitre [pu'pitre] nm desk

puré [pu're] nm puree; (sopa) (thick) soup; ~ **de patatas** mashed potatoes

pureza [pu'reθa] nf purity

purga ['purɣa] nf purge; **purgante** adj, nm purgative; **purgar** vt to purge

purgatorio [purɣa'torjo] nm purgatory

purificar [purifi'kar] vt to purify; (refinar) to refine

puritano, a [puri'tano, a] adj (actitud) puritanical; (iglesia, tradición) puritan ♦ nm/f puritan

puro, a ['puro, a] adj (gen) pure; (verdad) simple, plain ♦ adv: **de** ~ **cansado** out of sheer tiredness ♦ nm cigar

púrpura ['purpura] nf purple; **purpúreo, a** adj purple

pus [pus] nm pus

puse etc vb ver **poner**

pusiera etc vb ver **poner**

pústula ['pustula] nf pimple, sore

puta ['puta] (fam!) nf whore, prostitute

putrefacción [putrefak'θjon] nf rotting, putrefaction

PVP abr (ESP: = precio venta al público) RRP

pyme, PYME ['pime] nf abr (= Pequeña y Mediana Empresa) SME

Q, q

PALABRA CLAVE
---

que [ke] conj 1 (con oración subordinada: muchas veces no se traduce): **dijo** ~ **vendría** he said (that) he would come; **espero** ~ **lo encuentres** I hope (that) you find it; ver tb **el**

2 (en oración independiente): **¡**~ **entre!** send him in; **¡**~ **se mejore tu padre!** I hope your father gets better

3 (enfático): **¿me quieres? – ¡**~ **sí!** do you love me? – of course!

4 (consecutivo: muchas veces no se traduce): **es tan grande** ~ **no lo puedo levantar** it's so big (that) I can't lift it

5 (comparaciones) than: **yo** ~ **tú/él** if I were you/him; ver tb **más; menos; mismo**

6 (valor disyuntivo): ~ **le guste o no** whether he likes it or not; ~ **venga o** ~ **no venga** whether he comes or not

7 (porque): **no puedo, ~ tengo** ~ **quedarme en casa** I can't, I've got to stay in

♦ pron 1 (cosa) that, which; (+ prep) which; **el sombrero** ~ **te compraste** the hat (that o which) you bought; **la cama en la** ~ **dormí** the bed (that o which) I slept in

2 (persona: suj) that, who; (: objeto)

that, whom; **el amigo ~ me
acompañó al museo** the friend that
o who went to the museum with me:
la chica ~ invité the girl (that o
whom) I invited

qué [ke] adj what?, which? ♦ pron
what?; **¡~ divertido!** how funny!;
¿~ edad tienes? how old are you?;
¿de ~ me hablas? what are you
saying to me?; **¿~ tal?** how are you?,
how are things?; **¿~ hay (de nuevo)?**
what's new?

quebradizo, a [keβra'ðiθo, a] adj
fragile, (persona) frail

quebrado, a [ke'βraðo, a] adj (roto)
broken ♦ nm/f bankrupt ♦ nm (MAT)
fraction

quebrantar [keβran'tar] vt (infringir)
to violate, transgress; **~se** vr (persona)
to fail in health

quebranto [ke'βranto] nm damage,
harm; (dolor) grief, pain

quebrar [ke'βrar] vt to break, smash
♦ vi to go bankrupt; **~se** vr to break,
get broken; (MED) to be ruptured

quedar [ke'ðar] vi to stay, remain;
(encontrarse: sitio) to be; (haber aún) to
remain, be left; **~se** vr to remain, stay
(behind); **~se (con) algo** to keep sth;
~ en (acordar) to agree on/to; **~ en
nada** to come to nothing; **~ por
hacer** to be still to be done; **~ ciego/
mudo** to be left blind/dumb; **no te
queda bien ese vestido** that dress
doesn't suit you; **eso queda muy
lejos** that's a long way (away);
quedamos a las seis we agreed to
meet at six

quedo, a [ke'ðo, a] adj still ♦ adv
softly, gently

quehacer [kea'θer] nm task, job; **~es
(domésticos)** nmpl household chores

queja [kexa] nf complaint; **quejarse**
vr (enfermo) to moan, groan; (protestar)
to complain; **quejarse de que** to
complain (about the fact) that;

quejido nm moan

quemado, a [ke'maðo, a] adj burnt

quemadura [kema'ðura] nf burn,
scald

quemar [ke'mar] vt to burn; (fig:
malgastar) to squander ♦ vi to
be burning hot; **~se** vr (consumirse) to
burn (up); (del sol) to get sunburnt

quemarropa [kema'rropa]: **a ~** adv
point-blank

quepo etc vb ver **caber**

querella [ke'reʎa] nf (JUR) charge;
(disputa) dispute; **~rse** vr (JUR) to file a
complaint

┌─────────────────────────┐
│ PALABRA CLAVE │
└─────────────────────────┘

querer [ke'rer] vt **1** (desear) to want;
quiero más dinero I want more
money; **quisiera** o **querría un té** I'd
like a tea; **sin ~** unintentionally;
quiero ayudar/que vayas I want to
help/you to go
2 (preguntas: para pedir algo): **¿quiere
abrir la ventana?** could you open the
window?; **¿quieres echarme una
mano?** can you give me a hand?
3 (amar) to love; (tener cariño a) to be
fond of; **quiere mucho a sus hijos**
he's very fond of his children
4 (requerir): **esta planta quiere más
luz** this plant needs more light
5: **le pedí que me dejara ir pero no
quiso** I asked him to let me go but he
refused

querido, a [ke'riðo, a] adj dear ♦ nm/f
darling; (amante) lover

queso [keso] nm cheese

quicio [kiθjo] nm hinge; **sacar a uno
de ~** to get on sb's nerves

quiebra [kjeβra] nf break, split; (COM)
bankruptcy; (ECON) slump

quiebro [kjeβro] nm (del cuerpo)
swerve

quien [kjen] pron who; **hay ~ piensa
que** there are those who think that;
no hay ~ lo haga no-one will do it

quién [kjen] *pron* who, whom; ¿~ **es?** who's there?

quienquiera [kjen'kjera] (*pl* **quienesquiera**) *pron* whoever

quiero *etc vb ver* **querer**

quieto, a ['kjeto, a] *adj* still; (*carácter*) placid; **quietud** *nf* stillness

quilate [ki'late] *nm* carat

quilla ['kiʎa] *nf* keel

quimera [ki'mera] *nf* chimera; **quimérico, a** *adj* fantastic

químico, a ['kimiko, a] *adj* chemical ♦ *nm/f* chemist ♦ *nf* chemistry

quincalla [kin'kaʎa] *nf* hardware, ironmongery

quince ['kinθe] *num* fifteen; ~ **días** a fortnight; **~añero, a** *nm/f* teenager; **~na** *nf* fortnight; (*pago*) fortnightly pay; **~nal** *adj* fortnightly

quiniela [ki'njela] *nf* football pools *pl*; **~s** *nfpl* (*impreso*) pools coupon *sg*

quinientos, as [ki'njentos, as] *adj, num* five hundred

quinina [ki'nina] *nf* quinine

quinto, a ['kinto, a] *adj* fifth ♦ *nf* country house; (*MIL*) call-up, draft

quiosco ['kjosko] *nm* (*de música*) bandstand; (*de periódicos*) news stand

quirófano [ki'rofano] *nm* operating theatre

quirúrgico, a [ki'rurxiko, a] *adj* surgical

quise *etc vb ver* **querer**

quisiera *etc vb ver* **querer**

quisquilloso, a [kiski'ʎoso, a] *adj* (*susceptible*) touchy; (*meticuloso*) pernickety

quiste ['kiste] *nm* cyst

quitaesmalte [kitaes'malte] *nm* nail-polish remover

quitamanchas [kita'mantʃas] *nm inv* stain remover

quitanieves [kita'njeßes] *nm inv* snowplough (*BRIT*), snowplow (*US*)

quitar [ki'tar] *vt* to remove, take away; (*ropa*) to take off; (*dolor*) to relieve; ¡**quita de ahí!** get away!; **~se** *vr* to

withdraw; (*ropa*) to take off; **se quitó el sombrero** he took off his hat

quite ['kite] *nm* (*esgrima*) parry; (*evasión*) dodge

Quito ['kito] *n* Quito

quizá(s) [ki'θa(s)] *adv* perhaps, maybe

R, r

rábano ['raßano] *nm* radish; **me importa un ~** I don't give a damn

rabia ['raßja] *nf* (*MED*) rabies *sg*; (*ira*) fury, rage; **rabiar** *vi* to have rabies; to rage, be furious; **rabiar por algo** to long for sth

rabieta [ra'ßjeta] *nf* tantrum, fit of temper

rabino [ra'ßino] *nm* rabbi

rabioso, a [ra'ßjoso, a] *adj* rabid; (*fig*) furious

rabo ['raßo] *nm* tail

racha ['ratʃa] *nf* gust of wind: **buena/mala ~** spell of good/bad luck

racial [ra'θjal] *adj* racial, race *cpd*

racimo [ra'θimo] *nm* bunch

raciocinio [raθjo'θinjo] *nm* reason

ración [ra'θjon] *nf* portion; **raciones** *nfpl* rations

racional [raθjo'nal] *adj* (*razonable*) reasonable; (*lógico*) rational; **~izar** *vt* to rationalize

racionar [raθjo'nar] *vt* to ration (out)

racismo [ra'θismo] *nm* racism; **racista** *adj, nm/f* racist

radar [ra'ðar] *nm* radar

radiactivo, a [raðiak'tißo, a] *adj* = **radioactivo**

radiador [raðja'ðor] *nm* radiator

radiante [ra'ðjante] *adj* radiant

radical [raði'kal] *adj, nm/f* radical

radicar [raði'kar] *vi*: **~ en** (*dificultad, problema*) to lie in; (*solución*) to consist in; **~se** *vr* to establish o.s., put down (one's) roots

radio ['raðjo] *nf* radio; (*aparato*) radio (set) ♦ *nm* (*MAT*) radius; (*QUÍM*) radium;

ráfaga   239   **raspadura**

~actividad nf radioactivity; **~activo, a** adj radioactive; **~difusión** nf broadcasting; **~emisora** nf transmitter, radio station; **~escucha** nm/f listener; **~grafía** nf X-ray; **~grafiar** vt to X-ray; **~terapia** nf radiotherapy; **~yente** nm/f listener

ráfaga ['rafaɣa] nf gust; (de luz) flash; (de tiros) burst

raído, a [ra'iðo, a] adj (ropa) threadbare

raigambre [rai'ɣambre] nf (BOT) roots pl; (fig) tradition

raíz [ra'iθ] nf root; **~ cuadrada** square root; **a ~ de** as a result of

raja ['raxa] nf (de melón etc) slice; (grieta) crack; **rajar** vt to split; (fam) to slash; **rajarse** vr to split, crack; **rajarse de** to back out of

rajatabla [raxa'taβla]: **a ~** adv (estrictamente) strictly, to the letter

rallador [raʎa'ðor] nm grater

rallar [ra'ʎar] vt to grate

rama ['rama] nf branch; **~je** nm branches pl, foliage; **ramal** nm (de cuerda) strand; (FERRO) branch line (BRIT); (AUTO) branch (road) (BRIT)

rambla ['rambla] nf (avenida) avenue

ramificación [ramifika'θjon] nf ramification

ramificarse [ramifi'karse] vr to branch out

ramillete [rami'ʎete] nm bouquet

ramo ['ramo] nm branch; (sección) department, section

rampa ['rampa] nf ramp

ramplón, ona [ram'plon, ona] adj uncouth, coarse

rana ['rana] nf frog; **salto de ~** leapfrog

ranchero [ran'tʃero] nm (AM) rancher; smallholder

rancho ['rantʃo] nm (grande) ranch; (pequeño) small farm

rancio, a ['ranθjo, a] adj (comestibles) rancid; (vino) aged, mellow; (fig) ancient

rango ['rango] nm rank, standing

ranura [ra'nura] nf (de teléfono etc) slot

rapar [ra'par] vt to shave; (los cabellos) to crop

rapaz [ra'paθ] (nf: **rapaza**) nm/f young boy/girl ♦ adj (ZOOL) predatory

rape ['rape] nm (pez) monkfish; **al ~** cropped

rapé [ra'pe] nm snuff

rapidez [rapi'ðeθ] nf speed, rapidity; **rápido, a** adj fast, quick ♦ adv quickly ♦ nm (FERRO) express; **rápidos** nmpl rapids

rapiña [ra'piɲa] nm robbery; **ave de ~** bird of prey

raptar [rap'tar] vt to kidnap; **rapto** nm kidnapping; (impulso) sudden impulse; (éxtasis) ecstasy, rapture

raqueta [ra'keta] nf racquet

raquítico, a [ra'kitiko, a] adj stunted; (fig) poor, inadequate; **raquitismo** nm rickets sg

rareza [ra'reθa] nf rarity; (fig) eccentricity

raro, a ['raro, a] adj (poco común) rare; (extraño) odd, strange; (excepcional) remarkable

ras [ras] nm: **a ~ de** level with; **a ~ de tierra** at ground level

rasar [ra'sar] vt (igualar) to level

rascacielos [raska'θjelos] nm inv skyscraper

rascar [ras'kar] vt (con las uñas etc) to scratch; (raspar) to scrape; **~se** vr to scratch (o.s.)

rasgar [ras'ɣar] vt to tear, rip (up)

rasgo ['rasɣo] nm (con pluma) stroke; **~s** nmpl (facciones) features, characteristics; **a grandes ~s** in outline, broadly

rasguñar [rasɣu'ɲar] vt to scratch; **rasguño** nm scratch

raso, a ['raso, a] adj (liso) flat, level; (a baja altura) very low ♦ nm satin; **cielo ~** clear sky

raspadura [raspa'ðura] nf (acto)

scrape, scraping; (*marca*) scratch; **~s**
nfpl (*de papel etc*) scrapings

raspar [ras'par] *vt* to scrape; (*arañar*)
to scratch; (*limar*) to file

rastra ['rastra] *nf* (AGR) rake; **a ~s by**
dragging; (*fig*) unwillingly

rastreador [rastrea'ðor] *nm* tracker;
~ de minas minesweeper

rastrear [rastre'ar] *vt* (*seguir*) to track

rastrero, a [ras'trero, a] *adj* (BOT,
ZOOL) creeping; (*fig*) despicable, mean

rastrillo [ras'triʎo] *nm* rake

rastro ['rastro] *nm* (AGR) rake; (*pista*)
track, trail; (*vestigio*) trace; **el R~** the
Madrid fleamarket

rastrojo [ras'troxo] *nm* stubble

rasurador [rasura'ðor] (AM) *nm*
electric shaver

rasuradora [rasura'ðora] (AM) *nf* =
rasurador

rasurarse [rasu'rarse] *vr* to shave

rata ['rata] *nf* rat

ratear [rate'ar] *vt* (*robar*) to steal

ratero, a [ra'tero, a] *adj* light-fingered
♦ *nm/f* (*carterista*) pickpocket; (AM: *de
casas*) burglar

ratificar [ratifi'kar] *vt* to ratify

rato ['rato] *nm* while, short time; **a ~s**
from time to time; **hay para ~** there's
still a long way to go; **al poco ~** soon
afterwards; **pasar el ~** to kill time;
pasar un buen/mal ~ to have a
good/rough time; **en mis ~s libres** in
my spare time

ratón [ra'ton] *nm* mouse; **ratonera** *nf*
mousetrap

raudal [rau'ðal] *nm* torrent; **a ~es** in
abundance

raya ['raja] *nf* line; (*marca*) scratch; (*en
tela*) stripe; (*de pelo*) parting; (*límite*)
boundary; (*pez*) ray; (*puntuación*) dash;
a ~s striped; **pasarse de la ~** to go
too far: **tener a ~** to keep in check;

rayar [ra'jar] *vt* to line; to scratch; (*subrayar*)
to underline ♦ *vi*: **rayar en o con** to
border on

rayo ['rajo] *nm* (*del sol*) ray, beam; (*de*

luz) shaft; (*en una tormenta*) (flash of)
lightning; **~s X** X-rays

raza ['raθa] *nf* race; **~ humana** human
race

razón [ra'θon] *nf* reason; (*justicia*)
right, justice; (*razonamiento*) reasoning;
(*motivo*) reason, motive; (MAT) ratio; **a
~ de 10 cada día** at the rate of 10 a
day; **"~: ..."** "inquiries to ..."; **en ~ de**
with regard to; **dar ~ a uno** to agree
that sb is right; **tener ~** to be right;
~ directa/inversa direct/inverse
proportion; **~ de ser** raison d'être;
razonable *adj* reasonable; (*justo,
moderado*) fair; **razonamiento** *nm*
(*juicio*) judg(e)ment; (*argumento*)
reasoning; **razonar** *vt, vi* to reason,
argue

reacción [reak'θjon] *nf* reaction;
avión a ~ jet plane; **~ en cadena**
chain reaction; **reaccionar** *vi* to react;
reaccionario, a *adj* reactionary

reacio, a [re'aθjo, a] *adj* stubborn

reactivar [reakti'βar] *vt* to revitalize

reactor [reak'tor] *nm* reactor

readaptación [reaðapta'θjon] *nf*:
~ profesional industrial retraining

reajuste [rea'xuste] *nm* readjustment

real [re'al] *adj* real; (*del rey, fig*) royal

realce [re'alθe] *nm* (*lustre, fig*)
splendour; **poner de ~** to emphasize

realidad [reali'ðað] *nf* reality, fact;
(*verdad*) truth

realista [rea'lista] *nm/f* realist

realización [realiθa'θjon] *nf* fulfilment

realizador, a [realiθa'ðor, a] *nm/f*
film-maker

realizar [reali'θar] *vt* (*objetivo*) to
achieve; (*plan*) to carry out; (*viaje*) to
make, undertake; **~se** *vr* to come
about, come true

realmente [real'mente] *adv* really,
actually

realquilar [realki'lar] *vt* to sublet

realzar [real'θar] *vt* to enhance; to
(*acentuar*) to highlight

reanimar [reani'mar] *vt* to revive;

(*alentar*) to encourage; **~se** *vr* to revive

reanudar |reanu'ðar| *vt* (*renovar*) to renew; (*historia, viaje*) to resume

reaparición |reapari'θjon| *nf* reappearance

rearme |re'arme| *nm* rearmament

rebaja |re'βaxa| *nf* (COM) reduction; (: *descuento*) discount; **~s** *nfpl* (COM) sale; **rebajar** *vt* (*bajar*) to lower; (*reducir*) to reduce; (*disminuir*) to lessen; (*humillar*) to humble

rebanada |reβa'naða| *nf* slice

rebañar |reβa'ɲar| *vt* (*comida*) to scrape up; (*plato*) to scrape clean

rebaño |re'βaɲo| *nm* herd; (*de ovejas*) flock

rebasar |reβa'sar| *vt* (*tb: ~ de*) to exceed

rebatir |reβa'tir| *vt* to refute

rebeca |re'βeka| *nf* cardigan

rebelarse |reβe'larse| *vr* to rebel, revolt

rebelde |re'βelde| *adj* rebellious; (*niño*) unruly ♦ *nm/f* rebel; **rebeldía** *nf* rebelliousness; (*desobediencia*) disobedience

rebelión |reβe'ljon| *nf* rebellion

reblandecer |reβlande'θer| *vt* to soften

rebobinar |reβoβi'nar| *vt* (*cinta, película de video*) to rewind

rebosante |reβo'sante| *adj* overflowing

rebosar |reβo'sar| *vi* (*liquido, recipiente*) to overflow; (*abundar*) to abound, be plentiful

rebotar |reβo'tar| *vt* to bounce; (*rechazar*) to repel ♦ *vi* (*pelota*) to bounce; (*bala*) to ricochet; **rebote** *nm* rebound; **de rebote** on the rebound

rebozado, a |reβo'θaðo, a| *adj* fried in batter *o* breadcrumbs

rebozar |reβo'θar| *vt* to wrap up; (*CULIN*) to fry in batter *o* breadcrumbs

rebuscado, a |reβus'kaðo, a| *adj* (*amanerado*) affected; (*palabra*) recherché; (*idea*) far-fetched

rebuscar |reβus'kar| *vi*: **~ (en/por)** to search carefully (in/for)

rebuznar |reβuθ'nar| *vi* to bray

recado |re'kaðo| *nm* (*mensaje*) message; (*encargo*) errand; **tomar un ~** (*TEL*) to take a message

recaer |reka'er| *vi* to relapse; **~ en** to fall to *o* on; (*criminal etc*) to fall back into, relapse into; **recaída** *nf* relapse

recalcar |rekal'kar| *vt* (*fig*) to stress, emphasize

recalcitrante |rekalθi'trante| *adj* recalcitrant

recalentar |rekalen'tar| *vt* (*volver a calentar*) to reheat; (*calentar demasiado*) to overheat

recámara |re'kamara| (*AM*) *nf* bedroom

recambio |re'kambjo| *nm* spare; (*de pluma*) refill

recapacitar |rekapaθi'tar| *vi* to reflect

recargado, a |rekar'xaðo, a| *adj* overloaded

recargar |rekar'xar| *vt* to overload; (*batería*) to recharge; **recargo** *nm* surcharge; (*aumento*) increase

recatado, a |reka'taðo, a| *adj* (*modesto*) modest, demure; (*prudente*) cautious

recato |re'kato| *nm* (*modestia*) modesty, demureness; (*cautela*) caution

recaudación |rekauða'θjon| *nf* (*acción*) collection; (*cantidad*) takings *pl*; (*en deporte*) gate; **recaudador, a** *nm/f* tax collector

recelar |reθe'lar| *vt*: **~ que** (*sospechar*) to suspect that; (*temer*) to fear that ♦ *vi*: **~ de** to distrust; **recelo** *nm* distrust, suspicion; **receloso, a** *adj* distrustful, suspicious

recepción |reθep'θjon| *nf* reception; **recepcionista** *nm/f* receptionist

receptáculo |reθep'takulo| *nm* receptacle

receptivo, a |reθep'tiβo, a| *adj* receptive

receptor, a |reθep'tor, a| *nm/f*

recipient ♦ *nm* (TEL) receiver

recesión [reθe'sjon] *nf* (COM) recession

receta [re'θeta] *nf* (CULIN) recipe; (MED) prescription

rechazar [retʃa'θar] *vt* to reject; (oferta) to turn down; (ataque) to repel

rechazo [re'tʃaθo] *nm* rejection

rechifla [re'tʃifla] *nf* hissing, booing; (fig) derision

rechinar [retʃi'nar] *vi* to creak; (dientes) to grind

rechistar [retʃis'tar] *vi*: **sin ~** without a murmur

rechoncho, a [re'tʃontʃo, a] (fam) adj thickset (BRIT), heavy-set (US)

rechupete [retʃu'pete]: **de ~** (comida) delicious, scrumptious

recibidor [reθiβi'ðor, a] *nm* entrance hall

recibimiento [reθiβi'mjento] *nm* reception, welcome

recibir [reθi'βir] *vt* to receive; (dar la bienvenida) to welcome ♦ *vi* to entertain; **~se** *vr*: **~se de** to qualify as; **recibo** *nm* receipt

reciclar [reθi'klar] *vt* to recycle

recién [re'θjen] *adv* recently, newly; **los ~ casados** the newly-weds; **el ~ llegado** the newcomer; **el ~ nacido** the newborn child

reciente [re'θjente] *adj* recent; (fresco) fresh; **~mente** *adv* recently

recinto [re'θinto] *nm* enclosure; (área) area, place

recio, a [r're θjo, a] adj strong, tough; (voz) loud ♦ *adv* hard; loud(ly)

recipiente [reθi'pjente] *nm* receptacle

reciprocidad [reθiproθi'ðað] *nf* reciprocity; **recíproco, a** adj reciprocal

recital [reθi'tal] *nm* (MUS) recital; (LITERATURA) reading

recitar [reθi'tar] *vt* to recite

reclamación [reklama'θjon] *nf* claim, demand; (queja) complaint

reclamar [rekla'mar] *vt* to claim, demand ♦ *vi*: **~ contra** to complain about; **~ a uno en justicia** to take sb

to court; **reclamo** *nm* (anuncio) advertisement; (tentación) attraction

reclinar [rekli'nar] *vt* to recline, lean; **~se** *vr* to lean back

recluir [reklu'ir] *vt* to intern, confine

reclusión [reklu'sjon] *nf* (prisión) prison; (refugio) seclusion; **~ perpetua** life imprisonment

recluta [re'kluta] *nm/f* recruit ♦ *nf* recruitment; **reclutar** *vt* (datos) to collect; (dinero) to collect up; **~miento** [rekluta'mjento] *nm* recruitment

recobrar [reko'βrar] *vt* (salud) to recover; (rescatar) to get back; **~se** *vr* to recover

recodo [re'koðo] *nm* (de río, camino) bend

recogedor [rekoxe'ðor] *nm* dustpan

recoger [reko'xer] *vt* to collect; (AGR) to harvest; (levantar) to pick up; (juntar) to gather; (pasar a buscar) to come for, get; (dar asilo) to give shelter to; (faldas) to gather up; (pelo) to put up; **~se** *vr* (retirarse) to retire; **recogido, a** adj (lugar) quiet, secluded; (pequeño) small ♦ *nf* (CORREOS) collection; (AGR) harvest

recolección [rekolek'θjon] *nf* (AGR) harvesting; (colecta) collection

recomendación [rekomenda'θjon] *nf* (sugerencia) suggestion, recommendation; (referencia) reference

recomendar [rekomen'dar] *vt* to suggest, recommend; (confiar) to entrust

recompensa [rekom'pensa] *nf* reward, recompense; **recompensar** *vt* to reward, recompense

recomponer [rekompo'ner] *vt* to mend

reconciliación [rekonθilja'θjon] *nf* reconciliation

reconciliar [rekonθi'ljar] *vt* to reconcile; **~se** *vr* to become reconciled

recóndito, a [re'kondito, a] adj (lugar) hidden, secret

reconfortar [rekonfor'tar] *vt* to

comfort

reconocer [rekono'θer] vt to recognize; (registrar) to search; (MED) to examine; **reconocido, a** adj recognized; (agradecido) grateful; **reconocimiento** nm recognition; search; examination; gratitude; (confesión) admission

reconquista [rekon'kista] nf reconquest; **la R~** the Reconquest (of Spain)

reconstituyente [rekonstitu'jente] nm tonic

reconstruir [rekonstru'ir] vt to reconstruct

reconversión [rekonßer'sjon] nf: **~ industrial** industrial rationalization

recopilación [rekopila'θjon] nf (resumen) summary; (compilación) compilation; **recopilar** vt to compile

récord ['rekorð] (pl **~s**) adj inv, nm record

recordar [rekor'ðar] vt (acordarse de) to remember; (acordar a otro) to remind ♦ vi to remember

recorrer [reko'rrer] vt (país) to cross, travel through; (distancia) to cover; (registrar) to search; (repasar) to look over; **recorrido** nm run, journey; **tren de largo recorrido** main-line train

recortado, a [rekor'taðo, a] adj uneven, irregular

recortar [rekor'tar] vt to cut out; **recorte** nm (acción, de prensa) cutting; (de telas, chapas) trimming; **recorte presupuestario** budget cut

recostado, a [rekos'taðo, a] adj leaning; **estar ~** to be lying down

recostar [rekos'tar] vt to lean; **~se** vr to lie down

recoveco [reko'ßeko] nm (de camino, río etc) bend; (en casa) cubby hole

recreación [rekrea'θjon] nf recreation

recrear [rekre'ar] vt (entretener) to entertain; (volver a crear) to recreate; **recreativo, a** adj recreational; **recreo** nm recreation; (ESCOL) break, playtime

recriminar [rekrimi'nar] vt to reproach ♦ vi to recriminate; **~se** vr to reproach each other

recrudecer [rekruðe'θer] vt, vi to worsen; **~se** vr to worsen

recrudecimiento [rekruðeθi'mjento] nm upsurge

recta ['rekta] nf straight line

rectángulo, a [rek'tangulo, a] adj rectangular ♦ nm rectangle

rectificar [rektifi'kar] vt to rectify; (volverse recto) to straighten ♦ vi to correct o.s.

rectitud [rekti'tuð] nf straightness

recto, a ['rekto, a] adj straight; (persona) honest, upright ♦ nm rectum

rector, a [rek'tor, a] adj governing

recuadro [re'kwaðro] nm box; (TIPOGRAFÍA) inset

recubrir [reku'ßrir] vt: **~ (con)** (pintura, crema) to cover (with)

recuento [re'kwento] nm inventory; **hacer el ~ de** to count o reckon up

recuerdo [re'kwerðo] nm souvenir; **~s** nmpl (memorias) memories; **¡~s a tu madre!** give my regards to your mother!

recular [reku'lar] vi to back down

recuperable [rekupe'raßle] adj recoverable

recuperación [rekupera'θjon] nf recovery

recuperar [rekupe'rar] vt to recover; (tiempo) to make up; **~se** vr to recuperate

recurrir [reku'rrir] vi (JUR) to appeal; **~ a** to resort to; (persona) to turn to; **recurso** nm resort; (medios) means pl, resources pl; (JUR) appeal

recusar [reku'sar] vt to reject, refuse

red [reð] nf net, mesh; (FERRO etc) network; (trampa) trap; **la R~** (Internet) the Net

redacción [reðak'θjon] nf (acción) editing; (personal) editorial staff; (ESCOL) essay, composition

redactar [reðak'tar] vt to draw up,

draft; (periódico) to edit
redactor, a |reðak'tor, a| nm/f editor
redada |re'ðaða| nf: ~ **policial** police
raid, round-up
rededor |reðe'ðor| nm: **al** o **en** ~
around, round about
redención |reðen'θjon| nf redemption
redicho, a |re'ðitʃo, a| adj affected
redil |re'ðil| nm sheepfold
redimir |reði'mir| vt to redeem
rédito |'reðito| nm interest, yield
redoblar |reðo'ßlar| vt to redouble
♦ vi (tambor) to roll
redomado, a |reðo'maðo, a| adj
(astuto) sly, crafty; (perfecto) utter
redonda |re'ðonda| nf: **a la** ~ around,
round about
redondear |reðonde'ar| vt to round,
round off
redondel |reðon'del| nm (círculo)
circle; (TAUR) bullring, arena
redondo, a |re'ðondo, a| adj (circular)
round; (completo) complete
reducción |reðuk'θjon| nf reduction
reducido, a |reðu'θiðo, a| adj
reduced; (limitado) limited; (pequeño)
small
reducir |reðu'θir| vt to reduce; to limit;
~**se** vr to diminish
redundancia |reðun'danθja| nf
redundancy
reembolsar |re(e)mbol'sar| vt
(persona) to reimburse; (dinero) to
repay, pay back; (depósito) to refund;
reembolso nm reimbursement;
refund
reemplazar |re(e)mpla'θar| vt to
replace; **reemplazo** nm replacement;
de reemplazo (MIL) reserve
reencuentro |re(e)n'kwentro| nm
reunion
referencia |refe'renθja| nf reference;
con ~ a with reference to
referéndum |refe'rendum| (pl ~**s**) nm
referendum
referente |refe'rente| adj: ~ a
concerning, relating to

referir |refe'rir| vt (contar) to tell,
recount; (relacionar) to refer, relate;
~**se** vr: ~**se a** to refer to
refilón |refi'lon|: **de** ~ adv obliquely
refinado, a |refi'naðo, a| adj refined
refinamiento |refina'mjento| nm
refinement
refinar |refi'nar| vt to refine; **refinería**
nf refinery
reflejar |refle'xar| vt to reflect; **reflejo,
a** adj reflected; (movimiento) reflex
♦ nm reflection; (ANAT) reflex
reflexión |reflek'sjon| nf reflection;
reflexionar vt to reflect on ♦ vi to
reflect; (detenerse) to pause (to think)
reflexivo, a |reflek'sißo, a| adj
thoughtful; (LING) reflexive
reflujo |re'fluxo| nm ebb
reforma |re'forma| nf reform; (ARQ etc)
repair; ~ **agraria** agrarian reform
reformar |refor'mar| vt to reform;
(modificar) to change, alter; (ARQ) to
repair; ~**se** vr to mend one's ways
reformatorio |reforma'torjo| nm
reformatory
reforzar |refor'θar| vt to strengthen;
(ARQ) to reinforce; (fig) to encourage
refractario, a |refrak'tarjo, a| adj
(TEC.) heat-resistant
refrán |re'fran| nm proverb, saying
refregar |refre'var| vt to scrub
refrenar |refre'nar| vt to check,
restrain
refrendar |refren'dar| vt (firma) to
endorse, countersign; (ley) to approve
refrescante |refres'kante| adj
refreshing, cooling
refrescar |refres'kar| vt to refresh ♦ vi
to cool down; ~**se** vr to get cooler;
(tomar aire fresco) to go out for a
breath of fresh air; (beber) to have a
drink
refresco |re'fresko| nm soft drink, cool
drink; "~**s**" "refreshments"
refriega |re'frjeva| nf scuffle, brawl
refrigeración |refrixera'θjon| nf
refrigeration; (de sala) air-conditioning

refrigerador |refrixera'ðor| nm
refrigerator (BRIT), icebox (US)

refrigerar |refrixe'rar| vt to refrigerate;
(sala) to air-condition

refuerzo |re'fwerθo| nm
reinforcement; (TEC) support

refugiado, a |refu'xjaðo, a| nm/f
refugee

refugiarse |refu'xjarse| vr to take
refuge, shelter

refugio |re'fuxjo| nm refuge;
(protección) shelter

refunfuñar |refunfu'ɲar| vi to grunt,
growl; (quejarse) to grumble

refutar |refu'tar| vt to refute

regadera |reɣa'ðera| nf watering can

regadío |reɣa'ðio| nm irrigated land

regalado, a |reɣa'laðo, a| adj
comfortable, luxurious; (gratis) free, for
nothing

regalar |reɣa'lar| vt (dar) to give (as a
present); (entregar) to give away;
(mimar) to pamper, make a fuss of

regaliz |reɣa'liθ| nm liquorice

regalo |re'ɣalo| nm (obsequio) gift,
present; (gusto) pleasure

regañadientes |reɣaɲa'ðjentes|: **a ~**
adv reluctantly

regañar |reɣa'ɲar| vt to scold ♦ vi to
grumble; **regañón, ona** adj nagging

regar |re'ɣar| vt to water, irrigate; (fig)
to scatter, sprinkle

regatear |reɣate'ar| vt (COM) to
bargain over; (escatimar) to be mean
with ♦ vi to bargain, haggle; (DEPORTE)
to dribble; **regateo** nm bargaining;
(dribbling); (del cuerpo) swerve, dodge

regazo |re'ɣaθo| nm lap

regeneración |rexenera'θjon| nf
regeneration

regenerar |rexene'rar| vt to
regenerate

regentar |rexen'tar| vt to direct,
manage; **regente** nm (COM) manager;
(POL) regent

régimen |'reximen| (pl regímenes)
nm regime; (MED) diet

regimiento |rexi'mjento| nm
regiment

regio, a |'rexjo, a| adj royal, regal; (fig:
suntuoso) splendid; (AM: fam) great,
terrific

región |re'xjon| nf region

regir |re'xir| vt to govern, rule; (dirigir)
to manage, run ♦ vi to apply, be in
force

registrar |rexis'trar| vt (buscar) to
search; (: en cajón) to look through;
(inspeccionar) to inspect; (anotar) to
register, record; (INFORM) to log; **~se** vr
to register; (ocurrir) to happen

registro |re'xistro| nm (acto)
registration; (MUS, libro) register;
(inspección) inspection, search; **~ civil**
registry office

regla |'reɣla| nf (ley) rule, regulation;
(de medir) ruler, rule; (MED: período)
period

reglamentación |reɣlamenta'θjon| nf
(acto) regulation; (lista) rules pl

reglamentar |reɣlamen'tar| vt to
regulate; **reglamentario, a** adj
statutory; **reglamento** nm rules pl,
regulations pl

regocijarse |reɣoθi'xarse| vr: to
rejoice at, be happy about; **regocijo**
nm joy, happiness

regodearse |reɣoðe'arse| vr to be
glad, be delighted; **regodeo** nm
delight

regresar |reɣre'sar| vi to come back,
go back, return; **regresivo, a** adj
backward; (fig) regressive; **regreso** nm
return

reguero |re'ɣero| nm (de sangre etc)
trickle; (de humo) trail

regulador |reɣula'ðor| nm regulator;
(de radio etc) knob, control

regular |reɣu'lar| adj regular; (normal)
normal, usual; (común) ordinary;
(organizado) regular, orderly; (mediano)
average; (fam) not bad, so-so ♦ adv
so-so, alright ♦ vt (controlar) to control,
regulate; (TEC) to adjust; **por lo ~** as a

rule; **~idad** nf regularity; **~izar** vt to regularize

regusto [re'vusto] nm aftertaste

rehabilitación [reaßilita'θjon] nf rehabilitation; (ARQ) restoration

rehabilitar [reaßili'tar] vt to rehabilitate; (ARQ) to restore; (reintegrar) to reinstate

rehacer [rea'θer] vt (reparar) to mend, repair; (volver a hacer) to redo, repeat; **~se** vr (MED) to recover

rehén [re'en] nm hostage

rehuir [reu'ir] vt to avoid, shun

rehusar [reu'sar] vt, vi to refuse

reina ['reina] nf queen; **~do** nm reign

reinante [rei'nante] adj (fig) prevailing

reinar [rei'nar], vi to reign

reincidir [reinθi'ðir] vi to relapse

reincorporarse [reinkorpo'rarse] vr: **~ a** to rejoin

reino ['reino] nm kingdom; **el R~ Unido** the United Kingdom

reintegrar [reinte'xrar] vt (reconstituir) to reconstruct; (persona) to reinstate; (dinero) to refund, pay back; **~se** vr: **~se a** to return to

reír [re'ir] vi to laugh; **~se** vr to laugh; **~se de** to laugh at

reiterar [reite'rar] vt to reiterate

reivindicación [reißindika'θjon] nf (demanda) claim, demand; (justificación) vindication

reivindicar [reißindi'kar] vt to claim

reja ['rexa] nf (de ventana) grille, bars pl; (en la calle) grating

rejilla [re'xiʎa] nf grating, grille; (muebles) wickerwork; (de ventilación) vent; (de coche etc) luggage rack

rejoneador [rexonea'ðor] nm mounted bullfighter

rejuvenecer [rexuße'neθer] vt, vi to rejuvenate

relación [rela'θjon] nf relation, relationship; (MAT) ratio; (narración) report; **relaciones públicas** public relations; **con ~ a, en ~ con** in relation to; **relacionar** vt to relate,

connect; **relacionarse** vr to be connected, be linked

relajación [relaxa'θjon] nf relaxation

relajado, a [rela'xaðo, a] adj (disoluto) loose; (cómodo) relaxed; (MED) ruptured

relajar [rela'xar] vt to relax; **~se** vr to relax

relamerse [rela'merse] vr to lick one's lips

relamido, a [rela'miðo, a] adj (pulcro) overdressed; (afectado) affected

relámpago [re'lampaxo] nm flash of lightning; **visita/huelga ~** lightning visit/strike; **relampaguear** vi to flash

relatar [rela'tar] vt to tell, relate

relativo, a [rela'tißo, a] adj relative; **en lo ~ a** concerning

relato [re'lato] nm (narración) story, tale

relegar [rele'xar] vt to relegate

relevante [rele'ßante] adj eminent, outstanding

relevar [rele'ßar] vt (sustituir) to relieve; **~se** vr to relay; **~ a uno de un cargo** to relieve sb of his post

relevo [re'leßo] nm relief; **carrera de ~s** relay race

relieve [re'ljeße] nm (ARTE, TEC) relief; (fig) prominence, importance; **bajo ~** bas-relief

religión [reli'xjon] nf religion; **religioso, a** adj religious ♦ nm/f monk/nun

relinchar [relin'tʃar] vi to neigh; **relincho** nm neigh; (acto) neighing

reliquia [re'likja] nf relic; **~ de familia** heirloom

rellano [re'ʎano] nm (ARQ) landing

rellenar [reʎe'nar] vt (llenar) to fill up; (CULIN) to stuff; (COSTURA) to pad; **relleno, a** adj full up; stuffed ♦ nm stuffing; (de tapicería) padding

reloj [re'lo(x)] nm clock; **~ (de pulsera)** wristwatch; **~ despertador** alarm (clock); **poner el ~** to set one's watch (o the clock); **~ero, a** nm/f clockmaker; watchmaker

reluciente |relu'θjente| adj brilliant, shining

relucir |relu'θir| vi to shine; (fig) to excel

relumbrar |relum'brar| vi to dazzle, shine brilliantly

remachar |rema'tʃar| vt to rivet; (fig) to hammer home, drive home; **remache** nm rivet

remanente |rema'nente| nm remainder; (COM) balance; (de producto) surplus

remangar |reman'gar| vt to roll up

remanso |re'manso| nm pool

remar |re'mar| vi to row

rematado, a |rema'taðo, a| adj complete, utter

rematar |rema'tar| vt to finish off; (COM) to sell off cheap ♦ vi to end, finish off; (DEPORTE) to shoot

remate |re'mate| nm end, finish; (punta) tip; (DEPORTE) shot; (ARQ) top; **de** o **para ~** to crown it all (BRIT), to top it off

remedar |reme'ðar| vt to imitate

remediar |reme'ðjar| vt to remedy; (subsanar) to make good, repair; (evitar) to avoid

remedio |re'meðjo| nm remedy; (alivio) relief, help; (JUR) recourse, remedy; **poner ~ a** to correct, stop; **no tener más ~** to have no alternative; **¡qué ~!** there's no choice!; **sin ~** hopeless

remedo |re'meðo| nm imitation; (pey) parody

remendar |remen'dar| vt to repair; (con parche) to patch

remesa |re'mesa| nf remittance; (COM) shipment

remiendo |re'mjendo| nm mend; (con parche) patch; (cosido) darn

remilgado, a |remil'gaðo, a| adj prim; (afectado) affected

remilgo |re'milvo| nm primness; (afectación) affectation

reminiscencia |reminis'θenθja| nf reminiscence

remiso, a |re'miso, a| adj slack, slow

remite |re'mite| nm (en sobre) name and address of sender

remitir |remi'tir| vt to remit, send ♦ vi to slacken; (en carta): **remite: X** sender: X; **remitente** nm/f sender

remo |'remo| nm (de barco) oar; (DEPORTE) rowing

remojar |remo'xar| vt to steep, soak; (galleta etc) to dip, dunk

remojo |re'moxo| nm: **dejar la ropa en ~** to leave clothes to soak

remolacha |remo'latʃa| nf beet, beetroot

remolcador |remolka'ðor| nm (NAUT) tug; (AUTO) breakdown lorry

remolcar |remol'kar| vt to tow

remolino |remo'lino| nm eddy; (de agua) whirlpool; (de viento) whirlwind; (de gente) crowd

remolque |re'molke| nm tow, towing; (cuerda) towrope; **llevar a ~** to tow

remontar |remon'tar| vt to mend; **~se** vr to soar; **~se a** (COM) to amount to; **~ el vuelo** to soar

remorder |remor'ðer| vt to distress, disturb; **~le la conciencia a uno** to have a guilty conscience; **remordimiento** nm remorse

remoto, a |re'moto, a| adj remote

remover |remo'βer| vt to stir; (tierra) to turn over; (objetos) to move round

remozar |remo'θar| vt (ARQ) to refurbish

remuneración |remunera'θjon| nf remuneration

remunerar |remune'rar| vt to remunerate; (premiar) to reward

renacer |rena'θer| vi to be reborn; (fig) to revive; **renacimiento** nm rebirth; **el Renacimiento** the Renaissance

renacuajo |rena'kwaxo| nm (ZOOL) tadpole

renal |re'nal| adj renal, kidney cpd

rencilla |ren'θiʎa| nf quarrel

rencor [reŋ'kor] nm rancour, bitterness; **~oso, a** adj spiteful

rendición [rendi'θjon] nf surrender

rendido, a [ren'diðo, a] adj (sumiso) submissive; (cansado) worn-out, exhausted

rendija [ren'dixa] nf (hendedura) crack, cleft

rendimiento [rendi'mjento] nm (producción) production; (TEC, COM) efficiency

rendir [ren'dir] vt (vencer) to defeat; (producir) to produce; (dar beneficio) to yield; (agotar) to exhaust ♦ vi to pay; **~se** vr (someterse) to surrender; (cansarse) to wear o.s. up; **~ homenaje o culto a** to pay homage to

renegar [rene'var] vi (renunciar) to renounce; (blasfemar) to blaspheme; (quejarse) to complain

RENFE ['renfe] nf abr (= Red Nacional de los Ferrocarriles Españoles) ≈ BR (BRIT)

renglón [reŋ'glon] nm (línea) line; (COM) item, article; **a ~ seguido** immediately after

renombrado, a [renom'braðo, a] adj renowned

renombre [re'nombre] nm renown

renovación [renoβa'θjon] nf (de contrato) renewal; (ARQ) renovation

renovar [reno'βar] vt to renew; (ARQ) to renovate

renta ['renta] nf (ingresos) income; (beneficio) profit; (alquiler) rent; **~ vitalicia** annuity; **rentable** adj profitable; **rentar** vt to produce, yield

renuncia [re'nunθja] nf resignation

renunciar [renun'θjar] vt to renounce; (tabaco, alcohol etc): **~ a** to give up; (oferta, oportunidad) to turn down; (puesto) to resign ♦ vi to resign

reñido, a [re'niðo, a] adj (batalla) bitter, hard-fought; **estar ~ con uno** to be on bad terms with sb

reñir [re'nir] vt (regañar) to scold ♦ vi

(estar peleado) to quarrel, fall out; (combatir) to fight

reo ['reo] nm/f culprit, offender; **~ de muerte** prisoner condemned to death

reojo [re'oxo]: **de ~** adv out of the corner of one's eye

reparación [repara'θjon] nf (acto) mending, repairing; (TEC) repair; (fig) amends, reparation

reparar [repa'rar] vt to repair; (fig) to make amends for; (observar) to observe ♦ vi: **~ en** (darse cuenta de) to notice; (prestar atención a) to pay attention to

reparo [re'paro] nm (advertencia) observation; (duda) doubt; (dificultad) difficulty; **poner ~s (a)** to raise objections (to)

repartición [reparti'θjon] nf distribution; (división) division; **repartidor, a** nm/f distributor

repartir [repar'tir] vt to distribute, share out; (CORREOS) to deliver; **reparto** nm distribution; delivery; (TEATRO, CINE) cast; (AM: urbanización) housing estate (BRIT), real estate development (US)

repasar [repa'sar] vt (ESCOL) to revise; (MECÁNICA) to check, overhaul; (COSTURA) to mend; **repaso** nm revision; overhaul, checkup; mending

repatriar [repa'trjar] vt to repatriate

repecho [re'petʃo] nm steep incline

repelente [repe'lente] adj repellent, repulsive

repeler [repe'ler] vt to repel

repensar [repen'sar] vt to reconsider

repente [re'pente] nm: **de ~** suddenly; **~ de ira** fit of anger

repentino, a [repen'tino, a] adj sudden

repercusión [reperku'sjon] nf repercussion

repercutir [reperku'tir] vi (objeto) to rebound; (sonido) to echo; **~ en** (fig) to have repercussions on

repertorio [reper'torjo] nm list; (TEATRO) repertoire

repetición [repeti'θjon] nf repetition
repetir [repe'tir] vt to repeat; (plato) to have a second helping of ♦ vi to repeat; (sabor) to come back; **~se** vr (volver a un tema) to repeat o.s.
repetitivo, a [repeti'tiβo, a] adj repetitive, repetitious
repicar [repi'kar] vt (campanas) to ring
repique [re'pike] nm pealing, ringing; **~teo** nm pealing; (de tambor) drumming
repisa [re'pisa] nf ledge, shelf; (de ventana) windowsill; **~ de chimenea** mantelpiece
repito etc vb ver **repetir**
replantearse [replante'arse] vr: **~ un problema** to reconsider a problem
replegarse [reple'xarse] vr to fall back, retreat
repleto, a [re'pleto, a] adj replete, full up
réplica ['replika] nf answer; (ARTE) replica
replicar [repli'kar] vi to answer; (objetar) to argue, answer back
repliegue [re'pljexe] nm (MIL) withdrawal
repoblación [repoβla'θjon] nf repopulation; (de río) restocking; **~ forestal** reafforestation
repoblar [repo'βlar] vt to repopulate; (con árboles) to reafforest
repollo [re'poʎo] nm cabbage
reponer [repo'ner] vt to replace, put back; (TEATRO) to revive; **~se** vr to recover; **~ que** to reply that
reportaje [repor'taxe] nm report, article
reportero, a [repor'tero, a] nm/f reporter
reposacabezas [reposaka'βeθas] nm inv headrest
reposado, a [repo'saðo, a] adj (descansado) restful; (tranquilo) calm
reposar [repo'sar] vi to rest, repose
reposición [reposi'θjon] nf replacement; (CINE) remake

reposo [re'poso] nm rest
repostar [repos'tar] vt to replenish; (AUTO) to fill up (with petrol (BRIT) o gasoline (US))
repostería [reposte'ria] nf confectioner's (shop); **repostero, a** nm/f confectioner
reprender [repren'der] vt to reprimand
represa [re'presa] nf dam; (lago artificial) lake, pool
represalia [repre'salja] nf reprisal
representación [representa'θjon] nf representation; (TEATRO) performance; **representante** nm/f representative, performer
representar [represen'tar] vt to represent; (TEATRO) to perform; (edad) to look; **~se** vr to imagine; **representativo, a** adj representative
represión [repre'sjon] nf repression
reprimenda [repri'menda] nf reprimand, rebuke
reprimir [repri'mir] vt to repress
reprobar [repro'βar] vt to censure, reprove
reprochar [repro'tʃar] vt to reproach; **reproche** nm reproach
reproducción [reproðuk'θjon] nf reproduction
reproducir [reproðu'θir] vt to reproduce; **~se** vr to breed; (situación) to recur
reproductor, a [reproðuk'tor, a] adj reproductive
reptil [rep'til] nm reptile
república [re'puβlika] nf republic; **R~ Dominicana** Dominican Republic; **republicano, a** adj, nm/f republican
repudiar [repu'ðjar] vt to repudiate; (fe) to renounce
repuesto [re'pwesto] nm (pieza de recambio) spare (part); (abastecimiento) supply; **rueda de ~** spare wheel
repugnancia [repuɣ'nanθja] nf repugnance; **repugnante** adj repugnant, repulsive

repugnar |repuɣ'nar| vt to disgust

repulsa |re'pulsa| nf rebuff

repulsión |repul'sjon| nf repulsion, aversion; **repulsivo, a** adj repulsive

reputación |reputa'θjon| nf reputation

requemado, a |reke'maðo, a| adj (quemado) scorched; (bronceado) tanned

requerimiento |rekeri'mjento| nm request; (JUR) summons

requerir |reke'rir| vt (pedir) to ask, request; (exigir) to require; (llamar) to send for, summon

requesón |reke'son| nm cottage cheese

requete... |re'kete| prefijo extremely

réquiem |'rekjem| (pl **~s**) nm requiem

requisito |reki'sito| nm requirement, requisite

res |res| nf beast, animal

resaca |re'saka| nf (en el mar) undertow, undercurrent; (fam) hangover

resaltar |resal'tar| vi to project, stick out; (fig) to stand out

resarcir |resar'θir| vt to compensate; **~se** vr to make up for

resbaladizo, a |resβala'ðiθo, a| adj slippery

resbalar |resβa'lar| vi to slip, slide; (fig) to slip (up); **~se** vr to slip, slide; to slip (up); **resbalón** nm (acción) slip

rescatar |reska'tar| vt (salvar) to save, rescue; (objeto) to get back, recover; (cautivos) to ransom

rescate |res'kate| nm rescue; (de objeto) recovery; **pagar un ~** to pay a ransom

rescindir |resθin'dir| vt to rescind

rescisión |resθi'sjon| nf cancellation

rescoldo |res'koldo| nm embers pl

resecar |rese'kar| vt to dry thoroughly; (MED) to cut out, remove; **~se** vr to dry up

reseco, a |re'seko, a| adj very dry; (fig) skinny

resentido, a |resen'tiðo, a| adj resentful

resentimiento |resenti'mjento| nm resentment, bitterness

resentirse |resen'tirse| vr (debilitarse: persona) to suffer; **~ de** (consecuencias) to feel the effects of; **~ de (o por) algo** to resent sth, be bitter about sth

reseña |re'seɲa| nf (cuenta) account; (informe) report; (LITERATURA) review

reseñar |rese'ɲar| vt to describe; (LITERATURA) to review

reserva |re'serβa| nf reserve; (reservación) reservation; **a ~ de que ... unless ...**; **con toda ~** in strictest confidence

reservado, a |reser'βaðo, a| adj reserved; (retraído) cold, distant ♦ nm private room

reservar |reser'βar| vt (guardar) to keep; (habitación, entrada) to reserve; **~se** vr to save o.s.; (callar) to keep to o.s.

resfriado |resfri'aðo| nm cold; **resfriarse** vr to cool; (MED) to catch (a) cold

resguardar |resɣwar'ðar| vt to protect, shield; **~se** vr: **~se de** to guard against; **resguardo** nm defence; (vale) voucher; (recibo) receipt, slip

residencia |resi'ðenθja| nf residence; **~l** nf (urbanización) housing estate

residente |resi'ðente| adj, nm/f resident

residir |resi'ðir| vi to reside, live; **~ en** to reside in, lie in

residuo |re'siðwo| nm residue

resignación |resiɣna'θjon| nf resignation; **resignarse** vr: **resignarse a o con** to resign o.s. to, be resigned to

resina |re'sina| nf resin

resistencia |resis'tenθja| nf (dureza) endurance, strength; (oposición, ELEC) resistance; **resistente** adj strong, hardy; resistant

resistir |resis'tir| vt (soportar) to bear;

(*oponerse a*) to resist, oppose; (*aguantar*) to put up with ♦ *vi* to resist; (*aguantar*) to last, endure; **~se** *vr*: **~se a** to refuse to, resist

resolución |resolu'θjon| *nf* resolution; (*decisión*) decision; **resoluto, a** *adj* resolute

resolver |resol'βer| *vt* to resolve; (*solucionar*) to solve, resolve; (*decidir*) to decide, settle; **~se** *vr* to make up one's mind

resonancia |reso'nanθja| *nf* (*del sonido*) resonance; (*repercusión*) repercussion

resonar |reso'nar| *vi* to ring, echo

resoplar |reso'plar| *vi* to snort; **resoplido** *nm* heavy breathing

resorte |re'sorte| *nm* spring; (*fig*) lever

respaldar |respal'dar| *vt* to back (up), support; **~se** *vr* to lean back; **~se con** o **en** (*fig*) to take one's stand on; **respaldo** *nm* (*de sillón*) back; (*fig*) support, backing

respectivo, a |respek'tiβo, a| *adj* respective; **en lo ~** with regard to

respecto |res'pekto| *nm*: **al ~** on this matter; **con ~ a, ~ de** with regard to, in relation to

respetable |respe'taβle| *adj* respectable

respetar |respe'tar| *vt* to respect; **respeto** *nm* respect; (*acatamiento*) deference; **respetos** *nmpl* respects; **respetuoso, a** *adj* respectful

respingo |res'pingo| *nm* start, jump

respiración |respira'θjon| *nf* breathing; (*MED*) respiration; (*ventilación*) ventilation

respirar |respi'rar| *vi* to breathe; **respiratorio, a** *adj* respiratory; **respiro** *nm* breathing; (*fig: descanso*) respite

resplandecer |resplande'θer| *vi* to shine; **resplandeciente** *adj* resplendent, shining; **resplandor** *nm* brilliance, brightness; (*de luz, fuego*) blaze

responder |respon'der| *vt* to answer ♦ *vi* to answer; (*fig*) to respond; (*pey*) to answer back; **~ de** o **por** to answer for; **respondón, ona** *adj* cheeky

responsabilidad |responsaβili'ðað| *nf* responsibility

responsabilizarse |responsaβili-'θarse| *vr* to make o.s. responsible, take charge

responsable |respon'saβle| *adj* responsible

respuesta |res'pwesta| *nf* answer, reply

resquebrajar |reskeβra'xar| *vt* to crack, split; **~se** *vr* to crack, split

resquemor |reske'mor| *nm* resentment

resquicio |res'kiθjo| *nm* chink; (*hendedura*) crack

resta |'resta| *nf* (*MAT*) remainder

restablecer |restaβle'θer| *vt* to re-establish, restore; **~se** *vr* to recover

restallar |resta'ʎar| *vi* to crack

restante |res'tante| *adj* remaining; **lo ~** the remainder

restar |res'tar| *vt* (*MAT*) to subtract; (*fig*) to take away ♦ *vi* to remain, be left

restauración |restaura'θjon| *nf* restoration

restaurante |restau'rante| *nm* restaurant

restaurar |restau'rar| *vt* to restore

restitución |restitu'θjon| *nf* return, restitution

restituir |restitu'ir| *vt* (*devolver*) to return, give back; (*rehabilitar*) to restore

resto |'resto| *nm* (*residuo*) rest, remainder; (*apuesta*) stake; **~s** *nmpl* remains

restregar |restre'ɣar| *vt* to scrub, rub

restricción |restrik'θjon| *nf* restriction

restrictivo, a |restrik'tiβo, a| *adj* restrictive

restringir |restrin'xir| *vt* to restrict, limit

resucitar [resuθi'tar] vt, vi to resuscitate, revive

resuello [re'sweʎo] nm (aliento) breath; **estar sin ~** to be breathless

resuelto, a [re'swelto, a] pp de **resolver ♦** adj resolute, determined

resultado [resul'taðo] nm result; (conclusión) outcome; **resultante** adj resulting, resultant

resultar [resul'tar] vi (ser) to be; (llegar a ser) to turn out to be; (salir bien) to turn out well; (COM) to amount to; **~ de** to stem from; **me resulta difícil hacerlo** it's difficult for me to do it

resumen [re'sumen] (pl resúmenes) nm summary, résumé; **en ~** in short

resumir [resu'mir] vt to sum up; (cortar) to abridge, cut down; (condensar) to summarize

resurgir [resur'xir] vi (reaparecer) to reappear

resurrección [resurre(k)'θjon] nf resurrection

retablo [re'taβlo] nm altarpiece

retaguardia [reta'ɣwarðja] nf rearguard

retahíla [reta'ila] nf series, string

retal [re'tal] nm remnant

retar [re'tar] vt to challenge; (desafiar) to defy, dare

retardar [retar'ðar] vt (demorar) to delay; (hacer más lento) to slow down; (retener) to hold back

retazo [re'taθo] nm snippet (BRIT), fragment

retener [rete'ner] vt (intereses) to withhold

reticente [reti'θente] adj (tono) insinuating; (postura) reluctant; **ser ~ a hacer algo** to be reluctant o unwilling to do sth

retina [re'tina] nf retina

retintín [retin'tin] nm jangle, jingle

retirada [reti'raða] nf (MIL, refugio) retreat; (de dinero) withdrawal; (de embajador) recall; **retirado, a** adj (lugar) remote; (vida) quiet; (jubilado) retired

retirar [reti'rar] vt to withdraw; (quitar) to remove; (jubilar) to retire, pension off; **~se** vr to retreat, withdraw; to retire; (acostarse) to retire, go to bed; **retiro** nm retreat; retirement; (pago) pension

reto [reto] nm dare, challenge

retocar [reto'kar] vt (fotografía) to touch up, retouch

retoño [re'toɲo] nm sprout, shoot; (fig) offspring, child

retoque [re'toke] nm retouching

retorcer [retor'θer] vt to twist; (manos, lavado) to wring; **~se** vr to become twisted; (mover el cuerpo) to writhe; **retorcido, a** [retor'θiðo, a] adj (persona) devious

retórica [re'torika] nf rhetoric; (pey) affectedness; **retórico, a** adj rhetorical

retornar [retor'nar] vt to return, give back ♦ vi to return, go/come back; **retorno** nm return

retortijón [retorti'xon] nm twist, twisting

retozar [reto'θar] vi (juguetear) to frolic, romp; (saltar) to gambol; **retozón, ona** adj playful

retracción [retrak'θjon] nf retraction

retractarse [retrak'tarse] vr to retract; **me retracto** I take that back

retraerse [retra'erse] vr to retreat, withdraw; **retraído, a** adj shy, retiring; **retraimiento** nm retirement; (timidez) shyness

retransmisión [retransmi'sjon] nf repeat (broadcast)

retransmitir [retransmi'tir] vt (mensaje) to relay; (TV etc) to repeat, retransmit; (: en vivo) to broadcast live

retrasado, a [retra'saðo, a] adj late; (MED) mentally retarded; (país etc) backward, underdeveloped

retrasar [retra'sar] vt (demorar) to postpone, put off; (retardar) to slow down ♦ vi (atrasarse) to be late; (reloj) to be slow; (producción) to fall (off);

(quedarse atrás) to lag behind; **~se** *vr* to be late; to be slow; to fall (off); to lag behind

retraso [re'traso] *nm (demora)* delay; *(lentitud)* slowness; *(tardanza)* lateness; *(atraso)* backwardness; **~s** *(FINANZAS) nmpl* arrears; **llegar con ~** to arrive late; **~ mental** mental deficiency

retratar [retra'tar] *vt (ARTE)* to paint the portrait of; *(fotografiar)* to photograph; *(fig)* to depict, describe; **~se** *vr* to have one's portrait painted; to have one's photograph taken; **retrato** *nm* portrait; *(fig)* likeness; **retrato-robot** *nm* Identikit ® picture

retreta [re'treta] *nf* retreat

retrete [re'trete] *nm* toilet

retribución [retriβu'θjon] *nf (recompensa)* reward; *(pago)* pay, payment

retribuir [retri'βwir] *vt (recompensar)* to reward; *(pagar)* to pay

retro... ['retro] *prefijo* retro...

retroactivo, a [retroak'tiβo, a] *adj* retroactive, retrospective

retroceder [retroθe'ðer] *vi (echarse atrás)* to move back(wards); *(fig)* to back down

retroceso [retro'θeso] *nm* backward movement; *(MED)* relapse; *(fig)* backing down

retrógrado, a [re'troɣraðo, a] *adj* retrograde, retrogressive; *(POL)* reactionary

retrospectivo, a [retrospek'tiβo, a] *adj* retrospective

retrovisor [retroβi'sor] *nm (tb: espejo ~)* rear-view mirror

retumbar [retum'bar] *vi* to echo, resound

reúma [re'uma], **reuma** ['reuma] *nm* rheumatism

reumatismo [reuma'tismo] *nm* = **reúma**

reunificar [reunifi'kar] *vt* to reunify

reunión [reu'njon] *nf (asamblea)* meeting; *(fiesta)* party

reunir [reu'nir] *vt (juntar)* to reunite, join (together); *(recoger)* to gather (together); *(personas)* to get together; *(cualidades)* to combine; **~se** *vr (personas: en asamblea)* to meet, gather

revalidar [reβali'ðar] *vt (ratificar)* to confirm, ratify

revalorizar [reβalori'θar] *vt* to revalue, reassess

revancha [re'βantʃa] *nf* revenge

revelación [reβela'θjon] *nf* revelation

revelado [reβe'laðo] *nm* developing

revelar [reβe'lar] *vt* to reveal; *(FOTO)* to develop

reventa [re'βenta] *nf (de entradas: para concierto)* touting

reventar [reβen'tar] *vt* to burst, explode

reventón [reβen'ton] *nm (AUTO)* blow-out *(BRIT)*, flat *(US)*

reverencia [reβe'renθja] *nf* reverence; **reverenciar** *vt* to revere

reverendo, a [reβe'rendo, a] *adj* reverend

reverente [reβe'rente] *adj* reverent

reversible [reβer'siβle] *adj (prenda)* reversible

reverso [re'βerso] *nm* back, other side; *(de moneda)* reverse

revertir [reβer'tir] *vi* to revert

revés [re'βes] *nm* back, wrong side; *(fig)* reverse, setback; *(DEPORTE)* backhand; **al ~** the wrong way round; *(de arriba abajo)* upside down; *(ropa)* inside out; **volver algo del ~** to turn sth round; *(ropa)* to turn sth inside out

revestir [reβes'tir] *vt (cubrir)* to cover, coat

revisar [reβi'sar] *vt (examinar)* to check; *(texto etc)* to revise; **revisión** *nf* revision

revisor, a [reβi'sor, a] *nm/f* inspector; *(FERRO)* ticket collector

revista [re'βista] *nf* magazine, review; *(TEATRO)* revue; *(inspección)* inspection; **pasar ~ a** to review, inspect

revivir [reβi'βir] *vi* to revive

revocación [reβoka'θjon] *nf* repeal

revocar [reβo'kar] *vt* to revoke

revolcarse [reβol'karse] *vr* to roll about

revolotear [reβolote'ar] *vi* to flutter

revoltijo [reβol'tixo] *nm* mess, jumble

revoltoso, a [reβol'toso, a] *adj* (*travieso*) naughty, unruly

revolución [reβolu'θjon] *nf* revolution; **revolucionar** *vt* to revolutionize; **revolucionario, a** *adj, nm/f* revolutionary

revolver [reβol'βer] *vt* (*desordenar*) to disturb, mess up; (*mover*) to move about ♦ *vi*: **~ en** to go through, rummage (about) in; **~se** *vr* (*volver contra*) to turn on against

revólver [re'βolβer] *nm* revolver

revuelo [re'βwelo] *nm* fluttering; (*fig*) commotion

revuelta [re'βwelta] *nf* (*motín*) revolt; (*agitación*) commotion

revuelto, a [re'βwelto, a] *pp de* **revolver** ♦ *adj* (*mezclado*) mixed-up, in disorder

rey [rei] *nm* king; **Día de R~es** Twelfth Night

┌─────────────────────────┐
│ **Reyes Magos** │

On the night before the 6th January (the Epiphany), children go to bed expecting **los Reyes Magos** (the Three Wise Men) to bring them presents. Twelfth Night processions, known as **cabalgatas**, take place that evening when 3 people dressed as **los Reyes Magos** arrive in the town by land or sea to the delight of the children.
└─────────────────────────┘

reyerta [re'jerta] *nf* quarrel, brawl

rezagado, a [reθa'xaðo, a] *nm/f* straggler

rezagar [reθa'xar] *vt* (*dejar atrás*) to leave behind; (*retrasar*) to delay, postpone

rezar [re'θar] *vi* to pray; **~ con** (*fam*) to concern, have to do with; **rezo** *nm* prayer

rezongar [reθon'gar] *vi* to grumble

rezumar [reθu'mar] *vt* to ooze

ría ['ria] *nf* estuary

riada [ri'aða] *nf* flood

ribera [ri'βera] *nf* (*de río*) bank; (: *área*) riverside

ribete [ri'βete] *nm* (*de vestido*) border; (*fig*) addition; **~ar** *vt* to edge, border

ricino [ri'θino] *nm*: **aceite de ~** castor oil

rico, a ['riko, a] *adj* rich; (*adinerado*) wealthy, rich; (*lujoso*) luxurious; (*comida*) delicious; (*niño*) lovely, cute ♦ *nm/f* rich person

rictus ['riktus] *nm* (*mueca*) sneer, grin

ridiculez [riðiku'leθ] *nf* absurdity

ridiculizar [riðikuliθar] *vt* to ridicule

ridículo, a [ri'ðikulo, a] *adj* ridiculous; **hacer el ~** to make a fool of o.s.; **poner a uno en ~** to make a fool of sb

riego ['rjeɣo] *nm* (*aspersión*) watering; (*irrigación*) irrigation

riel [rjel] *nm* rail

rienda ['rjenda] *nf* rein; **dar ~ suelta a** to give free rein to

riesgo ['rjesɣo] *nm* risk; **correr el ~ de** to run the risk of

rifa ['rifa] *nf* (*lotería*) raffle; **rifar** *vt* to raffle

rifle ['rifle] *nm* rifle

rigidez [rixi'ðeθ] *nf* rigidity, stiffness; (*fig*) strictness; **rígido, a** *adj* rigid, stiff; strict, inflexible

rigor [ri'xor] *nm* strictness, rigour; (*inclemencia*) harshness; **de ~ de** rigueur, essential; **riguroso, a** *adj* rigorous; harsh; (*severo*) severe

rimar [ri'mar] *vi* to rhyme

rimbombante [rimbom'bante] *adj* pompous

rímel ['rimel] *nm* mascara

rimmel ['rimel] *nm* = **rímel**

rincón [rin'kon] *nm* corner (inside)

rinoceronte [rinoθe'ronte] *nm* rhinoceros

riña ['riɲa] *nf (disputa)* argument; *(pelea)* brawl

riñón [ri'ɲon] *nm* kidney

río *etc* ['rio] *vb ver* **reír** ♦ *nm* river; *(fig)* torrent, stream; **~ abajo/arriba** downstream/upstream; **~ de la Plata** River Plate

rioja [ri'oxa] *nm (vino)* rioja (wine)

rioplatense [riopla'tense] *adj* of o from the River Plate region

riqueza [ri'keθa] *nf* wealth, riches *pl*; *(cualidad)* richness

risa ['risa] *nf* laughter; *(una ~)* laugh; **¡qué ~!** what a laugh!

risco ['risko] *nm* crag, cliff

risible [ri'siβle] *adj* ludicrous, laughable

risotada [riso'taða] *nf* guffaw, loud laugh

ristra ['ristra] *nf* string

risueño, a [ri'sweɲo, a] *adj (sonriente)* smiling; *(contento)* cheerful

ritmo ['ritmo] *nm* rhythm; **a ~ lento** slowly; **trabajar a ~ lento** to go slow

rito ['rito] *nm* rite

ritual [ri'twal] *adj, nm* ritual

rival [ri'βal] *nm/f* rival; **~idad** *nf* rivalry; **~izar** *vi*: **~izar con** to rival, vie with

rizado, a [ri'θaðo, a] *adj* curly ♦ *nm* curls *pl*

rizar [ri'θar] *vt* to curl; **~se** *vr (pelo)* to curl; *(agua)* to ripple; **rizo** *nm* curl; ripple

RNE *nf abr* = **Radio Nacional de España**

robar [ro'βar] *vt* to rob; *(objeto)* to steal; *(casa etc)* to break into; *(NAIPES)* to draw

roble ['roβle] *nm* oak; **~dal** *nm* oakwood

robo ['roβo] *nm* robbery, theft

robot [ro'βot] *nm* robot; **~ (de cocina)** food processor

robustecer [roβuste'θer] *vt* to strengthen

robusto, a [ro'βusto, a] *adj* robust, strong

roca [ro'ka] *nf* rock

roce ['roθe] *nm (caricia)* brush; *(TEC)* friction; *(en la piel)* graze; **tener ~ con** to be in close contact with

rociar [ro'θjar] *vt* to spray

rocín [ro'θin] *nm* nag, hack

rocío [ro'θio] *nm* dew

rocoso, a [ro'koso, a] *adj* rocky

rodaballo [roða'βaʎo] *nm* turbot

rodado, a [ro'ðaðo, a] *adj (con ruedas)* wheeled

rodaja [ro'ðaxa] *nf* slice

rodaje [ro'ðaxe] *nm (CINE)* shooting, filming; *(AUTO)*: **en ~** running in

rodar [ro'ðar] *vt (vehículo)* to wheel (along); *(escalera)* to roll down; *(viajar por)* to travel (over) ♦ *vi* to roll; *(coche)* to go, run; *(CINE)* to shoot, film

rodear [roðe'ar] *vt* to surround ♦ *vi* to go round; **~se** *vr*: **~se de amigos** to surround o.s. with friends

rodeo [ro'ðeo] *nm (ruta indirecta)* detour; *(evasión)* evasion; *(AM)* rodeo; **hablar sin ~s** to come to the point, speak plainly

rodilla [ro'ðiʎa] *nf* knee; **de ~s** kneeling; **ponerse de ~s** to kneel (down)

rodillo [ro'ðiʎo] *nm* roller; *(CULIN)* rolling-pin

roedor, a [roe'ðor, a] *adj* gnawing ♦ *nm* rodent

roer [ro'er] *vt (masticar)* to gnaw; *(corroer, fig)* to corrode

rogar [ro'ɣar] *vt, vi (pedir)* to ask for; *(suplicar)* to beg, plead; **se ruega no fumar** please do not smoke

rojizo, a [ro'xiθo, a] *adj* reddish

rojo, a ['roxo, a] *adj, nm* red; **al ~ vivo** red-hot

rol [rol] *nm* list, roll; *(papel)* role

rollito [ro'ʎito] *nm*: **~ de primavera** spring roll

rollizo, a [ro'ʎiθo, a] *adj (objeto)* cylindrical; *(persona)* plump

rollo ['roʎo] nm roll; (de cuerda) coil; (madera) log; (fam) bore; **¡qué ~!** what a carry-on!

Roma ['roma] n Rome

romance [ro'manθe] nm (amoroso) romance; (LITERATURA) ballad

romano, a [ro'mano, a] adj, nm/f Roman; **a la romana** in batter

romanticismo [romanti'θismo] nm romanticism

romántico, a [ro'mantiko, a] adj romantic

rombo ['rombo] nm (GEOM) rhombus

romería [rome'ria] nf (REL) pilgrimage; (excursión) trip, outing

----
Romería

Originally a pilgrimage to a shrine or church to express devotion to the Virgin Mary or a local Saint, the romería has also become a rural festival which accompanies the pilgrimage. People come from all over to attend, bringing their own food and drink, and spend the day in celebration.

----

romero, a [ro'mero, a] nm/f pilgrim ♦ nm rosemary

romo, a ['romo, a] adj blunt; (fig) dull

rompecabezas [rompeka'βeθas] nm inv riddle, puzzle; (juego) jigsaw (puzzle)

rompeolas [rompe'olas] nm inv breakwater

romper [rom'per] vt to break; (hacer pedazos) to smash; (papel, tela etc) to tear, rip ♦ vi (olas) to break; (sol, diente) to break through; **~ un contrato** to break a contract; **~ a** (empezar a) to start (suddenly) to; **~ a llorar** to burst into tears; **~ con uno** to fall out with sb

ron [ron] nm rum

roncar [ron'kar] vi to snore

ronco, a ['ronko, a] adj (afónico) hoarse; (áspero) raucous

ronda ['ronda] nf (gen) round; (patrulla) patrol; **rondar** vt to patrol ♦ vi to patrol; (fig) to prowl round

ronquido [ron'kiðo] nm snore, snoring

ronronear [ronrone'ar] vi to purr; **ronroneo** nm purr

roña ['roɲa] nf (VETERINARIA) mange; (mugre) dirt, grime; (óxido) rust

roñoso, a [ro'ɲoso, a] adj (mugriento) filthy; (tacaño) mean

ropa ['ropa] nf clothes pl, clothing; **~ blanca** linen; **~ de cama** bed linen; **~ interior** underwear; **~ para lavar** washing; **~je** nm gown, robes pl

ropero [ro'pero] nm linen cupboard; (guardarropa) wardrobe

rosa ['rosa] adj pink ♦ nm rose; **~ de los vientos** the compass

rosado, a [ro'saðo, a] adj pink ♦ nm rosé

rosal [ro'sal] nm rosebush

rosario [ro'sarjo] nm (REL) rosary; **rezar el ~** to say the rosary

rosca ['roska] nf (de tornillo) thread; (de humo) coil, spiral; (pan, postre) ring-shaped roll/pastry

rosetón [rose'ton] nm rosette; (ARQ) rose window

rosquilla [ros'kiʎa] nf doughnut-shaped fritter

rostro ['rostro] nm (cara) face

rotación [rota'θjon] nf rotation; **~ de cultivos** crop rotation

rotativo, a [rota'tiβo, a] adj rotary

roto, a ['roto, a] pp de **romper** ♦ adj broken

rotonda [ro'tonda] nf roundabout

rótula ['rotula] nf kneecap; (TEC) ball-and-socket joint

rotulador [rotula'ðor] nm felt-tip pen

rotular [rotu'lar] vt (carta, documento) to head, entitle; (objeto) to label; **rótulo** nm heading, title; label; (letrero) sign

rotundamente [rotunda'mente] adv (negar) flatly; (responder, afirmar) emphatically; **rotundo, a** adj round;

(enfático) emphatic

rotura [ro'tura] nf (acto) breaking; (MED) fracture

roturar [rotu'rar] vt to plough

rozadura [roθa'ðura] nf abrasion, graze

rozar [ro'θar] vt (frotar) to rub; (arañar) to scratch; (tocar ligeramente) to shave, touch lightly; **~se** vr to rub (together); **~se con** (fam) to rub shoulders with

rte. abr (= remite, remitente) sender

RTVE nf abr = **Radiotelevisión Española**

rubí [ru'βi] nm ruby; (de reloj) jewel

rubio, a [ru'βjo, a] adj fair-haired, blond(e) ♦ nm/f blond/blonde; **tabaco ~** Virginia tobacco

rubor [ru'βor] nm (sonrojo) blush; (timidez) bashfulness; **~izarse** vr to blush

rúbrica [ru'βrika] nf (de la firma) flourish; **rubricar** vt (firmar) to sign with a flourish; (concluir) to sign and seal

rudimentario, a [ruðimen'tarjo, a] adj rudimentary; **rudimento** nm rudiment

rudo, a [ruðo, a] adj (sin pulir) unpolished; (grosero) coarse; (violento) violent; (sencillo) simple

rueda ['rweða] nf wheel; (círculo) ring, circle; (rodaja) slice, round; **~ delantera/trasera/de repuesto** front/back/spare wheel; **~ de prensa** press conference

ruedo ['rweðo] nm (círculo) circle; (TAUR) arena, bullring

ruego etc ['rweyo] vb ver **rogar** ♦ nm request

rufián [ru'fjan] nm scoundrel

rugby ['ruɣβi] nm rugby

rugido [ru'xiðo] nm roar

rugir [ru'xir] vi to roar

rugoso, a [ru'xoso, a] adj (arrugado) wrinkled; (áspero) rough; (desigual) ridged

ruido ['rwiðo] nm noise; (sonido)

sound; (alboroto) racket; row; (escándalo) commotion, rumpus; **~so, a** adj noisy, loud; (fig) sensational

ruin [rwin] adj contemptible, mean

ruina ['rwina] nf ruin; (colapso) collapse; (de persona) ruin, downfall

ruindad [rwin'dað] nf lowness, meanness; (acto) low o mean act

ruinoso, a [rwi'noso, a] adj ruinous; (destartalado) dilapidated, tumbledown; (COM) disastrous

ruiseñor [rwise'nor] nm nightingale

ruleta [ru'leta] nf roulette

rulo ['rulo] nm (para el pelo) curler

Rumanía [ruma'nia] nf Rumania

rumba ['rumba] nf rumba

rumbo ['rumbo] nm (ruta) route, direction; (ángulo de dirección) course, bearing; (fig) course of events; **ir con ~ a** to be heading for

rumboso, a [rum'boso, a] adj generous

rumiante [ru'mjante] nm ruminant

rumiar [ru'mjar] vt to chew; (fig) to chew over ♦ vi to chew the cud

rumor [ru'mor] nm (ruido sordo) low sound; (murmuración) murmur, buzz

rumorearse vr: **se rumorea que** it is rumoured that

runrún [run'run] nm (voces) murmur, sound of voices; (fig) rumour

rupestre [ru'pestre] adj rock cpd

ruptura [rup'tura] nf rupture

rural [ru'ral] adj rural

Rusia ['rusja] nf Russia; **ruso, a** adj, nm/f Russian

rústica [rustika] nf: **libro en ~** paperback (book); ver tb **rústico**

rústico, a [rustiko, a] adj rustic; (ordinario) coarse, uncouth ♦ nm/f yokel

ruta ['ruta] nf route

rutina [ru'tina] nf routine; **~rio, a** adj routine

S, s

S *abr* (= *santo, a*) St; (= *sur*) S

s. *abr* (= *siglo*) C.; (= *siguiente*) sig

S.A. *abr* (= *Sociedad Anónima*) Ltd. (*BRIT*), Inc. (*US*)

sábado ['saβaðo] *nm* Saturday

sábana ['saβana] *nf* sheet

sabandija [saβan'dixa] *nf* bug, insect

sabañón [saβa'ɲon] *nm* chilblain

saber [sa'βer] *vt* to know; (*llegar a conocer*) to find out, learn; (*tener capacidad de*) to know how to ♦ *vi*: **~ a** to taste of, taste like ♦ *nm* knowledge, learning; **a ~** namely; **¿sabes conducir/nadar?** can you drive/ swim?; **¿sabes francés?** do you speak French?; **~ de memoria** to know by heart; **hacer ~ algo a algn** to inform sb of sth, let sb know sth

sabiduría [saβiðu'ria] *nf* (*conocimientos*) wisdom; (*instrucción*) learning

sabiendas [sa'βjendas]: **a ~** *adv* knowingly

sabio, a ['saβjo,a] *adj* (*docto*) learned; (*prudente*) wise, sensible

sable [sa'βer] *etc vb ver* **saber**

sabor [sa'βor] *nm* taste, flavour; **~ear** *vt* to taste, savour; (*fig*) to relish

sabotaje [saβo'taxe] *nm* sabotage

saboteador, a [saβotea'ðor, a] *nm/f* saboteur

sabotear [saβote'ar] *vt* to sabotage

sabré etc *vb ver* **saber**

sabroso, a [sa'βroso, a] *adj* tasty; (*fig: fam*) racy, salty

sacacorchos [saka'kortʃos] *nm inv* corkscrew

sacapuntas [saka'puntas] *nm inv* pencil sharpener

sacar [sa'kar] *vt* to take out; (*fig: extraer*) to get (out); (*quitar*) to remove, get out; (*hacer salir*) to bring out; (*conclusión*) to draw; (*novela etc*) to publish, bring out; (*ropa*) to take off;

(*obra*) to make; (*premio*) to receive; (*entradas*) to get; (*TENIS*) to serve; **~ adelante** (*niño*) to bring up; (*negocio*) to carry on, go on with; **~ a uno a bailar** to get sb up to dance; **~ una foto** to take a photo; **~ la lengua** to stick out one's tongue; **~ buenas/malas notas** to get good/ bad marks

sacarina [saka'rina] *nf* saccharin(e)

sacerdote [saθer'ðote] *nm* priest

saciar [sa'θjar] *vt* (*hambre, sed*) to satisfy; **~se** *vr* (*de comida*) to get full up; **comer hasta ~se** to eat one's fill

saco ['sako] *nm* bag; (*grande*) sack; (*su contenido*) bagful; (*AM*) jacket; **~ de dormir** sleeping bag

sacramento [sakra'mento] *nm* sacrament

sacrificar [sakrifi'kar] *vt* to sacrifice

sacrificio *nm* sacrifice

sacrilegio [sakri'lexjo] *nm* sacrilege; **sacrílego, a** *adj* sacrilegious

sacristía [sakris'tia] *nf* sacristy

sacro, a ['sakro, a] *adj* sacred

sacudida [saku'ðiða] *nf* (*agitación*) shake, shaking; (*sacudimiento*) jolt, bump; **~ eléctrica** electric shock

sacudir [saku'ðir] *vt* to shake; (*golpear*) to hit

sádico, a ['saðiko, a] *adj* sadistic ♦ *nm/f* sadist; **sadismo** *nm* sadism

saeta [sa'eta] *nf* (*flecha*) arrow

sagacidad [saɣaθi'ðað] *nf* shrewdness, cleverness; **sagaz** *adj* shrewd, clever

sagitario [saxi'tarjo] *nm* Sagittarius

sagrado, a [sa'ɣraðo, a] *adj* sacred, holy

Sáhara ['saara] *nm*: **el ~** the Sahara (desert)

sal [sal] *vb ver* **salir** ♦ *nf* salt

sala ['sala] *nf* room; (**~ de estar**) living room; (*TEATRO*) house, auditorium; (*de hospital*) ward; **~ de apelación** court; **~ de espera** waiting room; **~ de estar** living room; **~ de fiestas** dance hall

salado, a |sa'laðo, a| *adj* salty; *(fig)* witty, amusing; **agua salada** salt water

salar |sa'lar| *vt* to salt, add salt to

salarial |sala'rjal| *adj (aumento, revisión)* wage *cpd*, salary *cpd*

salario |sa'larjo| *nm* wage, pay

salchicha |sal'tʃitʃa| *nf (pork)* sausage; **salchichón** *nm (salami-type)* sausage

saldar |sal'dar| *vt* to pay; *(vender)* to sell off; *(fig)* to settle, resolve; **saldo** *nm (pago)* settlement; *(de una cuenta)* balance; *(lo restante)* remnant(s) *(pl)*, remainder; **saldos** *nmpl (en tienda)* sale

saldré *etc vb ver* **salir**

salero |sa'lero| *nm* salt cellar

salgo *etc vb ver* **salir**

salida |sa'liða| *nf (puerta etc)* exit, way out; *(acto)* leaving, going out; *(de tren, AVIAT)* departure; *(TEC)* output, production; *(COM)* opening; *(GEO, válvula)* outlet; *(de gas)* leak; **calle sin ~** cul-de-sac; **~ de incendios** fire escape

saliente |sa'ljente| *adj (ARQ)* projecting; *(sol)* rising; *(fig)* outstanding

┌─────────────────
│ *PALABRA CLAVE*
└─────────────────

salir |sa'lir| *vi* **1** *(partir: tb: ~ de)* to leave; **Juan ha salido** Juan is out; **salió de la cocina** he came out of the kitchen

2 *(aparecer)* to appear; *(disco, libro)* to come out; **anoche salió en la tele** she appeared o was on TV last night; **salió en todos los periódicos** it was in all the papers

3 *(resultar)*: **la muchacha nos salió muy trabajadora** the girl turned out to be a very hard worker; **la comida te ha salido exquisita** the food was delicious; **sale muy caro** it's very expensive

4: **~le a uno algo: la entrevista que hice me salió bien/mal** the interview I did went o turned out well/badly

5: **~ adelante: no sé como haré para ~ adelante** I don't know how I'll get by

♦ **~se** *vr (líquido)* to spill; *(animal)* to escape

saliva |sa'liβa| *nf* saliva

salmo |'salmo| *nm* psalm

salmón |sal'mon| *nm* salmon

salmonete |salmo'nete| *nm* red mullet

salmuera |sal'mwera| *nf* pickle, brine

salón |sa'lon| *nm (de casa)* living room, lounge; *(muebles)* lounge suite; **~ de belleza** beauty parlour; **~ de baile** dance hall

salpicadero |salpika'ðero| *nm (AUTO)* dashboard

salpicar |salpi'kar| *vt (rociar)* to sprinkle, spatter; *(esparcir)* to scatter

salpicón |salpi'kon| *nm:* **~ de mariscos** seafood salad

salsa |'salsa| *nf* sauce; *(con carne asada)* gravy; *(fig)* spice

saltamontes |salta'montes| *nm inv* grasshopper

saltar |sal'tar| *vt* to jump (over), leap (over); *(dejar de lado)* to skip, miss out ♦ *vi* to jump, leap; *(pelota)* to bounce; *(al aire)* to fly up; *(quebrarse)* to break; *(al agua)* to dive; *(fig)* to explode, blow up

salto |'salto| *nm* jump, leap; *(al agua)* dive; **~ de agua** waterfall; **~ de altura** high jump

saltón, ona |sal'ton, ona| *adj (ojos)* bulging, popping; *(dientes)* protruding

salud |sa'luð| *nf* health; **¡(a su) ~!** cheers!, good health!; **~able** *adj (de buena ~)* healthy; *(provechoso)* good, beneficial

saludar |salu'ðar| *vt* to greet; *(MIL)* to salute; **saludo** *nm* greeting; **"saludos"** *(en carta)* "best wishes", "regards"

salva ['salβa] *nf*: **~ de aplausos** ovation

salvación [salβa'θjon] *nf* salvation; (*rescate*) rescue

salvado [sal'βaðo] *nm* bran

salvaguardar [salβaɣwar'ðar] *vt* to safeguard

salvajada [salβa'xaða] *nf* atrocity

salvaje [sal'βaxe] *adj* wild; (*tribu*) savage; **salvajismo** *nm* savagery

salvamento [salβa'mento] *nm* rescue

salvar [sal'βar] *vt* (*rescatar*) to save, rescue; (*resolver*) to overcome, resolve; (*cubrir distancias*) to cover, travel; (*hacer excepción*) to except, exclude; (*barco*) to salvage

salvavidas [salβa'βiðas] *adj inv*: **bote/chaleco/cinturón ~** lifeboat/life jacket/life belt

salvo, a ['salβo, a] *adj* safe ♦ *adv* except (for), save; **a ~** out of danger; **~ que** unless; **~conducto** *nm* safe-conduct

san [san] *adj* saint; **S~ Juan** St John

sanar [sa'nar] *vt* (*herida*) to heal; (*persona*) to cure ♦ *vi* (*persona*) to get well, recover; (*herida*) to heal

sanatorio [sana'torjo] *nm* sanatorium

sanción [san'θjon] *nf* sanction; **sancionar** *vt* to sanction

sandalia [san'dalja] *nf* sandal

sandez [san'deθ] *nf* foolishness

sandía [san'dia] *nf* watermelon

sandwich ['sandwitʃ] (*pl* **~s**, **~es**) *nm* sandwich

saneamiento [sanea'mjento] *nm* sanitation

sanear [sane'ar] *vt* to clean up; (*terreno*) to drain

The **Sanfermines** *is a week-long festival in Pamplona made famous by Ernest Hemingway. From the 7th July, the feast of "San Fermín", crowds of mainly young people take to the streets drinking, singing and*

dancing. Early in the morning bulls are released along the narrow streets leading to the bullring, and young men risk serious injury to show their bravery by running out in front of them, a custom which is also typical of many Spanish villages.

sangrar [san'grar] *vt, vi* to bleed; **sangre** *nf* blood

sangría [san'gria] *nf* sangria, sweetened drink of red wine with fruit

sangriento, a [san'grjento, a] *adj* bloody

sanguijuela [sangi'xwela] *nf* (ZOOL, *fig*) leech

sanguinario, a [sangi'narjo, a] *adj* bloodthirsty

sanguíneo, a [san'gineo, a] *adj* blood *cpd*

sanidad [sani'ðað] *nf*: **~ (pública)** public health

San Isidro *is the patron saint of Madrid, and gives his name to the week-long festivities which take place around the 15th May. Originally an 18th-century trade fair, the San Isidro celebrations now include music, dance, a famous romería, theatre and bullfighting.*

sanitario, a [sani'tarjo, a] *adj* health *cpd*; **~s** *nmpl* toilets (*BRIT*), washroom (*US*)

sano, a ['sano, a] *adj* healthy; (*sin daños*) sound; (*comida*) wholesome; (*entero*) whole, intact; **~ y salvo** safe and sound

Santiago [san'tjaɣo] *nm*: **~ (de Chile)** Santiago

santiamén [santja'men] *nm*: **en un ~** in no time at all

santidad [santi'ðað] *nf* holiness, sanctity

santiguarse [santi'ɣwarse] *vr* to make

the sign of the cross

santo, a ['santo, a] *adj* holy; (*fig*) wonderful, miraculous ♦ *nm/f* saint ♦ *nm* saint's day; **~ y seña** password

santuario [san'twarjo] *nm* sanctuary, shrine

saña ['sapa] *nf* rage, fury

sapo ['sapo] *nm* toad

saque ['sake] *nm* (*TENIS*) service, serve; (*FÚTBOL*) throw-in; **~ de esquina** corner (kick)

saquear [sake'ar] *vt* (*MIL*) to sack; (*robar*) to loot, plunder; **saqueo** *nm* sacking; looting, plundering; ransacking

sarampión [saram'pjon] *nm* measles *sg*

sarcasmo [sar'kasmo] *nm* sarcasm; **sarcástico, a** *adj* sarcastic

sardina [sar'ðina] *nf* sardine

sargento [sar'xento] *nm* sergeant

sarmiento [sar'mjento] *nm* (*BOT*) vine shoot

sarna ['sarna] *nf* itch; (*MED*) scabies

sarpullido [sarpu'ʎiðo] *nm* (*MED*) rash

sarro ['sarro] *nm* (*en dientes*) tartar, plaque

sartén [sar'ten] *nf* frying pan

sastre ['sastre] *nm* tailor; **~ría** *nf* (*arte*) tailoring; (*tienda*) tailor's (shop)

Satanás [sata'nas] *nm* Satan

satélite [sa'telite] *nm* satellite

sátira ['satira] *nf* satire

satisfacción [satisfak'θjon] *nf* satisfaction

satisfacer [satisfa'θer] *vt* to satisfy; (*gastos*) to meet; (*pérdida*) to make good; **~se** *vr* to satisfy o.s., be satisfied; (*vengarse*) to take revenge; **satisfecho, a** *adj* satisfied; (*contento*) content(ed), happy; (*tb*: **satisfecho de sí mismo**) self-satisfied, smug

saturar [satu'rar] *vt* to saturate; **~se** *vr* (*mercado, aeropuerto*) to reach saturation point

sauce ['sauθe] *nm* willow; **~ llorón** weeping willow

sauna ['sauna] *nf* sauna

savia ['saβja] *nf* sap

saxofón [sakso'fon] *nm* saxophone

sazonar [saθo'nar] *vt* to ripen; (*CULIN*) to flavour, season

SE *abr* (= *sudeste*) SE

PALABRA CLAVE
---

se [se] *pron* **1** (*reflexivo: sg: m*) himself; (*: f*) herself; (*: cosa*) itself; (*: de Vd*) yourself; (*: de Vds*) yourselves; **~ está preparando** she's preparing herself; *para usos léxicos del pron ver el vb en cuestión, p.ej.* **arrepentirse**

2 (*con complemento indirecto*) to him; to her; to them; to it; to you; **a usted ~ lo dije ayer** I told you yesterday; **~ compró un sombrero** he bought himself a hat; **~ rompió la pierna** he broke his leg

3 (*uso recíproco*) each other, one another; **~ miraron (el uno al otro)** they looked at each other o one another

4 (*en oraciones pasivas*): **se han vendido muchos libros** a lot of books have been sold

5 (*impers*): **~ dice que** people say that, it is said that; **allí ~ come muy bien** the food there is very good, you can eat very well there

---

sé *vb ver* **saber**; **ser**

sea *etc vb ver* **ser**

sebo ['seβo] *nm* fat, grease

secador [seka'ðor] *nm*: **~ de pelo** hair-dryer

secadora [seka'ðora] *nf* tumble dryer

secar [se'kar] *vt* to dry; **~se** *vr* to dry (off); (*río, planta*) to dry up

sección [sek'θjon] *nf* section

seco, a ['seko, a] *adj* dry; (*carácter*) cold; (*respuesta*) sharp, curt; **habrá pan a secas** there will be just bread; **decir algo a secas** to say sth curtly; **parar en ~** to stop dead

secretaría |sekreta'ria| nf secretariat
secretario, a |sekre'tarjo, a| nm/f
secretary
secreto, a |se'kreto, a| adj secret;
(persona) secretive ♦ nm secret;
(calidad) secrecy
secta |'sekta| nf sect; **~rio, a** adj
sectarian
sector |sek'tor| nm sector
secuela |se'kwela| nf consequence
secuencia |se'kwenθja| nf sequence
secuestrar |sekwes'trar| vt to kidnap;
(bienes) to seize, confiscate; **secuestro**
nm kidnapping; seizure, confiscation
secular |seku'lar| adj secular
secundar |sekun'dar| vt to second,
support
secundario, a |sekun'darjo, a| adj
secondary
sed |seð| nf thirst; **tener ~** to be thirsty
seda |'seða| nf silk
sedal |se'ðal| nm fishing line
sedante |se'ðante| nm sedative
sede |'seðe| nf (de gobierno) seat; (de
compañía) headquarters pl; **Santa S~**
Holy See
sedentario, a |seðen'tarjo, a| adj
sedentary
sediento, a |se'ðjento, a| adj thirsty
sedimento |seði'mento| nm sediment
sedoso, a |se'ðoso, a| adj silky, silken
seducción |seðuk'θjon| nf seduction
seducir |seðu'θir| vt to seduce;
(cautivar) to charm, fascinate; (atraer)
to attract; **seductor, a** adj seductive;
charming, fascinating; attractive ♦ nm/f
seducer
segar |se'xar| vt (mies) to reap, cut;
(hierba) to mow, cut
seglar |se'xlar| adj secular, lay
segregación |sexrexa'θjon| nf
segregation. **~ racial** racial segregation
segregar |sexre'xar| vt to segregate,
separate
seguida |se'xiða| nf: **en ~** at once,
right away
seguido, a |se'xiðo, a| adj (continuo)

continuous, unbroken; (recto) straight
♦ adv (directo) straight (on); (después)
after; (AM: a menudo) often; **~s**
consecutive, successive; **5 días ~s** 5
days running, 5 days in a row
seguimiento |sexi'mjento| nm chase,
pursuit; (continuación) continuation
seguir |se'xir| vt to follow; (venir
después) to follow on, come after;
(proseguir) to continue; (perseguir) to
chase, pursue ♦ vi (gen) to follow;
(continuar) to continue, carry o go on;
~se vr to follow; **sigo sin**
comprender I still don't understand;
sigue lloviendo it's still raining
según |se'xun| prep according to
♦ adv: **¿irás?** — ~ are you going? — it
all depends ♦ conj as; **~ caminamos**
while we walk
segundo, a |se'xundo, a| adj second
♦ nm second ♦ nf second meaning; **de**
segunda mano second-hand; **de**
segunda (clase) second class;
segunda enseñanza secondary
education; **segunda (marcha)** (AUT)
second (gear)
seguramente |sexura'mente| adv
surely; (con certeza) for sure, with
certainty
seguridad |sexuri'ðað| nf safety; (del
estado, de casa etc) security;
(certidumbre) certainty; (confianza)
confidence; (estabilidad) stability;
~ social social security
seguro, a |se'xuro, a| adj (cierto) sure,
certain; (fiel) trustworthy; (libre de
peligro) safe; (bien defendido, firme)
secure ♦ adv for sure, certainly ♦ nm
(COM) insurance; **~ contra terceros/a**
todo riesgo third party/
comprehensive insurance; **~s sociales**
social security sg
seis |seis| num six
seísmo |se'ismo| nm tremor,
earthquake
selección |selek'θjon| nf selection;
seleccionar vt to pick, choose, select

selectividad |selektiβi'ðað| (ESP) nf university entrance examination

selecto, a |se'lekto, a| adj select, choice; (escogido) selected

sellar |se'ʎar| vt (documento oficial) to seal; (pasaporte, visado) to stamp

sello |'seʎo| nm stamp; (precinto) seal

selva |'selβa| nf (bosque) forest, woods pl; (jungla) jungle

semáforo |se'maforo| nm (AUTO) traffic lights pl; (FERRO) signal

semana |se'mana| nf week; **entre ~** during the week; **S~ Santa** Holy Week; **semanal** adj weekly; **~rio** nm weekly magazine

---

Semana Santa

In Spain celebrations for **Semana Santa** *(Holy Week) are often spectacular. "Viernes Santo", "Sábado Santo" and "Domingo de Resurrección" (Good Friday, Holy Saturday, Easter Sunday) are all national public holidays, with additional days being given as local holidays. There are fabulous* procesiones *all over the country, with members of "cofradías" (brotherhoods) dressing in hooded robes and parading their "pasos" (religious floats and sculptures) through the streets. Seville has the most famous Holy Week processions.*

---

semblante |sem'blante| nm face; (fig) look

sembrar |sem'brar| vt to sow; (objetos) to sprinkle, scatter about; (noticias etc) to spread

semejante |seme'xante| adj (parecido) similar ♦ nm fellow man, fellow creature; **~s** alike, similar; **nunca hizo cosa ~** he never did any such thing; **semejanza** nf similarity, resemblance

semejar |seme'xar| vi to seem like, resemble; **~se** vr to look alike, be similar

semen |'semen| nm semen

semestral |semes'tral| adj half-yearly, bi-annual

semicírculo |semi'θirkulo| nm semicircle

semidesnatado, a |semiðesna'taðo, a| adj semi-skimmed

semifinal |semifi'nal| nf semifinal

semilla |se'miʎa| nf seed

seminario |semi'narjo| nm (REL) seminary; (ESCOL) seminar

sémola |'semola| nf semolina

Sena |'sena| nm: **el ~** the (river) Seine

senado |se'naðo| nm senate; **senador, a** nm/f senator

sencillez |senθi'ʎeθ| nf simplicity; (de persona) naturalness; **sencillo, a** adj simple; natural, unaffected

senda |'senda| nf path, track

senderismo |sende'rismo| nm hiking

sendero |sen'dero| nm path, track

sendos, as |'sendos, as| adj pl: **les dio ~ golpes** he hit both of them

senil |se'nil| adj senile

seno |'seno| nm (ANAT) bosom, bust; (fig) bosom; **~s** breasts

sensación |sensa'θjon| nf sensation; (sentido) sense; (sentimiento) feeling; **sensacional** adj sensational

sensato, a |sen'sato, a| adj sensible

sensible |sen'sible| adj sensitive; (apreciable) perceptible, appreciable; (pérdida) considerable; **~ro, a** adj sentimental

sensitivo, a |sensi'tiβo, a| adj sense cpd

sensorial |senso'rjal| adj sensory

sensual |sen'swal| adj sensual

sentada |sen'taða| nf sitting; (protesta) sit-in

sentado, a |sen'taðo, a| adj: **estar ~** to sit, be sitting (down); **dar por ~** to take for granted, assume

sentar |sen'tar| vt to sit, seat; (fig) to establish ♦ vi (vestido) to suit; (alimento): **~ bien/mal a** to agree/ disagree with; **~se** vr (persona) to sit, sit down; (los depósitos) to settle

sentencia |sen'tenθja| nf (máxima)
maxim, saying; (JUR) sentence;
sentenciar vt to sentence

sentido, a |sen'tiðo, a| adj (pérdida)
regrettable; (carácter) sensitive ♦ nm
sense; (sentimiento) feeling; (significado)
sense, meaning; (dirección) direction;
mi más ~ pésame my deepest
sympathy; **~ del humor** sense of
humour; **~ único** one-way (street);
tener ~ to make sense

sentimental |sentimen'tal| adj
sentimental; **vida ~** love life

sentimiento |senti'mjento| nm
feeling

sentir |sen'tir| vt to feel; (percibir) to
perceive, sense; (lamentar) to regret,
be sorry for ♦ vi (tener la sensación) to
feel; (lamentarse) to feel sorry ♦ nm
opinion, judgement; **~se bien/mal** to
feel well/ill; **lo siento** I'm sorry

seña |'seɲa| nf sign; (MIL) password; **~s**
nfpl (dirección) address sg; **~s
personales** personal description sg

señal |se'ɲal| nf sign; (síntoma)
symptom; (FERRO, TELEC) signal;
(marca) mark; (COM) deposit; **en ~ de**
as a token of, as a sign of; **~ar** vt to
mark; (indicar) to point out, indicate

señor |se'ɲor| nm (hombre) man;
(caballero) gentleman; (dueño) owner,
master; (trato: antes de nombre propio)
Mr; (: hablando directamente) sir; **muy
~ mío** Dear Sir; **el ~ alcalde/
presidente** the mayor/president

señora |se'ɲora| nf (dama) lady; (trato:
antes de nombre propio) Mrs;
(: hablando directamente) madam;
(esposa) wife; **Nuestra S~** Our Lady

señorita |seɲo'rita| nf (con nombre y/o
apellido) Miss; (mujer joven) young lady

señorito |seɲo'rito| nm young
gentleman; (pey) rich kid

señuelo |se'ɲwelo| nm decoy

sepa etc vb ver **saber**

separación |separa'θjon| nf
separation; (división) division; (hueco)
gap

separar |sepa'rar| vt to separate;
(dividir) to divide; **~se** vr (parte) to
come away; (partes) to come apart;
(persona) to leave, go away;
(matrimonio) to separate;
separatismo nm separatism

sepia |'sepja| nf cuttlefish

septentrional |septentrjo'nal| adj
northern

septiembre |sep'tjembre| nm
September

séptimo, a |'septimo, a| adj, nm
seventh

sepulcral |sepul'kral| adj (fig: silencio,
atmósfera) deadly; **sepulcro** nm tomb,
grave

sepultar |sepul'tar| vt to bury;
sepultura nf (acto) burial; (tumba)
grave, tomb

sequedad |seke'ðað| nf dryness; (fig)
brusqueness, curtness

sequía |se'kia| nf drought

séquito |'sekito| nm (de rey etc)
retinue; (seguidores) followers pl

PALABRA CLAVE

---

ser |ser| vi **1** (descripción) to be; **es
médica/muy alta** she's a doctor/very
tall; **la familia es de Cuzco** his (o her
etc) family is from Cuzco; **soy Ana**
(TELEC) Ana speaking o here

2 (propiedad): **es de Joaquín** it's
Joaquín's, it belongs to Joaquín

3 (horas, fechas, números): **es la una**
it's one o'clock; **son las seis y media**
it's half-past six; **es el 1 de junio** it's
the first of June; **somos/son seis**
there are six of us/them

4 (en oraciones pasivas): **ha sido
descubierto ya** it's already been
discovered

5: **es de esperar que ...** it is to be
hoped o I etc hope that ...

6 (locuciones con sub): **o sea** that is to
say; **sea él sea su hermana** either
him or his sister

7: a no ~ por él ... but for him ...
8: a no ~ que: a no ~ que tenga uno ya unless he's got one already
♦ *nm* being; **~ humano** human being

serenarse [sere'narse] *vr* to calm down

sereno, a [se'reno, a] *adj* (*persona*) calm, unruffled; (*el tiempo*) fine, settled; (*ambiente*) calm, peaceful ♦ *nm* night watchman

serial [ser'jal] *nm* serial

serie ['serje] *nf* series; (*cadena*) sequence, succession; **fuera de ~** out of order; (*fig*) special, out of the ordinary; **fabricación en ~** mass production

seriedad [serje'ðað] *nf* seriousness; (*formalidad*) reliability; **serio, a** *adj* serious; reliable, dependable; grave, serious; **en serio** adv seriously

serigrafía [seriɣra'fia] *nf* silk-screen printing

sermón [ser'mon] *nm* (*REL*) sermon

seropositivo, a [seroposi'tiβo] *adj* HIV positive

serpentear [serpente'ar] *vi* to wriggle; (*camino, río*) to wind, snake

serpentina [serpen'tina] *nf* streamer

serpiente [ser'pjente] *nf* snake; **~ de cascabel** rattlesnake

serranía [serra'nia] *nf* mountainous area

serrar [se'rrar] *vt* = **aserrar**

serrín [se'rrin] *nm* = **aserrín**

serrucho [se'rrutʃo] *nm* saw

servicio [ser'βiθjo] *nm* service; **~s** *nmpl* toilet(s); **~ incluido** service charge included; **~ militar** military service

servidumbre [serβi'ðumbre] *nf* (*sujeción*) servitude; (*criados*) servants *pl*, staff

servil [ser'βil] *adj* servile

servilleta [serβi'ʎeta] *nf* serviette, napkin

servir [ser'βir] *vt* to serve ♦ *vi* to serve;

(*tener utilidad*) to be of use, be useful; **~se** *vr* to serve o help o.s.; **~se de algo** to make use of sth, use sth; **sírvase pasar** please come in

sesenta [se'senta] *num* sixty

sesgo ['sesɣo] *nm* slant; (*fig*) slant, twist

sesión [se'sjon] *nf* (*POL*) session, sitting; (*CINE*) showing

seso ['seso] *nm* brain; **sesudo, a** *adj* sensible, wise

seta ['seta] *nf* mushroom; **~ venenosa** toadstool

setecientos, as [sete'θjentos, as] *adj, num* seven hundred

setenta [se'tenta] *num* seventy

seto ['seto] *nm* hedge

seudónimo [seu'ðonimo] *nm* pseudonym

severidad [seβeri'ðað] *nf* severity; **severo, a** *adj* severe

Sevilla [se'βiʎa] *n* Seville, **sevillano, a** *adj* o from Seville ♦ *nm/f* native o inhabitant of Seville

sexo ['sekso] *nm* sex

sexto, a ['seksto, a] *adj, num* sixth

sexual [sek'swal] *adj* sexual; **vida ~** sex life

si [si] *conj* if; **me pregunto ~** ... I wonder if o whether ...

sí [si] *adv* yes ♦ *nm* consent ♦ *pron* (*uso impersonal*) oneself; (*sg: m*) himself; (*: f*) herself; (*: de cosa*) itself; (*de usted*) yourself; (*pl*) themselves; (*de ustedes*) yourselves; (*recíproco*) each other; **él no quiere pero sí yo** he doesn't want to but I do; **ella ~ vendrá** she will certainly come, she is sure to come; **claro que ~** of course; **creo que ~** I think so

siamés, esa [sja'mes, esa] *adj, nm/f* Siamese

SIDA ['siða] *nm abr* (= *Síndrome de Inmunodeficiencia Adquirida*) AIDS

siderúrgico, a [siðe'rurxico, a] *adj* iron and steel *cpd*

sidra ['siðra] *nf* cider

siembra ['sjembra] nf sowing

siempre ['sjempre] adv always; (todo el tiempo) all the time; ~ que (cada vez) whenever; (dado que) provided.that; como ~ as usual; para ~ for ever

sien [sjen] nf temple

siento etc vb ver **sentar**; **sentir**

sierra ['sjerra] nf (TEC) saw; (cadena de montañas) mountain range

siervo, a ['sjerβo, a] nm/f slave

siesta ['sjesta] nf siesta, nap; echar la ~ to have an afternoon nap o a siesta

siete ['sjete] num seven

sífilis ['sifilis] nf syphilis

sifón [si'fon] nm syphon; **whisky con ~** whisky and soda

sigla ['sixla] nf abbreviation; acronym

siglo ['sixlo] nm century; (fig) age

significación [sixnifika'θjon] nf significance

significado [sixnifi'kaðo] nm (de palabra etc) meaning

significar [sixnifi'kar] vt to mean, signify; (notificar) to make known, express; **significativo, a** adj significant

signo ['sixno] nm sign; ~ de admiración o exclamación exclamation mark; ~ de interrogación question mark

sigo etc vb ver **seguir**

siguiente [si'xjente] adj next, following

siguió etc vb ver **seguir**

sílaba ['silaβa] nf syllable

silbar [sil'βar] vt, vi to whistle; **silbato** [sil'βato] nm whistle; **silbido** nm whistle, whistling

silenciador [silenθja'ðor] nm silencer

silenciar [silen'θjar] vt (persona) to silence; (escándalo) to hush up; **silencio** nm silence, quiet; **silencioso, a** adj silent, quiet

silla ['siʎa] nf (asiento) chair; (tb: ~ de montar) saddle; ~ de ruedas wheelchair

sillón [si'ʎon] nm armchair, easy chair

silueta [si'lweta] nf silhouette; (de edificio) outline; (figura) figure

silvestre [sil'βestre] adj wild

simbólico, a [sim'βoliko, a] adj symbolic(al)

simbolizar [simboli'θar] vt to symbolize

símbolo ['simbolo] nm symbol

simetría [sime'tria] nf symmetry

simiente [si'mjente] nf seed

similar [simi'lar] adj similar

simio ['simjo] nm ape

simpatía [simpa'tia] nf liking; (afecto) affection; (amabilidad) kindness; **simpático, a** adj nice, pleasant; kind

simpatizante [simpati'θante] nm/f sympathizer

simpatizar [simpati'θar] vi: ~ con to get on well with

simple ['simple] adj simple; (elemental) simple, easy; (mero) mere; (puro) pure, sheer ♦ nm/f simpleton; **~za** nf simpleness; (necedad) silly thing; **simplificar** vt to simplify

simposio [sim'posjo] nm symposium

simular [simu'lar] vt to simulate

simultáneo, a [simul'taneo, a] adj simultaneous

sin [sin] prep without; la ropa está ~ lavar the clothes are unwashed; ~ que without; ~ embargo however, still

sinagoga [sina'xoɣa] nf synagogue

sinceridad [sinθeri'ðað] nf sincerity; **sincero, a** adj sincere

sincronizar [sinkroni'θar] vt to synchronize

sindical [sindi'kal] adj union cpd, trade-union cpd; **~ista** adj, nm/f trade unionist

sindicato [sindi'kato] nm (de trabajadores) trade(s) union; (de negociantes) syndicate

síndrome ['sindrome] nm (MED) syndrome; ~ de abstinencia (MED) withdrawal symptoms

sinfín [sin'fin] nm: un ~ de a great

many, no end of

sinfonía [siɱfo'nia] nf symphony

singular [singu'lar] adj singular; (fig) outstanding, exceptional; (raro) peculiar, odd; **~idad** nf singularity, peculiarity; **~izarse** vr to distinguish o.s., stand out

siniestro, a [si'njestro, a] adj sinister ♦ nm (accidente) accident

sinnúmero [si'numero] nm = **sinfín**

sino ['sino] nm fate, destiny ♦ conj (pero) but; (salvo) except, save

sinónimo, a [si'nonimo, a] adj synonymous ♦ nm synonym

síntesis ['sintesis] nf synthesis;
 sintético, a adj synthetic

sintetizar [sinteti'θar] vt to synthesize

sintió vb ver **sentir**

síntoma ['sintoma] nm symptom

sintonía [sinto'nia] nf (RADIO, MUS: de programa) tuning; **sintonizar** vt (RADIO: emisora) to tune (in)

sinvergüenza [simber'ɣwenθa] nm/f rogue, scoundrel; **¡es un ~!** he's got a nerve!

siquiera [si'kjera] conj even if, even though ♦ adv at least; **ni ~** not even

Siria ['sirja] nf Syria

sirviente, a [sir'βjente, a] nm/f servant

sirvo etc vb ver **servir**

sisear [sise'ar] vt, vi to hiss

sistema [sis'tema] nm system;
 (método) method; **sistemático, a** adj systematic

Sistema educativo

The reform of the Spanish **sistema educativo** (education system) begun in the early 90s has replaced the courses EGB, BUP and COU with the following: "Primaria" a compulsory 6 years; "Secundaria" a compulsory 4 years and "Bachillerato" an optional 2-year secondary school course, essential for those wishing to go on to higher education.

---

sitiar [si'tjar] vt to besiege, lay siege to

sitio ['sitjo] nm (lugar) place; (espacio) room, space; (MIL) siege; **~ Web** (INFORM) website

situación [sitwa'θjon] nf situation, position; (estatus) position, standing

situado, a [situ'aðo] adj situated, placed

situar [si'twar] vt to place, put; (edificio) to locate, situate

slip [slip] nm pants pl, briefs pl

smoking ['smokin, es'mokin] (pl **~s**) nm dinner jacket (BRIT), tuxedo (US)

snob [es'nob] = **esnob**

SO abr (= suroeste) SW

sobaco [so'βako] nm armpit

sobar [so'βar] vt (ropa) to rumple; (comida) to play around with

soberanía [soßera'nia] nf sovereignty;
 soberano, a adj sovereign; (fig) supreme ♦ nm/f sovereign

soberbia [so'βerßja] nf pride; haughtiness, arrogance; magnificence

soberbio, a [so'βerßjo, a] adj (orgulloso) proud; (altivo) arrogant; (estupendo) magnificent, superb

sobornar [soßor'nar] vt to bribe;
 soborno nm bribe

sobra ['soßra] nf excess, surplus; **~s** nfpl left-overs, scraps; **de ~** surplus, extra; **tengo de ~** I've more than enough; **~do, a** adj (más que suficiente) more than enough; (superfluo) excessive; **sobrante** adj remaining, extra ♦ nm surplus, remainder

sobrar [so'βrar] vt to exceed, surpass ♦ vi (tener de más) to be more than enough; (quedar) to remain, be left (over)

sobrasada [soßra'saða] nf pork sausage spread

sobre ['soßre] prep (gen) on; (encima) on (top of); (por encima de, arriba de)

over, above; (más que) more than;
(además) in addition to, besides;
(alrededor de) about ♦ nm envelope;
~ **todo** above all

sobrecama |soβre'kama| nf
bedspread

sobrecargar |soβrekar'xar| vt
(camión) to overload; (COM) to
surcharge

sobredosis |soβre'ðosis| nf inv
overdose

sobreentender |soβre(e)nten'der| vt
to deduce, infer; **~se** vr: **se
sobreentiende que ...** it is implied
that ...

sobrehumano, a |soβreu'mano, a|
adj superhuman

sobrellevar |soβreλe'βar| vt to bear,
endure

sobremesa |soβre'mesa| nf: **durante
la ~** after dinner; **ordenador de ~**
desktop computer

sobrenatural |soβrenatu'ral| adj
supernatural

sobrenombre |soβre'nombre| nm
nickname

sobrepasar |soβrepa'sar| vt to exceed,
surpass

sobreponerse |soβrepo'nerse| vr: **~ a**
to overcome

sobresaliente |soβresa'ljente| adj
outstanding, excellent

sobresalir |soβresa'lir| vi to project,
jut out; (fig) to stand out, excel

sobresaltar |soβresal'tar| vt (asustar)
to scare, frighten; (sobrecoger) to
startle; **sobresalto** nm (movimiento)
start; (susto) scare; (turbación) sudden
shock

sobretodo |soβre'toðo| nm overcoat

sobrevenir |soβreβe'nir| vi (ocurrir) to
happen (unexpectedly); (resultar) to
follow, ensue

sobreviviente |soβreβi'βjente| adj
surviving ♦ nm/f survivor

sobrevivir |soβreβi'βir| vi to survive

sobrevolar |soβreβo'lar| vt to fly over

sobriedad |soβrje'ðað| nf sobriety,
soberness; (moderación) moderation,
restraint

sobrino, a |so'βrino, a| nm/f
nephew/niece

sobrio, a |'soβrjo, a| adj sober;
(moderado) moderate, restrained

socarrón, ona |soka'rron, ona| adj
(sarcástico) sarcastic, ironic(al)

socavar |soka'βar| vt (tb fig) to
undermine

socavón |soka'βon| nm (hoyo) hole

sociable |so'θjaβle| adj (persona)
sociable, friendly; (animal) social

social |so'θjal| adj social; (COM)
company cpd

socialdemócrata |soθjalde'mokrata|
nm/f social democrat

socialista |soθja'lista| adj, nm/f
socialist

socializar |soθjali'θar| vt to socialize

sociedad |soθje'ðað| nf society; (COM)
company; **~ anónima** limited
company; **~ de consumo** consumer
society

socio, a |'soθjo, a| nm/f (miembro)
member; (COM) partner

sociología |soθjolo'xia| nf sociology;
sociólogo, a nm/f sociologist

socorrer |soko'rrer| vt to help;
socorrista nm/f first aider; (en piscina,
playa) lifeguard; **socorro** nm (ayuda)
help, aid; (MIL) relief; **¡socorro!** help!

soda |'soða| nf (sosa) soda; (bebida)
soda (water)

sofá |so'fa| nm (pl **~s**) nm sofa, settee; **~-
cama** nm studio couch; sofa bed

sofisticación |sofistika'θjon| nf
sophistication

sofocar |sofo'kar| vt to suffocate;
(apagar) to smother, put out; **~se** vr to
suffocate; (fig) to blush, feel
embarrassed; **sofoco** nm suffocation;
embarrassment

sofreír |sofre'ir| vt (CULIN) to fry lightly

soga |'soxa| nf rope

sois vb ver **ser**

soja ['soxa] *nf* soya

sol [sol] *nm* sun; (*luz*) sunshine, sunlight; **hace ~** it is sunny

solamente [sola'mente] *adv* only, just

solapa [so'lapa] *nf* (*de chaqueta*) lapel; (*de libro*) jacket

solapado, a [sola'paðo, a] *adj* (*intenciones*) underhand; (*gestos, movimientos*) sly

solar [so'lar] *adj* solar, sun *cpd*

solaz [so'laθ] *nm* recreation, relaxation; **~ar** *vt* (*divertir*) to amuse

soldado [sol'daðo] *nm* soldier; **~ raso** private

soldador [solda'ðor] *nm* soldering iron; (*persona*) welder

soldar [sol'dar] *vt* to solder, weld

soleado, a [sole'aðo, a] *adj* sunny

soledad [sole'ðað] *nf* solitude; (*estado infeliz*) loneliness

solemne [so'lemne] *adj* solemn; **solemnidad** *nf* solemnity

soler [so'ler] *vi* to be in the habit of, be accustomed to; **suele salir a las ocho** she usually goes out at 8 o'clock

solfeo [sol'feo] *nm* solfa

solicitar [soliθi'tar] *vt* (*permiso*) to ask for, seek; (*puesto*) to apply for; (*votos*) to canvass for; (*atención*) to attract

solícito, a [so'liθito, a] *adj* (*diligente*) diligent; (*cuidadoso*) careful; **solicitud** *nf* (*calidad*) great care; (*petición*) request; (*a un puesto*) application

solidaridad [soliðari'ðað] *nf* solidarity; **solidario, a** *adj* (*participación*) joint, common; (*compromiso*) mutually binding

solidez [soli'ðeθ] *nf* solidity; **sólido, a** *adj* solid

soliloquio [soli'lokjo] *nm* soliloquy

solista [so'lista] *nm/f* soloist

solitario, a [soli'tarjo, a] *adj* (*persona*) lonely, solitary; (*lugar*) lonely, desolate ♦ *nm/f* (*reclusa*) recluse; (*en la sociedad*) loner ♦ *nm* solitaire

sollozar [soλo'θar] *vi* to sob; **sollozo** *nm* sob

solo, a ['solo, a] *adj* (*único*) single, sole; (*sin compañía*) alone; (*solitario*) lonely; **hay una sola dificultad** there is just one difficulty; **a solas** alone, by oneself

sólo ['solo] *adv* only, just

solomillo [solo'miλo] *nm* sirloin

soltar [sol'tar] *vt* (*dejar ir*) to let go of; (*desprender*) to unfasten, loosen; (*librar*) to release, set free; (*risa etc*) to let out

soltero, a [sol'tero, a] *adj* single, unmarried ♦ *nm/f* bachelor/single woman; **solterón, ona** *nm/f* old bachelor/spinster

soltura [sol'tura] *nf* looseness, slackness; (*de los miembros*) agility, ease of movement; (*en el hablar*) fluency, ease

soluble [so'luβle] *adj* (*QUÍM*) soluble; (*problema*) solvable; **~ en agua** soluble in water

solución [solu'θjon] *nf* solution; **solucionar** *vt* (*problema*) to solve; (*asunto*) to settle, resolve

solventar [solβen'tar] *vt* (*pagar*) to settle, pay; (*resolver*) to resolve;

solvente *adj* (*ECON: empresa, persona*) solvent

sombra ['sombra] *nf* shadow; (*como protección*) shade; **~s** *nfpl* (*oscuridad*) darkness *sg*, shadows; **tener buena/ mala ~** to be lucky/unlucky

sombrero [som'brero] *nm* hat

sombrilla [som'briλa] *nf* parasol, sunshade

sombrío, a [som'brio, a] *adj* (*oscuro*) dark; (*triste*) sombre, sad; (*persona*) gloomy

somero, a [so'mero, a] *adj* superficial

someter [some'ter] *vt* (*país*) to conquer; (*persona*) to subject to one's will; (*informe*) to present, submit; **~se** *vr* to give in, yield, submit; **~ a** to subject to

somier [so'mjer] (*pl* **somiers**) *n* spring mattress

somnífero [som'nifero] *nm* sleeping

pill

somnolencia [somno'lenθja] nf
sleepiness, drowsiness

somos vb ver **ser**

son [son] vb ver **ser** ♦ nm sound; **en
~ de broma** as a joke

sonajero [sona'xero] nm (baby's)
rattle

sonambulismo [sonambu'lismo] nm
sleepwalking; **sonámbulo, a** nm/f
sleepwalker

sonar [so'nar] vt to ring ♦ vi to sound;
(hacer ruido) to make a noise;
(pronunciarse) to be sounded, be
pronounced; (ser conocido) to sound
familiar; (campana) to ring; (reloj) to
strike, chime; **~se** vr: **~se (las
narices)** to blow one's nose; **me
suena ese nombre** that name rings a
bell

sonda ['sonda] nf (NAUT) sounding;
(TEC) bore, drill; (MED) probe

sondear [sonde'ar] vt to sound; to
bore (into), drill; to probe, sound; (fig)
to sound out; **sondeo** nm sounding;
boring, drilling; (fig) poll, enquiry

sonido [so'niðo] nm sound

sonoro, a [so'noro, a] adj sonorous;
(resonante) resonant, resounding

sonreír [sonre'ir] vi to smile; **~se** vr to
smile; **sonriente** adj smiling; **sonrisa**
nf smile

sonrojarse [sonro'xarse] vr to blush,
go red; **sonrojo** nm blush

soñador, a [soɲa'ðor, a] nm/f dreamer

soñar [so'ɲar] vt, vi to dream; **~ con**
to dream about o of

soñoliento, a [soɲo'ljento, a] adj
sleepy, drowsy

sopa ['sopa] nf soup

sopesar [sope'sar] vt to consider,
weigh up

soplar [so'plar] vt (polvo) to blow
away, blow off; (inflar) to blow up;
(vela) to blow out ♦ vi to blow; **soplo**
nm blow, puff; (de viento) puff, gust

soplón, ona [so'plon, ona] (fam),

nm/f (niño) telltale; (de policía) grass
(fam)

sopor [so'por] nm drowsiness

soporífero [sopo'rifero] nm sleeping
pill

soportable [sopor'taßle] adj bearable

soportar [sopor'tar] vt to bear, carry;
(fig) to bear, put up with; **soporte** nm
support; (fig) pillar, support

soprano [so'prano] nf soprano

sorber [sor'ßer] vt (chupar) to sip;
(absorber) to soak up, absorb

sorbete [sor'ßete] nm iced fruit drink

sorbo ['sorßo] nm (trago: grande) gulp,
swallow; (: pequeño) sip

sordera [sor'ðera] nf deafness

sórdido, a ['sorðiðo, a] adj dirty,
squalid

sordo, a ['sorðo, a] adj (persona) deaf
♦ nm/f deaf person; **~mudo, a** adj
deaf and dumb

sorna ['sorna] nf sarcastic tone

soroche [so'rotʃe] (AM) nm mountain
sickness

sorprendente [sorpren'dente] adj
surprising

sorprender [sorpren'der] vt to
surprise; **sorpresa** nf surprise

sortear [sorte'ar] vt to draw lots for;
(rifar) to raffle; (dificultad) to avoid;
sorteo nm (en lotería) draw; (rifa)
raffle

sortija [sor'tixa] nf ring; (rizo) ringlet,
curl

sosegado, a [sose'xaðo, a] adj quiet,
calm

sosegar [sose'var] vt to quieten, calm;
(el ánimo) to reassure ♦ vi to rest;
sosiego nm quiet(ness), calm(ness)

soslayo [sos'lajo]: **de ~** adv obliquely,
sideways

soso, a ['soso, a] adj (CULIN) tasteless;
(aburrido) dull, uninteresting

sospecha [sos'petʃa] nf suspicion;
sospechar vt to suspect;
sospechoso, a adj suspicious;
(testimonio, opinión) suspect ♦ nm/f

suspect
sostén [sos'ten] *nm* (apoyo) support; (sujetador) bra; (alimentación) sustenance, food
sostener [soste'ner] *vt* to support; (mantener) to keep up, maintain; (alimentar) to sustain, keep going; **~se** *vr* to support o.s.; (seguir) to continue, remain; **sostenido, a** *adj* continuous, sustained; (prolongado) prolonged
sotana [so'tana] *nf* (REL) cassock
sótano ['sotano] *nm* basement
soviético, a [so'βjetiko, a] *adj* Soviet; **los ~s** the Soviets
soy *vb ver* **ser**
Sr. *abr* (= Señor) Mr
Sra. *abr* (= Señora) Mrs
S.R.C. *abr* (= se ruega contestación) R.S.V.P.
Sres. *abr* (= Señores) Messrs
Srta. *abr* (= Señorita) Miss
Sta. *abr* (= Santa) St
status ['status, e'status] *nm inv* status
Sto. *abr* (= Santo) St
su [su] *pron* (de él) his; (de ella) her; (de una cosa) its; (de ellos, ellas) their; (de usted, ustedes) your
suave ['swaβe] *adj* gentle; (superficie) smooth; (trabajo) easy; (música, voz) soft, sweet; **suavidad** *nf* gentleness; smoothness; softness, sweetness;
suavizante *nm* (de ropa) softener; (del pelo) conditioner; **suavizar** *vt* to soften; (quitar la aspereza) to smooth (out)
subalimentado, a [suβalimen'taðo, a] *adj* undernourished
subasta [su'βasta] *nf* auction; **subastar** *vt* to auction (off)
subcampeón, a [suβkampe'on, ona] *nm/f* runner-up
subconsciente [suβkon'sθjente] *adj, nm* subconscious
subdesarrollado, a [suβðesarro'λaðo, a] *adj* underdeveloped
subdesarrollo [suβðesa'rroλo] *nm* underdevelopment

subdirector, a [suβðirek'tor, a] *nm/f* assistant director
súbdito, a ['suβðito, a] *nm/f* subject
subestimar [suβesti'mar] *vt* to underestimate, underrate
subida [su'βiða] *nf* (de montaña etc) ascent, climb; (de precio) rise, increase; (pendiente) slope, hill
subir [su'βir] *vt* (objeto) to raise, lift up; (cuesta, calle) to go up; (colina, montaña) to climb; (precio) to raise, put up ♦ *vi* to go up, come up; (a un coche) to get in; (a un autobús, tren o avión) to get on, board; (precio) to rise, go up; (río, marea) to rise; **~se** *vr* to get up, climb
súbito, a ['suβito, a] *adj* (repentino) sudden; (imprevisto) unexpected
subjetivo, a [suβxe'tiβo, a] *adj* subjective
sublevación [suβleβa'θjon] *nf* revolt, rising
sublevar [suβle'βar] *vt* to rouse to revolt; **~se** *vr* to revolt, rise
sublime [su'βlime] *adj* sublime
submarinismo [suβmari'nismo] *nm* scuba diving
submarino, a [suβma'rino, a] *adj* underwater ♦ *nm* submarine
subnormal [suβnor'mal] *adj* subnormal ♦ *nm/f* subnormal person
subordinado, a [suβorði'naðo, a] *adj, nm/f* subordinate
subrayar [suβra'jar] *vt* to underline
subsanar [suβsa'nar] *vt* to rectify
subscribir [suβskri'βir] *vt* = **suscribir**
subsidio [suβ'siðjo] *nm* (ayuda) aid, financial help; (subvención) subsidy, grant; (de enfermedad, paro etc) benefit, allowance
subsistencia [suβsis'tenθja] *nf* subsistence
subsistir [suβsis'tir] *vi* to subsist; (sobrevivir) to survive, endure
subterráneo, a [suβte'rraneo, a] *adj* underground, subterranean ♦ *nm*

underpass, underground passage

subtítulo [suß'titulo] nm (CINE) subtitle

suburbano, a [sußur'ßano, a] adj suburban

suburbio [su'ßurßjo] nm (barrio) slum quarter

subvención [sußßen'θjon] nf (ECON) subsidy, grant; **subvencionar** vt to subsidize

subversión [sußßer'sjon] nf subversion; **subversivo, a** adj subversive

subyugar [sußju'var] vt (país) to subjugate, subdue; (enemigo) to overpower; (voluntad) to dominate

sucedáneo, a [suθe'ðaneo, a] adj substitute ♦ nm substitute (food)

suceder [suθe'ðer] vt, vi to happen; (seguir) to succeed, follow; **lo que sucede es que ...** the fact is that ...;

sucesión nf succession; (serie) sequence, series

sucesivamente [suθesißa'mente] adv: **y así** ~ and so on

sucesivo, a [suθe'sißo, a] adj successive, following; **en lo** ~ in future, from now on

suceso [su'θeso] nm (hecho) event, happening; (incidente) incident

suciedad [suθje'ðað] nf (estado) dirtiness; (mugre) dirt, filth

sucinto, a [su'θinto, a] adj (conciso) succinct, concise

sucio, a [su'θjo, a] adj dirty

suculento, a [suku'lento, a] adj succulent

sucumbir [sukum'bir] vi to succumb

sucursal [sukur'sal] nf branch (office)

sudadera [suða'ðera] nf sweatshirt

Sudáfrica [suð'afrika] nf South Africa

Sudamérica [suða'merika] nf South America; **sudamericano, a** adj, nm/f South American

sudar [su'ðar] vt, vi to sweat

sudeste [su'ðeste] nm south-east

sudoeste [suðo'este] nm south-west

sudor [su'ðor] nm sweat; **~oso, a** adj sweaty, sweating

Suecia ['sweθja] nf Sweden; **sueco, a** adj Swedish ♦ nm/f Swede

suegro, a ['swevro, a] nm/f father-/mother-in-law

suela ['swela] nf sole

sueldo ['sweldo] nm pay, wage(s) (pl)

suele etc vb ver **soler**

suelo ['swelo] nm (tierra) ground; (de casa) floor

suelto, a ['swelto, a] adj loose; (libre) free; (separado) detached; (ágil) quick, agile ♦ nm (loose) change, small change

sueño etc ['sweɲo] vb ver **soñar** ♦ nm sleep; (somnolencia) sleepiness, drowsiness; (lo soñado, fig) dream; **tener** ~ to be sleepy

suero ['swero] nm (MED) serum; (de leche) whey

suerte ['swerte] nf (fortuna) luck; (azar) chance; (destino) fate, destiny; (especie) sort, kind; **tener** ~ to be lucky; **de otra** ~ otherwise, if not; **de** ~ **que** so that, in such a way that

suéter ['sweter] nm sweater

suficiente [sufi'θjente] adj enough, sufficient ♦ nm (ESCOL) pass

sufragio [su'fraxjo] nm (voto) vote; (derecho de voto) suffrage

sufrido, a [su'friðo, a] adj (persona) tough; (paciente) long-suffering, patient

sufrimiento [sufri'mjento] nm (dolor) suffering

sufrir [su'frir] vt (padecer) to suffer; (soportar) to bear, put up with; (apoyar) to hold up, support ♦ vi to suffer

sugerencia [suxe'renθja] nf suggestion

sugerir [suxe'rir] vt to suggest; (sutilmente) to hint

sugestión [suxes'tjon] nf suggestion; (sutil) hint; **sugestionar** vt to influence

sugestivo, a [suxes'tiβo, a] *adj* stimulating; *(fascinante)* fascinating

suicida [sui'θiða] *adj* suicidal ♦ *nm/f* suicidal person; *(muerto)* suicide, person who has committed suicide; **suicidarse** *vr* to commit suicide, kill o.s.; **suicidio** *nm* suicide

Suiza ['swiθa] *nf* Switzerland; **suizo, a** *adj, nm/f* Swiss

sujeción [suxe'θjon] *nf* subjection

sujetador [suxeta'ðor] *nm (sostén)* bra

sujetar [suxe'tar] *vt (fijar)* to fasten; *(detener)* to hold down; **~se** *vr* to subject o.s.; **sujeto, a** *adj* fastened, secure ♦ *nm* subject; *(individuo)* individual; **sujeto a** subject to

suma ['suma] *nf (cantidad)* total, sum; *(de dinero)* sum; *(acto)* adding (up), addition; **en ~** in short

sumamente [suma'mente] *adv* extremely, exceedingly

sumar [su'mar] *vt* to add (up) ♦ *vi* to add up

sumario, a [su'marjo, a] *adj* brief, concise ♦ *nm* summary

sumergir [sumer'xir] *vt* to submerge; *(hundir)* to sink

suministrar [sumini'strar] *vt* to supply, provide; **suministro** *nm* supply; *(acto)* supplying, providing

sumir [su'mir] *vt* to sink, submerge; *(fig)* to plunge

sumisión [sumi'sjon] *nf (acto)* submission; *(calidad)* submissiveness, docility; **sumiso, a** *adj* submissive, docile

sumo, a [su'mo, a] *adj* great, extreme; *(autoridad)* highest, supreme

suntuoso, a [sun'twoso, a] *adj* sumptuous, magnificent

supe *etc vb ver* **saber**

supeditar [supeði'tar] *vt*: **~ algo a algo** to subordinate sth to sth

super... [super] *prefijo* super..., over...; **~bueno** *adj* great, fantastic

súper ['super] *nf (gasolina)* three-star (petrol)

superar [supe'rar] *vt (sobreponerse a)* to overcome; *(rebasar)* to surpass, do better than; *(pasar)* to go beyond; **~se** *vr* to excel o.s.

superávit [supe'raβit] *nm inv* surplus

superficial [superfi'θjal] *adj* superficial; *(medida)* surface *cpd*, of the surface

superficie [super'fiθje] *nf* surface; *(área)* area

superfluo, a [su'perflwo, a] *adj* superfluous

superior [supe'rjor] *adj (piso, clase)* upper; *(temperatura, número, nivel)* higher; *(mejor: calidad, producto)* superior, better ♦ *nm/f* superior; **~idad** *nf* superiority

supermercado [supermer'kaðo] *nm* supermarket

superponer [superpo'ner] *vt* to superimpose

supersónico, a [super'soniko, a] *adj* supersonic

superstición [supersti'θjon] *nf* superstition; **supersticioso, a** *adj* superstitious

supervisar [superβi'sar] *vt* to supervise

supervivencia [superβi'βenθja] *nf* survival

superviviente [superβi'βjente] *adj* surviving

supiera *etc vb ver* **saber**

suplantar [suplan'tar] *vt* to supplant

suplemento [suple'mento] *nm* supplement

suplente [su'plente] *adj, nm/f* substitute

supletorio, a [suple'torjo, a] *adj* supplementary ♦ *nm* supplement; **teléfono ~** extension

súplica [su'plika] *nf* request; *(JUR)* petition

suplicar [supli'kar] *vt (cosa)* to beg (for), plead for; *(persona)* to beg, plead with

suplicio [su'pliθjo] *nm* torture

suplir [su'plir] vt (compensar) to make good, make up for; (reemplazar) to replace, substitute ♦ vi: ~ a to take the place of, substitute for

supo etc vb ver **saber**

suponer [supo'ner] vt to suppose; **suposición** nf supposition

supremacía [suprema'θia] nf supremacy

supremo, a [su'premo, a] adj supreme

supresión [supre'sjon] nf suppression; (de derecho) abolition; (de palabra etc) deletion; (de restricción) cancellation, lifting

suprimir [supri'mir] vt to suppress; (derecho, costumbre) to abolish; (palabra etc) to delete; (restricción) to cancel, lift

supuesto, a [su'pwesto, a] pp de **suponer** ♦ adj (hipotético) supposed ♦ nm assumption, hypothesis; ~ **que** since; **por** ~ of course

sur [sur] nm south

surcar [sur'kar] vt to plough; **surco** nm (en metal, disco) groove; (AGR) furrow

surgir [sur'xir] vi to arise, emerge; (dificultad) to come up, crop up

suroeste [suro'este] nm south-west

surtido, a [sur'tiðo, a] adj mixed, assorted ♦ nm (selección) selection, assortment; (abastecimiento) supply, stock; ~**r** nm (also: ~**r de gasolina**) petrol pump (BRIT), gas pump (US)

surtir [sur'tir] vt to supply, provide ♦ vi to spout, spurt

susceptible [susθep'tiβle] adj susceptible; (sensible) sensitive; ~ **de** capable of

suscitar [susθi'tar] vt to cause, provoke; (interés, sospechas) to arouse

suscribir [suskri'βir] vt (firmar) to sign; (respaldar) to subscribe to, endorse; ~**se** to subscribe; **suscripción** nf subscription

susodicho, a [suso'ðitʃo, a] adj above-mentioned

suspender [suspen'der] vt (objeto) to hang (up), suspend; (trabajo) to stop, suspend; (ESCOL) to fail; (interrumpir) to adjourn; (atrasar) to postpone; **suspensión** nf suspension; (fig) stoppage, suspension

suspenso, a [sus'penso, a] adj hanging, suspended; (ESCOL) failed ♦ nm (ESCOL) fail; **quedar** o **estar en** ~ to be pending

suspicacia [suspi'kaθja] nf suspicion, mistrust; **suspicaz** adj suspicious, distrustful

suspirar [suspi'rar] vi to sigh; **suspiro** nm sigh

sustancia [sus'tanθja] nf substance

sustentar [susten'tar] vt (alimentar) to sustain, nourish; (objeto) to hold up, support; (idea, teoría) to maintain, uphold; (fig) to sustain, keep going; **sustento** nm support; (alimento) sustenance, food

sustituir [sustitu'ir] vt to substitute, replace; **sustituto, a** nm/f substitute, replacement

susto ['susto] nm fright, scare

sustraer [sustra'er] vt to remove, take away; (MAT) to subtract

susurrar [susu'rrar] vi to whisper; **susurro** nm whisper

sutil [su'til] adj (aroma, diferencia) subtle; (tenue) thin; (inteligencia, persona) sharp; ~**eza** nf subtlety; thinness

suyo, a ['sujo, a] (con artículo o después del verbo **ser**) adj (de él) his; (de ella) hers; (de ellos, ellas) theirs; (de Ud, Uds) yours; **un amigo** ~ a friend of his (o hers o theirs o yours)

T, t

tabacalera [taβaka'lera] nf: **T~** Spanish state tobacco monopoly

tabaco [ta'βako] nm tobacco; (fam)

cigarettes *pl*

taberna [ta'βerna] *nf* bar, pub (BRIT)

tabique [ta'βike] *nm* partition (wall)

tabla ['taβla] *nf* (de madera) plank; (estante) shelf; (de vestido) pleat; (ARTE) panel; ~s *nfpl*: **estar** o **quedar en ~s** to draw; **~do** *nm* (plataforma) platform; (TEATRO) stage

tablao [ta'βlao] *nm* (tb: ~ *flamenco*) flamenco show

tablero [ta'βlero] *nm* (de madera) plank, board; (de ajedrez, damas) board; ~ **de anuncios** notice (BRIT) o bulletin (US)

tableta [ta'βleta] *nf* (MED) tablet; (de chocolate) bar

tablón [ta'βlon] *nm* (de suelo) plank; (de techo) beam; ~ **de anuncios** notice board (BRIT), bulletin board (US)

tabú [ta'βu] *nm* taboo

tabular [taβu'lar] *vt* to tabulate

taburete [taβu'rete] *nm* stool

tacaño, a [ta'kaɲo, a] *adj* mean

tacha ['tatʃa] *nf* flaw; (TEC) stud; **tachar** *vt* (borrar) to cross out; **tachar de** to accuse of

tácito, a ['taθito, a] *adj* tacit

taciturno, a [taθi'turno, a] *adj* silent

taco ['tako] *nm* (BILLAR) cue; (libro de billetes) book; (AM: de zapato) heel; (tarugo) peg; (palabrota) swear word

tacón [ta'kon] *nm* heel; **de ~ alto** high-heeled; **taconeo** [ta'koneo] *nm* (heel) stamping

táctica ['taktika] *nf* tactics *pl*

táctico, a [ta'ktiko, a] *adj* tactical

tacto ['takto] *nm* touch; (fig) tact

taimado, a [tai'maðo, a] *adj* (astuto) sly

tajada [ta'xaða] *nf* slice

tajante [ta'xante] *adj* sharp

tajo ['taxo] *nm* (corte) cut; (GEO) cleft

tal [tal] *adj* such; ~ **vez** perhaps ♦ *pron* (persona) someone, such a one; (cosa) something, such a thing; ~ **como** such as; ~ **para cual** (dos iguales) two of a kind ♦ *adv*: ~ **como** (igual) just as; ~

cual (como es) just as it is; ¿**qué ~**? how are things?; ¿**qué ~ te gusta**? how do you like it? ♦ *conj*: **con ~ de que** provided that

taladrar [tala'ðrar] *vt* to drill; **taladro** *nm* drill

talante [ta'lante] *nm* (humor) mood; (voluntad) will, willingness

talar [ta'lar] *vt* to fell, cut down; (devastar) to devastate

talco ['talko] *nm* (polvos) talcum powder

talego [ta'levo] *nm* sack

talento [ta'lento] *nm* talent; (capacidad) ability

TALGO ['talvo] (ESP) *nm abr* (= *tren articulado ligero Goicoechea-Oriol*) ≈ HST (BRIT)

talismán [talis'man] *nm* talisman

talla ['taʎa] *nf* (estatura, fig, MED) height, stature; (palo) measuring rod; (ARTE) carving; (medida) size

tallado, a [ta'ʎaðo, a] *adj* carved ♦ *nm* carving

tallar [ta'ʎar] *vt* (madera) to carve; (metal etc) to engrave; (medir) to measure

tallarines [taʎa'rines] *nmpl* noodles

talle ['taʎe] *nm* (ANAT) waist; (fig) appearance

taller [ta'ʎer] *nm* (TEC) workshop; (de artista) studio

tallo ['taʎo] *nm* (de planta) stem; (de hierba) blade; (brote) shoot

talón [ta'lon] *nm* (ANAT) heel; (COM) counterfoil; (cheque) cheque (BRIT), check (US)

talonario [talo'narjo] *nm* (de cheques) chequebook (BRIT), checkbook (US); (de recibos) receipt book

tamaño, a [ta'maɲo, a] *adj* (tan grande) such a big; (tan pequeño) such a small ♦ *nm* size; **de ~ natural** full-size

tamarindo [tama'rindo] *nm* tamarind

tambalearse [tambale'arse] *vr* (persona) to stagger; (vehículo) to sway

también [tam'bjen] *adv* (*igualmente*) also, too, as well; (*además*) besides

tambor [tam'bor] *nm* drum; (*ANAT*) eardrum; ~ **del freno** brake drum

tamiz [ta'miθ] *nm* sieve; **~ar** *vt* to sieve

tampoco [tam'poko] *adv* nor, neither; **yo ~ lo compré** I didn't buy it either

tampón [tam'pon] *nm* tampon

tan [tan] *adv* so; **~ es así que ...** so much so that ....

tanda ['tanda] *nf* (*gen*) series; (*turno*) shift

tangente [tan'xente] *nf* tangent

Tánger [tanxer] *n* Tangier(s)

tangible [tan'xiβle] *adj* tangible

tanque ['tanke] *nm* (*cisterna, MIL*) tank; (*AUTO*) tanker

tantear [tante'ar] *vt* (*calcular*) to reckon (up); (*medir*) to take the measure of; (*probar*) to test, try out; (*tomar la medida: persona*) to take the measurements of; (*situación*) to weigh up; (*persona: opinión*) to sound out ♦ *vi* (*DEPORTE*) to score; **tanteo** [tan'teo] *nm* (*cálculo*) (rough) calculation; (*prueba*) test, trial; (*DEPORTE*) scoring

tanto, a ['tanto, a] *adj* (*cantidad*) so much, as much; **~s** so many, as many; **20 y ~s** 20-odd ♦ *adv* (*cantidad*) so much, as much; (*tiempo*) so long, as long ♦ *conj*: **en ~ que** while; **hasta ~ (que)** until such time as ♦ *pron*: **cado uno paga** ~ each one pays so much; **~ tú como yo** both you and I; **~ como eso** as much as that; **~ más ... cuanto que** all the more ... because; **~ mejor/peor** so much the better/the worse; **~ si viene como si va** whether he comes or whether he goes; **~ es así que** so much so that; **por o por lo** ~ therefore; **me he vuelto ronco de o con** ~ **hablar** I have become hoarse with so much

talking; **a ~s de agosto** on such and such a day in August

tapa ['tapa] *nf* (*de caja, olla*) lid; (*de botella*) top; (*de libro*) cover; (*comida*) snack

tapadera [tapa'ðera] *nf* lid, cover

tapar [ta'par] *vt* (*cubrir*) to cover; (*envolver*) to wrap o cover up; (*la vista*) to obstruct; (*persona, falta*) to conceal; (*AM*) to fill; **~se** *vr* to wrap o.s. up

taparrabo [tapa'rraβo] *nm* loincloth

tapete [ta'pete] *nm* table cover

tapia ['tapja] *nf* (garden) wall; **tapiar** *vt* to wall in

tapicería [tapiθe'ria] *nf* tapestry; (*para muebles*) upholstery; (*tienda*) upholsterer's (shop)

tapiz [ta'piθ] *nm* (*alfombra*) carpet; (*tela tejida*) tapestry; **~ar** *vt* (*muebles*) to upholster

tapón [ta'pon] *nm* (*de botella*) top; (*de lavabo*) plug; **~ de rosca** screw-top

taquigrafía [takixra'fia] *nf* shorthand; **taquígrafo, a** *nm/f* shorthand writer, stenographer

taquilla [ta'kiʎa] *nf* (*donde se compra*) booking office; (*suma recogida*) takings *pl*; (*casillero*) **taquillero, a** *adj*: **función taquillera** box office success ♦ *nm/f* ticket clerk

tara ['tara] *nf* (*defecto*) defect; (*COM*) tare

tarántula [ta'rantula] *nf* tarantula

tararear [tarare'ar] *vi* to hum

tardar [tar'ðar] *vi* (*tomar tiempo*) to take a long time; (*llegar tarde*) to be late; (*demorar*) to delay; **¿tarda mucho el tren?** does the train take (very) long?; **a más** ~ at the latest; **no tardes en venir** come soon

tarde ['tarðe] *adv* late ♦ *nf* (*de día*) afternoon; (*al anochecer*) evening; **de ~ en ~** from time to time; **¡buenas ~s!** good afternoon!; **a o por la ~** in the afternoon, in the evening

tardío, a [tar'ðio, a] *adj* (*retrasado*) late; (*lento*) slow (to arrive)

tarea [ta'rea] *nf* task; (*faena*) chore; (*ESCOL*) homework

tarifa [ta'rifa] *nf* (*lista de precios*) price list; (*precio*) tariff

tarima [ta'rima] *nf* (*plataforma*) platform

tarjeta [tar'xeta] *nf* card; ~ **postal/de crédito/de Navidad** postcard/credit card/Christmas card

tarro ['tarro] *nm* jar, pot

tarta ['tarta] *nf* (*pastel*) cake; (*de base dura*) tart

tartamudear [tartamuðe'ar] *vi* to stammer; **tartamudo, a** *adj* stammering ♦ *nm/f* stammerer

tártaro, a ['tartaro, a] *adj*: **salsa tártara** tartar(e) sauce

tasa ['tasa] *nf* (*precio*) (fixed) price, rate; (*valoración*) valuation; (*medida, norma*) measure, standard; ~ **de cambio/interés** exchange/interest rate; ~**s universitarias** university fees; ~**ción** *nf* valuation; ~**dor, a** *nm/f* valuer

tasar [ta'sar] *vt* (*arreglar el precio*) to fix a price for; (*valorar*) to value, assess

tasca ['taska] *nf* (*fam*) pub

tatarabuelo, a [tatara'ßwelo, a] *nm/f* great-great-grandfather/mother

tatuaje [ta'twaxe] *nm* (*dibujo*) tattoo; (*acto*) tattooing

tatuar [ta'twar] *vt* to tattoo

taurino, a [tau'rino, a] *adj* bullfighting *cpd*

Tauro ['tauro] *nm* Taurus

tauromaquia [tauro'makja] *nf* tauromachy, (art of) bullfighting

taxi ['taksi] *nm* taxi

taxista [tak'sista] *nm/f* taxi driver

taza ['taθa] *nf* cup; (*de retrete*) bowl; ~ **para café** coffee cup; **tazón** *nm* (*taza grande*) mug, large cup; (*de fuente*) basin

te [te] *pron* (*complemento de objeto*) you; (*complemento indirecto*) (to) you; (*reflexivo*) (to) yourself; ¿~ **duele mucho el brazo?** does your arm hurt

a lot?; ~ **equivocas** you're wrong; ¡**cálma**~! calm down!

té [te] *nm* tea

tea ['tea] *nf* torch

teatral [tea'tral] *adj* theatre *cpd*; (*fig*) theatrical

teatro [te'atro] *nm* theatre; (*LITERATURA*) plays *pl*, drama

tebeo [te'ßeo] *nm* comic

techo ['tetʃo] *nm* (*externo*) roof; (*interno*) ceiling; ~ **corredizo** sunroof

tecla ['tekla] *nf* key; ~**do** *nm* keyboard; **teclear** *vi* (*MUS*) to strum; (*con los dedos*) to tap ♦ *vt* (*INFORM*) to key in

técnica ['teknika] *nf* technique; (*tecnología*) technology; *ver tb* **técnico**

técnico, a ['tekniko, a] *adj* technical ♦ *nm/f* technician; (*experto*) expert

tecnología [teknolo'xia] *nf* technology; **tecnológico, a** *adj* technological

tedio ['teðjo] *nm* boredom, tedium; ~**so, a** *adj* boring, tedious

teja ['texa] *nf* tile; (*BOT*) lime (tree); ~**do** *nm* (tiled) roof

tejemaneje [texema'nexe] *nm* (*lío*) fuss; (*intriga*) intrigue

tejer [te'xer] *vt* to weave; (*hacer punto*) to knit; (*fig*) to fabricate; **tejido** *nm* (*tela*) material, fabric; (*telaraña*) web; (*ANAT*) tissue

tel [tel] *abr* (= *teléfono*) tel

tela ['tela] *nf* (*tejido*) material; (*telaraña*) web; (*en líquido*) skin; **telar** *nm* (*máquina*) loom

telaraña [tela'raɲa] *nf* cobweb

tele ['tele] (*fam*) *nf* telly (*BRIT*), tube (*US*)

tele... ['tele] *pref* tele...; ~**comunicación** *nf* telecommunication; ~**control** *nm* remote control; ~**diario** *nm* television news; ~**difusión** *nf* (television) broadcast; ~**dirigido, a** *adj* remote-controlled

teléf *abr* (= *teléfono*) tel

teleférico [tele'feriko] *nm* (*de esquí*)

ski-lift

telefonear [telefone'ar] vi to telephone

telefónico, a [tele'foniko, a] adj telephone cpd

telefonillo [telefo'niʎo] nm (de puerta) intercom

telefonista [telefo'nista] nm/f telephonist

teléfono [te'lefono] nm (tele)phone; **estar hablando al ~** to be on the phone; **llamar a uno por ~** to ring sb (up) o phone sb (up); **~ móvil** car phone; **~ portátil** mobile phone

telegrafía [teleɣra'fia] nf telegraphy

telégrafo [te'leɣrafo] nm telegraph

telegrama [tele'ɣrama] nm telegram

tele: ~impresor nm teleprinter (BRIT), teletype (US); **~novela** nf soap (opera); **~objetivo** nm telephoto lens; **~patía** nf telepathy; **~pático, a** adj telepathic; **~scópico, a** adj telescopic; **~scopio** nm telescope; **~silla** nm chairlift; **~spectador, a** nm/f viewer; **~squí** nm ski-lift; **~tarjeta** nf phonecard; **~tipo** nm teletype; **~ventas** nfpl telesales

televidente [teleβi'ðente] nm/f viewer

televisar [teleβi'sar] vt to televise

televisión [teleβi'sjon] nf television; **~ digital** digital television

televisor [teleβi'sor] nm television set

télex ['teleks] nm inv telex

telón [te'lon] nm curtain; **~ de acero** (POL) iron curtain; **~ de fondo** backcloth, background

tema ['tema] nm (asunto) subject, topic; (MUS) theme; **temática** nf (social, histórica, artística) range of topics; **temático, a** adj thematic

temblar [tem'blar] vi to shake, tremble; (de frío) to shiver; **temblón, ona** adj shaking; **temblor** nm trembling; (de tierra) earthquake; **tembloroso, a** adj trembling

temer [te'mer] vt to fear ♦ vi to be afraid; **temo que llegue tarde** I am

afraid he may be late

temerario, a [teme'rarjo, a] adj (descuidado) reckless; (irreflexivo) hasty; **temeridad** nf (imprudencia) rashness; (audacia) boldness

temeroso, a [teme'roso, a] adj (miedoso) fearful; (que inspira temor) frightful

temible [te'miβle] adj fearsome

temor [te'mor] nm (miedo) fear; (duda) suspicion

témpano ['tempano] nm: **~ de hielo** ice-floe

temperamento [tempera'mento] nm temperament

temperatura [tempera'tura] nf temperature

tempestad [tempes'taθ] nf storm; **tempestuoso, a** adj stormy

templado, a [tem'plaðo, a] adj (moderado) moderate; (frugal) frugal; (agua) lukewarm; (clima) mild; (MUS) well-tuned; **templanza** nf moderation; mildness

templar [tem'plar] vt (moderar) to moderate; (furia) to restrain; (calor) to reduce; (afinar) to tune (up); (acero) to temper; (tuerca) to tighten up; **temple** nm (ajuste) tempering; (afinación) tuning; (pintura) tempera

templo ['templo] nm (iglesia) church; (pagano etc) temple

temporada [tempo'raða] nf time, period; (estación) season

temporal [tempo'ral] adj (no permanente) temporary ♦ nm storm

temprano, a [tem'prano, a] adj (BOT) early; (persona) early-rising

temprano, a [tem'prano, a] adj early; (demasiado pronto) too soon, too early

ten vb ver **tener**

tenaces [te'naθes] adj pl ver **tenaz**

tenacidad [tenaθi'ðað] nf tenacity; (dureza) toughness; (terquedad) stubbornness

tenacillas [tena'θiʎas] nfpl tongs; (para el pelo) curling tongs (BRIT) o iron sg (US); (MED) forceps

tenaz [te'naθ] adj (material) tough; (persona) tenacious; (creencia, resistencia) stubborn

tenaza(s) [te'naθa(s)] nf(pl) (MED) forceps; (TEC) pliers; (ZOOL) pincers

tendedero [tende'ðero] nm (para ropa) drying place; (cuerda) clothes line

tendencia [ten'denθja] nf tendency; **tener ~ a** to tend to, have a tendency to; **tendencioso, a** adj tendentious

tender [ten'der] vt (extender) to spread out; (colgar) to hang out; (vía férrea, cable) to lay; (estirar) to stretch ♦ vi: **~ a** to tend to, have a tendency towards; **~se** vr to lie down; **~ la cama/la mesa** (AM) to make the bed/lay (BRIT) o set (US) the table

tenderete [tende'rete] nm (puesto) stall; (exposición) display of goods

tendero, a [ten'dero, a] nm/f shopkeeper

tendido, a [ten'diðo, a] adj (acostado) lying down, flat; (colgado) hanging ♦ nm (TAUR) front rows of seats; **a galope ~** flat out

tendón [ten'don] nm tendon

tendré etc vb ver **tener**

tenebroso, a [tene'βroso, a] adj (oscuro) dark; (fig) gloomy

tenedor [tene'ðor] nm (CULIN) fork; **~ de libros** book-keeper

tenencia [te'nenθja] nf (de casa) tenancy; (de oficio) tenure; (de propiedad) possession

---

PALABRA CLAVE

tener [te'ner] vt 1 (poseer, gen) to have; (en la mano) to hold; **¿tienes un boli?** have you got a pen?; **va a ~ un niño** she's going to have a baby; **¡ten** (o **tenga**)!, **¡aquí tienes** (o **tiene**)! here you are!

2 (edad, medidas) to be; **tiene 7 años** she's 7 (years old); **tiene 15 cm de largo** it's 15 cm long; ver **calor; hambre** etc

3 (considerar): **lo tengo por brillante** I consider him to be brilliant; **~ en mucho a uno** to think very highly of sb

4 (+ pp: = pretérito): **tengo terminada ya la mitad del trabajo** I've done half the work already

5: **~ que hacer algo** to have to do sth; **tengo que acabar este trabajo hoy** I have to finish this job today

6: **¿qué tienes, estás enfermo?** what's the matter with you, are you ill?

♦ **~se** vr 1: **~se en pie** to stand up

2: **~se por** to think o.s.; **se tiene por muy listo** he thinks himself very clever

---

tengo etc vb ver **tener**

tenia ['tenja] nf tapeworm

teniente [te'njente] nm (rango) lieutenant; (ayudante) deputy

tenis ['tenis] nm tennis; **~ de mesa** table tennis; **~ta** nm/f tennis player

tenor [te'nor] nm (sentido) meaning; (MUS) tenor; **a ~ de** on the lines of

tensar [ten'sar] vt to tighten; (arco) to draw

tensión [ten'sjon] nf tension; (TEC) stress; (MED): **~ arterial** blood pressure; **tener la ~ alta** to have high blood pressure

tenso, a ['tenso, a] adj tense

tentación [tenta'θjon] nf temptation

tentáculo [ten'takulo] nm tentacle

tentador, a [tenta'ðor, a] adj tempting

tentar [ten'tar] vt (seducir) to tempt; (atraer) to attract; **tentativa** nf attempt; **tentativa de asesinato** attempted murder

tentempié [tentem'pje] nm snack

tenue ['tenwe] adj (delgado) thin, slender; (neblina) light; (lazo, vínculo) slight

teñir [te'ɲir] vt to dye; (fig) to tinge; **~se** vr to dye; **~se el pelo** to dye one's hair

teología [teolo'xia] nf theology

teoría |teo'ria| nf theory; **en ~** in theory; **teóricamente** adv theoretically; **teórico, a** adj theoretic(al) ♦ nm/f theoretician, theorist; **teorizar** vi to theorize

terapéutico, a |tera'peutiko, a| adj therapeutic

terapia |te'rapja| nf therapy

tercer |ter'θer| adj ver **tercero**

tercermundista |terθermun'dista| adj Third World cpd

tercero, a |ter'θero, a| adj (delante de nmsg: **tercer**) third ♦ nm (JUR) third party

terceto |ter'θeto| nm trio

terciar |ter'θjar| vi (participar) to take part; (hacer de árbitro) to mediate; **~se** vr to come up; **~io, a** adj tertiary

tercio |'terθjo| nm third

terciopelo |terθjo'pelo| nm velvet

terco, a |'terko, a| adj obstinate

tergal ® |ter'xal| nm type of polyester

tergiversar |terxiβer'sar| vt to distort

termal |ter'mal| adj thermal

termas |'termas| nfpl hot springs

térmico, a |'termiko, a| adj thermal

terminación |termina'θjon| nf (final) end; (conclusión) conclusion, ending

terminal |termi'nal| adj, nm, nf terminal

terminante |termi'nante| adj (final) final, definitive; (tajante) categorical; **~mente** adv: **~mente** prohibido strictly forbidden

terminar |termi'nar| vt (completar) to complete, finish; (concluir) to end ♦ vi (llegar a su fin) to end; (parar) to stop; (acabar) to finish; **~se** vr to come to an end; **~ por hacer algo** to end up (by) doing sth

término |'termino| nm end, conclusion; (parada) terminus; (límite) boundary; **~ medio** average; (fig) middle way; **en último ~** (a fin de cuentas) in the last analysis; (como último recurso) as a last resort

terminología |terminolo'xia| nf terminology

termodinámico, a |termoði'namiko, a| adj thermodynamic

termómetro |ter'mometro| nm thermometer

termonuclear |termonukle'ar| adj thermonuclear

termo(s) ® |'termo(s)| nm Thermos ® (flask)

termostato |termo'stato| nm thermostat

ternero, a |ter'nero, a| nm/f (animal) calf ♦ nf (carne) veal

ternura |ter'nura| nf (trato) tenderness; (palabra) endearment; (cariño) fondness

terquedad |terke'ðað| nf obstinacy

terrado |te'rraðo| nm terrace

terraplén |terra'plen| nm embankment

terrateniente |terrate'njente| nm/f landowner

terraza |te'rraθa| nf (balcón) balcony; (tejado) (flat) roof; (AGR) terrace

terremoto |terre'moto| nm earthquake

terrenal |terre'nal| adj earthly

terreno |te'rreno| nm (tierra) land; (parcela) plot; (suelo) soil; (fig) field; **un ~** a piece of land

terrestre |te'rrestre| adj terrestrial; (ruta) land cpd

terrible |te'rriβle| adj terrible, awful

territorio |terri'torjo| nm territory

terrón |te'rron| nm (de azúcar) lump; (de tierra) clod, lump

terror |te'rror| nm terror; **~ífico, a** adj terrifying; **~ista** adj, nm/f terrorist

terso, a |'terso, a| adj (liso) smooth; (pulido) polished; **tersura** nf smoothness

tertulia |ter'tulja| nf (reunión informal) social gathering; (grupo) group, circle

tesis |'tesis| nf inv thesis

tesón |te'son| nm (firmeza) firmness; (tenacidad) tenacity

tesorero, a |teso'rero, a| nm/f

treasurer

tesoro |te'soro| nm treasure; (COM, POL) treasury

testaferro |testa'ferro| nm figurehead

testamentario, a |testamen'tarjo, a| adj testamentary ♦ nm/f executor/ executrix

testamento |testa'mento| nm will

testar |tes'tar| vi to make a will

testarudo, a |testa'ruðo, a| adj stubborn

testículo |tes'tikulo| nm testicle

testificar |testifi'kar| vt to testify; (fig) to attest ♦ vi to give evidence

testigo |tes'tixo| nm/f witness; **~ de cargo/descargo** witness for the prosecution/defence; **~ ocular** eye witness

testimoniar |testimo'njar| vt to testify to; (fig) to show; **testimonio** nm testimony

teta |'teta| nf (de biberón) teat; (ANAT: fam) breast

tétanos |'tetanos| nm tetanus

tetera |te'tera| nf teapot

tétrico, a |'tetriko, a| adj gloomy, dismal

textil |teks'til| adj textile

texto |'teksto| nm text; **textual** adj textual

textura |teks'tura| nf (de tejido) texture

tez |teθ| nf (cutis) complexion

ti |ti| pron you; (reflexivo) yourself

tía |'tia| nf (pariente) aunt; (fam) chick, bird

tibieza |ti'βjeθa| nf (temperatura) tepidness; (actitud) coolness; **tibio, a** adj lukewarm

tiburón |tiβu'ron| nm shark

tic |tik| nm (ruido) click; (de reloj) tick; (MED): **~ nervioso** nervous tic

tictac |tik'tak| nm (de reloj) tick tock

tiempo |'tjempo| nm time; (época, período) age, period; (METEOROLOGÍA) weather; (LING) tense; (DEPORTE) half; **a ~** in time; **a un** o **al mismo ~** at the same time; **al poco ~** very soon

(after); **se quedó poco ~** he didn't stay very long; **hace poco ~** not long ago; **mucho ~** a long time; **de ~ en ~** from time to time; **hace buen/mal ~** the weather is fine/bad; **estar a ~** to be in time; **hace ~** some time ago; **hacer ~** to while away the time; **motor de 2 ~s** two-stroke engine; **primer ~** first half

tienda |'tjenda| nf shop, store; **~ (de campaña)** tent; **~ de alimentación** o **comestibles** grocer's (BRIT), grocery store (US)

tienes etc vb ver **tener**

tienta etc |'tjenta| vb ver **tentar** ♦ nf: **andar a ~s** to grope one's way along

tiento |'tjento| vb ver **tentar** ♦ nm (tacto) touch; (precaución) wariness

tierno, a |'tjerno, a| adj (blando) tender; (fresco) fresh; (amable) sweet

tierra |'tjerra| nf earth; (suelo) soil; (mundo) earth, world; (país) country, land; **~ adentro** inland

tieso, a |'tjeso, a| adj (rígido) rigid; (duro) stiff; (fam: orgulloso) conceited

tiesto |'tjesto| nm flowerpot

tifoidea |tifoi'ðea| nf typhoid

tifón |ti'fon| nm typhoon

tifus |'tifus| nm typhus

tigre |'tixre| nm tiger

tijera |ti'xera| nf scissors pl; (ZOOL) claw; **~s** nfpl scissors; (para plantas) shears

tijeretear |tixerete'ar| vt to snip

tila |'tila| nf lime blossom tea

tildar |til'dar| vt: **~ de** to brand as

tilde |'tilde| nf (TIP) tilde

tilín |ti'lin| nm tinkle

tilo |'tilo| nm lime tree

timar |ti'mar| vt (estafar) to swindle

timbal |tim'bal| nm small drum

timbrar |tim'brar| vt to stamp

timbre |'timbre| nm (sello) stamp; (campanilla) bell; (tono) timbre; (COM) stamp duty

timidez |timi'ðeθ| nf shyness; **tímido, a** adj shy

timo ['timo] nm swindle

timón [ti'mon] nm helm, rudder; **timonel** nm helmsman

tímpano ['timpano] nm (ANAT) eardrum; (MUS) small drum

tina ['tina] nf tub; (baño) bath(tub); **tinaja** nf large jar

tinglado [tin'glaðo] nm (cobertizo) shed; (fig: truco) trick; (intriga) intrigue

tinieblas [ti'njeßlas] nfpl darkness sg; (sombras) shadows

tino ['tino] nm (habilidad) skill; (juicio) insight

tinta ['tinta] nf ink; (TEC) dye; (ARTE) colour

tinte ['tinte] nm dye

tintero [tin'tero] nm inkwell

tintinear [tintine'ar] vt to tinkle

tinto ['tinto] nm red wine

tintorería [tintore'ria] nf dry cleaner's

tintura [tin'tura] nf (QUÍM) dye; (farmacéutico) tincture

tío ['tio] nm (pariente) uncle; (fam: individuo) bloke (BRIT), guy

tiovivo [tio'ßißo] nm merry-go-round

típico, a ['tipiko, a] adj typical

tipo ['tipo] nm (clase) type, kind; (hombre) fellow; (ANAT: de hombre) build; (: de mujer) figure; (IMPRENTA) type; **~ bancario/de descuento/de interés/de cambio** bank/discount/ interest/exchange rate

tipografía [tipoɣra'fia] nf printing cpd; **tipográfico, a** adj printing cpd

tiquet ['tiket] (pl **~s**) nm ticket; (en tienda) cash slip

tiquismiquis [tikis'mikis] nm inv fussy person ♦ nmpl (querellas) squabbling sg; (escrúpulos) silly scruples

tira ['tira] nf strip; (fig) abundance; **~ y afloja** give and take

tirabuzón [tiraßu'θon] nm (rizo) curl

tirachinas [tira'tʃinas] nm inv catapult

tirada [ti'raða] nf (acto) cast, throw; (serie) series; (TIP) printing, edition; **de una ~** at one go

tirado, a [ti'raðo, a] adj (barato) dirt-

cheap; (fam: fácil) very easy

tirador [tira'ðor] nm (mango) handle

tiranía [tira'nia] nf tyranny; **tirano, a** adj tyrannical ♦ nm/f tyrant

tirante [ti'rante] adj (cuerda etc) tight, taut; (relaciones) strained ♦ nm (ARQ) brace; (TEC) stay; **~s** nmpl (de pantalón) braces (BRIT), suspenders (US); **tirantez** nf tightness; (fig) tension

tirar [ti'rar] vt to throw; (dejar caer) to drop; (volcar) to upset; (derribar) to knock down o over; (desechar) to throw out o away; (dinero) to squander; (imprimir) to print ♦ vi (disparar) to shoot; (de la palanca) to pull; (fam: andar) to go; (tender a, buscar realizar) to tend to; (DEPORTE) to shoot; **~se** vr to throw o.s.; **~ abajo** to bring down, destroy; **tira más a su padre** he takes more after his father; **ir tirando** to manage; **a todo ~** at the most

tirita [ti'rita] nf (sticking plaster (BRIT), bandaid (US)

tiritar [tiri'tar] vi to shiver

tiro ['tiro] nm (lanzamiento) throw; (disparo) shot; (DEPORTE) shot; (GOLF, TENIS) drive; (alcance) range; **~ al blanco** target practice; **caballo de ~** cart-horse; **andar de ~s largos** to be all dressed up; **al ~** (AM) at once

tirón [ti'ron] nm (sacudida) pull, tug; **de un ~** in one go, all at once

tiroteo [tiro'teo] nm exchange of shots, shooting

tísico, a ['tisiko, a] adj consumptive

tisis ['tisis] nf inv consumption, tuberculosis

títere ['titere] nm puppet

titiritero, a [titiri'tero, a] nm/f puppeteer

titubeante [tituße'ante] adj (al andar) shaky, tottering; (al hablar) stammering; (dudoso) hesitant

titubear [tituße'ar] vi to stagger; to stammer; (fig) to hesitate; **titubeo** nm staggering; stammering; hesitation

titulado, a |titu'laðo, a| *adj (libro)* entitled; *(persona)* titled

titular |titu'lar| *adj* titular ♦ *nm/f* holder ♦ *nm* headline ♦ *vt*: **~se** *vr* to be entitled; **título** *nm* title; *(de diario)* headline; *(certificado)* professional qualification; *(universitario)* (university) degree; **a título de** in the capacity of

tiza |'tiθa| *nf* chalk

tiznar |tiθ'nar| *vt* to blacken

tizón |ti'θon| *nm* brand

toalla |to'aʎa| *nf* towel

tobillo |to'βiʎo| *nm* ankle

tobogán |toβo'van| *nm (montaña rusa)* roller-coaster; *(de niños)* chute, slide

tocadiscos |toka'ðiskos| *nm inv* record player

tocado, a |to'kaðo, a| *adj (fam)* touched ♦ *nm* headdress

tocador |toka'ðor| *nm (mueble)* dressing table; *(cuarto)* boudoir; *(fam)* ladies' toilet *(BRIT)* o room *(US)*

tocante |to'kante|: **~ a** *prep* with regard to

tocar |to'kar| *vt* to touch; *(MUS)* to play; *(referirse a)* to allude to; *(timbre)* to ring ♦ *vi (a la puerta)* to knock (on o at the door); *(ser de turno)* to fall to, be the turn of; *(ser hora)* to be up; **~se** *vr (cubrirse la cabeza)* to cover one's head; *(tener contacto)* to touch (each other); **por lo que a mí me toca** as far as I am concerned; **te toca a ti** it's your turn

tocayo, a |to'kajo, a| *nm/f* namesake

tocino |to'θino| *nm* bacon

todavía |toða'βia| *adv (aun)* even; *(aún)* still, yet; **~ más** yet more; **~ no** not yet

---

todo, a |'toðo, a| *adj* **1** *(con artículo sg)* all; **toda la carne** all the meat; **toda la noche** all night, the whole night; **~ el libro** the whole book; **toda una**

botella a whole bottle; **~ lo contrario** quite the opposite; **está toda sucia** she's all dirty; **por ~ el país** throughout the whole country **2** *(con artículo pl)* all; every; **~s los libros** all the books; **todas las noches** every night; **~s los que quieran salir** all those who want to leave

♦ *pron* **1** everything, all; **~s** everyone, everybody; **lo sabemos** ~ we know everything; **~ querían más tiempo** everybody o everyone wanted more time; **nos marchamos ~s** all of us left

2: **con ~**: **con ~ él me sigue gustando** even so I still like him

♦ *adv* all; **vaya ~ seguido** keep straight on o ahead

♦ *nm*: **como un ~** as a whole; **del ~**: **no me agrada del ~** I don't entirely like it

---

todopoderoso, a |toðopoðe'roso, a| *adj* all powerful; *(REL)* almighty

toga |'toγa| *nf* toga; *(ESCOL)* gown

Tokio |'tokjo| *n* Tokyo

toldo |'toldo| *nm (para el sol)* sunshade *(BRIT)*, parasol; *(tienda)* marquee

tolerancia |tole'ranθja| *nf* tolerance;

tolerante *adj (sociedad)* liberal; *(persona)* open-minded

tolerar |tole'rar| *vt* to tolerate; *(resistir)* to endure

toma |'toma| *nf (acto)* taking; *(MED)* dose; **~ de corriente** socket

tomar |to'mar| *vt* to take; *(aspecto)* to take on; *(beber)* to drink ♦ *vi* to take; *(AM)* to drink; **~se** *vr* to take; **~se por** to consider o.s. to be; **~ a bien/a mal** to take well/badly; **~ en serio** to take seriously; **~ el pelo a alguien** to pull sb's leg; **~la con uno** to pick a quarrel with sb; **¡tome!** here you are!; **~ el sol** to sunbathe

tomate |to'mate| *nm* tomato

tomillo |to'miʎo| *nm* thyme

tomo ['tomo] nm (libro) volume

ton [ton] abr = **tonelada** ♦ nm: **sin ~ ni son** without rhyme or reason

tonada [to'naða] nf tune

tonalidad [tonali'ðað] nf tone

tonel [to'nel] nm barrel

tonelada [tone'laða] nf ton; **tonelaje** nm tonnage

tónica ['tonika] nf (MUS) tonic; (fig) keynote

tónico, a ['toniko, a] adj tonic ♦ nm (MED) tonic

tonificar [tonifi'kar] vt to tone up

tono ['tono] nm tone; **fuera de ~** inappropriate; **darse ~** to put on airs

tontería [tonte'ria] nf (estupidez) foolishness; (cosa) stupid thing; (acto) foolish act; **~s** nfpl (disparates) rubbish sg, nonsense sg

tonto, a ['tonto, a] adj stupid, silly ♦ nm/f fool

topar [to'par] vi: **~ contra** o **en** to run into; **~ con** to run up against

tope ['tope] adj maximum ♦ nm (fin) end; (límite) limit; (FERRO) buffer; (AUTO) bumper; **al ~** end to end

tópico, a ['topiko, a] adj topical ♦ nm platitude

topo ['topo] nm (ZOOL) mole; (fig) blunderer

topografía [topoɣra'fia] nf topography; **topógrafo, a** nm/f topographer

toque etc ['toke] vb ver **tocar** ♦ nm touch; (MUS) beat; (de campana) peal; **dar un ~ a** to warn; **~ de queda** curfew

toqué vb ver **tocar**

toquetear [tokete'ar] vt to finger

toquilla [to'kiʎa] nf (pañuelo) headscarf; (chal) shawl

tórax ['toraks] nm thorax

torbellino [torbe'ʎino] nm whirlwind; (fig) whirl

torcedura [torθe'ðura] nf twist; (MED) sprain

torcer [tor'θer] vt to twist; (la esquina)

to turn; (MED) to sprain ♦ vi (desviar) to turn off; **~se** vr (ladearse) to bend; (desviarse) to go astray; (fracasar) to go wrong; **torcido, a** adj twisted; (fig) crooked ♦ nm curl

tordo, a ['torðo, a] adj dappled ♦ nm thrush

torear [tore'ar] vt (fig: evadir) to avoid; (jugar con) to tease ♦ vi to fight bulls; **toreo** nm bullfighting; **torero, a** nm/f bullfighter

tormenta [tor'menta] nf storm; (fig: confusión) turmoil

tormento [tor'mento] nm torture; (fig) anguish

tornar [tor'nar] vt (devolver) to return, give back; (transformar) to transform ♦ vi to go back; **~se** vr (ponerse) to become

tornasolado, a [tornaso'laðo, a] adj (brillante) iridescent; (reluciente) shimmering

torneo [tor'neo] nm tournament

tornillo [tor'niʎo] nm screw

torniquete [torni'kete] nm (MED) tourniquet

torno ['torno] nm (TEC) winch; (tambor) drum; **en ~ (a)** round, about

toro ['toro] nm bull; (fam) he-man; **los ~s** bullfighting

toronja [to'ronxa] nf grapefruit

torpe ['torpe] adj (poco hábil) clumsy, awkward; (necio) dim; (lento) slow

torpedo [tor'peðo] nm torpedo

torpeza [tor'peθa] nf (falta de agilidad) clumsiness; (lentitud) slowness; (error) mistake

torre ['torre] nf tower; (de petróleo) derrick

torrefacto, a [torre'facto, a] adj roasted

torrente [to'rrente] nm torrent

tórrido, a ['torriðo, a] adj torrid

torrija [to'rrixa] nf French toast

torsión [tor'sjon] nf twisting

torso ['torso] nm torso

torta ['torta] nf cake; (fam) slap

tortícolis [tor'tikolis] *nm inv* stiff neck

tortilla [tor'tiʎa] *nf* omelette; (*AM*) maize pancake; ~ **francesa/española** plain/potato omelette

tórtola ['tortola] *nf* turtledove

tortuga [tor'tuɣa] *nf* tortoise

tortuoso, a [tor'twoso, a] *adj* winding

tortura [tor'tura] *nf* torture; **torturar** *vt* to torture

tos [tos] *nf* cough; ~ **ferina** whooping cough

tosco, a ['tosko, a] *adj* coarse

toser [to'ser] *vi* to cough

tostada [tos'taða] *nf* piece of toast; **tostado, a** *adj* toasted; (*por el sol*) dark brown; (*piel*) tanned

tostador [tosta'ðor] *nm* toaster

tostar [tos'tar] *vt* to toast; (*café*) to roast; (*persona*) to tan; ~**se** *vr* to get brown

total [to'tal] *adj* total ♦ *adv* in short; (*al fin y al cabo*) when all is said and done ♦ *nm* total; ~ **que** to cut (*BRIT*) o make (*US*) a long story short

totalidad [totali'ðað] *nf* whole

totalitario, a [totali'tarjo, a] *adj* totalitarian

tóxico, a ['toksiko, a] *adj* toxic ♦ *nm* poison; **toxicómano, a** *nm/f* drug addict

toxina [to'ksina] *nf* toxin

tozudo, a [to'θuðo, a] *adj* obstinate

traba ['traβa] *nf* bond, tie; (*cadena*) shackle

trabajador, a [traβaxa'ðor, a] *adj* hard-working ♦ *nm/f* worker

trabajar [traβa'xar] *vt* to work; (*AGR*) to till; (*empeñarse en*) to work at; (*convencer*) to persuade ♦ *vi* to work; (*esforzarse*) to strive; **trabajo** *nm* work; (*tarea*) task; (*POL*) labour; (*fig*) effort; **tomarse el trabajo de** to take the trouble to; **trabajo por turno/a destajo** shift work/piecework; **trabajoso, a** *adj* hard

trabalenguas [traβa'lengwas] *nm inv* tongue twister

trabar [tra'βar] *vt* (*juntar*) to join, unite; (*atar*) to tie down, fetter; (*agarrar*) to seize; (*amistad*) to strike up; ~**se** *vr* to become entangled; **trabársele a uno la lengua** to be tongue-tied

tracción [trak'θjon] *nf* traction; ~ **delantera/trasera** front-wheel/rear-wheel drive

tractor [trak'tor] *nm* tractor

tradición [traði'θjon] *nf* tradition; **tradicional** *adj* traditional

traducción [traðuk'θjon] *nf* translation

traducir [traðu'θir] *vt* to translate; **traductor, a** *nm/f* translator

traer [tra'er] *vt* to bring; (*llevar*) to carry; (*llevar puesto*) to wear; (*incluir*) to carry; (*causar*) to cause; ~**se** *vr*: ~**se algo** to be up to sth

traficar [trafi'kar] *vi* to trade

tráfico ['trafiko] *nm* (*COM*) trade; (*AUTO*) traffic

tragaluz [traɣa'luθ] *nm* skylight

tragaperras [traɣa'perras] *nm o f inv* slot machine

tragar [tra'ɣar] *vt* to swallow; (*devorar*) to devour, bolt down; ~**se** *vr* to swallow

tragedia [tra'xeðja] *nf* tragedy; **trágico, a** *adj* tragic

trago ['traɣo] *nm* (*líquido*) drink; (*bocado*) gulp; (*fam: de bebida*) swig; (*desgracia*) blow

traición [trai'θjon] *nf* treachery; (*JUR*) treason; (*una* ~) act of treachery; **traicionar** *vt* to betray

traicionero, a [traiθjo'nero, a] *adj* treacherous

traidor, a [trai'ðor, a] *adj* treacherous ♦ *nm/f* traitor

traigo *etc vb ver* **traer**

traje ['traxe] *vb ver* **traer** ♦ *nm* (*de hombre*) suit; (*de mujer*) dress; (*vestido típico*) costume; ~ **de baño** swimsuit; ~ **de luces** bullfighter's costume

trajera *etc vb ver* **traer**

trajín [tra'xin] *nm* (*fam: movimiento*) bustle; **trajinar** *vi* (*moverse*) to bustle about

trama ['trama] *nf* (*intriga*) plot; (*de tejido*) weft (*BRIT*), woof (*US*); **tramar** *vt* to plot; (*TEC*) to weave

tramitar [trami'tar] *vt* (*asunto*) to transact; (*negociar*) to negotiate

trámite ['tramite] *nm* (*paso*) step; (*JUR*) transaction; **~s** *nmpl* (*burocracia*) procedure *sg*; (*JUR*) proceedings

tramo ['tramo] *nm* (*de tierra*) plot; (*de escalera*) flight; (*de vía*) section

tramoya [tra'moja] *nf* (*TEATRO*) piece of stage machinery; (*fig*) scene shifter; (*fig*) trickster

tramoyista [tramo'jista] *nm/f* scene shifter; (*fig*) trickster

trampa ['trampa] *nf* trap; (*en el suelo*) trapdoor; (*truco*) trick; (*engaño*) fiddle; **trampear** *vt*, *vi* to cheat

trampolín [trampo'lin] *nm* (*de piscina etc*) diving board

tramposo, a [tram'poso, a] *adj* crooked, cheating ♦ *nm/f* crook, cheat

tranca ['tranka] *nf* (*palo*) stick; (*de puerta, ventana*) bar; **trancar** *vt* (*puerta*) to bar

trance ['tranθe] *nm* (*momento difícil*) difficult moment *o* juncture; (*estado hipnotizado*) trance

tranquilidad [trankili'ðað] *nf* (*calma*) calmness, stillness; (*paz*) peacefulness

tranquilizar [trankili'θar] *vt* (*calmar*) to calm (down); (*asegurar*) to reassure; **~se** *vr* to calm down; **tranquilo, a** [tran'kilo, a] *adj* (*calmado*) calm; (*apacible*) peaceful; (*mar*) calm; (*mente*) untroubled

transacción [transak'θjon] *nf* transaction

transbordador [transβorða'ðor] *nm* ferry

transbordar [transβor'ðar] *vt* to transfer; **transbordo** *nm* transfer; **hacer transbordo** to change (trains *etc*)

transcurrir [transku'rrir] *vi* (*tiempo*) to pass; (*hecho*) to take place

transcurso [trans'kurso] *nm*: **~ del tiempo** lapse (of time)

transeúnte [transe'unte] *nm/f* passerby

transferencia [transfe'renθja] *nf* transference; (*COM*) transfer

transferir [transfe'rir] *vt* to transfer

transformador [transforma'ðor] *nm* (*ELEC*) transformer

transformar [transfor'mar] *vt* to transform; (*convertir*) to convert

tránsfuga ['transfuɣa] *nm/f* (*MIL*) deserter; (*POL*) turncoat

transfusión [transfu'sjon] *nf* transfusion

transgénico, a [trans'xeniko, a] *adj* genetically modified, GM

transición [transi'θjon] *nf* transition

transigir [transi'xir] *vi* to compromise, make concessions

transitar [transi'tar] *vi* to go (from place to place); **tránsito** *nm* transit; (*AUTO*) traffic; **transitorio, a** *adj* transitory

transmisión [transmi'sjon] *nf* (*TEC*) transmission; (*transferencia*) transfer; **~ en directo/exterior** live/outside broadcast

transmitir [transmi'tir] *vt* to transmit; (*RADIO, TV*) to broadcast

transparencia [transpa'renθja] *nf* transparency; (*claridad*) clearness, clarity; (*foto*) slide

transparentar [transparen'tar] *vt* to reveal ♦ *vi* to be transparent; **transparente** *adj* transparent; (*claro*) clear

transpirar [transpi'rar] *vi* to perspire

transportar [transpor'tar] *vt* to transport; (*llevar*) to carry; **transporte** *nm* transport; (*COM*) haulage

transversal [transβer'sal] *adj* transverse, cross

tranvía [tram'bia] *nm* tram

trapecio [tra'peθjo] *nm* trapeze; **trapecista** *nm/f* trapeze artist

trapero, a [tra'pero, a] *nm/f* ragman

trapicheo [trapi'tʃeo] (*fam*) *nm* scheme, fiddle

trapo ['trapo] *nm* (*tela*) rag; (*de cocina*)

cloth

tráquea |'trakea| nf windpipe

traqueteo |trake'teo| nm rattling

tras |tras| prep (detrás) behind; (después) after

trasatlántico |trasat'lantiko| nm (barco) (cabin) cruiser

trascendencia |trasθen'denθja| nf (importancia) importance; (FILOSOFÍA) transcendence

trascendental |trasθenden'tal| adj important; (FILOSOFÍA) transcendental

trascender |trasθen'der| vi (noticias) to come out; (suceso) to have a wide effect

trasero, a |tra'sero, a| adj back, rear ♦ nm (ANAT) bottom

trasfondo |tras'fondo| nm background

trasgredir |trasɣre'ðir| vt to contravene

trashumante |trasu'mante| adj (animales) migrating

trasladar |trasla'ðar| vt to move; (persona) to transfer; (postergar) to postpone; (copiar) to copy; ~se vr (mudarse) to move; (mudanza) move, removal

traslúcir |traslu'θir| vt to show; ~se vr to be translucent; (fig) to be revealed

trasluz |tras'luθ| nm reflected light; **al ~** against o up to the light

trasnochado, a |trasnot∫a'ðor, a| nm/f night owl

trasnochar |trasno't∫ar| vi (acostarse tarde) to stay up late

traspapelar |traspape'lar| vt (document, carta) to mislay, misplace

traspasar |traspa'sar| vt (suj: bala etc) to pierce, go through; (propiedad) to sell, transfer; (calle) to cross over; (límites) to go beyond; (ley) to break; **traspaso** nm (venta) transfer, sale

traspié |tras'pje| nm (tropezón) trip; (error) blunder

trasplantar |trasplan'tar| vt to transplant

traste |'traste| nm (MUS) fret; **dar al ~ con algo** to ruin sth

trastero |tras'tero| nm storage room

trastienda |tras'tjenda| nf back of shop

trasto |'trasto| (pey) nm (cosa) piece of junk; (persona) dead loss

trastornado, a |trastor'naðo, a| adj (loco) mad, crazy

trastornar |trastor'nar| vt (fig: planes) to disrupt; (: nervios) to shatter; (: persona) to drive crazy; ~se vr (volverse loco) to go mad o crazy; **trastorno** nm (acto) overturning; (confusión) confusion

tratable |tra'taβle| adj friendly

tratado |tra'taðo| nm (POL) treaty; (COM) agreement

tratamiento |trata'mjento| nm treatment; **~ de textos** (INFORM) word processing cpd

tratar |tra'tar| vt (ocuparse de) to treat; (manejar, TEC) to handle; (MED) to treat; (dirigirse a: persona) to address ♦ vi: **~ de** (hablar sobre) to deal with, be about; (intentar) to try to; ~se vr to treat each other; **~ con** (COM) to trade in; (negociar) to negotiate with; (tener contactos) to have dealings with; **¿de qué se trata?** what's it about?; **trato** nm dealings pl; (relaciones) relationship; (comportamiento) manner; (COM) agreement

trauma |'trauma| nm trauma

través |tra'βes| nm (fig) reverse; **al ~** across, crossways; **a ~ de** across; (sobre) over; (por) through

travesaño |traβe'saɲo| nm (ARQ) crossbeam; (DEPORTE) crossbar

travesía |traβe'sia| nf (calle) cross-street; (NAUT) crossing

travesura |traβe'sura| nf (broma) prank; (ingenio) wit

traviesa |tra'βjesa| nf (ARQ) crossbeam

travieso, a |tra'βjeso, a| adj (niño) naughty

trayecto |tra'jekto| nm (ruta) road,

way; (*viaje*) journey; (*tramo*) stretch;
~ria nf trajectory; (fig) path

traza ['traθa] nf (*aspecto*) looks pl;
(*señal*) sign; (fig) path

trazar [tra'θar] vt (ARQ) to plan; (ARTE)
to sketch; (fig) to trace; (*plan*) to draw
up; **trazo** nm (*línea*) line; (*bosquejo*)
sketch

trébol ['treβol] nm (BOT) clover

trece ['treθe] num thirteen

trecho ['tretʃo] nm (*distancia*) distance;
(*de tiempo*) while; **de ~ en ~** at
intervals

tregua ['treɣwa] nf (MIL) truce; (fig)
respite

treinta ['treinta] num thirty

tremendo, a [tre'mendo, a] adj
(*terrible*) terrible; (*imponente: cosa*)
imposing; (fam: *fabuloso*) tremendous

trémulo, a ['tremulo, a] adj quiver-
ing

tren [tren] nm train; **~ de aterrizaje**
undercarriage

trenca ['trenka] nf duffel coat

trenza ['trenθa] nf (*de pelo*) plait
(BRIT), braid (US); **trenzar** vt (*pelo*) to
plait, braid; **trenzarse** vr (AM) to
become involved

trepadora [trepa'ðora] nf (BOT)
climber

trepar [tre'par] vt, vi to climb

trepidante [trepi'ðante] adj (*acción*)
fast; (*ritmo*) hectic

tres [tres] num three

tresillo [tre'siʎo] nm three-piece suite;
(MUS) triplet

treta ['treta] nf trick

triángulo ['trjangulo] nm triangle

tribu ['triβu] nf tribe

tribuna [tri'βuna] nf (*plataforma*)
platform; (DEPORTE) (grand)stand

tribunal [triβu'nal] nm (JUR) court;
(*comisión, fig*) tribunal

tributar [triβu'tar] vt (gen) to pay;
tributo nm (COM) tax

tricotar [triko'tar] vi to knit

trigal [tri'ɣal] nm wheat field

trigo ['triɣo] nm wheat

trigueño, a [tri'ɣeɲo, a] adj (*pelo*)
corn-coloured

trillado, a [tri'ʎaðo, a] adj threshed;
(*asunto*) trite, hackneyed; **trilladora** nf
threshing machine

trillar [tri'ʎar] vt (AGR) to thresh

trimestral [trimes'tral] adj quarterly;
(ESCOL) termly

trimestre [tri'mestre] nm (ESCOL) term

trinar [tri'nar] vi (*pájaros*) to sing;
(*rabiar*) to fume, be angry

trinchar [trin'tʃar] vt to carve

trinchera [trin'tʃera] nf (*fosa*) trench

trineo [tri'neo] nm sledge

trinidad [trini'ðað] nf trio; (REL): **la T~**
the Trinity

trino ['trino] nm trill

tripa ['tripa] nf (ANAT) intestine; (fam:
tb: **~s**) insides pl

triple ['triple] adj triple

triplicado, a [tripli'kaðo, a] adj: **por ~**
in triplicate

tripulación [tripula'θjon] nf crew

tripulante [tripu'lante] nm/f
crewman/woman

tripular [tripu'lar] vt (*barco*) to man;
(AUTO) to drive

triquiñuela [triki'nwela] nf trick

tris [tris] nm inv crack; **en un ~** in an
instant

triste ['triste] adj sad; (*lamentable*)
sorry, miserable; **~za** nf (*aflicción*)
sadness; (*melancolía*) melancholy

triturar [tritu'rar] vt (*moler*) to grind;
(*mascar*) to chew

triunfar [tʃjun'far] vi (*tener éxito*) to
triumph; (*ganar*) to win; **triunfo** nm
triumph

trivial [tri'βjal] adj trivial; **~izar** vt to
minimize, play down

triza ['triθa] nf: **hacer ~s** to smash to
bits; (*papel*) to tear to shreds

trocar [tro'kar] vt to exchange

trocear [troθe'ar] vt (*carne, manzana*)

to cut up, cut into pieces

trocha ['trotʃa] nf short cut

troche ['trotʃe]: **a ~ y moche** adv helter-skelter, pell-mell

trofeo [tro'feo] nm (premio) trophy; (éxito) success

tromba ['tromba] nf downpour

trombón [trom'bon] nm trombone

trombosis [trom'bosis] nf inv thrombosis

trompa ['trompa] nf horn; (trompo) humming top; (hocico) snout; (fam): **cogerse una ~** to get tight

trompazo [trom'paθo] nm bump, bang

trompeta [trom'peta] nf trumpet; (clar.:) bugle

trompicón [trompi'kon]: **a ~es** adv in fits and starts

trompo ['trompo] nm spinning top

trompón [trom'pon] nm bump

tronar [tro'nar] vt (AM) to shoot ♦ vi to thunder; (fig) to rage

tronchar [tron'tʃar] vt (árbol) to chop down; (fig: vida) to cut short; (: esperanza) to shatter; (persona) to tire out; **~se** vr to fall down

tronco ['tronko] nm (de árbol, ANAT) trunk

trono ['trono] nm throne

tropa ['tropa] nf (MIL) troop; (soldados) soldiers pl

tropel [tro'pel] nm (muchedumbre) crowd

tropezar [trope'θar] vi to trip, stumble; (error) to slip up; **~ con** to run into; (topar con) to bump into; **tropezón** nm trip; (fig) blunder

tropical [tropi'kal] adj tropical

trópico ['tropiko] nm tropic

tropiezo [tro'pjeθo] vb ver **tropezar** ♦ nm (error) slip, blunder; (desgracia) misfortune; (obstáculo) snag

trotamundos [trota'mundos] nm inv globetrotter

trotar [tro'tar] vi to trot; **trote** nm trot; (fam) travelling; **de mucho trote**

hard-wearing

trozo ['troθo] nm bit, piece

trucha ['trutʃa] nf trout

truco ['truko] nm (habilidad) knack; (engaño) trick

trueno ['trweno] nm thunder; (estampido) bang

trueque etc ['trweke] vb ver **trocar** ♦ nm exchange; (COM) barter

trufa ['trufa] nf (BOT) truffle

truhán, ana [tru'an, ana] nm/f rogue

truncar [trun'kar] vt (cortar) to truncate; (fig: la vida etc) to cut short; (: el desarrollo) to stunt

tu [tu] adj your

tú [tu] pron you

tubérculo [tu'βerkulo] nm (BOT) tuber

tuberculosis [tußerku'losis] nf inv tuberculosis

tubería [tuße'ria] nf pipes pl; (conducto) pipeline

tubo ['tußo] nm tube, pipe; **~ de ensayo** test tube; **~ de escape** exhaust (pipe)

tuerca ['twerka] nf nut

tuerto, a ['twerto, a] adj blind in one eye ♦ nm/f one-eyed person

tuerza etc vb ver **torcer**

tuétano ['twetano] nm marrow; (BOT) pith

tufo ['tufo] nm (hedor) stench

tul [tul] nm tulle

tulipán [tuli'pan] nm tulip

tullido, a [tu'ʎiðo, a] adj crippled

tumba ['tumba] nf (sepultura) tomb

tumbar [tum'bar] vt to knock down; **~se** vr (echarse) to lie down; (extenderse) to stretch out

tumbo ['tumbo] nm: **dar ~s** to stagger

tumbona [tum'bona] nf (butaca) easy chair; (de playa) deckchair (BRIT), beach chair (US)

tumor [tu'mor] nm tumour

tumulto [tu'multo] nm turmoil

tuna ['tuna] nf (MUS) student music group; ver tb **tuno**

Tuna

A **tuna** is a musical group made up
of university students or former
students who dress up in costumes
from the "Edad de Oro", the Spanish
Golden Age. These groups go through
the town playing their guitars, lutes
and tambourines and serenade the
young ladies in the halls of residence
or make impromptu appearances at
weddings or parties singing traditional
Spanish songs for a few pesetas.

tunante [tu'nante] *nm/f* rascal
tunda ['tunda] *nf (golpea)* beating
túnel ['tunel] *nm* tunnel
Túnez ['tuneθ] *nm* Tunisia; *(ciudad)*
Tunis
tuno, a [tuno, a] *nm/f (fam)* rogue
♦ *nm* member of student music group
tupido, a [tu'piðo, a] *adj (denso)*
dense; *(tela)* close-woven
turba ['turßa] *nf* crowd
turbante [tur'ßante] *nm* turban
turbar [tur'ßar] *vt (molestar)* to disturb;
(incomodar) to upset; **~se** *vr* to be
disturbed
turbina [tur'ßina] *nf* turbine
turbio, a ['turßjo, a] *adj* cloudy; *(tema
etc)* confused
turbulencia [turßu'lenθja] *nf*
turbulence; *(fig)* restlessness;
turbulento, a *adj* turbulent; *(fig:
intranquilo)* restless; *(: ruidoso)* noisy
turco, a ['turko, a] *adj* Turkish ♦ *nm/f*
Turk
turismo [tu'rismo] *nm* tourism; *(coche)*
car; **turista** *nm/f* tourist; **turístico, a**
adj tourist *cpd*
turnar [tur'nar] *vi* to take (it in) turns;
~se *vr* to take (it in) turns; **turno** *nm*
(de trabajo) shift; *(juegos etc)* turn
turquesa [tur'kesa] *nf* turquoise
Turquía [tur'kia] *nf* Turkey
turrón [tu'rron] *nm (dulce)* nougat
tutear [tute'ar] *vt* to address as familiar

"tú"; **~se** *vr* to be on familiar terms
tutela [tu'tela] *nf (legal)* guardianship;
tutelar *adj* tutelary ♦ *vt* to protect
tutor, a [tu'tor, a] *nm/f (legal)*
guardian; *(ESCOL)* tutor
tuve *etc vb ver* **tener**
tuviera *etc vb ver* **tener**
tuyo, a ['tujo, a] *adj* yours, of yours
♦ *pron* yours; **un amigo ~** a friend of
yours; **los ~s** *(fam)* your relations, your
family
TV ['te'ße] *nf abr (= television)* TV
TVE *nf abr* = **Televisión Española**

U, u

u [u] *conj* or
ubicar [ußi'kar] *vt* to place, situate;
(AM: encontrar) to find; **~se** *vr* to lie,
be located
ubre ['ußre] *nf* udder
UCI *nf abr (= Unidad de Cuidados
Intensivos)* ICU
Ud(s) *abr* = **usted(es)**
UE *nf abr (= Unión Europea)* EU
ufanarse [ufa'narse] *vr* to boast; **~ de**
to pride o.s. on; **ufano, a** *adj
(arrogante)* arrogant; *(presumido)*
conceited
UGT *nf abr* = **Unión General de
Trabajadores**
ujier [u'xjer] *nm* usher; *(portero)*
doorkeeper
úlcera ['ulθera] *nf* ulcer
ulcerar [ulθe'rar] *vt* to make sore; **~se**
vr to ulcerate
ulterior [ulte'rjor] *adj (más allá)*
farther, further; *(subsecuente, siguiente)*
subsequent
últimamente ['ultimamente] *adv
(recientemente)* lately, recently
ultimar [ulti'mar] *vt* to finish;
(finalizar) to finalize; *(AM: rematar)* to
finish off
ultimátum [ulti'matum] *(pl* **~s)**
ultimatum

último, a ['ultimo, a] *adj* last; (*más reciente*) latest, most recent; (*más bajo*) bottom; (*más alto*) top; **en las últimas** on one's last legs; **por ~** finally

ultra ['ultra] *adj ultra* ♦ *nm/f* extreme right-winger

ultrajar [ultra'xar] *vt* (*ofender*) to outrage; (*insultar*) to insult, abuse; **ultraje** *nm* outrage; insult

ultramar [ultra'mar] *nm*: **de o en ~** abroad, overseas

ultramarinos [ultrama'rinos] *nmpl* groceries; **tienda de ~** grocer's (shop)

ultranza [ul'tranθa]: **a ~** *adv* (*a toda trance*) at all costs; (*completo*) outright

ultratumba [ultra'tumba] *nf*: **la vida de ~** the next life

umbral [um'bral] *nm* (*gen*) threshold

umbrío, a [um'brio, a], **umbroso, a** [um'broso, a] *adj* shady

---

PALABRA CLAVE

un, una [un, 'una] *art indef* a; (*antes de vocal*) an; **una mujer/naranja** a woman/an orange
♦ *adj*: **unos** (o **unas**): **hay unos regalos para ti** there are some presents for you; **hay unas cervezas en la nevera** there are some beers in the fridge

---

unánime [u'nanime] *adj* unanimous; **unanimidad** *nf* unanimity

undécimo, a [un'deθimo, a] *adj* eleventh

ungir [un'xir] *vt* to anoint

ungüento [un'gwento] *nm* ointment

únicamente [u'nikamente] *adv* solely, only

único, a ['uniko, a] *adj* only, sole; (*sin par*) unique

unidad [uni'ðað] *nf* unity; (*COM, TEC etc*) unit

unido, a [u'niðo, a] *adj* joined, linked; (*fig*) united

unificar [unifi'kar] *vt* to unite, unify

uniformar [unifor'mar] *vt* to make

uniform, level up; (*persona*) to put into uniform

uniforme [uni'forme] *adj* uniform, equal; (*superficie*) even ♦ *nm* uniform; **uniformidad** *nf* uniformity; (*de terreno*) levelness, evenness

unilateral [unilate'ral] *adj* unilateral

unión [u'njon] *nf* union; (*acto*) uniting, joining; (*unidad*) unity; (*TEC*) joint; **la U~ Europea** the European Union; **la U~ Soviética** the Soviet Union

unir [u'nir] *vt* (*juntar*) to join, unite; (*atar*) to tie, fasten; (*combinar*) to combine; **~se** *vr* to join together, unite; (*empresas*) to merge

unísono [u'nisono] *nm*: **al ~** in unison

universal [uniβer'sal] *adj* universal; (*mundial*) world *cpd*

universidad [uniβersi'ðað] *nf* university

universitario, a [uniβersi'tarjo, a] *adj* university *cpd* ♦ *nm/f* (*profesor*) lecturer; (*estudiante*) (university) student; (*graduado*) graduate

universo [uni'βerso] *nm* universe

PALABRA CLAVE

uno, a ['uno, a] *adj* one; **es todo ~** it's all one and the same; **~s pocos** a few; **~s cien** about a hundred
♦ *pron* 1 one; **quiero sólo ~** I only want one; **~ de ellos** one of them
2 (*alguien*) somebody, someone; **conozco a ~ que se te parece** I know somebody o someone who looks like you; **~ mismo** oneself; **~s querían quedarse** some (people) wanted to stay
3: (**los**) **~s ... (los) otros ...** some ... others; **una y otra son muy agradables** they're both very nice
♦ *nf* one; **es la una** it's one o'clock
♦ *nm* (number) one

---

untar [un'tar] *vt* (*mantequilla*) to spread; (*engrasar*) to grease, oil

uña [u'ɲa] *nf* (*ANAT*) nail; (*garra*) claw;

(casco) hoof; (arrancaclavos) claw

uranio [u'ranjo] nm uranium

urbanidad [urßani'ðað] nf courtesy, politeness

urbanismo [urßa'nismo] nm town planning

urbanización [urßaniθa'θjon] nf (barrio, colonia) housing estate

urbanizar [urßani'θar] vt (zona) to develop, urbanize

urbano, a [ur'ßano, a] adj (de ciudad) urban; (cortés) courteous, polite

urbe ['urße] nf large city

urdimbre [ur'ðimbre] nf (de tejido) warp; (intriga) intrigue

urdir [ur'ðir] vt to warp; (complot) to plot, contrive

urgencia [ur'xenθja] nf urgency; (prisa) haste, rush; (emergencia) emergency; **servicios de ~** emergency services; "**Urgencias**" "Casualty"; **urgente** adj urgent

urgir [ur'xir] vi to be urgent; **me urge** I'm in a hurry for it

urinario, a [uri'narjo, a] adj urinary ♦ nm urinal

urna ['urna] nf urn; (POL) ballot box

urraca [u'rraka] nf magpie

URSS nf: **la ~** the USSR

Uruguay [uru'ɣwai] nm: **el ~** Uruguay; **uruguayo, a** adj, nm/f Uruguayan

usado, a [u'saðo, a] adj used; (de segunda mano) secondhand

usar [u'sar] vt to use; (ropa) to wear; (tener costumbre) to be in the habit of; **~se** vr to be used; **uso** nm use; wear; (costumbre) usage, custom; (moda) fashion; **al uso** in keeping with custom; **al uso de** in the style of

usted [us'teð] pron (sg) you sg; (pl): **~es** you pl

usual [u'swal] adj usual

usuario, a [u'swarjo, a] nm/f user

usura [u'sura] nf usury; **usurero, a** nm/f usurer

usurpar [usur'par] vt to usurp

utensilio [uten'siljo] nm tool; (CULIN) utensil

útero ['utero] nm uterus, womb

útil ['util] adj useful ♦ nm tool; **utilidad** nf usefulness; (COM) profit; **utilizar** vt to use, utilize

utopía [uto'pia] nf Utopia; **utópico, a** adj Utopian

uva ['ußa] nf grape

Las Uvas

In Spain Las uvas play a big part on New Year's Eve (**Nochevieja**), when on the stroke of midnight people gather at home, in restaurants or in the **plaza mayor** and eat a grape for each stroke of the clock of the **Puerta del Sol** in Madrid. It is said to bring luck for the following year.

V, v

v abr (= voltio) v

va vb ver **ir**

vaca ['baka] nf (animal) cow; **carne de ~** beef

vacaciones [baka'θjones] nfpl holidays

vacante [ba'kante] adj vacant, empty ♦ nf vacancy

vaciar [ba'θjar] vt to empty out; (ahuecar) to hollow out; (moldear) to cast; **~se** vr to empty

vacilante [baθi'lante] adj unsteady; (habla) faltering; (dudoso) hesitant

vacilar [baθi'lar] vi to be unsteady; (al hablar) to falter; (dudar) to hesitate, waver; (memoria) to fail

vacío, a [ba'θio, a] adj empty; (puesto) vacant; (desocupado) idle; (vano) vain ♦ nm emptiness; (FÍSICA) vacuum; (un ~) (empty) space

vacuna [ba'kuna] nf vaccine; **vacunar** vt to vaccinate

vacuno, a [ba'kuno, a] adj cow cpd; **ganado ~** cattle

vacuo, a ['bakwo, a] adj empty

vadear [baðe'ar] vt (río) to ford; **vado** nm ford

vagabundo, a [baɣa'ßundo, a] adj wandering ♦ nm tramp

vagamente [baxa'mente] adv vaguely

vagancia [ba'xanθja] nf (pereza) idleness, laziness

vagar [ba'xar] vi to wander; (no hacer nada) to idle

vagina [ba'xina] nf vagina

vago, a [' baxo, a] adj vague; (perezoso) lazy ♦ nm/f (vagabundo) tramp; (flojo) lazybones sg, idler

vagón [ba'xon] nm (FERRO: de pasajeros) carriage; (: de mercancías) wagon

vaguedad [baxwe'ðað] nf vagueness

vaho [' bao] nm (vapor) vapour, steam; (respiración) breath

vaina [' baina] nf sheath

vainilla [bai'niλa] nf vanilla

vainita [bai'nita] nf (AM) green o French bean

vais vb ver **ir**

vaivén [bai'ßen] nm to-and-fro movement; (de tránsito) coming and going; **vaivenes** nmpl (fig) ups and downs

vajilla [ba'xiλa] nf crockery, dishes pl; **lavar la ~** to do the washing-up (BRIT), wash the dishes (US)

valdré etc vb ver **valer**

vale [' bale] nm voucher; (recibo) receipt; (pagaré) IOU

valedero, a [bale'ðero, a] adj valid

valenciano, a [balen'θjano, a] adj Valencian

valentía [balen'tia] nf courage, bravery

valer [ba'ler] vt to be worth; (MAT) to equal; (costar) to cost ♦ vi (ser útil) to be useful; (ser válido) to be valid; **~se** vr to take care of oneself; **~se de** to make use of, take advantage of; **~ la pena** to be worthwhile; **¿vale?** (ESP) OK?

valeroso, a [bale'roso, a] adj brave, valiant

valgo etc vb ver **valer**

valía [ba'lia] nf worth, value

validar [bali'ðar] vt to validate; **validez** [bali'ðeθ] nf validity; **válido, a** adj valid

valiente [ba'ljente] adj brave, valiant ♦ nm hero

valioso, a [ba'ljoso, a] adj valuable

valla [' baλa] nf fence; (DEPORTE) hurdle; **~ publicitaria** hoarding; **vallar** vt to fence in

valle [' baλe] nm valley

valor [ba'lor] nm value, worth; (precio) price; (valentía) valour, courage; (importancia) importance; **~es** nmpl (COM) securities; **~ar** vt to value

vals [bals] nm inv waltz

válvula [' balßula] nf valve

vamos vb ver **ir**

vampiro, resa [bam'piro, 'resa] nm/f vampire

van vb ver **ir**

vanagloriarse [banaxlo'rjarse] vr to boast

vandalismo [banda'lismo] nm vandalism; **vándalo, a** nm/f vandal

vanguardia [ban'gwarðja] nf vanguard; (ARTE etc) avant-garde

vanidad [bani'ðað] nf vanity; **vanidoso, a** adj vain, conceited

vano, a [' bano, a] adj vain

vapor [ba'por] nm vapour; (vaho) steam; **al ~** (CULIN) steamed; **~izador** nm atomizer; **~izar** vt to vaporize; **~oso, a** adj vaporous

vapulear [bapule'ar] vt to beat, thrash

vaquero, a [ba'kero, a] adj cattle cpd ♦ nm cowboy; **~s** nmpl (pantalones) jeans

vaquilla [ba'kiλa] nf (ZOOL) heifer

vara [' bara] nf stick; (TEC) rod; **~ mágica** magic wand

variable [ba'rjaßle] adj, nf variable

variación [barja'θjon] nf variation

variar [bar'jar] vt to vary; (modificar) to modify; (cambiar de posición) to switch around ♦ vi to vary

varicela [bari'θela] nf chickenpox

varices |baˈriθes| nfpl varicose veins

variedad |barjeˈðað| nf variety

varilla |baˈriʎa| nf stick; (BOT) twig; (TEC) rod; (de rueda) spoke

vario, a |ˈbarjo, a| adj varied; **~s** various, several

varita |baˈrita| nf: **~ mágica** magic wand

vas vb ver **ir**

vasco, a |ˈbasko, a| adj, nm/f Basque

vascongado, a |baskonˈgaðo, a| adj Basque; **las Vascongadas** the Basque Country

vascuence |basˈkwenθe| adj = **vascongado**

vaselina |baseˈlina| nf Vaseline ®

vasija |baˈsixa| nf container, vessel

vaso |ˈbaso| nm glass, tumbler; (ANAT) vessel

vástago |ˈbastaxo| nm (BOT) shoot; (TEC) rod; (fig) offspring

vasto, a |ˈbasto, a| adj vast, huge

Vaticano |batiˈkano| nm: **el ~** the Vatican

vatio |ˈbatjo| nm (ELEC) watt

vaya etc vb ver **ir**

Vd(s) abr = **usted(es)**

ve vb ver **ir; ver**

vecindad |beθinˈdað| nf neighbourhood; (habitantes) residents pl

vecindario |beθinˈdarjo| nm neighbourhood; residents pl

vecino, a |beˈθino, a| adj neighbouring ♦ nm/f neighbour; (residente) resident

veda |ˈbeða| nf prohibition

vedar |beˈðar| vt (prohibir) to ban, prohibit; (impedir) to stop, prevent

vegetación |bexetaˈθjon| nf vegetation

vegetal |bexeˈtal| adj, nm vegetable

vegetariano, a |bexetaˈrjano, a| adj, nm/f vegetarian

vehemencia |be(e)ˈmenθja| nf vehemence; **vehemente** adj vehement

vehículo |beˈikulo| nm vehicle; (MED) carrier

veía etc vb ver **ver**

veinte |ˈbeinte| num twenty

vejación |bexaˈθjon| nf vexation; (humillación) humiliation

vejar |beˈxar| vt (irritar) to annoy, vex; (humillar) to humiliate

vejez |beˈxeθ| nf old age

vejiga |beˈxixa| nf (ANAT) bladder

vela |ˈbela| nf (de cera) candle; (NAUT) sail; (insomnio) sleeplessness; (vigilia) vigil; (MIL) sentry duty; **estar a dos ~s** (fam: sin dinero) to be skint

velado, a |beˈlaðo, a| adj veiled; (sonido) muffled; (FOTO) blurred ♦ nf soirée

velar |beˈlar| vt (vigilar) to keep watch over ♦ vi to stay awake; **~ por** to watch over, look after

velatorio |belaˈtorjo| nm (funeral) wake

veleidad |beleiˈðað| nf (ligereza) fickleness; (capricho) whim

velero |beˈlero| nm (NAUT) sailing ship; (AVIA t) glider

veleta |beˈleta| nf weather vane

veliz |beˈliθ| nm (AM) suitcase

vello |ˈbeʎo| nm down, fuzz

velo |ˈbelo| nm veil

velocidad |beloθiˈðað| nf speed; (TEC, AUTO) gear

velocímetro |beloˈθimetro| nm speedometer

veloz |beˈloθ| adj fast

ven vb ver **venir**

vena |ˈbena| nf vein

venado |beˈnaðo| nm deer

vencedor, a |benθeˈðor, a| adj victorious ♦ nm/f victor, winner

vencer |benˈθer| vt (dominar) to defeat, beat; (derrotar) to vanquish; (superar, controlar) to overcome, master ♦ vi (triunfar) to win (through),

triumph; (*plazo*) to expire; **vencido, a**
adj (*derrotado*) defeated, beaten; (COM)
due ♦ *adv*: **pagar vencido** to pay in
arrears; **vencimiento** *nm* (COM)
maturity

venda ['benda] *nf* bandage; **vendaje**
nm bandage, dressing; **vendar** *vt* to
bandage; **vendar los ojos** to
blindfold

vendaval [benda'βal] *nm* (*viento*) gale

vendedor, a [bende'ðor, a] *nm/f* seller

vender [ben'der] *vt* to sell; **~ al
contado/al por mayor/al por
menor** to sell for cash/wholesale/retail

vendimia [ben'dimja] *nf* grape harvest

vendré *etc vb ver* **venir**

veneno [be'neno] *nm* poison; (*de
serpiente*) venom; **~so, a** *adj*
poisonous; venomous

venerable [bene'raβle] *adj* venerable;
venerar *vt* (*respetar*) to revere;
(*adorar*) to worship

venéreo, a [be'nereo, a] *adj*:
enfermedad venérea venereal
disease

venezolano, a [beneθo'lano, a] *adj*
Venezuelan

Venezuela [bene'θwela] *nf* Venezuela

venganza [ben'ganθa] *nf* vengeance,
revenge; **vengar** *vt* to avenge;
vengarse *vr* to take revenge;
vengativo, a *adj* (*persona*) vindictive

vengo *etc vb ver* **venir**

venia ['benja] *nf* (*perdón*) pardon;
(*permiso*) consent

venial [be'njal] *adj* venial

venida [be'niða] *nf* (*llegada*) arrival;
(*regreso*) return

venidero, a [beni'ðero, a] *adj* coming,
future

venir [be'nir] *vi* to come; (*llegar*) to
arrive; (*ocurrir*) to happen; (*fig*): **~ de**
to stem from; **~ bien/mal** to be
suitable/unsuitable; **el año que viene**
next year; **~se abajo** to collapse

venta ['benta] *nf* (COM) sale; **~ a
plazos** hire purchase; **~ al contado/**

al por mayor/al por menor o **al
detalle** cash sale/wholesale/retail;
~ con derecho a retorno sale or
return; **"en ~"** "for sale"

ventaja [ben'taxa] *nf* advantage;
ventajoso, a *adj* advantageous

ventana [ben'tana] *nf* window;
ventanilla *nf* (*de taquilla*) window (*of
booking office etc*)

ventilación [bentila'θjon] *nf*
ventilation; (*corriente*) draught

ventilador [bentila'ðor] *nm* fan

ventilar [benti'lar] *vt* to ventilate;
(*para secar*) to put out to dry; (*asunto*)
to air, discuss

ventisca [ben'tiska] *nf* blizzard

ventrílocuo, a [ben'trilokwo, a] *nm/f*
ventriloquist

ventura [ben'tura] *nf* (*felicidad*)
happiness; (*buena suerte*) luck; (*destino*)
fortune; **a la (buena) ~** at random;
venturoso, a *adj* happy; (*afortunado*)
lucky, fortunate

veo *etc vb ver* **ver**

ver [ber] *vt* to see; (*mirar*) to look at,
watch; (*entender*) to understand;
(*investigar*) to look into; ♦ *vi* to see; to
understand; **~se** *vr* (*encontrarse*) to
meet; (*dejarse ~*) to be seen; (*hallarse:
en un apuro*) to find o.s.; **a ~** let's
see; **no tener nada que ~ con** to
have nothing to do with; **a mi modo
de ~** as I see it

vera ['bera] *nf* edge, verge; (*de río*) bank

veracidad [beraθi'ðað] *nf* truthfulness

veranear [berane'ar] *vi* to spend the
summer; **veraneo** *nm* summer
holiday; **veraniego, a** *adj* summer *cpd*

verano [be'rano] *nm* summer

veras ['beras] *nfpl* truth *sg*; **de ~** really,
truly

veraz [be'raθ] *adj* truthful

verbal [ber'βal] *adj* verbal

verbena [ber'βena] *nf* (*baile*) open-air
dance

verbo ['berβo] *nm* verb; **~so, a** *adj*
verbose

verdad [ber'ðað] *nf* truth; *(fiabilidad)* reliability; **de** ~ real, proper; **a decir** ~ to tell the truth; **~ero, a** *adj (veraz)* true, truthful; *(fiable)* reliable; *(fig)* real

verde ['berðe] *adj* green; *(chiste)* blue, dirty ♦ *nm* green; **viejo** ~ dirty old man; **~ar** *vi* to turn green; **verdor** *nm* greenness

verdugo [ber'ðuɣo] *nm* executioner

verdulero, a [berðu'lero, a] *nm/f* greengrocer

verduras [ber'ðuras] *nfpl (CULIN)* greens

vereda [be'reða] *nf* path; *(AM)* pavement *(BRIT)*, sidewalk *(US)*

veredicto [bere'ðikto] *nm* verdict

vergonzoso, a [berɣon'θoso, a] *adj* shameful; *(tímido)* timid, bashful

vergüenza [ber'ɣwenθa] *nf* shame, sense of shame; *(timidez)* bashfulness; *(pudor)* modesty; **me da** ~ I'm ashamed

verídico, a [be'riðiko, a] *adj* true, truthful

verificar [berifi'kar] *vt* to check; *(corroborar)* to verify; *(llevar a cabo)* to carry out; **~se** *vr (predicción)* to prove to be true

verja ['berxa] *nf (cancela)* iron gate; *(valla)* iron railings *pl*; *(de ventana)* grille

vermut [ber'mut] *(pl* **~s)** *nm* vermouth

verosímil [bero'simil] *adj* likely, probable; *(relato)* credible

verruga [be'rruɣa] *nf* wart

versado, a [ber'saðo, a] *adj*: ~ **en** versed in

versátil [ber'satil] *adj* versatile

versión [ber'sjon] *nf* version

verso ['berso] *nm* verse; **un** ~ a line of poetry

vértebra ['bertebra] *nf* vertebra

verter [ber'ter] *vt (líquido: adrede)* to empty, pour (out); *(: sin querer)* to spill; *(basura)* to dump ♦ *vi* to flow

vertical [berti'kal] *adj* vertical

vértice ['bertiθe] *nm* vertex, apex

vertidos [ber'tiðos] *nmpl* waste *sg*

vertiente [ber'tjente] *nf* slope; *(fig)* aspect

vertiginoso, a [bertixi'noso, a] *adj* giddy, dizzy

vértigo ['bertixo] *nm* vertigo; *(mareo)* dizziness

vesícula [be'sikula] *nf* blister

vespino ® [bes'pino] *nm o nf* moped

vestíbulo [bes'tiβulo] *nm* hall; *(de teatro)* foyer

vestido [bes'tiðo] *pp de* **vestir** ♦ *nm* *(de persona)* clothing, clothes *pl*; *(ropa)* dress, frock ♦ *adj* ~ **de azul/marinero** dressed in blue/as a sailor ♦ *nm (ropa)* clothes *pl*, clothing; *(de mujer)* dress, frock

vestigio [bes'tixjo] *nm (huella)* trace; **~s** *nmpl (restos)* remains

vestimenta [besti'menta] *nf* clothing

vestir [bes'tir] *vt (poner: ropa)* to put on; *(llevar: ropa)* to wear; *(proveer de ropa a)* to clothe; *(suj: sastre)* to make clothes for ♦ *vi* to dress; *(verse bien)* to look good; **~se** *vr* to get dressed, dress o.s.

vestuario [bes'twarjo] *nm* clothes *pl*, wardrobe; *(TEATRO: cuarto)* dressing room; *(DEPORTE)* changing room

veta ['beta] *nf (vena)* vein, seam; *(en carne)* streak; *(de madera)* grain

vetar [be'tar] *vt* to veto

veterano, a [bete'rano, a] *adj, nm* veteran

veterinaria [beteri'narja] *nf* veterinary science; *ver tb* **veterinario**

veterinario, a [beteri'narjo, a] *nm/f* vet(erinary surgeon)

veto ['beto] *nm* veto

vez [beθ] *nf* time; *(turno)* turn; **a la** ~ **que** at the same time as; **a su** ~ in its turn; **otra** ~ again; **una** ~ once; **de una** ~ in one go; **de una** ~ **para siempre** once and for all; **en** ~ **de** instead of; **a** *o* **algunas veces** sometimes; **una y otra** ~ repeatedly; **de** ~ **en cuando** from time to time; **7 veces 9** 7 times 9; **hacer las veces de** to stand in for; **tal** ~ perhaps

vía |'bia| nf track, route; (FERRO) line; (fig) way; (ANAT) passage, tube ♦ prep via, by way of; **por ~ judicial** by legal means; **por ~ oficial** through official channels; **en ~s de** in the process of; **~ aérea** airway; **V~ Láctea** Milky Way; **~ pública** public road o thoroughfare

viable |'bjaßle| adj (solución, plan, alternativa) feasible

viaducto |bja'ðukto| nm viaduct

viajante |bja'xante| nm commercial traveller

viajar |bja'xar| vi to travel; **viaje** nm journey; (gira) tour; (NAUT) voyage; **estar de viaje** to be on a trip; **viaje de ida y vuelta** round trip; **viaje de novios** honeymoon; **viajero, a** adj travelling; (ZOOL) migratory ♦ nm/f (quien viaja) traveller; (pasajero) passenger

vial |bjal| adj road cpd, traffic cpd

víbora |'bißora| nf viper; (AM) poisonous snake

vibración |bißra'θjon| nf vibration

vibrar |bi'ßrar| vt, vi to vibrate

vicario |bi'karjo| nm curate

vicepresidente |biθepresi'ðente| nm/f vice-president

viceversa |biθe'ßersa| adv vice versa

viciado, a |bi'θjaðo, a| adj (corrompido) corrupt; (contaminado) foul, contaminated; **viciar** vt (pervertir) to pervert; (JUR) to nullify; (estropear) to spoil; **viciarse** vr to become corrupted

vicio |'biθjo| nm vice; (mala costumbre) bad habit; **~so, a** adj (muy malo) vicious; (corrompido) depraved ♦ nm/f depraved person

vicisitud |biθisi'tuð| nf vicissitude

víctima |'biktima| nf victim

victoria |bik'torja| nf victory; **victorioso, a** adj victorious

vid |bið| nf vine

vida |'biða| nf (gen) life; (duración) lifetime; **de por ~** for life; **en la/mi ~** never; **estar con ~** to be still alive; **ganarse la ~** to earn one's living

video |'biðeo| nm video ♦ adj inv: **película ~** video film; **~cámara** nf camcorder; **~casete** nm video cassette, videotape; **~club** nm video club; **~juego** nm video game

vidriero, a |bi'ðrjero, a| nm/f glazier ♦ nf (ventana) stained-glass window; (AM: de tienda) shop window; (puerta) glass door

vidrio |'biðrjo| nm glass

vieira |'bjeira| nf scallop

viejo, a |'bjexo, a| adj old ♦ nm/f old man/woman; **hacerse ~** to get old

Viena |'bjena| n Vienna

vienes etc vb ver **venir**

vienés, esa |bje'nes, esa| adj Viennese

viento |'bjento| nm wind; **hacer ~** to be windy

vientre |'bjentre| nm belly; (matriz) womb

viernes |'bjernes| nm inv Friday; **V~ Santo** Good Friday

Vietnam |bjet'nam| nm: **el ~** Vietnam; **vietnamita** adj Vietnamese

viga |'biɣa| nf beam, rafter; (de metal) girder

vigencia |bi'xenθja| nf validity; **estar en ~** to be in force; **vigente** adj valid, in force; (imperante) prevailing

vigésimo, a |bi'xesimo, a| adj twentieth

vigía |bi'xia| nm look-out

vigilancia |bixi'lanθja| nf: **tener a uno bajo ~** to keep watch on sb

vigilar |bixi'lar| vt to watch over ♦ vi (gen) to be vigilant; (hacer guardia) to keep watch; **~ por** to take care of

vigilia |vi'xilja| nf wakefulness, being awake; (REL) fast

vigor |bi'ɣor| nm vigour, vitality; **en ~** in force; **entrar/poner en ~** to come/put into effect; **~oso, a** adj vigorous

VIH nm abr (= virus de la inmunodeficiencia humana) HIV;

~ positivo/negativo HIV-positive/-negative

vil |bil| *adj* vile, low; **~eza** *nf* vileness; *(acto)* base deed

vilipendiar |bilipen'djar| *vt* to vilify, revile

villa |'biʎa| *nf (casa)* villa; *(pueblo)* small town; *(municipalidad)* municipality; **~ miseria** *(AM)* shantytown

villancico |biʎan'θiko| *nm* (Christmas) carol

villorrio |bi'ʎorrjo| *nm* shantytown

vilo |'bilo|: **en ~** *adv* in the air, suspended; *(fig)* on tenterhooks, in suspense

vinagre |bi'naɣre| *nm* vinegar

vinagreta |bina'ɣreta| *nf* vinaigrette, French dressing

vinculación |binkula'θjon| *nf (lazo)* link, bond; *(acción)* linking

vincular |binku'lar| *vt* to link, bind; **vínculo** *nm* link, bond

vine *etc vb ver* **venir**

vinicultura |binikul'tura| *nf* wine growing

viniera *etc vb ver* **venir**

vino |'bino| *vb ver* **venir ♦** *nm* wine; **~ blanco/tinto** white/red wine

viña |'biɲa| *nf* vineyard; **viñedo** *nm* vineyard

viola |'bjola| *nf* viola

violación |bjola'θjon| *nf* violation; **~ (sexual)** rape

violar |bjo'lar| *vt* to violate; *(sexualmente)* to rape

violencia |bjo'lenθja| *nf* violence, force; *(incomodidad)* embarrassment; *(acto injusto)* unjust act; **violentar** *vt* to force; *(casa)* to break into; *(agredir)* to assault; *(violar)* to violate; **violento, a** *adj* violent; *(furioso)* furious; *(situación)* embarrassing; *(acto)* forced, unnatural

violeta |bjo'leta| *nf* violet

violín |bjo'lin| *nm* violin

violón |bjo'lon| *nm* double bass

viraje |bi'raxe| *nm* turn; *(de vehículo)* swerve; *(fig)* change of direction; **virar** *vi* to change direction

virgen |'birxen| *adj*, *nf* virgin

Virgo |'birxo| *nm* Virgo

viril |bi'ril| *adj* virile; **~idad** *nf* virility

virtud |bir'tuð| *nf* virtue; **en ~ de** by virtue of; **virtuoso, a** *adj* virtuous ♦ *nm/f* virtuoso

viruela |bi'rwela| *nf* smallpox

virulento, a |biru'lento, a| *adj* virulent

virus |'birus| *nm inv* virus

visa |'bisa| *(AM)* *nf* = **visado**

visado |bi'saðo| *nm* visa

víscera |'bisθera| *nf (ANAT, ZOOL)* gut, bowel; **~s** *nfpl* entrails

visceral |bisθe'ral| *adj (odio)* intense; **reacción ~** gut reaction

viscoso, a |bis'koso, a| *adj* viscous

visera |bi'sera| *nf* visor

visibilidad |bisiβili'ðað| *nf* visibility; **visible** *adj* visible; *(fig)* obvious

visillos |bi'siʎos| *nmpl* lace curtains

visión |bi'sjon| *nf (ANAT)* vision, (eye)sight; *(fantasía)* vision, fantasy

visita |bi'sita| *nf (acto)* visit; *(persona)* visitor; **hacer una ~** to pay a visit

visitar |bisi'tar| *vt* to visit, call on

vislumbrar |bislum'brar| *vt* to glimpse, catch a glimpse of

viso |'biso| *nm (del metal)* glint, gleam; *(de tela)* sheen; *(aspecto)* appearance

visón |bi'son| *nm* mink

visor |bi'sor| *nm (FOTO)* viewfinder

víspera |'bispera| *nf*: **la ~ de ...** the day before ...

vista |'bista| *nf* sight, vision; *(capacidad de ver)* (eye)sight; *(mirada)* look's *(pl)*; **a primera ~** at first glance; **volver la ~ gorda** to turn a blind eye; **volver la ~** to look back; **está a la ~ que** it's obvious that; **en ~ de** in view of; **en ~ de que** in view of the fact that; **¡hasta la ~!** so long!, see you!; **con ~s a** with a view to; **~zo** *nm* glance; **dar o echar un ~zo a** to glance at

visto, a |'bisto, a| *pp de* **ver ♦** *vb ver*

tb **vestir ♦** *adj* seen; *(considerado)* considered **♦** *nm:* **~ bueno** approval; **"~ bueno"** "approved"; **por lo ~** apparently; **está ~ que** it's clear that; **está bien/mal ~** it's acceptable/ unacceptable; **~ que** since, considering that

vistoso, a [bis'toso, a] *adj* colourful

visual [bi'swal] *adj* visual

vital [bi'tal] *adj* life *cpd*, living *cpd*; *(fig)* vital; *(persona)* lively, vivacious; **~icio, a** *adj* for life; **~idad** *nf (de persona, negocio)* energy; *(de ciudad)* liveliness

vitamina [bita'mina] *nf* vitamin

viticultor, a [bitikul'tor, a] *nm/f* wine grower; **viticultura** *nf* wine growing

vitorear [bitore'ar] *vt* to cheer, acclaim

vitrina [bi'trina] *nf* show case; *(AM)* shop window

viudez *nf* widowhood

viudo, a ['bjuðo, a] *nm/f* widower/ widow

viva ['biβa] *excl* hurrah!; **¡~ el rey!** long live the king!

vivacidad [biβaθi'ðað] *nf (vigor)* vigour; *(vida)* liveliness

vivaracho, a [biβa'ratʃo, a] *adj* jaunty, lively; *(ojos)* bright, twinkling

vivaz [bi'βaθ] *adj* lively

víveres ['biβeres] *nmpl* provisions

vivero [bi'βero] *nm (para plantas)* nursery; *(para peces)* fish farm; *(fig)* hotbed

viveza [bi'βeθa] *nf* liveliness; *(agudeza: mental)* sharpness

vivienda [bi'βjenda] *nf* housing; *(una ~)* house; *(piso)* flat *(BRIT)*, apartment *(US)*

viviente [bi'βjente] *adj* living

vivir [bi'βir] *vt, vi* to live **♦** *nm* life, living

vivo, a ['biβo, a] *adj* living, alive; *(fig: descripción)* vivid; *(persona)* astuto: smart, clever; **en ~** *(transmisión etc)* live

vocablo [bo'kaβlo] *nm (palabra)* word; *(término)* term

vocabulario [bokaβu'larjo] *nm* vocabulary

vocación [boka'θjon] *nf* vocation;

vocacional *(AM)* *nf* ≈ technical college

vocal [bo'kal] *adj* vocal **♦** *nf* vowel; **~izar** *vt* to vocalize

vocear [boθe'ar] *vt (para vender)* to cry; *(aclamar)* to acclaim; *(fig)* to proclaim **♦** *vi* to yell; **vocerío** *nm* shouting

vocero [bo'θero] *nm/f* spokesman/ woman

voces ['boθes] *pl de* **voz**

vociferar [boθife'rar] *vt* to shout **♦** *vi* to yell

vodka ['boðka] *nm o f* vodka

vol *abr* = **volumen**

volador, a [bola'ðor, a] *adj* flying

volandas [bo'landas]: **en ~** *adv* in the air

volante [bo'lante] *adj* flying **♦** *nm (de coche)* steering wheel; *(de reloj)* balance

volar [bo'lar] *vt (edificio)* to blow up **♦** *vi* to fly

volátil [bo'latil] *adj* volatile

volcán [bol'kan] *nm* volcano; **~ico, a** *adj* volcanic

volcar [bol'kar] *vt* to upset, overturn; *(tumbar, derribar)* to knock over; *(vaciar)* to empty out **♦** *vi* to overturn; **~se** *vr* to tip over

voleibol [bolei'βol] *nm* volleyball

volqué *etc vb ver* **volcar**

voltaje [bol'taxe] *nm* voltage

voltear [bolte'ar] *vt* to turn over; *(volcar)* to turn upside down

voltereta [bolte'reta] *nf* somersault

voltio ['boltjo] *nm* volt

voluble [bo'luβle] *adj* fickle

volumen [bo'lumen] *nm (pl* **volúmenes)** *nm* volume; **voluminoso, a** *adj* voluminous; *(enorme)* massive

voluntad [bolun'tað] *nf* will; *(resolución)* willpower; *(deseo)* desire, wish

voluntario, a [bolun'tarjo, a] *adj*

voluntary ♦ nm/f volunteer
voluntarioso, a [bolunta'rjoso, a] adj
headstrong
voluptuoso, a [bolup'twoso, a] adj
voluptuous
volver [bol'ßer] vt (gen) to turn; (dar
vuelta a) to turn (over); (voltear) to
turn round, turn upside down; (poner
al revés) to turn inside out; (devolver)
to return ♦ vi to return, come
back; ~se vr to turn round; ~ la
espalda to turn one's back; ~ triste
etc a uno to make sb sad etc; ~ a
hacer to do again; ~ en sí to come
to; ~se insoportable/muy caro to
get o become unbearable/very
expensive; ~se loco to go mad
vomitar [bomi'tar] vt, vi to vomit;
vómito nm vomit
voraz [bo'raθ] adj voracious
vos [bos] (AM) pron you
vosotros, as [bo'sotros, as] pron you;
(reflexivo): entre/para ~ among/for
yourselves
votación [bota'θjon] nf (acto) voting;
(voto) vote
votar [bo'tar] vi to vote; **voto** nm
vote; (promesa) vow; **votos** (good)
wishes
voy vb ver **ir**
voz [boθ] nf voice; (grito) shout;
(rumor) rumour; (LING) word; **dar
voces** to shout, yell; **a media ~** in a
low voice; **a ~ en cuello o en grito** at
the top of one's voice; **de viva ~**
verbally; **en ~ alta** aloud; **~ de
mando** command
vuelco etc vb ver **volcar**
vuelco ['bwelko] vb ver **volcar** ♦ nm
spill, overturning
vuelo ['bwelo] vb ver **volar** ♦ nm
flight; (encaje) lace, frill; **coger al ~** to
catch in flight; **~ charter/regular**
charter/scheduled flight; **~ libre**
(DEPORTE) hang-gliding
vuelque etc vb ver **volcar**
vuelta ['bwelta] nf (gen) turn; (curva)
bend, curve; (regreso) return;

(revolución) revolution; (de circuito) lap;
(de papel, tela) reverse; (cambio)
change; **a la ~** on one's return; **a ~ de
correo** by return of post; **dar ~s** (suj:
cabeza) to spin; **dar ~s a una idea** to
turn over an idea in one's mind;
estar de ~ to be back; **dar una ~** to
go for a walk; (en coche) to go for a
drive; **~ ciclista** (DEPORTE) (cycle) tour
vuelto pp de **volver**
vuelvo etc vb ver **volver**
vuestro, a ['bwestro, a] adj your; **un
amigo ~** a friend of yours ♦ pron: **el
~/la vuestra, los ~s/las vuestras**
yours
vulgar [bul'xar] adj (ordinario) vulgar;
(común) common; **~idad** nf
commonness; (acto) vulgarity;
(expresión) coarse expression; **~izar** vt
to popularize
vulgo ['bulxo] nm common people
vulnerable [bulne'raßle] adj
vulnerable
vulnerar [bulne'rar] vt (ley, acuerdo) to
violate, breach; (derechos, intimidad) to
violate; (reputación) to damage

W, w

Walkman ® [wak'man] nm Walkman
®
wáter ['bater] nm toilet
whisky ['wiski] nm whisky, whiskey

X, x

xenofobia [kseno'foßja] nf
xenophobia
xilófono [ksi'lofono] nm xylophone

Y, y

y [i] conj and
ya [ja] adv (gen) already; (ahora) now;

(en seguida) at once; (pronto) soon ♦ excl all right! ♦ conj (ahora que) now that; ~ lo sé I know; ~ que since

yacer [ja'θer] vi to lie

yacimiento [jaθi'mjento] nm (de mineral) deposit; (arqueológico) site

yanqui ['jaŋki] adj, nm/f Yankee

yate ['jate] nm yacht

yazco etc vb ver **yacer**

yedra ['jeðra] nf ivy

yegua ['jeɣwa] nf mare

yema ['jema] nf (del huevo) yolk; (BOT) leaf bud; (fig) best part; ~ del dedo fingertip

yergo etc vb ver **erguir**

yermo, a ['jermo, a] adj (estéril, fig) barren ♦ nm wasteland

yerno ['jerno] nm son-in-law

yerro etc vb ver **errar**

yeso ['jeso] nm plaster

yo [jo] pron I; **soy ~** it's me, it is I

yodo ['joðo] nm iodine

yoga ['joɣa] nm yoga

yogur(t) [jo'ɣur(t)] nm yoghurt

yugo ['juɣo] nm yoke

Yugoslavia [juɣos'laßja] nf Yugoslavia

yugular [juɣu'lar] adj jugular

yunque ['juŋke] nm anvil

yunta ['junta] nf yoke

yuxtaponer [jukstapo'ner] vt to juxtapose; **yuxtaposición** nf juxtaposition

Z, z

zafar [θa'far] vt (soltar) to untie; (superficie) to clear; **~se** vr (escaparse) to escape; (TEC) to slip off

zafio [θa'fjo, a] adj coarse

zafiro [θa'firo] nm sapphire

zaga ['θaɣa] nf: **a la ~** behind, in the rear

zaguán [θa'ɣwan] nm hallway

zaherir [θae'rir] vt (criticar) to criticize

zaino, a ['θaino, a] adj (caballo) chestnut

zalamería [θalame'ria] nf flattery; **zalamero, a** adj flattering; (cobista) suave

zamarra [θa'marra] nf (chaqueta) sheepskin jacket

zambullirse [θambu'ʎirse] vr to dive

zampar [θam'par] vt to gobble down

zanahoria [θana'orja] nf carrot

zancada [θan'kaða] nf stride

zancadilla [θanka'ðiʎa] nf trip

zanco ['θanko] nm stilt

zancudo, a [θan'kuðo, a] adj long-legged ♦ nm (AM) mosquito

zángano ['θangano] nm drone

zanja ['θanxa] nf ditch; **zanjar** vt (resolver) to resolve

zapata [θa'pata] nf (MECÁNICA) shoe

zapatear [θapate'ar] vi to tap with one's feet

zapatería [θapate'ria] nf (oficio) shoemaking; (tienda) shoe shop; (fábrica) shoe factory; **zapatero, a** nm/f shoemaker

zapatilla [θapa'tiʎa] nf slipper; ~ de deporte training shoe

zapato [θa'pato] nm shoe

zapping [θapin] nm channel-hopping; **hacer ~** to flick through the channels

zar [θar] nm tsar, czar

zarandear [θarande'ar] (fam) vt to shake vigorously

zarpa ['θarpa] nf (garra) claw

zarpar [θar'par] vi to weigh anchor

zarza ['θarθa] nf (BOT) bramble; **zarzal** nm (matorral) bramble patch

zarzamora [θarθa'mora] nf blackberry

zarzuela [θar'θwela] nf Spanish light opera

zigzag [θix'θaɣ] nm zigzag; **zigzaguear** vi to zigzag

zinc [θiŋk] nm zinc

zócalo ['θokalo] nm (ARQ) plinth, base

zodíaco [θo'ðiako] nm (ASTRO) zodiac

zona ['θona] nf zone; ~ **fronteriza** border area

zoo ['θoo] nm zoo

zoología [θoolo'xia] nf zoology;

zoológico, a adj zoological ♦ nm (tb: parque ~) zoo; **zoólogo, a** nm/f zoologist

zoom [θum] nm zoom lens

zopilote [θopi'lote] (AM) nm buzzard

zoquete [θo'kete] nm (fam) blockhead

zorro, a ['θorro, a] adj crafty ♦ nm/f fox/vixen

zozobra [θo'θoßra] nf (fig) anxiety; **zozobrar** vi (hundirse) to capsize; (fig) to fail

zueco ['θweko] nm clog

zumbar [θum'bar] vt (golpear) to hit ♦ vi to buzz; **zumbido** nm buzzing

zumo ['θumo] nm juice

zurcir [θur'θir] vt (coser) to darn

zurdo, a ['θurðo, a] adj (persona) left-handed

zurrar [θu'rrar] (fam) vt to wallop

ENGLISH · SPANISH
INGLÉS · ESPAÑOL

ENGLISH-SPANISH
INGLÉS-ESPAÑOL

A, a

A [eɪ] n (MUS) la m

a [ə] indef art (before vowel or silent h: an) **1** un(a); ~ **book** un libro; an **apple** una manzana; she's ~ **doctor** (ella) es médica
2 (instead of the number "one") un(a); ~ **year ago** hace un año; ~ **hundred/thousand** etc **pounds** cien/mil etc libras
3 (in expressing ratios, prices etc): **3** ~ **day/week** 3 al día/a la semana; **10 km an hour** 10 km por hora; **£5** ~ **person** £5 por persona; **30p** ~ **kilo** 30p el kilo

A.A. n abbr (= Automobile Association: BRIT) ≈ RACE m (SP); (= Alcoholics Anonymous) Alcohólicos Anónimos
A.A.A. (US) n abbr (= American Automobile Association) ≈ RACE m (SP)
aback [ə'bæk] adv: **to be taken** ~ quedar desconcertado
abandon [ə'bændən] vt abandonar; (give up) renunciar a
abate [ə'beɪt] vi (storm) amainar; (anger) aplacarse; (terror) disminuir
abattoir ['æbətwɑːʳ] (BRIT) n matadero m
abbey ['æbɪ] n abadía f
abbot ['æbət] n abad m
abbreviation [əbriːvɪ'eɪʃən] n (short form) abreviatura f
abdicate ['æbdɪkeɪt] vt renunciar a ♦ vi abdicar
abdomen ['æbdəmən] n abdomen m
abduct [æb'dʌkt] vt raptar, secuestrar
abeyance [ə'beɪəns] n: **in** ~ (law) en

desuso; (matter) en suspenso
abide [ə'baɪd] vt: **I can't** ~ **it/him** no lo/le puedo ver; ~ **by** vt fus atenerse a
ability [ə'bɪlɪtɪ] n habilidad f, capacidad f; (talent) talento
abject ['æbdʒekt] adj (poverty) miserable; (apology) rastrero
ablaze [ə'bleɪz] adj en llamas, ardiendo
able ['eɪbl] adj capaz; (skilled) hábil; **to be** ~ **to do sth** poder hacer algo; ~**bodied** adj sano; **ably** adv hábilmente
abnormal [æb'nɔːməl] adj anormal
aboard [ə'bɔːd] adv a bordo ♦ prep a bordo de
abode [ə'bəud] n: **of no fixed** ~ sin domicilio fijo
abolish [ə'bɒlɪʃ] vt suprimir, abolir
aborigine [æbə'rɪdʒɪnɪ] n aborigen m/f
abort [ə'bɔːt] vt, vi abortar; ~**ion** [ə'bɔːʃən] n aborto; **to have an** ~**ion** abortar, hacerse abortar; ~**ive** adj malogrado

about [ə'baut] adv **1** (approximately) más o menos, aproximadamente; ~ **a hundred/thousand** etc unos(unas) cien/mil etc; **it takes** ~ **10 hours** se tarda unas o más o menos 10 horas; **at** ~ **2 o'clock** sobre las dos; **I've just** ~ **finished** casi he terminado
2 (referring to place) por todas partes; **to leave things lying** ~ dejar las cosas (tiradas) por ahí; **to run** ~ correr por todas partes; **to walk** ~ pasearse, ir y venir
3: **to be** ~ **to do sth** estar a punto de hacer algo

♦ prep 1 (relating to) de, sobre, acerca de; **a book ~ London** un libro sobre or acerca de Londres; **what is it ~?** ¿de qué se trata?, ¿qué pasa?; **we talked ~ it** hablamos de eso or ello; **what** or **how ~ doing this?** ¿qué tal si hacemos esto?

2 (referring to place) por; **to walk ~ the town** caminar por la ciudad

above [ə'bʌv] adv encima, por encima, arriba **♦ prep** encima de; (greater than: in number) más de; (: in rank) superior a; **mentioned ~** susodicho; **~ all** sobre todo; **~ board** adj legítimo

abrasive [ə'breɪzɪv] adj abrasivo; (manner) brusco

abreast [ə'brest] adv de frente; **to keep ~ of** (fig) mantenerse al corriente de

abroad [ə'brɔːd] adv (to be) en el extranjero; (to go) al extranjero

abrupt [ə'brʌpt] adj (sudden) brusco; (curt) áspero

abruptly [ə'brʌptlɪ] adv (leave) repentinamente; (speak) bruscamente

abscess ['æbsɪs] n absceso

abscond [əb'skɒnd] vi (thief): **to ~ with** fugarse con; (prisoner): **to ~ (from)** escaparse (de)

absence ['æbsəns] n ausencia

absent ['æbsənt] adj ausente; **~ee** [-'tiː] n ausente m/f; **~-minded** adj distraído

absolute ['æbsəluːt] adj absoluto; **~ly** [-'luːtlɪ] adv (totally) totalmente; (certainly!) ¡por supuesto (que sí)!

absolve [əb'zɒlv] vt: **to ~ sb (from)** absolver a alguien de

absorb [əb'zɔːb] vt absorber; **to be ~ed in a book** estar absorto en un libro; **~ent cotton** (US) n algodón m hidrófilo; **~ing** adj absorbente

absorption [əb'zɔːpʃən] n absorción f

abstain [əb'steɪn] vi: **to ~ (from)** abstenerse (de)

abstinence ['æbstɪnəns] n abstinencia

abstract ['æbstrækt] adj abstracto

absurd [əb'sɜːd] adj absurdo

abundance [ə'bʌndəns] n abundancia

abuse [n ə'bjuːs, vb ə'bjuːz] n (insults) insultos mpl, injurias fpl; (ill-treatment) malos tratos mpl; (misuse) abuso **♦ vt** insultar; maltratar; abusar de; **abusive** adj ofensivo

abysmal [ə'bɪzməl] adj pésimo; (failure) garrafal; (ignorance) supino

abyss [ə'bɪs] n abismo

AC abbr (= alternating current) corriente f alterna

academic [ækə'demɪk] adj académico, universitario; (pej: issue) puramente teórico **♦ n** estudioso/a; profesor(a) m/f universitario/a

academy [ə'kædəmɪ] n (learned body) academia; (school) instituto, colegio; **~ of music** conservatorio

accelerate [æk'seləreɪt] vt, vi acelerar; **accelerator** (BRIT) n acelerador m

accent ['æksənt] n acento; (fig) énfasis m

accept [ək'sept] vt aceptar; (responsibility, blame) admitir; **~able** adj aceptable; **~ance** n aceptación f

access ['ækses] n acceso; **to have ~ to** tener libre acceso a; **~ible** [-'sesəbl] adj (place, person) accesible; (knowledge etc) asequible

accessory [æk'sesərɪ] n accesorio; (LAW): **~ to** cómplice de

accident ['æksɪdənt] n accidente m; (chance event) casualidad f; **by ~** (unintentionally) sin querer; (by chance) por casualidad; **~al** [-'dentl] adj accidental, fortuito; **~ally** [-'dentlɪ] adv sin querer; por casualidad; **~ insurance** n seguro contra accidentes; **~-prone** adj propenso a los accidentes

acclaim [ə'kleɪm] vt aclamar, aplaudir **♦ n** aclamación f, aplausos mpl

acclimatize [ə'klaɪmətaɪz] (US: **acclimate**) vt: **to become ~d** aclimatarse

accommodate [əˈkɔmədeɪt] vt (subj: person) alojar, hospedar; (: car, hotel etc) tener cabida para; (oblige, help) complacer; **accommodating** adj servicial, complaciente

accommodation [əkɔməˈdeɪʃən] n (US **accommodations** npl) alojamiento

accompany [əˈkʌmpənɪ] vt acompañar

accomplice [əˈkʌmplɪs] n cómplice m/f

accomplish [əˈkʌmplɪʃ] vt (finish) concluir; (achieve) lograr; **~ed** adj experto, hábil; **~ment** n (skill: gen pl) talento; (completion) realización f

accord [əˈkɔːd] n acuerdo ♦ vt conceder; **of his own ~** espontáneamente; **~ance** n: **in ~ance with** de acuerdo con; **~ing:** **~ing to** prep según; (in accordance with) conforme a; **~ingly** adv (appropriately) de acuerdo con esto; (as a result) en consecuencia

accordion [əˈkɔːdɪən] n acordeón m

accost [əˈkɔst] vt abordar, dirigirse a

account [əˈkaʊnt] n (COMM) cuenta; (report) informe m; **~s** npl (COMM) cuentas fpl; **of no ~** de ninguna importancia; **on ~** a cuenta; **on no ~** bajo ningún concepto; **on ~ of** a causa de, por motivo de; **to take into ~, take ~ of** tener en cuenta; **~ for** vt fus (explain) explicar; (represent) representar; **~able** adj: **~able (to)** responsable (ante); **~ancy** n contabilidad f; **~ant** n contable m/f, contador(a) m/f; **~ number** n (at bank etc) número de cuenta

accrued interest [əˈkruːd-] n interés m acumulado

accumulate [əˈkjuːmjuleɪt] vt acumular ♦ vi acumularse

accuracy [ˈækjurəsɪ] n (of total) exactitud f; (of description etc) precisión f

accurate [ˈækjurɪt] adj (total) exacto;

(description) preciso; (person) cuidadoso; (device) de precisión; **~ly** adv con precisión

accusation [ækjuˈzeɪʃən] n acusación f

accuse [əˈkjuːz] vt: **to ~ sb (of sth)** acusar a uno (de algo); **~d** n (LAW) acusado/a

accustom [əˈkʌstəm] vt acostumbrar; **~ed** adj: **~ed to** acostumbrado a

ace [eɪs] n as m

ache [eɪk] n dolor m ♦ vi doler; **my head ~s** me duele la cabeza

achieve [əˈtʃiːv] vt (aim, result) alcanzar; (success) lograr, conseguir; **~ment** n (completion) realización f; (success) éxito

acid [ˈæsɪd] adj ácido; (taste) agrio ♦ n (CHEM, also: LSD) ácido; **~ rain** n lluvia ácida

acknowledge [əkˈnɔlɪdʒ] vt (letter: also: ~ receipt of) acusar recibo de; (fact, situation, person) reconocer; **~ment** n acuse m de recibo

acne [ˈæknɪ] n acné m

acorn [ˈeɪkɔːn] n bellota

acoustic [əˈkuːstɪk] adj acústico; **~s** n, npl acústica sg

acquaint [əˈkweɪnt] vt: **to ~ sb with sth** (inform) poner a uno al corriente de algo; **to be ~ed with** conocer; **~ance** n (person) conocido/a; (with person, subject) conocimiento

acquire [əˈkwaɪə*] vt adquirir; **acquisition** [ækwɪˈzɪʃən] n adquisición f

acquit [əˈkwɪt] vt absolver, exculpar; **to ~ o.s. well** salir con éxito

acre [ˈeɪkə*] n acre m

acrid [ˈækrɪd] adj acre

acrobat [ˈækrəbæt] n acróbata m/f

across [əˈkrɔs] prep (on the other side of) al otro lado de, del otro lado de; (crosswise) a través de ♦ adv de un lado a otro, de una parte a otra; a través, al través; (measurement): **the road is 10m ~** la carretera tiene 10m de ancho; **to run/swim ~** atravesar corriendo/nadando; **~ from** enfrente de

acrylic [ə'krɪlɪk] *adj* acrílico ♦ *n* acrílica

act [ækt] *n* acto, acción f; (*of play*) acto; (*in music hall etc*) número; (LAW) decreto, ley f ♦ *vi* (*behave*) comportarse; (*have effect: drug, chemical*) hacer efecto; (THEATRE) actuar; (*pretend*) fingir; (*take action*) obrar ♦ *vt* (*part*) hacer el papel de; **in the ~ of: to catch sb in the ~ of ...** pillar a uno en el momento en que ...; **to ~ as** actuar or hacer de; **~ing** *adj* suplente ♦ *n* (*activity*) actuación f; (*profession*) profesión f de actor

action ['ækʃən] *n* acción f, acto; (MIL) acción f, batalla; (LAW) proceso, demanda; **out of ~** (*person*) fuera de combate; (*thing*) estropeado; **to take ~** tomar medidas; **~ replay** *n* (TV) repetición f

activate ['æktɪveɪt] *vt* activar

active ['æktɪv] *adj* activo, enérgico; (*volcano*) en actividad; **~ly** *adv* (*participate*) activamente; (*discourage, dislike*) enérgicamente; **activity** [-'tɪvɪtɪ] *n* actividad f; **activity holiday** *n* vacaciones *fpl* con actividades organizadas

actor ['æktə*] *n* actor m

actress ['æktrɪs] *n* actriz f

actual ['æktjuəl] *adj* verdadero, real; (*emphatic use*) propiamente dicho; **~ly** *adv* realmente, en realidad; (*even*) incluso

acumen ['ækjumən] *n* perspicacia

acute [ə'kjuːt] *adj* agudo

ad [æd] *n abbr* = **advertisement**

A.D. *adv abbr* (= *anno Domini*) A.C.

adamant ['ædəmənt] *adj* firme, inflexible

adapt [ə'dæpt] *vt* adaptar ♦ *vi*: **to ~ (to)** adaptarse (a), ajustarse (a); **~able** *adj* adaptable; **~er, ~or** *n* (ELEC) adaptador m

add [æd] *vt* añadir, agregar; (*figures: also: ~ up*) sumar ♦ *vi*: **to ~ to**

(*increase*) aumentar, acrecentar; **it doesn't ~ up** (*fig*) no tiene sentido

adder ['ædə*] *n* víbora

addict ['ædɪkt] *n* adicto/a; (*enthusiast*) entusiasta *m/f*; **~ed** [ə'dɪktɪd] *adj*: **to be ~ed to** ser adicto a; (*football etc*) ser fanático de; **~ion** [ə'dɪkʃən] *n* (*to drugs etc*) adicción f; **~ive** [ə'dɪktɪv] *adj* que causa adicción

addition [ə'dɪʃən] *n* (*adding up*) adición f; (*thing added*) añadidura, añadido; **in ~** además, por añadidura; **in ~ to** además de; **~al** *adj* adicional

additive ['ædɪtɪv] *n* aditivo

address [ə'drɛs] *n* dirección f, señas *fpl*; (*speech*) discurso ♦ *vt* (*letter*) dirigir; (*speak to*) dirigirse a, dirigir la palabra a; (*problem*) tratar

adept ['ædɛpt] *adj*: **~ at** experto or hábil en

adequate ['ædɪkwɪt] *adj* (*satisfactory*) adecuado; (*enough*) suficiente

adhere [əd'hɪə*] *vi*: **to ~ to** (*stick to*) pegarse a; (*fig: abide by*) observar; (: *belief etc*) ser partidario de

adhesive [əd'hiːzɪv] *n* adhesivo; **~ tape** *n* (BRIT) cinta adhesiva; (US: MED) esparadrapo

ad hoc [æd'hɒk] *adj* ad hoc

adjacent [ə'dʒeɪsənt] *adj*: **~ to** contiguo a, inmediato a

adjective ['ædʒɛktɪv] *n* adjetivo

adjoining [ə'dʒɔɪnɪŋ] *adj* contiguo, vecino

adjourn [ə'dʒəːn] *vt* aplazar ♦ *vi* suspenderse

adjudicate [ə'dʒuːdɪkeɪt] *vi* sentenciar

adjust [ə'dʒʌst] *vt* (*change*) modificar; (*clothing*) arreglar; (*machine*) ajustar ♦ *vi*: **to ~ (to)** adaptarse (a); **~able** *adj* ajustable; **~ment** *n* adaptación f; (: *to machine, prices*) ajuste m

ad-lib [æd'lɪb] *vt, vi* improvisar; **ad lib** *adv* de forma improvisada

administer [əd'mɪnɪstə*] *vt* administrar; **administration** [-'treɪʃən] *n* (*management*) administración f; (government) gobierno; **administrative** [-trətɪv] adj administrativo

admiral ['ædmərəl] n almirante m; **A~ty** (BRIT) n Ministerio de Marina, Almirantazgo

admiration [ædmə'reɪʃən] n admiración f

admire [əd'maɪə*] vt admirar; **~r** n (fan) admirador(a) m/f

admission [əd'mɪʃən] n (to university, club) ingreso; (entry fee) entrada; (confession) confesión f

admit [əd'mɪt] vt (confess) confesar; (permit to enter) dejar entrar, dar entrada a; (to club, organization) admitir; (accept: defeat) reconocer; **to be ~ted to hospital** ingresar en el hospital; **~ to** vt fus confesarse culpable de; **~tance** n entrada; **~tedly** adv es cierto or verdad que

admonish [əd'mɒnɪʃ] vt amonestar

ad nauseam [æd'nɔ:sɪæm] adv hasta el cansancio

ado [ə'du:] n: **without (any) more ~** sin más (ni más)

adolescent [ædəu'lesnt] adj, n adolescente m/f

adopt [ə'dɒpt] vt adoptar; **~ed** adj adoptivo; **~ion** [ə'dɒpʃən] n adopción f

adore [ə'dɔ:*] vt adorar

Adriatic [eɪdrɪ'ætɪk] n: **the ~ (Sea)** el (Mar) Adriático

adrift [ə'drɪft] adv a la deriva

adult ['ædʌlt] n adulto/a ♦ adj (grown-up) adulto; (for adults) para adultos

adultery [ə'dʌltərɪ] n adulterio

advance [əd'vɑ:ns] n (progress) adelanto, progreso; (money) anticipo, préstamo; (MIL) avance m ♦ adj: **~ booking** venta anticipada; **~ notice, ~ warning** previo aviso ♦ vt (money) anticipar; (theory, idea) proponer (para la discusión) ♦ vi avanzar, adelantarse; **to make ~s (to sb)** hacer proposiciones (a alguien); **in**

~ por adelantado; **~d** adj avanzado; (SCOL: studies) adelantado

advantage [əd'vɑ:ntɪdʒ] n (also TENNIS) ventaja; **to take ~ of** (person) aprovecharse de; (opportunity) aprovechar

Advent ['ædvənt] n (REL) Adviento

adventure [əd'ventʃə*] n aventura; **adventurous** [-tʃərəs] adj atrevido; aventurero

adverb ['ædvə:b] n adverbio

adverse ['ædvə:s] adj adverso, contrario

adversity [əd'və:sɪtɪ] n infortunio

advert ['ædvə:t] (BRIT) n abbr = **advertisement**

advertise ['ædvətaɪz] vi (in newspaper etc) anunciar, hacer publicidad; **to ~ for** (staff, accommodation etc) buscar por medio de anuncios ♦ vt anunciar; **~ment** [əd'və:tɪsmənt] n (COMM) anuncio; **~r** n anunciante m/f

advertising n publicidad f, anuncios mpl; (industry) industria publicitaria

advice [əd'vaɪs] n consejo, consejos mpl; (notification) aviso; **a piece of ~** un consejo; **to take legal ~** consultar con un abogado

advisable [əd'vaɪzəbl] adj aconsejable, conveniente

advise [əd'vaɪz] vt aconsejar; (inform): **to ~ sb of sth** informar a uno de algo; **to ~ sb against sth/doing sth** desaconsejar algo a uno/aconsejar a uno que no haga algo; **~dly** [əd'vaɪzɪdlɪ] adv (deliberately) deliberadamente; **~r** n = **advisor**; **advisor** n consejero/a; (consultant) asesor(a) m/f; **advisory** adj consultivo

advocate [əd'vɒkeɪt] vt abogar por ♦ ['-kɪt] (lawyer) abogado/a; (supporter): **~ of** defensor/a m/f de

Aegean [i:'dʒi:ən] n: **the ~ (Sea)** el (Mar) Egeo

aerial ['ɛərɪəl] n antena ♦ adj aéreo

aerobics [ɛə'rəubɪks] n aerobic m

aeroplane ['ɛərəpleɪn] (BRIT) n

avión *m*

aerosol ['eərəsɒl] *n* aerosol *m*

aesthetic [i:s'θetɪk] *adj* estético

afar [ə'fɑ:*] *adv*: **from ~** desde lejos

affair [ə'feə*] *n* asunto; (*also: love ~*) aventura (amorosa)

affect [ə'fekt] *vt* (*influence*) afectar, influir en; (*afflict, concern*) afectar; (*move*) conmover; **~ed** *adj* afectado

affection [ə'fekʃən] *n* afecto, cariño; **~ate** *adj* afectuoso, cariñoso

affinity [ə'fɪnɪtɪ] *n* (*bond, rapport*): **to feel an ~ with** sentirse identificado con; (*resemblance*) afinidad *f*

afflict [ə'flɪkt] *vt* afligir

affluence ['æfluəns] *n* opulencia, riqueza

affluent ['æfluənt] *adj* (*wealthy*) acomodado; **the ~ society** la sociedad opulenta

afford [ə'fɔ:d] *vt* (*provide*) proporcionar; **can we ~ (to buy) it?** ¿tenemos bastante dinero para comprarlo?

Afghanistan [æf'gænɪstæn] *n* Afganistán *m*

afield [ə'fi:ld] *adv*: **far ~** muy lejos

afloat [ə'fləut] *adv* (*floating*) a flote

afoot [ə'fut] *adv*: **there is something ~** algo se está tramando

afraid [ə'freɪd] *adj*: **to be ~ of** (*person*) tener miedo de; (*thing*) tener miedo de; **to be ~ to** tener miedo, temer; **I am ~ that** me temo que; **I am ~ not/so** lo siento, pero no/es así

afresh [ə'freʃ] *adv* de nuevo, otra vez

Africa ['æfrɪkə] *n* África; **~n** *adj, n* africano/a *m/f*

after ['ɑ:ftə*] *prep* (*time*) después de; (*place, order*) detrás de, tras ♦ *adv* después ♦ *conj* después de (que); **what/who are you ~?** ¿qué/a quién busca usted?; **~ having done/he left** después de haber hecho/después de que se marchó; **to name sb ~ sb** llamar a uno por uno; **it's twenty ~ eight** (*US*) son las ocho y veinte; **to**

ask ~ sb preguntar por alguien; **~ all** después de todo, al fin y al cabo; **~ you!** ¡pase usted!; **~-effects** *npl* consecuencias *fpl*, efectos *mpl*; **~math** *n* consecuencias *fpl*, resultados *mpl*; **~noon** *n* tarde *f*; **~s** (*inf*) *n* (*dessert*) postre *m*; **~-sales service** (*BRIT*) *n* servicio de asistencia pos-venta; **~shave (lotion)** *n* aftershave *m*; **~sun (lotion/cream)** *n* loción *f*/crema para después del sol, aftersun *m*; **~thought** *n* ocurrencia (tardía); **~wards** (*US* **~ward**) *adv* después, más tarde

again [ə'gen] *adv* otra vez, de nuevo; **to do sth ~** volver a hacer algo; **~ and ~** una y otra vez

against [ə'genst] *prep* (*in opposition to*) en contra de; (*leaning on, touching*) contra, junto a

age [eɪdʒ] *n* edad *f*; (*period*) época ♦ *vi* envejecer(se) ♦ *vt* envejecer; **she is 20 years of ~** tiene 20 años; **to come of ~** llegar a la mayoría de edad; **it's been ~s since I saw you** hace siglos que no te veo; **~d 10** de 10 años de edad; **the ~d** ['eɪdʒɪd] *npl* los ancianos; **~ group** *n*: **to be in the same ~ group** tener la misma edad; **~ limit** *n* edad *f* mínima (or máxima)

agency ['eɪdʒənsɪ] *n* agencia

agenda [ə'dʒendə] *n* orden *m* del día

agent ['eɪdʒənt] *n* agente *m/f*; (*COMM: holding concession*) representante *m/f*, delegado/a *m/f*; (*CHEM, fig*) agente *m*

aggravate ['ægrəveɪt] *vt* (*situation*) agravar; (*person*) irritar

aggregate ['ægrɪgət] *n* conjunto

aggressive [ə'gresɪv] *adj* (*belligerent*) agresivo; (*assertive*) enérgico

aggrieved [ə'gri:vd] *adj* ofendido, agraviado

aghast [ə'gɑ:st] *adj* horrorizado

agile ['ædʒaɪl] *adj* ágil

agitate ['ædʒɪteɪt] *vt* (*trouble*) inquietar ♦ *vi*: **to ~ for/against** hacer campaña pro or en favor de/en contra de

AGM *n abbr* (= *annual general meeting*)

asamblea anual

ago [ə'gəu] adv: **2 days ~** hace 2 días; **not long ~** hace poco; **how long ~?** ¿hace cuánto tiempo?

agog [ə'gɔg] adj (eager) ansioso; (excited) emocionado

agonizing ['ægənaızıŋ] adj (pain) atroz; (decision, wait) angustioso

agony ['ægənı] n (pain) dolor m agudo; (distress) angustia; **to be in ~** retorcerse de dolor

agree [ə'gri:] vt (price, date) acordar, quedar en ♦ vi (have same opinion): **to ~ (with/that)** estar de acuerdo (con/que); (correspond) coincidir, concordar; (consent) acceder; **to ~ with** (subj: person) estar de acuerdo con, ponerse de acuerdo con; (: food) sentar bien a; (LING) concordar con; **to ~ to sth/to do sth** consentir en algo/aceptar hacer algo; **to ~ that** (admit) estar de acuerdo en que; **~able** adj (sensation) agradable; (person) simpático; (willing) de acuerdo, conforme; **~d** adj (time, place) convenido; **~ment** n acuerdo; (contract) contrato; **in ~ment** de acuerdo, conforme

agricultural [ægrı'kʌltʃərəl] adj agrícola

agriculture ['ægrıkʌltʃə*] n agricultura

aground [ə'graund] adv: **to run ~** (NAUT) encallar, embarrancar

ahead [ə'hed] adv (in front) delante; (into the future): **she had no time to think ~** no tenía tiempo de hacer planes para el futuro; **~ of** delante de; (in advance of) antes de; **~ of time** antes de la hora; **go right** or **straight ~** (direction) siga adelante; (permission) hazlo (or hágalo)

aid [eıd] n ayuda, auxilio; (device) aparato ♦ vt ayudar, auxiliar; **in ~ of** a beneficio de

aide [eıd] n (person, also: MIL) ayudante m/f

AIDS [eıdz] n abbr (= acquired immune deficiency syndrome) SIDA m

ailment ['eılmənt] n enfermedad f, achaque m

aim [eım] vt (gun, camera) apuntar; (missile, remark) dirigir; (blow) asestar ♦ vi (also: take ~) apuntar ♦ n (in shooting: skill) puntería; (objective) propósito, meta; **to ~ at** (with weapon) apuntar a; (objective) aspirar a, pretender; **to ~ to do** tener la intención de hacer; **~less** adj sin propósito, sin objeto

ain't [eınt] (inf) = **am not**; **aren't**; **isn't**

air [ɛə*] n aire m; (appearance) aspecto ♦ vt (room) ventilar; (clothes, ideas) airear ♦ cpd aéreo; **to throw sth into the ~** (ball etc) lanzar algo al aire; **by ~** (travel) en avión; **to be on the ~** (RADIO, TV) estar en antena; **~bed** (BRIT) n colchón m neumático; **~-conditioned** adj climatizado; **~-conditioning** n aire acondicionado; **~craft** n inv avión m; **~craft carrier** n porta(a)viones m inv; **~field** n campo de aviación; **A~ Force** n fuerzas fpl aéreas, aviación f; **~ freshener** n ambientador m; **~gun** n escopeta de aire comprimido; **~ hostess** (BRIT) n azafata; **~ letter** (BRIT) n carta aérea; **~lift** n puente m aéreo; **~line** n línea aérea; **~liner** n avión m de pasajeros; **~mail** n: **by ~mail** por avión; **~plane** (US) n avión m; **~port** n aeropuerto; **~ raid** n ataque m aéreo; **~sick** adj: **to be ~sick** marearse (en avión); **~space** n espacio aéreo; **~tight** adj hermético; **~-traffic controller** n controlador(a) m/f aéreo/a; **~y** adj (room) bien ventilado; (fig: manner) desenfadado

aisle [aıl] n (of church) nave f; (of theatre, supermarket) pasillo; **~ seat** n (on plane) asiento de pasillo

ajar [ə'dʒɑ:*] adj entreabierto

alarm [ə'lɑ:m] n alarma; (anxiety) inquietud f ♦ vt asustar, inquietar; **~ call** n (in hotel etc) alarma; **~ clock** n despertador m

alas [ə'læs] adv desgraciadamente

albeit [ɔːl'biːɪt] conj aunque

album ['ælbəm] n álbum m; (L.P.) elepé m

alcohol ['ælkəhɔl] n alcohol m; **~ic** [-'hɔlɪk] adj, n alcohólico/a m/f

ale [eɪl] n cerveza

alert [ə'ləːt] adj (attentive) atento; (to danger, opportunity) alerta ♦ n alerta m, alarma f ♦ vt poner sobre aviso; **to be on the ~** (also MIL.) estar alerta o sobre aviso

algebra ['ældʒɪbrə] n álgebra

Algeria [æl'dʒɪərɪə] n Argelia

alias ['eɪlɪəs] adv alias, conocido por ♦ n (of criminal) apodo; (of writer) seudónimo

alibi ['ælɪbaɪ] n coartada

alien ['eɪlɪən] n (foreigner) extranjero/a; (extraterrestrial) extraterrestre m/f ♦ adj: **~ to** ajeno a; **~ate** vt enajenar, alejar

alight [ə'laɪt] adj ardiendo; (eyes) brillante ♦ vi (person) apearse, bajar; (bird) posarse

align [ə'laɪn] vt alinear

alike [ə'laɪk] adj semejantes, iguales ♦ adv igualmente, del mismo modo; **to look ~** parecerse

alimony ['ælɪmənɪ] n manutención f

alive [ə'laɪv] adj vivo; (lively) alegre

─── KEYWORD ───

all [ɔːl] adj (sg) todo/a; (pl) todos/as; **~ day** todo el día; **~ night** toda la noche; **~ men** todos los hombres; **~ five came** vinieron los cinco; **~ the books** todos los libros; **~ his life** toda su vida

♦ pron **1** todo; **I ate it ~**, **I ate ~ of it** me lo comí todo; **~ of us went** fuimos todos; **~ the boys went** fueron todos los chicos; **is that ~?** ¿eso es todo? ¿algo más?; (in shop) ¿algo más?, ¿alguna cosa más?

2 (in phrases): **above ~** sobre todo; por encima de todo; **after ~** después

de todo; **at ~: not at ~** (in answer to question) en absoluto; (in answer to thanks) ¡de nada!, ¡no hay de qué!; **I'm not at ~ tired** no estoy nada cansado/a; **anything at ~ will do** cualquier cosa viene bien; **~ in ~** a fin de cuentas

♦ adv: **~ alone** completamente solo/a; **it's not as hard as ~ that** no es tan difícil como la pintas; **~ the more/the better** tanto más/mejor; **~ but** casi; **the score is 2 ~** están empatados a 2

all clear n (after attack etc) fin m de la alerta; (fig) luz f verde

allege [ə'ledʒ] vt pretender; **~dly** [ə'ledʒɪdlɪ] adv supuestamente, según se afirma

allegiance [ə'liːdʒəns] n lealtad f

allergy ['ælədʒɪ] n alergia

alleviate [ə'liːvɪeɪt] vt aliviar

alley ['ælɪ] n callejuela

alliance [ə'laɪəns] n alianza

allied ['ælaɪd] adj aliado

alligator ['ælɪɡeɪtə*] n (ZOOL) caimán m

all-in (BRIT) adj (charge) todo incluido

all-night adj (café, shop) abierto toda la noche; (party) que dura toda la noche

allocate ['æləkeɪt] vt (money etc) asignar

allot [ə'lɔt] vt asignar; **~ment** n ración f; (garden) parcela

all-out adj (effort etc) supremo; **all out** adv con todas las fuerzas

allow [ə'laʊ] vt permitir, dejar; (a claim) admitir; (sum, time etc) dar, conceder; (concede): **to ~ that** reconocer que; **to ~ sb to do** permitir a alguien hacer; **he is ~ed to ...** se le permite ...; **~ for** vt fus tener en cuenta; **~ance** n subvención f; (welfare payment) subsidio, pensión f; (pocket money) dinero de bolsillo; (tax ~ance) desgravación f; **to make ~ances for** (person) disculpar a; (thing) tener en cuenta

alloy ['ælɔɪ] n mezcla

all: ~ **right** adv bien; (as answer) ¡conforme!, ¡está bien!; **~-rounder** n: **he's a good ~-rounder** se le da bien todo; **~-time** adj (record) de todos los tiempos

alluring [ə'ljʊərɪŋ] adj atractivo, tentador(a)

ally ['ælaɪ] n aliado/a ♦ vt: **to ~ o.s. with** aliarse con

almighty [ɔːl'maɪtɪ] adj todopoderoso; (row etc) imponente

almond ['ɑːmənd] n almendra

almost ['ɔːlməʊst] adv casi

alone [ə'ləʊn] adj, adv solo; **to leave sb ~** dejar a uno en paz; **to leave sth ~** no tocar algo, dejar algo sin tocar; **let ~ ...** y mucho menos ...

along [ə'lɒŋ] prep a lo largo de, por ♦ adv: **is he coming ~ with us?** ¿viene con nosotros?; **he was limping ~** iba cojeando; **~ with** junto con; **all ~** (all the time) desde el principio; **~side** prep al lado de ♦ adv al lado

aloof [ə'luːf] adj reservado ♦ adv: **to stand ~** mantenerse apartado

aloud [ə'laʊd] adv en voz alta

alphabet ['ælfəbet] n alfabeto

Alps [ælps] npl: **the ~** los Alpes

already [ɔːl'redɪ] adv ya

alright [ɔːl'raɪt] (BRIT) adv = **all right**

Alsatian [æl'seɪʃən] n (dog) pastor m alemán

also ['ɔːlsəʊ] adv también, además

altar ['ɔːltə*] n altar m

alter ['ɔːltə*] vt cambiar, modificar ♦ vi cambiar; **~ation** [ɔːltə'reɪʃən] n cambio; (to clothes) arreglo; (to building) arreglos mpl

alternate [adj ɔːl'tɜːnɪt, vb 'ɔːltəneɪt] adj (actions etc) alternativo; (events) alterno; (US) = **alternative** ♦ vi: **to ~ (with)** alternar (con); **on ~ days** un día sí y otro no; **alternating current** [-neɪtɪŋ] n corriente f alterna

alternative [ɔːl'tɜːnətɪv] adj alternativo

♦ n alternativa; **~ medicine** n medicina alternativa; **~ly** adv: **~ly one could ...** por otra parte se podría ...

although [ɔːl'ðəʊ] conj aunque

altitude ['æltɪtjuːd] n altura

alto ['æltəʊ] n (female) contralto f; (male) alto

altogether [ɔːltə'geðə*] adv completamente, del todo; (on the whole) en total, en conjunto

aluminium [ælju'mɪnɪəm] (BRIT), **aluminum** [ə'luːmɪnəm] (US) n aluminio

always ['ɔːlweɪz] adv siempre

Alzheimer's (disease) ['æltshaɪməz-] n enfermedad f de Alzheimer

AM n abbr (= Assembly Member) parlamentario/a m/f

am [æm] vb see **be**

a.m. adv abbr (= ante meridiem) de la mañana

amalgamate [ə'mælgəmeɪt] vi amalgamarse ♦ vt amalgamar, unir

amateur ['æmətə*] n aficionado/a, amateur m/f; **~ish** adj inexperto

amaze [ə'meɪz] vt asombrar, pasmar; **to be ~d (at)** quedar pasmado (de); **~ment** n asombro, sorpresa; **amazing** adj extraordinario; (fantastic) increíble

Amazon ['æməzən] n (GEO) Amazonas m

ambassador [æm'bæsədə*] n embajador/a m/f

amber ['æmbə*] n ámbar m; **at ~** (BRIT: AUT) en el amarillo

ambiguous [æm'bɪgjuəs] adj ambiguo

ambition [æm'bɪʃən] n ambición f; **ambitious** [-ʃəs] adj ambicioso

ambulance ['æmbjuləns] n ambulancia

ambush ['æmbuʃ] n emboscada ♦ vt tender una emboscada a

amenable [ə'miːnəbl] adj: **to be ~ to** dejarse influir por

amend [ə'mend] vt enmendar; **to make ~s** dar cumplida satisfacción

amenities [ə'miːnɪtɪz] npl

comodidades *fpl*

America [əˈmerɪkə] *n* (*USA*) Estados *mpl* Unidos; **~n** *adj*, *n* norteamericano/a *m/f*; estadounidense *m/f*

amiable [ˈeɪmɪəbl] *adj* amable, simpático

amicable [ˈæmɪkəbl] *adj* amistoso, amigable

amid(st) [əˈmɪd(st)] *prep* entre, en medio de

amiss [əˈmɪs] *adv*: **to take sth ~** tomar algo a mal; **there's something ~** pasa algo

ammonia [əˈməunɪə] *n* amoníaco

ammunition [æmjuˈnɪʃən] *n* municiones *fpl*

amnesty [ˈæmnɪstɪ] *n* amnistía

amok [əˈmɔk] *adv*: **to run ~** enloquecerse, desbocarse

among(st) [əˈmʌŋ(st)] *prep* entre, en medio de

amorous [ˈæmərəs] *adj* amoroso

amount [əˈmaunt] *n* (*gen*) cantidad; (*of bill etc*) suma, importe *m* ♦ *vi*: **to ~ to** sumar; (*be same as*) equivaler a, significar

amp(ere) [ˈæmp(εəˈ)] *n* amperio

ample [ˈæmpl] *adj* (*large*) grande; (*abundant*) abundante; (*enough*) bastante, suficiente

amplifier [ˈæmplɪfaɪəˈ] *n* amplificador *m*

amuse [əˈmjuːz] *vt* divertir; (*distract*) distraer, entretener; **~ment** *n* diversión *f*; (*pastime*) pasatiempo; (*laughter*) risa; **~ment arcade** *n* salón *m* de juegos; **~ment park** *n* parque *m* de atracciones

an [æn] *indef art see* **a**

anaemic [əˈniːmɪk] (*US* **anemic**) *adj* anémico; (*fig*) soso, insípido

anaesthetic [ænɪsˈθetɪk] *n* (*US* **anesthetic**) anestesia

analog(ue) [ˈænəlɔg] *adj* (*computer, watch*) analógico

analyse [ˈænəlaɪz] (*US* **analyze**) *vt*

analizar; **analysis** [əˈnæləsɪs] (*pl* **analyses**) *n* análisis *m inv*; **analyst** [-lɪst] *n* (*political analyst, psychoanalyst*) analista *m/f*

analyze [ˈænəlaɪz] (*US*) *vt* = **analyse**

anarchist [ˈænəkɪst] *n* anarquista *m/f*

anatomy [əˈnætəmɪ] *n* anatomía

ancestor [ˈænsɪstəˈ] *n* antepasado

anchor [ˈæŋkəˈ] *n* ancla, áncora ♦ *vi* (*also: to drop ~*) anclar ♦ *vt* anclar; **to weigh ~** levar anclas

anchovy [ˈæntʃəvɪ] *n* anchoa

ancient [ˈeɪnʃənt] *adj* antiguo

ancillary [ænˈsɪlərɪ] *adj* auxiliar

and [ænd] *conj* y; (*before i-, hi- + consonant*) e; **men ~ women** hombres y mujeres; **father ~ son** padre e hijo; **trees ~ grass** árboles y hierba; **~ so on** etcétera, y así sucesivamente; **try ~ come** procura venir; **he talked ~ talked** habló sin parar; **better ~ better** cada vez mejor

Andes [ˈændiːz] *npl*: **the ~** los Andes

anemic *etc* [əˈniːmɪk] (*US*) = **anaemic** *etc*

anesthetic *etc* [ænɪsˈθetɪk] (*US*) = **anaesthetic** *etc*

anew [əˈnjuː] *adv* de nuevo, otra vez

angel [ˈeɪndʒəl] *n* ángel *m*

anger [ˈæŋgəˈ] *n* cólera

angina [ænˈdʒaɪnə] *n* angina (del pecho)

angle [ˈæŋgl] *n* ángulo; **from their ~** desde su punto de vista

angler [ˈæŋgləˈ] *n* pescador(a) *m/f* (de caña)

Anglican [ˈæŋglɪkən] *adj*, *n* anglicano/a *m/f*

angling [ˈæŋglɪŋ] *n* pesca con caña

Anglo- [ˈæŋgləu] *prefix* anglo-

angrily [ˈæŋgrɪlɪ] *adv* coléricamente, airadamente

angry [ˈæŋgrɪ] *adj* enfadado, airado; (*wound*) inflamado; **to be ~ with sb/ at sth** estar enfadado con alguien/por algo; **to get ~** enfadarse, enojarse

anguish [ˈæŋgwɪʃ] *n* (*physical*)

tormentos *mpl*; (*mental*) angustia
animal ['ænɪməl] *n* animal *m*; (*pej: person*) bestia ♦ *adj* animal
animate ['ænɪmeɪt] *adj* vivo; **~d** [-meɪtɪd] *adj* animado
aniseed ['ænɪsiːd] *n* anís *m*
ankle ['æŋkl] *n* tobillo *m*; **~ sock** *n* calcetín *m* corto
annex [*n* 'æneks, *vb* æ'neks] *n* (*also: BRIT: annexe*) (*building*) edificio anexo ♦ *vt* (*territory*) anexionar
annihilate [ə'naɪəleɪt] *vt* aniquilar
anniversary [ænɪ'vɜːsərɪ] *n* aniversario *m*
announce [ə'nauns] *vt* anunciar; **~ment** *n* anuncio; **~r** *n* (RADIO) locutor(a) *m/f*; (TV) presentador(a) *m/f*
annoy [ə'nɔɪ] *vt* molestar, fastidiar; **don't get ~ed!** ¡no se enfade!; **~ance** *n* enojo; **~ing** *adj* molesto, fastidioso; (*person*) pesado
annual ['ænjuəl] *adj* anual ♦ *n* (BOT) anual *m*; (*book*) anuario; **~ly** *adv* anualmente, cada año
annul [ə'nʌl] *vt* anular
annum ['ænəm] *n* see **per**
anonymous [ə'nɒnɪməs] *adj* anónimo
anorak ['ænəræk] *n* anorak *m*
anorexia [ænə'reksɪə] *n* (MED: also: **~ nervosa**) anorexia
another [ə'nʌðə*] *adj* (*one more, a different one*) otro ♦ *pron* otro; see **one**
answer ['ɑːnsə*] *n* contestación *f*, respuesta; (*to problem*) solución *f* ♦ *vi* contestar, responder ♦ *vt* (*reply to*) contestar a, responder a; (*problem*) resolver; (*prayer*) escuchar; **in ~ to your letter** contestando o en contestación a su carta; **to ~ the phone** contestar o coger el teléfono; **to ~ the bell** o **the door** acudir a la puerta; **~ back** *vi* replicar, ser respondón/ona; **~ for** *vt fus* responder de o por; **~ to** *vt fus* (*description*) corresponder a; **~able** *adj*: **~able to sb for sth** responsable ante uno de algo; **~ing machine** *n* contestador *m*

automático
ant [ænt] *n* hormiga
antagonism [æn'tægənɪzm] *n* antagonismo, hostilidad *f*
antagonize [æn'tægənaɪz] *vt* provocar la enemistad de
Antarctic [ænt'ɑːktɪk] *n*: **the ~** el Antártico
antelope ['æntɪləup] *n* antílope *m*
antenatal ['æntɪ'neɪtl] *adj* antenatal, prenatal; **~ clinic** *n* clínica prenatal
anthem ['ænθəm] *n*: **national ~** himno nacional
anthropology [ænθrə'pɒlədʒɪ] *n* antropología
anti... [æntɪ] *prefix* anti...; **~aircraft** [-'eəkrɑːft] *adj* antiaéreo; **~biotic** [-baɪ'ɒtɪk] *n* antibiótico; **~body** ['æntɪbɒdɪ] *n* anticuerpo
anticipate [æn'tɪsɪpeɪt] *vt* prever; (*expect*) esperar, contar con; (*look forward to*) esperar con ilusión; (*do first*) anticiparse a, adelantarse a
anticipation [-'peɪʃən] *n* (*expectation*) previsión *f*; (*eagerness*) ilusión *f*, expectación *f*
anticlimax [æntɪ'klaɪmæks] *n* decepción *f*
anticlockwise [æntɪ'klɒkwaɪz] (BRIT) *adv* en dirección contraria a la de las agujas del reloj
antics ['æntɪks] *npl* gracias *fpl*
anticyclone [æntɪ'saɪkləun] *n* anticiclón *m*
antidepressant ['æntɪdɪ'presnt] *n* antidepresivo
antidote ['æntɪdəut] *n* antídoto
antifreeze ['æntɪfriːz] *n* anticongelante *m*
antihistamine [æntɪ'hɪstəmiːn] *n* antihistamínico
antiquated ['æntɪkweɪtɪd] *adj* anticuado
antique [æn'tiːk] *n* antigüedad *f* ♦ *adj* antiguo; **~ dealer** *n* anticuario/a; **~ shop** *n* tienda de antigüedades
antiquity [æn'tɪkwɪtɪ] *n* antigüedad *f*

antiseptic [æntɪˈsɛptɪk] *adj, n* antiséptico

antlers [ˈæntləz] *npl* cuernas *fpl*, cornamenta *sg*

anus [ˈeɪnəs] *n* ano

anvil [ˈænvɪl] *n* yunque *m*

anxiety [æŋˈzaɪətɪ] *n* inquietud *f*; (MED) ansiedad *f*; **~ to do** deseo de hacer

anxious [ˈæŋkʃəs] *adj* inquieto, preocupado; (*worrying*) preocupante; (*keen*): **to be ~ to do** tener muchas ganas de hacer

---
KEYWORD
---

any [ˈɛnɪ] *adj* **1** (*in questions etc*) algún/alguna; **have you ~ butter/children?** ¿tienes mantequilla/hijos?; **if there are ~ tickets left** si quedan billetes, si queda algún billete

2 (*with negative*): **I haven't ~ money/books** no tengo dinero/libros

3 (*no matter which*) cualquier; **~ excuse will do** valdrá o servirá cualquier excusa; **choose ~ book you like** escoge el libro que quieras; **~ teacher you ask will tell you** cualquier profesor al que preguntes te lo dirá

4 (*in phrases*): **in ~ case** de todas formas, en cualquier caso; **~ day now** cualquier día (de estos); **at ~ moment** en cualquier momento, de un momento a otro; **at ~ rate** en todo caso; **~ time: come (at) ~ time** ven cuando quieras; **he might come (at) ~ time** podría llegar de un momento a otro

♦ *pron* **1** (*in questions etc*): **have you got ~?** ¿tienes alguno(s)/a(s)?; **can ~ of you sing?** ¿sabe cantar alguno de vosotros/ustedes?

2 (*with negative*): **I haven't ~ (of them)** no tengo ninguno

3 (*no matter which one(s)*): **take ~ of those books (you like)** toma el libro que quieras de ésos

♦ *adv* **1** (*in questions etc*): **do you want ~ more soup/sandwiches?** ¿quieres más sopa/bocadillos?; **are you feeling ~ better?** ¿te sientes algo mejor?

2 (*with negative*): **I can't hear him ~ more** ya no le oigo; **don't wait ~ longer** no esperes más

---

anybody [ˈɛnɪbɔdɪ] *pron* cualquiera; (*in interrogative sentences*) alguien; (*in negative sentences*): **I don't see ~** no veo a nadie; **if ~ should phone ...** si llama alguien ...

anyhow [ˈɛnɪhau] *adv* (*at any rate*) de todos modos, de todas formas; (*haphazard*): **do it ~ you like** hazlo como quieras; **she leaves things just ~** deja las cosas como quiera or de cualquier modo; **I shall go ~** de todos modos iré

anyone [ˈɛnɪwʌn] *pron* = **anybody**

anything [ˈɛnɪθɪŋ] *pron* (*in questions etc*) algo, alguna cosa; (*with negative*) nada; **can you see ~?** ¿ves algo?; **if ~ happens to me ...** si algo me ocurre ...; (*no matter what*): **you can say ~ you like** puedes decir lo que quieras; **~ will do** vale todo or cualquier cosa; **he'll eat ~** come de todo or lo que sea

anyway [ˈɛnɪweɪ] *adv* (*at any rate*) de todos modos, de todas formas; **I shall go ~** iré de todos modos; (*besides*): **~, I couldn't come even if I wanted to** además, no podría venir aunque quisiera; **why are you phoning, ~?** ¿entonces, por qué llamas?, ¿por qué llamas, pues?

anywhere [ˈɛnɪwɛə] *adv* (*in questions etc*): **can you see him ~?** ¿le ves por algún lado?; **are you going ~?** ¿vas a algún sitio?; (*with negative*): **I can't see him ~** no le veo por ninguna parte; **~ in the world** en cualquier parte (del mundo); **put the books down ~** deja los libros donde quieras

apart [əˈpɑːt] adv (aside) aparte; (situation): ~ **(from)** separado (de); (movement): ~ **(from)** separado (de); (movement): ~ separar; **10 miles** ~ separados por 10 millas; **to take** ~ desmontar; ~ **from** prep aparte de

apartheid [əˈpɑːteɪt] n apartheid m

apartment [əˈpɑːtmənt] n (US) piso (SP), departamento (AM), apartamento; (room) cuarto; ~ **building** (US) n edificio de apartamentos

apathetic [æpəˈθetɪk] adj apático, indiferente

ape [eɪp] n mono ♦ vt imitar, remedar

aperitif [əˈperɪtɪf] n aperitivo

aperture [ˈæpətʃjuə*] n rendija, resquicio; (PHOT) abertura

APEX [ˈeɪpeks] n abbr (= Advanced Purchase Excursion Fare) tarifa APEX f

apex n ápice m; (fig) cumbre f

apiece [əˈpiːs] adv cada uno

aplomb [əˈplɒm] n aplomo

apologetic [əpɒləˈdʒetɪk] adj de disculpa; (person) arrepentido

apologize [əˈpɒlədʒaɪz] vi: **to** ~ **(for sth to sb)** disculparse (con alguien de algo)

apology [əˈpɒlədʒɪ] n disculpa, excusa

apostrophe [əˈpɒstrəfɪ] n apóstrofo m

appal [əˈpɔːl] vt horrorizar, espantar; ~**ling** adj espantoso; (awful) pésimo

apparatus [æpəˈreɪtəs] n (equipment) equipo, (organization) aparato; (in gymnasium) aparatos mpl

apparel [əˈpærəl] (US) n ropa

apparent [əˈpærənt] adj aparente; (obvious) evidente; ~**ly** adv por lo visto, al parecer

appeal [əˈpiːl] vi (LAW) apelar ♦ n (LAW) apelación f; (request) llamamiento; (plea) petición f; (charm) atractivo; **to** ~ **for** reclamar; **to** ~ **to** (be attractive to) atraer; **it doesn't** ~ **to me** no me atrae, no me llama la atención; ~**ing** adj (attractive) atractivo

appear [əˈpɪə*] vi aparecer;

presentarse; (LAW) comparecer; (publication) salir (a luz), publicarse; (seem) parecer; **to** ~ **on TV/in "Hamlet"** salir por la tele/hacer un papel en "Hamlet"; **it would** ~ **that** parecería que; ~**ance** n aparición f; (look) apariencia, aspecto

appease [əˈpiːz] vt (pacify) apaciguar; (satisfy) satisfacer

appendices [əˈpendɪsiːz] npl of **appendix**

appendicitis [əpendɪˈsaɪtɪs] n apendicitis f

appendix [əˈpendɪks] (pl **appendices**) n apéndice m

appetite [ˈæpɪtaɪt] n apetito; (fig) deseo, anhelo

appetizer [ˈæpɪtaɪzə*] n (drink) aperitivo; (food) tapas fpl (SP)

applaud [əˈplɔːd] vt, vi aplaudir

applause [əˈplɔːz] n aplausos mpl

apple [ˈæpl] n manzana; ~ **tree** n manzano

appliance [əˈplaɪəns] n aparato

applicable [əˈplɪkəbl] adj (relevant): **to be** ~ **(to)** referirse (a)

applicant [ˈæplɪkənt] n candidato/a; solicitante m/f

application [æplɪˈkeɪʃən] n aplicación f; (for a job etc) solicitud f, petición f; ~ **form** n solicitud f

applied [əˈplaɪd] adj aplicado

apply [əˈplaɪ] vt (paint etc) poner; (law etc: put into practice) poner en vigor ♦ vi: **to** ~ **to** (ask) dirigirse a; (be applicable) ser aplicable a; **to** ~ **for** (permit, grant, job) solicitar; **to** ~ **o.s. to** aplicarse a, dedicarse a

appoint [əˈpɔɪnt] vt (to post) nombrar; ~**ed** adj: **at the** ~**ed time** a la hora señalada; ~**ment** n (with client) cita; (act) nombramiento; (post) puesto; (at hairdresser etc): **to have an** ~**ment** tener hora; **to make an** ~**ment (with sb)** citarse (con uno)

appraisal [əˈpreɪzl] n valoración f

appreciate [əˈpriːʃieɪt] vt apreciar,

tener en mucho; (*be grateful for*) agradecer; (*be aware of*) comprender ♦ vi (COMM) aumentar(se) en valor;

appreciation [-'eɪʃən] n apreciación f; (*gratitude*) reconocimiento, agradecimiento; (COMM) aumento en valor

appreciative [ə'priːʃɪətɪv] adj apreciativo; (*comment*) agradecido

apprehensive [æprɪ'hensɪv] adj aprensivo

apprentice [ə'prentɪs] n aprendiz/a m/f; **~ship** n aprendizaje m

approach [ə'prəʊtʃ] vi acercarse ♦ vt acercarse a; (*ask, apply to*) dirigirse a; (*situation, problem*) abordar ♦ n acercamiento; (*access*) acceso; (*to problem, situation*): **~ (to)** actitud f (*ante*); **~able** adj (*person*) abordable; (*place*) accesible

appropriate [adj ə'prəʊprɪɪt, vb ə'prəʊprɪeɪt] adj apropiado, conveniente ♦ vt (*take*) apropiarse de

approval [ə'pruːvəl] n aprobación f, visto bueno; (*permission*) consentimiento; **on ~** (COMM) a prueba

approve [ə'pruːv] vt aprobar; **~ of** vt fus (*thing*) aprobar; (*person*): **they don't ~ of her** (*ella*) no les parece bien

approximate [ə'prɒksɪmɪt] adj aproximado; **~ly** adv aproximadamente, más o menos

apricot ['eɪprɪkɒt] n albaricoque m (SP), damasco (AM)

April ['eɪprəl] n abril m; **~ Fools' Day** n el primero de abril m; ≈ día m de los Inocentes (*28 December*)

apron ['eɪprən] n delantal m

apt [æpt] adj acertado, apropiado; (*likely*): **~ to** propenso a hacer

aquarium [ə'kweərɪəm] n acuario

Aquarius [ə'kweərɪəs] n Acuario

Arab ['ærəb] adj, n árabe m/f

Arabian [ə'reɪbɪən] adj árabe

Arabic ['ærəbɪk] adj árabe; (*numerals*) arábigo ♦ n árabe m

arable ['ærəbl] adj cultivable

Aragon ['ærəgən] n Aragón m

arbitrary ['ɑːbɪtrərɪ] adj arbitrario

arbitration [ɑːbɪ'treɪʃən] n arbitraje m

arcade [ɑː'keɪd] n (*round a square*) soportales mpl; (*shopping mall*) galería comercial

arch [ɑːtʃ] n arco; (*of foot*) arco del pie ♦ vt arquear

archaeologist [ɑːkɪ'ɒlədʒɪst] (US **archeologist**) n arqueólogo/a

archaeology [ɑːkɪ'ɒlədʒɪ] (US **archeology**) n arqueología

archbishop [ɑːtʃ'bɪʃəp] n arzobispo

archeology etc [ɑːkɪ'ɒlədʒɪ] (US) = **archaeology** etc

archery ['ɑːtʃərɪ] n tiro al arco

architect ['ɑːkɪtekt] n arquitecto/a; **~ure** n arquitectura

archives ['ɑːkaɪvz] npl archivo

Arctic ['ɑːktɪk] adj ártico ♦ n: **the ~** el Ártico

ardent ['ɑːdənt] adj ardiente, apasionado

arduous ['ɑːdjuəs] adj (*task*) arduo; (*journey*) agotador(a)

are [ɑː*] vb see **be**

area ['eərɪə] n área, región f; (*part of place*) zona; (MATH etc) área, superficie f; (*in room: e.g. dining ~*) parte f; (*of knowledge, experience*) campo

arena [ə'riːnə] n estadio; (*of circus*) pista

aren't [ɑːnt] = **are not**

Argentina [ɑːdʒən'tiːnə] n Argentina; **Argentinian** [-'tɪnɪən] adj, n argentino/a m/f

arguably ['ɑːgjuəblɪ] adv posiblemente

argue ['ɑːgjuː] vi (*quarrel*) discutir, pelearse; (*reason*) razonar, argumentar; **to ~ that** sostener que

argument ['ɑːgjumənt] n discusión f, pelea; (*reasons*) argumento; **~ative** [-'mentətɪv] adj discutidor(a)

Aries ['eərɪz] n Aries m

arise [ə'raɪz] (*pt* **arose**, *pp* **arisen**) vi surgir, presentarse

arisen [ə'rɪzn] *pp of* **arise**

aristocrat ['ærɪstəkræt] *n* aristócrata *m/f*

arithmetic [ə'rɪθmətɪk] *n* aritmética

ark [ɑːk] *n*: **Noah's A~** el Arca *f* de Noé

arm [ɑːm] *n* brazo ♦ *vt* armar; **~s** *npl* armas *fpl*; **~ in ~** = cogidos del brazo

armaments ['ɑːməmənts] *npl* armamento

armchair ['ɑːmtʃɛə*] *n* sillón *m*, butaca

armed [ɑːmd] *adj* armado; **~ robbery** *n* robo a mano armada

armour ['ɑːmə*] (*US* **armor**) *n* armadura; (*MIL*: *tanks*) blindaje *m*; **~ed car** *n* coche *m* (*SP*) o carro (*AM*) blindado

armpit ['ɑːmpɪt] *n* sobaco, axila

armrest ['ɑːmrest] *n* apoyabrazos *m inv*

army ['ɑːmɪ] *n* ejército; (*fig*) multitud *f*

aroma [ə'rəumə] *n* aroma *m*, fragancia; **~therapy** *n* aromaterapia

arose [ə'rəuz] *pt of* **arise**

around [ə'raund] *adv* alrededor; (*in the area*): **there is no one else ~** no hay nadie más por aquí ♦ *prep* alrededor de

arouse [ə'rauz] *vt* despertar; (*anger*) provocar

arrange [ə'reɪndʒ] *vt* arreglar, ordenar; (*organize*) organizar; **to ~ to do sth** quedar en hacer algo; **~ment** *n* arreglo; (*agreement*) acuerdo; **~ments** *npl* (*preparations*) preparativos *mpl*

array [ə'reɪ] *n*: **~ of** (*things*) serie *f* de; (*people*) conjunto de

arrears [ə'rɪəz] *npl* atrasos *mpl*; **to be in ~ with one's rent** estar retrasado en el pago del alquiler

arrest [ə'rest] *vt* detener; (*sb's attention*) llamar ♦ *n* detención *f*; **under ~** detenido

arrival [ə'raɪvl] *n* llegada; **new ~** recién llegado/a; (*baby*) recién nacido

arrive [ə'raɪv] *vi* llegar; (*baby*) nacer

arrogant ['ærəgənt] *adj* arrogante

arrow ['ærəu] *n* flecha

arse [ɑːs] (*BRIT*: *inf!*) *n* culo, trasero

arson ['ɑːsn] *n* incendio premeditado

art [ɑːt] *n* arte *m*; (*skill*) destreza; **A~s** *npl* (*SCOL*) Letras *fpl*

art gallery *n* pinacoteca; (*saleroom*) galería de arte

artery ['ɑːtərɪ] *n* arteria

arthritis [ɑː'θraɪtɪs] *n* artritis *f*

artichoke ['ɑːtɪtʃəuk] *n* alcachofa; **Jerusalem ~** aguaturma

article ['ɑːtɪkl] *n* artículo; (*BRIT*: *LAW*: *training*) **~s** *npl* contrato de aprendizaje; **~ of clothing** prenda de vestir

articulate [*adj* ɑː'tɪkjulɪt, *vb* ɑː'tɪkjuleɪt] *adj* claro, bien expresado ♦ *vt* expresar; **~d lorry** (*BRIT*) *n* trailer *m*

artificial [ɑːtɪ'fɪʃəl] *adj* artificial; (*affected*) afectado

artillery [ɑː'tɪlərɪ] *n* artillería

artisan ['ɑːtɪzæn] *n* artesano

artist ['ɑːtɪst] *n* artista *m/f*; (*MUS*) intérprete *m/f*; **~ic** [ɑː'tɪstɪk] *adj* artístico; **~ry** *n* arte *m*, habilidad *f* (artística)

art school *n* escuela de bellas artes

KEYWORD

as [æz] *conj* **1** (*referring to time*) cuando, mientras; a medida que; **~ the years went by** con el paso de los años; **he came in ~ I was leaving** entró cuando me marchaba; **~ from tomorrow** desde o a partir de mañana

2 (*in comparisons*): **~ big ~** tan grande como; **twice ~ big ~** el doble de grande que; **~ much money/many books ~** tanto dinero/tantos libros como; **~ soon ~** en cuanto

3 (*since, because*) como, ya que; **he left early ~ he had to be home by 10** se fue temprano ya que tenía que estar en casa a las 10

4 (*referring to manner, way*): **do ~ you**

wish haz lo que quieras; ~ **she said** como dijo; **he gave it to me** ~ **a present** me lo dio de regalo
5 (*in the capacity of*): **he works** ~ **a barman** trabaja de barman; ~ **chairman of the company, he ...** como presidente de la compañía, ...
6 (*concerning*): ~ **for** or **to that** por or en lo que respecta a eso
7: ~ **if** or **though** como si; **he looked** ~ **if he was ill** parecía como si estuviera enfermo, tenía aspecto de enfermo; *see also* **long; such; well**

a.s.a.p. *abbr* (= *as soon as possible*) cuanto antes

asbestos [æz'bestəs] *n* asbesto, amianto

ascend [ə'send] *vt* subir; (*throne*) ascender or subir a

ascent [ə'sent] *n* subida; (*slope*) cuesta, pendiente f

ascertain [æsə'teɪn] *vt* averiguar

ash [æʃ] *n* ceniza; (*tree*) fresno

ashamed [ə'feɪmd] *adj* avergonzado, apenado (*AM*); **to be** ~ **of** avergonzarse de

ashore [ə'ʃɔ:*] *adv* en tierra; (*swim etc*) a tierra

ashtray [æʃtreɪ] *n* cenicero

Ash Wednesday *n* miércoles *m* de Ceniza

Asia [ˈeɪʃə] *n* Asia; ~**n** *adj*, *n* asiático/a *m/f*

aside [ə'saɪd] *adv* a un lado ♦ *n* aparte *m*

ask [ɑːsk] *vt* (*question*) preguntar; (*invite*) invitar; **to** ~ **sb sth/to do sth** preguntar algo a alguien/pedir a alguien que haga algo; **to** ~ **sb about sth** preguntar algo a alguien; **to** ~ **(sb) a question** hacer una pregunta (a alguien); **to** ~ **sb out to dinner** invitar a cenar a uno; ~ **after** *vt fus* preguntar por; ~ **for** *vt fus* pedir; (*trouble*) buscar

asking price *n* precio inicial

asleep [ə'sliːp] *adj* dormido; **to fall** ~ dormirse, quedarse dormido

asparagus [əs'pærəgəs] *n* (*plant*) espárrago; (*food*) espárragos *mpl*

aspect [ˈæspekt] *n* aspecto, apariencia; (*direction in which a building etc faces*) orientación f

aspersions [əs'pɜ:ʃənz] *npl*: **to cast** ~ **on** difamar a, calumniar a

asphyxiation [æsfɪksi'eɪʃən] *n* asfixia

aspire [əs'paɪə*] *vi*: **to** ~ **to** aspirar a, ambicionar

aspirin [ˈæsprɪn] *n* aspirina

ass [æs] *n* asno, burro; (*inf*: *idiot*) imbécil *m/f*; (*US*: *inf*: *bottom*) culo, trasero

assailant [ə'seɪlənt] *n* asaltador/a *m/f*, agresor(a) *m/f*

assassinate [ə'sæsɪneɪt] *vt* asesinar; **assassination** [əsæsɪ'neɪʃən] *n* asesinato

assault [ə'sɔːlt] *n* asalto; (*LAW*) agresión f ♦ *vt* asaltar, atacar; (*sexually*) violar

assemble [ə'sembl] *vt* reunir, juntar; (*TECH*) montar ♦ *vi* reunirse, juntarse

assembly [ə'semblɪ] *n* reunión f, asamblea; (*parliament*) parlamento; (*construction*) montaje *m*; ~ **line** *n* cadena de montaje

assent [ə'sent] *n* asentimiento, aprobación f

assert [ə'sɜːt] *vt* afirmar; (*authority*) hacer valer; ~**ion** [-ʃən] *n* afirmación f

assess [ə'ses] *vt* valorar, calcular; (*tax, damages*) fijar; (*for tax*) gravar; ~**ment** *n* valoración f; (*for tax*) gravamen *m*; ~**or** *n* asesor(a) *m/f*

asset [ˈæset] *n* ventaja; ~**s** *npl* (*COMM*) activo; (*property, funds*) fondos *mpl*

assign [ə'saɪn] *vt*: **to** ~ **(to)** (*date*) fijar (para); (*task*) asignar (a); (*resources*) destinar (a); ~**ment** *n* tarea

assist [ə'sɪst] *vt* ayudar; ~**ance** *n* ayuda, auxilio; ~**ant** *n* ayudante *m/f*; (*BRIT*: *also*: **shop** ~**ant**) dependiente/a *m/f*

associate [*adj*, *n* ə'səʊʃɪɪt, *vb*

əˈsəʊʃɪeɪt] adj asociado ♦ n (at work) colega m/f ♦ vt asociar; (ideas) relacionar ♦ vi: to ~ with sb tratar con alguien

association [əsəʊsɪˈeɪʃən] n asociación f

assorted [əˈsɔːtɪd] adj surtido, variado

assortment [əˈsɔːtmənt] n (of shapes, colours) surtido; (of books) colección f; (of people) mezcla

assume [əˈsjuːm] vt suponer; (responsibilities) asumir; (attitude) adoptar, tomar

assumption [əˈsʌmpʃən] n suposición f, presunción f; (of power etc) toma

assurance [əˈʃʊərəns] n garantía, promesa; (confidence) confianza, aplomo; (insurance) seguro

assure [əˈʃʊə*] vt asegurar

asthma [ˈæsmə] n asma

astonish [əˈstɒnɪʃ] vt asombrar, pasmar; **~ment** n asombro, sorpresa

astound [əˈstaʊnd] vt asombrar, pasmar

astray [əˈstreɪ] adv: **to go ~** extraviarse; **to lead ~** (morally) llevar por mal camino

astride [əˈstraɪd] prep a caballo or horcajadas sobre

astrology [æsˈtrɒlədʒɪ] n astrología

astronaut [ˈæstrənɔːt] n astronauta m/f

astronomy [əsˈtrɒnəmɪ] n astronomía

asylum [əˈsaɪləm] n (refuge) asilo; (mental hospital) manicomio

KEYWORD

at [æt] prep 1 (referring to position: in) en; (direction) a; **~ the top** en lo alto; **~ home/school** en casa/la escuela; **to look ~ sth/sb** mirar algo/a uno
2 (referring to time): **~ 4 o'clock** a las 4; **~ night** por la noche; **~ Christmas** en Navidad; **~ times** a veces
3 (referring to rate, speed etc): **~ £1 a kilo** a una libra el kilo; **two ~ a time** de dos en dos; **~ 50 km/h** a 50 km/h

4 (referring to manner): **~ a stroke** de un golpe; **~ peace** en paz
5 (referring to activity): **to be ~ work** estar trabajando; (in the office etc) estar en el trabajo; **to play ~ cowboys** jugar a los vaqueros; **to be good ~ sth** ser bueno en algo
6 (referring to cause): **shocked/ surprised/annoyed ~ sth** asombrado/sorprendido/fastidiado por algo; **I went ~ his suggestion** fui a instancias suyas

ate [eɪt] pt of **eat**

atheist [ˈeɪθɪɪst] n ateo/a

Athens [ˈæθɪnz] n Atenas

athlete [ˈæθliːt] n atleta m/f

athletic [æθˈletɪk] adj atlético; **~s** n atletismo

Atlantic [ətˈlæntɪk] adj atlántico ♦ n: **the ~ (Ocean)** el (Océano) Atlántico

atlas [ˈætləs] n atlas m

A.T.M. n abbr (= automated telling machine) cajero automático

atmosphere [ˈætməsfɪə*] n atmósfera; (of place) ambiente m

atom [ˈætəm] n átomo; **~ic** [əˈtɒmɪk] adj atómico; **~ic bomb** n bomba atómica; **~izer** [ˈætəmaɪzə*] n atomizador m

atone [əˈtəʊn] vi: **to ~ for** expiar

atrocious [əˈtrəʊʃəs] adj atroz

attach [əˈtætʃ] vt (fasten) atar; (join) unir, sujetar; (document, letter) adjuntar; (importance etc) dar, conceder; **to be ~ed to sb/sth** (to like) tener cariño a alguien/algo

attaché case [əˈtæʃeɪ-] n maletín m

attachment [əˈtætʃmənt] n (tool) accesorio; (love): **~ (to)** apego a

attack [əˈtæk] vt (MIL) atacar; (subj: criminal) agredir, asaltar; (criticize) criticar; (task) emprender ♦ n ataque m, asalto; (on sb's life) atentado; (fig: criticism) crítica; (of illness) ataque m; **heart ~** infarto (de miocardio); **~er** n agresor(a) m/f, asaltante m/f

attain [ə'teɪn] vt (also: ~ to) alcanzar; (achieve) lograr, conseguir

attempt [ə'tɛmpt] n tentativa, intento; (attack) atentado ♦ vt intentar; ~ed adj: ~ed burglary/murder/suicide tentativa or intento de robo/asesinato/ suicidio

attend [ə'tɛnd] vt asistir a; (patient) atender; ~ to vt fus ocuparse de; (customer, patient) atender a; ~ance n asistencia, presencia; (people present) concurrencia; ~ant n ayudante m/f; (in garage etc) encargado/a ♦ adj (dangers) concomitante

attention [ə'tɛnʃən] n atención f; (care) atenciones fpl ♦ excl (MIL) ¡firme(s)!; for the ~ of (ADMIN) atención ...

attentive [ə'tɛntɪv] adj atento

attic ['ætɪk] n desván m

attitude ['ætɪtjuːd] n actitud f; (disposition) disposición f

attorney [ə'tɜːnɪ] n (lawyer) abogado/ a; A~ General n (BRIT) ≈ Presidente m del Consejo del Poder Judicial (SP); (US) ≈ ministro de justicia

attract [ə'trækt] vt atraer; (sb's attention) llamar; ~ion [ə'trækʃən] n encanto; (gen pl: amusements) diversiones fpl; (PHYSICS) atracción f; (fig: towards sb, sth) atractivo; ~ive adj guapo; (interesting) atrayente

attribute [n 'ætrɪbjuːt, vb ə'trɪbjuːt] n atributo ♦ vt: to ~ sth to atribuir algo a

attrition [ə'trɪʃən] n: war of ~ guerra de agotamiento

aubergine ['əʊbəʒiːn] (BRIT) n berenjena; (colour) morado

auburn ['ɔːbən] adj color castaño rojizo

auction ['ɔːkʃən] n (also: sale by ~) subasta ♦ vt subastar; ~eer [-'nɪə*] n subastador(a) m/f

audible ['ɔːdɪbl] adj audible, que se puede oír

audience ['ɔːdɪəns] n público, (RADIO)

radioescuchas mpl; (TV) telespectadores mpl; (interview) audiencia

audio-visual [ɔːdɪəʊ'vɪzjuəl] adj audiovisual; ~ aid n ayuda audiovisual.

audit ['ɔːdɪt] vt revisar, intervenir

audition [ɔː'dɪʃən] n audición f

auditor ['ɔːdɪtə*] n interventor(a) m/f, censor(a) m/f de cuentas

augment [ɔːg'mɛnt] vt aumentar

augur ['ɔːgə*] vi: it ~s well es un buen augurio

August ['ɔːgəst] n agosto

aunt [ɑːnt] n tía; ~ie, ~y n diminutive of aunt; ~y n diminutive of aunt

au pair ['əʊ'pɛə*] n (also: ~ girl) (chica) au pair f

auspicious [ɔːs'pɪʃəs] adj propicio, de buen augurio

Australia [ɔs'treɪlɪə] n Australia; ~n adj, n australiano/a m/f

Austria ['ɔstrɪə] n Austria; ~n adj, n austríaco/a m/f

authentic [ɔː'θɛntɪk] adj auténtico

author ['ɔːθə] n autor(a) m/f

authoritarian [ɔːθɔrɪ'tɛərɪən] adj autoritario

authoritative [ɔː'θɔrɪtətɪv] adj autorizado; (manner) autoritario

authority [ɔː'θɔrɪtɪ] n autoridad f; (official permission) autorización f; the authorities npl las autoridades

authorize ['ɔːθəraɪz] vt autorizar

auto ['ɔːtəʊ] (US) n coche m (SP), carro (AM), automóvil m

auto- ~**biography** [ɔːtəbaɪ'ɔgrəfɪ] n autobiografía; ~**graph** ['ɔːtəgrɑːf] n autógrafo ♦ vt (photo etc) dedicar; (programme) firmar; ~**mated** ['ɔːtəmeɪtɪd] adj automatizado; ~**matic** [ɔːtə'mætɪk] adj automático ♦ n (gun) pistola automática; (car) coche m automático; ~**matically** adv automáticamente; ~**mation** [ɔːtə'meɪʃən] n reconversión f; ~**mobile** ['ɔːtəməbiːl] (US) n coche m (SP), carro (AM), automóvil m; ~**nomy** [ɔː'tɔnəmɪ] n autonomía

autumn ['ɔːtəm] n otoño

auxiliary [ɔːg'zɪlɪəri] adj, n auxiliar m/f

avail [ə'veɪl] vt: **to ~ o.s. of** aprovechar(se) de ♦ n: **to no ~** en vano, sin resultado

available [ə'veɪləbl] adj disponible; (unoccupied) libre; (person: unattached) soltero y sin compromiso

avalanche ['ævəlɑːnʃ] n alud m, avalancha

avant-garde ['ævãŋ'gɑːd] adj de vanguardia

Ave. abbr = **avenue**

avenge [ə'vendʒ] vt vengar

avenue ['ævənjuː] n avenida; (fig) camino

average ['ævərɪdʒ] n promedio, término medio ♦ adj medio, de término medio; (ordinary) regular, corriente ♦ vt sacar un promedio de; **on ~** por regla general; **~ out** vi: **to ~ out at** salir en un promedio de

averse [ə'vɜːs] adj: **to be ~ to sth/ doing** sentir aversión or antipatía por algo/por hacer

avert [ə'vɜːt] vt prevenir; (blow) desviar; (one's eyes) apartar

aviary ['eɪvɪərɪ] n pajarera, avería

avocado [ævə'kɑːdəu] n (also: BRIT: ~ pear) aguacate m (SP), palta (AM)

avoid [ə'vɔɪd] vt evitar, eludir

await [ə'weɪt] vt esperar, aguardar

awake [ə'weɪk] (pt awoke, pp awoken or awaked) adj despierto ♦ vt despertar ♦ vi despertarse; **to be ~** estar despierto; **~ning** el despertar

award [ə'wɔːd] n premio; (LAW: damages) indemnización ♦ vt otorgar, conceder; (LAW: damages) adjudicar

aware [ə'wεə*] adj: **~ (of)** consciente (de); **to become ~ of/that** (realize) darse cuenta de/de que; (learn) enterarse de/de que; **~ness** n conciencia; (knowledge) conocimiento

away [ə'weɪ] adv fuera; (movement): **she went ~** se marchó; (far~): lejos; **two kilometres ~** a dos kilómetros

de distancia; **two hours ~ by car** a dos horas en coche; **the holiday was two weeks ~** faltaban dos semanas para las vacaciones; **he's ~ for a week** estará ausente una semana; **to take ~ (from)** quitar (a); (subtract) substraer (de); **to work/pedal ~** seguir trabajando/pedaleando; **to fade ~** (colour) desvanecerse; (sound) apagarse; **~ game** n (SPORT) partido de fuera

awe [ɔː] n admiración f respetuosa; **~-inspiring** adj imponente

awful ['ɔːfəl] adj horroroso; (quantity): **an ~ lot (of)** cantidad (de); **~ly** adv (very) terriblemente

awkward ['ɔːkwəd] adj desmañado, torpe; (shape) incómodo; (embarrassing) delicado, difícil

awning ['ɔːnɪŋ] n (of tent, caravan, shop) toldo

awoke [ə'wəuk] pt of **awake**

awoken [ə'wəukən] pp of **awake**

awry [ə'raɪ] adv: **to be ~** estar descolocado or mal puesto

axe [æks] (US **ax**) n hacha ♦ vt (project) cortar; (jobs) reducir

axes ['æksiːz] npl of **axis**

axis ['æksɪs] (pl **axes**) n eje m

axle ['æksl] n eje m, árbol m

ay(e) [aɪ] excl sí

B, b

B [biː] n (MUS) si m

B.A. abbr = **Bachelor of Arts**

baby ['beɪbɪ] n bebé m/f; (US: inf: darling) mi amor; **~ carriage** n (US) cochecito; **~-sit** vi hacer de canguro; **~-sitter** n canguro/a; **~ wipe** n toallita húmeda (para bebés)

bachelor ['bætʃələ*] n soltero; **B~ of Arts/Science** licenciado/a en Filosofía y Letras/Ciencias

back [bæk] n (of person) espalda; (of animal) lomo; (of hand) dorso; (as opposed to front) parte f de atrás; (of chair) respaldo; (of page) reverso; (of book) final m; (FOOTBALL) defensa m; (of crowd): **the ones at the ~** los del fondo ♦ vt (candidate: also: ~ **up**) respaldar, apoyar; (horse: at races) apostar a; (car) dar marcha atrás a o con ♦ vi (car) ir (o salir o entrar) marcha atrás ♦ adj (payment, rent) atrasado; (seats, wheels) de atrás ♦ adv (not forward) (hacia) atrás; (returned): **he's ~** está de vuelta, ha vuelto; **he ran ~** volvió corriendo; (restitution): **throw the ball ~** devuelve la pelota; **can I have it ~?** ¿me lo devuelve?; (again): **he called ~** llamó de nuevo; **~ down** vi echarse atrás; **~ out** vi (of promise) volverse atrás; **~ up** vt (person) apoyar, respaldar; (theory) defender; (COMPUT) hacer una copia preventiva o de reserva; **~bencher** (BRIT) n miembro del parlamento sin cargo relevante; **~bone** n columna vertebral; **~date** vt (pay rise) dar efecto retroactivo a; (letter) poner fecha atrasada a; **~drop** n telón m de fondo; **~fire** vi (AUT) petardear; (plans) fallar, salir mal; **~ground** n fondo; (of events) antecedentes mpl; (basic knowledge) bases fpl; (experience) conocimientos mpl, educación f; **~ family ~ground** origen m, antecedentes mpl; **~hand** n (TENNIS: also: **~hand stroke**) revés m; **~hander** (BRIT) n (bribe) soborno; **~ing** n (fig) apoyo, respaldo; **~lash** n reacción f; **~log** n: **~log of work** trabajo atrasado; **~ number** n (of magazine etc) número atrasado; **~pack** n mochila; **~packer** n mochilero(a); **~ pay** n pago atrasado; **~side** (inf) n trasero, culo; **~stage** adv entre bastidores; **~stroke** n espalda; **~up** adj suplementario; (COMPUT) de reserva ♦ n (support) apoyo; (also: **~up file**) copia preventiva o de reserva; **~ward** adj (person, country) atrasado; **~wards** adv hacia atrás; (read a list) al revés;

(fall) de espaldas; **~yard** n traspatio

bacon ['beɪkən] n tocino, beicon m

bad [bæd] adj malo; (mistake, accident) grave; (food) podrido, pasado; **his ~ leg** su pierna lisiada; **to go ~** (food) pasarse

badge [bædʒ] n insignia; (policeman's) chapa, placa

badger ['bædʒə*] n tejón m

badly ['bædlɪ] adv mal; **to reflect ~ on sb** influir negativamente en la reputación de uno; **~ wounded** gravemente herido; **he needs it ~** le hace gran falta; **to be ~ off (for money)** andar mal de dinero

badminton ['bædmɪntən] n bádminton m

bad-tempered adj de mal genio o carácter; (temporarily) de mal humor

bag [bæg] n bolsa; (handbag) bolso; (satchel) mochila; (case) maleta; **~s of** (inf) un montón de; **~gage** n equipaje m; **~gage allowance** n límite m de equipaje; **~gage reclaim** n recogida de equipajes; **~gy** adj amplio; **~pipes** npl gaita

Bahamas [bə'hɑːməz] npl: **the ~** las Islas Bahamas

bail [beɪl] n fianza ♦ vt (prisoner: gen: grant ~) poner en libertad bajo fianza; (boat: also: ~ **out**) achicar; **on ~** (prisoner) bajo fianza; **to ~ sb out** obtener la libertad de uno bajo fianza; see also **bale**

bailiff ['beɪlɪf] n alguacil m

bait [beɪt] n cebo ♦ vt poner cebo en; (tease) tomar el pelo a

bake [beɪk] vt cocer (al horno) ♦ vi cocerse; **~d beans** npl judías fpl en salsa de tomate; **~d potato** n patata al horno; **~r** n panadero; **~ry** n panadería; (for cakes) pastelería; **baking** n (act) amasar m; (batch) hornada; **baking powder** n levadura (en polvo)

balance ['bæləns] n equilibrio; (COMM: sum) balance m; (remainder) resto;

(scales) balanza ♦ vt equilibrar; (budget) nivelar; (account) saldar; (make equal) equilibrar; ~ **of trade/payments** balanza de comercio/pagos; **~d** adj (personality, diet) equilibrado; (report) objetivo; ~ **sheet** n balance m

balcony ['bælkənɪ] n (open) balcón m; (closed) galería; (in theatre) anfiteatro

bald [bɔːld] adj calvo; (tyre) liso

bale [beɪl] n (AGR) paca, fardo; (of papers etc) fajo; ~ **out** vi lanzarse en paracaídas

Balearics [bælɪ'æɪks] npl: **the** ~ las Baleares

ball [bɔːl] n pelota; (football) balón m; (of wool, string) ovillo; (dance) baile m; **to play** ~ (fig) cooperar

ballast ['bæləst] n lastre m

ball bearings npl cojinetes mpl de bolas

ballerina [bælə'riːnə] n bailarina

ballet ['bæleɪ] n ballet m; ~ **dancer** n bailarín/ina m/f

balloon [bə'luːn] n globo

ballot ['bælət] n votación f; ~ **paper** n papeleta (para votar)

ballpoint (pen) ['bɔːlpɔɪnt-] n bolígrafo

ballroom ['bɔːlrum] n salón m de baile

Baltic ['bɔːltɪk] n: **the** ~ **(Sea)** el (Mar) Báltico

ban [bæn] n prohibición f, proscripción f ♦ vt prohibir, proscribir

banal [bə'nɑːl] adj banal, vulgar

banana [bə'nɑːnə] n plátano (SP), banana (AM)

band [bænd] n grupo; (strip) faja, tira; (stripe) lista; (MUS: jazz) orquesta; (: rock) grupo; (: MIL) banda; ~ **together** vi juntarse, asociarse

bandage ['bændɪdʒ] n venda, vendaje m ♦ vt vendar

Bandaid ® ['bændeɪd] (US) n tirita

bandit ['bændɪt] n bandido

bandy-legged ['bændɪ'legd] adj estevado

bang [bæŋ] n (of gun, exhaust)

estallido, detonación f; (of door) portazo; (blow) golpe m ♦ vt (door) cerrar de golpe; (one's head) golpear ♦ vi estallar; (door) cerrar de golpe

Bangladesh [bɑːŋglə'deʃ] n Bangladesh m

bangs [bæŋz] (US) npl flequillo

banish ['bænɪʃ] vt desterrar

banister(s) ['bænɪstə(z)] n(pl) barandilla, pasamanos m inv

bank [bæŋk] n (COMM) banco; (of river, lake) ribera, orilla; (of earth) terraplén m ♦ vi (AVIAT) ladearse; ~ **on** vt fus contar con; ~ **account** n cuenta de banco; ~ **card** n tarjeta bancaria; ~er n banquero; ~**er's card** (BRIT) n = ~ **card**; **B**~ **holiday** (BRIT) n día m festivo; ~**ing** n banca; ~**note** n billete m de banco; ~ **rate** n tipo de interés bancario

---
bank holiday

El término **bank holiday** *se aplica en el Reino Unido a todo día festivo oficial en el que cierran bancos y comercios. Los más importantes son en Navidad, Semana Santa, finales de mayo y finales de agosto y, al contrario que en los países de tradición católica, no coinciden necesariamente con una celebración religiosa.*

---

bankrupt ['bæŋkrʌpt] adj quebrado, insolvente; **to go** ~ hacer bancarrota; **to be** ~ estar en quiebra; ~**cy** n quiebra

bank statement n balance m or detalle m de cuenta

banner ['bænə*] n pancarta

bannister(s) ['bænɪstə(z)] n(pl) = **banister(s)**

baptism ['bæptɪzəm] n bautismo; (act) bautizo

bar [bɑː*] n (pub) bar m; (counter) mostrador m; (rod) barra; (of window, cage) reja; (of soap) pastilla; (of chocolate) tableta; (fig: hindrance) obstáculo; (prohibition) proscripción f; (MUS) barra ♦ vt (road) obstruir; (person) excluir; (activity) prohibir; the B~ (LAW) la abogacía; **behind ~s** entre rejas; **~ none** sin excepción

barbaric [ba:'bærɪk] adj bárbaro

barbecue ['ba:bɪkju:] n barbacoa

barbed wire ['ba:bd-] n alambre m de púas

barber ['ba:bə*] n peluquero, barbero

bar code n código de barras

bare [beə*] adj desnudo; (trees) sin hojas; (necessities etc) básico ♦ vt desnudar; (teeth) enseñar; **~back** adv a pelo, sin silla; **~faced** adj descarado; **~foot** adj, adv descalzo; **~ly** adv apenas

bargain ['ba:gɪn] n pacto, negocio; (good buy) ganga ♦ vi negociar; (haggle) regatear; **into the ~** además, por añadidura; **~ for** vt fus: **he got more than he ~ed for** le resultó peor de lo que esperaba

barge [ba:dʒ] n barcaza; **~ in** vi irrumpir; (interrupt: conversation) interrumpir

bark [ba:k] n (of tree) corteza; (of dog) ladrido ♦ vi ladrar

barley ['ba:lɪ] n cebada

barmaid ['ba:meɪd] n camarera

barman ['ba:mən] n camarero, barman m

barn [ba:n] n granero

barometer [bə'rɔmɪtə*] n barómetro

baron ['bærən] n barón m; (press · etc) magnate m; **~ess** n baronesa

barracks ['bærəks] npl cuartel m

barrage ['bæra:ʒ] n (MIL.) descarga, bombardeo; (dam) presa; (of criticism) lluvia, aluvión m

barrel ['bærəl] n barril m; (of gun) cañón m

barren ['bærən] adj estéril

barricade [bærɪ'keɪd] n barricada

barrier ['bærɪə*] n barrera

barring ['ba:rɪŋ] prep excepto, salvo

barrister ['bærɪstə*] (BRIT) n abogado/a

barrow ['bærəu] n (cart) carretilla (de mano)

bartender ['ba:tendə*] (US) n camarero, barman m

barter ['ba:tə*] vt: **to ~ sth for sth** trocar algo por algo

base [beɪs] n base f ♦ vt: **to ~ sth on** basar or fundar algo en ♦ adj bajo, infame

baseball ['beɪsbɔ:l] n béisbol m

basement ['beɪsmənt] n sótano

bases¹ ['beɪsi:z] npl of **basis**

bases² ['beɪsɪz] npl of **base**

bash [bæʃ] (inf) vt golpear

bashful ['bæʃful] adj tímido, vergonzoso

basic ['beɪsɪk] adj básico; **~ally** adv fundamentalmente, en el fondo; (simply) sencillamente; **~s** npl: **the ~s** los fundamentos

basil ['bæzl] n albahaca

basin ['beɪsn] n cuenco, tazón m; (GEO) cuenca; (also: wash~) lavabo

basis ['beɪsɪs] (pl **bases**) n base f; **on a part-time/trial ~** a tiempo parcial/a prueba

bask [ba:sk] vi: **to ~ in the sun** tomar el sol

basket ['ba:skɪt] n cesta, cesto, canasta; **~ball** n baloncesto

Basque [bæsk] adj, n vasco/a m/f; **~ Country** n Euskadi m, País m Vasco

bass [beɪs] n (MUS: instrument) bajo; (double ~) contrabajo; (singer) bajo

bassoon [bə'su:n] n fagot m

bastard ['ba:stəd] n bastardo; (inf!) hijo de puta (!)

bat [bæt] n (ZOOL) murciélago; (for ball games) palo; (BRIT: for table tennis) pala ♦ vt: **he didn't ~ an eyelid** ni pestañeó

batch [bætʃ] n (of bread) hornada; (of letters etc) lote m

bated ['beɪtɪd] adj: **with ~ breath** sin respirar

bath [bɑ:θ, pl bɑ:ðz] n (action) baño; (~tub) baño (SP), bañera (SP), tina (AM) ♦ vt bañar; **to have a ~** bañarse, tomar un baño; see also **bathe**

bathe [beɪð] vi bañarse ♦ vt (wound) lavar; ~ n bañista m/f

bathing ['beɪðɪŋ] n el bañarse; **~ costume** (US ~ **suit**) n traje m de baño

bath: ~**robe** n (man's) batín m; (woman's) bata; ~**room** n (cuarto de) baño; **~s** [bɑ:ðz] npl (also: swimming ~s) piscina; ~ **towel** n toalla de baño

baton ['bætən] n (MUS) batuta; (ATHLETICS) testigo; (weapon) porra

batter ['bætə*] vt maltratar; (subj: rain etc) azotar ♦ n masa (para rebozar); ~**ed** adj (hat, pan) estropeado

battery ['bætərɪ] n (AUT) batería; (of torch) pila

battle ['bætl] n batalla; (fig) lucha ♦ vi luchar; ~**ship** n acorazado

bawl [bɔ:l] vi chillar, gritar; (child) berrear

bay [beɪ] n (GEO) bahía; **B~ of Biscay** ≈ mar Cantábrico; **to hold sb at ~** mantener a alguien a raya; ~ **leaf** n hoja de laurel

bay window n ventana saladiza

bazaar [bə'zɑ:*] n bazar m; (fete) venta con fines benéficos

B. & B. n abbr (= bed and breakfast) cama y desayuno

BBC n abbr (= British Broadcasting Corporation) cadena de radio y televisión estatal británica

B.C. adv abbr (= before Christ) a. de C.

KEYWORD

be [bi:] (pt was, were, pp been) aux vb 1 (with present participle: forming continuous tenses): **what are you doing?** ¿qué estás haciendo?, ¿qué haces?; **they're coming tomorrow** vienen mañana; **I've been waiting for you for hours** llevo horas esperándote

2 (with pp: forming passives) ser (but often replaced by active or reflective constructions); **to ~ murdered** ser asesinado; **the box had been opened** habían abierto la caja; **the thief was nowhere to ~ seen** no se veía al ladrón por ninguna parte

3 (in tag questions): **it was fun, wasn't it?** fue divertido, ¿no? or ¿verdad?; **he's good-looking, isn't he?** es guapo, ¿no te parece?; **she's back again, is she?** entonces, ¿ha vuelto?

4 (+ to + infin): **the house is to ~ sold** (necessity) hay que vender la casa; (future) van a vender la casa; **he's not to open it** no tiene que abrirlo

♦ vb + complement 1 (with n or num complement, but see also 3, 4, 5 and impers vb below) ser; **he's a doctor** es médico; **2 and 2 are 4** 2 y 2 son 4

2 (with adj complement: expressing permanent or inherent quality) ser; (: expressing state as temporary or reversible) estar; **I'm English** soy inglés/esa; **he's tall/pretty** es alto/ bonita; **he's young** es joven; ~ **careful/good/quiet** ten cuidado/ pórtate bien/cállate; **I'm tired** estoy cansado/a; **it's dirty** está sucio/a

3 (of health) estar; **how are you?** ¿cómo estás?; **he's very ill** está muy enfermo; **I'm better now** ya estoy mejor

4 (of age) tener; **how old are you?** ¿cuántos años tienes?; **I'm sixteen (years old)** tengo dieciséis años

5 (cost) costar; **how much was the meal?** ¿cuánto fue or costó la comida?; **that'll ~ £5.75, please** son £5.75, por favor; **this shirt is £17** esta camisa cuesta £17

♦ vi 1 (exist, occur etc) existir, haber; **the best singer that ever was** el mejor cantante que existió jamás; **is there a God?** ¿hay un Dios?, ¿existe

Dios?; **~ that as it may** sea como sea; **so ~ it** así sea
2 (referring to place) estar; **I won't ~ here tomorrow** no estaré aquí mañana
3 (referring to movement): **where have you been?** ¿dónde has estado?
♦ impers vb **1** (referring to time): **it's 5 o'clock** son las 5; **it's the 28th of April** estamos a 28 de abril
2 (referring to distance): **it's 10 km to the village** el pueblo está a 10 km
3 (referring to the weather): **it's too hot/cold** hace demasiado calor/frío; **it's windy today** hace viento hoy
4 (emphatic): **it's me** soy yo; **it was Maria who paid the bill** fue María la que pagó la cuenta

beach [biːtʃ] n playa ♦ vt varar
beacon ['biːkən] n (lighthouse) faro; (marker) guía
bead [biːd] n cuenta; (of sweat etc) gota
beak [biːk] n pico
beaker ['biːkə*] n vaso de plástico
beam [biːm] n (ARCH) viga, travesaño; (of light) rayo, haz m de luz ♦ vi brillar; (smile) sonreír
bean [biːn] n judía; **runner/broad ~** habichuela/haba; **coffee ~** grano de café; **~sprouts** npl brotes mpl de soja
bear [bɛə*] n (pt bore, pp borne) n oso ♦ vt (weight etc) llevar; (cost) pagar; (responsibility) tener; (endure) soportar, aguantar; (children) parir, tener; (fruit) dar ♦ vi: **to ~ right/left** torcer a la derecha/izquierda; **~ out** (suspicions) corroborar, confirmar; (person) dar la razón a; **~ up** (remain cheerful) mantenerse animado
beard [biəd] n barba; **~ed** adj con barba, barbudo
bearer ['bɛərə*] n portador(a) m/f
bearing ['bɛərɪŋ] n porte m, comportamiento; (connection) relación

f; **~s** npl (also: **ball ~s**) cojinetes mpl a bolas; **to take a ~** tomar marcaciones; **to find one's ~s** orientarse
beast [biːst] n bruto, salvaje m; **~ly** (inf) adj horrible
beat [biːt] n (pt **beat**, pp **beaten**) n (of heart) latido; (MUS) ritmo, compás m; (of policeman) ronda ♦ vt pegar, golpear; (eggs) batir; (defeat: opponent) vencer, derrotar; (: record) sobrepasar ♦ vi (heart) latir; (drum) redoblar; (rain, wind) azotar; **off the ~en track** aislado; **to ~ it** (inf) largarse; **~ off** rechazar; **~ up** (attack) dar una paliza a; **~ing** n paliza
beautiful ['bjuːtɪful] adj precioso, hermoso, bello; **~ly** adv maravillosamente
beauty ['bjuːtɪ] n belleza; **~ salon** n salón m de belleza; **~ spot** n (TOURISM) lugar m pintoresco
beaver ['biːvə*] n castor m
became [bɪ'keɪm] pt of **become**
because [bɪ'kɔz] conj porque; **~ of** debido a, a causa de
beckon ['bekən] vt (also: **~ to**) llamar con señas
become [bɪ'kʌm] (irreg: like **come**) vt (suit) favorecer, sentar bien a ♦ vi (+ n) hacerse, llegar a ser; (+ adj) ponerse, volverse; **to ~ fat** engordar
becoming [bɪ'kʌmɪŋ] adj (behaviour) decoroso; (clothes) favorecedor(a)
bed [bed] n cama; (of flowers) macizo; (of coal, clay) capa; (of river) lecho; (of sea) fondo; **to go to ~** acostarse; **~ and breakfast** n (place) pensión f; (terms) cama y desayuno; **~clothes** npl ropa de cama; **~ding** n ropa de cama

---

Bed and Breakfast

Se llama **Bed and Breakfast** a una forma de alojamiento, en el campo o la ciudad, que ofrece cama y desayuno a precios inferiores a los de un hotel. El servicio se suele anunciar con carteles en los que a menudo se usa únicamente la abreviatura B. & B.

bedraggled [bɪ'drægld] adj (untidy: person) desastrado; (clothes, hair) desordenado

bed: ~**ridden** adj postrado (en cama); ~**room** n dormitorio; ~**side** n: **at the** ~**side of** a la cabecera de; ~**sit(ter)** (BRIT) n estudio (SP), suite m (AM); ~**spread** n cubrecama m, colcha; ~**time** n hora de acostarse

bee [bi:] n abeja

beech [bi:tʃ] n haya

beef [bi:f] n carne f de vaca; **roast** ~ rosbif m; ~**burger** n hamburguesa; **B~eater** n alabardero de la Torre de Londres

beehive ['bi:haɪv] n colmena

beeline ['bi:laɪn] n: **to make a** ~ **for** ir derecho a

been [bi:n] pp of **be**

beer [bɪə*] n cerveza

beet [bi:t] (US) n (also: red ~) remolacha

beetle ['bi:tl] n escarabajo

beetroot ['bi:tru:t] (BRIT) n remolacha

before [bɪ'fɔ:*] prep (of time) antes de; (of space) delante de ♦ conj antes (de) que ♦ adv antes, anteriormente; delante, adelante; ~ **going** antes de marcharse; ~ **she goes** antes de que se vaya; **the week** ~ la semana anterior; **I've never seen it** ~ no lo he visto nunca; ~**hand** adv antes de antemano, con anticipación

beg [beg] vi pedir limosna ♦ vt pedir, rogar; (entreat) suplicar; **to** ~ **sb to do sth** rogar a uno que haga algo; see also **pardon**

began [bɪ'gæn] pt of **begin**

beggar ['begə*] n mendigo/a

begin [bɪ'gɪn] (pt **began**, pp **begun**) vt, vi empezar, comenzar; **to** ~ **doing** or **to do sth** empezar a hacer algo; ~**ner** n principiante m/f; ~**ning** n principio, comienzo

begun [bɪ'gʌn] pp of **begin**

behalf [bɪ'hɑ:f] n: **on** ~ **of** en nombre de, por; (for benefit of) en beneficio de; **on my/his** ~ por mí/él

behave [bɪ'heɪv] vi (person) portarse, comportarse; (well: also: ~ o.s.) portarse bien; **behaviour** (US **behavior**) n comportamiento, conducta

behind [bɪ'haɪnd] prep detrás de; (supporting): **to be** ~ **sb** apoyar a alguien ♦ adv detrás, por detrás, atrás ♦ n trasero; **to be** ~ (schedule) ir retrasado; ~ **the scenes** (fig) entre bastidores

behold [bɪ'həʊld] (irreg: like **hold**) vt contemplar

beige [beɪʒ] adj color beige

Beijing ['beɪ'dʒɪŋ] n Pekín m

being ['bi:ɪŋ] n ser m; (existence): **in** ~ existente; **to come into** ~ aparecer

Beirut [beɪ'ru:t] n Beirut m

Belarus [bɛlə'ru:s] n Bielorrusia

belated [bɪ'leɪtɪd] adj atrasado, tardío

belch [bɛltʃ] vi eructar ♦ vt (gen: ~ out: smoke etc) arrojar

Belgian ['bɛldʒən] adj, n belga m/f

Belgium ['bɛldʒəm] n Bélgica

belief [bɪ'li:f] n opinión f; (faith) fe f

believe [bɪ'li:v] vt, vi creer; **to** ~ **in** creer en; ~**r** n partidario/a; (REL) creyente m/f, fiel m/f

belittle [bɪ'lɪtl] vt quitar importancia a

bell [bɛl] n campana; (small) campanilla; (on door) timbre m

belligerent [bɪ'lɪdʒərənt] adj agresivo

bellow ['bɛləʊ] vi bramar; (person) rugir

belly ['bɛlɪ] n barriga, panza

belong [bɪ'lɒŋ] vi: **to** ~ **to** pertenecer a; (club etc) ser socio de; **this book** ~**s here** este libro va aquí; ~**ings** npl pertenencias fpl

beloved [bɪ'lʌvɪd] adj querido/a

below [bɪ'ləʊ] prep bajo, debajo de; (less than) inferior a ♦ adv abajo, (por) debajo; **see** ~ véase más abajo

belt [belt] n cinturón m; (TECH) correa, cinta ♦ vt (thrash) pegar con correa; **~way** (US) n (AUT) carretera de circunvalación

bench [bentʃ] n banco; (BRIT: POL): **the Government/Opposition ~es** (los asientos de) los miembros del Gobierno/de la Oposición; **the B~** (LAW: judges) magistratura

bend [bend] (pt, pp bent) vt doblar ♦ vi inclinarse ♦ n (BRIT: in road, river) curva; (in pipe) codo; **~ down** vi inclinarse, doblarse; **~ over** vi inclinarse

beneath [bɪ'niːθ] prep bajo, debajo de; (unworthy of) indigno de ♦ adv abajo, (por) debajo

benefactor ['benɪfæktə*] n bienhechor m

beneficial [benɪ'fɪʃəl] adj beneficioso

benefit ['benɪfɪt] n beneficio; (allowance of money) subsidio ♦ vt beneficiar ♦ vi: **he'll ~ from it** le sacará provecho

benevolent [bɪ'nevələnt] adj (person) benévolo

benign [bɪ'naɪn] adj benigno; (smile) afable

bent [bent] pt, pp of bend ♦ n inclinación ♦ adj: **to be ~ on** estar empeñado en

bequest [bɪ'kwest] n legado

bereaved [bɪ'riːvd] npl: **the ~** los íntimos de una persona afligidos por su muerte

beret ['bereɪ] n boina

Berlin [bɜː'lɪn] n Berlín

berm [bɜːm] (US) n (AUT) arcén m

Bermuda [bɜː'mjuːdə] n las Bermudas

berry ['berɪ] n baya

berserk [bə'sɜːk] adj: **to go ~** perder los estribos

berth [bɜːθ] n (bed) litera; (cabin) camarote m; (for ship) amarradero ♦ vi atracar, amarrar

beseech [bɪ'siːtʃ] (pt, pp besought) vt suplicar

beset [bɪ'set] (pt, pp beset) vt (person) acosar

beside [bɪ'saɪd] prep junto a, al lado de; **to be ~ o.s. with anger** estar fuera de sí; **that's ~ the point** eso no tiene nada que ver; **~s** adv además ♦ prep además de

besiege [bɪ'siːdʒ] vt sitiar; (fig) asediar

best [best] adj (el/la) mejor ♦ adv (lo) mejor; **the ~ part of** (quantity) la mayor parte de; **at ~** en el mejor de los casos; **to make the ~ of sth** sacar el mejor partido de algo; **to do one's ~** hacer lo posible; **to the ~ of my knowledge** que yo sepa; **to the ~ of my ability** como mejor puedo; **~-before date** n fecha de consumo preferente; **~ man** n padrino de boda

bestow [bɪ'stəʊ] vt (title) otorgar

bestseller ['best'selə*] n éxito de librería, bestseller m

bet [bet] (pt, pp bet or betted) n apuesta ♦ vt, vi: **to ~ money on** apostar dinero por; **to ~ sb sth** apostar algo a uno ♦ vi apostar

betray [bɪ'treɪ] vt traicionar; (trust) faltar a; **~al** n traición f

better ['betə*] adj, adv mejor ♦ vt superar ♦ n: **to get the ~ of sb** quedar por encima de alguien; **you had ~ do it** más vale que lo hagas; **he thought ~ of it** cambió de parecer; **to get ~** (MED) mejorar(se); **~ off** adj mejor; (wealthier) más acomodado

betting ['betɪŋ] n juego, el apostar; **~ shop** (BRIT) n agencia de apuestas

between [bɪ'twiːn] prep entre ♦ adv (time) mientras tanto; (place) en medio

beverage ['bevərɪdʒ] n bebida

beware [bɪ'weə*] vi: **to ~ (of)** tener cuidado (con); **"~ of the dog"** "perro peligroso"

bewildered [bɪ'wɪldəd] adj aturdido, perplejo

beyond [bɪ'jɒnd] prep más allá de; (past: understanding) fuera de; (after:

date) después de, más allá de; (above) superior a ♦ adv (in space) más allá; (in time) posteriormente; ~ **doubt** fuera de toda duda; ~ **repair** irreparable

bias ['baɪəs] n (prejudice) prejuicio, pasión f; (preference) predisposición f; ~**(s)ed** adj parcial

bib [bɪb] n babero

Bible ['baɪbl] n Biblia

bicarbonate of soda [baɪ'kɑːbənɪt-] n bicarbonato sódico

bicker ['bɪkə*] vi pelearse

bicycle ['baɪsɪkl] n bicicleta

bid [bɪd] (pt **bade** or **bid**, pp **bidden** or **bid**) n oferta, postura; (in tender) licitación f; (attempt) tentativa, conato ♦ vi hacer una oferta ♦ vt (offer) ofrecer; **to ~ sb good day** dar a uno los buenos días; ~**der** n: **the highest** ~**der** el mejor postor; ~**ding** n (at auction) ofertas fpl

bide [baɪd] vt: **to ~ one's time** esperar el momento adecuado

bifocals [baɪ'fəʊklz] npl gafas fpl (SP) or anteojos mpl (AM) bifocales

big [bɪg] adj grande; (brother, sister) mayor

bigheaded ['bɪg'hedɪd] adj engreído

bigot ['bɪgət] n fanático/a, intolerante m/f; ~**ed** adj fanático, intolerante; ~**ry** n fanatismo, intolerancia

big top n (at circus) carpa

bike [baɪk] n bici f

bikini [bɪ'kiːnɪ] n bikini m

bilingual [baɪ'lɪŋgwəl] adj bilingüe

bill [bɪl] n cuenta; (invoice) factura; (POL) proyecto de ley; (US: banknote) billete m; (of bird) pico; (of show) programa m; **"post no ~s"** "prohibido fijar carteles"; **to fit** or **fill the ~** (fig) cumplir con los requisitos; ~**board** (US) n cartelera

billet ['bɪlɪt] n alojamiento

billfold ['bɪlfəʊld] (US) n cartera

billiards ['bɪljədz] n billar m

billion ['bɪljən] n (BRIT) billón m (millón de millones); (US) mil millones mpl

bimbo ['bɪmbəʊ] (inf) n tía buena sin seso

bin [bɪn] n (for rubbish) cubo (SP) or bote m (AM) de la basura; (container) recipiente m

bind [baɪnd] (pt, pp **bound**) vt atar; (book) encuadernar; (oblige) obligar ♦ n (inf: nuisance) lata; ~**ing** adj (contract) obligatorio

binge [bɪndʒ] (inf) n: **to go on a ~** ir de juerga

bingo ['bɪŋgəʊ] n bingo m

binoculars [bɪ'nɔkjuləz] npl prismáticos mpl

bio... [baɪə*] prefix: ~**chemistry** n bioquímica; ~**degradable** [baɪəʊdɪ'greɪdəbl] adj biodegradable; ~**graphy** [baɪ'ɔgrəfɪ] n biografía; ~**logical** [baɪə'lɔdʒɪkl] adj biológico; ~**logy** [baɪ'ɔlədʒɪ] n biología

birch [bɜːtʃ] n (tree) abedul m

bird [bɜːd] n ave f, pájaro; (BRIT: inf: girl) chica; ~'**s eye view** n (aerial view) vista de pájaro; (overview) visión f de conjunto; ~ **watcher** n ornitólogo/a

Biro ® ['baɪrəʊ] n bolígrafo

birth [bɜːθ] n nacimiento; **to give ~ to** parir, dar a luz; ~ **certificate** n partida de nacimiento; ~ **control** n (policy) control m de natalidad; (methods) métodos mpl anticonceptivos; ~**day** n cumpleaños m inv ♦ cpd (cake, card etc) de cumpleaños; ~**place** n lugar m de nacimiento; ~ **rate** n (tasa de) natalidad f

biscuit ['bɪskɪt] (BRIT) n galleta, bizcocho (AM)

bisect [baɪ'sekt] vt bisecar

bishop ['bɪʃəp] n obispo; (CHESS) alfil m

bit [bɪt] pt of **bite** ♦ n trozo, pedazo, pedacito; (COMPUT) bit m, bitio; (for horse) freno, bocado; **a ~ of** un poco de; **a ~ mad** un poco loco; ~ **by ~** poco a poco

bitch [bɪtʃ] n perra; (inf!: woman) zorra (!)

bite [baɪt] (pt **bit**, pp **bitten**) vt, vi
morder; (insect etc) picar ♦ n (insect ~)
picadura; (mouthful) bocado; **to
~ one's nails** comerse las uñas; **let's
have a ~ (to eat)** (inf) vamos a comer
algo

bitter ['bɪtə*] adj amargo; (wind)
cortante, penetrante; (battle) encarnizado ♦ n (BRIT: beer) cerveza típica
británica a base de lúpulos; **~ness** n lo
amargo, amargura; (anger) rencor m

bizarre [bɪ'zɑ:*] adj raro, extraño

black [blæk] adj negro; (tea, coffee)
solo ♦ n color m negro; (person): **B~**
negro/a ♦ vt (BRIT: INDUSTRY) boicotear;
to give sb a ~ eye ponerle a uno el
ojo morado; **~ and blue** (bruised)
amoratado; **to be in the ~** (bank
account) estar en números negros;
~berry n zarzamora; **~bird** n mirlo;
~board n pizarra; **~ coffee** n café m
solo; **~currant** n grosella negra; **~en**
vt (fig) desacreditar; **~ ice** n hielo
invisible en la carretera; **~leg** (BRIT) n
esquirol m, rompehuelgas m inv; **~list**
n lista negra; **~mail** n chantaje m ♦ vt
chantajear; **~ market** n mercado
negro; **~out** n (MIL) oscurecimiento;
(power cut) apagón m; (TV, RADIO)
interrupción f de programas; (fainting)
desvanecimiento; **B~ Sea** n: **the
B~ Sea** el Mar Negro; **~ sheep** n (fig)
oveja negra; **~smith** n herrero; **~ spot**
n (AUT) lugar m peligroso; (for
unemployment etc) punto negro

bladder ['blædə*] n vejiga

blade [bleɪd] n hoja; (of propeller)
paleta; **a ~ of grass** una brizna de
hierba

blame [bleɪm] n culpa ♦ vt: **to ~ sb
for sth** echar a uno la culpa de algo;
to be to ~ tener la culpa de

bland [blænd] adj (music, taste) soso

blank [blæŋk] adj en blanco; (look) sin
expresión ♦ n (of memory): **my mind
is a ~** no puedo recordar nada; (on
form) blanco, espacio en blanco;

(cartridge) cartucho sin bala or de
foguo; **~ cheque** n cheque m en
blanco

blanket ['blæŋkɪt] n manta (SP), cobija
(AM); (of snow) capa; (of fog) manto

blare [blɛə*] vi sonar estrepitosamente

blasé ['blɑ:zeɪ] adj hastiado

blast [blɑ:st] n (of wind) ráfaga, soplo;
(of explosive) explosión f ♦ vt (blow up)
volar; **~-off** n (SPACE) lanzamiento

blatant ['bleɪtənt] adj descarado

blaze [bleɪz] n (fire) fuego; (fig: of
colour) despliegue m; (: of glory)
esplendor m ♦ vi arder en llamas; (fig)
brillar ♦ vt: **to ~ a trail** (fig) abrir un
camino; **in a ~ of publicity** con gran
publicidad

blazer ['bleɪzə*] n chaqueta de uniforme
de colegial o de socio de club

bleach [bli:tʃ] n (also: household ~) lejía
♦ vt blanquear; **~ed** adj (hair) teñido
(de rubio); **~ers** (US) npl (SPORT) gradas
fpl al sol

bleak [bli:k] adj (countryside) desierto;
(prospect) poco prometedor/a;
(weather) crudo; (smile) triste

bleat [bli:t] vi balar

bleed [bli:d] (pt, pp **bled**) vt, vi
sangrar; **my nose is ~ing** me está
sangrando la nariz

bleeper ['bli:pə*] n busca m

blemish ['blemɪʃ] n marca, mancha;
(on reputation) tacha

blend [blend] n mezcla ♦ vt mezclar;
(colours etc) combinar, mezclar ♦ vi
(colours etc: also: ~ in) combinarse,
mezclarse

bless [bles] (pt, pp **blessed** or **blest**)
vt bendecir; **~ you!** (after sneeze)
¡Jesús!, ¡salud!; **~ing** n (approval) aprobación f;
(godsend) don m del cielo, bendición f;
(advantage) beneficio, ventaja

blew [blu:] pt of **blow**

blind [blaɪnd] adj ciego, (fig): **~ (to)**
ciego (a) ♦ n (for window) persiana ♦ vt
cegar; (dazzle) deslumbrar; (deceive):
to ~ sb to ... cegar a uno a ...; **the ~**

blink [blɪŋk] vi parpadear, pestañear; (light) oscilar; **~ers** npl anteojeras fpl

bliss [blɪs] n felicidad f

blister ['blɪstə*] n ampolla ♦ vi (paint) ampollarse

blizzard ['blɪzəd] n ventisca

bloated ['bləʊtɪd] adj hinchado; (person: full) ahíto

blob [blɒb] n (drop) gota; (indistinct object) bulto

bloc [blɒk] n (POL) bloque m

block [blɒk] n bloque m; (in pipes) obstáculo; (of buildings) manzana (SP), cuadra (AM) ♦ vt obstruir, cerrar; (progress) estorbar; **~ of flats** (BRIT) bloque m de pisos; **mental ~** bloqueo mental; **~ade** [-'keɪd] n bloqueo ♦ vt bloquear; **~age** n estorbo, obstrucción f; **~buster** n (book) bestseller m; (film) éxito de público; **~ letters** npl letras fpl de molde

bloke [bləʊk] (BRIT: inf) n tipo, tío

blond(e) [blɒnd] adj, n rubio/a m/f

blood [blʌd] n sangre f; **~ donor** n donante m/f de sangre; **~ group** n grupo sanguíneo; **~hound** n sabueso; **~ poisoning** n envenenamiento de la sangre; **~ pressure** n presión f sanguínea; **~shed** n derramamiento de sangre; **~shot** adj inyectado en sangre; **~stream** n corriente f sanguínea; **~ test** n análisis m inv de sangre; **~thirsty** adj sanguinario; **~ vessel** n vaso sanguíneo; **~y** adj sangriento; (nose etc) lleno de sangre; (BRIT: inf!): **this ~y...** este condenado o puñetero ... (!) ♦ adv: **~y strong/good** (BRIT: inf!) terriblemente fuerte/bueno; **~y-minded** (BRIT: inf) adj puñetero (!)

blink npl los ciegos; **~ alley** n callejón m sin salida; **~ corner** (BRIT) n esquina escondida; **~fold** n venda ♦ adv con los ojos vendados ♦ vt vendar los ojos a; **~ly** adv a ciegas, ciegamente; **~ness** n ceguera; **~ spot** n (AUT) ángulo ciego

bliss → above

bloom [bluːm] n flor f ♦ vi florecer

blossom ['blɒsəm] n flor f ♦ vi (also fig) florecer

blot [blɒt] n borrón m; (fig) mancha ♦ vt (stain) manchar; **~ out** vt (view) tapar

blotchy ['blɒtʃɪ] adj (complexion) lleno de manchas

blotting paper ['blɒtɪŋ-] n papel m secante

blouse [blauz] n blusa

blow [bləʊ] (pt blew, pp blown) n golpe m; (with sword) espadazo ♦ vi soplar; (dust, sand etc) volar; (fuse) fundirse ♦ vt (subj: wind) llevarse; (fuse) quemar; (instrument) tocar; **to ~ one's nose** sonarse; **~ away** vt llevarse, arrancar; **~ down** vt derribar; **~ off** vt arrebatar; **~ out** vi apagarse; **~ over** vi amainar; **~ up** vi estallar ♦ vt volar; (tyre) inflar; (PHOT) ampliar; **~-dry** n moldeado (con secador); **~lamp** (BRIT) n soplete m, lámpara de soldar; **~-out** n (of tyre) pinchazo; **~torch** n = **~lamp**

blue [bluː] adj azul; (depressed) deprimido; **~ film/joke** película/chiste m verde; **out of the ~** (fig) de repente; **~bell** n campanilla, campánula azul; **~bottle** n moscarda, mosca azul; **~print** n (fig) anteproyecto

bluff [blʌf] vi tirarse un farol, farolear ♦ n farol m; **to call sb's ~** coger a uno la palabra

blunder ['blʌndə*] n patinazo, metedura de pata ♦ vi cometer un error, meter la pata

blunt [blʌnt] adj (pencil) despuntado; (knife) desafilado, romo; (person) franco, directo

blur [blɜː*] n (in shape): **to become a ~** hacerse borroso ♦ vt (vision) enturbiar; (distinction) borrar

blush [blʌʃ] vi ruborizarse, ponerse colorado ♦ n rubor m

blustery ['blʌstərɪ] adj (weather)

tempestuoso, tormentoso

boar [bɔ:*] n verraco, cerdo

board [bɔ:d] n (card-) cartón m; (wooden) tabla, tablero; (on wall) tablón m; (for chess etc) tablero; (committee) junta, consejo; (in firm) mesa o junta directiva; (NAUT, AVIAT): **on ~** a bordo ♦ vt (ship) embarcar en; (train) subir a; **full ~** (BRIT) pensión completa; **half ~** (BRIT) media pensión; **to go by the ~** (fig) ser abandonado or olvidado; **~ up** vt (door) tapiar; **~ and lodging** n casa y comida; **~er** n (SCOL) interno/a; **~ing card** (BRIT) n tarjeta de embarque; **~ing house** n casa de huéspedes; **~ing pass** (US) n = **~ing card**; **~ing school** n internado; **~ room** n sala de juntas

boast [bəust] vi: **to ~ (about** or **of)** alardear (de)

boat [bəut] n barco, buque m; (small) barca, bote m

bob [bɔb] vi (also: ~ **up and down)** menearse, balancearse; **~ up** vi (re)aparecer de repente

bobby ['bɔbɪ] (BRIT: inf) n poli m

bobsleigh ['bɔbsleɪ] n bob m

bode [bəud] vi: **to ~ well/ill (for)** ser prometedor/poco prometedor (para)

bodily ['bɔdɪlɪ] adj corporal ♦ adv (move: person) en peso

body ['bɔdɪ] n cuerpo; (corpse) cadáver m; (of car) caja, carrocería; (fig: group) grupo; (: organization) organismo; **~-building** n culturismo; **~guard** n guardaespaldas m inv; **~work** n carrocería

bog [bɔg] n pantano, ciénaga ♦ vt: **to get ~ged down** (fig) empantanarse, atascarse

bogus ['bəugəs] adj falso, fraudulento

boil [bɔɪl] vt (water) hervir; (eggs) pasar por agua, cocer ♦ vi hervir; (fig: with anger) estar furioso; (: with heat) asfixiarse ♦ n (MED) furúnculo, divieso; **to come to the ~, to come to a ~** (US) comenzar a hervir; **to ~ down to**

(fig) reducirse a; **~ over** vi salirse, rebosar; (anger etc) llegar al colmo; **~ed egg** n huevo cocido (SP) or pasado (AM); **~ed potatoes** npl patatas fpl (SP) or papas fpl (AM) hervidas; **~er** n caldera; **~ing point** n punto de ebullición

boisterous ['bɔɪstərəs] adj (noisy) bullicioso; (excitable) exuberante; (crowd) tumultuoso

bold [bəuld] adj valiente, audaz; (pej) descarado; (colour) llamativo

Bolivia [bə'lɪvɪə] n Bolivia; **~n** adj, n boliviano/a m/f

bollard ['bɔləd] n (AUT) poste m

bolt [bəult] n (lock) cerrojo; (with nut) perno, tornillo ♦ adv: **~ upright** rígido, erguido ♦ vt (door) echar el cerrojo a; (also: ~ **together**) sujetar con tornillos; (food) engullir ♦ vi fugarse; (horse) desbocarse

bomb [bɔm] n bomba ♦ vt bombardear; **~ disposal** n desmontaje m de explosivos; **~er** n (AVIAT) bombardero; **~shell** n (fig) bomba

bond [bɔnd] n (promise) fianza; (FINANCE) bono; (link) vínculo, lazo; (COMM): **in ~** en depósito bajo fianza

bondage ['bɔndɪdʒ] n esclavitud f

bone [bəun] n hueso; (of fish) espina ♦ vt deshuesar; quitar las espinas a; **~ idle** adj gandul; **~ marrow** n médula

bonfire ['bɔnfaɪə*] n hoguera, fogata

bonnet ['bɔnɪt] n gorra; (BRIT: of car) capó m

bonus ['bəunəs] n (payment) paga extraordinaria, plus m; (fig) bendición f

bony ['bəunɪ] adj (arm, face) huesudo; (MED: tissue) óseo; (meat) lleno de huesos; (fish) lleno de espinas

boo [bu:] excl ¡uh! ♦ vt abuchear, rechiflar

booby trap ['bu:bɪ-] n trampa explosiva

book [buk] n libro; (of tickets) taco; (of

stamps etc) librito ♦ *vt* (*ticket*) sacar; (*seat, room*) reservar; **~s** *npl* (COMM) cuentas *fpl*, contabilidad *f*; **~case** *n* librería, estante *m* para libros; **~ing office** *n* (BRIT: RAIL) despacho de billetes (SP) or boletos (AM); (THEATRE) taquilla (SP), boletería (AM); **~keeping** *n* contabilidad *f*; **~let** *n* folleto; **~maker** *n* corredor *m* de apuestas; **~seller** *n* librero; **~shop, ~ store** *n* librería

boom [buːm] *n* (*noise*) trueno, estampido; (*in prices etc*) alza rápida; (ECON, *in population*) boom *m* ♦ *vi* (*cannon*) hacer gran estruendo, retumbar; (ECON) estar en alza

boon [buːn] *n* favor *m*, beneficio

boost [buːst] *n* estímulo, empuje *m* ♦ *vt* estimular, empujar; **~er** *n* (MED) reinyección *f*

boot [buːt] *n* bota; (BRIT: *of car*) maleta, maletero *m* (COMPUT) arrancar; **to ~** (*in addition*) además, por añadidura

booth [buːð] *n* (*telephone ~, voting ~*) cabina

booze [buːz] (*inf*) *n* bebida

border ['bɔːdə*] *n* borde *m*, margen *m*; (*of a country*) frontera; (*for flowers*) arriate *m* ♦ *vt* (*road*) bordear; (*another country: also: ~ on*) lindar con; **B~s** *n* the **B~s** región fronteriza entre Escocia e Inglaterra; **~ on** *vt fus* (*insanity etc*) rayar en; **~line** *n*: on the **~line** en el límite; **~line case** *n* caso dudoso

bore [bɔː*] *pt of* **bear** ♦ *vt* (*hole*) hacer un agujero, (*well*) perforar; (*person*) aburrir ♦ *n* (*person*) pelmazo, pesado; (*of gun*) calibre *m*; **to be ~d** estar aburrido; **~dom** *n* aburrimiento

boring ['bɔːrɪŋ] *adj* aburrido

born [bɔːn] *adj*: **to be ~** nacer; **I was ~ in 1960** nací en 1960

borne [bɔːn] *pp of* **bear**

borough ['bʌrə] *n* municipio

borrow ['bɔrəu] *vt*: **to ~ sth (from sb)** tomar algo prestado (a alguien)

Bosnia(-Herzegovina) ['bɔːsnɪə (herzə'gəuvɪːnə)] *n* Bosnia (-Herzegovina)

bosom ['buzəm] *n* pecho

boss [bɔs] *n* jefe *m* ♦ *vt* (*also: ~ about or around*) mangonear; **~y** *adj* mandón/ona

bosun ['bəusn] *n* contramaestre *m*

botany ['bɔtənɪ] *n* botánica

botch [bɔtʃ] *vt* (*also: ~ up*) arruinar, estropear

both [bəuθ] *adj, pron* ambos/as, los/las dos; **~ of us went, we ~ went** fuimos los dos, ambos fuimos ♦ *adv*: **~ A and B** tanto A como B

bother ['bɔðə*] *vt* (*worry*) preocupar; (*disturb*) molestar, fastidiar ♦ *vi* (*also: ~ o.s.*) molestarse ♦ *n* (*trouble*) dificultad *f*; (*nuisance*) molestia, lata; **to ~ doing** tomarse la molestia de hacer

bottle ['bɔtl] *n* botella; (*small*) frasco; (*baby's*) biberón *m* ♦ *vt* embotellar; **~ up** *vt* suprimir; **~ bank** *n* contenedor *m* de vidrio; **~neck** *n* (AUT) embotellamiento; (*in supply*) obstáculo; **~opener** *n* abrebotellas *m inv*

bottom ['bɔtəm] *n* (*of box, sea*) fondo; (*buttocks*) trasero, culo; (*of page*) pie *m*; (*of list*) final *m*; (*of class*) último/a *adj* (*lowest*) más bajo; (*last*) último

bough [bau] *n* rama

bought [bɔːt] *pt, pp of* **buy**

boulder ['bəuldə*] *n* canto rodado

bounce [bauns] *vi* (*ball*) (re)botar; (*cheque*) ser rechazado ♦ *vt* hacer (re)botar ♦ *n* (*rebound*) (re)bote *m*; **~r** (*inf*) *n* gorila *m* (*que echa a los alborotadores de un bar, club etc*)

bound [baund] *pt, pp of* **bind** ♦ *n* (*leap*) salto; (*gen pl: limit*) límite *m* ♦ *vi* (*leap*) saltar ♦ *vt* (*border*) rodear ♦ *adj*: **~ by** rodeado de; **to be ~ to do sth** (*obliged*) tener el deber de hacer algo; **he's ~ to come** es seguro que vendrá; **out of ~s** prohibido el paso; **~ for** con destino a

boundary [ˈbaundrɪ] n límite m

bouquet [ˈbukeɪ] n (of flowers) ramo

bourgeois [ˈbuəʒwɑː] adj burgués/esa m/f

bout [baut] n (of malaria etc) ataque m; (of activity) período; (BOXING etc) combate m, encuentro

bow¹ [bau] n (knot) lazo; (weapon, MUS) arco

bow² [bau] n (of the head) reverencia; (NAUT: also: ~s) proa ♦ vi inclinarse, hacer una reverencia; (yield): **to ~ to** or **before** ceder ante, someterse a

bowels [bauəlz] npl intestinos mpl, vientre m; (fig) entrañas fpl

bowl [baul] n tazón m, cuenco; (ball) bola ♦ vi (CRICKET) arrojar la pelota; see also **bowls**

bow-legged [ˈbəuˈlegɪd] adj estevado

bowler [ˈbəulə*] n (CRICKET) lanzador m (de la pelota); (BRIT: also: ~ hat) hongo, bombín m

bowling [ˈbəulɪŋ] n (game) bochas fpl, bolos mpl; ~ **alley** n bolera; ~ **green** n pista para bochas

bowls [bəulz] n juego de las bochas, bolos mpl

bow tie [ˈbəu-] n corbata de lazo, pajarita

box [bɒks] n (also: cardboard ~) caja, cajón m; (THEATRE) palco ♦ vt encajonar ♦ vi (SPORT) boxear; **~er** [ˈbɒksə*] n (person) boxeador m; **~ing** [ˈbɒksɪŋ] n (SPORT) boxeo; **B~ing Day** (BRIT) n día en que se dan los aguinaldos, 26 de diciembre; **~ing gloves** npl guantes mpl de boxeo; **~ing ring** n ring m, cuadrilátero; **~ office** n taquilla (SP), boletería (AM); **~room** n trastero

El día 26 de diciembre se conoce como Boxing Day y es día festivo en todo el Reino Unido. En el siglo XIX era tradición entregar "Christmas boxes" (aguinaldos) a empleados,

carteros y otros proveedores en este día, y de ahí el nombre.

boy [bɔɪ] n (young) niño; (older) muchacho, chico; (son) hijo

boycott [ˈbɔɪkɔt] n boicot m ♦ vt boicotear

boyfriend [ˈbɔɪfrend] n novio

boyish [ˈbɔɪʃ] adj juvenil; (girl) con aspecto de muchacho

B.R. n abbr (formerly = British Rail) ≈ RENFE f (SP)

bra [brɑː] n sostén m, sujetador m

brace [breɪs] n (BRIT: also: ~s: on teeth) corrector m, aparato; (tool) berbiquí m; (on knees, shoulders) tensionar; **~s** npl (BRIT) tirantes mpl; **to ~ o.s.** (fig) prepararse

bracelet [ˈbreɪslɪt] n pulsera, brazalete m

bracing [ˈbreɪsɪŋ] adj vigorizante, tónico

bracket [ˈbrækɪt] n (TECH) soporte m, puntal m; (group) clase f, categoría; (also: brace ~) soporte m, abrazadera; (also: round ~) paréntesis m inv; (also: square ~) corchete m ♦ vt (word etc) poner entre paréntesis

brag [bræg] vi jactarse

braid [breɪd] n (trimming) galón m; (of hair) trenza

brain [breɪn] n cerebro; **~s** npl sesos mpl; **she's got ~s** es muy lista; **~wash** vt lavar el cerebro; **~wave** n idea luminosa; **~y** adj muy inteligente

braise [breɪz] vt cocer a fuego lento

brake [breɪk] n (on vehicle) freno ♦ vi frenar; **~ light** n luz f de frenado

bran [bræn] n salvado

branch [brɑːntʃ] n rama; (COMM) sucursal f; **~ out** vi (fig) extenderse

brand [brænd] n marca; (fig: type) tipo ♦ vt (cattle) marcar con hierro candente; **~-new** adj flamante, completamente nuevo

brandy [ˈbrændɪ] n coñac m

brash [bræʃ] adj (forward) descarado

brass [brɑːs] n latón m; **the ~** (MUS) los cobres; **~ band** n banda de metal

brat [bræt] (pej) n mocoso/a

brave [breɪv] adj valiente, valeroso ♦ vt (face up to) desafiar; **~ry** n valor m, valentía

brawl [brɔːl] n pelea, reyerta

brazen ['breɪzn] adj descarado, cínico ♦ vt: **to ~ it out** echarle cara

Brazil [brə'zɪl] n (el) Brasil; **~ian** adj, n brasileño/a m/f

breach [briːtʃ] vt abrir brecha en ♦ n (gap) brecha; (breaking): **~ of contract** infracción f de contrato; **~ of the peace** perturbación f del órden público

bread [bred] n pan m; **~ and butter** n pan con mantequilla; (fig) pan de cada día); **~bin** n panera; **~crumbs** npl migajas fpl; (CULIN) pan rallado; **~line** n: **on the ~line** en la miseria

breadth [bretθ] n anchura; (fig) amplitud f

breadwinner ['bredwɪnə*] n sustento m de la familia

break [breɪk] (pt **broke**, pp **broken**) vt romper; (promise) faltar a; (law) violar, infringir; (record) batir ♦ vi romperse, quebrarse; (storm) estallar; (weather) cambiar; (dawn) despuntar; (news etc) darse a conocer ♦ n (gap) abertura; (fracture) fractura; (time) intervalo; (: at school) (período de) recreo; (chance) oportunidad f; **to ~ the news to sb** comunicar la noticia a uno; **~ down** vt (figures, data) analizar, descomponer ♦ vi (machine) estropearse; (AUT) averiarse; (person) romper a llorar; (talks) fracasar; **~ even** vi cubrir los gastos; **~ free** o **loose** vi escaparse; **~ in** vt (horse etc) domar ♦ vi (burglar) forzar una entrada; (interrupt) interrumpir; **~ into** vt fus (house) forzar; **~ off** vi (speaker) pararse, detenerse; (branch) partir; **~ open** vt (door etc) abrir por la fuerza, forzar; **~ out** vi estallar; (prisoner) escaparse;

to ~ out in spots salirle a uno granos; **~ up** vi (ship) hacerse pedazos; (crowd, meeting) disolverse; (marriage) deshacerse; (SCOL) terminar (el curso) ♦ vt (rocks etc) partir; (journey) partir; (fight etc) acabar con; **~age** n rotura; **~down** n (AUT) avería; (in communications) interrupción f; (MED: also: nervous ~down) colapso, crisis f nerviosa; (of marriage, talks) fracaso; (of statistics) análisis m inv; **~down van** (BRIT) n (camión m) grúa; **~er** n (ola) rompiente f

breakfast ['brekfəst] n desayuno

break: **~-in** n robo con allanamiento de morada; **~ing and entering** n (LAW) violación f de domicilio, allanamiento de morada; **~through** n (also fig) avance m; **~water** n rompeolas m inv

breast [brest] n (of woman) pecho, seno; (chest) pecho; (of bird) pechuga; **~-feed** (irreg: like **feed**) vt, vi amamantar, criar a los pechos; **~-stroke** n braza (de pecho)

breath [breθ] n aliento, respiración f; **to take a deep ~** respirar hondo; **out of ~** sin aliento, sofocado

Breathalyser ® ['breθəlaɪzə*] (BRIT) n alcoholímetro m

breathe [briːð] vt, vi respirar; **~ in** vt, vi aspirar; **~ out** vt, vi espirar; **~r** n respiro; **breathing** n respiración f

breath: **~less** adj sin aliento, jadeante; **~taking** adj imponente, pasmoso

breed [briːd] (pt, pp **bred**) vt criar ♦ vi reproducirse, procrear ♦ n (ZOOL) raza, casta; (type) tipo m; **~ing** n (of person) educación f

breeze [briːz] n brisa

breezy ['briːzɪ] adj de mucho viento, ventoso; (person) despreocupado

brevity ['brevɪtɪ] n brevedad f

brew [bruː] vt (tea) hacer; (beer) elaborar ♦ vi (fig: trouble) prepararse; (storm) amenazar; **~ery** n fábrica de cerveza, cervecería

bribe [braɪb] n soborno ♦ vt sobornar, cohechar; **~ry** n soborno, cohecho

bric-a-brac ['brɪkəbræk] n inv baratijas fpl

brick [brɪk] n ladrillo; **~layer** n albañil m

bridal ['braɪdl] adj nupcial

bride [braɪd] n novia; **~groom** n novio; **~smaid** n dama de honor

bridge [brɪdʒ] n puente m; (NAUT) puente m de mando; (of nose) caballete m; (CARDS) bridge m ♦ vt (fig): **to ~ a gap** llenar un vacío

bridle ['braɪdl] n brida, freno; **~ path** n camino de herradura

brief [briːf] adj breve, corto ♦ n (LAW) escrito; (task) cometido, encargo ♦ vt informar; **~s** npl (for men) calzoncillos mpl; (for women) bragas fpl; **~case** n cartera (SP), portafolio (AM); **~ing** n (PRESS) informe m; **~ly** adv (glance) fugazmente; (say) en pocas palabras

brigadier [brɪɡə'dɪə*] n general m de brigada

bright [braɪt] adj brillante; (room) luminoso; (day) de sol; (person: clever) listo, inteligente; (: lively) alegre; (colour) vivo; (future) prometedor(a); **~en** (also: **~en up**) vt (room) hacer más alegre; (event) alegrar ♦ vi (weather) despejarse; (person) animarse, alegrarse; (prospects) mejorar

brilliance ['brɪljəns] n brillo, brillantez f; (of talent etc) brillantez

brilliant ['brɪljənt] adj brillante; (inf) fenomenal

brim [brɪm] n borde m; (of hat) ala

brine [braɪn] n (CULIN) salmuera

bring [brɪŋ] (pt, pp **brought**) vt (thing, person: with you) traer; (: to sb) llevar, conducir; (trouble, satisfaction) causar; **~ about** vt ocasionar, producir; **~ back** vt volver a traer; (return) devolver; **~ down** vt (government, plane) derribar; (price) rebajar; **~ forward** vt adelantar; **~ off** vt (task, plan) lograr, conseguir; **~ out** vt sacar;

(book etc) publicar; (meaning) subrayar; **~ round** vt (unconscious person) hacer volver en sí; **~ up** vt subir; (person) educar, criar; (question) sacar a colación; (food: vomit) devolver, vomitar

brink [brɪŋk] n borde m

brisk [brɪsk] adj (abrupt: tone) brusco; (person) enérgico, vigoroso; (pace) rápido; (trade) activo

bristle ['brɪsl] n cerda ♦ vi: **to ~ in anger** temblar de rabia

Britain ['brɪtən] n (also: **Great ~**) Gran Bretaña

British ['brɪtɪʃ] adj británico ♦ npl: **the ~** los británicos; **~ Isles** npl: **the ~ Isles** las Islas Británicas; **~ Rail** n ≈ RENFE f (SP)

Briton ['brɪtən] n británico/a

brittle ['brɪtl] adj quebradizo, frágil

broach [brəʊtʃ] vt (subject) abordar

broad [brɔːd] adj ancho; (range) amplio; (smile) abierto; (general: outlines etc) general; (accent) cerrado; **in ~ daylight** en pleno día; **~cast** (irreg: like **cast**) n emisión f ♦ vt (RADIO) emitir; (TV) transmitir ♦ vi emitir; transmitir; **~en** vt ampliar ♦ vi ensancharse; **to ~en one's mind** hacer más tolerante a uno; **~ly** adv en general; **~-minded** adj tolerante, liberal

broccoli ['brɔkəlɪ] n brécol n

brochure ['brəʊʃjuə*] n folleto

broil [brɔɪl] vt (CULIN) asar a la parrilla

broke [brəʊk] pt of **break** ♦ adj (inf) pelado, sin blanca

broken ['brəʊkən] pp of **break** ♦ adj roto; (machine: also: **~ down**) averiado; **~ leg** pierna rota; **in ~ English** un inglés imperfecto; **~-hearted** adj con el corazón partido

broker ['brəʊkə*] n agente m/f, bolsista m/f; (insurance) ~ agente de seguros

brolly ['brɔlɪ] n (BRIT: inf) paraguas m inv

bronchitis [brɔŋ'kaɪtɪs] n bronquitis f

bronze [brɔnz] n bronce m

brooch [brəʊtʃ] n prendedor m, broche m

brood [bru:d] n camada, cría ♦ vi (person) dejarse obsesionar

broom [brum] n escoba; (BOT) retama

Bros. abbr (= Brothers) Hnos

broth [brɔθ] n caldo

brothel ['brɔθl] n burdel m

brother ['brʌðə*] n hermano; **~-in-law** n cuñado

brought [brɔ:t] pt, pp of **bring**

brow [braʊ] n (forehead) frente m; (eye~) ceja; (of hill) cumbre f

brown [braʊn] adj (colour) marrón; (hair) castaño; (tanned) moreno ♦ n (colour) color m marrón o pardo ♦ vt (CULIN) dorar; **~ bread** n pan integral

Brownie ['braʊnɪ] n niña exploradora; **b~** (US: cake) pastel de chocolate con nueces

brown paper n papel m de estraza

brown sugar n azúcar m terciado

browse [braʊz] vi (through book) hojear; (in shop) mirar; **~r** n (COMPUT) navegador m

bruise [bru:z] n cardenal m (SP), moretón m (AM) ♦ vt magullar

brunch [brʌntʃ] n desayuno-almuerzo

brunette [bru:'net] n morena

brunt [brʌnt] n: **to bear the ~ of** llevar el peso de

brush [brʌʃ] n cepillo; (for painting, shaving etc) brocha; (artist's) pincel m; (with police etc) roce m ♦ vt (sweep) barrer; (groom) cepillar; (also: ~ against) rozar al pasar; **~ aside** vt rechazar, no hacer caso a; **~ up** vt (knowledge) repasar, refrescar; **~wood** n (sticks) leña

Brussels ['brʌslz] n Bruselas; **~ sprout** n col f de Bruselas

brute [bru:t] n bruto; (person) bestia ♦ adj: **by ~ force** a fuerza bruta

B.Sc. abbr (= Bachelor of Science) licenciado en Ciencias

BSE n abbr (= bovine spongiform encephalopathy) encefalopatía espongiforme bovina

bubble ['bʌbl] n burbuja ♦ vi burbujear, borbotar; **~ bath** n espuma para el baño; **~ gum** n chicle m de globo

buck [bʌk] n (rabbit) conejo macho; (deer) gamo; (US: inf) dólar m ♦ vi corcovear; **to pass the ~** (US: inf) echar (a uno) el muerto; **~ up** vi (cheer up) animarse, cobrar ánimo

Buckingham Palace

Buckingham Palace es la residencia oficial del monarca británico en Londres. El palacio se concluyó en 1703 y fue residencia del Duque de Buckingham hasta que, en 1762, pasó a manos de Jorge III. Fue reconstruido en el siglo XIX y posteriormente reformado a principios de este siglo. Una parte del palacio está actualmente abierta al público.

bucket ['bʌkɪt] n cubo, balde m

buckle ['bʌkl] n hebilla ♦ vt abrochar con hebilla ♦ vi combarse

bud [bʌd] n (of plant) brote m, yema; (of flower) capullo ♦ vi brotar, echar brotes

Buddhism ['bʊdɪzm] n Budismo

budding ['bʌdɪŋ] adj en ciernes

buddy ['bʌdɪ] n (US) compañero, compinche m

budge [bʌdʒ] vt mover; (fig) hacer ceder ♦ vi moverse, ceder

budgerigar ['bʌdʒərɪɡɑ:*] n periquito

budget ['bʌdʒɪt] n presupuesto ♦ vi: **to ~ for sth** presupuestar algo

budgie ['bʌdʒɪ] n = **budgerigar**

buff [bʌf] adj (colour) color de ante ♦ n (inf: enthusiast) entusiasta m/f

buffalo ['bʌfələʊ] n (pl ~ or ~es) (BRIT) búfalo; (US: bison) bisonte m

buffer ['bʌfə*] n (COMPUT) memoria

intermedia; (RAIL) tope m

buffet[1] ['bufei] n (BRIT: in station) bar m, cafetería; (food) buffet m; ~ **car** (BRIT) (RAIL) coche-comedor m

buffet[2] ['bʌfit] vt golpear

bug [bʌg] n (esp US: insect) bicho, sabandija; (COMPUT) error m; (germ) microbio, bacilo; (spy device) micrófono oculto ♦ vt (inf: annoy) fastidiar; (room) poner micrófono oculto en

buggy ['bʌgi] n cochecito de niño

bugle ['bju:gl] n corneta, clarín m

build [bild] (pt, pp built) n (of person) tipo ♦ vt construir, edificar; ~ **up** vt (morale, forces, production) acrecentar; (stocks) acumular; ~**er** n (contractor) contratista m/f; ~**ing** n construcción f; (structure) edificio; ~**ing society** (BRIT) n sociedad f inmobiliaria

built [bilt] pt, pp of **build** ♦ adj: ~**-in** (wardrobe etc) empotrado; ~**-up area** n zona urbanizada

bulb [bʌlb] n (BOT) bulbo; (ELEC) bombilla (SP), foco (AM)

Bulgaria [bʌlˈgeəriə] n Bulgaria; ~**n** adj, n búlgaro/a m/f

bulge [bʌldʒ] n bombeo, protuberancia ♦ vi bombearse, pandearse; (pocket etc): **to ~ (with)** rebosar (de)

bulk [bʌlk] n masa, mole f; **in ~** (COMM) a granel; **the ~ of** la mayor parte de; ~**y** adj voluminoso, abultado

bull [bul] n toro; (male elephant, whale) macho; ~**dog** n dogo

bulldozer ['buldəuzə*] n bulldozer m

bullet ['bulit] n bala

bulletin ['bulitin] n anuncio, parte m; (journal) boletín m; ~ **board** n (US) tablón m de anuncios; (COMPUT) tablero de noticias

bulletproof ['bulitpru:f] adj a prueba de balas

bullfight ['bulfait] n corrida de toros; ~**er** n torero; ~**ing** n los toros, el toreo

bullion ['buljən] n oro (or plata) en barras

bullock ['bulək] n novillo

bullring ['bulriŋ] n plaza de toros

bull's-eye n centro del blanco

bully ['buli] n valentón m, matón m ♦ vt intimidar, tiranizar

bum [bʌm] n (inf: backside) culo; (esp US: tramp) vagabundo

bumblebee ['bʌmblbi:] n abejorro

bump [bʌmp] n (blow) tope m, choque m; (jolt) sacudida; (on road etc) bache m; (on head etc) chichón m ♦ vt (strike) chocar contra; ~ **into** vt fus chocar contra, tropezar con; (person) topar con; ~**er** n (AUT) parachoques m inv ♦ adj: ~**er crop/harvest** cosecha abundante; ~**er cars** npl coches mpl de choque; ~**y** adj (road) lleno de baches

bun [bʌn] n (BRIT: cake) pastel m; (US: bread) bollo; (of hair) moño

bunch [bʌntʃ] n (of flowers) ramo; (of keys) manojo; (of bananas) piña; (of people) grupo; (pej) pandilla; ~**es** npl (in hair) coletas fpl

bundle ['bʌndl] n bulto, fardo; (of sticks) haz m; (of papers) legajo ♦ vt (also: ~ **up**) atar, envolver; **to ~ sth/sb into** meter algo/a alguien precipitadamente en

bungalow ['bʌŋgələu] n bungalow m, chalé m

bungle ['bʌŋgl] vt hacer mal

bunion ['bʌnjən] n juanete m

bunk [bʌŋk] n litera; ~ **beds** npl literas fpl

bunker ['bʌŋkə*] n (coal store) carbonera; (MIL) refugio; (GOLF) bunker m

bunny ['bʌni] n (also: ~ **rabbit**) conejito

buoy [bɔi] n boya; ~**ant** adj (ship) capaz de flotar; (economy) boyante; (person) optimista

burden ['bə:dn] n carga ♦ vt cargar

bureau [bjuəˈrəu] n (pl **bureaux**) n (BRIT: writing desk) escritorio, buró m; (US: chest of drawers) cómoda; (office) oficina, agencia

bureaucracy [bjuəˈrɔkrəsi] n

burocracia

burglar ['bɜːglə*] n ladrón/ona m/f;
~ **alarm** n alarma f antirrobo; ~**y** n
robo con allanamiento, robo de una
casa

burial ['bɜɹɪəl] n entierro

burly ['bɜːlɪ] adj fornido, membrudo

Burma ['bɜːmə] n Birmania

burn [bɜːn] (pt, pp **burned** or **burnt**)
vt quemar; (house) incendiar ♦ vi
quemarse, arder; incendiarse; (sting)
escocer ♦ n quemadura; ~ **down** vt
incendiar; ~**er** n (on cooker etc)
quemador m; ~**ing** adj (building etc) en
llamas; (hot: sand etc) abrasador(a);
(ambition) ardiente

burrow ['bʌrəu] n madriguera ♦ vi
hacer una madriguera; (rummage)
hurgar

bursary ['bɜːsərɪ] (BRIT) n beca

burst [bɜːst] (pt, pp **burst**) vt reventar;
(subj: river. banks etc) romper ♦ vi
reventarse; (tyre) pincharse ♦ n (of
gunfire) ráfaga; (also: ~ pipe) reventón
m; **a** ~ **of energy/speed/**
enthusiasm una explosión de
energía/un ímpetu de velocidad/un
arranque de entusiasmo; **to** ~ **into**
flames estallar en llamas; **to** ~ **into**
tears deshacerse en lágrimas; **to** ~
out laughing soltar la carcajada; **to**
~ **open** abrirse de golpe; **to be** ~**ing**
with (subj: container) estar lleno a
rebosar de; (person) reventar por or de;
~ **into** vt fus (room etc) irrumpir en

bury ['berɪ] vt enterrar; (body) enterrar,
sepultar

bus [bʌs] (pl ~**es**) n autobús m

bush [buʃ] n arbusto; (scrub land)
monte m; **to beat about the** ~
andar(se) con rodeos

bushy ['buʃɪ] adj (thick) espeso,
poblado

busily ['bɪzɪlɪ] adv afanosamente

business ['bɪznɪs] n (matter) asunto;
(trading) comercio, negocios mpl; (firm)
empresa, casa; (occupation) oficio; **to**

be away on ~ estar en viaje de
negocios; **it's my** ~ **to** ... me toca or
corresponde ...; **it's none of my** ~ yo
no tengo nada que ver; **he means** ~
habla en serio; ~**like** adj eficiente;
~**man** n hombre m de negocios;
~ **trip** n viaje m de negocios;
~**woman** n mujer f de negocios

busker ['bʌskə*] (BRIT) n músico/a
ambulante

bus: ~ **shelter** n parada cubierta;
~ **station** n estación f de autobuses;
~**stop** n parada de autobús

bust [bʌst] n (ANAT) pecho; (sculpture)
busto ♦ adj (inf: broken) roto,
estropeado; **to go** ~ quebrar

bustle ['bʌsl] n bullicio, movimiento
♦ vi menearse, apresurarse; **bustling**
adj (town) animado, bullicioso

busy ['bɪzɪ] adj ocupado, atareado;
(shop, street) concurrido, animado;
(TEL: line) comunicando ♦ vt: **to** ~ **o.s.**
with ocuparse en; ~**body** n
entrometido/a; ~ **signal** (US) n (TEL)
señal f de comunicando

┌─────────────┐
│ **KEYWORD** │
└─────────────┘

but [bʌt] conj **1** pero; **he's not very**
bright, ~ **he's hard-working** no es
muy inteligente, pero es trabajador
2 (in direct contradiction) sino; **he's**
not English ~ **French** no es inglés
sino francés; **he didn't sing** ~ **he**
shouted no cantó sino que gritó
3 (showing disagreement, surprise etc):
~ **that's far too expensive!** ¡pero
eso es carísimo!; ~ **it does work!**
¡(pero) sí que funciona!
♦ prep (apart from, except) menos,
salvo; **we've had nothing** ~ **trouble**
no hemos tenido más que problemas;
no-one ~ **him can do it** nadie más
que él puede hacerlo; **who** ~ **a**
lunatic would do such a thing?
¿sólo un loco haría una cosa así?; ~
for you/your help si no fuera por ti/tu
ayuda; **anything** ~ **that** cualquier

cosa menos eso
♦ *adv* (*just, only*): **she's ~ a child** no es más que una niña; **had I ~ known** si lo hubiera sabido; **I can ~ try** al menos lo puedo intentar; **it's all ~ finished** está casi acabado

butcher ['butʃə*] *n* carnicero ♦ *vt* hacer una carnicería con; (*cattle etc*) matar; **~'s (shop)** *n* carnicería

butler ['bʌtlə*] *n* mayordomo

butt [bʌt] *n* (*barrel*) tonel *m*; (*of gun*) culata; (*of cigarette*) colilla; (BRIT: *fig: target*) blanco ♦ *vt* dar cabezadas contra, top(et)ar; **~ in** *vi* (*interrupt*) interrumpir

butter ['bʌtə*] *n* mantequilla ♦ *vt* untar con mantequilla; **~cup** *n* botón *m* de oro

butterfly ['bʌtəflaɪ] *n* mariposa; (SWIMMING: *also*: **~ stroke**) braza de mariposa

buttocks ['bʌtəks] *npl* nalgas *fpl*

button ['bʌtn] *n* botón *m*; (US) placa, chapa ♦ *vt* (*also*: **~ up**) abotonar, abrochar ♦ *vi* abrocharse

buttress ['bʌtris] *n* contrafuerte *m*

buy [baɪ] (*pt, pp* bought) *vt* comprar ♦ *n* compra; **to ~ sb sth/sth from sb** comprarle algo a alguien; **to ~ sb a drink** invitar a alguien a tomar algo; **~er** *n* comprador(a) *m/f*

buzz [bʌz] *n* zumbido; (*inf: phone call*) llamada (por teléfono) ♦ *vi* zumbar; **~er** *n* timbre *m*; **~ word** *n* palabra que está de moda

KEYWORD

by [baɪ] *prep* 1 (*referring to cause, agent*) por; de; **killed ~ lightning** muerto por un relámpago; **a painting ~ Picasso** un cuadro de Picasso
2 (*referring to method, manner, means*): **~ bus/car/train** en autobús/coche/tren; **to pay ~ cheque** pagar con un cheque; **~ moonlight/candlelight** a la luz de la luna/una vela; **~ saving**

hard, he ... ahorrando, ...
3 (*via, through*) por; **we came ~ Dover** vinimos por Dover
4 (*close to, past*): **the house ~ the river** la casa junto al río; **she rushed ~ me** pasó a mi lado como una exhalación; **I go ~ the post office every day** paso por delante de Correos todos los días
5 (*time: not later than*) para; (: *during*): **~ daylight** de día; **~ 4 o'clock** para las cuatro; **~ this time tomorrow** mañana a estas horas; **~ the time I got here it was too late** cuando llegué ya era demasiado tarde
6 (*amount*): **~ the metre/kilo** por metro/kilo; **paid ~ the hour** pagado por hora
7 (MATH, *measure*): **to divide/multiply ~ 3** dividir/multiplicar por 3; **a room 3 metres ~ 4** una habitación de 3 metros por 4; **it's broader ~ a metre** es un metro más ancho
8 (*according to*) según, de acuerdo con; **it's 3 o'clock ~ my watch** según mi reloj, son las tres; **it's all right ~ me** por mí, está bien
9: (**all**) **~ oneself** *etc* todo solo; **he did it** (**all**) **~ himself** lo hizo él solo; **he was standing** (**all**) **~ himself in a corner** estaba de pie solo en un rincón
10: **~ the way** a propósito, por cierto; **this wasn't my idea, ~ the way** pues, no fue idea mía
♦ *adv* 1 *see* **go**; **pass** *etc*
2: **~ and ~** finalmente; **they'll come back ~ and ~** acabarán volviendo; **~ and large** en líneas generales, en general

bye(-bye) ['baɪ('baɪ)] *excl* adiós, hasta luego

bye(-)law *n* ordenanza municipal

by-: ~-election (BRIT) *n* elección *f* parcial; **~gone** ['baɪgɔn] *adj* pasado, del pasado ♦ *n*: **let ~gones be**

~gones lo pasado, pasado está;
~pass ['baipɑ:s] n carretera de
circunvalación; (MED) (operación f de)
by-pass m ♦ vt evitar; **~-product** n
subproducto, derivado; (of situation)
consecuencia; **~stander** ['baistændə*]
n espectador(a) m/f
byte [bait] n (COMPUT) byte m, octeto
byword ['baiwɜːd] n: **to be a ~ for**
ser conocidísimo por

C, c

C [si:] n (MUS) do m
C. abbr (= centigrade) C.
C.A. abbr = chartered accountant
cab [kæb] n taxi m; (of truck) cabina
cabbage ['kæbidʒ] n col f, berza
cabin ['kæbin] n cabaña; (on ship)
camarote m; (on plane) cabina; **~ crew**
n tripulación f de cabina; **~ cruiser** n
yate m de motor
cabinet ['kæbinit] n (POL) consejo de
ministros; (furniture) armario; (also:
display ~) vitrina
cable ['keibl] n cable m ♦ vt
cablegrafiar; **~-car** n teleférico;
~ television n televisión f por cable
cache [kæʃ] n (of arms, drugs etc) alijo
cackle ['kækl] vi lanzar risotadas; (hen)
cacarear
cactus ['kæktəs] (pl **cacti**) n cacto
cadge [kædʒ] (inf) vt gorronear
Caesarean [si:'zɛəriən] adj:
~ (section) cesárea
café ['kæfei] n café m
cafeteria [kæfi'tiəriə] n cafetería
cage [keidʒ] n jaula
cagey ['keidʒi] (inf) adj cauteloso,
reservado
cagoule [kə'gu:l] n chubasquero
cajole [kə'dʒəul] vt engatusar
cake [keik] n (CULIN: large) tarta;
(: small) pastel m; (of soap) pastilla; **~d**
adj: **~d with** cubierto de
calculate ['kælkjuleit] vt calcular;

calculation [-'leiʃən] n cálculo,
cómputo; **calculator** n calculadora
calendar ['kæləndə*] n calendario;
~ month/year n mes m/año civil
calf [kɑ:f] (pl **calves**) n (of cow)
ternero, becerro; (of other animals) cría;
(also: ~skin) piel f de becerro; (ANAT)
pantorrilla
calibre ['kælibə*] (US **caliber**) n calibre m
call [kɔ:l] vt llamar; (meeting) convocar
♦ vi (shout) llamar; (TEL) llamar (por
teléfono), telefonear (esp AM); (visit:
also: ~ in, ~ round) hacer una visita ♦ n
llamada; (of bird) canto; **to be ~ed**
llamarse; **on ~** (on duty) de guardia;
~ back vi (return) volver; (TEL) volver a
llamar; **~ for** vt fus (demand) pedir,
exigir; (fetch) venir por (SP), pasar por
(AM); **~ off** vt (cancel) anular; (: strike)
cancelar; (: deal) anular; **~ on** vt fus
(visit) visitar; (turn to) acudir a; **~ out** vi
gritar; **~ up** vt (MIL) llamar al servicio militar; (TEL)
llamar; **~box** (BRIT) n cabina telefónica;
~ centre n (BRIT) centro de atención
al cliente; **~er** n visita; (TEL) usuario/a;
~ girl n prostituta; **~-in** (US) n (programa m) coloquio (por teléfono); **~ing** n
vocación f; (occupation) profesión f;
~ing card (US) n tarjeta de visita
callous ['kæləs] adj insensible, cruel
calm [kɑ:m] adj tranquilo; (sea) liso, en
calma ♦ n calma, tranquilidad f ♦ vt
calmar, tranquilizar; **~ down** vi
calmarse, tranquilizarse ♦ vt calmar,
tranquilizar
Calor gas ® ['kælə*-] n butano
calorie ['kæləri] n caloría
calves [kɑ:vz] npl of **calf**
Cambodia [kæm'bəudiə] n Camboya
camcorder ['kæmkɔ:də*] n
videocámara
came [keim] pt of **come**
camel ['kæməl] n camello
camera ['kæmərə] n máquina
fotográfica; (CINEMA, TV) cámara; **in ~**
(LAW) a puerta cerrada; **~man** n

cámara m

camouflage ['kæməflɑ:ʒ] n camuflaje m ♦ vt camuflar

camp [kæmp] n campamento, camping m; (MIL) campamento; (for prisoners) campo; (fig: faction) bando ♦ vi acampar ♦ adj afectado, afeminado

campaign [kæm'peɪn] n (MIL, POL etc) campaña ♦ vi hacer campaña

camp: ~**bed** (BRIT) n cama de campaña; ~**er** n campista m/f; (vehicle) caravana; ~**ing** n camping m; **to go** ~**ing** hacer camping; ~**site** n camping m

campus ['kæmpəs] n ciudad f universitaria

can[1] [kæn] n (of oil, water) bidón m; (tin) lata, bote m ♦ vt enlatar

---
KEYWORD
---

can[2] [kæn] (negative **cannot**, **can't**; conditional and pt **could**) aux vb **1** (be able to) poder; **you** ~ **do it if you try** puedes hacerlo si lo intentas; **I** ~**'t see you** no te veo

2 (know how to) saber; **I** ~ **swim/play tennis/drive** sé nadar/jugar al tenis/ conducir; ~ **you speak French?** ¿hablas o sabes hablar francés?

3 (may) poder; ~ **I use your phone?** ¿me dejas or puedo usar tu teléfono?

4 (expressing disbelief, puzzlement etc): **it** ~**'t be true!** ¡no puede ser (verdad)!; **what** CAN **he want?** ¿qué querrá?

5 (expressing possibility, suggestion etc): **he could be in the library** podría estar en la biblioteca; **she could have been delayed** pudo haberse retrasado

---

Canada ['kænədə] n (el) Canadá; **Canadian** [kə'neɪdɪən] adj, n canadiense m/f

canal [kə'næl] n canal m

canary [kə'neərɪ] n canario; **the C~ Islands** npl las (Islas) Canarias

cancel ['kænsəl] vt cancelar; (train) suprimir; (cross out) tachar, borrar; ~**lation** [-'leɪʃən] n cancelación f; supresión f

cancer ['kænsə*] n cáncer m; **C~** (ASTROLOGY) Cáncer m

candid ['kændɪd] adj franco, abierto

candidate ['kændɪdeɪt] n candidato/a

candle ['kændl] n vela; (in church) cirio; ~**light** n: **by** ~**light** a la luz de una vela; ~**stick** n (single) candelero; (low) palmatoria; (bigger, ornate) candelabro

candour ['kændə*] (US **candor**) n franqueza

candy ['kændɪ] n azúcar m cande; (US) caramelo; ~**floss** (BRIT) n algodón m (azucarado)

cane [keɪn] n (BOT) caña; (stick) vara, palmeta; (for furniture) mimbre f ♦ (BRIT) vt (SCOL) castigar (con vara)

canister ['kænɪstə*] n bote m, lata; (of gas) bombona

cannabis ['kænəbɪs] n marijuana

canned [kænd] adj en lata, de lata

cannon ['kænən] (pl ~ or ~**s**) n cañón m

cannot ['kænɔt] = **can not**

canoe [kə'nu:] n canoa; (SPORT) piragua; ~**ing** n piragüismo

canon ['kænən] n (clergyman) canónigo; (standard) canon m

can-opener n abrelatas m inv

canopy ['kænəpɪ] n dosel m; toldo

can't [kænt] = **can not**

canteen [kæn'ti:n] n (eating place) cantina; (BRIT: of cutlery) juego

canter ['kæntə*] vi ir a medio galope

canvas ['kænvəs] n (material) lona; (painting) lienzo; (NAUT) velas fpl

canvass ['kænvəs] vi (POL): **to** ~ **for** solicitar votos por ♦ vt (COMM) sondear

canyon ['kænjən] n cañón m

cap [kæp] n (hat) gorra; (of pen) capuchón m; (of bottle) tapa, tapón m; (contraceptive) diafragma m; (for toy gun) cápsula ♦ vt (outdo) superar;

(*limit*) recortar

capability [keɪpə'bɪlɪtɪ] *n* capacidad *f*

capable ['keɪpəbl] *adj* capaz

capacity [kə'pæsɪtɪ] *n* capacidad *f*; (*position*) calidad *f*

cape [keɪp] *n* capa; (*GEO*) cabo

caper ['keɪpə*] *n* (*CULIN: gen: ~s*) alcaparra; (*prank*) broma

capital ['kæpɪtl] *n* (*also: ~ city*) capital *f*; (*money*) capital *m*; (*also: ~ letter*) mayúscula; **~ gains tax** *n* impuesto sobre las ganancias de capital; **~ism** *n* capitalismo; **~ist** *adj*, *n* capitalista *m/f*; **~ize** *vt fus* aprovechar; **~ punishment** *n* pena de muerte

Capitol

El Capitolio (**Capitol**) es el edificio del Congreso (**Congress**) de los Estados Unidos, situado en la ciudad de Washington. Por extensión, también se suele llamar así al edificio en el que tienen lugar las sesiones parlamentarias de la cámara de representantes de muchos de los estados.

Capricorn ['kæprɪkɔːn] *n* (*ASTROLOGY*) Capricornio

capsize [kæp'saɪz] *vt* volcar, hacer zozobrar ♦ *vi* volcarse, zozobrar

capsule ['kæpsjuːl] *n* cápsula

captain ['kæptɪn] *n* capitán *m*

caption ['kæpʃən] *n* (*heading*) título; (*to picture*) leyenda

captive ['kæptɪv] *adj*, *n* cautivo/a *m/f*

capture ['kæptʃə*] *vt* prender, apresar; (*animal, COMPUT*) capturar; (*place*) tomar; (*attention*) captar, llamar ♦ *n* apresamiento; captura; toma; (*data ~*) formulación *f* de datos

car [kɑː*] *n* coche *m*, carro (*AM*), automóvil *m*; (*US: RAIL*) vagón *m*

carafe [kə'ræf] *n* jarra

carat ['kærət] *n* quilate *m*

caravan ['kærəvæn] *n* (*BRIT*) caravana, ruló *f*; (*in desert*) caravana; **~ning** *n*: **to**

go ~ning ir de vacaciones en caravana, viajar en caravana; **~ site** (*BRIT*) *n* camping *m* para caravanas

carbohydrate [kɑːbəʊ'haɪdreɪt] *n* hidrato de carbono; (*food*) fécula

carbon ['kɑːbən] *n* carbono; **~ paper** *n* papel *m* carbón

car boot sale *n* mercadillo organizado en un aparcamiento, en el que se exponen las mercancías en el maletero del coche

carburettor [kɑːbju'rɛtə*] (*US* **carburetor**) *n* carburador *m*

card [kɑːd] *n* (*material*) cartulina; (*index ~ etc*) ficha; (*playing ~*) carta, naipe *m*; (*visiting ~, greetings ~ etc*) tarjeta; **~board** *n* cartón *m*

cardiac ['kɑːdɪæk] *adj* cardíaco

cardigan ['kɑːdɪgən] *n* rebeca

cardinal ['kɑːdɪnl] *adj* cardinal; (*importance, principal*) esencial ♦ *n* cardenal *m*

card index *n* fichero

care [kɛə*] *n* cuidado; (*worry*) inquietud *f*; (*charge*) cargo, custodia ♦ *vi*: **to ~ about** (*person, animal*) tener cariño a; (*thing, idea*) preocuparse por; **~ of** en casa de, al cuidado de; **in sb's ~** a cargo de uno; **to take ~** to cuidarse de, tener cuidado de; **to take ~ of** cuidar; (*problem etc*) ocuparse de; **I don't ~** no me importa; **I couldn't ~ less** eso me trae sin cuidado; **~ for** *vt fus* cuidar a; (*like*) querer

career [kə'rɪə*] *n* profesión *f*; (*in work, school*) carrera ♦ *vi* (*also: ~ along*) correr a toda velocidad; **~ woman** *n* mujer *f* dedicada a su profesión

care: ~free *adj* despreocupado; **~ful** *adj* cuidadoso; (*cautious*) cauteloso; (**be**) **~ful!** ¡tenga cuidado!; **~fully** *adv* con cuidado, cuidadosamente; con cautela; **~less** *adj* descuidado; (*heedless*) poco atento; **~lessness** *n* descuido; falta de atención; **~r** ['kɛərə*] *n* enfermero/a *m/f* (*official*); (*unpaid*) persona que cuida a un pariente o vecino

caress [kə'res] n caricia ♦ vt acariciar

caretaker ['keəteɪkə*] n portero/a, conserje m/f

car-ferry n transbordador m para coches

cargo ['kɑːgəu] (pl ~es) n cargamento, carga

car hire n alquiler m de automóviles

Caribbean [kærɪ'biːən] n: **the ~ (Sea)** el (Mar) Caribe

caring ['keərɪŋ] adj humanitario; (behaviour) afectuoso

carnation [kɑː'neɪʃən] n clavel m

carnival ['kɑːnɪvəl] n carnaval m; (US: funfair) parque m de atracciones

carol ['kærəl] n: (Christmas) ~ villancico

carp [kɑːp] n (fish) carpa

car park (BRIT) n aparcamiento, parking m

carpenter ['kɑːpɪntə*] n carpintero/a

carpet ['kɑːpɪt] n alfombra; (fitted) moqueta ♦ vt alfombrar

car phone n teléfono movil

car rental (US) n alquiler m de coches

carriage ['kærɪdʒ] n (BRIT: RAIL) vagón m; (horse-drawn) coche m; (of goods) transporte m; (: cost) porte m, flete m; **~way** (BRIT) n (part of road) calzada

carrier ['kærɪə*] n (transport company) transportista, empresa de transportes; (MED) portador m; ~ **bag** (BRIT) n bolsa de papel or plástico

carrot ['kærət] n zanahoria

carry ['kærɪ] vt (subj: person) llevar; (transport) transportar; (involve: responsibilities etc) entrañar, implicar; (MED) ser portador de ♦ vi (sound) oírse; **to get carried away** (fig) entusiasmarse; ~ **on** vi (continue) seguir (adelante), continuar ♦ vt proseguir, continuar; ~ **out** vt (orders) cumplir; (investigation) llevar a cabo, realizar; ~ **cot** (BRIT) n cuna portátil; **~-on** (inf) n (fuss) lío

cart [kɑːt] n carro, carreta ♦ vt (inf: transport) acarrear

carton ['kɑːtən] n (box) caja (de cartón); (of milk etc) bote m; (of yogurt) tarrina

cartoon [kɑː'tuːn] n (PRESS) caricatura; (comic strip) tira cómica; (film) dibujos mpl animados

cartridge ['kɑːtrɪdʒ] n cartucho; (of pen) recambio; (of record player) cápsula

carve [kɑːv] vt (meat) trinchar; (wood, stone) cincelar, esculpir; (initials etc) grabar; ~ **up** vt dividir, repartir; **carving** n (object) escultura; (design) talla; (art) tallado; **carving knife** n trinchante m

car wash n lavado de coches

case [keɪs] n (container) caja; (MED) caso; (for jewels etc) estuche m; (LAW) causa, proceso; (BRIT: also: suit~) maleta; **in ~ of** en caso de; **in any ~** en todo caso; **just in ~** por si acaso

cash [kæʃ] n en efectivo, dinero contante ♦ vt cobrar, hacer efectivo; **to pay (in) ~** pagar al contado; ~ **on delivery** cóbrese al entregar; ~**book** n libro de caja; ~ **card** n tarjeta f dinero; ~ **desk** n BRIT caja; ~ **dispenser** n cajero automático

cashew [kæ'ʃuː] n (also: ~ **nut**) anacardo

cash flow n flujo de fondos, cash-flow m

cashier [kæ'ʃɪə*] n cajero/a

cashmere ['kæʃmɪə*] n cachemira

cash register n caja

casing ['keɪsɪŋ] n revestimiento

casino [kə'siːnəu] n casino

casket ['kɑːskɪt] n cofre, estuche m; (US: coffin) ataúd m

casserole ['kæsərəul] n (food, pot) cazuela

cassette [kæ'set] n cassette f; ~ **player/recorder** n tocacassettes m inv, cassette m

cast [kɑːst] (pt, pp cast) vt (throw) echar, arrojar, lanzar; (glance, eyes) dirigir; (THEATRE): **to ~ sb as Othello**

dar a uno el papel de Otelo ♦ vi (FISHING) lanzar ♦ n (THEATRE) reparto; (also: plaster ~) vaciado; **to ~ one's vote** votar; **to ~ doubt on** suscitar dudas acerca de; **~ off** vi (NAUT) desamarrar; (KNITTING) cerrar (los puntos); **~ on** vi (KNITTING) poner los puntos

castanets [kæstə'nɛts] npl castañuelas fpl

castaway ['kɑːstəwei] n náufrago/a f

caster sugar ['kɑːstə*-] (BRIT) n azúcar m extrafino

Castile [kæs'tiːl] n Castilla; **Castilian** adj, n castellano/a m/f

casting vote ['kɑːstɪŋ-] (BRIT) n voto decisivo

cast iron n hierro fundido

castle ['kɑːsl] n castillo; (CHESS) torre f

castor oil ['kɑːstə*-] n aceite m de ricino

casual ['kæʒjul] adj fortuito; (irregular: work etc) eventual, temporero; (unconcerned) despreocupado; (clothes) de sport; **~ly** adv de manera despreocupada; (dress) de sport

casualty ['kæʒjultɪ] n víctima, herido; (dead) muerto; (MED: department) urgencias fpl

cat [kæt] n gato; (big ~) felino

Catalan ['kætəlæn] adj, n catalán/ana m/f

catalogue ['kætəlɒg] (US **catalog**) n catálogo ♦ vt catalogar

Catalonia [kætə'ləunɪə] n Cataluña

catalyst ['kætəlɪst] n catalizador m

catalytic convertor [kætə'lɪtɪk kən'vɜːtə*] n catalizador m

catapult ['kætəpʌlt] n tirachinas m inv

catarrh [kə'tɑː*] n catarro

catastrophe [kə'tæstrəfɪ] n catástrofe f

catch [kætʃ] (pt, pp **caught**) vt coger (SP), agarrar (AM); (arrest) detener; (grasp) asir; (breath) contener; (surprise: person) sorprender; (attract: attention) captar; (hear) oír; (MED) contagiarse de; coger; (also: ~ up) alcanzar ♦ vi (fire)

encenderse; (in branches etc) enredarse ♦ n (fish etc) pesca; (act of catching) cogida; (hidden problem) dificultad f; (game) pilla-pilla; (of lock) pestillo, cerradura; **to ~ fire** encenderse; **to ~ sight of** divisar; **~ on** vi (understand) caer en la cuenta; (grow popular) hacerse popular; **~ up** vi (fig) ponerse al día; **~ing** ['kætʃɪŋ] adj (MED) contagioso; **~ment area** ['kætʃmənt-] (BRIT) n zona de captación; **~phrase** ['kætʃfreɪz] n lema m, eslogan m; **~y** ['kætʃɪ] adj (tune) pegadizo

category ['kætɪgərɪ] n categoría, clase f

cater ['keɪtə*] vi: **to ~ for** (BRIT) abastecer a; (needs) atender a; (COMM: parties etc) proveer comida a; **~er** n abastecedor(a) m/f, proveedor(a) m/f; **~ing** (trade) hostelería

caterpillar ['kætəpɪlə*] n oruga, gusano

cathedral [kə'θiːdrəl] n catedral f

catholic ['kæθəlɪk] adj (tastes etc) amplio; **C~** adj, n (REL) católico/a m/f

CAT scan [kæt-] n TAC f, tomografía

Cat'seye ® ['kæts'aɪ] (BRIT) n (AUT) catafoto

cattle ['kætl] npl ganado

catty ['kætɪ] adj malicioso, rencoroso

caucus ['kɔːkəs] n (POL) camarilla política; (: US: to elect candidates) comité m electoral

caught [kɔːt] pt, pp of **catch**

cauliflower ['kɒlɪflauə*] n coliflor f

cause [kɔːz] n causa, motivo, razón f; (principle: also: POL) causa ♦ vt causar

caution ['kɔːʃən] n cautela, prudencia; (warning) advertencia, amonestación f ♦ vt amonestar; **cautious** adj cauteloso, prudente, precavido

cavalry ['kævəlrɪ] n caballería

cave [keɪv] n cueva, caverna; **~ in** vi (roof etc) derrumbarse, hundirse

caviar(e) ['kævɪɑː*] n caviar m

CB n abbr (= Citizens' Band (Radio))

banda ciudadana

CBI *n abbr* (= Confederation of British Industry) ≈ C.E.O.E. *f* (*SP*)

cc *abbr* = **cubic centimetres**; = **carbon copy**

CCTV *n abbr* (= closed-circuit television) circuito cerrado de televisión

CD *n abbr* (= compact disc) DC *m*; (*player*) (reproductor *m* de) disco compacto; ~ **player** *n* lector *m* de discos compactos; ~**-ROM** [siːdiːˈrɔm] *n abbr* CD-ROM *m*

cease [siːs] *vt, vi* cesar; **~-fire** *n* alto *m* el fuego; **~less** *adj* incesante

cedar [ˈsiːdəˀ] *n* cedro

ceiling [ˈsiːlɪŋ] *n* techo; (*fig*) límite *m*

celebrate [ˈsɛlɪbreɪt] *vt* celebrar ♦ *vi* divertirse; **~d** *adj* célebre; **celebration** [-ˈbreɪʃən] *n* fiesta, celebración *f*

celery [ˈsɛlərɪ] *n* apio

cell [sɛl] *n* celda; (*BIOL*) célula; (*ELEC*) elemento

cellar [ˈsɛləˀ] *n* sótano; (*for wine*) bodega

cello [ˈtʃɛləʊ] *n* violoncelo

Cellophane ® [ˈsɛləfeɪn] *n* celofán *m*

cellphone [ˈsɛlfəʊn] *n* teléfono celular

Celt [kɛlt, sɛlt] *adj, n* celta *m/f*; **~ic** *adj* celta

cement [səˈmɛnt] *n* cemento; ~ **mixer** *n* hormigonera

cemetery [ˈsɛmɪtrɪ] *n* cementerio

censor [ˈsɛnsəˀ] *n* censor *m* ♦ *vt* (*cut*) censurar; **~ship** *n* censura

censure [ˈsɛnʃəˀ] *vt* censurar

census [ˈsɛnsəs] *n* censo

cent [sɛnt] *n* (unit of dollar) centavo, céntimo; (unit of euro) céntimo; see also per

centenary [sɛnˈtiːnərɪ] *n* centenario

center [ˈsɛntəˀ] *n* (*US*) = **centre**

centi... [sɛntɪ] *prefix*: **~grade** *adj* centígrado; **~litre** (*US* **~liter**) *n* centilitro; **~metre**, (*US* **~meter**) *n* centímetro

centipede [ˈsɛntɪpiːd] *n* ciempiés *m inv*

central [ˈsɛntrəl] *adj* central; (*of house etc*) céntrico; **C~ America** *n* Centroamérica; **~ heating** *n* calefacción *f* central; **~ize** *vt* centralizar

centre [ˈsɛntəˀ] *n* (*US* **center**) *n* centro; (*fig*) núcleo ♦ *vt* centrar; **~-forward** *n* (*SPORT*) delantero centro; **~-half** *n* (*SPORT*) medio centro

century [ˈsɛntjʊrɪ] *n* siglo; **20th ~** siglo veinte

ceramic [sɪˈræmɪk] *adj* cerámico; **~s** *n* cerámica

cereal [ˈsiːrɪəl] *n* cereal *m*

ceremony [ˈsɛrɪmənɪ] *n* ceremonia; **to stand on ~** hacer ceremonias, estar de cumplido

certain [ˈsəːtən] *adj* seguro; (*person*): **a ~ Mr Smith** un tal Sr Smith; (*particular, some*) cierto; **for ~** a ciencia cierta; **~ly** *adv* (*undoubtedly*) ciertamente; (*of course*) desde luego, por supuesto; **~ty** *n* certeza, certidumbre *f*, seguridad *f*; (*inevitability*) certeza

certificate [səˈtɪfɪkɪt] *n* certificado

certified [ˈsəːtɪfaɪd] *adj*: **~ mail** (*US*) *n* correo certificado; **~ public accountant** (*US*) *n* contable *m/f* diplomado/a

certify [ˈsəːtɪfaɪ] *vt* certificar; (*award diploma to*) conceder un diploma a; (*declare insane*) declarar loco

cervical [ˈsəːvɪkl] *adj* cervical

cervix [ˈsəːvɪks] *n* cuello del útero

cf. *abbr* (= compare) cfr

CFC *n abbr* (= chlorofluorocarbon) CFC *m*

ch. *abbr* (= chapter) cap

chain [tʃeɪn] *n* cadena; (*of mountains*) cordillera; (*of events*) sucesión *f* ♦ *vt* (*also:* ~ **up**) encadenar; **~ reaction** *n* reacción *f* en cadena; **~-smoke** *n* fumar un cigarrillo tras otro; **~ store** *n* tienda de una cadena; ≈ gran almacén

chair [tʃɛəˀ] *n* silla; (*armchair*) sillón *m*, butaca; (*of university*) cátedra; (*of meeting etc*) presidencia ♦ *vt* (*meeting*)

presidir; **~lift** n telesilla; **~man** n
presidente m

chalk [tʃɔːk] n (GEO) creta; (for writing)
tiza (SP), gis m (AM)

challenge ['tʃælɪndʒ] n desafío, reto
♦ vt desafiar, retar; (statement, right)
poner en duda; **to ~ sb to do sth**
retar a uno a que haga algo; **challenging** adj exigente; (tone) de desafío

chamber ['tʃeɪmbə*] n cámara, sala;
(POL) cámara; (BRIT: LAW: gen pl)
despacho; **~ of commerce** cámara de
comercio; **~maid** n camarera

chamois ['ʃæmwɑː] n gamuza

champagne [ʃæm'peɪn] n champaña
m, champán m

champion ['tʃæmpɪən] n campeón/
ona m/f; (of cause) defensor(a) m/f;
~ship n campeonato

chance [tʃɑːns] n (opportunity) ocasión
f, oportunidad f; (likelihood) posibilidad
f; (risk) riesgo ♦ vt arriesgar, probar
♦ adj fortuito, casual; **to ~ it**
arriesgarse, intentarlo; **to take a ~**
arriesgarse; **by ~** por casualidad

chancellor ['tʃɑːnsələ*] n canciller m;
C~ of the Exchequer (BRIT) n
Ministro de Hacienda

chandelier [ʃændə'lɪə*] n araña (de
luces)

change [tʃeɪndʒ] vt cambiar; (replace)
cambiar, reemplazar; (gear, clothes, job)
cambiar de; (transform) transformar
♦ vi cambiar(se); (trains) hacer
transbordo; (traffic lights) cambiar de
color; (be transformed): **to ~ into**
transformarse en ♦ n cambio;
(alteration) modificación f,
transformación f; (of clothes) muda;
(coins) suelto, sencillo; (money returned)
vuelta; **to ~ gear** (AUT) cambiar de
marcha; **to ~ one's mind** cambiar de
opinión o idea; **to ~** para variar;
~able adj (weather) cambiable;
~ machine n máquina de cambio;
~over n (to new system) cambio;
changing adj cambiante; **changing**

room (BRIT) n vestuario

channel ['tʃænl] n (TV) canal m; (of
river) cauce m; (groove) conducto; (fig:
medium) medio ♦ vt (fig: energies)
encauzar; **the (English) C~** el Canal
(de la Mancha); **the C~ Islands** las
Islas Normandas; **the C~ Tunnel** el
túnel del Canal de la Mancha, el
Eurotúnel; **~-hopping** n (TV) zapping m

chant [tʃɑːnt] n (of crowd) gritos mpl;
(REL) canto ♦ vt (slogan, word) repetir a
gritos

chaos ['keɪɔs] n caos m

chap [tʃæp] (BRIT: inf) n (man) tío, tipo

chapel ['tʃæpl] n capilla

chaperone ['ʃæpərəun] n carabina

chaplain ['tʃæplɪn] n capellán m

chapped [tʃæpt] adj agrietado

chapter ['tʃæptə*] n capítulo

char [tʃɑː*] vt (burn) carbonizar,
chamuscar

character ['kærɪktə*] n carácter m,
naturaleza, índole f; (moral strength,
personality) carácter; (in novel, film)
personaje m; **~istic** [-'rɪstɪk] adj
característico ♦ característica

charcoal ['tʃɑːkəul] n carbón m
vegetal; (ART) carboncillo

charge [tʃɑːdʒ] n (LAW) cargo,
acusación f; (cost) precio, coste m;
(responsibility) cargo ♦ vt (LAW): **to
~ (with)** acusar (de); (battery) cargar;
(price) pedir; (customer) cobrar ♦ vi
precipitarse; (MIL) cargar, atacar; **~s**
npl: **to reverse the ~s** (BRIT: TEL)
revertir el cobro; **to take ~ of** hacerse
cargo de, encargarse de; **to be in ~ of**
estar encargado de; (business) dirigir;
how much do you ~? ¿cuánto cobra
usted?; **to ~ an expense (up) to**
sb's account cargar algo a cuenta de
alguien; **~ card** n tarjeta de cuenta

charity ['tʃærɪtɪ] n caridad f;
(organization) sociedad f benéfica;
(money, gifts) limosnas fpl

charm [tʃɑːm] n encanto, atractivo;
(talisman) hechizo; (on bracelet) dije m

chart 348 chestnut

chart [tʃɑːt] n (diagram) cuadro; (graph) gráfica; (map) carta de navegación ♦ vt (course) trazar; (progress) seguir; ~s npl (Top 40): the ~s ≈ los 40 principales (SP)

charter ['tʃɑːtə*] vt (plane) alquilar; (ship) fletar ♦ n (document) carta; (of university, company) estatutos mpl; ~ed accountant (BRIT) n contable m/f diplomado/a; ~ flight n vuelo m chárter

chase [tʃeɪs] vt (pursue) perseguir; (also: ~ away) ahuyentar ♦ n persecución f

chasm ['kæzəm] n sima

chassis ['ʃæsɪ] n chasis m

chat [tʃæt] vi (also: have a ~) charlar ♦ n charla; ~ show (BRIT) n programa m de entrevistas

chatter ['tʃætə*] vi (person) charlar; (teeth) castañetear ♦ n (of birds) parloteo; (of people) charla, cháchara; ~box (inf) n parlanchín/ina m/f

chatty ['tʃætɪ] adj (style) informal; (person) hablador/a

chauffeur ['ʃəʊfə*] n chófer m

chauvinist ['ʃəʊvɪnɪst] n (male ~) machista m; (nationalist) chovinista m/f

cheap [tʃiːp] adj barato; (joke) de mal gusto; (poor quality) de mala calidad ♦ adv barato; ~ day return n billete m de ida y vuelta el mismo día; ~er más barato; ~ly adv barato, a bajo precio

cheat [tʃiːt] vi hacer trampa ♦ vt: to ~ sb (out of sth) estafar (algo) a uno ♦ n (person) tramposo/a

check [tʃek] vt (examine) controlar; (facts) comprobar; (halt) parar, detener; (restrain) refrenar, restringir ♦ n (inspection) control m, inspección f; (curb) freno; (US: bill) nota, cuenta, (US) = **cheque**; (pattern: gen pl) cuadro ♦ adj (also: ~ed: pattern, cloth) a cuadros; ~ in vi (at hotel) firmar el registro; (at airport) facturar el equipaje ♦ vt (luggage) facturar; ~ out vi (of hotel) marcharse; ~ up vi: to ~ up on

sth comprobar algo; to ~ up on sb investigar a alguien; ~ered (US) adj = **check**; ~ered (US) adj = **chequered**; ~ers (US) n juego de damas; ~-in (desk) n mostrador m de facturación; ~ing account (US) n cuenta corriente; ~mate n jaque m mate; ~out n caja; ~point n (punto de) control m; ~room (US) n consigna; ~up n (MED) reconocimiento general

cheek [tʃiːk] n mejilla; (impudence) descaro; **what a ~!** ¡qué cara!; ~bone n pómulo; ~y adj fresco, descarado

cheep [tʃiːp] vi piar

cheer [tʃɪə*] vt vitorear, aplaudir; (gladden) alegrar, animar ♦ vi dar vivas ♦ n viva m; ~s npl aplausos mpl; ~s! ¡salud!; ~ up vi animarse ♦ vt alegrar, animar; ~ful adj alegre

cheerio [tʃɪərɪ'əʊ] (BRIT) excl ¡hasta luego!

cheese [tʃiːz] n queso; ~board n tabla de quesos

cheetah ['tʃiːtə] n leopardo cazador

chef [ʃef] n jefe/a m/f de cocina

chemical ['kemɪkəl] adj químico ♦ n producto químico

chemist ['kemɪst] n (BRIT: pharmacist) farmacéutico/a; (scientist) químico/a; ~ry n química; ~'s (shop) (BRIT) n farmacia

cheque [tʃek] (US **check**) n cheque m; ~book n talonario de cheques (SP), chequera (AM); ~ card n tarjeta de cheque

chequered ['tʃekəd] (US **checkered**) adj (fig) accidentado

cherish ['tʃerɪʃ] vt (love) querer, apreciar; (protect) cuidar; (hope etc) abrigar

cherry ['tʃerɪ] n cereza; (also: ~ tree) cerezo

chess [tʃes] n ajedrez m; ~board n tablero (de ajedrez)

chest [tʃest] n (ANAT) pecho, (box) cofre m, cajón m; ~ of drawers n cómoda

chestnut ['tʃesnʌt] n castaña; ~ (tree)

n castaño

chew [tʃuː] *vt* mascar, masticar; **~ing gum** *n* chicle *m*

chic [ʃiːk] *adj* elegante

chick [tʃik] *n* pollito, polluelo; (*inf: girl*) chica

chicken ['tʃikɪn] *n* gallina, pollo; (*food*) pollo; (*inf: coward*) gallina *m/f*; **~ out** (*inf*) *vi* rajarse; **~pox** *n* varicela

chicory ['tʃikərɪ] *n* (*for coffee*) achicoria; (*salad*) escarola

chief [tʃiːf] *n* jefe/a *m/f* ♦ *adj* principal; **~ executive** *n* director(a) *m/f* general; **~ly** *adv* principalmente

chilblain ['tʃilbleɪn] *n* sabañón *m*

child [tʃaɪld] (*pl* **children**) *n* niño/a; (*offspring*) hijo/a; **~birth** *n* parto; **~hood** *n* niñez *f*, infancia; **~ish** *adj* pueril, aniñado; **~like** *adj* de niño; **~ minder** (*BRIT*) *n* madre *f* de día; **~ren** ['tʃildrən] *npl of* **child**

Chile ['tʃili] *n* Chile *m*; **~an** *adj*, *n* chileno/a *m/f*

chill [tʃil] *n* frío; (*MED*) resfriado ♦ *vt* enfriar; (*CULIN*) congelar

chil(l)i ['tʃili] (*BRIT*) *n* chile *m* (*SP*), ají *m* (*AM*)

chilly ['tʃili] *adj* frío

chime [tʃaɪm] *n* repique *m*; (*of clock*) campanada ♦ *vi* repicar; sonar

chimney ['tʃimni] *n* chimenea; **~ sweep** *n* deshollinador *m*

chimpanzee [tʃimpæn'ziː] *n* chimpancé *m*

chin [tʃin] *n* mentón *m*, barbilla

china ['tʃaɪnə] *n* porcelana; (*crockery*) loza

China ['tʃaɪnə] *n* China; **Chinese** [tʃaɪ'niːz] *adj* chino ♦ *n inv* chino/a; (*LING*) chino

chink [tʃiŋk] *n* (*opening*) grieta, hendedura; (*noise*) tintineo

chip [tʃip] *n* (*gen pl: CULIN: BRIT*) patata (*SP*) *or* papa (*AM*) frita; (: *US: also: potato* ~) patata *or* papa frita; (*of wood*) astilla; (*of glass, stone*) lasca; (*at poker*) ficha; (*COMPUT*) chip *m* ♦ *vt* (*cup, plate*) desconchar

┌─────────────┐
│ **chip shop** │
└─────────────┘

Se denomina **chip shop** *o* "**fish-and-chip shop**" *a un establecimiento en el que se sirven algunas especialidades de comida rápida, muy populares entre los británicos, sobre todo pescado rebozado y patatas fritas.*

chiropodist [kɪ'rɔpədɪst] (*BRIT*) *n* pedicuro/a, callista *m/f*

chirp [tʃəːp] *vi* (*bird*) gorjear, piar

chisel ['tʃizl] *n* (*for wood*) escoplo; (*for stone*) cincel *m*

chit [tʃit] *n* nota

chitchat ['tʃitʃæt] *n* chismes *mpl*, habladurías *fpl*

chivalry ['ʃivəlrɪ] *n* caballerosidad *f*

chives [tʃaɪvz] *npl* cebollinos *mpl*

chlorine ['klɔːriːn] *n* cloro

chock-a-block ['tʃɔk'blɔk] *adj* atestado

chock-full ['tʃɔk'ful] *adj* atestado

chocolate ['tʃɔklɪt] *n* chocolate *m*; (*sweet*) bombón *m*

choice [tʃɔis] *n* elección *f*, selección *f*; (*option*) opción *f*; (*preference*) preferencia *f* ♦ *adj* escogido

choir ['kwaɪə*] *n* coro; **~boy** *n* niño de coro

choke [tʃəuk] *vi* ahogarse; (*on food*) atragantarse ♦ *vt* estrangular, ahogar; (*block*): **to be ~d with** estar atascado de ♦ *n* (*AUT*) estárter *m*

cholesterol [kə'lestərɔl] *n* colesterol *m*

choose [tʃuːz] (*pt* **chose**, *pp* **chosen**) *vt* escoger, elegir; (*team*) seleccionar; **to ~ to do sth** optar por hacer algo

choosy ['tʃuːzi] *adj* delicado

chop [tʃɔp] *vt* (*wood*) cortar, tajar; (*CULIN: also:* ~ **up**) picar ♦ *n* (*CULIN*) chuleta; **~s** *npl* (*jaws*) boca, labios *mpl*

chopper ['tʃɔpə*] *n* (*helicopter*) helicóptero

choppy ['tʃɔpi] *adj* (*sea*) picado, agitado

chopsticks ['tʃɒpstɪks] npl palillos mpl

chord [kɔːd] n (MUS) acorde m

chore [tʃɔː*] n faena, tarea; (routine task) trabajo rutinario

chorus ['kɔːrəs] n coro; (repeated part of song) estribillo

chose [tʃəuz] pt of **choose**

chosen ['tʃəuzn] pp of **choose**

chowder ['tʃaudə*] n (esp US) sopa de pescado

Christ [kraɪst] n Cristo

christen ['krɪsn] vt bautizar

Christian ['krɪstɪən] adj, n cristiano/a m/f; **~ity** [-'ænɪtɪ] n cristianismo; **~ name** n nombre m de pila

Christmas ['krɪsməs] n Navidad f; **Merry ~!** ¡Felices Pascuas!; **~ card** n crismas m inv, tarjeta de Navidad; **~ Day** n día m de Navidad; **~ Eve** n Nochebuena; **~ tree** n árbol m de Navidad

chrome [krəum] n cromo

chronic ['krɒnɪk] adj crónico

chronological [krɒnə'lɒdʒɪkəl] adj cronológico

chubby ['tʃʌbɪ] adj regordete

chuck [tʃʌk] (inf) vt lanzar, arrojar; (BRIT: also: ~ up) abandonar; **~ out** vt (person) echar (fuera); (rubbish etc) tirar

chuckle ['tʃʌkl] vi reírse entre dientes

chug [tʃʌg] vi resoplar; (car, boat: also: ~ along) avanzar traqueteando

chum [tʃʌm] n compañero/a

chunk [tʃʌŋk] n pedazo, trozo

church [tʃəːtʃ] n iglesia; **~yard** n cementerio

churn [tʃəːn] n (for butter) mantequera; (for milk) lechera; **~ out** vt producir en serie

chute [ʃuːt] n (also: rubbish ~) vertedero; (for coal etc) rampa de caída

chutney ['tʃʌtnɪ] n condimento a base de frutas de la India

CIA (US) n abbr (= Central Intelligence Agency) CIA f

CID (BRIT) n abbr (= Criminal Investigation Department) ≈ B.I.C. f (SP)

cider ['saɪdə*] n sidra

cigar [sɪ'gɑː*] n puro

cigarette [sɪgə'ret] n cigarrillo (SP), cigarro (AM); pitillo; **~ case** n pitillera; **~ end** n colilla

Cinderella [sɪndə'relə] n Cenicienta

cine camera ['sɪnɪ-] (BRIT) n cámara cinematográfica

cinema ['sɪnəmə] n cine m

cinnamon ['sɪnəmən] n canela

circle ['səːkl] n círculo; (in theatre) anfiteatro ♦ vi dar vueltas ♦ vt (surround) rodear, cercar; (move round) dar la vuelta a

circuit ['səːkɪt] n circuito; (tour) gira; (track) pista; (lap) vuelta; **~ous** [səː'kjuːtəs] adj indirecto

circular ['səːkjulə*] adj circular ♦ n circular f

circulate ['səːkjuleɪt] vi circular; (person: at party etc) hablar con los invitados ♦ vt poner en circulación; **circulation** [-'leɪʃən] n circulación f; (of newspaper) tirada

circumstances ['səːkəmstənsɪz] npl circunstancias fpl; (financial condition) situación f económica

circus ['səːkəs] n circo

CIS n abbr (= Commonwealth of Independent States) CEI f

cistern ['sɪstən] n tanque m, depósito; (in toilet) cisterna

citizen ['sɪtɪzn] n (POL) ciudadano/a; (of city) vecino/a, habitante m/f; **~ship** n ciudadanía

citrus fruits ['sɪtrəs-] npl agrios mpl

city ['sɪtɪ] n ciudad f; **the C~** centro financiero de Londres

civic ['sɪvɪk] adj cívico; (authorities) municipal; **~ centre** (BRIT) n centro público

civil ['sɪvɪl] adj civil; (polite) atento, cortés; **~ engineer** n ingeniero de caminos, canales y puertos); **~ian** [sɪ'vɪlɪən] adj civil (no militar) ♦ n m/f, paisano/a

civilization |sıvılaı'zeıʃən| *n* civilización *f*

civilized |'sıvılaızd| *adj* civilizado

civil: ~ **law** *n* derecho civil; ~ **servant** *n* funcionario/a del Estado; **C~ Service** *n* administración *f* pública; ~ **war** *n* guerra civil

claim |kleım| *vt* exigir, reclamar; (*rights etc*) reivindicar; (*assert*) pretender ♦ *vi* (*for insurance*) reclamar ♦ *n* reclamación *f*; pretensión *f*; ~**ant** *n* demandante *m/f*

clairvoyant |kleə'vɔıənt| *n* clarividente *m/f*

clam |klæm| *n* almeja

clamber |'klæmbə*| *vi* trepar

clammy |'klæmı| *adj* frío y húmedo

clamour |'klæmə*| (*US* **clamor**) *vi:* to ~ **for** clamar por, pedir a voces

clamp |klæmp| *n* abrazadera, grapa ♦ *vt* (2 *things together*) cerrar fuertemente; (*one thing on another*) afianzar (con abrazadera); (*AUT: wheel*) poner el cepo a; ~ **down on** *vt fus* (*subj: government, police*) reforzar la lucha contra

clang |klæŋ| *vi* sonar, hacer estruendo

clap |klæp| *vi* aplaudir; ~**ping** *n* aplausos *mpl*

claret |'klærət| *n* burdeos *m inv*

clarify |'klærıfaı| *vt* aclarar

clarinet |klærı'nɛt| *n* clarinete *m*

clash |klæʃ| *n* enfrentamiento; choque *m*; desacuerdo; estruendo ♦ *vi* (*fight*) enfrentarse; (*beliefs*) chocar; (*disagree*) estar en desacuerdo; (*colours*) desentonar; (*two events*) coincidir

clasp |klɑːsp| *n* (*hold*) apretón *m*; (*of necklace, bag*) cierre *m* ♦ *vt* apretar; abrazar

class |klɑːs| *n* clase *f* ♦ *vt* clasificar

classic |'klæsık| *adj, n* clásico; ~**al** *adj* clásico

classified |'klæsıfaıd| *adj* (*information*) reservado; ~ **advertisement** *n* anuncio por palabras

classmate |'klɑːsmeıt| *n* compañero/a de clase

classroom |'klɑːsrum| *n* aula

clatter |'klætə*| *n* estrépito ♦ *vi* hacer ruido o estrépito

clause |klɔːz| *n* cláusula; (*LING*) oración *f*

claw |klɔː| *n* (*of cat*) uña; (*of bird of prey*) garra; (*of lobster*) pinza

clay |kleı| *n* arcilla

clean |kliːn| *adj* limpio; (*record, reputation*) bueno, intachable; (*joke*) decente ♦ *vt* limpiar; (*hands etc*) lavar; ~ **out** *vt* limpiar; ~ **up** *vt* limpiar, asear; ~**-cut** *adj* (*person*) bien parecido; ~**er** *n* (*person*) asistenta; (*substance*) producto para la limpieza; ~**er's** *n* tintorería; ~**ing** *n* limpieza; ~**liness** |'klɛnlınıs| *n* limpieza

cleanse |klɛnz| *vt* limpiar; ~**r** *n* (*for face*) crema limpiadora

clean-shaven *adj* sin barba, afeitado

cleansing department (*BRIT*) *n* departamento de limpieza

clear |klıə*| *adj* claro; (*road, way*) libre; (*conscience*) limpio, tranquilo; (*skin*) terso; (*sky*) despejado ♦ *vt* (*space*) despejar, limpiar; (*LAW: suspect*) absolver; (*obstacle*) salvar, saltar por encima de; (*cheque*) aceptar ♦ *vi* (*fog etc*) despejarse ♦ *adv:* ~ **of** a distancia de; to ~ **the table** recoger o levantar la mesa; ~ **up** *vt* limpiar; (*mystery*) aclarar, resolver; ~**ance** *n* (*removal*) despeje *m*; (*permission*) acreditación *f*; ~**-cut** *adj* bien definido, nítido; ~**ing** *n* (*in wood*) claro *m*; ~**ing bank** (*BRIT*) *n* cámara de compensación; ~**ly** *adv* claramente; (*evidently*) sin duda; ~**way** (*BRIT*) *n* carretera donde no se puede parar

clef |klɛf| *n* (*MUS*) clave *f*

cleft |klɛft| *n* (*in rock*) grieta, hendedura

clench |klɛntʃ| *vt* apretar, cerrar

clergy |'klɑːdʒı| *n* clero; ~**man** *n* clérigo

clerical |'klɛrıkəl| *adj* de oficina; (*REL*)

clerical

clerk [klɑːk, (US) klɜːrk] n (BRIT) oficinista m/f, (US) dependiente/a m/f

clever ['klevə*] adj (intelligent) inteligente, listo; (skilful) hábil; (device, arrangement) ingenioso

click [klɪk] vt (tongue) chasquear; (heels) taconear ♦ vi (COMPUT) hacer clic; **to ~ on an icon** hacer clic en un icono

client ['klaɪənt] n cliente m/f

cliff [klɪf] n acantilado

climate ['klaɪmɪt] n clima m

climax ['klaɪmæks] n (of battle, career) apogeo; (of film, book) punto culminante; (sexual) orgasmo

climb [klaɪm] vi subir; (plant) trepar; (move with effort): **to ~ over a wall/into a car** trepar a una tapia/subir a un coche ♦ vt (stairs) subir; (tree) trepar a; (mountain) escalar ♦ n subida; **~down** n vuelta atrás; **~er** n alpinista m/f (SP), andinista m/f (AM); **~ing** n alpinismo (SP), andinismo (AM)

clinch [klɪntʃ] vt (deal) cerrar; (argument) remachar

cling [klɪŋ] (pt, pp **clung**) vi: **to ~ to** agarrarse a; (clothes) pegarse a

clinic ['klɪnɪk] n clínica; **~al** adj clínico; (fig) frío

clink [klɪŋk] vi tintinar

clip [klɪp] n (for hair) horquilla; (also: paper ~) sujetapapeles m inv, clip m; (TV, CINEMA) fragmento ♦ vt (cut) cortar; (also: ~ together) unir; **~pers** npl (for gardening) tijeras fpl; **~ping** n (newspaper) recorte m

cloak [kləuk] n capa, manto ♦ vt (fig) encubrir, disimular; **~room** n guardarropa; (BRIT: WC) lavabo (SP), aseos mpl (SP), baño (AM)

clock [klɒk] n reloj m; **~ in** or **on** vi fichar, picar; **~ off** or **out** vi fichar or picar la salida; **~wise** adv en el sentido de las agujas del reloj; **~work** n aparato de relojería ♦ adj (toy) de cuerda

clog [klɒg] n zueco, chanclo ♦ vt atascar ♦ vi (also: ~ up) atascarse

cloister ['klɔɪstə*] n claustro

clone [kləun] n clon m ♦ vt clonar

close¹ [kləus] adj (near): **~ (to)** cerca (de); (friend) íntimo; (connection) estrecho; (examination) detallado, minucioso; (weather) bochornoso; **to have a ~ shave** (fig) escaparse por un pelo ♦ adv cerca; **~ by**, **~ at hand** muy cerca; **~ to** prep cerca de

close² [kləuz] vt (shut) cerrar; (end) concluir, terminar ♦ vi (shop etc) cerrarse; (end) concluirse, terminarse ♦ n (end) fin m, final m, conclusión f; **~ down** vi cerrarse definitivamente; **~d** adj (shop etc) cerrado; **~d shop** n taller m gremial

close-knit [kləus'nɪt] adj (fig) muy unido

closely ['kləuslɪ] adv (study) con detalle; (watch) de cerca; (resemble) estrechamente

closet ['klɒzɪt] n armario

close-up ['kləusʌp] n primer plano

closure ['kləuʒə*] n cierre m

clot [klɒt] n (gen) coágulo; (inf: idiot) imbécil m/f ♦ vi (blood) coagularse

cloth [klɒθ] n (material) tela, paño; (rag) trapo

clothe [kləuð] vt vestir; **~s** npl ropa; **~s brush** n cepillo (para la ropa); **~s line** n cuerda (para tender la ropa); **~s peg** (US **~s pin**) n pinza

clothing ['kləuðɪŋ] n = **clothes**

cloud [klaud] n nube f; **~burst** n aguacero; **~y** adj nublado, nubloso; (liquid) turbio

clout [klaut] vt dar un tortazo a

clove [kləuv] n clavo; **~ of garlic** diente m de ajo

clover ['kləuvə*] n trébol m

clown [klaun] n payaso ♦ vi (also: ~ about, ~ around) hacer el payaso

cloying ['klɔɪɪŋ] adj empalagoso

club [klʌb] n (society) club m; (weapon) porra, cachiporra; (also: golf ~) palo

♦ vt aporrear ♦ vi: **to ~ together** (for gift) comprar entre todos; **~s** (CARDS) tréboles mpl; **~ class** n (AVIAT) clase f preferente; **~house** n local social, sobre todo en clubs deportivos

cluck [klʌk] vi cloquear

clue [klu:] n pista; (in crosswords) indicación f; **I haven't a ~** no tengo ni idea

clump [klʌmp] n (of trees) grupo

clumsy [ˈklʌmzi] adj (person) torpe, desmañado; (tool) difícil de manejar; (movement) desgarbado

clung [klʌŋ] pt, pp of **cling**

cluster [ˈklʌstə*] n grupo ♦ vi agruparse, apiñarse

clutch [klʌtʃ] n (AUT) embrague m; (grasp): **~es** garras fpl ♦ vt asir; agarrar

clutter [ˈklʌtə*] vt atestar

cm abbr (= centimetre) cm

CND n abbr (= Campaign for Nuclear Disarmament) plataforma pro desarme nuclear

Co. abbr = **county**; **company**

c/o abbr (= care of) c/a, a/c

coach [kəutʃ] n autocar m (SP), coche m de línea; (horse-drawn) coche m; (of train) vagón m, coche m; (SPORT) entrenador/a m/f, instructor/a m/f; (tutor) profesor/a m/f particular ♦ vt (SPORT) entrenar; (student) preparar, enseñar; **~ trip** n excursión f en autocar

coal [kəul] n carbón m; **~ face** n frente m de carbón; **~field** n yacimiento de carbón

coalition [kəuəˈlɪʃən] n coalición f

coalman [ˈkəulmən] (irreg) n carbonero

coalmine [ˈkəulmaɪn] n mina de carbón

coarse [kɔːs] adj basto, burdo; (vulgar) grosero, ordinario

coast [kəust] n costa, litoral m ♦ vi (AUT) ir en punto muerto; **~al** adj costero, costanero; **~guard** n guardacostas m inv; **~line** n litoral m

coat [kəut] n abrigo; (of animal) pelaje m, lana; (of paint) mano f, capa ♦ vt cubrir, revestir; **~ of arms** n escudo de armas; **~ hanger** n percha (SP), gancho (AM); **~ing** n capa, baño

coax [kəuks] vt engatusar

cobbler [ˈkɔblə] n zapatero (remendón)

cobbles [ˈkɔblz] npl, **cobblestones** [ˈkɔblstəunz] npl adoquines mpl

cobweb [ˈkɔbweb] n telaraña

cocaine [kəˈkeɪn] n cocaína

cock [kɔk] n (rooster) gallo; (male bird) macho ♦ vt (gun) amartillar; **~erel** n gallito

cockle [ˈkɔkl] n berberecho

cockney [ˈkɔkni] n habitante de ciertos barrios de Londres

cockpit [ˈkɔkpit] n cabina

cockroach [ˈkɔkrəutʃ] n cucaracha

cocktail [ˈkɔkteɪl] n coctel m, cóctel m; **~ cabinet** n mueble-bar m; **~ party** n coctel m, cóctel m

cocoa [ˈkəukəu] n cacao; (drink) chocolate m

coconut [ˈkəukənʌt] n coco

cod [kɔd] n bacalao

C.O.D. abbr (= cash on delivery) C.A.E.

code [kəud] n código; (cipher) clave f; (dialling) n prefijo; (post ~) código postal

cod-liver oil [ˈkɔdlɪvər-] n aceite de hígado de bacalao

coercion [kəuˈə:ʃən] n coacción f

coffee [ˈkɔfi] n café m; **~ bar** (BRIT) n cafetería; **~ bean** n grano de café; **~ break** n descanso (para tomar café); **~pot** n cafetera; **~ table** n mesita (para servir el café)

coffin [ˈkɔfin] n ataúd m

cog [kɔg] n (wheel) rueda dentada; (tooth) diente m

cogent [ˈkəudʒənt] adj convincente

cognac [ˈkɔnjæk] n coñac m

coil [kɔil] n rollo; (ELEC) bobina, carrete m; (contraceptive) espiral f ♦ vt enrollar

coin [kɔin] n moneda ♦ vt (word)

inventar, idear; **~age** n moneda; **~box** (BRIT) n cabina telefónica

coincide [kəun'saɪd] vi coincidir; (agree) estar de acuerdo; **coincidence** [kəu'ɪnsɪdəns] n casualidad f

Coke ® [kəuk] n Coca-Cola ®

coke [kəuk] n (coal) coque m

colander ['kɔləndə*] n colador m, escurridor m

cold [kəuld] adj frío ♦ n frío; (MED) resfriado; **it's ~** hace frío; **to be ~** (person) tener frío; **to catch ~** enfriarse; **to catch a ~** resfriarse, acatarrarse; **in ~ blood** a sangre fría; **~-shoulder** vt dar or volver la espalda a; **~ sore** n herpes mpl or fpl

coleslaw ['kəulslɔ:] n especie de ensalada de col

colic ['kɔlɪk] n cólico

collapse [kə'læps] vi hundirse, derrumbarse; (MED) sufrir un colapso ♦ n hundimiento, derrumbamiento; (MED) colapso; **collapsible** adj plegable

collar ['kɔlə*] n (of coat, shirt) cuello; (of dog etc) collar; **~bone** n clavícula

collateral [kə'lætərəl] n garantía colateral

colleague ['kɔli:g] n colega m/f; (at work) compañero, a

collect [kə'lekt] vt (litter, mail etc) recoger; (as a hobby) coleccionar; (BRIT: call and pick up) recoger; (debts, subscriptions etc) recaudar ♦ vi reunirse; (dust) acumularse; **to call ~** (US: TEL) llamar a cobro revertido; **~ion** [kə'lekʃən] n colección f; (of mail, for charity) recogida; **~or** n coleccionista m/f

college ['kɔlɪdʒ] n colegio mayor; (of agriculture, technology) escuela universitaria

collide [kə'laɪd] vi chocar

colliery ['kɔlɪərɪ] (BRIT) n mina de carbón

collision [kə'lɪʒən] n choque m

colloquial [kə'ləukwɪəl] adj familiar,

coloquial

Colombia [kə'lɔmbɪə] n Colombia; **~n** adj, n colombiano/a

colon ['kəulən] n (sign) dos puntos; (MED) colon m

colonel ['kə:nl] n coronel m

colonial [kə'ləunɪəl] adj colonial

colony ['kɔlənɪ] n colonia

colour ['kʌlə*] (US color) n color m ♦ vt color(e)ar; (dye) teñir; (fig: account) distorsionar ♦ vi (blush) sonrojarse; **~s** npl (of party, club) colores mpl; **in ~** en color; **~ in** vt colorear; **~ bar** n segregación f racial; **~-blind** adj daltónico; **~ed** adj de color; (photo) en color; **~ film** n película en color; **~ful** adj lleno de color; (story) fantástico; (person) excéntrico; **~ing** n (complexion) tez f; (in food) colorante m; **~ scheme** n combinación f de colores; **~ television** n televisión f en color

colt [kəult] n potro

column ['kɔləm] n columna; **~ist** ['kɔləmnɪst] n columnista m/f

coma ['kəumə] n coma m

comb [kəum] n peine m; (ornamental) peineta ♦ vt (hair) peinar; (area) registrar a fondo

combat ['kɔmbæt] n combate m ♦ vt combatir

combination [kɔmbɪ'neɪʃən] n combinación f

combine [vb kəm'baɪn, n 'kɔmbaɪn] vt combinar; (qualities) reunir ♦ vi combinarse ♦ n (ECON) cartel m; **~ (harvester)** n cosechadora

KEYWORD

come [kʌm] (pt came, pp come) vi 1 (movement towards) venir; **to ~ running** venir corriendo
2 (arrive) llegar; **he's ~ here to work** ha venido aquí para trabajar; **to ~ home** volver a casa
3 (reach): **to ~ to** llegar a; **the bill**

came to £40 la cuenta ascendía a cuarenta libras
4 (occur): **an idea came to me** se me ocurrió una idea
5 (be, become): **to ~ loose/undone** etc aflojarse/desabrocharse, desatarse etc; **I've ~ to like him** por fin ha llegado a gustarme
come about vi suceder, ocurrir
come across vt fus (person) topar con; (thing) dar con
come away vi (leave) marcharse; (become detached) desprenderse
come back vi (return) volver
come by vt fus (acquire) conseguir
come down vi (price) bajar; (tree, building) ser derribado
come forward vi presentarse
come from vt fus (place, source) ser de
come in vi (visitor) entrar; (train, report) llegar; (fashion) ponerse de moda; (on deal etc) entrar
come in for vt fus (criticism etc) recibir
come into vt fus (money) heredar; (be involved) tener que ver con; **to ~ into fashion** ponerse de moda
come off vi (button) soltarse, desprenderse; (attempt) salir bien
come on vi (pupil) progresar; (work, project) desarrollarse; (lights) encenderse; (electricity) volver; **~ on!** ¡vamos!
come out vi (fact) salir a la luz; (book, sun) salir; (stain) quitarse
come round vi (after faint, operation) volver en sí
come to vi (wake) volver en sí
come up vi (sun) salir; (problem) surgir; (event) aproximarse; (in conversation) mencionarse
come up against vt fus (resistance etc) tropezar con
come up with vt fus (idea) sugerir; (money) conseguir
come upon vt fus (find) dar con

comeback ['kʌmbæk] n: **to make a ~** (THEATRE) volver a las tablas
comedian [kə'miːdɪən] n cómico;
comedienne [-'en] n cómica
comedy ['kɒmɪdɪ] n comedia; (humour) comicidad f
comet ['kɒmɪt] n cometa m
comeuppance [kʌm'ʌpəns] n: **to get one's ~** llevar su merecido
comfort ['kʌmfət] n bienestar m; (relief) alivio ♦ vt consolar; **~s** npl (of home etc) comodidades fpl; **~able** adj cómodo; (financially) acomodado; (easy) fácil; **~ably** adv (sit) cómodamente; (live) holgadamente; **~ station** (US) n servicios mpl
comic ['kɒmɪk] adj (also: ~al) cómico ♦ n (comedian) cómico; (BRIT: for children) tebeo; (BRIT: for adults) comic m; **~ strip** n tira cómica
coming ['kʌmɪŋ] n venida, llegada ♦ adj que viene; **~(s) and going(s)** n(pl) ir y venir, ajetreo
comma ['kɒmə] n coma
command [kə'mɑːnd] n orden f, mandato; (MIL: authority) mando; (mastery) dominio ♦ vt (troops) mandar; (give orders to): **to ~ sb to do** mandar or ordenar a uno hacer; **~eer** [kɒmən'dɪə*] vt requisar; **~er** n (MIL) comandante m/f, jefe/a m/f
commemorate [kə'meməreɪt] vt conmemorar
commence [kə'mens] vt, vi comenzar, empezar
commend [kə'mend] vt elogiar, alabar; (recommend) recomendar
commensurate [kə'menʃərɪt] adj: **~ with** en proporción a, que corresponde a
comment ['kɒment] n comentario ♦ vi: **to ~ on** hacer comentarios sobre; **"no ~"** (written) "sin comentarios"; (spoken) "no tengo nada que decir"; **~ary** ['kɒməntəri] n comentario; **~ator** ['kɒmənteɪtə*] n comentarista m/f

commerce ['kɔmə:s] n comercio

commercial [kə'mə:ʃəl] adj comercial ♦ n (TV, RADIO) anuncio

commiserate [kə'mɪzəreɪt] vi: **to ~ with** compadecerse de, condolerse de

commission [kə'mɪʃən] n (committee, fee) comisión f ♦ vt (work of art) encargar; **out of ~** fuera de servicio; **~aire** [kəmɪʃə'neə*] (BRIT) n portero; **~er** n (POLICE) comisario de policía

commit [kə'mɪt] vt (act) cometer; (resources) dedicar; (to sb's care) entregar; **to ~ o.s. (to do)** comprometerse a hacer; **to ~ suicide** suicidarse; **~ment** n compromiso; (to ideology etc) entrega

committee [kə'mɪtɪ] n comité m

commodity [kə'mɔdɪtɪ] n mercancía

common ['kɔmən] adj común; (pej) ordinario ♦ n campo común; **the C~s** npl (BRIT) la Cámara de) los Comunes mpl; **in ~** en común; **~er** n plebeyo; **~ law** n ley f consuetudinaria; **~ly** adv comúnmente; **C~ Market** n Mercado Común; **~place** adj de lo más común; **~room** n sala común; **~ sense** n sentido común; **the C~wealth** n la Commonwealth

commotion [kə'məʊʃən] n tumulto, confusión f

commune [n 'kɔmju:n, vb kə'mju:n] n (group) comuna ♦ vi: **to ~ with** comulgar o conversar con

communicate [kə'mju:nɪkeɪt] vt comunicar ♦ vi: **to ~ (with)** comunicarse (con); (in writing) estar en contacto (con)

communication [kəmju:nɪ'keɪʃən] n comunicación f; **~ cord** (BRIT) n timbre m de alarma

communion [kə'mju:nɪən] n (also: Holy C~) comunión f

communiqué [kə'mju:nɪkeɪ] n comunicado, parte f

communism ['kɔmjunɪzəm] n comunismo; **communist** adj, n

comunista m/f

community [kə'mju:nɪtɪ] n comunidad f; (large group) colectividad f; **~ centre** n centro social; **~ chest** (US) n arca comunitaria, fondo común

commutation ticket [kɔmju:'teɪʃən-] (US) n billete m de abono

commute [kə'mju:t] vi viajar a diario de la casa al trabajo ♦ vt conmutar; **~r** n persona (que viaja ... see vi)

compact [adj kəm'pækt, n 'kɔmpækt] adj compacto ♦ n (also: powder ~) polvera; **~ disc** n compact disc m; **~ disc player** n reproductor m de disco compacto, compact disc m

companion [kəm'pænɪən] n compañero/a; **~ship** n compañerismo

company ['kʌmpənɪ] n compañía; (COMM) sociedad f, compañía; **to keep sb ~** acompañar a uno; **~ secretary** (BRIT) n secretario/a de compañía

comparative [kəm'pærətɪv] adj relativo; (study) comparativo; **~ly** adv (relatively) relativamente

compare [kəm'peə*] vt: **to ~ sth/sb with/to** comparar algo/a uno con ♦ vi: **to ~ (with)** compararse (con); **comparison** [-'pærɪsn] n comparación f

compartment [kəm'pɑ:tmənt] n (also: RAIL) compartim(i)ento

compass ['kʌmpəs] n brújula; **~es** npl (MATH) compás m

compassion [kəm'pæʃən] n compasión f; **~ate** adj compasivo

compatible [kəm'pætɪbl] adj compatible

compel [kəm'pel] vt obligar

compensate ['kɔmpənseɪt] vt compensar ♦ vi: **to ~ for** compensar; **compensation** [-'seɪʃən] n (for loss) indemnización f

compère ['kɔmpeə*] n presentador m

compete [kəm'pi:t] vi (take part) tomar parte, concurrir; (vie with): **to ~ with** competir con, hacer competencia a

competent ['kɔmpɪtənt] *adj*
competente, capaz

competition [kɔmpɪ'tɪʃən] *n* (*contest*)
concurso; (*rivalry*) competencia *f*

competitive [kəm'petɪtɪv] *adj* (*ECON*,
SPORT) competitivo

competitor [kəm'petɪtə*] *n* (*rival*)
competidor/a *m/f*; (*participant*)
concursante *m*

complacency [kəm'pleɪsnsɪ] *n*
autosatisfacción *f*

complacent [kəm'pleɪsənt] *adj*
autocomplaciente

complain [kəm'pleɪn] *vi* quejarse;
(*COMM*) reclamar; **~t n** queja;
reclamación *f*; (*MED*) enfermedad *f*

complement [*n* 'kɔmplɪmənt, *vb*
'kɔmplɪment] *n* complemento; (*esp of
ship's crew*) dotación ♦ *vt* (*enhance*)
complementar; **~ary** [kɔmplɪ'mentərɪ]
adj complementario

complete [kəm'pliːt] *adj* (*full*)
completo; (*finished*) acabado ♦ *vt*
(*fulfil*) completar; (*finish*) acabar; (*a
form*) llenar; **~ly** completamente;
completion [-'pliːʃən] *n* terminación
f; (*of contract*) realización *f*

complex ['kɔmpleks] *adj*, *n* complejo

complexion [kəm'plekʃən] *n* (*of face*)
tez *f*, cutis *m*

compliance [kəm'plaɪəns] *n*
(*submission*) sumisión *f*; (*agreement*)
conformidad *f*; **in ~ with** de acuerdo
con

complicate ['kɔmplɪkeɪt] *vt* complicar;
~d *adj* complicado; **complication**
[-'keɪʃən] *n* complicación *f*

compliment ['kɔmplɪmənt] *n* (*formal*)
cumplido ♦ *vt* felicitar; **~s** *npl* (*regards*)
saludos *mpl*; **to pay sb a ~** hacer
cumplidos a uno; **~ary** [-'mentərɪ] *adj*
lisonjero; (*free*) de favor

comply [kəm'plaɪ] *vi*: **to ~ with**
cumplir con

component [kəm'pəunənt] *adj*
componente ♦ *n* (*TECH*) pieza

compose [kəm'pəuz] *vt*: **to be ~d of**

componerse de; (*music etc*) componer;
to ~ o.s. tranquilizarse; **~d** *adj*
sosegado; **~r n** (*MUS*) compositor(a)
m/f; **composition** [kɔmpə'zɪʃən] *n*
composición *f*

compost ['kɔmpɔst] *n* abono (vegetal)

composure [kəm'pəuʒə*] *n* serenidad
f, calma

compound ['kɔmpaund] *n* (*CHEM*)
compuesto; (*LING*) palabra compuesta;
(*enclosure*) recinto ♦ *adj* compuesto;
(*fracture*) complicado

comprehend [kɔmprɪ'hend] *vt*
comprender; **comprehension**
[-'henʃən] *n* comprensión *f*

comprehensive [kɔmprɪ'hensɪv] *adj*
exhaustivo; (*INSURANCE*) contra todo
riesgo; **~ (school)** *n* centro estatal de
enseñanza secundaria; ≈ Instituto
Nacional de Bachillerato (*SP*)

compress [*vb* kəm'pres, *n* 'kɔmpres]
vt comprimir; (*information*) condensar
♦ *n* (*MED*) compresa

comprise [kəm'praɪz] *vt* (*also*: **be ~d
of**) comprender, constar de; (*constitute*)
constituir

compromise ['kɔmprəmaɪz] *n*
(*agreement*) arreglo ♦ *vt* comprometer
♦ *vi* transigir

compulsion [kəm'pʌlʃən] *n*
compulsión *f*; (*force*) obligación *f*

compulsive [kəm'pʌlsɪv] *adj*
compulsivo; (*viewing, reading*) obligado

compulsory [kəm'pʌlsərɪ] *adj*
obligatorio

computer [kəm'pjuːtə*] *n* ordenador
m, computador *m*, computadora;
~ game *n* juego para ordenador; **~-
generated** *adj* realizado por
ordenador, creado por ordenador; **~-
ize** *vt* (*data*) computerizar; (*system*)
informatizar; **~ programmer** *n*
programador(a) *m/f*; **~ programming**
n programación *f*; **~ science** *n*
informática; **computing** [kəm'pjuːtɪŋ]
n (*activity, science*) informática

comrade ['kɔmrɪd] *n* (*POL, MIL*)

camarada; (friend) compañero/a;
~ship n camaradería, compañerismo
con [kɔn] vt (deceive) engañar; (cheat)
estafar ♦ n estafa
conceal [kən'siːl] vt ocultar
conceit [kən'siːt] n presunción f; ~ed
adj presumido
conceive [kən'siːv] vt, vi concebir
concentrate ['kɔnsəntreɪt] vi
concentrarse ♦ vt concentrar
concentration [kɔnsən'treɪʃən] n
concentración f
concept ['kɔnsept] n concepto
concern [kən'sɜːn] n (matter) asunto;
(COMM) empresa; (anxiety)
preocupación f ♦ vt (worry) preocupar;
(involve) afectar; (relate to) tener que
ver con; to be ~ed (about)
interesarse (por), preocuparse (por);
~ing prep sobre, acerca de
concert ['kɔnsət] n concierto; ~ed
[kən'sɜːtəd] adj (efforts etc)
concertado; ~ hall n sala de conciertos
concerto [kən'tʃɜːtəu] n concierto
concession [kən'sɛʃən] n concesión f;
tax ~ privilegio fiscal
conclude [kən'kluːd] vt concluir;
(treaty etc) firmar; (agreement) llegar a;
(decide) llegar a la conclusión de;
conclusion [-'kluːʒən] n conclusión f;
firma; conclusive [-'kluːsɪv] adj
decisivo, concluyente
concoct [kən'kɔkt] vt confeccionar;
(plot) tramar; ~ion [-'kɔkʃən] n mezcla
concourse ['kɔnkɔːs] n vestíbulo
concrete ['kɔnkriːt] n hormigón m
♦ adj de hormigón; (fig) concreto
concur [kən'kɜː'] vi estar de acuerdo,
asentir
concurrently [kən'kʌrntlɪ] adv al
mismo tiempo
concussion [kən'kʌʃən] n conmoción
f cerebral
condemn [kən'dɛm] vt condenar;
(building) declarar en ruina
condense [kən'dɛns] vi condensarse
♦ vt condensar, abreviar; ~d milk n

leche f condensada
condition [kən'dɪʃən] n condición f,
estado; (requirement) condición f ♦ vt
condicionar; on ~ that a condición
(de) que; ~er n suavizante
condolences [kən'dəulənsɪz] npl
pésame m
condom ['kɔndəm] n condón m
condone [kən'dəun] vt condonar
conducive [kən'djuːsɪv] adj: ~ to
conducente a
conduct [n 'kɔndʌkt, vb kən'dʌkt] n
conducta, comportamiento ♦ vt (lead)
conducir; (manage) llevar a cabo,
dirigir; (MUS) dirigir; to ~ o.s.
comportarse; ~ed tour (BRIT) n visita
acompañada; ~or n (of orchestra)
director m; (US: on train) revisor/a m/f;
(on bus) cobrador m; (ELEC) conductor
m; ~ress n (on bus) cobradora
cone [kəun] n cono; (pine ~) piña; (on
road) pivote m; (for ice-cream)
cucurucho
confectioner [kən'fɛkʃənə'] n
repostero/a; ~'s (shop) n confitería;
~y n dulces mpl
confer [kən'fɜː'] vt: to ~ sth on
otorgar algo a ♦ vi conferenciar
conference ['kɔnfərns] n (meeting)
reunión f; (convention) congreso
confess [kən'fɛs] vt confesar ♦ vi
admitir; ~ion [-'fɛʃən] n confesión f
confetti [kən'fɛtɪ] n confeti m
confide [kən'faɪd] vi: to ~ in confiar
en
confidence ['kɔnfɪdns] n (also: self-~)
confianza; (secret) confidencia; in ~
(speak, write) en confianza; ~ trick n
timo; confident adj seguro de sí
mismo; (certain) seguro; confidential
[kɔnfɪ'dɛnʃəl] adj confidencial
confine [kən'faɪn] vt (limit) limitar;
(shut up) encerrar; ~d adj (space)
reducido; ~ment n (prison) prisión f;
~s ['kɔnfaɪnz] npl confines mpl
confirm [kən'fɜːm] vt confirmar;
~ation [kɔnfə'meɪʃən] n confirmación

f; **~ed** adj empedernido

confiscate ['kɒnfɪskeɪt] vt confiscar

conflict [n 'kɒnflɪkt, vb kən'flɪkt] n conflicto ♦ vi (opinions) chocar; **~ing** adj contradictorio

conform [kən'fɔːm] vi conformarse; **to ~ to** ajustarse a

confound [kən'faund] vt confundir

confront [kən'frʌnt] vt (problems) hacer frente a; (enemy, danger) enfrentarse con; **~ation** [kɒnfrən'teɪʃən] n enfrentamiento

confuse [kən'fjuːz] vt (perplex) aturdir, desconcertar; (mix up) confundir; (complicate) complicar; **~d** adj confuso; (person) perplejo; **confusing** adj confuso; **confusion** [-'fjuːʒən] n confusión f

congeal [kən'dʒiːl] vi (blood) coagularse; (sauce etc) cuajarse

congested [kən'dʒestɪd] adj congestionado; **congestion** n congestión f

congratulate [kən'grætjuleɪt] vt: **to ~ sb (on)** felicitar a uno (por); **congratulations** [-'leɪʃənz] npl felicitaciones fpl; **congratulations!** ¡enhorabuena!

congregate ['kɒŋgrɪgeɪt] vi congregarse; **congregation** [-'geɪʃən] n (of a church) feligreses mpl

congress ['kɒŋgres] n congreso; (US): **C~** Congreso; **C~man** (irreg) (US) n miembro del Congreso

conifer ['kɒnɪfə*] n conífera

conjunctivitis [kəndʒʌŋktɪ'vaɪtɪs] n conjuntivitis f

conjure ['kʌndʒə*] vi hacer juegos de manos; **~ up** vt (ghost, spirit) hacer aparecer; (memories) evocar; **~r** n ilusionista m/f

con man n estafador m

connect [kə'nekt] vt juntar, unir; (ELEC) conectar; (TEL: subscriber) poner; (: caller) poner al habla; (fig) relacionar, asociar ♦ vi: **to ~ with** (train) enlazar con; **to be ~ed with** (associated) estar

relacionado con; **~ion** [-ʃən] n juntura, unión f; (ELEC) conexión f; (RAIL) empalme m; (TEL) comunicación f; (fig) relación f

connive [kə'naɪv] vi: **to ~ at** hacer la vista gorda a

connoisseur [kɒnɪ'sə*] n experto/a, entendido/a

conquer ['kɒŋkə*] vt (territory) conquistar; (enemy, feelings) vencer; **~or** n conquistador m

conquest ['kɒŋkwest] n conquista

cons [kɒnz] npl see **convenience**; **pro**

conscience ['kɒnʃəns] n conciencia

conscientious [kɒnʃɪ'enʃəs] adj concienzudo; (objection) de conciencia

conscious ['kɒnʃəs] (deliberate) deliberado; (awake, aware) consciente; **~ness** n conciencia; (MED) conocimiento

conscript ['kɒnskrɪpt] n recluta m; **~ion** [kən'skrɪpʃən] n servicio militar (obligatorio)

consensus [kən'sensəs] n consenso

consent [kən'sent] n consentimiento ♦ vi: **to ~ (to)** consentir (en)

consequence ['kɒnsɪkwəns] n consecuencia; (significance) importancia

consequently ['kɒnsɪkwəntlɪ] adv por consiguiente

conservation [kɒnsə'veɪʃən] n conservación f

conservative [kən'sɜːvətɪv] adj conservador(a); (estimate etc) cauteloso; **C~** (BRIT) adj, n (POL) conservador(a) m/f

conservatory [kən'sɜːvətrɪ] n invernadero; (MUS) conservatorio

conserve [kən'sɜːv] vt conservar ♦ n conserva

consider [kən'sɪdə*] vt considerar; (take into account) tener en cuenta; (study) estudiar, examinar; **to ~ doing sth** pensar en (la posibilidad de) hacer algo; **~able** adj considerable; **~ably** adv notablemente; **~ate** adj considerado; **consideration** [-'reɪʃən] n consideración f; (factor) factor m; **to**

give sth further consideration estudiar algo más a fondo; **~ing** prep teniendo en cuenta

consign [kən'saɪn] vt: **to ~ to** (sth unwanted) relegar a; (person) destinar a; **~ment** n envío

consist [kən'sɪst] vi: **to ~ of** consistir en

consistency [kən'sɪstənsɪ] n (of argument etc) coherencia; consecuencia; (thickness) consistencia

consistent [kən'sɪstənt] adj (person) consecuente; (argument etc) coherente

consolation [kɒnsə'leɪʃən] n consuelo

console[1] [kən'səʊl] vt consolar

console[2] ['kɒnsəʊl] n consola

consonant ['kɒnsənənt] n consonante f

consortium [kən'sɔːtɪəm] n consorcio

conspicuous [kən'spɪkjʊəs] adj (visible) visible

conspiracy [kən'spɪrəsɪ] n conjura, complot m

constable ['kʌnstəbl] (BRIT) n policía m/f; **chief ~** jefe m de policía

constabulary [kən'stæbjʊlərɪ] n ≈ policía

constant ['kɒnstənt] adj constante; **~ly** adv constantemente

constipated ['kɒnstɪpeɪtɪd] adj estreñido; **constipation** [kɒnstɪ'peɪʃən] n estreñimiento

constituency [kən'stɪtjʊənsɪ] n (POL: area) distrito electoral; (: electors) electorado; **constituent** [-ənt] n (POL) elector/a m/f; (part) componente m

constitution [kɒnstɪ'tjuːʃən] n constitución f; **~al** adj constitucional

constraint [kən'streɪnt] n obligación f; (limit) restricción f

construct [kən'strʌkt] vt construir; **~ion** [-ʃən] n construcción f; **~ive** adj constructivo

consul ['kɒnsl] n cónsul m/f; **~ate** ['kɒnsjʊlɪt] n consulado

consult [kən'sʌlt] vt consultar; **~ant** n (BRIT: MED) especialista m/f; (other

specialist) asesor(a) m/f; **~ation** [kɒnsəl'teɪʃən] n consulta; **~ing room** (BRIT) n consultorio

consume [kən'sjuːm] vt (eat) comerse; (drink) beberse; (fire etc, COMM) consumir; **~r** n consumidor(a) m/f; **~r goods** npl bienes mpl de consumo

consummate ['kɒnsʌmeɪt] vt consumar

consumption [kən'sʌmpʃən] n consumo

cont. abbr (= continued) sigue

contact ['kɒntækt] n contacto; (person) contacto; (: pej) enchufe m ♦ vt ponerse en contacto con; **~ lenses** npl lentes fpl de contacto

contagious [kən'teɪdʒəs] adj contagioso

contain [kən'teɪn] vt contener; **to ~ o.s.** contenerse; **~er** n recipiente m; (for shipping etc) contenedor m

contaminate [kən'tæmɪneɪt] vt contaminar

cont'd abbr (= continued) sigue

contemplate ['kɒntəmpleɪt] vt contemplar; (reflect upon) considerar

contemporary [kən'tɛmpərərɪ] adj, n contemporáneo/a m/f

contempt [kən'tɛmpt] n desprecio; **~ of court** (LAW) desacato (a los tribunales); **~ible** adj despreciable; **~uous** adj desdeñoso

contend [kən'tɛnd] vt (argue) afirmar ♦ vi: **to ~ with/for** luchar contra/por; **~er** n (SPORT) contendiente f

content [adj, vb kən'tɛnt, n 'kɒntɛnt] adj (happy) contento; (satisfied) satisfecho ♦ vt satisfacer ♦ n contenido; **~s** npl contenido; (table of) **~s** índice m de materias; **~ed** adj contento; satisfecho

contention [kən'tɛnʃən] n (assertion) aseveración f; (disagreement) discusión f

contest [n 'kɒntɛst, vb kən'tɛst] n lucha; (competition) concurso ♦ vt (dispute) impugnar; (POL) presentarse como candidato/a en; **~ant**

context [ˈkɒntekst] n contexto m

continent [ˈkɒntɪnənt] n continente m; **the C~** (BRIT) el continente europeo; **~al** [-ˈnentl] adj continental; **~al breakfast** n desayuno estilo europeo; **~al quilt** (BRIT) n edredón m

contingency [kənˈtɪndʒənsɪ] n contingencia

continual [kənˈtɪnjuəl] adj continuo; **~ly** adv constantemente

continuation [kəntɪnjuˈeɪʃən] n prolongación f; (after interruption) reanudación f

continue [kənˈtɪnjuː] vi, vt seguir, continuar

continuous [kənˈtɪnjuəs] adj continuo

contort [kənˈtɔːt] vt retorcer

contour [ˈkɒntuə*] n contorno m; (also: ~ line) curva de nivel

contraband [ˈkɒntrəbænd] n contrabando

contraceptive [kɒntrəˈseptɪv] adj, n anticonceptivo

contract [n ˈkɒntrækt, vb kənˈtrækt] n contrato m (COMM): **to ~ to do sth** comprometerse por contrato a hacer algo; (become smaller) contraerse, encogerse ♦ vt contraer; **~ion** [kənˈtrækʃən] n contracción f; **~or** n contratista m/f

contradict [kɒntrəˈdɪkt] vt contradecir; **~ion** [-ʃən] n contradicción f

contraption [kənˈtræpʃən] (pej) n artilugio m

contrary¹ [ˈkɒntrərɪ] adj contrario ♦ n lo contrario; **on the ~** al contrario; **unless you hear to the ~** a no ser que le digan lo contrario

contrary² [kənˈtreərɪ] adj (perverse) terco

contrast [n ˈkɒntrɑːst, vt kənˈtrɑːst] n contraste m ♦ vt comparar; **in ~ to** en contraste con

contravene [kɒntrəˈviːn] vt infringir

contribute [kənˈtrɪbjuːt] vi contribuir ♦ vt: **to ~ £10/an article to** contribuir con 10 libras/un artículo a; **to ~ to** (charity) donar a; (newspaper) escribir para; (discussion) intervenir en; **contribution** [kɒntrɪˈbjuːʃən] n (donation) donativo; (BRIT: for social security) cotización f; (to debate) intervención f; (to journal) colaboración f; **contributor** n contribuyente m/f; (to newspaper) colaborador(a) m/f

contrive [kənˈtraɪv] vt (invent) idear ♦ vi: **to ~ to do** lograr hacer

control [kənˈtrəul] vt (process etc) dirigir; (machinery) manejar; (temper) dominar; (disease) contener ♦ n control m; **~s** npl (of vehicle) instrumentos mpl de mando; (of radio) controles mpl; (governmental) medidas fpl de control; **under ~** bajo control; **to be in ~ of** tener el mando de; **the car went out of ~** se perdió el control del coche; **~led substance** n sustancia controlada; **~ panel** n tablero de instrumentos; **~ room** n sala de mando; **~ tower** n (AVIAT) torre f de control

controversial [kɒntrəˈvɜːʃl] adj polémico

controversy [ˈkɒntrəvɜːsɪ] n polémica

convalesce [kɒnvəˈles] vi convalecer

convector [kənˈvektə*] n calentador m de aire

convene [kənˈviːn] vt convocar ♦ vi reunirse

convenience [kənˈviːnɪəns] n (easiness) comodidad f; (suitability) idoneidad f; (advantage) ventaja; **at your ~** cuando le sea conveniente; **all modern ~s, all mod cons** (BRIT) todo confort

convenient [kənˈviːnɪənt] adj (useful) útil; (place, time) conveniente

convent [ˈkɒnvənt] n convento m

convention [kənˈvenʃən] n convención f; (meeting) asamblea; (agreement) convenio; **~al** adj convencional

converge [kən'vɜːdʒ] vi convergir; (people): to ~ on dirigirse todos a
conversant [kən'vɜːsnt] adj: to be ~ with estar al tanto de
conversation [kɒnvə'seɪʃən] n conversación f; **~al** adj familiar; **~al skill** facilidad f de palabra
converse [n 'kɒnvɜːs, vb kən'vɜːs] n inversa f ♦ vi conversar; **~ly** ['-'vɜːslɪ] adv a la inversa
conversion [kən'vɜːʃən] n conversión f
convert [vb kən'vɜːt, n 'kɒnvɜːt] vt (REL, COMM) convertir; (alter): to ~ sth into/to transformar algo o ♦ n converso/a; **~ible** adj convertible ♦ n descapotable m
convey [kən'veɪ] vt llevar; (thanks) comunicar; (idea) expresar; **~or belt** n cinta transportadora
convict [vb kən'vɪkt, n 'kɒnvɪkt] vt (find guilty) declarar culpable a ♦ n presidiario/a; **~ion** [-ʃən] n condena; (belief, certainty) convicción f
convince [kən'vɪns] vt convencer; **~d** adj: **~d of/that** convencido de/de que; **convincing** adj convincente
convoluted ['kɒnvəlutɪd] adj (argument etc) enrevesado
convoy ['kɒnvɔɪ] n convoy m
convulse [kən'vʌls] vt: to be **~d with** laughter desternillarse de risa; **convulsion** [-'vʌlʃən] n convulsión f
cook [kuk] vt (stew etc) guisar; (meal) preparar ♦ vi cocer; (person) cocinar ♦ n cocinero/a; **~ book** n libro de cocina; **~er** n cocina; **~ery** n cocina; **~ery book** (BRIT) n = **~ book**; **~ie** (US) n galleta; **~ing** n cocina
cool [kuːl] adj fresco; (not afraid) tranquilo; (unfriendly) frío ♦ vt enfriar ♦ vi enfriarse; **~ness** n frescura; tranquilidad f; (indifference) falta de entusiasmo
coop [kuːp] n gallinero ♦ vt: to ~ up (fig) encerrar
cooperate [kəu'ɔpəreɪt] vi cooperar,

colaborar; **cooperation** [-'reɪʃən] n cooperación f, colaboración f
cooperative [-rətɪv] adj (business) cooperativo; (person) servicial ♦ n cooperativa f
coordinate [vb kəu'ɔːdɪneɪt, n kəu'ɔːdɪnət] vt coordinar ♦ n (MATH) coordenada; **~s** npl (clothes) coordinados mpl; **coordination** [-'neɪʃən] n coordinación f
co-ownership [kəu'əunəʃɪp] n co-propiedad f
cop [kɒp] (inf) n poli m (SP), tira m (AM)
cope [kəup] vi: to ~ with (problem) hacer frente a
copper ['kɒpə*] n (metal) cobre m; (BRIT: inf) poli m; **~s** npl (money) calderilla (SP), centavos mpl (AM)
copulate ['kɒpjuleɪt] vi copularse
copy ['kɒpɪ] n copia; (of book) ejemplar m ♦ vt copiar; **~right** n derechos mpl de autor
coral ['kɒrəl] n coral m
cord [kɔːd] n cuerda; (ELEC) cable m; (fabric) pana
cordial ['kɔːdɪəl] adj cordial ♦ n cordial m
cordon ['kɔːdn] n cordón m; ~ off vt acordonar
corduroy ['kɔːdərɔɪ] n pana
core [kɔː*] n centro, núcleo; (of fruit) corazón m; (of problem) meollo ♦ vt quitar el corazón de
coriander [kɒrɪ'ændə*] n culantro
cork [kɔːk] n corcho; (tree) alcornoque m; **~screw** n sacacorchos m inv
corn [kɔːn] n (BRIT: cereal crop) trigo; (US: maize) maíz m; (on foot) callo; ~ **on the cob** (CULIN) maíz en la mazorca (SP), choclo (AM)
corned beef ['kɔːnd-] n carne f acecinada (en lata)
corner ['kɔːnə*] n (outside) esquina; (inside) rincón m; (in road) curva; (FOOTBALL) córner m; (BOXING) esquina ♦ vt (trap) arrinconar; (COMM) acaparar ♦ vi (in car) tomar las curvas; **~stone** n

(also fig) piedra angular

cornet ['kɔ:nɪt] n (MUS) corneta; (BRIT: ice-cream) cucurucho

cornflakes ['kɔ:nfleɪks] npl copos mpl de maíz, cornflakes mpl

cornflour ['kɔ:nflauə*] (BRIT), **cornstarch** ['kɔ:nstɑ:tʃ] (US) n harina de maíz

Cornwall ['kɔ:nwəl] n Cornualles m

corny ['kɔ:nɪ] (inf) adj gastado

coronary ['kɔrənərɪ] n (also: ~ thrombosis) infarto

coronation [kɔrə'neɪʃən] n coronación f

coroner ['kɔrənə*] n juez m (de instrucción)

corporal ['kɔ:pərl] n cabo ♦ adj: ~ **punishment** castigo corporal

corporate ['kɔ:pərɪt] adj (action, ownership) colectivo; (finance, image) corporativo

corporation [kɔ:pə'reɪʃən] n (of town) ayuntamiento; (COMM) corporación f

corps [kɔ:*, pl kɔ:z] n inv cuerpo; **diplomatic** ~ cuerpo diplomático; **press** ~ gabinete m de prensa

corpse [kɔ:ps] n cadáver m

correct [kə'rɛkt] adj justo, exacto; (proper) correcto ♦ vt (exam) corregir, calificar; **~ion** [-ʃən] n (act) corrección f; (instance) rectificación f

correspond [kɔrɪs'pɔnd] vi (write): **to** ~ (**with**) escribirse (con); (be equivalent to): **to** ~ (**to**) corresponder (a); (be in accordance): **to** ~ (**with**) corresponder (con); **~ence** n correspondencia; **~ence course** n curso por correspondencia; **~ent** n corresponsal m/f

corridor ['kɔrɪdɔ:*] n pasillo

corrode [kə'rəud] vt corroer ♦ vi corroerse

corrugated ['kɔrəgeɪtɪd] adj ondulado; ~ **iron** n chapa ondulada

corrupt [kə'rʌpt] adj (person) corrupto; (COMPUT) corrompido ♦ vt corromper; (COMPUT) degradar

Corsica ['kɔ:sɪkə] n Córcega

cosmetic [kɔz'mɛtɪk] adj, n cosmético

cosmopolitan [kɔzmə'pɔlɪtn] adj cosmopolita

cost [kɔst] (pt, pp **cost**) n (price) precio; **~s** npl (COMM) costes mpl; (LAW) costas fpl ♦ vi costar, valer ♦ vt preparar el presupuesto de; **how much does it ~?** ¿cuánto cuesta?; **to ~ sb time/effort** costarle a uno tiempo/esfuerzo; **it ~ him his life** le costó la vida; **at all ~s** cueste lo que cueste

co-star ['kəustɑ:*] n coprotagonista m/f

Costa Rica ['kɔstə'ri:kə] n Costa Rica; **~n** adj, n costarriqueño/a m/f

cost-effective [kɔstɪ'fɛktɪv] adj rentable

costly ['kɔstlɪ] adj costoso

cost-of-living [kɔstəv'lɪvɪŋ] adj: **~ allowance** plus m de carestía de vida; **~ index** índice m del costo de vida

cost price (BRIT) n precio de coste

costume ['kɔstju:m] n traje m; (BRIT: also: swimming ~) traje de baño; **~ jewellery** n bisutería

cosy ['kəuzɪ] (US **cozy**) adj (person) cómodo; (room) acogedor(a)

cot [kɔt] n (BRIT: child's) cuna; (US: campbed) cama de campaña

cottage ['kɔtɪdʒ] n casita de campo; (rustic) barraca; **~ cheese** n requesón m

cotton ['kɔtn] n algodón m; (thread) hilo; **~ on to** (inf) vt fus caer en la cuenta de; **~ candy** (US) n algodón m (azucarado); **~ wool** (BRIT) n algodón m (hidrófilo)

couch [kautʃ] n sofá m; (doctor's etc) diván m

couchette [ku:'ʃet] n litera

cough [kɔf] vi toser ♦ n tos f; **~ drop** n pastilla para la tos

could [kud] pt of **can²**; **~n't** = **could not**

council ['kaʊnsl] *n* consejo; **city** *or* **town** ~ consejo municipal; **~ estate** *(BRIT)* *n* urbanización *f* de viviendas municipales de alquiler; **~ house** *(BRIT)* *n* vivienda municipal de alquiler; **~lor** *n* concejal/a *m/f*

counsel ['kaʊnsl] *n (advice)* consejo; *(lawyer)* abogado/a ♦ *vt* aconsejar; **~lor** *n* consejero/a; **~or** *(US)* *n* abogado/a

count [kaʊnt] *vt* contar; *(include)* incluir ♦ *vi* contar ♦ *n* cuenta; *(of votes)* escrutinio; *(level)* nivel *m*; *(nobleman)* conde *m*; **~ on** *vt fus* contar con; **~down** *n* cuenta atrás

countenance ['kaʊntɪnəns] *n* semblante *m*, rostro ♦ *vt (tolerate)* aprobar, tolerar

counter ['kaʊntə*] *n (in shop)* mostrador *m*; *(in games)* ficha ♦ *vt* contrarrestar ♦ *adv*: **to run ~ to** ser contrario a, ir en contra de; **~act** *vt* contrarrestar

counterfeit ['kaʊntəfɪt] *n* falsificación *f*, simulación *f* ♦ *vt* falsificar ♦ *adj* falso, falsificado

counterfoil ['kaʊntəfɔɪl] *n* talón *m*

counterpart ['kaʊntəpɑːt] *n* homólogo/a

counter-productive [kaʊntəprə'dʌktɪv] *adj* contraproducente

countersign ['kaʊntəsaɪn] *vt* refrendar

countess ['kaʊntɪs] *n* condesa

countless ['kaʊntlɪs] *adj* innumerable

country ['kʌntrɪ] *n* país *m*; *(native land)* patria; *(as opposed to town)* campo; *(region)* región *f*, tierra; **~ dancing** *(BRIT)* *n* baile *m* regional; **~ house** *n* casa de campo; **~man** *n (irreg) (compatriot)* compatriota *m*; *(rural)* campesino, paisano; **~side** *n* campo

county ['kaʊntɪ] *n* condado

coup [kuː] *(pl ~s)* *n (also:* ~ *d'état)* golpe *m* (de estado); *(achievement)* éxito

couple ['kʌpl] *n (of things)* par *m*; *(of*

people) pareja; *(married ~)* matrimonio; **a ~ of** un par de

coupon ['kuːpɔn] *n* cupón *m*; *(voucher)* valé *m* f

courage ['kʌrɪdʒ] *n* valor *m*, valentía; **~ous** [kə'reɪdʒəs] *adj* valiente

courgette [kuə'ʒɛt] *(BRIT)* *n* calabacín *m (SP)*, calabacita *(AM)*

courier ['kʊrɪə*] *n* mensajero/a; *(for tourists)* guía *m/f* de turismo

course [kɔːs] *n (direction)* dirección *f*; *(of river, SCOL)* curso; *(process)* transcurso; *(MED.):* **of ~ treatment** tratamiento; *(of ship)* rumbo; *(part of meal)* plato; *(GOLF)* campo; **of ~** desde luego, naturalmente; **of ~!** ¡claro!

court [kɔːt] *n (royal)* corte *f*; *(LAW)* tribunal *m*, juzgado; *(TENNIS etc)* pista, cancha ♦ *vt (woman)* cortejar a; **to take to ~** demandar

courteous ['kɜːtɪəs] *adj* cortés

courtesy ['kɜːtəsɪ] *n* cortesía; **(by) ~ of** por cortesía de; **~ bus, ~ coach** *n* autobús *m* gratuito

court-house ['kɔːthaʊs] *(US)* *n* palacio de justicia

courtier ['kɔːtɪə*] *n* cortesano

court-martial *(pl* **courts-martial)** *n* consejo de guerra

courtroom ['kɔːtrʊm] *n* sala de justicia

courtyard ['kɔːtjɑːd] *n* patio

cousin ['kʌzn] *n* primo/a; **first ~** primo/a carnal, primo/a hermano/a

cove [kəʊv] *n* cala, ensenada

covenant ['kʌvənənt] *n* pacto

cover ['kʌvə*] *vt* cubrir; *(feelings, mistake)* ocultar; *(with lid)* tapar; *(book etc)* forrar; *(distance)* recorrer; *(include)* abarcar; *(protect: also: INSURANCE)* cubrir; *(PRESS)* informar; *(discuss)* tratar ♦ *n* cubierta; *(lid)* tapa; *(for chair etc)* funda; *(envelope)* sobre *m*; *(for book)* forro; *(of magazine)* portada; *(shelter)* abrigo; *(INSURANCE)* cobertura; *(of spy)* cobertura; **~s** *npl* (on bed) sábanas; mantas; **to take ~** *(shelter)* protegerse, resguardarse; **under ~** *(indoors)* bajo techo; **under ~ of darkness** al amparo de la oscuridad; **under separate ~** (COMM) por separado; **~ up** vt: **to ~ up for sb** encubrir a uno; **~age** n (TV, PRESS) cobertura; **~alls** (US) npl mono; **~ charge** n precio del cubierto; **~ing** n capa; **~ing letter** (US ~ **letter**) n carta de explicación; **~ note** n (INSURANCE) póliza provisional

covert ['kʌvət] adj secreto, encubierto

cover-up n encubrimiento

cow [kau] n vaca; (inf!: woman) bruja ♦ vt intimidar

coward ['kauəd] n cobarde m/f; **~ice** [-ıs] n cobardía; **~ly** adj cobarde

cowboy ['kaubɔı] n vaquero

cower ['kauə*] vi encogerse (de miedo)

coy [kɔı] adj tímido

cozy ['kəuzı] (US) adj = **cosy**

CPA (US) n abbr = **certified public accountant**

crab [kræb] n cangrejo; **~ apple** n manzana silvestre

crack [kræk] n grieta; (noise) crujido; (drug) crack m ♦ vt agrietar, romper; (nut) cascar; (solve: problem) resolver; (: code) descifrar; (whip etc) chasquear; (knuckles) crujir; (joke) contar ♦ adj (expert) de primera; **~ down on** vt fus adoptar fuertes medidas contra; **~ up** vi (MED) sufrir una crisis nerviosa; **~er** n (biscuit) cráquer m; (Christmas ~) petardo sorpresa

crackle ['krækl] vi crepitar

cradle ['kreıdl] n cuna

craft [krɑːft] n (skill) arte m; (trade) oficio; (cunning) astucia; (boat: pl inv) barco; (plane: pl inv) avión m

craftsman ['krɑːftsmən] n artesano; **~ship** n (quality) destreza

crafty ['krɑːftı] adj astuto

crag [kræg] n peñasco

cram [kræm] vt (fill): **to ~ sth with** llenar algo (a reventar) de; (put): **to ~ sth into** meter algo a la fuerza en ♦ vi (for exams) empollar

cramp [kræmp] n (MED) calambre m; **~ed** adj apretado, estrecho

cranberry ['krænbərı] n arándano agrio

crane [kreın] n (TECH) grúa; (bird) grulla

crank [kræŋk] n manivela; (person) chiflado

cranny ['krænı] n see **nook**

crash [kræʃ] n (noise) estrépito; (of cars etc) choque m; (of plane) accidente m de aviación; (COMM) quiebra ♦ vt (car, plane) estrellar ♦ vi (car, plane) estrellarse; (two cars) chocar; (COMM) quebrar; **~ course** n curso acelerado; **~ helmet** n casco (protector); **~ landing** n aterrizaje m forzado

crass [kræs] adj grosero, maleducado

crate [kreıt] n cajón m de embalaje; (for bottles) caja

cravat(e) [krə'væt] n pañuelo

crave [kreıv] vt, vi: **to ~ (for)** ansiar, anhelar

crawl [krɔːl] vi (drag o.s.) arrastrarse; (child) andar a gatas, gatear; (vehicle) avanzar (lentamente) ♦ n (SWIMMING) crol m

crayfish ['kreıfıʃ] n inv (freshwater) cangrejo de río; (saltwater) cigala

crayon ['kreıən] n lápiz m de color

craze [kreız] n (fashion) moda

crazy ['kreızı] adj (person) loco; (idea) disparatado; (inf: keen): **~ about sb/ sth** loco por uno/algo

creak [kri:k] vi (floorboard) crujir; (hinge etc) chirriar, rechinar

cream [kri:m] n (of milk) nata, crema; (lotion) crema; (fig) flor f y nata ♦ adj (colour) color crema; **~ cake** n pastel m de nata; **~ cheese** n queso blanco; **~y** adj cremoso; (colour) color crema

crease [kri:s] n (fold) pliegue m; (in trousers) raya; (wrinkle) arruga ♦ vt (wrinkle) arrugar ♦ vi (wrinkle up) arrugarse

create [kri:'eıt] vt crear; **creation**

[-ʃən] *n* creación f; **creative** *adj*
creativo; **creator** *n* creador(a) *m/f*
creature ['kri:tʃə*] *n* (*animal*) animal
m, bicho; (*person*) criatura
crèche [kreʃ] *n* guardería (infantil)
credence ['kri:dəns] *n*: **to lend** or
give ~ to creer en, dar crédito a
credentials [krɪ'denʃlz] *npl* (*references*)
referencias *fpl*; (*identity papers*)
documentos *mpl* de identidad
credible ['kredɪbl] *adj* creíble;
(*trustworthy*) digno de confianza
credit ['kredɪt] *n* crédito; (*merit*) honor
m, mérito ♦ *vt* (COMM) abonar; (*believe:
also: give ~ to*) creer, prestar fe a ♦ *adj*
crediticio; **~s** *npl* (CINEMA) fichas *fpl*
técnicas; **to be in ~** (*person*) tener
saldo a favor; **to ~ sb with** (*fig*)
reconocer a uno el mérito de; **~ card**
n tarjeta de crédito; **~or** *n* acreedor(a)
m/f
creed [kri:d] *n* credo
creek [kri:k] *n* cala, ensenada; (US)
riachuelo
creep [kri:p] (*pt, pp* **crept**) *vi*
arrastrarse; **~er** *n* enredadera; **~y** *adj*
(*frightening*) horripilante
cremate [krɪ'meɪt] *vt* incinerar
crematorium [kremə'tɔ:rɪəm] (*pl*
crematoria) *n* crematorio
crêpe [kreɪp] *n* (*fabric*) crespón *m*;
(*also: ~ rubber*) crepé *m*; **~ bandage**
(BRIT) *n* venda de crepé
crept [krept] *pt, pp of* **creep**
crescent ['kresnt] *n* media luna;
(*street*) calle f (en forma de semicírculo)
cress [kres] *n* berro
crest [krest] *n* (*of bird*) cresta; (*of hill*)
cima, cumbre f; (*of coat of arms*)
blasón *m*; **~fallen** *adj* alicaído
crevice ['krevɪs] *n* grieta, hendedura
crew [kru:] *n* (*of ship etc*) tripulación f;
(TV, CINEMA) equipo; **~-cut** *n* corte *m*
al rape; **~-neck** *n* cuello a la caja
crib [krɪb] *n* cuna ♦ *vt* (*inf*) plagiar
crick [krɪk] *n* (*in neck*) tortícolis f
cricket ['krɪkɪt] *n* (*insect*) grillo; (*game*)

críquet *m*
crime [kraɪm] *n* (*no pl: illegal activities*)
crimen *m*; (*illegal action*) delito;
criminal ['krɪmɪnl] *n* criminal *m/f*,
delincuente *m/f* ♦ *adj* criminal; (*illegal*)
delictivo; (*law*) penal
crimson ['krɪmzn] *adj* carmesí
cringe [krɪndʒ] *vi* agacharse, encogerse
crinkle ['krɪŋkl] *vt* arrugar
cripple ['krɪpl] *n* lisiado/a, cojo/a ♦ *vt*
lisiar, mutilar
crisis ['kraɪsɪs] (*pl* **crises**) *n* crisis f *inv*
crisp [krɪsp] *adj* fresco; (*manner*) seco;
~s (BRIT) *npl*
patatas *fpl* (SP) or papas *fpl* (AM) fritas
crisscross ['krɪskrɔs] *adj* entrelazado
criterion [kraɪ'tɪərɪən] (*pl* **criteria**) *n*
criterio
critic ['krɪtɪk] *n* crítico/a; **~al** *adj*
crítico; (*illness*) grave; **~ally** *adv* (*speak
etc*) en tono crítico; (*ill*) gravemente;
~ism ['krɪtɪsɪzm] *n* crítica; **~ize**
['krɪtɪsaɪz] *vt* criticar
croak [krəʊk] *vi* (*frog*) croar; (*raven*)
graznar; (*person*) gruñir
Croatia [krəʊ'eɪʃə] *n* Croacia
crochet ['krəʊʃeɪ] *n* ganchillo
crockery ['krɒkərɪ] *n* loza, vajilla
crocodile ['krɒkədaɪl] *n* cocodrilo
crocus ['krəʊkəs] *n* croco, crocus *m*
croft [krɒft] *n* granja pequeña
crony ['krəʊnɪ] (*inf: pej*) *n* compinche
m/f
crook [krʊk] *n* ladrón/ona *m/f*; (*of
shepherd*) cayado; **~ed** ['krʊkɪd] *adj*
torcido; (*dishonest*) nada honrado
crop [krɒp] *n* (*produce*) cultivo; (*amount
produced*) cosecha; (*riding ~*) látigo de
montar ♦ *vt* cortar, recortar; **~ up** *vi*
surgir, presentarse
cross [krɒs] *n* cruz f; (*hybrid*) cruce *m*
♦ *vt* (*street etc*) cruzar, atravesar ♦ *adj*
de mal humor, enojado; **~ out** *vt*
tachar; **~ over** *vi* cruzar; **~bar** *n*
travesaño; **~country** (*race*) *n* carrera
a campo traviesa, cross *m*; **~-examine**
vt interrogar; **~-eyed** *adj* bizco; **~fire**

n fuego cruzado; **~ing** *n* (*sea passage*) travesía; (*also: pedestrian ~ing*) paso para peatones; **~ing guard** (*US*) *n* persona encargada de ayudar a los niños a cruzar la calle; **~ purposes** *npl*: **to be at ~ purposes** no comprenderse uno a otro; **~reference** *n* referencia, llamada; **~roads** *n* cruce *m*, encrucijada; **~ section** *n* corte *m* transversal; (*of population*) muestra (representativa); **~walk** (*US*) *n* paso de peatones; **~wind** *n* viento de costado; **~word** *n* crucigrama *m*

crotch [krɔtʃ] *n* (*ANAT, of garment*) entrepierna

crotchet ['krɔtʃit] *n* (*MUS*) negra

crouch [krautʃ] *vi* agacharse, acurrucarse

crow [krəu] *n* (*bird*) cuervo; (*of cock*) canto, cacareo ♦ *vi* (*cock*) cantar

crowbar ['krəubɑ:*] *n* palanca

crowd [kraud] *n* muchedumbre *f*, multitud *f* ♦ *vt* (*fill*) llenar ♦ *vi* (*gather*): **to ~ round** reunirse en torno a; (*cram*): **to ~ in** entrar en tropel; **~ed** *adj* (*full*) atestado; (*densely populated*) superpoblado

crown [kraun] *n* corona; (*of head*) coronilla; (*for tooth*) funda; (*of hill*) cumbre *f* ♦ *vt* coronar; (*fig*) completar, rematar; **~ jewels** *npl* joyas *fpl* reales; **~ prince** *n* príncipe *m* heredero

crow's feet *npl* patas *fpl* de gallo

crucial ['kru:ʃl] *adj* decisivo

crucifix ['kru:sifiks] *n* crucifijo; **~ion** [-'fikʃən] *n* crucifixión *f*

crude [kru:d] *adj* (*materials*) bruto; (*fig: basic*) tosco; (: *vulgar*) ordinario; **~ (oil)** *n* (*petróleo*) crudo

cruel ['kruəl] *adj* cruel; **~ty** *n* crueldad *f*

cruise [kru:z] *n* crucero ♦ *vi* (*ship*) hacer un crucero; (*car*) ir a velocidad de crucero; **~r** *n* (*motorboat*) yate *m* de motor; (*warship*) crucero

crumb [krʌm] *n* miga, migaja

crumble ['krʌmbl] *vt* desmenuzar ♦ *vi*

(*building, also fig*) desmoronarse; **crumbly** *adj* que se desmigaja fácilmente

crumpet ['krʌmpit] *n* ≈ bollo para tostar

crumple ['krʌmpl] *vt* (*paper*) estrujar; (*material*) arrugar

crunch [krʌntʃ] *vt* (*with teeth*) mascar; (*underfoot*) hacer crujir ♦ *n* (*fig*) hora or momento de la verdad; (*drink*): **~y** *adj* crujiente

crusade [kru:'seid] *n* cruzada

crush [krʌʃ] *n* (*crowd*) aglomeración *f*; (*infatuation*): **to have a ~ on sb** estar loco por uno; (*drink*): **lemon ~** limonada ♦ *vt* aplastar; (*paper*) estrujar; (*cloth*) arrugar; (*fruit*) exprimir; (*opposition*) aplastar; (*hopes*) destruir

crust [krʌst] *n* corteza; (*of snow, ice*) costra

crutch [krʌtʃ] *n* muleta

crux [krʌks] *n*: **the ~ of** lo esencial de, el quid de

cry [krai] *vi* llorar; (*shout: also: ~ out*) gritar ♦ *n* (*shriek*) chillido; (*shout*) grito; **~ off** *vi* echarse atrás

cryptic ['kriptik] *adj* enigmático, secreto

crystal ['kristl] *n* cristal *m*; **~-clear** *adj* claro como el agua

cub [kʌb] *n* cachorro; (*also: ~ scout*) niño explorador

Cuba ['kju:bə] *n* Cuba; **~n** *adj*, *n* cubano/a *m/f*

cube [kju:b] *n* cubo ♦ *vt* (*MATH*) cubicar; **cubic** *adj* cúbico

cubicle ['kju:bikl] *n* (*at pool*) caseta; (*for bed*) cubículo

cuckoo ['kuku:] *n* cuco; **~ clock** *n* reloj *m* de cucú

cucumber ['kju:kʌmbə*] *n* pepino

cuddle ['kʌdl] *vt* abrazar ♦ *vi* abrazarse

cue [kju:] *n* (*snooker ~*) taco; (*THEATRE etc*) señal *f*

cuff [kʌf] *n* (*of sleeve*) puño; (*US: of trousers*) vuelta; (*blow*) bofetada; **off the ~** *adv* de improviso; **~links** *npl* gemelos *mpl*

cuisine [kwɪˈziːn] *n* cocina

cul-de-sac [ˈkʌldəsæk] *n* callejón *m* sin salida

cull [kʌl] *vt* (*idea*) sacar ♦ *n* (*of animals*) matanza selectiva

culminate [ˈkʌlmɪneɪt] *vi*: **to ~ in** terminar en; **culmination** [-ˈneɪʃən] *n* culminación *f*, colmo

culottes [kuːˈlɒts] *npl* falda pantalón *f*

culprit [ˈkʌlprɪt] *n* culpable *m/f*

cult [kʌlt] *n* culto

cultivate [ˈkʌltɪveɪt] *vt* (*also fig*) cultivar; **~d** *adj* culto; **cultivation** [-ˈveɪʃən] *n* cultivo

cultural [ˈkʌltʃərəl] *adj* cultural

culture [ˈkʌltʃə*] *n* (*also fig*) cultura; (*BIO*) cultivo; **~d** *adj* culto

cumbersome [ˈkʌmbəsəm] *adj* de mucho bulto, voluminoso; (*process*) enrevesado

cunning [ˈkʌnɪŋ] *n* astucia ♦ *adj* astuto

cup [kʌp] *n* taza; (*as prize*) copa

cupboard [ˈkʌbəd] *n* armario, (*kitchen*) alacena

cup tie (*BRIT*) *n* partido de copa

curate [ˈkjuərɪt] *n* cura *m*

curator [kjuəˈreɪtə*] *n* director(a) *m/f*

curb [kəːb] *vt* refrenar; (*person*) reprimir ♦ *n* freno; (*US*) bordillo

curdle [ˈkəːdl] *vi* cuajarse

cure [kjuə*] *vt* curar ♦ *n* cura, curación *f*; (*fig: solution*) remedio

curfew [ˈkəːfjuː] *n* toque *m* de queda

curiosity [kjuərɪˈɒsɪtɪ] *n* curiosidad *f*

curious [ˈkjuərɪəs] *adj* curioso; (*person: interested*): **to be ~** sentir curiosidad

curl [kəːl] *n* rizo ♦ *vt* (*hair*) rizar ♦ *vi* rizarse; **~ up** (*person*) hacerse un ovillo; (*animal*) enroscarse ♦ *n* rulo; **~er** *n* rulo; **~y** *adj* rizado

currant [ˈkʌrnt] *n* pasa de Corinto; (*black~, red~*) grosella

currency [ˈkʌrnsɪ] *n* moneda; **to gain ~** (*fig*) difundirse

current [ˈkʌrnt] *n* corriente *f* ♦ *adj* (*accepted*) corriente; (*present*) actual; **~ account** (*BRIT*) *n* cuenta corriente;

~ affairs *npl* noticias *fpl* de actualidad; **~ly** *adv* actualmente

curriculum [kəˈrɪkjuləm] (*pl* **~s** *or* **curricula**) *n* plan *m* de estudios; **~ vitae** *n* currículum *m*

curry [ˈkʌrɪ] *n* curry *m* ♦ *vt*: **to ~ favour with** buscar favores con; **~ powder** *n* curry *m* en polvo

curse [kəːs] *vi* soltar tacos ♦ *vt* maldecir ♦ *n* maldición *f*; (*swearword*) palabrota, taco

cursor [ˈkəːsə*] *n* (*COMPUT*) cursor *m*

cursory [ˈkəːsərɪ] *adj* rápido, superficial

curt [kəːt] *adj* corto, seco

curtail [kəːˈteɪl] *vt* (*visit etc*) acortar; (*freedom*) restringir; (*expenses etc*) reducir

curtain [ˈkəːtn] *n* cortina; (*THEATRE*) telón *m*

curts(e)y [ˈkəːtsɪ] *vi* hacer una reverencia

curve [kəːv] *n* curva ♦ *vi* (*road*) hacer una curva; (*line etc*) curvarse

cushion [ˈkuʃən] *n* cojín *m*, (*of air*) colchón *m* ♦ *vt* (*shock*) amortiguar

custard [ˈkʌstəd] *n* natillas *fpl*

custody [ˈkʌstədɪ] *n* custodia; **to take into ~** detener

custom [ˈkʌstəm] *n* costumbre *f*; (*COMM*) clientela; **~ary** *adj* acostumbrado

customer [ˈkʌstəmə*] *n* cliente *m/f*

customized [ˈkʌstəmaɪzd] *adj* (*car etc*) hecho a encargo

custom-made *adj* hecho a la medida

customs [ˈkʌstəmz] *npl* aduana; **~ officer** *n* aduanero/a

cut [kʌt] (*pt, pp* **cut**) *vt* cortar; (*price*) rebajar; (*text, programme*) acortar; (*reduce*) reducir ♦ *vi* cortar ♦ *n* (*of garment*) corte *m*; (*in skin*) cortadura; (*in salary etc*) rebaja; (*in spending*) reducción *f*, recorte *m*; (*slice of meat*) tajada; **to ~ a tooth** echar un diente; **~ down** *vt* (*tree*) derribar; (*reduce*) reducir; **~ off** *vt* cortar; (*person, place*) aislar, (*TEL*) desconectar; **~ out** *vt* (*shape*) recortar; (*stop: activity etc*) dejar; (remove) quitar; ~ **up** vt cortar (en pedazos); ~**back** n reducción f

cute [kju:t] adj mono

cuticle ['kju:tɪkl] n cutícula

cutlery ['kʌtlərɪ] n cubiertos mpl

cutlet ['kʌtlɪt] n chuleta; (nut etc ~) plato vegetariano hecho con nueces y verdura en forma de chuleta

cut: ~out n (switch) dispositivo de seguridad, disyuntor m; (plano ~out) recortable m; ~**-price** (US ~**-rate**) adj a precio reducido; ~**throat** n asesino/a ♦ adj feroz

cutting ['kʌtɪŋ] adj (remark) mordaz ♦ n (BRIT: from newspaper) recorte m; (from plant) esqueje m

CV n abbr = **curriculum vitae**

cwt abbr = **hundredweight(s)**

cyanide ['saɪənaɪd] n cianuro

cybercafé ['saɪbəkæfeɪ] n cibercafé m

cycle ['saɪkl] n ciclo; (bicycle) bicicleta ♦ vi ir en bicicleta; ~ **lane** n carril-bici m; ~ **path** n carril-bici m; **cycling** n ciclismo; **cyclist** n ciclista m/f

cyclone ['saɪkləun] n ciclón m

cygnet ['sɪgnɪt] n pollo de cisne

cylinder ['sɪlɪndə*] n cilindro; (of gas) bombona; ~**-head gasket** n junta de culata

cymbals ['sɪmblz] npl platillos mpl

cynic ['sɪnɪk] n cínico/a; ~**al** adj cínico; ~**ism** ['sɪnɪsɪzəm] n cinismo

Cyprus ['saɪprəs] n Chipre f

cyst [sɪst] n quiste m; ~**itis** [-'taɪtɪs] n cistitis f

czar [zɑ:*] n zar m

Czech [tʃek] adj, n checo/a m/f; ~ **Republic** n la República Checa

D, d

D [di:] n (MUS) re m

dab [dæb] vt (eyes, wound) tocar (ligeramente); (paint, cream) poner un poco de

dabble ['dæbl] vi: **to ~ in** ser algo aficionado a

dad [dæd] n = **daddy**

daddy ['dædɪ] n papá m

daffodil ['dæfədɪl] n narciso

daft [dɑ:ft] adj tonto

dagger ['dægə*] n puñal m, daga

daily ['deɪlɪ] adj diario, cotidiano ♦ adv todos los días, cada día

dainty ['deɪntɪ] adj delicado

dairy ['dɛərɪ] n (shop) lechería; (on farm) vaquería; ~ **farm** n granja; ~ **products** npl productos mpl lácteos; ~ **store** (US) n lechería

daisy ['deɪzɪ] n margarita

dale [deɪl] n valle m

dam [dæm] n presa ♦ vt construir una presa sobre, represar

damage ['dæmɪdʒ] n lesión f; daño; (dents etc) desperfectos mpl; (fig) perjuicio ♦ vt dañar, perjudicar; (spoil, break) estropear; ~**s** npl (LAW) daños mpl y perjuicios

damn [dæm] vt condenar; (curse) maldecir ♦ n (inf): **I don't give a ~** me importa un pito ♦ adj (inf: also: ~ed) maldito; (it)! ¡maldito sea!; ~**ing** adj (evidence) irrecusable

damp [dæmp] adj húmedo, mojado ♦ n humedad f ♦ vt (also: ~**en**: cloth, rag) mojar; (: enthusiasm) enfriar

damson ['dæmzən] n ciruela damascena

dance [dɑ:ns] n baile m ♦ vi bailar; ~ **hall** n salón m de baile; ~**r** n bailador/a m/f; (professional) bailarín/ina m/f; **dancing** n baile m

dandelion ['dændɪlaɪən] n diente de león

dandruff ['dændrəf] n caspa

Dane [deɪn] n danés/esa m/f

danger ['deɪndʒə*] n peligro; (risk) riesgo; ~! (on sign) ¡peligro de muerte!; **to be in ~** correr riesgo de; ~**ous** adj peligroso; ~**ously** adv peligrosamente

dangle ['dæŋgl] vt colgar ♦ vi pender, colgar

Danish [ˈdeɪnɪʃ] adj danés/esa ♦ n
(LING) danés m

dare [deə*] vt: **to ~ sb to do** desafiar
a uno a hacer ♦ vi: **to ~ (to) do sth**
atreverse a hacer algo; **I ~ say** (I
suppose) puede ser (que); **daring** adj
atrevido, osado ♦ n atrevimiento,
osadía

dark [dɑːk] adj oscuro; (hair,
complexion) moreno ♦ n: **in the ~** a
oscuras; **to be in the ~ about** (fig) no
saber nada de; **after ~** después del
anochecer; **~en** vt (of colour) hacer más
oscuro ♦ vi oscurecerse; **~ glasses** npl
gafas fpl negras (SP), anteojos mpl
negros (AM); **~ness** n oscuridad f,
~room n cuarto oscuro

darling [ˈdɑːlɪŋ] adj, n querido/a m/f

darn [dɑːn] vt zurcir

dart [dɑːt] n dardo; (in sewing) sisa ♦ vi
precipitarse; **~ away/along** vi salir/
marchar disparado; **~board** n diana;
~s n dardos mpl

dash [dæʃ] n (small quantity: of liquid)
gota, chorrito; (: of solid) pizca; (sign)
raya ♦ vt (throw) tirar; (hopes)
defraudar ♦ vi precipitarse, ir de prisa;
~ away or **off** vi marcharse
apresuradamente

dashboard [ˈdæʃbɔːd] n (AUT)
salpicadero

dashing [ˈdæʃɪŋ] adj gallardo

data [ˈdeɪtə] npl datos mpl; **~base** n
base f de datos; **~ processing** n.
proceso de datos

date [deɪt] n (day) fecha; (with friend)
cita; (fruit) dátil m ♦ vt fechar; (person)
salir con; **~ of birth** fecha de
nacimiento; **to ~** adv hasta la fecha;
~d adj anticuado; **~ rape** n violación
ocurrida durante una cita con un
conocido

daub [dɔːb] vt embadurnar

daughter [ˈdɔːtə*] n hija; **~-in-law** n
nuera, hija política

daunting [ˈdɔːntɪŋ] adj
desalentador(a)

dawdle [ˈdɔːdl] vi (go slowly) andar
muy despacio

dawn [dɔːn] n alba, amanecer m; (fig)
nacimiento ♦ vi (day) amanecer; (fig):
it ~ed on him that ... cayó en la
cuenta de que ...

day [deɪ] n día m; (working ~) jornada;
(hey~) tiempos mpl, días mpl; **the
~ before/after** el día anterior/
siguiente; **the ~ after tomorrow**
pasado mañana; **the ~ before
yesterday** anteayer; **the following ~**
el día siguiente; **by ~** de día; **~break** n
amanecer m; **~dream** vi soñar
despierto; **~light** n luz f (del día);
~ return (BRIT) n billete m de ida y
vuelta (en un día); **~time** n día m; **~-
to~** adj cotidiano

daze [deɪz] vt (stun) aturdir ♦ n: **in a ~**
aturdido

dazzle [ˈdæzl] vt deslumbrar

DC abbr (= direct current) corriente f
continua

dead [ded] adj muerto; (limb) dormido;
(telephone) cortado; (battery) agotado
♦ adv (completely) totalmente; (exactly)
exactamente; **to shoot sb ~** matar a
uno a tiros; **~ tired** muerto de
cansancio); **to stop ~** parar en seco;
the ~ npl los muertos; **to be a ~ loss**
(inf: person) ser un inútil; **~en** vt (blow,
sound) amortiguar; (pain etc) aliviar;
~ end n callejón m sin salida; **~ heat**
n (SPORT) empate m; **~line** n fecha (or
hora) tope; **~lock** n punto muerto;
~ly adj mortal, fatal; **~pan** adj sin
expresión; **the D~ Sea** n el Mar Muerto

deaf [def] adj sordo; **~en** vt
ensordecer; **~ness** n sordera

deal [diːl] n (pt, pp dealt) n (agreement)
pacto, convenio; (business ~) trato ♦ vt
dar; (card) repartir; **a great ~ (of)**
bastante, mucho; **~ in** vt fus tratar en,
comerciar en; **~ with** vt fus (people)
tratar con; (problem) ocuparse de;
(subject) tratar de; **~ings** npl (COMM)

transacciones *fpl*; (*relations*) relaciones *fpl*

dealt [dɛlt] *pt, pp of* **deal**

dean [diːn] *n* (*REL*) deán *m*; (*SCOL: BRIT*) decano; (: *US*) decano; rector *m*

dear [dɪə*] *adj* querido; (*expensive*) caro ♦ *n*: **my** ~ mi querido/a ♦ *excl*: ~ **me!** ¡Dios mío!; **D~ Sir/Madam** (*in letter*) Muy Señor Mío, Estimado Señor/ Estimada Señora; **D~ Mr/Mrs X** Estimado/a Señor(a) X; ~**ly** *adv* (*love*) mucho; (*pay*) caro

death [dɛθ] *n* muerte *f*; ~ **certificate** *n* partida de defunción; ~**ly** *adj* (*white*) como un muerto; (*silence*) sepulcral; ~ **penalty** *n* pena de muerte; ~ **rate** *n* mortalidad *f*; ~ **toll** *n* número de víctimas

debacle [deɪˈbɑːkl] *n* desastre *m*

debase [dɪˈbeɪs] *vt* degradar

debatable [dɪˈbeɪtəbl] *adj* discutible

debate [dɪˈbeɪt] *n* debate *m* ♦ *vt* discutir

debit [ˈdɛbɪt] *n* debe *m* ♦ *vt*: **to ~ a sum to sb** *or* **to sb's account** cargar una suma en cuenta a alguien

debris [ˈdɛbriː] *n* escombros *mpl*

debt [dɛt] *n* deuda; **to be in ~** tener deudas; ~**or** *n* deudor/a *m/f*

début [ˈdeɪbjuː] *n* presentación *f*

decade [ˈdɛkeɪd] *n* decenio, década

decadence [ˈdɛkədəns] *n* decadencia

decaff [ˈdiːkæf] (*inf*) *n* descafeinado

decaffeinated [diːˈkæfɪneɪtɪd] *adj* descafeinado

decanter [dɪˈkæntə*] *n* garrafa

decay [dɪˈkeɪ] *n* (*of building*) desmoronamiento; (*of tooth*) caries *f inv* ♦ *vi* (*rot*) pudrirse

deceased [dɪˈsiːst] *adj*: **the ~** el/la difunto/a

deceit [dɪˈsiːt] *n* engaño; ~**ful** *adj* engañoso; **deceive** [dɪˈsiːv] *vt* engañar

December [dɪˈsɛmbə*] *n* diciembre *m*

decent [ˈdiːsnt] *adj* (*proper*) decente; (*person: kind*) amable, bueno

deception [dɪˈsɛpʃən] *n* engaño

deceptive [dɪˈsɛptɪv] *adj* engañoso

decibel [ˈdɛsɪbɛl] *n* decibel(io) *m*

decide [dɪˈsaɪd] *vt* (*person*) decidir; (*question, argument*) resolver ♦ *vi* decidir; **to ~ to do/that** decidir hacer/que; **to ~ on sth** decidirse por algo; ~**d** *adj* (*resolute*) decidido; (*clear, definite*) indudable; ~**dly** [-dɪdlɪ] *adv* decididamente; (*emphatically*) con resolución

deciduous [dɪˈsɪdjuəs] *adj* de hoja caduca

decimal [ˈdɛsɪməl] *adj* decimal ♦ *n* decimal *m*; ~ **point** *n* coma decimal

decipher [dɪˈsaɪfə*] *vt* descifrar

decision [dɪˈsɪʒən] *n* decisión *f*

decisive [dɪˈsaɪsɪv] *adj* decisivo; (*person*) decidido

deck [dɛk] *n* (*NAUT*) cubierta; (*of bus*) piso; (*record* ~) platina; (*of cards*) baraja; ~**chair** *n* tumbona

declaration [dɛkləˈreɪʃən] *n* declaración *f*

declare [dɪˈklɛə*] *vt* declarar

decline [dɪˈklaɪn] *n* disminución *f*, descenso ♦ *vt* rehusar ♦ *vi* (*person, business*) decaer; (*strength*) disminuir

decoder [diːˈkəʊdə*] *n* (*TV*) decodificador *m*

décor [ˈdeɪkɔː*] *n* decoración *f*; (*THEATRE*) decorado

decorate [ˈdɛkəreɪt] *vt* (*adorn*): **to ~ (with)** adornar (de), decorar (de); (*paint*) pintar; (*paper*) empapelar; **decoration** [-ˈreɪʃən] *n* adorno; (*act*) decoración *f*; (*medal*) condecoración *f*; **decorator** *n* (*workman*) pintor *m* (decorador)

decorum [dɪˈkɔːrəm] *n* decoro

decoy [ˈdiːkɔɪ] *n* señuelo

decrease [*n* ˈdiːkriːs, *vb* diːˈkriːs] *n*: ~ **(in)** disminución *f* (de) ♦ *vt* disminuir, reducir ♦ *vi* reducirse

decree [dɪˈkriː] *n* decreto; ~ **nisi** *n* sentencia provisional de divorcio

dedicate [ˈdɛdɪkeɪt] *vt* dedicar; **dedication** [-ˈkeɪʃən] *n* (*devotion*)

dedicación f; (in book) dedicatoria
deduce [dɪ'djuːs] vt deducir
deduct [dɪ'dʌkt] vt restar; descontar; **~ion** [dɪ'dʌkʃən] n (amount deducted) descuento; (conclusion) deducción f, conclusión f
deed [diːd] n hecho, acto; (feat) hazaña; (LAW) escritura
deep [diːp] adj profundo; (expressing measurements) de profundidad; (voice) bajo; (breath) profundo; (colour) intenso ♦ adv: **the spectators stood 20 ~** los espectadores se formaron de 20 en fondo; **to be 4 metres ~** tener 4 metros de profundidad; **~en** vt ahondar, profundizar ♦ vi aumentar, crecer; **~-freeze** n congelador m; **~-fry** vt freír en aceite abundante; **~ly** adv (breathe) a pleno pulmón; (interested, moved, grateful) profundamente, hondamente; **~-sea diving** n buceo de altura; **~-seated** adj (beliefs) (profundamente) arraigado
deer [dɪə*] n inv ciervo
deface [dɪ'feɪs] vt (wall, surface) estropear, pintarrajear
default [dɪ'fɔːlt] n: **by ~** (win) por incomparecencia ♦ adj (COMPUT) por defecto
defeat [dɪ'fiːt] n derrota ♦ vt derrotar, vencer; **~ist** adj, n derrotista m/f
defect [n 'diːfekt, vb dɪ'fekt] n defecto ♦ vi: **to ~ to the enemy** pasarse al enemigo; **~ive** [dɪ'fektɪv] adj defectuoso
defence [dɪ'fens] (US **defense**) n defensa; **~less** adj indefenso
defend [dɪ'fend] vt defender; **~ant** n acusado/a; (in civil case) demandado/a; **~er** n defensor(a) m/f; (SPORT) defensa m/f
defense [dɪ'fens] (US) n = **defence**
defensive [dɪ'fensɪv] adj defensivo ♦ n: **on the ~** a la defensiva
defer [dɪ'fəː*] vt aplazar
defiance [dɪ'faɪəns] n desafío; **in ~ of** en contra de; **defiant** [dɪ'faɪənt] adj

(challenging) desafiante, retador(a)
deficiency [dɪ'fɪʃənsɪ] n (lack) falta; (defect) defecto; **deficient** [dɪ'fɪʃənt] adj deficiente
deficit ['defɪsɪt] n déficit m
define [dɪ'faɪn] vt (word etc) definir; (limits etc) determinar
definite ['defɪnɪt] adj (fixed) determinado; (obvious) claro; (certain) indudable; **he was ~ about it** no dejó lugar a dudas (sobre ello); **~ly** adv desde luego, por supuesto
definition [defɪ'nɪʃən] n definición f; (clearness) nitidez f
deflate [diː'fleɪt] vt desinflar
deflect [dɪ'flekt] vt desviar
defraud [dɪ'frɔːd] vt: **to ~ sb of sth** estafar algo a uno
defrost [diː'frɔst] vt descongelar; **~er** (US) n (demister) eliminador m de vaho
deft [deft] adj diestro, hábil
defunct [dɪ'fʌŋkt] adj difunto; (organization etc) ya que no existe
defuse [diː'fjuːz] vt desactivar; (situation) calmar
defy [dɪ'faɪ] vt (resist) oponerse a; (challenge) desafiar; (fig): **it defies description** resulta imposible describirlo
degenerate [vb dɪ'dʒenəreɪt, adj dɪ'dʒenərɪt] vi degenerar ♦ adj degenerado
degree [dɪ'griː] n grado; (SCOL) título; **to have a ~ in maths** tener una licenciatura en matemáticas; **by ~s** (gradually) poco a poco, por etapas; **to some ~** hasta cierto punto
dehydrated [diːhaɪ'dreɪtɪd] adj deshidratado; (milk) en polvo
de-ice [diː'aɪs] vt deshelar
deign [deɪn] vi: **to do** dignarse hacer
dejected [dɪ'dʒektɪd] adj abatido, desanimado
delay [dɪ'leɪ] vt demorar, aplazar; (person) entretener; (train) retrasar ♦ vi tardar ♦ n demora, retraso; **to be ~ed**

retrasarse; **without ~** en seguida, sin tardar

delectable [dɪ'lektəbl] adj (person) encantador(a); (food) delicioso

delegate [n 'delɪgɪt, vb 'delɪgeɪt] n delegado/a ♦ vt (person) delegar en; (task) delegar

delete [dɪ'liːt] vt suprimir, tachar

deliberate [adj dɪ'lɪbərɪt, vb dɪ'lɪbəreɪt] adj (intentional) intencionado; (slow) pausado, lento ♦ vi deliberar; **~ly** adv (on purpose) a propósito

delicacy ['delɪkəsɪ] n delicadeza; (choice food) manjar m

delicate ['delɪkɪt] adj delicado; (fragile) frágil

delicatessen [delɪkə'tesn] n ultramarinos mpl finos

delicious [dɪ'lɪʃəs] adj delicioso

delight [dɪ'laɪt] n (feeling) placer m, deleite m; (person, experience etc) encanto, delicia ♦ vt encantar, deleitar; **to take ~ in** deleitarse en; **~ed** adj: **~ed (at** or **with/to do)** encantado (con/de hacer); **~ful** adj encantador(a), delicioso

delinquent [dɪ'lɪŋkwənt] adj, n delincuente m/f

delirious [dɪ'lɪrɪəs] adj (MED) delirar, desvariar; **to be ~ with** estar loco de

deliver [dɪ'lɪvə*] vt (distribute) repartir; (hand over) entregar; (message) comunicar; (speech) pronunciar; (MED) asistir al parto de; **~y** n reparto; entrega; (of speaker) modo de expresarse; (MED) parto, alumbramiento; **to take ~y of** recibir

delude [dɪ'luːd] vt engañar

deluge ['deljuːdʒ] n diluvio

delusion [dɪ'luːʒən] n ilusión f, engaño

de luxe [də'lʌks] adj de lujo

demand [dɪ'mɑːnd] vt (gen) exigir; (rights) reclamar ♦ n exigencia; (claim) reclamación f; (ECON) demanda; **to be in ~** ser muy solicitado; **on ~** a

solicitud; **~ing** adj (boss) exigente; (work) absorbente

demean [dɪ'miːn] vt: **to ~ o.s.** rebajarse

demeanour [dɪ'miːnə*] (US **demeanor**) n porte m, conducta

demented [dɪ'mentɪd] adj demente

demise [dɪ'maɪz] n (death) fallecimiento

demister [diː'mɪstə*] n (AUT) eliminador m de vaho

demo ['deməu] (inf) n abbr (= demonstration) manifestación f

democracy [dɪ'mɔkrəsɪ] n democracia; **democrat** ['deməkræt] n demócrata m/f; **democratic** [demə'krætɪk] adj democrático; (US) demócrata

demolish [dɪ'mɔlɪʃ] vt derribar, demoler; (fig: argument) destruir

demon ['diːmən] n (evil spirit) demonio

demonstrate ['demənstreɪt] vt demostrar; (skill, appliance) mostrar ♦ vi manifestarse; **demonstration** [-'streɪʃən] n (POL) manifestación f; (proof, exhibition) demostración f; **demonstrator** n (POL) manifestante m/f; (COMM) demostrador(a) m/f; vendedor(a) m/f

demote [dɪ'məut] vt degradar

demure [dɪ'mjuə*] adj recatado

den [den] n (of animal) guarida; (room) habitación f

denial [dɪ'naɪəl] n (refusal) negativa; (of report etc) negación f

denim ['denɪm] n tela vaquera; **~s** npl vaqueros mpl

Denmark ['denmɑːk] n Dinamarca

denomination [dɪnɔmɪ'neɪʃən] n valor m; (REL) confesión f

denounce [dɪ'nauns] vt denunciar

dense [dens] adj (crowd) denso; (thick) espeso; (: foliage etc) tupido; (inf: stupid) torpe; **~ly** adv: **~ly populated** con una alta densidad de población

density ['densɪtɪ] n densidad f; **single/double-~ disk** n (COMPUT)

disco de densidad sencilla/doble
densidad

dent [dent] *n* abolladura ♦ *vt* (*also*:
make a ~ in) abollar

dental ['dentl] *adj* dental; **~ surgeon**
n odontólogo/a

dentist ['dentist] *n* dentista *m/f*

dentures ['dentʃəz] *npl* dentadura
(postiza)

deny [di'nai] *vt* negar; (*charge*)
rechazar

deodorant [di:'əudərənt] *n*
desodorante *m*

depart [di'pa:t] *vi* irse, marcharse;
(*train*) salir; **to ~ from** (*fig: differ from*)
apartarse de

department [di'pa:tmənt] *n* (*COMM*)
sección *f*; (*SCOL*) departamento; (*POL*)
ministerio; **~ store** *n* gran almacén *m*

departure [di'pa:tʃə*] *n* partida, ida;
(*of train*) salida; (*of employee*) marcha;
a new ~ un nuevo rumbo; **~ lounge**
n (*at airport*) sala de embarque

depend [di'pend] *vi*: **to ~ on**
depender de; (*rely on*) contar con; **it**
~s depende, según; **~ing on the**
result según el resultado; **~able** *adj*
(*person*) formal, serio; (*watch*) exacto;
(*car*) seguro; **~ant** *n* dependiente *m/f*;
~ent *adj*: **to be ~ent on** depender de
♦ *n* = **dependant**

depict [di'pikt] *vt* (*in picture*) pintar;
(*describe*) representar

depleted [di'pli:tid] *adj* reducido

deploy [di'plɔi] *vt* desplegar

deport [di'pɔ:t] *vt* deportar

deposit [di'pɔzit] *n* depósito; (*CHEM*)
sedimento; (*of ore, oil*) yacimiento ♦
(*gen*) depositar; **~ account** (*BRIT*) *n*
cuenta de ahorros

depot ['depəu] *n* (*storehouse*) depósito;
(*for vehicles*) parque *m*; (*US*) estación *f*

depreciate [di'pri:ʃieit] *vi* depreciarse,
perder valor

depress [di'pres] *vt* deprimir; (*wages*
etc) hacer bajar; (*press down*) apretar;
~ed *adj* deprimido; **~ing** *adj*

deprimente; **~ion** [di'preʃən] *n*
depresión *f*

deprivation [depri'veiʃən] *n* privación
f

deprive [di'praiv] *vt*: **to ~ sb of** privar
a uno de; **~d** *adj* necesitado

depth [depθ] *n* profundidad *f*; (*of*
cupboard) fondo; **to be in the ~s of**
despair sentir la mayor desesperación;
to be out of one's ~ (*in water*) no
hacer pie; (*fig*) sentirse totalmente
perdido

deputize ['depjutaiz] *vi*: **to ~ for sb**
suplir a uno

deputy ['depjuti] *adj*: **~ head**
subdirector(a) *m/f* ♦ *n* sustituto/a,
suplente *m/f*; (*US: POL*) diputado/a; (*US*:
also: **~ sheriff**) agente *m* (del sheriff)

derail [di'reil] *vt*: **to be ~ed**
descarrilarse

deranged [di'reindʒd] *adj* trastornado

derby ['da:bi] (*US*) *n* (*hat*) hongo

derelict ['derilikt] *adj* abandonado

derisory [di'raizəri] *adj* (*sum*) irrisorio

derive [di'raiv] *vt* (*benefit etc*) obtener
♦ *vi*: **to ~ from** derivarse de

derogatory [di'rɔgətəri] *adj*
despectivo

descend [di'send] *vt*, *vi* descender,
bajar; **to ~ from** descender de; **to**
~ to rebajarse a; **~ant** *n* descendiente
m/f

descent [di'sent] *n* descenso; (*origin*)
descendencia

describe [dis'kraib] *vt* describir;
description [-'kripʃən] *n* descripción
f; (*sort*) clase *f*, género

desecrate ['desikreit] *vt* profanar

desert [*n* 'dezət, *vb* di'zə:t] *n* desierto
♦ *vt* abandonar ♦ *vi* (*MIL*) desertar; **~er**
[di'zə:tə*] *n* desertor/a *m/f*; **~ion**
[di'zə:ʃən] *n* deserción *f*; (*LAW*)
abandono; **~ island** *n* isla desierta; **~s**
[di'zə:ts] *npl*: **to get one's just ~s**
llevar su merecido

deserve [di'zə:v] *vt* merecer, ser digno
de; **deserving** *adj* (*person*) digno;

(action, cause) meritorio

design [dɪ'zaɪn] n *(sketch)* bosquejo; *(layout, shape)* diseño; *(pattern)* dibujo; *(intention)* intención f ♦ vt diseñar

designate [vb 'dezɪgneɪt, adj 'dezɪgnɪt] vt *(appoint)* nombrar; *(destine)* designar ♦ adj designado

designer [dɪ'zaɪnə*] n diseñador(a) m/f; *(fashion ~)* modisto/a, diseñador(a) m/f de moda

desirable [dɪ'zaɪərəbl] adj *(proper)* deseable; *(attractive)* atractivo

desire [dɪ'zaɪə*] n deseo ♦ vt desear

desk [dɛsk] n *(in office)* escritorio; *(for pupil)* pupitre m; *(in hotel, at airport)* recepción f; *(BRIT: in shop, restaurant)* caja

desk-top publishing ['dɛsktɒp-] n autoedición f

desolate ['dɛsəlɪt] adj *(place)* desierto; *(person)* afligido

despair [dɪs'pɛə*] n desesperación f ♦ vi: **to ~ of** perder la esperanza de

despatch [dɪs'pætʃ] n, vt = **dispatch**

desperate ['dɛspərɪt] adj desesperado; *(fugitive)* peligroso; **to be ~ for sth/to do** necesitar urgentemente algo/hacer; **~ly** adv desesperadamente; *(very)* terriblemente, gravemente

desperation [dɛspə'reɪʃən] n desesperación f; **in (sheer) ~** (absolutamente) desesperado

despicable [dɪs'pɪkəbl] adj vil, despreciable

despise [dɪs'paɪz] vt despreciar

despite [dɪs'paɪt] prep a pesar de, pese a

despondent [dɪs'pɒndənt] adj deprimido, abatido

dessert [dɪ'zɜ:t] n postre m; **~spoon** n cuchara (de postre)

destination [dɛstɪ'neɪʃən] n destino

destiny ['dɛstɪnɪ] n destino

destitute ['dɛstɪtjuːt] adj desamparado, indigente

destroy [dɪs'trɔɪ] vt destruir; *(animal)* sacrificar; **~er** n *(NAUT)* destructor m

destruction [dɪs'trʌkʃən] n destrucción f

detach [dɪ'tætʃ] vt separar; *(unstick)* despegar; **~ed** adj *(attitude)* objetivo, imparcial; **~ed house** n ≈ chalé m, ≈ chalet m; **~ment** n *(aloofness)* frialdad f; *(MIL)* destacamento

detail [dɪ'teɪl] n detalle m; *(no pl: in picture etc)* detalles mpl; *(trifle)* pequeñez f ♦ vt detallar; **in ~** detalladamente; **~ed** adj detallado

detain [dɪ'teɪn] vt retener; *(in captivity)* detener

detect [dɪ'tɛkt] vt descubrir; *(MED, POLICE)* identificar; *(MIL, RADAR, TECH)* detectar; **~ion** [dɪ'tɛkʃən] n descubrimiento; identificación f; **~ive** n detective m/f; **~ive story** n novela policíaca; **~or** n detector m

detention [dɪ'tɛnʃən] n detención f, arresto; *(SCOL)* castigo

deter [dɪ'tɜ:*] vt *(dissuade)* disuadir

detergent [dɪ'tɜ:dʒənt] n detergente m

deteriorate [dɪ'tɪərɪəreɪt] vi deteriorarse; **deterioration** [-'reɪʃən] n deterioro

determination [dɪtɜ:mɪ'neɪʃən] n resolución f

determine [dɪ'tɜ:mɪn] vt determinar; **~d** adj *(person)* resuelto, decidido; **~d to do** resuelto a hacer

deterrent [dɪ'tɛrənt] n *(MIL)* fuerza de disuasión

detest [dɪ'tɛst] vt aborrecer

detonate ['dɛtəneɪt] vi estallar ♦ vt hacer detonar

detour ['diːtuə*] n *(gen, US: AUT)* desviación f

detract [dɪ'trækt] vt: **to ~ from** quitar mérito a, desvirtuar

detriment ['dɛtrɪmənt] n: **to the ~ of** en perjuicio de; **~al** [dɛtrɪ'mɛntl] adj: **~al (to)** perjudicial (a)

devaluation [dɪvælju'eɪʃən] n devaluación f

devalue [di:'vælju:] vt (currency) devaluar; (fig) quitar mérito a

devastate ['devəsteɪt] vt devastar; (fig): **to be ~d by** quedar destrozado por; **devastating** adj devastador(a); (fig) arrollador(a)

develop [dɪ'veləp] vt desarrollar; (PHOT) revelar; (disease) coger; (habit) adquirir; (fault) empezar a tener ♦ vi desarrollarse; (advance) progresar; (facts, symptoms) aparecer; **~er** n promotor m; **~ing country** n país m en (vías de) desarrollo; **~ment** n desarrollo; (advance) progreso; (of affair, case) desenvolvimiento; (of land) urbanización f

deviation [di:vɪ'eɪʃən] n desviación f

device [dɪ'vaɪs] n (apparatus) aparato, mecanismo

devil ['devl] n diablo, demonio

devious ['di:vɪəs] adj taimado

devise [dɪ'vaɪz] vt idear, inventar

devoid [dɪ'vɔɪd] adj: **~ of** desprovisto de

devolution [di:və'lu:ʃən] n (POL) descentralización f

devote [dɪ'vəut] vt: **to ~ sth to** dedicar algo a; **~d** adj (loyal) leal, fiel; **to be ~d to sb** querer con devoción a alguien; **the book is ~d to politics** el libro trata de la política; **~e** [devəu'ti:] n entusiasta m/f; (REL) devoto/a; **devotion** n dedicación f; (REL) devoción f

devour [dɪ'vauə*] vt devorar

devout [dɪ'vaut] adj devoto

dew [dju:] n rocío

diabetes [daɪə'bi:ti:z] n diabetes f; **diabetic** [-'betɪk] adj, n diabético/a m/f

diabolical [daɪə'bɔlɪkəl] (inf) adj (weather, behaviour) pésimo

diagnosis [daɪəg'nəusɪs] (pl **-ses**) n diagnóstico

diagonal [daɪ'ægənl] adj, n diagonal f

diagram ['daɪəgræm] n diagrama m, esquema m

dial ['daɪəl] n esfera, cuadrante m, cara (AM); (on radio etc) selector m; (of phone) disco ♦ vt (number) marcar

dialling ['daɪəlɪŋ]: **~ code** n prefijo; **~ tone** (US **dial tone**) n (BRIT) señal f or tono de marcar

dialogue ['daɪəlɔg] (US **dialog**) n diálogo

diameter [daɪ'æmɪtə*] n diámetro

diamond ['daɪəmənd] n diamante m; (shape) rombo; **~s** npl (CARDS) diamantes mpl

diaper ['daɪəpə*] (US) n pañal m

diaphragm ['daɪəfræm] n diafragma m

diarrhoea [daɪə'ri:ə] (US **diarrhea**) n diarrea

diary ['daɪərɪ] n (daily account) diario; (book) agenda

dice [daɪs] n inv dados mpl ♦ vt (CULIN) cortar en cuadritos

Dictaphone ® ['dɪktəfəun] n dictáfono ®

dictate [dɪk'teɪt] vt dictar; (conditions) imponer; **dictation** [-'teɪʃən] n dictado; (giving of orders) órdenes fpl

dictator [dɪk'teɪtə*] n dictador m; **~ship** n dictadura

dictionary ['dɪkʃənrɪ] n diccionario

did [dɪd] pt of **do**

didn't ['dɪdənt] = **did not**

die [daɪ] vi morir; (fig: fade) desvanecerse, desaparecer; **to be dying for sth/to do sth** morirse por algo/de ganas de hacer algo; **~ away** vi (sound, light) perderse; **~ down** vi apagarse; (wind) amainar; **~ out** vi desaparecer

diesel ['di:zəl] n vehículo con motor Diesel; **~ engine** n motor m Diesel; **~ (oil)** n gasoil m

diet ['daɪət] n dieta; (restricted food) régimen m ♦ vi (also: **be on a ~**) estar a dieta, hacer régimen

differ ['dɪfə*] vi: **to ~ (from)** (be different) ser distinto a, diferenciarse (de); (disagree) discrepar (de); **~ence** n diferencia; (disagreement) desacuerdo;

~ent adj diferente, distinto; **~entiate**
[-'renʃɪeɪt] vt: **to ~entiate (between)**
distinguir (entre); (differ) distinguirse
(entre); **~ently** adv de otro
modo, en forma distinta

difficult ['dɪfɪkəlt] adj difícil; **~y** n
dificultad f

diffident ['dɪfɪdənt] adj tímido

dig [dɪg] (pt, pp dug) vt (hole, ground)
cavar ♦ n (prod) empujón m;
(archaeological) excavación f; (remark)
indirecta; **to ~ one's nails into** clavar
las uñas en; **~ into** vt fus (savings)
consumir; **~ up** vt (information)
desenterrar; (plant) desarraigar

digest [vb daɪ'dʒest, n 'daɪdʒest] vt
(food) digerir; (facts) asimilar ♦ n
resumen m; **~ion** [dɪ'dʒestʃən] n
digestión f

digit ['dɪdʒɪt] n (number) dígito; (finger)
dedo; **~al** adj digital; **~al camera** n
cámara digital; **~al TV** n televisión f
digital

dignified ['dɪgnɪfaɪd] adj grave,
solemne

dignity ['dɪgnɪtɪ] n dignidad f

digress [daɪ'gres] vi: **to ~ from**
apartarse de

digs [dɪgz] (BRIT: inf) npl pensión f,
alojamiento

dilapidated [dɪ'læpɪdeɪtɪd] adj
desmoronado, ruinoso

dilemma [daɪ'lemə] n dilema m

diligent ['dɪlɪdʒənt] adj diligente

dilute [daɪ'luːt] vt diluir

dim [dɪm] adj (light) débil; (memory)
indistinto; (room) oscuro; (inf: stupid)
lerdo ♦ vt (light) bajar

dime [daɪm] (US) n moneda de diez
centavos

dimension [dɪ'menʃən] n dimensión f

diminish [dɪ'mɪnɪʃ] vt, vi disminuir

diminutive [dɪ'mɪnjutɪv] adj diminuto
♦ n (LING) diminutivo

dimmers ['dɪməz] (US) npl (AUT: dipped
headlights) luces fpl cortas; (: parking
lights) luces fpl de posición

dimple ['dɪmpl] n hoyuelo

din [dɪn] n estruendo, estrépito

dine [daɪn] vi cenar; **~r** n (person)
comensal m/f

dinghy ['dɪŋgɪ] n bote m; (also: rubber
~) lancha (neumática)

dingy ['dɪndʒɪ] adj (room) sombrío;
(colour) sucio

dining car ['daɪnɪŋ-] (BRIT) n (RAIL)
coche-comedor m

dining room n comedor m

dinner ['dɪnə*] n (evening meal) cena;
(lunch) comida; (public) cena, banquete
m; **~ jacket** n smoking m; **~ party** n
cena; **~ time** n (evening) hora de
cenar; (midday) hora de comer

dinosaur ['daɪnəsɔː*] n dinosaurio

dip [dɪp] n (slope) pendiente f; (in sea)
baño; (CULIN) salsa ♦ vt (in water)
mojar; (ladle etc) meter; (BRIT: AUT): **to**
~ one's lights poner luces de cruce
♦ vi (road etc) descender, bajar

diploma [dɪ'pləumə] n diploma m

diplomacy [dɪ'pləuməsɪ] n diplomacia

diplomat ['dɪpləmæt] n diplomático/a;
~ic [dɪplə'mætɪk] adj diplomático

diprod ['dɪprəd] (US) n = **dipstick**

dipstick ['dɪpstɪk] (BRIT) n (AUT) varilla
de nivel (del aceite)

dipswitch ['dɪpswɪtʃ] (BRIT) n (AUT)
interruptor m

dire [daɪə*] adj calamitoso

direct [daɪ'rekt] adj directo; (challenge)
claro; (person) franco ♦ vt dirigir;
(order): **to ~ sb to do sth** mandar a
uno hacer algo ♦ adv derecho; **can**
you ~ me to...? ¿puede indicarme
dónde está...?; **~ debit** (BRIT) n
domiciliación f bancaria de recibos

direction [dɪ'rekʃən] n dirección f;
sense of ~ sentido de la dirección; **~s**
npl (instructions) instrucciones fpl; **~s**
for use modo de empleo

directly [dɪ'rektlɪ] adv (in straight line)
directamente; (at once) en seguida

director [dɪ'rektə*] n director(a) m/f

directory [dɪ'rektərɪ] n (TEL) guía
(telefónica); (COMPUT) directorio;

~ enquiries, ~ assistance (US) n (servicio de) información f

dirt [dɜːt] n suciedad f; (earth) tierra; **~-cheap** adj baratísimo; **~y** adj sucio; (joke) verde (SP), colorado (AM) ♦ vt ensuciar; (stain) manchar; **~y trick** n juego sucio

disability [dɪsə'bɪlɪtɪ] n incapacidad f

disabled [dɪs'eɪbld] adj: **to be physically ~** ser minusválido/a; **to be mentally ~** ser deficiente mental

disadvantage [dɪsəd'vɑːntɪdʒ] n desventaja, inconveniente m

disagree [dɪsə'griː] vi (differ) discrepar; **to ~ (with)** no estar de acuerdo (con); **~able** adj desagradable; (person) antipático; **~ment** n desacuerdo

disallow [dɪsə'laʊ] vt (goal) anular; (claim) rechazar

disappear [dɪsə'pɪə*] vi desaparecer; **~ance** n desaparición f

disappoint [dɪsə'pɔɪnt] vt decepcionar, defraudar; **~ed** adj decepcionado; **~ing** adj decepcionante; **~ment** n decepción f

disapproval [dɪsə'pruːvəl] n desaprobación f

disapprove [dɪsə'pruːv] vi: **to ~ of** ver mal

disarmament [dɪs'ɑːməmənt] n desarme m

disarray [dɪsə'reɪ] n: **in ~** (army, organization) desorganizado; (hair, clothes) desarreglado

disaster [dɪ'zɑːstə*] n desastre m

disband [dɪs'bænd] vt disolver ♦ vi desbandarse

disbelief [dɪsbə'liːf] n incredulidad f

disc [dɪsk] n disco; (COMPUT) = **disk**

discard [dɪs'kɑːd] vt (old things) tirar; (fig) descartar

discern [dɪ'sɜːn] vt percibir, discernir; (understand) comprender; **~ing** adj perspicaz

discharge [vb dɪs'tʃɑːdʒ, n 'dɪstʃɑːdʒ] vt (task, duty) cumplir; (waste) verter; (patient) dar de alta; (employee)

despedir; (soldier) licenciar; (defendant) poner en libertad ♦ n (ELEC) descarga; (MED) supuración f; (dismissal) despedida; (of duty) desempeño; (of debt) pago, descargo

discipline ['dɪsɪplɪn] n disciplina ♦ vt disciplinar; (punish) castigar

disc jockey [dɪs'dʒɒkɪ] n pinchadiscos m/f inv

disclaim [dɪs'kleɪm] vt negar

disclose [dɪs'kləʊz] vt revelar; **disclosure** [-'kləʊʒə*] n revelación f

disco ['dɪskəʊ] n abbr = **discothèque**

discomfort [dɪs'kʌmfət] n incomodidad f; (unease) inquietud f; (physical) malestar m

disconcert [dɪskən'sɜːt] vt desconcertar

disconnect [dɪskə'nekt] vt separar; (ELEC etc) desconectar

discontent [dɪskən'tent] n descontento; **~ed** adj descontento

discontinue [dɪskən'tɪnjuː] vt interrumpir; (payments) suspender; **'"~d"** (COMM) "ya no se fabrica"

discord ['dɪskɔːd] n discordia; (MUS) disonancia

discothèque ['dɪskəʊtek] n discoteca

discount [n 'dɪskaʊnt, vb dɪs'kaʊnt] n descuento ♦ vt descontar

discourage [dɪs'kʌrɪdʒ] vt desalentar; (advise against) desaconsejar; **to ~ sb from doing** disuadir a uno de hacer

discover [dɪs'kʌvə*] vt descubrir; (error) darse cuenta de; **~y** n descubrimiento

discredit [dɪs'kredɪt] vt desacreditar

discreet [dɪ'skriːt] adj (tactful) discreto; (careful) circunspecto, prudente

discrepancy [dɪ'skrepənsɪ] n diferencia

discretion [dɪ'skreʃən] n (tact) discreción f; **at the ~ of** a criterio de

discriminate [dɪ'skrɪmɪnet] vi: **to ~ between** distinguir entre; **to ~ against** discriminar contra; **discriminating** adj entendido; **discrimination** [-'neɪʃən] n (*discernment*) perspicacia; (*bias*) discriminación f

discuss [dɪsˈkʌs] vt discutir; (*a theme*) tratar; **~ion** [dɪˈskʌʃən] n discusión f

disdain [dɪsˈdeɪn] n desdén m

disease [dɪˈziːz] n enfermedad f

disembark [dɪsɪmˈbɑːk] vt, vi desembarcar

disentangle [dɪsɪnˈtæŋgl] vt soltar; (*wire, thread*) desenredar

disfigure [dɪsˈfɪgə*] vt (*person*) desfigurar; (*object*) afear

disgrace [dɪsˈgreɪs] n ignominia; (*shame*) vergüenza, escándalo ♦ vt deshonrar; **~ful** adj vergonzoso

disgruntled [dɪsˈgrʌntld] adj disgustado, descontento

disguise [dɪsˈgaɪz] n disfraz m ♦ vt disfrazar; **in ~** disfrazado

disgust [dɪsˈgʌst] n repugnancia ♦ vt repugnar, dar asco a; **~ing** adj repugnante, asqueroso; (*behaviour etc*) vergonzoso

dish [dɪʃ] n (*gen*) plato; **to do** or **wash the ~es** fregar los platos; **~ out** vt repartir; **~ up** vt servir; **~cloth** n estropajo

dishearten [dɪsˈhɑːtn] vt desalentar

dishevelled [dɪˈʃevəld] (*US* **disheveled**) adj (*hair*) despeinado; (*appearance*) desarreglado

dishonest [dɪsˈɒnɪst] adj (*person*) poco honrado, tramposo; (*means*) fraudulento; **~y** n falta de honradez

dishonour [dɪsˈɒnə*] (*US* **dishonor**) n deshonra; **~able** adj deshonroso

dishtowel [ˈdɪʃtauəl] (*US*) n estropajo

dishwasher [ˈdɪʃwɔʃə*] n lavaplatos m inv

disillusion [dɪsɪˈluːʒən] vt desilusionar

disinfect [dɪsɪnˈfekt] vt desinfectar; **~ant** n desinfectante m

disintegrate [dɪsˈɪntɪgreɪt] vi disgregarse, desintegrarse

disinterested [dɪsˈɪntrəstɪd] adj desinteresado

disjointed [dɪsˈdʒɔɪntɪd] adj inconexo

disk [dɪsk] n (*esp US*) = **disc**; (*COMPUT*) disco, disquete m; **single-/double-sided ~** disco de una cara/dos caras; **~ drive** n disc drive m; **~ette** n = **disk**

dislike [dɪsˈlaɪk] n antipatía, aversión f ♦ vt tener antipatía a

dislocate [ˈdɪsləkeɪt] vt dislocar

dislodge [dɪsˈlɒdʒ] vt sacar

disloyal [dɪsˈlɔɪəl] adj desleal

dismal [ˈdɪzml] adj (*gloomy*) deprimente, triste; (*very bad*) malísimo, fatal

dismantle [dɪsˈmæntl] vt desmontar, desarmar

dismay [dɪsˈmeɪ] n consternación f ♦ vt consternar

dismiss [dɪsˈmɪs] vt (*worker*) despedir; (*pupils*) dejar marchar; (*soldiers*) dar permiso para irse; (*idea, LAW*) rechazar; (*possibility*) descartar; **~al** n despido

dismount [dɪsˈmaunt] vi apearse

disobedient [dɪsəˈbiːdɪənt] adj desobediente

disobey [dɪsəˈbeɪ] vt desobedecer

disorder [dɪsˈɔːdə*] n desorden m; (*rioting*) disturbios mpl; (*MED*) trastorno; **~ly** adj desordenado; (*meeting*) alborotado; (*conduct*) escandaloso

disorientated [dɪsˈɔːrɪɛnteɪtəd] adj desorientado

disown [dɪsˈəun] vt (*action*) renegar de; (*person*) negar cualquier tipo de relación con

disparaging [dɪsˈpærɪdʒɪŋ] adj despreciativo

dispassionate [dɪsˈpæʃənɪt] adj (*unbiased*) imparcial

dispatch [dɪsˈpætʃ] vt enviar ♦ n (*sending*) envío; (*PRESS*) informe m; (*MIL*) parte m

dispel [dɪsˈpel] vt disipar

dispense [dɪsˈpens] vt (*medicines*) preparar; **~ with** vt fus prescindir de; **~r** n (*container*) distribuidor m automático; **dispensing chemist** (*BRIT*) n farmacia

disperse [dɪs'pə:s] vt dispersar ♦ vi dispersarse

dispirited [dɪ'spɪrɪtɪd] adj desanimado, desalentado

displace [dɪs'pleɪs] vt desplazar, reemplazar; **~d person** n (POL) desplazado/a

display [dɪs'pleɪ] n (in shop window) escaparate m; (exhibition) exposición f; (COMPUT) visualización f; (of feeling) manifestación f ♦ vt exponer; manifestar; (ostentatiously) lucir

displease [dɪs'pli:z] vt (offend) ofender; (annoy) fastidiar; **~d** adj: **~d with** disgustado con; **displeasure** [-'pleʒə*] n disgusto

disposable [dɪs'pəuzəbl] adj desechable; (income) disponible; **~ nappy** n pañal m desechable

disposal [dɪs'pəuzl] n (of rubbish) destrucción f; **at one's ~** a su disposición

dispose [dɪs'pəuz] vi: **to ~ of** (unwanted goods) deshacerse de; (problem etc) resolver; **~d** adj: **~d to do** dispuesto a hacer; **to be well-~d towards sb** estar bien dispuesto hacia uno; **disposition** [dɪspə'zɪʃən] n (nature) temperamento m; (inclination) propensión f

disprove [dɪs'pru:v] vt refutar

dispute [dɪs'pju:t] n disputa; (also: industrial ~) conflicto (laboral) ♦ vt (argue) disputar, discutir; (question) cuestionar

disqualify [dɪs'kwɔlɪfaɪ] vt (SPORT) descalificar; **to ~ sb for sth/from doing sth** incapacitar a alguien para algo/hacer algo

disquiet [dɪs'kwaɪət] n preocupación f, inquietud f

disregard [dɪsrɪ'gɑ:d] vt (ignore) no hacer caso de

disrepair [dɪsrɪ'pεə*] n: **to fall into ~** (building) desmoronarse

disreputable [dɪs'rεpjutəbl] adj (person) de mala fama; (behaviour) vergonzoso

disrespectful [dɪsrɪ'spεktful] adj irrespetuoso

disrupt [dɪs'rʌpt] vt (plans) desbaratar, trastornar; (conversation) interrumpir

dissatisfaction [dɪssætɪs'fækʃən] n disgusto, descontento

dissect [dɪ'sεkt] vt disecar

dissent [dɪ'sεnt] n disensión f

dissertation [dɪsə'teɪʃən] n tesina

disservice [dɪs'sə:vɪs] n: **to do sb a ~** perjudicar a alguien

dissimilar [dɪ'sɪmɪlə*] adj distinto

dissipate ['dɪsɪpeɪt] vt disipar; (waste) desperdiciar

dissolve [dɪ'zɔlv] vt disolver ♦ vi disolverse; **to ~ into tears** deshacerse en lágrimas

dissuade [dɪ'sweɪd] vt: **to ~ sb (from)** disuadir a uno (de)

distance ['dɪstəns] n distancia; **in the ~** a lo lejos

distant ['dɪstənt] adj lejano; (manner) reservado, frío

distaste [dɪs'teɪst] n repugnancia; **~ful** adj repugnante, desagradable

distended [dɪs'tεndɪd] adj (stomach) hinchado

distil [dɪs'tɪl] (US **distill**) vt destilar; **~lery** n destilería

distinct [dɪs'tɪŋkt] adj (different) distinto; (clear) claro; (unmisteakable) inequívoco; **as ~ from** a diferencia de; **~ion** [dɪs'tɪŋkʃən] n distinción f; (honour) honor m; (in exam) sobresaliente m; **~ive** adj distintivo

distinguish [dɪs'tɪŋgwɪʃ] vt distinguir; **to ~ o.s.** destacarse; **~ed** adj (eminent) distinguido; **~ing** adj (feature) distintivo

distort [dɪs'tɔ:t] vt distorsionar; (shape, image) deformar; **~ion** [dɪs'tɔ:ʃən] n distorsión f; deformación f

distract [dɪs'trækt] vt distraer; **~ed** adj distraído; **~ion** [dɪs'trækʃən] n distracción f; (confusion) aturdimiento

distraught [dɪs'trɔ:t] adj loco de

inquietud

distress [dɪsˈtrɛs] n (anguish) angustia, aflicción f ♦ vt afligir; **~ing** adj angustioso; doloroso; **~ signal** n señal f de socorro

distribute [dɪsˈtrɪbjuːt] vt distribuir; (share out) repartir; **distribution** [-ˈbjuːʃən] n distribución f, reparto; **distributor** n (AUT) distribuidor m; (COMM) distribuidora

district [ˈdɪstrɪkt] n (of country) zona, región f; (of town) barrio; (ADMIN) distrito; **~ attorney** (US) n fiscal m/f; **~ nurse** (BRIT) n enfermera que atiende a pacientes a domicilio

distrust [dɪsˈtrʌst] n desconfianza ♦ vt desconfiar de

disturb [dɪsˈtɜːb] vt (person: bother, interrupt) molestar; (: upset) perturbar, inquietar; (disorganize) alterar; **~ance** n (upheaval) perturbación f; (political etc: gen act) disturbio; (of mind) trastorno; **~ed** adj (worried, upset) preocupado, angustiado; **emotionally ~ed** trastornado; (childhood) inseguro; **~ing** adj inquietante, perturbador(a)

disuse [dɪsˈjuːs] n: **to fall into ~** caer en desuso

disused [dɪsˈjuːzd] adj abandonado

ditch [dɪtʃ] n zanja; (irrigation ~) acequia ♦ vt (inf: partner) deshacerse de; (: plan, car etc) abandonar

dither [ˈdɪðə*] (pej) vi vacilar

ditto [ˈdɪtəu] adv ídem, lo mismo

divan [dɪˈvæn] n (also: ~ bed) cama turca

dive [daɪv] n (from board) salto; (underwater) buceo; (of submarine) sumersión f ♦ vi (swimmer: into water) saltar; (: under water) bucear; (fish, submarine) sumergirse; (bird) lanzarse en picado; **to ~ into** (bag etc) meter la mano en; (place) meterse de prisa en; **~r** n (underwater) buzo

diverse [daɪˈvɜːs] adj diversos/as, varios/as

diversion [daɪˈvɜːʃən] n (BRIT: AUT) desviación f; (distraction, MIL) diversión f; (of funds) distracción f

divert [daɪˈvɜːt] vt (turn aside) desviar

divide [dɪˈvaɪd] vt dividir; (separate) separar ♦ vi dividirse; (road) bifurcarse; **~d highway** (US) n carretera de doble calzada

dividend [ˈdɪvɪdɛnd] n dividendo; (fig): **to pay ~s** proporcionar beneficios

divine [dɪˈvaɪn] adj (also fig) divino

diving [ˈdaɪvɪŋ] n (SPORT) salto; (underwater) buceo; **~ board** n trampolín m

divinity [dɪˈvɪnɪtɪ] n divinidad f; (SCOL) teología

division [dɪˈvɪʒən] n división f; (sharing out) reparto; (disagreement) diferencias fpl; (COMM) sección f

divorce [dɪˈvɔːs] n divorcio ♦ vt divorciarse de; **~d** adj divorciado; **~e** [-ˈsiː] n divorciado/a

divulge [daɪˈvʌldʒ] vt divulgar, revelar

D.I.Y. (BRIT) adj, n abbr = **do-it-yourself**

dizzy [ˈdɪzɪ] adj (spell) de mareo; **to feel ~** marearse

DJ n abbr = **disc jockey**

KEYWORD

do [duː] (pt did, pp done) n (inf: party etc): **we're having a little ~ on Saturday** damos una fiestecita el sábado; **it was rather a grand ~** fue un acontecimiento a lo grande
♦ aux vb **1** (in negative constructions: not translated) **I don't understand** no entiendo
2 (to form questions: not translated) **didn't you know?** ¿no lo sabías?; **what ~ you think?** ¿qué opinas?
3 (for emphasis, in polite expressions): **people ~ make mistakes sometimes** sí que se cometen errores a veces; **she does seem rather late** a mí también me parece que se ha

retrasado; **~ sit down/help yourself** siéntate/sírvete por favor; **~ take care!** ¡ten cuidado(, te pido)!

4 (used to avoid repeating vb): **she sings better than I ~** canta mejor que yo; **~ you agree? — yes, I ~/no, I don't** ¿estás de acuerdo? — sí (lo estoy)/no (lo estoy); **she lives in Glasgow — so ~ I** vive en Glasgow — yo también; **he didn't like it and neither did we** no le gustó a él ni a nosotros tampoco; **who made this mess? — I did** ¿quién hizo esta chapuza? — yo; **he asked me to help him and I did** me pidió que le ayudara y lo hice

5 (in question tags): **you like him, don't you?** te gusta, ¿verdad? or ¿no?; **I don't know him, ~ I?** creo que no le conozco

♦ vt **1** (gen, carry out, perform etc): **what are you ~ing tonight?** ¿qué haces esta noche?; **what can I ~ for you?** ¿en qué puedo servirle?; **to ~ the washing-up/cooking** fregar los platos/cocinar; **to ~ one's teeth/hair/nails** lavarse los dientes/arreglarse el pelo/arreglarse las uñas **2** (AUT etc): **the car was ~ing 100** el coche iba a 100; **we've done 200 km already** ya hemos hecho 200 km; **he can ~ 100 in that car** puede ir a 100 en ese coche

♦ vi **1** (act, behave) hacer; **~ as I ~** haz como yo

2 (get on, fare): **he's ~ing well/badly at school** va bien/mal en la escuela; **the firm is ~ing well** la empresa anda or va bien; **how ~ you ~?** mucho gusto; (less formal) ¿qué tal? **3** (suit): **will it ~?** ¿sirve?, ¿está or va bien?

4 (be sufficient) bastar; **will £10 ~?** ¿será bastante con £10?; **that'll ~** así está bien; **that'll ~!** (in annoyance) ¡ya está bien!, ¡basta ya!; **to make ~ (with)** arreglárselas (con)

do away with vt fus (kill, disease) eliminar; (abolish: law etc) abolir; (withdraw) retirar

do up vt (laces) atar; (zip, dress, shirt) abrochar; (renovate: room, house) renovar

do with vt fus (need): **I could ~ with a drink/some help** no me vendría mal un trago/un poco de ayuda; (be connected) tener que ver con; **what has it got to ~ with you?** ¿qué tiene que ver contigo?

do without vi pasar sin; **if you're late for tea then you'll ~ without** si llegas tarde tendrás que quedarte sin cenar ♦ vt fus pasar sin; **I can ~ without a car** puedo pasar sin coche

---

dock [dɔk] n (NAUT) muelle m; (LAW) banquillo (de los acusados); ~ **s** npl (NAUT) muelles mpl, puerto sg ♦ vt (enter ~) atracar (la) muelle; (SPACE) acoplarse; **~er** n trabajador m portuario, estibador m; **~yard** n astillero

doctor ['dɔktə*] n médico/a; (Ph.D. etc) doctor(a) m/f ♦ vt (drink etc) adulterar; **D~ of Philosophy** n Doctor en Filosofía y Letras

document ['dɔkjʊmənt] n documento; **~ary** [-'mentərɪ] adj documental ♦ n documental m

dodge [dɔdʒ] n (fig) truco ♦ vt evadir; (blow) esquivar

dodgems ['dɔdʒəmz] (BRIT) npl coches mpl de choque

doe [dəʊ] n (deer) cierva, gama; (rabbit) coneja

does [dʌz] vb see do; **~n't = does not**

dog [dɔg] n perro ♦ vt seguir los pasos de; (subj: bad luck) perseguir; **~ collar** n collar m de perro; (fig: clergyman) alzacuellos m inv; **~-eared** adj sobado

dogged ['dɔgɪd] adj tenaz, obstinado

dogsbody ['dɔgzbɔdɪ] (BRIT: inf) n

burro de carga

doings ['duɪŋz] npl (activities) actividades fpl

do-it-yourself n bricolaje m

doldrums ['dɔldrəmz] npl: **to be in the ~** (person) estar abatido; (business) estar estancado

dole [dəul] (BRIT) n (payment) subsidio de paro; **on the ~** parado; **~ out** vt repartir

doll [dɔl] n muñeca; (US: inf: woman) muñeca, gachí f*

dollar ['dɔlə*] n dólar m

dolled up (inf) adj arreglado

dolphin ['dɔlfin] n delfín m

domain [də'meɪn] n (fig) campo, competencia; (land) dominios mpl

dome [dəum] n (ARCH) cúpula

domestic [də'mestɪk] adj (animal, duty) doméstico; (flight, policy) nacional; **~ated** adj domesticado; (home-loving) casero, hogareño

dominate ['dɔmineɪt] vt dominar; **domineering** [dɔmi'nɪərɪŋ] adj dominante

dominion [də'mɪnɪən] n dominio

domino ['dɔminəu] (pl **~es**) n ficha de dominó; **~es** n (game) dominó

don [dɔn] (BRIT) n profesor(a) m/f universitario/a

donate [də'neɪt] vt donar; **donation** [də'neɪʃən] n donativo

done [dʌn] pp of **do**

donkey ['dɔŋkɪ] n burro

donor ['dəunə*] n donante m/f; **~ card** n carnet m de donante

don't [dəunt] = do not

donut ['dəunʌt] (US) n = **doughnut**

doodle ['du:dl] vi hacer dibujitos or garabatos

doom [du:m] n (fate) suerte f ♦ vt: **to be ~ed to failure** estar condenado al fracaso

door [dɔ:*] n puerta; **~bell** n timbre m; **~ handle** n tirador m; (of car) manija; **~man** (irreg) n (in hotel) portero; **~mat** n felpudo, estera; **~step** n

peldaño; **~-to-~** adj de puerta en puerta; **~way** n entrada, puerta

dope [dəup] n (inf: illegal drug) droga; (: person) imbécil m/f ♦ vt (horse etc) drogar

dormant ['dɔ:mənt] adj inactivo

dormitory ['dɔ:mitri] n (BRIT) dormitorio; (US) colegio mayor

dormouse ['dɔ:maus] n (pl **-mice**) n lirón m

DOS n abbr (= disk operating system) DOS m

dosage ['dəusɪdʒ] n dosis f inv

dose [dəus] n dosis f inv

doss house ['dɔs-] (BRIT) n pensión f de mala muerte

dossier ['dɔsɪeɪ] n expediente m, dosier m

dot [dɔt] n punto ♦ vi: **~ted** with salpicado de; **on the ~** en punto

double ['dʌbl] adj doble ♦ adv (twice): **to cost ~** costar el doble ♦ n doble m ♦ vt doblar ♦ vi doblarse; **on the ~**, **at the ~** (BRIT) corriendo; **~ bass** n contrabajo; **~ bed** n cama de matrimonio; **~ bend** n (BRIT) doble curva; **~breasted** adj cruzado; **~-click** vi (COMPUT) hacer doble clic; **~cross** vt (trick) engañar; (betray) traicionar; **~decker** n autobús m de dos pisos; **~ glazing** n (BRIT) doble acristalamiento; **~ room** n habitación f doble; **~s** n (TENNIS) juego de dobles; **doubly** adv doblemente

doubt [daut] n duda ♦ vt dudar; (suspect) dudar de; **to ~ that** dudar que; **~ful** adj dudoso; (person): **to be ~ful about sth** tener dudas sobre algo; **~less** adv sin duda

dough [dəu] n masa, pasta; **~nut** (US **donut**) n ≈ rosquilla

dove [dʌv] n paloma

dovetail ['dʌvteɪl] vi (fig) encajar

dowdy ['daudɪ] adj (person) mal vestido; (clothes) pasado de moda

down [daun] n (feathers) plumón m, flojel m ♦ adv (~wards) abajo, hacia abajo; (*on the ground*) por o en tierra ♦ *prep* abajo ♦ *vt* (*inf:* drink) beberse; ~ **with X!** ¡abajo X!; **~-and-out** *n* vagabundo/a; **~-at-heel** *adj* venido a menos; (*appearance*) desaliñado; **~cast** *adj* abatido; **~fall** *n* caída, ruina; **~hearted** *adj* desanimado; **~hill** *adv:* **to go ~hill** (*also fig*) ir cuesta abajo; **~load** *vt* (*COMPUT*) bajar; ♦ **payment** *n* entrada, pago al contado; **~pour** *n* aguacero; **~right** *adj* (*nonsense, lie*) manifiesto; (*refusal*) terminante; **~size** *vi* (*ECON: company*) reducir la plantilla de

---

Downing Street

Downing Street *es la calle de Londres en la que están las residencias oficiales del Presidente del Gobierno (Prime Minister), tradicionalmente en el No. 10, y del Ministro de Economía (Chancellor of the Exchequer). La calle está situada en el céntrico barrio londinense de Westminster y está cerrada al tráfico de peatones y vehículos. En lenguaje periodístico, se usa también* Downing Street *para referirse al primer ministro o al Gobierno.*

Down's syndrome ['daunz-] *n* síndrome *m* de Down

down: **~stairs** *adv* (*below*) (en la casa de) abajo; (*~wards*) escaleras abajo; **~stream** *adv* aguas o río abajo; **~ to-earth** *adj* práctico; **~town** *adv* en el centro de la ciudad; **~ under** *adv* en Australia (*or* Nueva Zelanda); **~ward** [-wəd] *adj, adv* hacia abajo; **~wards** [-wədz] *adv* hacia abajo

dowry ['dauri] *n* dote *f*

doz. *abbr* = **dozen**

doze [dauz] *vi* dormitar; **~ off** *vi* quedarse medio dormido

dozen ['dʌzn] *n* docena; **a ~ books** una docena de libros; **~s of** cantidad de

Dr. *abbr* = **doctor**; **drive**

drab [dræb] *adj* gris, monótono

draft [drɑːft] *n* (*first copy*) borrador *m*; (*POL: of bill*) anteproyecto; (*US: call-up*) quinta ♦ *vt* (*plan*) hacer un borrador de; (*write roughly*) hacer un borrador de; *see also* **draught**

draftsman ['drɑːftsmən] (*US*) *n* = **draughtsman**

drag [dræg] *vt* arrastrar; (*river*) dragar, rastrear ♦ *vi* (*time*) pasar despacio; (*play, film etc*) hacerse pesado ♦ *n* (*inf*) lata; (*women's clothing*): **in ~** vestido de travestí; **~ on** *vi* ser interminable; **~ and drop** *vt* (*COMPUT*) arrastrar y soltar

dragonfly ['drægənflaɪ] *n* libélula

drain [dreɪn] *n* desaguadero; (*in street*) sumidero; (*source of loss*): **to be a ~ on** consumir, agotar ♦ *vt* (*land, marshes*) desaguar; (*reservoir*) desecar; (*vegetables*) escurrir ♦ *vi* escurrirse; **~age** *n* (*act*) desagüe *m*; (*MED, AGR*) drenaje *m*; (*sewage*) alcantarillado; **~ing board** (*US* **~board**) *n* escurridera, escurridor *m*; **~pipe** *n* tubo de desagüe

drama ['drɑːmə] *n* (*art*) teatro; (*play*) drama *m*; (*excitement*) emoción *f*; **~tic** [drə'mætɪk] *adj* dramático; (*sudden, marked*) espectacular; **~tist** ['dræmətɪst] *n* dramaturgo/a; **~tize** ['dræmətaɪz] *vt* (*events*) dramatizar

drank [dræŋk] *pt of* **drink**

drape [dreɪp] *vt* (*cloth*) colocar; (*flag*) colgar; **~s** (*US*) *npl* cortinas *fpl*

drastic ['dræstɪk] *adj* (*measure*) severo; (*change*) radical, drástico

draught [drɑːft] (*US* **draft**) *n* (*of air*) corriente *f* de aire; (*NAUT*) calado; **on ~** (*beer*) de barril; **~ beer** *n* cerveza de barril; **~board** (*BRIT*) *n* tablero de damas; **~s** (*BRIT*) *n* (*game*) juego de damas

draughtsman ['drɑːftsmən] (*US* **draftsman**) (*irreg*) *n* delineante *m*

draw [drɔː] (*pt* **drew**, *pp* **drawn**) *vt*

(picture) dibujar; (cart) tirar de; (curtain) correr; (take out) sacar; (attract) atraer; (money) retirar; (wages) cobrar ♦ vi (SPORT) empatar ♦ n (SPORT) empate m; (lottery) sorteo; ~ **near** vi acercarse; ~ **out** vi (lengthen) alargarse ♦ vt sacar; ~ **up** vi (stop) pararse ♦ vt (chair) acercar; (document) redactar; **~back** n inconveniente m, desventaja; **~bridge** n puente m levadizo

drawer [drɔː*] n cajón m

drawing ['drɔːɪŋ] n dibujo; ~ **board** n tablero de dibujante); ~ **pin** n (BRIT) chincheta; ~ **room** n salón m

drawl [drɔːl] n habla lenta y cansina

drawn [drɔːn] pp of draw

dread [dred] n pavor m, terror m ♦ vt temer, tener miedo or pavor a; **~ful** adj horroroso

dream [driːm] (pt, pp **dreamed** or **dreamt**) n sueño ♦ vt, vi soñar; **~y** adj (distracted) soñador(a), distraído; (music) suave

dreary ['drɪərɪ] adj monótono

dredge [dredʒ] vt dragar

dregs [dregz] npl posos mpl; (of humanity) hez f

drench [drentʃ] vt empapar

dress [dres] n vestido; (clothing) ropa ♦ vt vestir; (wound) vendar ♦ vi vestirse; **to get ~ed** vestirse; ~ **up** vi vestirse de etiqueta; (in fancy dress) disfrazarse; ~ **circle** n (BRIT) n principal m; **~er** n (furniture) aparador m; (: US) cómoda (con espejo); **~ing** n (MED) vendaje m; (CULIN) aliño; **~ing gown** n (BRIT) n bata; **~ing room** n (THEATRE) camarín m; (SPORT) vestuario; **~ing table** n tocador m; **~maker** n modista, costurera; ~ **rehearsal** n ensayo general

drew [druː] pt of draw

dribble ['drɪbl] vi (baby) babear ♦ vt (ball) regatear

dried [draɪd] adj (fruit) seco; (milk) en polvo

drier ['draɪə*] n = **dryer**

drift [drɪft] n (of current etc) flujo; (of snow) ventisquero; (meaning) significado ♦ vi (boat) ir a la deriva; (sand, snow) amontonarse; **~wood** n madera de deriva

drill [drɪl] n (~ bit) broca; (tool for DIY etc) taladro; (of dentist) fresa; (for mining etc) perforadora, barrena; (MIL) instrucción f ♦ vt perforar, taladrar; (troops) enseñar la instrucción a ♦ vi (for oil) perforar

drink [drɪŋk] n (pt **drank**, pp **drunk**) n bebida; (sip) trago ♦ vt, vi beber; **to have a ~** tomar algo; tomar una copa or un trago; **a ~ of water** un trago de agua; **~er** n bebedor(a) m/f; **~ing water** n agua potable

drip [drɪp] n (act) goteo; (one ~) gota; (MED) gota a gota m ♦ vi gotear; **~-dry** adj (shirt) inarrugable; **~-ping** n (animal fat) pringue m

drive [draɪv] n (pt **drove**, pp **driven**) n (journey) viaje m (en coche); (also: **~way**) entrada; (energy) energía, vigor m; (COMPUT: also: disk ~) drive m ♦ vt (car) conducir (SP), manejar (AM); (nail) clavar; (push) empujar; (TECH: motor) impulsar ♦ vi (AUT: at controls) conducir; (: travel) pasearse en coche; **left-/right-hand ~** conducción f a la izquierda/derecha; **to ~ sb mad** volverle loco a uno

drivel ['drɪvl] (inf) n tonterías fpl

driven ['drɪvn] pp of drive

driver ['draɪvə*] n conductor(a) m/f (SP), chofer m (AM); (of taxi, bus) chofer; **~'s license** (US) n carnet m de conducir

driveway ['draɪvweɪ] n entrada

driving ['draɪvɪŋ] n el conducir (SP), el manejar (AM); ~ **instructor** n instructor(a) m/f de conducción or manejo; ~ **lesson** n clase f de conducción or manejo; ~ **licence** (BRIT) n permiso de conducir; ~ **school** n autoescuela; ~ **test** n examen m de conducción or manejo

drizzle |'drɪzl| n llovizna

drool |dru:l| vi babear

droop |dru:p| vi (flower) marchitarse; (shoulders) encorvarse; (head) inclinarse

drop |drɔp| n (of water) gota; (lessening) baja; (fall) caída ♦ vt dejar caer; (voice, eyes, price) bajar; (passenger) dejar; (omit) omitir ♦ vi (object) caer; (wind) amainar; ~s npl (MED) gotas fpl; ~ **off** vi (sleep) dormirse ♦ vt (passenger) dejar; ~ **out** vi (withdraw) retirarse; ~**out** n marginado/a (SCOL) estudiante que abandona los estudios; ~**per** n cuentagotas m inv; ~**pings** npl excremento

drought |draut| n sequía

drove |drəuv| pt of **drive**

drown |draun| vt ahogar ♦ vi ahogarse

drowsy |'drauzɪ| adj soñoliento; **to be ~** tener sueño

drug |drʌg| n medicamento; (narcotic) droga ♦ vt drogar; **to be on ~s** drogarse; ~ **addict** n drogadicto/a; ~**gist** (US) n farmacéutico; ~**store** (US) n farmacia

drum |drʌm| n tambor m; (for oil, petrol) bidón m; ~**s** npl batería; ~**mer** n tambor m

drunk |drʌŋk| pp of **drink** ♦ adj borracho ♦ n (also: ~**ard**) borracho/a; ~**en** adj borracho; (laughter, party) de borrachos

dry |draɪ| adj seco; (day) sin lluvia; (climate) árido, seco ♦ vt secar; (tears) enjugarse ♦ vi secarse; ~ **up** vi (river) secarse; ~~**cleaner's** n tintorería; ~~**cleaning** n lavado en seco; ~~**er** n (for hair) secador m; (US: for clothes) secadora; ~ **rot** n putrefacción f fungoide

DSS n abbr = Department of Social Security

DTP n abbr (= desk-top publishing) autoedición f

dual |'djuəl| adj doble; ~ **carriageway** (BRIT) n carretera de

doble calzada; ~**purpose** adj de doble uso

dubbed |dʌbd| adj (CINEMA) doblado

dubious |'dju:bɪəs| adj indeciso, (reputation, company) sospechoso

duchess |'dʌtʃɪs| n duquesa

duck |dʌk| n pato ♦ vi agacharse; ~**ling** n patito

duct |dʌkt| n conducto, canal m

dud |dʌd| n (object, tool) engaño, engañifa ♦ adj: ~ **cheque** (BRIT) cheque m sin fondos

due |dju:| adj (owed): **he is ~ £10** se le deben 10 libras; (expected: event): **the meeting is ~ on Wednesday** la reunión tendrá lugar el miércoles; (: arrival) **the train is ~ at 8am** el tren tiene su llegada para las 8; (proper) debido ♦ n: **to give sb his** (or **her**) ~ ser justo con alguien ♦ adv: ~ **north** derecho al norte; ~**s** npl (for club, union) cuota; (in harbour) derechos mpl; **in ~ course** a su debido tiempo; ~ **to** debido a; **to be ~ to** deberse a

duet |dju:'et| n dúo

duffel bag |'dʌfəl| n bolsa de lona

duffel coat n trenca, abrigo de tres cuartos

dug |dʌg| pt, pp of **dig**

duke |dju:k| n duque m

dull |dʌl| adj (light) débil; (stupid) torpe; (boring) pesado; (sound, pain) sordo; (weather, day) gris ♦ vt (pain, grief) aliviar; (mind, senses) entorpecer

duly |'dju:lɪ| adv debidamente; (on time) a su debido tiempo

dumb |dʌm| adj mudo; (pej: stupid) estúpido; ~**founded** |dʌm'faundɪd| adj pasmado

dummy |'dʌmɪ| n (tailor's ~) maniquí m; (mock-up) maqueta; (BRIT: for baby) chupete m ♦ adj falso, postizo

dump |dʌmp| n (also: rubbish ~) basurero, vertedero; (inf: place) cuchitril m ♦ vt (put down) dejar; (get rid of) deshacerse de; (COMPUT: data) transferir

dumpling ['dʌmplɪŋ] n bola de masa hervida

dumpy ['dʌmpi] adj regordete/a

dunce [dʌns] n zopenco

dung [dʌŋ] n estiércol m

dungarees [dʌŋgə'ri:z] npl mono

dungeon ['dʌndʒən] n calabozo

duplex ['dju:pleks] n dúplex m

duplicate n ['dju:plikət, vb 'dju:plikeit] n duplicado ♦ vt duplicar; (photocopy) fotocopiar; (repeat) repetir; **in ~** por duplicado

durable ['djuərəbl] adj duradero

duration [djuə'reɪʃən] n duración f

during ['djuərɪŋ] prep durante

dusk [dʌsk] n crepúsculo, anochecer m

dust [dʌst] n polvo ♦ vt quitar el polvo a, desempolvar; (cake etc): **to ~ with** espolvorear de; **~bin** (BRIT) n cubo de la basura (SP), balde m (AM); **~er** n paño, trapo; **~man** (BRIT irreg) n basurero; **~y** adj polvoriento

Dutch [dʌtʃ] adj holandés/esa ♦ n (LING) holandés m; **the ~** npl los holandeses; **to go ~** (inf) pagar cada uno lo suyo; **~man/woman** (irreg) n holandés/esa m/f

duty ['dju:tɪ] n deber m; (tax) derechos mpl de aduana; **on ~** de servicio; (at night etc) de guardia; **off ~** libre de servicio; **~-free** adj libre de impuestos

duvet ['du:veɪ] (BRIT) n edredón m

DVD n abbr (= digital versatile or video disc) DVD m

dwarf [dwɔ:f] (pl **dwarves**) n enano/a ♦ vt empequeñecer

dwell [dwel] (pt, pp **dwelt**) vi morar; **~ on** vt fus explayarse en

dwindle ['dwɪndl] vi disminuir

dye [daɪ] n tinte m ♦ vt teñir

dying ['daɪɪŋ] adj moribundo

dyke [daɪk] (BRIT) n dique m

dynamic [daɪ'næmɪk] adj dinámico

dynamite ['daɪnəmaɪt] n dinamita

dynamo ['daɪnəməu] n dínamo f

dynasty ['dɪnəstɪ] n dinastía

E, e

E [i:] n (MUS) mi m

each [i:tʃ] adj cada inv ♦ pron cada uno; **~ other** el uno al otro; **they hate ~ other** se odian (entre ellos or mutuamente); **they have 2 books ~** tienen 2 libros por persona

eager ['i:gə*] adj (keen) entusiasmado; **to be ~ to do sth** tener muchas ganas de hacer algo, impacientarse por hacer algo; **to be ~ for** tener muchas ganas de

eagle ['i:gl] n águila

ear [ɪə*] n oreja; oído; (of corn) espiga; **~ache** n dolor m de oídos; **~drum** n tímpano

earl [ə:l] n conde m

earlier ['ə:lɪə*] adj anterior ♦ adv antes

early ['ə:lɪ] adv temprano; (before time) con tiempo, con anticipación ♦ adj temprano; (settlers etc) primitivo; (death, departure) prematuro; (reply) pronto; **to have an ~ night** acostarse temprano; **in the ~** or **~ in the spring/19th century** a principios de primavera/del siglo diecinueve; **~ retirement** n jubilación f anticipada

earmark ['ɪəmɑ:k] vt: **to ~ (for)** reservar (para), destinar (a)

earn [ə:n] vt (salary) percibir; (interest) devengar; (praise) merecerse

earnest ['ə:nɪst] adj (wish) fervoroso; (person) serio, formal; **in ~** en serio

earnings ['ə:nɪŋz] npl (personal) sueldo, ingresos mpl; (company) ganancias fpl

ear: **~phones** npl auriculares mpl; **~ring** n pendiente m, arete m; **~shot** n: **within ~shot** al alcance del oído

earth [ə:θ] n tierra; (BRIT: ELEC) cable m de toma de tierra ♦ vt (BRIT: ELEC) conectar a tierra; **~enware** n loza (de barro); **~quake** n terremoto; **~y** adj (fig: vulgar) grosero

ease [iːz] n facilidad f; (comfort) comodidad f ♦ vt (lessen: problem) mitigar; (: pain) aliviar; (: tension) reducir; **to ~ sth in/out** meter/sacar algo con cuidado; **at ~!** (MIL) ¡descansen!; **~ off** or **up** vi (wind, rain) amainar; (slow down) aflojar la marcha

easel ['iːzl] n caballete m

easily ['iːzɪlɪ] adv fácilmente

east [iːst] n este m ♦ adj del este, oriental; (wind) este ♦ adv al este, hacia el este; **the E~** el Oriente; (POL) los países del Este

Easter ['iːstə*] n Pascua (de Resurrección); **~ egg** n huevo de Pascua

east: ~erly ['iːstəlɪ] adj (to the east) al este; (from the east) del este; **~ern** ['iːstən] adj del este, oriental; (oriental) oriental; **~ward(s)** ['iːstwəd(z)] adv hacia el este

easy ['iːzɪ] adj fácil; (simple) sencillo; (comfortable) holgado, cómodo; (relaxed) tranquilo ♦ adv: **to take it** or **things ~** (not worry) tomarlo con calma; (rest) descansar; **~ chair** n sillón m; **~-going** adj acomodadizo

eat [iːt] (pt **ate**, pp **eaten**) vt comer; **~ away** at vt fus corroer; mermar; **~ into** vt fus corroer; (savings) mermar

eaves [iːvz] npl alero

eavesdrop ['iːvzdrɔp] vi: **to ~ (on)** escuchar a escondidas

ebb [eb] n reflujo ♦ vi bajar; (fig: also: **~ away**) decaer

ebony ['ebənɪ] n ébano

EC n abbr (= European Community) CE f

ECB n abbr (= European Central Bank) BCE m

eccentric [ɪk'sentrɪk] adj, n excéntrico/a m/f

echo ['ekəʊ] (pl **~es**) n eco m ♦ vt (sound) repetir ♦ vi resonar, hacer eco

éclair [ɪ'kleə*] n pastelillo relleno de crema y con chocolate por encima

eclipse [ɪ'klɪps] n eclipse m

ecology [ɪ'kɔlədʒɪ] n ecología

e-commerce n abbr (= electronic

commerce) comercio electrónico

economic [iːkə'nɔmɪk] adj económico; (business etc) rentable; **~al** adj económico; **~s** n (SCOL) economía ♦ npl (of project etc) rentabilidad f

economize [ɪ'kɔnəmaɪz] vi economizar, ahorrar

economy [ɪ'kɔnəmɪ] n economía; **~ class** n (AVIAT) clase f económica; **~ size** n tamaño económico

ecstasy ['ekstəsɪ] n éxtasis m inv; (drug) éxtasis m inv; **ecstatic** [eks'tætɪk] adj extático

ECU ['eɪkjuː] n (= European Currency Unit) ECU m

Ecuador ['ekwədɔː*] n Ecuador m; **~ian** adj, n ecuatoriano/a m/f

eczema ['eksɪmə] n eczema m

edge [edʒ] n (of knife) filo; (of object) borde m; (of lake) orilla ♦ vt (SEWING) ribetear; on **~** (fig) = **edgy**; **to ~ away from** alejarse poco a poco de; **~ways** adv: **he couldn't get a word in ~ways** no pudo meter ni baza

edgy ['edʒɪ] adj nervioso, inquieto

edible ['edɪbl] adj comestible

Edinburgh ['edɪnbərə] n Edimburgo

edit ['edɪt] vt (be editor of) dirigir; (text, report) corregir, preparar; **~ion** [ɪ'dɪʃən] n edición f; **~or** n (of newspaper) director/a m/f; (of column): **foreign/political ~or** encargado de la sección de extranjero/política; (of book) redactor(a) m/f; **~orial** [-'tɔːrɪəl] adj editorial ♦ n editorial m

educate ['edjʊkeɪt] vt (gen) educar; (instruct) instruir

education [edjʊ'keɪʃən] n educación f; (schooling) enseñanza; (SCOL) pedagogía; **~al** adj (policy etc) educacional; (experience) docente; (toy) educativo

EEC n abbr (= European Economic Community) CEE f

eel [iːl] n anguila

eerie ['ɪərɪ] adj misterioso.

effect [ɪ'fekt] n efecto ♦ vt efectuar, llevar a cabo; **to take ~** (law) entrar en vigor or vigencia; (drug) surtir efecto; **in ~** en realidad; **~ive** adj eficaz; (actual) verdadero; **~ively** adv eficazmente; (in reality) efectivamente; **~iveness** n eficacia

effeminate [ɪ'femɪnɪt] adj afeminado

efficiency [ɪ'fɪʃənsɪ] n eficiencia; rendimiento

efficient [ɪ'fɪʃənt] adj eficiente; (machine) de buen rendimiento

effort ['efət] n esfuerzo; **~less** adj sin ningún esfuerzo; (style) natural

effusive [ɪ'fju:sɪv] adj efusivo

e.g. adv abbr (= exempli gratia) p. ej.

egg [eɡ] n huevo; **hard-boiled/soft-boiled ~** huevo duro/pasado por agua; **~ on** vt incitar; **~cup** n huevera; **~ plant** (esp US) n berenjena; **~shell** n cáscara de huevo

ego ['i:ɡəʊ] n ego; **~tism** n egoísmo; **~tist** n egoísta m/f

Egypt ['i:dʒɪpt] n Egipto; **~ian** [ɪ'dʒɪpʃən] adj, n egipcio/a m/f

eiderdown ['aɪdədaʊn] n edredón m

eight [eɪt] num ocho; **~een** num dieciocho; **eighth** [eɪtθ] num octavo; **~y** num ochenta

Eire ['eərə] n Eire m

either ['aɪðə*] adj cualquiera de los dos; (both, each) cada ♦ pron: **~ (of them)** cualquiera (de los dos) ♦ adv tampoco; **on ~ side** en ambos lados; **I don't like ~** no me gusta ninguno/a de los/las dos; **no, I don't ~** no, yo tampoco ♦ conj: **~ yes or no** o sí o no

eject [ɪ'dʒekt] vt echar, expulsar; (tenant) desahuciar; **~or seat** n asiento proyectable

elaborate [adj ɪ'læbərɪt, vb ɪ'læbəreɪt] adj (complex) complejo ♦ vt (expand) ampliar; (refine) refinar ♦ vi explicar con más detalles

elastic [ɪ'læstɪk] n elástico ♦ adj elástico; (fig) flexible; **~ band** (BRIT) n gomita

elated [ɪ'leɪtɪd] adj: **to be ~** regocijarse

elbow ['elbəʊ] n codo

elder ['eldə*] adj mayor ♦ n (tree) saúco; (person) mayor; **~ly** adj de edad, mayor ♦ npl: **the ~ly** los mayores

eldest ['eldɪst] adj, n el/la mayor

elect [ɪ'lekt] vt elegir ♦ adj: **the president ~** el presidente electo; **to ~ to do** optar por hacer; **~ion** [ɪ'lekʃən] n elección f; **~ioneering** [ɪlekʃə'nɪərɪŋ] n campaña electoral; **~or** n elector(a) m/f; **~oral** adj electoral; **~orate** n electorado

electric [ɪ'lektrɪk] adj eléctrico; **~al** adj eléctrico; **~ blanket** n manta eléctrica; **~ fire** n estufa eléctrica; **~ian** [ɪlek'trɪʃən] n electricista m/f; **~ity** [ɪlek'trɪsɪtɪ] n electricidad f; **electrify** [ɪ'lektrɪfaɪ] vt (RAIL) electrificar; (fig: audience) electrizar

electronic [ɪlek'trɒnɪk] adj electrónico; **~ mail** n correo electrónico; **~s** n electrónica

elegant ['elɪɡənt] adj elegante

element ['elɪmənt] n elemento; (of kettle etc) resistencia; **~ary** [-'mentərɪ] adj elemental; (primitive) rudimentario; (school) primario

elephant ['elɪfənt] n elefante m

elevation [elɪ'veɪʃən] n elevación f; (height) altura

elevator ['elɪveɪtə*] n (US) ascensor m; (in warehouse etc) montacargas m inv

eleven [ɪ'levn] num once; **~ses** (BRIT) npl café m de las once; **~th** num undécimo

elicit [ɪ'lɪsɪt] vt: **to ~ (from)** sacar (de)

eligible ['elɪdʒəbl] adj: **an ~ young man/woman** un buen partido; **to be ~ for sth** llenar los requisitos para algo

elm [elm] n olmo

elongated ['i:lɒŋɡeɪtɪd] adj alargado

elope [ɪ'ləʊp] vi fugarse (para casarse)

eloquent ['eləkwənt] adj elocuente

else [els] adv: **something ~** otra cosa; **somewhere ~** en otra parte; **everywhere ~** en todas partes menos aquí; **where ~?** ¿dónde más?, ¿en qué

otra parte?; **there was little ~ to do**
apenas quedaba otra cosa que hacer;
nobody ~ spoke no habló nadie más;
~where adv (be) en otra parte; (go) a
otra parte

elude [ɪ'luːd] vt (subj: idea etc)
escaparse a; (capture) esquivar

elusive [ɪ'luːsɪv] adj esquivo; (quality)
difícil de encontrar

emaciated [ɪ'meɪsɪeɪtɪd] adj
demacrado

E-mail, e-mail ['iːmeɪl] n abbr
(= electronic mail) correo electrónico,
e-mail m

emancipate [ɪ'mænsɪpeɪt] vt
emancipar

embankment [ɪm'bæŋkmənt] n
terraplén m

embark [ɪm'bɑːk] vi embarcarse ♦ vt
embarcar; **to ~ on** (journey)
emprender; (course of action) lanzarse
a; **~ation** [embɑː'keɪʃən] n (people)
embarco; (goods) embarque m

embarrass [ɪm'bærəs] vt avergonzar;
(government etc) dejar en mal lugar;
~ed adj (laugh, silence) embarazoso;
~ing adj (situation) violento; (question)
embarazoso; **~ment** n (shame)
vergüenza; (problem): **to be an
~ment for sb** poner en un aprieto a
uno

embassy ['embəsɪ] n embajada

embedded [ɪm'bedɪd] adj (object)
empotrado; (thorn etc) clavado

embellish [ɪm'belɪʃ] vt embellecer;
(story) adornar

embers ['embəz] npl rescoldo, ascua

embezzle [ɪm'bezl] vt desfalcar,
malversar

embitter [ɪm'bɪtə*] vt (fig: sour)
amargar

embody [ɪm'bɒdɪ] vt (spirit) encarnar;
(include) incorporar

embossed [ɪm'bɒst] adj realzado

embrace [ɪm'breɪs] vt abrazar, dar un
abrazo a; (include) abarcar ♦ vi
abrazarse ♦ n abrazo

embroider [ɪm'brɔɪdə*] vt bordar; **~y**
n bordado

embryo ['embrɪəu] n embrión m

emerald ['emərəld] n esmeralda

emerge [ɪ'mɜːdʒ] vi salir; (arise) surgir

emergency [ɪ'mɜːdʒənsɪ] n crisis f inv;
in an ~ en caso de urgencia; **state of
~** estado de emergencia; **~ cord** (US) n
timbre m de alarma; **~ exit** n salida de
emergencia; **~ landing** n aterrizaje m
forzoso; **~ services** npl (fire, police,
ambulance) servicios mpl de urgencia or
emergencia

emery board ['emərɪ-] n lima de uñas

emigrate ['emɪɡreɪt] vi emigrar

emissions [ɪ'mɪʃənz] npl emisión f

emit [ɪ'mɪt] vt emitir; (smoke) arrojar;
(smell) despedir; (sound) producir

emotion [ɪ'məuʃən] n emoción f; **~al**
adj (needs) emocional; (person)
sentimental; (scene) conmovedor(a),
emocionante; (speech) emocionado

emperor ['empərə*] n emperador m

emphasis ['emfəsɪs] (pl **-ses**) n énfasis
m inv

emphasize ['emfəsaɪz] vt (word, point)
subrayar, recalcar; (feature) hacer
resaltar

emphatic [em'fætɪk] adj (reply)
categórico; (person) insistente

empire ['empaɪə*] n (also fig) imperio

employ [ɪm'plɔɪ] vt emplear; **~ee** [-'iː]
n empleado/a; **~er** n patrón/ona m/f;
empresario; **~ment** n (work) trabajo;
~ment agency n agencia de
colocaciones

empower [ɪm'pauə*] vt: **to ~ sb to
do sth** autorizar a uno para hacer algo

empress ['emprɪs] n emperatriz f

emptiness ['emptɪnɪs] n vacío; (of life
etc) vaciedad f

empty ['emptɪ] adj vacío; (place)
desierto; (house) desocupado; (threat)
vano ♦ vt vaciar; (place) dejar vacío ♦ vi
vaciarse; (house etc) quedar
desocupado; **~-handed** adj con las
manos vacías

EMU n abbr (= European Monetary Union) UME f

emulate ['emjuleɪt] vt emular

emulsion [ɪ'mʌlʃən] n emulsión f; (also: ~ paint) pintura emulsión

enable [ɪ'neɪbl] vt: **to ~ sb to do sth** permitir a uno hacer algo

enamel [ɪ'næməl] n esmalte m; (also: ~ paint) pintura esmaltada

enchant [ɪn'tʃɑːnt] vt encantar; **~ing** adj encantador(a)

encl. abbr (= enclosed) adj

enclose [ɪn'kləʊz] vt (land) cercar; (letter etc) adjuntar; **please find ~d** le mandamos adjunto

enclosure [ɪn'kləʊʒə*] n cercado, recinto

encompass [ɪn'kʌmpəs] vt abarcar

encore [ɔŋ'kɔː*] excl ¡otra!, ¡bis! ♦ n bis m

encounter [ɪn'kaʊntə*] n encuentro ♦ vt encontrar, encontrarse con; (difficulty) tropezar con

encourage [ɪn'kʌrɪdʒ] vt alentar, animar; (activity) fomentar; (growth) estimular; **~ment** n estímulo; (of industry) fomento

encroach [ɪn'krəʊtʃ] vi: **to ~ (up)on** invadir; (rights) usurpar; (time) adueñarse de

encyclop(a)edia [ɛnsaɪkləʊ'piːdɪə] n enciclopedia

end [end] n (gen, also aim) fin m; (of table) extremo; (of street) final m; (SPORT) lado ♦ vt terminar, acabar; (also: bring to an ~, put an ~ to) acabar con ♦ vi terminar, acabar; **in the ~** al fin; **on ~** (object) de punta, de cabeza; **to stand on ~** (hair) erizarse; **for hours on ~** hora tras hora; **~ up** vi: **to ~ up in** terminar en; (place) ir a parar en

endanger [ɪn'deɪndʒə*] vt poner en peligro; **an ~ed species** una especie en peligro de extinción

endearing [ɪn'dɪərɪŋ] adj simpático, atractivo

endeavour [ɪn'devə*] (US **endeavor**) n esfuerzo; (attempt) tentativa ♦ vi: **to ~ to do** esforzarse por hacer; (try) procurar hacer

ending ['endɪŋ] n (of book) desenlace m; (LING) terminación f

endive ['endaɪv] n (chicory) endibia; (curly) escarola

endless ['endlɪs] adj interminable, inacabable

endorse [ɪn'dɔːs] vt (cheque) endosar; (approve) aprobar; **~ment** n (on driving licence) nota de inhabilitación

endure [ɪn'djʊə*] vt (bear) aguantar, soportar ♦ vi (last) durar

enemy ['enəmɪ] adj, n enemigo/a m/f

energetic [enə'dʒetɪk] adj enérgico

energy ['enədʒɪ] n energía

enforce [ɪn'fɔːs] vt (LAW) hacer cumplir

engage [ɪn'geɪdʒ] vt (attention) llamar; (interest) ocupar; (in conversation) abordar; (AUT) contratar; (AUT): **to ~ the clutch** embragar ♦ vi (TECH) engranar; **to ~ in** dedicarse a, ocuparse en; **~d** adj (betrothed) prometido; (BRIT: busy, in use) ocupado; (betrothed) prometido; **to get ~d** prometerse; **~d tone** (BRIT) n (TEL) señal f de comunicando; **~ment** n (appointment) compromiso, cita; (booking) contratación f; (to marry) compromiso; (period) noviazgo; **~ment ring** n anillo de prometida

engaging [ɪn'geɪdʒɪŋ] adj atractivo

engine ['endʒɪn] n (AUT) motor m; (RAIL) locomotora; **~ driver** n (RAIL) maquinista m/f

engineer [endʒɪ'nɪə*] n ingeniero, (BRIT: for repairs) mecánico; (on ship, US: RAIL) maquinista m/f; **~ing** n ingeniería

England ['ɪŋglənd] n Inglaterra

English ['ɪŋglɪʃ] adj inglés/esa ♦ n (LING) inglés m; **the ~** npl los ingleses mpl; **the ~ Channel** n (el Canal de) la Mancha; **~man/woman** (irreg) n inglés/esa m/f

engraving [ɪn'greɪvɪŋ] n grabado

engrossed [ɪn'grəust] adj: ~ **in** absorto en

engulf [ɪn'gʌlf] vt (subj: water) sumergir, hundir; (: fire) prender; (: fear) apoderarse de

enhance [ɪn'hɑːns] vt (gen) aumentar; (beauty) realzar

enjoy [ɪn'dʒɔɪ] vt (health, fortune) disfrutar de, gozar de; (like) gustarle a uno; **to ~ o.s.** divertirse; **~able** adj agradable; (amusing) divertido; **~ment** n (joy) placer m; (activity) diversión f

enlarge [ɪn'lɑːdʒ] vt aumentar; (broaden) extender; (PHOT) ampliar ♦ vi: **to ~ on** (subject) tratar con más detalles; **~ment** n (PHOT) ampliación f

enlighten [ɪn'laɪtn] vt (inform) informar; **~ed** adj comprensivo; **the E~ment** n (HISTORY) la Ilustración, ≈ el Siglo de las Luces

enlist [ɪn'lɪst] vt alistar; (support) conseguir ♦ vi alistarse

enmity ['enmɪtɪ] n enemistad f

enormous [ɪ'nɔːməs] adj enorme

enough [ɪ'nʌf] adj: **~ time/books** bastante tiempo/bastantes libros ♦ pron bastante(s) ♦ adv: **big ~** bastante grande; **he has not worked ~** no ha trabajado bastante; **have you got ~?** ¿tiene usted bastante(s)?; **~ to eat** (lo) suficiente or (lo) bastante para comer; **~!** ¡basta ya!; **that's ~, thanks** con eso basta, gracias; **I've had ~ of him** estoy harto de él; **... which, funnily or oddly ~ ...** ... lo que, por extraño que parezca ...

enquire [ɪn'kwaɪə*] vt, vi = **inquire**

enrage [ɪn'reɪdʒ] vt enfurecer

enrol [ɪn'rəul] (US **enroll**) vt (members) inscribir; (SCOL) matricular ♦ vi inscribirse; matricularse; **~ment** (US **enrollment**) n inscripción f; matriculación f

en route [ɒn'ruːt] adv durante el viaje

en suite [ɒn'swiːt] adj: **with ~ bathroom** con baño

ensure [ɪn'ʃuə*] vt asegurar

entail [ɪn'teɪl] vt suponer

entangled [ɪn'tæŋgld] adj: **to become ~ (in)** quedarse enredado (en) or enmarañado (en)

enter ['entə*] vt (room) entrar en; (club) hacerse socio de; (army) alistarse en; (sb for a competition) inscribir; (write down) anotar, apuntar; (COMPUT) meter ♦ vi entrar; **~ for** vt fus presentarse para; **~ into** vt fus (discussion etc) entablar; (agreement) llegar a, firmar

enterprise ['entəpraɪz] n empresa; (spirit) iniciativa; **free ~** la libre empresa; **private ~** la iniciativa privada; **enterprising** adj emprendedor(a)

entertain [entə'teɪn] vt (amuse) divertir; (invite: guest) invitar a (casa); (idea) abrigar; **~er** n artista m/f; **~ing** adj divertido, entretenido; **~ment** n (amusement) diversión f; (show) espectáculo

enthralled [ɪn'θrɔːld] adj encantado

enthusiasm [ɪn'θuːzɪæzəm] n entusiasmo

enthusiast [ɪn'θuːzɪæst] n entusiasta m/f; **~ic** [-'æstɪk] adj entusiasta; **to be ~ic about** entusiasmarse por

entire [ɪn'taɪə*] adj entero; **~ly** adv totalmente; **~ty** [ɪn'taɪərətɪ] n: **in its ~ty** en su totalidad

entitle [ɪn'taɪtl] vt: **to ~ sb to sth** dar a uno derecho a algo; **~d** adj (book) titulado; **to be ~d to do** tener derecho a hacer

entrance [n 'entrəns, vb ɪn'trɑːns] n entrada ♦ vt encantar, hechizar; **to gain ~** (university etc) ingresar en; **~ examination** n examen m de ingreso; **~ fee** n cuota; **~ ramp** (US) n (AUT) rampa de acceso

entrant ['entrənt] n (in race, competition) participante m/f; (in examination) candidato/a

entrenched [en'trentʃd] adj inamovible

entrepreneur [ɔntrəprə'nə:] *n* empresario

entrust [ɪn'trʌst] *vt:* **to ~ sth to sb** confiar algo a uno

entry ['entrɪ] *n* entrada; *(in competition)* participación *f*; *(in register)* apunte *m*; *(in account)* partida; *(in reference book)* artículo; **"no ~"** "prohibido el paso"; *(AUT)* "dirección prohibida"; **~ form** *n* hoja de inscripción; **~ phone** *n* portero automático

envelop [ɪn'veləp] *vt* envolver

envelope ['envələup] *n* sobre *m*

envious ['envɪəs] *adj* envidioso; *(look)* de envidia

environment [ɪn'vaɪərnmənt] *n* *(surroundings)* entorno; *(natural world):* **the ~** el medio ambiente; **~al** [-'mentl] *adj* ambiental; medioambiental; **~friendly** *adj* no perjudicial para el medio ambiente

envisage [ɪn'vɪzɪdʒ] *vt* prever

envoy ['envɔɪ] *n* enviado

envy ['envɪ] *n* envidia ♦ *vt* tener envidia a; **to ~ sb sth** envidiar algo a uno

epic ['epɪk] *n* épica ♦ *adj* épico

epidemic [epɪ'demɪk] *n* epidemia

epilepsy ['epɪlepsɪ] *n* epilepsia

episode ['epɪsəud] *n* episodio

epitomize [ɪ'pɪtəmaɪz] *vt* epitomar, resumir

equal ['i:kwl] *adj* igual; *(treatment)* equitativo ♦ *n* igual *m/f* ♦ *vt* ser igual a; *(fig)* igualar; **to be ~ to** *(task)* estar a la altura de; **~ity** [i:'kwɔlɪtɪ] *n* igualdad *f*; **~ize** *vi* *(SPORT)* empatar; **~ly** *adv* igualmente; *(share etc)* a partes iguales

equate [ɪ'kweɪt] *vt:* **to ~ sth with** equiparar algo con; **equation** [ɪ'kweɪʒən] *n* *(MATH)* ecuación *f*

equator [ɪ'kweɪtə*] *n* ecuador *m*

equilibrium [i:kwɪ'lɪbrɪəm] *n* equilibrio

equip [ɪ'kwɪp] *vt* equipar; *(person)* proveer; **to be well ~ped** estar bien

equipado; **~ment** *n* equipo; *(tools)* avíos *mpl*

equities ['ekwɪtɪz] *(BRIT)* *npl* *(COMM)* derechos *mpl* sobre *or* en el activo

equivalent [ɪ'kwɪvələnt] *adj:* **~ (to)** equivalente (a) ♦ *n* equivalente *m*

era ['ɪərə] *n* era, época

eradicate [ɪ'rædɪkeɪt] *vt* erradicar

erase [ɪ'reɪz] *vt* borrar; **~r** *n* goma de borrar

erect [ɪ'rekt] *adj* erguido ♦ *vt* erigir, levantar; *(assemble)* montar; **~ion** [-ʃən] *n* construcción *f*; *(assembly)* montaje *m*; *(PHYSIOL)* erección *f*

ERM *n abbr* (= *Exchange Rate Mechanism*) tipo de cambio europeo

erode [ɪ'rəud] *vt* *(GEO)* erosionar; *(metal)* corroer, desgastar; *(fig)* desgastar

erotic [ɪ'rɔtɪk] *adj* erótico

errand ['ernd] *n* recado *(SP)*, mandado *(AM)*

erratic [ɪ'rætɪk] *adj* desigual, poco uniforme

error ['erə*] *n* error *m*, equivocación *f*

erupt [ɪ'rʌpt] *vi* entrar en erupción; *(fig)* estallar; **~ion** [ɪ'rʌpʃən] *n* erupción *f*; *(of war)* estallido

escalate ['eskəleɪt] *vi* extenderse, intensificarse

escalator ['eskəleɪtə*] *n* escalera móvil

escapade [eskə'peɪd] *n* travesura

escape [ɪ'skeɪp] *n* fuga ♦ *vi* escapar; *(flee)* huir, evadirse; *(leak)* fugarse ♦ *vt* *(responsibility etc)* evitar, eludir; *(consequences)* escapar a; *(elude)*: **his name ~s me** no me sale su nombre; **to ~ from** *(place)* escaparse de; *(person)* escaparse a

escort [*n* 'eskɔ:t, *vb* ɪ'skɔ:t] *n* acompañante *m/f*; *(MIL)* escolta ♦ *vt* acompañar

Eskimo ['eskɪməu] *n* esquimal *m/f*

especially [ɪ'speʃlɪ] *adv* sobre todo; *(particularly)* en particular, especialmente

espionage ['espɪənɑ:ʒ] *n* espionaje *m*

esplanade [ɛspləˈneɪd] n (by sea) paseo marítimo

Esquire [ɪˈskwaɪə] (abbr **Esq.**) n: **J. Brown, ~ Sr.** D. J. Brown

essay [ˈɛseɪ] n (LITERATURE) ensayo; (SCOL: short) redacción f; (: long) trabajo

essence [ˈɛsns] n esencia

essential [ɪˈsɛnʃl] adj (necessary) imprescindible; (basic) esencial; **~s** npl lo imprescindible, lo esencial; **~ly** adv esencialmente

establish [ɪˈstæblɪʃ] vt establecer; (prove) demostrar; (relations) entablar; (reputation) ganarse; **~ed** adj (business) conocido; (practice) arraigado; **~ment** n establecimiento; **the E~ment** n la clase dirigente

estate [ɪˈsteɪt] n (land) finca, hacienda; (inheritance) herencia; (BRIT: also: housing ~) urbanización f; **~ agent** (BRIT) n agente m/f inmobiliario/a; **~ car** (BRIT) n furgoneta

esteem [ɪˈstiːm] n: **to hold sb in high ~** estimar en mucho a uno

esthetic [ɪsˈθɛtɪk] (US) adj = **aesthetic**

estimate [n ˈɛstɪmət, vb ˈɛstɪmeɪt] n estimación f, apreciación f; (assessment) tasa, cálculo; (COMM) presupuesto ♦ vt estimar, tasar; calcular; **estimation** [-ˈmeɪʃən] n opinión f, juicio; cálculo

estranged [ɪˈstreɪndʒd] adj separado

estuary [ˈɛstjuərɪ] n estuario, ría

etc abbr (= et cetera) etc

eternal [ɪˈtəːnl] adj eterno

eternity [ɪˈtəːnɪtɪ] n eternidad f

ethical [ˈɛθɪkl] adj ético; **ethics** [ˈɛθɪks] n ética ♦ npl moralidad f

Ethiopia [iːθɪˈəupɪə] n Etiopía

ethnic [ˈɛθnɪk] adj étnico; **~ minority** n minoría étnica

ethos [ˈiːθɒs] n genio, carácter m

EU n abbr (= European Union) UE f

euro [ˈjuərəu] n euro

Eurocheque [ˈjuərəutʃɛk] n Eurocheque m

Euroland [ˈjuərəulænd] n zona (del)

euro

Europe [ˈjuərəp] n Europa; **~an** [-ˈpiːən] adj, n europeo/a m/f; **~an Community** n Comunidad f Europea; **~an Union** n Unión f Europea

evacuate [ɪˈvækjueɪt] vt (people) evacuar; (place) desocupar

evade [ɪˈveɪd] vt evadir, eludir

evaporate [ɪˈvæpəreɪt] vi evaporarse; (fig) desvanecerse; **~d milk** n leche f evaporada

evasion [ɪˈveɪʒən] n evasión f

eve [iːv] n: **on the ~ of** en vísperas de

even [ˈiːvn] adj (level) llano; (smooth) liso; (speed, temperature) uniforme; (number) par ♦ adv hasta, incluso; (introducing a comparison) aún, todavía; **~ if, ~ though** aunque + sub; **~ more** aún más; **~ so** aun así; **not ~** ni siquiera; **~ he was there** hasta él estuvo allí; **~ on Sundays** incluso los domingos; **to get ~ with sb** ajustar cuentas con uno

evening [ˈiːvnɪŋ] n tarde f; (late) noche f; **in the ~** por la tarde; **~ class** n clase f nocturna; **~ dress** n (no pl: formal clothes) traje m de etiqueta; (woman's) traje m de noche

event [ɪˈvɛnt] n suceso, acontecimiento; (SPORT) prueba; **in the ~ of** en caso de; **~ful** adj (life) activo; (day) ajetreado

eventual [ɪˈvɛntʃuəl] adj final; **~ity** [-ˈælɪtɪ] n eventualidad f; **~ly** adv (finally) finalmente; (in time) con el tiempo

ever [ˈɛvə*] adv (at any time) nunca, jamás; (at all times) siempre; (in question) **why ~ not?** ¿y por qué no?; **the best ~** lo nunca visto; **have you ~ seen it?** ¿lo ha visto usted alguna vez?; **better than ~** mejor que nunca; **~ since** adv desde entonces ♦ conj después de que; **~green** n árbol m de hoja perenne; **~lasting** adj eterno, perpetuo

KEYWORD

every ['ɛvrɪ] adj **1** (each) cada; **~ one of them** (persons) todos ellos/as; (objects) cada uno de ellos/as; **~ shop in the town was closed** todas las tiendas de la ciudad estaban cerradas **2** (all possible) todo/a; **I gave you ~ assistance** te di toda la ayuda posible; **I have ~ confidence in him** tiene toda mi confianza; **we wish you ~ success** te deseamos toda suerte de éxitos **3** (showing recurrence) todo/a; **~ day/ week** todos los días/todas las semanas; (usual) acostumbrado/a; **~ other car had been broken into** habían forzado uno de cada dos coches; **she visits me ~ other/third day** me visita cada dos/tres días; **~ now and then** de vez en cuando

every: ~body pron = **everyone; ~day** adj (daily) cotidiano, de todos los días; (usual) acostumbrado/a; **~one** pron todos/as, todo el mundo; **~thing** pron todo; **this shop sells ~thing** esta tienda vende de todo; **~where** adv: **I've been looking for you ~where** te he estado buscando por todas partes; **~where you go you meet ...** en todas partes encuentras ...

evict [ɪ'vɪkt] vt desahuciar; **~ion** [ɪ'vɪkʃən] n desahucio

evidence ['ɛvɪdəns] n (proof) prueba; (of witness) testimonio; (sign) indicios mpl; **to give ~** prestar declaración, dar testimonio

evident ['ɛvɪdənt] adj evidente, manifiesto; **~ly** adv por lo visto

evil ['iːvl] adj malo; (influence) funesto ♦ n mal m

evoke [ɪ'vəuk] vt evocar

evolution [iːvə'luːʃən] n evolución f

evolve [ɪ'vɒlv] vt desarrollar ♦ vi evolucionar, desarrollarse

ewe [juː] n oveja

ex- [ɛks] prefix ex

exact [ɪg'zækt] adj exacto; (person) meticuloso ♦ vt: **to ~ sth (from)** exigir algo (de); **~ing** adj exigente; (conditions) arduo; **~ly** adv exactamente; (indicating agreement) exacto

exaggerate [ɪg'zædʒəreɪt] vt, vi exagerar; **exaggeration** [-'reɪʃən] n exageración f

exalted [ɪg'zɔːltɪd] adj eminente

exam [ɪg'zæm] n abbr (SCOL) = **examination**

examination [ɪgzæmɪ'neɪʃən] n examen m; (MED) reconocimiento

examine [ɪg'zæmɪn] vt examinar; (inspect) inspeccionar, escudriñar; (MED) reconocer; **~r** n examinador(a) m/f

example [ɪg'zɑːmpl] n ejemplo; **for ~** por ejemplo

exasperate [ɪg'zɑːspəreɪt] vt exasperar, irritar; **exasperation** [-ʃən] n exasperación f, irritación f

excavate ['ɛkskəveɪt] vt excavar

exceed [ɪk'siːd] vt (amount) exceder; (number) pasar de; (speed limit) sobrepasar; (powers) excederse en; (hopes) superar; **~ingly** adv sumamente, sobremanera

excellent ['ɛksələnt] adj excelente

except [ɪk'sɛpt] prep (also: ~ **for, ~ing**) excepto, salvo ♦ vt exceptuar, excluir; **~ if/when** excepto si/cuando; **~ that** salvo que; **~ion** [ɪk'sɛpʃən] n excepción f; **to take ~ion to** ofenderse por; **~ional** [ɪk'sɛpʃənl] adj excepcional

excerpt ['ɛksɜːpt] n extracto

excess [ɪk'sɛs] n exceso; **~es** npl (of cruelty etc) atrocidades fpl; **~ baggage** n exceso de equipaje; **~ fare** n suplemento; **~ive** adj excesivo

exchange [ɪks'tʃeɪndʒ] n intercambio; (conversation) diálogo; (also: telephone ~) central f (telefónica) ♦ vt: **to ~ (for)** cambiar (por); **~ rate** n tipo de

cambio
exchequer [ɪks'tʃekə*] (BRIT) n: **the E~** la Hacienda del Fisco
excise ['eksaɪz] n impuestos mpl sobre el alcohol y el tabaco
excite [ɪk'saɪt] vt (stimulate) estimular; (arouse) excitar; **~d** adj: **to get ~d** emocionarse; **~ment** n (agitation) excitación f; (exhilaration) emoción f; **exciting** adj emocionante
exclaim [ɪk'skleɪm] vi exclamar; **exclamation** [eksklə'meɪʃən] n exclamación f; **exclamation mark** n punto de admiración
exclude [ɪk'sklu:d] vt excluir; exceptuar
exclusive [ɪk'sklu:sɪv] adj exclusivo; (club, district) selecto; **~ of tax** excluyendo impuestos; **~ly** adv únicamente
excruciating [ɪk'skru:ʃɪeɪtɪŋ] adj (pain) agudísimo, atroz; (noise, embarrassment) horrible
excursion [ɪk'skɜ:ʃən] n (tourist ~) excursión f
excuse [n ɪk'skju:s, vb ɪk'skju:z] n disculpa, excusa; (pretext) pretexto ♦ vt (justify) justificar; (forgive) disculpar, perdonar; **to ~ sb from doing sth** dispensar a uno de hacer algo; **~ me!** (attracting attention) ¡por favor!; (apologizing) ¡perdón!; **if you will ~ me** con su permiso
ex-directory ['eksdɪ'rektərɪ] (BRIT) adj que no consta en la guía
execute ['eksɪkju:t] vt (plan) realizar; (order) cumplir; (person) ajusticiar, ejecutar; **execution** [-'kju:ʃən] n realización f; cumplimiento; ejecución f
executive [ɪg'zekjʊtɪv] n (person, committee) ejecutivo; (POL: committee) poder m ejecutivo ♦ adj ejecutivo
exemplify [ɪg'zemplɪfaɪ] vt ejemplificar; (illustrate) ilustrar
exempt [ɪg'zempt] adj: **~ from** exento de ♦ vt: **to ~ sb from** eximir a uno de; **~ion** [-ʃən] n exención f

exercise ['eksəsaɪz] n ejercicio ♦ vt (patience) usar de; (right) valerse de; (dog) llevar de paseo; (mind) preocupar ♦ vi (also: **to take ~**) hacer ejercicio(s); **~ bike** n ciclostático ® m, bicicleta estática; **~ book** n cuaderno
exert [ɪg'zɜ:t] vt ejercer; **to ~ o.s.** esforzarse; **~ion** [-ʃən] n esfuerzo
exhale [eks'heɪl] vt despedir ♦ vi exhalar
exhaust [ɪg'zɔ:st] n (AUT: also: **~ pipe**) escape m; (: fumes) gases mpl de escape ♦ vt agotar; **~ed** adj agotado; **~ion** [ɪg'zɔ:stʃən] n agotamiento; **nervous ~ion** postración f nerviosa; **~ive** adj exhaustivo
exhibit [ɪg'zɪbɪt] n (ART) obra expuesta; (LAW) objeto expuesto ♦ vt (show: emotions) manifestar; (: courage, skill) demostrar; (paintings) exponer; **~ion** [eksɪ'bɪʃən] n exposición f; (of talent etc) demostración f
exhilarating [ɪg'zɪləreɪtɪŋ] adj estimulante, tónico
exile ['eksaɪl] n exilio; (person) exiliado/a ♦ vt desterrar, exiliar
exist [ɪg'zɪst] vi existir; (live) vivir; **~ence** n existencia; **~ing** adj existente, actual
exit ['eksɪt] n salida ♦ vi (THEATRE) hacer mutis; (COMPUT) salir (al sistema); **~ poll** n encuesta a la salida de los colegios electorales; **~ ramp** (US) n (AUT) vía de acceso
exodus ['eksədəs] n éxodo
exonerate [ɪg'zɒnəreɪt] vt: **to ~ from** exculpar de
exotic [ɪg'zɒtɪk] adj exótico
expand [ɪk'spænd] vt ampliar; (number) aumentar ♦ vi (population) aumentar; (trade etc) expandirse; (gas, metal) dilatarse
expanse [ɪk'spæns] n extensión f
expansion [ɪk'spænʃən] n (of population) aumento; (of trade) expansión f
expect [ɪk'spekt] vt esperar; (require)

contar con; *(suppose)* suponer ♦ *vi*: **to be ~ing** *(pregnant woman)* estar embarazada; **~ancy** *n (anticipation)* esperanza de; **life ~ancy** esperanza de vida; **~ant mother** *n* futura madre *f*; **~ation** [ɛkspek'teɪʃən] *n (hope)* esperanza; *(belief)* expectativa
expedient [ɪk'spi:dɪənt] *adj* conveniente, oportuno ♦ *n* recurso, expediente *m*
expedition [ɛkspə'dɪʃən] *n* expedición *f*
expel [ɪk'spɛl] *vt* arrojar; *(from place)* expulsar
expend [ɪk'spɛnd] *vt (money)* gastar; *(time, energy)* consumir; **~iture** *n* gastos *mpl*, desembolso; consumo
expense [ɪk'spɛns] *n* gasto, gastos *mpl*; *(high cost)* costa; **~s** *npl* (COMM) gastos *mpl*; **at the ~ of** a costa de; **~ account** *n* cuenta de gastos
expensive [ɪk'spɛnsɪv] *adj* caro, costoso
experience [ɪk'spɪərɪəns] *n* experiencia ♦ *vt* experimentar; *(suffer)* sufrir; **~d** *adj* experimentado
experiment [ɪk'spɛrɪmənt] *n* experimento ♦ *vi* hacer experimentos
expert ['ɛkspɜ:t] *adj* experto, perito ♦ *n* experto/a, perito/a; *(specialist)* especialista *m/f*; **~ise** [-'tiːz] *n* pericia
expire [ɪk'spaɪə*] *vi* caducar, vencer; **expiry** *n* vencimiento
explain [ɪk'spleɪn] *vt* explicar; **explanation** [ɛksplə'neɪʃən] *n* explicación *f*; **explanatory** [ɪk'splænətrɪ] *adj* explicativo; aclaratorio
explicit [ɪk'splɪsɪt] *adj* explícito
explode [ɪk'spləud] *vi* estallar, explotar; *(population)* crecer rápidamente; *(with anger)* reventar
exploit [*n* 'ɛksplɔɪt, *vb* ɪk'splɔɪt] *n* hazaña ♦ *vt* explotar; **~ation** [-'teɪʃən] *n* explotación *f*
exploratory [ɪk'splɔrətrɪ] *adj* de exploración; *(fig: talks)* exploratorio,

preliminar
explore [ɪk'splɔː*] *vt* explorar; *(fig)* examinar; investigar; **~r** *n* explorador/a *m/f*
explosion [ɪk'spləuʒən] *n (also fig)* explosión *f*; **explosive** [ɪks'pləusɪv] *adj, n* explosivo
exponent [ɪk'spəunənt] *n (of theory etc)* partidario/a; *(of skill etc)* exponente *m/f*
export [*vb* ɛk'spɔːt, *n* 'ɛkspɔːt] *vt* exportar ♦ *n (process)* exportación *f*; *(product)* producto de exportación ♦ *cpd* de exportación; **~er** *n* exportador *m*
expose [ɪk'spəuz] *vt* exponer; *(unmask)* desenmascarar; **~d** *adj* expuesto
exposure [ɪk'spəuʒə*] *n* exposición *f*; *(publicity)* publicidad *f*; *(PHOT: speed)* velocidad *f* de obturación; *(: shot)* fotografía *f*; **to die from ~** *(MED)* morir de frío; **~ meter** *n* fotómetro
express [ɪk'sprɛs] *adj (definite)* expreso, explícito; *(train)* rápido ♦ *vt* expresar; **~ion** [ɪk'sprɛʃən] *n* expresión *f*; *(of actor etc)* sentimiento; **~ly** *adv* expresamente; **~way** *(US)* *n (urban motorway)* autopista
exquisite [ɛk'skwɪzɪt] *adj* exquisito
extend [ɪk'stɛnd] *vt (visit, street)* prolongar; *(building)* ampliar; *(invitation)* ofrecer ♦ *vi (land)* extenderse; *(period of time)* prolongarse
extension [ɪk'stɛnʃən] *n* extensión *f*; *(building)* ampliación *f*; *(of time)* prolongación *f*; *(TEL: in private house)* línea derivada; *(: in office)* extensión *f*
extensive [ɪk'stɛnsɪv] *adj* extenso; *(damage)* importante; *(knowledge)* amplio; **~ly** *adv*: **he's travelled ~ly** ha viajado por muchos países
extent [ɪk'stɛnt] *n (breadth)* extensión *f*; *(scope)* alcance *m*; **to some ~** hasta cierto punto; **to the ~ of...** hasta el punto de...; **to such an ~ that...** hasta tal punto que...; **to what ~?**

¿hasta qué punto?

extenuating [ɪk'stɛnjueɪtɪŋ] adj:
~ **circumstances** circunstancias fpl
atenuantes

exterior [ɛk'stɪərɪə*] adj exterior,
externo ♦ n exterior m

external [ɛk'stɜːnl] adj externo

extinct [ɪk'stɪŋkt] adj (volcano)
extinguido; (race) extinto

extinguish [ɪk'stɪŋgwɪʃ] vt extinguir,
apagar; **~er** n extintor m

extort [ɪk'stɔːt] vt obtener por fuerza;
~ionate adj excesivo, exorbitante

extra ['ɛkstrə] adj adicional ♦ adv (in
addition) de más ♦ n (luxury, addition)
extra m; (CINEMA, THEATRE) extra m/f,
comparsa m/f

extra... ['ɛkstrə] prefix extra...

extract [vb ɪk'strækt, n 'ɛkstrækt] vt
sacar; (tooth) extraer; (money, promise)
obtener ♦ n extracto

extracurricular ['ɛkstrəkə'rɪkjulə*] adj
extraescolar, extra-académico

extradite ['ɛkstrədaɪt] vt extraditar

extra: **~marital** adj extramatrimonial;
~mural [ɛkstrə'mjuərl] adj
extraescolar; **~ordinary** [ɪk'strɔːdnrɪ]
adj extraordinario; (odd) raro

extravagance [ɪk'strævəgəns] n
derroche m, despilfarro; (thing bought)
extravagancia

extravagant [ɪk'strævəgənt] adj
(lavish: person) pródigo, (: gift)
(demasiado) caro; (wasteful)
despilfarrador(a)

extreme [ɪk'striːm] adj extremo,
extremado ♦ n extremo; **~ly** adv
sumamente, extremadamente

extricate ['ɛkstrɪkeɪt] vt: **to ~ sth/sb
from** librar algo/a uno de

extrovert ['ɛkstrəvɜːt] n extrovertido,-a

eye [aɪ] n ojo vt mirar de soslayo,
ojear; **to keep an ~ on** vigilar; **~bath**
n ojera; **~brow** n ceja; **~drops** npl
gotas fpl para los ojos, colirio; **~lash** n
pestaña; **~lid** n párpado; **~liner** n lápiz
m de ojos; **~-opener** n revelación f,

gran sorpresa; **~shadow** [n]
sombreador m de ojos; **~sight** n vista;
~sore n monstruosidad f; **~ witness**
n testigo m/f presencial

F, f

F [ɛf] n (MUS) fa m

F. abbr = **Fahrenheit**

fable ['feɪbl] n fábula

fabric ['fæbrɪk] n tejido, tela

fabulous ['fæbjuləs] adj fabuloso

façade [fə'sɑːd] n fachada

face [feɪs] n (ANAT) cara, rostro; (of
clock) esfera (SP), cara (AM); (of
mountain) cara, ladera; (of building)
fachada ♦ vt (direction) estar de cara a;
(situation) hacer frente a; (facts)
aceptar; **~ down** (person, card) boca
abajo; **to lose ~** desprestigiarse; **to
make or pull a ~** hacer muecas; **in
the ~ of** (difficulties etc) ante; **on the
~ of it** a primera vista; **~ to ~** cara a
cara; **~ up to** vt fus hacer frente a,
arrostrar; **~ cloth** (BRIT) n manopla;
~ cream n crema (de belleza); **~ lift** n
estirado facial; (of building) renovación
f; **~ powder** n polvos mpl; **~-saving**
adj para salvar las apariencias; **~ value**
n (of stamp) valor m nominal; **to take
sth at ~ value** (fig) tomar algo en
sentido literal

facilities [fə'sɪlɪtɪz] npl (buildings)
instalaciones fpl; (equipment) servicios
mpl; **credit ~** facilidades fpl de crédito

facing ['feɪsɪŋ] prep frente a

facsimile [fæk'sɪmɪlɪ] n (replica)
facsímil(e) m; (machine) telefax m; (fax)
fax m

fact [fækt] n hecho; **in ~** en realidad

factor ['fæktə*] n factor m

factory ['fæktərɪ] n fábrica

factual ['fæktjuəl] adj basado en los
hechos

faculty ['fækltɪ] n facultad f; (US:
teaching staff) personal m docente

fad [fæd] *n* novedad *f*, moda

fade [feɪd] *vi* desteñirse; (*sound, smile*) desvanecerse; (*light*) apagarse; (*flower*) marchitarse; (*hope, memory*) perderse

fag [fæg] (*BRIT: inf*) *n* (*cigarette*) pitillo (*SP*), cigarro

fail [feɪl] *vt* (*candidate*) suspender; (*exam*) no aprobar (*SP*), reprobar (*AM*); (*subj: memory*) fallar a ♦ *vi* suspender; (*be unsuccessful*) fracasar; (*strength, brakes*) fallar; (*light*) acabarse; **to ~ to do sth** (*neglect*) dejar de hacer algo; (*be unable*) no poder hacer algo; **without ~** sin falta; **~ing** *n* falta, defecto ♦ *prep* a falta de; **~ure** ['feɪljə*] *n* fracaso; (*person*) fracasado/a; (*mechanical etc*) fallo

faint [feɪnt] *adj* débil; (*recollection*) vago; (*mark*) apenas visible ♦ *n* desmayo ♦ *vi* desmayarse; **to feel ~** estar mareado, marearse

fair [fɛə*] *adj* justo; (*hair, person*) rubio; (*weather*) bueno; (*good enough*) regular; (*considerable*) considerable ♦ *adv* (*play*) limpio ♦ *n* feria; (*BRIT: funfair*) parque *m* de atracciones; **~ly** *adv* (*justly*) con justicia; (*quite*) bastante; **~ness** *n* justicia, imparcialidad *f*; **~ play** *n* juego limpio

fairy ['fɛərɪ] *n* hada; **~ tale** *n* cuento de hadas

faith [feɪθ] *n* fe *f*; (*trust*) confianza; (*sect*) religión *f*; **~ful** *adj* (*dsur: troops etc*) leal; (*spouse*) fiel; (*account*) exacto; **~fully** *adv* fielmente; **yours ~fully** (*BRIT: in letters*) le saluda atentamente

fake [feɪk] *n* (*painting etc*) falsificación *f*; (*person*) impostor(a) *m/f* ♦ *adj* falso ♦ *vt* fingir; (*painting etc*) falsificar

falcon ['fɔːlkən] *n* halcón *m*

fall [fɔːl] (*pt* **fell**, *pp* **fallen**) *n* caída; (*in price etc*) descenso; (*US*) otoño ♦ *vi* caer(se); (*price*) bajar, descender; **~s** *npl* (*water~*) cascada, salto de agua; **to ~ flat** (*on one's face*) caerse (boca abajo); (*plan*) fracasar; (*joke, story*) no hacer gracia; **~ back** *vi* retroceder;

~ back on *vt fus* (*remedy etc*) recurrir a; **~ behind** *vi* quedarse atrás; **~ down** *vi* (*person*) caerse; (*building, hopes*) derrumbarse; **~ for** *vt fus* (*trick*) dejarse engañar por; (*person*) enamorarse de; **~ in** *vi* (*roof*) hundirse; (*MIL*) alinearse; **~ off** *vi* caerse; (*diminish*) disminuir; **~ out** *vi* (*friends etc*) reñir; (*hair, teeth*) caerse; **~ through** *vi* (*plan, project*) fracasar

fallacy ['fæləsɪ] *n* error *m*

fallen ['fɔːlən] *pp* of **fall**

fallout ['fɔːlaut] *n* lluvia radioactiva

fallow ['fæləu] *adj* en barbecho

false [fɔːls] *adj* falso; **under ~ pretences** con engaños; **~ alarm** *n* falsa alarma; **~ teeth** (*BRIT*) *npl* dentadura postiza

falter ['fɔːltə*] *vi* vacilar; (*engine*) fallar

fame [feɪm] *n* fama

familiar [fə'mɪlɪə*] *adj* conocido, familiar; (*tone*) de confianza; **to be ~ with** (*subject*) conocer (bien)

family ['fæmɪlɪ] *n* familia; **~ business** *n* negocio familiar; **~ doctor** *n* médico/a de cabecera

famine ['fæmɪn] *n* hambre *f*, hambruna

famished ['fæmɪʃt] *adj* hambriento

famous ['feɪməs] *adj* famoso, célebre; **~ly** *adv* (*get on*) estupendamente

fan [fæn] *n* abanico; (*ELEC*) ventilador *m*; (*of pop star etc*) fan *m/f*; (*SPORT*) hincha *m/f* ♦ *vt* abanicar; (*fire, quarrel*) atizar

fanatic [fə'nætɪk] *n* fanático/a

fan belt *n* correa del ventilador

fanciful ['fænsɪful] *adj* (*design, name*) fantástico

fancy ['fænsɪ] *n* (*whim*) capricho, antojo; (*imagination*) imaginación *f* ♦ *adj* (*luxury*) lujoso, de lujo ♦ *vt* (*feel like, want*) tener ganas de; (*imagine*) imaginarse; (*think*) creer; **to take a ~ to sb** tomar cariño a uno; **he fancies her** (*inf*) le gusta (ella) mucho; **~ dress** *n* disfraz *m*; **~-dress ball** *n* baile *m* de disfraces

fanfare ['fænfɛə*] n fanfarria (de trompeta)

fang [fæŋ] n colmillo

fantastic [fæn'tæstɪk] adj (enormous) enorme; (strange, wonderful) fantástico

fantasy ['fæntəzɪ] n (dream) sueño; (unreality) fantasía

far [fɑ:*] adj (distant) lejano ♦ adv lejos; (much, greatly) mucho; ~ away, ~ off (a lo) lejos; ~ better mucho mejor; ~ from lejos de; by ~ con mucho; as ~ as the farm vaya hasta la granja; as ~ as I know que yo sepa; how ~? ¿hasta dónde?; (fig) ¿hasta qué punto?; ~away adj remoto; (look) distraído

farce [fɑ:s] n farsa

fare [fɛə*] n (on trains, buses) precio (del billete); (in taxi: cost) tarifa; (food) comida; half ~ medio pasaje m; full ~ pasaje completo

Far East n: the ~ el Extremo Oriente

farewell [fɛə'wɛl] excl, n adiós m

farm [fɑ:m] n granja (SP), finca (AM), estancia (AM) ♦ vt cultivar; ~er n granjero (SP), estanciero (AM); ~hand n peón m; ~house n granja, casa de hacienda (AM); ~ing n agricultura; (of crops) cultivo; (of animals) cría; ~land n tierra de cultivo; ~ worker n = ~hand; ~yard n corral m

far-reaching [fɑ:'ri:tʃɪŋ] adj (reform, effect) de gran alcance

fart [fɑ:t] (inf!) vi tirarse un pedo (!)

farther ['fɑ:ðə*] adv más lejos, más allá ♦ adj más lejano

farthest ['fɑ:ðɪst] superlative of far

fascinate ['fæsɪneɪt] vt fascinar; **fascination** [-'neɪʃən] n fascinación f

fascism ['fæʃɪzəm] n fascismo

fashion ['fæʃən] n moda; (~ industry) industria de la moda; (manner) manera ♦ vt formar; in ~ a la moda; out of ~ pasado de moda; ~able adj de moda; ~ show n desfile m de modelos

fast [fɑ:st] adj rápido; (dye, colour) resistente; (clock): **to be ~** estar adelantado ♦ adv rápidamente, de

prisa; (stuck, held) firmemente ♦ n ayuno ♦ vi ayunar; ~ asleep profundamente dormido

fast food n comida rápida, platos mpl preparados

fastidious [fæs'tɪdɪəs] adj (fussy) quisquilloso

fat [fæt] adj gordo; (book) grueso; (profit) grande, pingüe ♦ n grasa; (on person) carnes fpl; (lard) manteca

fatal ['feɪtl] adj (mistake) fatal; (injury) mortal; ~ity [fə'tælɪtɪ] n (road death etc) víctima; ~ly adv fatalmente; mortalmente

fate [feɪt] n destino; (of person) suerte f; ~ful adj fatídico

father ['fɑ:ðə*] n padre m; ~-in-law n suegro; ~ly adj paternal

fathom ['fæðəm] n braza ♦ vt (mystery) desentrañar; (understand) lograr comprender

fatigue [fə'ti:g] n fatiga, cansancio

fatten ['fætn] vt, vi engordar

fatty ['fætɪ] adj (food) graso ♦ n (inf) gordito/a, gordinflón/ona m/f

fatuous ['fætjuəs] adj fatuo, necio

faucet ['fɔ:sɪt] (US) n grifo (SP), llave f (AM)

fault [fɔ:lt] n (blame) culpa; (defect: in person, machine) defecto; (GEO) falla ♦ vt criticar; it's my ~ es culpa mía; to find ~ with criticar, poner peros a; at ~ culpable; ~y adj defectuoso

fauna ['fɔ:nə] n fauna

favour ['feɪvə*] (US favor) n favor m; (approval) aprobación f ♦ vt (proposition) estar a favor de, aprobar; (assist) ser propicio a; to do sb a ~ hacer un favor a uno; to find ~ with sb caer en gracia a uno; in ~ of a favor de; ~able adj favorable; ~ite ['feɪvrɪt] adj, n favorito, preferido

fawn [fɔ:n] n cervato ♦ adj (also: ~-

coloured) color de cervato, leonado
♦ vi: to ~ (up)on adular

fax [fæks] n (document) fax m;
(machine) telefax m ♦ vt mandar por
telefax

FBI (US) n abbr (= Federal Bureau of
Investigation) ≈ BIC f (SP)

fear [fɪə*] n miedo, temor m ♦ vt tener
miedo de, temer; **for ~ of** por si; **~ful**
adj temeroso, miedoso; (awful) terrible;
~less adj audaz

feasible ['fiːzəbl] adj factible

feast [fiːst] n banquete m; (REL: also:
~ day) fiesta ♦ vi festejar

feat [fiːt] n hazaña

feather ['feðə*] n pluma

feature ['fiːtʃə*] n característica;
(article) artículo de fondo ♦ vt (subj:
film) presentar ♦ vi: **to ~ in** tener un
papel destacado en; **~s** npl (of face)
facciones fpl; **~ film** n largometraje m

February ['februərɪ] n febrero

fed [fed] pt, pp of **feed**

federal ['fedərəl] adj federal

fed up [fed'ʌp] adj: **to be ~ (with)**
estar harto de

fee [fiː] n pago; (professional) derechos
mpl, honorarios mpl; (of club) cuota;
school ~s matrícula

feeble ['fiːbl] adj débil; (joke) flojo

feed [fiːd] (pt, pp **fed**) n comida; (of
animal) pienso; (on printer) dispositivo
de alimentación ♦ vt alimentar; (BRIT:
baby: breast~) dar el pecho a; (animal)
dar de comer a; (data, information): **to
~ into** meter en; **~ on** vt fus
alimentarse de; **~back** n reacción f,
feedback m

feel [fiːl] (pt, pp **felt**) n (sensation)
sensación f; (sense of touch) tacto;
(impression): **to have the ~ of**
parecerse a ♦ vt tocar; (pain etc) sentir;
(think, believe) creer; **to ~ hungry/
cold** tener hambre/frío; **to ~ lonely/
better** sentirse solo/mejor; **I don't
~ well** no me siento bien; **it ~s soft**
es suave al tacto; **to ~ like** (want)

tener ganas de; **~ about** or **around** vi
tantear; **~er** n (of insect) antena; **~ing**
n (physical) sensación f; (foreboding)
presentimiento; (emotion) sentimiento

feet [fiːt] npl of **foot**

feign [feɪn] vt fingir

fell [fel] pt of **fall** ♦ vt (tree) talar

fellow ['feləu] n tipo, tío (SP);
(comrade) compañero; (of learned
society) socio/a ♦ cpd: **~ citizen** n
conciudadano/a; **~ countryman**
(irreg) n compatriota m; **~ men** npl
semejantes mpl; **~ship** n
compañerismo; (grant) beca

felony ['felənɪ] n crimen m

felt [felt] pt, pp of **feel** ♦ n fieltro; **~-tip
pen** n rotulador m

female ['fiːmeɪl] n (pej: woman) mujer
f, tía; (ZOOL) hembra ♦ adj femenino;
hembra

feminine ['femɪnɪn] adj femenino

feminist ['femɪnɪst] n feminista

fence [fens] n valla, cerca ♦ vt (also:
~ in) cercar ♦ vi (SPORT) hacer esgrima;
fencing n esgrima

fend [fend] vi: **to ~ for o.s.** valerse por
sí mismo; **~ off** vt (attack) rechazar;
(questions) evadir

fender ['fendə*] n guardafuego; (US:
AUT) parachoques m inv

ferment [vb fə'ment, n 'fɜːment] vi
fermentar ♦ n (fig) agitación f

fern [fɜːn] n helecho

ferocious [fə'rəuʃəs] adj feroz

ferret ['ferɪt] n hurón m

ferry ['ferɪ] n (small) barca de (pasaje),
balsa; (large: also: ~boat) transbordador
m (SP), embarcadero (AM) ♦ vt
transportar

fertile ['fɜːtaɪl] adj fértil; (BIOL)
fecundo; **fertilize** ['fɜːtɪlaɪz] vt (BIOL)
fecundar; (AGR) abonar; **fertilizer** n
abono

fester ['festə*] vi ulcerarse

festival ['festɪvəl] n (REL) fiesta; (ART,
MUS) festival m

festive ['festɪv] adj festivo; **the**

~ **season** (BRIT: *Christmas*) las Navidades

festivities [fes'tɪvɪtɪz] *npl* fiestas *fpl*

festoon [fes'tuːn] *vt*: **to ~ with** engalanar de

fetch [fetʃ] *vt* ir a buscar; (*sell for*) venderse por

fête [feɪt] *n* fiesta

fetus ['fiːtəs] (US) *n* = **foetus**

feud [fjuːd] *n* (*hostility*) enemistad *f*, (*quarrel*) disputa

fever ['fiːvəʳ] *n* fiebre *f*; **~ish** *adj* febril

few [fjuː] *adj* (*not many*) pocos ♦ *pron* pocos; algunos; **a ~** unos pocos, algunos; **~er** *adj* menos; **~est** *adj* los/ las menos

fiancé [fɪ'ãːnseɪ] *n* novio, prometido; **~e** *n* novia, prometida

fib [fɪb] *n* mentirijilla

fibre ['faɪbəʳ] (US **fiber**) *n* fibra; **~glass** (**Fiberglass** (R) (US) *n* fibra de vidrio

fickle ['fɪkl] *adj* inconstante

fiction ['fɪkʃən] *n* ficción *f*; **~al** *adj* novelesco; **fictitious** [fɪk'tɪʃəs] *adj* ficticio

fiddle ['fɪdl] *n* (MUS) violín *m*; (*cheating*) trampa ♦ *vt* (BRIT: *accounts*) falsificar; **~ with** *vt fus* juguetear con

fidget ['fɪdʒɪt] *vi* enredar; **stop ~ing!** ¡estáte quieto!

field [fiːld] *n* campo; (*fig*) campo, esfera; (SPORT) campo, cancha (AM); **~ marshal** *n* mariscal *m*; **~work** *n* trabajo de campo

fiend [fiːnd] *n* demonio

fierce [fɪəs] *adj* feroz; (*wind, heat*) fuerte; (*fighting, enemy*) encarnizado

fiery ['faɪərɪ] *adj* (*burning*) ardiente; (*temperament*) apasionado

fifteen [fɪf'tiːn] *num* quince

fifth [fɪfθ] *num* quinto

fifty ['fɪftɪ] *num* cincuenta; **~-~** *adj* (*deal, split*) a medias ♦ *adv* a medias, mitad por mitad

fig [fɪg] *n* higo

fight [faɪt] (*pt, pp* **fought**) *n* (*gen*) pelea; (MIL) combate *m*; (*struggle*)

lucha ♦ *vt* luchar contra; (*cancer, alcoholism*) combatir; (*election*) intentar ganar; (*emotion*) resistir ♦ *vi* pelear, luchar; **~er** *n* combatiente *m/f*; (*plane*) caza *m*; **~ing** *n* combate *m*, pelea

figment ['fɪgmənt] *n*: **a ~ of the imagination** una quimera

figurative ['fɪgjʊrətɪv] *adj* (*meaning*) figurado; (*style*) figurativo

figure ['fɪgəʳ] *n* (DRAWING, GEOM) figura, dibujo; (*number, cipher*) cifra; (*body, outline*) tipo; (*personality*) figura ♦ *vt* (*esp US*) imaginar ♦ *vi* (*appear*) figurar; **~ out** *vt* (*work out*) resolver; **~head** *n* (NAUT) mascarón *m* de proa; (*pej: leader*) figura decorativa; **~ of speech** *n* figura retórica

file [faɪl] *n* (*tool*) lima; (*dossier*) expediente *m*; (*folder*) carpeta; (COMPUT) fichero; (*row*) fila ♦ *vt* limar; (LAW: *claim*) presentar; (*store*) archivar; **~ in/out** *vi* entrar/salir en fila; **filing cabinet** *n* fichero, archivador *m*

fill [fɪl] *vt* (*space*): **to ~ (with)** llenar (de); (*vacancy, need*) cubrir ♦ *n*: **to eat one's ~** llenarse; **~ in** *vt* rellenar; **~ up** *vt* llenar (hasta el borde) ♦ *vi* (AUT) poner gasolina

fillet ['fɪlɪt] *n* filete *m*; **~ steak** *n* filete *m* de ternera

filling ['fɪlɪŋ] *n* (CULIN) relleno; (*for tooth*) empaste *m*; **~ station** *n* estación *f* de servicio

film [fɪlm] *n* película ♦ *vt* (*scene*) filmar ♦ *vi* rodar (una película); **~ star** *n* astro, estrella de cine

filter ['fɪltəʳ] *n* filtro ♦ *vt* filtrar; **~ lane** (BRIT) *n* carril *m* de selección; **~-tipped** *adj* con filtro

filth [fɪlθ] *n* suciedad *f*; **~y** *adj* sucio; (*language*) obsceno

fin [fɪn] *n* (*gen*) aleta

final ['faɪnl] *adj* (*last*) final, último; (*definitive*) definitivo, terminante ♦ *n* (BRIT: SPORT) final *f*; **~s** *npl* (SCOL) examen *m* final; (US: SPORT) final *f*

finale [fɪ'nɑːlɪ] *n* final *m*

final ['faɪnl] *adj* final; **~ist** *n* (SPORT) finalista *m/f*; **~ize** *vt* concluir, completar; **~ly** *adv* (lastly) por último, finalmente; (eventually) por fin

finance [faɪˈnæns] *n* (money) fondos *mpl*, **~s** *npl* finanzas *fpl*; (personal ~s) situación *f* económica ♦ *vt* financiar; **financial** [-ˈnænʃəl] *adj* financiero

find [faɪnd] (*pt, pp* found) *vt* encontrar, hallar; (come upon) descubrir ♦ *n* hallazgo; descubrimiento; **to ~ sb guilty** (LAW) declarar culpable a uno; **~ out** *vt* averiguar; (truth, secret) descubrir; **to ~ out about** (subject) informarse sobre; (by chance) enterarse de; **~ings** *npl* (LAW) veredicto, fallo; (of report) recomendaciones *fpl*

fine [faɪn] *adj* excelente; (thin) fino ♦ *adv* (well) bien ♦ *n* (LAW) multa ♦ *vt* (LAW) multar; **to be ~** (person) estar bien; (weather) hacer buen tiempo; **~ arts** *npl* bellas artes *fpl*

finery ['faɪnərɪ] *n* adornos *mpl*

finger ['fɪŋgə*] *n* dedo ♦ *vt* (touch) manosear; **little/index ~** dedo meñique/índice *m*; **~nail** *n* uña; **~print** *n* huella dactilar; **~tip** *n* yema del dedo

finish ['fɪnɪʃ] *n* (end) fin *m*; (SPORT) meta; (polish etc) acabado ♦ *vt, vi* terminar; **to ~ doing sth** acabar de hacer algo; **to ~ third** llegar el tercero; **~ off** *vt* acabar, terminar; (kill) acabar con; **~ up** *vt* acabar, terminar ♦ *vi* ir a parar, terminar; **~ing line** *n* línea de llegada or meta

finite ['faɪnaɪt] *adj* finito; (verb) conjugado

Finland ['fɪnlənd] *n* Finlandia

Finn [fɪn] *n* finlandés/esa *m/f*; **~ish** *adj* finlandés/esa *n* ♦ *n* (LING) finlandés *m*

fir [fə:*] *n* abeto

fire ['faɪə*] *n* fuego; (in hearth) lumbre *f*; (accidental) incendio; (heater) estufa ♦ *vt* (gun) disparar; (interest) despertar ♦ *vi* (shoot) disparar; **on ~** ardiendo, en llamas; **~ alarm** *n* alarma de incendios; **~arm** *n* arma de fuego; **~ brigade** (US **~ department**) *n* (cuerpo de) bomberos *mpl*; **~ engine** *n* coche *m* de bomberos; **~ escape** *n* escalera de incendios; **~ extinguisher** *n* extintor *m* (de incendios); **~guard** *n* rejilla de protección; **~man** (*irreg*) *n* bombero; **~place** *n* chimenea; **~side** *n*: **by the ~side** al lado de la chimenea; **~ station** *n* parque *m* de bomberos; **~wood** *n* leña; **~works** *npl* fuegos *mpl* artificiales

firing squad ['faɪrɪŋ-] *n* pelotón *m* de ejecución

firm [fə:m] *adj* firme; (look, voice) resuelto ♦ *n* firma, empresa; **~ly** *adv* firmemente; resueltamente

first [fə:st] *adj* primero ♦ *adv* (before others) primero; (when listing reasons etc) en primer lugar, primeramente ♦ *n* (person: in race) primero/a; (AUT) primera; (BRIT: SCOL) título de licenciado con calificación de sobresaliente; **at ~** al principio; **~ of all** ante todo; **~ aid** *n* primera ayuda, primeros auxilios *mpl*; **~-aid kit** *n* botiquín *m*; **~-class** *adj* (excellent) de primera (categoría); (ticket etc) de primera clase; **~-hand** *adj* de primera mano; **F~ Lady** (esp US) *n* primera dama; **~ly** *adv* en primer lugar; **~ name** *n* nombre *m* (de pila); **~-rate** *adj* estupendo

fish [fɪʃ] *n inv* pez *m*; (food) pescado ♦ *vt, vi* pescar; **to go ~ing** ir de pesca; **~erman** (*irreg*) *n* pescador *m*; **~ farm** *n* criadero de peces; **~ fingers** (BRIT) *npl* croquetas *fpl* de pescado; **~ing boat** *n* barca de pesca; **~ing line** *n* sedal *m*; **~ing rod** *n* caña (de pescar); **~monger's (shop)** (BRIT) *n* pescadería; **~ sticks** (US) *npl* = **~ fingers**; **~y** (*inf*) *adj* sospechoso

fist [fɪst] *n* puño

fit [fɪt] *adj* (healthy) en buena forma; (proper) adecuado, apropiado ♦ *vt* (subj: clothes) estar or sentar bien a; (instal) poner; (equip) proveer; dotar; (facts) cuadrar or corresponder con ♦ vi (clothes) sentar bien; (in space, gap) caber; (facts) coincidir n (MED) ataque m; ~ **to** (ready) a punto de; ~ **for** apropiado para; **a ~ of anger/ pride** un arranque de cólera/orgullo; **this dress is a good ~** este vestido me sienta bien; **by ~s and starts a** rachas; ~ **in** vi (fig: person) llevarse bien (con todos); ~**ful** adj espasmódico, intermitente; ~**ment** n modo adosable; ~**ness** n (MED) salud f; ~**ted carpet** n moqueta, ~**ted kitchen** n cocina amueblada; ~**ter** n ajustador m; ~**ting** adj apropiado ♦ n (of dress) prueba; (of piece of equipment) instalación f; ~**ting room** n probador m; ~**tings** npl instalaciones f

five [faɪv] num cinco; ~**r** (inf) n (BRIT) billete m de cinco libras; (US) billete m de cinco dólares

fix [fɪks] vt (secure) fijar, asegurar; (mend) arreglar; (prepare) preparar ♦ n: **to be in a ~** estar en un aprieto; ~ **up** vt (meeting) arreglar; **to ~ sb up with sth** proveer a uno de algo; ~**ation** [fɪk'seɪʃən] n obsesión f; ~**ed** adj (prices etc) fijo; ~**ture** n (SPORT) encuentro; ~**tures** npl (cupboards etc) instalaciones fpl fijas

fizzy ['fɪzɪ] adj (drink) gaseoso

fjord [fjɔːd] n fiordo

flabbergasted ['flæbəgɑːstɪd] adj pasmado, alucinado

flabby ['flæbɪ] adj gordo

flag [flæg] n bandera; (stone) losa ♦ vi decaer; **to ~ sb down** hacer señas a uno para que se pare; ~**pole** n asta de bandera; ~**ship** n buque m insignia; (fig) bandera

flair [flɛə*] n aptitud f especial

flak [flæk] n (MIL) fuego antiaéreo; (inf: criticism) lluvia de críticas

flake [fleɪk] n (of rust, paint) escama; (of snow, soap powder) copo ♦ vi (also:

~ **off**) desconcharse

flamboyant [flæm'bɔɪənt] adj (dress) vistoso; (person) extravagante

flame [fleɪm] n llama

flamingo [flə'mɪŋgəu] n flamenco

flammable ['flæməbl] adj inflamable

flan [flæn] n (BRIT) tarta

flank [flæŋk] n (of animal) ijar m; (of army) flanco ♦ vt flanquear

flannel ['flænl] n (BRIT: also: face ~) manopla; (fabric) franela

flap [flæp] n (of pocket, envelope) solapa ♦ vt (wings, arms) agitar ♦ vi (sail, flag) ondear

flare [flɛə*] n llamarada; (MIL) bengala; (in skirt etc) vuelo; ~ **up** vi encenderse; (fig: person) encolerizarse; (: revolt) estallar

flash [flæʃ] n relámpago; (also: news ~) noticias fpl de última hora; (PHOT) flash m ♦ vt (light, headlights) lanzar un destello con; (news, message) transmitir; (smile) lanzar vi brillar; (hazard light etc) lanzar destellos; **in a ~** en un instante; **he ~ed by or past** pasó como un rayo; ~**back** n (CINEMA) flashback m; ~**bulb** n bombilla fusible; ~ **cube** n cubo de flash; ~**light** n linterna

flashy ['flæʃɪ] (pej) adj ostentoso

flask [flɑːsk] n frasco; (also: vacuum ~) termo

flat [flæt] adj llano; (smooth) liso; (tyre) desinflado; (battery) descargado; (beer) muerto; (refusal etc) rotundo; (MUS) desafinado; (rate) fijo ♦ n (BRIT: apartment) piso (SP), departamento (AM), apartamento; (AUT) pinchazo; (MUS) bemol m; **to work ~ out** trabajar a toda mecha; ~**ly** adv terminantemente, de plano; ~**ten** vt (also: ~**ten out**) allanar; (smooth out) alisar; (building, plants) arrasar

flatter ['flætə*] vt adular, halagar; ~**ing** adj halagüeño; (dress) que favorece; ~**y** n adulación f

flaunt [flɔːnt] vt ostentar, lucir

flavour ['fleɪvə*] (US **flavor**) n sabor m, gusto ♦ vt sazonar, condimentar; **strawberry-~ed** con sabor a fresa; **~ing** n (in product) aromatizante m

flaw [flɔː] n defecto m; **~less** adj impecable

flax [flæks] n lino

flea [fliː] n pulga

fleck [flɛk] n (mark) mota

flee [fliː] (pt, pp **fled**) vt huir de ♦ vi huir, fugarse

fleece [fliːs] n vellón m; (wool) lana ♦ vt (inf) desplumar

fleet [fliːt] n flota; (of lorries etc) escuadra

fleeting ['fliːtɪŋ] adj fugaz

Flemish ['flemɪʃ] adj flamenco

flesh [fleʃ] n carne f; (skin) piel f; (of fruit) pulpa; **~ wound** n herida superficial

flew [fluː] pt of **fly**

flex [fleks] n cordón m ♦ vt (muscles) tensar; **~ible** adj flexible

flick [flɪk] n capirotazo; chasquido ♦ vt (with hand) dar un capirotazo a; (whip etc) chasquear; (switch) accionar; **~ through** vt fus hojear

flicker ['flɪkə*] vi (light) parpadear; (flame) vacilar

flier ['flaɪə*] n aviador(a) m/f

flight [flaɪt] n vuelo; (escape) huida, fuga; (also: **~ of steps**) tramo (de escaleras); **~ attendant** (US) n camarero/azafata; **~ deck** n (AVIAT) cabina de mandos; (NAUT) cubierta de aterrizaje

flimsy ['flɪmzɪ] adj (thin) muy ligero; (building) endeble; (excuse) flojo

flinch [flɪntʃ] vi encogerse; **to ~ from** retroceder ante

fling [flɪŋ] (pt, pp **flung**) vt arrojar

flint [flɪnt] n pedernal m; (in lighter) piedra

flip [flɪp] vt dar la vuelta a; (switch: turn on) encender; (: turn off) apagar; (coin) echar a cara o cruz

flippant ['flɪpənt] adj poco serio

flipper ['flɪpə*] n aleta

flirt [flɜːt] vi coquetear, flirtear ♦ n coqueta

float [fləʊt] n flotador m; (in procession) carroza; (money) reserva ♦ vi flotar; (swimmer) hacer la plancha

flock [flɒk] n (of sheep) rebaño; (of birds) bandada ♦ vi: **to ~ to** acudir en tropel a

flog [flɒg] vt azotar

flood [flʌd] n inundación f; (of letters, imports etc) avalancha ♦ vt inundar ♦ vi (place) inundarse; (people): **to ~ into** inundar; **~ing** n inundaciones fpl; **~light** n foco

floor [flɔː*] n suelo; (storey) piso; (of sea) fondo ♦ vt (question) dejar sin respuesta; (: blow) derribar; **ground ~, first ~** (US) planta baja; **first ~, second ~** (US) primer piso; **~board** n tabla; **~ show** n cabaret m

flop [flɒp] n fracaso ♦ vi (fail) fracasar; (fall) derrumbarse; **~py** adj flojo ♦ n (COMPUT: also: **~py disk**) floppy m

flora ['flɔːrə] n flora

floral ['flɔːrl] adj (pattern) floreado

florid ['flɒrɪd] adj florido; (complexion) rubicundo

florist ['flɒrɪst] n florista m/f; **~'s (shop)** n florería

flounder ['flaʊndə*] vi (swimmer) patalear; (fig: economy) estar en dificultades ♦ n (ZOOL) platija

flour ['flaʊə*] n harina

flourish ['flʌrɪʃ] vi florecer ♦ n ademán m, movimiento (ostentoso)

flout [flaʊt] vt burlarse de

flow [fləʊ] n (movement) flujo; (of traffic) circulación f; (tide) corriente f ♦ vi (river, blood) fluir; (traffic) circular; **~ chart** n organigrama m

flower ['flaʊə*] n flor f ♦ vi florecer; **~ bed** n macizo; **~pot** n tiesto; **~y** adj (fragrance) floral; (pattern) floreado; (speech) florido

flown [fləʊn] pp of **fly**

flu [fluː] n: **to have ~** tener la gripe

fluctuate ['flʌktjueɪt] vi fluctuar

fluent ['fluːənt] adj (linguist) que habla perfectamente; (speech) elocuente; he **speaks ~ French**, he's **~ in French** domina el francés; **~ly** adv con fluidez

fluff [flʌf] n pelusa; **~y** adj de pelo suave

fluid ['fluːɪd] adj (movement) fluido, líquido; (situation) inestable ♦ n fluido, líquido

fluke [fluːk] (inf) n chiripa

flung [flʌŋ] pt, pp of **fling**

fluoride ['fluəraɪd] n fluoruro

flurry ['flʌrɪ] n (of snow) temporal m; **~ of activity** frenesí m de actividad

flush [flʌʃ] n rubor m; (fig: of youth etc) resplandor m ♦ vt limpiar con agua ♦ vi ruborizarse ♦ adj: **~ with** a ras de; **to ~ the toilet** hacer funcionar la cisterna; **~ed** adj ruborizado

flustered ['flʌstəd] adj aturdido

flute [fluːt] n flauta

flutter ['flʌtə*] n (of wings) revoloteo, aleteo; **a ~ of panic/excitement** una oleada de pánico/excitación ♦ vi revolotear

flux [flʌks] n: **to be in a state of ~** estar continuamente cambiando

fly [flaɪ] (pt **flew**, pp **flown**) n mosca; (on trousers: also: **flies**) bragueta ♦ vt (plane) pilot(e)ar; (cargo) transportar (en avión) ♦ vi volar; (passengers) ir en avión; (escape) evadirse; (flag) ondear; **~ away** or **off** vi emprender el vuelo; **~drive** n: **~-drive holiday** vacaciones que incluyen vuelo y alquiler de coche; **~ing** n (activity) (el) volar; (action) vuelo ♦ adj: **~ing visit** visita relámpago; **with ~ing colours** con lucimiento; **~ing saucer** n platillo volante; **~ing start** n: **to get off to a ~ing start** empezar con buen pie; **~over** (BRIT) n paso a desnivel or superior; **~sheet** n (for tent) doble techo

foal [fəul] n potro

foam [fəum] n espuma ♦ vi hacer espuma; **~ rubber** n goma espuma

fob [fɔb] vt: **to ~ sb off with sth** despachar a uno con algo

focal point ['fəukl-] n (fig) centro de atención

focus ['fəukəs] (pl **~es**) n foco; (centre) centro ♦ vt (field glasses etc) enfocar ♦ vi: **to ~ (on)** enfocar (a); (issue etc) centrarse en; **in/out of ~** enfocado/ desenfocado

fodder ['fɔdə*] n forraje m

foetus ['fiːtəs] (US **fetus**) n feto

fog [fɔg] n niebla; **~gy** adj: **it's ~gy** hay niebla, está brumoso; **~ lamp** (US **~ light**) n (AUT) faro de niebla

foil [fɔɪl] vt frustrar ♦ n hoja; (kitchen ~) papel m (de) aluminio; (complement) complemento; (FENCING) florete m

fold [fəuld] n (bend, crease) pliegue m; (AGR) redil m ♦ vt doblar; (arms) cruzar; **~ up** vi plegarse, doblarse; (business) quebrar ♦ vt (map etc) plegar; **~er** n (for papers) carpeta; (COMPUT) directorio; **~ing** adj (chair, bed) plegable

foliage ['fəulɪdʒ] n follaje m

folk [fəuk] npl gente f ♦ adj popular, folklórico; **~s** npl (family) familia sg, parientes mpl; **~lore** ['fəuklɔː*] n folklore m; **~ song** n canción f popular

follow ['fɔləu] vt seguir ♦ vi seguir; (result) resultar; **to ~ suit** hacer lo mismo; **~ up** vt (letter, offer) responder a; (case) investigar; **~er** n (of person, belief) partidario/a; **~ing** adj siguiente ♦ n afición f, partidarios mpl

folly ['fɔlɪ] n locura

fond [fɔnd] adj (memory, smile etc) cariñoso; (hopes) ilusorio; **to be ~ of** tener cariño a; (pastime, food) ser aficionado a

fondle ['fɔndl] vt acariciar

font [fɔnt] n pila bautismal; (TYP) fundición f

food [fuːd] n comida; **~ mixer** n batidora; **~ poisoning** n intoxicación f alimenticia; **~ processor** n robot m de cocina; **~stuffs** npl comestibles mpl

fool [fu:l] n tonto/a; (CULIN) puré m de frutas con nata ♦ vt engañar ♦ vi (gen: ~ around) bromear; **~hardy** adj temerario; **~ish** adj tonto; (careless) imprudente; **~proof** adj (plan etc) infalible

foot [fut] (pl **feet**) n pie m; (measure) pie m (= 304 mm); (of animal) pata ♦ vt (bill) pagar; **on ~** a pie; **~age** n (CINEMA) imágenes fpl; **~ball** n balón m; (game: BRIT) fútbol m; (: US) fútbol m americano; **~ball player** (BRIT: also: **~baller**) n futbolista m de fútbol m americano; **~brake** n freno de pie; **~bridge** n puente m para peatones; **~hills** npl estribaciones fpl; **~hold** n pie m firme; **~ing** n (fig) posición f; **to lose one's ~ing** perder el pie; **~lights** npl candilejas fpl; **~note** n nota (al pie de la página); **~path** n sendero; **~print** n huella, pisada; **~step** n paso; **~wear** n calzado

---

KEYWORD

---

for [fɔ:] prep **1** (indicating destination, intention) para; **the train ~ London** el tren con destino a or de Londres; **he left ~ Rome** marchó para Roma; **he went ~ the paper** fue por el periódico; **is this ~ me?** ¿es esto para mí?; **it's time ~ lunch** es la hora de comer

2 (indicating purpose) para; **what's it ~?** ¿para qué (es)?; **to pray ~ peace** rezar por la paz

3 (on behalf of, representing): **the MP ~ Hove** el diputado por Hove; **he works ~ the government/a local firm** trabaja para el gobierno/en una empresa local; **I'll ask him ~ you** se lo pediré por ti; **G ~ George** G de Gerona

4 (because of) por esta razón; **~ fear of being criticized** por temor a ser criticado

5 (with regard to) para; **it's cold ~ July** hace frío para julio; **he has a gift ~ languages** tiene don de lenguas

6 (in exchange for) por; **I sold it ~ £5** lo vendí por £5; **to pay 50 pence ~ a ticket** pagar 50 peniques por un billete

7 (in favour of): **are you ~ or against us?** ¿estás con nosotros o contra nosotros?; **I'm all ~ it** estoy totalmente a favor; **vote ~ X** vote (a) X

8 (referring to distance): **there are roadworks ~ 5 km** hay obras en 5 km; **we walked ~ miles** caminamos kilómetros y kilómetros

9 (referring to time): **he was away ~ 2 years** estuvo fuera (durante) dos años; **it hasn't rained ~ 3 weeks** no ha llovido durante or en 3 semanas; **I have known her ~ years** la conozco desde hace años; **can you do it ~ tomorrow?** ¿lo podrás hacer para mañana?

10 (with infinitive clauses): **it is not ~ me to decide** la decisión no es cosa mía; **it would be best ~ you to leave** sería mejor que te fueras; **there is still time ~ you to do it** todavía te queda tiempo para hacerlo; **~ this to be possible ...** para que esto sea posible ...

11 (in spite of) a pesar de; **~ all his complaints** a pesar de sus quejas ♦ conj (since, as: rather formal) puesto que

---

forage ['fɔrɪdʒ] vi (animal) forrajear; (person): **to ~ for** hurgar en busca de

foray ['fɔreɪ] n incursión f

forbid [fə'bɪd] (pt **forbad(e)**, pp **forbidden**) vt prohibir; **to ~ sb to do sth** prohibir a uno hacer algo; **~ding** adj amenazador(a)

force [fɔ:s] n fuerza ♦ vt forzar; (push)

meter a la fuerza; **to ~ o.s.** to do hacer un esfuerzo por hacer; **the F~s** *npl* (*BRIT*) las Fuerzas Armadas; **in ~** en vigor; **~d** [fɔːst] *adj* forzado; **~-feed** *vt* alimentar a la fuerza; **~ful** *adj* enérgico

forcibly ['fɔːsəblɪ] *adv* a la fuerza; (*speak*) enérgicamente

ford [fɔːd] *n* vado

fore [fɔː*] *n*: **to come to the ~** empezar a destacar

fore: ~arm *n* antebrazo; **~boding** *n* presentimiento; **~cast** *n* pronóstico ♦ *vt* (*irreg: like cast*) pronosticar; **~court** *n* patio; **~finger** *n* (dedo) índice *m*; **~front** *n*: **in the ~front of** en la vanguardia de

forego *vt* = **forgo**

foregone ['fɔːgɒn] *pp of* **forego** ♦ *adj*: **it's a ~ conclusion** es una conclusión evidente

foreground ['fɔːgraund] *n* primer plano

forehead ['fɒrɪd] *n* frente *f*

foreign ['fɒrɪn] *adj* extranjero; (*trade*) exterior; (*object*) extraño; **~er** *n* extranjero/a; **~ exchange** *n* divisas *fpl*; **F~ Office** (*BRIT*) *n* Ministerio de Asuntos Exteriores; **F~ Secretary** (*BRIT*) *n* Ministro de Asuntos Exteriores

fore: ~leg *n* pata delantera; **~man** (*irreg*) *n* capataz *m*; (*in construction*) maestro *m* de obras; **~most** *adj* principal ♦ *adv*: **first and ~most** ante todo

forensic [fə'rɛnsɪk] *adj* forense

fore: ~runner *n* precursor/a *m/f*; **~see** (*pt* **foresaw**, *pp* **foreseen**) *vt* prever; **~seeable** *adj* previsible; **~shadow** *vt* prefigurar, anunciar; **~sight** *n* previsión *f*

forest ['fɒrɪst] *n* bosque *m*

forestry ['fɒrɪstrɪ] *n* silvicultura

foretaste ['fɔːteɪst] *n* muestra

foretell [fɔː'tɛl] (*pt, pp* **foretold**) *vt* predecir, pronosticar

forever [fə'rɛvə*] *adv* para siempre; (*endlessly*) constantemente

foreword ['fɔːwəːd] *n* prefacio

forfeit ['fɔːfɪt] *vt* perder

forgave [fə'geɪv] *pt of* **forgive**

forge [fɔːdʒ] *n* herrería ♦ *vt* (*signature, money*) falsificar; (*metal*) forjar; **~ ahead** *vi* avanzar mucho; **~ry** *n* falsificación *f*

forget [fə'gɛt] (*pt* **forgot**, *pp* **forgotten**) *vt* olvidar ♦ *vi* olvidarse; **~ful** *adj* despistado; **~-me-not** *n* nomeolvides *f inv*

forgive [fə'gɪv] (*pt* **forgave**, *pp* **forgiven**) *vt* perdonar; **to ~ sb for sth** perdonar algo a uno; **~ness** *n* perdón *m*

forgo [fɔː'gəu] (*pt* **forwent**, *pp* **forgone**) *vt* (*give up*) renunciar a; (*go without*) privarse de

forgot [fə'gɒt] *pt of* **forget**

forgotten [fə'gɒtn] *pp of* **forget**

fork [fɔːk] *n* (*for eating*) tenedor *m*; (*for gardening*) horca; (*of roads*) bifurcación *f* ♦ *vi* (*road*) bifurcarse; **~ out** (*inf*) *vt* (*pay*) desembolsar; **~lift truck** *n* máquina elevadora

forlorn [fə'lɔːn] *adj* (*person*) triste, melancólico; (*place*) abandonado; (*attempt, hope*) desesperado

form [fɔːm] *n* forma; (*BRIT: SCOL*) clase *f*; (*document*) formulario ♦ *vt* formar; (*idea*) concebir; (*habit*) adquirir; **in top ~** en plena forma; **to ~ a queue** hacer cola

formal ['fɔːmal] *adj* (*offer, receipt*) por escrito; (*person etc*) correcto; (*occasion, dinner*) de etiqueta; (*dress*) correcto; (*garden*) (de estilo) clásico; **~ity** [-'mælɪtɪ] *n* (*procedure*) trámite *m*; corrección *f*, etiqueta; **~ly** *adv* oficialmente

format ['fɔːmæt] *n* formato ♦ *vt* (*COMPUT*) formatear

formative ['fɔːmətɪv] *adj* (*years*) de formación; (*influence*) formativo

former ['fɔːmə*] *adj* anterior; (*earlier*) antiguo; (*ex*) ex; **the ~ ... the latter ...** aquél ... éste ...; **~ly** *adv* antes

formula ['fɔːmjulə] *n* fórmula

forsake [fə'seɪk] (*pt* **forsook**, *pp* **forsaken**) *vt* (*gen*) abandonar; (*plan*) renunciar a

fort [fɔːt] *n* fuerte *m*

forte ['fɔːtɪ] *n* fuerte *m*

forth [fɔːθ] *adv*: **back and ~** de acá para allá; **and so ~** y y así sucesivamente; **~coming** *adj* próximo, venidero; (*help, information*) disponible; (*character*) comunicativo; **~right** *adj* franco; **~with** *adv* en el acto

fortify ['fɔːtɪfaɪ] *vt* (*city*) fortificar; (*person*) fortalecer

fortitude ['fɔːtɪtjuːd] *n* fortaleza

fortnight ['fɔːtnaɪt] (*BRIT*) *n* quince días *mpl*; quincena; **~ly** *adj* de cada quince días, quincenal ♦ *adv* cada quince días, quincenalmente

fortress ['fɔːtrɪs] *n* fortaleza

fortunate ['fɔːtʃənɪt] *adj* afortunado; **it is ~ that ...** (es una) suerte que ...; **~ly** *adv* afortunadamente

fortune ['fɔːtʃən] *n* suerte *f*; (*wealth*) fortuna; **~-teller** *n* adivino/a

forty ['fɔːtɪ] *num* cuarenta

forum ['fɔːrəm] *n* foro

forward ['fɔːwəd] *adj* (*movement, position*) avanzado; (*front*) delantero; (*in time*) adelantado; (*not shy*) atrevido ♦ *n* (*SPORT*) delantero *m* ♦ *vt* (*letter*) remitir; (*career*) promocionar; **to move ~** avanzar; **~(s)** *adv* (hacia) adelante

fossil ['fɔsl] *n* fósil *m*

foster ['fɔstə*] *vt* (*child*) acoger en una familia; fomentar; **~ child** *n* hijo/a adoptivo/a

fought [fɔːt] *pt*, *pp* of **fight**

foul [faul] *adj* sucio, puerco; (*weather, smell etc*) asqueroso; (*language*) grosero; (*temper*) malísimo ♦ *n* (*SPORT*) falta ♦ *vt* (*dirty*) ensuciar; **~ play** *n* (*LAW*) muerte *f* violenta

found [faund] *pt*, *pp* of **find** ♦ *vt* fundar; **~ation** [-'deɪʃən] *n* (*act*) fundación *f*; (*basis*) base *f*; (*also*: **~ation cream**) crema base; **~ations** *npl* (*of building*) cimientos *mpl*

founder ['faundə*] *n* fundador(a) *m/f* ♦ *vi* hundirse

foundry ['faundrɪ] *n* fundición *f*

fountain ['fauntɪn] *n* fuente *f*; **~ pen** *n* pluma (estilográfica) (*SP*), plumafuente *f* (*AM*)

four [fɔː*] *num* cuatro; **on all ~s** a gatas; **~-poster (bed)** *n* cama de dosel; **~teen** *num* catorce; **~th** *num* cuarto

fowl [faul] *n* ave *f* (de corral)

fox [fɔks] *n* zorro ♦ *vt* confundir

foyer ['fɔɪeɪ] *n* vestíbulo

fraction ['frækʃən] *n* fracción *f*

fracture ['fræktʃə*] *n* fractura

fragile ['frædʒaɪl] *adj* frágil

fragment ['frægmənt] *n* fragmento

fragrant ['freɪgrənt] *adj* fragante, oloroso

frail [freɪl] *adj* frágil; (*person*) débil

frame [freɪm] *n* (*TECH*) armazón *m*; (*of picture, door etc*) marco; (*of spectacles: also*: **~s**) montura ♦ *vt* enmarcar; **~ of mind** *n* estado de ánimo; **~work** *n* marco

France [frɑːns] *n* Francia

franchise ['fræntʃaɪz] *n* (*POL*) derecho de votar, sufragio; (*COMM*) licencia, concesión *f*

frank [fræŋk] *adj* franco ♦ *vt* (*letter*) franquear; **~ly** *adv* francamente

frantic ['fræntɪk] *adj* (*distraught*) desesperado; (*hectic*) frenético

fraternity [frə'tɜːnɪtɪ] *n* (*feeling*) fraternidad *f*; (*group of people*) círculos *mpl*

fraud [frɔːd] *n* fraude *m*; (*person*) impostor/a *m/f*

fraught [frɔːt] *adj*: **~ with** lleno de

fray [freɪ] *vi* deshilacharse

freak [friːk] *n* (*person*) fenómeno; (*event*) suceso anormal

freckle ['frekl] *n* peca

free [friː] *adj* libre; (*gratis*) gratuito ♦ *vt* (*prisoner etc*) poner en libertad; (*jammed object*) soltar; **~ (of charge)**, **for ~** gratis; **~dom** ['friːdəm] *n*

libertad f; **F~fone** ® ['fri:fəun] n
número gratuito; **~for-all** n riña
general; **~ gift** n prima; **~hold** n
propiedad f vitalicia; **~ kick** n tiro libre;
~lance adj independiente ♦ adv por
cuenta propia; **~ly** adv libremente;
(liberally) generosamente; **F~mason** n
francmasón m; **F~post** ® n porte m
pagado; **~-range** adj (hen, eggs) de
granja; **~ trade** n libre comercio;
~way (US) n autopista f; **~ will** n libre
albedrío; **of one's own ~ will** por su
propia voluntad

freeze [fri:z] (pt **froze**, pp **frozen**) vi
(weather) helar; (liquid, pipe, person)
helarse, congelarse ♦ vt helar; (food,
prices, salaries) congelar ♦ n helada;
(on arms, wages) congelación f; **~-
dried** adj liofilizado; **~r** n congelador
m (SP), congeladora (AM)

freezing ['fri:zɪŋ] adj helado; **3
degrees below ~** tres grados bajo
cero; **~ point** n punto de congelación

freight [freit] n (goods) carga; (money
charged) flete m; **~ train** (US) n tren m
de mercancías

French [frentʃ] adj francés/esa ♦ n
(LING) francés m; **the ~** npl los
franceses; **~ bean** n judía verde;
~ fried potatoes npl patatas fpl (SP)
or papas fpl (AM) fritas; **~ fries** (US) npl
= **~ fried potatoes**; **~man/woman**
(irreg) n francés/esa m/f; **~ window** n
puerta de cristal

frenzy ['frenzɪ] n frenesí m

frequent [adj 'fri:kwənt, vb frɪ'kwent]
adj frecuente ♦ vt frecuentar; **~ly**
[-əntlɪ] adv frecuentemente, a menudo

fresh [freʃ] adj fresco; (bread) tierno;
(new) nuevo; **~en** vi (wind, air) soplar
más recio; **~en up** vi (person)
arreglarse, lavarse; **~er** n (BRIT: inf)
(UNIV) estudiante m/f de primer año;
~ly adv (made, painted etc) recién;
~man (US irreg) n = **~er**; **~ness** n
frescura; **~water** adj (fish) de agua
dulce

fret [fret] vi inquietarse

friar ['fraɪə*] n fraile m; (before name)
fray m

friction ['frɪkʃən] n fricción f

Friday ['fraɪdɪ] n viernes m inv

fridge [frɪdʒ] (BRIT) n nevera (SP),
refrigeradora (AM)

fried [fraɪd] adj frito

friend [frend] n amigo/a; **~ly** adj
simpático; (government) amigo; (place)
acogedor/a; (match) amistoso; **~ly
fire** fuego amigo, disparos mpl del
propio bando; **~ship** n amistad f

frieze [fri:z] n friso

fright [fraɪt] n (terror) terror m; (scare)
susto; **to take ~** asustarse; **~en** vt
asustar; **~ened** adj asustado; **~ening**
adj espantoso; **~ful** adj espantoso,
horrible

frill [frɪl] n volante m

fringe [frɪndʒ] n (BRIT: of hair) flequillo;
(on lampshade etc) flecos mpl; (of forest
etc) borde m, margen m; **~ benefits**
npl beneficios mpl marginales

frisk [frɪsk] vt cachear, registrar

frisky ['frɪskɪ] adj juguetón/ona

fritter ['frɪtə*] n buñuelo; **~ away** vt
desperdiciar

frivolous ['frɪvələs] adj frívolo

frizzy ['frɪzɪ] adj rizado

fro [frəu] see **to**

frock [frɔk] n vestido

frog [frɔg] n rana; **~man** n hombre-
rana m

frolic ['frɔlɪk] vi juguetear

from [frɔm] prep 1 (indicating starting
place) de, desde; **where do you
come ~?** ¿de dónde eres?; **~
London to Glasgow** de Londres a Glasgow;
to escape ~ sth/sb escaparse de
algo/alguien
2 (indicating origin etc) de; **a letter/
telephone call ~ my sister** una
carta/llamada de mi hermana; **tell
him ~ me that ...** dígale de mi

parte que ...
3 (*indicating time*): ~ **one o'clock to** or **until** or **till two** de la una a or hasta las dos; ~ **January (on)** a partir de enero

4 (*indicating distance*) de; **the hotel is 1 km ~ the beach** el hotel está a 1 km de la playa

5 (*indicating price, number etc*) de; **prices range ~ £10 to £50** los precios van desde £10 a or hasta £50; **the interest rate was increased ~ 9% to 10%** el tipo de interés fue incrementado de un 9% a un 10%

6 (*indicating difference*) de; **he can't tell red ~ green** no sabe distinguir el rojo del verde; **to be different ~ sb/sth** ser diferente a algo/alguien

7 (*because of, on the basis of*): ~ **what he says** por lo que dice; **weak ~ hunger** debilitado por el hambre

front [frʌnt] *n* (*foremost part*) parte *f* delantera; (*of house*) fachada; (*of dress*) delantero; (*promenade: also: sea ~*) paseo marítimo; (MIL, POL, METEOROLOGY) frente *m*; (*fig: appearances*) apariencias *fpl* ♦ *adj* (*wheel, leg*) delantero; (*row, line*) primero; **in ~ (of)** delante (de); ~ **door** *n* puerta principal; ~**ier** ['frʌntɪə*] *n* frontera; ~ **page** *n* primera plana; ~ **room** (BRIT) *n* salón *m*, sala; ~**-wheel drive** *n* tracción *f* delantera

frost [frɔst] *n* helada; (*also: hoar~*) escarcha; ~**bite** *n* congelación *f*; ~**ed** *adj* (*glass*) deslustrado; ~**y** *adj* (*weather*) de helada; (*welcome etc*) glacial

froth [frɔθ] *n* espuma

frown [fraun] *vi* fruncir el ceño

froze [frəuz] *pt of* **freeze**

frozen ['frəuzn] *pp of* **freeze**

fruit [fruːt] *n inv* fruta; fruto; (*fig*) fruto; resultados *mpl*; ~**erer** *n* frutero/a; ~**erer's (shop)** *n* frutería; ~**ful** *adj*

provechoso; ~**ion** [fruːˈɪʃən] *n*: **to come to ~ion** realizarse; ~ **juice** *n* zumo (SP) or jugo (AM) de fruta; ~ **machine** (BRIT) *n* máquina *f* tragaperras; ~ **salad** *n* macedonia (SP) or ensalada (AM) de frutas

frustrate [frʌsˈtreɪt] *vt* frustrar

fry [fraɪ] (*pt, pp* **fried**) *vt* freír; **small ~** *gente* f *menuda*; ~**ing pan** *n* sartén *f*.

ft. *abbr* = **foot**; **feet**

fudge [fʌdʒ] *n* (CULIN) caramelo blando

fuel [fjuəl] *n* (*for heating*) combustible *m*; (*coal*) carbón *m*; (*wood*) leña; (*for engine*) carburante *m*; ~ **oil** *n* fuel oil *m*; ~ **tank** *n* depósito (de combustible)

fugitive ['fjuːdʒɪtɪv] *n* fugitivo/a

fulfil [fulˈfɪl] *vt* (*function*) cumplir con; (*condition*) satisfacer; (*wish, desire*) realizar; ~**ment** (US **fulfillment** *n*) satisfacción *f*; (*of promise, desire*) realización *f*

full [ful] *adj* lleno; (*fig*) pleno; (*complete*) completo; (*maximum*) máximo; (*information*) detallado; (*price*) íntegro; (*skirt*) amplio ♦ *adv*: **to know ~ well** that saber perfectamente que; **I'm ~ (up)** no puedo más; ~ **employment** pleno empleo; **a ~ two hours** dos horas completas; **at ~ speed** a máxima velocidad; **in ~** (*reproduce, quote*) íntegramente; ~**-length** *adj* (*novel etc*) entero; (*coat*) largo; (*portrait*) de cuerpo entero; ~ **moon** *n* luna llena; ~**-scale** *adj* (*attack, war*) en gran escala; (*model*) de tamaño natural; ~ **stop** *n* punto; ~**-time** *adj* (*work*) de tiempo completo ♦ *adv*: **to work ~-time** trabajar a tiempo completo; ~**y** *adv* completamente; (*at least*) por lo menos; ~**y-fledged** *adj* (*teacher, barrister*) diplomado

fumble ['fʌmbl] *vi*: **to ~ with** manejar torpemente

fume [fjuːm] *vi* (*rage*) estar furioso; ~**s** *npl* humo, gases *mpl*

fun [fʌn] *n* (*amusement*) diversión *f*; **to**

have ~ divertirse; **for** ~ en broma; **to make** ~ **of** burlarse de

function ['fʌŋkʃən] *n* función *f* ♦ *vi* funcionar; ~**al** *adj* (*operational*) en buen estado; (*practical*) funcional

fund [fʌnd] *n* fondo; (*reserve*) reserva; ~**s** *npl* (*money*) fondos *mpl*

fundamental [fʌndəˈmentl] *adj* fundamental

funeral ['fjuːnərəl] *n* (*burial*) entierro; (*ceremony*) funerales *mpl*; ~ **parlour** (*BRIT*) *n* funeraria; ~ **service** *n* misa de difuntos, funeral *m*

funfair ['fʌnfɛə*] (*BRIT*) *n* parque *m* de atracciones

fungus ['fʌŋgəs] (*pl* **fungi**) *n* hongo; (*mould*) moho

funnel ['fʌnl] *n* embudo; (*of ship*) chimenea

funny ['fʌnɪ] *adj* gracioso, divertido; (*strange*) curioso, raro

fur [fə:*] *n* piel *f*; (*BRIT*: *in kettle etc*) sarro; ~ **coat** *n* abrigo de pieles

furious ['fjuərɪəs] *adj* furioso; (*effort*) violento

furlong ['fə:lɔŋ] *n* octava parte de una milla, = 201.17 m

furnace ['fə:nɪs] *n* horno

furnish ['fə:nɪʃ] *vt* amueblar; (*supply*) suministrar; (*information*) facilitar; ~**ings** *npl* muebles *mpl*

furniture ['fə:nɪtʃə*] *n* muebles *mpl*; **piece of** ~ mueble *m*

furrow ['fʌrəu] *n* surco

furry ['fə:rɪ] *adj* peludo

further ['fə:ðə*] *adj* (*new*) nuevo, adicional ♦ *adv* más lejos; (*more*) más; (*moreover*) además ♦ *vt* promover, adelantar; ~ **education** *n* educación *f* superior; ~**more** [fə:ðə'mɔ:*] *adv* además

furthest ['fə:ðɪst] *superlative of* **far**

fury ['fjuərɪ] *n* furia

fuse [fjuːz] (*US* **fuze**) *n* fusible *m*; (*for bomb etc*) mecha ♦ *vt* (*metal*) fundir; (*fig*) fusionar ♦ *vi* fundirse; fusionarse; (*BRIT*: *ELEC*): **to** ~ **the lights** fundir los

plomos; ~ **box** *n* caja de fusibles

fuss [fʌs] *n* (*excitement*) conmoción *f*; (*trouble*) alboroto; **to make a** ~ armar un lío or jaleo; **to make a** ~ **of sb** mimar a uno; ~**y** *adj* (*person*) exigente; (*too ornate*) recargado

futile ['fjuːtaɪl] *adj* vano

future ['fjuːtʃə*] *adj* futuro; (*coming*) venidero ♦ *n* futuro; (*prospects*) porvenir; **in** ~ de ahora en adelante

fuze [fjuːz] (*US*) = **fuse**

fuzzy ['fʌzɪ] *adj* (*PHOT*) borroso; (*hair*) muy rizado

G, g

G [dʒiː] *n* (*MUS*) sol *m*

g. *abbr* (= *gram(s)*) gr.

G7 *abbr* (= *Group of Seven*) el grupo de los 7

gabble ['gæbl] *vi* hablar atropelladamente

gable ['geɪbl] *n* aguilón *m*

gadget ['gædʒɪt] *n* aparato

Gaelic ['geɪlɪk] *adj*, *n* (*LING*) gaélico

gag [gæg] *n* (*on mouth*) mordaza; (*joke*) chiste *m* ♦ *vt* amordazar

gaiety ['geɪətɪ] *n* alegría

gaily ['geɪlɪ] *adv* alegremente

gain [geɪn] *n*: ~ (**in**) aumento (de); (*profit*) ganancia ♦ *vt* ganar ♦ *vi* (*watch*) adelantarse; **to** ~ **from/by sth** sacar provecho de algo; **to** ~ **on sb** ganar terreno a uno; **to** ~ **3 lbs** (**in weight**) engordar 3 libras

gal. *abbr* = **gallon**

gala ['gɑːlə] *n* fiesta

gale [geɪl] *n* (*wind*) vendaval *m*

gallant ['gælənt] *adj* valiente; (*towards ladies*) atento

gall bladder ['gɔːl-] *n* vesícula biliar

gallery ['gælərɪ] *n* (*also*: *art* ~: *public*) pinacoteca; (: *private*) galería de arte; (*for spectators*) tribuna

gallon ['gælən] *n* galón *m* (*BRIT* = 4,546 litros, *US* = 3,785 litros)

gallop ['gæləp] n galope m ♦ vi galopar

gallows ['gæləuz] n horca

gallstone ['gɔːlstəun] n cálculo biliario

galore [gə'lɔː*] adv en cantidad, en abundancia

gambit ['gæmbɪt] n (fig): (opening) ~ estrategia (inicial)

gamble ['gæmbl] n (risk) riesgo m ♦ vt jugar, apostar ♦ vi (take a risk) jugárselas; (bet) apostar; to ~ on apostar a; (success etc) contar con; ~ n jugador/a m/f; **gambling** n juego

game [geɪm] n juego; (match) partido; (of cards) partida; (HUNTING) caza ♦ adj (willing): to be ~ for anything atreverse a todo; big ~ caza mayor; ~keeper n guardabosques m inv

gammon ['gæmən] n (bacon) tocino ahumado; (ham) jamón m ahumado

gamut ['gæmət] n gama

gang [gæŋ] n (of criminals) pandilla; (of friends etc) grupo; (of workmen) brigada; ~ up vi: to ~ up on sb aliarse contra uno

gangster ['gæŋstə*] n gángster m

gangway ['gæŋweɪ] n (on ship) pasarela; (BRIT: in theatre, bus etc) pasillo

gaol [dʒeɪl] (BRIT) n, vt = **jail**

gap [gæp] n vacío, hueco (AM); (in trees, traffic) claro; (in time) intervalo; (difference): ~ (between) intervalo (entre)

gape [geɪp] vi mirar boquiabierto; (shirt etc) abrirse (completamente); **gaping** adj (completamente) abierto

garage ['gæraːʒ] n garaje m; (for repairs) taller m

garbage ['gɑːbɪdʒ] (US) n basura; (inf: nonsense) tonterías fpl; ~ can n cubo (SP) or bote m (AM) de la basura

garbled ['gɑːbld] adj (distorted) falsificado, amañado

garden ['gɑːdn] n jardín m; ~s npl (park) parque m (AM) de la basura; ~er n jardinero/a; ~ing n jardinería

gargle ['gɑːgl] vi hacer gárgaras, gargarear (AM)

garish ['gɛərɪʃ] adj chillón/ona

garland ['gɑːlənd] n guirnalda

garlic ['gɑːlɪk] n ajo

garment ['gɑːmənt] n prenda (de vestir)

garnish ['gɑːnɪʃ] vt (CULIN) aderezar

garrison ['gærɪsn] n guarnición f

garter ['gɑːtə*] n (for sock) liga; (US) liguero

gas [gæs] n gas m; (fuel) combustible m; (US: gasoline) gasolina ♦ vt asfixiar con gas; ~ cooker (BRIT) n cocina de gas; ~ cylinder n bombona de gas; ~ fire n estufa de gas

gash [gæʃ] n raja; (wound) cuchillada ♦ vt rajar; acuchillar

gasket ['gæskɪt] n (AUT) junta de culata

gas mask n careta antigás

gas meter n contador m de gas

gasoline ['gæsəliːn] (US) n gasolina

gasp [gɑːsp] n boqueada; (of shock etc) grito sofocado ♦ vi (pant) jadear

gas station (US) n gasolinera

gastric ['gæstrɪk] adj gástrico

gate [geɪt] n puerta; (iron ~) verja; ~crash (BRIT) vt colarse en; ~way n (also fig) puerta

gather ['gæðə*] vt (flowers, fruit) coger (SP), recoger; (assemble) reunir; (pick up) recoger; (SEWING) fruncir; (understand) entender ♦ vi (assemble) reunirse; to ~ speed ganar velocidad; ~ing n reunión f, asamblea

gaudy ['gɔːdɪ] adj chillón/ona

gauge [geɪdʒ] n (instrument) indicador m ♦ vt medir; (fig) juzgar

gaunt [gɔːnt] adj (haggard) demacrado; (stark) desolado

gauntlet ['gɔːntlɪt] n (fig): to run the ~ of exponerse a; to throw down the ~ arrojar el guante

gauze [gɔːz] n gasa

gave [geɪv] pt of **give**

gay [geɪ] adj (homosexual) gay; (joyful)

alegre; (colour) vivo

gaze [geɪz] n mirada fija ♦ vi: **to ~ at sth** mirar algo fijamente

gazelle [gə'zɛl] n gacela

gazumping [gə'zʌmpɪŋ] (BRIT) n la subida del precio de una casa una vez que ya ha sido apalabrado

GB abbr = **Great Britain**

GCE n abbr (BRIT) = General Certificate of Education

GCSE (BRIT) n abbr (= General Certificate of Secondary Education) examen de reválida que se hace a los 16 años

gear [gɪə*] n equipo, herramientas fpl; (TECH) engranaje m; (AUT) velocidad f, marcha ♦ vt (fig: adapt): **to ~ sth to** adaptar or ajustar algo a; **top** or **high** (US)/**low ~** cuarta/primera velocidad; **in ~** en marcha; **~ box** n caja de cambios; **~ lever** n palanca de cambio; **~ shift** (US) n = **~ lever**

geese [giːs] npl of **goose**

gel [dʒɛl] n gel m

gem [dʒɛm] n piedra preciosa

Gemini ['dʒɛmɪnaɪ] n Géminis m, Gemelos mpl

gender ['dʒɛndə*] n género

gene [dʒiːn] n gen(e) m

general ['dʒɛnərəl] n general m ♦ adj general; **in ~** en general; **~ delivery** (US) n lista de correos; **~ election** n elecciones fpl generales; **~ly** adv generalmente, en general; **~ practitioner** n médico general

generate ['dʒɛnəreɪt] vt (ELEC) generar; (jobs, profits) producir

generation [dʒɛnə'reɪʃən] n generación f

generator ['dʒɛnəreɪtə*] n generador m

generosity [dʒɛnə'rɔsɪtɪ] n generosidad f

generous ['dʒɛnərəs] adj generoso

genetic [dʒɪ'nɛtɪk] adj: **~ engineering** ingeniería genética; **~ fingerprinting** identificación f genética

Geneva [dʒɪ'niːvə] n Ginebra

genial ['dʒiːnɪəl] adj afable, simpático

genitals ['dʒɛnɪtlz] npl (órganos mpl) genitales mpl

genius ['dʒiːnɪəs] n genio

genteel [dʒɛn'tiːl] adj fino, elegante

gentle ['dʒɛntl] adj apacible, dulce; (animal) manso; (breeze, curve etc) suave

gentleman ['dʒɛntlmən] (irreg) n señor m; (well-bred man) caballero

gently ['dʒɛntlɪ] adv dulcemente, suavemente

gentry ['dʒɛntrɪ] n alta burguesía

gents [dʒɛnts] n aseos mpl (de caballeros)

genuine ['dʒɛnjuɪn] adj auténtico; (person) sincero

geography [dʒɪ'ɔgrəfɪ] n geografía

geology [dʒɪ'ɔlədʒɪ] n geología

geometric(al) [dʒɪə'mɛtrɪk(l)] adj geométrico

geranium [dʒɪ'reɪnjəm] n geranio

geriatric [dʒɛrɪ'ætrɪk] adj, n geriátrico/a m/f

germ [dʒɜːm] n (microbe) microbio, bacteria; (seed, fig) germen m

German ['dʒɜːmən] adj alemán/ana ♦ n alemán/ana m/f; (LING) alemán m; **~ measles** n rubéola

Germany ['dʒɜːmənɪ] n Alemania

gesture ['dʒɛstjə*] n gesto; (symbol) muestra

KEYWORD

---

get [gɛt] (pt, pp **got**, pp **gotten** (US)) vi
1 (become, be) ponerse, volverse; **to ~ old/tired** envejecer/cansarse; **to ~ drunk** emborracharse; **to ~ dirty** ensuciarse; **to ~ married** casarse; **when do I ~ paid?** ¿cuándo me pagan or se me paga?; **it's ~ting late** se está haciendo tarde

2 (go): **to ~ to/from** llegar a/de; **to ~ home** llegar a casa

3 (begin) empezar a; **to ~ to know sb** (llegar a) conocer a uno; **I'm ~ting to**

like him me está empezando a gustar; **let's ~ going** or **started** ¡vamos (a empezar)!

4 (modal aux vb): **you've got to do it** tienes que hacerlo

♦ vt **1**: **to ~ sth done** (finish) terminar algo; (have done) mandar hacer algo; **to ~ one's hair cut** cortarse el pelo; **to ~ the car going** or **to go** arrancar el coche; **to ~ sb to do sth** conseguir or hacer que alguien haga algo; **to ~ sth/sb ready** preparar algo/a alguien

2 (obtain: money, permission, results) conseguir; (find: job, flat) encontrar; (fetch: person, doctor) buscar; (object) ir a buscar, traer; **to ~ sth for sb** conseguir algo para alguien; **~ me Mr Jones, please** (TEL) póngame or comuníqueme (AM) con el Sr. Jones, por favor; **can I ~ you a drink?** ¿quieres algo de beber?

3 (receive: present, letter) recibir; (acquire: reputation) alcanzar; (: prize) ganar; **what did you ~ for your birthday?** ¿qué te regalaron por tu cumpleaños?; **how much did you ~ for the painting?** ¿cuánto sacaste por el cuadro?

4 (catch) coger (SP), agarrar (AM); (hit: target etc) dar en; **to ~ sb by the arm/throat** coger or agarrar a uno por el brazo/cuello; **~ him!** ¡cógelo! (SP), ¡atrápalo! (AM); **the bullet got him in the leg** la bala le dio en la pierna

5 (take, move) llevar; **to ~ sth to sb** hacer llegar algo a alguien; **do you think we'll ~ it through the door?** ¿crees que lo podremos meter por la puerta?

6 (catch, take: plane, bus etc) coger (SP), tomar (AM); **where do I ~ the train for Birmingham?** ¿dónde se coge or se toma el tren para Birmingham?

7 (understand) entender; (hear) oír;

I've got it! ¡ya lo tengo!, ¡eureka!; **I don't ~ your meaning** no te entiendo; **I'm sorry, I didn't ~ your name** lo siento, no cogí su nombre

8 (have, possess): **to have got** tener

get about vi salir mucho; (news) divulgarse

get along vi (agree) llevarse bien; (depart) marcharse; (manage) = **get by**

get at vt fus (attack) atacar; (reach) alcanzar

get away vi marcharse; (escape) escaparse

get away with vt fus hacer impunemente

get back vi (return) volver ♦ vt recobrar

get by vi (pass) lograr pasar; (manage) arreglárselas

get down vi bajarse ♦ vt fus bajar ♦ vt bajar; (depress) deprimir

get down to vt fus (work) ponerse a

get in vi entrar; (train) llegar; (arrive home) volver a casa, regresar

get into vt fus entrar en; (vehicle) subir a; **to ~ into a rage** enfadarse

get off vi (from train etc) bajar; (depart: person, car) marcharse ♦ vt (remove) quitar ♦ vt fus (train, bus) bajar de

get on vi (at exam etc): **how are you ~ting on?** ¿cómo te va?; (agree): **to ~ on (with)** llevarse bien (con) ♦ vt fus subir a

get out vi salir; (of vehicle) bajar ♦ vt sacar

get out of vt fus salir de; (duty etc) escaparse de

get over vt fus (illness) recobrarse de

get round vt fus rodear; (fig: person) engatusar a

get through vi (TEL) lograr comunicarse

get through to vt fus (TEL) comunicar con

get together vi reunirse ♦ vt reunir,

juntar

get up vi (rise) levantarse ♦ vt fus subir
get up to vt fus (reach) llegar a; (prank) hacer

subsidio de desempleo
gist [dʒɪst] n lo esencial
give [gɪv] (pt **gave**, pp **given**) vt dar; (deliver) entregar; (as gift) regalar ♦ vt (break) romperse; (stretch: fabric) dar de sí; **to ~ sb sth, ~ sth to sb** dar algo a uno; **~ away** vt (give free) regalar; (betray) traicionar; (disclose) revelar; **~ back** vt devolver; **~ in** vi ceder ♦ vt entregar; **~ off** vt despedir; **~ out** vt distribuir; **~ up** vi rendirse, darse por vencido ♦ vt renunciar a; **to ~ up smoking** dejar de fumar; **to ~ o.s. up** entregarse; **~ way** vi ceder; (BRIT: AUT) ceder el paso

geyser ['giːzə*] n (water heater) calentador m de agua; (GEO) géiser m
ghastly ['gɑːstlɪ] adj horrible
gherkin ['gɜːkɪn] n pepinillo
ghetto blaster ['getəublɑːstə*] n cassette m portátil de gran tamaño
ghost [gəust] n fantasma m
giant ['dʒaɪənt] n gigante m/f ♦ adj gigantesco, gigante
gibberish ['dʒɪbərɪʃ] n galimatías m
giblets ['dʒɪblɪts] npl menudillos mpl
Gibraltar [dʒɪ'brɔːltə*] n Gibraltar m
giddy ['gɪdɪ] adj mareado
gift [gɪft] n regalo; (ability) talento; **~ed** adj dotado; **~ token** o **voucher** n vale m canjeable por un regalo
gigantic [dʒaɪ'gæntɪk] adj gigantesco
giggle ['gɪgl] vi reírse tontamente
gill [dʒɪl] n (measure) = 0.25 pints (BRIT = 0.148l, US = 0.118l)
gills [gɪlz] npl (of fish) branquias fpl, agallas fpl
gilt [gɪlt] adj, n dorado; **~-edged** adj (COMM) de máxima garantía
gimmick ['gɪmɪk] n truco
gin [dʒɪn] n ginebra
ginger ['dʒɪndʒə*] n jengibre m; **~ ale** = **~ beer** n; **~ beer** (BRIT) n gaseosa de jengibre; **~bread** n pan m (o galleta) de jengibre
gingerly ['dʒɪndʒəlɪ] adv con cautela
gipsy ['dʒɪpsɪ] n = gypsy
giraffe [dʒɪ'rɑːf] n jirafa
girder ['gɜːdə*] n viga
girl [gɜːl] n (small) niña; (young woman) chica, joven f, muchacha; (daughter) hija; **an English ~** una (chica) inglesa; **~friend** n (of girl) amiga; (of boy) novia; **~ish** adj de niña
giro ['dʒaɪrəu] n (BRIT: bank ~) giro bancario; (post office ~) giro postal; (state benefit) cheque quincenal del

glacier ['glæsɪə*] n glaciar m
glad [glæd] adj contento
gladly ['glædlɪ] adv con mucho gusto
glamorous ['glæmərəs] adj encantador(a), atractivo; **glamour** ['glæmə*] n encanto, atractivo
glance [glɑːns] n ojeada, mirada ♦ vi: **to ~ at** echar una ojeada a; **glancing** adj (blow) oblicuo
gland [glænd] n glándula
glare [glɛə*] n (of anger) mirada feroz; (of light) deslumbramiento, brillo; **to be in the ~ of publicity** ser el foco de la atención pública ♦ vi deslumbrar; **to ~ at** mirar con odio a; **glaring** adj (mistake) manifiesto
glass [glɑːs] n vidrio, cristal m; (for drinking) vaso; (: with stem) copa; **~es** npl (spectacles) gafas fpl; **~house** n invernadero; **~ware** n cristalería
glaze [gleɪz] vt (window) poner cristales a; (pottery) vidriar ♦ n vidriado; **glazier** ['gleɪzɪə*] n vidriero/a
gleam [gliːm] vi brillar
glean [gliːn] vt (information) recoger
glee [gliː] n alegría, regocijo
glen [glen] n cañada
glib [glɪb] adj de mucha labia; (promise, response) poco sincero
glide [glaɪd] vi deslizarse; (AVIAT, birds) planear; **~r** n (AVIAT) planeador m; **gliding** n (AVIAT) vuelo sin motor

glimmer ['glɪmə*] n luz f tenue; (of interest) muestra; (of hope) rayo
glimpse [glɪmps] n vislumbre m ♦ vt vislumbrar, entrever
glint [glɪnt] vi centellear
glisten ['glɪsn] vi relucir, brillar
glitter ['glɪtə*] vi relucir, brillar
gloat [gləut] vi: **to ~ over** recrearse en
global ['gləubl] adj mundial; **~ warming** (re)calentamiento global
globe [gləub] n globo; (model) globo terráqueo
gloom [glu:m] n oscuridad f; (sadness) tristeza; **~y** adj (dark) oscuro; (sad) triste; (pessimistic) pesimista
glorious ['glɔːrɪəs] adj glorioso; (weather etc) magnífico
glory ['glɔːrɪ] n gloria
gloss [glɔs] n (shine) brillo; (paint) pintura de aceite; **~ over** vt fus disimular
glossary ['glɔsərɪ] n glosario
glossy ['glɔsɪ] adj lustroso; (magazine) de lujo
glove [glʌv] n guante m; **~ compartment** n (AUT) guantera
glow [gləu] vi brillar
glower ['glauə*] vi: **to ~ at** mirar con ceño
glue [glu:] n goma (de pegar), cemento ♦ vt pegar
glum [glʌm] adj (person, tone) melancólico
glut [glʌt] n superabundancia
glutton ['glʌtn] n glotón/ona m/f; **a ~ for work** un(a) trabajador(a) incansable
GM adj abbr (= genetically modified) transgénico
GMO n abbr (= genetically-modified organism) organismo transgénico
gnat [næt] n mosquito
gnaw [nɔː] vt roer
gnome [nəum] n gnomo
go [gəu] (pt went, pp gone; pl ~es) vi ir; (travel) viajar; (depart) irse, marcharse; (work) funcionar, marchar; (be sold) venderse; (time) pasar; (fit,

suit): **to ~ with** hacer juego con; (become) ponerse; (break etc) estropearse, romperse ♦ n: **to have a ~ (at)** probar suerte (con); **to be on the ~** no parar; **whose ~ is it?** ¿a quién le toca?; **he's going to do it** va a hacerlo; **to ~ for a walk** ir de paseo; **to ~ dancing** ir a bailar; **how did it ~?** ¿qué tal salió or resultó?; ¿cómo ha ido?; **to ~ round the back** pasar por detrás; **~ about** vi (rumour) propagarse ♦ vt fus: **how do I ~ about this?** ¿cómo me las arreglo para hacer esto?; **~ ahead** vi seguir. adelante; **~ along** vi ir ♦ vt fus bordear; **to ~ along with** (agree) estar de acuerdo con; **~ away** vi irse, marcharse; **~ back** vi volver; **~ back on** vt fus (promise) faltar a; **~ by** vi (time) pasar ♦ vt fus guiarse por; **~ down** vi bajar; (ship) hundirse; (sun) ponerse ♦ vt fus bajar; **~ for** vt fus (fetch) ir por; (like) gustar; (attack) atacar; **~ in** vi entrar; **~ in for** vt fus (competition) presentarse a; **~ into** vt fus entrar en; (investigate) investigar; (embark on) dedicarse a; **~ off** vi irse, marcharse; (food) pasarse; (explode) estallar; (event) realizarse ♦ vt fus dejar de gustar; **I'm going off him/the idea** ya no me gusta tanto él/la idea; **~ on** vi (continue) seguir, continuar; (happen) pasar, ocurrir; **to ~ on doing sth** seguir haciendo algo; **~ out** vi salir; (fire, light) apagarse; **~ over** vi (ship) zozobrar ♦ vt fus (check) revisar; **~ through** vt fus (town etc) atravesar; **~ up** vi, vt fus subir; **~ without** vt fus pasarse sin
goad [gəud] vt aguijonear
go-ahead adj (person) dinámico; (firm) innovador(a) ♦ n luz f verde
goal [gəul] n meta; (score) gol m; **~keeper** n portero, m; **~post** n poste m (de la portería)
goat [gəut] n cabra
gobble ['gɔbl] vt (also: **~ down**, **~ up**) tragarse, engullir

go-between ['gəʊbɪtwiːn] n intermediario/a

god [gɒd] n dios m; **G~** n Dios m; **~child** n ahijado/a; **~daughter** n ahijada; **~dess** n diosa; **~father** n padrino; **~-forsaken** adj dejado de la mano de Dios; **~mother** n madrina; **~send** n don m del cielo; **~son** n ahijado

goggles ['gɒglz] npl gafas fpl

going ['gəʊɪŋ] n (conditions) estado del terreno ♦ adj: **the ~ rate** la tarifa corriente o en vigor

gold [gəʊld] n oro m ♦ adj de oro; **~en** adj (made of ~) de oro; (~ in colour) dorado; **~fish** n pez m de colores; **~mine** n (also fig) mina de oro; **~-plated** adj chapado en oro; **~smith** n orfebre m/f

golf [gɒlf] n golf m; **~ ball** n (for game) pelota de golf; (on typewriter) esfera; **~ club** n club m de golf; (stick) palo (de golf); **~ course** n campo de golf; **~er** n golfista m/f

gone [gɒn] pp of **go**

good [gʊd] adj bueno; (pleasant) agradable; (kind) bueno, amable; (well-behaved) educado ♦ n bien m, provecho; **~s** npl (COMM) mercancías fpl; **~!** ¡qué bien!; **to be ~ at** tener aptitud para; **to be ~ for** servir para; **it's ~ for you** te hace bien; **would you be ~ enough to ...?** ¿podría hacerme el favor de ...?, ¿sería tan amable de ...?; **a ~ deal (of)** mucho; **a ~ many** muchos; **to make ~** reparar; **it's no ~ complaining** no vale la pena (de) quejarse; **for ~** para siempre, definitivamente; **~ morning/afternoon!** ¡buenos días/buenas tardes!; **~ evening!** ¡buenas noches!; **~ night!** ¡buenas noches!; **~-bye!** ¡adiós!; **to say ~bye** despedirse; **G~ Friday** n Viernes m Santo; **~-looking** adj guapo; **~-natured** adj amable, simpático; **~ness** n (of person) bondad f; **for ~ness sake!** ¡por Dios!; **~ness gracious!** ¡Dios mío!; **~s train**

(BRIT) n tren m de mercancías; **~will** n buena voluntad f

goose [guːs] (pl **geese**) n ganso, oca

gooseberry ['gʊzbərɪ] n grosella espinosa; **to play ~** hacer de carabina

gooseflesh ['guːsfleʃ] n = **goose pimples**

goose pimples npl carne f de gallina

gore [gɔː*] vt cornear ♦ n sangre f

gorge [gɔːdʒ] n barranco ♦ vr: **to ~ o.s. (on)** atracarse (de)

gorgeous ['gɔːdʒəs] adj (thing) precioso; (weather) espléndido; (person) guapísimo

gorilla [gə'rɪlə] n gorila m

gorse [gɔːs] n tojo

gory ['gɔːrɪ] adj sangriento

go-slow (BRIT) n huelga de manos caídas

gospel ['gɒspl] n evangelio

gossip ['gɒsɪp] n (scandal) cotilleo, chismes mpl; (chat) charla; (scandalmonger) cotilla m/f, chismoso/a ♦ vi cotillear

got [gɒt] pt, pp of **get**; **~ten** (US) pp of **get**

gout [gaʊt] n gota

govern ['gʌvən] vt gobernar; (influence) dominar; **~ess** n institutriz f; **~ment** n gobierno; **~or** n gobernador(a) m/f; (of school etc) miembro del consejo; (of jail) director(a) m/f

gown [gaʊn] n traje m; (of teacher, BRIT: of judge) toga

G.P. n abbr = **general practitioner**

grab [græb] vt coger (SP) or agarrar (AM), arrebatar ♦ vi: **to ~ at** intentar agarrar

grace [greɪs] n gracia ♦ vt honrar; (adorn) adornar; **5 days' ~** un plazo de 5 días; **~ful** adj grácil, ágil; (style, shape) elegante, gracioso; **gracious** ['greɪʃəs] adj amable

grade [greɪd] n (quality) clase f, calidad f; (in hierarchy) grado; (SCOL: mark) nota; (US: school class) curso ♦ vt clasificar; ~ **crossing** (US) n paso a nivel; ~ **school** (US) n escuela primaria

gradient ['greɪdɪənt] n pendiente f

gradual ['grædjuəl] adj paulatino; ~**ly** adv paulatinamente

graduate [n 'grædjuɪt, vb 'grædjueɪt] n (US: of high school) graduado/a; (of university) licenciado/a ♦ vi graduarse; licenciarse; **graduation** [-'eɪʃən] n (ceremony) entrega del título

graffiti [grə'fi:tɪ] n pintadas fpl

graft [grɑ:ft] n (AGR, MED) injerto; (BRIT: inf) trabajo duro; (bribery) corrupción f ♦ vt injertar

grain [greɪn] n (single particle) grano; (corn) granos mpl, cereales mpl; (of wood) fibra

gram [græm] n gramo

grammar ['græmə*] n gramática; ~ **school** (BRIT) n ≈ instituto de segunda enseñanza, liceo (SP)

grammatical [grə'mætɪkl] adj gramatical

gramme [græm] n = **gram**

gramophone ['græməfəʊn] (BRIT) n tocadiscos m inv

grand [grænd] adj magnífico, imponente; (wonderful) estupendo; (gesture etc) grandioso; ~**children** npl nieto mpl; ~**dad** (inf) n yayo, abuelito; ~**daughter** n nieta; ~**eur** [ɡrændjə*] n magnificencia, lo grandioso; ~**father** n abuelo; ~**ma** (inf) n yaya, abuela; ~**mother** n abuela; ~**pa** (inf) n = ~**dad**; ~**parents** npl abuelos mpl; ~ **piano** n piano de cola; ~**son** n nieto; ~**stand** n (SPORT) tribuna

granite ['grænɪt] n granito

granny ['grænɪ] (inf) n abuelita, yaya

grant [grɑ:nt] vt (concede) conceder; (admit) reconocer ♦ n (SCOL) beca; (ADMIN) subvención f; **to take sth ~ for ~ed** dar algo por sentado/no hacer ningún caso a uno

granulated sugar ['grænjuleɪtɪd-] (BRIT) n azúcar m blanquilla

grape [greɪp] n uva

grapefruit ['greɪpfru:t] n pomelo (SP), toronja (AM)

graph [grɑ:f] n gráfica; ~**ic** ['græfɪk] adj gráfico; ~**ics** n artes fpl gráficas ♦ npl (drawings) dibujos mpl

grapple ['græpl] vi: **to ~ with sth/sb** agarrar a algo/uno

grasp [grɑ:sp] vt agarrar, asir; (understand) comprender ♦ n (grip) asimiento; (understanding) comprensión f; ~**ing** adj (mean) avaro

grass [grɑ:s] n hierba; (lawn) césped m; ~**hopper** n saltamontes m inv; ~**roots** npl (fig) popular

grate [greɪt] n parrilla de chimenea ♦ vi: **to ~ (on)** chirriar (sobre) ♦ vt (CULIN) rallar

grateful ['greɪtful] adj agradecido

grater ['greɪtə*] n rallador m

gratifying ['grætɪfaɪɪŋ] adj grato

grating ['greɪtɪŋ] n (iron bars) reja ♦ adj (noise) áspero

gratitude ['grætɪtju:d] n agradecimiento

gratuity [grə'tju:ɪtɪ] n gratificación f

grave [greɪv] n tumba ♦ adj serio, grave

gravel ['grævl] n grava

gravestone ['greɪvstəʊn] n lápida

graveyard ['greɪvjɑ:d] n cementerio

gravity ['grævɪtɪ] n gravedad f

gravy ['greɪvɪ] n salsa de carne

gray [greɪ] adj = **grey**

graze [greɪz] vi pacer ♦ vt (touch lightly) rozar; (scrape) raspar ♦ n (MED) abrasión f

grease [gri:s] n (fat) grasa; (lubricant) lubricante m ♦ vt engrasar; lubrificar; ~**proof paper** (BRIT) n papel m apergaminado; **greasy** adj grasiento

great [greɪt] adj grande; (inf) magnífico, estupendo; **G~ Britain** n Gran Bretaña; ~**grandfather** n bisabuelo; ~**grandmother** n bisabuela; ~**ly** adv muy; (with verb) mucho; ~**ness** n grandeza

Greece [gri:s] n Grecia

greed [griːd] n (also: ~iness) codicia,
avaricia; (for food) gula; (for power etc)
avidez f; **~y** adj avaro; (for food)
glotón/ona

Greek [griːk] adj griego ♦ n griego/a;
(LING) griego

green [griːn] adj (also POL.) verde;
(inexperienced) novato ♦ n verde m;
(stretch of grass) césped m; (GOLF)
green m; **~s** npl (vegetables) verduras
fpl; **~ belt** n zona verde; **~ card** n
(AUT) carta verde; (US: work permit)
permiso de trabajo para los extranjeros
en EE. UU.; **~ery** n verdura; **~grocer**
(BRIT) n verdulero/a; **~house** n
invernadero; **~house effect** n efecto
invernadero; **~house gas** n gases m
de invernadero; **~ish** adj verdoso

Greenland ['griːnlənd] n Groenlandia

greet [griːt] vt (welcome) dar la
bienvenida a; (receive: news) recibir;
~ing n (welcome) bienvenida; **~ing(s)
card** n tarjeta de felicitación

grenade [grə'neɪd] n granada

grew [gruː] pt of **grow**

grey [greɪ] adj gris; (weather) sombrío;
~-haired adj canoso; **~hound** n galgo

grid [grɪd] n reja; (ELEC) red f; **~lock** n
(traffic jam) retención f

grief [griːf] n dolor m, pena

grievance ['griːvəns] n motivo de
queja, agravio

grieve [griːv] vi afligirse, acongojarse
♦ vt dar pena a; **to ~ for** llorar por

grievous ['griːvəs] adj: **~ bodily
harm** (LAW) daños mpl corporales
graves

grill [grɪl] n (on cooker) parrilla; (also:
mixed ~) parrillada ♦ vt (BRIT) asar a la
parrilla; (inf: question) interrogar

grille [grɪl] n reja; (AUT) rejilla

grim [grɪm] adj (place) sombrío;
(situation) triste; (person) ceñudo

grimace [grɪ'meɪs] n mueca ♦ vi hacer
muecas

grime [graɪm] n mugre f, suciedad f

grin [grɪn] n sonrisa abierta ♦ vi sonreír
abiertamente

grind [graɪnd] (pt, pp **ground**) vt
(coffee, pepper etc) moler; (US: meat)
picar; (make sharp) afilar ♦ n (work)
rutina

grip [grɪp] n (hold) asimiento; (control)
control m, dominio; (of tyre etc): **to
have a good/bad ~** agarrarse bien/
mal; (handle) asidero; (holdall) maletín
m ♦ vt agarrar; (viewer, reader) fascinar;
to get to ~s with enfrentarse con;
~ping adj absorbente

grisly ['grɪzlɪ] adj horripilante, horrible

gristle ['grɪsl] n ternilla

grit [grɪt] n gravilla; (courage) valor m
♦ vt (road) poner gravilla en; **to
~ one's teeth** apretar los dientes

groan [grəun] n gemido; quejido ♦ vi
gemir; quejarse

grocer ['grəusə*] n tendero (de
ultramarinos SP)); **~ies** npl comestibles
mpl; **~'s (shop)** n tienda de
ultramarinos or de abarrotes (AM)

groin [grɔɪn] n ingle f

groom [gruːm] n mozo/a de cuadra;
(also: bride~) novio ♦ vt (horse)
almohazar; (fig): **to ~ sb for** preparar
a uno para; **well-~ed** de buena
presencia

groove [gruːv] n ranura, surco

grope [grəup] vi: **to ~ for** vt fus buscar a
tientas

gross [grəus] adj (neglect, injustice)
grave; (vulgar: behaviour) grosero;
(: appearance) de mal gusto; (COMM)
bruto; **~ly** adv (greatly) enormemente

grotto ['grɔtəu] n gruta

grotty ['grɔtɪ] (inf) adj horrible

ground [graund] pt, pp of **grind** ♦ n
suelo, tierra; (SPORT) campo, terreno;
(reason: gen pl) causa, razón f; (US: also:
~ wire) tierra ♦ vt (plane) mantener en
tierra; (US: ELEC) conectar con tierra; **~s**
npl (of coffee etc) poso; (gardens etc)
jardines mpl, parque m; **on the ~** en el
suelo; **to the ~** al suelo; **to gain/lose
~** ganar/perder terreno; **~ cloth** (US) n

= **~sheet**; **~ing** n (in education) conocimientos mpl básicos; **~less** adj infundado; **~sheet** (BRIT) n tela impermeable; suelo; **~ staff** n personal m de tierra; **~work** n preparación f

group |gru:p| n grupo; (musical) conjunto ♦ vt (also: ~ together) agrupar ♦ vi (also: ~ together) agruparse

grouse |graus| n inv (bird) urogallo ♦ vi (complain) quejarse

grove |grəuv| n arboleda

grovel ['grɔvl] vi (fig): **to ~ before** humillarse ante

grow |grəu| (pt grew, pp grown) vi crecer; (increase) aumentar; (expand) desarrollarse; (become) volverse; **to ~ rich/weak** enriquecerse/debilitarse ♦ vt cultivar; (hair, beard) dejar crecer; **~ up** vi crecer, hacerse hombre/mujer; **~er** n cultivador(a) m/f, productor(a) m/f; **~ing** adj creciente

growl |graul| vi gruñir

grown |grəun| pp of **grow**; **~-up** n adulto, mayor m/f

growth |grəuθ| n crecimiento, desarrollo; (what has grown) brote m; (MED) tumor m

grub |grʌb| n larva, gusano; (inf: food) comida

grubby ['grʌbɪ] adj sucio, mugriento

grudge |grʌdʒ| n (motivo de) rencor m ♦ vt: **to ~ sb sth** dar algo a uno de mala gana; **to bear sb a ~** guardar rencor a uno

gruelling ['gruəlɪŋ] (US grueling) adj penoso, duro

gruesome ['gru:səm] adj horrible

gruff |grʌf| adj (voice) ronco; (manner) brusco

grumble ['grʌmbl] vi refunfuñar, quejarse

grumpy ['grʌmpɪ] adj gruñón/ona

grunt |grʌnt| vi gruñir

G-string |'dʒi:strɪŋ| n taparrabo

guarantee |gærən'ti:| n garantía ♦ vt garantizar

guard |ga:d| n (squad) guardia; (one

man) guardia m; (BRIT: RAIL) jefe m de tren; (on machine) dispositivo de seguridad; (also: fire~) rejilla de protección ♦ vt guardar; (prisoner) vigilar; **to be on one's ~** estar alerta; **~ against** vt fus (prevent) protegerse de; **~ed** adj (fig) cauteloso; **~ian** n guardián/ana m/f; (of minor) tutor(a) m/f; **~'s van** n (BRIT: RAIL) furgón m

Guatemala |gwætɪ'mɑːlə| n Guatemala; **~n** adj, n guatemalteco/a m/f

guerrilla |gə'rɪlə| n guerrillero/a

guess |gɛs| vi adivinar; (US) suponer ♦ vt adivinar; suponer ♦ n suposición f, conjetura; **to take** or **have a ~** tratar de adivinar; **~work** n conjeturas fpl

guest |gɛst| n invitado/a, (in hotel) huésped a m/f; **~ house** n casa de huéspedes, pensión f; **~ room** n cuarto de huéspedes

guffaw |gʌ'fɔ:| vi reírse a carcajadas

guidance |'gaɪdəns| n (advice) consejos mpl

guide |gaɪd| n (person) guía m/f; (book, fig) guía f ♦ vt (round museum etc) guiar; (lead) conducir; (direct) orientar; (girl) **~** n exploradora; **~book** n guía; **~ dog** n perro m guía; **~lines** npl (advice) directrices fpl

guild |gɪld| n gremio

guilt |gɪlt| n culpabilidad f; **~y** adj culpable

guinea pig ['gɪnɪ-] n cobaya; (fig) conejillo de Indias

guise |gaɪz| n: **in** or **under the ~ of** bajo apariencia de

guitar |gɪ'tɑ:*| n guitarra

gulf |gʌlf| n golfo; (abyss) abismo

gull |gʌl| n gaviota

gullible ['gʌlɪbl] adj crédulo

gully |'gʌlɪ| n barranco

gulp |gʌlp| vi tragar saliva ♦ vt (also: ~ down) tragarse

gum |gʌm| n (ANAT) encía; (glue) goma, cemento; (sweet) caramelo de goma; (also: chewing-~) chicle m ♦ vt

pegar con goma; **~boots** (BRIT) npl
botas fpl de goma

gun |gʌn| n (small) pistola, revólver m;
(shotgun) escopeta; (rifle) fusil m;
(cannon) cañón m; **~boat** n cañonero;
~fire n disparos mpl; **~man** n
pistolero; **~point** n: **at ~point** a mano
armada; **~powder** n pólvora; **~shot** n
escopetazo

gurgle |'gɔːgl| vi (baby) gorgotear;
(water) borbotear

gush |gʌʃ| vi salir a raudales; (person)
deshacerse en efusiones

gust |gʌst| n (of wind) ráfaga

gusto |'gʌstəu| n entusiasmo

gut |gʌt| n intestino; **~s** npl (ANAT)
tripas fpl; (courage) valor m

gutter |'gʌtə*| n (of roof) canalón m;
(in street) cuneta

guy |gaɪ| n (also: ~rope) cuerda; (inf:
man) tío (SP), tipo; (figure) monigote m

Guy Fawkes' Night

La noche del cinco de noviembre,
Guy Fawkes' Night, se celebra en el
Reino Unido el fracaso de la
conspiración de la pólvora
("Gunpowder Plot"), un intento
fallido de volar el parlamento de
Jaime I en 1605. Esa noche se lanzan
fuegos artificiales y se hacen hogueras
en las que se queman unos muñecos
de trapo que representan a Guy
Fawkes, uno de los cabecillas de la
revuelta. Días antes, los niños tienen
por costumbre pedir a los transeúntes
"a penny for the guy", dinero que
emplean en comprar cohetes y
petardos.

---

guzzle |'gʌzl| vi tragar ♦ vt engullir

gym |dʒɪm| n (also: gymnasium)
gimnasio; (also: gymnastics) gimnasia;
~nast n gimnasta m/f; **~ shoes**
zapatillas fpl (de deporte); **~ slip** (BRIT)
n túnica de colegiala

gynaecologist |gaɪnɪ'kɔlədʒɪst| (US

gynecologist) n ginecólogo/a

gypsy |'dʒɪpsɪ| n gitano/a

H, h

haberdashery |hæbə'dæʃərɪ| (BRIT) n
mercería

habit |'hæbɪt| n hábito, costumbre f;
(drug ~) adicción f; (costume) hábito

habitual |hə'bɪtjuəl| adj
acostumbrado, habitual; (drinker, liar)
empedernido

hack |hæk| vt (cut) cortar; (slice) tajar
♦ n (pej: writer) escritor(a) m/f a sueldo;
~er n (COMPUT) pirata m/f
informático/a

hackneyed |'hæknɪd| adj trillado

had |hæd| pt, pp of **have**

haddock |'hædək| (pl ~ or **~s**) n
especie de merluza

hadn't |'hædnt| = **had not**

haemorrhage |'hɛmərɪdʒ| (US
hemorrhage) n hemorragia

haemorrhoids |'hɛmərɔɪdz| (US
hemorrhoids) npl hemorroides fpl

haggle |'hægl| vi regatear

Hague |heɪg| n: **The ~ La Haya**

hail |heɪl| n granizo; (fig) lluvia ♦ vt
saludar; (taxi) llamar a; (acclaim)
aclamar ♦ vi granizar; **~stone** n
(piedra de) granizo

hair |hɛə*| n pelo, cabellos mpl; (one ~)
pelo, cabello; (on legs etc) vello; **to do
one's ~** arreglarse el pelo; **to have
grey ~** tener canas fpl; **~brush** n
cepillo para el pelo; **~cut** n corte m
(de pelo); **~do** n peinado; **~dresser** n
peluquero/a; **~dresser's** n peluquería ♦
~ dryer n secador m de pelo; **~grip** n
horquilla; **~net** n redecilla; **~piece** n
postizo; **~pin** n horquilla; **~pin bend**
(US **~pin curve**) n curva de horquilla;
~raising adj espeluznante;
~ removing cream n crema
depilatoria; **~ spray** n laca; **~style** n
peinado; **~y** adj peludo; velludo; (inf:

frightening) espeluznante

hake [heɪk] *(pl inv o ~s) n* merluza

half [hɑːf] *(pl halves) n* mitad f; *(of beer)* ≈ caña *(SP)*, media pinta; *(RAIL, BUS)* billete *m* de niño ♦ *adj* medio ♦ *adv* medio, a medias; **two and a ~** dos y media; **~ a dozen** media docena; **~ a pound** media libra; **to cut sth in ~** cortar algo por la mitad; **~-caste** [ˈhɑːfkɑːst] *n* mestizo/a; **~-hearted** *adj* indiferente, poco entusiasta; **~-hour** *n* media hora; **~-mast** *n:* **at ~-mast** *(flag)* a media asta; **~-price** *adj, adv* a mitad de precio; **~ term** *(BRIT) (SCOL) vacaciones de mediados del trimestre;* **~-time** *n* descanso; **~way** *adv* a medio camino; *(in period of time)* a mitad de

hall [hɔːl] *n (for concerts)* sala; *(entrance way)* hall *m;* vestíbulo; **~ of residence** *(BRIT) n* residencia

hallmark [ˈhɔːlmɑːk] *n* sello

hallo [həˈləʊ] *excl* = **hello**

Hallowe'en [hæləʊˈiːn] *n* víspera de Todos los Santos

Hallowe'en

La tradición anglosajona dice que en la noche del 31 de octubre, Hallowe'en, víspera de Todos los Santos, es posible ver a brujas y fantasmas. En este día los niños se disfrazan y van de puerta en puerta llevando un farol hecho con una calabaza en forma de cabeza humana. Cuando se les abre la puerta gritan "trick or treat", amenazando con gastar una broma a quien no les dé golosinas o algo de calderilla.

---

hallucination [həluːsɪˈneɪʃən] *n* alucinación f

hallway [ˈhɔːlweɪ] *n* vestíbulo

halo [ˈheɪləʊ] *n (of saint)* halo, aureola

halt [hɔːlt] *n (stop)* alto, parada f ♦ *vt* parar; interrumpir ♦ *vi* pararse

halve [hɑːv] *vt* partir por la mitad

halves [hɑːvz] *npl* de **half**

ham [hæm] *n* jamón *m (cocido)*

hamburger [ˈhæmbəːgə*] *n* hamburguesa

hamlet [ˈhæmlɪt] *n* aldea

hammer [ˈhæmə*] *n* martillo ♦ *vt (nail)* clavar; *(force)*: **to ~ an idea into sb/a message across** meter una idea en la cabeza a uno/machacar una idea ♦ *vi* dar golpes

hammock [ˈhæmək] *n* hamaca

hamper [ˈhæmpə*] *vt* estorbar ♦ *n* cesto

hand [hænd] *n* mano f; *(of clock)* aguja; *(writing)* letra; *(worker)* obrero ♦ *vt* dar, pasar; **to give** o **lend sb a ~** echar una mano a uno, ayudar a uno; **at ~** a mano; **in ~** *(time)* libre; *(job etc)* entre manos; **on ~** *(person, services)* a mano, al alcance; **to ~** *(information etc)* a mano; **on the one ~ ..., on the other ~ ...** por una parte ... por otra (parte) ...; **~ in** *vt* entregar; **~ out** *vt* distribuir; **~ over** *vt (deliver)* entregar; **~bag** *n* bolso *(SP)*, cartera *(AM)*; **~book** *n* manual *m;* **~brake** *n* freno de mano; **~cuffs** *npl* esposas *fpl;* **~ful** *n* puñado

handicap [ˈhændɪkæp] *n* minusvalía; *(disadvantage)* desventaja; *(SPORT)* handicap *m* ♦ *vt* estorbar; **mentally/ physically ~ped** deficiente *m/f* (mental)/minusválido/a (físico/a)

handicraft [ˈhændɪkrɑːft] *n* artesanía; *(object)* objeto de artesanía

handiwork [ˈhændɪwəːk] *n* obra

handkerchief [ˈhæŋkətʃɪf] *n* pañuelo

handle [ˈhændl] *n (of door etc)* tirador *m; (of cup etc)* asa; *(of knife etc)* mango; *(for winding)* manivela ♦ *vt (touch)* tocar; *(deal with)* encargarse de; *(treat: people)* manejar; **"~ with care"** "(manéjese) con cuidado"; **to fly off the ~** perder los estribos; **~bar(s)** *n(pl)* manillar f

hand: ~ luggage *n* equipaje *m* de

mano; **~made** adj hecho a mano; **~out** n (money etc) limosna; (leaflet) folleto; **~rail** n pasamanos m inv; **~shake** n apretón m de manos

handsome ['hænsəm] adj guapo; (building) bello; (fig: profit) considerable

handwriting ['hændraitiŋ] n letra

handy ['hændi] adj (close at hand) a la mano; (tool etc) práctico; (skilful) hábil, diestro

hang [hæŋ] (pt, pp hung) vt colgar; (criminal: pt, pp hanged) ahorcar ♦ vi (painting, coat etc) colgar; (hair, drapery) caer; **to get the ~ of sth** (inf) lograr dominar algo; **~ about** or **around** vi haraganear; **~ on** vi (wait) esperar; **~ up** vi (TEL) colgar ♦ vt colgar

hanger ['hæŋə*] n percha; **~on** n parásito

hang: ~-gliding ['-glaɪdɪŋ] n vuelo libre; **~over** n (after drinking) resaca; **~-up** n complejo

hanker ['hæŋkə*] vi: **to ~ after** añorar

hankie, **hanky** ['hæŋkɪ] n abbr = handkerchief

haphazard [hæp'hæzəd] adj fortuito

happen ['hæpən] vi suceder, ocurrir; (chance): **he ~ed to hear/see** dió la casualidad de que oyó/vió; **as it ~s** da la casualidad de que; **~ing** n suceso, acontecimiento

happily ['hæpɪlɪ] adv (luckily) afortunadamente; (cheerfully) alegremente

happiness ['hæpɪnɪs] n felicidad f; (cheerfulness) alegría

happy ['hæpɪ] adj feliz; (cheerful) alegre; **to be ~ (with)** estar contento (con); **to be ~ to do** estar encantado de hacer; **~ birthday!** ¡feliz cumpleaños!; **~-go-lucky** adj despreocupado; **~ hour** n horas en las que la bebida es más barata, happy hour f

harass ['hærəs] vt acosar, hostigar; **~ment** n persecución f

harbour ['hɑːbə*] (US **harbor**) n puerto ♦ vt (fugitive) dar abrigo a; (hope etc) abrigar

hard [hɑːd] adj duro; (difficult) difícil; (work) arduo; (person) severo; (fact) innegable ♦ adv (work) mucho, duro; (think) profundamente; **to look ~ at** clavar los ojos en; **to try ~** esforzarse; **no ~ feelings!** ¡sin rencor(es)!; **to be ~ of hearing** ser duro de oído; **to be ~ done by** ser tratado injustamente; **~back** n libro en cartoné; **~ cash** n dinero contante; **~ disk** n (COMPUT) disco duro or rígido; **~en** vt endurecer; (fig) curtir ♦ vi endurecerse; curtirse; **~-headed** adj realista; **~ labour** n trabajos mpl forzados

hardly ['hɑːdlɪ] adv apenas; **~ ever** casi nunca

hard: ~ship n privación f; **~ shoulder** (BRIT) n (AUT) arcén m; **~-up** (inf) adj sin un duro (SP), sin plata (AM); **~ware** n ferretería; (COMPUT) hardware m; (MIL) armamento; **~ware shop** n ferretería; **~-wearing** adj resistente, duradero; **~-working** adj trabajador(a)

hardy ['hɑːdɪ] adj fuerte; (plant) resistente

hare [hɛə*] n liebre f; **~-brained** adj descabellado

harm [hɑːm] n daño, mal m ♦ vt (person) hacer daño a; (health, interests) perjudicar; (thing) dañar; **out of ~'s way** a salvo; **~ful** adj dañino; **~less** adj (person) inofensivo; (joke etc) inocente

harmony ['hɑːmənɪ] n armonía

harness ['hɑːnɪs] n arreos mpl; (for child) arnés m; (safety ~) arneses mpl ♦ vt (horse) enjaezar; (resources) aprovechar

harp [hɑːp] n arpa ♦ vi: **to ~ on (about)** machacar (con)

harrowing ['hærəʊɪŋ] adj angustioso

harsh [hɑːʃ] adj (cruel) duro, cruel; (severe) severo; (sound) áspero; (light) deslumbrador(a)

harvest ['hɑ:vɪst] n (~ time) siega; (of cereals etc) cosecha; (of grapes) vendimia ♦ vt cosechar

has [hæz] vb see **have**

hash [hæʃ] n (CULIN) picadillo; (fig: mess) lío

hashish ['hæʃɪʃ] n hachís m

hasn't ['hæznt] = **has not**

hassle ['hæsl] (inf) n lata

haste [heɪst] n prisa; ~**n** ['heɪsn] vt acelerar ♦ vi darse prisa; **hastily** adv de prisa; precipitadamente; **hasty** adj apresurado; (rash) precipitado

hat [hæt] n sombrero

hatch [hætʃ] n (NAUT: also: ~way) escotilla; (also: service ~) ventanilla ♦ vi (bird) salir del cascarón ♦ vt incubar; (plot) tramar; **5 eggs have ~ed** han salido 5 pollos

hatchback ['hætʃbæk] n (AUT) tres or cinco puertas m

hatchet ['hætʃɪt] n hacha

hate [heɪt] vt odiar, aborrecer ♦ n odio; ~**ful** adj odioso; **hatred** ['heɪtrɪd] n odio

haughty ['hɔ:tɪ] adj altanero

haul [hɔ:l] vt tirar ♦ n (of fish) redada; (of stolen goods etc) botín m; ~**age** (BRIT) n transporte m; (costs) gastos mpl de transporte; ~**ier** (US ~**er**) n transportista m/f

haunch [hɔ:ntʃ] n anca; (of meat) pierna

haunt [hɔ:nt] vt (subj: ghost) aparecerse en; (obsess) obsesionar ♦ n guarida

---

KEYWORD

have [hæv] (pt, pp **had**) aux vb **1** (gen) haber; **to ~ arrived/eaten** haber llegado/comido; **having finished** or **when he had finished, he left** cuando hubo acabado, se fue

2 (in tag questions): **you've done it, ~n't you?** lo has hecho, ¿verdad? or ¿no?

3 (in short answers and questions): **I**

~**n't** no; **so I ~** pues, es verdad; **we ~n't paid — yes we ~!** no hemos pagado — ¡sí que hemos pagado!; **I've been there before, ~ you?** he estado allí antes, ¿y tú?

♦ modal aux vb (be obliged): **to ~ (got) to do sth** tener que hacer algo; **you ~n't to tell her** no hay que or no debes decírselo

♦ vt **1** (possess): **he has (got) blue eyes/dark hair** tiene los ojos azules/el pelo negro

2 (referring to meals etc): **to ~ breakfast/lunch/dinner** desayunar/comer/cenar; **to ~ a drink/a cigarette** tomar algo/fumar un cigarrillo

3 (receive) recibir; (obtain) obtener; **may I ~ your address?** ¿puedes darme tu dirección?; **you can ~ it for £5** te lo puedes quedar por £5; **I must ~ it by tomorrow** lo necesito para mañana; **to ~ a baby** tener un niño or bebé

4 (maintain, allow): **I won't ~ it/this nonsense!** ¡no lo permitiré!; ¡no permitiré estas tonterías!; **we can't ~ that** no podemos permitir eso

5: **to ~ sth done** hacer or mandar hacer algo; **to ~ one's hair cut** cortarse el pelo; **to ~ sb do sth** hacer que alguien haga algo

6 (experience, suffer): **to ~ a cold/flu** tener un resfriado/la gripe; **she had her bag stolen/her arm broken** le robaron el bolso/se rompió un brazo; **to ~ an operation** operarse

7 (+ noun): **to ~ a swim/walk/bath/rest** nadar/dar un paseo/darse un baño/descansar; **let's ~ a look** vamos a ver; **to ~ a meeting/party** celebrar una reunión/una fiesta; **let me ~ a try** déjame intentarlo

have out vt: **to ~ it out with sb** (settle a problem etc) dejar las cosas en claro con alguien

haven ['heɪvn] n puerto; (fig) refugio

haven't ['hævnt] = have not

havoc ['hævək] n estragos mpl

hawk [hɔːk] n halcón m

hay [heɪ] n heno; **~ fever** n fiebre f del heno; **~stack** n almiar m

haywire ['heɪwaɪə*] (inf) adj: **to go ~** (plan) embrollarse

hazard ['hæzəd] n peligro ♦ vt aventurar; **~ous** adj peligroso; **~ warning lights** npl (AUT) señales fpl de emergencia

haze [heɪz] n neblina

hazelnut ['heɪzlnʌt] n avellana

hazy ['heɪzɪ] adj brumoso; (idea) vago

he [hiː] pron él; **~ who ...** el que ..., quien ...

head [hed] n cabeza; (leader) jefe/a m/f; (of school) director(a) m/f ♦ vt (list) encabezar; (group) capitanear; (company) dirigir; **~s (or tails)** cara (o cruz); **~ first** de cabeza; **~ over heels** (in love) perdidamente; **to ~ the ball** cabecear (la pelota); **~ for** vt fus dirigirse a; (disaster) ir camino de; **~ache** n dolor m de cabeza; **~dress** n tocado; **~ing** n título; **~lamp** (BRIT) n = **~light**; **~land** n promontorio; **~light** n faro; **~line** n titular m; **~long** adv (fall) de cabeza; (rush) precipitadamente; **~master/mistress** n director(a) m/f (de escuela); **~ office** n oficina central, central f; **~-on** adj (collision) de frente; **~phones** npl auriculares mpl; **~quarters** npl sede f central; (MIL) cuartel m general; **~rest** n reposa-cabezas m inv; **~room** n (in car) altura interior; (under bridge) (límite m de) altura; **~scarf** n pañuelo; **~strong** adj testarudo; **~ waiter** n maître m; **~way** n: **to make ~way** (fig) hacer progresos; **~wind** n viento contrario; **~y** adj (experience, period) apasionante; (wine) cabezón; (atmosphere) embriagador(a)

heal [hiːl] vt curar ♦ vi cicatrizarse

health [helθ] n salud f; **~ food** n alimentos mpl orgánicos; **the H~ Service** (BRIT) n el servicio de salud pública; ≈ el Insalud (SP); **~y** adj sano, saludable

heap [hiːp] n montón m ♦ vt: **to ~ (up)** amontonar; **to ~ sth with** llenar algo hasta arriba de; **~s of** un montón de

hear [hɪə*] (pt, pp heard) vt (also LAW) oír; (news) saber ♦ vi oír; **to ~ about** oír hablar de; **to ~ from sb** tener noticias de uno; **~ing** n (sense) oído; (LAW) vista; **~ing aid** n audífono; **~say** n rumores mpl, hablillas fpl

hearse [hɜːs] n coche m fúnebre

heart [hɑːt] n corazón m; (fig) valor m; (of lettuce) cogollo; **~s** npl (CARDS) corazones mpl; **to lose/take ~** descorazonarse/cobrar ánimo; **at ~** en el fondo; **by ~** (learn, know) de memoria; **~ attack** n infarto (de miocardio); **~beat** n latido (del corazón); **~breaking** adj desgarrador(a); **~broken** adj: **she was ~broken about it** esto le partió el corazón; **~burn** n acedía; **~ failure** n fallo cardíaco; **~felt** adj (deeply felt) más sentido

hearth [hɑːθ] n (fireplace) chimenea

hearty ['hɑːtɪ] adj (person) campechano; (laugh) sano; (dislike, support) absoluto

heat [hiːt] n calor m; (SPORT: also: qualifying ~) prueba eliminatoria ♦ vt calentar; **~ up** vi calentarse ♦ vt calentar; **~ed** adj caliente; (fig) acalorado; **~er** n estufa; (in car) calefacción f

heath [hiːθ] (BRIT) n brezal m

heather ['heðə*] n brezo

heating ['hiːtɪŋ] n calefacción f

heatstroke ['hiːtstrəuk] n insolación f

heatwave ['hiːtweɪv] n ola de calor

heave [hiːv] vt (pull) tirar; (push) empujar con esfuerzo; (lift) levantar (con esfuerzo) ♦ vi (chest) palpitar; (retch) tener náuseas ♦ n tirón m;

empujón m; **to ~ a sigh** suspirar
heaven ['hɛvn] n cielo; (fig) una
maravilla; **~ly** adj celestial; (fig)
maravilloso
heavily ['hɛvɪlɪ] adv pesadamente;
(drink, smoke) con exceso; (sleep, sigh)
profundamente; (depend) mucho
heavy ['hɛvɪ] adj (blow, work, blow)
duro; (sea, rain, meal) fuerte; (drinker,
smoker) grande; (responsibility) grave;
(schedule) ocupado; (weather)
bochornoso; **~ goods vehicle** n
vehículo pesado; **~weight** n (SPORT)
peso pesado
Hebrew ['hi:bru:] adj, n (LING) hebreo
heckle ['hɛkl] vt interrumpir
hectic ['hɛktɪk] adj agitado
he'd [hi:d] = **he would; he had**
hedge [hɛdʒ] n seto ♦ vi contestar con
evasivas; **to ~ one's bets** cubrirse
hedgehog ['hɛdʒhɔg] n erizo
heed [hi:d] vt (also: **take ~ of**) (pay
attention to) hacer caso de; **~less** adj:
to be ~less (of) no hacer caso (de)
heel [hi:l] n talón m; (of shoe) tacón m
♦ vt (shoe) poner tacón a
hefty ['hɛftɪ] adj (person) fornido;
(parcel, profit) gordo
heifer ['hɛfə*] n novilla, ternera
height [haɪt] n (of person) estatura; (of
building) altura; (high ground) cerro;
(altitude) altura f; (fig: of season): **at
the ~ of summer** en los días más
calurosos del verano; (: of power etc)
cúspide f; (: of stupidity etc) colmo;
~en vt elevar; (fig) aumentar
heir [ɛə*] n heredero; **~ess** n heredera;
~loom n reliquia de familia
held [hɛld] pt, pp of **hold**
helicopter ['hɛlɪkɔptə*] n helicóptero
hell [hɛl] n infierno; **~!** (inf) ¡demonios!
he'll [hi:l] = **he will; he shall**
hello [hə'ləu] excl ¡hola!; (to attract
attention) ¡oiga!; (surprise) ¡caramba!
helm [hɛlm] n (NAUT) timón m
helmet ['hɛlmɪt] n casco
help [hɛlp] n ayuda; (cleaner etc)

criada, asistenta ♦ vt ayudar; **~!**
¡socorro!; **~ yourself** sírvete; **he can't
~ it** no es culpa suya; **~er** n ayudante
m/f; **~ful** adj útil; (person) servicial;
(advice) útil; **~ing** n ración f; **~less** adj
(incapable) incapaz; (defenceless)
indefenso
hem [hɛm] n dobladillo ♦ vt poner o
coser el dobladillo; **~ in** vt cercar
hemorrhage ['hɛmərɪdʒ] (US) n =
haemorrhage
hemorrhoids ['hɛmərɔɪdz] (US) npl =
haemorrhoids
hen [hɛn] n gallina; (female bird)
hembra
hence [hɛns] adv (therefore) por lo
tanto; **2 years ~** de aquí a 2 años;
~forth adv de hoy en adelante
hepatitis [hɛpə'taɪtɪs] n hepatitis f
her [hə:*] pron (direct) la; (indirect) le;
(stressed, after prep) ella ♦ adj su; see
also **me; my**
herald ['hɛrəld] n heraldo ♦ vt
anunciar; **~ry** n heráldica
herb [hə:b] n hierba
herd [hə:d] n rebaño
here [hɪə*] adv aquí; (at this point) en
este punto; **~!** (present) ¡presente!;
~ is/are aquí está/están; **~ she is** aquí
está; **~after** adv en el futuro; **~by** adv
(in letter) por la presente
heritage ['hɛrɪtɪdʒ] n patrimonio
hermit ['hə:mɪt] n ermitaño/a
hernia ['hə:nɪə] n hernia
hero ['hɪərəu] (pl **~es**) n héroe m; (in
book, film) protagonista m
heroin ['hɛrəuɪn] n heroína
heroine ['hɛrəuɪn] n heroína f; (in book,
film) protagonista
heron ['hɛrən] n garza
herring ['hɛrɪŋ] n arenque m
hers [hə:z] pron (el) suyo/(la) suya etc;
see also **mine¹**
herself [hə:'sɛlf] pron (reflexive) se;
(emphatic) ella misma; (after prep) sí
(misma); see also **oneself**
he's [hi:z] = **he is; he has**

hesitant [ˈhɛzɪtənt] *adj* vacilante

hesitate [ˈhɛzɪteɪt] *vi* vacilar; (*in speech*) titubear; (*be unwilling*) resistirse a; **hesitation** [-ˈteɪʃən] *n* indecisión *f*; titubeo; dudas *fpl*

heterosexual [hɛtərəʊˈsɛksjuəl] *adj* heterosexual

heyday [ˈheɪdeɪ] *n*: **the ~ of** el apogeo de

HGV *n abbr* = **heavy goods vehicle**

hi [haɪ] *excl* ¡hola!; (*to attract attention*) ¡oiga!

hiatus [haɪˈeɪtəs] *n* vacío

hibernate [ˈhaɪbəneɪt] *vi* invernar

hiccough [ˈhɪkʌp] = **hiccup**

hiccup [ˈhɪkʌp] *vi* hipar; **~s** *npl* hipo

hide [haɪd] (*pt* **hid**, *pp* **hidden**) *n* (*skin*) piel *f* ♦ *vt* esconder, ocultar ♦ *vi*: **to ~ (from sb)** esconderse or ocultarse (de uno); **~-and-seek** *n* escondite *m*

hideous [ˈhɪdɪəs] *adj* horrible

hiding [ˈhaɪdɪŋ] *n* (*beating*) paliza; **to be in ~** (*concealed*) estar escondido

hierarchy [ˈhaɪərɑːkɪ] *n* jerarquía

hi-fi [ˈhaɪfaɪ] *n* estéreo, hifi *m* ♦ *adj* de alta fidelidad

high [haɪ] *adj* alto; (*speed, number*) grande; (*price*) elevado; (*wind*) fuerte; (*voice*) agudo ♦ *adv* alto, a gran altura; **it is 20 m ~** tiene 20 m de altura; **~ in the air** en las alturas; **~brow** *adj* intelectual; **~chair** *n* silla alta; **~er education** *n* educación *f* or enseñanza superior; **~-handed** *adj* despótico; **~-heeled** *adj* de tacón alto; **~ jump** *n* (*SPORT*) salto de altura; **the H~lands** *npl* las tierras altas de Escocia; **~light** *n* (*fig: of event*) punto culminante; (*in hair*) reflejo ♦ *vt* subrayar; **~ly** *adv* (*paid*) muy bien; (*critical, confidential*) sumamente; (*a lot*) muy: **to speak/think ~ly of** hablar muy bien de/tener en mucho a; **~ly strung** *adj* hipertenso; **~ness** *n* altura; **Her** or **His H~ness** Su Alteza; **~-pitched** *adj* agudo; **~-rise block** *n* torre *f* de pisos; **~ school** *n* ≈ Instituto Nacional de Bachillerato (*SP*);

~ season (*BRIT*) *n* temporada alta; **~ street** (*BRIT*) *n* calle *f* mayor; **~way** *n* carretera; (*US*) carretera nacional; autopista; **H~way Code** (*BRIT*) *n* código de la circulación

hijack [ˈhaɪdʒæk] *vt* secuestrar; **~er** *n* secuestrador(a) *m/f*

hike [haɪk] *vi* (*go walking*) ir de excursión (a pie) ♦ *n* caminata; **~r** *n* excursionista *m/f*; **hiking** *n* senderismo

hilarious [hɪˈlɛərɪəs] *adj* divertidísimo

hill [hɪl] *n* colina, (*high*) montaña; (*slope*) cuesta; **~side** *n* ladera; **~ walking** *n* senderismo (de montaña); **~y** *adj* montañoso

hilt [hɪlt] *n* (*of sword*) empuñadura; **to the ~** (*fig: support*) incondicionalmente

him [hɪm] *pron* (*direct*) le, lo; (*indirect*) le; (*stressed, after prep*) él; *see also* **me**; **~self** *pron* (*reflexive*) se; (*emphatic*) él mismo; (*after prep*) sí (mismo); *see also* **oneself**

hinder [ˈhɪndə*] *vt* estorbar, impedir; **hindrance** [ˈhɪndrəns] *n* estorbo

hindsight [ˈhaɪndsaɪt] *n*: **with ~** en retrospectiva

Hindu [ˈhɪnduː] *n* hindú *m/f*

hinge [hɪndʒ] *n* bisagra, gozne *m* ♦ *vi* (*fig*): **to ~ on** depender de

hint [hɪnt] *n* indirecta; (*advice*) consejo; (*sign*) dejo ♦ *vt*: **to ~ that** insinuar que ♦ *vi*: **to ~** hacer alusión a

hip [hɪp] *n* cadera

hippopotamus [hɪpəˈpɒtəməs] (*pl* **~es** or **hippopotami**) *n* hipopótamo

hire [ˈhaɪə*] *vt* (*BRIT: car, equipment*) alquilar; (*worker*) contratar ♦ *n* alquiler *m*; **for ~** se alquila; (*taxi*) libre; **~(d) car** (*BRIT*) *n* coche *m* de alquiler; **~ purchase** (*BRIT*) *n* compra a plazos

his [hɪz] *pron* (el) suyo/(la) suya *etc* ♦ *adj* su; *see also* **mine¹**; **my**

Hispanic [hɪsˈpænɪk] *adj* hispánico

hiss [hɪs] *vi* silbar

historian [hɪˈstɔːrɪən] *n* historiador(a) *m/f*

historic(al) [hɪˈstɔrɪk(l)] *adj* histórico

history ['hɪstərɪ] n historia

hit [hɪt] (pt, pp **hit**) vt (strike) golpear, pegar; (reach: target) alcanzar; (collide with: car) chocar contra; (fig: affect) afectar ♦ n golpe m; (success) éxito; **to ~ it off with sb** llevarse bien con uno; **~-and-run driver** n conductor(a) que atropella y huye

hitch [hɪtʃ] vt (fasten) atar, amarrar; (also: **~ up**) remangar ♦ n (difficulty) dificultad f; **to ~ a lift** hacer autostop

hitch-hike vi hacer autostop; **~hiking** n autostop m

hi-tech [haɪ'tek] adj de alta tecnología

hitherto ['hɪðə'tu:] adv hasta ahora

HIV n abbr (= human immunodeficiency virus) VIH m; **~-negative/positive** adj VIH negativo/positivo

hive [haɪv] n colmena

HMS abbr = His (Her) Majesty's Ship

hoard [hɔːd] n (treasure) tesoro; (stockpile) provisión f ♦ vt acumular; (goods in short supply) acaparar; **~ing** n (for posters) cartelera

hoarse [hɔːs] adj ronco

hoax [həuks] n trampa

hob [hɔb] n quemador m

hobble ['hɔbl] vi cojear

hobby ['hɔbɪ] n pasatiempo, afición f

hobo ['həubəu] (US) n vagabundo

hockey ['hɔkɪ] n hockey m

hog [hɔg] n cerdo, puerco m ♦ vt (fig) acaparar; **to go the whole ~** poner toda la carne en el asador

hoist [hɔɪst] n (crane) grúa ♦ vt levantar, alzar; (flag, sail) izar

hold [həuld] (pt, pp **held**) vt sostener; (contain) contener; (have: power, qualification) tener; (keep back) retener; (believe) sostener; (consider) considerar; (keep in position) mantener; **to ~ one's head up** mantener la cabeza alta; (meeting) celebrar ♦ vi (withstand pressure) resistir; (be valid) valer ♦ n (grasp) asimiento; (fig) dominio; **~ the line!** (TEL) ¡no cuelgue!; **to ~ one's own**

(fig) defenderse; **to catch** or **get (a) ~ of** agarrarse or asirse de; **~ back** vt retener; (secret) ocultar; **~ down** vt (person) sujetar; (job) mantener; **~ off** vt (enemy) rechazar; **~ on** vi agarrarse bien; (wait) esperar; **~ on!** (TEL) ¡(espere) un momento!; **~ on to** vt fus agarrarse a; (keep) guardar; **~ out** vt ofrecer ♦ vi (resist) resistir; **~ up** vt (raise) levantar; (support) apoyar; (delay) retrasar; (rob) asaltar; **~-all** (BRIT) n bolsa; **~er** n (container) receptáculo; (of ticket, record) poseedor(a) m/f; (of office, title etc) titular m/f; **~ing** n (share) interés m; (farmland) parcela; **~up** n (robbery) atraco; (delay) retraso; (BRIT: in traffic) embotellamiento

hole [həul] n agujero

holiday ['hɔlɪdɪ] n vacaciones fpl; (public ~) (día m de) fiesta, día m feriado; **on ~** de vacaciones; **~ camp** n (BRIT: also: **~ centre**) centro de vacaciones; **~-maker** (BRIT) n turista m/f; **~ resort** n centro turístico

holiness ['həulɪnɪs] n santidad f

Holland ['hɔlənd] n Holanda

hollow ['hɔləu] adj hueco; (claim) vacío; (eyes) hundido; (sound) sordo ♦ n hueco; (in ground) hoyo ♦ vt: **to ~ out** excavar

holly ['hɔlɪ] n acebo

holocaust ['hɔləkɔːst] n holocausto

holy ['həulɪ] adj santo, sagrado; (water) bendito

homage ['hɔmɪdʒ] n homenaje m

home [həum] n casa; (country) patria; (institution) asilo ♦ cpd (domestic) casero, de casa; (ECON, POL) nacional ♦ adv (direction) a casa; (right in: nail etc) a fondo; **at ~** en casa; (fig) como pez en el agua; **to go/come ~** ir/volver a casa; **make yourself at ~** ¡estás en tu casa!; **~ address** n domicilio; **~land** n tierra natal; **~less** adj sin hogar, sin casa; **~ly** adj (simple) sencillo; **~made** adj casero; **H~ Office** (BRIT) n Ministerio

del Interior; **~ page** n página de inicio;
~ rule n autonomía; **H~ Secretary**
(BRIT) n Ministro del Interior; **~sick**
adj: **to be ~sick** tener morriña, sentir
nostalgia; **~ town** n ciudad f natal;
~ward ['həʊmwəd] adj (journey) hacia
casa; **~work** n deberes mpl
homoeopathic [ˌhəʊmɪə'pæθɪk] (US
homeopathic) adj homeopático
homosexual [hɔmə'seksjuəl] adj, n
homosexual m/f
Honduran [hɔn'djʊərən] adj, n
hondureño/a m/f
Honduras [hɔn'djʊərəs] n Honduras f
honest ['ɔnɪst] adj honrado; (sincere)
franco, sincero; **~ly** adv honradamente;
francamente; **~y** n honradez f
honey ['hʌnɪ] n miel f; **~comb** n
panal m; **~moon** n luna de miel;
~suckle n madreselva
honk [hɔŋk] vi (AUT) tocar el pito, pitar
honorary ['ɔnərərɪ] adj (member,
president) de honor; (title) honorífico;
~ degree n doctorado honoris causa
honour ['ɔnə*] (US **honor**) vt honrar;
(commitment, promise) cumplir con ♦ n
honor m, honra; **~able** adj honorable;
~s degree n (SCOL) título de licenciado
con calificación alta
hood [hʊd] n capucha; (BRIT: AUT)
capota; (US: AUT) capó m; (of cooker)
campana de humos
hoof [huːf] (pl **hooves**) n pezuña
hook [hʊk] n gancho; (on dress)
corchete m, broche m; (for fishing)
anzuelo ♦ vt enganchar; (fish) pescar
hooligan ['huːlɪɡən] n gamberro
hoop [huːp] n aro
hooray [huː'reɪ] excl = **hurray**
hoot [huːt] vi (BRIT: AUT) tocar el pito,
pitar; (siren) sonar la sirena; (owl)
ulular; **~er** n (BRIT) (AUT) pito, claxon
m; (NAUT) sirena
Hoover ® ['huːvə*] (BRIT) n aspiradora
♦ vt: **h~** pasar la aspiradora por
hooves [huːvz] npl of **hoof**
hop [hɔp] vi saltar, brincar; (on one

foot) saltar con un pie
hope [həʊp] vt, vi esperar ♦ n
esperanza; **I ~ so/not** espero que sí/
no; **~ful** adj (person) optimista;
(situation) prometedor(a); **~fully** adv
con esperanza, (one hopes): **~fully he
will recover** esperamos que se
recupere; **~less** adj desesperado;
(person): **to be ~less** un ser un desastre
hops [hɔps] npl lúpulo
horizon [hə'raɪzn] n horizonte m; **~tal**
[hɔrɪ'zɔntl] adj horizontal
hormone ['hɔːməʊn] n hormona
horn [hɔːn] n cuerno; (MUS: also: French
~) trompa; (AUT) pito, claxon m
hornet ['hɔːnɪt] n avispón m
horoscope ['hɔrəskəʊp] n horóscopo
horrible ['hɔrɪbl] adj horrible
horrid ['hɔrɪd] adj horrible, horroroso
horrify ['hɔrɪfaɪ] vt horrorizar
horror ['hɔrə*] n horror m; **~ film** n
película de horror
hors d'oeuvre [ɔː'dəːvrə] n entremeses
mpl
horse [hɔːs] n caballo; **~back** n: **on
~back** a caballo; **~ chestnut** n (tree)
castaño de Indias; (nut) castaña de
Indias; **~man/woman** (irreg) n
jinete/a m/f; **~power** n caballo (de
fuerza); **~racing** n carreras fpl de
caballos; **~radish** n rábano picante;
~shoe n herradura
hose [həʊz] n (also: **~pipe**) manguera
hospitable [hɔs'pɪtəbl] adj hospitalario
hospital ['hɔspɪtl] n hospital m
hospitality [hɔspɪ'tælɪtɪ] n
hospitalidad f
host [həʊst] n anfitrión m; (TV, RADIO)
presentador m; (REL) hostia; (large
number): **a ~ of** multitud de
hostage ['hɔstɪdʒ] n rehén m
hostel ['hɔstl] n hostal m; **(youth) ~**
albergue m juvenil
hostess ['həʊstɪs] n anfitriona; (BRIT:
air. ~) azafata; (TV, RADIO) presentadora
hostile ['hɔstaɪl] adj hostil
hot [hɔt] adj caliente; (weather)

caluroso, de calor; (*as opposed to warm*) muy caliente; (*spicy*) picante; **to be ~** (*person*) tener calor; (*object*) estar caliente; (*weather*) hacer calor; **~bed** n (fig) semillero; **~ dog** n perro caliente

hotel [hau'tɛl] n hotel m

hot: **~house** n invernadero; **~ line** n (POL) teléfono rojo; **~ly** adv con pasión, apasionadamente; **~water bottle** n bolsa de agua caliente

hound [haund] vt acosar ♦ n perro de (caza)

hour ['auə*] n hora; **~ly** adj (de) cada hora

house [n haus, pl 'hauzız, vb hauz] n (gen, firm) casa; (POL) cámara; (THEATRE) sala ♦ vt (person) alojar; (collection) albergar; **on the ~** (fig) la casa invita; **~ arrest** n arresto domiciliario; **~boat** n casa flotante; **~bound** adj confinado en casa; **~breaking** n allanamiento de morada; **~hold** n familia; (home) casa; **~keeper** n ama de llaves; **~keeping** n (work) trabajos mpl domésticos; **~keeping (money)** n dinero para gastos domésticos; **~warming party** n fiesta de estreno de una casa; **~wife** (irreg) n ama de casa; **~work** n faenas fpl (de la casa)

housing ['hauzıŋ] n (act) alojamiento; (houses) viviendas fpl; **~ development**, **~ estate** (BRIT) n urbanización f

hovel ['hɔvl] n casucha

hover ['hɔvə*] vi flotar (en el aire); **~craft** n aerodeslizador m

how [hau] adv (in what way) cómo; **~ are you?** ¿cómo estás?; **~ much milk/many people?** ¿cuánta leche/gente?; **~ much does it cost?** ¿cuánto cuesta?; **~ long have you been here?** ¿cuánto hace que estás aquí?; **~ old are you?** ¿cuántos años tienes?; **~ tall is he?** ¿cómo es de alto?; **~ is school?** ¿cómo (te) va en la escuela?; **~ was the film?** ¿qué tal la película?; **~ lovely/awful!** ¡qué

bonito/horror!

however [hau'ɛvə*] adv: **~ I do it** lo haga como lo haga; **~ cold it is** por mucho frío que haga; **~ fast he runs** por muy rápido que corra; **~ did you do it?** ¿cómo lo hiciste? ♦ conj sin embargo, no obstante

howl [haul] n aullido ♦ vi aullar; (person) dar alaridos; (wind) ulular

H.P. n abbr = **hire purchase**

h.p. abbr = **horse power**

HQ n abbr = **headquarters**

HTML n abbr (= hypertext markup language) lenguaje m de hipertexto

hub [hʌb] n (of wheel) cubo; (fig) centro

hubcap ['hʌbkæp] n tapacubos m inv

huddle ['hʌdl] vi: **to ~ together** acurrucarse

hue [hju:] n color m, matiz m

huff [hʌf] n: **in a ~** enojado

hug [hʌg] vt abrazar; (thing) apretar con los brazos

huge [hju:dʒ] adj enorme

hull [hʌl] n (of ship) casco

hullo [hʌ'ləu] excl = **hello**

hum [hʌm] vt tararear, canturrear ♦ vi tararear, canturrear; (insect) zumbar

human ['hju:mən] adj, n humano; **~e** [hju:'meɪn] adj humano, humanitario; **~itarian** [hju:mænı'tɛərıən] adj humanitario; **~ity** [hju:'mænıtı] n humanidad f

humble ['hʌmbl] adj humilde

humdrum ['hʌmdrʌm] adj (boring) monótono, aburrido

humid ['hju:mɪd] adj húmedo

humiliate [hju:'mılıeɪt] vt humillar

humorous ['hju:mərəs] adj gracioso, divertido

humour ['hju:mə*] (US **humor**) n humorismo, sentido del humor; (mood) humor m ♦ vt complacer

hump [hʌmp] n (in ground) montículo; (camel's) giba

hunch [hʌntʃ] n (premonition) presentimiento; **~back** n joroba m/f; **~ed** adj jorobado

hundred ['hʌndrəd] *num* ciento;
(*before n*) cien; **~s of** centenares de;
~weight *n* (*BRIT*) = 50.8 kg; 112 lb;
(*US*) = 45.3 kg; 100 lb

hung [hʌŋ] *pt, pp of* **hang**

Hungarian [hʌŋ'ɡeərɪən] *adj, n*
húngaro/a *m/f*

Hungary ['hʌŋɡərɪ] *n* Hungría

hunger ['hʌŋɡə*] *n* hambre *f* ♦ *vi*: **to
~ for** (*fig*) tener hambre de, anhelar;
~ strike *n* huelga de hambre

hungry ['hʌŋɡrɪ] *adj*: **~ (for)**
hambriento (de); **to be ~** tener
hambre

hunk [hʌŋk] *n* (*of bread etc*) trozo,
pedazo

hunt [hʌnt] *vt* (*seek*) buscar; (*SPORT*)
cazar ♦ *vi* (*search*): **to ~ (for)** buscar;
(*SPORT*) cazar ♦ *n* búsqueda, caza,
cacería; **~er** *n* cazador(a) *m/f*; **~ing** *n*
caza

hurdle ['hɜːdl] *n* (*in SPORT*) valla; (*fig*)
obstáculo

hurl [hɜːl] *vt* lanzar, arrojar

hurrah [hu'rɑː] *excl* = **hurray**

hurray [hu'reɪ] *excl* ¡viva!

hurricane ['hʌrɪkən] *n* huracán *m*

hurried ['hʌrɪd] *adj* (*rushed*) hecho de
prisa; **~ly** *adv* con prisa,
apresuradamente

hurry ['hʌrɪ] *n* prisa ♦ *vi* (*also: ~ up*)
apresurarse, darse prisa ♦ *vt* (*also: ~ up:
person*) dar prisa a; (*: work*) apresurar,
hacer de prisa; **to be in a ~** tener
prisa

hurt [hɜːt] (*pt, pp* **hurt**) *vt* hacer daño
a ♦ *vi* doler ♦ *adj* lastimado; **~ful** *adj*
(*remark etc*) hiriente

hurtle ['hɜːtl] *vi*: **to ~ past** pasar
como un rayo; **to ~ down** ir a toda
velocidad

husband ['hʌzbənd] *n* marido

hush [hʌʃ] *n* silencio ♦ *vt* hacer callar;
~! ¡chitón!, ¡cállate!; **~ up** *vt* encubrir

husk [hʌsk] *n* (*of wheat*) cáscara

husky ['hʌskɪ] *adj* ronco ♦ *n* perro
esquimal

hustle ['hʌsl] *vt* (*hurry*) dar prisa a ♦ *n*:
~ and bustle ajetreo

hut [hʌt] *n* cabaña; (*shed*) cobertizo

hutch [hʌtʃ] *n* conejera

hyacinth ['haɪəsɪnθ] *n* jacinto

hydrant ['haɪdrənt] *n* (*also: fire ~*)
boca de incendios

hydraulic [haɪ'drɔːlɪk] *adj* hidráulico

hydroelectric [haɪdrəʊɪ'lektrɪk] *adj*
hidroeléctrico

hydrofoil ['haɪdrəfɔɪl] *n* aerodeslizador
m

hydrogen ['haɪdrədʒən] *n* hidrógeno

hygiene ['haɪdʒiːn] *n* higiene *f*;
hygienic [-'dʒiːnɪk] *adj* higiénico

hymn [hɪm] *n* himno

hype [haɪp] (*inf*) *n* bombardeo
publicitario

hypermarket ['haɪpəmɑːkɪt] *n*
hipermercado

hyphen ['haɪfn] *n* guión *m*

hypnotize ['hɪpnətaɪz] *vt* hipnotizar

hypocrisy [hɪ'pɒkrɪsɪ] *n* hipocresía

hypocrite ['hɪpəkrɪt] *n* hipócrita *m/f*;
hypocritical [hɪpə'krɪtɪkl] *adj*
hipócrita

hypothesis [haɪ'pɒθɪsɪs] (*pl*
hypotheses) *n* hipótesis *f inv*

hysteria [hɪ'stɪərɪə] *n* histeria;
hysterical [-'sterɪkl] *adj* histérico;
(*funny*) para morirse de risa; **hysterics**
[-'sterɪks] *npl* histeria; **to be in**
hysterics (*fig*) morirse de risa

I, i

I [aɪ] *pron* yo

ice [aɪs] *n* hielo; (*~ cream*) helado ♦ *vt*
(*cake*) alcorzar ♦ *vi* (*also: ~ over, ~ up*)
helarse; **~berg** *n* iceberg *m*; **~box** *n*
(*BRIT*) congelador *m*; (*US*) nevera (*SP*),
refrigadora (*AM*); **~ cream** *n* helado;
~ cube *n* cubito de hielo; **~d** *adj*
(*cake*) escarchado; (*drink*) helado;
~ hockey *n* hockey *m* sobre hielo

Iceland ['aɪslənd] *n* Islandia

ice: ~ **lolly** (BRIT) n polo; ~ **rink** n pista de hielo; ~ **skating** n patinaje m sobre hielo

icicle ['aɪsɪkl] n carámbano

icing ['aɪsɪŋ] n (CULIN) alcorza; ~ **sugar** (BRIT) n azúcar m glas(eado)

icon ['aɪkɔn] n icono

icy ['aɪsɪ] adj helado

I'd [aɪd] = I would; I had

idea [aɪ'dɪə] n idea

ideal [aɪ'dɪəl] n ideal m ♦ adj ideal

identical [aɪ'dentɪkl] adj idéntico

identification [aɪdentɪfɪ'keɪʃən] n identificación f; (means of) ~ documentos mpl personales

identify [aɪ'dentɪfaɪ] vt identificar

Identikit ® [aɪ'dentɪkɪt] n: ~ (picture) retrato-robot m

identity [aɪ'dentɪtɪ] n identidad f; ~ **card** n carnet m de identidad

ideology [aɪdɪ'ɔlədʒɪ] n ideología f

idiom ['ɪdɪəm] n modismo; (style of speaking) lenguaje m

idiosyncrasy [ɪdɪəʊ'sɪŋkrəsɪ] n idiosincrasia

idiot ['ɪdɪət] n idiota m/f; ~**ic** [-'ɔtɪk] adj tonto

idle ['aɪdl] adj (inactive) ocioso; (lazy) holgazán/ana; (unemployed) parado, desocupado; (machinery etc) parado; (talk etc) frívolo ♦ vi (machine) marchar en vacío

idol ['aɪdl] n ídolo; ~**ize** vt idolatrar

i.e. abbr (= that is) esto es

if [ɪf] conj si; ~ **necessary** si fuera necesario, si hiciese falta; ~ **I were you** yo en tu lugar; ~ **so/not** de ser así/si no; ~ **only I could!** ¡ojalá pudiera!; see also as; even

igloo ['ɪgluː] n iglú m

ignite [ɪg'naɪt] vt (set fire to) encender ♦ vi encenderse

ignition [ɪg'nɪʃən] n (AUT: process) ignición f; (: mechanism) encendido; **to switch on/off the** ~ arrancar/apagar el motor; ~ **key** n (AUT) llave f de contacto

ignorant ['ɪgnərənt] adj ignorante; **to be** ~ **of** ignorar

ignore [ɪg'nɔːʳ] vt (person, advice) no hacer caso de; (fact) pasar por alto

I'll [aɪl] = I will; I shall

ill [ɪl] adj enfermo, malo ♦ n mal m ♦ adv mal; **to be taken** ~ ponerse enfermo; ~**-advised** adj (decision) imprudente; ~**-at-ease** adj incómodo

illegal [ɪ'liːgl] adj ilegal

illegible [ɪ'ledʒɪbl] adj ilegible

illegitimate [ɪlɪ'dʒɪtɪmət] adj ilegítimo

ill-fated adj malogrado

ill feeling n rencor m

illiterate [ɪ'lɪtərət] adj analfabeto

ill: ~**-mannered** adj mal educado; ~**ness** n enfermedad f; ~**-treat** vt maltratar

illuminate [ɪ'luːmɪneɪt] vt (room, street) iluminar, alumbrar;

illumination [-'neɪʃən] n alumbrado; **illuminations** npl (decorative lights) iluminaciones fpl, luces fpl

illusion [ɪ'luːʒən] n ilusión f; (trick) truco

illustrate ['ɪləstreɪt] vt ilustrar

illustration [ɪlə'streɪʃən] n (act of illustrating) ilustración f; (example) ejemplo, ilustración f; (in book) lámina

illustrious [ɪ'lʌstrɪəs] adj ilustre

I'm [aɪm] = I am

image ['ɪmɪdʒ] n imagen f; ~**ry** [-ərɪ] n imágenes fpl

imaginary [ɪ'mædʒɪnərɪ] adj imaginario

imagination [ɪmædʒɪ'neɪʃən] n imaginación f; (inventiveness) inventiva

imaginative [ɪ'mædʒɪnətɪv] adj imaginativo

imagine [ɪ'mædʒɪn] vt imaginarse

imbalance [ɪm'bæləns] n desequilibrio

imitate ['ɪmɪteɪt] vt imitar; **imitation** [ɪmɪ'teɪʃən] n imitación f; (copy) copia

immaculate [ɪ'mækjʊlət] adj inmaculado

immaterial [ɪmə'tɪərɪəl] adj (unimportant) sin importancia

immature [ˌɪməˈtjuəʳ] adj (person)
inmaduro

immediate [ɪˈmiːdɪət] adj inmediato;
(pressing) urgente, apremiante;
(nearest: family) próximo;
(: neighbourhood) inmediato; **~ly** adv
(at once) en seguida; (directly)
inmediatamente; **~ly next to** muy
junto a

immense [ɪˈmɛns] adj inmenso,
enorme; (importance) enorme

immerse [ɪˈmɜːs] vt (submerge)
sumergir; **to be ~d in** (fig) estar
absorto en

immersion heater [ɪˈmɜːʃən-] (BRIT)
n calentador m de inmersión

immigrant [ˈɪmɪɡrənt] n inmigrante
m/f; **immigration** [ɪmɪˈɡreɪʃən] n
inmigración f

imminent [ˈɪmɪnənt] adj inminente

immobile [ɪˈməubaɪl] adj inmóvil

immoral [ɪˈmɔrl] adj inmoral

immortal [ɪˈmɔːtl] adj inmortal

immune [ɪˈmjuːn] adj: **~ (to)** inmune
(a); **immunity** n (MED, of diplomat)
inmunidad f

immunize [ˈɪmjunaɪz] vt inmunizar

impact [ˈɪmpækt] n impacto

impair [ɪmˈpɛəʳ] vt perjudicar

impart [ɪmˈpɑːt] vt comunicar;
(flavour) proporcionar

impartial [ɪmˈpɑːʃl] adj imparcial

impassable [ɪmˈpɑːsəbl] adj (barrier)
infranqueable; (river, road) intransitable

impassive [ɪmˈpæsɪv] adj impasible

impatience [ɪmˈpeɪʃəns] n impaciencia

impatient [ɪmˈpeɪʃənt] adj impaciente;
to get or **grow ~** impacientarse

impeccable [ɪmˈpekəbl] adj impecable

impede [ɪmˈpiːd] vt estorbar

impediment [ɪmˈpedɪmənt] n
obstáculo, estorbo; (also: speech ~)
defecto (del habla)

impending [ɪmˈpendɪŋ] adj inminente

imperative [ɪmˈperətɪv] adj (tone)
imperioso; (need) imprescindible

imperfect [ɪmˈpɜːfɪkt] adj (goods etc)

defectuoso ♦ n (LING: also: ~ tense)
imperfecto

imperial [ɪmˈpɪərɪəl] adj imperial

impersonal [ɪmˈpɜːsnl] adj
impersonal

impersonate [ɪmˈpɜːsəneɪt] vt hacerse
pasar por; (THEATRE) imitar

impertinent [ɪmˈpɜːtɪnənt] adj
impertinente, insolente

impervious [ɪmˈpɜːvɪəs] adj
impermeable; (fig): **~ to** insensible a

impetuous [ɪmˈpetjuəs] adj impetuoso

impetus [ˈɪmpətəs] n ímpetu m; (fig)
impulso

impinge [ɪmˈpɪndʒ]: **to ~ on** vt fus
(affect) afectar a

implement [n ˈɪmplɪmənt, vb
ˈɪmplɪmənt] n herramienta; (for
cooking) utensilio ♦ vt (regulation)
hacer efectivo; (plan) realizar

implicit [ɪmˈplɪsɪt] adj implícito; (belief,
trust) absoluto

imply [ɪmˈplaɪ] vt (involve) suponer;
(hint) dar a entender que

impolite [ɪmpəˈlaɪt] adj mal educado

import [vb ɪmˈpɔːt, n ˈɪmpɔːt] vt
importar ♦ n (COMM) importación f;
(: article) producto importado;
(meaning) significado, sentido

importance [ɪmˈpɔːtəns] n
importancia

important [ɪmˈpɔːtənt] adj
importante; **it's not ~** no importa, no
tiene importancia

importer [ɪmˈpɔːtəʳ] n importador(a)
m/f

impose [ɪmˈpəuz] vt imponer ♦ vi: **to
~ on sb** abusar de uno; **imposing** adj
imponente, impresionante

imposition [ɪmpəˈzɪʃən] n (of tax etc)
imposición f; **to be an ~ on** (person)
molestar a

impossible [ɪmˈpɔsɪbl] adj imposible;
(person) insoportable

impotent [ˈɪmpətənt] adj impotente

impound [ɪmˈpaund] vt embargar

impoverished [ɪmˈpɔvərɪʃt] adj

necesitado

impractical [ɪmˈpræktɪkl] *adj* (person, plan) poco práctico

imprecise [ɪmprɪˈsaɪs] *adj* impreciso

impregnable [ɪmˈpregnəbl] *adj* (castle) inexpugnable

impress [ɪmˈpres] *vt* impresionar; (mark) estampar; **to ~ sth on sb** hacer entender algo a uno

impression [ɪmˈpreʃən] *n* impresión f; (imitation) imitación f; **to be under the ~ that** tener la impresión de que; **~ist** *n* impresionista *m/f*

impressive [ɪmˈpresɪv] *adj* impresionante

imprint [ˈɪmprɪnt] *n* (outline) huella; (PUBLISHING) pie *m* de imprenta

imprison [ɪmˈprɪzn] *vt* encarcelar; **~ment** *n* encarcelamiento; (term of ~ment) cárcel f

improbable [ɪmˈprɒbəbl] *adj* improbable, inverosímil

improper [ɪmˈprɒpə*] *adj* (unsuitable: conduct etc) incorrecto; (: activities) deshonesto

improve [ɪmˈpruːv] *vt* mejorar; (foreign language) perfeccionar ♦ *vi* mejorarse; **~ment** *n* mejoramiento; perfección f; progreso

improvise [ˈɪmprəvaɪz] *vt, vi* improvisar

impulse [ˈɪmpʌls] *n* impulso; **to act on ~** obrar sin reflexión; **impulsive** [-ˈpʌlsɪv] *adj* irreflexivo

impure [ɪmˈpjuə*] *adj* (adulterated) adulterado; (morally) impuro; **impurity** *n* impureza

---

KEYWORD

---

in [ɪn] *prep* **1** (indicating place, position, with place names) en; **~ the house/ garden** en (la) casa/el jardín; **~ here/ there** aquí/ahí o allí dentro; **~ London/England** en Londres/ Inglaterra

2 (indicating time) en; **~ spring** en (la) primavera; **~ the afternoon** por la

---

tarde; **at 4 o'clock ~ the afternoon** a las 4 de la tarde; **I did it ~ 3 hours/days** lo hice en 3 horas/días; **I'll see you ~ 2 weeks** *or* **~ 2 weeks' time** te veré dentro de 2 semanas

3 (indicating manner etc) en; **~ a loud/soft voice** en voz alta/baja; **~ pencil/ink** a lápiz/bolígrafo; **the boy ~ the blue shirt** el chico de la camisa azul

4 (indicating circumstances): **~ the sun/shade/rain** al sol/a la sombra/ bajo la lluvia; **a change ~ policy** un cambio de política

5 (indicating mood, state): **~ tears** en lágrimas, llorando; **~ anger/despair** enfadado/desesperado; **to live ~ luxury** vivir lujosamente

6 (with ratios, numbers): **1 ~ 10 households, 1 household ~ 10** una de cada 10 familias; **20 pence ~ the pound** 20 peniques por libra; **they lined up ~ twos** se alinearon de dos en dos

7 (referring to people, works) en; entre; **the disease is common ~ children** la enfermedad es común entre los niños; **~ (the works of) Dickens** en (las obras de) Dickens

8 (indicating profession etc): **to be ~ teaching** estar en la enseñanza

9 (after superlative) de; **the best pupil ~ the class** el/la mejor alumno/a de la clase

10 (with present participle): **~ saying this** al decir esto

♦ *adv*: **to be ~** (person: at home) estar en casa; (work) estar; (train, ship, plane) haber llegado; (in fashion) estar de moda; **she'll be ~ later today** llegará más tarde hoy; **to ask sb ~** hacer pasar a uno; **to run/limp** etc **~** entrar corriendo/cojeando etc

♦ *n*: **the ~s and outs** (of proposal, situation etc) los detalles

in. abbr = **inch**

inability [ɪnəˈbɪlɪtɪ] n: ~ **(to do)** incapacidad f (de hacer)

inaccurate [ɪnˈækjurət] adj inexacto, incorrecto

inadequate [ɪnˈædɪkwət] adj (income, reply etc) insuficiente; (person) incapaz

inadvertently [ɪnədˈvɜːtntlɪ] adv por descuido

inadvisable [ɪnədˈvaɪzəbl] adj poco aconsejable

inane [ɪˈneɪn] adj necio, fatuo

inanimate [ɪnˈænɪmət] adj inanimado

inappropriate [ɪnəˈprəuprɪət] adj inadecuado; (improper) poco oportuno

inarticulate [ɪnɑːˈtɪkjulət] adj (person) incapaz de expresarse; (speech) mal pronunciado

inasmuch as [ɪnəzˈmʌtʃ-] conj puesto que, ya que

inauguration [ɪnɔːgjuˈreɪʃən] n ceremonia de apertura

inborn [ɪnˈbɔːn] adj (quality) innato

inbred [ɪnˈbred] adj innato; (family) engendrado por endogamia

Inc. abbr (US: = incorporated) S.A.

incapable [ɪnˈkeɪpəbl] adj incapaz

incapacitate [ɪnkəˈpæsɪteɪt] vt: to ~ **sb** incapacitar a uno

incense [n ˈɪnsens, vb ɪnˈsens] n incienso ♦ vt (anger) indignar, encolerizar

incentive [ɪnˈsentɪv] n incentivo, estímulo

incessant [ɪnˈsesnt] adj incesante, continuo; **~ly** adv constantemente

incest [ˈɪnsest] n incesto

inch [ɪntʃ] n pulgada; **to be within an ~ of** estar a dos dedos de; **he didn't give an ~** no dio concesión alguna

incident [ˈɪnsɪdnt] n incidente m

incidental [ɪnsɪˈdentl] adj accesorio; ~ **to** relacionado con; **~ly** [-ˈdentəlɪ] adv (by the way) a propósito

incite [ɪnˈsaɪt] vt provocar

inclination [ɪnklɪˈneɪʃən] n (tendency) tendencia, inclinación f; (desire) deseo; (disposition) propensión f

incline [n ˈɪnklaɪn, vb ɪnˈklaɪn] n pendiente m, cuesta ♦ vt (head) poner de lado ♦ vi inclinarse; **to be ~d to** (tend) ser propenso a

include [ɪnˈkluːd] vt (incorporate) incluir; (in letter) adjuntar; **including** prep incluso, inclusive

inclusion [ɪnˈkluːʒən] n inclusión f

inclusive [ɪnˈkluːsɪv] adj inclusivo; ~ **of tax** incluidos los impuestos

income [ˈɪnkʌm] n (earned) ingresos mpl; (from property etc) renta; (from investment etc) rédito; ~ **tax** n impuesto sobre la renta

incoming [ˈɪnkʌmɪŋ] adj (flight, government etc) entrante

incomparable [ɪnˈkɒmpərəbl] adj incomparable, sin par

incompatible [ɪnkəmˈpætɪbl] adj incompatible

incompetent [ɪnˈkɒmpɪtənt] adj incompetente

incomplete [ɪnkəmˈpliːt] adj (partial: achievement etc) incompleto; (unfinished: painting etc) inacabado

incongruous [ɪnˈkɒŋgruəs] adj (strange) discordante; (inappropriate) incongruente

inconsiderate [ɪnkənˈsɪdərət] adj desconsiderado

inconsistent [ɪnkənˈsɪstənt] adj inconsecuente; (contradictory) incongruente; ~ **with** (que) no concuerda con

inconspicuous [ɪnkənˈspɪkjuəs] adj (colour, building etc) discreto; (person) que llama poco la atención

inconvenience [ɪnkənˈviːnjəns] n inconvenientes mpl; (trouble) molestia, incomodidad f ♦ vt incomodar

inconvenient [ɪnkənˈviːnjənt] adj incómodo, poco práctico; (time, place, visitor) inoportuno

incorporate [ɪnˈkɔːpəreɪt] vt incorporar; (contain) comprender;

(*add*) agregar; **~d** *adj*: **~d company** (*US*) ≈ sociedad *f* anónima

incorrect [ɪnkəˈrekt] *adj* incorrecto

increase [*n* ˈɪnkriːs, *vb* ɪnˈkriːs] *n* aumento ♦ *vi* aumentar; (*grow*) crecer; (*price*) subir ♦ *vt* aumentar; (*price*) subir; **increasing** *adj* creciente; **increasingly** *adv* cada vez más, más y más

incredible [ɪnˈkredɪbl] *adj* increíble

incubator [ˈɪnkjubeɪtə*] *n* incubadora

incumbent [ɪnˈkʌmbənt] *adj*: **it is ~ on him to ...** le incumbe ...

incur [ɪnˈkəː*] *vt* (*expenditure*) incurrir; (*loss*) sufrir; (*anger, disapproval*) provocar

indebted [ɪnˈdetɪd] *adj*: **to be ~ to sb** estar agradecido a uno

indecent [ɪnˈdiːsnt] *adj* indecente; **~ assault** (*BRIT*) *n* atentado contra el pudor; **~ exposure** *n* exhibicionismo

indecisive [ɪndɪˈsaɪsɪv] *adj* indeciso

indeed [ɪnˈdiːd] *adv* efectivamente, en realidad; (*in fact*) en efecto; (*furthermore*) es más; **yes ~!** ¡claro que sí!

indefinitely [ɪnˈdefɪnɪtlɪ] *adv* (*wait*) indefinidamente

indemnity [ɪnˈdemnɪtɪ] *n* (*insurance*) indemnidad *f*; (*compensation*) indemnización *f*

independence [ɪndɪˈpendns] *n* independencia

Independence Day

El cuatro de julio es **Independence Day**, *la fiesta nacional de Estados Unidos, que se celebra en conmemoración de la Declaración de Independencia, escrita por Thomas Jefferson y aprobada en 1776. En ella se proclamaba la independencia total de Gran Bretaña de las trece colonias americanas que serían el origen de los Estados Unidos de América.*

---

independent [ɪndɪˈpendənt] *adj* independiente

index [ˈɪndeks] (*pl* **~es**) *n* (*in book*) índice *m*; (: *in library etc*) catálogo; (*pl* **indices**: *ratio, sign*) exponente *m*; **~ card** *n* ficha; **~ed** (*US*) *adj*: **~-linked**; **~ finger** *n* índice *m*; **~-linked** (*BRIT*) *adj* vinculado al índice del coste de la vida

India [ˈɪndɪə] *n* la India; **~n** *adj, n* indio/a *m/f*; **Red ~n** piel roja *m/f*; **~n Ocean** *n*: **the ~n Ocean** el Océano Índico

indicate [ˈɪndɪkeɪt] *vt* indicar; **indication** [-ˈkeɪʃən] *n* indicio, señal *f*; **indicative** [ɪnˈdɪkətɪv] *adj*: **to be ~ of** indicativo de indicar; **indicator** *n* indicador *m*; (*AUT*) intermitente *m*

indices [ˈɪndɪsiːz] *npl* of **index**

indictment [ɪnˈdaɪtmənt] *n* acusación *f*

indifferent [ɪnˈdɪfrənt] *adj* indiferente; (*mediocre*) regular

indigenous [ɪnˈdɪdʒɪnəs] *adj* indígena

indigestion [ɪndɪˈdʒestʃən] *n* indigestión *f*

indignant [ɪnˈdɪgnənt] *adj*: **to be ~ at sth/with sb** indignarse por algo/con uno

indigo [ˈɪndɪgəu] *adj* de color añil ♦ *n* añil *m*

indirect [ɪndɪˈrekt] *adj* indirecto

indiscreet [ɪndɪˈskriːt] *adj* indiscreto, imprudente

indiscriminate [ɪndɪˈskrɪmɪnət] *adj* indiscriminado

indisputable [ɪndɪˈspjuːtəbl] *adj* incontestable

indistinct [ɪndɪˈstɪŋkt] *adj* (*noise, memory etc*) confuso

individual [ɪndɪˈvɪdjuəl] *n* individuo ♦ *adj* individual; (*personal*) personal; (*particular*) particular; **~ly** *adv* (*singly*) individualmente

indoctrinate [ɪnˈdɒktrɪneɪt] *vt* adoctrinar

indoor [ˈɪndɔː*] *adj* (*swimming pool*) cubierto; (*plant*) de interior; (*sport*) bajo cubierta; **~s** [ɪnˈdɔːz] adv dentro

induce [ɪnˈdjuːs] vt inducir, persuadir; (bring about) producir; (birth) provocar; **~ment** n (incentive) incentivo; (pej: bribe) soborno

indulge [ɪnˈdʌldʒ] vt (whim) satisfacer; (person) complacer; (child) mimar ♦ vi: **to ~ in** darse el gusto de; **~nce** n vicio; (leniency) indulgencia; **~nt** adj indulgente

industrial [ɪnˈdʌstrɪəl] adj industrial; **~ action** n huelga; **~ estate** (BRIT) n polígono (SP) or zona (AM) industrial; **~ist** n industrial m/f; **~ize** vt industrializar; **~ park** (US) n = **~ estate**

industrious [ɪnˈdʌstrɪəs] adj trabajador(a); (student) aplicado

industry [ˈɪndəstrɪ] n industria; (diligence) aplicación f

inebriated [ɪˈniːbrɪeɪtɪd] adj borracho

inedible [ɪnˈedɪbl] adj incomible; (poisonous) no comestible

ineffective [ɪnɪˈfektɪv] adj ineficaz, inútil

ineffectual [ɪnɪˈfektjuəl] adj = **ineffective**

inefficient [ɪnɪˈfɪʃənt] adj ineficaz, ineficiente

inept [ɪˈnept] adj incompetente

inequality [ɪnɪˈkwɔlɪtɪ] n desigualdad f

inert [ɪˈnəːt] adj inerte, inactivo; (immobile) inmóvil

inescapable [ɪnɪˈskeɪpəbl] adj ineludible

inevitable [ɪnˈevɪtəbl] adj inevitable; **inevitably** adv inevitablemente

inexcusable [ɪnɪksˈkjuːzəbl] adj imperdonable

inexpensive [ɪnɪkˈspensɪv] adj económico

inexperienced [ɪnɪkˈspɪərɪənst] adj inexperto

infallible [ɪnˈfælɪbl] adj infalible

infamous [ˈɪnfəməs] adj infame

infancy [ˈɪnfənsɪ] n infancia

infant [ˈɪnfənt] n niño/a; (baby) niño

pequeño, bebé m; (pej) aniñado

infantry [ˈɪnfəntrɪ] n infantería

infant school (BRIT) n parvulario

infatuated [ɪnˈfætjueɪtɪd] adj: **~ with** (in love) loco por

infatuation [ɪnfætuˈeɪʃən] n enamoramiento, pasión f

infect [ɪnˈfekt] vt (wound) infectar; (food) contaminar; (person, animal) contagiar; **~ion** [ɪnˈfekʃən] n infección f; (fig) contagio; **~ious** [ɪnˈfekʃəs] adj (also fig) contagioso

infer [ɪnˈfəːˀ] vt deducir, inferir

inferior [ɪnˈfɪərɪəˀ] adj, n inferior m/f; **~ity** [-rɪˈɔrɪtɪ] n inferioridad f

infertile [ɪnˈfəːtaɪl] adj estéril; (person) infecundo

infested [ɪnˈfestɪd] adj: **~ with** plagado de

in-fighting n (fig) lucha(s) f(pl) interna(s)

infinite [ˈɪnfɪnɪt] adj infinito

infinitive [ɪnˈfɪnɪtɪv] n infinitivo

infinity [ɪnˈfɪnɪtɪ] n infinito; (an ~) infinidad f

infirmary [ɪnˈfəːmərɪ] n hospital m

inflamed [ɪnˈfleɪmd] adj: **to become ~** inflamarse

inflammable [ɪnˈflæməbl] adj inflamable

inflammation [ɪnfləˈmeɪʃən] n inflación f?

inflatable [ɪnˈfleɪtəbl] adj (ball, boat) inflable

inflate [ɪnˈfleɪt] vt (tyre, price etc) inflar; (fig) hinchar; **inflation** [ɪnˈfleɪʃən] n (ECON) inflación f

inflexible [ɪnˈfleksəbl] adj (rule) rígido; (person) inflexible

inflict [ɪnˈflɪkt] vt: **to ~ sth on sb** infligir algo en uno

influence [ˈɪnfluəns] n influencia ♦ vt influir en, influenciar; **under the ~ of alcohol** en estado de embriaguez; **influential** [-ˈenʃl] adj influyente

influenza [ɪnfluˈenzə] n gripe f

influx [ˈɪnflʌks] n afluencia

inform [ɪnˈfɔːm] vt: **to ~ sb of sth**
informar a uno sobre or de algo ♦ vi:
to ~ on sb delatar a uno
informal [ɪnˈfɔːməl] adj (manner, tone)
familiar; (dress, interview, occasion)
informal; (visit, meeting) extraoficial;
~ity [-ˈmælɪtɪ] n informalidad f;
sencillez f
informant [ɪnˈfɔːmənt] n informante
m/f
information [ɪnfəˈmeɪʃən] n
información f; (knowledge)
conocimientos mpl; **a piece of ~** un
dato; **~ desk** n (mostrador m de)
información f; **~ office** n información f
informative [ɪnˈfɔːmətɪv] adj
informativo
informer [ɪnˈfɔːməˀ] n (also: police ~)
soplón/ona m/f
infra-red [ɪnfrəˈred] adj infrarrojo
infrastructure [ˈɪnfrəstrʌktʃəˀ] n (of
system etc) infraestructura
infringe [ɪnˈfrɪndʒ] vt infringir, violar
♦ vi: **to ~ on** abusar de; **~ment** n
infracción f; (of rights) usurpación f
infuriating [ɪnˈfjuərieɪtɪŋ] adj (habit,
noise) enloquecedor(a)
ingenious [ɪnˈdʒiːnjəs] adj ingenioso;
ingenuity [-dʒɪˈnjuːɪtɪ] n ingeniosidad f
ingenuous [ɪnˈdʒenjuəs] adj ingenuo
ingot [ˈɪŋgət] n lingote m, barra
ingrained [ɪnˈgreɪnd] adj arraigado
ingratiate [ɪnˈgreɪʃɪeɪt] vt: **to ~ o.s.
with** congraciarse con
ingredient [ɪnˈgriːdɪənt] n ingrediente
m
inhabit [ɪnˈhæbɪt] vt vivir en; **~ant** n
habitante m/f
inhale [ɪnˈheɪl] vt inhalar ♦ vi (breathe
in) aspirar; (in smoking) tragar
inherent [ɪnˈhɪərənt] adj: **~ in** or **to**
inherente a
inherit [ɪnˈherɪt] vt heredar; **~ance** n
herencia f; (fig) patrimonio
inhibit [ɪnˈhɪbɪt] vt inhibir, impedir;
~ed adj (PSYCH) cohibido; **~ion**

[-ˈbɪʃən] n cohibición f
inhospitable [ɪnhɔsˈpɪtəbl] adj
(person) inhospitalario; (place)
inhóspito
inhuman [ɪnˈhjuːmən] adj inhumano
initial [ɪˈnɪʃl] adj primero ♦ n inicial f
♦ vt firmar con las iniciales; **~s** npl (as
signature) iniciales fpl; (abbreviation)
siglas fpl; **~ly** adv al principio
initiate [ɪˈnɪʃɪeɪt] vt iniciar; **to
~ proceedings against sb** (LAW)
entablar proceso contra uno
initiative [ɪˈnɪʃətɪv] n iniciativa
inject [ɪnˈdʒekt] vt inyectar; **to ~ sb
with sth** inyectar algo a uno; **~ion**
[ɪnˈdʒekʃən] n inyección f
injunction [ɪnˈdʒʌŋkʃən] n interdicto
injure [ˈɪndʒəˀ] vt (hurt) herir, lastimar;
(fig: reputation etc) perjudicar; **~d** adj
(person, arm) herido, lastimado; **injury**
n herida, lesión f; (wrong) perjuicio,
daño; **injury time** n (SPORT) (tiempo
de) descuento
injustice [ɪnˈdʒʌstɪs] n injusticia
ink [ɪŋk] n tinta
inkling [ˈɪŋklɪŋ] n sospecha; (idea) idea
inlaid [ˈɪnleɪd] adj (with wood, gems
etc) incrustado
inland [adj ˈɪnlənd, adv ɪnˈlænd] adj
(waterway, port etc) interior ♦ adv tierra
adentro; **I~ Revenue** (BRIT) n
departamento de impuestos; ≈
Hacienda (SP)
in-laws npl suegros mpl
inlet [ˈɪnlet] n (GEO) ensenada, cala;
(TECH) admisión f, entrada
inmate [ˈɪnmeɪt] n (in prison) preso/a;
presidiario/a; (in asylum) internado/a
inn [ɪn] n posada, mesón m
innate [ɪˈneɪt] adj innato
inner [ˈɪnəˀ] adj (courtyard, calm)
interior; (feelings) íntimo; **~ city** n
barrios deprimidos del centro de una
ciudad; **~ tube** n (of tyre) cámara (SP),
llanta (AM)
innings [ˈɪnɪŋz] n (CRICKET) entrada,
turno

innocent |'ınəsnt| adj inocente

innocuous |ı'nɔkjuəs| adj inocuo

innovation |ınəu'veıʃən| n novedad f

innuendo |ınju'endəu| (pl **-es**) n indirecta

inoculation |ınɔkju'leıʃən| n inoculación f

in-patient n paciente m/f interno/a

input |'ınput| n entrada f, (of resources) inversión f; (COMPUT) entrada de datos

inquest |'ınkwest| n (coroner's) encuesta judicial

inquire |ın'kwaıə*| vi preguntar ♦ vt: **to ~ whether** preguntar si; **to ~ about** (person) preguntar por; (fact) informarse de; **~ into** vt fus investigar, indagar; **inquiry** n pregunta, pesquisa; (investigation) investigación f; "**Inquiries**" "Información"; **inquiry office** (BRIT) n oficina de información

inquisitive |ın'kwızıtıv| adj (curious) curioso

ins. abbr = inches

insane |ın'seın| adj loco; (MED) demente

insanity |ın'sænıtı| n demencia, locura

inscription |ın'skrıpʃən| n inscripción f; (in book) dedicatoria

inscrutable |ın'skru:təbl| adj inescrutable, insondable

insect |'ınsekt| n insecto; **~icide** |ın'sektısaıd| n insecticida m; **~ repellent** n loción f contra insectos

insecure |ınsı'kjuə*| adj inseguro

insemination |ınsemı'neıʃn| n: **artificial ~** inseminación f artificial

insensitive |ın'sensıtıv| adj insensible

insert |vb ın'sə:t, n 'ınsə:t| vt (into sth) introducir ♦ n encarte m; **~ion** |ın'sə:ʃən| n inserción f

in-service |'ınsə:vıs| adj (training, course) a cargo de la empresa

inshore |ın'fɔ:*| adj de bajura ♦ adv (be) cerca de la orilla; (move) hacia la orilla

inside |'ın'saıd| n interior m ♦ adj interior, interno ♦ adv (be) por

dentro; (go) hacia dentro ♦ prep dentro de; (of time): **~ 10 minutes** en menos de 10 minutos; **~s** npl (inf: stomach) tripas fpl; **~ information** n información f confidencial; **~ lane** n (AUT: in Britain) carril m izquierdo; (: in US, Europe etc) carril m derecho; **~ out** adv (turn) al revés; (know) a fondo

insider dealing, insider trading n (STOCK EXCHANGE) abuso de información privilegiada

insight |'ınsaıt| n perspicacia

insignificant |ınsıg'nıfıknt| adj insignificante

insincere |ınsın'sıə*| adj poco sincero

insinuate |ın'sınjueıt| vt insinuar

insipid |ın'sıpıd| adj soso, insulso

insist |ın'sıst| vi insistir; **to ~ on** insistir en; **to ~ that** insistir en que; (claim) exigir que; **~ent** adj insistente; (noise, action) persistente

insole |'ınsəul| n plantilla

insolent |'ınsələnt| adj insolente, descarado

insomnia |ın'sɔmnıə| n insomnio

inspect |ın'spekt| vt inspeccionar, examinar; (troops) pasar revista a; **~ion** |ın'spekʃən| n inspección f, examen m; (of troops) revista; **~or** n inspector(a) m/f; (BRIT: on buses, trains) revisor(a) m/f

inspiration |ınspə'reıʃən| n inspiración f; **inspire** |ın'spaıə*| vt inspirar

instability |ınstə'bılıtı| n inestabilidad f

install |ın'stɔ:l| vt instalar; (official) nombrar; **~ation** |ınstə'leıʃən| n instalación f

instalment |ın'stɔ:lmənt| (US **installment**) n plazo; (of story) entrega; (of TV serial etc) capítulo; **in ~s** (pay, receive) a plazos

instance |'ınstəns| n ejemplo, caso; **for ~** por ejemplo; **in the first ~** en primer lugar

instant |'ınstənt| n instante m, momento m ♦ adj inmediato; (coffee etc) instantáneo; **~ly** adv en seguida

instead [ɪnˈstɛd] adv en cambio; ~ of en lugar de, en vez de

instep [ˈɪnstɛp] n empeine m

instil [ɪnˈstɪl] vt: **to ~ sth into** inculcar algo a

instinct [ˈɪnstɪŋkt] n instinto

institute [ˈɪnstɪtjuːt] n instituto; (professional body) colegio ♦ vt (begin) iniciar, empezar; (proceedings) entablar; (system, rule) establecer

institution [ɪnstɪˈtjuːʃən] n institución f; (MED: home) asilo; (: asylum) manicomio; (of system etc) establecimiento; (of custom) iniciación f

instruct [ɪnˈstrʌkt] vt: **to ~ sb in sth** instruir a uno en or sobre algo; **to ~ sb to do sth** dar instrucciones a uno de hacer algo; **~ion** [ɪnˈstrʌkʃən] n (teaching) instrucción f; **~ions** npl (orders) órdenes fpl; **~ions (for use)** modo de empleo; **~or** n instructor(a) m/f

instrument [ˈɪnstrəmənt] n instrumento; **~al** [-ˈmɛntl] adj (MUS) instrumental; **to be ~al in** ser (el) artífice de; **~ panel** n tablero (de instrumentos)

insufficient [ɪnsəˈfɪʃənt] adj insuficiente

insular [ˈɪnsjʊlə*] adj insular; (person) estrecho de miras

insulate [ˈɪnsjʊleɪt] vt aislar; **insulation** [-ˈleɪʃən] n aislamiento

insulin [ˈɪnsjʊlɪn] n insulina

insult [n ˈɪnsʌlt, vb ɪnˈsʌlt] n insulto ♦ vt insultar; **~ing** adj insultante

insurance [ɪnˈʃʊərəns] n seguro; **fire/ life ~** seguro contra incendios/sobre la vida; **~ agent** n agente m/f de seguros; **~ policy** n póliza (de seguros)

insure [ɪnˈʃʊə*] vt asegurar

intact [ɪnˈtækt] adj íntegro, intacto; (unharmed) intacto

intake [ˈɪnteɪk] n (of food) ingestión f; (of air) consumo; (BRIT: SCOL): **an ~ of 200 a year** 200 matriculados al año

integral [ˈɪntɪɡrəl] adj (whole) íntegro; (part) integrante

integrate [ˈɪntɪɡreɪt] vt integrar ♦ vi integrarse

integrity [ɪnˈtɛɡrɪtɪ] n honradez f, rectitud f

intellect [ˈɪntəlɛkt] n intelecto; **~ual** [-ˈlɛktjuəl] adj, n intelectual m/f

intelligence [ɪnˈtɛlɪdʒəns] n inteligencia

intelligent [ɪnˈtɛlɪdʒənt] adj inteligente

intelligible [ɪnˈtɛlɪdʒɪbl] adj inteligible, comprensible

intend [ɪnˈtɛnd] vt (gift etc): **to ~ sth for** destinar algo a; **to ~ to do sth** tener intención or pensar hacer algo

intense [ɪnˈtɛns] adj intenso; **~ly** adv (extremely) sumamente

intensify [ɪnˈtɛnsɪfaɪ] vt intensificar; (increase) aumentar

intensive [ɪnˈtɛnsɪv] adj intensivo; **~ care unit** n unidad f de vigilancia intensiva

intent [ɪnˈtɛnt] n propósito; (LAW) premeditación f ♦ adj (absorbed) absorto; (attentive) atento; **to all ~s and purposes** prácticamente; **to be ~ on doing sth** estar resuelto a hacer algo

intention [ɪnˈtɛnʃən] n intención f, propósito; **~al** adj deliberado; **~ally** adv a propósito

intently [ɪnˈtɛntlɪ] adv atentamente, fijamente

interact [ɪntərˈækt] vi influirse mutuamente; **~ive** adj (COMPUT) interactivo

interchange [ˈɪntətʃeɪndʒ] n intercambio; (on motorway) intersección f; **~able** adj intercambiable

intercom [ˈɪntəkɔm] n interfono

intercourse [ˈɪntəkɔːs] n (sexual) relaciones fpl sexuales

interest [ˈɪntrɪst] n (also COMM) interés m ♦ vt interesar; **to be ~ed in**

interesarse por; **~ing** adj interesante; **~ rate** n tipo o tasa de interés

interface ['ɪntəfeɪs] n (COMPUT) junción f

interfere [ɪntə'fɪə*] vi: **to ~ in** entrometerse en; **to ~ with** (hinder) estorbar; (damage) estropear

interference [ɪntə'fɪərəns] n intromisión f; (RADIO, TV) interferencia f

interim ['ɪntərɪm] n: **in the ~** en el ínterin ♦ adj provisional

interior [ɪn'tɪərɪə*] n interior m ♦ adj interior; **~ designer** n interiorista m/f

interjection [ɪntə'dʒekʃən] n interposición f; (LING) interjección f

interlock [ɪntə'lɔk] vi entrelazarse

interlude ['ɪntəluːd] n intervalo; (THEATRE) intermedio

intermediate [ɪntə'miːdɪət] adj intermedio

intermission [ɪntə'mɪʃən] n intermisión f; (THEATRE) descanso

intern [vb ɪn'təːn, n 'ɪntəːn] vt internar ♦ n (US) interno/a

internal [ɪn'təːnl] adj (layout, pipes, security) interior; (injury, structure, memo) internal; **~ly** adv: "**not to be taken ~ly**" "uso externo"; **I~ Revenue Service** (US) n departamento de impuestos; ≈ Hacienda (SP)

international [ɪntə'næʃnl] adj internacional ♦ n (BRIT: match) partido internacional

Internet ['ɪntənet] n: **the ~** Internet m or f; **~ café** n cibercafé m; **~ Service Provider** n proveedor m de (acceso a) Internet

interplay ['ɪntəpleɪ] n interacción f

interpret [ɪn'təːprɪt] vt interpretar; (translate) traducir; (understand) entender ♦ vi hacer de intérprete; **~er** n intérprete m/f

interrogate [ɪn'terəɡeɪt] vt interrogar; **interrogation** [-'ɡeɪʃən] n interrogatorio

interrupt [ɪntə'rʌpt] vt, vi interrumpir;

~ion [-'rʌpʃən] n interrupción f

intersect [ɪntə'sekt] vi (roads) cruzarse; **~ion** [-'sekʃən] n (of roads) cruce m

intersperse [ɪntə'spəːs] vt: **to ~ with** salpicar de

intertwine [ɪntə'twaɪn] vt entrelazarse

interval ['ɪntəvl] n intervalo; (BRIT: THEATRE, SPORT) descanso; (: SCOL) recreo; **at ~s** a ratos, de vez en cuando

intervene [ɪntə'viːn] vi intervenir; (event) interponerse; (time) transcurrir; **intervention** n intervención f

interview ['ɪntəvjuː] n entrevista ♦ vt entrevistarse con; **~er** n entrevistador(a) m/f

intestine [ɪn'testɪn] n intestino

intimacy ['ɪntɪməsɪ] n intimidad f

intimate [adj 'ɪntɪmət, vb 'ɪntɪmeɪt] adj íntimo; (friendship) estrecho; (knowledge) profundo ♦ vt dar a entender

intolerable [ɪn'tɔlərəbl] adj intolerable, insoportable

intolerant [ɪn'tɔlərənt] adj: **~ (of)** intolerante (con or para)

intoxicated [ɪn'tɔksɪkeɪtɪd] adj embriagado

intractable [ɪn'træktəbl] adj (person) intratable; (problem) espinoso

intranet ['ɪntranet] n intranet f

intransitive [ɪn'trænsɪtɪv] adj intransitivo

intravenous [ɪntrə'viːnəs] adj intravenoso

in-tray n bandeja de entrada

intricate ['ɪntrɪkət] adj (design, pattern) intrincado

intrigue [ɪn'triːɡ] n intriga ♦ vt fascinar; **intriguing** adj fascinante

intrinsic [ɪn'trɪnsɪk] adj intrínseco

introduce [ɪntrə'djuːs] vt introducir; (speaker, TV show etc) presentar;

to ~ sb (to sb) presentar uno (a otro); **to ~ sb to** (*pastime, technique*) introducir a uno a; **introduction** [-'dʌkʃən] n introducción f; (*of person*) presentación f; **introductory** [-'dʌktəri] adj introductorio; (*lesson, offer*) de introducción

introvert ['ɪntrəvə:t] n introvertido/a ♦ adj (*also: ~ed*) introvertido

intrude [ɪn'tru:d] vi (*person*) entrometerse; **to ~ on** estorbar; **~r** n intruso/a; **intrusion** [-ʒən] n invasión f

intuition [ɪntju:'ɪʃən] n intuición f

inundate ['ɪnʌndeɪt] vt: **to ~ with** inundar de

invade [ɪn'veɪd] vt invadir

invalid [n 'ɪnvəlɪd, adj ɪn'vælɪd] n (*MED*) minusválido/a ♦ adj (*not valid*) inválido, nulo

invaluable [ɪn'væljuəbl] adj inestimable

invariable [ɪn'vɛərɪəbl] adj invariable

invent [ɪn'vent] vt inventar; **~ion** [ɪn'venʃən] n invento; (*lie*) ficción f, mentira; **~ive** adj inventivo; **~or** n inventor(a) m/f

inventory ['ɪnvəntri] n inventario

invert [ɪn'və:t] vt invertir

inverted commas (*BRIT*) npl comillas fpl

invest [ɪn'vest] vt invertir ♦ vi: **to ~ in** (*company etc*) invertir dinero en; (*fig: sth useful*) comprar

investigate [ɪn'vestɪgeɪt] vt investigar; **investigation** [-'geɪʃən] n investigación f, pesquisa

investment [ɪn'vestmənt] n inversión f

investor [ɪn'vestə*] n inversionista m/f

invigilator [ɪn'vɪdʒɪleɪtə*] n persona que vigila en un examen

invigorating [ɪn'vɪgəreɪtɪŋ] adj vigorizante

invisible [ɪn'vɪzɪbl] adj invisible

invitation [ɪnvɪ'teɪʃən] n invitación f

invite [ɪn'vaɪt] vt invitar; (*opinions etc*) solicitar, pedir; **inviting** adj atractivo;

(*food*) apetitoso

invoice ['ɪnvɔɪs] n factura ♦ vt facturar

involuntary [ɪn'vɔləntri] adj involuntario

involve [ɪn'vɔlv] vt suponer, implicar; tener que ver con; (*concern, affect*) corresponder; **to ~ sb (in sth)** comprometer a uno (con algo); **~d** adj complicado; **to be ~d in** (*take part*) tomar parte en; (*be engrossed*) estar muy metido en; **~ment** n participación f; dedicación f

inward ['ɪnwəd] adj (*movement*) interior, interno; (*thought, feeling*) íntimo; **~(s)** adv hacia dentro

I/O abbr (*COMPUT* = input/output) entrada/salida

iodine ['aɪəʊdi:n] n yodo

ion ['aɪən] n ion m; **ioniser** ['aɪənaɪzə*] n ionizador m

iota [aɪ'əʊtə] n jota, ápice m

IOU n abbr (= I owe you) pagaré m

IQ n abbr (= intelligence quotient) cociente m intelectual

IRA n abbr (= Irish Republican Army) IRA m

Iran [ɪ'rɑːn] n Irán m; **~ian** [ɪ'reɪnɪən] adj, n iraní m/f

Iraq [ɪ'rɑːk] n Iraq; **~i** adj, n iraquí m/f

irate [aɪ'reɪt] adj enojado, airado

Ireland ['aɪələnd] n Irlanda

iris ['aɪrɪs] (pl **~es**) n (*ANAT*) iris m; (*BOT*) lirio

Irish ['aɪrɪʃ] adj irlandés/esa ♦ npl: **the ~** los irlandeses; **~man/woman** (*irreg*) n irlandés/esa m/f; **~ Sea** n: **the ~ Sea** el mar de Irlanda

iron ['aɪən] n hierro; (*for clothes*) plancha ♦ cpd de hierro; (*clothes*) planchar; **~ out** vt (*fig*) allanar

ironic(al) [aɪ'rɔnɪk(l)] adj irónico

ironing ['aɪənɪŋ] n (*activity*) planchado; (*clothes: ironed*) ropa planchada; (: *to be ironed*) ropa por planchar; **~ board** n tabla de planchar

ironmonger's (shop) ['aɪənmʌŋgəz] (*BRIT*) n ferretería, quincallería

irony ['aɪrənɪ] n ironía

irrational [ɪ'ræʃənl] adj irracional

irreconcilable [ɪrekən'saɪləbl] adj (ideas) incompatible; (enemies) irreconciliable

irregular [ɪ'regjulə*] adj irregular; (surface) desigual; (action, event) anómalo; (behaviour) poco ortodoxo

irrelevant [ɪ'reləvənt] adj fuera de lugar, inoportuno

irresolute [ɪ'rezəluːt] adj indeciso

irrespective [ɪrɪ'spektɪv]: ~ of prep sin tener en cuenta, no importa

irresponsible [ɪrɪ'spɒnsɪbl] adj (act) irresponsable; (person) poco serio

irrigate ['ɪrɪgeɪt] vt regar; **irrigation** [-'geɪʃən] n riego

irritable ['ɪrɪtəbl] adj (person) de mal humor

irritate ['ɪrɪteɪt] vt fastidiar; (MED) picar; **irritating** adj fastidioso; **irritation** [-'teɪʃən] n fastidio; enfado; picazón f

IRS (US) n abbr = **Internal Revenue Service**

is [ɪz] vb see **be**

Islam ['ɪzlɑːm] n Islam m; ~**ic** [ɪz'læmɪk] adj islámico

island ['aɪlənd] n isla; ~**er** n isleño/a

isle [aɪl] n isla

isn't ['ɪznt] = **is not**

isolate ['aɪsəleɪt] vt aislar; ~**d** adj aislado; **isolation** [-'leɪʃən] n aislamiento

ISP n abbr = **Internet Service Provider**

Israel ['ɪzreɪl] n Israel m; ~**i** [ɪz'reɪlɪ] adj, n israelí m/f

issue ['ɪʃuː] n (problem, subject) cuestión f; (outcome) resultado; (of banknotes etc) emisión f; (of newspaper etc) edición f ♦ vt (rations, equipment) distribuir, repartir; (orders) dar; (certificate, passport) expedir; (decree) promulgar; (magazine) publicar; (cheques) extender; (banknotes, stamps) emitir; **at** ~ en cuestión; **to take** ~ **with sb (over)** estar en desacuerdo

con uno (sobre); **to make an** ~ **of sth** hacer una cuestión de algo

Istanbul [ɪstæn'buːl] n Estambul m

KEYWORD

it [ɪt] pron **1** (specific: subject: not generally translated) él/ella; (: direct object) lo, la; (: indirect object) le; (after prep) él/ella; (abstract concept) ello; ~'**s on the table** está en la mesa; **I can't find** ~ no lo (or la) encuentro; **give** ~ **to me** dámelo (or dámela); **I spoke to him about** ~ le hablé del asunto; **what did you learn from** ~? ¿qué aprendiste de él (or ella)?; **did you go to** ~? (party, concert etc) ¿fuiste?

2 (impersonal): ~'**s raining** llueve, está lloviendo; ~'**s 6 o'clock/the 10th of August** son las 6/es el 10 de agosto; **how far is** ~? — ~'**s 10 miles/2 hours on the train** ¿a qué distancia está? — a 10 millas/2 horas en tren; **who is** ~? — ~'**s me** ¿quién es? — soy yo

Italian [ɪ'tæljən] adj italiano ♦ n italiano/a; (LING) italiano

italics [ɪ'tælɪks] npl cursiva

Italy ['ɪtəlɪ] n Italia

itch [ɪtʃ] n picazón f ♦ vi (part of body) picar; **to ~ to do sth** rabiar por hacer algo; ~**y** adj: **my hand is ~y** me pica la mano

it'd ['ɪtd] = **it would; it had**

item ['aɪtəm] n artículo; (on agenda) asunto (a tratar); (also: news ~) noticia; ~**ize** vt detallar

itinerary [aɪ'tɪnərərɪ] n itinerario

it'll ['ɪtl] = **it will; it shall**

its [ɪts] adj su; sus pl

it's [ɪts] = **it is; it has**

itself [ɪt'self] pron (reflexive) sí mismo/a; (emphatic) él mismo/ella misma

ITV n abbr (BRIT: = Independent Television) cadena de televisión comercial independiente del Estado

I.U.D. n abbr (= intra-uterine device)

DIU m

I've [aɪv] = I **have**

ivory ['aɪvərɪ] n marfil m

ivy ['aɪvɪ] n (BOT) hiedra

J, j

jab [dʒæb] vt: **to ~ sth into sth** clavar algo en algo ♦ n (inf) (MED) pinchazo

jack [dʒæk] n (AUT) gato; (CARDS) sota; **~ up** vt (AUT) levantar con gato

jackal ['dʒækɔ:l] n (ZOOL) chacal m

jacket ['dʒækɪt] n chaqueta, americana, saco (AM); (of book) sobrecubierta

jack: ~-knife vi colear; **~ plug** n (ELEC) enchufe m de clavija; **~pot** n premio gordo

jaded ['dʒeɪdɪd] adj (tired) cansado; (fed-up) hastiado

jagged ['dʒægɪd] adj dentado

jail [dʒeɪl] n cárcel f ♦ vt encarcelar

jam [dʒæm] n mermelada; (also: traffic **~**) embotellamiento; (inf: difficulty) apuro m ♦ vt (passage etc) obstruir; (mechanism, drawer etc) atascar; (RADIO) interferir ♦ vi atascarse, trabarse; **to ~ sth into sth** meter algo a la fuerza en algo

Jamaica [dʒə'meɪkə] n Jamaica

jangle ['dʒæŋgl] vi entrechocar (ruidosamente)

janitor ['dʒænɪtə*] n (caretaker) portero, conserje m

January ['dʒænjuərɪ] n enero

Japan [dʒə'pæn] n (el) Japón; **~ese** [dʒæpə'ni:z] adj japonés/esa ♦ n inv japonés/esa m/f; (LING) japonés m

jar [dʒɑ:*] n tarro, bote m ♦ vi (sound) chirriar; (colours) desentonar

jargon ['dʒɑ:gən] n jerga

jasmine ['dʒæzmɪn] n jazmín m

jaundice ['dʒɔ:ndɪs] n ictericia

jaunt [dʒɔ:nt] n excursión f

javelin ['dʒævlɪn] n jabalina

jaw [dʒɔ:] n mandíbula

jay [dʒeɪ] n (ZOOL) arrendajo

jaywalker ['dʒeɪwɔ:kə*] n peatón/ona m/f imprudente

jazz [dʒæz] n jazz m; **~ up** vt (liven up) animar, avivar

jealous ['dʒeləs] adj celoso; (envious) envidioso; **~y** n celos mpl; envidia

jeans [dʒi:nz] npl vaqueros mpl, tejanos mpl

Jeep ® [dʒi:p] n jeep m

jeer [dʒɪə*] vi: **to ~ (at)** (mock) mofarse (de)

jelly ['dʒelɪ] n (jam) jalea; (dessert etc) gelatina; **~fish** n inv medusa (SP), aguaviva (AM)

jeopardy ['dʒepədɪ] n: **to be in ~** estar en peligro

jerk [dʒɜ:k] n (jolt) sacudida; (wrench) tirón m; (inf) imbécil m/f ♦ vt tirar bruscamente de ♦ vi (vehicle) traquetear

jersey ['dʒɜ:zɪ] n jersey m; (fabric) (tejido de) punto

Jesus ['dʒi:zəs] n Jesús m

jet [dʒet] n (of gas, liquid) chorro; (AVIAT) avión m a reacción; **~-black** adj negro como el azabache; **~ engine** n motor m a reacción; **~ lag** n desorientación f después de un largo vuelo

jettison ['dʒetɪsn] vt desechar

jetty ['dʒetɪ] n muelle m, embarcadero

Jew [dʒu:] n judío

jewel ['dʒu:əl] n joya; (in watch) rubí m; **~ler** (US **~er**) n joyero/a; **~ler's (shop)** (US **~ry store**) n joyería; **~lery** (US **~ry**) n joyas fpl, alhajas fpl

Jewess ['dʒu:ɪs] n judía

Jewish ['dʒu:ɪʃ] adj judío

jibe [dʒaɪb] n mofa

jiffy ['dʒɪfɪ] (inf) n: **in a ~** en un santiamén

jigsaw ['dʒɪgsɔ:] n (also: **~ puzzle**) rompecabezas m inv, puzle m

jilt [dʒɪlt] vt dejar plantado a

jingle ['dʒɪŋgl] n musiquilla ♦ vi tintinear

jinx [dʒɪŋks] n: **there's a ~ on it** está

gafado

jitters ['dʒɪtəz] (inf) npl: **to get the ~** ponerse nervioso

job [dʒɔb] n (task) tarea; (post) empleo; **it's not the ~** no me incumbe a mí; **it's a good ~ that** ... menos mal que ...; **just the ~!** ¡estupendo!; ~ **centre** (BRIT) n oficina estatal de colocaciones; **~less** adj sin trabajo

jockey ['dʒɔkɪ] n jockey m/f ♦ vi: **to ~ for position** maniobrar para conseguir una posición

jog [dʒɔg] vt empujar (ligeramente) ♦ vi (run) hacer footing; **to ~ sb's memory** refrescar la memoria a uno; **~ along** vi (fig) ir tirando; **~ging** n footing m

join [dʒɔɪn] vt (things) juntar, unir; (club) hacerse socio de; (POL: party) afiliarse a; (queue) ponerse en; (meet: people) reunirse con ♦ vi (roads) juntarse; (rivers) confluir ♦ n juntura; **~ in** vi tomar parte, participar ♦ vt fus tomar parte o participar en; **~ up** vi reunirse; (MIL) alistarse

joiner ['dʒɔɪnə*] (BRIT) n carpintero/a; **~y** n carpintería

joint [dʒɔɪnt] n (TECH) junta, unión f; (ANAT) articulación f; (BRIT: CULIN) pieza de carne (para asar); (inf: place) tugurio; (: of cannabis) porro ♦ adj (common) común; (combined) combinado; **~ account** (with bank etc) cuenta común

joke [dʒəuk] n chiste m; (also: practical ~) broma ♦ vi bromear; **to play a ~ on** gastar una broma a; **~r** n (CARDS) comodín m

jolly ['dʒɔlɪ] adj (merry) alegre; (enjoyable) divertido ♦ adv (BRIT: inf) muy, terriblemente

jolt [dʒəult] n (jerk) sacudida; (shock) susto ♦ vt (physically) sacudir; (emotionally) asustar

jostle ['dʒɔsl] vt dar empellones a, codear

jot [dʒɔt] n: **not one ~** ni jota, ni

pizca; **~ down** vt apuntar; **~ter** (BRIT) n bloc m

journal ['dʒəːnl] n (magazine) revista; (diary) periódico, diario; **~ism** n periodismo; **~ist** n periodista m/f, reportero/a

journey ['dʒəːnɪ] n viaje m; (distance covered) trayecto

jovial ['dʒəuvɪəl] adj risueño, jovial

joy [dʒɔɪ] n alegría; **~ful** adj alegre; **~ous** adj alegre; **~ ride** n (illegal) paseo en coche robado; **~rider** n gamberro que roba un coche para dar una vuelta y luego abandonarlo; **~ stick** n (AVIAT) palanca de mando; (COMPUT) palanca de control

JP n abbr = **Justice of the Peace**

Jr abbr = **junior**

jubilant ['dʒuːbɪlnt] adj jubiloso

judge [dʒʌdʒ] n juez m/f; (fig: expert) perito ♦ vt juzgar; (consider) considerar; **judg(e)ment** n juicio

judiciary [dʒuː'dɪʃiərɪ] n poder m judicial

judicious [dʒuː'dɪʃəs] adj juicioso

judo ['dʒuːdəu] n judo

jug [dʒʌg] n jarra

juggernaut ['dʒʌgənɔːt] n (BRIT) (huge truck) trailer m

juggle ['dʒʌgl] vi hacer juegos malabares; **~r** n malabarista m/f

juice [dʒuːs] n zumo, jugo (esp AM); **juicy** adj jugoso

jukebox ['dʒuːkbɔks] n máquina de discos

July [dʒuː'laɪ] n julio

jumble ['dʒʌmbl] n revoltijo ♦ vt (also: ~ up) revolver; **~ sale** (BRIT) n venta de objetos usados con fines benéficos

jumble sale

Los jumble sales son unos mercadillos que se organizan con fines benéficos en los locales de un colegio, iglesia u otro centro público. En ellos puede comprarse todo tipo de artículos baratos de segunda mano, sobre todo

ropa, juguetes, libros, vajillas o muebles.

jumbo (jet) ['dʒʌmbəʊ-] *n* jumbo
jump [dʒʌmp] *n* visaltar, dar saltos; *(with fear etc)* pegar un bote; *(increase)* aumentar ♦ *vt* saltar ♦ *n* salto; aumento; **to ~ the queue** (BRIT) colarse
jumper ['dʒʌmpə*] *n* (BRIT: *pullover*) suéter *m*, jersey *m*; (US: *dress*) mandil *m*; **~ cables** (US) *npl* = **jump leads**
jump leads (BRIT) *npl* cables *mpl* puente de batería
jumpy ['dʒʌmpɪ] (*inf*) *adj* nervioso
Jun. *abbr* = **junior**
junction ['dʒʌŋkʃən] *n* (BRIT: *of roads*) cruce *m*; (RAIL) empalme *m*
juncture ['dʒʌŋktʃə*] *n*: **at this ~** en este momento, en esta coyuntura
June [dʒuːn] *n* junio
jungle ['dʒʌŋgl] *n* selva, jungla
junior ['dʒuːnɪə*] *adj* (in age) menor, más joven; *(brother/sister etc)*: **7 years her ~** siete años menor que ella; *(position)* subalterno ♦ *n* menor *m/f*, joven *m/f*; **~ school** (BRIT) *n* escuela primaria
junk [dʒʌŋk] *n* (cheap goods) baratijas *fpl*; *(rubbish)* basura; **~ food** *n* alimentos preparados y envasados de escaso valor nutritivo
junkie ['dʒʌŋkɪ] (*inf*) *n* drogadicto/a, yonqui *m/f*
junk mail *n* propaganda de buzón
junk shop *n* tienda de objetos usados
Junr *abbr* = **junior**
juror ['dʒuərə*] *n* jurado
jury ['dʒuərɪ] *n* jurado
just [dʒʌst] *adj* justo ♦ *adv* (exactly) exactamente; (only) sólo, solamente; **he's ~ done it/left** acaba de hacerlo/irse; **~ right** correcto; **~ two o'clock** las dos en punto; **she's ~ as clever as you** (ella) es tan lista como tú; **~ as well as** ... menos mal que ...; **~ as he was leaving** en el momento en que se marchaba;

~ before/enough justo antes/lo suficiente; **~ here** aquí mismo; **he ~ missed** ha fallado por poco; **~ listen to this** escucha esto un momento
justice ['dʒʌstɪs] *n* justicia; (US: *judge*) juez *m*; **to do ~ to** (*fig*) hacer justicia a; **J~ of the Peace** *n* juez *m* de paz
justify ['dʒʌstɪfaɪ] *vt* justificar; *(text)* alinear
jut [dʒʌt] *vi* (*also*: **~ out**) sobresalir
juvenile ['dʒuːvənaɪl] *adj* (*court*) de menores; *(humour, mentality)* infantil ♦ *n* menor *m* de edad

K, k

K *abbr* (= *one thousand*) mil; (= *kilobyte*) kilobyte *m*, kilooocteto
kangaroo [kæŋgə'ruː] *n* canguro
karate [kə'rɑːtɪ] *n* karate *m*
kebab [kə'bæb] *n* pincho moruno
keel [kiːl] *n* quilla; **on an even ~** (*fig*) en equilibrio
keen [kiːn] *adj* (*interest, desire*) grande, vivo; (*eye, intelligence*) agudo; *(competition)* reñido; *(edge)* afilado; *(eager)* entusiasta; **to be ~ to do** *or* **on doing sth** tener muchas ganas de hacer algo; **to be ~ on sth/sb** interesarse por algo/uno
keep [kiːp] (*pt, pp* **kept**) *vt* (*preserve, store*) guardar; (*hold back*) quedarse con; *(maintain)* mantener; *(detain)* detener; *(shop)* ser propietario de; *(feed: family etc)* mantener; *(promise)* cumplir; *(chickens, bees etc)* criar; *(accounts)* llevar; *(diary)* escribir; *(prevent)*: **to ~ sb from doing sth** impedir a uno hacer algo ♦ *vi* (*food*) conservarse; *(remain)* seguir, continuar ♦ *n* (*of castle*) torreón *m*; *(food etc)* comida, subsistencia; (*inf*): **for ~s** para siempre; **to ~ doing sth** seguir haciendo algo; **to ~ sb happy** tener a uno contento; **to ~ a place tidy**

mantener un lugar limpio; **to ~ sth to o.s.** guardar algo para sí mismo; **to ~ sth (back) from sb** ocultar algo a uno; **to ~ time** (clock) mantener la hora exacta; **~ on** vi (stay out) permanecer fuera; **"~ out"** "prohibida la entrada"; **~ up** vt mantener, conservar ♦ vi no retrasarse; **to ~ up with** (pace) ir al paso de; (level) mantenerse a la altura de; **~er** n guardián/ana m/f; **~-fit** n gimnasia (para mantenerse en forma); **~ing** n (care) cuidado; **in ~ing with** de acuerdo con; **~sake** n recuerdo

kennel ['kɛnl] n perrera; **~s** npl residencia canina

Kenya ['kɛnjə] n Kenia

kept [kɛpt] pt, pp of **keep**

kerb [kə:b] (BRIT) n bordillo

kernel ['kə:nl] n (nut) almendra; (fig) meollo

ketchup ['kɛtʃəp] n salsa de tomate, catsup m

kettle ['kɛtl] n hervidor m de agua; **~ drum** n (MUS) timbal m

key [ki:] n llave f; (MUS) tono; (of piano, typewriter) tecla ♦ adj (issue etc) clave inv ♦ vt (also: **~ in**) teclear; **~board** n teclado; **~ed up** adj (person) nervioso; **~hole** n ojo (de la cerradura); **~hole surgery** n cirugía cerrada, cirugía no invasiva; **~note** n (MUS) tónica; (of speech) punto principal or clave; **~ring** n llavero

khaki ['kɑ:ki] n caqui

kick [kik] vt dar una patada or un puntapié a; (inf: habit) quitarse de ♦ n (of horse) coz f; (thrill): **he does it for ~s** lo hace por pura diversión; **~ off** vi (SPORT) hacer el saque inicial

kid [kid] n (inf: child) chiquillo m; (animal) cabrito; (leather) cabritilla ♦ vi (inf) bromear

kidnap ['kidnæp] vt secuestrar; **~per** n

secuestrador(a) m/f; **~ping** n secuestro

kidney ['kidni] n riñón m

kill [kil] vt matar; (murder) asesinar ♦ n matanza; **to ~ time** matar el tiempo; **~er** n asesino/a; **~ing** n (one) asesinato; (several) matanza; **to make a ~ing** (fig) hacer su agosto; **~joy** n (BRIT) n aguafiestas m/f inv

kiln [kiln] n horno

kilo ['ki:ləu] n kilo; **~byte** n (COMPUT) kilobyte m, kilocteto; **~gram(me)** ['kiləugræm] n kilo, kilogramo; (BRIT) n aguafiestas m/f inv
~metre ['kiləmi:tə*] (US **~meter**) n kilómetro; **~watt** ['kiləwɔt] n kilovatio

kilt [kilt] n falda escocesa

kin [kin] n see **next**

kind [kaind] adj amable, atento ♦ n clase f, especie f; (species) género m; **in ~** (COMM) en especie; **a ~ of** una especie de; **to be two of a ~** ser tal para cual

kindergarten ['kindəgɑ:tn] n jardín m de la infancia

kind-hearted adj bondadoso, de buen corazón

kindle ['kindl] vt encender; (arouse) despertar

kindly ['kaindli] adj bondadoso, cariñoso ♦ adv bondadosamente, amablemente; **will you ~ ...** sea usted tan amable de ...

kindness ['kaindnis] n (quality) bondad f, amabilidad f; (act) favor m

king [kin] n rey m; **~dom** n reino; **~fisher** n martín m pescador; **~-size** adj de tamaño extra

kiosk ['ki:ɔsk] n quiosco; (BRIT: TEL) cabina

kipper ['kipə*] n arenque m ahumado

kiss [kis] n beso ♦ vt besar; **to ~ (each other)** besarse; **~ of life** n respiración f boca a boca

kit [kit] n (equipment) equipo; (tools etc) (caja de herramientas fpl; (assembly ~) juego de armar

kitchen ['kitʃin] n cocina; **~ sink** n fregadero

kite [kaɪt] n (toy) cometa

kitten ['kɪtn] n gatito/a

kitty ['kɪtɪ] n (funds) fondo común

km abbr (= kilometre) km

knack [næk] n: **to have the ~ of doing sth** tener el don de hacer algo

knapsack ['næpsæk] n mochila

knead [niːd] vt amasar

knee [niː] n rodilla; **~cap** n rótula

kneel [niːl] (pt, pp **knelt**) vi (also: ~ **down**) arrodillarse

knew [njuː] pt of **know**

knickers ['nɪkəz] npl (BRIT) bragas fpl

knife [naɪf] (pl **knives**) n cuchillo ♦ vt acuchillar

knight [naɪt] n caballero; (CHESS) caballo; **~hood** n (BRIT) (title): **to receive a ~hood** recibir el título de Sir

knit [nɪt] vt tejer, tricotar ♦ vi hacer punto, tricotar; (bones) soldarse; **to ~ one's brows** fruncir el ceño; **~ting** n labor f de punto; **~ting machine** n máquina de tricotar; **~ting needle** n aguja de hacer punto; **~wear** n prendas fpl de punto

knives [naɪvz] npl of **knife**

knob [nɔb] n (of door) tirador m; (of stick) puño; (on radio, TV) botón m

knock [nɔk] vt (strike) golpear; (bump into) chocar contra; (inf) criticar ♦ vi (at door etc): **to ~ at/on** llamar a ♦ n golpe m; (on door) llamada; **~ down** vt atropellar; **~ off** vi (inf) (finish) salir del trabajo ♦ vt (from price) descontar; (inf: steal) birlar; **~ out** vt dejar sin sentido; (BOXING) poner fuera de combate, dejar K.O.; (in competition) eliminar; **~ over** vt (object) tirar; (person) atropellar; **~er** n (on door) aldabón m; **~out** n (BOXING) K.O. m, knockout m ♦ cpd (competition etc) eliminatorio

knot [nɔt] n nudo ♦ vt anudar

know [nəʊ] (pt **knew**, pp **known**) vt (facts) saber; (be acquainted with) conocer; (recognize) reconocer,

conocer; **to ~ how to swim** saber nadar; **to ~ about** or **of sb/sth** saber de uno/algo; **~-all** n sabelotodo m/f; **~-how** n conocimientos mpl; **~ing** adj (look) de complicidad; **~ingly** adv (purposely) adrede; (smile, look) con complicidad

knowledge ['nɔlɪdʒ] n conocimiento; (learning) saber m, conocimientos mpl; **~able** adj entendido

knuckle ['nʌkl] n nudillo

Koran [kɔ'rɑːn] n Corán m

Korea [kə'rɪə] n Corea f

kosher ['kəʊʃə*] adj autorizado por la ley judía

Kosovo ['kɔsəvəʊ] n Kosovo m

L, l

L (BRIT) abbr = **learner driver**

l. abbr (= litre) l

lab [læb] n abbr = **laboratory**

label ['leɪbl] n etiqueta ♦ vt poner etiqueta a

labor etc ['leɪbə*] (US) = **labour**

laboratory [lə'bɔrətəri] n laboratorio

laborious [lə'bɔːrɪəs] adj penoso

labour ['leɪbə*] (US **labor**) n (hard work) trabajo; (~ force) mano f de obra; (MED): **to be in ~** estar de parto ♦ vi: **to ~ (at)** sth trabajar (en algo) ♦ vt: **to ~ a point** insistir en un punto; **L~, the L~ party** (BRIT) el partido laborista, los laboristas mpl; **~ed** adj (breathing) fatigoso; **~er** n peón m; **farm ~er** peón m; (day ~er) jornalero

lace [leɪs] n encaje m; (of shoe) cordón m ♦ vt (shoes: also: ~ **up**) atarse (los zapatos)

lack [læk] n (absence) falta ♦ vt faltarle a uno, carecer de; **through** or **for ~ of** por falta de; **to be ~ing** faltar, no haber; **to be ~ing in sth** faltarle a uno algo

lacquer ['lækə*] n laca

lad [læd] n muchacho, chico

ladder ['lædə*] n escalera (de mano); (BRIT: in tights) carrera

laden ['leɪdn] adj: ~ (with) cargado (de)

ladle ['leɪdl] n cucharón m

lady ['leɪdɪ] n señora; (dignified, graceful) dama; "ladies and gentlemen ..." "señoras y caballeros ..."; **young ~** señorita; **the ladies' (room)** los servicios de señoras; **~bird** (US **~bug**) n mariquita; **~like** adj fino; **L~ship** n: **your L~ship** su Señoría

lag [læg] n retraso ♦ vi (also: ~ **behind**) retrasarse, quedarse atrás ♦ vt (pipes) revestir

lager ['lɑːgə*] n cerveza (rubia)

lagoon [lə'guːn] n laguna

laid [leɪd] pt, pp of **lay**; **~ back** (inf) adj relajado; **~ up** adj: **to be ~ up** (with) tener que guardar cama (a causa de)

lain [leɪn] pp of **lie**

lake [leɪk] n lago

lamb [læm] n cordero; (meat) (carne f de) cordero; **~ chop** n chuleta de cordero; **lambswool** n lana de cordero

lame [leɪm] adj cojo; (excuse) poco convincente

lament [lə'ment] n quejo ♦ vt lamentarse de

laminated ['læmɪneɪtɪd] adj (metal) laminado; (wood) contrachapado; (surface) plastificado

lamp [læmp] n lámpara; **~post** (BRIT) n (poste m de) farol m; **~shade** n pantalla

lance [lɑːns] vt (MED) abrir con lanceta

land [lænd] n tierra; (country) país m; (piece of ~) terreno; (estate) tierras fpl, finca ♦ vi (from ship) desembarcar; (AVIAT) aterrizar; (fig: fall) caer, terminar ♦ vt (passengers, goods) desembarcar; **to ~ sb with sth** (inf) hacer cargar a uno con algo; **~ up** vi: **to ~ up in/at** ir a parar a/en; **~fill site** ['lændfɪl-] n vertedero; **~ing** n aterrizaje m; (of staircase) rellano; **~ing**

gear n (AVIAT) tren m de aterrizaje; **~lady** n (of rented house, pub etc) dueña; (fig) patrón m (of pub etc) patrón; **~lord** n propietario; (of pub etc) patrón m; **~mark** n lugar m conocido; **to be a ~mark** (fig) marcar un hito histórico; **~owner** n terrateniente m/f; **~scape** n paisaje m; **~scape gardener** n arquitecto de jardines; **~slide** n (GEO) corrimiento de tierras; (fig: POL) victoria arrolladora

lane [leɪn] n (in country) camino; (AUT) carril m; (in race) calle f

language ['læŋgwɪdʒ] n lenguaje m; (national tongue) idioma m, lengua; **bad ~** palabrotas fpl; **~ laboratory** n laboratorio de idiomas

lank [læŋk] adj (hair) lacio

lanky ['læŋkɪ] adj larguirucho

lantern ['læntn] n linterna, farol m

lap [læp] n (of track) vuelta; (of body) regazo; **to sit on sb's ~** sentarse en las rodillas de uno ♦ vt (also: ~ **up**) beber a lengüetadas ♦ vi (waves) chapotear; **~ up** vt (fig) tragarse

lapel [lə'pel] n solapa

Lapland ['læplænd] n Laponia

lapse [læps] n fallo; (moral) desliz m; (of time) intervalo ♦ vi (expire) caducar; (time) pasar, transcurrir; **to ~ into bad habits** caer en malos hábitos

laptop (computer) ['læptɔp-] n (ordenador m) portátil m

larch [lɑːtʃ] n alerce m

lard [lɑːd] n manteca (de cerdo)

larder ['lɑːdə*] n despensa

large [lɑːdʒ] adj grande; **at ~** (free) en libertad; (generally) en general; **~ly** adv (mostly) en su mayor parte; (introducing reason) en gran parte; **~-scale** adj (map) en gran escala; (fig) importante

lark [lɑːk] n (bird) alondra; (joke) broma

laryngitis [lærɪn'dʒaɪtɪs] n laringitis f

laser ['leɪzə*] n láser m; **~ printer** n impresora (por) láser

lash [læʃ] n latigazo; (also: eye~) pestaña ♦ vt azotar; (tie): **to ~ to/ together** atar a/atar; **~ out** vi: **to**

lass [læs] (BRIT) n chica
lasso [læˈsuː] n lazo
last [lɑːst] adj último; (end: of series etc) final ♦ adv (most recently) la última vez; (finally) por último ♦ vi durar; (continue) continuar, seguir; ~ **night** anoche; ~ **week** la semana pasada; **at** ~ por fin; ~ **but one** penúltimo; ~**ditch** adj (attempt) último, desesperado; ~**ing** adj duradero; ~**ly** adv por último, finalmente; ~**-minute** adj de última hora
latch [lætʃ] n pestillo
late [leɪt] adj (far on: in time, process etc) al final de; (not on time) tarde, atrasado; (dead) fallecido ♦ adv tarde; (behind time, schedule) con retraso; **of** ~ últimamente; ~ **at night** a última hora de la noche; **in** ~ **May** hacia fines de mayo; **the** ~ **Mr X** el difunto Sr X; ~**comer** n recién llegado/a; ~**ly** adv últimamente; ~**r** adj (date etc) posterior; (version etc) más reciente ♦ adv más tarde, después; ~**st** [ˈleɪtɪst] adj último; **at the** ~**st** a más tardar
lathe [leɪð] n torno
lather [ˈlɑːðə*] n espuma (de jabón) ♦ vt enjabonar
Latin [ˈlætɪn] n latín m ♦ adj latino; ~ **America** n América latina; ~-**American** adj, n latinoamericano/a
latitude [ˈlætɪtjuːd] n latitud f; (fig) libertad f
latter [ˈlætə*] adj (second) segundo; **the** ~ el último, éste; ~**ly** adv últimamente
laudable [ˈlɔːdəbl] adj loable
laugh [lɑːf] n risa ♦ vi reír(se); (**to do sth**) **for a** ~ (hacer algo) en broma; ~ **at** vt fus reírse de; ~ **off** vt tomar algo a risa; ~**able** adj ridículo; ~**ing stock** n: **the** ~**ing stock of** el hazmerreír de; ~**ter** n risa
launch [lɔːntʃ] n lanzamiento m; (boat)

~ out (at sb) (hit) arremeter (contra uno); **to** ~ **out against sb** lanzar invectivas contra uno ♦ vt (ship) botar; (rocket etc) lanzar; (fig) comenzar; ~ **into** vt fus lanzarse a; ~(**ing**) **pad** n plataforma de lanzamiento
launder [ˈlɔːndə*] vt lavar
Launderette ® [lɔːnˈdret] (BRIT) n lavandería (automática)
Laundromat ® [ˈlɔːndrəmæt] (US) n = **Launderette**
laundry [ˈlɔːndrɪ] n (dirty) ropa sucia; (clean) colada; (room) lavadero
lavatory [ˈlævətərɪ] n wáter m
lavender [ˈlævəndə*] n lavanda
lavish [ˈlævɪʃ] adj (amount) abundante; (person): ~ **with** pródigo en ♦ vt: **to** ~ **sth on sb** colmar a uno de algo
law [lɔː] n ley f; (SCOL) derecho; (a rule) regla; (professions connected with ~) jurisprudencia; ~-**abiding** adj respetuoso de la ley; ~ **and order** n orden m público; ~ **court** n tribunal m (de justicia); ~**ful** adj legítimo, lícito; ~**less** adj (action) criminal
lawn [lɔːn] n césped m; ~**mower** n cortacésped m; ~ **tennis** n tenis m sobre hierba
law school (US) n (SCOL) facultad f de derecho
lawsuit [ˈlɔːsuːt] n pleito
lawyer [ˈlɔːjə*] n abogado/a; (for sales, wills etc) notario/a
lax [læks] adj laxo
laxative [ˈlæksətɪv] n laxante m
lay [leɪ] (pt, pp **laid**) pt de **lie** ♦ adj laico; (not expert) lego ♦ vt (place) colocar; (eggs, table) poner; (cable) tender; (carpet) extender; ~ **aside** or **by** vt dejar a un lado; ~ **down** vt (pen etc) dejar; (rules etc) establecer; **to** ~ **down the law** (pej) imponer las normas; ~ **off** vt (workers) despedir; ~ **on** vt (meal, facilities) proveer; ~ **out** vt (spread out) disponer, exponer; ~**about** (inf) n vago/a; ~**-by** n (BRIT: AUT) área de aparcamiento
layer [ˈleɪə*] n capa
layman [ˈleɪmən] (irreg) n lego

layout ['leɪaʊt] n (design) plan m, trazado; (PRESS) composición f

laze [leɪz] vi (also: ~ about) holgazanear

lazy ['leɪzɪ] adj perezoso, vago; (movement) lento

lb. abbr = **pound** (weight)

lead¹ [liːd] (pt, pp led) n (front position) delantera; (clue) pista; (ELEC) cable m; (for dog) correa; (THEATRE) papel m principal ♦ vt (walk etc in front of) ir a la cabeza de; (guide): **to ~ sb somewhere** conducir a uno a algún sitio; (be leader of) dirigir; (start, guide: activity) protagonizar ♦ vi (SPORT) ir primero; **to be in the ~** (SPORT) llevar la delantera; (fig) ir a la cabeza; **to ~ the way** (also fig) llevar la delantera; **~ away** vt llevar; **~ back** vi (person, route) llevar de vuelta; **~ on** vt (tease) engañar; **~ to** vt fus producir, provocar; **~ up to** vt fus (events) conducir a; (in conversation) preparar el terreno para

lead² [led] n (metal) plomo m; (in pencil) mina; **~ed petrol** n gasolina con plomo

leader ['liːdə*] n jefe/a m/f, líder m; (SPORT) líder m; **~ship** n dirección f; (position) mando; (quality) iniciativa f

leading ['liːdɪŋ] adj (main) principal; (first) primero; (front) delantero; **~ lady** n (THEATRE) primera actriz f; **~ light** n (person) figura principal; **~ man** (irreg) n (THEATRE) primer galán m

lead singer [liːd-] n cantante m/f

leaf [liːf] (pl **leaves**) n hoja f ♦ vi: **~ through** hojear; **to turn over a new ~** reformarse

leaflet ['liːflɪt] n folleto

league [liːg] n sociedad f; (FOOTBALL) liga; **to be in ~ with** haberse confabulado con

leak [liːk] n (of liquid, gas) escape m, fuga; (in pipe) agujero; (in roof) gotera; (in security) filtración f ♦ vi (shoes, ship) hacer agua; (pipe) tener (un) escape;

(roof) gotear; (liquid, gas) escaparse, fugarse; (fig) divulgarse ♦ vt (fig) filtrar

lean [liːn] (pt, pp **leaned** or **leant**) adj (thin) flaco; (meat) magro ♦ vt: **to ~ sth on sth** apoyar algo en algo ♦ vi (slope) inclinarse; **to ~ against** apoyarse contra; **to ~ on** apoyarse en; **~ back/forward** vi inclinarse hacia atrás/adelante; **~ out** vi asomarse; **~ over** vi inclinarse; **~ing** n: **~ing (towards)** inclinación f (hacia); **leant** [lent] pt, pp of **lean**

leap [liːp] (pt, pp **leaped** or **leapt**) n salto ♦ vi saltar; **~frog** n pídola; **~ year** n año bisiesto

learn [lɜːn] (pt, pp **learned** or **learnt**) vt aprender ♦ vi aprender; **to ~ about sth** enterarse de algo; **to ~ to do sth** aprender a hacer algo; **~ed** ['lɜːnɪd] adj erudito; **~er** n (BRIT: also: **~er driver**) principiante m/f; **~ing** n el saber m, conocimientos mpl

lease [liːs] n arriendo ♦ vt arrendar

leash [liːʃ] n correa

least [liːst] adj: **the ~** (slightest) el menor, el más pequeño; (smallest amount of) mínimo ♦ adv (+ vb) menos; (+ adj): **the ~ expensive** el/la menos costoso/a; **the ~ possible effort** el menor esfuerzo posible; **at ~** por lo menos, al menos; **you could at ~ have written** por lo menos podías haber escrito; **not in the ~** en absoluto

leather ['leðə*] n cuero

leave [liːv] (pt, pp **left**) vt dejar; (go away from) abandonar; (place etc: permanently) salir de ♦ vi irse; (train etc) salir ♦ n permiso; **to ~ sth to sb** (money etc) legar algo a uno; (responsibility) encargar a uno de algo; **to be left** quedar, sobrar; **there's some milk left over** sobra or queda algo de leche; **on ~** de permiso; **~ behind** vt (on purpose) dejar; (accidentally) dejarse; **~ out** vt omitir; **~ of absence** n permiso de ausentarse

leaves |liːvz| npl of **leaf**

Lebanon |'lebənən| n: **the ~** el Líbano

lecherous |'letʃərəs| (pej) adj lascivo

lecture |'lektʃə*| n conferencia; (SCOL) clase f ♦ vi dar una clase ♦ vt (scold): **to ~ sb on** or **about sth** echar una reprimenda a uno por algo; **to give a ~ on** dar una conferencia sobre; **~r** n conferenciante m/f; (BRIT: at university) profesor(a) m/f

led |led| pt, pp of **lead**

ledge |ledʒ| n repisa; (of window) alféizar m; (of mountain) saliente m

ledger |'ledʒə*| n libro mayor

leech |liːtʃ| n sanguijuela

leek |liːk| n puerro

leer |lɪə*| vi: **to ~ at sb** mirar de manera lasciva a uno

leeway |'liːweɪ| n (fig): **to have some ~** tener cierta libertad de acción

left |left| pt, pp of **leave** ♦ adj izquierdo; (remaining): **there are 2 ~** quedan dos ♦ n izquierda ♦ adv a la izquierda; **on** or **to the ~** a la izquierda; **the L~** (POL) la izquierda; **~-handed** adj zurdo; **the ~-hand side** n la izquierda; **~-luggage (office)** (BRIT) n consigna; **~-overs** npl sobras fpl; **~-wing** adj (POL) de izquierdas, izquierdista

leg |leg| n pierna; (of animal, chair) pata; (trouser ~) pernera; (CULIN: of lamb) pierna; (of chicken) pata; (of journey) etapa

legacy |'legəsɪ| n herencia

legal |'liːgl| adj (permitted by law) lícito; (of law) legal; **~ holiday** (US) n fiesta oficial; **~ize** vt legalizar; **~ly** adv legalmente; **~ tender** n moneda de curso legal

legend |'ledʒənd| n (also fig: person) leyenda

legislation |ledʒɪs'leɪʃən| n legislación f

legislature |'ledʒɪslətʃə*| n cuerpo legislativo

legitimate |lɪ'dʒɪtɪmət| adj legítimo

leg-room n espacio para las piernas

leisure |'leʒə*| n ocio, tiempo libre; **at ~** con tranquilidad; **~ centre** n centro de recreo; **~ly** adj sin prisa; lento

lemon |'lemən| n limón m; **~ade** n (fizzy) gaseosa; **~ tea** n té m con limón

lend |lend| (pt, pp lent) vt: **to ~ sth to sb** prestar algo a uno; **~ing library** n biblioteca de préstamo

length |leŋθ| n (size) largo, longitud f; (distance): **the ~ of** todo a lo largo de; (of swimming pool, cloth) largo; (of wood, string) trozo; (amount of time) duración f; **at ~** (at last) por fin, finalmente; (lengthily) largamente; **~en** vt alargar ♦ vi alargarse; **~ways** adv a lo largo; **~y** adj largo, extenso

lenient |'liːnɪənt| adj indulgente

lens |lenz| n (of spectacles) lente f; (of camera) objetivo

Lent |lent| n Cuaresma

lent |lent| pt, pp of **lend**

lentil |'lentl| n lenteja

Leo |'liːəu| n Leo

leotard |'liːətɑːd| n mallas fpl

leprosy |'leprəsɪ| n lepra

lesbian |'lezbɪən| n lesbiana

less |les| adj (in size, degree etc) menor (in quality) menos ♦ pron, adv menos ♦ prep: **~ tax/10% discount** menos impuestos/el 10 por ciento de descuento; **~ than half** menos de la mitad; **~ than ever** menos que nunca; **~ and ~** cada vez menos; **the ~ he works ...** cuanto menos trabaja ...; **~en** vi disminuir, reducirse ♦ vt disminuir, reducir; **~er** |'lesə*| adj menor; **to a ~er extent** en menor grado

lesson |'lesn| n clase f; (warning) lección f

let |let| (pt, pp **let**) vt (allow) dejar, permitir; (BRIT: lease) alquilar; **to ~ sb do sth** dejar que uno haga algo; **to ~ sb know sth** comunicar algo a uno; **~'s go** ¡vamos!; **~ him come** que venga; **"to ~"** "se alquila"; **~ down** vt *(tyre)* desinflar; *(disappoint)* defraudar; **~ go** *vi* tv soltar; **~ in** *vt* dejar entrar; *(visitor etc)* hacer pasar; **~ off** *vt (culprit)* dejar escapar; *(gun)* disparar; *(bomb)* accionar; *(firework)* hacer estallar; **~ on** *(inf)* vi divulgar; **~ out** *vt* dejar salir; *(sound)* soltar; **~ up** vi amainar, disminuir

lethal ['li:θl] *adj (weapon)* mortífero; *(poison, wound)* mortal

letter ['lɛtə*] *n (of alphabet)* letra; *(correspondence)* carta; **~ bomb** n carta-bomba; **~box** *(BRIT)* n buzón m; **~ing** n letras fpl

lettuce ['lɛtɪs] *n* lechuga

let-up n disminución f

leukaemia [lu:'ki:mɪə] *(US leukemia* n leucemia

level ['lɛvl] *adj (flat)* llano ♦ *adv*: **to draw ~ with** llegar a la altura de ♦ n nivel m; *(height)* altura ♦ *vt* nivelar; allanar; *(destroy: building)* derribar; *(: forest)* arrasar; **to be ~ with** estar a nivel de; **"A" ~s** *(BRIT)* npl = exámenes mpl de bachillerato superior, B.U.P.; **"O" ~s** *(BRIT)* npl = exámenes mpl de octavo de básica; **on the ~** *(fig: honest)* serio; **~ off** or **out** vi *(prices etc)* estabilizarse; **~ crossing** *(BRIT)* n paso a nivel; **~-headed** adj sensato

lever ['li:və*] n *(also fig)* palanca ♦ vt: **to ~ up** levantar con palanca; **~age** n *(using bar etc)* apalancamiento; *(fig: influence)* influencia

levy ['lɛvɪ] n impuesto ♦ vt exigir, recaudar

lewd [lu:d] *adj* lascivo; *(joke)* obsceno, colorado *(AM)*

liability [laɪə'bɪlɪtɪ] n *(pej: person, thing)* estorbo, lastre m; *(JUR: responsibility)* responsabilidad f; **liabilities** npl *(COMM)* pasivo

liable ['laɪəbl] *adj (subject)*: **~ to** sujeto a; *(responsible)*: **~ for** responsable de; *(likely)*: **~ to** propenso a hacer

liaise [lɪ'eɪz] *vi*: **to ~ with** enlazar con; **liaison** [lɪ:'eɪzɔn] n *(coordination)*

enlace m; *(affair)* relaciones fpl amorosas

liar ['laɪə*] n mentiroso/a

libel ['laɪbl] n calumnia ♦ vt calumniar

liberal ['lɪbərəl] adj liberal; *(offer, amount etc)* generoso

liberate ['lɪbəreɪt] vt *(people: from poverty etc)* librar; *(prisoner)* libertar; *(country)* liberar

liberty ['lɪbətɪ] n libertad f; *(criminal)*: **to be at ~** estar en libertad; **to be at ~ to do** estar libre para hacer; **to take the ~ of doing sth** tomarse la libertad de hacer algo

Libra ['li:brə] n Libra

librarian [laɪ'brɛərɪən] n bibliotecario/a

library ['laɪbrərɪ] n biblioteca

libretto [lɪ'brɛtəu] n libreto

Libya ['lɪbɪə] n Libia; **~n** adj, n libio/a m/f

lice [laɪs] npl of **louse**

licence ['laɪsəns] *(US* **license**) n licencia; *(permit)* licencia; *(also: driving ~, (US) driver's ~)* carnet m de conducir *(SP)*, permiso *(AM)*

license ['laɪsəns] n *(US)* = **licence** ♦ vt autorizar, dar permiso a; **~d** adj *(for alcohol)* autorizado para vender bebidas alcohólicas; *(car)* matriculado; **~ plate** *(US)* n placa *(de matrícula)*

lick [lɪk] vt lamer; *(inf: defeat)* dar una paliza a; **to ~ one's lips** relamerse

licorice ['lɪkərɪs] *(US)* n = **liquorice**

lid [lɪd] n *(of box, case)* tapa; *(of pan)* tapadera

lido ['laɪdəu] *(BRIT)* n piscina

lie [laɪ] *(pt* **lay,** *pp* **lain)** vi *(rest)* estar echado, estar acostado; *(of object: be situated)* estar, encontrarse; *(tell lies: pt, pp* **lied)** mentir ♦ n mentira; **to ~ low** *(fig)* mantenerse a escondidas; **~ about** or **around** vi *(things)* estar tirado; *(BRIT: people)* estar tumbado; **~-down** *(BRIT)* n: **to have a ~-down** echarse (una siesta); *(take a siesta)*; **~-in** *(BRIT)* n: **to have a ~-in** quedarse en la cama

lieu [lu:]: **in ~ of** prep en lugar de

lieutenant [lefˈtenənt, (US) luːˈtenənt] n (MIL) teniente m

life [laɪf] (pl **lives**) n vida; **to come to ~** animarse; **~ assurance** (BRIT) n seguro de vida; **~belt** (BRIT) n salvavidas m inv; **~boat** n lancha de socorro; **~guard** n vigilante m/f, socorrista m/f; **~ insurance** n = **~ assurance**; **~ jacket** n chaleco salvavidas; **~less** adj sin vida; (dull) soso; **~like** adj (model etc) que parece vivo; (realistic) realista; **~long** adj de toda la vida; **~ preserver** (US) n cinturón m/chaleco salvavidas; **~ sentence** n cadena perpetua; **~size** adj de tamaño natural; **~ span** n vida; **~style** n estilo de vida; **~ support system** n (MED) sistema m de respiración asistida; **~time** n (of person) vida; (of thing) período de vida

lift [lɪft] vt levantar; (end: ban, rule) levantar, suprimir ♦ vi (fog) disiparse ♦ n (BRIT: machine) ascensor m; **to give sb a ~** (BRIT) llevar a uno en el coche; **~-off** n despegue m

light [laɪt] (pt, pp **lighted** or **lit**) n luz f; (lamp) luz f, lámpara; (AUT) faro; (for cigarette etc): **have you got a ~?** ¿tienes fuego? ♦ vt (candle, cigarette, fire) encender (SP), prender (AM); (room) alumbrar ♦ adj (colour) claro; (not heavy, also fig) ligero; (room) con mucha luz; (gentle, graceful) ágil; **~s** npl (traffic ~s) semáforos mpl; **to come to ~** salir a luz; **in the ~ of** (new evidence etc) a la luz de; **~ up** vi (smoke) encender un cigarrillo; (face) iluminarse ♦ vt (illuminate) iluminar, alumbrar; (set fire to) encender; **~ bulb** n bombilla (SP), foco (AM); **~en** vt (make less heavy) aligerar; **~er** n (also: cigarette ~) encendedor m, mechero; **~-headed** adj (dizzy) mareado; (excited) exaltado; **~-hearted** adj (person) alegre; (remark etc) divertido; **~house** n faro; **~ing** n (system) alumbrado; **~ly** adv ligeramente; (not

seriously) con poca seriedad; **to get off ~ly** ser castigado con poca severidad; **~ness** n (in weight) ligereza

lightning [ˈlaɪtnɪŋ] n relámpago, rayo; **~ conductor** (US = **rod**) n pararrayos m inv

light: ~ pen n lápiz m óptico; **~weight** adj (suit) ligero ♦ n (BOXING) peso ligero; **~ year** n año luz

like [laɪk] vt gustarle a uno ♦ prep como ♦ adj parecido, semejante ♦ n: **and the ~** y otros por el estilo; **his ~s and dislikes** sus gustos y aversiones; **I would ~, I'd ~** me gustaría; (for purchase) quisiera; **would you ~ a coffee?** ¿te apetece un café?; **I ~ swimming** me gusta nadar; **she ~s apples** le gustan las manzanas; **to be or look ~ sb/sth** parecerse a alguien/ algo; **what does it look/taste/ sound ~?** ¿cómo es/a qué sabe/cómo suena?; **that's just ~ him** es muy de él, es característico de él; **do it ~ this** hazlo así; **it is nothing ~ ...** no tiene parecido alguno con ...; **~able** adj simpático, agradable

likelihood [ˈlaɪklɪhud] n probabilidad f

likely [ˈlaɪklɪ] adj probable; **he's ~ to leave** es probable que se vaya; **not ~!** ¡ni hablar!

likeness [ˈlaɪknɪs] n semejanza, parecido; **that's a good ~** se parece mucho

likewise [ˈlaɪkwaɪz] adv igualmente; **to do ~** hacer lo mismo

liking [ˈlaɪkɪŋ] n: **~ (for)** (person) cariño (a); (thing) afición (a); **to be to sb's ~** ser del gusto de uno

lilac [ˈlaɪlək] n (tree) lilo; (flower) lila

lily [ˈlɪlɪ] n lirio, azucena; **~ of the valley** n lirio de los valles

limb [lɪm] n miembro

limber [ˈlɪmbə*]: **to ~ up** vi (SPORT) hacer ejercicios de calentamiento

limbo [ˈlɪmbəu] n: **to be in ~** (fig) quedar a la expectativa

lime [laɪm] n (tree) limero; (fruit) lima;

(GEO) cal f

limelight ['laɪmlaɪt] n: **to be in the ~** (fig) ser el centro de atención

limerick ['lɪmərɪk] n especie de poema humorístico

limestone ['laɪmstəʊn] n piedra caliza

limit ['lɪmɪt] n límite m ♦ vt limitar; **~ed** limitado; **to be ~ed to** limitarse a; **~ed (liability) company** (BRIT) n sociedad f anónima

limousine ['lɪməziːn] n limusina

limp [lɪmp] n: **to have a ~** tener cojera ♦ vi cojear ♦ adj flojo; (material) fláccido

limpet ['lɪmpɪt] n lapa

line [laɪn] n línea; (rope) cuerda; (for fishing) sedal m; (wire) hilo; (row, series) fila, hilera; (of writing) renglón m, línea; (of song) verso; (on face) arruga; (RAIL) vía ♦ vt (road etc) llenar; (SEWING) forrar; **to ~ the streets** llenar las aceras; **in ~ with** alineado con; (according to) de acuerdo con; **~ up** vi hacer cola ♦ vt alinear; (prepare) preparar; organizar

lined [laɪnd] adj (face) arrugado; (paper) rayado

linen ['lɪnɪn] n ropa blanca; (cloth) lino

liner ['laɪnə*] n vapor m de línea, transatlántico; (for bin) bolsa (de basura)

linesman ['laɪnzmən] n (SPORT) juez m de línea

line-up n (US: queue) cola; (SPORT) alineación f

linger ['lɪŋgə*] vi retrasarse, tardar en marcharse; (smell, tradition) persistir

lingerie ['lænʒəriː] n lencería

linguist ['lɪŋgwɪst] n lingüista m/f; **~ics** n lingüística

lining ['laɪnɪŋ] n forro; (ANAT) (membrana) mucosa

link [lɪŋk] n (of a chain) eslabón m; (relationship) relación f, vínculo ♦ vt vincular, unir; (associate): **to ~ with** or **to** relacionar con; **~s** npl (GOLF) campo de golf; **~ up** vt acoplar ♦ vi unirse

lino ['laɪnəʊ] n = **linoleum**

linoleum [lɪ'nəʊlɪəm] n linóleo

lion ['laɪən] n león m; **~ess** n leona

lip [lɪp] n labio

liposuction ['lɪpəʊsʌkʃən] n liposucción f

lip: ~read vi leer los labios; **~ salve** n crema protectora para labios; **~ service** n: **to pay ~ service to sth** (pej) prometer algo de boquilla; **~stick** n lápiz m de labios, carmín m

liqueur [lɪ'kjʊə*] n licor m

liquid ['lɪkwɪd] adj, n líquido; **~ize** [-aɪz] vt (CULIN) licuar; **~izer** [-aɪzə*] n licuadora

liquor ['lɪkə*] n licor m, bebidas fpl alcohólicas

liquorice ['lɪkərɪs] (BRIT) n regaliz m

liquor store (US) n bodega, tienda de vinos y bebidas alcohólicas

Lisbon ['lɪzbən] n Lisboa

lisp [lɪsp] n ceceo ♦ vi cecear

list [lɪst] n lista ♦ vt (enumerate) enumerar; (put on a list) poner en una lista; **~ed building** (BRIT) n monumento declarado de interés histórico-artístico

listen ['lɪsn] vi escuchar, oír; **to ~ to sb/sth** escuchar a uno/algo; **~er** n oyente m/f; (RADIO) radioyente m/f

listless ['lɪstlɪs] adj apático, indiferente

lit [lɪt] pt, pp of **light**

liter ['liːtə*] (US) n = **litre**

literacy ['lɪtərəsɪ] n capacidad f de leer y escribir

literal ['lɪtərl] adj literal

literary ['lɪtərərɪ] adj literario

literate ['lɪtərət] adj que sabe leer y escribir; (educated) culto

literature ['lɪtərɪtʃə*] n literatura; (brochures etc) folletos mpl

lithe [laɪð] adj ágil

litigation [lɪtɪ'geɪʃən] n litigio

litre ['liːtə*] (US **liter**) n litro

litter ['lɪtə*] n (rubbish) basura; (young animals) camada, cría; **~ bin** (BRIT) n papelera; **~ed** adj: **~ed with**

(*scattered*) lleno de

little ['lɪtl] *adj* (*small*) pequeño; (*not much*) poco ♦ *adv* poco; **a ~** un poco (de); **~ house/bird** casita/pajarito; **a ~ bit** un poquito; **~ by ~** poco a poco; **~ finger** *n* dedo meñique

live¹ [laɪv] *adj* (*animal*) vivo; (*wire*) conectado; (*broadcast*) en directo; (*shell*) cargado

live² [lɪv] *vi* vivir; **~ down** *vt* hacer olvidar; **~ on** *vt fus* (*food, salary*) vivir de; **~ together** *vi* vivir juntos; **~ up to** *vt fus* (*fulfil*) cumplir con

livelihood ['laɪvlɪhud] *n* sustento

lively ['laɪvlɪ] *adj* vivo; (*interesting: place, book etc*) animado

liven up ['laɪvn-] *vt* animar ♦ *vi* animarse

liver ['lɪvə*] *n* hígado

lives [laɪvz] *npl of* **life**

livestock ['laɪvstɔk] *n* ganado

livid ['lɪvɪd] *adj* lívido; (*furious*) furioso

living ['lɪvɪŋ] *adj* (*alive*) vivo ♦ *n*: **to earn** *or* **make a ~** ganarse la vida; **~ conditions** *npl* condiciones *fpl* de vida; **~ room** *n* sala (de estar); **~ standards** *npl* nivel *m* de vida; **~ wage** *n* jornal *m* suficiente para vivir

lizard ['lɪzəd] *n* lagarto; (*small*) lagartija

load [ləud] *n* carga; (*weight*) peso ♦ *vt* (*COMPUT*) cargar; (*also: ~ up*): **to ~ (with)** cargar (con *or* de); **a ~ of rubbish** (*inf*) tonterías *fpl*; **a ~ of, ~s of** (*fig*) (gran) cantidad de, montones de; **~ed** *adj* (*vehicle*): **to be ~ed with** estar cargado de; (*question*) intencionado; (*inf: rich*) forrado (de dinero)

loaf [ləuf] (*pl* **loaves**) *n* (barra de) pan *m*

loan [ləun] *n* préstamo ♦ *vt* prestar; **on ~** prestado

loath [ləuθ] *adj*: **to be ~ to do sth** estar poco dispuesto a hacer algo

loathe [ləuð] *vt* aborrecer; (*person*) odiar; **loathing** *n* aversión *f*; odio

loaves [ləuvz] *npl of* **loaf**

lobby ['lɔbɪ] *n* vestíbulo, sala de

espera; (*POL: pressure group*) grupo de presión ♦ *vt* presionar

lobster ['lɔbstə*] *n* langosta

local ['ləukl] *adj* local ♦ *n* (*pub*) bar *m*; **the ~s** los vecinos, los del lugar; **~ anaesthetic** *n* (*MED*) anestesia local; **~ authority** *n* municipio, ayuntamiento (*SP*); **~ call** *n* (*TEL*) llamada local; **~ government** *n* gobierno municipal; **~ity** [-'kælɪtɪ] *n* localidad *f*; **~ly** [-kəlɪ] *adv* en la vecindad; por aquí

locate [ləu'keɪt] *vt* (*find*) localizar; (*situate*): **to be ~d in** estar situado en

location [ləu'keɪʃən] *n* situación *f*; **on ~** (*CINEMA*) en exteriores

loch [lɔx] *n* lago

lock [lɔk] *n* (*of door, box*) cerradura; (*of canal*) esclusa; (*of hair*) mechón *m* ♦ *vt* (*with key*) cerrar (con llave) ♦ *vi* (*door etc*) cerrarse (con llave); (*wheels*) trabarse; **~ in** *vt* encerrar; **~ out** *vt* (*person*) cerrar la puerta a; **~ up** *vt* (*criminal*) meter en la cárcel; (*mental patient*) encerrar; (*house*) cerrar (con llave) ♦ *vi* echar la llave

locker ['lɔkə*] *n* casillero

locket ['lɔkɪt] *n* medallón *m*

locksmith ['lɔksmɪθ] *n* cerrajero/a

lockup ['lɔkʌp] *n* (*jail, cell*) cárcel *f*

locum ['ləukəm] *n* (*MED*) interino/a

locust ['ləukəst] *n* langosta

lodge [lɔdʒ] *n* casita (del guarda) ♦ *vi* (*person*): **to ~ (with)** alojarse (en casa de); (*bullet, bone*) incrustarse ♦ *vt* presentar; **~r** *n* huésped(a) *m/f*

lodgings ['lɔdʒɪŋz] *npl* alojamiento

loft [lɔft] *n* desván *m*

lofty ['lɔftɪ] *adj* (*noble*) sublime; (*haughty*) altanero

log [lɔg] *n* (*of wood*) leño, tronco; (*written account*) diario ♦ *vt* anotar; **~ in** *or* **on** *vi* (*COMPUT*) entrar en el sistema; **~ off** *or* **out** *vi* (*COMPUT*) salir del sistema

logbook ['lɔgbuk] *n* (*NAUT*) diario de a bordo; (*AVIAT*) libro de vuelo; (*of car*) documentación f (del coche (SP) or carro (AM))

loggerheads ['lɔgəhɛdz] npl: **to be at ~ (with)** estar en desacuerdo (con)

logic ['lɔdʒɪk] n lógica; **~al** adj lógico

logo ['laugau] n logotipo

loin [lɔɪn] n (CULIN) lomo, solomillo

loiter ['lɔɪtə*] vi (linger) entretenerse

loll [lɔl] vi (also: ~ about) repantigarse

lollipop ['lɔlɪpɔp] n piruli m; **~ man/ lady** (BRIT irreg) persona encargada de ayudar a los niños a cruzar la calle

---

lollipop man/lollipop lady

En el Reino Unido, se llama **lollipop man** o **lollipop lady** a la persona que se ocupa de parar el tráfico en los alrededores de los colegios para que los niños crucen sin peligro. Suelen ser personas ya jubiladas, vestidas con una gabardina de color llamativo y llevan una señal de stop portátil, la cual recuerda por su forma a una piruleta, y de ahí su nombre.

London ['lʌndən] n Londres; **~er** n londinense m/f

lone [ləun] adj solitario

loneliness ['ləunlınıs] n soledad f, aislamiento

lonely ['ləunlı] adj (situation) solitario; (person) solo; (place) aislado

long [lɔŋ] adj largo ♦ adv mucho tiempo, largamente ♦ vi: **to ~ for sth** anhelar algo; **so** or **as ~ as** mientras, con tal que; **don't be ~!** ¡no tardes!, ¡vuelve pronto!; **how ~ is the street?** ¿cuánto tiene la calle de largo?; **how ~ is the lesson?** ¿cuánto dura la clase?; **6 metres ~** ¿que mide 6 metros, de 6 metros de largo; **6 months ~** que duran 6 meses, de 6 meses de duración; **all night ~** toda la noche; **he no ~er comes** ya no viene; **~ before** mucho antes; **before ~** (+ future) dentro de poco; (+ past)

poco tiempo después; **at ~ last** al fin, por fin; **~-distance** adj (race) de larga distancia; (call) interurbano; **~-ing** adj de pelo largo; **~-haired** adj de pelo largo; **~-hand** n escritura sin abreviaturas; **~-ing** n anhelo, ansia; (nostalgia) nostalgia ♦ adj anhelante

longitude ['lɔŋgıtjuːd] n longitud f

long: **~ jump** n salto de longitud; **~-life** adj (batteries) de larga duración; (milk) uperizado; **~-lost** adj desaparecido hace mucho tiempo; **~-range** adj (plan) de gran alcance; (missile) de largo alcance; **~-sighted** (BRIT) adj présbita; **~-standing** adj de mucho tiempo; **~-suffering** adj sufrido; **~-term** adj a largo plazo; **~ wave** n onda larga; **~-winded** adj prolijo

loo [luː] n (BRIT: inf) wáter m

look [luk] vi mirar; (seem) parecer; (building etc): **to ~ south/on to the sea** dar al sur/al mar ♦ n (gen): **to have a ~** mirar; (glance) mirada; (appearance) aire m, aspecto; **~s** npl (good ~s) belleza; **(here)!** (expressing annoyance etc) ¡oye!; **~!** (expressing surprise) ¡mira!; **~ after** vt fus (care for) cuidar a; (deal with) encargarse de; **~ at** vt fus mirar; (read quickly) echar un vistazo a; **~ back** vi mirar hacia atrás; **~ down on** vt fus (fig) despreciar, mirar con desprecio; **~ for** vt fus buscar; **~ forward to** vt fus esperar con ilusión; (in letters): **we ~ forward to hearing from you** quedamos a la espera de sus gratas noticias; **~ into** vt investigar; **~ on** vi mirar (como espectador); **~ out** vi (beware): **to ~ out (for)** tener cuidado (de); **~ out for** vt fus (seek) buscar; (await) esperar; **~ round** vi volver la cabeza; **~ through** vt fus (examine) examinar; **~ to** vt fus (rely on) contar con; **~ up** vi mirar hacia arriba; (improve) mejorar ♦ vt (word) buscar; **~ up to** vt fus admirar; **~-out** n (tower etc) puesto de observación; (person) vigía m/f; **to be on the ~-out for sth** estar al acecho de algo

loom [lu:m] vi: ~ **(up)** (threaten) surgir, amenazar; (event: approach) aproximarse

loony ['lu:nɪ] (inf) adj loco/a m/f

loop [lu:p] n lazo ♦ vt: **to ~ sth round sth** pasar algo alrededor de algo; **~hole** n escapatoria

loose [lu:s] adj suelto; (clothes) ancho; (morals, discipline) relajado; **to be on the ~** estar en libertad; **to be at a ~ end** or **at ~ ends** (US) no saber qué hacer; **~ change** n cambio; **~ chippings** npl (on road) gravilla suelta; **~ly** adv libremente, aproximadamente; **~n** vt aflojar

loot [lu:t] n botín m ♦ vt saquear

lop off [lɔp-] vt (branches) podar

lop-sided adj torcido

lord [lɔːd] n señor m; **L~ Smith** Lord Smith; **the L~** el Señor; **my ~** (to bishop) Ilustrísima; (to noble etc) Señor; **good L~!** ¡Dios mío!; **the (House of) L~s** (BRIT) la Cámara de los Lores; **~ship** n: **your L~ship** su Señoría

lore [lɔː*] n tradiciones fpl

lorry ['lɔrɪ] (BRIT) n camión m; **~ driver** n camionero/a m/f

lose [lu:z] (pt, pp lost) vt perder ♦ vi perder, ser vencido; **to ~ (time)** (clock) atrasarse; **~r** n perdedor(a) m/f

loss [lɔs] n pérdida; **heavy ~es** (MIL.) grandes pérdidas; **to be at a ~** no saber qué hacer; **to make a ~** sufrir pérdidas

lost [lɔst] pt, pp of **lose** ♦ adj perdido; **~ property** (US **~ and found**) n objetos mpl perdidos

lot [lɔt] n (group: of things) grupo m; (at auctions) lote m; **the ~** el todo, todos; **a ~** (large number: of books etc) muchos; (a great deal) mucho, bastante; **a ~ of**, **~s of** mucho(s) (pl); **I read a ~** leo bastante; **to draw ~s (for sth)** echar suertes (para decidir algo)

lotion ['ləuʃən] n loción f

lottery ['lɔtərɪ] n lotería

loud [laud] adj (voice, sound) fuerte; (laugh, shout) estrepitoso; (condemnation etc) enérgico; (gaudy) chillón/ona ♦ adv (speak etc) fuerte; **out** ~ en voz alta; **~hailer** (BRIT) n megáfono; **~ly** adv (noisily) fuerte; (aloud) en voz alta; **~speaker** n altavoz m

lounge [laundʒ] n salón m, sala (de estar); (at airport etc) sala; (BRIT: also: ~-bar) salón-bar m ♦ vi (also: ~ about or around) reposar, holgazanear

louse [laus] (pl lice) n piojo

lousy ['lauzɪ] (inf) adj (bad quality) malísimo, asqueroso; (ill) fatal

lout [laut] n gamberro/a

lovable ['lʌvəbl] adj amable, simpático

love [lʌv] n (romantic, sexual) amor m; (kind, caring) cariño ♦ vt amar, querer; (thing, activity) encantarle a uno; **"~ from Anne"** (on letter) "un abrazo (de) Anne"; **to ~** to do encantarle a uno hacer; **to be/fall in ~ with** estar enamorado/enamorarse de uno; **to make ~** hacer el amor; **for the ~ of** por amor de; **"15 ~"** (TENNIS) "15 a cero"; **I ~ paella** me encanta la paella; **~ affair** n aventura sentimental; **~ letter** n carta de amor; **~ life** n vida sentimental

lovely ['lʌvlɪ] adj (delightful) encantador(a); (beautiful) precioso

lover ['lʌvə*] n amante m/f; (person in love) enamorado; (amateur): **a ~ of** un(a) aficionado/a or un(a) amante de

loving ['lʌvɪŋ] adj amoroso, cariñoso; (action) tierno

low [ləu] adj, adv bajo ♦ n (METEOROLOGY) área de baja presión; **to be ~ on** (supplies etc) andar mal de; **to feel ~** sentirse deprimido; **to turn (down)** ~ bajar; **~-alcohol** adj de bajo contenido en alcohol; **~-calorie** adj bajo en calorías; **~-cut** adj (dress) escotado

lower ['ləuə*] adj más bajo; (less important) menos importante ♦ vt bajar; (reduce) reducir ♦ vr: to ~ o.s. to (fig) rebajarse a

low: ~-**fat** adj (milk, yoghurt) desnatado; (diet) bajo en calorías; ~**lands** npl (GEO) tierras fpl bajas; ~**ly** adj humilde, inferior; ~ **season** n la temporada baja

loyal ['lɔɪəl] adj leal; ~**ty** n lealtad f; ~**ty card** n tarjeta de cliente

lozenge ['lɔzɪndʒ] n (MED) pastilla

L.P. n abbr (= long-playing record) elepé m

L-plates ['el-] (BRIT) npl placas fpl de aprendiz de conductor

Ltd abbr (= limited company) S.A.

lubricate ['luːbrɪkeɪt] vt lubricar

luck [lʌk] n suerte f; **bad** ~ mala suerte; **good** ~! ¡que tengas suerte!, ¡suerte!; **bad** or **hard** or **tough** ~! ¡qué pena!; ~**ily** adv afortunadamente; ~**y** adj afortunado; (at cards etc) con suerte; (object) que trae suerte

ludicrous ['luːdɪkrəs] adj absurdo

lug [lʌg] vt (drag) arrastrar

luggage ['lʌgɪdʒ] n equipaje m; ~ **rack** n (on car) baca, portaequipajes m inv

lukewarm ['luːkwɔːm] adj tibio

lull [lʌl] n tregua ♦ vt: **to** ~ **sb to sleep** arrullar a uno; **to** ~ **sb into a false sense of security** dar a alguien una falsa sensación de seguridad

lullaby ['lʌləbaɪ] n nana

lumbago [lʌm'beɪgəu] n lumbago

lumber ['lʌmbə*] n (junk) trastos mpl viejos; (wood) maderos mpl; ~ **with** vt: **to be** ~**ed with** tener que cargar con algo; ~**jack** n maderero

luminous ['luːmɪnəs] adj luminoso

lump [lʌmp] n terrón m; (fragment) trozo; (swelling) bulto ♦ vt (also: ~ **together**) juntar; ~ **sum** n suma global; ~**y** adj (sauce) lleno de grumos; (mattress) lleno de bultos

lunatic ['luːnətɪk] adj loco

lunch [lʌntʃ] n almuerzo, comida ♦ vi almorzar

luncheon ['lʌntʃən] n almuerzo; ~ **voucher** (BRIT) n vale m de comida

lunch time n hora de comer

lung [lʌŋ] n pulmón m

lunge [lʌndʒ] vi (also: ~ **forward**) abalanzarse; **to** ~ **at** arremeter contra

lurch [lɜːtʃ] vi dar sacudidas ♦ n sacudida; **to leave sb in the** ~ dejar a uno plantado

lure [luə*] n (attraction) atracción f ♦ vt tentar

lurid ['luərɪd] adj (colour) chillón/ona; (account) espeluznante

lurk [lɜːk] vi (person, animal) estar al acecho; (fig) esconderse

luscious ['lʌʃəs] adj (attractive: person, thing) precioso; (food) delicioso

lush [lʌʃ] adj exuberante

lust [lʌst] n lujuria; (greed) codicia

lustre ['lʌstə*] (US **luster**) n lustre m, brillo

lusty ['lʌstɪ] adj robusto, fuerte

Luxembourg ['lʌksəmbɜːg] n Luxemburgo

luxuriant [lʌg'zjuərɪənt] adj exuberante

luxurious [lʌg'zjuərɪəs] adj lujoso

luxury ['lʌkʃəri] n lujo ♦ cpd de lujo
lying ['laɪɪŋ] n mentiras fpl ♦ adj mentiroso
lyrical ['lɪrɪkl] adj lírico
lyrics ['lɪrɪks] npl (of song) letra

M, m

m. abbr = **metre; mile; million**
M.A. abbr = **Master of Arts**
mac [mæk] n (BRIT) n impermeable m
macaroni [mækə'rəʊnɪ] n macarrones mpl
machine [mə'ʃiːn] n máquina ♦ vt (dress etc) coser a máquina; (TECH) hacer a máquina; **~ gun** n ametralladora; **~ language** n (COMPUT) lenguaje m máquina; **~ry** n maquinaria; (fig) mecanismo
macho ['mætʃəʊ] adj machista
mackerel ['mækrl] n inv caballa
mackintosh ['mækɪntɒʃ] (BRIT) n impermeable m
mad [mæd] adj loco; (idea) disparatado; (angry) furioso; (keen): **to be ~ about** sth volverse loco a uno algo
madam ['mædəm] n señora
madden ['mædn] vt volver loco
made [meɪd] pt, pp of **make**
Madeira [mə'dɪərə] n (GEO) Madera; (wine) vino de Madera
made-to-measure (BRIT) adj hecho a la medida
madly ['mædlɪ] adv locamente
madman ['mædmən] (irreg) n loco
madness ['mædnɪs] n locura
Madrid [mə'drɪd] n Madrid
magazine [mægə'ziːn] n revista; (RADIO, TV) programa m magazina
maggot ['mægət] n gusano
magic ['mædʒɪk] n magia ♦ adj mágico; **~ian** [mə'dʒɪʃən] n mago/a; (conjurer) prestidigitador(a) m/f
magistrate ['mædʒɪstreɪt] n juez m/f (municipal)

magnet ['mægnɪt] n imán m; **~ic** [-'netɪk] adj magnético; (personality) atrayente
magnificent [mæg'nɪfɪsənt] adj magnífico
magnify ['mægnɪfaɪ] vt (object) ampliar; (sound) aumentar; **~ing glass** n lupa
magpie ['mægpaɪ] n urraca
mahogany [mə'hɒgənɪ] n caoba
maid [meɪd] n criada; **old ~** (pej) solterona
maiden ['meɪdn] n doncella ♦ adj (aunt etc) solterona; (speech, voyage) inaugural; **~ name** n nombre m de soltera
mail [meɪl] n correo; (letters) cartas fpl ♦ vt echar al correo; **~box** (US) n buzón m; **~ing list** n lista de direcciones; **~-order** n pedido postal
maim [meɪm] vt mutilar, lisiar
main [meɪn] adj principal, mayor ♦ n (pipe) cañería maestra; (US) red f eléctrica; **the ~s** npl (BRIT: ELEC) la red eléctrica; **in the ~** en general; **~frame** n (COMPUT) ordenador m central; **~land** n tierra firme; **~ly** adv principalmente; **~ road** n carretera; **~stay** n (fig) pilar m; **~stream** n corriente f principal
maintain [meɪn'teɪn] vt mantener; **maintenance** ['meɪntənəns] n mantenimiento; (LAW) manutención f
maize [meɪz] (BRIT) n maíz m (SP), choclo (AM)
majestic [mə'dʒestɪk] adj majestuoso
majesty ['mædʒɪstɪ] n majestad f; (title): **Your M~** Su Majestad
major ['meɪdʒər] n (MIL) comandante m ♦ adj principal; (MUS) mayor
Majorca [mə'jɔːkə] n Mallorca
majority [mə'dʒɒrɪtɪ] n mayoría
make [meɪk] (pt, pp **made**) vt hacer; (manufacture) fabricar; (mistake) cometer; (speech) pronunciar; (cause to be): **to ~ sb sad** poner triste a alguien; (force): **to ~ sb do sth**

obligar a alguien a hacer algo; (earn)
ganar; (equal): **2 and 2 ~ 4** 2 y 2 son
4 ♦ n marca; **to ~ the bed** hacer la
cama; **to ~ a fool of sb** poner a
alguien en ridículo; **to ~ a profit/loss**
obtener ganancias/sufrir pérdidas; **to
~ it** (arrive) llegar; (achieve sth) tener
éxito; **what time do you ~ it?** ¿qué
hora tienes?; **to ~ do with**
contentarse con; **~ for** vt fus (place)
dirigirse a; **~ out** vt (decipher) descifrar;
(understand) entender; (see) distinguir;
(cheque) extender; **~ up** vt (invent)
inventar; (prepare) hacer; (constitute)
constituir ♦ vi reconciliarse; (with
cosmetics) maquillarse; **~ up for** vt fus
compensar; **~-believe** n ficción f,
invención f; **~r** n fabricante m/f; (of
film, programme) autor(a) m/f; **~shift**
adj improvisado; **~-up** n maquillaje m;
~-up remover n desmaquillador m

making ['meɪkɪŋ] n (fig): **in the ~** en
vías de formación; **to have the ~s of** (of
person) tener madera de

Malaysia [mə'leɪzɪə] n Malasia,
Malaysia

male [meɪl] n (BIOL) macho ♦ adj (sex,
attitude) masculino; (child etc) varón

malfunction [mæl'fʌŋkʃən] n mal
funcionamiento

malice ['mælɪs] n malicia; **malicious**
[mə'lɪʃəs] adj malicioso; rencoroso

malignant [mə'lɪɡnənt] adj (MED)
maligno

mall [mɔːl] n (also: shopping ~)
centro comercial

mallet ['mælɪt] n mazo

malnutrition [mælnjuː'trɪʃən] n
desnutrición f

malpractice [mæl'præktɪs] n
negligencia profesional

malt [mɔːlt] n (also: (whisky) whisky m
de malta

Malta ['mɔːltə] n Malta; **Maltese**
[-'tiːz] adj, n inv maltés/esa m/f

mammal ['mæml] n mamífero

mammoth ['mæməθ] n mamut m

♦ adj gigantesco

man [mæn] (pl **men**) n hombre m;
(~kind) el hombre ♦ vt (NAUT) tripular;
(MIL) guarnecer; (operate: machine)
manejar; **an old ~** un viejo; **~ and
wife** marido y mujer

manage ['mænɪdʒ] vi arreglárselas, ir
tirando ♦ vt (be in charge of) dirigir;
(control: person) manejar; (: ship)
gobernar; **~able** adj manejable;
~ment n dirección f; **~r** n director(a)
m/f; (of pop star) mánayer m/f; (SPORT)
entrenador(a) m/f; **~ress** n directora;
entrenadora; **~rial** [-ə'dʒɪərɪəl] adj
directivo; **managing director** n
director(a) m/f general

mandarin ['mændərɪn] n (also:
~ orange) mandarina; (person)
mandarín m

mandatory ['mændətərɪ] adj
obligatorio

mane [meɪn] n (of horse) crin f; (of
lion) melena

maneuver [mə'nuːvə*] (US) =
manoeuvre

manfully ['mænfəlɪ] adv valientemente

mangle ['mæŋɡl] vt mutilar, destrozar

man-: ~handle vt maltratar; **~hole** n
agujero de acceso; **~hood** n edad f
viril; (state) virilidad f; **~hour** n hora-
hombre f; **~hunt** n (POLICE) búsqueda
y captura

mania ['meɪnɪə] n manía; **~c**
['meɪnɪæk] n maníaco/a; (fig)
maniático

manic ['mænɪk] adj frenético; **~-
depressive** n maníaco/a depresivo/a

manicure ['mænɪkjʊə*] n manicura

manifest ['mænɪfest] vt manifestar,
mostrar ♦ adj manifiesto

manifesto [mænɪ'festəʊ] n manifiesto

manipulate [mə'nɪpjʊleɪt] vt
manipular

man-: ~kind [mæn'kaɪnd] n
humanidad f, género humano; **~ly** adj
varonil; **~-made** adj artificial

manner ['mænə*] n manera, modo;

(*behaviour*) conducta, manera de ser; (*type*): **all ~ of things** toda clase de cosas; **~s** *npl* (*behaviour*) modales *mpl*; **bad ~s** mala educación; **~ism** *n* peculiaridad f de lenguaje (*or de comportamiento*)

manoeuvre [məˈnuːvə*] (*US* **maneuver**) *vt, vi* maniobrar ♦ *n* maniobra

manor [ˈmænə*] *n* (*also*: ~ **house**) casa solariega

manpower [ˈmænpauə*] *n* mano f de obra

mansion [ˈmænʃən] *n* palacio, casa grande

manslaughter [ˈmænslɔːtə*] *n* homicidio no premeditado

mantelpiece [ˈmæntlpiːs] *n* repisa, chimenea

manual [ˈmænjuəl] *adj* manual ♦ *n* manual *m*

manufacture [mænjuˈfæktʃə*] *vt* fabricar ♦ *n* fabricación f; **~r** *n* fabricante *m/f*

manure [məˈnjuə*] *n* estiércol *m*

manuscript [ˈmænjuskrɪpt] *n* manuscrito

many [ˈmenɪ] *adj, pron* muchos/as; **a great ~** muchísimos, un buen número de; **~ a time** muchas veces

map [mæp] *n* mapa *m*; **to ~ out** *vt* proyectar

maple [ˈmeɪpl] *n* arce *m* (*SP*), maple *m* (*AM*)

mar [mɑː*] *vt* estropear

marathon [ˈmærəθən] *n* maratón *m*

marble [ˈmɑːbl] *n* mármol *m*; (*toy*) canica

March [mɑːtʃ] *n* marzo

march [mɑːtʃ] *vi* (*MIL*) marchar; (*demonstrators*) manifestarse ♦ *n* marcha; (*demonstration*) manifestación f

mare [meə*] *n* yegua

margarine [mɑːdʒəˈriːn] *n* margarina

margin [ˈmɑːdʒɪn] *n* margen *m*; (*COMM*: *profit ~*) margen m de

beneficios; **~al** *adj* marginal; **~ seat** *n* (*POL*) escaño electoral difícil de asegurar

marigold [ˈmærɪɡəʊld] *n* caléndula

marijuana [mærɪˈwɑːnə] *n* marijuana

marina [məˈriːnə] *n* puerto deportivo

marinate [ˈmærɪneɪt] *vt* marinar

marine [məˈriːn] *adj* marino ♦ *n* soldado de marina

marital [ˈmærɪtl] *adj* matrimonial; **~ status** estado civil

marjoram [ˈmɑːdʒərəm] *n* mejorana

mark [mɑːk] *n* marca, señal f; (*in snow, mud etc*) huella; (*stain*) mancha; (*BRIT: SCOL*) nota; (*currency*) marco ♦ *vt* marcar; manchar; (*damage: furniture*) rayar; (*indicate: place etc*) señalar; (*BRIT: SCOL*) calificar, corregir; **to ~ time** marcar el paso; (*fig*) marcar(se) un ritmo; **~ed** *adj* (*obvious*) marcado, acusado; **~er** *n* (*sign*) marcador *m*; (*bookmark*) señal f (de libro)

market [ˈmɑːkɪt] *n* mercado ♦ *vt* (*COMM*) comercializar; **~ garden** (*BRIT*) *n* huerto; **~ing** *n* márketing *m*; **~place** *n* mercado; **~ research** *n* análisis *m inv* de mercados

marksman [ˈmɑːksmən] *n* tirador m

marmalade [ˈmɑːməleɪd] *n* mermelada de naranja

maroon [məˈruːn] *vt*: **to be ~ed** quedar aislado; (*fig*) quedar abandonado

marquee [mɑːˈkiː] *n* entoldado

marriage [ˈmærɪdʒ] *n* (*relationship, institution*) matrimonio; (*wedding*) boda; (*act*) casamiento; **~ certificate** *n* partida de casamiento

married [ˈmærɪd] *adj* casado; (*life, love*) conyugal

marrow [ˈmærəʊ] *n* médula; (*vegetable*) calabacín *m*

marry [ˈmærɪ] *vt* casarse con; (*subj: father, priest etc*) casar ♦ *vi* (*also: get married*) casarse

Mars [mɑːz] *n* Marte *m*

marsh [mɑːʃ] *n* pantano; (*salt ~*)

marisma

marshal ['mɑːʃl] n (MIL) mariscal m;
(at sports meeting etc) oficial m; (US: of
police, fire department) jefe/a m/f ♦ vt
(thoughts etc) ordenar; (soldiers) formar

marshy ['mɑːʃɪ] adj pantanoso

martial law ['mɑːʃl-] n ley f marcial

martyr ['mɑːtə*] n mártir m/f; **~dom** n
martirio

marvel ['mɑːvl] n maravilla, prodigio
♦ vi: **to ~ (at)** maravillarse (de); **~lous**
(US **~ous**) adj maravilloso

Marxist ['mɑːksɪst] adj, n marxista m/f

marzipan ['mɑːzɪpæn] n mazapán m

mascara [mæs'kɑːrə] n rímel m

masculine ['mæskjulɪn] adj masculino

mash [mæʃ] vt machacar; **~ed
potatoes** npl puré m de patatas (SP)
or papas (AM)

mask [mɑːsk] n máscara ♦ vt (cover):
to ~ one's face ocultarse la cara;
(hide: feelings) esconder

mason ['meɪsn] n (also: stone~) albañil
m; (also: free~) masón m; **~ry** n (in
building) mampostería

masquerade [mæskə'reɪd] vi: **to ~ as**
disfrazarse de, hacerse pasar por

mass [mæs] n (people) muchedumbre
f; (of air, liquid etc) masa; (of detail, hair
etc) gran cantidad f; (REL) misa ♦ cpd
masivo ♦ vi reunirse; concentrarse; **the
~es** npl las masas; **~es of** (inf)
montones de

massacre ['mæsəkə*] n masacre f

massage ['mæsɑːʒ] n masaje m ♦ vt
dar masaje en

masseur [mæ'sɜː*] n masajista m

masseuse [mæ'sɜːz] n masajista f

massive ['mæsɪv] adj enorme;
(support, changes) masivo

mass media npl medios mpl de
comunicación

mass production n fabricación f en
serie

mast [mɑːst] n (NAUT) mástil m; (RADIO
etc) torre f

master ['mɑːstə*] n (of servant) amo;

(of situation) dueño, maestro; (in
primary school) maestro; (in secondary
school) profesor m; (title for boys):
M~ X Señorito X ♦ vt dominar; **M~ of
Arts/Science** n licenciatura superior
en Letras/Ciencias; **~ly** adj magistral;
~mind n inteligencia superior ♦ vt
dirigir, planear; **~piece** n obra
maestra; **~y** n maestría

mat [mæt] n estera; (also: door~)
felpudo; (also: table ~) salvamanteles m
inv, posavasos m inv ♦ adj = **matt**

match [mætʃ] n cerilla, fósforo; (game)
partido; (equal) igual m/f ♦ vt (go well
with) hacer juego con; (equal) igualar;
(correspond to) corresponder con;
(pair: also: ~ up) casar con ♦ vi hacer
juego; **to be a good ~** hacer juego;
~box n caja de cerillas; **~ing** adj que
hace juego

mate [meɪt] n (work~) colega m/f; (inf:
friend) amigo/a; (animal) macho m/
hembra f; (in merchant navy) segundo
a bordo ♦ vi acoplarse, aparearse
♦ vt aparear

material [mə'tɪərɪəl] n (substance)
materia; (information) material m;
(cloth) tela, tejido ♦ adj (important)
(important) esencial; **~s** npl materiales
mpl

maternal [mə'tɜːnl] adj maternal

maternity [mə'tɜːnɪtɪ] n maternidad f;
~ dress n vestido premamá

math [mæθ] (US) n = **mathematics**

mathematical [mæθə'mætɪkl] adj
matemático

mathematician [mæθəmə'tɪʃən] n
matemático/a

mathematics [mæθə'mætɪks] n
matemáticas fpl

maths [mæθs] (BRIT) n =
mathematics

matinée ['mætɪneɪ] n sesión f de tarde

matrices ['meɪtrɪsiːz] npl of **matrix**

matriculation [mətrɪkju'leɪʃən] n
(formalización f de) matrícula

matrimony ['mætrɪmənɪ] n

matrimonio

matrix ['meɪtrɪks] (pl **matrices**) n
matriz f

matron ['meɪtrən] n enfermera f jefe;
(in school) ama de llaves

mat(t) [mæt] adj mate

matted ['mætɪd] adj enmarañado

matter ['mætə*] n cuestión f, asunto;
(PHYSICS) sustancia, materia; (reading ~)
material m; (MED: pus) pus m ♦ vi
importar; ~s npl (affairs) asuntos mpl,
temas mpl; **it doesn't** ~ no importa;
what's the ~? ¿qué pasa?; **no**
~ **what** pase lo que pase; **as a** ~ **of**
course por rutina; **as a** ~ **of fact** de
hecho; ~**-of-fact** adj prosaico, práctico

mattress ['mætrɪs] n colchón m

mature [mə'tjuə*] adj maduro ♦ vi
madurar; **maturity** n madurez f

maul [mɔːl] vt magullar

mauve [məuv] adj de color malva (SP)
or guinda (AM)

maximum ['mæksɪməm] (pl **maxima**)
adj máximo ♦ n máximo

May [meɪ] n mayo

may [meɪ] (conditional: **might**) vi
(indicating possibility): **he** ~ **come**
puede que venga; (be allowed to): ~ **I**
smoke? ¿puedo fumar?; (wishes):
~ **God bless you!** ¡que Dios le
bendiga!; **you** ~ **as well go** bien
puedes irte

maybe ['meɪbiː] adv quizá(s)

May Day n el primero de Mayo

mayhem ['meɪhem] n caos m total

mayonnaise [meɪə'neɪz] n mayonesa f

mayor [mɛə*] n alcalde m; ~**ess** n
alcaldesa

maze [meɪz] n laberinto

M.D. abbr = **Doctor of Medicine**

me [miː] pron (direct) me; (stressed,
after pron) mí; can you hear ~? ¿me
oyes?; **he heard ME!** me oyó a mí; **it's**
~ soy yo; **give them to** ~ dámelos;
las; **with/without** ~ conmigo/sin mí

meadow ['mɛdəu] n prado, pradera

meagre ['miːgə*] (US **meager**) adj

escaso, pobre

meal [miːl] n comida; (flour) harina;
~**time** n hora de comer

mean [miːn] (pt, pp **meant**) adj (with
money) tacaño; (unkind) mezquino,
malo; (shabby) humilde; (average)
medio ♦ vt (signify) querer decir,
significar; (refer to) referirse a; (intend):
to ~ **to do sth** pensar o pretender
hacer algo ♦ n medio, término medio;
~**s** npl (way) medio, manera; (money)
recursos mpl, medios mpl; **by** ~**s of**
mediante, por medio de; **by all** ~**s!**
¡naturalmente!, ¡claro que sí!; **do you**
~ **it?** ¿lo dices en serio?; **what do**
you ~? ¿qué quiere decir?; **to be**
meant for sb/sth ser para uno/algo

meander [mi'ændə*] vi (river)
serpentear

meaning ['miːnɪŋ] n significado,
sentido; (purpose) sentido, propósito;
~**ful** adj significativo; ~**less** adj sin
sentido

meanness ['miːnnɪs] n (with money)
tacañería; (unkindness) maldad f,
mezquindad f; (shabbiness) humildad f

meant [ment] pt, pp of **mean**

meantime ['miːntaɪm] adv (also: **in**
the ~) mientras tanto

meanwhile ['miːnwaɪl] adv =
meantime

measles ['miːzlz] n sarampión m

measure ['meʒə*] vt, vi medir ♦ n
medida; (ruler) regla; ~**ments** npl
medidas fpl

meat [miːt] n carne f; **cold** ~ fiambre
m; ~**ball** n albóndiga; ~ **pie** n pastel
m de carne

Mecca ['mekə] n La Meca

mechanic [mɪ'kænɪk] n mecánico/a;
~**s** n mecánica ♦ npl mecanismo; ~**al**
adj mecánico

mechanism ['mekənɪzəm] n
mecanismo

medal ['medl] n medalla; ~**lion**
[mɪ'dælɪən] n medallón m; ~**list** (US
~**ist**) n (SPORT) medallista m/f

meddle

meddle ['medl] vi: to ~ in entrometerse en; to ~ with sth manosear algo

media ['mi:dɪə] npl medios mpl de comunicación ♦ npl of **medium**

mediaeval [medɪ'i:vl] adj = **medieval**

mediate ['mi:dɪeɪt] vi mediar; **mediator** n intermediario/a, mediador(a) m/f

Medicaid ® ['medɪkeɪd] (US) n programa de ayuda médica para los pobres

medical ['medɪkl] adj médico ♦ n reconocimiento médico

Medicare ® ['medɪkeə*] (US) n programa de ayuda médica para los ancianos

medication [medɪ'keɪʃən] n medicación f

medicine ['medsɪn] n medicina; (drug) medicamento

medieval [medɪ'i:vl] adj medieval

mediocre [mi:dɪ'əukə*] adj mediocre

meditate ['medɪteɪt] vi meditar

Mediterranean [medɪtə'reɪnɪən] adj mediterráneo; **the ~ (Sea)** el (Mar) Mediterráneo

medium ['mi:dɪəm] (pl media) adj mediano, regular ♦ n (means) medio; (pl mediums: person) médium m/f; ~ **wave** n onda media

meek [mi:k] adj manso, sumiso

meet [mi:t] (pt, pp met) vt encontrar; (accidentally) encontrarse con, tropezar con; (by arrangement) reunirse con; (for the first time) conocer; (go and fetch) ir a buscar; (opponent) enfrentarse con; (obligations) cumplir; (encounter: problem) hacer frente a; (need) satisfacer ♦ vi encontrarse; (in session) reunirse; (join: objects) unirse; (for the first time) conocerse; ~ **with** vt fus (difficulty) tropezar con; to ~ **with success** tener éxito; ~**ing** n encuentro; (arranged) cita, compromiso; (business ~ing) reunión f; (POL) mitin m

meningitis

megabyte ['megabaɪt] n (COMPUT) megabyte m, megaocteto

megaphone ['megafəun] n megáfono

melancholy ['melənkəlɪ] n melancolía ♦ adj melancólico

mellow ['meləu] adj (wine) añejo; (sound, colour) suave ♦ vi (person) ablandar

melody ['melədɪ] n melodía

melon ['melən] n melón m

melt [melt] vi (metal) fundirse; (snow) derretirse ♦ vt fundir; ~**down** n (in nuclear reactor) fusión f de un reactor (nuclear); ~**ing pot** n (fig) crisol m

member ['membə*] n (gen, ANAT) miembro; (of club) socio/a; **M~ of Parliament** (BRIT) diputado/a; **M~ of the European Parliament** (BRIT) eurodiputado/a; **M~ of the Scottish Parliament** (BRIT) diputado/a del Parlamento escocés; ~**ship** n (members) número de miembros; (state) filiación f; ~**ship card** n carnet m de socio

memento [mə'mentəu] n recuerdo

memo ['meməu] n apunte m, nota

memoirs ['memwa:z] npl memorias fpl

memorandum [memə'rændəm] (pl **memoranda**) n apunte m, nota; (official note) acta

memorial [mɪ'mɔ:rɪəl] n monumento conmemorativo ♦ adj conmemorativo

memorize ['meməraɪz] vt aprender de memoria

memory ['memərɪ] n (also: COMPUT) memoria; (instance) recuerdo; (of dead person): **in ~ of** a la memoria de

men [men] npl of **man**

menace ['menəs] n amenaza ♦ vt amenazar; **menacing** adj amenazador(a)

mend [mend] vt reparar, arreglar; (darn) zurcir ♦ vi reponerse ♦ n arreglo, reparación f; zurcido ♦ n: **to be on the ~** ir mejorando; to ~ **one's ways** enmendarse; ~**ing** n reparación f; (clothes) ropa por remendar

meningitis [menɪn'dʒaɪtɪs] n meningitis f

menopause ['menəupɔːz] n
menopausia

menstruation [menstru'eɪʃən] n
menstruación f

mental ['mentl] adj mental; **~ity**
[-'tælɪtɪ] n mentalidad f

mention ['menʃən] n mención f ♦ vt
mencionar; (speak of) hablar de; **don't
~ it!** ¡de nada!

menu ['menjuː] n (set ~) menú m;
(printed) carta; (COMPUT) menú m

MEP n abbr = **Member of the
European Parliament**

merchandise ['mɜːtʃəndaɪz] n
mercancías fpl

merchant ['mɜːtʃənt] n comerciante
m/f; **~ bank** (BRIT) n banco comercial;
~ navy (US **~ marine**) n marina
mercante

merciful ['mɜːsɪful] adj compasivo;
(fortunate) afortunado

merciless ['mɜːsɪlɪs] adj despiadado

mercury ['mɜːkjurɪ] n mercurio

mercy ['mɜːsɪ] n compasión f; (REL)
misericordia; **at the ~ of** a la merced
de

merely ['mɪəlɪ] adv simplemente, sólo

merge [mɜːdʒ] vt (join) unir ♦ vi
unirse; (COMM) fusionarse; (colours etc)
fundirse; **~r** n (COMM) fusión f

meringue [mə'ræŋ] n merengue m

merit ['merɪt] n mérito ♦ vt merecer

mermaid ['mɜːmeɪd] n sirena

merry ['merɪ] adj alegre;
M~ Christmas! ¡Felices Pascuas!; **~-
go-round** n tiovivo

mesh [meʃ] n malla

mesmerize ['mezməraɪz] vt hipnotizar

mess [mes] n (muddle: of situation)
confusión f; (: of room) revoltijo; (dirt)
porquería; (MIL) comedor m; **~ about
or around** (inf) vi perder el tiempo;
(pass the time) entretenerse; **~ about
or around with** (inf) vt fus divertirse
con; **~ up** vt (spoil) estropear; (dirty)
ensuciar

message ['mesɪdʒ] n recado, mensaje

m

messenger ['mesɪndʒə*] n
mensajero/a

Messrs abbr (on letters: = Messieurs)
Sres

messy ['mesɪ] adj (dirty) sucio; (untidy)
desordenado

met [met] pt, pp of **meet**

metal ['metl] n metal m; **~lic** [-'tælɪk]
adj metálico

metaphor ['metəfə*] n metáfora

meteor ['miːtɪə*] n meteoro; **~ite**
[-aɪt] n meteorito

meteorology [miːtɪə'rɔlədʒɪ] n
meteorología

meter ['miːtə*] n (instrument) contador
m; (US: unit) = **metre** ♦ vt (US: POST)
franquear

method ['meθəd] n método

meths [meθs] (BRIT) n, **methylated
spirit** ['meθɪleɪtɪd] (BRIT) n alcohol m
metilado or desnaturalizado

metre ['miːtə*] (US **meter**) n metro

metric ['metrɪk] adj métrico

metropolitan [metrə'pɔlɪtən] adj
metropolitano; **the M~ Police** (BRIT) n
la policía londinense

mettle ['metl] n: **to be on one's ~**
estar dispuesto a mostrar todo lo que
uno vale

mew [mjuː] vi (cat) maullar

mews [mjuːz] n: **~ flat** (BRIT) piso
acondicionado en antiguos establos o
cocheras

Mexican ['meksɪkən] adj, n mejicano/a
m/f, mexicano/a m/f

Mexico ['meksɪkəu] n Méjico (SP),
México (AM); **~ City** n Ciudad f de
Méjico or México

miaow [miː'au] vi maullar

mice [maɪs] npl of **mouse**

micro... ['maɪkrəu] prefix micro...;
~chip n microplaqueta; **~(computer)**
n microordenador m; **~phone** n
micrófono; **~processor** n
microprocesador m; **~scope** n
microscopio; **~wave** n (also: ~**wave**

oven) horno microondas

mid [mɪd] adj: in ~ May a mediados de mayo; in ~ afternoon a media tarde; in ~ air en el aire; ~day n mediodía m

middle ['mɪdl] n centro; (half-way point) medio; (waist) cintura ♦ adj de en medio; (course, way) intermedio; in the ~ of the night en plena noche; ~aged adj de mediana edad; the M~ Ages npl la Edad Media; ~class adj de clase media; the ~ class(es) n(pl) la clase media; M~ East n Oriente m Medio; ~man n intermediario m segundo nombre; ~of-the-road adj moderado; ~weight n (BOXING) peso medio

middling ['mɪdlɪŋ] adj mediano

midge [mɪdʒ] n mosquito

midget ['mɪdʒɪt] n enano/a

Midlands ['mɪdləndz] npl: the ~ la región central de Inglaterra

midnight ['mɪdnaɪt] n medianoche f

midst [mɪdst] n: in the ~ of (crowd) en medio de; (situation, action) en mitad de

midsummer [mɪd'sʌmə*] n: in ~ en pleno verano

midway [mɪd'weɪ] adj, adv: ~ (between) a medio camino (entre); ~ through a la mitad de

midweek [mɪd'wiːk] adv entre semana

midwife ['mɪdwaɪf] (pl **midwives**) n comadrona, partera

might [maɪt] vb see **may** ♦ n fuerza, poder m; ~y adj fuerte, poderoso

migraine ['miːɡreɪn] n jaqueca

migrant ['maɪɡrənt] n adj (bird) migratorio; (worker) emigrante

migrate [maɪ'ɡreɪt] vi emigrar

mike [maɪk] n abbr (= microphone) micro

mild [maɪld] adj (person) apacible; (climate) templado; (slight) ligero; (taste) suave; (illness) leve; ~ly adv ligeramente; suavemente; to put it

~ly para no decir más

mile [maɪl] n milla; ~age n número de millas, ≈ kilometraje m; ~ometer [maɪ'lɔmɪtə*] n ≈ cuentakilómetros m inv; ~stone n mojón m.

militant ['mɪlɪtnt] adj, n militante m/f

military ['mɪlɪtəri] adj militar

militia [mɪ'lɪʃə] n milicia

milk [mɪlk] n leche f ♦ vt (cow) ordeñar; (fig) chupar; ~ chocolate n chocolate m con leche; ~man (irreg) n lechero; ~ shake n batido, malteada (AM); ~y adj lechoso; M~y Way n Vía Láctea

mill [mɪl] n (windmill etc) molino; (coffee ~) molinillo; (factory) fábrica ♦ vt moler ♦ vi (also: ~ about) arremolinarse

millennium [mɪ'lenɪəm] (pl ~s or **millennia**) n milenio, milenario

miller ['mɪlə*] n molinero

milli... ['mɪlɪ] prefix: ~gram(me) n miligramo; ~metre (US ~meter) n milímetro

million ['mɪljən] n millón m; a ~ times un millón de veces; ~aire [-jə'neə*] n millonario/a

milometer [maɪ'lɔmɪtə*] (BRIT) n = **mileometer**

mime [maɪm] n mímica; (actor) mimo/a ♦ vt remedar ♦ vi actuar de mimo

mimic ['mɪmɪk] n imitador(a) m/f ♦ adj mímico ♦ vt remedar, imitar

min. abbr = **minimum**; **minute(s)**

mince [mɪns] vt picar ♦ n (BRIT: CULIN) carne f picada; ~meat n conserva de fruta picada; (US: meat) carne f picada; ~ pie n empanadilla rellena de fruta picada; ~r n picadora de carne

mind [maɪnd] n mente f; (intellect) intelecto; (contrasted with matter) espíritu m ♦ vt (attend to, look after) ocuparse de, cuidar; (be careful of) tener cuidado con; (object to): I don't ~ the noise no me molesta el ruido; it is on my ~ me preocupa; to bear

sth in ~ tomar or tener algo en
cuenta; **to make up one's ~**
decidirse; **I don't ~** me es igual;
~ you, ... te advierto que ...;
never ~! ¡es igual!, ¡no importa!; (don't worry)
¡no te preocupes!; **"~ the step"**
"cuidado con el escalón"; **~er** n
guardaespaldas m inv; (child ~er) ≈
niñera; **~ful** adj: **~ful of** consciente de;
~less adj (crime) sin motivo; (work) de
autómata

mine¹ [maɪn] pron el mío/la mía etc; **a
friend of ~** un(a) amigo/a mío/mía
♦ adj: **this book is ~** = este libro es mío
mine² [maɪn] n mina ♦ vt (coal)
extraer; (bomb: beach etc) minar;
~field n campo de minas; **miner** n
minero/a

mineral ['mɪnərəl] adj mineral ♦ n
mineral m; **~s** npl (BRIT: soft drinks)
refrescos mpl; **~ water** n agua mineral
mingle ['mɪŋɡl] vi: **to ~ with**
mezclarse con
miniature ['mɪnətʃə*] adj (en)
miniatura ♦ n miniatura
minibus ['mɪnɪbʌs] n microbús m
Minidisc ® ['mɪnɪdɪsk] n minidisco
minimal ['mɪnɪml] adj mínimo
minimize ['mɪnɪmaɪz] vt minimizar;
(play down) empequeñecer
minimum ['mɪnɪməm] (pl **minima**) n,
adj mínimo
mining ['maɪnɪŋ] n explotación f
minera
miniskirt ['mɪnɪskə:t] n minifalda
minister ['mɪnɪstə*] n (BRIT: POL)
ministro/a (SP), secretario/a (AM); (REL)
pastor m ♦ vi: **to ~ to** atender a
ministry ['mɪnɪstrɪ] n (BRIT: POL)
ministerio (SP), secretaría (AM); (REL)
sacerdocio
mink [mɪŋk] n visón m
minnow ['mɪnəu] n pececillo (de agua
dulce)
minor ['maɪnə*] adj (repairs, injuries)
leve; (poet, planet) menor; (MUS) menor
♦ n (LAW) menor m de edad

Minorca [mɪˈnɔːkə] n Menorca
minority [maɪˈnɔrɪtɪ] n minoría
mint [mɪnt] n (plant) menta, hierba-
buena; (sweet) caramelo de menta ♦ vt
(coins) acuñar; **the (Royal) M~, the
(US) M~** la Casa de la Moneda; **in
~ condition** en perfecto estado
minus ['maɪnəs] n (also: **~ sign**) signo
de menos ♦ prep menos; **12 ~ 6
equals 6** 12 menos 6 son 6; **~ 24°C**
menos 24 grados
minute¹ ['mɪnɪt] n minuto; (fig)
momento; **~s** npl (of meeting) actas fpl;
at the last ~ a última hora
minute² [maɪˈnjuːt] adj diminuto;
(search) minucioso
miracle ['mɪrəkl] n milagro
mirage ['mɪrɑːʒ] n espejismo
mirror ['mɪrə*] n espejo; (in car)
retrovisor m
mirth [mə:θ] n alegría
misadventure [mɪsədˈventʃə*] n
desgracia
misapprehension [mɪsæprɪˈhenʃən]
n equivocación f
misappropriate [mɪsəˈprəuprɪeɪt] vt
malversar
misbehave [mɪsbɪˈheɪv] vi portarse
mal
miscalculate [mɪsˈkælkjuleɪt] vt
calcular mal
miscarriage ['mɪskærɪdʒ] n (MED)
aborto; **~ of justice** error m judicial
miscellaneous [mɪsɪˈleɪnɪəs] adj
varios/as, diversos/as
mischief ['mɪstʃɪf] n travesuras fpl,
diabluras fpl; (maliciousness) malicia;
mischievous [-ʃɪvəs] adj travieso
misconception [mɪskənˈsepʃən] n
idea equivocada; equivocación f
misconduct [mɪsˈkɔndʌkt] n mala
conducta; **professional ~** falta
profesional
misdemeanour [mɪsdɪˈmiːnə*] (US
misdemeanor) n delito, ofensa
miser ['maɪzə*] n avaro/a
miserable ['mɪzərəbl] adj (unhappy)

triste, desgraciado; (*unpleasant, contemptible*) miserable

miserly ['maɪzəlɪ] *adj* avariento, tacaño

misery ['mɪzərɪ] *n* tristeza; (*wretchedness*) miseria, desdicha

misfire [mɪs'faɪə*] *vi* fallar

misfit ['mɪsfɪt] *n* inadaptado/a

misfortune [mɪs'fɔːtʃən] *n* desgracia

misgiving [mɪs'gɪvɪŋ] *n* (*apprehension*) presentimiento; **to have ~s about sth** tener dudas acerca de algo

misguided [mɪs'gaɪdɪd] *adj* equivocado

mishandle [mɪs'hændl] *vt* (*mismanage*) manejar mal

mishap ['mɪshæp] *n* desgracia, contratiempo

misinform [mɪsɪn'fɔːm] *vt* informar mal

misinterpret [mɪsɪn'tɜːprɪt] *vt* interpretar mal

misjudge [mɪs'dʒʌdʒ] *vt* juzgar mal

mislay [mɪs'leɪ] (*irreg*) *vt* extraviar, perder

mislead [mɪs'liːd] (*irreg*) *vt* llevar a conclusiones erróneas; **~ing** *adj* engañoso

mismanage [mɪs'mænɪdʒ] *vt* administrar mal

misplace [mɪs'pleɪs] *vt* extraviar

misprint ['mɪsprɪnt] *n* errata, error *m* de imprenta

Miss [mɪs] *n* Señorita

miss [mɪs] *vt* (*train etc*) perder; (*fail to hit: target*) errar; (*regret the absence of*): **I ~ him** (yo) le echo de menos *or* a faltar; (*fail to see*): **you can't ~ it** no tiene pérdida ♦ *vi* fallar ♦ *n* (*shot*) tiro fallido *or* perdido; **~ out** (*BRIT*) *vt* omitir

misshapen [mɪs'ʃeɪpən] *adj* deforme

missile ['mɪsaɪl] *n* (*AVIAT*) mísil *m*; (*object thrown*) proyectil *m*

missing ['mɪsɪŋ] *adj* (*pupil*) ausente; (*thing*) perdido; (*MIL*): **~ in action** desaparecido en combate

mission ['mɪʃən] *n* misión *f*; (*official representation*) delegación *f*; **~ary** *n* misionero/a

mist [mɪst] *n* (*light*) neblina; (*heavy*) niebla; (*at sea*) bruma ♦ *vi* (*eyes: also: ~ over, ~ up*) llenarse de lágrimas; (*BRIT: windows: also: ~ over, ~ up*) empañarse

mistake [mɪs'teɪk] (*vt: irreg*) *n* error *m* ♦ *vt* entender mal; **by ~** por equivocación; **to make a ~** equivocarse; **to ~ A for B** confundir A con B; **mistaken** *pp* of **mistake** ♦ *adj* equivocado; **to be mistaken** equivocarse, engañarse

mister ['mɪstə*] (*inf*) *n* señor *m*; *see* **Mr**

mistletoe ['mɪsltəʊ] *n* muérdago

mistook [mɪs'tʊk] *pt* of **mistake**

mistress ['mɪstrɪs] *n* (*lover*) amante *f*; (*of house*) señora (de la casa); (*BRIT: in primary school*) maestra; (*in secondary school*) profesora; (*of situation*) dueña

mistrust [mɪs'trʌst] *vt* desconfiar de

misty ['mɪstɪ] *adj* (*day*) de niebla; (*glasses etc*) empañado

misunderstand [mɪsʌndə'stænd] (*irreg*) *vt, vi* entender mal; **~ing** *n* malentendido

misuse [*n* mɪs'juːs, *vb* mɪs'juːz] *n* mal uso; (*of power*) abuso; (*of funds*) malversación *f* ♦ *vt* abusar de; malversar

mitt(en) ['mɪt(n)] *n* manopla

mix [mɪks] *vt* mezclar; (*combine*) unir ♦ *vi* mezclarse; (*people*) llevarse bien ♦ *n* mezcla; **~ up** *vt* mezclar; (*confuse*) confundir; **~ed** *adj* mixto; (*feelings etc*) encontrado; **~ed-up** *adj* (*confused*) confuso, revuelto; **~er** *n* (*for food*) licuadora; (*for drinks*) coctelera; (*person*): **he's a good ~er** tiene don de gentes; **~ture** *n* mezcla; (*also: cough ~ture*) jarabe *m*; **~-up** *n* confusión *f*

mm *abbr* (= *millimetre*) mm

moan [məʊn] *n* gemido ♦ *vi* gemir; (*inf: complain*): **to ~ (about)** quejarse (de)

moat |məut| n foso

mob |mɔb| n multitud f ♦ vt acosar

mobile |'məubaıl| adj móvil ♦ n móvil m; ~ **home** n caravana; ~ **phone** n teléfono portátil

mock |mɔk| vt (ridicule) ridiculizar; (laugh at) burlarse de ♦ adj fingido; ~ **exam** examen preparatorio antes de los exámenes oficiales; ~**ery** n burla; ~-**up** n maqueta

mod |mɔd| adj see **convenience**

mode |məud| n modo

model |'mɔdl| n modelo; (fashion ~, artist's ~) modelo m/f ♦ adj modelo ♦ vt (with clay etc) modelar (copy): to ~ **o.s. on** tomar como modelo a ♦ vi ser modelo; to ~ **clothes** pasar modelos, ser modelo; ~ **railway** n ferrocarril m de juguete

modem |'məudəm| n modem m

moderate |adj 'mɔdərət, vb 'mɔdəreıt| adj moderado/a ♦ vi moderarse, calmarse ♦ vt moderar

modern |'mɔdən| adj moderno; ~**ize** vt modernizar

modest |'mɔdıst| adj modesto; (small) módico; ~**y** n modestia

modify |'mɔdıfaı| vt modificar

mogul |'məugəl| n (fig) magnate m

mohair |'məuheə*| n mohair m

moist |mɔıst| adj húmedo; ~**en** |'mɔısn| vt humedecer; ~**ure** |'mɔıstʃə*| n humedad f; ~**urizer** |'mɔıstʃəraızə*| n crema hidratante

molar |'məulə*| n muela

mold |məuld| (US) n, vt = **mould**

mole |məul| n (animal, spy) topo; (spot) lunar m

molest |mə'lest| vt importunar; (assault sexually) abusar sexualmente de

mollycoddle |'mɔlıkɔdl| vt mimar

molt |məult| (US) vi = **moult**

molten |'məultən| adj fundido; (lava) líquido

mom |mɔm| (US) n = **mum**

moment |'məumənt| n momento; at

the ~ de momento, por ahora; ~**ary** adj momentáneo; ~**ous** |-'mentəs| adj trascendental, importante

momentum |məu'mentəm| n momento; (fig) ímpetu m; to **gather** ~ cobrar velocidad; (fig) ganar fuerza

mommy |'mɔmı| (US) n = **mummy**

Monaco |'mɔnəkəu| n Mónaco

monarch |'mɔnək| n monarca m/f; ~**y** n monarquía

monastery |'mɔnəstərı| n monasterio

Monday |'mʌndı| n lunes m inv

monetary |'mʌnıtərı| adj monetario

money |'mʌnı| n dinero; (currency) moneda; to **make** ~ ganar dinero; ~ **order** n giro; ~-**spinner** (inf) n: to **be a** ~-**spinner** dar mucho dinero

mongrel |'mʌŋgrəl| n (dog) perro mestizo

monitor |'mɔnıtə*| n (SCOL) monitor m; (also: television ~) receptor m de control; (of computer) monitor m ♦ vt controlar

monk |mʌŋk| n monje m

monkey |'mʌŋkı| n mono; ~ **nut** (BRIT) n cacahuete m (SP), maní m (AM); ~ **wrench** n llave f inglesa

monopoly |mə'nɔpəlı| n monopolio

monotone |'mɔnətəun| n voz f (or tono) monocorde

monotonous |mə'nɔtənəs| adj monótono

monsoon |mɔn'su:n| n monzón m

monster |'mɔnstə*| n monstruo

monstrous |'mɔnstrəs| adj (huge) enorme; (atrocious, ugly) monstruoso

month |mʌnθ| n mes m; ~**ly** adj mensual ♦ adv mensualmente

monument |'mɔnjumənt| n monumento

moo |mu:| vi mugir

mood |mu:d| n humor m; (of crowd, group) clima m; to **be in a good/bad** ~ estar de buen/mal humor; ~**y** adj (changeable) de humor variable; (sullen) malhumorado

moon |mu:n| n luna; ~**light** n luz f de

la luna; **~lighting** n pluriempleo; **~lit**
adj: a **~lit night** una noche de luna
Moor [muə*] n moro/a
moor [muə*] n páramo ♦ vt (ship)
amarrar ♦ vi echar las amarras
Moorish [ˈmuərɪʃ] adj moro;
(architecture) árabe, morisco
moorland [ˈmuələnd] n páramo,
brezal m
moose [muːs] n inv alce m
mop [mɒp] n fregona; (of hair) greña,
melena ♦ vt fregar; **~ up** vt limpiar
mope [məup] vi estar o andar
deprimido
moped [ˈməupɛd] n ciclomotor m
moral [ˈmɒrl] adj moral ♦ n moraleja;
~s npl moralidad f, moral f
morale [mɒˈrɑːl] n moral f
morality [məˈrælɪtɪ] n moralidad f

more [mɔː*] adj 1 (greater in number
etc) más; **~ people/work than
before** más gente/trabajo que antes
2 (additional) más; **do you want
(some) ~ tea?** ¿quieres más té?; **is
there any ~ wine?** ¿queda vino?; **it'll
take a few ~ weeks** tardará unas
semanas más; **it's 2 kms ~ to the
house** faltan 2 kms para la casa;
~ time/letters than we expected
más tiempo del que/más cartas de las
que esperábamos
♦ pron (greater amount, additional
amount) más; **~ than 10** más de 10; **it
cost ~ than the other one/than we
expected** costó más que el otro/más
de lo que esperábamos; **is there any
~?** ¿hay más?; **many/much ~**
muchos(as)/mucho(a) más
♦ adv más; **~ dangerous/easily
(than)** más peligroso/fácilmente (que);
~ and ~ expensive cada vez más
caro; **~ or less** más o menos; **~ than
ever** más que nunca

moreover [mɔːˈrəuvə*] adv además,
por otra parte
morning [ˈmɔːnɪŋ] n mañana; (early ~)
madrugada ♦ cpd matutino, de la
mañana; **in the ~** por la mañana; **7
o'clock in the ~** las 7 de la mañana;
~ sickness n náuseas fpl matutinas
Morocco [məˈrɒkəu] n Marruecos m
moron [ˈmɔːrɒn] (inf) n imbécil
m/f
morphine [ˈmɔːfiːn] n morfina
Morse [mɔːs] n (also: **~ code**) (código)
Morse
morsel [ˈmɔːsl] n (of food) bocado
mortar [ˈmɔːtə*] n argamasa
mortgage [ˈmɔːɡɪdʒ] n hipoteca ♦ vt
hipotecar; **~ company** (US) n ≈ banco
hipotecario
mortuary [ˈmɔːtjuərɪ] n depósito de
cadáveres
Moscow [ˈmɒskəu] n Moscú
Moslem [ˈmɒzləm] adj, n = **Muslim**
mosque [mɒsk] n mezquita
mosquito [mɒsˈkiːtəu] (pl **~es**) n
mosquito (SP), zancudo (AM)
moss [mɒs] n musgo
most [məust] adj la mayor parte de, la
mayoría de ♦ pron la mayor parte, la
mayoría ♦ adv el más; (very) muy; **the
~** (also: + adj) el más; la mayor
parte de ellos; **I saw the ~** yo
vi el que más; **at the (very) ~** a lo
sumo, todo lo más; **to make the ~ of**
aprovechar (al máximo); **a
~ interesting book** un libro
interesantísimo; **~ly** adv en su mayor
parte, principalmente
MOT (BRIT) n abbr (= Ministry of
Transport): **the ~ (test)** inspección
(anual) obligatoria de coches y camiones
motel [məuˈtel] n motel m
moth [mɒθ] n mariposa nocturna;
(clothes) polilla
mother [ˈmʌðə*] n madre f ♦ adj
materno ♦ vt (care for) cuidar (como
una madre); **~hood** n maternidad f;
~-in-law n suegra; **~ly** adj maternal;

~-of-pearl n nácar m; **~-to-be** n futura madre f; **~ tongue** n lengua materna

motion ['məʊʃən] n movimiento; (gesture) ademán m, señal f; (at meeting) moción f ♦ vt, vi: **to ~ (to) sb to do sth** hacer señas a uno para que haga algo; **~less** adj inmóvil; **~ picture** n película

motivated ['məʊtɪveɪtɪd] adj motivado

motive ['məʊtɪv] n motivo

motley ['mɒtlɪ] adj variado

motor ['məʊtə*] n motor m; (BRIT: inf: vehicle) coche m (SP), carro (AM), automóvil m ♦ adj motor (f: motora or motriz); **~bike** n moto f; **~boat** n lancha motora; **~car** (BRIT) n coche m, carro, automóvil m; **~cycle** n motocicleta; **~cycle racing** n motociclismo; **~cyclist** n motociclista m/f; **~ing** (BRIT) n automovilismo; **~ist** n conductor(a) m/f, automovilista m/f; **~ racing** (BRIT) n carreras fpl de coches, automovilismo; **~ vehicle** n automóvil m; **~way** (BRIT) n autopista

mottled ['mɒtld] adj abigarrado

motto ['mɒtəʊ] (pl **~es**) n lema m, (watchword) consigna

mould [məʊld] (US **mold**) n molde m; (mildew) moho ♦ vt moldear; (fig) formar; **~y** adj enmohecido

moult [məʊlt] (US **molt**) vi mudar la piel (or las plumas)

mound [maʊnd] n montón m, montículo

mount [maʊnt] n monte m ♦ vt montar, subir a; (jewel) engarzar; (picture) enmarcar; (exhibition etc) organizar ♦ vi (increase) aumentar; **~ up** vi aumentar

mountain ['maʊntɪn] n montaña ♦ cpd de montaña; **~ bike** n bicicleta de montaña; **~eer** [-'nɪə*] n montañero/a (SP), andinista m/f (AM), **~eering** [-'nɪərɪŋ] n montañismo, andinismo; **~ous** adj montañoso

~ rescue team n equipo de rescate de montaña; **~side** n ladera de la montaña

mourn [mɔːn] vt llorar, lamentar ♦ vi: **to ~ for** llorar la muerte de; **~er** n doliente m/f; doloroso; **~ing** n luto; **in ~ing** de luto

mouse [maʊs] (pl **mice**) n (ZOOL, COMPUT) ratón m; **~ mat** n (COMPUT) alfombrilla; **~trap** n ratonera

mousse [muːs] n (CULIN) crema batida; (for hair) espuma (moldeadora)

moustache [məs'tɑːʃ] (US **mustache**) n bigote m

mousy ['maʊsɪ] adj (hair) pardusco

mouth [maʊθ, pl maʊðz] n boca; (of river) desembocadura; **~ful** n bocado; **~ organ** n armónica; **~piece** n (of musical instrument) boquilla; (spokesman) portavoz m/f; **~wash** n enjuague m; **~watering** adj apetitoso

movable ['muːvəbl] adj movible

move [muːv] n (movement) movimiento; (in game) jugada, (: turn to play) turno; (change: of house) mudanza; (: of job) cambio de trabajo ♦ vt mover, (emotionally) conmover; (POL: resolution etc) proponer ♦ vi moverse; (traffic) circular; (also: ~ house) trasladarse, mudarse; **to ~ sb to do sth** mover a uno a hacer algo; **to get a ~ on** darse prisa; **~ about or around** vi (travel) viajar; **~ along** vi avanzar, adelantarse; **~ away** vi alejarse; **~ back** vi retroceder; **~ forward** vi avanzar; **~ in** vi (to a house) instalarse; (police, soldiers) intervenir; **~ on** vi ponerse en camino; **~ out** vi (of house) mudarse; **~ over** vi apartarse, hacer sitio; **~ up** vi (employee) ser ascendido

moveable ['muːvəbl] adj = **movable**

movement ['muːvmənt] n movimiento

movie ['muːvɪ] n película; **to go to the ~s** ir al cine

moving ['muːvɪŋ] adj (emotional)

conmovedor(a); *(that moves)* móvil

mow [məu] *(pt mowed, pp mowed or mown)* vt *(grass, corn)* cortar, segar; ~ **down** vt *(shoot)* acribillar; ~**er** n *(also: lawn~er)* cortacéspedes m inv

MP n abbr = **Member of Parliament**

m.p.h. abbr = *miles per hour* (60 m.p.h. = 96 k.p.h.)

Mr ['mɪstə*] *(US **Mr.**)* n: ~ **Smith** (el) Sr. Smith

Mrs ['mɪsɪz] *(US **Mrs.**)* n: ~ **Smith** (la) Sra. Smith

Ms [mɪz] *(US **Ms.**)* n (= *Miss or Mrs*): ~ **Smith** (la) Sr(t)a. Smith

M.Sc. abbr = **Master of Science**

MSP n abbr = **Member of the Scottish Parliament**

much [mʌtʃ] adj mucho ♦ adv mucho; *(before pp)* muy ♦ n or pron mucho; **how** ~ **is it?** ¿cuánto es?, ¿cuánto cuesta?; **too** ~ demasiado; **it's not** ~ no es mucho; **as** ~ **as** tanto como; **however** ~ **he tries** por mucho que se esfuerce

muck [mʌk] n suciedad f; ~ **about** or **around** *(inf)* vi perder el tiempo; *(enjoy o.s.)* entretenerse; ~ **up** *(inf)* vt arruinar, estropear

mud [mʌd] n barro, lodo

muddle ['mʌdl] n desorden m, confusión f; *(mix-up)* embrollo, lío ♦ vt *(also: ~ up)* embrollar, confundir; ~ **through** vi salir del paso

muddy ['mʌdɪ] adj fangoso, cubierto de lodo

mudguard ['mʌdgɑːd] n guardabarros m inv

muffin ['mʌfɪn] n panecillo dulce

muffle ['mʌfl] vt *(sound)* amortiguar; *(against cold)* embozar; ~**d** adj *(noise etc)* amortiguado, apagado; ~**r** *(US)* n *(AUT)* silenciador m

mug [mʌg] n taza grande *(sin platillo)*; *(for beer)* jarra; *(inf: face)* jeta ♦ vt *(assault)* asaltar; ~**ging** n asalto

muggy ['mʌgɪ] adj bochornoso

mule [mjuːl] n mula

multi... [mʌltɪ] prefix multi...

multi-level ['mʌltɪ'levl] *(US)* adj = **multistorey**

multiple ['mʌltɪpl] adj múltiple ♦ n múltiplo; ~ **sclerosis** n esclerosis f múltiple

multiplex cinema ['mʌltɪpleks-] n multicines mp

multiplication [mʌltɪplɪ'keɪʃən] n multiplicación f

multiply ['mʌltɪplaɪ] vt multiplicar ♦ vi multiplicarse

multistorey [mʌltɪ'stɔːrɪ] *(BRIT)* adj de muchos pisos

multitude ['mʌltɪtjuːd] n multitud f

mum [mʌm] *(BRIT: inf)* n mamá ♦ adj: **to keep** ~ mantener la boca cerrada

mumble ['mʌmbl] vt, vi hablar entre dientes, refunfuñar

mummy ['mʌmɪ] n *(BRIT: mother)* mamá; *(embalmed)* momia

mumps [mʌmps] n paperas fpl

munch [mʌntʃ] vt, vi mascar

mundane [mʌn'deɪn] adj trivial

municipal [mjuːˈnɪsɪpl] adj municipal

murder ['mɜːdə*] n asesinato; *(in law)* homicidio ♦ vt asesinar, matar; ~**er/ ess** n asesino/a; ~**ous** adj homicida

murky ['mɜːkɪ] adj *(water)* turbio; *(street, night)* lóbrego

murmur ['mɜːmə*] n murmullo ♦ vt, vi murmurar

muscle ['mʌsl] n músculo; *(fig: strength)* garra, fuerza; ~ **in** vi entrometerse; **muscular** ['mʌskjulə*] adj muscular; *(person)* musculoso

muse [mjuːz] vi meditar ♦ n musa

museum [mjuːˈzɪəm] n museo

mushroom ['mʌʃrum] n seta, hongo; *(CULIN)* champiñón m ♦ vi crecer de la noche a la mañana

music ['mjuːzɪk] n música; ~**al** adj musical; *(sound)* melodioso; *(person)* con talento musical ♦ n *(show)* comedia musical; ~**al instrument** n instrumento musical; ~ **hall** n teatro de variedades; ~**ian** [-'zɪʃən] músico/a

Muslim ['mʌzlɪm] adj, n musulmán/ana m/f

muslin ['mʌzlɪn] n muselina

mussel ['mʌsl] n mejillón m

must [mʌst] aux vb (obligation): **I ~ do it** debo hacerlo, tengo que hacerlo; (probability): **he ~ be there by now** ya debe (de) estar allí ♦ n: **it's a ~** es imprescindible

mustache ['mʌstæʃ] (US) n = **moustache**

mustard ['mʌstəd] n mostaza

muster ['mʌstə*] vt juntar, reunir

mustn't ['mʌsnt] = **must not**

mute [mjuːt] adj, n mudo/a m/f

muted ['mjuːtɪd] adj (person) callado; (colour) apagado

mutiny ['mjuːtɪnɪ] n motín m ♦ vi amotinarse

mutter ['mʌtə*] vt, vi murmurar

mutton ['mʌtn] n carne f de cordero

mutual ['mjuːtʃuəl] adj mutuo; (interest) común; **~ly** adv mutuamente

muzzle ['mʌzl] n hocico; (for dog) bozal m; (of gun) boca ♦ vt (dog) poner un bozal a

my [maɪ] adj mi(s); **~ house/brother/sisters** mi casa/mi hermano/mis hermanas; **I've washed ~ hair/cut ♦ finger** me he lavado el pelo/cortado un dedo; **is this ~ pen or yours?** ¿es este bolígrafo mío o tuyo?

myself [maɪˈself] pron (reflexive) me; (emphatic) yo mismo; (after prep) mí (mismo); see also **oneself**

mysterious [mɪsˈtɪərɪəs] adj misterioso

mystery ['mɪstərɪ] n misterio

mystify ['mɪstɪfaɪ] vt (perplex) dejar perplejo

myth [mɪθ] n mito

N, n

n/a abbr (= not applicable) no interesa

nag [næg] vt (scold) regañar; **~ging** adj (doubt) persistente; (pain) continuo

nail [neɪl] n (human) uña; (metal) clavo ♦ vt clavar; **to ~ sth to sth** clavar algo en algo; **to ~ sb down to doing sth** comprometer a uno a que haga algo; **~brush** n cepillo para las uñas; **~file** n lima para las uñas; **~ polish** n esmalte m or laca para las uñas; **~ polish remover** n quitaesmalte m; **~ scissors** npl tijeras fpl para las uñas; **~ varnish** (BRIT) n = **~ polish**

naïve [naɪˈiːv] adj ingenuo

naked ['neɪkɪd] adj (nude) desnudo; (flame) expuesto al aire

name [neɪm] n nombre m; (surname) apellido; (reputation) fama, renombre m ♦ vt (child) poner nombre a; (criminal) identificar; (price, date etc) fijar; **what's your ~?** ¿cómo se llama?; **by ~** de nombre; **in the ~ of** en nombre de; **to give one's ~ and address** dar sus señas; **~ly** adv a saber; **~sake** n tocayo/a

nanny ['nænɪ] n niñera

nap [næp] n (sleep) sueñecito, siesta

nape [neɪp] n: **~ of the neck** nuca, cogote m

napkin ['næpkɪn] n (also: table ~) servilleta

nappy ['næpɪ] (BRIT) n pañal m; **~ rash** n prurito

narcotic [nɑːˈkɔtɪk] adj, n narcótico

narrow ['nærəu] adj estrecho, angosto; (fig: majority etc) corto; (: ideas etc) estrecho ♦ vi (road) estrecharse; (diminish) reducirse; **to have a ~ escape** escaparse por los pelos; **to ~ sth down** reducir algo; **~ly** adv (miss) por poco; **~-minded** adj de miras estrechas

nasty ['nɑːstɪ] adj (remark) feo;

(person) antipático; *(revolting: taste,
smell)* asqueroso; *(wound, disease etc)*
peligroso, grave
nation ['neɪʃən] n nación f
national ['næʃənl] adj, n nacional m/f;
~ **dress** n vestido nacional;
N~ Health Service *(BRIT)* n servicio
nacional de salud pública; ≈ Insalud m
(SP); **N~ Insurance** *(BRIT)* n seguro
social nacional; ~**ism** n nacionalismo;
~**ist** adj, n nacionalista m/f; ~**ity**
[-'nælɪtɪ] n nacionalidad f; ~**ize** vt
nacionalizar; ~**ly** adv *(nationwide)* en
escala nacional; *(as a nation)*
nacionalmente, como nación; ~ **park**
(BRIT) n parque m nacional
nationwide ['neɪʃənwaɪd] adj en
escala or a nivel nacional
native ['neɪtɪv] n *(local inhabitant)*
natural m/f, *(country)* natal;
(innate) natural, innato; a ~ **of Russia**
un(a) natural m/f de Rusia; a
~ **speaker of French** un hablante
nativo de francés; **N~ American** adj,
n americano/a indígena, amerindio/a;
~ **language** n lengua materna
Nativity [nə'tɪvɪtɪ] n: **the** ~ la Navidad f
NATO ['neɪtəʊ] n abbr (= North
Atlantic Treaty Organization) OTAN f
natural ['nætʃrəl] adj natural; ~**ly** adv
(speak etc) naturalmente; *(of course)*
desde luego, por supuesto
nature ['neɪtʃə*] n *(also: N~)*
naturaleza f; *(group, sort)* género, clase f;
(character) carácter m, genio; **by** ~ por
or de naturaleza
naught [nɔːt] = **nought**
naughty ['nɔːtɪ] adj *(child)* travieso
nausea ['nɔːsɪə] n náuseas fpl
nautical ['nɔːtɪkl] adj náutico,
marítimo; *(mile)* marino
naval ['neɪvl] adj naval, de marina;
~ **officer** n oficial m/f de marina
nave [neɪv] n nave f
navel ['neɪvl] n ombligo
navigate ['nævɪgeɪt] vt gobernar ♦ vi

navegar; *(AUT)* ir de copiloto;
navigation [-'geɪʃən] n *(action)*
navegación f; *(science)* náutica.
navigator n navegador(a) m/f,
navegante m/f; *(AUT)* copiloto m/f
navvy ['nævɪ] *(BRIT)* n peón m
caminero
navy ['neɪvɪ] n marina de guerra;
(ships) armada, flota; ~(**-blue**) adj azul
marino
Nazi ['nɑːtsɪ] n nazi m/f
NB abbr (= nota bene) nótese
near [nɪə*] adj *(place, relation)* cercano;
(time) próximo ♦ adv cerca ♦ prep
(also: ~ to: space) cerca de, junto a;
(: time) cerca de ♦ vt acercarse a,
aproximarse a; ~**by** [nɪə'baɪ] adj
cercano, próximo ♦ adv cerca; ~**ly** adv
casi, por poco; **I ~ly fell** por poco me
caigo; ~ **miss** n tiro cercano; ~**side** n
(AUT: in Britain) lado izquierdo; *(: in US,
Europe etc)* lado derecho; ~**sighted**
adj miope, corto de vista
neat [niːt] adj *(place)* ordenado, bien
cuidado; *(person)* pulcro; *(plan)*
ingenioso; *(spirits)* solo; ~**ly** adv *(tidily)*
con esmero; *(skilfully)* ingeniosamente
necessarily ['nesɪsrɪlɪ] adv
necesariamente
necessary ['nesɪsrɪ] adj necesario,
preciso
necessitate [nɪ'sesɪteɪt] vt hacer
necesario
necessity [nɪ'sesɪtɪ] n necesidad f;
necessities npl artículos mpl de
primera necesidad
neck [nek] n *(of person, garment, bottle)*
cuello; *(of animal)* pescuezo ♦ vi *(inf)*
besuquearse; ~ **and** ~ parejos; ~**lace**
['neklɪs] n collar m; ~**line** n escote m;
~**tie** ['nektaɪ] n corbata
née [neɪ] adj: ~ **Scott** de soltera Scott
need [niːd] n *(lack)* escasez f, falta;
(necessity) necesidad f ♦ vt *(require)*
necesitar; **I ~ to do it** tengo que or
debo hacerlo; **you don't ~ to go** no
hace falta que (te) vayas

needle ['niːdl] n aguja ♦ vt (fig: inf) picar, fastidiar

needless ['niːdlɪs] adj innecesario; ~ **to say** huelga decir que

needlework ['niːdlwəːk] n (activity) costura, labor f de aguja

needn't ['niːdnt] = **need not**

needy ['niːdɪ] adj necesitado

negative ['negətɪv] n (PHOT) negativo; (LING) negación f ♦ adj negativo; ~ **equity** n situación que se da cuando el valor de la vivienda es menor que el de la hipoteca que pesa sobre ella

neglect [nɪ'glekt] vt (one's duty) faltar a, no cumplir con; (child) descuidar, desatender ♦ n (of house, garden etc) abandono; (of child) desatención f; (of duty) incumplimiento

negligee ['neglɪʒeɪ] n (nightgown) salto de cama

negotiate [nɪ'gəʊʃɪeɪt] vt (treaty, loan) negociar; (obstacle) franquear; (bend in road) tomar ♦ vi: **to ~ (with)** negociar (con); **negotiation** n -'eɪʃən] n negociación f, gestión f

neigh [neɪ] vi relinchar

neighbour ['neɪbə*] (US **neighbor**) n vecino/a; **~hood** n (place) vecindad f, barrio; (people) vecindario; **~ing** adj vecino; **~ly** adj (person) amable; (attitude) de buen vecino

neither ['naɪðə*] adj, conj: **I didn't move and ~ did John** no me he movido, ni Juan tampoco ♦ pron ninguno (de los dos) ♦ adv: ~ **good nor bad** ni bueno ni malo; ~ **is true** ninguno/a de los/las dos es cierto/a

neon ['niːɔn] n neón m; ~ **light** n lámpara de neón

nephew ['nevjuː] n sobrino

nerve [nəːv] n (ANAT) nervio; (courage) valor m; (impudence) descaro, frescura; **a fit of ~s** un ataque de nervios; **~-racking** adj desquiciante

nervous ['nəːvəs] adj (anxious, ANAT) nervioso; (timid) tímido, miedoso; ~ **breakdown** n crisis f nerviosa

nest [nest] n (of bird) nido; (wasps' ~) avispero ♦ vi anidar; ~ **egg** n (fig) ahorros mpl

nestle ['nesl] vi: **to ~ down** acurrucarse

net [net] n (gen) red f; (fabric) tul m ♦ adj (COMM) neto, líquido ♦ vt coger (SP) or agarrar (AM) con red; (SPORT) marcar; **the N~** (Internet) la Red; **~ball** n básquet m

Netherlands ['neðələndz] npl: **the ~** los Países Bajos

nett [net] adj = **net**

netting ['netɪŋ] n red f, redes fpl

nettle ['netl] n ortiga

network ['netwəːk] n red f

neurotic [njuə'rɔtɪk] adj neurótico/a

neuter ['njuːtə*] adj (LING) neutro ♦ vt castrar, capar

neutral ['njuːtrəl] adj (person) neutral; (colour etc, ELEC) neutro ♦ n (AUT) punto muerto; **~ize** vt neutralizar

never ['nevə*] adv nunca, jamás; **I ~ went** no fui nunca; ~ **in my life** jamás en la vida; see also **mind**; **~-ending** adj interminable, sin fin; **~theless** [nevəðə'les] adv sin embargo, no obstante

new [njuː] adj nuevo; (brand new) a estrenar; (recent) reciente; **N~ Age** n Nueva Era; **~born** ['njuːkʌmə*] n recién venido/a or llegado/a; **~-fangled** (pej) adj modernísimo; **~-found** adj (friend) nuevo; (enthusiasm) recién adquirido; **~ly** adv nuevamente, recién; **~ly-weds** npl recién casados mpl

news [njuːz] n noticias fpl; **a piece of ~** una noticia; **the ~** (RADIO, TV) las noticias fpl; ~ **agency** n agencia de noticias; **~agent** (BRIT) n vendedor(a) m/f de periódicos; **~caster** n presentador(a) m/f, locutor(a) m/f; ~ **flash** n noticia de última hora; **~letter** n hoja informativa, boletín m; **~paper** n periódico, diario; **~print** n papel m de periódico; **~reader** n =

~caster; ~reel n noticiario; **~ stand** n quiosco or puesto de periódicos

newt [njuːt] n tritón m

New Year n Año Nuevo; **~'s Day** n Día m de Año Nuevo; **~'s Eve** n Nochevieja

New York ['njuː'jɔːk] n Nueva York

New Zealand [njuː'ziːlənd] n Nueva Zelanda; **~er** n neozelandés/esa m/f

next [nɛkst] adj (house, room) próximo; (bus stop, meeting) próximo; (following: page etc) siguiente ♦ adv después; the **~ day** el día siguiente; **~ time** la próxima vez; **~ year** el año próximo or que viene; **~ to** junto a, al lado de; **~ to nothing** casi nada; **~ please!** ¡el siguiente! **~ door** adv en la casa de al lado ♦ adj vecino, de al lado; **~-of-kin** n pariente m más cercano

NHS n abbr = **National Health Service**

nib [nɪb] n plumilla

nibble ['nɪbl] vt mordisquear, mordiscar

Nicaragua [nɪka'ræɡjuə] n Nicaragua; **~n** adj, n nicaragüense m/f

nice [naɪs] adj (likeable) simpático; (kind) amable; (pleasant) agradable; (attractive) bonito, mono, lindo (AM); **~ly** adv amablemente; bien

nick [nɪk] n (wound) rasguño; (cut, indentation) mella, muesca ♦ vt (inf) birlar, robar; **in the ~ of time** justo a tiempo

nickel ['nɪkl] n níquel m; (US) moneda de 5 centavos

nickname ['nɪkneɪm] n apodo, mote m ♦ vt apodar

nicotine ['nɪkətiːn] n nicotina

niece [niːs] n sobrina

Nigeria [naɪ'dʒɪərɪə] n Nigeria; **~n** adj, n nigeriano/a m/f

niggling ['nɪɡlɪŋ] adj (trifling) nimio, insignificante; (annoying) molesto

night [naɪt] n noche f; (evening) tarde f; **the ~ before last** anteanoche; **at ~**, **by ~** de noche, por la noche; **~cap** n

(drink) bebida que se toma antes de acostarse; **~ club** n cabaret m; **~dress** (BRIT) n camisón m; **~fall** n anochecer m; **~gown** n = **~dress**; **~ie** ['naɪtɪ] n = **~dress**

nightingale n ['naɪtɪŋɡeɪl] n ruiseñor m

night: ~life n vida nocturna; **~ly** adj de todas las noches ♦ adv todas las noches, cada noche; **~mare** n pesadilla; **~ porter** n portero de noche; **~ school** n clase(s) f(pl) nocturna(s); **~ shift** n turno nocturno or de noche; **~time** n noche f; **~ watchman** n vigilante m nocturno

nil [nɪl] (BRIT) n (SPORT) cero, nada

Nile [naɪl] n: **the ~** el Nilo

nimble ['nɪmbl] adj (agile) ágil, ligero; (skilful) diestro

nine [naɪn] num nueve; **~teen** num diecinueve, diez y nueve; **~ty** num noventa

ninth [naɪnθ] adj noveno

nip [nɪp] vt (pinch) pellizcar; (bite) morder

nipple ['nɪpl] n (ANAT) pezón m

nitrogen ['naɪtrədʒən] n nitrógeno

KEYWORD

no [nəʊ] (pl **~es**) adv (opposite of "yes") no; **are you coming?** — **~ (I'm not)** ¿vienes? — no; **would you like some more?** — **~ thank you** ¿quieres más? — no gracias ♦ adj (not any): **I have ~ money/time/books** no tengo dinero/tiempo/libros; **~ other man would have done it** ningún otro lo hubiera hecho; **"~ entry"** "prohibido el paso"; **"~ smoking"** "prohibido fumar" ♦ n no m

nobility [nəʊ'bɪlɪtɪ] n nobleza

noble ['nəʊbl] adj noble

nobody ['nəʊbədɪ] pron nadie

nod [nɒd] vi saludar con la cabeza; (in agreement) decir que sí con la cabeza; (doze) dar cabezadas ♦ vt: **to ~ one's**

head inclinar la cabeza ♦ n inclinación f de cabeza; **~ off** vi dar cabezadas

noise [nɔɪz] n ruido; (din) escándalo, estrépito; **noisy** adj ruidoso; (child) escandaloso

nominate ['nɔmɪneɪt] vt (propose) proponer; (appoint) nombrar; **nominee** [-'niː] n candidato/a

non... [nɔn] prefix no, des..., in...; **~-alcoholic** adj no alcohólico; **~chalant** adj indiferente; **~committal** adj evasivo; **~descript** adj soso

none [nʌn] pron ninguno/a ♦ adv de ninguna manera; **~ of you** ninguno de vosotros; **I've ~ left** no me queda ninguno/a; **he's ~ the worse for it** no le ha hecho ningún mal

nonentity [nɔ'nentɪtɪ] n cero a la izquierda, nulidad f

nonetheless [nʌnðə'les] adv sin embargo, no obstante

non-existent adj inexistente

non-fiction n literatura no novelesca

nonplussed [nɔn'plʌst] adj perplejo

nonsense ['nɔnsəns] n tonterías fpl, disparates fpl; **~!** ¡qué tonterías!

non: ~-smoker n no fumador(a) m/f; **~-smoking** adj (de) no fumador; **~-stick** adj (pan, surface) antiadherente; **~-stop** adj continuo; (RAIL) directo ♦ adv sin parar

noodles ['nuːdlz] npl tallarines mpl

nook [nuk] n: **~s and crannies** escondrijos mpl

noon [nuːn] n mediodía m

no-one pron = **nobody**

noose [nuːs] n (hangman's) dogal m

nor [nɔː*] conj = **neither** ♦ adv see **neither**

norm [nɔːm] n norma

normal ['nɔːml] adj normal; **~ly** adv normalmente

north [nɔːθ] n norte m ♦ adj del norte, norteño ♦ adv al o hacia el norte; **N~ Africa** n África del Norte; **N~ America** n América del Norte; **~east** n nor(d)este m; **~erly** ['nɔːðəlɪ]

adj (point, direction) norteño; **~ern** ['nɔːðən] adj norteño, del norte; **N~ern Ireland** n Irlanda del Norte; **N~ Pole** n Polo Norte; **N~ Sea** n Mar m del Norte; **~ward(s)** ['nɔːθwəd(z)] adv hacia el norte; **~-west** n nor(d)oeste m

Norway ['nɔːweɪ] n Noruega

Norwegian [-'wiːdʒən] adj noruego/a ♦ n noruego/a; (LING) noruego

nose [nəuz] n (ANAT) nariz f; (ZOOL) hocico; (sense of smell) olfato ♦ vi: to **~ about** curiosear; **~bleed** n hemorragia nasal; **~-dive** n (of plane: deliberate) picado vertical; (: involuntary) caída en picado; **~y** (inf) adj curioso, fisgón/ona

nostalgia [nɔs'tældʒɪə] n nostalgia

nostril ['nɔstrɪl] n ventana de la nariz

nosy ['nəuzɪ] (inf) adj = **nosey**

not [nɔt] adv no; **~ that ...** no es que ...; **it's too late, isn't it?** es demasiado tarde, ¿verdad o no?; **~ yet/now** todavía/ahora no; **why ~?** ¿por qué no?; see also **all**; **only**

notably ['nəutəblɪ] adv especialmente

notary ['nəutərɪ] n notario/a

notch [nɔtʃ] n muesca, corte m

note [nəut] n (MUS, record, letter) nota; (banknote) billete m; (tone) tono ♦ vt (observe) notar, observar; (write down) apuntar, anotar; **~book** n libreta, cuaderno; **~d** ['nəutɪd] adj célebre, conocido; **~pad** n bloc m; **~paper** n papel m para cartas

nothing ['nʌθɪŋ] n nada; (zero) cero; **he does ~** no hace nada; **~ new** nuevo; **~ much** no mucho; **for ~** (free) gratis, sin pago; (in vain) en balde

notice ['nəutɪs] n (announcement) anuncio; (warning) aviso; (dismissal) despido; (resignation) dimisión f; (period of time) plazo ♦ vt (observe) notar, observar; **to bring sth to sb's ~** (attention) llamar la atención de uno sobre algo; **to take ~ of** tomar nota de, prestar atención a; **at short ~** con

poca anticipación; **until further ~**
hasta nuevo aviso; **to hand in one's
~** dimitir; **~able** adj evidente, obvio;
~ board (BRIT) n tablón m de anuncios
notify ['nəutifai] vt: **to ~ sb (of sth)**
comunicar (algo) a uno
notion ['nəuʃən] n idea; (opinion)
opinión f
notorious [nəu'tɔ:riəs] adj notorio
nougat ['nu:ga:] n turrón m
nought [nɔ:t] n cero
noun [naun] n nombre m, sustantivo
m
nourish ['nʌriʃ] vt nutrir; (fig)
alimentar; **~ing** adj nutritivo; **~ment** n
alimento, sustento
novel ['nɔvl] n novela ♦ adj (new)
nuevo, original; (unexpected) insólito;
~ist n novelista m/f; **~ty** n novedad f
November [nəu'vɛmbə*] n noviembre
m
novice ['nɔvis] n (REL) novicio/a
now [nau] adv (at the present time)
ahora; (these days) actualmente, hoy
día ♦ conj: **~ (that)** ya que, ahora que;
right ~ ahora mismo; **by ~** ya; **just ~**
ahora mismo; **~ and then, ~ and
again** de vez en cuando; **from ~ on**
de ahora en adelante; **~adays**
['nauədeiz] adv hoy (en) día,
actualmente
nowhere ['nəuwεə*] adv (direction) a
ninguna parte; (location) en ninguna
parte
nozzle ['nɔzl] n boquilla
nuance ['nju:ɑ:ns] n matiz m
nuclear ['nju:kliə*] adj nuclear
nucleus ['nju:kliəs] (pl nuclei) n
núcleo
nude [nju:d] adj, n desnudo/a m/f; **in
the ~** desnudo
nudge [nʌdʒ] vt dar un codazo a
nudist ['nju:dist] n nudista m/f
nuisance ['nju:sns] n molestia,
fastidio; (person) pesado, latoso; **what
a ~!** ¡qué lata!
null [nʌl] adj: **~ and void** nulo y sin
efecto

numb [nʌm] adj: **~ with cold/fear**
entumecido por el frío/paralizado de
miedo
number ['nʌmbə*] n número;
(quantity) cantidad f ♦ vt (pages etc)
numerar, poner número a; (amount to)
sumar, ascender a; **to be ~ed among**
figurar entre; **a ~ of** varios, algunos;
they were ten in ~ eran diez;
~ plate (BRIT) n matrícula, placa
numeral ['nju:mərəl] n número, cifra
numerate ['nju:mərit] adj competente
en la aritmética
numerous ['nju:mərəs] adj numeroso
nun [nʌn] n monja, religiosa
nurse [nə:s] n (institution) enfermero/a; (also:
~maid) niñera ♦ vt (patient) cuidar,
atender
nursery ['nə:səri] n (institution)
guardería infantil; (room) cuarto de los
niños; (for plants) criadero, semillero;
~ rhyme n canción f infantil;
~ school n parvulario, escuela de
párvulos; **~ slope** (BRIT) n (SKI) cuesta
para principiantes
nursing ['nə:siŋ] n (profession)
profesión f de enfermera; (care)
asistencia, cuidado; **~ home** n clínica
de reposo
nut [nʌt] n (TECH) tuerca; (BOT) nuez f;
~crackers npl cascanueces m inv
nutmeg ['nʌtmeg] n nuez f moscada
nutritious [nju:'triʃəs] adj nutritivo,
alimenticio
nuts [nʌts] (inf) adj loco
nutshell ['nʌtʃel] n: **in a ~** en
resumidas cuentas
nylon ['nailɔn] n nilón m ♦ adj de
nilón

O, o

oak [əuk] n roble m ♦ adj de roble
O.A.P. (BRIT) n abbr = **old-age
pensioner**
oar [ɔ:*] n remo

oasis [əu'eɪsɪs] (pl **oases**) n oasis m inv

oath [əuθ] n juramento; (swear word) palabrota; **on** (BRIT) or **under** ~ bajo juramento

oatmeal ['əutmi:l] n harina de avena

oats [əuts] n avena

obedience [ə'bi:dɪəns] n obediencia

obedient [ə'bi:dɪənt] adj obediente

obey [ə'beɪ] vt obedecer; (instructions, regulations) cumplir

obituary [ə'bɪtjuərɪ] n necrología

object [n 'ɔbdʒɪkt, vb əb'dʒekt] n objeto; (purpose) objeto, propósito; (LING) complemento ♦ vi: **to** ~ **to** estar en contra de; (proposal) oponerse a; **to** ~ **that** objetar que; **expense is no** ~ no importa cuánto cuesta; **I** ~! ¡yo protesto!; **~ion** [əb'dʒekʃən] n protesta; **I have no ~ion to ...** no tengo inconveniente en que ...; **~ionable** [əb'dʒekʃənəbl] adj desagradable; (conduct) censurable; **~ive** adj, n objetivo

obligation [ɔblɪ'geɪʃən] n obligación f; (debt) deber m; **without** ~ sin compromiso

oblige [ə'blaɪdʒ] vt (do a favour for) complacer, hacer un favor a; **to** ~ **sb to do sth** forzar o obligar a uno a hacer algo; **to be** ~**d to sb for sth** estarle agradecido a uno por algo; **obliging** adj servicial, atento

oblique [ə'bli:k] adj oblicuo; (allusion) indirecto

obliterate [ə'blɪtəreɪt] vt borrar

oblivion [ə'blɪvɪən] n olvido

oblivious [-ɪəs] adj: **oblivious of** inconsciente de

oblong ['ɔblɔŋ] adj rectangular ♦ n rectángulo

obnoxious [əb'nɔkʃəs] adj odioso, detestable; (smell) nauseabundo

oboe ['əubəu] n oboe m

obscene [əb'si:n] adj obsceno

obscure [əb'skjuə*] adj oscuro ♦ vt oscurecer; (hide: sun) esconder

observant [əb'zə:vnt] adj

observador(a)

observation [ɔbzə'veɪʃən] n observación f; (MED) examen m

observe [əb'zə:v] vt observar; (rule) cumplir; **~r** n observador(a) m/f

obsess [əb'ses] vt obsesionar; **~ive** adj obsesivo; obsesionante

obsolete ['ɔbsəli:t] adj: **to be** ~ estar en desuso

obstacle ['ɔbstəkl] n obstáculo; (nuisance) estorbo; ~ **race** n carrera de obstáculos

obstinate ['ɔbstɪnɪt] adj terco, porfiado; (determined) empeñado

obstruct [əb'strʌkt] vt obstruir; (hinder) estorbar, obstaculizar; **~ion** [əb'strʌkʃən] n (action) obstrucción f; (object) estorbo, obstáculo

obtain [əb'teɪn] vt obtener; (achieve) conseguir

obvious ['ɔbvɪəs] adj obvio, evidente; **~ly** adv evidentemente, naturalmente; **~ly not** por supuesto que no

occasion [ə'keɪʒən] n oportunidad f, ocasión f; (event) acontecimiento; **~al** adj poco frecuente, ocasional; **~ally** adv de vez en cuando

occupant ['ɔkjupənt] n (of house) inquilino/a; (of car) ocupante m/f

occupation [ɔkju'peɪʃən] n ocupación f; (job) trabajo; (pastime) ocupaciones fpl; **~al hazard** n riesgo profesional

occupier ['ɔkjupaɪə*] n inquilino/a

occupy ['ɔkjupaɪ] vt (seat, post, time) ocupar; (house) habitar; **to** ~ **o.s. in doing** pasar el tiempo haciendo

occur [ə'kə:*] vi pasar, suceder; **to** ~ **to sb** ocurrírsele a uno; **~rence** [ə'kʌrəns] n acontecimiento; (existence) existencia

ocean ['əuʃən] n océano

o'clock [ə'klɔk] adv: **it is 5** ~ son las 5

OCR n abbr = **optical character recognition/reader**

October [ɔk'təubə*] n octubre m

octopus ['ɔktəpəs] n pulpo

odd [ɔd] adj extraño, raro; (number)

impar; (*sock, shoe etc*) suelto; **60~** 60 y pico; **at ~ times** de vez en cuando; **to be the ~ one** out estar de más; **~ity** n rareza; (*person*) excéntrico; **~ job man** n chico para todo; **~s** npl bricolaje m; **~ly** adv curiosamente, extrañamente; *see also* **enough**; **~ments** n (COMM) retales mpl; **~s** npl (*in betting*) puntos mpl de ventaja; **it makes no ~s** da lo mismo; **at ~s** reñidos/as; **~s and ends** minucias fpl

odometer [ɔ'dɔmitə*] (US) n cuentakilómetros m inv

odour ['audə*] (US **odor**) n olor m; (*unpleasant*) hedor m

---

of [ɔv, əv] prep **1** (*gen*) de; **a friend ~ ours** un amigo nuestro; **a boy ~ 10** un chico de 10 años; **that was kind ~ you** eso fue muy amable por de tu parte

2 (*expressing quantity, amount, dates etc*) de; **a kilo ~ flour** un kilo de harina; **there were 3 ~ them** había tres; **3 ~ us went** tres de nosotros fuimos; **the 5th ~ July** el 5 de julio

3 (*from, out of*) de; **made ~ wood** (hecho) de madera

---

off [ɔf] adj, adv (*engine*) desconectado; (*light*) apagado; (*tap*) cerrado; (BRIT: *food: bad*) pasado, malo; (: *milk*) cortado; (*cancelled*) cancelado ♦ prep de; **to be ~** (*to leave*) irse, marcharse; **to be ~ sick** estar enfermo o de baja; **a day ~** un día libre o sin trabajar; **to have an ~ day** tener un día malo; **he had his coat ~** se había quitado el abrigo; **10% ~** (COMM) (con el) 10% de descuento; **5 km ~ (the road)** a 5 km (de la carretera); **~ the coast** frente a la costa; **I'm ~ meat** (*no longer eat/like it*) dejo de comer la carne; **on the ~ chance** por si acaso; **~ and on** de vez en cuando

offal ['ɔfl] (BRIT) n (CULIN) menudencias fpl

off-colour [ɔf'kʌlə*] (BRIT) adj (*ill*) indispuesto

offence [ə'fɛns] (US **offense**) n (*crime*) delito; **to take ~ at** ofenderse por

offend [ə'fɛnd] vt (*person*) ofender; **~er** n delincuente m/f

offensive [ə'fɛnsıv] adj ofensivo; (*smell etc*) repugnante ♦ n (MIL) ofensiva

offer ['ɔfə*] n oferta, ofrecimiento; (*proposal*) propuesta ♦ vt ofrecer; (*opportunity*) facilitar; **"on ~"** (COMM) "en oferta"; **~ing** n ofrenda

offhand [ɔf'hænd] adj informal ♦ adv de improviso

office ['ɔfıs] n (*place*) oficina; (*room*) despacho; (*position*) carga, oficio; **doctor's ~** (US) consultorio; **to take ~** entrar en funciones; **~ automation** n ofimática, buromática; **~ block** (US **~ building**) n bloque m de oficinas; **~ hours** npl horas fpl de oficina; (US: MED) horas fpl de consulta

officer ['ɔfısə*] n (MIL etc) oficial m/f; (*also: police ~*) agente m/f de policía; (*of organization*) director(a) m/f

office worker n oficinista m/f

official [ə'fıʃl] adj oficial, autorizado ♦ n funcionario, oficial m

offing ['ɔfıŋ] n: **in the ~** (*fig*) en perspectiva

off-: ~licence (BRIT) n (*shop*) bodega, tienda de vinos y bebidas alcohólicas; **~line** adj, adv (COMPUT) fuera de línea; **~peak** adj (*electricity*) de banda económica; (*ticket*) billete de precio reducido por viajar fuera de las horas punta; **~putting** (BRIT) adj (*person*) asqueroso; (*remark*) desalentador(a); **~season** adj, adv fuera de temporada

---

En el Reino Unido la venta de bebidas alcohólicas está estrictamente regulada y se necesita una licencia especial, con la que cuentan los bares, restaurantes y los establecimientos de

off-licence, los únicos lugares en donde se pueden adquirir bebidas alcohólicas para su consumo fuera del local, de donde viene su nombre. También venden bebidas no alcohólicas, tabaco, chocolatinas, patatas fritas, etc. y a menudo forman parte de una cadena nacional.

offset ['ɔfset] (*irreg*) *vt* contrarrestar, compensar

offshoot ['ɔfʃu:t] *n* (*fig*) ramificación *f*

offshore [ɔf'ʃɔ:ᵊ] *adj* (*breeze, island*) costera; (*fishing*) de bajura

offside ['ɔf'said] *adj* (*SPORT*) fuera de juego; (*AUT: in UK*) del lado derecho; (*: in US, Europe etc*) del lado izquierdo

offspring ['ɔfspriŋ] *n inv* descendencia

off-: ~stage *adv* entre bastidores; **~-the-peg** (*US* **~-the-rack**) *adv* confeccionado; **~-white** *adj* color crudo

often ['ɔfn] *adv* a menudo, con frecuencia; **how ~ do you go?** ¿cada cuánto vas?

oh [əu] *excl* ¡ah!

oil [ɔil] *n* aceite *m*; (*petroleum*) petróleo; (*for heating*) aceite *m* combustible ♦ *vt* engrasar; **~can** *n* lata de aceite; **~field** *n* campo petrolífero; **~ filter** *n* (*AUT*) filtro de aceite; **~ painting** *n* pintura al óleo; **~ rig** *n* torre *f* de perforación; **~ tanker** *n* petrolero; (*truck*) camión *m* cisterna; **~ well** *n* pozo de (petróleo); **~y** *adj* aceitoso; (*food*) grasiento

ointment ['ɔintmənt] *n* ungüento

O.K., okay [əu'kei] *excl* O.K., ¡está bien!, ¡vale! (*SP*) ♦ *adj* bien ♦ *vt* dar el visto bueno a

old [əuld] *adj* viejo; (*former*) antiguo; **how ~ are you?** ¿cuántos años tienes?, ¿qué edad tienes?; **he's 10 years ~** tiene 10 años; **~er brother** hermano mayor; **~ age** vejez *f*; **~-age pensioner** (*BRIT*) *n* jubilado/a; **~-fashioned** *adj* anticuado, pasado de

moda

olive ['ɔliv] *n* (*fruit*) aceituna; (*tree*) olivo ♦ *adj* (*also:* **~-green**) verde oliva; **~ oil** *n* aceite *m* de oliva

Olympic [əu'limpik] *adj* olímpico; **the ~ Games**, **the ~s** las Olimpíadas

omelet(te) ['ɔmlit] *n* tortilla (*SP*), tortilla de huevo (*AM*)

omen ['əumən] *n* presagio

ominous ['ɔminəs] *adj* de mal agüero, amenazador(a)

omit [əu'mit] *vt* omitir

on [ɔn] **KEYWORD**

prep **1** (*indicating position*) en; sobre; **~ the wall** en la pared; **it's ~ the table** está sobre *or* en la mesa; **~ the left** a la izquierda

2 (*indicating means, method, condition etc*): **~ foot** a pie; **~ the train/plane** (*go*) en tren/avión; (*be*) en el tren/el avión; **~ the radio/television/telephone** por *or* en la radio/televisión/al teléfono; **to be ~ drugs** drogarse; (*MED*) estar a tratamiento; **to be ~ holiday/business** estar de vacaciones/en viaje de negocios

3 (*referring to time*): **~ Friday** el viernes; **~ Fridays** los viernes; **~ June 20th** el 20 de junio; **a week ~ Friday** del viernes en una semana; **~ arrival** al llegar; **~ seeing this** al ver esto

4 (*about, concerning*) sobre, acerca de; **a book ~ physics** un libro de *or* sobre física

♦ *adv* **1** (*referring to dress*): **to have one's coat ~** tener *or* llevar el abrigo puesto; **she put her gloves ~** se puso los guantes

2 (*referring to covering*): **"screw the lid ~ tightly"** "cerrar bien la tapa"

3 (*further, continuously*): **to walk** *etc* **~** seguir caminando *etc*

♦ *adv* **1** (*functioning, in operation*): *machine, radio, TV, light*) encendido/a (*SP*), prendido/a (*AM*); (*: tap*) abierto/a; (*: brakes*) echado/a, puesto/a; **is the**

meeting still ~? (*in progress*) ¿todavía continúa la reunión?; (*not cancelled*) ¿va a haber reunión al fin?; **there's a good film ~ at the cinema** ponen una buena película en el cine
2: that's not ~! (*inf: not possible*) ¡eso ni hablar!; (: *not acceptable*) ¡eso no se hace!

once [wʌns] *adv* una vez; (*formerly*) antiguamente ♦ *conj* una vez que; **~ he had left/it was done** una vez que se había marchado/se hizo; **at ~** en seguida, inmediatamente; (*simultaneously*) a la vez; **~ a week** una vez por semana; **~ more** otra vez; **~ and for all** de una vez por todas; **~ upon a time** érase una vez

oncoming ['ɔnkʌmɪŋ] *adj* (*traffic*) que viene de frente

KEYWORD

one [wʌn] *num* un(o)/una; **~ hundred and fifty** ciento cincuenta; **~ by ~** uno a uno
♦ *adj* **1** (*sole*) único; **the ~ book which** el único libro que; **the ~ man who** el único que
2 (*same*) mismo/a; **they came in the ~ car** vinieron en un solo coche
♦ *pron* **1: this ~** éste/ésta; **that ~** ése/ésa; (*more remote*) aquél/aquella; **I've already got a (red) ~** ya tengo uno/a (rojo/a); **~ by ~** uno/a por una/a
2: ~ another o (*SP*), se (*+ el uno al otro, unos a otros etc*); **do you two ever see ~ another?** ¿vosotros dos os veis alguna vez?, (*SP*), ¿se ven ustedes dos alguna vez?; **the boys didn't dare look at ~ another** los chicos no se atrevieron a mirarse (el uno al otro); **they all kissed ~ another** se besaron unos a otros
3 (*impers*) **~ never knows** nunca se sabe; **to cut ~'s finger** cortarse el dedo; **~ needs to eat** hay que comer

one: ~-day excursion (*US*) *n* billete *m* de ida y vuelta en un día; **~-man** *adj* (*business*) individual; **~-man band** *n* hombre-orquesta *m*; **~-off** (*BRIT: inf*) *n* (*event*) acontecimiento único

oneself [wʌn'sɛlf] *pron* (*reflexive*) se; (*after prep*) sí; (*emphatic*) uno/a mismo/a; **to hurt ~** hacerse daño; **to keep sth for ~** guardarse algo; **to talk to ~** hablar solo

one: ~-sided *adj* (*argument*) parcial; **~-to-~** *adj* (*relationship*) de dos; **~-way** *adj* (*street*) de sentido único

ongoing ['ɔngəʊɪŋ] *adj* continuo

onion ['ʌnjən] *n* cebolla

on-line *adj, adv* (*COMPUT*) en línea

onlooker ['ɔnluːkə*] *n* espectador(a) *m/f*

only ['əʊnlɪ] *adv* solamente, sólo ♦ *adj* único, solo ♦ *conj* solamente que, pero; **an ~ child** un hijo único; **not ~ ... but also ...** no sólo ... sino también ...

onset ['ɔnset] *n* comienzo

onshore ['ɔnʃɔː*] *adj* (*wind*) que sopla del mar hacia la tierra

onslaught ['ɔnslɔːt] *n* ataque *m*, embestida

onto ['ɔntʊ] *prep* = **on to**

onward(s) ['ɔnwəd(z)] *adv* (*move*) (hacia) adelante; **from that time ~** desde entonces en adelante

onyx ['ɔnɪks] *n* ónice *m*

ooze [uːz] *vi* rezumar

opaque [əu'peɪk] *adj* opaco

OPEC ['əupɛk] *n abbr* (= *Organization of Petroleum-Exporting Countries*) OPEP *f*

open ['əupn] *adj* abierto; (*car*) descubierto; (*road, view*) despejado; (*meeting*) público; (*admiration*) manifiesto ♦ *vt* abrir ♦ *vi* abrirse; (*book etc: commence*) comenzar; **in the ~ (air)** al aire libre; **~ on to** *vt fus* (*subj: room, door*) dar a; **~ up** *vt* abrir; (*blocked road*) despejar ♦ *vi* abrirse, empezar; **~ing** *n* abertura; (*start*) comienzo; (*opportunity*) oportunidad *f*

~ing hours npl horario de apertura;
~ learning n enseñanza flexible a
tiempo parcial; **~ly** adv abiertamente;
~-minded adj imparcial; **~-necked**
adj (shirt) desabrochado, sin corbata;
~-plan adj: **~-plan office** gran oficina
sin particiones

Open University

La **Open University**, fundada en
1969, está especializada en impartir
cursos a distancia que no exigen una
dedicación exclusiva. Cuenta con sus
propios materiales de apoyo, entre
ellos programas de radio y televisión
emitidos por la BBC y para conseguir
los créditos de la licenciatura es
necesaria la presentación de unos
trabajos y la asistencia a los cursos de
verano.

---

opera ['ɔpərə] n ópera; **~ house** n
teatro de la ópera
operate ['ɔpəreɪt] vt (machine) hacer
funcionar; (company) dirigir ♦ vi
funcionar; **to ~ on sb** (MED) operar a
uno
operatic [ɔpə'rætɪk] adj de ópera
operating table ['ɔpəreɪtɪŋ-] n mesa
de operaciones
operating theatre n sala de
operaciones
operation [ɔpə'reɪʃən] n operación f;
(of machine) funcionamiento; **to be in
~** estar funcionando or en
funcionamiento; **to have an ~** (MED)
ser operado(a); **~al** adj operacional, en
buen estado
operative ['ɔpərətɪv] adj en vigor
operator ['ɔpəreɪtə*] n (of machine)
maquinista m/f, operario/a; (TEL)
operador(a) m/f, telefonista m/f
opinion [ə'pɪnjən] n opinión f; **in my
~** en mi opinión, a mi juicio; **~ated**
adj testarudo; **~ poll** n encuesta, sondeo
opponent [ə'pəunənt] n adversario/a,
contrincante m/f

opportunity [ɔpə'tjuːnɪtɪ] n
oportunidad f; **to take the ~ of
doing** aprovechar la ocasión para
hacer
oppose [ə'pəuz] vt oponerse a; **to be
~d to sth** oponerse a algo; **as ~d to**
a diferencia de; **opposing** adj
opuesto, contrario
opposite ['ɔpəzɪt] adj opuesto,
contrario a; (house etc) de enfrente
♦ adv en frente ♦ prep en frente de,
frente a ♦ n lo contrario
opposition [ɔpə'zɪʃən] n oposición f
oppressive [ə'presɪv] adj opresivo;
(weather) agobiante
opt [ɔpt] vi: **to ~ for** optar por; **to
~ to do** optar por hacer; **~ out** vi: **to
~ out of** optar por no hacer
optical ['ɔptɪkl] adj óptico
optician [ɔp'tɪʃən] n óptico m/f
optimist ['ɔptɪmɪst] n optimista m/f;
~ic [-'mɪstɪk] adj optimista
option ['ɔpʃən] n opción f; **~al** adj
facultativo, discrecional
or [ɔː*] conj o; (before o, ho) u; (with
negative): **he hasn't seen ~ heard
anything** no ha visto ni oído nada;
~ else lo mismo
oral ['ɔːrəl] adj oral ♦ n examen m oral
orange ['ɔrɪndʒ] n (fruit) naranja ♦ adj
color naranja
orbit ['ɔːbɪt] n órbita ♦ vt, vi orbitar
orchard ['ɔːtʃəd] n huerto
orchestra ['ɔːkɪstrə] n orquesta; (US:
seating) platea
orchid ['ɔːkɪd] n orquídea
ordain [ɔː'deɪn] vt (REL) ordenar,
decretar
ordeal [ɔː'diːl] n experiencia horrorosa
order ['ɔːdə*] n orden m; (command)
orden f; (good ~) buen estado; (COMM)
pedido ♦ vt (also: put in ~) arreglar,
poner en orden; (COMM) pedir;
(command) mandar, ordenar; **in ~** en
orden; (of document) en regla; **in
(working) ~** en funcionamiento; **in
~ to do/that** para hacer/que; **on ~**

(COMM) pedido; **to be out of ~** estar desordenado; (not working) no funcionar; **to ~ sb to do sth** mandar a uno hacer algo; **~ form** hoja de pedido; **~ly** n (MIL) ordenanza m; (MED) enfermero/a (auxiliar) ♦ adj ordenado

ordinary ['ɔːdnrɪ] adj corriente, normal; (pej) común y corriente; **out of the ~** fuera de lo común

Ordnance Survey ['ɔːdnəns-] (BRIT) n servicio oficial de topografía

ore [ɔː*] n mineral m

organ ['ɔːɡən] n órgano; **~ic** [ɔː'ɡænɪk] adj orgánico; **~ism** [-ɪzəm] n organismo

organization [ɔːɡənaɪ'zeɪʃən] n organización f

organize ['ɔːɡənaɪz] vt organizar; **~r** n organizador(a) m/f

orgasm ['ɔːɡæzəm] n orgasmo

orgy ['ɔːdʒɪ] n orgía

Orient ['ɔːrɪənt] n Oriente m; **oriental** [-'entl] adj oriental

orientate ['ɔːrɪənteɪt] vt: **to ~ o.s.** orientarse

origin ['ɒrɪdʒɪn] n origen m

original [ə'rɪdʒɪnl] adj original; (first) primero; (earlier) primitivo ♦ n original m; **~ly** adv al principio

originate [ə'rɪdʒɪneɪt] vi: **to ~ from, to ~ in** surgir de, tener su origen en

Orkneys ['ɔːknɪz] npl: **the ~** (also: the Orkney Islands) las Orcadas

ornament ['ɔːnəmənt] n adorno; (trinket) chuchería; **~al** [-'mentl] adj decorativo, de adorno

ornate [ɔː'neɪt] adj muy ornado, vistoso

orphan ['ɔːfn] n huérfano/a

orthopaedic [ɔːθə'piːdɪk] (US **orthopedic**) adj ortopédico

ostensibly [ɔs'tensɪblɪ] adv aparentemente

ostentatious [ɒsten'teɪʃəs] adj ostentoso

osteopath ['ɔstɪəpæθ] n osteópata m/f

ostracize ['ɔstrəsaɪz] vt hacer el vacío a

ostrich ['ɔstrɪtʃ] n avestruz m

other ['ʌðə*] adj otro ♦ pron: **the ~ (one)** el/la otro/a ♦ adv: **~ than** aparte de; **~s** (~ people) otros; **the ~ day** el otro día; **~wise** adv de otra manera ♦ conj (if not) si no

otter ['ɔtə*] n nutria

ouch [autʃ] excl ¡ay!

ought [ɔːt] (pt ought) aux vb: **I ~ to do it** debería hacerlo; **this ~ to have been corrected** esto debiera haberse corregido; **he ~ to win** (probability) debe or debiera ganar

ounce [auns] n onza (28.35g)

our ['auə*] adj nuestro; see also **my**; **~s** pron (el) nuestro/(la) nuestra etc; see also **mine**[1]; **~selves** pron pl (reflexive, after prep) nosotros; (emphatic) nosotros mismos; see also **oneself**

oust [aust] vt desalojar

out [aut] adv fuera, afuera; (not at home) fuera (de casa); (light, fire) apagado; **~ there** allí (fuera); **he's ~** (absent) no está, ha salido; **to be in one's calculations** equivocarse (en sus cálculos); **to run ~** salir corriendo; **~ loud** en alta voz; **~ of** (outside) fuera de; (because of: anger etc) por; **~ of petrol** sin gasolina; **"~ of order"** "no funciona"; **~-and-~** adj (liar, thief etc) redomado, empedernido; **~back** n interior m; **~board** adj: **~board motor** (motor m) fuera borda m; **~break** n (of war) comienzo; (of disease) epidemia; (of violence etc) ola; **~burst** n explosión f, arranque m; **~cast** n paria m/f; **~come** n resultado; **~crop** n (of rock) afloramiento f; **~cry** n protestas fpl; **~dated** adj anticuado, fuera de moda; **~do** (irreg) vt superar; **~door** adj exterior, de aire libre; (clothes) de calle; **~doors** adv al aire libre

outer ['autə*] adj exterior, externo; **~ space** n espacio exterior

outfit ['autfɪt] n (clothes) conjunto
m

out: **~going** adj (character)
extrovertido; (retiring: president etc)
saliente; **~goings** (BRIT) npl gastos
mpl; **~grow** (irreg) vt: **he has
~grown his clothes** su ropa le queda
pequeña ya; **~house** n dependencia;
~ing ['autɪŋ] n excursión f, paseo

out: **~law** n proscrito ♦ vt proscribir;
~lay n inversión f; **~let** n salida; (of
pipe) desagüe m; (US: ELEC) toma de
corriente; (also: retail **~**) punto de
venta; **~line** n (shape) contorno, perfil
m; (sketch, plan) esbozo ♦ vt (plan etc)
esbozar; **in ~line** (fig) a grandes
rasgos; **~live** vt sobrevivir a; **~look** n
(fig) perspectivas fpl; (: for
weather) pronóstico; **~lying** adj
remoto, aislado; **~moded** adj
anticuado, pasado de moda;
~number vt superar en número; **~-
of-date** adj (passport) caducado;
(clothes) pasado de moda; **~-of-the-
way** adj apartado; **~patient** n
paciente m/f externo/a; **~post** n
puesto avanzado; **~put** n (volumen m
de) producción f, rendimiento m
(COMPUT) salida

outrage ['autreɪdʒ] n escándalo; m
(atrocity) atrocidad f ♦ vt ultrajar; **~ous**
[-'reɪdʒəs] adj monstruoso

outright [adv aut'raɪt, adj 'autraɪt] adv
(ask, deny) francamente; (win) de manera
absoluta; (refuse)
rotundamente; (be killed) en el acto ♦ adj
franco; rotundo

outset ['autsɛt] n principio

outside [aut'saɪd] n exterior m ♦ adj
exterior, externo ♦ adv fuera ♦ prep
fuera de; (beyond) más allá de; **at the
~** (fig) a lo sumo; **~ lane** n (AUT: in
Britain) carril m de la derecha; (: in US,
Europe etc) carril m de la izquierda;
~ line n (TEL) línea (exterior); **~r** n
(stranger) extraño, forastero

out: **~size** adj (clothes) de talla grande;
~skirts npl alrededores mpl, afueras

fpl; **~spoken** adj muy franco;
~standing adj excepcional,
destacado; (unfinished) pendiente;
~stay vt: **to ~stay one's welcome**
quedarse más de la cuenta;
~stretched adj (hand) extendido;
~strip vt (competitors, demand) dejar
atrás, aventajar; **~-tray** n bandeja de
salida

outward ['autwəd] adj exterior,
(journey) de ida

outweigh [aut'weɪ] vt pesar más que

outwit [aut'wɪt] vt ser más listo que

oval ['əuvl] adj ovalado ♦ n óvalo

ovary ['əuvərɪ] n ovario

oven ['ʌvn] n horno; **~proof** adj
resistente al horno

over ['əuvə*] adv encima, por encima
♦ adj (or adv) (finished) terminado;
(surplus) de sobra ♦ prep (por) encima
de; (above) sobre; (on the other side of)
al otro lado de; (more than) más de;
(during) durante; **~ here** (por) aquí;
~ there (por) allí or allá; **all ~**
(everywhere) por todas partes; **~ and
~ (again)** una y otra vez; **~ and
above** además de; **to ask sb ~** invitar
a uno a casa; **to bend ~** inclinarse

overall [adj 'əuvərɔ:l, adv əuvər'ɔ:l]
adj (length etc) total; (study) de
conjunto ♦ adv en conjunto ♦ n (BRIT)
guardapolvo; **~s** npl mono (SP), overol
m (AM)

over: **~awe** vt: **to be ~awed (by)**
quedar impresionado (con); **~balance**
vi perder el equilibrio; **~board** adv
(NAUT) por la borda; **~book**
[əuvə'buk] vt sobrereservar

overcast ['əuvəka:st] adj encapotado

overcharge [əuvə'tʃɑ:dʒ] vt: **to ~ sb**
cobrar un precio excesivo a uno

overcoat ['əuvəkəut] n abrigo,
sobretodo

overcome [əuvə'kʌm] (irreg) vt
vencer; (difficulty) superar

over: **~crowded** adj atestado de
gente; (city, country) superpoblado;

~do (irreg) vt exagerar; (overcook) cocer demasiado; **to ~do it** (work etc) pasarse; **~dose** n sobredosis f inv; **~draft** n saldo deudor; **~drawn** adj (account) en descubierto; **~due** adj retrasado; **~estimate** [əuvə'estɪmeɪt] vt sobreestimar

overflow [vb əuvə'fləu, n 'əuvəfləu] vi desbordarse ♦ n (also: ~ pipe) (cañería de) desagüe m

overgrown [əuvə'grəun] adj (garden) invadido por la vegetación

overhaul [vb əuvə'hɔːl, n 'əuvəhɔːl] vt revisar, repasar ♦ n revisión f

overhead [adv əuvə'hed, adj, n 'əuvəhed] adv por arriba or encima ♦ adj (cable) aéreo ♦ n (US) = **~s**; **~s** npl (expenses) gastos mpl generales

over: ~hear (irreg) vt oír por casualidad; **~heat** vi (engine) recalentarse; **~joyed** adj encantado, lleno de alegría

overland ['əuvəlænd] adj, adv por tierra

overlap [əuvə'læp] vi traslaparse

over: ~leaf adv al dorso; **~load** vt sobrecargar; **~look** vt (have view of) dar a, tener vistas a; (miss: by mistake) pasar por alto; (excuse) perdonar

overnight [əuvə'naɪt] adv durante la noche; (fig) de la noche a la mañana ♦ adj de noche; **to stay ~** pasar la noche

overpass ['əuvəpɑːs] (US) n paso superior

overpower [əuvə'pauə*] vt dominar; (fig) embargar; **~ing** adj (heat) agobiante; (smell) penetrante

over: ~rate vt sobreestimar; **~riding** (irreg) vt no hacer caso de; **~riding** adj predominante; **~rule** vt (decision) anular; (claim) denegar; **~run** vt (country) invadir; (time limit) rebasar, exceder

overseas [əuvə'siːz] adv (abroad: live) en el extranjero; (: travel) al extranjero ♦ adj (trade) exterior; (visitor) extranjero

overshadow [əuvə'ʃædəu] vt: **to be ~ed by** estar a la sombra de

overshoot [əuvə'ʃuːt] (irreg) vt exceder

oversight ['əuvəsaɪt] n descuido

oversleep [əuvə'sliːp] (irreg) vi quedarse dormido

overstep [əuvə'step] vt: **to ~ the mark** pasarse de la raya

overt [əu'vɜːt] adj abierto

overtake [əuvə'teɪk] (irreg) vt sobrepasar; (BRIT: AUT) adelantar

over: ~throw (irreg) vt (government) derrocar; **~time** n horas fpl extraordinarias; **~tone** n (fig) tono

overture ['əuvətʃuə*] n (MUS) obertura; (fig) preludio

over: ~turn vt volcar; (fig: plan) desbaratar; (: government) derrocar ♦ vi volcar; **~weight** adj demasiado gordo or pesado; **~whelm** vt aplastar; (subj: emotion) sobrecoger; **~whelming** adj (victory, defeat) arrollador(a); (feeling) irresistible; **~work** vi trabajar demasiado; **~wrought** [əuvə'rɔːt] adj sobreexcitado

owe [əu] vt: **to ~ sb sth, to ~ sth to sb** deber algo a uno; **owing to** prep debido a, por causa de

owl [aul] n búho, lechuza

own [əun] vt tener, poseer ♦ adj propio; **a room of my ~** una habitación propia; **to get one's ~ back** tomar revancha; **on one's ~** solo, a solas; **to ~ up** vi confesar; **~er** n dueño/a; **~ership** n posesión f

ox [ɔks] (pl **~en**) n buey m; **~tail** n: **~tail soup** sopa de rabo de buey

oxygen ['ɔksɪdʒən] n oxígeno

oyster ['ɔɪstə*] n ostra

oz. abbr = **ounce**(s)

ozone ['əuzəun]: **~ friendly** adj que no daña la capa de ozono; **~ hole** n agujero m de/en la capa de ozono; **~ layer** n capa f de ozono

P, p

p |piː| abbr = **penny; pence**

P.A. n abbr = **personal assistant; public address system**

p.a. abbr = **per annum**

pa |pɑː| (inf) n papá m

pace |peɪs| n paso m; **to ~ up and down** pasearse de un lado a otro; **to keep ~ with** llevar el mismo paso que; **~maker** n (MED) regulador m cardíaco, marcapasos m inv; (SPORT: also: ~setter) liebre f

Pacific |pəˈsɪfɪk| n: **the ~ (Ocean)** el (Océano) Pacífico

pack |pæk| n (packet) paquete m; (of hounds) jauría; (of people) manada, bando; (of cards) baraja; (bundle) fardo; (US: of cigarettes) paquete m; (back ~) mochila ♦ vt (fill) llenar; (in suitcase etc) meter, poner; (cram) llenar, atestar; **to ~ (one's bags)** hacerse la maleta; **to ~ sb off** despachar a uno; **~ it in!** (inf) ¡déjalo!

package |ˈpækɪdʒ| n paquete m; (bulky) bulto; (also: ~ deal) acuerdo global; **~ holiday** n vacaciones fpl organizadas; **~ tour** n viaje m organizado

packed lunch n almuerzo frío

packet |ˈpækɪt| n paquete m

packing |ˈpækɪŋ| n embalaje m; **~ case** n cajón m de embalaje

pact |pækt| n pacto m

pad |pæd| n (of paper) bloc m; (cushion) cojinete m, (inf: home) casa ♦ vt rellenar; **~ding** n (material) relleno m

paddle |ˈpædl| n (oar) canalete m; (US: for table tennis) paleta ♦ vt impulsar con canalete ♦ vi (with feet) chapotear; **paddling pool** (BRIT) n estanque m de juegos

paddock |ˈpædək| n corral m

padlock |ˈpædlɔk| n candado m

paediatrics |piːdɪˈætrɪks| (US

pediatrics) n pediatría

pagan |ˈpeɪɡən| adj, n pagano/a m/f

page |peɪdʒ| n (of book) página; (of newspaper) plana; (also: ~ boy) paje m ♦ vt (in hotel etc) llamar por altavoz a

pageant |ˈpædʒənt| n (procession) desfile m; (show) espectáculo; **~ry** n pompa

pager |ˈpeɪdʒə*| (TEL) busca m

paging device |ˈpeɪdʒɪŋ-| n = **pager**

paid |peɪd| pt, pp of **pay** ♦ adj (work) remunerado; (holiday) pagado; (official etc) a sueldo; **to put ~ to** (BRIT) acabar con

pail |peɪl| n cubo, balde m

pain |peɪn| n dolor m; **to be in ~** sufrir; **to take ~s to do sth** tomarse grandes molestias en hacer algo; **~ed** adj (expression) afligido; **~ful** adj doloroso; (difficult) penoso; (disagreeable) desagradable; **~fully** adv (fig: very) terriblemente; **~killer** n analgésico; **~less** adj que no causa dolor; **~staking** |ˈpeɪnzteɪkɪŋ| adj (person) concienzudo, esmerado

paint |peɪnt| n pintura ♦ vt pintar; **to ~ the door blue** pintar la puerta de azul; **~brush** n (artist's) pincel m; (decorator's) brocha; **~er** n pintor(a) m/f; **~ing** n pintura; **~work** n pintura

pair |peə*| n (of shoes, gloves etc) par m; (of people) pareja; **a ~ of scissors** unas tijeras; **a ~ of trousers** unos pantalones, un pantalón

pajamas |pəˈdʒɑːməz| (US) npl pijama m

Pakistan |pɑːkɪˈstɑːn| n Paquistán m; **~i** adj, n paquistaní m/f

pal |pæl| (inf) n compinche m/f, compañero/a

palace |ˈpæləs| n palacio

palatable |ˈpælɪtəbl| adj sabroso

palate |ˈpælɪt| n paladar m

pale |peɪl| adj (gen) pálido; (colour) claro ♦ n: **to be beyond the ~** pasarse de la raya

Palestine |ˈpælɪstaɪn| n Palestina;

Palestinian [-'tɪnɪən] adj, n palestino/a m/f

palette ['pælɪt] n paleta

pall [pɔ:l] vi perder el sabor

pallet ['pælɪt] n (for goods) pallet m

pallid ['pælɪd] adj pálido

palm [pɑ:m] n (ANAT) palma; (also: ~ tree) palmera, palma ♦ vt: **to ~ sth off on sb** (inf) encajar algo a uno; **P~ Sunday** n Domingo de Ramos

paltry ['pɔ:ltrɪ] adj irrisorio

pamper ['pæmpə*] vt mimar

pamphlet ['pæmflət] n folleto

pan [pæn] n (also: sauce~) cacerola, cazuela, olla; (also: frying ~) sartén f

Panama ['pænəmɑ:] n Panamá m; **the ~ Canal** el Canal de Panamá

pancake ['pænkeɪk] n crepe f

panda ['pændə] n panda m; **~ car** (BRIT) n coche m Z (BRIT)

pandemonium [pændɪ'məunɪəm] n jaleo

pander ['pændə*] vi: **to ~** complacer a

pane [peɪn] n cristal m

panel ['pænl] n (of wood etc) panel m; (RADIO, TV) panel m de invitados; **~ling** (US **~ing**) n paneles m

pang [pæŋ] n: **a ~ of regret** una (punzada de) remordimiento; **hunger ~s** dolores mpl del hambre

panic ['pænɪk] n (terror m) pánico ♦ vi dejarse llevar por el pánico; **~ky** adj (person) asustadizo; **~-stricken** adj preso de pánico

pansy ['pænzɪ] n (BOT) pensamiento; (inf: pej) maricón m

pant [pænt] vi jadear

panther ['pænθə*] n pantera

panties ['pæntɪz] npl bragas fpl, pantis mpl

pantihose ['pæntɪhəuz] (US) n pantimedias fpl

pantomime ['pæntəmaɪm] (BRIT) n revista musical representada en Navidad, basada en cuentos de hadas

---

Pantomime

En época navideña se ponen en escena en los teatros británicos las llamadas **pantomimes**, que son versiones libres de cuentos tradicionales como Aladino o El gato con botas. En ella nunca faltan personajes como la dama ("dame"), papel que siempre interpreta un actor, el protagonista joven ("principal boy"), normalmente interpretado por una actriz, y el malvado ("villain"). Es un espectáculo familiar en el que se anima al público a participar y aunque va dirigido principalmente a los niños, cuenta con grandes dosis de humor para adultos.

---

pantry ['pæntrɪ] n despensa

pants [pænts] n (BRIT: underwear: woman's) bragas fpl; (: man's) calzoncillos mpl; (US: trousers) pantalones mpl

paper ['peɪpə*] n papel m; (also: news~) periódico, diario; (academic essay) ensayo; (exam) examen m ♦ adj de papel ♦ vt empapelar (SP), tapizar (AM); **~s** npl (also: identity ~s) papeles mpl, documentos mpl; **~back** n libro en rústica; **~ bag** n bolsa de papel; **~ clip** n clip m; **~ hankie** n pañuelo de papel; **~weight** n pisapapeles m inv; **~work** n trabajo administrativo

paprika ['pæprɪkə] n pimentón m

par [pɑ:*] n par f, (GOLF) par m; **to be on a ~ with** estar a la par con

parachute ['pærəʃu:t] n paracaídas m inv

parade [pə'reɪd] n desfile m ♦ vt (show off) hacer alarde de ♦ vi desfilar; (MIL) pasar revista

paradise ['pærədaɪs] n paraíso

paradox ['pærədɔks] n paradoja; **~ically** [-'dɔksɪklɪ] adv paradójicamente

paraffin ['pærəfɪn] (BRIT) n (also: ~ oil)

parafina

paragon ['pærəgən] n modelo

paragraph ['pærəgra:f] n párrafo

parallel ['pærəlel] adj en paralelo; (fig) semejante ♦ n (line) paralela; (fig, GEO) paralelo

paralyse ['pærəlaiz] vt paralizar

paralysis [pə'rælisis] n parálisis f inv

paralyze ['pærəlaiz] (US) vt = **paralyse**

paramount ['pærəmaunt] adj: **of ~ importance** de suma importancia

paranoid ['pærənɔid] adj (person, feeling) paranoico

paraphernalia [pærəfə'neiliə] n (gear) avíos mpl

parasite ['pærəsait] n parásito/a

parasol ['pærəsɔl] n sombrilla, quitasol m

paratrooper ['pærətru:pə*] n paracaidista m/f

parcel ['pa:sl] n paquete m ♦ vt (also: ~ up) empaquetar, embalar

parched [pa:tʃt] adj (person) muerto de sed

parchment ['pa:tʃmənt] n pergamino

pardon ['pa:dn] n (LAW) indulto ♦ vt perdonar; **~ me!, I beg your ~!** (I'm sorry!) ¡perdone usted!; **(I beg your) ~?, ~ me?** (US) (what did you say?) ¿cómo?

parent ['pɛərənt] n (mother) madre f; (father) padre m; **~s** npl padres mpl; **~al** [pə'rentl] adj paternal/maternal

parenthesis [pə'renθisis] (pl **parentheses**) n paréntesis m inv

Paris ['pæris] n París

parish ['pæriʃ] n parroquia

Parisian [pə'riziən] adj, n parisiense m/f

park [pa:k] n parque m ♦ vt aparcar, estacionar ♦ vi aparcar, estacionarse

parking ['pa:kiŋ] n aparcamiento, estacionamiento; **"no ~"** "prohibido estacionarse"; **~ lot** (US) n parking m; **~ meter** n parquímetro; **~ ticket** n multa de aparcamiento

parliament ['pa:ləmənt] n parlamento; (Spanish) Cortes fpl; **~ary** [-'mentəri] adj parlamentario

Parliament

*El Parlamento británico (**Parliament**) tiene como sede el palacio de Westminster, también llamado "Houses of Parliament" y consta de dos cámaras. La Cámara de los Comunes ("House of Commons"), compuesta por 650 diputados (**Members of Parliament**) elegidos por sufragio universal en su respectiva circunscripción electoral (**constituency**), se reúne 175 días al año y sus sesiones son moderadas por el Presidente de la Cámara (**Speaker**). La cámara alta es la Cámara de los Lores ("House of Lords") y está formada por miembros que han sido nombrados por el monarca o que han heredado su escaño. Su poder es limitado, aunque actúa como tribunal supremo de apelación, excepto en Escocia.*

parlour ['pa:lə*] (US **parlor**) n sala de recibo, salón m, living m (AM)

parochial [pə'rəukiəl] (pej) adj de miras estrechas

parole [pə'rəul] n: **on ~** libre bajo palabra

parquet ['pa:kei] n: **~ floor(ing)** parquet m

parrot ['pærət] n loro, papagayo

parry ['pæri] vt parar

parsley ['pa:sli] n perejil m

parsnip ['pa:snip] n chirivía

parson ['pa:sn] n cura m

part [pa:t] n (gen, MUS) parte f; (bit) trozo; (of machine) pieza; (THEATRE etc) papel m; (of serial) entrega; (US: in hair) raya ♦ adv = **partly** ♦ vt separar ♦ vi (people) separarse; (crowd) apartarse; **to take ~ in** tomar parte or participar en; **to take sth in good ~** tomar algo en buena parte; **to take sb's ~** defender a uno; **for my ~** por mi parte; **for the most ~** en su mayor parte; **to ~ one's hair** hacerse la raya; **~ with** vt fus ceder, entregar; (money) pagar; **~ exchange** (BRIT) n: **in ~ exchange** como parte del pago

partial ['pɑːʃl] adj parcial; **to be ~ to** ser aficionado a

participant [pɑː'tɪsɪpənt] n (in competition) concursante m/f; (in campaign etc) participante m/f

participate [pɑː'tɪsɪpeɪt] vi: **to ~ in** participar en; **participation** [-'peɪʃən] n participación f

participle ['pɑːtɪsɪpl] n participio

particle ['pɑːtɪkl] n partícula; (of dust) grano

particular [pə'tɪkjulə*] adj (special) particular; (concrete) concreto; (given) determinado; (fussy) quisquilloso; (demanding) exigente; **~s** npl (information) datos mpl; (details) pormenores mpl; **in ~** en particular; **~ly** adv (in particular) sobre todo; (difficult, good etc) especialmente

parting ['pɑːtɪŋ] n (act of leaving) separación f; (farewell) despedida; (BRIT: in hair) raya ♦ adj de despedida

partisan [pɑːtɪ'zæn] adj partidista ♦ n partidario/a

partition [pɑː'tɪʃən] n (POL) división f; (wall) tabique m

partly ['pɑːtlɪ] adv en parte

partner ['pɑːtnə*] n (COMM) socio/a; (SPORT, at dance) pareja; (spouse) cónyuge m/f; (lover) compañero/a; **~ship** n asociación f; (COMM) sociedad f

partridge ['pɑːtrɪdʒ] n perdiz f

part-time adj, adv a tiempo parcial

party ['pɑːtɪ] n (POL) partido; (celebration) fiesta; (group) grupo; (LAW) parte f interesada ♦ cpd (POL) de partido; **~ dress** n vestido de fiesta

pass [pɑːs] vt (time, object) pasar; (place) pasar por; (overtake) rebasar;

(exam) aprobar; (approve) aprobar ♦ vi pasar; (SCOL) aprobar, ser aprobado ♦ n (of person) permiso; (membership card) carnet m; (in mountains) puerto, desfiladero; (SPORT) pase m; (SCOL: also: ~ mark): **to get a ~ in** aprobar en; **to ~ sth through sth** pasar algo por algo; **to make a ~ at sb** (inf) hacer proposiciones a uno; **~ away** vi fallecer; **~ by** vi (ignore) pasar por alto; **~ for** vt fus pasar por; **~ on** vt transmitir; **~ out** vi desmayarse; **~ up** vt (opportunity) renunciar a; **~able** adj (road) transitable; (tolerable) pasable

passage ['pæsɪdʒ] n (also: ~way) pasillo; (act of passing) tránsito; (fare, in book) pasaje m; (by boat) travesía; (ANAT) tubo

passbook ['pɑːsbuk] n libreta de banco

passenger ['pæsɪndʒə*] n pasajero/a, viajero/a

passer-by [pɑːsə'baɪ] n transeúnte m/f

passing ['pɑːsɪŋ] adj pasajero; **in ~** de paso; **~ place** n (AUT) apartadero

passion ['pæʃən] n pasión f; **~ate** adj apasionado

passive ['pæsɪv] adj (gen, also LING) pasivo; **~ smoking** n efectos del tabaco en fumadores pasivos

Passover ['pɑːsəuvə*] n Pascua (de los judíos)

passport ['pɑːspɔːt] n pasaporte m; **~ control** n control m de pasaporte; **~ office** n oficina de pasaportes

password ['pɑːswɜːd] n contraseña

past [pɑːst] prep (in front of) por delante de; (further than) más allá de; (later than) después de ♦ adj pasado; (president etc) antiguo ♦ n (time) pasado; (of person) antecedentes mpl; **he's ~ forty** tiene más de cuarenta años; **ten/quarter ~ eight** las ocho y diez/cuarto; **for the ~ few/3 days** durante los últimos días/últimos 3 días; **to run ~ sb** pasar a uno corriendo

pasta ['pæstə] n pasta

paste [peɪst] n pasta; (glue) engrudo ♦ vt pegar

pasteurized ['pæstəraɪzd] adj pasteurizado

pastille ['pæstl] n pastilla

pastime ['pɑːstaɪm] n pasatiempo

pastry ['peɪstrɪ] n (dough) pasta; (cake) pastel m

pasture ['pɑːstʃə*] n pasto

pasty¹ ['pæstɪ] n empanada

pasty² ['peɪstɪ] adj (complexion) pálido

pat [pæt] vt dar una palmadita a; (dog etc) acariciar

patch [pætʃ] n (of material, eye ~) parche m; (mended part) remiendo; (of land) terreno ♦ vt remendar; (to go through) a bad ~ (pasar por) una mala racha; ~ up vt reparar; (quarrel) hacer las paces en; ~work n labor m de retazos; ~y adj desigual

pâté ['pæteɪ] n paté m

patent ['peɪtnt] n patente f ♦ vt patentar ♦ adj patente, evidente; ~ leather n charol m

paternal [pə'tɜːnl] adj paternal; (relation) paterno

path [pɑːθ] n camino, sendero; (trail, track) pista; (of missile) trayectoria

pathetic [pə'θetɪk] adj patético, lastimoso; (very bad) malísimo

pathological [pæθə'lɒdʒɪkəl] adj patológico

pathway ['pɑːθweɪ] n sendero, vereda

patience ['peɪʃns] n paciencia; (BRIT: CARDS) solitario

patient ['peɪʃnt] n paciente m/f ♦ adj paciente, sufrido

patio ['pætɪəʊ] n patio

patriot ['peɪtrɪət] n patriota m/f; ~ic [pætrɪ'ɒtɪk] adj patriótico

patrol [pə'trəʊl] n patrulla ♦ vt patrullar por; ~ car n coche m patrulla; ~man (US irreg) n policía m

patron ['peɪtrən] n (in shop) cliente m/f; (of charity) patrocinador(a) m/f; ~ of the arts mecenas m; ~ize

['pætrənaɪz] vt (shop) ser cliente de; (artist etc) proteger; (look down on) condescender con; ~ saint n santo/a patrón/ona m/f

patter ['pætə*] n golpeteo; (sales talk) labia ♦ vi (rain) tamborilear

pattern ['pætən] n (SEWING) patrón m; (design) dibujo

pauper ['pɔːpə*] n pobre m/f

pause [pɔːz] n pausa ♦ vi hacer una pausa

pave [peɪv] vt pavimentar; to ~ the way for preparar el terreno para

pavement ['peɪvmənt] n (BRIT) acera (SP), vereda (AM)

pavilion [pə'vɪlɪən] n (SPORT) caseta

paving ['peɪvɪŋ] n pavimento, enlosado; ~ stone n losa

paw [pɔː] n pata

pawn [pɔːn] n (CHESS) peón m; (fig) instrumento ♦ vt empeñar; ~ broker n prestamista m/f; ~shop n monte m de piedad

pay [peɪ] (pt, pp paid) n (wage etc) sueldo, salario ♦ vt pagar ♦ vi (be profitable) rendir; to ~ attention (to) prestar atención (a); to ~ sb a visit hacer una visita a uno; to ~ one's respects to sb presentar sus respetos a uno; ~ back vt (money) reembolsar; ~ for vt fus pagar; ~ in vt ingresar; ~ off vt saldar ♦ vi (scheme, decision) dar resultado; ~ up vt pagar (de mala gana); ~able adj: ~able to pagadero a; ~ day n día m de paga; ~ee n portador(a) m/f; ~ envelope (US) n = ~ packet; ~ment n pago; monthly ~ment mensualidad f; ~ packet (BRIT) n sobre m (de paga); ~ phone n teléfono público; ~roll n nómina; ~ slip n recibo de sueldo; ~ television n televisión f de pago

PC n abbr = **personal computer**; (BRIT) = **police constable** ♦ adv abbr = **politically correct**

p.c. abbr = **per cent**

pea [piː] n guisante m (SP), chícharo

(AM), arveja (AM)

peace |piːs| n paz f; (calm) tranquilidad f; **~ful** adj (gentle) pacífico; (calm) tranquilo, sosegado

peach |piːtʃ| n melocotón m (SP), durazno (AM)

peacock |'piːkɔk| n pavo real

peak |piːk| n (of mountain) cumbre f, cima; (of cap) visera; (fig) cumbre f; **~ hours** npl, **~ period** n horas fpl punta

peal |piːl| n (of bells) repique m; **~ of laughter** carcajada

peanut |'piːnʌt| n cacahuete m (SP), maní m (AM); **~ butter** manteca de cacahuete or maní

pear |pɛə*| n pera

pearl |pɜːl| n perla

peasant |'pɛznt| n campesino/a

peat |piːt| n turba

pebble |'pɛbl| n guijarro

peck |pɛk| vt (also: ~ at) picotear ♦ n picotazo; (kiss) besito; **~ing order** n orden m de jerarquía; **~ish** (BRIT: inf) adj: **I feel ~ish** tengo ganas de picar algo

peculiar |pɪ'kjuːlɪə*| adj (odd) extraño, raro; (typical) propio, característico; **~ to** propio de

pedal |'pɛdl| n pedal m ♦ vi pedalear

pedantic |pɪ'dæntɪk| adj pedante

peddler |'pɛdlə*| n: **drug ~** traficante m/f; camello

pedestrian |pɪ'dɛstrɪən| n peatón/ona m/f ♦ adj pedestre; **~ crossing** (BRIT) n paso de peatones; **~ precinct** (BRIT), **~ zone** (US) n zona peatonal

pediatrics |piːdɪ'ætrɪks| (US) n = **paediatrics**

pedigree |'pɛdɪɡriː| n genealogía; (of animal) raza, pedigrí m ♦ cpd (animal) de raza, de casta

pee |piː| (inf) vi mear

peek |piːk| vi mirar a hurtadillas

peel |piːl| n piel f; (of orange, lemon) cáscara; (: removed) peladuras fpl ♦ vt pelar ♦ vi (paint etc) desconcharse;

(wallpaper) despegarse, desprenderse; (skin) pelar

peep |piːp| n (BRIT: look) mirada furtiva; (sound) pío ♦ vi (BRIT: look) mirar furtivamente; **~ out** vi salir (un poco); **~hole** n mirilla

peer |pɪə*| vi: **to ~ at** escudriñar ♦ n (noble) par m; (equal) igual m; (contemporary) contemporáneo/a; **~age** n nobleza

peeved |piːvd| adj enojado

peg |pɛɡ| n (for coat etc) gancho, colgador(a); (BRIT: also: clothes ~) pinza

Pekingese |piːkɪ'niːz| n (dog) pequinés/esa m/f

pelican |'pɛlɪkən| n pelícano; **~ crossing** (BRIT) n (AUT) paso de peatones señalizado

pellet |'pɛlɪt| n bolita; (bullet) perdigón m

pelt |pɛlt| vt: **to ~ sb with sth** arrojarle algo a uno ♦ vi (rain) llover a cántaros; (inf: run) correr ♦ n pellejo

pen |pɛn| n (for writing) pluma; (ballpoint ~) bolígrafo; (for sheep) redil m

penal |'piːnl| adj penal; **~ize** vt castigar

penalty |'pɛnltɪ| n (gen) pena; (fine) multa; **~ (kick)** n (FOOTBALL) penalty m; (RUGBY) golpe m de castigo

penance |'pɛnəns| n penitencia

pence |pɛns| npl of **penny**

pencil |'pɛnsl| n lápiz m, lapicero (AM); **~ case** n estuche m; **~ sharpener** n sacapuntas m inv

pendant |'pɛndnt| n pendiente m

pending |'pɛndɪŋ| prep antes de ♦ adj pendiente

pendulum |'pɛndjuləm| n péndulo

penetrate |'pɛnɪtreɪt| vt penetrar

penfriend |'pɛnfrɛnd| (BRIT) n amigo/a por carta

penguin |'pɛŋɡwɪn| n pingüino

penicillin |pɛnɪ'sɪlɪn| n penicilina

peninsula |pə'nɪnsjulə| n península

penis |'piːnɪs| n pene m

penitentiary [penɪ'tenʃərɪ] (US) n cárcel f, presidio

penknife ['pennaɪf] n navaja

pen name n seudónimo

penniless ['penɪlɪs] adj sin dinero

penny ['penɪ] (pl **pennies** or (BRIT) **pence**) n penique m; (US) centavo

penpal ['penpæl] n amigo/a por carta

pension ['penʃən] n (state benefit) jubilación f; **~er** (BRIT) n (state benefit) jubilado/a; **~ fund** n caja or fondo de pensiones

pentagon ['pentəgən] n: **the P~** (US: POL) el Pentágono

Pentecost ['pentɪkɒst] n Pentecostés m

penthouse ['penthaus] n ático de lujo

pent-up ['pentʌp] adj reprimido

people ['piːpl] npl gente f; (citizens) pueblo, ciudadanos mpl; (POL): **the ~** el pueblo ♦ n (nation, race) pueblo, nación f; **several ~ came** vinieron varias personas; **~ say that ...** dice la gente que ...

pep [pep] (inf): **~ up** vt animar

pepper ['pepə*] n (spice) pimienta; (vegetable) pimiento ♦ vt: **to ~ with** (fig) salpicar de; **~mint** n (sweet) pastilla de menta

peptalk ['peptɔːk] n: **to give sb a ~** darle a uno una inyección de ánimo

per [pɜː*] prep por; **~ day/person** al día/persona; **~ annum** al año; **~ capita** adj, adv per cápita

perceive [pə'siːv] vt percibir; (realize) darse cuenta de

per cent n, por ciento

percentage [pə'sentɪdʒ] n porcentaje m

perception [pə'sepʃən] n percepción f; (insight) perspicacia; (opinion etc) opinión f; **perceptive** [-'septɪv] adj perspicaz

perch [pɜːtʃ] n (fish) perca; (for bird) percha ♦ vi: **to ~ (on)** (bird) posarse (en); (person) encaramarse (en)

percolator ['pɜːkəleɪtə*] n (also: coffee ~) cafetera de filtro

perennial [pə'renɪəl] adj perenne

perfect [adj, n 'pɜːfɪkt, vb pə'fekt] adj perfecto ♦ n (also: **~ tense**) perfecto ♦ vt perfeccionar; **~ly** ['pɜːfɪktlɪ] adv perfectamente

perforate ['pɜːfəreɪt] vt perforar

perform [pə'fɔːm] vt (carry out) realizar, llevar a cabo; (THEATRE) representar; (piece of music) interpretar ♦ vi (well, badly) funcionar; **~ance** n (of a play) representación f; (of actor, athlete etc) actuación f; (of car, engine, company) rendimiento; (of economy) resultados mpl; **~er** n (actor) actor m, actriz f

perfume ['pɜːfjuːm] n perfume m

perhaps [pə'hæps] adv quizá(s), tal vez

peril ['perɪl] n peligro, riesgo

perimeter [pə'rɪmɪtə*] n perímetro

period ['pɪərɪəd] n periodo; (SCOL) clase f; (full stop) punto; (MED) regla ♦ adj (costume, furniture) de época; **~ic(al)** [-'ɒdɪk(l)] adj periódico; **~ical** [-'ɒdɪkl] n periódico; **~ically** [-'ɒdɪklɪ] adv de vez en cuando, cada cierto tiempo

peripheral [pə'rɪfərəl] adj periférico ♦ n (COMPUT) periférico, unidad f periférica

perish ['perɪʃ] vi perecer; (decay) echarse a perder; **~able** adj perecedero

perjury ['pɜːdʒərɪ] n (LAW) perjurio

perk [pɜːk] n extra m; **~ up** vi (cheer up) animarse

perm [pɜːm] n permanente f

permanent |'pɜːmənənt| adj
permanente

permeate |'pɜːmɪeɪt| vi penetrar,
trascender ♦ vt penetrar, trascender a

permissible |pə'mɪsɪbl| adj permisible,
lícito

permission |pə'mɪʃən| n permiso

permissive |pə'mɪsɪv| adj permisivo

permit |n 'pɜːmɪt, vt pə'mɪt| n
permiso, licencia ♦ vt permitir

perplex |pə'plɛks| vt dejar perplejo

persecute |'pɜːsɪkjuːt| vt perseguir

persevere |pɜːsɪ'vɪə*| vi persistir

Persian |'pɜːʃən| adj, n persa m/f; the
~ Gulf el Golfo Pérsico

persist |pə'sɪst| vi: to ~ (in doing
sth) persistir (en hacer algo); ~ence n
empeño; ~ent adj persistente;
(determined) porfiado

person |'pɜːsn| n persona; in ~ en
persona; ~al adj personal; individual;
(visit) en persona; ~al assistant n
ayudante m/f personal; ~al column n
anuncios mpl personales; ~al
computer n ordenador m personal;
~ality |-'nælɪtɪ| n personalidad f; ~ally
adv personalmente; (in person) en
persona; to take sth ~ally tomarse
algo a mal; ~al organizer n agenda;
~al stereo n Walkman ® m; ~ify
|-'sɒnɪfaɪ| vt encarnar

personnel |pɜːsə'nɛl| n personal m

perspective |pə'spɛktɪv| n perspectiva

Perspex ® |'pɜːspɛks| n plexiglás ® n

perspiration |pɜːspɪ'reɪʃən| n
transpiración f

persuade |pə'sweɪd| vt: to ~ sb to
do sth persuadir a uno para que haga
algo

Peru |pə'ruː| n el Perú; **Peruvian** adj,
n peruano/a m/f

perverse |pə'vɜːs| adj perverso;
(wayward) travieso

pervert |n 'pɜːvɜːt, vb pə'vɜːt| n
pervertido/a ♦ vt pervertir; (truth, sb's
words) tergiversar

pessimist |'pɛsɪmɪst| n pesimista m/f;

~ic |-'mɪstɪk| adj pesimista

pest |pɛst| n (insect) insecto nocivo;
(fig) lata, molestia

pester |'pɛstə*| vt molestar, acosar

pesticide |'pɛstɪsaɪd| n pesticida m

pet |pɛt| n animal m doméstico ♦ cpd
favorito ♦ vt acariciar; **teacher's ~**
favorito/a (del profesor); ~ **hate** manía

petal |'pɛtl| n pétalo

peter |'piːtə*|: **to ~ out** vi agotarse,
acabarse

petite |pə'tiːt| adj chiquita

petition |pə'tɪʃən| n petición f

petrified |'pɛtrɪfaɪd| adj horrorizado

petrol |'pɛtrəl| (BRIT) n gasolina; **two/
four-star ~** gasolina normal/súper;
~ **can** n bidón m de gasolina

petroleum |pə'trəʊlɪəm| n petróleo

petrol: ~ **pump** (BRIT) n (in car)
surtidor m de gasolina; (in garage)
~ **station** (BRIT) n gasolinera; ~ **tank**
(BRIT) n depósito (de gasolina)

petticoat |'pɛtɪkəʊt| n enaguas fpl

petty |'pɛtɪ| adj (mean) mezquino;
(unimportant) insignificante; ~ **cash** n
dinero para gastos menores; ~ **officer**
n contramaestre m

petulant |'pɛtjʊlənt| adj malhumorado

pew |pjuː| n banco

pewter |'pjuːtə*| n peltre m

phantom |'fæntəm| n fantasma m

pharmacist |'fɑːməsɪst| n
farmacéutico/a

pharmacy |'fɑːməsɪ| n farmacia

phase |feɪz| n fase f ♦ vt: **to ~ sth in/
out** introducir/retirar algo por etapas

Ph.D. abbr = **Doctor of Philosophy**

pheasant |'fɛznt| n faisán m

phenomenon |fə'nɒmɪnən| (pl
phenomena) n fenómeno

philanthropist |fɪ'lænθrəpɪst| n
filántropo/a

Philippines |'fɪlɪpiːnz| npl: **the ~** las
Filipinas

philosopher |fɪ'lɒsəfə*| n filósofo/a

philosophy |fɪ'lɒsəfɪ| n filosofía

phobia |'fəʊbɪə| n fobia

phone [fəun] n teléfono ♦ vt telefonear, llamar por teléfono; **to be on the ~** tener teléfono; (be calling) estar hablando por teléfono; **~ back** vt, vi volver a llamar; **~ up** vt, vi llamar por teléfono; **~ book** n guía telefónica; **~ booth** n cabina telefónica; **~ box** (BRIT) n = **~ booth**; **~ call** n llamada (telefónica); **~card** n teletarjeta; **~-in** (BRIT) n (RADIO, TV) programa de participación (telefónica)

phonetics [fəˈnetɪks] n fonética

phoney [ˈfəunɪ] adj falso

photo [ˈfəutəu] n foto f; **~copier** n fotocopiadora; **~copy** n fotocopia ♦ vt fotocopiar

photograph [ˈfəutəgrɑːf] n fotografía ♦ vt fotografiar; **~er** [fəˈtɔgrəfə*] n fotógrafo; **~y** [fəˈtɔgrəfɪ] n fotografía

phrase [freɪz] n frase f ♦ vt expresar; **~ book** n libro de frases

physical [ˈfɪzɪkl] adj físico; **~ education** n educación f física; **~ly** adv físicamente

physician [fɪˈzɪʃən] n médico/a

physicist [ˈfɪzɪsɪst] n físico/a

physics [ˈfɪzɪks] n física

physiotherapy [fɪzɪəuˈθerəpɪ] n fisioterapia

physique [fɪˈziːk] n físico

pianist [ˈpiːənɪst] n pianista m/f

piano [pɪˈænəu] n piano

pick [pɪk] n (tool: also: ~-axe) pico, piqueta ♦ vt (select) elegir, escoger; (gather) coger (sp), recoger; (remove, take out) sacar, quitar; (lock) abrir con ganzúa; **take your ~** escoja lo que quiera; **the ~ of** lo mejor de; **to ~ one's nose/teeth** hurgarse las narices/limpiarse los dientes; **to ~ a quarrel with sb** meterse con alguien; **~ at** vt fus: **to ~ at one's food** comer con poco apetito; **~ on** vt fus (person) meterse con; **~ out** vt escoger; (distinguish) identificar; **~ up** vi (improve: sales) ir mejor; (: patient) reponerse; (: FINANCE) recobrarse ♦ vt

recoger; (learn) aprender; (POLICE: arrest) detener; (person: for sex) ligar; (RADIO) captar; **to ~ up speed** acelerarse; **to ~ o.s. up** levantarse

picket [ˈpɪkɪt] n piquete m ♦ vt piquetear

pickle [ˈpɪkl] n (also: ~s: as condiment) escabeche m; (fig: mess) apuro ♦ vt encurtir

pickpocket [ˈpɪkpɔkɪt] n carterista m/f

pickup [ˈpɪkʌp] n (small truck) furgoneta

picnic [ˈpɪknɪk] n merienda ♦ vi ir de merienda; **~ area** n zona de picnic, (AUT) área de descanso

picture [ˈpɪktʃə*] n cuadro; (painting) pintura; (photograph) fotografía; (TV) imagen f; (film) película; (fig: description) descripción f; (: situation) situación f ♦ vt (imagine) imaginar; **~s** npl: **the ~s** (BRIT) el cine; **~ book** n libro de dibujos

picturesque [pɪktʃəˈresk] adj pintoresco

pie [paɪ] n pastel m; (open) tarta; (small: of meat) empanada

piece [piːs] n pedazo, trozo; (of cake) trozo; (item): **a ~ of clothing/furniture/advice** una prenda (de vestir)/un mueble/un consejo ♦ vt: **to ~ together** juntar; (TECH) armar; **to take to ~s** desmontar; **~meal** adv poco a poco; **~work** n trabajo a destajo

pie chart n gráfico de sectores or tarta

pier [pɪə*] n muelle m, embarcadero

pierce [pɪəs] vt perforar

piercing [ˈpɪəsɪŋ] adj penetrante

pig [pɪg] n cerdo (sp), puerco (sp), chancho (AM); (pej: unkind person) asqueroso; (: greedy person) glotón/ona m/f

pigeon [ˈpɪdʒən] n paloma; (as food) pichón m; **~hole** n casilla

piggy bank [ˈpɪgɪ-] n hucha (en forma de cerdito)

pig-headed [ˈpɪgˈhedɪd] adj terco,

testarudo; **~let** [ˈpɪglɪt] n cochinillo;
~skin n piel f de cerdo; **~sty** [ˈpɪgstaɪ]
n pocilga; **~tail** n (girl's) trenza;
(Chinese, TAUR) coleta

pike [paɪk] n (fish) lucio

pilchard [ˈpɪltʃəd] n sardina

pile [paɪl] n montón m; (of carpet,
cloth) pelo ♦ vt (also: ~ up) amontonar;
(fig) acumular ♦ vi (also: ~ up)
amontonarse; acumularse; **~ into** vt
fus (car) meterse en; **~s** [paɪlz] npl
(MED) almorranas fpl, hemorroides mpl;
~-up n (AUT) accidente m múltiple

pilfering [ˈpɪlfərɪŋ] n ratería

pilgrim [ˈpɪlgrɪm] n peregrino/a; **~age**
n peregrinación f, romería

pill [pɪl] n píldora; **the ~** la píldora

pillage [ˈpɪlɪdʒ] vt pillar, saquear

pillar [ˈpɪlə*] n pilar m; **~ box** (BRIT) n
buzón m

pillion [ˈpɪljən] n (of motorcycle)
asiento trasero

pillow [ˈpɪləu] n almohada; **~case** n
funda

pilot [ˈpaɪlət] n piloto ♦ cpd (scheme
etc) piloto ♦ vt pilotar; **~ light** n piloto

pimp [pɪmp] n chulo (SP), cafiche m
(AM)

pimple [ˈpɪmpl] n grano

PIN n abbr (= personal identification
number) número personal

pin [pɪn] n alfiler m ♦ vt prender (con
alfiler); **~s and needles** npl hormigueo;
to ~ sb down (fig) hacer que uno
concrete; **to ~ sth on sb** (fig) colgarle
a uno el sambenito de algo

pinafore [ˈpɪnəfɔː*] n delantal m;
~ dress (BRIT) n mandil m

pinball [ˈpɪnbɔːl] n mesa americana

pincers [ˈpɪnsəz] npl pinzas fpl, tenazas
fpl

pinch [pɪntʃ] n (of salt etc) pizca ♦ vt
pellizcar; (inf: steal) birlar; **at ~** en
caso de apuro

pincushion [ˈpɪnkuʃən] n acerico

pine [paɪn] n (also: ~ tree, wood) pino
♦ vi: **to ~ for** suspirar por; **~ away** vi

morirse de pena

pineapple [ˈpaɪnæpl] n piña, ananás m

ping [pɪŋ] n (noise) sonido agudo; **~-
pong** ® n pingpong ® m

pink [pɪŋk] adj rosado, (color de) rosa
♦ n (colour) rosa; (BOT) clavel m,
clavellina

pinpoint [ˈpɪnpɔɪnt] vt precisar

pint [paɪnt] n pinta (BRIT = 568cc; US
= 473cc); (BRIT: inf: of beer) pinta de
cerveza; **≈ jarra** (SP)

pin-up n fotografía erótica

pioneer [paɪəˈnɪə*] n pionero/a

pious [ˈpaɪəs] adj piadoso, devoto

pip [pɪp] n (seed) pepita; **the ~s** (BRIT)
la señal

pipe [paɪp] n tubo, caño; (for smoking)
pipa ♦ vt conducir en cañerías; **~s** npl
(gen) cañería; (also: bag-~s) gaita;
~ cleaner n limpiapipas m inv;
~ dream n sueño imposible; **~line** n
(for oil) oleoducto; (for gas) gasoducto;
~r n gaitero/a

piping [ˈpaɪpɪŋ] adv: **to be ~ hot** estar
que quema

piquant [ˈpiːkənt] adj picante; (fig)
agudo

pique [piːk] n pique m, resentimiento

pirate [ˈpaɪərət] n pirata m/f ♦ vt
(cassette, book) piratear; **~ radio** (BRIT)
n emisora pirata

Pisces [ˈpaɪsiːz] n Piscis m

piss [pɪs] (inf!) vi mear; **~ed** (inf!) adj
(drunk) borracho

pistol [ˈpɪstl] n pistola

piston [ˈpɪstən] n pistón m, émbolo

pit [pɪt] n hoyo; (also: coal ~) mina; (in
garage) foso de inspección; (also:
orchestra ~) platea ♦ vt: **to ~ one's
wits against sb** medir fuerzas con
uno; **~s** npl (AUT) box m

pitch [pɪtʃ] n (MUS) tono; (fig) punto; (tar) brea
♦ vt (throw) arrojar, lanzar ♦ vi (fall)
caer(se); **to ~ a tent** montar una
tienda (de campaña); **~-black** adj
negro como boca de lobo; **~ed battle**

n batalla campal

pitfall ['pɪtfɔ:l] *n* riesgo

pith [pɪθ] *n* (*of orange*) médula

pithy ['pɪθɪ] *adj* (*fig*) jugoso

pitiful ['pɪtɪful] *adj* (*touching*) lastimoso, conmovedor(a)

pitiless ['pɪtɪlɪs] *adj* despiadado

pittance ['pɪtns] *n* miseria

pity ['pɪtɪ] *n* compasión *f*, piedad *f* ♦ *vt* compadecer(se de); **what a ~!** ¡qué pena!

pizza ['pi:tsə] *n* pizza

placard ['plækɑ:d] *n* letrero; (*in march etc*) pancarta

placate [plə'keɪt] *vt* apaciguar

place [pleɪs] *n* lugar *m*, sitio; (*seat*) asiento; (*post*) puesto; (*home*): **at/to his ~** en/a su casa; (*role: in society etc*) papel *m* ♦ *vt* (*object*) poner, colocar; (*identify*) reconocer; **to take ~** tener lugar; **to be ~d** (*in race, exam*) colocarse; **out of ~** (*not suitable*) fuera de lugar; **in the first ~** en primer lugar; **to change ~s with sb** cambiarse de sitio con uno; **~ of birth** *n* lugar *m* de nacimiento

placid ['plæsɪd] *adj* apacible

plague [pleɪg] *n* plaga; (*MED*) peste *f* ♦ *vt* (*fig*) acosar, atormentar

plaice [pleɪs] *n inv* platija

plaid [plæd] *n* (*material*) tartán *m*

plain [pleɪn] *adj* (*unpatterned*) liso; (*clear*) claro, evidente; (*simple*) sencillo; (*not handsome*) poco atractivo ♦ *adv* claramente ♦ *n* llano, llanura; **~ chocolate** *n* chocolate *m* amargo; **~-clothes** *adj* (*police*) vestido de paisano; **~ly** *adv* claramente

plaintiff ['pleɪntɪf] *n* demandante *m/f*

plait [plæt] *n* trenza

plan [plæn] *n* (*drawing*) plano; (*scheme*) plan *m*, proyecto ♦ *vt* proyectar, planificar ♦ *vi* hacer proyectos; **to ~ to do** pensar hacer

plane [pleɪn] *n* (*AVIAT*) avión *m*; (*MATH, fig*) plano; (*also: ~ tree*) plátano; (*tool*) cepillo

planet ['plænɪt] *n* planeta *m*

plank [plæŋk] *n* tabla

planner ['plænə*] *n* planificador(a) *m/f*

planning ['plænɪŋ] *n* planificación *f*; **family ~** planificación familiar; **~ permission** *n* permiso para realizar obras

plant [plɑ:nt] *n* planta; (*machinery*) maquinaria; (*factory*) fábrica ♦ *vt* plantar; (*field*) sembrar; (*bomb*) colocar

plaster ['plɑ:stə*] *n* (*for walls*) yeso; (*also: ~ of Paris*) yeso mate; (*BRIT: also: sticking ~*) tirita (*SP*), esparadrapo, curita (*AM*) ♦ *vt* enyesar; (*cover*): **to ~ with** llenar or cubrir de; **~ed** (*inf*) *adj* borracho; **~er** *n* yesero

plastic ['plæstɪk] *n* plástico ♦ *adj* de plástico; **~ bag** *n* bolsa de plástico

Plasticine ® ['plæstɪsi:n] (*BRIT*) *n* plastilina ®

plastic surgery *n* cirujía plástica

plate [pleɪt] *n* (*dish*) plato; (*metal, in book*) lámina; (*dental ~*) placa de dentadura postiza

plateau ['plætəʊ] (*pl* **~s** *or* **~x**) *n* meseta, altiplanicie *f*

plateaux ['plætəʊz] *npl of* **plateau**

plate glass *n* vidrio cilindrado

platform ['plætfɔ:m] *n* (*RAIL*) andén *m*; (*stage, BRIT: on bus*) plataforma; (*at meeting*) tribuna; (*POL*) programa *m* (electoral)

platinum ['plætɪnəm] *adj, n* platino

platoon [plə'tu:n] *n* pelotón *m*

platter ['plætə*] *n* fuente *f*

plausible ['plɔ:zɪbl] *adj* verosímil; (*person*) convincente

play [pleɪ] *n* (*THEATRE*) obra, comedia ♦ *vt* (*game*) jugar; (*compete against*) jugar contra; (*instrument*) tocar; (*part: in play etc*) hacer el papel de; (*tape, record*) poner ♦ *vi* jugar; (*band*) tocar; (*tape, record*) sonar; **to ~ safe** ir a lo seguro; **~ down** *vt* quitar importancia a; **~ up** *vi* (*cause trouble*) dar guerra; **~boy** *n* playboy *m*, **~er** *n* jugador(a) *m/f*; (*THEATRE*) actor/actriz *m/f*; (*MUS*) músico/a; **~ful** adj juguetón/ona; **~ground** n (in school) patio de recreo; (in park) parque m infantil; **~group** n (LAW) acuerdo entre fiscal y defensor para agilizar los trámites judiciales

jardín m de niños; **~ing card** n naipe m, carta; **~ing field** n campo de deportes; **~mate** n compañero/a de juego; **~-off** n (SPORT) (partido de) desempate m; **~pen** n corral m; **~thing** n juguete m; **~time** n (SCOL) recreo; **~wright** n dramaturgo/a

plc abbr (= public limited company) ≈ S.A.

plea [pliː] n súplica, petición f; (LAW) alegato, defensa; **~ bargaining** n (LAW) acuerdo entre fiscal y defensor para agilizar los trámites judiciales

plead [pliːd] vt (LAW): **to ~ sb's case** defender a uno; (give as excuse) poner como pretexto ♦ vi (LAW) declararse; (beg): **to ~ with sb** suplicar o rogar a uno

pleasant ['plɛznt] adj agradable; **~ries** npl cortesías fpl

please [pliːz] excl ¡por favor! ♦ vt (give pleasure to) dar gusto a, agradar ♦ vi (think fit): **do as you ~** haz lo que quieras; **~ yourself!** (inf) ¡haz lo que quieras!, ¡como quieras!; **~d** adj (happy) alegre, contento; **~d (with)** satisfecho (de); **~d to meet you** ¡encantado!, ¡tanto gusto!; **pleasing** adj agradable, grato

pleasure ['plɛʒə*] n placer m, gusto; **"it's a ~"** "el gusto es mío"

pleat [pliːt] n pliegue m

pledge [plɛdʒ] n (promise) promesa, voto ♦ vt prometer

plentiful ['plɛntɪful] adj copioso, abundante

plenty ['plɛntɪ] n: **~ of** mucho(s)/a(s)

pliable ['plaɪəbl] adj flexible

pliers ['plaɪəz] npl alicates mpl, tenazas fpl

plight [plaɪt] n situación f difícil

plimsolls ['plɪmsɔlz] (BRIT) npl zapatos mpl de tenis

plinth [plɪnθ] n plinto

plod [plɔd] vi caminar con paso pesado; (fig) trabajar laboriosamente

plonk [plɔŋk] (inf) n (BRIT: wine) vino peleón ♦ vt: **to ~ sth down** dejar caer algo

plot [plɔt] n (scheme) complot m, conjura; (of story, play) argumento; (of land) terreno, lote m (AM) ♦ vt (mark out) trazar; (conspire) tramar, urdir ♦ vi conspirar

plough [plau] (US **plow**) n arado ♦ vt (earth) arar; **to ~ money into** invertir dinero en; **~ through** vt fus (crowd) abrirse paso por la fuerza por; **~man's lunch** (BRIT) n almuerzo de pub a base de pan, queso y encurtidos

pluck [plʌk] vt (fruit) coger (SP), recoger (AM); (musical instrument) puntear; (bird) desplumar; (eyebrows) depilar; **to ~ up courage** hacer de tripas corazón

plug [plʌg] n tapón m; (ELEC) enchufe m, clavija; (AUT: also: spark(ing) ~ bujía ♦ vt (hole) tapar; (inf: advertise) dar publicidad a; **~ in** vt (ELEC) enchufar

plum [plʌm] n (fruit) ciruela

plumb [plʌm] vt: **to ~ the depths of** alcanzar los mayores extremos de

plumber ['plʌmə*] n fontanero/a (SP), plomero/a (AM)

plumbing ['plʌmɪŋ] n (trade) fontanería, plomería; (piping) cañería

plummet ['plʌmɪt] vi: **to ~ (down)** caer a plomo

plump [plʌmp] adj rechoncho, rollizo ♦ vi: **to ~ for** (inf: choose) optar por; **~ up** vt mullir

plunder ['plʌndə*] n pillaje, saqueo

plunge [plʌndʒ] n zambullida ♦ vt sumergir, hundir ♦ vi (fall) caer; (dive) saltar; (person) arrojarse; **to take the ~** lanzarse; **plunging** adj: **plunging neckline** escote m pronunciado

pluperfect [pluː'pəːfɪkt] n pluscuamperfecto

plural ['pluərl] adj plural ♦ n plural m

plus [plʌs] n (also: ~ sign) signo más

♦ prep más, y, además de; **ten/
twenty ~** más de diez/veinte

plush [plʌʃ] adj lujoso

plutonium [pluː'təʊnɪəm] n plutonio

ply [plaɪ] vt (a trade) ejercer ♦ vi (ship)
ir y venir ♦ n (of wool, rope) cabo; **to
~ sb with drink** insistir en ofrecer a
uno muchas copas; **~wood** n madera
contrachapada

P.M. n abbr = **Prime Minister**

p.m. adv abbr (= post meridiem) de la
tarde or noche

pneumatic [njuː'mætɪk] adj
neumático; **~ drill** n martillo
neumático

pneumonia [njuː'məʊnɪə] n pulmonía

poach [pəʊtʃ] vt (cook) escalfar; (steal)
cazar (or pescar) en vedado ♦ vi cazar
(or pescar) en vedado; **~ed** adj
escalfado; **~er** n cazador/a m/f
furtivo/a

P.O. Box n abbr = **Post Office Box**

pocket ['pɒkɪt] n bolsillo; (fig: small
area) bolsa ♦ vt meter en el bolsillo;
(steal) embolsar; **to be out of ~** (BRIT)
salir perdiendo; **~book** (US) n cartera;
~ calculator n calculadora de bolsillo;
~ knife n navaja; **~ money** n
asignación f

pod [pɒd] n vaina

podgy ['pɒdʒɪ] adj gordinflón/ona

podiatrist [pɒ'diːətrɪst] (US) n
pedicuro/a

poem ['pəʊɪm] n poema m

poet ['pəʊɪt] n poeta m/f; **~ic** [-'etɪk]
adj poético; **~ry** n poesía

poignant ['pɔɪnjənt] adj
conmovedor/a

point [pɔɪnt] n punto; (tip) punta;
(purpose) fin m, propósito; (use)
utilidad f; (significant part) lo
significativo; (moment) momento;
(ELEC) toma de corriente; (also:
decimal ~): **2 ~ 3 (2.3)** dos coma tres
(2,3) ♦ vt señalar; (gun etc) to **~ sth
at sb** apuntar algo a uno ♦ vi: **to ~ at**
señalar; **~s** npl (AUT) contactos mpl;

(RAIL) agujas fpl; **to be on the ~ of
doing sth** estar a punto de hacer
algo; **to make a ~ of** poner empeño
en; **to get/miss the ~** comprender/
no comprender; **to come to the ~** ir
al meollo; **there's no ~ (in doing)** no
tiene sentido (hacer); **~ out** vt señalar;
~ to vt fus (fig) indicar, señalar; **~-
blank** adv (say, refuse) sin más hablar;
(also: at ~-blank range) a quemarropa;
~ed adj (shape) puntiagudo, afilado;
(remark) intencionado; **~edly** adv
intencionadamente; **~er** n (needle)
aguja, indicador m; **~less** adj sin
sentido; **~ of view** n punto de vista

poise [pɔɪz] n aplomo, elegancia

poison ['pɔɪzn] n veneno ♦ vt
envenenar; **~ing** n envenenamiento;
~ous adj venenoso; (fumes etc) tóxico

poke [pəʊk] vt (jab with finger, stick
etc) empujar; (put): **to ~ sth in(to)**
introducir algo en; **~ about** vi
fisgonear

poker ['pəʊkə*] n atizador m; (CARDS)
póker m

poky ['pəʊkɪ] adj estrecho

Poland ['pəʊlənd] n Polonia

polar ['pəʊlə*] adj polar; **~ bear** n oso
polar

Pole [pəʊl] n polaco/a

pole [pəʊl] n palo; (fixed) poste m;
(GEO) polo; **~ bean** (US) n ≈ judía
verde; **~ vault** n salto con pértiga

police [pə'liːs] n policía ♦ vt vigilar;
~ car n coche-patrulla m; **~man** (irreg)
n policía, guardia m; **~ state** n
estado policial; **~ station** n comisaría;
~woman (irreg) n mujer f policía

policy ['pɒlɪsɪ] n política; (also:
insurance ~) póliza

polio ['pəʊlɪəʊ] n polio f

Polish ['pəʊlɪʃ] adj polaco ♦ n (LING)
polaco

polish ['pɒlɪʃ] n (for shoes) betún m;
(for floor) cera de (lustrar); (shine)
brillo, lustre m; (fig: refinement)
educación f ♦ vt (shoes) limpiar; (make

shiny) pulir, sacar brillo a; **~ off** vt (food) despachar; **~ed** adj (fig: person) elegante

polite [pə'laɪt] adj cortés, atento; **~ness** n cortesía

political [pə'lɪtɪkl] adj político; **~ly** adv políticamente; **~ly correct** políticamente correcto

politician [pɒlɪ'tɪʃən] n político/a

politics [ˈpɒlɪtɪks] n política

poll [pəul] n (election) votación f; (also: opinion ~) sondeo, encuesta ♦ vt encuestar; (votes) obtener

pollen [ˈpɒlən] n polen m

polling day [ˈpəulɪŋ-] n día m de elecciones

polling station n centro electoral

pollute [pə'luːt] vt contaminar

pollution [pə'luːʃən] n polución f, contaminación f del medio ambiente

polo [ˈpəuləu] n (sport) polo; **~ necked** adj de cuello vuelto; **~ shirt** n polo, niqui m

polyester [pɒlɪ'estə*] n poliéster m

polystyrene [pɒlɪ'staɪriːn] n poliestireno

polythene [ˈpɒlɪθiːn] (BRIT) n politeno

pomegranate [ˈpɒmɪɡrænɪt] n granada

pomp [pɒmp] n pompa

pompous [ˈpɒmpəs] adj pomposo

pond [pɒnd] n (natural) charca; (artificial) estanque m

ponder [ˈpɒndə*] vt meditar

ponderous [ˈpɒndərəs] adj pesado

pong [pɒŋ] (BRIT: inf) n hedor m

pony [ˈpəunɪ] n poney m, jaca, potro (AM); **~tail** n cola de caballo; **~ trekking** (BRIT) n excursión f a caballo

poodle [ˈpuːdl] n caniche m

pool [puːl] n (natural) charca; (also: swimming ~) piscina (SP), alberca (AM); (fig: of light etc) charco; (SPORT) chapolín m ♦ vt juntar; **~s** npl (football ~s) quinielas fpl; **typing ~** servicio de mecanografía

poor [puə*] adj pobre; (bad) de mala calidad ♦ npl: **the ~** los pobres; **~ly** adj mal, enfermo ♦ adv mal

pop [pɒp] n (sound) ruido seco; (MUS) (música) pop m; (US: inf: father) papá m; (drink) gaseosa ♦ vt (put quickly) meter (de prisa) ♦ vi reventar; (cork) saltar; **~ in/out** vi entrar/salir un momento; **~ up** vi aparecer inesperadamente; **~corn** n palomitas fpl

pope [pəup] n papa m

poplar [ˈpɒplə*] n álamo

popper [ˈpɒpə*] (BRIT) n automático

poppy [ˈpɒpɪ] n amapola

Popsicle ® [ˈpɒpsɪkl] (US) n polo

pop star n estrella del pop

populace [ˈpɒpjuləs] n pueblo, plebe f

popular [ˈpɒpjulə*] adj popular

population [pɒpju'leɪʃən] n población f

porcelain [ˈpɔːslɪn] n porcelana

porch [pɔːtʃ] n pórtico, entrada; (US) veranda

porcupine [ˈpɔːkjupaɪn] n puerco m espín

pore [pɔː*] n poro ♦ vi: **to ~ over** engolfarse en

pork [pɔːk] n carne f de cerdo (SP) or chancho (AM)

pornography [pɔː'nɒɡrəfɪ] n pornografía

porpoise [ˈpɔːpəs] n marsopa

porridge [ˈpɒrɪdʒ] n gachas fpl de avena

port [pɔːt] n puerto; (NAUT: left side) babor m; (wine) vino de Oporto; **~ of call** puerto de escala

portable [ˈpɔːtəbl] adj portátil

porter [ˈpɔːtə*] n (for luggage) maletero; (doorkeeper) portero/a, conserje m/f

portfolio [pɔːt'fəulɪəu] n cartera

porthole [ˈpɔːthəul] n portilla

portion [ˈpɔːʃən] n porción f; (of food) ración f

portrait [ˈpɔːtreɪt] n retrato

portray [pɔː'treɪ] vt retratar; (subj:

αctor) representar

Portugal ['pɔːtjugl] n Portugal m

Portuguese [pɔːtju'giːz] adj portugués/esa ♦ n inv portugués/esa m/f; (LING) portugués m

pose [pəuz] n postura, actitud f ♦ vi (pretend): **to ~ as** hacerse pasar por ♦ vt (question) plantear; **to ~ for** posar para

posh [pɔʃ] (inf) adj elegante, de lujo

position [pə'zɪʃən] n posición f; (job) puesto; (situation) situación f ♦ vt colocar

positive ['pɔzɪtɪv] adj positivo; (certain) seguro; (definite) definitivo

possess [pə'zɛs] vt poseer; **~ion** [pə'zɛʃən] n posesión f; **~ions** npl (belongings) pertenencias fpl

possibility [pɔsɪ'bɪlɪtɪ] n posibilidad f

possible ['pɔsɪbl] adj posible; **as big as ~** lo más grande posible; **possibly** adv posiblemente; **I cannot possibly come** me es imposible venir

post [pəust] n (BRIT: system) correos mpl; (BRIT: letters, delivery) correo m; (job, situation) puesto; (pole) poste m ♦ vt (BRIT: appoint): **to ~** to enviar a; **~age** n porte m, franqueo; **~age stamp** n sello de correos; **~al** adj postal, de correos; **~al order** n giro postal; **~box** (BRIT) n buzón m; **~card** n tarjeta postal; **~code** n código postal

postdate [pəust'deɪt] vt (cheque) poner fecha adelantada a

poster ['pəustə*] n cartel m

poste restante [pəust'rɛstɔnt] (BRIT) n lista de correos

postgraduate ['pəust'grædjuət] n posgraduado/a

posthumous ['pɔstjuməs] adj póstumo

postman ['pəustmən] (irreg) n cartero

postmark ['pəustmɑːk] n matasellos m inv

post-mortem [-'mɔːtəm] n autopsia f

post office n (building) oficina f de

correos m; (organization): **the Post Office** Administración f General de Correos; **Post Office Box** n apartado postal (SP), casilla de correos (AM)

postpone [pəs'pəun] vt aplazar

postscript ['pəustskrɪpt] n posdata

posture ['pɔstʃə*] n postura, actitud f

postwar [pəust'wɔː*] adj de la posguerra

posy ['pəuzɪ] n ramillete m (de flores)

pot [pɔt] n (for cooking) olla; (tea~) tetera; (coffee~) cafetera; (for flowers) maceta; (for jam) tarro, pote m; (inf: marijuana) chocolate m ♦ vt (plant) poner en tiesto; **to go to ~** (inf) irse al traste

potato [pə'teɪtəu] (pl **~es**) n patata (SP), papa (AM); **~ peeler** n pelapatatas m inv

potent ['pəutnt] adj potente, poderoso; (drink) fuerte

potential [pə'tenʃl] adj potencial, posible ♦ n potencial m; **~ly** adv en potencia

pothole ['pɔthəul] n (in road) bache m; (BRIT: underground) gruta; **potholing** (BRIT) n: **to go potholing** dedicarse a la espeleología

potluck [pɔt'lʌk] n: **to take ~** tomar lo que haya

potted ['pɔtɪd] adj (food) en conserva; (plant) en tiesto o maceta; (shortened) resumido

potter ['pɔtə*] n alfarero/a ♦ vi: **to ~ around, ~ about** (BRIT) hacer trabajitos; **~y** n cerámica; (factory) alfarería

potty ['pɔtɪ] n orinal m de niño

pouch [pautʃ] n (ZOOL) bolsa; (for tobacco) petaca

poultry ['pəultrɪ] n aves fpl de corral; (meat) pollo

pounce [pauns] vi: **to ~ on** precipitarse sobre

pound [paund] n (money = libra (weight = 453g or 16oz; money = 100 pence) ♦ vt (beat) golpear; (crush) machacar ♦ vi (*heart*) latir; **~ sterling** n libra esterlina

pour [pɔː*] vt echar; (*tea etc*) servir ♦ vi correr, fluir; **to ~ sb a drink** servirle a uno una copa; **~ away** o **off** vt vaciar, verter; **~ in** vi (*people*) entrar en tropel; **~ out** vi salir en tropel ♦ vt (*drink*) echar, servir; (*fig*): **to ~ out one's feelings** desahogarse; **~ing** adj: **~ing rain** lluvia torrencial

pout [paut] vi hacer pucheros

poverty ['pɔvətɪ] n pobreza, miseria; **~-stricken** adj necesitado

powder ['paudə*] n polvo; (*face ~*) polvos m/pl ♦ vt polvorear; **to ~ one's face** empolvarse la cara; **~ compact** n polvera; **~ed milk** n leche f en polvo; **~ room** n aseos mpl

power ['pauə*] n poder m; (*strength*) fuerza; (*nation, TECH*) potencia; (*drive*) empuje m; (*ELEC*) fuerza, energía ♦ vt impulsar; **to be in ~** (*POL*) estar en el poder; **~ cut** (*BRIT*) n apagón m; **~ed** adj: **~ed by** impulsado por; **~ failure** n = **~ cut**; **~ful** adj poderoso; (*engine*) potente; (*speech etc*) convincente; **~less** adj: **~less (to do)** incapaz (de hacer); **~ point** (*BRIT*) n enchufe m; **~ station** n central f eléctrica

p.p. abbr (= per procurationem): **~ J. Smith** p.p. (por poder de) J. Smith; (= *pages*) págs

PR n abbr = **public relations**

practical ['præktɪkl] adj práctico; **~ity** [-'kælɪtɪ] n factibilidad f; **~ joke** n broma pesada; **~ly** adv (*almost*) casi

practice ['præktɪs] n (*habit*) costumbre f; (*exercise*) práctica, ejercicio; (*training*) adiestramiento; (*MED: of profession*) práctica, ejercicio; (*MED, LAW: business*) consulta ♦ vt, vi (*US*) = **practise**; **in ~** (*in reality*) en la práctica; **out of ~** desentrenado

practise ['præktɪs] (*US* **practice**) vt (*carry out*) practicar; (*profession*) ejercer; (*train at*) practicar ♦ vi ejercer; (*train*) practicar; **practising** adj (*Christian etc*) practicante; (*lawyer*) en

ejercicio

practitioner [præk'tɪʃənə*] n (*MED*) médico/a

prairie ['prɛərɪ] n pampa

praise [preɪz] n alabanza(s) f(pl), elogio(s) m(pl) ♦ vt alabar, elogiar; **~worthy** adj loable

pram [præm] (*BRIT*) n cochecito de niño

prank [præŋk] n travesura

prawn [prɔːn] n gamba; **~ cocktail** n cóctel m de gambas

pray [preɪ] vi rezar

prayer [prɛə*] n oración f, rezo; (*entreaty*) ruego, súplica

preach [priːtʃ] vi (*also fig*) predicar; **~er** n predicador(a) m/f

precaution [prɪ'kɔːʃən] n precaución f

precede [prɪ'siːd] vt, vi preceder

precedent ['presɪdənt] n precedente m

preceding [prɪ'siːdɪŋ] adj anterior

precinct ['priːsɪŋkt] n recinto; **~s** npl contornos mpl; **pedestrian ~** (*BRIT*) zona peatonal; **shopping ~** (*BRIT*) centro comercial

precious ['preʃəs] adj precioso

precipitate [prɪ'sɪpɪteɪt] vt precipitar

precise [prɪ'saɪs] adj preciso, exacto; **~ly** adv precisamente, exactamente

precocious [prɪ'kəuʃəs] adj precoz

precondition [priːkən'dɪʃən] n condición f previa

predecessor ['priːdɪsesə*] n antecesor/a m/f

predicament [prɪ'dɪkəmənt] n apuro

predict [prɪ'dɪkt] vt pronosticar; **~able** adj previsible; **~ion** [-'dɪkʃən] n predicción f

predominantly [prɪ'dɔmɪnəntlɪ] adv en su mayoría

pre-empt [prɪː'emt] vt adelantarse a

preen [priːn] vt: **to ~ itself** (*bird*) limpiarse (las plumas); **to ~ o.s.** pavonearse

preface ['prefəs] n prefacio

prefect ['priːfekt] (*BRIT*) n (*in school*)

monitor(a) m/f
prefer [prɪˈfəː*] vt preferir; **to ~ doing** or **to do** preferir hacer; **~able** [ˈprefrəbl] adj preferible; **~ably** [ˈprefrəblɪ] adv de preferencia; **~ence** [ˈprefrəns] n preferencia; (priority) prioridad f; **~ential** [prefəˈrenʃəl] adj preferente
prefix [ˈpriːfɪks] n prefijo
pregnancy [ˈpregnənsɪ] n (of woman) embarazo; (of animal) preñez f
pregnant [ˈpregnənt] adj (woman) embarazada; (animal) preñada
prehistoric [ˈpriːhɪsˈtɔrɪk] adj prehistórico
prejudice [ˈpredʒudɪs] n prejuicio; **~d** adj (person) predispuesto
premarital [ˈpriːˈmærɪtl] adj premarital
premature [ˈpremətʃuə*] adj prematuro
premier [ˈpremɪə*] adj primero, principal ♦ n (POL) primer(a) ministro/a
première [ˈpremɪə*] n estreno
premise [ˈpremɪs] n premisa; **~s** npl (of business etc) local m; **on the ~s** en el lugar mismo
premium [ˈpriːmɪəm] n premio; (insurance) prima; **to be at a ~** ser muy solicitado; **~ bond** (BRIT) n bono del estado que participa en una lotería nacional
premonition [premǝˈnɪʃən] n presentimiento
preoccupied [priːˈɔkjupaɪd] adj ensimismado
prep [prep] n (SCOL: study) deberes m
prepaid [priːˈpeɪd] adj porte pagado
preparation [prepəˈreɪʃən] n preparación f; **~s** npl preparativos mpl
preparatory [prɪˈpærətərɪ] adj preparatorio, preliminar; **~ school** n escuela preparatoria
prepare [prɪˈpɛə*] vt preparar, disponer, (CULIN) preparar ♦ vi: **to ~ for** (action) prepararse o disponerse para; (event) hacer preparativos para; **~d to** dispuesto a; **~d for** listo para

preposition [prepəˈzɪʃən] n preposición f
preposterous [prɪˈpɔstərəs] adj absurdo, ridículo
prep school n = **preparatory school**
prerequisite [priːˈrekwɪzɪt] n requisito
Presbyterian [prezbɪˈtɪərɪən] adj, n presbiteriano/a m/f
preschool [ˈpriːˈskuːl] adj preescolar
prescribe [prɪˈskraɪb] vt (MED) recetar
prescription [prɪˈskrɪpʃən] n (MED) receta
presence [ˈprezns] n presencia; **in sb's ~** en presencia de uno; **~ of mind** aplomo
present [adj, n ˈpreznt, vb prɪˈzent] adj (in attendance) presente; (current) actual ♦ n (gift) regalo; (actuality): **the ~** la actualidad, el presente ♦ vt (introduce, describe) presentar; (expound) exponer; (give) presentar, dar, ofrecer; (THEATRE) representar; **to give sb a ~** regalar algo a uno; **at ~** actualmente; **~able** [prɪˈzentəbl] adj: **to make o.s. ~able** arreglarse; **~ation** [-ˈteɪʃən] n presentación f; (of report etc) exposición f; (formal ceremony) entrega de un regalo; **~day** adj actual; **~er** [prɪˈzentə*] n (RADIO, TV) locutor(a) m/f; **~ly** adv (soon) dentro de poco; (now) ahora
preservative [prɪˈzəːvətɪv] n conservante m
preserve [prɪˈzəːv] vt (keep safe) preservar, proteger; (maintain) mantener; (food) conservar ♦ n (for game) coto, vedado; (often pl: jam) conserva, confitura
president [ˈprezɪdənt] n presidente m/f; **~ial** [-ˈdenʃl] adj presidencial
press [pres] n (newspapers): **the P~** la prensa; (printer's) imprenta; (of button) pulsación f ♦ vt empujar; (button etc) apretar; (clothes: iron) planchar; (put pressure on: person) presionar; (insist): **to ~ sth on sb** insistir en que uno acepte algo ♦ vi (squeeze) apretar;

(*pressurize*): **to ~ for** presionar por; **we are ~ed for time/money** estamos apurados de tiempo/dinero; **~ on** vi avanzar; (*hurry*) apretar el paso; **~ agency** n agencia de prensa; **~ conference** n rueda de prensa; **~ing** adj apremiante; **~ stud** (BRIT) n botón m de presión; **~-up** (BRIT) n plancha

pressure ['prɛʃə*] n presión f; **to put ~ on sb** presionar a uno; **~ cooker** n olla a presión; **~ gauge** n manómetro; **~ group** n grupo de presión; **pressurized** (*container*) adj presurizado

prestige [prɛs'ti:ʒ] n prestigio
presumably [prɪ'zju:məblɪ] adv es de suponer que, cabe presumir que
presume [prɪ'zju:m] vi: **to ~ (that)** presumir (que), suponer (que)
pretence [prɪ'tɛns] (US **pretense**) n fingimiento; **under false ~s** con engaños
pretend [prɪ'tɛnd] vt, vi (*feign*) fingir
pretentious [prɪ'tɛnʃəs] adj presumido; (*ostentatious*) ostentoso, aparatoso
pretext ['pri:tɛkst] n pretexto
pretty ['prɪtɪ] adj bonito (SP), lindo (AM) ♦ adv bastante
prevail [prɪ'veɪl] vi (*gain mastery*) prevalecer; (*be current*) predominar; **~ing** adj (*dominant*) predominante
prevalent ['prɛvələnt] adj (*widespread*) extendido
prevent [prɪ'vɛnt] vt: **to ~ sb from doing sth** impedir a uno hacer algo; **to ~ sth from happening** evitar que ocurra algo; **~ative** adj = **preventive**; **~ive** adj preventivo
preview ['pri:vju:] n (*of film*) preestreno
previous ['pri:vɪəs] adj previo, anterior; **~ly** adv antes
prewar [pri:'wɔ:] adj de antes de la guerra
prey [preɪ] n presa ♦ vi: **to ~ on** (*feed on*) alimentarse de; **it was ~ing on**

his mind le preocupaba, le obsesionaba
price [praɪs] n precio ♦ vt (*goods*) fijar el precio de; **~less** adj que no tiene precio; **~ list** n tarifa
prick [prɪk] n (*sting*) picadura ♦ vt pinchar; (*hurt*) picar; **to ~ up one's ears** aguzar el oído
prickle ['prɪkl] n (*sensation*) picor m; (BOT) espina; **prickly** adj espinoso; (*fig: person*) enojadizo; **prickly heat** n sarpullido causado por exceso de calor
pride [praɪd] n orgullo; (*pej*) soberbia ♦ vt: **to ~ o.s. on** enorgullecerse de
priest [pri:st] n sacerdote m; **~hood** n sacerdocio
prim [prɪm] adj (*demure*) remilgado; (*prudish*) gazmoño
primarily ['praɪmərɪlɪ] adv ante todo
primary ['praɪmərɪ] adj (*first in importance*) primordial ♦ n (US: POL) (*elección f*) primaria; **~ school** (BRIT) n escuela primaria
prime [praɪm] adj primero, principal; (*excellent*) selecto, de primera clase ♦ n: **in the ~ of life** en la flor de la vida ♦ vt (*wood, fig*) preparar; **~ example** ejemplo típico; **P~ Minister** n primer(a) ministro(a)
primeval [praɪ'mi:vəl] adj primitivo
primitive ['prɪmɪtɪv] adj primitivo; (*crude*) rudimentario
primrose ['prɪmrəuz] n primavera, prímula
Primus (stove) ® ['praɪməs-] (BRIT) n hornillo de camping
prince [prɪns] n príncipe m
princess [prɪn'sɛs] n princesa
principal ['prɪnsɪpl] adj principal, mayor ♦ n director(a) m/f; **~ity** [-'pælɪtɪ] n principado
principle ['prɪnsɪpl] n principio; **in ~** en principio; **on ~** por principio
print [prɪnt] n (*foot~*) huella; (*finger~*) huella dactilar; (*letters*) letra de molde; (*fabric*) estampado; (ART) grabado; (PHOT) impresión f ♦ vt imprimir; (*cloth*)

estampar; (*write in capitals*) escribir en letras de molde; **out of ~** agotado; **~d matter** n impresos *mpl*; **~er** n (*person*) impresor(a) *m/f*; (*machine*) impresora; **~ing** n (*art*) imprenta; (*act*) impresión *f*; **~out** n (COMPUT) impresión *f*

prior ['praɪə*] *adj* anterior, previo; (*more important*) más importante; **~ to** antes de

priority [praɪ'ɒrɪtɪ] n prioridad *f*; **to have ~ (over)** tener prioridad (sobre)

prison ['prɪzn] n cárcel *f*, prisión *f* ♦ *cpd* carcelario; **~er** n (*in prison*) preso/a; (*captured person*) prisionero/a; **~er-of-war** n prisionero de guerra

privacy ['prɪvəsɪ] n intimidad *f*

private ['praɪvɪt] *adj* (*personal*) particular; (*property, industry, discussion etc*) privado; (*person*) reservado; (*place*) tranquilo ♦ n soldado raso; **"~"** (*on envelope*) "confidencial"; (*on door*) "prohibido el paso"; **in ~** en privado; **~ enterprise** n empresa privada; **~ eye** n detective *m/f* privado/a; **~ property** n propiedad *f* privada; **~ school** n colegio particular

privet ['prɪvɪt] n alheña

privilege ['prɪvɪlɪdʒ] n privilegio; (*prerogative*) prerrogativa

privy ['prɪvɪ] *adj*: **to be ~ to** estar enterado de

prize [praɪz] n premio ♦ *adj* de primera clase ♦ *vt* apreciar, estimar; **~-giving** n distribución *f* de premios; **~winner** n premiado/a

pro [prəʊ] n (SPORT) profesional *m/f* ♦ *prep* a favor de; **the ~s and cons** los pros y los contras

probability [prɒbə'bɪlɪtɪ] n probabilidad *f*; **in all ~** con toda probabilidad

probable ['prɒbəbl] *adj* probable

probably ['prɒbəblɪ] *adv* probablemente

probation [prə'beɪʃən] n: **on ~** (*employee*) a prueba; (LAW) en libertad condicional

probe [prəʊb] n (MED, SPACE) sonda; (*enquiry*) encuesta, investigación *f* ♦ *vt* sondar; (*investigate*) investigar

problem ['prɒbləm] n problema *m*

procedure [prə'siːdʒə*] n procedimiento; (*bureaucratic*) trámites *mpl*

proceed [prə'siːd] vi (*do afterwards*): **to ~ to do sth** proceder a hacer algo; (*continue*): **to ~ (with)** continuar or seguir (con); **~ings** npl acto(s) (*pl*); (LAW) proceso; **~s** ['prəʊsiːdz] npl (*money*) ganancias *fpl*, ingresos *mpl*

process ['prəʊses] n proceso ♦ *vt* tratar, elaborar; **~ing** n tratamiento, elaboración *f*; (PHOT) revelado

procession [prə'seʃən] n desfile *m*; **funeral ~** cortejo fúnebre

pro-choice [prəʊ'tʃɔɪs] *adj* en favor del derecho a elegir de la madre

proclaim [prə'kleɪm] *vt* (*announce*) anunciar

procrastinate [prəʊ'kræstɪneɪt] vi demorarse

procure [prə'kjʊə*] *vt* conseguir

prod [prɒd] *vt* empujar ♦ n empujón *m*

prodigy ['prɒdɪdʒɪ] n prodigio

produce [n 'prɒdjuːs, vt prə'djuːs] (AGR) productos *mpl* agrícolas ♦ *vt* producir; (*play, film, programme*) presentar; **~r** n productor(a) *m/f*; (*of film, programme*) director(a) *m/f*; (*of record*) productor(a) *m/f*

product ['prɒdʌkt] n producto

production [prə'dʌkʃən] n producción *f*; (THEATRE) presentación *f*; **~ line** n línea de producción

productivity [prɒdʌk'tɪvɪtɪ] n productividad *f*

profession [prə'feʃən] n profesión *f*; **~al** *adj* profesional ♦ n profesional *m/f*; (*skilled person*) perito

professor [prə'fesə*] n catedrático/a; (US, Canada) profesor(a) *m/f*

proficient [prə'fɪʃənt] *adj* experto,

hábil

profile ['prəufaɪl] n perfil m

profit ['prɒfɪt] n (COMM) ganancia ♦ vi: **to ~ by** or **from** aprovechar or sacar provecho de; **~ability** [-ə'bɪlɪtɪ] n rentabilidad f; **~able** adj (ECON) rentable

profound [prə'faund] adj profundo

profusely [prə'fju:slɪ] adv profusamente

programme ['prəugræm] (US **program**) n programa m ♦ vt programar; **~r** (US **programer**) n programador(a) m/f; **programming** (US **programing**) n programación f

progress [n 'prəugres, vi prə'gres] n progreso, (development) desarrollo m ♦ vi progresar, avanzar; **in ~** en curso; **~ive** [-'gresɪv] adj progresivo; (person) progresista

prohibit [prə'hɪbɪt] vt prohibir; **to ~ sb from doing sth** prohibir a uno hacer algo; **~ion** [-'bɪʃən] n prohibición f; (US): **P~ion** Ley f Seca

project [n 'prɒdʒekt, vb prə'dʒekt] n proyecto ♦ vt proyectar ♦ vi (stick out) salir, sobresalir; **~ion** [prə'dʒekʃən] n proyección f; (overhang) saliente m; **~or** [prə'dʒektə*] n proyector m

pro-life [prəu'laɪf] adj pro-vida

prolong [prə'lɒŋ] vt prolongar, extender

prom [prɒm] n abbr = **promenade**; (US: ball) baile m de gala

---

Prom

El ciclo de conciertos de música clásica más conocido de Londres es el llamado los **Proms** (promenade concerts), que se celebra anualmente en el Royal Albert Hall. Su nombre se debe a que originalmente el público paseaba durante las actuaciones, costumbre que en la actualidad se mantiene de forma simbólica, permitiendo que parte de los asistentes permanezcan de pie. En Estados Unidos se llama **prom** a un baile de gala en un centro de educación secundaria o universitaria.

---

promenade [prɒmə'nɑːd] n (by sea) paseo marítimo; **~ concert** (BRIT) n concierto (en que parte del público permanece de pie)

prominence ['prɒmɪnəns] n importancia

prominent ['prɒmɪnənt] adj (standing out) saliente; (important) eminente, importante

promiscuous [prə'mɪskjuəs] adj (sexually) promiscuo

promise ['prɒmɪs] n promesa ♦ vt, vi prometer; **promising** adj prometedor(a)

promote [prə'məut] vt (employee) ascender; (product, pop star) hacer propaganda por; (ideas) fomentar; **~r** n (of event) promotor/a m/f; (of cause etc) impulsor(a) m/f; **promotion** [-'məuʃən] n (advertising campaign) campaña de promoción f; (in rank) ascenso

prompt [prɒmpt] adj rápido ♦ adv: **at 6 o'clock ~** a las seis en punto ♦ n (COMPUT) aviso ♦ vt (urge) mover, incitar; (when talking) instar; (THEATRE) apuntar; **to ~ sb to do sth** instar a uno a hacer algo; **~ly** adv rápidamente; (exactly) puntualmente

prone [prəun] adj (lying) postrado; **~ to** propenso a

prong [prɒŋ] n diente m, punta

pronoun ['prəunaun] n pronombre m

pronounce [prə'nauns] vt pronunciar; **~d** adj (marked) marcado

pronunciation [prənʌnsɪ'eɪʃən] n pronunciación f

proof [pru:f] n prueba ♦ adj: **~ against** a prueba de

prop [prɒp] n apoyo, (fig) sostén m ♦ vt (also: ~ up) apoyar; (lean): **to ~ sth against** apoyar algo contra

propaganda [prɒpə'gændə] n

propaganda

propel [prə'pɛl] vt impulsar, propulsar; **~ler** n hélice f

propensity [prə'pɛnsɪtɪ] n propensión f

proper ['prɒpə*] adj (suited, right) propio; (exact) justo; (seemly) correcto, decente; (authentic) verdadero; (referring to place): **the village ~ el** pueblo mismo; **~ly** adv (adequately) correctamente; (decently) decentemente; **~ noun** n nombre m propio

property ['prɒpətɪ] n propiedad f; (personal) bienes mpl muebles; **~ owner** n dueño/a de propiedades

prophecy ['prɒfɪsɪ] n profecía

prophesy ['prɒfɪsaɪ] vt (fig) predecir

prophet ['prɒfɪt] n profeta m

proportion [prə'pɔːʃən] n proporción f; (share) parte f; **~al** adj: **~al (to)** en proporción (con); **~al representation** n representación f proporcional; **~ate** adj: **~ate (to)** en proporción (con)

proposal [prə'pəuzl] n (offer of marriage) oferta de matrimonio; (plan) proyecto

propose [prə'pəuz] vt proponer ♦ vi declararse; **to ~ to do** tener intención de hacer

proposition [prɒpə'zɪʃən] n propuesta

proprietor [prə'praɪətə*] n propietario/a, dueño/a

propriety [prə'praɪətɪ] n decoro

pro rata ['rɑːtə] adv a prorrateo

prose [prəuz] n prosa

prosecute ['prɒsɪkjuːt] vt (LAW) procesar; **prosecution** [-'kjuːʃən] n proceso, causa; (accusing side) acusación f; **prosecutor** n acusador(a) m/f; (also: public prosecutor) fiscal m

prospect [n 'prɒspɛkt, vb prə'spɛkt] n (possibility) posibilidad f; (outlook) perspectiva f vi: **to ~ for** buscar; **~s** npl (for work etc) perspectivas fpl; **~ing** n prospección f; **~ive** [prə'spɛktɪv] adj futuro

prospectus [prə'spɛktəs] n prospecto

prosper ['prɒspə*] vi prosperar; **~ity** [-'spɛrɪtɪ] n prosperidad f; **~ous** adj próspero

prostitute ['prɒstɪtjuːt] n prostituta; (male) hombre que se dedica a la prostitución

protect [prə'tɛkt] vt proteger; **~ion** [-'tɛkʃən] n protección f; **~ive** adj protector(a)

protein ['prəutiːn] n proteína

protest [n 'prəutɛst, vb prə'tɛst] n protesta ♦ vi: **to ~ about** or **at/ against** protestar de/contra ♦ vt (insist): **to ~ (that)** insistir en (que)

Protestant ['prɒtɪstənt] adj, n protestante m/f

protester [prə'tɛstə*] n manifestante m/f

protracted [prə'træktɪd] adj prolongado

protrude [prə'truːd] vi salir, sobresalir

proud [praud] adj orgulloso; (pej) soberbio, altanero

prove [pruːv] vt probar; (show) demostrar ♦ vi: **to ~ (to be) correct** resultar correcto; **to ~ o.s.** probar su valía

proverb ['prɒvɜːb] n refrán m

provide [prə'vaɪd] vt proporcionar, dar; **to ~ sb with sth** proveer a uno de algo; **~d (that)** conj con tal de que, a condición de que; **~ for** vt fus (person) mantener a; (problem etc) tener en cuenta; **providing** [prə'vaɪdɪŋ] conj: a condición de que, con tal de que

province ['prɒvɪns] n provincia; (fig) esfera; **provincial** [prə'vɪnʃəl] adj provincial; (pej) provinciano

provision [prə'vɪʒən] n (supplying) suministro, abastecimiento; (of contract etc) disposición f; **~s** npl (food) comestibles mpl; **~al** adj provisional

proviso [prə'vaɪzəu] n condición f, estipulación f

provocative [prə'vɔkətɪv] adj

provoke   510   pull

provocativo

provoke [prə'vəʊk] vt (*cause*) provocar, incitar; (*anger*) enojar

prowess ['praʊɪs] n destreza

prowl [praʊl] vi (*also: ~ about, ~ around*) merodear ♦ n: **on the ~** de merodeo; **~er** n merodeador(a) m/f

proxy ['prɒksɪ] n: **by ~** por poderes

prudent ['pruːdənt] adj prudente

prune [pruːn] n ciruela pasa ♦ vt podar

pry [praɪ] vi: **to ~ (into)** entrometerse (en)

PS n abbr (= *postscript*) P.D.

psalm [sɑːm] n salmo

pseudonym ['sjuːdənɪm] n seudónimo

psyche ['saɪkɪ] n psique f

psychiatric [saɪkɪ'ætrɪk] adj psiquiátrico

psychiatrist [saɪ'kaɪətrɪst] n psiquiatra m/f

psychic ['saɪkɪk] adj (*also: ~al*) psíquico

psychoanalyse [saɪkəʊ'ænəlaɪz] vt psicoanalizar; **psychoanalysis** [-ə'næləsɪs] n psicoanálisis m inv

psychological [saɪkə'lɒdʒɪkl] adj psicológico

psychologist [saɪ'kɒlədʒɪst] n psicólogo/a

psychology [saɪ'kɒlədʒɪ] n psicología

PTO abbr (= *please turn over*) sigue

pub [pʌb] n abbr (= *public house*) pub m, bar m

---

puberty ['pjuːbətɪ] n pubertad f

public ['pʌblɪk] adj público ♦ n: **the ~** el público; **in ~** en público; **to make ~** hacer público; **~ address system** n megafonía

publican ['pʌblɪkən] n tabernero/a

publication [pʌblɪ'keɪʃən] n publicación f

public: **~ company** n sociedad f anónima; **~ convenience** n aseos mpl públicos (SP), sanitarios mpl (AM); **~ holiday** n día de fiesta (SP), (día) feriado (AM); **~ house** (BRIT) n bar m, pub m

publicity [pʌb'lɪsɪtɪ] n publicidad f

publicize ['pʌblɪsaɪz] vt publicitar

publicly ['pʌblɪklɪ] adv públicamente, en público

public: **~ opinion** n opinión f pública; **~ relations** n relaciones fpl públicas; **~ school** (BRIT) n escuela privada; (US) instituto; **~-spirited** adj que tiene sentido del deber ciudadano; **~ transport** n transporte m público

publish ['pʌblɪʃ] vt publicar; **~er** n (*person*) editor(a) m/f; (*firm*) editorial f; **~ing** n (*industry*) industria del libro

pub lunch n almuerzo que se sirve en un pub; **to go for a ~** almorzar o comer en un pub

pucker ['pʌkə*] vt (*pleat*) arrugar; (*brow etc*) fruncir

pudding ['pʊdɪŋ] n pudín m; (BRIT: *dessert*) postre m; **black ~** morcilla

puddle ['pʌdl] n charco

puff [pʌf] n soplo; (*of smoke, air*) bocanada; (*of breathing*) resoplido ♦ vt: **to ~ one's pipe** chupar la pipa ♦ vi (*pant*) jadear; **~ out** vt hinchar; **~ pastry** n hojaldre m; **~y** adj hinchado

pull [pʊl] n (*tug*): **to give sth a ~** dar un tirón a algo ♦ vt (*press: trigger*) apretar; (*haul*) tirar, arrastrar; (*close: curtain*) echar ♦ vi tirar; **to ~ to pieces** hacer pedazos; **to not ~ one's**

punches no andarse con bromas; **to ~ one's weight** hacer su parte; **to ~ o.s. together** sobreponerse; **to ~ sb's leg** tomar el pelo a uno; **~ apart** vt (break) romper; **~ down** vt (building) derribar; **~ in** vi (car etc) parar (junto a la acera); (train) llegar a la estación; **~ off** vi (MED etc) cerrar; **~ out** vi (car, train etc) salir ♦ vt sacar, arrancar; **~ over** vi (AUT) hacerse a un lado; **~ through** vi (MED) reponerse; **~ up** vi (stop) parar ♦ vt (raise) levantar; (uproot) arrancar, desarraigar

pulley ['puli] n polea

pullover ['puləʊvə*] n jersey m, suéter m

pulp [pʌlp] n (of fruit) pulpa

pulpit ['pulpit] n púlpito

pulsate [pʌl'seɪt] vi pulsar, latir

pulse [pʌls] n (ANAT) pulso; (rhythm) pulsación f; (BOT) legumbre f

pump [pʌmp] n bomba; (shoe) zapatilla ♦ vt sacar con una bomba; **~ up** vt inflar

pumpkin ['pʌmpkɪn] n calabaza

pun [pʌn] n juego de palabras

punch [pʌntʃ] n (blow) golpe m, puñetazo; (tool) punzón m; (drink) ponche m ♦ vt (hit): **to ~ sb/sth** dar un puñetazo a o golpear a uno/algo; **~line** n palabras que rematan un chiste; **~-up** n (BRIT: inf) riña

punctual ['pʌŋktjuəl] adj puntual

punctuation [pʌŋktju'eɪʃən] n puntuación f

puncture ['pʌŋktʃə*] (BRIT) n pinchazo ♦ vt pinchar

pungent ['pʌndʒənt] adj acre

punish ['pʌnɪʃ] vt castigar; **~ment** n castigo

punk [pʌŋk] n (also: ~ rocker) punki m/f; (also: ~ rock) música punk; (US: inf: hoodlum) rufián m

punt [pʌnt] n (boat) batea

punter ['pʌntə*] (BRIT) n (gambler) jugador(a) m/f; (inf) cliente m/f

puny ['pjuːnɪ] adj débil

pup [pʌp] n cachorro

pupil ['pjuːpl] n alumno/a; (of eye) pupila

puppet ['pʌpɪt] n títere m

puppy ['pʌpɪ] n cachorro, perrito

purchase ['pəːtʃɪs] n compra ♦ vt comprar; **~r** n comprador(a) m/f

pure [pjuə*] adj puro

purée ['pjuəreɪ] n puré m

purely ['pjuəlɪ] adv puramente

purge [pəːdʒ] n (MED, POL) purga ♦ vt purgar

purify ['pjuərɪfaɪ] vt purificar, depurar

purple ['pəːpl] adj purpúreo; morado

purpose ['pəːpəs] n propósito; **on ~** a propósito, adrede; **~ful** adj resuelto, determinado

purr [pəː*] vi ronronear

purse [pəːs] n monedero; (US) bolsa (SP), cartera (AM) ♦ vt fruncir

pursue [pə'sjuː] vt seguir; **~r** n perseguidor(a) m/f

pursuit [pə'sjuːt] n (chase) caza; (occupation) actividad f

push [puʃ] n empuje m, empujón m; (of button) presión f; (drive) empuje m ♦ vt empujar; (button) apretar; (promote) promover ♦ vi empujar; (demand): **to ~ for** luchar por; **~ aside** vt apartar con la mano; **~ off** vi (inf) largarse; **~ on** vi seguir adelante; **~ through** vi (crowd) abrirse paso a empujones ♦ vt (measure) despachar; **~ up** vt (total, prices) hacer subir; **~chair** (BRIT) n sillita de ruedas; **~er** n (drug ~er) traficante m/f de drogas; **~over** (inf) n: **it's a ~over** está tirado; **~-up** (US) n plancha; **~y** (pej) adj agresivo

puss [pus] (inf) n minino

pussy(-cat) ['pusɪ-] (inf) n = **puss**

put [put] (pt, pp **put**) vt (place) poner, colocar; (~ into) meter; (say) expresar; (a question) hacer; (estimate) estimar; **~ about** o **around** vt (rumour) diseminar; **~ across** vt (ideas etc) comunicar; **~ away** vt (store) guardar;

~ back vt (replace) devolver a su lugar; (postpone) aplazar; **~ by** vt (money) guardar; **~ down** vt (on ground) poner en el suelo; (animal) sacrificar; (in writing) apuntar; (revolt etc) sofocar; (attribute): **to ~ sth down to** atribuir algo a; **~ forward** vt (ideas) presentar, proponer; **~ in** vt (complaint) presentar; (time) dedicar; **~ off** vt (postpone) aplazar; (discourage) desanimar; **~ on** vt ponerse; (light etc) encender; (play etc) presentar; (gain): **to ~ on weight** engordar; (brake) echar; (record, kettle etc) poner; (assume) adoptar; **~ out** vt (fire, light) apagar; (rubbish etc) sacar; (cat etc) echar; (one's hand) alargar; (inf: person): **to be ~ out** alterarse; **~ through** vt (TEL) poner; (plan etc) hacer aprobar; **~ up** vt (raise) levantar, alzar; (hang) colgar; (build) construir; (increase) aumentar; (accommodate) alojar; **~ up with** vt fus aguantar

putt [pʌt] n putt m, golpe m corto; **~ing green** n green m; minigolf m

putty ['pʌtɪ] n masilla

put-up ['pʊtʌp] adj: **~ job** (BRIT) amaño

puzzle ['pʌzl] n rompecabezas m inv; (also: crossword ~) crucigrama m; (mystery) misterio ♦ vt dejar perplejo, confundir ♦ vi: **to ~ over sth** devanarse los sesos con algo; **puzzling** adj misterioso, extraño

pyjamas [pɪ'dʒɑːməz] (BRIT) npl pijama m

pylon ['paɪlən] n torre f de conducción eléctrica

pyramid ['pɪrəmɪd] n pirámide f

Pyrenees [pɪrə'niːz] npl: **the ~** los Pirineos

python ['paɪθən] n pitón m

Q, q

quack [kwæk] n graznido; (pej: doctor) curandero/a

quad [kwɒd] n abbr = **quadrangle**; **quadruplet**

quadrangle ['kwɒdræŋgl] n patio

quadruple [kwɒ'druːpl] vt, vi cuadruplicar

quadruplets [kwɒ'druːplɪts] npl cuatrillizos/as

quail [kweɪl] n codorniz f ♦ vi: **to ~ at** or **before** amedrentarse ante

quaint [kweɪnt] adj extraño; (picturesque) pintoresco

quake [kweɪk] vi temblar ♦ n abbr = **earthquake**

Quaker ['kweɪkə*] n cuáquero/a

qualification [kwɒlɪfɪ'keɪʃən] n (ability) capacidad f; (often pl: diploma etc) título; (reservation) salvedad f

qualified ['kwɒlɪfaɪd] adj capacitado; (professionally) titulado; (limited) limitado

qualify ['kwɒlɪfaɪ] vt (make competent) capacitar; (modify) modificar ♦ vi (in competition): **to ~ (for)** calificarse (para); (pass examination): **to ~ (as)** calificarse, graduarse (en); (be eligible): **to ~ (for)** reunir los requisitos (para)

quality ['kwɒlɪtɪ] n calidad f; (of person) cualidad f; **~ time** n tiempo dedicado a la familia y a los amigos

quality press

La expresión **quality press** se refiere a los periódicos que dan un tratamiento serio de las noticias, ofreciendo información detallada sobre un amplio espectro de temas y un análisis en profundidad de la actualidad. Por su tamaño, considerablemente mayor que el de los *periódicos sensacionalistas, se les conoce también como "broadsheets".*

qualm [kwɑːm] n escrúpulo

quandary ['kwɒndrɪ] n: **to be in a ~** tener dudas

quantity ['kwɒntɪtɪ] n cantidad f; **in ~** en grandes cantidades; **~ surveyor** n aparejador(a) m/f

quarantine ['kwɒrəntiːn] n cuarentena

quarrel ['kwɒrəl] n riña, pelea ♦ vi reñir, pelearse

quarry ['kwɒrɪ] n cantera

quart [kwɔːt] n ≈ litro

quarter ['kwɔːtə*] n cuarto, cuarta parte f; (US: coin) moneda de 25 centavos; (of year) trimestre m; (district) barrio ♦ vt dividir en cuartos; (MIL: lodge) alojar; **~s** npl (barracks) cuartel m; (living ~s) alojamiento; **a ~ of an hour** un cuarto de hora; **~ final** n cuarto de final; **~ly** adj trimestral ♦ adv cada 3 meses, trimestralmente

quartet(te) [kwɔːˈtet] n cuarteto

quartz [kwɔːts] n cuarzo

quash [kwɒʃ] vt (verdict) anular

quaver ['kweɪvə*] (BRIT) n (MUS) corchea ♦ vi temblar

quay [kiː] n (also: **~side**) muelle m

queasy ['kwiːzɪ] adj: **to feel ~** tener náuseas

queen [kwiːn] n reina; (CARDS etc) dama; **~ mother** n reina madre

queer [kwɪə*] adj raro, extraño ♦ n (inf: highly offensive) maricón m

quell [kwel] vt (feeling) calmar; (rebellion etc) sofocar

quench [kwentʃ] vt: **to ~ one's thirst** apagar la sed

query ['kwɪərɪ] n (question) pregunta ♦ vt dudar de

quest [kwest] n busca, búsqueda

question ['kwestʃən] n pregunta; (doubt) duda; (matter) asunto, cuestión f ♦ vt (doubt) dudar de; (interrogate) interrogar, hacer preguntas a; **beyond ~** fuera de toda duda; **out of the ~**

imposible; ni hablar; **~able** adj dudoso; **~ mark** n punto de interrogación; **~naire** [-ˈnɛə*] n cuestionario

queue [kjuː] (BRIT) n cola ♦ vi (also: **~ up**) hacer cola

quibble ['kwɪbl] vi sutilizar

quick [kwɪk] adj rápido; (agile) ágil; (mind) listo ♦ n: **cut to the ~** (fig) herido en lo vivo; **be ~!** ¡date prisa!; **~en** vt apresurar ♦ vi apresurarse, darse prisa; **~ly** adv rápidamente, de prisa; **~sand** n arenas fpl movedizas; **~-witted** adj perspicaz

quid [kwɪd] (BRIT: inf) n inv libra

quiet ['kwaɪət] adj (voice, music etc) bajo; (person, place) tranquilo; (ceremony) íntimo ♦ n silencio; (calm) tranquilidad f ♦ vt, vi (US) = **~en**; **~en** (also: **~en down**) vi calmarse; (grow silent) callarse ♦ vt calmar, hacer callar; **~ly** adv tranquilamente, (silently) silenciosamente; **~ness** n silencio; tranquilidad f

quilt [kwɪlt] n edredón ♦ vt

quin [kwɪn] n abbr = **quintuplet**

quintet(te) [kwɪnˈtet] n quinteto

quintuplets [kwɪnˈtjuːplɪts] npl quintillizos/as

quip [kwɪp] n pulla

quit [kwɪt] (pt, pp **quit** or **quitted**) vt dejar, abandonar; (premises) desocupar ♦ vi (give up) renunciar; (resign) dimitir

quite [kwaɪt] adv (rather) bastante; (entirely) completamente; **that's not ~ big enough** no acaba de ser lo bastante grande; **~ a few of them** un buen número de ellos; **~ (so)!** ¡así es!, ¡exactamente!

quits [kwɪts] adj: **~ (with)** en paz (con); **let's call it ~** dejémoslo en tablas

quiver ['kwɪvə*] vi estremecerse

quiz [kwɪz] n concurso ♦ vt interrogar; **~zical** adj burlón(ona)

quota ['kwəʊtə] *n* cuota

quotation [kwəʊ'teɪʃən] *n* cita; (*estimate*) presupuesto; **~ marks** *npl* comillas *fpl*

quote [kwəʊt] *n* cita; (*estimate*) presupuesto ♦ *vt* citar; (*price*) cotizar ♦ *vi*: **to ~ from** citar de; **~s** *npl* (*inverted commas*) comillas *fpl*

R, r

rabbi ['ræbaɪ] *n* rabino

rabbit ['ræbɪt] *n* conejo; **~ hutch** *n* conejera

rabble ['ræbl] (*pej*) *n* chusma, populacho

rabies ['reɪbiːz] *n* rabia

RAC (*BRIT*) *n abbr* = **Royal Automobile Club**

rac(c)oon [rə'kuːn] *n* mapache *m*

race [reɪs] *n* carrera; (*species*) raza ♦ *vt* (*horse*) hacer correr; (*engine*) acelerar ♦ *vi* (*compete*) competir; (*run*) correr; (*pulse*) latir a ritmo acelerado; **~ car** (*US*) *n* = **racing car**; **~ car driver** (*US*) *n* = **racing driver**; **~course** *n* hipódromo; **~horse** *n* caballo de carreras; **~track** *n* pista; (*for cars*) autódromo

racial ['reɪʃl] *adj* racial

racing ['reɪsɪŋ] *n* carreras *fpl*; **~ car** (*BRIT*) *n* coche *m* de carreras; **~ driver** (*BRIT*) *n* corredor(a) *m/f* de coches

racism ['reɪsɪzəm] *n* racismo; **racist** [-sɪst] *adj, n* racista *m/f*

rack [ræk] *n* (*also*: *luggage* ~) rejilla; (*shelf*) estante *m*; (*also*: *roof* ~) baca, portaequipajes *m inv*; (*dish* ~) escurreplatos *m inv*; (*clothes* ~) percha ♦ *vt* atormentar; **to ~ one's brains** devanarse los sesos

racket ['rækɪt] *n* (*for tennis*) raqueta; (*noise*) ruido, estrépito; (*swindle*) estafa, timo

racquet ['rækɪt] *n* raqueta

racy ['reɪsɪ] *adj* picante, salado

radar ['reɪdɑː*] *n* radar *m*

radiant ['reɪdɪənt] *adj* radiante (de felicidad)

radiate ['reɪdɪeɪt] *vt* (*heat*) radiar; (*emotion*) irradiar ♦ *vi* (*lines*) extenderse

radiation [reɪdɪ'eɪʃən] *n* radiación *f*

radiator ['reɪdɪeɪtə*] *n* radiador *m*

radical ['rædɪkl] *adj* radical

radii ['reɪdɪaɪ] *npl of* **radius**

radio ['reɪdɪəʊ] *n* radio *f*; **on the ~** por radio

radio... [reɪdɪəʊ] *prefix*: **~active** *adj* radioactivo; **~graphy** [reɪdɪ'ɔgrəfɪ] *n* radiografía; **~logy** [reɪdɪ'ɔlədʒɪ] *n* radiología

radio station *n* emisora

radiotherapy [-'θerəpɪ] *n* radioterapia

radish ['rædɪʃ] *n* rábano

radius ['reɪdɪəs] (*pl* **radii**) *n* radio

RAF *n abbr* = **Royal Air Force**

raffle ['ræfl] *n* rifa, sorteo

raft [rɑːft] *n* balsa; (*also*: *life* ~) balsa salvavidas

rafter ['rɑːftə*] *n* viga

rag [ræg] *n* (*piece of cloth*) trapo; (*torn cloth*) harapo; (*pej*: *newspaper*) periodicucho; (*for charity*) actividades estudiantiles benéficas; **~s** *npl* (*torn clothes*) harapos *mpl*; **~ doll** *n* muñeca de trapo

rage [reɪdʒ] *n* rabia, furor *m* ♦ *vi* (*person*) rabiar, estar furioso; (*storm*) bramar; **it's all the ~** (*very fashionable*) está muy de moda

ragged ['rægɪd] *adj* (*edge*) desigual, mellado; (*appearance*) andrajoso, harapiento

raid [reɪd] *n* (*MIL*) incursión *f*; (*criminal*) asalto; (*by police*) redada ♦ *vt* invadir, atacar; asaltar

rail [reɪl] *n* (*on stair*) barandilla, pasamanos *m inv*; (*on bridge, balcony*) pretil *m*; (*of ship*) barandilla; (*also*: *towel* ~) toallero; **~s** *npl* (*RAIL*) vía; **by ~** por ferrocarril; **~ing(s)** *n(pl)* vallado; **~road** (*US*) *n* = **~way**; **~way** (*BRIT*) *n* ferrocarril *m*, vía férrea; **~way line**

(BRIT) n línea (de ferrocarril);
~wayman (BRIT irreg) n ferroviario;
~way station (BRIT) n estación f de
ferrocarril

rain [reɪn] n lluvia ♦ vi llover; **in the ~**
bajo la lluvia; **it's ~ing** llueve, está
lloviendo; **~bow** n arco iris; **~coat** n
impermeable m; **~drop** n gota de
lluvia; **~fall** n lluvia; **~forest** n selvas
fpl tropicales; **~y** adj lluvioso

raise [reɪz] n aumento ♦ vt levantar;
(increase) aumentar; (improve: morale)
subir; (: standards) mejorar; (doubts)
suscitar; (a question) plantear; (cattle,
family) criar; (crop) cultivar; (army)
reclutar; (loan) obtener; **to ~ one's
voice** alzar la voz

raisin ['reɪzn] n pasa de Corinto

rake [reɪk] n (tool) rastrillo; (person)
libertino ♦ vt (garden) rastrillar

rally ['rælɪ] n (POL etc) reunión f, mitin
m; (AUT) rallye m; (TENNIS) peloteo ♦ vt
reunir ♦ vi recuperarse; **~ round** vt fus
(fig) dar apoyo a

RAM [ræm] n abbr (= random access
memory) RAM f

ram [ræm] n carnero; (also: battering ~)
ariete m ♦ vt (crash into) dar contra,
chocar con; (push: fist etc) empujar con
fuerza

ramble ['ræmbl] n caminata, excursión
f en el campo ♦ vi (pej: also: ~ on)
divagar; **~r** n excursionista m/f; (BOT)
trepadora; **rambling** adj (speech)
inconexo; (house) laberíntico; (BOT)
trepador(a)

ramp [ræmp] n rampa; **on/off ~** (US:
AUT) vía de acceso/salida

rampage [ræm'peɪdʒ] n: **to be on
the ~** desmandarse ♦ vi: **they went
rampaging through the town**
recorrieron la ciudad armando alboroto

rampant ['ræmpənt] adj (disease etc):
to be ~ estar extendiéndose mucho

ram raid vt atracar (rompiendo el
escaparate con un coche)

ramshackle ['ræmʃækl] adj
destartalado

ran [ræn] pt of **run**

ranch [rɑːntʃ] n hacienda, estancia;
~er n ganadero

rancid ['rænsɪd] adj rancio

rancour ['ræŋkə*] (US rancor) n rencor
m

random ['rændəm] adj fortuito, sin
orden; (COMPUT, MATH) aleatorio ♦ n:
at ~ al azar

randy ['rændɪ] (BRIT: inf) adj cachondo

rang [ræŋ] pt of **ring**

range [reɪndʒ] n (of mountains) cadena
de montañas, cordillera; (of missile)
alcance m; (of voice) registro; (series)
serie f; (of products) surtido; (MIL: also:
shooting ~) campo de tiro; (also:
kitchen ~) fogón m ♦ vt (place) colocar;
(arrange) arreglar ♦ vi: **to ~ over**
(extend) extenderse por; **to ~ from ...
to ...** oscilar entre ... y ...

ranger [reɪndʒə*] n guardabosques m
inv

rank [ræŋk] n (row) fila; (MIL) rango;
(status) categoría; (BRIT: also: taxi ~)
parada de taxis ♦ vi: **to ~ among**
figurar entre ♦ adj fétido, rancio; **the
~ and file** (fig) la base

ransack ['rænsæk] vt (search) registrar;
(plunder) saquear

ransom ['rænsəm] n rescate m; **to
hold to ~** (fig) hacer chantaje a

rant [rænt] vi divagar, desvariar

rap [ræp] vt golpear, dar un golpecito
en ♦ n (music) rap m

rape [reɪp] n violación f; (BOT) colza
♦ vt violar; **~ (seed) oil** n aceite m de
colza

rapid ['ræpɪd] adj rápido; **~ity**
[rə'pɪdɪtɪ] n rapidez f; **~s** npl (GEO)
rápidos mpl

rapist ['reɪpɪst] n violador m

rapport [ræ'pɔː*] n simpatía

rapturous ['ræptʃərəs] adj extático

rare [reə*] adj raro, poco común;
(CULIN: steak) poco hecho

rarely ['reəlɪ] adv pocas veces

raring ['reərɪŋ] adj: **to be ~ to go** (inf) tener muchas ganas de empezar

rascal ['rɑːskl] n pillo, pícaro

rash [ræʃ] adj imprudente, precipitado ♦ n (MED) sarpullido, erupción f (cutánea); (of events) serie f

rasher ['ræʃə*] n lonja

raspberry ['rɑːzbərɪ] n frambuesa

rasping ['rɑːspɪŋ] adj: **a ~ noise** un ruido áspero

rat [ræt] n rata

rate [reɪt] n razón f; (price) precio; (: of hotel etc) tarifa; (of interest) tipo; (speed) velocidad f ♦ vt (value) tasar; (estimate) estimar; **~s** npl (BRIT: property tax) impuesto municipal; (fees) tarifa; **to ~ sth/sb as** considerar algo/a uno como; **~able value** (BRIT) n valor m impuesto; **~payer** (BRIT) n contribuyente m/f

rather ['rɑːðə*] adv: **it's ~ expensive** es algo caro; (too much) es demasiado caro; (to some extent) más bien; **there's ~ a lot** hay bastante; **I would** or **I'd ~ go** preferiría ir; **or ~** mejor dicho

rating ['reɪtɪŋ] n tasación f; (score) índice m; (of ship) clase f; **~s** npl (RADIO, TV) niveles mpl de audiencia

ratio ['reɪʃɪəʊ] n razón f; **in the ~ of 100 to 1** a razón de 100 a 1

ration ['ræʃən] n ración f ♦ vt racionar; **~s** npl víveres mpl

rational ['ræʃənl] adj (solution, reasoning) lógico, razonable; (person) cuerdo, sensato; **~e** [-'nɑːl] n razón f fundamental; **~ize** vt justificar

rat race n lucha incesante por la supervivencia

rattle ['rætl] n golpeteo; (of train etc) traqueteo; (for baby) sonaja, sonajero ♦ vi castañetear; (car, bus): **to ~ along** traquetear ♦ vt hacer sonar agitando; **~snake** n serpiente f de cascabel

raucous ['rɔːkəs] adj estridente, ronco

ravage ['rævɪdʒ] vt hacer estragos en, destrozar; **~s** npl estragos mpl

rave [reɪv] vi (in anger) encolerizarse; (with enthusiasm) entusiasmarse; (MED) delirar, desvariar ♦ n (inf: party) rave m

raven ['reɪvən] n cuervo

ravenous ['rævənəs] adj hambriento

ravine [rə'viːn] n barranco

raving ['reɪvɪŋ] adj: **~ lunatic** loco/a de atar

ravishing ['rævɪʃɪŋ] adj encantador(a)

raw [rɔː] adj crudo; (not processed) bruto; (sore) vivo; (inexperienced) novato, inexperto; **~ deal** (inf) n injusticia; **~ material** n materia prima

ray [reɪ] n rayo; **~ of hope** (rayo de) esperanza

raze [reɪz] vt arrasar

razor ['reɪzə*] n (open) navaja; (safety ~) máquina de afeitar; (electric ~) máquina (eléctrica) de afeitar; **~ blade** n hoja de afeitar

Rd abbr = **road**

re [riː] prep con referencia a

reach [riːtʃ] n alcance m; (of river etc) extensión f entre dos recodos ♦ vt alcanzar, llegar a; (achieve) lograr ♦ vi extenderse; **within ~** al alcance (de la mano); **out of ~** fuera del alcance; **~ out** vt (hand) tender ♦ vi: **to ~ out for sth** alargar o tender la mano para tomar algo

react [riː'ækt] vi reaccionar; **~ion** [-'ækʃən] n reacción f

reactor [riː'æktə*] n (also: nuclear ~) reactor m (nuclear)

read [riːd, pt, pp red] (pt, pp **read**) vi leer ♦ vt leer; (understand) entender; (study) estudiar; **~ out** vt leer en alta voz; **~able** adj (writing) legible; (book) leíble; **~er** n lector(a) m/f; (BRIT: at university) profesor/a m/f adjunto/a; **~ership** n (of paper etc) (número de) lectores mpl

readily ['redɪlɪ] adv (willingly) de buena gana; (easily) fácilmente; (quickly) en seguida

readiness ['redɪnɪs] n buena voluntad f; (preparedness) preparación f; **in ~**

(*prepared*) listo, preparado

reading ['ri:dɪŋ] n lectura; (*on instrument*) indicación f

ready ['rɛdɪ] adj listo, preparado; (*willing*) dispuesto, (*available*) disponible ♦ adv: ~-**cooked** listo para comer ♦ n: **at the ~** (MIL) listo para tirar; **to get ~** vi prepararse ♦ vt preparar; ~-**made** adj confeccionado; ~-**to-wear** adj confeccionado

real [rɪəl] adj verdadero, auténtico; **in ~ terms** en términos reales; ~ **estate** n bienes mpl raíces; ~**istic** [-'lɪstɪk] adj realista

reality [ri:'ælɪtɪ] n realidad f

realization [rɪəlaɪ'zeɪʃən] n comprensión f; (*fulfilment*, COMM) realización f

realize ['rɪəlaɪz] vt (*understand*) darse cuenta de

really ['rɪəlɪ] adv realmente; (*for emphasis*) verdaderamente; (*actually*): **what ~ happened** lo que pasó en realidad; **~?** (*de veras?*); **~!** (*annoyance*) ¡vamos!, ¡por favor!

realm [rɛlm] n reino; (*fig*) esfera

realtor ® ['rɪəltə:*] (US) n corredor(a) m/f de bienes raíces

reap [ri:p] vt segar, (*fig*) cosechar, recoger

reappear [ri:ə'pɪə*] vi reaparecer

rear [rɪə*] adj trasero ♦ n parte f trasera ♦ vt (*cattle, family*) criar ♦ vi (*also: ~ up*) (*animal*) encabritarse; ~**guard** n retaguardia

rearmament [ri:'ɑ:məmənt] n rearme m

rearrange [ri:ə'reɪndʒ] vt ordenar or arreglar de nuevo

rear-view mirror n (AUT) (espejo) retrovisor m

reason ['ri:zn] n razón f ♦ vi: **to ~ with sb** tratar de que uno entre en razón; **it stands to ~ that** es lógico que; ~**able** adj razonable; (*sensible*) sensato; ~**ably** adv razonablemente; ~**ing** n razonamiento, argumentos mpl

reassurance [ri:ə'ʃuərəns] n consuelo

reassure [ri:ə'ʃuə*] vt tranquilizar, alentar; **to ~ sb that** tranquilizar a uno asegurando que

rebate ['ri:beɪt] n (*on tax etc*) desgravación f

rebel [n 'rɛbl, vi rɪ'bɛl] n rebelde m/f ♦ vi rebelarse, sublevarse; ~**lious** [rɪ'bɛljəs] adj rebelde; (*child*) revoltoso

rebirth ['ri:bə:θ] n renacimiento

rebound [vi rɪ'baund, n 'ri:baund] vi (*ball*) rebotar ♦ n rebote m; **on the ~** (*also fig*) de rebote

rebuff [rɪ'bʌf] n desaire m, rechazo

rebuild [ri:'bɪld] (*irreg*) vt reconstruir

rebuke [rɪ'bju:k] n reprimenda ♦ vt reprender

rebut [rɪ'bʌt] vt rebatir

recall [vb rɪ'kɔ:l, n 'ri:kɔl] vt (*remember*) recordar; (*ambassador etc*) retirar ♦ n recuerdo; retirada

recap ['ri:kæp], **recapitulate** [ri:kə'pɪtjuleɪt] vt, vi recapitular

rec'd abbr (= *received*) rbdo

recede [rɪ'si:d] vi (*memory*) ir borrándose; (*hair*) retroceder; **receding** adj (*forehead, chin*) huidizo; **to have a receding hairline** tener entradas

receipt [rɪ'si:t] n (*document*) recibo; (*for payment etc*) acuse m de recibo; (*act of receiving*) recepción f; ~**s** npl (COMM) ingresos mpl

receive [rɪ'si:v] vt recibir; (*guest*) acoger; (*wound*) sufrir; ~**r** n (TEL) auricular m; (RADIO) receptor m; (*of stolen goods*) perista m/f; (COMM) administrador m jurídico

recent ['ri:snt] adj reciente; ~**ly** adv recientemente; ~**ly arrived** recién llegado

receptacle [rɪ'sɛptɪkl] n receptáculo

reception [rɪ'sɛpʃən] n recepción f; (*welcome*) acogida; ~ **desk** n recepción f; ~**ist** n recepcionista f

recess [rɪ'sɛs] n (*in room*) hueco; (*for bed*) nicho; (*secret place*) escondrijo;

*(POL etc: holiday) clausura
recession [rɪ'seʃən] n recesión f
recipe ['resɪpɪ] n receta; (for disaster, success) fórmula
recipient [rɪ'sɪpɪənt] n recibidor(a) m/f; (of letter) destinatario/a
recital [rɪ'saɪtl] n recital m
recite [rɪ'saɪt] vt (poem) recitar
reckless ['rekləs] adj temerario, imprudente; (driving, driver) peligroso; **~ly** adv imprudentemente; de modo peligroso
reckon ['rekən] vt calcular; (consider) considerar; (think) **I ~ that ...** me parece que ...; **~ on** vt fus contar con; **~ing** n cálculo
reclaim [rɪ'kleɪm] vt (land, waste) recuperar; (land: from sea) rescatar; (demand back) reclamar
reclamation [reklə'meɪʃən] n (of land) acondicionamiento de tierras
recline [rɪ'klaɪn] vi reclinarse; **reclining** adj (seat) reclinable
recluse [rɪ'kluːs] n recluso/a
recognition [rekəg'nɪʃən] n reconocimiento f; **transformed beyond ~** irreconocible
recognizable ['rekəgnaɪzəbl] adj: **~ (by)** reconocible (por)
recognize ['rekəgnaɪz] vt: **to ~ (by/as)** reconocer (por/como)
recoil [vi rɪ'kɔɪl, n 'riːkɔɪl] vi (person): **to ~ from doing sth** retraerse de hacer algo ♦ n (of gun) retroceso
recollect [rekə'lekt] vt recordar, acordarse de; **~ion** [-'lekʃən] n recuerdo
recommend [rekə'mend] vt recomendar
reconcile ['rekənsaɪl] vt (two people) reconciliar; (two facts) compaginar; **to ~ o.s. to sth** conformarse a algo
recondition [riːkən'dɪʃən] vt (machine) reacondicionar
reconnoitre [rekə'nɔɪtə*] (US **reconnoiter**) vt, vi (MIL) reconocer
reconsider [riːkən'sɪdə*] vt repensar

reconstruct [riːkən'strʌkt] vt reconstruir
record [n 'rekɔːd, vt rɪ'kɔːd] n (MUS) disco; (of meeting etc) acta; (register) registro, partida; (file) archivo; (also: criminal ~) antecedentes mpl; (written) expediente m; (SPORT, COMPUT) récord m ♦ vt registrar; (MUS: song etc) grabar; **in ~ time** en un tiempo récord; **off the ~** adj no oficial ♦ adv confidencialmente; **~ card** n (in file) ficha; **~ed delivery** (BRIT) n (POST) entrega con acuse de recibo; **~er** n (MUS) flauta de pico; (SPORT) actual poseedor/a m/f del récord; **~ing** n (MUS) grabación f; **~ player** n tocadiscos m inv
recount [rɪ'kaunt] vt contar
re-count [rɪ'kaunt] n (POL: of votes) segundo escrutinio
recoup [rɪ'kuːp] vt: **to ~ one's losses** recuperar las pérdidas
recourse [rɪ'kɔːs] n: **to have ~ to** recurrir a
recover [rɪ'kʌvə*] vt recuperar ♦ vi (from illness, shock) recuperarse; **~y** n recuperación f
recreation [rekrɪ'eɪʃən] n recreo; **~al** adj de recreo; **~al drug** droga recreativa
recruit [rɪ'kruːt] n recluta m/f ♦ vt reclutar; (staff) contratar
rectangle ['rektæŋgl] n rectángulo; **rectangular** [-'tæŋgjulə*] adj rectangular
rectify ['rektɪfaɪ] vt rectificar
rector ['rektə*] n (REL) párroco; **~y** n casa del párroco
recuperate [rɪ'kuːpəreɪt] vi reponerse, restablecerse
recur [rɪ'kə:*] vi repetirse; (pain, illness) producirse de nuevo; **~rence** [rɪ'kʌrəns] n repetición f; **~rent** [rɪ'kʌrənt] adj repetido
recycle [riː'saɪkl] vt reciclar
red [red] n rojo ♦ adj rojo; (hair) pelirrojo; (wine) tinto; **to be in the ~**

(*account*) estar en números rojos; (*business*) tener un saldo negativo; **to give sb the ~ carpet treatment** recibir a uno con todos los honores; **R~ Cross** n Cruz f Roja; **~currant** n grosella roja; **~den** vt enrojecer ♦ vi enrojecerse

redeem [rɪ'diːm] vt redimir; (*promises*) cumplir; (*sth in pawn*) desempeñar; (*fig, also* REL) rescatar; **~ing** adj: **~ing feature** rasgo bueno o favorable

redeploy [riːdɪ'plɔɪ] vt (*resources*) reorganizar

red: ~-haired adj pelirrojo; **~-handed** adj: **to be caught ~-handed** cogerse (SP) or pillarse (AM) con las manos en la masa; **~head** n pelirrojo/a; **~ herring** n (*fig*) pista falsa; **~-hot** adj candente

redirect [riːdaɪ'rekt] vt (*mail*) reexpedir

red light n: **to go through a ~** (AUT) pasar la luz roja; **red-light district** n barrio chino

redo [riː'duː] (*irreg*) vt rehacer

redress [rɪ'dres] vt reparar

Red Sea n: **the ~** el mar Rojo

redskin ['redskɪn] n piel roja m/f

red tape n (*fig*) trámites mpl

reduce [rɪ'djuːs] vt reducir; **to ~ sb to tears** hacer llorar a uno; **to be ~d to begging** no quedarle a uno otro remedio que pedir limosna; **"~ speed now"** (AUT) "reduzca la velocidad"; **at a ~d price** (*of goods*) (a precio) rebajado; **reduction** [rɪ'dʌkʃən] n reducción f; (*of price*) rebaja f, (*discount*) descuento; (*smaller-scale copy*) copia reducida

redundancy [rɪ'dʌndənsɪ] n (*dismissal*) despido; (*unemployment*) desempleo

redundant [rɪ'dʌndnt] adj (BRIT: *worker*) parado, sin trabajo; (*detail, object*) superfluo; **to be made ~** quedar(se) sin trabajo

reed [riːd] n (BOT) junco, caña; (MUS) lengüeta

reef [riːf] n (*at sea*) arrecife m

reek [riːk] vi: **to ~ (of)** apestar (a)

reel [riːl] n carrete m, bobina; (*of film*) rollo; (*dance*) baile m escocés ♦ vt (*also: ~ up*) devanar; (*also: ~ in*) sacar ♦ vi (*sway*) tambalear(se)

ref [ref] (*inf*) n abbr = **referee**

refectory [rɪ'fektərɪ] n comedor m

refer [rɪ'fɜː*] vt (*send: patient*) referir; (: *matter*) remitir ♦ vi: **to ~ to** (*allude to*) referirse a, aludir a; (*apply to*) relacionarse con; (*consult*) consultar

referee [refə'riː] n árbitro; (BRIT: *for job application*): **to be a ~ for sb** proporcionar referencias a uno ♦ vt (*match*) arbitrar en

reference ['refrəns] n referencia; (*for job application: letter*) carta de recomendación f; **with ~ to** (COMM: *in letter*) me remito a; **~ book** n libro de consulta; **~ number** n número de referencia

refill [vt riː'fɪl, n 'riːfɪl] vt rellenar ♦ n repuesto, recambio

refine [rɪ'faɪn] vt refinar; **~d** adj (*person*) fino; **~ment** n cultura, educación f; (*of system*) refinamiento

reflect [rɪ'flekt] vt reflejar ♦ vi (*think*) reflexionar, pensar; **it ~s badly/well on him** le perjudica/le hace honor; **~ion** [-'flekʃən] n (*act*) reflexión f; (*image*) reflejo; (*criticism*) crítica; **on ~ion** pensándolo bien; **~or** n (AUT) captafaros m inv; (*of light, heat*) reflector m

reflex ['riːfleks] adj, n reflejo; **~ive** [rɪ'fleksɪv] adj (LING) reflexivo

reform [rɪ'fɔːm] n reforma ♦ vt reformar; **~atory** (US) n reformatorio

refrain [rɪ'freɪn] vi: **to ~ from doing** abstenerse de hacer ♦ n estribillo

refresh [rɪ'freʃ] vt refrescar; **~er course** (BRIT) n curso de repaso; **~ing** adj refrescante; **~ments** npl refrescos mpl

refrigerator [rɪ'frɪdʒəreɪtə*] n nevera (SP), refrigeradora (AM)

refuel [riː'fjuəl] vi repostar (combustible)

refuge ['refju:dʒ] n refugio, asilo; **to take ~ in** refugiarse en

refugee [refju'dʒi:] n refugiado/a

refund [n 'ri:fʌnd, vb rɪ'fʌnd] n reembolso ♦ vt devolver, reembolsar

refurbish [ri:'fɜ:bɪʃ] vt restaurar, renovar

refusal [rɪ'fju:zəl] n negativa; **to have first ~ on** tener la primera opción a

refuse[1] ['refju:s] n basura; **~ collection** n recolección f de basuras

refuse[2] [rɪ'fju:z] vt rechazar; (invitation) declinar; (permission) denegar ♦ vi: **to ~ to do sth** negarse a hacer algo; (horse) rehusar

regain [rɪ'geɪn] vt recobrar, recuperar

regal ['ri:gl] adj regio, real

regard [rɪ'gɑ:d] n mirada; (esteem) respeto; (attention) consideración f ♦ vt (consider) considerar; **to give one's ~s to** saludar de su parte a; "**with kindest ~s**" "con muchos recuerdos"; **~ing, as ~s, with ~ to** con respecto a, en cuanto a; **~less** adv a pesar de todo; **~less of** sin reparar en

régime [reɪ'ʒi:m] n régimen m

regiment ['redʒɪmənt] n regimiento; **~al** [-'mentl] adj militar

region ['ri:dʒən] n región f; **in the ~ of** (fig) alrededor de; **~al** adj regional

register ['redʒɪstə*] n registro ♦ vt registrar; (birth) declarar; (car) matricular; (letter) certificar; (subj: instrument) marcar, indicar ♦ vi (at hotel) registrarse; (as student) matricularse; (make impression) producir impresión; **~ed** adj (letter, parcel) certificado; **~ed trademark** n marca registrada

registrar ['redʒɪstrɑ:*] n secretario/a (del registro civil)

registration [redʒɪs'treɪʃən] n (act) declaración f; (AUT: also: ~ number) matrícula

registry ['redʒɪstrɪ] n registro; **~ office** (BRIT) n registro civil; **to get married**

in a ~ office casarse por lo civil

regret [rɪ'gret] n sentimiento, pesar m ♦ vt sentir, lamentar; **~fully** adv con pesar; **~table** adj lamentable

regular ['regjulə*] adj regular; (soldier) profesional; (usual) habitual; (: doctor) de cabecera ♦ n (client etc) cliente/a m/f habitual; **~ly** adv con regularidad; (often) repetidas veces

regulate ['regjuleɪt] vt controlar; **regulation** [-'leɪʃən] n (rule) regla, reglamento

rehearsal [rɪ'hɜ:səl] n ensayo

rehearse [rɪ'hɜ:s] vt ensayar

reign [reɪn] n reinado; (fig) predominio ♦ vi reinar; (fig) imperar

reimburse [ri:ɪm'bɜ:s] vt reembolsar

rein [reɪn] n (for horse) rienda

reindeer ['reɪndɪə*] n inv reno

reinforce [ri:ɪn'fɔ:s] vt reforzar; **~d concrete** n hormigón m armado; **~ments** npl (MIL) refuerzos mpl

reinstate [ri:ɪn'steɪt] vt reintegrar; (tax, law) reinstaurar

reiterate [ri:'ɪtəreɪt] vt reiterar, repetir

reject [n 'ri:dʒekt, vb rɪ'dʒekt] n (thing) desecho ♦ vt rechazar; (suggestion) descartar; (coin) expulsar; **~ion** [rɪ'dʒekʃən] n rechazo

rejoice [rɪ'dʒɔɪs] vi: **to ~ at or over** regocijarse or alegrarse de

rejuvenate [rɪ'dʒu:vəneɪt] vt rejuvenecer

relapse [rɪ'læps] n recaída

relate [rɪ'leɪt] vt (tell) contar, relatar; (connect) relacionar ♦ vi relacionarse; **~d** adj afín; (person) emparentado; **~d to** (subject) relacionado con; **relating to** prep referente a

relation [rɪ'leɪʃən] n (person) familiar m/f, pariente/a m/f; (link) relación f; **~s** npl (relatives) familiares mpl; **~ship** n relación f; (personal) relaciones fpl; (also: family ~ship) parentesco

relative ['relətɪv] n pariente m/f, familiar m/f ♦ adj relativo; **~ly** adv (comparatively) relativamente

relax [rɪˈlæks] vi descansar; (unwind)
relajarse ♦ vt (one's grip) soltar, aflojar;
(control) relajar; (mind, person)
descansar; ~**ation** [riːlækˈseɪʃən] n
descanso; (of rule, control) relajamiento;
(entertainment) diversión f; ~**ed** adj
relajado; (tranquil) tranquilo; ~**ing** adj
relajante

relay [ˈriːleɪ] n (race) carrera de relevos
♦ vt (RADIO, TV) retransmitir

release [rɪˈliːs] n (liberation) liberación
f; (from prison) puesta en libertad; (of
gas etc) escape m; (of film) estreno;
(of record) lanzamiento ♦ vt (prisoner)
poner en libertad; (gas) despedir,
arrojar; (from wreckage) soltar; (catch,
spring etc) desenganchar; (film)
estrenar; (book) publicar; (news)
difundir

relegate [ˈrelɪgeɪt] vt relegar; (BRIT:
SPORT): **to be ~d to** bajar a

relent [rɪˈlent] vi ablandarse; ~**less** adj
implacable

relevant [ˈreləvənt] adj (fact)
pertinente; ~ **to** relacionado con

reliable [rɪˈlaɪəbl] adj (person, firm) de
confianza, de fiar; (method, machine)
seguro; (source) fidedigno; **reliably**
adv: **to be reliably informed that ...**
saber de fuente fidedigna que ...

reliance [rɪˈlaɪəns] n: ~ **(on)**
dependencia (de)

relic [ˈrelɪk] n (REL) reliquia; (of the
past) vestigio

relief [rɪˈliːf] n (from pain, anxiety)
alivio; (help, supplies) socorro, ayuda;
(ART, GEO) relieve m

relieve [rɪˈliːv] vt (pain) aliviar; (bring
help to) ayudar, socorrer; (take over
from) sustituir a; (: guard) relevar; **to
~ sb of sth** quitar algo a uno; **to
~ o.s.** hacer sus necesidades

religion [rɪˈlɪdʒən] n religión f;
religious adj religioso

relinquish [rɪˈlɪŋkwɪʃ] vt abandonar;
(plan, habit) renunciar a

relish [ˈrelɪʃ] n (CULIN) salsa;

(enjoyment) entusiasmo ♦ vt (food etc)
saborear; (enjoy): **to ~ sth** hacerle
mucha ilusión a uno algo

relocate [riːləʊˈkeɪt] vt cambiar de
lugar, mudar ♦ vi mudarse

reluctance [rɪˈlʌktəns] n renuncia

reluctant [rɪˈlʌktənt] adj renuente; ~**ly**
adv de mala gana

rely on [rɪˈlaɪ-] vt fus depender de;
(trust) contar con

remain [rɪˈmeɪn] vi (survive) quedar;
(be left) sobrar; (continue) quedar(se),
permanecer; ~**der** n resto; ~**ing** adj
que queda(n); (surviving) restante(s);
~**s** npl restos mpl

remand [rɪˈmɑːnd] n: **on ~** detenido
(bajo custodia) ♦ vt: **to be ~ed in
custody** quedar detenido bajo
custodia; ~ **home** (BRIT) n
reformatorio

remark [rɪˈmɑːk] n comentario ♦ vt
comentar; ~**able** adj (outstanding)
extraordinario

remarry [riːˈmærɪ] vi volver a casarse

remedial [rɪˈmiːdɪəl] adj de
recuperación

remedy [ˈremədɪ] n remedio ♦ vt
remediar, curar

remember [rɪˈmembə*] vt recordar,
acordarse de; (bear in mind) tener
presente; (send greetings to): ~ **me to
him** dale recuerdos de mi parte;
remembrance n recuerdo; **R~ Day** n
≈ día en el que se recuerda a los
caídos en las dos guerras mundiales

Remembrance Day

En el Reino Unido el domingo más
próximo al 11 de noviembre se conoce
como Remembrance Sunday *o*
Remembrance Day, *aniversario de*
la firma del armisticio de 1918 que
puso fin a la Primera Guerra
Mundial. Ese día, a las once de la
mañana (hora en que se firmó el
armisticio), se recuerda a los que
murieron en las dos guerras

*mundiales con dos minutos de
silencio ante los monumentos a los
caídos. Allí se colocan coronas de
amapolas, flor que también se suele
llevar prendida en el pecho tras pagar
un donativo destinado a los inválidos
de guerra.*

remind [rɪ'maɪnd] vt: **to ~ sb to do
sth** recordar a uno que haga algo; **to
~ sb of sth** (of fact) recordar algo a
uno; **she ~s me of her mother** me
recuerda a su madre; **~er** n
notificación f; (memento) memento m
reminisce [remɪ'nɪs] vi recordar (viejas
historias); **reminiscent** adj: **to be
reminiscent of sth** recordar algo
remiss [rɪ'mɪs] adj descuidado; **it was
~ of him** fue un descuido de su parte
remission [rɪ'mɪʃən] n remisión f; (of
prison sentence) disminución f de pena;
(REL) perdón m
remit [rɪ'mɪt] vt (send: money) remitir,
enviar; **~tance** n remesa, envío
remnant ['remnənt] n resto; (of cloth)
retal m; **~s** npl (COMM) restos mpl de
serie
remorse [rɪ'mɔːs] n remordimientos
mpl; **~ful** adj arrepentido; **~less** adj
(fig) implacable, inexorable
remote [rɪ'məut] adj (distant) lejano;
(person) distante; **~ control** n
telecontrol m; **~ly** adv remotamente;
(slightly) levemente
remould ['riːməuld] (BRIT) n (tyre)
neumático or llanta (AM)
recauchutado/a
removable [rɪ'muːvəbl] adj
(detachable) separable
removal [rɪ'muːvl] n (taking away) el
quitar; (BRIT: from house) mudanza;
(from office: dismissal) destitución f;
(MED) extirpación f; **~ van** (BRIT) n
camión m de mudanzas
remove [rɪ'muːv] vt quitar; (employee)
destituir; (name: from list) tachar,
borrar; (doubt) disipar; (abuse)

suprimir, acabar con; (MED) extirpar
Renaissance [rɪ'neɪsɑːns] n: **the ~** el
Renacimiento
render ['rendə*] vt (thanks) dar; (aid)
proporcionar, prestar; (make): **to ~ sth
useless** hacer algo inútil; **~ing** n (MUS
etc) interpretación f
rendezvous ['rɔndɪvuː] n cita
renew [rɪ'njuː] vt (resume) reanudar;
(loan etc) prorrogar; **~able** adj
renovable; **~al** n reanudación f;
prórroga
renounce [rɪ'nauns] vt renunciar a;
(right, inheritance) renunciar
renovate ['renəveɪt] vt renovar
renown [rɪ'naun] n renombre m; **~ed**
adj renombrado
rent [rent] n (for house) arriendo, renta
♦ vt alquilar; **~al** n (for television, car)
alquiler m
rep [rep] n abbr = **representative**;
repertory
repair [rɪ'peə*] n reparación f,
compostura ♦ vt reparar, componer;
(shoes) remendar; **in good/bad ~** en
buen/mal estado; **~ kit** n caja de
herramientas
repatriate [riː'pætrɪeɪt] vt repatriar
repay [riː'peɪ] (irreg) vt (money)
devolver, reembolsar; (person) pagar;
(debt) liquidar; (sb's efforts) devolver,
corresponder a; **~ment** n reembolso,
devolución f; (sum of money)
recompensa
repeal [rɪ'piːl] n revocación f ♦ vt
revocar
repeat [rɪ'piːt] n (RADIO, TV) reposición
f ♦ vt repetir ♦ vi repetirse; **~edly** adv
repetidas veces
repel [rɪ'pel] vt (drive away) rechazar;
(disgust) repugnar; **~lent** adj
repugnante ♦ n: **insect ~lent** crema
(or loción f) anti-insectos
repent [rɪ'pent] vt: **to ~ (of)**
arrepentirse (de); **~ance** n
arrepentimiento
repercussions [riːpə'kʌʃənz] npl

consecuencias *fpl*
repertory ['repǝtǝrɪ] *n (also:* ~ *theatre)* teatro de repertorio
repetition [repɪ'tɪʃǝn] *n* repetición *f*
repetitive [rɪ'petɪtɪv] *adj* repetitivo
replace [rɪ'pleɪs] *vt (put back)* devolver a su sitio; *(take the place of)* reemplazar, sustituir; ~**ment** *n (act)* reposición *f*; *(thing)* recambio; *(person)* suplente *m/f*
replay ['riːpleɪ] *n (SPORT)* desempate *m*; *(of tape, film)* repetición *f*
replenish [rɪ'plenɪʃ] *vt* rellenar; *(stock etc)* reponer
replica ['replɪkǝ] *n* copia, reproducción *f (exacta)*
reply [rɪ'plaɪ] *n* respuesta, contestación *f* ♦ *vi* contestar, responder
report [rɪ'pɔːt] *n* informe *m*; *(PRESS etc)* reportaje *m*; *(BRIT: also: school* ~) boletín *m* escolar; *(of gun)* estallido ♦ *vt* informar de; *(PRESS etc)* hacer un reportaje sobre; *(notify: accident, culprit)* denunciar ♦ *vi (make a report)* presentar un informe; *(present o.s.)*: **to** ~ **(to sb)** presentarse (ante uno); ~ **card** *n (US, Scottish)* cartilla escolar; ~**edly** *adv* según se dice; ~**er** *n* periodista *m/f*
repose [rɪ'pǝuz] *n*: **in** ~ *(face, mouth)* en reposo
reprehensible [reprɪ'hensɪbl] *adj* reprensible, censurable
represent [reprɪ'zent] *vt* representar; *(COMM)* ser agente de; *(describe)*: **to** ~ **sth as** describir algo como; ~**ation** [-'teɪʃǝn] *n* representación *f*; ~**ations** *npl (protest)* quejas *fpl*; ~**ative** *n* representante *m/f*; *(US: POL)* diputado/a *m/f* ♦ *adj* representativo
repress [rɪ'pres] *vt* reprimir; ~**ion** [-'preʃǝn] *n* represión *f*
reprieve [rɪ'priːv] *n (LAW)* indulto; *(fig)* alivio
reprisals [rɪ'praɪzlz] *npl* represalias *fpl*
reproach [rɪ'prǝutʃ] *n* reproche *m* ♦ *vt*: **to** ~ **sb for sth** reprochar algo a uno;

~**ful** *adj* de reproche, de acusación
reproduce [riːprǝ'djuːs] *vt* reproducir ♦ *vi* reproducirse; **reproduction** [-'dʌkʃǝn] *n* reproducción *f*
reprove [rɪ'pruːv] *vt*: **to** ~ **sb for sth** reprochar algo a uno
reptile ['reptaɪl] *n* reptil *m*
republic [rɪ'pʌblɪk] *n* república; ~**an** *adj, n* republicano/a *m/f*
repudiate [rɪ'pjuːdɪeɪt] *vt* rechazar, *(violence etc)* repudiar
repulsive [rɪ'pʌlsɪv] *adj* repulsivo
reputable ['repjutǝbl] *adj (make etc)* de renombre
reputation [repju'teɪʃǝn] *n* reputación *f*
reputed [rɪ'pjuːtɪd] *adj* supuesto; ~**ly** *adv* según dicen or se dice
request [rɪ'kwest] *n* petición *f*; *(formal)* solicitud *f* ♦ *vt*: **to** ~ **sth of** *or* **from sb** solicitar algo a uno; ~ **stop** *(BRIT)* *n* parada discrecional
require [rɪ'kwaɪǝ*] *vt (need: subj: person)* necesitar, tener necesidad de; *(: thing, situation)* exigir; *(want)* pedir; **to** ~ **sb to do sth** pedir a uno que haga algo; ~**ment** *n* requisito; *(need)* necesidad *f*
requisition [rekwɪ'zɪʃǝn] *n*: ~ **(for)** solicitud *f* (de) ♦ *vt (MIL)* requisar
rescue ['reskjuː] *n* rescate *m* ♦ *vt* rescatar; ~ **party** *n* expedición *f* de salvamento; ~**r** *n* salvador(a) *m/f*
research [rɪ'sɜːtʃ] *n* investigación *fpl* ♦ *vt* investigar; ~**er** *n* investigador(a) *m/f*
resemblance [rɪ'zemblǝns] *n* parecido
resemble [rɪ'zembl] *vt* parecerse a
resent [rɪ'zent] *vt* tomar a mal; ~**ful** *adj* resentido; ~**ment** *n* resentimiento
reservation [rezǝ'veɪʃǝn] *n* reserva
reserve [rɪ'zɜːv] *n* reserva; *(SPORT)* suplente *m/f* ♦ *vt (seats etc)* reservar; ~**s** *npl (MIL)* reserva; **in** ~ de reserva; ~**d** *adj* reservado
reshuffle [riː'ʃʌfl] *n*: **Cabinet** ~ *(POL)* remodelación *f* del gabinete

residence ['rezidəns] n (formal: home)
domicilio; (length of stay) permanencia;
~ permit (BRIT) n permiso de
permanencia

resident ['rezidənt] n (of area) vecino/
a; (in hotel) huésped(a) m/f ♦ adj
(population) permanente; (doctor)
residente; **~ial** [-'denʃəl] adj residencial

residue ['rezidju:] n resto

resign [rɪ'zaɪn] vt renunciar a ♦ vi
dimitir; **to ~ o.s. to** (situation)
resignarse a; **~ation** [rezɪg'neɪʃən] n
dimisión f; (state of mind) resignación f;
~ed adj resignado

resilient [rɪ'zɪlɪənt] adj (material)
elástico; (person) resistente

resist [rɪ'zɪst] vt resistir, oponerse a;
~ance n resistencia

resolute ['rezəlu:t] adj resuelto,
(refusal) tajante

resolution [rezə'lu:ʃən] n (gen)
resolución f

resolve [rɪ'zɔlv] vi: **to ~ to do** resolver
hacer ♦ vt resolver ♦ vi; **~d** adj resuelto

resort [rɪ'zɔ:t] n (town) centro turístico;
(recourse) recurso ♦ vi: **to ~ to** recurrir
a; **in the last ~** como último recurso

resounding [rɪ'zaundɪŋ] adj sonoro,
(fig) clamoroso

resource [rɪ'sɔ:s] n recurso; **~s** npl
recursos mpl; **~ful** adj despabilado,
ingenioso

respect [rɪs'pekt] n respeto ♦ vt
respetar; **~s** npl recuerdos mpl, saludos
mpl; **with ~ to** con respecto a; **in this
~** en cuanto a eso; **~able** adj
respetable; (large: amount) apreciable;
(passable) tolerable; **~ful** adj
respetuoso

respective [rɪs'pektɪv] adj respectivo;
~ly adv respectivamente

respite ['respaɪt] n respiro

respond [rɪs'pɔnd] vi responder;
(react) reaccionar; **response** [-'pɔns] n
respuesta; reacción f

responsibility [rɪspɔnsɪ'bɪlɪtɪ] n

responsabilidad f

responsible [rɪs'pɔnsɪbl] adj
(character) serio, formal; (job) de
confianza; (liable): **~ (for)** responsable
(de)

responsive [rɪs'pɔnsɪv] adj sensible

rest [rest] n descanso, reposo; (MUS,
pause) pausa, silencio; (support) apoyo;
(remainder) resto ♦ vi descansar; (be
supported): **to ~ on** descansar sobre
♦ vt (lean): **to ~ sth on/against**
apoyar algo en or sobre/contra; **the
~ of them** (people, objects) los demás;
it ~s with him to ... depende de él lo
que ...

restaurant ['restərɔŋ] n restaurante m;
~ car (BRIT) n (RAIL) coche-comedor m

restful ['restful] adj descansado,
tranquilo

rest home n residencia para jubilados

restive ['restɪv] adj inquieto; (horse)
rebelón(ona)

restless ['restlɪs] adj inquieto

restoration [restə'reɪʃən] n
restauración f; devolución f

restore [rɪ'stɔ:] vt (building) restaurar;
(sth stolen) devolver; (health)
restablecer; (to power) volver a poner a

restrain [rɪs'treɪn] vt (feeling) contener,
refrenar; (person): **to ~ (from doing)**
disuadir (de hacer); **~ed** adj reservado;
~t n (restriction) restricción f;
(moderation) moderación f; (of manner)
reserva

restrict [rɪs'trɪkt] vt restringir, limitar;
~ion [-kʃən] n restricción f, limitación
f; **~ive** adj restrictivo

rest room (US) n aseos mpl

result [rɪ'zʌlt] n resultado ♦ vi: **to ~ in**
terminar en, tener por resultado; **as a
~ of** a consecuencia de

resume [rɪ'zju:m] vt reanudar ♦ vi
comenzar de nuevo

résumé ['reɪzju:meɪ] n resumen m;
(US) currículum m

resumption [rɪ'zʌmpʃən] n
reanudación f

resurgence [rɪˈsɜːdʒəns] n resurgimiento

resurrection [rezəˈrekʃən] n resurrección f

resuscitate [rɪˈsʌsɪteɪt] vt (MED) resucitar

retail [ˈriːteɪl] adj, adv al por menor; **~er** n detallista mf; **~ price** n precio de venta al público

retain [rɪˈteɪn] vt (keep) retener, conservar; **~er** n (fee) anticipo

retaliate [rɪˈtælɪeɪt] vi: **to ~ (against)** tomar represalias (contra); **retaliation** [-ˈeɪʃən] n represalias fpl

retarded [rɪˈtɑːdɪd] adj retrasado

retch [retʃ] vi dársele a uno arcadas

retentive [rɪˈtentɪv] adj (memory) retentivo

retire [rɪˈtaɪə*] vi (give up work) jubilarse; (withdraw) retirarse; (go to bed) acostarse; **~d** adj (person) jubilado; **~ment** n (giving up work: state) retiro; (: act) jubilación f;

retiring [rɪˈtaɪərɪŋ] adj (leaving) saliente; (shy) retraído

retort [rɪˈtɔːt] vi contestar

retrace [riːˈtreɪs] vt: **to ~ one's steps** volver sobre sus pasos, desandar lo andado

retract [rɪˈtrækt] vt (statement) retirar; (claws) retraer; (undercarriage, aerial) replegar

retrain [riːˈtreɪn] vt reciclar; **~ing** n readaptación f profesional

retread [ˈriːtred] n neumático (SP) or llanta (AM) recauchutado/a

retreat [rɪˈtriːt] n (place) retiro; (MIL) retirada ♦ vi retirarse

retribution [retrɪˈbjuːʃən] n desquite m

retrieval [rɪˈtriːvəl] n recuperación f

retrieve [rɪˈtriːv] vt recobrar; (situation, honour) salvar; (COMPUT) recuperar; (error) reparar; **~r** n perro cobrador

retrospect [ˈretrəspekt] n: **in ~** retrospectivamente; **~ive** [-ˈspektɪv] adj retrospectivo; (law) retroactivo

return [rɪˈtɜːn] n (going or coming back) vuelta, regreso; (of sth stolen etc) devolución f; (FINANCE: from land, shares) ganancia, ingresos mpl ♦ cpd (journey) de regreso; (BRIT: ticket) de ida y vuelta; (match) de vuelta ♦ vi (person etc: come or go back) volver, regresar; (symptoms etc) reaparecer; (regain): **to ~ to** recuperar ♦ vt devolver; (favour, love etc) corresponder a; (verdict) pronunciar; (POL: candidate) elegir; **~s** npl (COMM) ingresos mpl; **in ~ (for)** a cambio (de); **by ~ of post** a vuelta de correo; **many happy ~s (of the day)!** ¡feliz cumpleaños!

reunion [riːˈjuːnɪən] n (of family) reunión f; (of two people, school) reencuentro

reunite [riːjuːˈnaɪt] vt reunir; (reconcile) reconciliar

rev [rev] (AUT) n abbr (= revolution) revolución f ♦ vt (also: **~ up**) acelerar

reveal [rɪˈviːl] vt revelar; **~ing** adj revelador(a)

revel [ˈrevl] vi: **to ~ in sth/in doing sth** gozar de algo/con hacer algo

revenge [rɪˈvendʒ] n venganza; **to take ~ on** vengarse de

revenue [ˈrevənjuː] n ingresos mpl, rentas fpl

reverberate [rɪˈvɜːbəreɪt] vi (sound) resonar, retumbar; (fig: shock) repercutir

reverence [ˈrevərəns] n reverencia

Reverend [ˈrevərənd] adj (in titles): **the ~ John Smith** (Anglican) el Reverendo John Smith; (Catholic) el Padre John Smith; (Protestant) el Pastor John Smith

reversal [rɪˈvɜːsl] n (of order) inversión f; (of direction, policy) cambio; (of decision) revocación f

reverse [rɪˈvɜːs] n (opposite) contrario; (back: of cloth) revés m; (: of coin) reverso; (: of paper) dorso; (AUT: also: **~ gear**) marcha atrás; (setback) revés m

♦ adj (order) inverso; (direction) contrario; (process) opuesto **♦** vt (decision, AUT) marcha atrás a; (position, function) invertir **♦** vi (BRIT: AUT) dar marcha atrás; **~-charge call** (BRIT) n llamada a cobro revertido; **reversing lights** (BRIT) npl (AUT) luces fpl de retroceso

revert |rɪ'vɜːt| vi: **to ~ to** volver a

review |rɪ'vjuː| n (magazine, MIL) revista; (of book, film) reseña; (US: examination) repaso, examen m **♦** vt repasar, examinar, (MIL) pasar revista a; (book, film) reseñar; **~er** n crítico/a

revise |rɪ'vaɪz| vt (manuscript) corregir; (opinion) modificar; (price, procedure) revisar **♦** vi (study) repasar; **revision** |rɪ'vɪʒən| n corrección f; modificación f; (for exam) repaso

revival |rɪ'vaɪvəl| n (recovery) reanimación f; (of interest) renacimiento m; (THEATRE) reestreno m; (of faith) despertar m

revive |rɪ'vaɪv| vt resucitar; (custom) restablecer; (hope) despertar; (play) reestrenar **♦** vi (person) volver en sí; (business) reactivarse

revolt |rɪ'vəult| n rebelión f ♦ vi rebelarse, sublevarse ♦ vt dar asco a, repugnar; **~ing** adj asqueroso, repugnante

revolution |revə'luːʃən| n revolución f; **~ary** adj, n revolucionario/a m/f; **~ize** vt revolucionar

revolve |rɪ'vɒlv| vi dar vueltas, girar; (life, discussion): **to ~ (a)round** girar en torno a

revolver |rɪ'vɒlvə*| n revólver m

revolving |rɪ'vɒlvɪŋ| adj (chair, door etc) giratorio

revue |rɪ'vjuː| n (THEATRE) revista

revulsion |rɪ'vʌlʃən| n asco, repugnancia

reward |rɪ'wɔːd| n premio, recompensa **♦** vt: **to ~ (for)** recompensar or premiar (por); **~ing** adj (fig) valioso

rewind |riː'waɪnd| (irreg) vt rebobinar

rewire |riː'waɪə*| vt (house) renovar la instalación eléctrica de

rheumatism |'ruːmətɪzm| n reumatismo, reúma m

Rhine |raɪn| n: **the ~** el (río) Rin

rhinoceros |raɪ'nɔsərəs| n rinoceronte m

rhododendron |rəudə'dendrn| n rododendro

Rhone |rəun| n: **the ~** el (río) Ródano

rhubarb |'ruːbɑːb| n ruibarbo

rhyme |raɪm| n rima; (verse) poesía

rhythm |'rɪðm| n ritmo

rib |rɪb| n (ANAT) costilla **♦** vt (mock) tomar el pelo a

ribbon |'rɪbən| n cinta; **in ~s** (torn) hecho trizas

rice |raɪs| n arroz m; **~ pudding** n arroz m con leche

rich |rɪtʃ| adj rico; (soil) fértil; (food) pesado; (: sweet) empalagoso; (abundant): **~ in** (minerals etc) rico en; **the ~** npl los ricos; **~es** npl riqueza; **~ly** adv ricamente; (deserved, earned) bien

rickets |'rɪkɪts| n raquitismo

rid |rɪd| (pt, pp rid) vt: **to ~ sb of sth** librar a uno de algo; **to get ~ of sth** deshacerse or desembarazarse de

ridden |'rɪdn| pp of ride

riddle |'rɪdl| n (puzzle) acertijo; (mystery) enigma m, misterio **♦** vt: **to be ~d with** ser lleno o plagado de

ride |raɪd| (pt rode, pp ridden) n paseo; (distance covered) viaje m, recorrido **♦** vi (as sport) montar; (go somewhere: on horse, bicycle) dar un paseo, pasearse; (travel: on bicycle, motorcycle, bus) viajar **♦** vt (a horse) montar a; (a bicycle, motorcycle) andar en; (distance) recorrer; **to take sb for a ~** (fig) engañar a uno; **~r** n (on horse) jinete/a m/f; (on bicycle) ciclista m/f; (on motorcycle) motociclista m/f

ridge |rɪdʒ| n (of hill) cresta; (of roof) caballete m; (wrinkle) arruga

ridicule [ˈrɪdɪkjuːl] n irrisión f, burla
♦ vt poner en ridículo, burlarse de;
ridiculous [-ˈdɪkjuləs] adj ridículo

riding [ˈraɪdɪŋ] n equitación f; **I like** ~
me gusta montar a caballo; ~ **school**
n escuela de equitación

rife [raɪf] adj: **to be** ~ ser muy común;
to be ~ **with** abundar en

riffraff [ˈrɪfræf] n gentuza

rifle [ˈraɪfl] n rifle m, fusil m ♦ vt
saquear; ~ **through** vt (papers)
registrar; ~ **range** n campo de tiro; (at
fair) tiro al blanco

rift [rɪft] n (in clouds) claro m; (fig:
disagreement) desavenencia

rig [rɪg] n (also: **oil** ~: at sea) plataforma
petrolera f; (election etc) amañar;
~ **out** (BRIT) vt disfrazar; ~ **up** vt
improvisar; ~**ging** n (NAUT) aparejo

right [raɪt] adj (correct) correcto,
exacto; (suitable) indicado, debido;
(proper) apropiado; (just) justo; (morally
good) bueno; (not left) derecho ♦ n
bueno; (title, claim) derecho; (not left)
derecha ♦ adv bien, correctamente;
(not left) a la derecha; (exactly): ~ **now**
ahora mismo ♦ vt enderezar; (correct)
corregir ♦ excl ¡bueno!, ¡está bien!; **to
be** ~ (person) tener razón; (answer) ser
correcto; **is that the** ~ **time?** ¿es esa la hora buena? ¿de
clock) ¿es esa la hora buena?; **by** ~**s** en
justicia; **on the** ~ a la derecha; **to be
in the** ~ tener razón; ~ **away** en
seguida; ~ **in the middle**
exactamente en el centro; ~ **angle** n
ángulo recto; ~**eous** [ˈraɪtʃəs] adj
justado, honrado; (anger) justificado;
~**ful** adj legítimo; ~**handed** adj
diestro; ~**hand man** n brazo
derecho; ~**hand side** n derecha; ~**ly**
adv correctamente, debidamente; (with
reason) con razón; ~ **of way** n (on
path etc) derecho de paso; (AUT)
prioridad f; ~**wing** adj (POL)
derechista

rigid [ˈrɪdʒɪd] adj rígido; (person, ideas)
inflexible

rigmarole [ˈrɪgmərəʊl] n galimatías m
inv

rigorous [ˈrɪgərəs] adj riguroso

rile [raɪl] vt irritar

rim [rɪm] n borde m; (of spectacles) aro;
(of wheel) llanta

rind [raɪnd] n (of bacon) corteza; (of
lemon etc) cáscara; (of cheese) costra

ring [rɪŋ] (pt **rang**, pp **rung**) n (of
metal) aro; (on finger) anillo; (of people)
corro; (of objects) círculo; (gang)
banda; (for boxing) cuadrilátero; (of
circus) pista; (bull ~) ruedo, plaza;
(sound of bell) toque m ♦ vi (on
telephone) llamar por teléfono; (bell)
repicar; (doorbell, phone) sonar; (also:
~ **out**) sonar; (ears) zumbar ♦ vt (BRIT:
TEL) llamar, telefonear; (bell etc) hacer
sonar; (doorbell) tocar; **to give sb a** ~
(BRIT: TEL) llamar o telefonear a
alguien; ~ **back** (BRIT) vt, vi (TEL)
devolver la llamada; ~ **off** (BRIT) vi
(TEL) colgar, cortar la comunicación;
~ **up** (BRIT) vt (TEL) llamar, telefonear;
~**ing** n (of bell) repique m; (of phone)
el sonar; (in ears) zumbido; ~**ing tone**
n (TEL) tono de llamada; ~**leader** n (of
gang) cabecilla m; ~**lets** [ˈrɪŋlɪts] npl
rizos mpl, bucles mpl; ~ **road** (BRIT) n
carretera periférica o de circunvalación

rink [rɪŋk] n (also: **ice** ~) pista de hielo

rinse [rɪns] n aclarado; (dye) tinte m
♦ vt aclarar; (mouth) enjuagar

riot [ˈraɪət] n motín m, disturbio ♦ vi
amotinarse; **to run** ~ desmandarse;
~**ous** adj alborotado; (party) bullicioso

rip [rɪp] n rasgón m, rasgadura ♦ vt
rasgar, desgarrar ♦ vi rasgarse,
desgarrarse; ~**cord** n cabo de desgarre

ripe [raɪp] adj maduro; ~**n** vt madurar;
(cheese) curar ♦ vi madurar

ripple [ˈrɪpl] n onda, rizo; (sound)
murmullo ♦ vi rizarse

rise [raɪz] (pt **rose**, pp **risen**) n (slope)
cuesta, pendiente f; (hill) altura; (BRIT:
in wages) aumento; (in prices,
temperature) subida; (fig: to power etc)

ascenso ♦ vi subir; (waters) crecer; (sun, moon) salir; (person: from bed etc) levantarse; (also: ~ up: rebel) sublevarse; (in rank) ascender; **to give ~ to** dar lugar o origen a; **to ~ the occasion** ponerse a la altura de las circunstancias; **risen** ['rɪzn] pp of **rise**; **rising** (increasing: number) creciente; (: prices) en aumento or alza; (tide) creciente; (sun, moon) naciente

risk [rɪsk] n riesgo, peligro ♦ vt arriesgar; (run the ~ of) exponerse a; **to take** or **run the ~ of doing** correr el riesgo de hacer; **at ~** en peligro; **at one's own ~** bajo su propia responsabilidad; **~y** adj arriesgado, peligroso

rissole ['rɪsəʊl] n croqueta

rite [raɪt] n rito; **last ~s** exequias fpl

ritual ['rɪtjuəl] adj ritual ♦ n ritual m, rito

rival ['raɪvl] n rival m/f; (in business) competidor(a) m/f ♦ adj rival, opuesto ♦ vt competir con; **~ry** n competencia

river ['rɪvə*] n río ♦ cpd (port) de río; (traffic) fluvial; **up/down ~** río arriba/abajo; **~bank** n orilla (del río); **~bed** n lecho, cauce m

rivet ['rɪvɪt] n roblón m, remache m ♦ vt (fig) captar

Riviera [rɪvɪ'eərə] n: **the (French) ~** la Costa Azul (francesa)

road [rəʊd] n camino; (motorway etc) carretera; (in town) calle f ♦ cpd (accident) de tráfico; **major/minor ~** carretera principal/secundaria; **~ accident** n accidente m de tráfico; **~block** n barricada; **~hog** n loco/a del volante; **~ map** n mapa m de carreteras; **~ rage** n agresividad en la carretera; **~ safety** n seguridad f vial; **~side** n borde m (del camino); **~sign** n señal f de tráfico; **~ user** n usuario/a de la vía pública; **~way** n calzada; **~works** npl obras fpl; **~worthy** adj (car) en buen estado para circular

roam [rəʊm] vi vagar

roar [rɔ:*] n rugido; (of vehicle, storm) estruendo; (of laughter) carcajada ♦ vi rugir; (engine) hacer estruendo; **to ~ with laughter** reírse a carcajadas; **to do a ~ing trade** hacer buen negocio

roast [rəʊst] n carne f asada, asado ♦ vt asar; (coffee) tostar; **~ beef** n rosbif m

rob [rɔb] vt robar; **to ~ sb of sth** robar algo a uno; (fig: deprive) quitar algo a uno; **~ber** n ladrón/ona m/f; **~bery** n robo

robe [rəʊb] n (for ceremony etc) toga; (also: bath~, US) albornoz m

robin ['rɔbɪn] n petirrojo

robot ['rəʊbɔt] n robot m

robust [rəʊ'bʌst] adj robusto, fuerte

rock [rɔk] n roca; (boulder) peña, peñasco; US: small stone) piedrecita; (BRIT: sweet) ≈ pirulí ♦ vt (swing gently: cradle) balancear, mecer; (: child) arrullar; (shake) sacudir ♦ vi mecerse, balancearse; sacudirse; **on the ~s** (drink) con hielo; (marriage etc) en ruinas; **~ and roll** n rocanrol m; **~-bottom** (fig) punto más bajo; **~ery** n cuadro alpino

rocket ['rɔkɪt] n cohete m

rocking ['rɔkɪŋ]: **~ chair** n mecedora; **~ horse** n caballo de balancín

rocky ['rɔkɪ] adj rocoso

rod [rɔd] n vara, varilla; (also: fishing ~) caña

rode [rəʊd] pt of **ride**

rodent ['rəʊdnt] n roedor m

roe [rəʊ] n (species: also: ~ deer) corzo; (of fish): **hard/soft ~** hueva/lecha

rogue [rəʊg] n pícaro, pillo

role [rəʊl] n papel m

roll [rəʊl] n rollo; (of bank notes) fajo; (also: bread ~) panecillo; (register, list) lista, nómina; (sound: of drums etc) redoble m ♦ vt hacer rodar; (also: ~ up: string) enrollar; (: sleeves) arremangar; (cigarette) liar; (also: ~ out: pastry) aplanar; (flatten: road, lawn) apisonar ♦ vi rodar; (drum) redoblar; (ship) balancearse; **~ about** or **around** vi (person) revolcarse; (object) rodar (por); **~ by** vi (time) pasar; **~ over** vi dar una vuelta; **~ up** vi (inf: arrive) aparecer ♦ vt (carpet) arrollar; **~ call** n: **to take a ~ call** pasar lista; **~er** n rodillo; (wheel) rueda; (for road) apisonadora; (for hair) rulo; **~erblade** n patín m (en línea); **~er coaster** n montaña rusa; **~er skates** npl patines mpl de rueda

rolling ['rəulɪŋ] adj (landscape) ondulado; **~ pin** n rodillo (de cocina); **~ stock** n (RAIL) material m rodante

ROM [rɔm] n abbr (COMPUT: = read only memory) ROM f

Roman ['rəumən] adj romano/a; **~ Catholic** adj, n católico/a m/f (romano/a)

romance [rə'mæns] n (love affair) amor m; (charm) lo romántico; (novel) novela de amor

Romania [ru:'meɪnɪə] n = **Rumania**

Roman numeral n número romano

romantic [rə'mæntɪk] adj romántico

Rome [rəum] n Roma

romp [rɔmp] n retozo, juego ♦ vi (also: **~ about**) jugar, brincar

rompers ['rɔmpəz] npl pelele m

roof [ru:f] (pl **~s**) n (gen) techo; (of house) techo, tejado ♦ vt techar, poner techo a; **the ~ of the mouth** el paladar; **~ing** n techumbre f; **~ rack** n (AUT) baca, portaequipajes m inv

rook [ruk] n (bird) graja; (CHESS) torre f

room [ru:m] n cuarto, habitación f, pieza (esp AM); (also: **bed~**) dormitorio; (in school etc) sala; (space, scope) sitio, cabida; **~s** npl (lodging) alojamiento; **"~s to let"**, **"~s for rent"** (US) "se alquilan cuartos"; **single/double ~** habitación individual/doble or para dos personas; **~ing house** (US) n pensión f; **~mate** n compañero/a de cuarto; **~ service** n servicio de habitaciones; **~y** adj espacioso; (garment) amplio

roost [ru:st] vi pasar la noche

rooster ['ru:stə*] n gallo

root [ru:t] n raíz f ♦ vi arraigarse; **~ about** vi (fig) buscar y rebuscar; **~ for** vt fus (support) apoyar a; **~ out** vt desarraigar

rope [rəup] n cuerda; (NAUT) cable m ♦ vt (tie) atar o amarrar con (una) cuerda; (climbers: also: **~ together**) encordarse; (an area: also: **~ off**) acordonar; **to know the ~s** (fig) conocer los trucos (del oficio); **~ in** vt (fig): **to ~ sb in** persuadir a uno a tomar parte

rosary ['rəuzərɪ] n rosario

rose [rəuz] pt of **rise** ♦ n rosa; (shrub) rosal m; (on watering can) roseta

rosé ['rəuzeɪ] n vino rosado

rosebud ['rəuzbʌd] n capullo de rosa

rosebush ['rəuzbuʃ] n rosal m

rosemary ['rəuzmərɪ] n romero

roster ['rɔstə*] n: **duty ~** lista de deberes

rostrum ['rɔstrəm] n tribuna

rosy ['rəuzɪ] adj rosa, sonrosado; **a ~ future** un futuro prometedor

rot [rɔt] n podredumbre f, (fig: pej) tonterías fpl ♦ vt pudrir ♦ vi pudrirse

rota ['rəutə] n (sistema m de) turnos mpl

rotary ['rəutərɪ] adj rotativo

rotate [rəu'teɪt] vt (revolve) hacer girar, dar vueltas a; (jobs) alternar ♦ vi girar, dar vueltas; **rotating** adj rotativo; **rotation** [-'teɪʃən] n rotación f

rotten ['rɔtn] adj podrido; (dishonest) corrompido; (inf: bad) pocho; **to feel ~** (ill) sentirse fatal

rotund [rəu'tʌnd] adj regordete

rouble ['ru:bl] (US **ruble**) n rublo

rough [rʌf] adj (skin, surface) áspero; (terrain) quebrado; (road) desigual; (voice) bronco; (person, manner) tosco, grosero; (weather) borrascoso; (treatment) brutal; (sea) picado; (town, area) peligroso; (plan) básico; (plan) preliminar; (guess) aproximado ♦ n (GOLF): **in the ~** en las hierbas altas; **to ~ it** vivir sin comodidades; **to sleep ~**

(BRIT) pasar la noche al raso; **~age** n fibra(s) f(pl); **~-and-ready** adj improvisado; **~ copy** n borrador m; **~ draft** n = **~ copy**; **~ly** adv (handle) torpemente; (make) toscamente; (speak) groseramente; (approximately) aproximadamente; **~ness** n (of surface) aspereza; (of person) rudeza

roulette [ruː'let] n ruleta

Roumania [ruː'meɪnɪə] n = Rumania

round [raund] adj redondo ♦ n círculo; (BRIT: of toast) rebanada; (of policeman) ronda; (of milkman) recorrido; (of doctor) visitas fpl; (game: of cards, in competition) partida; (of ammunition) cartucho; (BOXING) asalto; (of talks) ronda ♦ vt doblar ♦ prep alrededor de; (surrounding): **~ his neck/the table** en su cuello/alrededor de la mesa; (in a circular movement): **to move ~ the room/sail ~ the world** dar una vuelta a la habitación/ circunnavigar el mundo; (in various directions): **to move ~ a room/house** moverse por toda la habitación/casa; (approximately) alrededor de ♦ adv: **all ~** por todos lados; **the long way ~** por el camino menos directo; **all the year ~** durante todo el año; **it's just ~ the corner** (fig) está a la vuelta de la esquina; **~ the clock** adv las 24 horas; **to go ~ to sb's (house)** ir a casa de uno; **to go ~ the back** pasar por atrás; **enough to go ~** bastante (para todos); **a ~ of applause** una salva de aplausos; **a ~ of drinks/ sandwiches** una ronda de bebidas/ bocadillos; **~ off** vt (speech etc) acabar, poner término a; **~ up** vt (cattle) acorralar; (people) reunir; (price) redondear; **~about** (BRIT) n (AUT) isleta; (at fair) tiovivo ♦ adj (route, means) indirecto; **~ers** n (game) juego similar al béisbol; **~ly** adv (fig) rotundamente; **~ trip** n viaje m de ida y vuelta; **~up** n rodeo; (of criminals) redada; (of news) resumen m

rouse [rauz] vt (wake up) despertar; (stir up) suscitar; **rousing** adj (cheer, welcome) caluroso

route [ruːt] n ruta, camino; (of bus) recorrido; (of shipping) derrota

routine [ruː'tiːn] adj rutinario ♦ n rutina; (THEATRE) número

rove [rauv] vt vagar o errar por

row¹ [rau] n (line) fila, hilera; (KNITTING) pasada ♦ vi (in boat) remar ♦ vt conducir remando; **4 days in a ~** 4 días seguidos

row² [rau] n (racket) escándalo; (dispute) bronca, pelea; (scolding) regaño ♦ vi pelear(se)

rowboat ['raubaut] (US) n bote m de remos

rowdy ['raudɪ] adj (person: noisy) ruidoso; (occasion) alborotado

rowing ['rauɪŋ] n remo; **~ boat** (BRIT) n bote m de remos

royal ['rɔɪəl] adj real; **R~ Air Force** n Fuerzas fpl Aéreas Británicas; **~ty** n (~ persons) familia real; (payment to author) derechos mpl de autor

rpm abbr (= revs per minute) r.p.m.

R.S.V.P. abbr (= répondez s'il vous plaît) SRC

Rt. Hon. abbr (BRIT: = Right Honourable) título honorífico de diputado

rub [rʌb] vt frotar; (scrub) restregar ♦ n: **to give sth a ~** frotar algo; **to ~ sb up** or **~ sb** (US) **the wrong way** entrarle uno por mal ojo; **~ off** vi borrarse; **~ off on** vt fus influir en; **~ out** vt borrar

rubber ['rʌbə*] n caucho, goma; (BRIT: eraser) goma de borrar; **~ band** n goma, gomita; **~ plant** n ficus m

rubbish ['rʌbɪʃ] n basura; (waste) desperdicios mpl; (fig: pej) tonterías fpl; (junk) pacotilla; **~ bin** (BRIT) n cubo (SP) or bote m (AM) de la basura; **~ dump** n vertedero, basurero

rubble ['rʌbl] n escombros mpl

ruble ['ruːbl] (US) n = **rouble**

ruby ['ruːbɪ] n rubí m

rucksack ['rʌksæk] n mochila
rudder ['rʌdə*] n timón m
ruddy ['rʌdɪ] adj (face) rubicundo; (inf: damned) condenado
rude [ruːd] adj (impolite: person) mal educado; (: word, manners) grosero; (crude) crudo; (indecent) indecente; **~ness** n descortesía
ruffle ['rʌfl] vt (hair) despeinar; (clothes) arrugar; **to get ~d** (fig: person) alterarse
rug [rʌg] n alfombra; (BRIT: blanket) manta
rugby ['rʌgbɪ] n (also: ~ football) rugby m
rugged ['rʌgɪd] adj (landscape) accidentado; (features) robusto
ruin ['ruːɪn] n ruina ♦ vt arruinar; (spoil) estropear; **~s** npl ruinas fpl, restos mpl
rule [ruːl] n (norm) norma, costumbre f; (regulation, ruler) regla; (government) dominio ♦ vt (country, person) gobernar ♦ vi gobernar; (LAW) fallar; **as a ~** por regla general; **~ out** vt excluir; **~d** adj (paper) rayado; **~r** n (sovereign) soberano; (for measuring) regla; **ruling** adj (party) gobernante; (class) dirigente ♦ n (LAW) fallo, decisión f
rum [rʌm] n ron m
Rumania [ruːˈmeɪnɪə] n Rumanía; **~n** adj rumano/a ♦ n rumano/a m/f; (LING) rumano
rumble ['rʌmbl] n (noise) ruido sordo ♦ vi retumbar, hacer un ruido sordo; (stomach, pipe) sonar
rummage ['rʌmɪdʒ] vi (search) hurgar
rumour ['ruːmə*] (US rumor) n rumor m ♦ vt: **it is ~ed that ...** se rumorea que ...
rump [rʌmp] n (of animal) ancas fpl, grupa; **~ steak** n filete m de lomo
rumpus ['rʌmpəs] n lío, jaleo
run [rʌn] (pt ran, pp run) n (fast pace): **at a ~** corriendo; (SPORT, in tights) carrera; (outing) paseo, excursión f; (distance travelled) trayecto; (series)

serie f; (THEATRE) temporada; (SKI) pista ♦ vt correr; (operate: business) dirigir; (: competition, course) organizar; (: hotel, house) administrar, llevar; (COMPUT) ejecutar; (pass: hand) pasar; (PRESS: feature) publicar ♦ vi correr; (work: machine) funcionar, marchar; (bus, train: operate) circular, ir; (: travel) ir; (continue: play) seguir; (: contract) ser válido; (flow: river) fluir; (colours, washing) desteñirse; (in election) ser candidato; **there was a ~ on** (meat, tickets) hubo mucha demanda de; **in the long ~** a la larga; **on the ~** en fuga; **I'll ~ you to the station** te llevaré a la estación (en coche); **to ~ a risk** correr un riesgo; **to ~ a bath** llenar la bañera; **~ about** or **around** vi (children) correr por todos lados; **~ across** vt fus (find) dar o topar con; **~ away** vi huir; **~ down** vt (production) ir reduciendo; (factory) ir restringiendo la producción en; (subj: car) atropellar; (criticize) criticar; **to be ~ down** (person: tired) estar debilitado; **~ in** (BRIT) vt (car) rodar; **~ into** vt fus (meet: person, trouble) tropezar con; (collide with) chocar con; **~ off** vt (water) dejar correr; (copies) sacar ♦ vi huir corriendo; **~ out** vi (person) salir corriendo; (liquid) irse; (lease) caducar, vencer; (money etc) acabarse; **~ out of** vt fus quedar sin; **~ over** vt (AUT) atropellar ♦ vt fus (revise) repasar; **~ through** vt fus (instructions) repasar; **~ up** vt (debt) contraer; **to ~ up against** (difficulties) tropezar con; **~away** adj (horse) desbocado; (truck) sin frenos; (child) escapado de casa
rung [rʌŋ] pp of **ring** ♦ n (of ladder) escalón m, peldaño
runner ['rʌnə*] n (in race: person) corredor(a) m/f; (: horse) caballo; (on sledge) patín m; (≈ bean (BRIT) n ≈ judía verde; **~up** n subcampeón/ona m/f
running ['rʌnɪŋ] n (sport) atletismo;

(*business*) administración f ♦ adj (*water, costs*) corriente; (*commentary*) continuo; **to be in/out of the ~** for sth tener/no tener posibilidades de ganar algo; **6 days ~** 6 días seguidos; **~ commentary** n (*TV, RADIO*) comentario en directo; (*on guided tour etc*) comentario detallado; **~ costs** npl gastos mpl corrientes

runny ['rʌnɪ] adj fluido; (*nose, eyes*) gastante

run-of-the-mill adj común y corriente

runt [rʌnt] n (*also pej*) redrojo, enano

run-up n: **~ to** (*election etc*) período previo a

runway ['rʌnweɪ] n (*AVIAT*) pista de aterrizaje

rural ['ruərl] adj rural

rush [rʌʃ] n ímpetu m; (*hurry*) prisa; (*COMM*) demanda repentina; (*current*) corriente f fuerte; (*of feeling*) torrente; (*BOT*) junco ♦ vt apresurar; (*work*) hacer de prisa ♦ vi correr, precipitarse; **~ hour** n horas fpl punta

rusk [rʌsk] n bizcocho tostado

Russia ['rʌʃə] n Rusia; **~n** adj ruso/a ♦ n ruso/a m/f; (*LING*) ruso

rust [rʌst] n herrumbre f, moho f ♦ vi oxidarse

rustic ['rʌstɪk] adj rústico

rustle ['rʌsl] vi susurrar ♦ vt (*paper*) hacer crujir

rustproof ['rʌstpru:f] adj inoxidable

rusty ['rʌstɪ] adj oxidado

rut [rʌt] n surco, (*ZOOL*) celo; **to be in a ~** ser esclavo de la rutina

ruthless ['ru:θlɪs] adj despiadado

rye [raɪ] n centeno

S, s

Sabbath ['sæbəθ] n domingo; (*Jewish*) sábado

sabotage ['sæbətɑ:ʒ] n sabotaje m ♦ vt sabotear

saccharin(e) ['sækərɪn] n sacarina

sachet ['sæʃeɪ] n sobrecito

sack [sæk] n (*bag*) saco, costal m ♦ vt (*dismiss*) despedir; (*plunder*) saquear; **to get the ~** ser despedido; **~ing** n despido; (*material*) arpillera

sacred ['seɪkrɪd] adj sagrado, santo

sacrifice ['sækrɪfaɪs] n sacrificio ♦ vt sacrificar

sad [sæd] adj (*unhappy*) triste; (*deplorable*) lamentable

saddle ['sædl] n silla (de montar); (*of cycle*) sillín m ♦ vt (*horse*) ensillar; **to be ~d with sth** (*inf*) quedar cargado con algo; **~bag** n alforja

sadistic [sə'dɪstɪk] adj sádico

sadly ['sædlɪ] adv lamentablemente; **to be ~ lacking** in estar por desgracia carente de

sadness ['sædnɪs] n tristeza

s.a.e. abbr (= *stamped addressed envelope*) sobre con las propias señas de uno y con sello

safari [sə'fɑ:rɪ] n safari m

safe [seɪf] adj (*out of danger*) fuera de peligro; (*not dangerous, sure*) seguro; (*unharmed*) ileso ♦ n caja de caudales, caja fuerte; **~ and sound** sano y salvo; (*just*) **to be on the ~ side** para mayor seguridad; **~-conduct** n salvoconducto; **~-deposit** n (*vault*) cámara acorazada; (*box*) caja de seguridad; **~guard** n protección f, garantía ♦ vt proteger, defender; **~keeping** n custodia; **~ly** adv seguramente, con seguridad; **to arrive ~ly** llegar bien; **~ sex** n sexo seguro o sin riesgo

safety ['seɪftɪ] n seguridad f; **~ belt** n cinturón m (de seguridad); **~ pin** n imperdible m (*SP*), seguro (*AM*); **~ valve** n válvula de seguridad

saffron ['sæfrən] n azafrán m

sag [sæg] vi aflojarse

sage [seɪdʒ] n (*herb*) salvia; (*man*) sabio

Sagittarius [sædʒɪ'tɛərɪəs] n Sagitario

Sahara [sə'hɑ:rə] n: **the ~** (*Desert*) el (desierto del) Sáhara

said [sɛd] pt, pp of **say**

sail [seɪl] n (on boat) vela; (trip): **to go for a ~** dar un paseo en barco ♦ vt (boat) gobernar ♦ vi (travel: ship) navegar; (SPORT) hacer vela; **~ing** n (boat voyage) salir; **they ~ed into Copenhagen** arribaron a Copenhague; **~ through** vt fus (exam) aprobar sin ningún problema; **~boat** (US) n velero, barco de vela; **~ing** n (SPORT) vela; **to go ~ing** hacer vela ♦ **~ing boat** n barco de vela; **~ing ship** n velero; **~or** n marinero, marino

saint [seɪnt] n santo; **~ly** adj santo

sake [seɪk] n: **for the ~ of** por

~lad ['sæləd] n ensalada; **~ bowl** n ensaladera; **~ cream** (BRIT) n (especie de) mayonesa; **~ dressing** n aliño

salary ['sælərɪ] n salario

sale [seɪl] n venta; (at reduced prices) liquidación f, saldo; (auction) subasta; **~s** npl (total amount sold) ventas fpl, facturación f; **"for ~"** "se vende"; **on ~** en venta; **on ~ or return** (goods) venta por reposición; **~room** n sala de subastas; **~s assistant** (US **~s clerk**) n dependiente/a m/f; **salesman/woman** (irreg) n (in shop) dependiente/a m/f; (representative) viajante m/f

salmon ['sæmən] n inv salmón m

salon ['sælɒn] n (hairdressing ~) peluquería; (beauty ~) salón m de belleza

saloon [sə'luːn] n (US) bar m, taberna; (BRIT: AUT) (coche m de) turismo; (ship's lounge) cámara, salón m

salt [sɔːlt] n sal f ♦ vt salar; (put ~ on) poner sal en; **~ cellar** n salero; **~water** adj de agua salada; **~y** adj salado

salute [sə'luːt] n saludo; (of guns) salva ♦ vt saludar

salvage ['sælvɪdʒ] n (saving) salvamento, recuperación f; (things saved) objetos mpl salvados ♦ vt salvar

salvation [sæl'veɪʃən] n salvación f;

S~ Army n Ejército de Salvación

same [seɪm] adj mismo ♦ pron: **the ~** el/la mismo/a, los/las mismos/as; **the ~ book as** el mismo libro que; **at the ~ time** (at the ~ moment) al mismo tiempo; (yet) sin embargo; **all or just the ~** sin embargo, aun así; **to do the ~ (as sb)** hacer lo mismo (que uno); **the ~ to you!** ¡igualmente!

sample ['sɑːmpl] n muestra ♦ vt (food) probar; (wine) catar

sanction ['sæŋkʃən] n aprobación f ♦ vt sancionar; aprobar; **~s** npl (POL) sanciones fpl

sanctity ['sæŋktɪtɪ] n santidad f; (inviolability) inviolabilidad f

sanctuary ['sæŋktjuərɪ] n santuario; (refuge) asilo, refugio; (for wildlife) reserva

sand [sænd] n arena; (beach) playa ♦ vt (also: ~ down) lijar

sandal ['sændl] n sandalia

sand: **~box** (US) n = **~pit**; **~castle** n castillo de arena; **~ dune** n duna; **~paper** n papel m de lija; **~pit** n (for children) cajón m de arena; **~stone** n piedra arenisca

sandwich ['sændwɪtʃ] n bocadillo (SP), sandwich m, emparedado (AM) ♦ vt intercalar; **~ed between** apretujado entre; **cheese/ham ~** sandwich de queso/jamón; **~ course** (BRIT) n curso de medio tiempo

sandy ['sændɪ] adj arenoso; (colour) rojizo

sane [seɪn] adj cuerdo; (sensible) sensato

sang [sæŋ] pt of **sing**

sanitary ['sænɪtərɪ] adj sanitario; (clean) higiénico; **~ towel** (US **~ napkin**) n paño higiénico, compresa

sanitation [sænɪ'teɪʃən] n (in house) servicios mpl higiénicos; (in town) servicio de desinfección; **~ department** (US) n departamento de limpieza y recogida de basuras

sanity ['sænɪtɪ] n cordura; (of

judgment) sensatez f
sank [sæŋk] *pt of* **sink**
Santa Claus [sæntə'klɔ:z] *n* San Nicolás, Papá Noel
sap [sæp] *n (of plants)* savia ♦ *vt (strength)* minar, agotar
sapling ['sæplıŋ] *n* árbol nuevo *or* joven
sapphire ['sæfaıə*] *n* zafiro
sarcasm ['sɑ:kæzm] *n* sarcasmo
sardine [sɑ:'di:n] *n* sardina
Sardinia [sɑ:'dınıə] *n* Cerdeña
sash [sæʃ] *n* faja
sat [sæt] *pt, pp of* **sit**
Satan ['seıtn] *n* Satanás
satchel ['sætʃl] *n (child's)* cartera (SP), mochila (AM)
satellite ['sætəlaıt] *n* satélite *m*; **~ dish** *n* antena de televisión por satélite; **~ television** *n* televisión *f* vía satélite
satin ['sætın] *n* raso ♦ *adj* de raso
satire ['sætaıə*] *n* sátira
satisfaction [sætıs'fækʃən] *n* satisfacción *f*
satisfactory [sætıs'fæktərı] *adj* satisfactorio
satisfy ['sætısfaı] *vt* satisfacer; *(convince)* convencer; **~ing** *adj* satisfactorio
Saturday ['sætədı] *n* sábado
sauce [sɔ:s] *n* salsa; *(sweet)* crema; jarabe *m*; **~pan** *n* cacerola, olla
saucer ['sɔ:sə*] *n* platillo
Saudi ['saudı]: **~ Arabia** *n* Arabia Saudí *or* Saudita; **~ (Arabian)** *adj, n* saudí *m/f*, saudita *m/f*
sauna ['sɔ:nə] *n* sauna
saunter ['sɔ:ntə*] *vi*: **to ~ in/out** entrar/salir sin prisa
sausage ['sɔsıdʒ] *n* salchicha; **~ roll** *n* empanadita de salchicha
sauté ['səuteı] *adj* salteado
savage ['sævıdʒ] *adj (cruel, fierce)* feroz, furioso; *(primitive)* salvaje ♦ *n* salvaje *m/f* ♦ *vt (attack)* embestir
save [seıv] *vt (rescue)* salvar, rescatar; *(money, time)* ahorrar; *(put by, keep;*

seat) guardar; *(COMPUT)* salvar (y guardar); *(avoid: trouble)* evitar; *(SPORT)* parar ♦ *vi (also: ~ up)* ahorrar ♦ *n (SPORT)* parada ♦ *prep* salvo, excepto
saving ['seıvıŋ] *n (on price etc)* economía ♦ *adj*: **the ~ grace of** el único mérito de; **~s** *npl* ahorros *mpl*; **~s account** *n* cuenta de ahorros; **~s bank** *n* caja de ahorros
saviour ['seıvjə*] *(US* **savior**) *n* salvador(a) *m/f*
savour ['seıvə*] *(US* **savor**) *vt* saborear; **~y** *adj* sabroso; *(dish: not sweet)* salado
saw [sɔ:] *(pt* sawed, *pp* sawed *or* sawn) *pt of* **see** ♦ *n (tool)* sierra ♦ *vt* serrar; **~dust** *n* (a)serrín; **~mill** *n* aserradero; **~n-off shotgun** *n* escopeta de cañones recortados
saxophone ['sæksəfəun] *n* saxófono
say [seı] *(pt, pp* said) *n*: **to have one's ~** expresar su opinión ♦ *vt* decir; **to have a** *or* **some ~ in sth** tener voz *or* tener que ver en algo; **to ~ yes/no** decir que sí/no; **could you ~ that again?** ¿podría repetir eso?; **that is to ~** es decir; **that goes without ~ing** ni que decir tiene; **~ing** *n* dicho, refrán *m*
scab [skæb] *n* costra; *(pej)* esquirol *m*
scaffold ['skæfəuld] *n* cadalso; **~ing** *n* andamio, andamiaje *m*
scald [skɔ:ld] *n* escaldadura ♦ *vt* escaldar
scale [skeıl] *n (gen, MUS)* escala; *(of fish)* escama; *(of salaries, fees etc)* escalafón *m* ♦ *vt (mountain)* escalar; *(tree)* trepar; **~s** *npl (for weighing: small)* balanza; *(: large)* báscula; **on a large ~** en gran escala; **~ of charges** tarifa, lista de precios; **~ down** *vt* reducir a escala
scallop ['skɔləp] *n (ZOOL)* venera; *(SEWING)* festón *m*
scalp [skælp] *n* cabellera ♦ *vt* escalpar
scampi ['skæmpı] *npl* gambas *fpl*
scan [skæn] *vt (examine)* escudriñar; *(glance at quickly)* dar un vistazo a; *(TV,*

RADAR) explorar, registrar ♦ n (MED.): **to have a ~** pasar por el escáner

scandal |'skændl| n escándalo; (gossip) chismes mpl

Scandinavia |skændɪ'neɪvɪə| n Escandinavia; **~n** adj, n escandinavo/a m/f

scant |skænt| adj escaso; **~y** adj (meal) insuficiente; (clothes) ligero

scapegoat |'skeɪpgəʊt| n cabeza de turco, chivo expiatorio

scar |skɑ:| n cicatriz f; (fig) señal f ♦ vt dejar señales en

scarce |skɛəs| adj escaso; **to make o.s. ~** (inf) esfumarse; **~ly** adv apenas; **scarcity** n escasez f

scare |skɛə*| n susto, sobresalto; (panic) pánico ♦ vt asustar, espantar; **to ~ sb stiff** dar a uno un susto de muerte; **bomb ~** amenaza de bomba; **~ off o away** vt ahuyentar; **~crow** n espantapájaros m inv; **~d** adj: **to be ~d** estar asustado

scarf |skɑ:f| (pl **~s** o **scarves**) n (long) bufanda; (square) pañuelo

scarlet |'skɑ:lɪt| adj escarlata; **~ fever** n escarlatina

scarves |skɑ:vz| npl of **scarf**

scary |'skɛərɪ| (inf) adj espeluznante

scathing |'skeɪðɪŋ| adj mordaz

scatter |'skætə*| vt (spread) esparcir, desparramar; (put to flight) dispersar ♦ vi desparramarse; dispersarse; **~brained** adj ligero de cascos

scavenger |'skævəndʒə*| n (person) basurero/a

scenario |sɪ'nɑ:rɪəʊ| n (THEATRE) argumento; (CINEMA) guión m; (fig) escenario

scene |si:n| n (THEATRE, fig etc) escena; (of crime etc) escenario; (view) panorama m; (fuss) escándalo; **~ry** n (THEATRE) decorado; (landscape) paisaje m; **scenic** adj pintoresco

scent |sent| n perfume m, olor m; (fig: track) rastro, pista

sceptic |'skɛptɪk| n (US **skeptic**) n

escéptico/a; **~al** adj escéptico

sceptre |'sɛptə*| (US **scepter**) n cetro

schedule |'ʃɛdju:l, (US) 'skɛdju:l| n (timetable) horario; (of events) programa m; (list) lista ♦ vt (visit) fijar la hora de; **to arrive on ~** llegar a la hora debida; **to be ahead of/behind ~** estar adelantado/en retraso; **~d flight** n vuelo regular

scheme |ski:m| n (plan) plan m, proyecto; (plot) intriga; (arrangement) disposición f; (pension ~ etc) sistema m ♦ vi (intrigue) intrigar; **scheming** adj intrigante ♦ n intrigas fpl

schizophrenic |skɪtsə'frɛnɪk| adj esquizofrénico

scholar |'skɒlə*| n (pupil) alumno/a; (learned person) sabio/a, erudito/a; **~ship** n erudición f; (grant) beca

school |sku:l| n escuela, colegio; (in university) facultad f ♦ cpd escolar; **~ age** n edad f escolar; **~book** n libro de texto; **~boy** n alumno; **~ children** npl alumnos mpl; **~girl** n alumna; **~ing** n enseñanza; **~master/mistress** n (primary) maestro/a; (secondary) profesor(a) m/f; **~teacher** n (primary) maestro/a; (secondary) profesor(a) m/f

schooner |'sku:nə*| n (ship) goleta

sciatica |saɪ'ætɪkə| n ciática

science |'saɪəns| n ciencia; **~ fiction** n ciencia-ficción f; **scientific** |-'tɪfɪk| adj científico; **scientist** n científico/a

scissors |'sɪzəz| npl tijeras fpl; **a pair of ~** unas tijeras

scoff |skɒf| vt (BRIT: inf: eat) engullir ♦ vi: **to ~ (at)** (mock) mofarse (de)

scold |skəʊld| vt regañar

scone |skɒn| n pastel de pan

scoop |sku:p| n (for flour etc) pala; (PRESS) exclusiva; **~ out** vt excavar; **~ up** vt recoger

scooter |'sku:tə*| n moto f; (toy) patinete m

scope |skəʊp| n (of plan) ámbito; (of person) competencia; (opportunity) libertad f (de acción)

scorch [skɔːtʃ] vt (clothes) chamuscar; (earth, grass) quemar, secar

score [skɔː*] n (points etc) puntuación f; (MUS) partitura f; (twenty) veintena ♦ vt (goal, point) ganar; (mark) rayar; (achieve: success) conseguir ♦ vi marcar un tanto; (FOOTBALL) marcar (un) gol; (keep score) llevar el tanteo; ~s of (lots) decenas de; **on that** ~ en lo que se refiere a eso; **to** ~ **6 out of 10** obtener una puntuación de seis sobre 10; ~ **out** vt tachar; ~ **over** vt fus obtener una victoria sobre; ~**board** n marcador m

scorn [skɔːn] n desprecio; ~**ful** adj desdeñoso, despreciativo

Scorpio ['skɔːpɪəu] n Escorpión m

scorpion ['skɔːpɪən] n alacrán m

Scot [skɒt] n escocés/esa m/f

Scotch [skɒtʃ] n whisky m escocés

Scotland ['skɒtlənd] n Escocia

Scots [skɒts] adj escocés/esa; ~**man/woman** (irreg) n escocés/esa m/f; **Scottish** ['skɒtɪʃ] adj escocés/esa; **Scottish Parliament** n Parlamento escocés

scoundrel ['skaundrl] n canalla m/f, sinvergüenza m/f

scout [skaut] n (MIL, also: boy ~) explorador m; **girl** ~ (US) niña exploradora; ~ **around** vi reconocer el terreno

scowl [skaul] vi fruncir el ceño; **to** ~ **at sb** mirar con ceño a uno

scrabble ['skræbl] vi (claw): **to** ~ (**at**) arañar; (also: ~ **around**: search) revolver todo buscando ♦ n: **S**~ ® Scrabble ® m

scraggy ['skrægɪ] adj descarnado

scram [skræm] (inf) vi largarse

scramble ['skræmbl] n (climb) subida (difícil); (struggle) pelea ♦ vi: **to** ~ **through/out** abrirse paso/salir con dificultad; **to** ~ **for** pelear por; ~**d eggs** npl huevos mpl revueltos

scrap [skræp] n (bit) pedacito; (fig) pizca; (fight) riña, bronca; (also: ~ **iron**) chatarra, hierro viejo ♦ vt (discard) desechar, descartar ♦ vi reñir, armar

(una) bronca; ~**s** npl (waste) sobras fpl, desperdicios mpl; ~**book** n álbum m de recortes; ~ **dealer** n chatarrero/a

scrape [skreɪp] n: **to get into a** ~ meterse en un lío ♦ vt raspar; (skin etc) rasguñar; (~ **against**) rozar ♦ vi: **to** ~ **through** (exam) aprobar por los pelos; ~ **together** vt (money) ahorrar, juntar

scrap: ~ heap n (fig): **to be on the** ~ **heap** estar acabado; (BRIT) chatarrero/a; ~ **merchant** (BRIT) n chatarrero/a; ~ **paper** n pedazos mpl de papel

scratch [skrætʃ] n rasguño; (from claw) arañazo ♦ cpd: ~ **team** equipo improvisado ♦ vt (paint, car) rayar; (with claw, nail) rasguñar, arañar; (rub: nose etc) rascarse ♦ vi rascarse; **to start from** ~ partir de cero; **to be up to** ~ cumplir con los requisitos

scrawl [skrɔːl] n garabatos mpl ♦ vi hacer garabatos

scrawny ['skrɔːnɪ] adj flaco

scream [skriːm] n chillido ♦ vi chillar

screech [skriːtʃ] vi chirriar

screen [skriːn] n (CINEMA, TV) pantalla; (movable barrier) biombo ♦ vt (conceal) tapar; (from the wind etc) proteger; (film) proyectar; (candidates etc) investigar a; ~**ing** n (MED) investigación f médica; ~**play** n guión m; ~ **saver** n (COMPUT) protector m de pantalla

screw [skruː] n tornillo ♦ vt (also: ~ **in**) atornillar; ~ **up** vt (paper) arrugar; **to** ~ **up one's eyes** arrugar el entrecejo; ~**driver** n destornillador m

scribble ['skrɪbl] n garabatos mpl ♦ vt, vi garabatear

script [skrɪpt] n (CINEMA etc) guión m; (writing) escritura, letra

Scripture(s) ['skrɪptʃə*(z)] n(pl) Sagrada Escritura

scroll [skrəul] n rollo

scrounge [skraundʒ] (inf) vt: **to** ~ **sth off or from sb** obtener algo de uno de gorra ♦ n: **on the** ~ de gorra; ~**r** n gorrón/ona m/f

scrub [skrʌb] n (land) maleza ♦ vt fregar, restregar; (inf: reject) cancelar, anular

scruff [skrʌf] n: by the ~ of the neck por el pescuezo

scruffy ['skrʌfɪ] adj desaliñado, piojoso

scrum(mage) ['skrʌm(mɪdʒ)] n (RUGBY) melée f

scruple ['skruːpl] n (gen pl) escrúpulo

scrutinize ['skruːtɪnaɪz] vt escudriñar; (votes) escrutar; **scrutiny** ['skruːtɪnɪ] n escrutinio, examen m

scuff [skʌf] vt (shoes, floor) rayar

scuffle ['skʌfl] n refriega

sculptor ['skʌlptə*] n escultor(a) m/f

sculpture ['skʌlptʃə*] n escultura

scum [skʌm] n (on liquid) espuma; (pej: people) escoria

scurry ['skʌrɪ] vi correr; **to ~ off** escabullirse

scuttle ['skʌtl] n (also: coal ~) cubo, carbonera ♦ vt (ship) barrenar ♦ vi to **~ away, ~ off** escabullirse

scythe [saɪð] n guadaña

SDP (BRIT) n abbr = **Social Democratic Party**

sea [siː] n mar m ♦ cpd de mar, marítimo; **by ~** (travel) en barco; **on the ~** (boat) en el mar; (town) junto al mar; **to be all at ~** (fig) estar despistado; **out to ~, at ~** en alta mar; **~board** n litoral m; **~food** n mariscos mpl; **~ front** n paseo marítimo; **~-going** adj de altura; **~gull** n gaviota

seal [siːl] n (animal) foca; (stamp) sello ♦ vt (close) cerrar; **~ off** vt (area) acordonar

sea level n nivel m del mar

sea lion n león m marino

seam [siːm] n (in cloth) costura; (of metal) juntura; (of coal) veta, filón m

seaman ['siːmən] (irreg) n marinero

seance ['seɪɔns] n sesión f de espiritismo

seaplane ['siːpleɪn] n hidroavión m

seaport ['siːpɔːt] n puerto de mar

search [sɜːtʃ] n (for person, thing) busca, búsqueda; (COMPUT) búsqueda; (inspection: of sb's home) registro ♦ vt (look in) buscar en; (examine) examinar; (person, place) registrar ♦ vi: **to ~ for** buscar; **in ~ of** en busca de; **~ through** vt fus registrar; **~ engine** n (COMPUT) buscador m; **~ing** adj penetrante; **~light** n reflector m; **~ party** n pelotón m de salvamento; **~ warrant** n mandamiento (judicial)

sea: ~shore n playa, orilla del mar; **~sick** adj mareado; **~side** n playa, orilla del mar; **~side resort** n centro turístico costero

season ['siːzn] n (of year) estación f; (sporting etc) temporada; (of films etc) ciclo ♦ vt (food) sazonar; **in/out of ~** en sazón/fuera de temporada; **~al** adj estacional; **~ed** adj (fig) experimentado; **~ing** n condimento, aderezo; **~ ticket** n abono

seat [siːt] n (in bus, train) asiento; (chair) silla; (PARLIAMENT) escaño; (buttocks) culo, trasero; (of trousers) culera ♦ vt sentar; (have room for) tener cabida para; **to be ~ed** sentarse; **~ belt** n cinturón m de seguridad

sea: ~ water n agua del mar; **~weed** n alga marina; **~worthy** adj en condiciones de navegar

sec. abbr = **second(s)**

secluded [sɪ'kluːdɪd] adj retirado

seclusion [sɪ'kluːʒən] n reclusión f

second ['sɛkənd] adj segundo ♦ adv en segundo lugar ♦ n segundo; (AUT: also: ~ gear) segunda; (COMM) artículo con algún desperfecto; (BRIT: SCOL: degree) título de licenciado con calificación de notable ♦ vt (motion) apoyar; **~ary** adj secundario; **~ary school** n escuela secundaria; **~-class** adj de segunda clase ♦ adv (RAIL) en segunda; **~hand** adj de segunda mano, usado; **~ hand** n (on clock) segundero; **~ly** adv en segundo lugar; **~ment** [sɪ'kɔndmənt] (BRIT) n traslado

temporal; **~-rate** adj de segunda
categoría; **~ thoughts** npl: **to have
~ thoughts** cambiar de opinión; **on
~ thoughts** or **thought** (US)
pensándolo bien

secrecy ['si:krəsɪ] n secreto

secret ['si:krɪt] adj, n secreto; **in ~** n
secreto

secretarial [sekrɪ'teərɪəl] adj de
secretario; (course, staff) de
secretariado

secretary ['sekrətərɪ] n secretario/a;
S~ of State (for) (BRIT: POL) Ministro
(de)

secretive ['si:krətɪv] adj reservado,
·sigiloso

secretly ['si:krɪtlɪ] adv en secreto

sect [sekt] n secta; **~arian** [-'teərɪən]
adj sectario

section ['sekʃən] n sección f; (part)
parte f; (of document) artículo; (of
opinion) sector m; (cross~) corte m
transversal

sector ['sektə*] n sector m

secular ['sekjulə*] adj secular, seglar

secure [sɪ'kjuə*] adj seguro; (firmly
fixed) firme, fijo ♦ vt (fix) asegurar,
afianzar; (get) conseguir

security [sɪ'kjuərɪtɪ] n seguridad f; (for
loan) fianza; (: object) prenda

sedate [sɪ'deɪt] adj tranquilo ♦ vt tratar
con sedantes

sedation [sɪ'deɪʃən] n (MED) sedación f

sedative ['sedɪtɪv] n sedante m,
sedativo

seduce [sɪ'djuːs] vt seducir; **seduction**
[-'dʌkʃən] n seducción f; **seductive**
[-'dʌktɪv] adj seductor(a)

see [si:] (pt **saw**, pp **seen**) vt ver;
(accompany): **~ sb to the door**
acompañar a uno a la puerta;
(understand) ver, comprender ♦ vi ver
♦ n (arz)obispado; **to ~ that** (ensure)
asegurar que; **~ you soon!** ¡hasta
pronto!; **~ about** vt fus atender a,
encargarse de; **~ off** vt despedir;
~ through vt fus (fig) calar ♦ vt (plan)

llevar a cabo; **~ to** vt fus atender a,
encargarse de

seed [si:d] n semilla; (in fruit) pepita;
(fig: gen pl) germen m; (TENNIS etc)
preseleccionado/a; **to go to ~** (plant)
granar; (fig) descuidarse; **~ling** n
planta de semillero; **~y** adj (shabby)
desaseado, raído

seeing ['si:ɪŋ] conj: **~ (that)** visto que,
en vista de que

seek [si:k] (pt, pp **sought**) vt buscar;
(post) solicitar

seem [si:m] vi parecer; **there ~s to be
... parece que hay ...**; **~ingly** adv
aparentemente, según parece

seen [si:n] pp of **see**

seep [si:p] vi filtrarse

seesaw ['si:sɔ:] n subibaja

seethe [si:ð] vi hervir; **to ~ with
anger** estar furioso

see-through adj transparente

segment ['segmənt] n (part) sección f,
(of orange) gajo

segregate ['segrɪgeɪt] vt segregar

seize [si:z] vt (grasp) agarrar, asir; (take
possession of) secuestrar; (: territory)
apoderarse de; (opportunity)
aprovecharse de; **~ up** vi (TECH) agarrotarse

seizure ['si:ʒə*] n (MED) ataque m,
(LAW, of power) incautación f

seldom ['seldəm] adv rara vez

select [sɪ'lekt] adj selecto, escogido
♦ vt escoger, elegir; (SPORT)
seleccionar; **~ion** [-'lekʃən] n selección
f, elección f; (COMM) surtido

self [self] (pl **selves**) n uno mismo; **the
~** el yo ♦ prefix auto...; **~-assured** adj
seguro de sí mismo; **~-catering** (BRIT)
adj (flat etc) con cocina; **~-centred** (US
~-centered) adj egocéntrico; **~-
confidence** n confianza en sí mismo;
~-conscious adj cohibido; **~-
contained** (BRIT) adj (flat) con entrada
particular; **~-control** n autodominio;
~-defence (US **~-defense**) n defensa
propia; **~-discipline** n autodisciplina;

~-employed adj que trabaja por cuenta propia; **~-evident** adj patente; **~-governing** adj autónomo; **~-indulgent** adj autocomplaciente; **~-interest** n egoísmo; **~-ish** adj egoísta; **~ishness** n egoísmo; **~-less** adj desinteresado; **~-made** adj: **~-made man** hombre m que se ha hecho a sí mismo; **~-pity** n lástima de sí mismo; **~-portrait** n autorretrato; **~-possessed** adj sereno, dueño de sí mismo; **~-preservation** n propia conservación f; **~-respect** n amor m propio; **~-righteous** adj santurrón/ona; **~-sacrifice** n abnegación f; **~-satisfied** adj satisfecho de sí mismo; **~-service** n de autoservicio; **~-sufficient** adj autosuficiente; **~-taught** adj autodidacta

sell [sel] (pt, pp **sold**) vt vender ♦ vi venderse; **to ~ at** or **for £10** venderse a 10 libras; **~ off** vt liquidar; **~ out** vi: **to ~ out of tickets/milk** vender todas las entradas/toda la leche; **~-by date** n fecha de caducidad; **~er** n vendedor(a) m/f; **~ing price** n precio de venta

Sellotape ® ['seləʊteɪp] (BRIT) n cinta adhesiva, celo (SP), scotch m (AM)

selves [selvz] npl of **self**

semblance ['sembləns] n apariencia f

semen ['siːmən] n semen m

semester [sɪ'mestə*] n (US) n semestre m

semi... [semɪ] prefix semi..., medio...; **~circle** n semicírculo; **~colon** n punto y coma; **~conductor** n semiconductor m; **~detached (house)** n (casa) semiseparada; **~-final** n semi-final m

seminar ['semɪnɑː*] n seminario

seminary ['semɪnərɪ] n (REL) seminario

semiskilled ['semɪskɪld] adj (work, worker) semi-cualificado

semi-skimmed (milk) n leche semidesnatada

senate ['senɪt] n senado; **senator** n senador(a) m/f

send [send] (pt, pp **sent**) vt mandar,

enviar; (signal) transmitir; **~ away** vt despachar; **~ away for** vt fus pedir; **~ back** vt devolver; **~ for** vt fus mandar traer; **~ off** vt (goods) despachar; (BRIT: SPORT: player) expulsar; **~ out** vt (invitation) mandar; (signal) emitir; **~ up** vt (person, price) hacer subir; (BRIT: parody) parodiar; **~er** n remitente m/f; **~off** n: **a good ~off** una buena despedida

senior ['siːnɪə*] adj (older) mayor, más viejo; (: on staff) de más antigüedad; (of higher rank) superior; **~ citizen** n persona de la tercera edad; **~ity** [-'ɒrɪtɪ] n antigüedad f

sensation [sen'seɪʃən] n sensación f; **~al** adj sensacional

sense [sens] n (faculty, meaning) sentido; (feeling) sensación f; (good ~) sentido común, juicio ♦ vt sentir, percibir; **it makes ~** tiene sentido; **~less** adj estúpido, insensato; (unconscious) sin conocimiento; **~ of humour** n sentido del humor

sensible ['sensɪbl] adj sensato; (reasonable) razonable, lógico

sensitive ['sensɪtɪv] adj sensible; (touchy) susceptible

sensual ['sensjuəl] adj sensual

sensuous ['sensjuəs] adj sensual

sent [sent] pt, pp of **send**

sentence ['sentns] n (LING) oración f; (LAW) sentencia, fallo ♦ vt: **to ~ sb to death/to 5 years (in prison)** condenar a una muerte/a 5 años de cárcel

sentiment ['sentɪmənt] n sentimiento; (opinion) opinión f; **~al** [-'mentl] adj sentimental

sentry ['sentrɪ] n centinela m

separate [adj 'seprɪt, vb 'sepəreɪt] adj separado; (distinct) distinto ♦ vt separar; (part) dividir ♦ vi separarse; **~s** npl (clothes) coordinados mpl; **~ly** adv por separado; **separation** [-'reɪʃən] n separación f

September [sep'tembə*] n

se(p)tiembre m

septic ['sɛptɪk] adj séptico; ~ **tank** n fosa séptica

sequel ['siːkwl] n consecuencia, resultado; (of story) continuación f

sequence ['siːkwəns] n sucesión f, serie f; (CINEMA) secuencia

sequin ['siːkwɪn] n lentejuela

serene [sɪˈriːn] adj sereno, tranquilo

sergeant ['sɑːdʒənt] n sargento

serial ['sɪərɪəl] n (TV) telenovela, serie f televisiva; (BOOK) serie f editada como serial; ~ **killer** n asesino/a múltiple; ~**ize** vt emitir como serial; ~ **number** n número de serie

series ['sɪəriːz] n inv serie f

serious ['sɪərɪəs] adj serio; (grave) grave; ~**ly** adv en serio; (ill, wounded etc) gravemente

sermon ['sɜːmən] n sermón m

serrated [sɪˈreɪtɪd] adj serrado, dentellado

serum ['sɪərəm] n suero

servant ['sɜːvənt] n servidor(a) m/f; (house ~) criado/a

serve [sɜːv] vt servir; (customer) atender; (subj: train) pasar por; (apprenticeship) hacer; (prison term) cumplir ♦ vi (at table) servir; (TENNIS) sacar; **to** ~ **as/for/to do** servir de/para/para hacer ♦ n (TENNIS) saque m; **it** ~**s him right** se lo tiene merecido; ~ **out** vt (food) servir; ~ **up** vt = ~ **out**

service ['sɜːvɪs] n servicio; (REL) misa; (AUT) mantenimiento; (dishes etc) juego ♦ vt (car etc) revisar; (: repair) reparar; **the S~s** npl las fuerzas armadas; **to be of** ~ **to sb** ser útil a uno; ~ **included/not included** servicio incluido/no incluido; ~**able** adj servible, utilizable; ~ **area** n (on motorway) área de servicio; ~ **charge** n (BRIT) n servicio; ~**man** n militar m; ~ **station** n estación f de servicio

serviette [sɜːvɪˈet] n (BRIT) n servilleta

session ['sɛʃən] n sesión f; **to be in** ~ estar en sesión

set [sɛt] (pt, pp **set**) n juego; (RADIO)

aparato; (TV) televisor m; (of utensils) batería; (of cutlery) cubierto; (of books) colección f; (TENNIS) set m; (group of people) grupo; (CINEMA) plató m; (THEATRE) decorado; (HAIRDRESSING) marcado ♦ adj (fixed) fijo; (ready) listo ♦ vt (place) poner, colocar; (fix) fijar; (adjust) ajustar, arreglar; (decide: rules etc) establecer, decidir ♦ vi (sun) ponerse; (jam, jelly) cuajarse; (concrete) fraguar; (bone) componerse; **to be** ~ **on doing sth** estar empeñado en hacer algo; **to** ~ **to music** poner música a; **to** ~ **on fire** incendiar, poner fuego a; **to** ~ **free** poner en libertad; **to** ~ **sth going** poner algo en marcha; **to** ~ **sail** zarpar, hacerse a la vela; ~ **about** vt fus ponerse a; ~ **aside** vt poner aparte, dejar de lado; (money, time) reservar; ~ **back** vt (cost): **to** ~ **sb back £5** costar a uno cinco libras; (: in time) retrasar (por); ~ **off** vi partir ♦ vt (bomb) hacer estallar; (events) poner en marcha; (show up well) hacer resaltar; ~ **out** vi partir ♦ vt (arrange) disponer; (state) exponer; **to** ~ **out to do sth** proponerse hacer algo; ~ **up** vt establecer; ~**back** n revés m, contratiempo; ~ **menu** n menú m

settee [sɛˈtiː] n sofá m

setting ['sɛtɪŋ] n (scenery) marco; (position) disposición f; (of sun) puesta; (of jewel) engaste m, montadura

settle ['sɛtl] vt (argument) resolver; (accounts) ajustar, liquidar; (MED: calm) calmar, sosegar ♦ vi (dust etc) depositarse; (weather) serenarse; (also: ~ **down**) instalarse; tranquilizarse; **to** ~ **for sth** convenir en aceptar algo; **to** ~ **on sth** decidirse por algo; ~ **in** vi instalarse; ~ **up** vi: **to** ~ **up with sb** ajustar cuentas con uno; ~**ment** n (payment) liquidación f; (agreement) acuerdo, convenio; (village place) pueblo; ~**r** n colono/a, colonizador/a m/f

setup ['sɛtʌp] n sistema m; (situation)

situación f

seven ['sɛvn] num siete; **~teen** num diez y siete, diecisiete; **~th** num séptimo; **~ty** num setenta

sever ['sɛvə*] vt cortar; (relations) romper

several ['sɛvrl] adj, pron varios/as m/fpl, algunos/as m/fpl; **~ of us** varios de nosotros

severance ['sɛvərəns] n (of relations) ruptura; **~ pay** n indemnización f por despido

severe [sɪ'vɪə*] adj severo; (serious) grave; (hard) duro; (pain) intenso; **severity** [sɪ'vɛrɪtɪ] n severidad f; gravedad f; intensidad f

sew [səu] (pt sewed, pp sewn) vt, vi coser; **~ up** vt coser, zurcir

sewage ['su:ɪdʒ] n aguas fpl residuales

sewer ['su:ə*] n alcantarilla, cloaca

sewing ['səuɪŋ] n costura; **~ machine** n máquina de coser

sewn [səun] pp of **sew**

sex [sɛks] n sexo; (lovemaking): **to have ~** hacer el amor; **~ist** adj, n sexista m/f; **~ual** ['sɛksjuəl] adj sexual; **~y** adj sexy

shabby ['ʃæbɪ] adj (person) desharrapado; (clothes) raído, gastado; (behaviour) ruin inv

shack [ʃæk] n choza, chabola

shackles ['ʃæklz] npl grillos mpl, grilletes mpl

shade [ʃeɪd] n sombra; (for lamp) pantalla; (for eyes) visera; (of colour) matiz m, tonalidad f; (small quantity): **a ~ (too big/more)** un poquitín (grande/más) ♦ vt dar sombra a; (eyes) proteger del sol; **in the ~** en la sombra

shadow ['ʃædəu] n sombra ♦ vt (follow) seguir y vigilar; **~ cabinet** n (BRIT) (POL) gabinete paralelo formado por el partido de oposición; **~y** adj oscuro; (dim) indistinto

shady ['ʃeɪdɪ] adj sombreado; (fig: dishonest) sospechoso; (: deal) turbio

shaft [ʃɑːft] n (of arrow, spear) astil m;

(AUT, TECH) eje m, árbol m; (of mine) pozo; (of lift) hueco, caja; (of light) rayo

shaggy ['ʃægɪ] adj peludo

shake [ʃeɪk] (pt shook, pp shaken) vt sacudir; (building) hacer temblar; (bottle, cocktail) agitar ♦ vi (tremble) temblar; **to ~ one's head** (in refusal) negar con la cabeza; (in dismay) mover or menear la cabeza, incrédulo; **to ~ hands with sb** estrechar la mano a uno; **~ off** vt sacudirse; (fig) deshacerse de; **~ up** vt agitar; (fig) reorganizar; **shaky** adj (hand, voice) trémulo; (building) inestable

shall [ʃæl] aux vb: **~ I help you?** ¿quieres que te ayude?; **I'll buy three, ~ I?** compro tres, ¿no te parece?

shallow ['ʃæləu] adj poco profundo; (fig) superficial

sham [ʃæm] n fraude m, engaño ♦ vt fingir, simular

shambles ['ʃæmblz] n confusión f

shame [ʃeɪm] n vergüenza ♦ vt avergonzar; **it is a ~ that/to do** es una lástima que/hacer; **what a ~!** ¡qué lástima!; **~ful** adj vergonzoso; **~less** adj desvergonzado

shampoo [ʃæm'puː] n champú m ♦ vt lavar con champú; **~ and set** n lavado y marcado

shamrock ['ʃæmrɔk] n trébol m (emblema nacional irlandés)

shandy ['ʃændɪ] n mezcla de cerveza con gaseosa

shan't [ʃɑːnt] = **shall not**

shantytown ['ʃæntɪtaun] n barrio de chabolas

shape [ʃeɪp] n forma ♦ vt formar, dar forma a; (sb's ideas) formar; (sb's life) determinar; **to take ~** tomar forma, formarse; **~ up** vi (events) desarrollarse; (person) formarse; **~-d** suffix: **heart-~d** en forma de corazón; **~less** adj informe, sin forma definida; **~ly** adj (body etc) esbelto

share [ʃɛə*] n (part) parte f, porción f; (contribution) cuota; (COMM) acción f

♦ *vt* dividir; *(have in common)*
compartir; **to ~ out (among** or
between) repartir (entre); **~holder**
(*BRIT*) *n* accionista *m/f*

shark [ʃɑːk] *n* tiburón *m*

sharp [ʃɑːp] *adj (blade, nose)* afilado;
(point) puntiagudo; *(outline)* definido;
(pain) intenso; *(MUS)* desafinado;
(contrast) marcado; *(voice)* agudo;
(person: quick-witted) astuto;
(: dishonest) poco escrupuloso ♦ *n*
(*MUS*) sostenido ♦ *adv*: **at 2 o'clock**
a las 2 en punto; **~en** *vt* afilar; *(pencil)*
sacar punta a; *(fig)* aguzar; **~ener** *n*
(also: pencil ~ener) sacapuntas *m inv*;
~-eyed *adj* de vista aguda; **~ly** *adv*
(turn, stop) bruscamente; *(stand out,
contrast)* claramente; *(criticize, retort)*
severamente

shatter [ˈʃætə*] *vt* hacer añicos or
pedazos; *(fig: ruin)* destruir, acabar con
♦ *vi* hacerse añicos

shave [ʃeɪv] *vt* afeitar, rasurar ♦ *vi*
afeitarse, rasurarse ♦ *n*: **to have a ~**
afeitarse; **~r** *n* *(also: electric ~r)*
máquina de afeitar (eléctrica)

shaving [ˈʃeɪvɪŋ] *n* *(action)* el afeitarse,
rasurado; **~s** *npl* *(of wood etc)* virutas
fpl; **~ brush** *n* brocha (de afeitar);
~ cream *n* crema de afeitar; **~ foam**
n espuma de afeitar

shawl [ʃɔːl] *n* chal *m*

she [ʃiː] *pron* ella; **~-cat** *n* gata

sheaf [ʃiːf] *(pl* **sheaves)** *n (of corn)*
gavilla; *(of papers)* fajo

shear [ʃɪə*] *vt (pt* **sheared,** *pp* **sheared**
or **shorn)** *vt* esquilar, trasquilar; **~s** *npl*
(for hedge) tijeras *fpl* de jardín

sheath [ʃiːθ] *n* vaina; *(contraceptive)*
preservativo

sheaves [ʃiːvz] *npl of* **sheaf**

shed [ʃed] *(pt, pp* **shed)** *n* cobertizo
♦ *vt (skin)* mudar; *(tears, blood)*
derramar; *(load)* desprenderse de; *(workers)*
despedir

she'd [ʃiːd] **= she had; she would**

sheen [ʃiːn] *n* brillo, lustre *m*

sheep [ʃiːp] *n inv* oveja; **~dog** *n* perro
pastor; **~skin** *n* piel *f* de carnero

sheer [ʃɪə*] *adj (utter)* puro, completo;
(steep) escarpado; *(material)* diáfano
♦ *adv* verticalmente

sheet [ʃiːt] *n (on bed)* sábana; *(of
paper)* hoja; *(of glass, metal)* lámina; *(of
ice)* capa

sheik(h) [ʃeɪk] *n* jeque *m*

shelf [ʃelf] *(pl* **shelves)** *n* estante *m*

shell [ʃel] *n (on beach)* concha; *(of egg,
nut etc)* cáscara; *(explosive)* proyectil *m*,
obús *m*; *(of building)* armazón *f* ♦ *vt
(peas)* desenvainar; *(MIL)* bombardear

she'll [ʃiːl] **= she will; she shall**

shellfish [ˈʃelfɪʃ] *n inv* crustáceo; *(as
food)* mariscos *mpl*

shell suit *n* chándal *m* de calle

shelter [ˈʃeltə*] *n* abrigo, refugio ♦ *vt
(aid)* amparar, proteger; *(give lodging
to)* abrigar ♦ *vi* abrigarse, refugiarse;
~ed *adj (life)* protegido; *(spot)*
abrigado; **~ed housing** *n* viviendas
vigiladas para ancianos y minusválidos

shelve [ʃelv] *vt (fig)* aplazar; **~s** *npl of*
shelf

shepherd [ˈʃepəd] *n* pastor *m* ♦ *vt
(guide)* guiar, conducir; **~'s pie** (*BRIT*)
n pastel de carne y patatas

sherry [ˈʃerɪ] *n* jerez *m*

she's [ʃiːz] **= she is; she has**

Shetland [ˈʃetlənd] *n (also: the ~s, the
~ Isles)* las Islas de Zetlandia

shield [ʃiːld] *n* escudo; *(protection)*
blindaje *m* ♦ *vt*: **to ~ (from)** proteger
(de)

shift [ʃɪft] *n (change)* cambio; *(at work)*
turno ♦ *vt* trasladar; *(remove)* quitar
♦ *vi* moverse; **~ work** *n* trabajo a
turnos; **~y** *adj* tramposo; *(eyes)* furtivo

shimmer [ˈʃɪmə*] *n* reflejo trémulo

shin [ʃɪn] *n* espinilla

shine [ʃaɪn] *(pt, pp* **shone)** *n* brillo,
lustre *m* ♦ *vi* brillar, relucir ♦ *vt (shoes)*
lustrar, sacar brillo a; **to ~ a torch on
sth** dirigir una linterna hacia algo

shingle [ˈʃɪŋgl] *n (on beach)* guijarros

mpl; **~s** n (MED) herpes mpl or fpl

shiny |'ʃaɪnɪ| adj brillante, lustroso

ship |ʃɪp| n buque m, barco ♦ vt (goods) embarcar; (send) transportar o enviar por vía marítima; **~building** n construcción f de buques; **~ment** n (goods) envío; **~ping** n (act) embarque m; (traffic) buques mpl; **~wreck** n naufragio ♦ vt: **to be ~wrecked** naufragar; **~yard** n astillero

shire |'ʃaɪə*| (BRIT) n condado

shirt |ʃɜːt| n camisa; **in (one's) ~ sleeves** en mangas de camisa

shit |ʃɪt| (inf!) excl ¡mierda! (!)

shiver |'ʃɪvə*| n escalofrío ♦ vi temblar, estremecerse; (with cold) tiritar

shoal |ʃəʊl| n (of fish) banco; (fig: also: ~s) tropel m

shock |ʃɔk| n (impact) choque m, (ELEC.) descarga (eléctrica); (emotional) conmoción f; (start) sobresalto, susto; (MED) postración f nerviosa ♦ vt dar un susto a; (offend) escandalizar; **~ absorber** n amortiguador m; **~ing** adj (awful) espantoso; (outrageous) escandaloso

shoddy |'ʃɔdɪ| adj de pacotilla

shoe |ʃuː| (pt, pp **shod**) n zapato; (for horse) herradura ♦ vt (horse) herrar; **~brush** n cepillo para zapatos; **~lace** n cordón m; **~ polish** n betún m; **~shop** n zapatería; **~string** n (fig: on a **~string** con muy poco dinero

shone |ʃɔn| pt, pp of **shine**

shook |ʃʊk| pt of **shake**

shoot |ʃuːt| (pt, pp **shot**) n (on branch, seedling) retoño, vástago ♦ vt disparar; (kill) matar a tiros; (wound) pegar un tiro a; (execute) fusilar; (film) rodar, filmar ♦ vi (FOOTBALL) chutar; **~ down** vt (plane) derribar; **~ in/out** vi entrar corriendo/salir disparado; **~ up** vi (prices) dispararse; **~ing** n (shots) tiros mpl; (HUNTING) caza con escopeta; **~ing star** n estrella fugaz

shop |ʃɔp| n tienda; (workshop) taller m ♦ vi (also: go **~ping**) ir de compras;

~ assistant (BRIT) n dependiente/a m/f; **~ floor** (BRIT) n (fig) taller m, fábrica; **~keeper** n tendero/a; **~lifting** n mechería; **~per** n comprador(a) m/f; **~ping** (goods) compras fpl; **~ping bag** n bolsa (de compras); **~ping centre** (US **~ping center**) n centro comercial; **~-soiled** adj deteriorado; **~ steward** n (INDUSTRY) enlace m sindical; **~ window** n escaparate m (SP), vidriera (AM)

shore |ʃɔː*| n orilla ♦ vt: **to ~ (up)** reforzar; **on ~** en tierra

shorn |ʃɔːn| pp of **shear**

short |ʃɔːt| adj corto; (in time) breve, de corta duración; (person) bajo; (curt) brusco, seco; (insufficient) insuficiente; **(a pair of) ~s** (unos) pantalones mpl cortos; **to be ~ of sth** estar falto de algo; **in ~** en pocas palabras; **to be ~ of doing ...** fuera de hacer ...; **it is ~ for** es la forma abreviada de; **to cut ~** (speech, visit) interrumpir, terminar inesperadamente; **everything ~ of ...** todo menos ...; **to fall ~ of** no alcanzar; **to run ~ of** quedarle a uno pocos; **to stop ~** parar en seco; **to stop ~ of** detenerse antes de; **~age** n escasez f; **~bread** n especie de mantecada; **~change** vt no dar el cambio completo a; **~circuit** n cortocircuito; **~coming** n defecto, deficiencia; **~(crust) pastry** (BRIT) n pasta quebradiza; **~cut** n atajo; **~en** vt acortar; (visit) interrumpir; **~fall** n déficit m; **~hand** (BRIT) n taquigrafía; **~hand typist** (BRIT) n taquimecanógrafo/a; **~ list** (BRIT) n (for job) lista de candidatos escogidos; **~lived** adj efímero; **~ly** adv en breve, dentro de poco; **~sighted** (BRIT) adj miope; (fig) imprudente; **~staffed** adj: **to be ~staffed** estar falto de personal; **~ story** n cuento; **~tempered** adj enojadizo; **~term** adj (effect) a corto plazo; **~wave** n (RADIO) onda corta

shot |ʃɔt| pt, pp of **shoot** ♦ n (sound)

tiro, disparo; (*try*) tentativa; (*injection*) inyección f; (PHOT) toma, fotografía; **to be a good/poor ~** (*person*) tener buena/mala puntería; **like a ~** (*without any delay*) como un rayo; **~gun** n escopeta

should [ʃud] *aux vb*: **I ~ go now** debo irme ahora; **he ~ be there now** debe de haber llegado (ya); **I ~ go if I were you** yo en tu lugar me iría; **I ~ like to** me gustaría

shoulder ['ʃəuldə*] n hombro ♦ *vt* (*fig*) cargar con; **~ bag** n cartera de bandolera; **~ blade** n omóplato

shouldn't ['ʃudnt] = **should not**

shout [ʃaut] n grito ♦ *vt* gritar ♦ *vi* gritar, dar voces; **~ down** *vt* acallar a gritos; **~ing** n griterío

shove [ʃʌv] n empujón m ♦ *vt* empujar; (*inf*: *put*): **to ~ sth in** meter algo a empellones; **~ off** (*inf*) *vi* largarse

shovel ['ʃʌvl] n pala; (*mechanical*) excavadora ♦ *vt* mover con pala

show [ʃəu] (*pt* showed, *pp* shown) n (*of emotion*) demostración f; (*semblance*) apariencia; (*exhibition*) exposición f; (THEATRE) función f, espectáculo; (TV) show m ♦ *vt* mostrar, enseñar; (*courage etc*) mostrar, manifestar; (*exhibit*) exponer; (*film*) proyectar ♦ *vi* mostrarse; (*appear*) aparecer ♦ *vt*; **for ~** para impresionar; **on ~** (*exhibits etc*) expuesto; **~ in** *vt* (*person*) hacer pasar; **~ off** (*pej*) *vi* presumir ♦ *vt* (*display*) lucir; **~ out** *vt*: **to ~ sb out** acompañar a uno a la puerta; **~ up** *vi* (*stand out*) destacar; (*inf*: *turn up*) aparecer ♦ *vt* (*unmask*) desenmascarar; **~ business** n mundo del espectáculo; **~down** n enfrentamiento (final)

shower ['ʃauə*] n (*rain*) chaparrón m, chubasco; (*of stones etc*) lluvia; (*for bathing*) ducha (SP), regadera (AM) ♦ *vi* llover ♦ *vt* (*fig*): **to ~ sb with sth** colmar a uno de algo; **to have a ~** ducharse; **~proof** *adj* impermeable

showing ['ʃəuiŋ] n (*of film*) proyección f

show jumping n hípica

shown [ʃəun] *pp of* **show**

show: **~-off** (*inf*) n (*person*) presumido/a; **~-piece** n (*of exhibition etc*) objeto cumbre; **~room** n sala de muestras

shrank [ʃræŋk] *pt of* **shrink**

shrapnel ['ʃræpnl] n metralla

shred [ʃred] n (*gen pl*) triza, jirón m ♦ *vt* hacer trizas; (CULIN) desmenuzar; **~der** n (*vegetable ~*) picadora; (*document ~der*) trituradora (de papel)

shrewd [ʃru:d] *adj* astuto

shriek [ʃri:k] n chillido ♦ *vi* chillar

shrill [ʃril] *adj* agudo, estridente

shrimp [ʃrimp] n camarón m

shrine [ʃrain] n santuario, sepulcro

shrink [ʃriŋk] (*pt* shrank, *pp* shrunk) *vi* encogerse; (*be reduced*) reducirse; (*also: ~ away*) retroceder ♦ *vt* encoger ♦ n (*inf*: *pej*) loquero/a; **to ~ from (doing) sth** no atreverse a hacer algo; **~wrap** *vt* embalar con película de plástico

shrivel ['ʃrivl] (*also: ~ up*) *vt* (*dry*) secar ♦ *vi* secarse

shroud [ʃraud] n sudario ♦ *vt*: **~ed in mystery** envuelto en el misterio

Shrove Tuesday ['ʃrəuv-] n martes m de carnaval

shrub [ʃrʌb] n arbusto; **~bery** n arbustos *mpl*

shrug [ʃrʌg] n encogimiento de hombros ♦ *vt*, *vi*: **to ~ (one's shoulders)** encogerse de hombros; **~ off** *vt* negar importancia a

shrunk [ʃrʌŋk] *pp of* **shrink**

shudder ['ʃʌdə*] n estremecimiento, escalofrío ♦ *vi* estremecerse

shuffle ['ʃʌfl] *vt* (*cards*) barajar ♦ *vi*: **to ~ (one's feet)** arrastrar los pies

shun [ʃʌn] *vt* rehuir, esquivar

shunt [ʃʌnt] *vt* (*train*) maniobrar; (*object*) empujar

shut [ʃʌt] (*pt*, *pp* shut) *vt* cerrar ♦ *vi*

cerrarse; ~ **down** vt, vi cerrar; ~ **off** vt
(supply etc) cortar; ~ **up** vi (inf: keep
quiet) callarse ♦ vt (close) cerrar;
(silence) hacer callar; ~**ter** n
contraventana; (PHOT) obturador m

shuttle ['ʃʌtl] n lanzadera; (also:
~ **service**) servicio rápido y continuo
entre dos puntos: (: AVIAT) puente m
aéreo; ~**cock** n volante m;
~ **diplomacy** n viajes mpl
diplomáticos

shy [ʃaɪ] adj tímido; ~**ness** n timidez f

Sicily ['sɪsɪlɪ] n Sicilia

sick [sɪk] adj (ill) enfermo; (nauseated)
mareado; (humour) negro; (vomiting):
to be ~ (BRIT) vomitar; **to feel** ~ tener
náuseas; **to be** ~ **of** (fig) estar harto
de; ~ **bay** n enfermería; ~**en** vt dar
asco a; ~**ening** adj (fig) asqueroso

sickle ['sɪkl] n hoz f

sick: ~ **leave** n baja por enfermedad;
~**ly** adj enfermizo; (smell)
nauseabundo; ~**ness** n enfermedad f,
mal m; (vomiting) náuseas fpl; ~ **pay** n
subsidio de enfermedad

side [saɪd] n (gen) lado; (of body)
costado; (of lake) orilla; (of hill) ladera;
(team) equipo; ♦ adj (door, entrance)
lateral ♦ vi: **to** ~ **with sb** tomar el
partido de uno; **by** ~ **of the** ~ **of** al lado
de; ~ **by** ~ juntos/as; **from** ~ **to** ~ de
un lado para otro; **from all** ~**s** de
todos lados; **to take** ~**s (with)** tomar
partido (con); ~**board** n aparador m;
~**boards** (BRIT) npl = ~**burns**;
~**burns** npl patillas fpl; ~ **drum** n
tambor m; ~ **effect** n efecto
secundario; ~**light** n (AUT) luz f lateral;
~**line** n (SPORT) línea de banda; (fig)
empleo suplementario; ~**long** adj de
soslayo; ~ **order** n plato de
acompañamiento; ~**show** n (stall)
caseta; ~**step** vt (fig) esquivar;
~ **street** n calle f lateral; ~**track** vt
(fig) desviar (de su propósito); ~**walk**
(US) n acera; ~**ways** adv de lado

siding ['saɪdɪŋ] n (RAIL) apartadero, vía

muerta

siege [siːdʒ] n cerco, sitio

sieve [sɪv] n colador m ♦ vt cribar

sift [sɪft] vt cribar; (fig: information)
escudriñar

sigh [saɪ] n suspiro ♦ vi suspirar

sight [saɪt] n (faculty) vista; (spectacle)
espectáculo; (on gun) mira, alza ♦ vt
divisar; **in** ~ a la vista; **out of** ~ fuera
de (la) vista; **on** ~ (shoot) sin previo
aviso; ~**seeing** n excursionismo,
turismo; **to go** ~**seeing** hacer turismo

sign [saɪn] n (with hand) señal f, seña;
(trace) huella, rastro; (notice) letrero;
(written) signo ♦ vt firmar; (SPORT)
fichar; **to** ~ **sth over to sb** firmar el
traspaso de algo a uno; ~ **on** vi (BRIT:
as unemployed) registrarse como
desempleado; (for course) inscribirse
♦ vt (MIL) alistar; (employee) contratar;
~ **up** vi (MIL) alistarse; (for course)
inscribirse ♦ vt (player) fichar

signal ['sɪgnl] n señal f ♦ vi señalizar
♦ vt (person) hacer señas a; (message)
comunicar por señales; ~**man** (irreg) n
(RAIL) guardavía m

signature ['sɪgnətʃə*] n firma; ~ **tune**
n sintonía de apertura de un programa

signet ring ['sɪgnət-] n anillo de sello

significance [sɪg'nɪfɪkəns] n
(importance) trascendencia

significant [sɪg'nɪfɪkənt] adj
significativo; (important) trascendente

signify ['sɪgnɪfaɪ] vt significar

sign language n lenguaje m para
sordomudos

signpost ['saɪnpəust] n indicador m

silence ['saɪləns] n silencio ♦ vt acallar;
(guns) reducir al silencio; ~**r** n (on gun,
BRIT: AUT) silenciador m

silent ['saɪlnt] adj silencioso; (not
speaking) callado; (film) mudo; **to
remain** ~ guardar silencio; ~ **partner**
n (COMM) socio/a comanditario/a

silhouette [sɪluː'ɛt] n silueta

silicon chip ['sɪlɪkən-] n plaqueta de
silicio

silk [sɪlk] n seda ♦ adj de seda; **~y** adj sedoso

silly ['sɪlɪ] adj (person) tonto; (idea) absurdo

silt [sɪlt] n sedimento

silver ['sɪlvə*] n plata; (money) moneda suelta ♦ adj de plata; (colour) plateado; **~ paper** (BRIT) n papel m de plata; **~-plated** adj plateado; **~smith** n platero/a; **~ware** n plata; **~y** adj argentino

similar ['sɪmɪlə*] adj: **~ (to)** parecido or semejante (a); **~ity** [-'lærɪtɪ] n semejanza; **~ly** adv del mismo modo

simmer ['sɪmə*] vi hervir a fuego lento

simple ['sɪmpl] adj (easy) sencillo; (foolish, COMM: interest) simple; **simplicity** [-'plɪsɪtɪ] n sencillez f; **simplify** ['sɪmplɪfaɪ] vt simplificar

simply ['sɪmplɪ] adv (live, talk) sencillamente; (just, merely) solo

simulate ['sɪmjʊleɪt] vt fingir, simular; **~d** adj simulado; (fur) de imitación

simultaneous [sɪmal'teɪnɪəs] adj simultáneo; **~ly** adv simultáneamente

sin [sɪn] n pecado ♦ vi pecar

since [sɪns] adv desde entonces, después ♦ prep desde ♦ conj (time) desde que; (because) ya que, puesto que; **~ then, ever ~** desde entonces

sincere [sɪn'sɪə*] adj sincero; **~ly** adv: **yours ~ly** (in letters) le saluda atentamente; **sincerity** [-'serɪtɪ] n sinceridad f

sinew ['sɪnju:] n tendón m

sing [sɪŋ] (pt **sang**, pp **sung**) vt, vi cantar

Singapore [sɪŋə'pɔ:*] n Singapur m

singe [sɪndʒ] vt chamuscar

singer ['sɪŋə*] n cantante m/f

singing ['sɪŋɪŋ] n canto

single ['sɪŋgl] adj único, solo; (unmarried) soltero; (not double) simple, sencillo ♦ n (also: ~ ticket) billete m sencillo; (record) sencillo, single m; **~s** npl (TENNIS) individual m; **~ out** vt (choose) escoger; **~ bed** cama

individual; **~-breasted** adj recto; **~ file** n: **in ~ file** en fila de uno; **~-handed** adv sin ayuda; **~-minded** adj resuelto, firme; **~ parent** n padre m soltero, madre f soltera (o divorciado etc); **~ parent family** familia monoparental; **~ room** n cuarto individual

singly ['sɪŋglɪ] adv uno por uno

singular ['sɪŋgjʊlə*] adj (odd) raro, extraño; (outstanding) excepcional ♦ n (LING) singular m

sinister ['sɪnɪstə*] adj siniestro

sink [sɪŋk] (pt **sank**, pp **sunk**) n fregadero ♦ vt (ship) hundir, echar a pique; (foundations) excavar ♦ vi (gen) hundirse; **to ~ sth into** hundir algo en; **~ in** vi (fig) penetrar, calar

sinner ['sɪnə*] n pecador/a m/f

sinus ['saɪnəs] n (ANAT) seno

sip [sɪp] n sorbo ♦ vt sorber, beber a sorbitos

siphon ['saɪfən] n sifón m; **~ off** vt desviar

sir [sə*] n señor m; S~ John Smith Sir John Smith; **yes ~** sí, señor

siren ['saɪərn] n sirena

sirloin ['sə:lɔɪn] n (also: ~ steak) solomillo

sister ['sɪstə*] n hermana; (BRIT: nurse) enfermera jefe; **~-in-law** n cuñada

sit [sɪt] (pt, pp **sat**) vi sentarse; (be sitting) estar sentado; (assembly) reunirse; (for painter) posar ♦ vt (exam) presentarse a; **~ down** vi sentarse; **~ on** vt fus asistir a; **~ up** vi incorporarse; (not go to bed) velar

sitcom ['sɪtkɔm] n abbr (= situation comedy) comedia de situación

site [saɪt] n sitio; (also: building ~) solar m ♦ vt situar

sit-in n (demonstration) sentada

sitting ['sɪtɪŋ] n (of assembly etc) sesión f; (in canteen) turno; **~ room** n sala de estar

situated ['sɪtjʊeɪtɪd] adj situado

situation [sɪtjʊ'eɪʃən] n situación f;

"~s vacant" (BRIT) "ofrecen trabajo"

six |sɪks| num seis; **~teen** num diez y seis, dieciséis; **~th** num sexto; **~ty** num sesenta

size |saɪz| n tamaño; (extent) extensión f; (of clothing) talla; (of shoes) número; **~ up** vt formarse una idea de; **~able** adj importante, considerable

sizzle |'sɪzl| vi crepitar

skate |skeɪt| n patín m; (fish: pl inv) raya ♦ vi patinar; **~board** n monopatín m; **~boarding** n monopatín m; **~r** n patinador(a) m/f; **skating** n patinaje m, **skating rink** n pista de patinaje

skeleton |'skelɪtn| n esqueleto; (TECH) armazón f; (outline) esquema m; **~ staff** n personal m reducido

skeptic etc |'skeptɪk| (US) = **sceptic**

sketch |sketʃ| n (drawing) dibujo; (outline) esbozo, bosquejo; (THEATRE) sketch m ♦ vt dibujar; (plan etc: also: **~ out**) esbozar; **~ book** n libro de dibujos; **~y** adj incompleto

skewer |'skjuːə*| n broqueta

ski |skiː| n esquí m ♦ vi esquiar; **~ boot** n bota de esquí

skid |skɪd| n patinazo ♦ vi patinar

ski: **~er** n esquiador(a) m/f; **~ing** n esquí m; **~ jump** n salto con esquís

skilful |'skɪlful| (BRIT) adj diestro, experto

ski lift n telesilla m, telesquí m

skill |skɪl| n destreza, pericia; técnica; **~ed** adj hábil, diestro; (worker) cualificado; **~full** (US) adj = **skilful**

skim |skɪm| vt (milk) desnatar; (glide over) rozar, rasar ♦ vi: **~ through** (book) hojear; **~med milk** n leche f desnatada

skimp |skɪmp| vt (also: **~ on**: work) chapucear; (cloth etc) escatimar; **~y** adj escaso; (skirt) muy corto

skin |skɪn| n piel f; (complexion) cutis m ♦ vt (fruit etc) pelar; (animal) despellejar; **~ cancer** n cáncer m de piel; **~-deep** adj superficial; **~ diving** n buceo; **~ny** adj flaco; **~tight** adj

(dress etc) muy ajustado

skip |skɪp| n brinco, salto; (BRIT: container) contenedor m ♦ vi brincar; (with rope) saltar a la comba ♦ vt saltarse

ski: **~ pass** n forfait m (de esquí); **~ pole** n bastón m de esquiar

skipper |'skɪpə*| n (NAUT, SPORT) capitán m

skipping rope |'skɪpɪŋ-| (BRIT) n comba

skirmish |'skɜːmɪʃ| n escaramuza

skirt |skɜːt| n falda (SP), pollera (AM) ♦ vt (go round) ladear; **~ing board** (BRIT) n rodapié m

ski slope n pista de esquí

ski suit n traje m de esquiar

ski tow n remonte m

skittle |'skɪtl| n bolo; **~s** n (game) boliche m

skive |skaɪv| (BRIT: inf) vi gandulear

skull |skʌl| n calavera; (ANAT) cráneo

skunk |skʌŋk| n mofeta

sky |skaɪ| n cielo; **~light** n tragaluz m, claraboya; **~scraper** n rascacielos m inv

slab |slæb| n (stone) bloque m; (flat) losa; (of cake) trozo

slack |slæk| adj (loose) flojo; (slow) de poca actividad; (careless) descuidado; **~s** npl pantalones mpl; **~en** (also: **~en off**) vi aflojarse ♦ vt aflojar; (speed) disminuir

slag heap |'slæg-| n escorial m, escombrera

slag off (BRIT: inf) vt poner como un trapo

slam |slæm| vt (throw) arrojar (violentamente); (criticize) criticar duramente ♦ vt (door) cerrarse de golpe; **to ~ the door** dar un portazo

slander |'slɑːndə*| n calumnia, difamación f

slang |slæŋ| n argot m; (jargon) jerga

slant |slɑːnt| n sesgo, inclinación f; (fig) interpretación f; **~ed** adj (fig) parcial; **~ing** adj inclinado; (eyes) rasgado

slap |slæp| n palmada; (in face) bofetada ♦ vt dar una palmada or bofetada a; (paint etc): **to ~ sth on sth** embadurnar algo con algo ♦ adv (directly) exactamente, directamente; **~dash** adj descuidado; **~stick** n comedia de golpe y porrazo; **~-up** adj: **a ~-up meal** (BRIT) un banquetazo, una comilona

slash |slæʃ| vt acuchillar; (fig: prices) fulminar

slat |slæt| n tablilla, listón m

slate |sleɪt| n pizarra ♦ vt (fig: criticize) criticar duramente

slaughter |'slɔ:tə*| n (of animals) matanza; (of people) carnicería ♦ vt matar; **~house** n matadero

Slav |slɑːv| adj eslavo

slave |sleɪv| n esclavo/a ♦ vi (also: **~ away**) sudar tinta; **~ry** n esclavitud f

slay |sleɪ| (pt slew, pp slain) vt matar

sleazy |'sliːzɪ| adj de mala fama

sledge |sledʒ| n trineo; **~hammer** n mazo

sleek |sliːk| adj (shiny) lustroso; (car etc) elegante

sleep |sliːp| (pt, pp slept) n sueño ♦ vi dormir; **to go to ~** quedarse dormido; **~ around** vi acostarse con cualquiera; **~ in** vi (oversleep) quedarse dormido; **~er** n (person) durmiente m/f; (BRIT RAIL: on track) traviesa; (: train) coche-cama m; **~ing bag** n saco de dormir; **~ing car** n coche-cama m; **~ing partner** (BRIT) n (COMM) socio comanditario; **~ing pill** n somnífero; **~less** adj: **a ~less night** una noche en blanco; **~walker** n sonámbulo/a; **~y** adj soñoliento; (place) soporífero

sleet |sliːt| n aguanieve f

sleeve |sliːv| n manga; (TECH) manguito; (of record) portada; **~less** adj sin mangas

sleigh |sleɪ| n trineo

sleight |slaɪt| n: **~ of hand** escamoteo

slender |'slendə*| adj delgado; (means)

escaso

slept |slept| pt, pp of **sleep**

slew |sluː| pt of **slay** ♦ vi (BRIT: veer) torcerse

slice |slaɪs| n (of meat) tajada; (of bread) rebanada; (of lemon) rodaja; (utensil) pala ♦ vt cortar (en tajos); rebanar

slick |slɪk| adj (skilful) hábil, diestro; (clever) astuto ♦ n (also: oil ~) marea negra

slide |slaɪd| (pt, pp slid) n (movement) descenso, desprendimiento; (in playground) tobogán m; (PHOT) diapositiva; (BRIT: also: hair ~) pasador m ♦ vt correr, deslizar ♦ vi (slip) resbalarse; (glide) deslizarse; **sliding** adj (door) corredizo; **sliding scale** n escala móvil

slight |slaɪt| adj (slim) delgado; (frail) delicado; (pain etc) leve; (trivial) insignificante; (small) pequeño ♦ n desaire m ♦ vt (insult) ofender, desairar; **not in the ~est** en absoluto; **~ly** adv ligeramente, un poco

slim |slɪm| adj delgado, esbelto; (fig: chance) remoto ♦ vi adelgazar

slime |slaɪm| n limo, cieno

slimming |'slɪmɪŋ| n adelgazamiento

slimy |'slaɪmɪ| adj cenagoso

sling |slɪŋ| (pt, pp slung) n (MED) cabestrillo; (weapon) honda ♦ vt tirar, arrojar

slip |slɪp| n (slide) resbalón m; (mistake) descuido; (underskirt) combinación f; (of paper) papelito ♦ vt (slide) deslizar ♦ vi deslizarse; (stumble) resbalar(se); (decline) decaer; (move smoothly): **to ~ into/out of** (room etc) introducirse en/salirse de; **to give sb the ~** eludir a uno; **a ~ of the tongue** un lapsus; **to ~ sth on/off** ponerse/quitarse algo; **~ away** vi escabullirse; **~ in** vt meter ♦ vi meterse; **~ out** vi (go out) salir (un momento); **~ up** vi (make mistake) equivocarse; meter la pata; **~ped disc** n vértebra dislocada

slipper [ˈslɪpəʳ] n zapatilla, pantufla

slippery [ˈslɪpərɪ] adj resbaladizo

slip: ~ **road** (BRIT) n carretera de acceso; ~-**up** n (error) desliz m; ~**way** n grada, gradas fpl

slit [slɪt] (pt, pp **slit**) n raja; (cut) corte m ♦ vt rajar; cortar

slither [ˈslɪðəʳ] vi deslizarse

sliver [ˈslɪvəʳ] n (of glass, wood) astilla; (of cheese etc) raja

slob [slɔb] (inf) n abandonado/a

slog [slɔg] (BRIT) vi sudar tinta; **it was a** ~ costó trabajo (hacerlo)

slogan [ˈsləʊgən] n eslogan m, lema m

slope [sləʊp] n (up) cuesta, pendiente f; (down) declive m; (side of mountain) falda, vertiente m ♦ vi: **to** ~ **down** estar en declive; **to** ~ **up** inclinarse

sloping adj en pendiente; en declive; (writing) inclinado

sloppy [ˈslɔpɪ] adj (work) descuidado; (appearance) desaliñado

slot [slɔt] n ranura ♦ vt: **to** ~ **into** encajar en

slot machine n (BRIT: vending machine) distribuidor m automático; (for gambling) tragaperras m inv

slouch [slaʊtʃ] vi andar etc con los hombros caídos

Slovenia [sləʊˈviːnɪə] n Eslovenia

slovenly [ˈslʌvənlɪ] adj desaliñado, desaseado; (careless) descuidado

slow [sləʊ] adj lento; (not clever) lerdo; (watch): **to be** ~ atrasar ♦ adv lentamente, despacio ♦ vt, vi (also: ~ **down**, ~ **up**) retardar; "~" (road sign) "disminuir velocidad"; ~**down** (US) n huelga de manos caídas; ~**ly** adv lentamente, despacio; ~ **motion** n: **in** ~ **motion** a cámara lenta

sludge [slʌdʒ] n lodo, fango

slug [slʌg] n babosa; (bullet) posta; ~**gish** adj lento; (person) perezoso

sluice [sluːs] n (gate) esclusa; (channel) canal m

slum [slʌm] n casucha

slump [slʌmp] n (economic) depresión

f ♦ vi hundirse; (prices) caer en picado

slung [slʌŋ] pt, pp of **sling**

slur [sləːʳ] n: **to cast a** ~ **on** insultar ♦ vt (speech) pronunciar mal

slush [slʌʃ] n nieve f a medio derretir

slut [slʌt] n putona

sly [slaɪ] adj astuto; (smile) taimado

smack [smæk] n bofetada ♦ vt dar en la mano a; (child, on face) abofetear ♦ vi: **to** ~ **of** saber a, oler a

small [smɔːl] adj pequeño; ~ **ads** (BRIT) npl anuncios mpl por palabras; ~ **change** n suelto, cambio; ~**holder** (BRIT) n granjero/a, parcelero/a; ~ **hours** npl: **in the** ~ **hours** a las altas horas de (la noche); ~**pox** n viruela; ~ **talk** n cháchara

smart [smaːt] adj elegante; (clever) listo, inteligente; (quick) rápido, vivo ♦ vi escocer, picar; ~**en up** vi arreglarse ♦ vt arreglar

smash [smæʃ] n (also: ~-**up**) choque m; (MUS) exitazo ♦ vt (break) hacer pedazos; (car etc) estrellar; (SPORT: record) batir ♦ vi hacerse pedazos; (against wall etc) estrellarse; ~**ing** (inf) adj estupendo

smattering [ˈsmætərɪŋ] n: **a** ~ **of** algo de

smear [smɪəʳ] n mancha; (MED) frotis m inv ♦ vt untar; ~ **campaign** n campaña de desprestigio

smell [smel] (pt, pp **smelt** or **smelled**) n olor m; (sense) olfato ♦ vt, vi oler; ~**y** adj maloliente

smile [smaɪl] n sonrisa ♦ vi sonreír

smirk [sməːk] n sonrisa falsa or afectada

smith [smɪθ] n herrero; ~**y** [ˈsmɪðɪ] n herrería

smog [smɔg] n esmog m

smoke [sməʊk] n humo ♦ vi fumar; (chimney) echar humo ♦ vt (cigarettes) fumar; ~**d** adj (bacon, glass) ahumado; ~**r** n fumador(a) m/f; (RAIL) coche m fumador; ~ **screen** n cortina de humo; ~ **shop** (US) n estanco (SP), tabaquería (AM); **smoking** n: "no smoking" "prohibido fumar";

smoky adj (room) lleno de humo; (taste) ahumado

smolder ['smǝuldǝ*] (US) vi = **smoulder**

smooth [smuːð] adj liso; (sea) tranquilo; (flavour, movement) suave; (sauce) fino; (person: pej) meloso ♦ vt (also: ~ out) alisar; (creases, difficulties) allanar

smother ['smʌðǝ*] vt sofocar; (repress) contener

smoulder ['smǝuldǝ*] (US **smolder**) vi arder sin llama

smudge [smʌdʒ] n mancha ♦ vt manchar

smug [smʌg] adj presumido; orondo

smuggle ['smʌgl] vt pasar de contrabando; **~r** n contrabandista m/f; **smuggling** n contrabando

smutty ['smʌtɪ] adj (fig) verde, obsceno

snack [snæk] n bocado; **~ bar** n cafetería

snag [snæg] n problema m

snail [sneɪl] n caracol m

snake [sneɪk] n serpiente f

snap [snæp] n (sound) chasquido; (photograph) foto f ♦ adj (decision) instantáneo ♦ vt (break) quebrar; (fingers) castañetear ♦ vi quebrarse; (fig: speak sharply) contestar bruscamente; **to ~ shut** cerrarse de golpe; **~ at** vt fus (subj: dog) intentar morder; **~ off** vi partirse; **~ up** vt agarrar; **~ fastener** (US) n botón m de presión; **~py** (inf) adj (answer) instantáneo; (slogan) conciso; **make it ~py!** (hurry up) ¡date prisa!; **~shot** n foto f (instantánea)

snare [snɛǝ*] n trampa

snarl [snɑːl] vi gruñir

snatch [snætʃ] n (small piece) fragmento ♦ vt (~ away) arrebatar; (fig) agarrar; **to ~ some sleep** encontrar tiempo para dormir

sneak [sniːk] (pt (US) **snuck**) vi: to **~ in/out** entrar/salir a hurtadillas ♦ n (inf) soplón/ona m/f; **to ~ up on sb** aparecérsele de improviso a uno; **~ers** npl zapatos mpl de lona; **~y** adj furtivo

sneer [snɪǝ*] vi reír con sarcasmo; (mock): **to ~ at** burlarse de

sneeze [sniːz] vi estornudar

sniff [snɪf] vi sollozar ♦ vt husmear, oler; (drugs) esnifar

snigger ['snɪgǝ*] vi reírse con disimulo

snip [snɪp] n tijeretazo; (BRIT: inf: bargain) ganga ♦ vt tijeretear

sniper ['snaɪpǝ*] n francotirador(a) m/f

snippet ['snɪpɪt] n retazo

snob [snɔb] n (e)snob m/f; **~bery** n (e)snobismo; **~bish** adj (e)snob

snooker ['snuːkǝ*] n especie de billar

snoop [snuːp] vi: **to ~ about** fisgonear

snooze [snuːz] n siesta ♦ vi echar una siesta

snore [snɔː*] n ronquido ♦ vi roncar

snorkel ['snɔːkl] n (tubo) respirador m

snort [snɔːt] n bufido ♦ vi bufar

snout [snaut] n hocico, morro

snow [snǝu] n nieve f ♦ vi nevar; **~ball** n bola de nieve ♦ vi (fig) agrandarse, ampliarse; **~bound** adj bloqueado por la nieve; **~drift** n ventisquero; **~drop** n campanilla; **~fall** n nevada; **~flake** n copo de nieve; **~man** (irreg) n figura de nieve; **~plough** (US **~plow**) n quitanieves m inv; **~shoe** n raqueta (de nieve); **~storm** n nevada, nevasca

snub [snʌb] vt (person) desairar ♦ n desaire m, repulsa; **~-nosed** adj chato

snuff [snʌf] n rapé m

snug [snʌg] adj (cosy) cómodo; (fitted) ajustado

snuggle ['snʌgl] vi: **to ~ up to sb** arrimarse a uno

KEYWORD

so [sǝu] adv **1** (thus, likewise) así, de este modo; **if ~** de ser así; **I like swimming — ~ do I** a mí me gusta nadar — a mí también; **I've got work**

to do — ~ has Paul tengo trabajo que hacer — Paul también; **it's 5 o'clock — ~ it is!** son las cinco — ¡pues es verdad!; **I hope/think ~** espero/creo que sí; **~ far** hasta ahora; (in past) hasta ese momento
2 (in comparisons etc: to such a degree) tan; **~ quickly (that)** tan rápido (que); **~ big (that)** tan grande (que); **she's not ~ clever as her brother** no es tan lista como su hermano; **we were ~ worried** estábamos preocupadísimos
3: **~ much** adj, adv tanto; **~ many** tantos/as
4 (phrases): **10 or ~** unos 10, 10 o así; **~ long!** (inf: goodbye) ¡hasta luego!
♦ conj **1** (expressing purpose): **~ as to do sth** para hacer; **~ (that)** para que + sub **2** (expressing result) así que; **~ you see, I could have gone** así que ya ves, (yo) podría haber ido

soak [səuk] vt (drench) empapar; (steep in water) remojar ♦ vi remojarse, estar a remojo; **~ in** vi penetrar; **~ up** vt absorber
soap [səup] n jabón m; **~flakes** npl escamas fpl de jabón; **~ opera** n telenovela; **~ powder** n jabón m en polvo; **~y** adj jabonoso
soar [sɔː*] vi (on wings) remontarse; (rocket, prices) disparrarse; (building etc) elevarse
sob [sɔb] n sollozo ♦ vi sollozar
sober ['səubə*] adj (serious) serio; (not drunk) sobrio; (colour, style) discreto; **~ up** vt quitar la borrachera
so-called adj así llamado
soccer ['sɔkə*] n fútbol m
social ['səuʃl] adj social ♦ n velada, fiesta; **~ club** n club m; **~ism** n socialismo; **~ist** adj, n socialista; **~ize** vi: **to ~ize (with)** alternar (con); **~ly** adv socialmente; **~ security** n seguridad f social; **~ work** n asistencia social; **~ worker** n asistente/a m/f

social
society [sə'saɪətɪ] n sociedad f; (club) asociación f; (also: high ~) alta sociedad
sociology [səusɪ'ɒlədʒɪ] n sociología
sock [sɔk] n calcetín m (SP), media (AM)
socket ['sɔkɪt] n cavidad f; (BRIT: ELEC) enchufe m
sod [sɔd] n (of earth) césped m; (BRIT: inf!) cabrón/ona m/f (!)
soda ['səudə] n (CHEM) sosa; (also: ~ water) soda; (US: also: ~ pop) gaseosa
sofa ['səufə] n sofá m
soft [sɔft] adj (lenient, not hard) blando; (gentle, not bright) suave; **~ drink** n bebida no alcohólica; **~en** ['sɔfn] vt ablandar; suavizar; (effect) amortiguar ♦ vi ablandarse; suavizarse; **~ly** adv suavemente; (gently) con delicadeza, con delicadeza; **~ness** n blandura; suavidad f; **~ware** n (COMPUT) software m
soggy ['sɔgɪ] adj empapado
soil [sɔɪl] n (earth) tierra, suelo ♦ vt ensuciar; **~ed** adj sucio
solar ['səulə*] adj: **~ energy** n energía solar; **~ panel** n panel m solar
sold [səuld] pt, pp of **sell**; **~ out** adj (COMM) agotado
solder ['səuldə*] vt soldar ♦ n soldadura
soldier ['səuldʒə*] n soldado m; (army man) militar m
sole [səul] n (of foot) planta; (of shoe) suela; (fish: pl inv) lenguado ♦ adj único
solemn ['sɔləm] adj solemne
sole trader n (COMM) comerciante m exclusivo
solicit [sə'lɪsɪt] vt (request) solicitar ♦ vi (prostitute) importunar
solicitor [sə'lɪsɪtə*] n (BRIT) (for wills etc) ≈ notario/a; (in court) ≈ abogado/a
solid ['sɔlɪd] adj sólido; (gold etc) macizo ♦ n sólido; **~s** npl (food) alimentos mpl sólidos

solidarity [sɔlɪˈdærɪtɪ] n solidaridad f

solitary [ˈsɔlɪtərɪ] adj solitario, solo; **~ confinement** n incomunicación f

solo [ˈsəʊləʊ] n solo ♦ adv (fly) en solitario; **~ist** n solista m/f

soluble [ˈsɔljʊbl] adj soluble

solution [səˈluːʃən] n solución f

solve [sɔlv] vt resolver, solucionar

solvent [ˈsɔlvənt] adj (COMM) solvente ♦ n (CHEM) solvente m

KEYWORD

some [sʌm] adj 1 (a certain amount or number of): **~ tea/water/biscuits** té/agua/(unas) galletas; **there's ~ milk in the fridge** hay leche en el frigo; **there were ~ people outside** había algunas personas fuera; **I've got ~ money, but not much** tengo algo de dinero, pero no mucho

2 (certain: in contrasts) algunos/as; **~ people say that ...** hay quien dice que ...; **~ films were excellent, but most were mediocre** hubo algunas películas excelentes, pero la mayoría fueron mediocres

3 (unspecified): **~ woman was asking for you** una mujer estuvo preguntando por ti; **he was asking for ~ book (or other)** pedía un libro; **~ day** algún día; **~ day next week** un día de la semana que viene

♦ pron 1 (a certain number): **I've got ~** (books etc) tengo algunos/as

2 (a certain amount) algo; **I've got ~** (money, milk) tengo algo; **could I have ~ of that cheese?** ¿me puede dar un poco de ese queso?; **I've read ~ of the book** he leído parte del libro

♦ adv: **~ 10 people** unas 10 personas, una decena de personas

---

some: ~body [ˈsʌmbədɪ] pron = **someone**; **~how** adv de alguna manera; (for some reason) por una u otra razón; **~one** pron alguien; **~place** (US) adv = **somewhere**

somersault [ˈsʌməsɔːlt] n (deliberate) salto mortal; (accidental) vuelco ♦ vi dar un salto mortal; dar vueltas

some: ~thing pron algo; **would you like ~thing to eat/drink?** ¿te gustaría cenar/tomar algo?; **~time** adv (in future) algún día, en algún momento; (in past): **~time last month** durante el mes pasado; **~times** adv a veces; **~what** adv algo; **~where** adv (be) en alguna parte; (go) a alguna parte; **~where else** (be) en otra parte; (go) a otra parte

son [sʌn] n hijo

song [sɔŋ] n canción f

son-in-law n yerno

soon [suːn] adv pronto, dentro de poco; **~ afterwards** poco después; see also as; **~er** adv (time) antes, más temprano; (preference): **I would ~er do that** preferiría hacer eso; **~er or later** tarde o temprano

soot [sʊt] n hollín m

soothe [suːð] vt tranquilizar; (pain) aliviar

sophisticated [səˈfɪstɪkeɪtɪd] adj sofisticado

sophomore [ˈsɔfəmɔː*] (US) n estudiante m/f de segundo año

sopping [ˈsɔpɪŋ] adj: **~ (wet)** empapado

soppy [ˈsɔpɪ] (pej) adj tonto

soprano [səˈprɑːnəʊ] n soprano f

sorcerer [ˈsɔːsərə*] n hechicero

sore [sɔː*] adj (painful) doloroso, que duele ♦ n llaga; **~ly** adv: **I am ~ly tempted to** estoy muy tentado a

sorrow [ˈsɔrəʊ] n pena, dolor m; **~s** npl pesares mpl; **~ful** adj triste

sorry [ˈsɔrɪ] adj (regretful) arrepentido; (condition, excuse) lastimoso; **~!** ¡perdón!, ¡perdone!; **~?** ¿cómo?; **to feel ~ for sb** tener lástima a uno; **I feel ~ for him** me da lástima

sort [sɔːt] n clase f, género, tipo ♦ vt (also: **~ out**: papers) clasificar; (: problems) arreglar, solucionar; **~ing**

office n sala de batalla
SOS n SOS m
so-so adv regular, así así
soufflé ['su:fleɪ] n suflé m
sought [sɔːt] pt, pp of **seek**
soul [səul] n alma; **~ful** adj lleno de sentimiento
sound [saund] n (noise) sonido, ruido; (volume: on TV etc) volumen m; (GEO) estrecho ♦ adj (healthy) sano; (safe, not damaged) en buen estado; (reliable: person) digno de confianza; (sensible) sensato, razonable; (secure: investment) seguro ♦ adv: **~ asleep** profundamente dormido ♦ vt (alarm) sonar ♦ vi sonar, resonar; (fig: seem) parecer; **to ~ like** sonar a; **~ out** vt sondear; **~ barrier** n barrera del sonido; **~bite** n cita jugosa; **~ effects** npl efectos mpl sonoros; **~ly** adv (sleep) profundamente; (defeated) completamente; **~proof** adj insonorizado; **~track** n (of film) banda sonora
soup [su:p] n (thick) sopa; (thin) caldo; **~ plate** n plato sopero; **~spoon** n cuchara sopera
sour ['sauə*] adj agrio; (milk) cortado; **it's ~ grapes** (fig) están verdes
source [sɔːs] n fuente f
south [sauθ] n sur m ♦ adj del sur, sureño ♦ adv al sur, hacia el sur; **S~ Africa** n África del Sur; **S~ African** adj, n sudafricano/a m/f; **S~ America** n América del Sur, Sudamérica; **S~ American** adj, n sudamericano/a m/f; **~east** n sudeste m; **~erly** ['sʌðəlɪ] adj sur; (from the ~) del sur; **~ern** ['sʌðən] adj del sur, meridional; **S~ Pole** n Polo Sur; **~ward(s)** adv hacia el sur; **~-west** n suroeste m
souvenir [su:və'nɪə*] n recuerdo
sovereign ['sɒvrɪn] adj, n soberano/a m/f; **~ty** n soberanía
soviet ['səuvɪət] adj soviético; **the S~ Union** la Unión Soviética

sow¹ [səu] (pt **sowed**, pp **sown**) vt sembrar
sow² [sau] n cerda (SP), puerca (SP), chancha (AM)
soy [sɔɪ] (US) n = **soya**
soya ['sɔɪə] (BRIT) n soja; **~ bean** n haba de soja; **~ sauce** n salsa de soja
spa [spɑː] n balneario
space [speɪs] n espacio; (room) sitio ♦ cpd espacial ♦ vt (also: **~ out**) espaciar; **~craft** n nave f espacial; **~man/woman** (irreg) n astronauta m/f, cosmonauta m/f; **~ship** n = **~craft**; **spacing** n espaciado
spacious ['speɪʃəs] adj amplio
spade [speɪd] n (tool) pala, laya; **~s** npl (CARDS: British) picas fpl; (: Spanish) espadas fpl
spaghetti [spə'getɪ] n espaguetis mpl, fideos mpl
Spain [speɪn] n España
span [spæn] n (of bird, plane) envergadura; (of arch) luz f; (in time) lapso ♦ vt extenderse sobre, cruzar; (fig) abarcar
Spaniard ['spænjəd] n español(a) m/f
spaniel ['spænjəl] n perro de aguas
Spanish ['spænɪʃ] adj español(a) ♦ n (LING) español m, castellano; **the ~** npl los españoles
spank [spæŋk] vt zurrar
spanner ['spænə*] (BRIT) n llave f (inglesa)
spare [speə*] adj de reserva; (surplus) sobrante, de más ♦ n = **~ part** ♦ vt (do without) pasarse sin; (refrain from hurting) perdonar; **to ~** (surplus) sobrante, de sobra; **~ part** n pieza de repuesto; **~ time** n tiempo libre; **~ wheel** n (AUT) rueda de recambio
sparingly ['speərɪŋlɪ] adv con moderación
spark [spɑːk] n chispa; (fig) chispazo; **~(ing) plug** n bujía
sparkle ['spɑːkl] n centelleo, destello ♦ vi (shine) relucir, brillar; **sparkling** adj (eyes, conversation) brillante; (wine)

espumoso; *(mineral water)* con gas
sparrow ['spærəʊ] n gorrión m
sparse [spɑːs] adj esparcido, escaso
spartan ['spɑːtən] adj *(fig)* espartano
spasm ['spæzəm] n *(MED)* espasmo
spastic ['spæstɪk] n espástico/a
spat [spæt] pt, pp of **spit**
spate [speɪt] n *(fig)*: **a ~ of** un torrente de
spawn [spɔːn] vi desovar, frezar ♦ n huevas *fpl*
speak [spiːk] *(pt* **spoke**, *pp* **spoken)** vt *(language)* hablar; *(truth)* decir ♦ vi hablar; *(make a speech)* intervenir; **to ~ to sb/of or about sth** hablar con uno/de or sobre algo; **~ up!** ¡habla fuerte!; **~er** n *(in public)* orador(a) m/f; *(also:* **loud~er)** altavoz m; *(for stereo etc)* bafle m; *(POL):* **the S~er** *(BRIT)* el Presidente de la Cámara de los Comunes; *(US)* el Presidente del Congreso
spear [spɪə*] n lanza ♦ vt alancear; **~head** n *(attack etc)* encabezar
spec [spek] *(inf)* n: **on ~** como especulación
special ['speʃl] adj especial; *(edition etc)* extraordinario; *(delivery)* urgente; **~ist** n especialista m/f; **~ity** [speʃi'ælɪtɪ] *(BRIT)* n especialidad f; **~ize** vi: **to ~ize (in)** especializarse (en); **~ly** adv sobre todo, en particular, en particular; **~ty** *(US)* n = **~ity**
species ['spiːʃiːz] n inv especie f
specific [spə'sɪfɪk] adj específico; **~ally** adv específicamente
specify ['spesɪfaɪ] vt, vi especificar, precisar
specimen ['spesɪmən] n ejemplar m; *(MED: of urine)* espécimen m; *(: of blood)* muestra
speck [spek] n grano, mota
speckled ['spekld] adj moteado
specs [speks] *(inf)* npl gafas *fpl (SP)*, anteojos *mpl*
spectacle ['spektəkl] n espectáculo; **~s** npl *(BRIT: glasses)* gafas *fpl (SP)*, anteojos *mpl*; **spectacular** [-'tækjulə*] adj espectacular; *(success)*

imprimesionante
spectator [spek'teɪtə*] n espectador(a) m/f
spectrum ['spektrəm] *(pl* **spectra)** n espectro
speculate ['spekjuleɪt] vi: **to ~ (on)** especular (en); **speculation** [spekju'leɪʃən] n especulación f
speech [spiːtʃ] n *(faculty)* habla; *(formal talk)* discurso; *(spoken language)* lenguaje m; **~less** adj mudo, estupefacto; **~ therapist** n especialista que corrige defectos de pronunciación en los niños
speed [spiːd] n velocidad f; *(haste)* prisa; *(promptness)* rapidez f; **at full or top ~** a máxima velocidad; **to ~ up** vi acelerarse ♦ vt acelerar; **~boat** n lancha motora; **~ily** adv rápida, rápidamente; **~ing** n *(AUT)* exceso de velocidad; **~ limit** n límite m de velocidad, velocidad f máxima; **~ometer** [spi'dɒmɪtə*] n velocímetro; **~way** n *(sport)* pista de carrera; **~y** adj *(fast)* veloz, rápido; *(prompt)* pronto
spell [spel] *(pt, pp* **spelt** *(BRIT)* or **spelled)** n *(also:* **magic ~)** encanto, hechizo; *(period of time)* rato, período ♦ vt deletrear; *(fig)* anunciar, presagiar; **to cast a ~ on sb** hechizar a uno; **can't ~** pone faltas de ortografía; **~bound** adj embelesado, hechizado; **~ing** n ortografía
spend [spend] *(pt, pp* **spent)** vt *(money)* gastar; *(time)* pasar; *(life)* dedicar; **~thrift** n derrochador(a) m/f, pródigo/a
sperm [spɜːm] n esperma
sphere [sfɪə*] n esfera
sphinx [sfɪŋks] n esfinge f
spice [spaɪs] n especia ♦ vt condimentar
spicy ['spaɪsɪ] adj picante
spider ['spaɪdə*] n araña
spike [spaɪk] n *(point)* punta; *(BOT)* espiga
spill [spɪl] *(pt, pp* **spilt** or **spilled)** vt

spin [spɪn] (pt, pp spun) n (AVIAT)
barrena; (trip in car) paseo (en coche);
(on ball) efecto ♦ vt (wool etc) hilar;
(ball etc) hacer girar ♦ vi girar, dar
vueltas

spinach ['spɪnɪtʃ] n espinaca; (as food)
espinacas fpl

spinal ['spaɪnl] adj espinal; ~ **cord** n
columna vertebral

spin doctor (BRIT) n informador(a) parcial al
servicio de un partido político etc

spin-dryer (BRIT) n secador m
centrífugo

spine [spaɪn] n espinazo, columna
vertebral; (thorn) espina; ~**less** adj (fig)
débil, pusilánime

spinning ['spɪnɪŋ] n hilandería; ~ **top**
n peonza

spin-off n derivado, producto
secundario

spinster ['spɪnstə*] n soltera

spiral ['spaɪrl] n espiral f ♦ vi (fig:
prices) subir desorbitadamente;
~ **staircase** n escalera de caracol

spire [spaɪə*] n aguja, chapitel m

spirit ['spɪrɪt] n (soul) alma f; (ghost)
fantasma m; (attitude, sense) espíritu m;
(courage) valor m, ánimo; ~s npl (drink)
licor(es) m(pl); **in good** ~**s** alegre, de
buen ánimo; ~**ed** adj enérgico,
vigoroso

spiritual ['spɪrɪtjuəl] adj espiritual ♦ n
espiritual m

spit [spɪt] (pt, pp **spat**) n (for roasting)
asador m, espetón m; (saliva) saliva ♦ vi
escupir; (sound) chisporrotear; (rain)
lloviznar

spite [spaɪt] n rencor m, ojeriza ♦ vt
causar pena a, mortificar; **in ~ of** a
pesar de, pese a; ~**ful** adj rencoroso,
malévolo

spittle ['spɪtl] n saliva, baba

splash [splæʃ] n (sound) chapoteo; (of
colour) mancha ♦ vt salpicar ♦ vi (also:
~ **about**) chapotear

spleen [spliːn] n (ANAT) bazo

splendid ['splendɪd] adj espléndido

splint [splɪnt] n tablilla

splinter ['splɪntə*] n (of wood etc)
astilla; (in finger) espigón m ♦ vi
astillarse, hacer astillas

split [splɪt] (pt, pp **split**) n hendedura,
raja; (fig) división f; (POL) escisión f ♦ vt
partir, rajar; (party) dividir; (share)
repartir ♦ vi dividirse, escindirse; ~ **up**
vi (couple) separarse; (meeting)
acabarse

spoil [spɔɪl] (pt, pp **spoilt** or **spoiled**)
vt (damage) dañar; (mar) estropear;
(child) mimar, consentir; ~**s** npl
despojo, botín m; ~**sport** n aguafiestas
m inv

spoke [spəuk] pt of **speak** ♦ n rayo,
radio

spoken ['spəukn] pp of **speak**

spokesman ['spəuksmən] (irreg) n
portavoz m; **spokeswoman**
['spəukswumən] (irreg) n portavoz f

sponge [spʌndʒ] n esponja; (also:
~ **cake**) bizcocho ♦ vt (wash) lavar con
esponja ♦ vi: **to ~ off** or **on sb** vivir a
costa de uno; ~ **bag** (BRIT) n esponjera

sponsor ['spɒnsə*] n patrocinador(a)
m/f ♦ vt (applicant, proposal etc)
proponer; ~**ship** n patrocinio

spontaneous [spɒn'teɪnɪəs] adj
espontáneo

spooky ['spuːkɪ] (inf) adj espeluznante,
horripilante

spool [spuːl] n carrete m

spoon [spuːn] n cuchara; ~**-feed** vt
dar de comer con cuchara a; (fig) tratar
como un niño a; ~**ful** n cucharada

sport [spɔːt] n deporte m; (person): **to
be a good ~** ser muy majo ♦ vt (wear)
lucir, ostentar; ~**ing** adj deportivo;
(generous) caballeroso; **to give sb a**
~**ing chance** darle a uno una (buena)
oportunidad; ~ **jacket** (US) n = ~**s**
jacket; ~**s car** n deportivo; ~**s jacket**
(BRIT) n chaqueta deportiva;
~**sman** (irreg) n deportista m;

~smanship n deportividad f; **~swear** n trajes mpl de deporte or sport; **~swoman** (irreg) n deportista; **~y** adj deportista

spot [spɔt] n sitio, lugar m; (dot: on pattern) punto, mancha; (pimple) grano; (RADIO) cuña publicitaria; (TV) espacio publicitario; (small amount): **a ~ of** un poquito de ♦ vt (notice) notar, observar; **on the ~** allí mismo; **~ check** n reconocimiento rápido; **~less** adj perfectamente limpio; **~light** n foco, reflector m; (AUT) faro auxiliar; **~ted** adj (pattern) de puntos; **~ty** (face) con granos

spouse [spauz] n cónyuge m/f

spout [spaut] n (of jug) pico; (of pipe) caño ♦ vi salir en chorro

sprain [sprein] n torcedura f ♦ vt: **to ~ one's ankle/wrist** torcerse el tobillo/la muñeca

sprang [spræŋ] pt of **spring**

sprawl [sprɔːl] vi tumbarse

spray [sprei] n rociada; (of sea) espuma; (container) atomizador m; (for paint etc) pistola rociadora; (of flowers) ramita ♦ vt rociar; (crops) regar

spread [spred] (pt, pp **spread**) n extensión f; (for bread etc) pasta para untar; (inf: food) comilona ♦ vt extender; (butter) untar; (wings, sails) desplegar; (work, wealth) repartir; (scatter) esparcir ♦ vi (also: ~ out: stain) extenderse; (news) diseminarse; **~ out** vi (move apart) separarse; **~-eagled** adj a pata tendida; **~sheet** n hoja electrónica or de cálculo

spree [spriː] n: **to go on a ~** ir de juerga

sprightly [ˈspraitli] adj vivo, enérgico

spring [spriŋ] (pt **sprang**, pp **sprung**) n (season) primavera; (leap) salto, brinco; (coiled metal) resorte m; (of water) fuente f, manantial m ♦ vi saltar, brincar; **~ up** vi (thing: appear) aparecer; (problem) surgir; **~board** n trampolín m; **~-clean(ing)** n limpieza

general; **~time** n primavera

sprinkle [ˈspriŋkl] vt (pour: liquid) rociar; (: salt, sugar) espolvorear; **to ~ water** etc **on, ~ with water** etc rociar or salpicar de agua etc; **~r** n (for lawn) rociadera; (: to put out fire) aparato de rociadura automática

sprint [sprint] n esprint m ♦ vi esprintar

sprout [spraut] vi brotar, retoñar; **(Brussels) ~s** npl coles fpl de Bruselas

spruce [spruːs] n inv (BOT) pícea ♦ adj aseado, pulcro

sprung [sprʌŋ] pp of **spring**

spun [spʌn] pt, pp of **spin**

spur [spəː*] n espuela; (fig) estímulo, aguijón m ♦ vt (also: ~ on) estimular, incitar; **on the ~ of the moment** de improviso

spurious [ˈspjuəriəs] adj falso

spurn [spəːn] vt desdeñar, rechazar

spurt [spəːt] n chorro; (of energy) arrebato ♦ vi chorrear

spy [spai] n espía m/f ♦ vi: **to ~ on** espiar a ♦ vt (see) divisar, lograr ver; **~ing** n espionaje m

sq. abbr = **square**

squabble [ˈskwɔbl] vi reñir, pelear

squad [skwɔd] n (MIL) pelotón m; (POLICE) brigada; (SPORT) equipo

squadron [ˈskwɔdrən] n (MIL) escuadrón m; (AVIAT, NAUT) escuadra

squalid [ˈskwɔlid] adj vil; (fig: sordid) sórdido

squall [skwɔːl] n (storm) chubasco; (wind) ráfaga

squalor [ˈskwɔlə*] n miseria

squander [ˈskwɔndə*] vt (money) derrochar, despilfarrar; (chances) desperdiciar

square [skwɛə*] n cuadro; (in town) plaza; (inf: person) carca m/f ♦ adj cuadrado; (inf: ideas, tastes) trasnochado ♦ vt (arrange) arreglar; (MATH) cuadrar; (reconcile) compaginar; **all ~** igual(es); **to have a ~ meal** comer caliente; **2 metres ~** 2 metros

en cuadro; **2 ~ metres** 2 metros
cuadrados; **~ly** adv de lleno

squash [skwɔʃ] n (BRIT: drink):
lemon/orange ~ zumo (SP) or jugo
(AM) de limón/naranja; (US: BOT)
calabacín m; (SPORT) squash m,
frontenis m ♦ vt aplastar

squat [skwɔt] adj achaparrado ♦ vi
(also: ~ down) agacharse, sentarse en
cuclillas; **~ter** n persona que ocupa
ilegalmente una casa

squeak [skwi:k] vi (hinge) chirriar,
rechinar; (mouse) chillar

squeal [skwi:l] vi chillar, dar gritos
agudos

squeamish ['skwi:mɪʃ] adj delicado,
remilgado

squeeze [skwi:z] n presión f; (of hand)
apretón m; (COMM) restricción f ♦ vt
(hand, arm) apretar; **~ out** vt exprimir

squelch [skweltʃ] vi chapotear

squid [skwɪd] n inv calamar m; (CULIN)
calamares mpl

squiggle ['skwɪgl] n garabato

squint [skwɪnt] vi bizquear, ser bizco
♦ n (MED) estrabismo

squirm [skwə:m] vi retorcerse,
revolverse

squirrel ['skwɪrəl] n ardilla

squirt [skwə:t] vi salir a chorros ♦ vi
chiscar

Sr abbr = **senior**

St abbr = **saint; street**

stab [stæb] n (with knife) puñalada; (of
pain) pinchazo; (inf: try): **to have a
~ at (doing)** sth intentar (hacer) algo
♦ vt apuñalar

stable ['steɪbl] adj estable ♦ n cuadra,
caballeriza

stack [stæk] n montón m, pila ♦ vt
amontonar, apilar

stadium ['steɪdɪəm] n estadio

staff [stɑ:f] n (work force) personal m,
plantilla; (BRIT: SCOL) cuerpo docente
♦ vt proveer de personal

stag [stæg] n ciervo, venado

stage [steɪdʒ] n escena; (point) etapa;

(platform) plataforma; (profession): **the
~** el teatro ♦ vt (play) poner en escena,
representar; (organize) montar,
organizar; **in ~s** por etapas; **~coach** n
diligencia; **~ manager** n director(a)
m/f de escena

stagger ['stægə*] vi tambalearse ♦ vt
(amaze) asombrar; (hours, holidays)
escalonar; **~ing** adj asombroso

stagnant ['stægnənt] adj estancado

stag party n despedida de soltero

staid [steɪd] adj serio, formal

stain [steɪn] n mancha; (colouring)
tintura ♦ vt manchar; (wood) teñir; **~ed
glass window** n vidriera de colores;
~less steel n acero inoxidable;
~ remover n quitamanchas m inv

stair [steə*] n (step) peldaño, escalón
m; **~s** npl escaleras fpl; **~case** n =
~way; ~way n escalera

stake [steɪk] n estaca, poste m; (COMM)
interés m; (BETTING) apuesta ♦ vt
(money) apostar; (life) arriesgar;
(reputation) poner en juego; (claim)
presentar una reclamación; **to be at ~**
estar en juego

stale [steɪl] adj (bread) duro; (food)
pasado; (smell) rancio; (beer) agrio

stalemate ['steɪlmeɪt] n tablas fpl (por
ahogado); (fig) estancamiento

stalk [stɔ:k] n tallo, caña ♦ vt acechar,
cazar al acecho; **~ off** vi irse airado

stall [stɔ:l] n (in market) puesto; (in
stable) casilla (de establo) ♦ vt (AUT)
calar; (fig) dar largas a ♦ vi (AUT)
calarse; (fig) andarse con rodeos; **~s**
npl (BRIT: in cinema, theatre) butacas fpl

stallion ['stælɪən] n semental m

stamina ['stæmɪnə] n resistencia

stammer ['stæmə*] n tartamudeo ♦ vi
tartamudear

stamp [stæmp] n sello (SP), estampilla
(AM); (mark, also fig) marca, huella; (on
document) timbre m ♦ vi (also: **~ one's
foot**) patear ♦ vt (mark) marcar; (letter)
poner sellos or estampillas en; (with
rubber ~) sellar; **~ album** n álbum de

para sellos or estampillas; **~ collecting** n filatelia

stampede [stæm'pi:d] n estampida

stance [stæns] n postura

stand [stænd] (pt, pp **stood**) n (position) posición f, postura; (for taxis) parada; (hall ~) perchero; (music ~) atril m; (SPORT) tribuna; (at exhibition) stand m ♦ vi (be) estar, encontrarse; (be on foot) estar de pie; (rise) levantarse; (remain) quedar en pie; (in election) presentar candidatura ♦ vt (place) poner, colocar; (withstand) aguantar, soportar; (invite to) invitar; **to make a ~** (fig) mantener una postura firme; **to ~ for parliament** (BRIT) presentarse (como candidato) a las elecciones; **~ by** vi (be ready) estar listo ♦ vt fus (opinion) aferrarse a; (person) apoyar; **~ down** vi (withdraw) ceder el puesto; **~ for** vt fus (signify) significar; (tolerate) aguantar, permitir; **~ in for** vt fus suplir a; **~ out** vi destacarse; **~ up** vi levantarse, ponerse de pie; **~ up for** vt fus defender; **~ up to** vt fus hacer frente a

standard ['stændəd] n patrón m, norma; (level) nivel m; (flag) estandarte m ♦ adj (size etc) normal, corriente; (text) básico; **~s** npl (morals) valores mpl morales; **~ lamp** n lámpara de pie; **~ of living** n nivel m de vida

stand-by ['stændbai] n (reserve) recurso seguro; **to be on ~** estar sobre aviso; **~ ticket** n (AVIAT) (billete m) standby m

stand-in ['stændɪn] n suplente m/f

standing ['stændɪŋ] adj (on foot) de pie, en pie; (permanent) permanente ♦ n reputación f; **of many years' ~** que lleva muchos años; **~ joke** n broma permanente; **~ order** (BRIT) n (at bank) orden f de pago permanente; **~ room** n sitio para estar de pie

stand: **~point** n punto de vista; **~still** n: **at a ~still** (industry, traffic) paralizado; (car) parado; **to come to**

a **~still** quedar paralizado; pararse

stank [stæŋk] pt of **stink**

staple ['steɪpl] n (for papers) grapa ♦ adj (food etc) básico ♦ vt grapar; **~r** n grapadora

star [sta:*] n estrella; (celebrity) estrella, astro ♦ vt (THEATRE, CINEMA) ser el/la protagonista de; **the ~s** npl (ASTROLOGY) el horóscopo

starboard ['sta:bəd] n estribor m

starch [sta:tʃ] n almidón m

stardom ['sta:dəm] n estrellato

stare [steə*] n mirada fija ♦ vi: **to ~ at** mirar fijo

starfish ['sta:fɪʃ] n estrella de mar

stark [sta:k] adj (bleak) severo, escueto ♦ adv: **~ naked** en cueros

starling ['sta:lɪŋ] n estornino

starry ['sta:rɪ] adj estrellado; **~-eyed** adj (innocent) inocentón/ona, ingenuo

start [sta:t] n principio, comienzo; (departure) salida; (sudden movement) salto, sobresalto; (advantage) ventaja ♦ vt empezar, comenzar; (cause) causar; (found) fundar; (engine) poner en marcha ♦ vi comenzar, empezar; (with fright) asustarse, sobresaltarse; (train etc) salir; **to ~ doing** or **to do sth** empezar a hacer algo; **~ off** vi empezar, comenzar; (leave) salir, ponerse en camino; **~ up** vi comenzar; (car) ponerse en marcha ♦ vt comenzar; poner en marcha; **~er** n (AUT) botón m de arranque; (SPORT: official) juez m/f de salida; (BRIT: CULIN) entrada; **~ing point** n punto de partida

startle ['sta:tl] vt asustar, sobrecoger; **startling** adj alarmante

starvation [sta:'veɪʃən] n hambre f

starve [sta:v] vi tener mucha hambre; (to death) morir de hambre ♦ vt hacer pasar hambre

state [steɪt] n estado ♦ vt (say, declare) afirmar; **the S~s** los Estados Unidos; **to be in a ~** estar agitado; **~ly** adj majestuoso, imponente; **~ly home** n casa señorial, casa solariega; **~ment** n afirmación f; **~sman** (irreg) n estadista m

static ['stætɪk] n (RADIO) parásitos mpl ♦ adj estático; **~ electricity** n estática f

station ['steɪʃən] n (gen) estación f; (RADIO) emisora f; (rank) posición f social ♦ vt colocar, situar; (MIL) apostar

stationary ['steɪʃnərɪ] adj estacionario, fijo

stationer ['steɪʃənə*] n papelero/a; **~'s (shop)** (BRIT) n papelería; **~y** [-nərɪ] n papel m de escribir, artículos mpl de escritorio

station master n (RAIL) jefe m de estación

station wagon (US) n ranchera

statistic [stə'tɪstɪk] n estadística; **~s** n (science) estadística

statue ['stætju:] n estatua

status ['steɪtəs] n estado; (reputation) estatus m; **~ symbol** n símbolo de prestigio

statute ['stætju:t] n estatuto, ley f; **statutory** adj estatutario

staunch [stɔ:ntʃ] adj leal, incondicional

stay [steɪ] n estancia ♦ vi quedar(se); (as guest) hospedarse; **to ~ put** seguir en el mismo sitio; **to ~ the night/5 days** pasar la noche/cinco 5 días; **~ behind** vi quedar atrás; **~ in** vi quedarse en casa; **~ on** vi quedarse; **~ out** vi (of house) no volver a casa; (on strike) permanecer en huelga; **~ up** vi (at night) velar, no acostarse; **~ing power** n aguante m

stead [sted] n: **in sb's ~** en lugar de uno; **to stand sb in good ~** ser muy útil a uno

steadfast ['stedfɑ:st] adj firme, resuelto

steadily ['stedɪlɪ] adv constantemente; (firmly) firmemente; (work, walk) sin parar; (gaze) fijamente

steady ['stedɪ] adj (firm) firme; (regular) regular; (person, character) sensato, juicioso; (boyfriend) formal; (look, voice)

tranquilo ♦ vt (stabilize) estabilizar; (nerves) calmar

steak [steɪk] n (gen) filete m; (beef) bistec m

steal [sti:l] (pt **stole**, pp **stolen**) vt robar ♦ vi robar; (move secretly) andar a hurtadillas

stealth [stelθ] n: **by ~** a escondidas, sigilosamente; **~y** adj cauteloso, sigiloso

steam [sti:m] n vapor m; (mist) vaho, humo ♦ vt (CULIN) cocer al vapor ♦ vi echar vapor; **~ engine** n máquina de vapor; **~er** n (buque m de) vapor m; **~roller** n apisonadora; **~ship** n = **~er**; **~y** adj (room) lleno de vapor; (window) empañado; (heat, atmosphere) bochornoso

steel [sti:l] n acero ♦ adj de acero; **~works** n acería

steep [sti:p] adj escarpado, abrupto; (stair) empinado; (price) exorbitante, excesivo ♦ vt empapar, remojar

steeple ['sti:pl] n aguja; **~chase** n carrera de obstáculos

steer [stɪə*] vt (car) conducir (SP), manejar (AM); (person) dirigir ♦ vi conducir, manejar; **~ing** n (AUT) dirección f; **~ing wheel** n volante m

stem [stem] n (of plant) tallo; (of glass) pie m ♦ vt detener; (blood) restañar; **~ from** vt fus ser consecuencia de

stench [stentʃ] n hedor m

stencil ['stensl] n (pattern) plantilla ♦ vt hacer un cliché de

stenographer [ste'nɔgrəfə*] (US) n taquígrafo/a

step [step] n paso; (on stair) peldaño, escalón m ♦ vi: **to ~ forward/back** dar un paso adelante/hacia atrás; **~s** npl (BRIT) = **~ladder**; **in/out of** (with) acorde/en disonancia (con); **~ down** vi (fig) retirarse; **~ on** vt fus pisar; **~ up** vt (increase) aumentar; **~brother** n hermanastro; **~daughter** n hijastra; **~father** n padrastro; **~ladder** n escalera doble or de tijera;

~mother n madrastra; **~ping stone** n pasadera; **~sister** n hermanastra; **~son** n hijastro

stereo ['stɛrɪəʊ] n estéreo ♦ adj (also: ~phonic) estéreo, estereofónico

sterile ['stɛraɪl] adj estéril; **sterilize** ['stɛrɪlaɪz] vt esterilizar

sterling ['stə:lɪŋ] adj (silver) de ley 1 n (ECON) (libras fpl) esterlinas fpl; **one pound** ~ una libra esterlina

stern [stə:n] adj severo, austero ♦ n (NAUT) popa

stew [stju:] n cocido (SP), estofado (SP), guisado (AM) ♦ vt estofar, guisar; (fruit) cocer

steward ['stju:əd] n camarero; **~ess** n (esp on plane) azafata

stick [stɪk] (pt, pp stuck) n palo; (of dynamite) barreno; (as weapon) porra; (walking ~) bastón m ♦ vt (glue) pegar; (inf: put) meter; (: tolerate) aguantar, soportar; (thrust): **to ~ sth into** clavar or hincar algo en ♦ vi pegarse; (be unmoveable) quedarse parado; (in mind) quedarse grabado; **~ out** vi sobresalir; **~ up** vi sobresalir; **~ up for** vt fus defender; **~er** n (label) etiqueta engomada; (with slogan) pegatina; **~ing plaster** n esparadrapo

stick-up ['stɪkʌp] (inf) n asalto, atraco

sticky ['stɪkɪ] adj pegajoso; (label) engomado; (fig) difícil

stiff [stɪf] adj rígido, tieso; (hard) duro; (manner) estirado; (difficult) difícil; (person) inflexible; (price) exorbitante ♦ adv: scared/bored ~ muerto de miedo/aburrimiento; **~en** vi (muscles etc) agarrotarse; **~ neck** n torticolis m inv; **~ness** n rigidez f, tiesura

stifle ['staɪfl] vt ahogar, sofocar; **stifling** adj (heat) sofocante, bochornoso

stigma ['stɪgmə] n (fig) estigma m

stile [staɪl] n portillo, portilla

stiletto [stɪ'lɛtəʊ] (BRIT) n (also: ~ heel) tacón m de aguja

still [stɪl] adj inmóvil, quieto ♦ adv todavía; (even) aun; (nonetheless) sin embargo, aun así; **~born** adj nacido muerto; **~ life** n naturaleza muerta

stilt [stɪlt] n zanco; (pile) pilar m, soporte m

stilted ['stɪltɪd] adj afectado

stimulate ['stɪmjʊleɪt] vt estimular

stimulus ['stɪmjʊləs] (pl stimuli) n estímulo, incentivo

sting [stɪŋ] (pt, pp stung) n picadura; (pain) escozor m, picazón f; (organ) aguijón m ♦ vt, vi picar

stingy ['stɪndʒɪ] adj tacaño

stink [stɪŋk] (pt stank, pp stunk) n hedor m, tufo ♦ vi heder, apestar; **~ing** adj hediondo, fétido; (fig: inf) horrible

stint [stɪnt] n tarea, trabajo ♦ vi: **to ~ on** escatimar

stir [stə:*] n (fig: agitation) conmoción f ♦ vt (tea etc) remover; (fig: emotions) provocar ♦ vi moverse; **~ up** vt (trouble) fomentar

stirrup ['stɪrəp] n estribo

stitch [stɪtʃ] n (SEWING) puntada; (KNITTING) punto; (MED) punto (de sutura); (pain) punzada ♦ vt coser; (MED) suturar

stoat [stəʊt] n armiño

stock [stɔk] n (COMM: reserves) existencias fpl, stock m; (: selection) surtido; (AGR) ganado, ganadería; (CULIN) caldo; (descent) raza, estirpe f; (FINANCE) capital m ♦ adj (fig: reply etc) clásico ♦ vt (have in ~) tener existencias de; **~s and shares** acciones y valores; **in ~** en existencia or almacén; **out of ~** agotado; **to take ~ of** (fig) asesorar, examinar; **~ up with** vt fus abastecerse de; **~broker** ['stɔkbrəʊkə*] n agente m/f or corredor(a) m/f de bolsa; **~ cube** (BRIT) n pastilla de caldo; **~ exchange** n bolsa

stocking ['stɔkɪŋ] n media

stock: **~ market** n bolsa (de valores); **~pile** n reserva ♦ vt acumular, almacenar; **~taking** (BRIT) n (COMM) inventario

stocky ['stɔkı] adj (strong) robusto; (short) achaparrado

stodgy ['stɔdʒı] adj indigesto, pesado

stoke [stəuk] vt atizar

stole [stəul] pt of **steal** ♦ n estola

stolen ['stəuln] pp of **steal**

stomach ['stʌmək] n (ANAT) estómago; (belly) vientre m ♦ vt tragar, aguantar; **~ache** n dolor m de estómago

stone [stəun] n piedra; (in fruit) hueso; = 6.348 kg; 14 libras ♦ adj de piedra ♦ vt apedrear; (fruit) deshuesar; **~-cold** adj helado; **~-deaf** adj sordo como una tapia; **~work** n (art) cantería; **stony** adj pedregoso; (fig) frío

stood [stud] pt, pp of **stand**

stool [stu:l] n taburete m

stoop [stu:p] vi (also: ~ down) doblarse, agacharse; (also: have a ~) ser cargado de espaldas

stop [stɔp] n parada; (in punctuation) punto ♦ vt parar, detener; (break off) suspender; (block: pay) suspender; (: cheque) invalidar; (also: put a ~ to) poner término a ♦ vi pararse, detenerse; (end) acabarse; **to ~ doing sth** dejar de hacer algo; **~ dead** vi pararse en seco; **~ off** vi interrumpir el viaje; **~ up** vt (hole) tapar; **~gap** n (person) interino/a; (thing) recurso provisional; **~over** n parada; (AVIAT) escala

stoppage ['stɔpıdʒ] n (strike) paro; (blockage) obstrucción f

stopper ['stɔpə*] n tapón m

stop press n noticias fpl de última hora

stopwatch ['stɔpwɔtʃ] n cronómetro

storage ['stɔ:rıdʒ] n almacenaje m; **~ heater** n acumulador m

store [stɔ:*] n (stock) provisión f; (depot: BRIT: large shop) almacén m; (US) tienda; (reserve) reserva, repuesto ♦ vt almacenar; **~s** npl víveres mpl; **in ~** (fig): **to be in ~ for sb** esperarle a

uno; **~ up** vt acumular; **~room** n despensa

storey ['stɔ:rı] (US **story**) n piso

stork [stɔ:k] n cigüeña

storm [stɔ:m] n tormenta; (fig: of applause) salva; (: of criticism) nube f ♦ vi (fig) rabiar ♦ vt tomar por asalto; **~y** adj tempestuoso

story ['stɔ:rı] n historia; (lie) mentira; (US) = **storey**; **~book** n libro de cuentos

stout [staut] adj (strong) sólido; (fat) gordo, corpulento; (resolute) resuelto ♦ n cerveza negra

stove [stəuv] n (for cooking) cocina; (for heating) estufa

stow [stəu] vt (also: ~ away) meter, poner; (NAUT) estibar; **~away** n polizón/ona m/f

straggle ['strægl] vi (houses etc) extenderse; (lag behind) rezagarse

straight [streıt] adj recto, derecho; (frank) franco, directo; (simple) sencillo ♦ adv derecho, directamente; (drink) sin mezcla; **to put o get sth ~** dejar algo en claro; **~ away, ~ off** en seguida; **~en** vt (also: ~en out) enderezar, poner derecho; **~-faced** adj serio; **~forward** adj (simple) sencillo; (honest) honrado, franco

strain [streın] n tensión f; (TECH) presión f; (MED) torcedura; (breed) tipo, variedad f ♦ vt (back etc) torcerse; (resources) agotar; (stretch) estirar; (food, tea) colar; **~s** npl (MUS) aires mpl; **~ed** adj (muscle) torcido; (laugh) forzado; (relations) tenso; **~er** n colador m

strait [streıt] n (GEO) estrecho; **to be in dire ~s** pasar grandes apuros; **~jacket** n camisa de fuerza; **~-laced** adj mojigato, gazmoño

strand [strænd] n (of thread) hebra; (of hair) trenza; (of rope) ramal m

stranded ['strændıd] adj (person: without money) desamparado; (: without transport) colgado

strange |streɪndʒ| *adj* (*not known*) desconocido; (*odd*) extraño, raro; **~ly** *adv* de un modo raro; *see also* **enough**; **~ r** *n* desconocido/a; (*from another area*) forastero/a

strangle |'stræŋgl| *vt* estrangular; **~hold** *n* (*fig*) dominio completo

strap |stræp| *n* correa; (*of slip, dress*) tirante *m*

strategic |strə'tiːdʒɪk| *adj* estratégico

strategy |'strætɪdʒɪ| *n* estrategia

straw |strɔː| *n* paja; (*drinking* ~) caña, pajita; **that's the last ~!** ¡eso es el colmo!

strawberry |'strɔːbərɪ| *n* fresa (SP), frutilla (AM)

stray |streɪ| *adj* (*animal*) extraviado; (*bullet*) perdido; (*scattered*) disperso ♦ *vi* extraviarse, perderse

streak |striːk| *n* raya; (*in hair*) raya ♦ *vt* rayar ♦ *vi*: **to ~ past** pasar como un rayo

stream |striːm| *n* riachuelo, arroyo; (*of people, vehicles*) riada, caravana; (*of smoke, insults etc*) chorro ♦ *vt* (SCOL) dividir en grupos por habilidad ♦ *vi* correr, fluir; **to ~ in/out** (*people*) entrar/salir en tropel

streamer |'striːmə*| *n* serpentina

streamlined |'striːmlaɪnd| *adj* aerodinámico

street |striːt| *n* calle *f*; **~car** *n* (US) *n* tranvía *m*; **~ lamp** *n* farol *m*; **~ plan** *n* plano; **~wise** (*inf*) *adj* que tiene mucha calle

strength |streŋθ| *n* fuerza; (*of girder, knot etc*) resistencia; (*fig: power*) poder *m*; **~en** *vt* fortalecer, reforzar

strenuous |'strenjuəs| *adj* (*energetic, determined*) enérgico

stress |stres| *n* presión *f*; (*mental strain*) estrés *m*; (*accent*) acento *m*; recalcar; (*syllable*) acentuar

stretch |stretʃ| *n* (*of sand*) trecho ♦ *vi* estirarse; (*extend*) **to ~ to or as far as** extenderse hasta ♦ *vt* extender, estirar; (*make demands of*) exigir el

máximo esfuerzo de; **~ out** *vi* tenderse ♦ *vt* (*arm etc*) extender; (*spread*) estirar

stretcher |'stretʃə*| *n* camilla

strewn |struːn| *adj*: **~ with** cubierto *or* sembrado de

stricken |'strɪkən| *adj* (*person*) herido; (*city, industry etc*) condenado; **~ with** (*disease*) afectado por

strict |strɪkt| *adj* severo; (*exact*) estricto; **~ly** *adv* severamente; estrictamente

stride |straɪd| (*pt* strode, *pp* **stridden**) *n* zancada, tranco ♦ *vi* dar zancadas, andar a trancos

strife |straɪf| *n* lucha

strike |straɪk| (*pt, pp* struck) *n* huelga; (*of oil etc*) descubrimiento; (*attack*) ataque *m* ♦ *vt* golpear, pegar; (*oil etc*) descubrir; (*bargain, deal*) cerrar ♦ *vi* declarar la huelga; (*attack*) atacar; (*clock*) dar la hora; *on* ~ (*workers*) en huelga; **to ~ a match** encender un fósforo; **~ down** *vt* derribar; **~ up** *vt* (MUS) empezar a tocar; (*conversation*) entablar; (*friendship*) trabar; **~r** *n* huelguista *m/f*; (SPORT) delantero

striking *adj* llamativo

string |strɪŋ| (*pt, pp* strung) *n* (*gen*) cuerda; (*row*) hilera ♦ *vt*: **to ~ together** ensartar; **to ~ out** extenderse; **the ~s** *npl* (MUS) los instrumentos de cuerda; **to pull ~s** (*fig*) mover palancas; **~ bean** *n* judía verde, habichuela; **~(ed) instrument** *n* (MUS) instrumento de cuerda

stringent |'strɪndʒənt| *adj* riguroso, severo

strip |strɪp| *n* tira; (*of land*) franja; (*of metal*) cinta, lámina ♦ *vt* desnudar; (*paint*) quitar; (*also*: **~ down**: *machine*) desmontar ♦ *vi* desnudarse; **~ cartoon** *n* tira cómica (SP), historieta (AM)

stripe |straɪp| *n* raya; (MIL) galón *m*; **~d** *adj* a rayas, rayado

strip lighting *n* alumbrado fluorescente

stripper |'strɪpə*| *n* artista *m/f* de

striptease
strive [straɪv] (pt **strove**, pp **striven**)
vi: **to ~ for sth/to do sth** luchar por
conseguir/hacer algo
strode [strəud] pt of **stride**
stroke [strəuk] n (blow) golpe m;
(SWIMMING) brazada; (MED) apoplejía;
(of paintbrush) toque m ♦ vt acariciar;
at a ~ de un solo golpe
stroll [strəul] n paseo, vuelta ♦ vi dar
un paseo o una vuelta; **~er** (US) n (for
child) sillita de ruedas
strong [strɔŋ] adj fuerte; **they are 50
~** son 50; **~hold** n fortaleza, (fig)
baluarte m; **~ly** adv fuertemente, con
fuerza; (believe) firmemente; **~room** n
cámara acorazada
strove [strəuv] pt of **strive**
struck [strʌk] pt, pp of **strike**
structure ['strʌktʃə*] n estructura;
(building) construcción f
struggle ['strʌgl] n lucha ♦ vi luchar
strum [strʌm] vt (guitar) rasguear
strung [strʌŋ] pt, pp of **string**
strut [strʌt] n puntal m ♦ vi pavonearse
stub [stʌb] n (of ticket etc) talón m (of
cigarette) colilla; **to ~ one's toe on
sth** dar con el dedo (del pie) contra
algo; **~ out** vt apagar
stubble ['stʌbl] n rastrojo; (on chin)
barba (incipiente)
stubborn ['stʌbən] adj terco, testarudo
stuck [stʌk] pt, pp of **stick** ♦ adj
(jammed) atascado; **~-up** adj engreído,
presumido
stud [stʌd] n (shirt ~) corchete m; (of
boot) taco; (earring) pendiente m (de
bolita); (also: ~ farm) caballeriza; (also:
~ horse) caballo semental ♦ vt (fig):
~ded with salpicado de
student ['stjuːdənt] n estudiante m/f
♦ adj estudiantil; **~ driver** (US) n
aprendiz(a) m/f
studio ['stjuːdɪəu] n estudio; (artist's)
taller m; **~ flat** (US = **apartment**) n
estudio
studious ['stjuːdɪəs] adj estudioso;

(studied) calculado; **~ly** adv (carefully)
con esmero
study ['stʌdɪ] n estudio ♦ vt estudiar;
(examine) examinar, investigar ♦ vi
estudiar
stuff [stʌf] n materia; (substance)
material m, sustancia; (things) cosas fpl
♦ vt llenar; (CULIN) rellenar; (animals)
disecar; (inf: push) meter; **~ing** n
relleno; **~y** adj (room) mal ventilado;
(person) de miras estrechas
stumble ['stʌmbl] vi tropezar, dar un
traspié; **to ~ across, ~ on** (fig)
tropezar con; **stumbling block** n
tropiezo, obstáculo
stump [stʌmp] n (of tree) tocón m; (of
limb) muñón m ♦ vt: **to be ~ed for
an answer** no saber qué contestar
stun [stʌn] vt dejar sin sentido
stung [stʌŋ] pt, pp of **sting**
stunk [stʌŋk] pp of **stink**
stunning ['stʌnɪŋ] adj (fig: news)
pasmoso; (: outfit etc) sensacional
stunt [stʌnt] n (in film) escena
peligrosa; (publicity ~) truco
publicitario; **~man** (irreg) n doble m
stupid ['stjuːpɪd] adj estúpido, tonto;
~ity [-'pɪdɪtɪ] n estupidez f
sturdy ['stɜːdɪ] adj robusto, fuerte
stutter ['stʌtə*] n tartamudeo ♦ vi
tartamudear
stye [staɪ] n (MED) orzuelo
style [staɪl] n estilo; **stylish** adj
elegante, a la moda
stylus ['staɪləs] n aguja
suave [swɑːv] adj cortés
sub... [sʌb] prefix sub...; **~conscious**
adj subconsciente; **~contract** vt
subcontratar; **~divide** vt subdividir
subdue [səb'djuː] vt sojuzgar;
(passions) dominar; **~d** adj (light)
tenue; (person) sumiso, manso
subject [n 'sʌbdʒɪkt, vb səb'dʒɛkt] n
súbdito; (SCOL) asignatura; (matter)
tema m; (GRAMMAR) sujeto ♦ vt: **to
~ sb to sth** someter a uno a algo; **to**

be ~ to (*law*) estar sujeto a; (*subj: person*) ser propenso a; **~ive** [-ˈdʒektɪv] *adj* subjetivo; **~ matter** *n* (*content*) contenido

sublet [sʌbˈlet] *vt* subarrendar

submarine [sʌbməˈriːn] *n* submarino

submerge [səbˈmɜːdʒ] *vt* sumergir ♦ *vi* sumergirse

submissive [səbˈmɪsɪv] *adj* sumiso

submit [səbˈmɪt] *vt* someter ♦ *vi*: **to ~ to sth** someterse a algo

subnormal [sʌbˈnɔːməl] *adj* anormal

subordinate [səˈbɔːdɪnət] *adj*, *n* subordinado/a *m/f*

subpoena [səbˈpiːnə] *n* (*LAW*) citación *f*

subscribe [səbˈskraɪb] *vi* suscribir; **to ~ to** (*opinion, fund*) suscribir, aprobar; (*newspaper*) suscribirse a; **~r** *n* (*to periodical*) subscriptor(a) *m/f*, (*to telephone*) abonado/a

subscription [səbˈskrɪpʃən] *n* abono; (*to magazine*) subscripción *f*

subsequent [ˈsʌbsɪkwənt] *adj* subsiguiente, posterior; **~ly** *adv* posteriormente, más tarde

subside [səbˈsaɪd] *vi* hundirse, (*flood*) bajar, (*wind*) amainar; **subsidence** [-ˈsaɪdns] *n* hundimiento; (*in road*) socavón *m*

subsidiary [səbˈsɪdɪərɪ] *adj* secundario ♦ *n* sucursal *f*, filial *f*

subsidize [ˈsʌbsɪdaɪz] *vt* subvencionar

subsidy [ˈsʌbsɪdɪ] *n* subvención *f*

subsistence [səbˈsɪstəns] *n* subsistencia; **~ allowance** *n* salario mínimo

substance [ˈsʌbstəns] *n* sustancia

substantial [səbˈstænʃl] *adj* sustancial, sustancioso; (*fig*) importante

substantiate [səbˈstænʃɪeɪt] *vt* comprobar

substitute [ˈsʌbstɪtjuːt] *n* (*person*) suplente *m/f*, (*thing*) sustituto ♦ *vt*: **to ~ A for B** sustituir A por B, reemplazar B por A

subtitle [ˈsʌbtaɪtl] *n* subtítulo

subtle [ˈsʌtl] *adj* sutil; **~ty** *n* sutileza

subtotal [sʌbˈtəʊtl] *n* total *m* parcial

subtract [səbˈtrækt] *vt* restar, sustraer; **~ion** [-ˈtrækʃən] *n* resta, sustracción *f*

suburb [ˈsʌbəːb] *n* barrio residencial; **the ~s** las afueras (de la ciudad); **~an** [səˈbəːbən] *adj* suburbano; (*train etc*) de cercanías; **~ia** [səˈbəːbɪə] *n* barrios *mpl* residenciales

subway [ˈsʌbweɪ] *n* (*BRIT*) paso subterráneo or inferior; (*US*) metro

succeed [səkˈsiːd] *vi* (*person*) tener éxito; (*plan*) salir bien ♦ *vt* suceder a; **to ~ in doing** lograr hacer; **~ing** *adj* (*following*) sucesivo

success [səkˈses] *n* éxito; **~ful** *adj* exitoso; (*business*) próspero; **to be ~ful (in doing)** lograr (hacer); **~fully** *adv* con éxito

succession [səkˈseʃən] *n* sucesión *f*, serie *f*

successive [səkˈsesɪv] *adj* sucesivo, consecutivo

succinct [səkˈsɪŋkt] *adj* sucinto

such [sʌtʃ] *adj* tal, semejante; (*of that kind*): **~ a book** tal libro; (*so much*): **~ courage** tanto valor ♦ *adv* tan; **~ a long trip** un viaje tan largo; **~ a lot of** tanto/a/s; **~ as** (*like*) tal como; **as ~** como tal; **~-and-~** *adj* tal o cual

suck [sʌk] *vt* chupar; (*bottle*) sorber; (*breast*) mamar; **~er** *n* (*ZOOL*) ventosa; (*inf*) bobo, primo

suction [ˈsʌkʃən] *n* succión *f*

Sudan [suˈdæn] *n* Sudán *m*

sudden [ˈsʌdn] *adj* (*rapid*) repentino, súbito; (*unexpected*) imprevisto; **all of a ~** de repente; **~ly** *adv* de repente

suds [sʌdz] *npl* espuma de jabón

sue [suː] *vt* demandar

suede [sweɪd] *n* ante *m* (*SP*), gamuza (*AM*)

suet [ˈsuɪt] *n* sebo

Suez [ˈsuːɪz] *n*: **the ~ Canal** el Canal de Suez

suffer [ˈsʌfə*] *vt* sufrir, padecer; (*tolerate*) aguantar, soportar ♦ *vi* sufrir;

to ~ from (*illness etc*) padecer; **~er** n víctima; (*MED*) enfermo/a; **~ing** n sufrimiento

sufficient [sə'fɪʃənt] adj suficiente, bastante; **~ly** ad suficientemente, bastante

suffocate ['sʌfəkeɪt] vt ahogarse, asfixiarse; **suffocation** [-'keɪʃən] n asfixia

sugar ['ʃugə*] n azúcar m ♦ vt echar azúcar a, azucarar; **~ beet** n remolacha; **~ cane** n caña de azúcar

suggest [sə'dʒɛst] vt sugerir; **~ion** [-'dʒɛstʃən] n sugerencia; **~ive** (*pej*) adj indecente

suicide ['suɪsaɪd] n suicidio; (*person*) suicida m/f; *see also* **commit**

suit [su:t] n (*man's*) traje m; (*woman's*) conjunto; (*LAW*) pleito m; (*CARDS*) palo ♦ vt convenir; (*clothes*) sentar a, ir bien a; (*adapt*): **to ~ sth to** adaptar o ajustar algo a; **well ~ed** (*well matched: couple*) hecho el uno para el otro; **~able** adj conveniente; (*apt*) indicado; **~ably** adv convenientemente, (*impressed*) apropiadamente

suitcase ['su:tkeɪs] n maleta (*SP*), valija (*AM*)

suite [swi:t] n (*of rooms, MUS*) suite f; (*furniture*): **bedroom/dining room ~** (juego de) dormitorio/comedor

suitor ['su:tə*] n pretendiente m

sulfur ['sʌlfə*] (*US*) n = **sulphur**

sulk [sʌlk] vi estar de mal humor; **~y** adj malhumorado

sullen ['sʌlən] adj hosco, malhumorado

sulphur ['sʌlfə*] (*US* **sulfur**) n azufre m

sultana [sʌl'tɑ:nə] n (*fruit*) pasa de Esmirna

sultry ['sʌltrɪ] adj (*weather*) bochornoso

sum [sʌm] n suma; (*total*) total m; **~ up** vt resumir ♦ vi hacer un resumen

summarize ['sʌməraɪz] vt resumir

summary ['sʌmərɪ] n resumen m ♦ adj (*justice*) sumario

summer ['sʌmə*] n verano ♦ cpd de verano; **in ~** en verano; **~ holidays** npl vacaciones fpl de verano; **~house** n (*in garden*) cenador m, glorieta; **~time** n (*season*) verano; **~ time** n (*by clock*) hora de verano

summit ['sʌmɪt] n cima, cumbre f; (*also: ~ conference, ~ meeting*) (conferencia) cumbre f

summon ['sʌmən] vt (*person*) llamar; (*meeting*) convocar; (*LAW*) citar; **~ up** vt (*courage*) armarse de; **~s** n llamamiento, llamada ♦ vt (*LAW*) citar

sump [sʌmp] (*BRIT*) n cárter m

sumptuous ['sʌmptjuəs] adj suntuoso

sun [sʌn] n sol m; **~bathe** vi tomar el sol; **~block** n filtro solar; **~burn** n (*painful*) quemadura; (*tan*) bronceado; **~burnt** adj quemado por el sol

Sunday ['sʌndɪ] n domingo; **~ school** n catequesis f dominical

sundial ['sʌndaɪəl] n reloj m de sol

sundown ['sʌndaun] n anochecer m

sundry ['sʌndrɪ] adj varios/as, diversos/as; **all and ~** todos sin excepción; **sundries** npl géneros mpl diversos

sunflower ['sʌnflauə*] n girasol m

sung [sʌŋ] pp of **sing**

sunglasses ['sʌnɡlɑ:sɪz] npl gafas fpl (*SP*) or anteojos mpl de sol

sunk [sʌŋk] pp of **sink**

sun: ~light n luz f del sol; **~lit** adj iluminado por el sol; **~ny** adj soleado; (*day*) de sol; (*fig*) alegre; **~rise** n salida del sol; **~ roof** n (*AUT*) techo corredizo; **~screen** n protector m solar; **~set** n puesta del sol; **~shade** n (*over table*) sombrilla; **~shine** n sol m; **~stroke** n insolación f; **~tan** n bronceado; **~tan oil** n aceite m bronceador

super ['su:pə*] (*inf*) adj genial

superannuation [su:pərænju'eɪʃən] n cuota de jubilación

superb [su:'pə:b] adj magnífico, espléndido

supercilious [su:pə'sɪlɪəs] adj altanero

superfluous [su'pə:fluəs] *adj*
superfluo, de sobra

superhuman [su:pə'hju:mən] *adj*
sobrehumano

superimpose ['su:pərɪm'pəuz] *vt*
sobreponer

superintendent [su:pərɪn'tendənt] *n*
director(a) *m/f*; (POLICE) subjefe/a *m/f*

superior [su'pɪərɪə*] *adj* superior;
(smug) desdeñoso ♦ *n* superior *m*; ~ity
[-'ɒrɪtɪ] *n* superioridad *f*

superlative [su'pə:lətɪv] *n* superlativo

superman ['su:pəmæn] (*irreg*) *n*
superhombre *m*

supermarket ['su:pəmɑ:kɪt] *n*
supermercado

supernatural [su:pə'nætʃərəl] *adj*
sobrenatural ♦ *n*: **the** ~ lo sobrenatural

superpower ['su:pəpauə*] *n* (POL)
superpotencia

supersede [su:pə'si:d] *vt* suplantar

superstar ['su:pəstɑ:*] *n* gran estrella

superstitious [su:pə'stɪʃəs] *adj*
supersticioso

supertanker ['su:pətæŋkə*] *n*
superpetrolero

supervise ['su:pəvaɪz] *vt* supervisar;
supervision [-'vɪʒən] *n* supervisión *f*;
supervisor *n* supervisor(a) *m/f*

supper ['sʌpə*] *n* cena

supple ['sʌpl] *adj* flexible

supplement [*n* 'sʌplɪmənt, *vb*
sʌplɪ'ment] *n* suplemento ♦ *vt* suplir;
~ary [-'mentərɪ] *adj* suplementario; ~ary
~ary benefit (BRIT) *n* subsidio
suplementario de la seguridad social

supplier [sə'plaɪə*] *n* (COMM)
distribuidor/a *m/f*

supply [sə'plaɪ] *vt* (provide) suministrar;
(equip): **to** ~ (**with**) proveer (de) ♦ *n*
provisión *f*; (gas, water etc) suministro;
supplies *npl* (food) víveres *mpl*; (MIL)
pertrechos *mpl*; ~ **teacher** *n*
profesor(a) *m/f* suplente

support [sə'pɔ:t] *n* apoyo; (TECH)
soporte *m* ♦ *vt* apoyar; (financially)
mantener; (uphold, TECH) sostener; ~er

n (POL etc) partidario/a; (SPORT)
aficionado/a

suppose [sə'pəuz] *vt* suponer;
(imagine) imaginarse; (duty): **to be** ~**d**
to do sth deber hacer algo; ~**dly**
[sə'pəuzɪdlɪ] *adv* según cabe suponer;
supposing *conj* en caso de que

suppress [sə'pres] *vt* suprimir; (yawn)
ahogar

supreme [su'pri:m] *adj* supremo

surcharge ['sə:tʃɑ:dʒ] *n* sobretasa,
recargo

sure [ʃuə*] *adj* seguro; (definite,
convinced) cierto; **to make** ~ **of sth/**
that asegurarse de algo/asegurar que;
~! (of course) ¡claro!, ¡por supuesto!;
~ **enough** efectivamente; ~**ly** *adv*
(certainly) seguramente

surf [sə:f] *n* olas *fpl*

surface ['sə:fɪs] *n* superficie *f* ♦ *vt*
(road) revestir ♦ *vi* (lit also fig) salir a la
superficie; **by** ~ **mail** por vía terrestre

surfboard ['sə:fbɔ:d] *n* tabla (de surf)

surfeit ['sə:fɪt] *n*: **a** ~ **of** un exceso de

surfing ['sə:fɪŋ] *n* surf *m*

surge [sə:dʒ] *n* oleada, oleaje *m* ♦ *vi*
(wave) romper; (people) avanzar en
tropel

surgeon ['sə:dʒən] *n* cirujano/a

surgery ['sə:dʒərɪ] *n* cirugía; (BRIT:
room) consultorio; ~ **hours** (BRIT) *npl*
horas *fpl* de consulta

surgical ['sə:dʒɪkl] *adj* quirúrgico;
~ **spirit** (BRIT) *n* alcohol *m* de 90°

surname ['sə:neɪm] *n* apellido

surpass [sə:'pɑ:s] *vt* superar, exceder

surplus ['sə:pləs] *n* excedente *m*;
(COMM) superávit *m* ♦ *adj* excedente,
sobrante

surprise [sə'praɪz] *n* sorpresa ♦ *vt*
sorprender; **surprising** *adj*
sorprendente; **surprisingly** *adv*: **it**
was surprisingly easy me *etc*
sorprendió lo fácil que fue

surrender [sə'rendə*] *n* rendición *f*,
entrega ♦ *vi* rendirse, entregarse

surreptitious [sʌrəp'tɪʃəs] *adj*

subrepticio

surrogate ['sʌrəgɪt] *n* sucedáneo; ~ **mother** *n* madre f portadora

surround [sə'raund] *vt* rodear, circundar; (MIL etc) cercar; **~ing** *adj* circundante; **~ings** *npl* alrededores *mpl*, cercanías *fpl*

surveillance [sə:'veɪləns] *n* vigilancia

survey [*n* 'sə:veɪ, *vb* sə:'veɪ] *n* inspección f, reconocimiento; (*inquiry*) encuesta ♦ *vt* examinar, inspeccionar; (*look at*) mirar, contemplar; **~or** *n* agrimensor/a *m/f*

survival [sə'vaɪvl] *n* supervivencia

survive [sə'vaɪv] *vi* sobrevivir; (*custom etc*) perdurar ♦ *vt* sobrevivir a; **survivor** *n* superviviente *m/f*

susceptible [sə'septəbl] *adj*: ~ (**to**) (*disease*) susceptible de; (*flattery*) sensible (a)

suspect [*adj*, *n* 'sʌspekt, *vb* səs'pekt] *adj*, *n* sospechoso/a *m/f* ♦ *vt* (*person*) sospechar de; (*think*) sospechar

suspend [səs'pend] *vt* suspender; **~ed sentence** *n* (LAW) libertad f condicional; **~er belt** *n* portaligas *m inv*; **~ers** *npl* (BRIT) ligas *fpl*; (US) tirantes *mpl*

suspense [səs'pens] *n* incertidumbre f, duda; (*in film etc*) suspense *m*; **to keep sb in** ~ mantener a uno en suspense

suspension [səs'penʃən] *n* (gen, AUT) suspensión f; (*of driving licence*) privación f; ~ **bridge** *n* puente *m* colgante

suspicion [səs'pɪʃən] *n* sospecha; (*distrust*) recelo; **suspicious** [-ʃəs] *adj* receloso; (*causing suspicion*) sospechoso

sustain [səs'teɪn] *vt* sostener, apoyar; (*suffer*) sufrir, padecer; **~able** *adj* sostenible; **~ed** *adj* (*effort*) sostenido

sustenance ['sʌstɪnəns] *n* sustento

swab [swɔb] *n* (MED) algodón *m*

swagger ['swægə*] *vi* pavonearse

swallow ['swɔləu] *n* (*bird*) golondrina ♦ *vt* tragar; (*fig: pride*) tragarse; ~ **up** *vt* (*savings etc*) consumir

swam [swæm] *pt* of **swim**

swamp [swɔmp] *n* pantano, ciénaga ♦ *vt* (*with water etc*) inundar; (*fig*) abrumar, agobiar; **~y** *adj* pantanoso

swan [swɔn] *n* cisne *m*

swap [swɔp] *n* canje *m*, intercambio ♦ *vt*: **to** ~ (**for**) cambiar (por)

swarm [swɔ:m] *n* (*of bees*) enjambre *m*; (*fig*) multitud f ♦ *vi* (*bees*) formar un enjambre; (*people*) pulular; **to be ~ing with** ser un hervidero de

swastika ['swɔstɪkə] *n* esvástika

swat [swɔt] *vt* aplastar

sway [sweɪ] *vi* mecerse, balancearse ♦ *vt* (*influence*) mover, influir en

swear [swɛə*] (*pt* **swore**, *pp* **sworn**) *vi* (*curse*) maldecir; (*promise*) jurar ♦ *vt* jurar; **~word** *n* taco, palabrota

sweat [swet] *n* sudor *m* ♦ *vi* sudar

sweater ['swetə*] *n* suéter *m*

sweatshirt ['swetʃə:t] *n* suéter *m*

sweaty ['swetɪ] *adj* sudoroso

Swede [swi:d] *n* sueco/a

swede [swi:d] *n* (BRIT) nabo

Sweden ['swi:dn] *n* Suecia; **Swedish** ['swi:dɪʃ] *adj* sueco ♦ *n* (LING) sueco

sweep [swi:p] (*pt*, *pp* **swept**) *n* (*act*) barrido; (*also: chimney* ~) deshollinador/a *m/f* ♦ *vt* barrer; (*with arm*) empujar; (*subj: current*) arrastrar ♦ *vi* barrer; (*arm etc*) moverse rápidamente; (*wind*) soplar con violencia; ~ **away** *vt* barrer; ~ **past** *vi* pasar majestuosamente; ~ **up** *vi* barrer; **~ing** *adj* (*gesture*) dramático; (*generalized: statement*) generalizado

sweet [swi:t] *n* (*candy*) dulce *m*, caramelo; (BRIT: *pudding*) postre *m* ♦ *adj* dulce; (*fig: kind*) dulce, amable; (: *attractive*) mono; **~corn** *n* maíz *m*; **~en** *vt* (*add sugar to*) poner azúcar a; (*person*) endulzar; **~heart** *n* novio/a; **~ness** *n* dulzura; ~ **pea** *n* guisante *m* de olor

swell [swel] (*pt* **swelled**, *pp* **swollen** or **swelled**) *n* (*of sea*) marejada, oleaje *m* ♦ *adj* (US: *inf: excellent*) estupendo,

fenomenal ♦ vt hinchar, inflar ♦ vi
(also: ~ up) hincharse; (numbers)
aumentar; (sound, feeling) ir
aumentando; ~ing n (MED) hinchazón
f.

sweltering ['sweltərɪŋ] adj sofocante,
de mucho calor

swept [swept] pt, pp of **sweep**

swerve [swɜːv] vi desviarse
bruscamente

swift [swɪft] n (bird) vencejo ♦ adj
rápido, veloz; ~**ly** adv rápidamente

swig [swɪg] (inf) n (drink) trago

swill [swɪl] vt (also: ~ out, ~ down)
lavar, limpiar con agua

swim [swɪm] (pt **swam**, pp **swum**) n:
to go for a ~ ir a nadar o a bañarse
♦ vi nadar; (head, room) dar vueltas
♦ vt nadar; (the Channel etc) cruzar a
nado; ~**mer** n nadador(a) m/f; ~**ming**
n natación f; ~**ming cap** n gorro de
baño; ~**ming costume** (BRIT) n
bañador m, traje m de baño; ~**ming
pool** n piscina (SP), alberca (AM);
~**ming trunks** n bañador m (de
hombre); ~**suit** n = ~**ming costume**

swindle ['swɪndl] n estafa ♦ vt estafar

swine [swaɪn] (inf!) canalla (!)

swing [swɪŋ] (pt, pp **swung**) n (in
playground) columpio; (movement)
balanceo, vaivén m; (change of
direction) viraje m; (rhythm) ritmo ♦ vt
balancear; (also: ~ round) voltear, girar
♦ vi balancearse, columpiarse; (also:
~ round) dar media vuelta; **to be in
full** ~ estar en plena marcha; ~ **bridge**
n puente m giratorio; ~ **door** (US ~**ing
door**) n puerta giratoria

swingeing ['swɪndʒɪŋ] (BRIT) adj (cuts)
atroz

swipe [swaɪp] vt (hit) golpear fuerte;
(inf: steal) guindar

swirl [swɜːl] vi arremolinarse

Swiss [swɪs] adj, n inv suizo/a m/f

switch [swɪtʃ] n (for light etc)
interruptor m; (change) cambio ♦ vt
(change) cambiar de; ~ **off** vt apagar;

(engine) parar; ~ **on** vt encender (SP),
prender (AM); (engine, machine)
arrancar; ~**board** n (TEL) centralita (de
teléfonos) (SP), conmutador m (AM)

Switzerland ['swɪtsələnd] n Suiza

swivel ['swɪvl] vt (also: ~ round) girar

swollen ['swəʊlən] pp of **swell**

swoon [swuːn] vi desmayarse

swoop [swuːp] n (by police etc) redada
♦ vi (also: ~ down) calarse

swop [swɒp] = **swap**

sword [sɔːd] n espada; ~**fish** n pez m
espada

swore [swɔː*] pt of **swear**

sworn [swɔːn] pp of **swear** ♦ adj
(statement) bajo juramento; (enemy)
implacable

swot [swɒt] (BRIT) vt, vi empollar

swum [swʌm] pp of **swim**

swung [swʌŋ] pt, pp of **swing**

sycamore ['sɪkəmɔː*] n sicomoro

syllable ['sɪləbl] n sílaba

syllabus ['sɪləbəs] n programa m de
estudios

symbol ['sɪmbl] n símbolo

symmetry ['sɪmɪtrɪ] n simetría

sympathetic [sɪmpə'θetɪk] adj
(understanding) comprensivo; (likeable)
simpático; (showing support):
~ **to(wards)** bien dispuesto hacia

sympathize ['sɪmpəθaɪz] vi: **to**
~ **with** (person) compadecerse de;
(feelings) comprender; (cause) apoyar;
~**r** n (POL) simpatizante m/f

sympathy ['sɪmpəθɪ] n (pity)
compasión f; **sympathies** npl
(tendencies) tendencias fpl; **with our
deepest** ~ nuestro más sentido
pésame; **in** ~ en solidaridad

symphony ['sɪmfənɪ] n sinfonía

symptom ['sɪmptəm] n síntoma m,
indicio

synagogue ['sɪnəgɒg] n sinagoga

syndicate ['sɪndɪkɪt] n (gen) sindicato;
(of newspapers) agencia de noticias

syndrome ['sɪndrəʊm] n síndrome m

synopsis [sɪ'nɒpsɪs] n (pl **synopses**) n

sinopsis f inv

synthesis ['sɪnθəsɪs] (pl **syntheses**) n síntesis f inv

synthetic [sɪn'θetɪk] adj sintético

syphilis ['sɪfɪlɪs] n sífilis f

syphon ['saɪfən] = **siphon**

Syria ['sɪrɪə] n Siria; **~n** adj, n sirio/a

syringe [sɪ'rɪndʒ] n jeringa

syrup ['sɪrəp] n jarabe m; (also: golden ~) almíbar m

system ['sɪstəm] n sistema m; (ANAT) organismo; **~atic** [-'mætɪk] adj sistemático, metódico; **~ disk** n (COMPUT) disco del sistema; **~s analyst** n analista m/f de sistemas

T, t

ta [tɑː] (BRIT: inf) excl ¡gracias!

tab [tæb] n lengüeta; (label) etiqueta; **to keep ~s on** (fig) vigilar

tabby ['tæbɪ] n (also: ~ cat) gato atigrado

table ['teɪbl] n mesa; (of statistics etc) cuadro, tabla ♦ vt (BRIT: motion etc) presentar; **to lay** or **set the ~** poner la mesa; **~cloth** n mantel m; **~ of contents** n índice m de materias; **~ d'hôte** [tɑːbl'dəʊt] adj del menú; **~ lamp** n lámpara de mesa; **~mat** n (for plate) posaplatos m inv; (for hot dish) salvamantel m; **~spoon** n cuchara de servir; (also: ~spoonful: as measurement) cucharada

tablet ['tæblɪt] n (MED) pastilla, comprimido; (of stone) lápida

table tennis n ping-pong m, tenis m de mesa

table wine n vino de mesa

tabloid ['tæblɔɪd] n periódico popular sensacionalista

---
tabloid press
---

*El término **tabloid press** o **tabloids** se usa para referirse a la prensa popular británica, por el tamaño más pequeño de los periódicos. A diferencia de los de la llamada **quality press**, estas publicaciones se caracterizan por un lenguaje sencillo, una presentación llamativa y un contenido sensacionalista, centrado a veces en los escándalos financieros y sexuales de los famosos, por lo que también reciben el nombre peyorativo de "gutter press".*

tack [tæk] n (nail) tachuela; (fig) rumbo ♦ vt (nail) clavar con tachuelas; (stitch) hilvanar ♦ vi virar

tackle ['tækl] n (fishing ~) aparejo (de pescar); (for lifting) aparejo ♦ vt (difficulty) enfrentarse con; (challenge: person) hacer frente a; (grapple with) agarrar; (FOOTBALL) cargar; (RUGBY) placar

tacky ['tækɪ] adj pegajoso; (pej) cutre

tact [tækt] n tacto, discreción f; **~ful** adj discreto, diplomático

tactics ['tæktɪks] n, npl táctica

tactless ['tæktlɪs] adj indiscreto

tadpole ['tædpəʊl] n renacuajo

tag [tæg] n (label) etiqueta; **~ along** vi ir (or venir) también

tail [teɪl] n cola; (of shirt, coat) faldón m ♦ vt (follow) vigilar a; **~s** npl (formal suit) levita; **~ away** vi (in size, quality etc) ir disminuyendo; **~ off** vi = **~ away**; **~back** (BRIT) n (AUT) cola; **~ end** n cola, parte f final; **~gate** n (AUT) puerta trasera

tailor ['teɪlə*] n sastre m; **~ing** n (cut) corte m; (craft) sastrería; **~-made** adj (also fig) hecho a la medida

tailwind ['teɪlwɪnd] n viento de cola

tainted ['teɪntɪd] adj (food) pasado; (water, air) contaminado; (fig) manchado

take [teɪk] (pt **took**, pp **taken**) vt tomar; (grab) coger (SP), agarrar (AM); (gain: prize) ganar; (require: effort, courage) exigir; (tolerate: pain etc) aguantar; (hold: passengers etc) tener cabida para; (*accompany, bring, carry*) llevar; (*exam*) presentarse a; **to ~ sth from** (*drawer etc*) sacar algo de; (*person*) quitar algo a; **I ~ it that ...** supongo que ...; **~ after** *vt fus* parecerse a; **~ apart** *vt* desmontar; **~ away** *vt* (*remove*) quitar; (*carry off*) llevar; (*MATH*) restar; **~ back** *vt* (*return*) devolver; (*one's words*) retractarse de; **~ down** *vt* (*building*) derribar; (*letter etc*) apuntar; **~ in** *vt* (*deceive*) engañar; (*understand*) entender; (*include*) abarcar; (*lodger*) acoger, recibir; **~ off** *vi* (*AVIAT*) despegar ♦ *vt* (*remove*) quitar; **~ on** *vt* (*work*) aceptar; (*employee*) contratar; (*opponent*) desafiar; **~ out** *vt* sacar; **~ over** *vt* (*business*) tomar posesión de; (*country*) tomar el poder ♦ *vi* **to ~ over from sb** reemplazar a uno; **~ to** *vt fus* (*person*) coger cariño a, encariñarse con; (*activity*) aficionarse a; **~ up** *vt* (*a dress*) acortar; (*occupy: time, space*) ocupar; (*engage in: hobby etc*) dedicarse a; (*accept*): **to ~ sb up on** aceptar; **~away** (*BRIT*) *adj* (*food*) para llevar ♦ *n* tienda *or* restaurante *m* de comida para llevar; **~off** *n* (*AVIAT*) despegue *m*; **~out** (*US*) *n* = **~away**; **~over** *n* (*COMM*) absorción *f*

takings ['teɪkɪŋz] *npl* (*COMM*) ingresos *mpl*

talc [tælk] *n* (*also: ~um powder*) polvos (de) talco

tale [teɪl] *n* (*story*) cuento; (*account*) relación *f*; **to tell ~s** (*fig*) chivarse

talent ['tælnt] *n* talento; **~ed** *adj* de talento

talk [tɔ:k] *n* charla; (*conversation*) conversación *f*; (*gossip*) habladurías *fpl*, chismes *mpl* ♦ *vi* hablar; **~s** *npl* (*POL etc*) conversaciones *fpl*; **to ~ about** hablar de; **to ~ sb into doing sth** convencer a uno para que haga algo; **to ~ sb out of doing sth** disuadir a uno de que haga algo; **to ~ shop** hablar del trabajo; **~ over** *vt* discutir;

~ative *adj* hablador(a); **~ show** *n* programa *m* de entrevistas

tall [tɔ:l] *adj* alto; (*object*) grande; **to be 6 feet ~** (*person*) ≈ medir 1 metro 80

tally ['tælɪ] *n* cuenta ♦ *vi:* **to ~ (with)** corresponder (con)

talon ['tælən] *n* garra

tambourine [tæmbə'ri:n] *n* pandereta

tame [teɪm] *adj* domesticado; (*fig*) mediocre

tamper ['tæmpə*] *vi:* **to ~ with** tocar, andar con

tampon ['tæmpɔn] *n* tampón *m*

tan [tæn] *n* (*also: sun~*) bronceado ♦ *vi* ponerse moreno ♦ *adj* (*colour*) marrón

tang [tæŋ] *n* sabor *m* fuerte

tangent ['tændʒənt] *n* (*MATH*) tangente *f*; **to go off at a ~** (*fig*) salirse por la tangente

tangerine [tændʒə'ri:n] *n* mandarina

tangle ['tæŋgl] *n* enredo; **to get in(to) a ~** enredarse

tank [tæŋk] *n* (*water ~*) depósito, tanque *m*; (*for fish*) acuario; (*MIL*) tanque *m*

tanker ['tæŋkə*] *n* (*ship*) buque *m* cisterna; (*truck*) camión *m* cisterna

tanned [tænd] *adj* (*skin*) moreno

tantalizing ['tæntəlaɪzɪŋ] *adj* tentador(a)

tantamount ['tæntəmaunt] *adj:* **~ to** equivalente a

tantrum ['tæntrəm] *n* rabieta

tap [tæp] *n* (*BRIT: on sink etc*) grifo (*SP*), canilla (*AM*); (*gas ~*) llave *f*; (*gentle blow*) golpecito ♦ *vt* (*hit gently*) dar golpecitos en; (*resources*) utilizar, explotar; (*telephone*) intervenir; **on ~** (*fig: resources*) a mano; **~ dancing** *n* claqué *m*

tape [teɪp] *n* (*also: magnetic ~*) cinta magnética; (*cassette*) cassette *f*, cinta; (*sticky ~*) cinta adhesiva; (*for tying*) cinta ♦ *vt* (*record*) grabar (en cinta); (*stick with ~*) pegar con cinta adhesiva; **~ deck** *n* grabadora; **~ measure** *n*

cinta métrica, metro
taper ['teɪpə*] n cirio ♦ vi afilarse
tape recorder n grabadora
tapestry ['tæpɪstrɪ] n (object) tapiz m; (art) tapicería
tar [tɑ:] n alquitrán m, brea
target ['tɑ:gɪt] n (gen) blanco
tariff ['tærɪf] n (on goods) arancel m; (BRIT: in hotels etc) tarifa
tarmac ['tɑ:mæk] n (BRIT: on road) asfaltado; (AVIAT) pista (de aterrizaje)
tarnish ['tɑ:nɪʃ] vt deslustrar
tarpaulin [tɑ:'pɔ:lɪn] n lona impermeabilizada
tarragon ['tærəgən] n estragón m
tart [tɑ:t] n (CULIN) tarta; (BRIT: inf: prostitute) puta ♦ adj ácido; ~ **up** (BRIT: inf) vt (building) remozar; **to ~ o.s. up** acicalarse
tartan ['tɑ:tn] n tejido escocés m
tartar ['tɑ:tə*] n (on teeth) sarro; **~(e) sauce** n salsa tártara
task [tɑ:sk] n tarea; **to take to ~** reprender; **~ force** n (MIL, POLICE) grupo de operaciones
taste [teɪst] n (sense) gusto; (flavour) sabor m; (also: after~) sabor m, dejo; (sample): **have a ~!** ¡prueba un poquito!; (fig) muestra, idea ♦ vt (also fig) probar ♦ vi: **to ~ of** or **like** (fish, garlic etc) saber a; **you can ~ the garlic (in it)** se nota al sabor a ajo; **in good/bad ~** de buen/mal gusto; **~ful** adj de buen gusto; **~less** adj (food) soso; (remark etc) de mal gusto; **tasty** adj sabroso, rico
tatters ['tætəz] npl: **in ~** hecho jirones
tattoo [tə'tu:] n tatuaje m; (spectacle) espectáculo militar ♦ vt tatuar
tatty ['tætɪ] (BRIT: inf) adj cochambroso
taught [tɔ:t] pt, pp of **teach**
taunt [tɔ:nt] n burla ♦ vt burlarse de
Taurus ['tɔ:rəs] n Tauro
taut [tɔ:t] adj tirante, tenso
tax [tæks] n impuesto ♦ vt gravar (con un impuesto); (fig: memory) poner a prueba (: patience) ponder a

(income) gravable; **~ation** [-'seɪʃən] n impuestos mpl; **~ avoidance** n evasión f de impuestos; **~ disc** (BRIT) n (AUT) pegatina del impuesto de circulación; **~ evasion** n evasión f fiscal; **~-free** adj libre de impuestos
taxi ['tæksɪ] n taxi m ♦ vi (AVIAT) rodar por la pista; **~ driver** n taxista m/f; **~ rank** (BRIT) n = **~ stand**; **~ stand** n parada de taxis
tax: ~ payer n contribuyente m/f; **~ relief** n desgravación f fiscal; **~ return** n declaración f de ingresos
TB n abbr = **tuberculosis**
tea [ti:] n té m; (BRIT: meal) ≈ merienda (SP); cena; **high ~** (BRIT) merienda-cena (SP); **~ bag** n bolsita de té; **~ break** (BRIT) n descanso para el té
teach [ti:tʃ] (pt, pp **taught**) vt: **to ~ sb sth, ~ sth to sb** enseñar algo a uno ♦ vi (be a teacher) ser profesor/a, enseñar; **~er** n (in secondary school) profesor/a m/f; (in primary school) maestro/a, profesor/a) de EGB; **~ing** n enseñanza
tea cosy n cubretetera m
teacup ['ti:kʌp] n taza para el té
teak [ti:k] n (madera de) teca
team [ti:m] n equipo; (of horses) tiro; **~work** n trabajo en equipo
teapot ['ti:pɔt] n tetera
tear¹ [tɪə*] n lágrima; **in ~s** llorando
tear² [tɛə*] (pt **tore**, pp **torn**) n rasgón m, desgarrón m ♦ vt romper, rasgar ♦ vi rasgarse; **~ along** n (rush) precipitarse; **~ up** vt (sheet of paper etc) romper
tearful ['tɪəful] adj lloroso
tear gas ['tɪə-] n gas m lacrimógeno
tearoom ['ti:ru:m] n salón m de té
tease [ti:z] vt tomar el pelo a
tea set n servicio de té
teaspoon ['ti:spu:n] n cucharita; (also: ~ful: as measurement) cucharadita
teat [ti:t] n (of bottle) tetina

tea towel (BRIT) n paño de cocina
technical ['tɛknɪkl] adj técnico;
~ **college** (BRIT) n = escuela de artes y
oficios (SP); ~**ity** [-'kælɪtɪ] n (point of
law) formalismo; (detail) detalle m
técnico; ~**ly** adv en teoría; (regarding
technique) técnicamente
technician [tɛk'nɪʃn] n técnico/a
technique [tɛk'niːk] n técnica
technological [tɛknə'lɒdʒɪkl] adj
tecnológico
technology [tɛk'nɒlədʒɪ] n tecnología
teddy (bear) ['tɛdɪ-] n osito de felpa
tedious ['tiːdɪəs] adj pesado, aburrido
teem [tiːm] vi: **to ~ with** rebosar de;
it is ~ing (with rain) llueve a
cántaros
teenage ['tiːneɪdʒ] adj (fashions etc)
juvenil; (children) quinceañero; ~**r** n
quinceañero/a
teens [tiːnz] npl: **to be in one's ~** ser
adolescente
tee-shirt ['tiːʃəːt] n = T-shirt
teeter ['tiːtə*] vi balancearse; (fig): **to
~ on the edge of** estar al borde de
teeth [tiːθ] npl of tooth
teethe [tiːð] vi echar los dientes
teething ['tiːðɪŋ]: ~ **ring** n mordedor
m; ~ **troubles** npl (fig) dificultades fpl
iniciales
teetotal ['tiː'təʊtl] adj abstemio
telegram ['tɛlɪɡræm] n telegrama m
telegraph ['tɛlɪɡrɑːf] n telégrafo;
~ **pole** n poste m telegráfico
telepathy [tə'lɛpəθɪ] n telepatía
telephone ['tɛlɪfəʊn] n teléfono ♦ vt
llamar por teléfono, telefonear;
(message) dar por teléfono; **to be on
the ~** (talking) hablar por teléfono;
(possessing) ~ tener teléfono; ~ **booth**
n cabina telefónica; ~ **box** (BRIT) n =
~ **booth**; ~ **call** n llamada (telefónica);
~ **directory** n guía (telefónica);
~ **number** n número de teléfono
telephonist [tə'lɛfənɪst] (BRIT) n
telefonista m/f
telesales ['tɛlɪseɪlz] npl televenta(s)

f(pl)
telescope ['tɛlɪskəʊp] n telescopio
television ['tɛlɪvɪʒən] n televisión f; **on
~** en la televisión; ~ **set** n televisor m
teleworking ['tɛlɪ,wɜːkɪŋ] n teletrabajo
tell [tɛl] (pt, pp **told**) vt decir; (relate:
story) contar; (distinguish): **to ~ sth
from** distinguir algo de ♦ vi (talk): **to
~ (of)** contar; (have effect) tener efecto;
to ~ sb to do sth mandar a uno
hacer algo; ~ **off** vt: **to ~ sb off**
regañar a uno; ~**er** n (in bank) cajero/
a; ~**ing** adj (remark, detail) revela-
dor(a); ~**tale** adj (sign) indicador(a)
telly ['tɛlɪ] (BRIT: inf) n abbr (=
television) tele f
temp [tɛmp] n abbr (BRIT: =
temporary) temporero/a
temper ['tɛmpə*] n (nature) carácter
m; (mood) humor m; (bad ~) (mal)
genio; (fit of anger) acceso de ira ♦ vt
(moderate) moderar; **to be in a ~**
estar furioso; **to lose one's ~**
enfadarse, enojarse
temperament ['tɛmprəmənt] n
(nature) temperamento
temperate ['tɛmprət] adj (climate etc)
templado
temperature ['tɛmprətʃə*] n temperatura; **to have** or **run a ~** tener fiebre
temple ['tɛmpl] n (building) templo;
(ANAT) sien f
tempo ['tɛmpəʊ] (pl **tempos** or
tempi) n (MUS) tempo, tiempo; (fig)
ritmo
temporarily ['tɛmpərərɪlɪ] adv
temporalmente
temporary ['tɛmpərərɪ] adj
provisional; (passing) transitorio;
(worker) temporero; (job) temporal
tempt [tɛmpt] vt tentar; **to ~ sb into
doing sth** tentar or inducir a uno a
hacer algo; ~**ation** [-'teɪʃən] n
tentación f; ~**ing** adj tentador(a);
(food) apetitoso/a
ten [tɛn] num diez
tenacity [tə'næsɪtɪ] n tenacidad f

tenancy ['tɛnənsɪ] n arrendamiento, alquiler m

tenant ['tɛnənt] n inquilino/a

tend [tɛnd] vt cuidar ♦ vi: **to ~ to do sth** tener tendencia a hacer algo

tendency ['tɛndənsɪ] n tendencia

tender ['tɛndə*] adj (person, care) tierno, cariñoso; (meat) tierno; (sore) sensible ♦ n (COMM: offer) oferta; (money): **legal ~** moneda de curso legal ♦ vt ofrecer; **~ness** n ternura; (of meat) blandura

tenement ['tɛnəmənt] n casa de pisos (SP)

tennis ['tɛnɪs] n tenis m; **~ ball** n pelota de tenis; **~ court** n cancha de tenis; **~ player** n tenista m/f; **~ racket** n raqueta de tenis

tenor ['tɛnə*] n (MUS) tenor m

tenpin bowling ['tɛnpɪn-] n (juego de los) bolos

tense [tɛns] adj (person) nervioso; (moment, atmosphere) tenso; (muscle) tenso, en tensión ♦ n (LING) tiempo

tension ['tɛnʃən] n tensión f

tent [tɛnt] n tienda (de campaña) (SP), carpa (AM)

tentative ['tɛntətɪv] adj (person, smile) indeciso; (conclusion, plans) provisional

tenterhooks ['tɛntəhʊks] npl: **on ~** sobre ascuas

tenth [tɛnθ] num décimo

tent peg n clavija, estaca

tent pole n mástil m

tenuous ['tɛnjʊəs] adj tenue

tenure ['tɛnjʊə*] n (of land etc) tenencia; (of office) ejercicio

tepid ['tɛpɪd] adj tibio

term [tɜːm] n (word) término; (period) período; (SCOL) trimestre m ♦ vt llamar; **~s** npl (conditions, COMM) condiciones fpl; **to be short/long ~** a corto/largo plazo; **to be on good ~s with sb** llevarse bien con uno; **to come to ~s with** (problem) aceptar

terminal ['tɜːmɪnl] adj (disease) mortal; (patient) terminal ♦ n (ELEC)
borne m; (COMPUT) terminal m; (also: air ~) terminal f; (BRIT: also: coach ~) (estación f) terminal f

terminate ['tɜːmɪneɪt] vt terminar

terminus ['tɜːmɪnəs] (pl **termini**) n término, (estación f) terminal f

terrace ['tɛrəs] n terraza; (BRIT: row of houses) hilera de casas adosadas; **the ~s** (BRIT: SPORT) las gradas fpl; **~d** adj (garden) en terrazas; (house) adosado

terrain [tɛ'reɪn] n terreno

terrible ['tɛrɪbl] adj terrible, horrible; (inf) atroz; **terribly** adv terriblemente; (very badly) malísimamente

terrier ['tɛrɪə*] n terrier m

terrific [tə'rɪfɪk] adj (very great) tremendo; (wonderful) fantástico, fenomenal

terrify ['tɛrɪfaɪ] vt aterrorizar

territory ['tɛrɪtərɪ] n (also fig) territorio

terror ['tɛrə*] n terror m; **~ism** n terrorismo; **~ist** n terrorista m/f

test [tɛst] n (gen, CHEM) prueba; (MED) examen m; (SCOL) examen m, test m; (also: driving ~) examen m de conducir ♦ vt probar, poner a prueba; (MED, SCOL) examinar

testament ['tɛstəmənt] n testamento; **the Old/New T~** el Antiguo/Nuevo Testamento

testicle ['tɛstɪkl] n testículo

testify ['tɛstɪfaɪ] vi (LAW) prestar declaración; **to ~ to sth** atestiguar algo

testimony ['tɛstɪmənɪ] n (LAW) testimonio

test: ~ match n (CRICKET, RUGBY) partido internacional; **~ tube** n probeta

tetanus ['tɛtənəs] n tétano

tether ['tɛðə*] vt atar (con una cuerda) ♦ n: **to be at the end of one's ~** no aguantar más

text [tɛkst] n texto; **~book** n libro de texto

textiles ['tɛkstaɪlz] npl textiles mpl; (textile industry) industria textil

texture ['tɛkstʃə*] n textura
Thailand ['taɪlænd] n Tailandia
Thames [tɛmz] n: the ~ el (río)
Támesis
than [ðæn] conj (in comparisons):
more ~ 10/once más de 10/una vez;
I have more/less ~ you/Paul tengo
más/menos que tú/Paul; **she is older
~ you think** es mayor de lo que
piensas
thank [θæŋk] vt dar las gracias a,
agradecer; **~ you (very much)**
muchas gracias; **~ God!** ¡gracias a
Dios!; **~s** npl gracias fpl ♦ excl (also:
many ~s, ~s a lot) ¡gracias!; **~s to** prep
gracias a; **~ful** adj: **~ful (for)**
agradecido (por); **~less** adj ingrato;
T~sgiving (Day) n día m de Acción
de Gracias

Thanksgiving (Day)

*En Estados Unidos el cuarto jueves de
noviembre es **Thanksgiving Day**,
fiesta oficial en la que se recuerda la
celebración que hicieron los primeros
colonos norteamericanos ("Pilgrims" o
"Pilgrim Fathers") tras la estupenda
cosecha de 1621, por la que se dan
gracias a Dios. En Canadá se celebra
una fiesta semejante el segundo lunes
de octubre, aunque no está
relacionada con dicha fecha histórica.*

KEYWORD

that [ðæt] (pl **those**) adj
(demonstrative) ese/a, pl esos/as;
(more remote) aquel/aquella, pl aquellos/as;
leave those books on the table
deja esos libros sobre la mesa; **~ one**
ése/ésa; (more remote) aquél/aquélla;
~ one over there aquél/aquélla de
allí
♦ pron 1 (demonstrative) ése/a, pl
ésos/as; (neuter) eso; (more remote)
aquél/aquélla, pl aquéllos/as; (neuter)
aquello; **what's ~?** ¿qué es eso (or

aquello)?; **who's ~?** ¿quién es ése/a
(or aquél/aquélla)?; **is ~ you?** ¿eres
tú?; **will you eat all ~?** ¿vas a comer
todo eso?; **~'s my house** ésa es mi
casa; **~'s what he said** eso es lo que
dijo; **~ is (to say)** es decir
2 (relative: subject, object) que; (with
preposition) (el/la) que etc, (el/la) cual
etc; **the book (~) I read** el libro que
leí; **the books ~ are in the library**
los libros que están en la biblioteca; **all
(~) I have** todo lo que tengo; **the
box (~) I put it in** la caja en la que o
donde lo puse; **the people (~) I
spoke to** la gente con la que hablé
3 (relative: of time) que; **the day (~)
he came** el día (en) que vino
♦ conj que; **he thought ~ I was ill**
creyó que yo estaba enfermo
♦ adv (demonstrative): **I can't work
~ much** no puedo trabajar tanto; **I
didn't realise it was ~ bad** no creí
que fuera tan malo; **~ high** así de alto

thatched [θætʃt] adj (roof) de paja;
(cottage) con tejado de paja
thaw [θɔ:] n deshielo ♦ vi (ice)
derretirse; (food) descongelarse ♦ vt
(food) descongelar

KEYWORD

the [ði:, ðə] def art 1 (gen) el, f la, pl
los, fpl las (NB = a + el = al; de + el =
del): (pl los) el, f la, pl los, fpl las (NB = a + el =
al; de + el = del); **the boy/girl** el chico/
la chica; **~ books/flowers** los libros/
las flores; **to ~ postman/from
~ drawer** el cartero/del cajón; **I
haven't ~ time/money** no tengo
tiempo/dinero
2 (+ adj to form it) los; lo; **~ rich and
~ poor** los ricos y los pobres; **to
attempt ~ impossible** intentar lo
imposible
3 (in titles): **Elizabeth ~ First** Isabel
primera; **Peter ~ Great** Pedro el
Grande

4 (in comparisons): ~ **more he works** ~ **more he earns** cuanto más trabaja más gana

theatre ['θɪətə*] (US **theater**) n teatro; (also: lecture ~) aula; (MED: also: operating ~) quirófano; **~goer** n aficionado/a al teatro

theatrical [θɪ'ætrɪk] adj teatral

theft [θeft] n robo

their [ðeə*] adj su; **~s** pron (el) suyo/(la) suya etc; see also **my; mine[1]**

them [ðem, ðəm] pron (direct) los/las; (indirect) les; (stressed, after prep) ellos/ellas; see also **me**

theme [θiːm] n tema m; ~ **park** n parque de atracciones (en torno a un tema central); ~ **song** n tema m (musical)

themselves [ðəm'selvz] pl pron (subject) ellos mismos/ellas mismas; (complement) se; (after prep) sí (mismos/as); see also **oneself**

then [ðen] adv (at that time) entonces; (next) después; (later) luego, después; (and also) además ♦ conj (therefore) en ese caso, entonces ♦ adj: **the** ~ **president** el entonces presidente; **by** ~ para entonces; **from** ~ **on** desde entonces

theology [θɪ'ɔlədʒɪ] n teología

theory ['θɪərɪ] n teoría

therapist ['θerəpɪst] n terapeuta m/f

therapy ['θerəpɪ] n terapia

KEYWORD

there ['ðeə*] adv **1**: ~ **is,** ~ **are** hay; ~ **is no-one here/no bread left** no hay nadie aquí/no queda pan; ~ **has been an accident** ha habido un accidente
2 (referring to place) ahí; (distant) allí; **it's** ~ está ahí; **put it in/on/up/down** ~ ponlo ahí dentro/encima/arriba/abajo; **I want that book** ~ quiero ese libro de ahí; ~ **he is!** ¡ahí

está!
3: ~, ~, (esp to child) ea, ea

there: ~**abouts** adv por ahí; ~**after** adv después; ~**by** adv así, de ese modo; ~**fore** adv por lo tanto; ~'**s** = **there is; there has**

thermal ['θɜːml] adj termal; (paper) térmico

thermometer [θə'mɔmɪtə*] n termómetro

Thermos ® ['θɜːməs] n (also: ~ **flask**) termo

thermostat ['θɜːməustæt] n termostato

thesaurus [θɪ'sɔːrəs] n tesoro

these [ðiːz] pl adj estos/as ♦ pl pron éstos/as

thesis ['θiːsɪs] (pl **theses**) n tesis f inv

they [ðeɪ] pl pron ellos/ellas; (stressed) ellos (mismos)/ellas (mismas); ~ **say that ...** (it is said that) se dice que ...; ~'**d** = **they had; they would;** ~'**ll** = **they shall; they will;** ~'**re** = **they are;** ~'**ve** = **they have**

thick [θɪk] adj (in consistency) espeso; (in size) grueso; (stupid) torpe ♦ n: **in the** ~ **of the battle** en lo más reñido de la batalla; **it's 20 cm** ~ tiene 20 cm de espesor; ~**en** vi espesarse ♦ vt (sauce etc) espesar; ~**ness** n espesor m; grueso; ~**set** adj fornido

thief [θiːf] (pl **thieves**) n ladrón/ona m/f

thigh [θaɪ] n muslo

thimble ['θɪmbl] n dedal m

thin [θɪn] adj (person, animal) flaco; (in size) delgado; (in consistency) poco espeso; (hair, crowd) escaso ♦ vt: **to** ~ (**down**) diluir

thing [θɪŋ] n cosa; (object) objeto, artículo; (matter) asunto; (mania): **to have a** ~ **about sb/sth** estar obsesionado con uno/algo; ~**s** npl (belongings) efectos mpl (personales); **the best** ~ **would be to ...** lo mejor sería ...; **how are** ~**s?** ¿qué tal?

think [θɪŋk] (pt, pp **thought**) vi pensar
♦ vt pensar, creer; **what did you ~ of
them?** ¿qué te parecieron?; **to
~ about sth/sb** pensar en algo/uno;
I'll ~ about it lo pensaré; **to ~ of
doing sth** pensar en hacer algo; **I ~
so/not** creo que sí/no; **to ~ well of
sb** tener buen concepto de uno;
~ over vt reflexionar sobre, meditar;
~ up vt (plan etc) idear; **~ tank** n
gabinete m de estrategia

thinly ['θɪnlɪ] adv (cut) fino; (spread)
ligeramente

third [θɜːd] adj (before n) tercer(a);
(following n) tercero/a ♦ n tercero/a;
(fraction) tercio; (BRIT: SCOL: degree)
título de licenciado con calificación de
aprobado; **~ly** adv en tercer lugar;
~ party insurance (BRIT) n seguro
contra terceros; **~-rate** adj (de calidad)
mediocre; **T~ World** n Tercer Mundo

thirst [θɜːst] n sed f; **~y** adj (person,
animal) sediento; (work) que da sed; **to
be ~y** tener sed

thirteen ['θɜː'tiːn] num trece

thirty ['θɜːtɪ] num treinta

this [ðɪs] (pl **these**) adj (demonstrative)
este/a; el pl estos/as; (neuter) esto;
~ man/woman este hombre/esta
mujer; **these children/flowers** estos
chicos/estas flores; **~ one (here)** éste/
a, esto (de aquí)
♦ pron (demonstrative) éste/a; el pl estos/
as; (neuter) esto; **who is ~?** ¿quién es
éste/ésta? **what is ~?** ¿qué es esto?;
~ is where I live aquí vivo; **~ is
what he said** esto es lo que dijo; **~ is
Mr Brown** (in introductions) le
presento al Sr. Brown; (photo) éste es
el Sr. Brown; (on telephone) habla el Sr.
Brown
♦ adv (demonstrative): **~ high/long** etc
así de alto/largo etc; **~ far** hasta aquí

thistle ['θɪsl] n cardo

thorn [θɔːn] n espina

thorough ['θʌrə] adj (search)
minucioso; (wash) a fondo; (knowledge,
research) profundo; (person)
meticuloso; **~bred** adj (horse) de pura
sangre; **~fare** n calle f; **"no ~fare"**
"prohibido el paso"; **~ly** adv (search)
minuciosamente; (study)
profundamente; (wash) a fondo;
(utterly: bad, wet etc) completamente,
totalmente

those [ðəuz] adj esos/esas; (more
remote) aquellos/as

though [ðəu] conj aunque ♦ adv sin
embargo

thought [θɔːt] pt, pp of **think** ♦ n
pensamiento; (opinion) opinión f; **~ful**
adj pensativo; (serious) serio;
(considerate) atento; **~less** adj
desconsiderado

thousand ['θauzənd] num mil; **two
~** dos mil; **~s of** miles de; **~th** num
milésimo

thrash [θræʃ] vt azotar; (defeat)
derrotar; **~ about** or **around** vi
debatirse; **~ out** vt discutir a fondo

thread [θred] n hilo; (of screw) rosca
♦ vt (needle) enhebrar; **~bare** adj raído

threat [θret] n amenaza; **~en** vi
amenazar ♦ vt: **to ~ sb with/to do**
amenazar a uno con/con hacer

three [θriː] num tres; **~-dimensional**
adj tridimensional; **~-piece suit** n traje
m de tres piezas; **~-piece suite** n
tresillo; **~-ply** adj (wool) de tres cabos

threshold ['θreʃhəuld] n umbral m

threw [θruː] pt of **throw**

thrifty ['θrɪftɪ] adj económico

thrill [θrɪl] n (excitement) emoción f;
(shudder) estremecimiento m ♦ vt
emocionar; **to be ~ed** (with gift etc)
estar encantado; **~er** n novela (or obra
or película) de suspense; **~ing** adj
emocionante

thrive [θraɪv] (pt, pp **thrived**) vi (grow)
crecer; (do well): **to ~ on sth** sentirse
muy bien uno algo; **thriving** adj

próspero

throat [θrəut] n garganta; **to have a sore ~** tener dolor de garganta

throb [θrɔb] vi latir; dar punzadas; vibrar

throes [θrəuz] npl: **in the ~ of** en medio de

throne [θrəun] n trono

throng [θrɔŋ] n multitud f, muchedumbre f ♦ vt agolparse en

throttle ['θrɔtl] n (AUT) acelerador m ♦ vt estrangular

through [θru:] prep por, a través de; (time) durante; (by means of) por medio de, mediante; (owing to) gracias a ♦ adj (ticket, train) directo ♦ adv completamente, de parte a parte; de principio a fin; **to put sb ~ to sb** (TEL) poner o pasar a uno con uno; **to be ~** (TEL) tener comunicación; (have finished) haber terminado; **"no ~ road"** (BRIT) "calle sin salida"; **~out** prep (place) por todas partes de, por todo; (time) durante todo ♦ adv por o en todas partes

throw [θrəu] (pt **threw**, pp **thrown**) n tiro; (SPORT) lanzamiento ♦ vt tirar, echar; (rider) lanzar; (fig) desconcertar; **to ~ a party** dar una fiesta; **~ away** vt tirar; (money) derrochar; **~ off** vt deshacerse de; **~ out** vt tirar; (person) echar; expulsar; **~ up** vi vomitar; **~away** adj para tirar, desechable; (remark) hecho de paso; **~-in** n (SPORT) saque m

thru [θru:] (US) = **through**

thrush [θrʌʃ] n zorzal m, tordo

thrust [θrʌst] (pt, pp **thrust**) n empujar (con fuerza)

thud [θʌd] n golpe m sordo

thug [θʌg] n gamberro/a

thumb [θʌm] n (ANAT) pulgar m; **to ~ a lift** hacer autostop; **~ through** vt fus (book) hojear; **~tack** (US) n. chincheta (SP)

thump [θʌmp] n golpe m; (sound) ruido seco o sordo ♦ vt golpear ♦ vi

(heart etc) palpitar

thunder ['θʌndə*] n trueno ♦ vi tronar; (train etc): **to ~ past** pasar como un trueno; **~bolt** n rayo; **~clap** n trueno; **~storm** n tormenta; **~y** adj tormentoso

Thursday ['θə:zdɪ] n jueves m inv

thus [ðʌs] adv así, de este modo

thyme [taɪm] n tomillo

thyroid ['θaɪrɔɪd] n (also: ~ gland) tiroides m inv

tic [tɪk] n tic m

tick [tɪk] n (sound: of clock) tictac m; (mark) palomita; (ZOOL) garrapata; (BRIT: inf): **in a ~** en un instante ♦ vi hacer tictac ♦ vt marcar; **~ off** vt marcar; (person) reñir; **~ over** vi (engine) girar en marcha lenta; (fig) ir tirando

ticket ['tɪkɪt] n billete m (SP), tíquet m, boleto (AM); (for cinema etc) entrada (SP), boleto (AM); (in shop: on goods) etiqueta; (for raffle) papeleta; (for library) tarjeta; (parking ~) multa por estacionamiento ilegal; **~ collector** n revisor(a) m/f; **~ office** n (THEATRE) taquilla (SP), boletería (AM); (RAIL) despacho de billetes (SP) or boletos (AM)

tickle ['tɪkl] vt hacer cosquillas a ♦ vi hacer cosquillas; **ticklish** adj (person) cosquilloso; (problem) delicado

tidal ['taɪdl] adj de marea; **~ wave** n maremoto

tidbit ['tɪdbɪt] (US) n = **titbit**

tiddlywinks ['tɪdlɪwɪŋks] n juego infantil con fichas de plástico

tide [taɪd] n marea; (fig: of events etc) curso, marcha; **~ over** vt (help out) ayudar a salir del apuro

tidy ['taɪdɪ] adj (room etc) ordenado; (dress, work) limpio; (person) (bien) arreglado ♦ vt (also: ~ up) poner en orden

tie [taɪ] n (string etc) atadura; (BRIT: also: neck~) corbata; (fig: link) vínculo, lazo; (SPORT etc: draw) empate m ♦ vt atar ♦ vi (SPORT etc) empatar; **to ~ in a bow** atar con un lazo; **to ~ a knot in sth** hacer un nudo en algo; **~ down** vt (fig: person: restrict) atar; (: to price, date etc) obligar a; **~ up** vt (parcel) envolver; (dog, person) atar; (arrangements) concluir; **to be ~d up** (busy) estar ocupado

tier [tɪə*] n grada; (of cake) piso

tiger [ˈtaɪgə*] n tigre m

tight [taɪt] adj (rope) tirante; (money) escaso; (clothes) ajustado; (bend) cerrado; (shoes, schedule) apretado; (budget) ajustado; (security) estricto; (inf: drunk) borracho ♦ adv (squeeze) muy fuerte; (shut) bien; **~en** vt (rope) estirar; (screw, grip) apretar; (security) reforzar ♦ vi estirarse; apretarse; **~-fisted** adj tacaño; **~ly** adv (grasp) muy fuerte; **~rope** n cuerda floja; **~s** (BRIT) npl panti mpl

tile [taɪl] n (on roof) teja; (on floor) baldosa; (on wall) azulejo; **~d** adj (de tejas; embaldosado; (wall) alicatado

till [tɪl] n caja (registradora) ♦ vt (land) cultivar ♦ prep, conj = **until**

tilt [tɪlt] vt inclinar ♦ vi inclinarse

timber [ˈtɪmbə*] n (material) madera

time [taɪm] n tiempo m; (epoch: often pl) época; (by clock) hora; (moment) momento; (occasion) vez f; (MUS) compás m ♦ vt calcular o medir el tiempo de; (race) cronometrar; (remark, visit etc) elegir el momento para; **a long ~** mucho tiempo; **4 at a ~** de 4 en 4; **4 a la vez**; **for the ~ being** de momento, por ahora; **from ~ to ~** de vez en cuando; **in ~** (soon enough) a tiempo; (after some time) con el tiempo; (MUS) al compás; **in a week's ~** dentro de una semana; **in no ~** en un abrir y cerrar de ojos; **any ~** cuando sea; **on ~** a la hora; **5 ~s 5** 5 por 5; **what ~ is it?** ¿qué hora es?; **to have a good ~** pasarlo bien, divertirse; **~ bomb** n bomba de efecto retardado; **~less** adj eterno; **~ limit** n

plazo; **~ly** adj oportuno; **~ off** n tiempo libre; **~r** n (in kitchen etc) programador m horario; **~ scale** (BRIT) n escala de tiempo; **~-share** n apartamento (o casa) a tiempo compartido; **~ switch** (BRIT) n interruptor m (horario); **~table** n horario; **~ zone** n huso horario

timid [ˈtɪmɪd] adj tímido

timing [ˈtaɪmɪŋ] n (SPORT) cronometraje m; **the ~ of his resignation** el momento que eligió para dimitir

tin [tɪn] n estaño; (also: ~ plate) hojalata; (BRIT: can) lata; **~foil** n papel m de estaño

tinge [tɪndʒ] n matiz m ♦ vt: **~d with** teñido de

tingle [ˈtɪŋgl] vi (person): **to ~ (with)** estremecerse (de); (hands etc) hormiguear

tinker [ˈtɪŋkə*] n: **~ with** vt fus jugar con, tocar

tinned [tɪnd] (BRIT) adj (food) en lata, en conserva

tin opener [-əupnə*] (BRIT) n abrelatas m inv

tinsel [ˈtɪnsl] n (guirnalda de) espumillón m

tint [tɪnt] n matiz m; (for hair) tinte m; **~ed** adj (hair) teñido; (glass, spectacles) ahumado

tiny [ˈtaɪnɪ] adj minúsculo, pequeñito

tip [tɪp] n (end) punta; (gratuity) propina; (BRIT: for rubbish) vertedero; (advice) consejo ♦ vt (waiter) dar una propina a; (tilt) inclinar; (empty: also: ~ out) vaciar, echar; (overturn: also: ~ over) volcar; **~-off** n (hint) advertencia; **~ped** (BRIT) adj (cigarette) con filtro

Tipp-Ex ® [ˈtɪpeks] n Tipp-Ex ® m

tipsy [ˈtɪpsɪ] (inf) adj alegre, mareado

tiptoe [ˈtɪptəu] n: **on ~** de puntillas

tire [ˈtaɪə*] n (US) = **tyre** ♦ vt cansar ♦ vi (gen) cansarse; (become bored) aburrirse; **~d** adj cansado; **to be ~d of**

sth estar harto de algo; **~less** adj incansable; **~some** adj aburrido; **tiring** adj cansado

tissue ['tɪʃuː] n tejido; (paper handkerchief) pañuelo de papel, kleenex ® n; **~ paper** n papel m de seda

tit [tɪt] n (bird) herrerillo común; **to give ~ for tat** dar ojo por ojo

titbit ['tɪtbɪt] (US **tidbit**) n (food) golosina; (news) noticia sabrosa

title ['taɪtl] n título; **~ deed** n (LAW) título de propiedad; **~ role** n papel m principal

TM abbr = **trademark**

┌─────────────────────────┐
│ **KEYWORD** │
└─────────────────────────┘

to [tuː, tə] prep **1** (direction) a; **to go ~ France/London/school/the station** ir a Francia/Londres/al colegio/a la estación; **to go ~ Claude's/the doctor's** ir a casa de Claude/al médico; **the road ~ Edinburgh** la carretera de Edimburgo

2 (as far as) hasta, a; **from here ~ London** de aquí a or hasta Londres; **to count ~ 10** contar hasta 10; **from 40 ~ 50 people** entre 40 y 50 personas

3 (with expressions of time): **a quarter/twenty ~ 5** las 5 menos cuarto/veinte

4 (for, of): **the key ~ the front door** la llave de la puerta principal; **she is secretary ~ the director** es la secretaria del director; **a letter ~ his wife** una carta or para su mujer

5 (expressing indirect object) a; **to give sth ~ sb** dar algo a alguien; **to talk ~ sb** hablar con alguien; **to be a danger ~ sb** ser un peligro para alguien; **to carry out repairs ~ sth** hacer reparaciones en algo

6 (in relation to): **3 goals ~ 2** 3 goles a 2; **30 miles ~ the gallon** ≈ 9,4 litros a los cien (kms)

7 (purpose, result): **to come ~ sb's aid** venir en auxilio or ayuda de alguien; **to sentence sb ~ death** condenar a uno a muerte; **~ my great surprise** con gran sorpresa mía

♦ with vb **1** (simple infin): **~ go/eat** ir/comer

2 (following another vb): **to want/try/start ~ do** querer/intentar/empezar a hacer; see also relevant vb

3 (with vb omitted): **I don't want ~** no quiero

4 (purpose, result) para; **I did it ~ help you** lo hice para ayudarte; **he came ~ see you** vino a verte

5 (equivalent to relative clause): **I have things ~ do** tengo cosas que hacer; **the main thing is ~ try** lo principal es intentarlo

6 (after adj etc): **ready ~ go** listo para irse; **too old ~ ...** demasiado viejo (como) para ...

♦ adv: **pull/push the door ~** tirar de/empujar la puerta

toad [təud] n sapo; **~stool** n hongo venenoso

toast [təust] n (CULIN) tostada; (drink, speech) brindis m ♦ vt (CULIN) tostar; (drink to) brindar por; **~er** n tostador m

tobacco [tə'bækəu] n tabaco; **~nist** n estanquero (SP), tabaquero (AM); **~nist's (shop)** (BRIT) n estanco (SP), tabaquería (AM)

toboggan [tə'bɔgən] n tobogán m

today [tə'deɪ] adv, n (also fig) hoy m

toddler ['tɔdlə*] n niño/a (que empieza a andar)

toe [təu] n dedo (del pie); (of shoe) punta; **to ~ the line** (fig) conformarse; **~nail** n uña del pie

toffee ['tɔfɪ] n toffee m; **~ apple** (BRIT) n manzana acaramelada

together [tə'gɛðə*] adv juntos; (at same time) al mismo tiempo, a la vez; **~ with** junto con

toil [tɔɪl] n trabajo duro, labor f ♦ vi trabajar duramente

toilet ['tɔɪlət] n retrete m; (BRIT: room) servicios mpl (SP), wáter m (SP), sanitario (AM) ♦ cpd (soap etc) de aseo; ~ **paper** n papel m higiénico; ~**ries** npl artículos mpl de tocador; ~ **roll** n rollo de papel higiénico

token ['təukən] n (sign) señal f, muestra; (souvenir) recuerdo; (disc) ficha ♦ adj (strike, payment etc) simbólico; **book/record/** (BRIT) **gift** ~ (BRIT) vale-regalo

Tokyo ['təukjəu] n Tokio, Tokío

told [təuld] pt, pp of **tell**

tolerable ['tɔlərəbl] adj (bearable) soportable; (fairly good) pasable

tolerant ['tɔlərnt] adj: ~ **of** tolerante con

tolerate ['tɔləreɪt] vt tolerar

toll [təul] n (of casualties) número de víctimas; (tax, charge) peaje m ♦ vi (bell) doblar

tomato [tə'mɑːtəu] (pl ~**es**) n tomate m

tomb [tuːm] n tumba

tomboy ['tɔmbɔɪ] n marimacho

tombstone ['tuːmstəun] n lápida

tomcat ['tɔmkæt] n gato (macho)

tomorrow [tə'mɔrəu] adv, n (also: fig) mañana; **the day after** ~ pasado mañana; ~ **morning** mañana por la mañana

ton [tʌn] n tonelada (BRIT = 1016 kg; US = 907 kg); (metric ~) tonelada métrica; ~**s of** (inf) montones de

tone [təun] n tono ♦ vi (also: ~ **in**) armonizar; ~ **down** vt (criticism) suavizar; (colour) atenuar; ~ **up** vt (muscles) tonificar; ~-**deaf** adj con mal oído

tongs [tɔŋz] npl (for coal) tenazas fpl; (curling ~) tenacillas fpl

tongue [tʌŋ] n lengua; ~ **in cheek** irónicamente; ~-**tied** adj (fig) mudo; ~-**twister** n trabalenguas m inv

tonic ['tɔnɪk] n (MED, also: fig) tónico; (also: ~ **water**) (agua) tónica

tonight [tə'naɪt] adv, n esta noche; esta tarde

tonsil ['tɔnsl] n amígdala; ~**litis** [-'laɪtɪs] n amigdalitis f

too [tuː] adv (excessively) demasiado; (also) también; ~ **much** adv demasiado; ~ **many** demasiados/as

took [tuk] pt of **take**

tool [tuːl] n herramienta; ~ **box** n caja de herramientas

toot [tuːt] n pitido ♦ vi tocar el pito

tooth [tuːθ] (pl **teeth**) n (ANAT, TECH) diente m; (molar) muela; ~**ache** n dolor m de muelas; ~**brush** n cepillo de dientes; ~**paste** n pasta de dientes; ~**pick** n palillo

top [tɔp] n (of mountain) cumbre f, cima; (of tree) copa; (of head) coronilla; (of ladder, page) parte f de arriba; (of table) superficie f; (of cupboard) parte f de arriba; (lid: of box) tapa; (: of bottle, jar) tapón m; (of list etc) cabeza; (toy) peonza; (garment) blusa; camiseta ♦ adj de arriba; (in rank) principal, primero; (best) mejor ♦ vt (exceed) exceder; (be first in) encabezar; **on** ~ **of** (above) sobre, encima de; (in addition to) además de; **from** ~ **to bottom** de pies a cabeza; ~ **off** (US) vt = ~ **up**; ~ **up** vt llenar; ~ **floor** n último piso; ~ **hat** n sombrero de copa; ~-**heavy** adj (object) mal equilibrado

topic ['tɔpɪk] n tema m; ~**al** adj actual

top: ~**less** adj (bather, bikini) topless inv; ~-**level** adj (talks) al más alto nivel; ~**most** adj más alto

topple ['tɔpl] vt derribar ♦ vi caerse

top-secret adj de alto secreto

topsy-turvy ['tɔpsɪ'təːvɪ] adj al revés ♦ adv patas arriba

torch [tɔːtʃ] n antorcha; (BRIT: electric) linterna

tore [tɔː⁻] pt of **tear²**

tormento ♦ vt atormentar; (fig: annoy) fastidiar

torn [tɔːn] pp of **tear²**

torrent ['tɔrnt] n torrente m

tortoise ['tɔːtəs] n tortuga; **~shell** ['tɔːtəʃɛl] adj de carey

torture ['tɔːtʃə*] n tortura ♦ vt torturar; (fig) atormentar

Tory ['tɔːrɪ] (BRIT) adj, n (POL) conservador(a) m/f

toss [tɔs] vt tirar, echar; (one's head) sacudir; **to ~ a coin** echar a cara o cruz; **to ~ up for sth** jugar a cara o cruz algo; **to ~ and turn** (in bed) dar vueltas

tot [tɔt] n (BRIT: drink) copita; (child) nene/a m/f

total ['təʊtl] adj total, entero; (emphatic: failure etc) completo, total ♦ n total m, suma ♦ vt (add up) sumar; (amount to) ascender a; **~ly** adv totalmente

touch [tʌtʃ] n tacto; (contact) contacto ♦ vt tocar; (emotionally) conmover; **a ~ of** (fig) un poquito de; **to get in ~ with sb** ponerse en contacto con uno; **to lose ~** (friends) perder contacto; **~ on** vt fus (topic) aludir (brevemente) a; **~ up** vt (paint) retocar; **~-and-go** adj arriesgado; **~down** n aterrizaje m; (on sea) amerizaje m; (US: FOOTBALL) ensayo; **~ed** adj (moved) conmovido; (inf) chiflado; **~ing** adj (moving) conmovedor(a); **~line** n (SPORT) línea de banda; **~y** adj (person) quisquilloso

tough [tʌf] adj (material) resistente; (meat) duro; (problem etc) difícil; (policy, stance) inflexible; (person) fuerte; **~en** vt endurecer

toupée ['tuːpeɪ] n peluca

tour ['tʊə*] n viaje m, vuelta; (also: package ~) viaje m todo comprendido; (of town, museum) visita; (by pop group) gira ♦ vt recorrer, visitar; **~ guide** n guía m turístico, guía f turística

tourism ['tʊərɪzm] n turismo

tourist ['tʊərɪst] n turista m/f ♦ cpd turístico; **~ office** n oficina de turismo

tousled ['taʊzld] adj (hair) despeinado

tout [taʊt] vi: **to ~ for business** solicitar clientes ♦ n (also: ticket ~) revendedor(a) m/f

tow [təʊ] vt remolcar; **"on** or **in** (US) **~"** (AUT) "a remolque"

toward(s) [tə'wɔːd(z)] prep hacia; (attitude) respecto a, con; (purpose) para

towel ['taʊəl] n toalla; **~ling** n (fabric) felpa; **~ rail** (US = **rack**) n toallero

tower ['taʊə*] n torre f; **~ block** (BRIT) n torre f (de pisos); **~ing** adj muy alto, imponente

town [taʊn] n ciudad f; **to go to ~** ir a la ciudad; (fig) echar la casa por la ventana; **~ centre** n centro de la ciudad; **~ council** n ayuntamiento, consejo municipal; **~ hall** n ayuntamiento; **~ plan** n plano de la ciudad; **~ planning** n urbanismo

towrope ['təʊrəʊp] n cable m de remolque

tow truck (US) n camión m grúa

toy [tɔɪ] n juguete m; **~ with** vt fus jugar con; (idea) acariciar; **~shop** n juguetería

trace [treɪs] n rastro ♦ vt (draw) trazar, delinear; (locate) encontrar; (follow) seguir la pista de; **tracing paper** n papel m de calco

track [træk] n (mark) huella, pista; (path: gen) camino, senda; (: of bullet etc) trayectoria; (: of suspect, animal) pista, rastro; (RAIL) vía; (SPORT) pista; (on tape, record) canción f ♦ vt seguir la pista de; **to keep ~ of** mantenerse al tanto de, seguir; **~ down** vt (prey) seguir el rastro de; (sth lost) encontrar; **~suit** n chandal m

tract [trækt] n (GEO) región f

traction ['trækʃən] n (power) tracción f; **in ~** (MED) en tracción

tractor ['træktə*] n tractor m

trade [treɪd] n comercio; (skill, job)

oficio ♦ vi negociar, comerciar ♦ vt
(exchange): **to ~ sth (for sth)** cambiar
algo (por algo); **~ in** vt (old car etc)
ofrecer como parte del pago; **~ fair** n
feria comercial; **~mark** n marca de
fábrica; **~ name** n marca registrada;
~r n comerciante m/f; **~sman** (irreg) n
(shopkeeper) tendero; **~ union** n
sindicato; **~ unionist** n sindicalista m/f

tradition [trə'dɪʃən] n tradición f; **~al**
adj tradicional

traffic ['træfɪk] n (gen, AUT) tráfico,
circulación f, tránsito (AM) ♦ vi: **to ~ in**
(pej: liquor, drugs) traficar en; **~ circle**
(US) n isleta; **~ jam** n embotellamiento;
~ lights npl semáforo; **~ warden** n
guardia m/f de tráfico

tragedy ['trædʒədɪ] n tragedia

tragic ['trædʒɪk] adj trágico

trail [treɪl] n (tracks) rastro, pista; (path)
camino, sendero; (dust, smoke) estela
♦ vt (drag) arrastrar; (follow) seguir la
pista de ♦ vi arrastrar; (in contest etc) ir
perdiendo; **~ behind** vi quedar a la
zaga; **~er** n (AUT) remolque m;
(caravan) caravana; (CINEMA) trailer m,
avance m; **~er truck** (US) n trailer m

train [treɪn] n tren m; (of dress) cola;
(series) serie f ♦ vt (educate, teach skills
to) formar; (sportsman) entrenar; (dog)
adiestrar; (point: gun etc): **to ~ on**
apuntar a ♦ vi (SPORT) entrenarse;
(learn a skill) formarse; **~ as a teacher** etc
estudiar para profesor etc; **one's ~ of
thought** el razonamiento de uno; **~ed**
adj (worker) cualificado; (animal)
amaestrado; **~ee** [treɪ'niː] n
aprendiz(a) m/f; **~er** n (SPORT: coach)
entrenador(a) m/f; (: shoe): **~ers**
zapatillas fpl (de deporte); (of animals)
domador(a) m/f; **~ing** n formación f;
entrenamiento; **to be in ~ing** (SPORT)
estar entrenando; **~ing college** n
(gen) colegio de formación profesional;
(for teachers) escuela de formación del
profesorado; **~ing shoes** npl zapatillas
fpl (de deporte)

trait [treɪt] n rasgo

traitor ['treɪtə*] n traidor(a) m/f

tram [træm] (BRIT) n (also: ~car) tranvía
m

tramp [træmp] n (person) vagabundo/
a; (inf: pej: woman) puta

trample ['træmpl] vt: **to ~ (underfoot)** pisotear

trampoline ['træmpəliːn] n trampolín f

tranquil ['træŋkwɪl] adj tranquilo;
~lizer n (MED) tranquilizante m

transact [træn'zækt] vt (business)
despachar; **~ion** [-'zækʃən] n
transacción f, operación f

transfer [n 'trænsfə:*, vb træns'fə:*] n
(of employees) traslado; (of money,
power) transferencia f; (SPORT) traspaso;
(picture, design) calcomanía ♦ vt
trasladar; transferir; **to ~ the charges**
(BRIT: TEL) llamar a cobro revertido

transform [træns'fɔːm] vt transformar

transfusion [træns'fjuːʒən] n
transfusión f

transient ['trænzɪənt] adj transitorio

transistor [træn'zɪstə*] n (ELEC)
transistor m; **~ radio** n transistor m

transit ['trænzɪt] n: **in ~** en tránsito

transitive ['trænzɪtɪv] adj (LING)
transitivo

transit lounge n sala de tránsito

translate [trænz'leɪt] vt traducir;
translation [-'leɪʃən] n traducción f;
translator n traductor(a) m/f

transmit [trænz'mɪt] vt transmitir;
~ter n transmisor m

transparency [træns'pɛərnsɪ] n
transparencia; (BRIT: PHOT) diapositiva

transparent [træns'pærnt] adj
transparente

transpire [træns'paɪə*] vi (turn out)
resultar; (happen) ocurrir, suceder; **it
~d that ...** se supo que ...

transplant [træns'plɑːnt] n (MED)
transplante m

transport [n 'trænspɔːt, vt træns'pɔːt]
n transporte m; (car) coche m (SP),

carro (*AM*), automóvil *m* ♦ *vt* transportar; **~ation** [-'teɪʃən] *n* transporte *m*; **~ café** (*BRIT*) *n* bar-restaurant *m* de carretera

transvestite [trænz'vestaɪt] *n* travestí *m/f*

trap [træp] *n* (*snare, trick*) trampa; (*carriage*) cabriolé *m* ♦ *vt* coger (*SP*) or agarrar (*AM*) en una trampa; (*trick*) engañar; (*confine*) atrapar; **~ door** *n* escotilla

trapeze [trə'piːz] *n* trapecio

trappings ['træpɪŋz] *npl* adornos *mpl*

trash [træʃ] *n* (*rubbish*) basura; (*pej*): **the book/film is ~** el libro/la película no vale nada; (*nonsense*) tonterías *fpl*; **~ can** (*US*) *n* cubo (*SP*) or balde *m* (*AM*) de la basura

travel ['trævl] *n* el viajar ♦ *vi* viajar ♦ *vt* (*distance*) recorrer; **~s** *npl* (*journeys*) viajes *mpl*; **~ agent** *n* agente *m/f* de viajes; **~ler** (*US* =**er**) *n* viajero/a; **~ler's cheque** (*US* =**er's check**) *n* cheque *m* de viajero; **~ling** (*US* =**ing**) *n* los viajes, el viajar; **~ sickness** *n* mareo

trawler ['trɔːlə*] *n* pesquero de arrastre

tray [treɪ] *n* bandeja, (*on desk*) cajón *m*

treacherous ['tretʃərəs] *adj* traidor, traicionero; (*dangerous*) peligroso

treacle ['triːkl] *n* melaza

tread [tred] (*pt* **trod**, *pp* **trodden**) *n* (*step*) paso, pisada; (*sound*) ruido de pasos; (*of stair*) escalón *m*; (*of tyre*) banda de rodadura ♦ *vi* pisar; **~ on** *vt fus* pisar

treason ['triːzn] *n* traición *f*

treasure ['treʒə*] *n* (*also fig*) tesoro ♦ *vt* (*value: object, friendship*) apreciar; (: *memory*) guardar

treasurer ['treʒərə*] *n* tesorero/a

treasury ['treʒərɪ] *n*: **the T~** el Ministerio de Hacienda

treat [triːt] *n* (*present*) regalo ♦ *vt* tratar; **to ~ sb to sth** invitar a uno a algo

treatment ['triːtmənt] *n* tratamiento

treaty ['triːtɪ] *n* tratado

treble ['trebl] *adj* triple ♦ *vt* triplicar ♦ *vi* triplicarse; **~ clef** *n* (*MUS*) clave *f* de sol

tree [triː] *n* árbol *m*; **~ trunk** tronco (de árbol)

trek [trek] *n* (*long journey*) viaje *m* largo y difícil; (*tiring walk*) caminata

trellis ['trelɪs] *n* enrejado

tremble ['trembl] *vi* temblar

tremendous [trɪ'mendəs] *adj* tremendo, enorme; (*excellent*) estupendo

tremor ['tremə*] *n* temblor *m*; (*also: earth ~*) temblor *m* de tierra

trench [trentʃ] *n* zanja

trend [trend] *n* (*tendency*) tendencia; (*of events*) curso; (*fashion*) moda; **~y** *adj* de moda

trespass ['trespəs] *vi*: **to ~ on** entrar sin permiso en; **"no ~ing"** "prohibido el paso"

trestle ['tresl] *n* caballete *m*

trial ['traɪəl] *n* (*LAW*) juicio, proceso; (*test: of machine etc*) prueba; **~s** *npl* (*hardships*) dificultades *fpl*; **by ~ and error** a fuerza de probar

triangle ['traɪæŋgl] *n* (*MATH, MUS*) triángulo

tribe [traɪb] *n* tribu *f*

tribunal [traɪ'bjuːnl] *n* tribunal *m*

tributary ['trɪbjutərɪ] *n* (*river*) afluente *m*

tribute ['trɪbjuːt] *n* homenaje *m*, tributo; **to pay ~ to** rendir homenaje a

trick [trɪk] *n* (*skill, knack*) truco; (*conjuring ~*) truco; (*joke*) broma; (*CARDS*) baza ♦ *vt* engañar; **to play a ~ on sb** gastar una broma a uno; **that should do the ~** a ver si funciona así; **~ery** *n* engaño

trickle ['trɪkl] *n* (*of water etc*) goteo ♦ *vi* gotear

tricky ['trɪkɪ] *adj* difícil; delicado

tricycle ['traɪsɪkl] *n* triciclo

trifle ['traɪfl] *n* bagatela; (*CULIN*) dulce

de bizcocho borracho, gelatina, fruta y
natillas ♦ *adv*: **a ~ long** un poquito
largo; (*stumble*) **trifling** *adj* insignificante
trigger ['trɪgə*] *n* (*of gun*) gatillo; **~ off**
vt desencadenar
trim [trɪm] *adj* (*house, garden*) en buen
estado; (*person, figure*) esbelto ♦ *n*
(*haircut etc*) recorte *m*; (*on car*)
guarnición *f* ♦ *vt* (*neaten*) arreglar; (*cut*)
recortar; (*decorate*) adornar; (*cut a
sail*) orientar; **~mings** (*CULIN*)
guarnición *f*
trip [trɪp] *n* viaje *m*; (*excursion*)
excursión *f*; (*stumble*) traspié *m* ♦ *vi*
(*stumble*) tropezar; (*go lightly*) andar a
paso ligero; **on a ~** de viaje; **~ up** *vi*
tropezar, caerse ♦ *vt* hacer tropezar o
caer
tripe [traɪp] *n* (*CULIN*) callos *mpl*
triple ['trɪpl] *adj* triple; **triplets**
['trɪplɪts] *npl* trillizos *as mpl/fpl*;
triplicate ['trɪplɪkət] *n*: **in triplicate**
por triplicado
trite [traɪt] *adj* trillado
triumph ['traɪʌmf] *n* triunfo ♦ *vi*: **to
~ (over)** vencer; **~ant** [traɪʌmfənt]
adj (*team etc*) vencedor(a); (*wave,
return*) triunfal
trivia ['trɪvɪə] *npl* trivialidades *fpl*
trivial ['trɪvɪəl] *adj* insignificante;
(*commonplace*) banal
trod [trɔd] *pt of* **tread**
trodden ['trɔdn] *pp of* **tread**
trolley ['trɔlɪ] *n* carrito; (*also: ~ bus*)
trolebús *m*
trombone [trɔm'bəun] *n* trombón *m*
troop [truːp] *n* grupo, banda; **~s** *npl*
(*MIL*) tropas *fpl*; **~ in/out** *vi* entrar/salir
en tropel; **~ing the colour** *n*
(*ceremony*) presentación *f* de la
bandera
trophy ['trəufɪ] *n* trofeo
tropical ['trɔpɪkl] *adj* tropical
trot [trɔt] *n* trote *m* ♦ *vi* trotar; **on the
~** (*BRIT: fig*) seguidos/as
trouble ['trʌbl] *n* problema *m*,
dificultad *f*; (*worry*) preocupación *f*;

(*bother, effort*) molestia, esfuerzo *f*;
(*unrest*) inquietud *f*; (*MED*): **stomach
etc ~** problemas *mpl* gástricos *etc* ♦ *vt*
(*disturb*) molestar; (*worry*) preocupar,
inquietar ♦ *vi*: **to ~ to do sth**
molestarse en hacer algo; **~s** *npl* (*POL
etc*) conflictos *mpl*; (*personal*)
problemas *mpl*; **to be in ~** estar en un
apuro; **it's no ~!** ¡no es molestia
(ninguna)!; **what's the ~?** (*with
broken TV etc*) ¿cuál es el problema?;
(*doctor to patient*) ¿qué pasa?; **~d** *adj*
(*person*) preocupado; (*country, epoch,
life*) agitado; **~maker** *n* agitador/a
m/f; (*child*) alborotador *m*; **~shooter** *n*
(*in conflict*) conciliador(a) *m/f*; **~some**
adj molesto
trough [trɔf] *n* (*also: drinking ~*)
abrevadero; (*also: feeding ~*) comedero;
(*depression*) depresión *f*
troupe [truːp] *n* grupo
trousers ['trauzəz] *npl* pantalones *mpl*;
short ~ pantalones *mpl* cortos
trousseau ['truːsəu] (*pl* **~x** *or* **~s**) *n*
ajuar *m*
trout [traut] *n inv* trucha *f*
trowel ['trauəl] *n* (*of gardener*) palita;
(*of builder*) paleta
truant ['truənt] *n*: **to play ~** (*BRIT*)
hacer novillos
truce [truːs] *n* tregua
truck [trʌk] *n* (*lorry*) camión *m*; (*RAIL*)
vagón *m*; **~ driver** *n* camionero;
~ farm (*US*) *n* huerto
true [truː] *adj* verdadero; (*accurate*)
exacto; (*genuine*) auténtico; (*faithful*)
fiel; **to come ~** realizarse
truffle ['trʌfl] *n* trufa
truly ['truːlɪ] *adv* (*really*) realmente;
(*truthfully*) verdaderamente; (*faithfully*):
yours ~ (*in letter*) le saluda
atentamente
trump [trʌmp] *n* triunfo
trumpet ['trʌmpɪt] *n* trompeta
truncheon ['trʌntʃən] *n* porra
trundle ['trʌndl] *vi*: **to ~ along** ir sin
prisas

trunk [trʌŋk] n (of tree, person) tronco; (of elephant) trompa; (case) baúl m; (US: AUT) maletero; **~s** npl (also: swimming ~s) bañador m (de hombre)

truss [trʌs] vt: **~ (up)** atar

trust [trʌst] n confianza f; (responsibility) responsabilidad f; (LAW) fideicomiso ♦ vt (rely on) tener confianza en; (hope) esperar; (entrust): **to ~ sth to sb** confiar algo a uno; **to take sth on ~** aceptar algo a ojos cerrados; **~ed** adj de confianza; **~ee** [trʌs'ti:] n (LAW) fideicomisario; (of school) administrador m; **~ful** adj confiado; **~ing** adj confiado; **~worthy** adj digno de confianza

truth [tru:θ, pl tru:ðz] n verdad f; **~ful** adj veraz

try [trai] n tentativa, intento; (RUGBY) ensayo ♦ vt (attempt) intentar; (test: also: ~ out) probar, someter a prueba; (LAW) juzgar, procesar; (strain: patience) hacer perder ♦ vi probar; **to have a ~** probar suerte; **to ~ to do sth** intentar hacer algo; **to ~ again!** ¡vuelve a probar!; **~ harder!** ¡esfuérzate más!; **well, I tried** al menos lo intenté; **~ on** vt (clothes) probarse; **~ing** adj (experience) cansado; (person) pesado

T-shirt [ˈtiːʃəːt] n camiseta

T-square n regla en T

tub [tʌb] n cubo (SP), balde m (AM); (bath) tina, bañera

tube [tjuːb] n tubo; (BRIT: underground) metro; (for tyre) cámara de aire

tuberculosis [tjubə:kjuˈləusɪs] n tuberculosis f inv

tube station (BRIT) n estación f de metro

tubular [ˈtjuːbjulə*] adj tubular

TUC (BRIT) n abbr (= Trades Union Congress) federación nacional de sindicatos

tuck [tʌk] vt (put) poner; **~ away** vt (money) guardar; (building): **to be ~ed away** esconderse; ocultarse; **~ in** vt

meter dentro; (child) arropar ♦ vi (eat) comer con apetito; **~ up** vt (child) arropar; **~ shop** n (SCOL) tienda; ≈ bar m (del colegio) (SP)

Tuesday [ˈtjuːzdɪ] n martes m inv

tuft [tʌft] n mechón m; (of grass etc) manojo

tug [tʌg] n (ship) remolcador m ♦ vt tirar de; **~-of-war** n lucha de tiro de cuerda; (fig) tira y afloja m

tuition [tjuˈɪʃən] n (BRIT) enseñanza; (: private ~) clases fpl particulares; (US: school fees) matrícula

tulip [ˈtjuːlɪp] n tulipán m

tumble [ˈtʌmbl] n (fall) caída ♦ vi caer; **to ~ to sth** (inf) caer en la cuenta de algo; **~down** adj destartalado; **~ dryer** (BRIT) n secadora

tumbler [ˈtʌmblə*] n (glass) vaso

tummy [ˈtʌmɪ] n (inf) barriga, tripa

tumour [ˈtjuːmə*] (US tumor) n tumor m

tuna [ˈtjuːnə] n inv (also: ~ fish) atún m

tune [tjuːn] n melodía ♦ vt (MUS) afinar; (RADIO, TV, AUT) sintonizar; **to be in/out of ~** (instrument) estar afinado/desafinado; (singer) cantar afinadamente/desafinar; **to be in/out of ~ with** (fig) estar de acuerdo/en desacuerdo con; **~ in** vi: **to ~ in (to)** (RADIO, TV) sintonizar (con); **~ up** vi (musician) afinar (su instrumento); **~ful** adj melodioso; **~r** n: **piano ~r** afinador(a) m/f de pianos

tunic [ˈtjuːnɪk] n túnica

Tunisia [tjuˈnɪzɪə] n Túnez m

tunnel [ˈtʌnl] n túnel m; (in mine) galería ♦ vi construir un túnel/una galería

turban [ˈtəːbən] n turbante m

turbulent [ˈtəːbjulənt] adj turbulento

tureen [təˈriːn] n sopera

turf [təːf] n césped m; (clod) tepe m ♦ vt cubrir con césped; **~ out** (inf) vt echar a la calle

Turk [təːk] n turco/a

Turkey [ˈtəːkɪ] n Turquía

turkey ['tɜːkɪ] n pavo

Turkish ['tɜːkɪʃ] adj, n turco

turmoil ['tɜːmɔɪl] n: **in ~** revuelto

turn [tɜːn] n turno; (in road) curva; (of mind, events) rumbo; (THEATRE) número; (MED) ataque m ♦ vt girar, volver; (collar, steak) dar la vuelta a; (page) pasar; (change): **to ~ sth into** convertir algo en ♦ vi volver; (person: look back) volverse; (reverse direction) dar la vuelta; (milk) cortarse; (become): **to ~ nasty/forty** ponerse feo/cumplir los cuarenta; **a good ~** un favor; **it gave me quite a ~** me dio un susto; **"no left ~"** "prohibido girar a la izquierda"; **it's your ~** te toca a ti; **in ~** por turnos; **to take ~s (at)** turnarse (en); **~ away** vi apartar la vista ♦ vt rechazar; **~ back** vi volverse atrás ♦ vt hacer retroceder; (clock) retrasar; **~ down** vt (refuse) rechazar; (reduce) bajar; (fold) doblar; **~ in** vi (inf: go to bed) acostarse ♦ vt (fold) doblar hacia dentro; **~ off** vi (from road) desviarse ♦ vt (light, radio etc) apagar; (tap) cerrar; (engine) parar; **~ on** vt (light, radio etc) encender (SP), prender (AM); (tap) abrir; (engine) poner en marcha; **~ out** vt (light, gas) apagar; (produce) producir ♦ vi (voters) concurrir; **to ~ out to be** ... resultar ser ...; **~ over** vi (person) volverse ♦ vt (object) dar la vuelta a; (page) volver; **~ round** vi volverse; (rotate) girar; **~ up** vi (person) llegar, presentarse; (lost object) aparecer ♦ vt (gen) subir; **~ing** n (in road) vuelta; **~ing point** n (fig) momento decisivo

turnip ['tɜːnɪp] n nabo

turn-: **~out** n concurrencia; **~over** n (COMM: amount of money) volumen m de ventas; (: of goods) movimiento; **~pike** (US) n autopista de peaje; **~stile** n torniquete m; **~table** n plato; **~up** (BRIT) n (on trousers) vuelta

turpentine ['tɜːpəntaɪn] n (also: turps) trementina

turquoise ['tɜːkwɔɪz] n (stone) turquesa ♦ adj color turquesa

turret ['tʌrɪt] n torreón m

turtle ['tɜːtl] n galápago; **~neck (sweater)** n jersey m de cuello vuelto

tusk [tʌsk] n colmillo

tutor ['tjuːtə*] n profesor(a) m/f; **~ial** [-'tɔːrɪəl] n (SCOL) seminario

tuxedo [tʌk'siːdəu] (US) n smóking m, esmoquin m

TV [tiː'viː] n abbr (= television) tele f

twang [twæŋ] n (of instrument) punteado; (of voice) timbre m nasal

tweezers ['twiːzəz] npl pinzas fpl (de depilar)

twelfth [twelfθ] num duodécimo

twelve [twelv] num doce; **at ~ o'clock** (midday) a mediodía; (midnight) a medianoche

twentieth ['twentɪəθ] adj vigésimo

twenty ['twentɪ] num veinte

twice [twaɪs] adv dos veces; **~ as much** dos veces más

twiddle ['twɪdl] vt: **to ~ (with) sth** dar vueltas a algo; **to ~ one's thumbs** (fig) estar mano sobre mano

twig [twɪg] n ramita

twilight ['twaɪlaɪt] n crepúsculo

twin [twɪn] adj, n gemelo/a m/f ♦ vt hermanar; **~-bedded room** n habitación f doble

twine [twaɪn] n bramante m ♦ vi (plant) enroscarse

twinge [twɪndʒ] n (of pain) punzada; (of conscience) remordimiento

twinkle ['twɪŋkl] vi centellear; (eyes) brillar

twirl [twɜːl] vt dar vueltas a ♦ vi dar vueltas

twist [twɪst] n (action) torsión f; (in road, coil) vuelta; (in wire, flex) doblez f; (in story) giro ♦ vt torcer; (weave) trenzar; (roll around) enrollar; (fig) deformar ♦ vi serpentear

twit [twɪt] (inf) n tonto

twitch [twɪtʃ] n (pull) tirón m; (nervous) tic m ♦ vi crisparse

two [tu:] *num* dos; **to put ~ and ~ together** (*fig*) atar cabos; **~door** *adj* (*AUT*) de dos puertas; **~faced** (*pej: person*) falso; **~fold** *adv*: **to increase ~fold** doblarse; **~piece** (*suit*) *n* traje *m* de dos piezas; **~piece** (**swimsuit**) *n* dos piezas *m inv*, bikini *m*; **~some** *n* (*people*) pareja; **~way** *adj*: **~way traffic** circulación *f* de dos sentidos

tycoon [taɪ'ku:n] *n*: (**business**) **~** magnate *m*

type [taɪp] *n* (*category*) tipo, género; (*model*) tipo; (*TYP*) tipo, letra ♦ *vt* (*letter etc*) escribir a máquina; **~cast** *adj* (*actor*) encasillado; **~face** *n* letra; **~script** *n* texto mecanografiado; **~writer** *n* máquina de escribir; **~written** *adj* mecanografiado

typhoid ['taɪfɔɪd] *n* tifoidea

typical ['tɪpɪkl] *adj* típico

typing ['taɪpɪŋ] *n* mecanografía

typist ['taɪpɪst] *n* mecanógrafo/a

tyrant ['taɪərnt] *n* tirano/a

tyre ['taɪə*] (*US* **tire**) *n* neumático (*SP*), llanta (*AM*); **~ pressure** *n* presión *f* de los neumáticos

U, u

U-bend ['ju:'bend] *n* (*AUT, in pipe*) recodo

udder ['ʌdə*] *n* ubre *f*

UFO ['ju:fəu] *n abbr* = (*unidentified flying object*) OVNI *m*

ugh [ə:h] *excl* ¡uf!

ugly ['ʌglɪ] *adj* feo; (*dangerous*) peligroso

UHT *abbr*: **~ milk** leche *f* UHT, leche *f* uperizada

UK *n abbr* = **United Kingdom**

ulcer ['ʌlsə*] *n* úlcera; (*mouth ~*) llaga

Ulster ['ʌlstə*] *n* Ulster *m*

ulterior [ʌl'tɪərɪə*] *adj*: **~ motive** segundas intenciones *fpl*

ultimate ['ʌltɪmət] *adj* último, final;

(*greatest*) máximo; **~ly** *adv* (*in the end*) por último, al final; (*fundamentally*) a or en fin de cuentas

umbilical cord [ʌm'bɪlɪkl-] *n* cordón *m* umbilical

umbrella [ʌm'brelə] *n* paraguas *m inv*; (*for sun*) sombrilla

umpire ['ʌmpaɪə*] *n* árbitro

umpteen [ʌmp'ti:n] *adj* enésimos/as; **~th** *adj*: **for the ~th time** por enésima vez

UN *n abbr* (= United Nations) NN. UU.

unable [ʌn'eɪbl] *adj*: **to be ~ to do sth** no poder hacer algo

unaccompanied [ʌnə'kʌmpənɪd] *adj* no acompañado; (*song*) sin acompañamiento

unaccustomed [ʌnə'kʌstəmd] *adj*: **to be ~ to** no estar acostumbrado a

unanimous [ju:'nænɪməs] *adj* unánime

unarmed [ʌn'ɑ:md] *adj* (*defenceless*) inerme; (*without weapon*) desarmado

unattached [ʌnə'tætʃt] *adj* (*person*) soltero y sin compromiso; (*part etc*) suelto

unattended [ʌnə'tendɪd] *adj* desatendido

unattractive [ʌnə'træktɪv] *adj* poco atractivo

unauthorized [ʌn'ɔ:θəraɪzd] *adj* no autorizado

unavoidable [ʌnə'vɔɪdəbl] *adj* inevitable

unaware [ʌnə'weə*] *adj*: **to be ~ of** ignorar; **~s** *adv* de improviso

unbalanced [ʌn'bælənst] *adj* (*report*) poco objetivo; (*mentally*) trastornado

unbearable [ʌn'bɛərəbl] *adj* insoportable

unbeatable [ʌn'bi:təbl] *adj* (*team*) invencible; (*price*) inmejorable; (*quality*) insuperable

unbelievable [ʌnbɪ'li:vəbl] *adj* increíble

unbend [ʌn'bend] (*irreg*) *vi* (*relax*) relajarse ♦ *vt* (*wire*) enderezar

unbiased [ʌnˈbaɪəst] adj imparcial
unborn [ʌnˈbɔːn] adj que va a nacer
unbroken [ʌnˈbrəʊkən] adj (seal) intacto; (series) continuo; (record) no batido; (spirit) indómito
unbutton [ʌnˈbʌtn] vt desabrochar
uncalled-for [ʌnˈkɔːldfɔː*] adj gratuito, inmerecido
uncanny [ʌnˈkænɪ] adj extraño
unceremonious [ˈʌnserɪˈməʊnɪəs] adj (abrupt, rude) brusco, hosco
uncertain [ʌnˈsɜːtn] adj incierto; (indecisive) indeciso
unchanged [ʌnˈtʃeɪndʒd] adj igual, sin cambios
uncivilized [ʌnˈsɪvɪlaɪzd] adj inculto; (fig: behaviour etc) bárbaro; (hour) inoportuno
uncle [ˈʌŋkl] n tío
uncomfortable [ʌnˈkʌmfətəbl] adj incómodo; (uneasy) inquieto
uncommon [ʌnˈkɒmən] adj poco común, raro
uncompromising [ʌnˈkɒmprəmaɪzɪŋ] adj intransigente
unconcerned [ʌnkənˈsɜːnd] adj indiferente, despreocupado
unconditional [ʌnkənˈdɪʃənl] adj incondicional
unconscious [ʌnˈkɒnʃəs] adj sin sentido; (unaware): **to be ~ of** no darse cuenta de ♦ n: **the ~** el inconsciente
uncontrollable [ʌnkənˈtrəʊləbl] adj (child etc) incontrolable; (temper) indomable; (laughter) incontenible
unconventional [ʌnkənˈvenʃənl] adj poco convencional
uncouth [ʌnˈkuːθ] adj grosero, inculto
uncover [ʌnˈkʌvə*] vt descubrir; (take lid off) destapar
undecided [ʌndɪˈsaɪdɪd] adj (character) indeciso; (question) no resuelto
under [ˈʌndə*] prep debajo de; (less than) menos de; (according to) según, de acuerdo con; (sb's leadership) bajo

♦ adv debajo, abajo; **~ there** allí abajo; **~ repair** en reparación
under... [ˈʌndə*] prefix sub; **~age** sub: menor de edad; (drinking etc) de los menores de edad; **~carriage** (BRIT) n (AVIAT) tren m de aterrizaje; **~charge** vt cobrar menos de la cuenta; **~clothes** npl ropa interior (SP) or íntima (AM); **~coat** n (paint) primera mano; **~cover** adj clandestino; **~current** n (fig) corriente f oculta; **~cut** vt irreg vender más barato que; **~developed** adj subdesarrollado; **~done** adj (CULIN) poco hecho; **~estimate** vt subestimar; **~exposed** adj (PHOT) subexpuesto; **~fed** adj subalimentado; **~foot** adv con los pies; **~go** vt irreg sufrir; (treatment) recibir; **~graduate** n estudiante m/f; **~ground** n (BRIT: railway) metro; (POL) movimiento clandestino ♦ adj (car park) subterráneo ♦ adv (work) en la clandestinidad; **~growth** n maleza; **~hand(ed)** adj (fig) socarrón; **~lie** vt irreg (fig) ser la razón fundamental de; **~line** vt subrayar; **~mine** vt socavar, minar; **~neath** [ʌndəˈniːθ] adv abajo ♦ prep debajo de, bajo; **~paid** adj mal pagado; **~pants** npl calzoncillos mpl; **~pass** (BRIT) n paso subterráneo; **~privileged** adj desposeído; **~rate** vt menospreciar, subestimar; **~shirt** (US) n camiseta; **~shorts** (US) npl calzoncillos mpl; **~side** n parte f inferior; **~skirt** (BRIT) n enaguas fpl
understand [ʌndəˈstænd] (irreg) vt, vi entender, comprender; (assume) tener entendido; **~able** adj comprensible; **~ing** adj comprensivo ♦ n comprensión f, entendimiento; (agreement) acuerdo
understatement [ˈʌndəsteɪtmənt] n modestia (excesiva); **that's an ~!** ¡eso es decir poco!
understood [ʌndəˈstʊd] pt, pp of **understand** ♦ adj (agreed) acordado,

(*implied*): **it is ~ that** se sobreentiende que

understudy |ˈʌndəstʌdɪ| n suplente m/f

undertake |ʌndəˈteɪk| (*irreg*) vt emprender; **to ~ to do sth** comprometerse a hacer algo

undertaker |ˈʌndəteɪkə| n director(a) m/f de pompas fúnebres

undertaking |ˈʌndəteɪkɪŋ| n empresa; (*promise*) promesa

under-: **~tone** n: **in an ~tone** en voz baja; **~water** adv bajo el agua ♦ adj submarino; **~wear** n ropa interior (SP) or íntima (AM); **~world** n (of crime) hampa, inframundo; **~writer** n (INSURANCE) asegurador(a) m/f

undesirable |ʌndɪˈzaɪrəbl| adj (*person*) indeseable; (*thing*) poco aconsejable

undo |ʌnˈduː| (*irreg*) vt (*laces*) desatar; (*button etc*) desabrochar; (*spoil*) deshacer; **~ing** n ruina, perdición f

undoubted |ʌnˈdaʊtɪd| adj indudable

undress |ʌnˈdres| vi desnudarse

undulating |ˈʌndjʊleɪtɪŋ| adj ondulante

unduly |ʌnˈdjuːlɪ| adv excesivamente, demasiado

unearth |ʌnˈɜːθ| vt desenterrar

unearthly |ʌnˈɜːθlɪ| adj (*hour*) inverosímil

uneasy |ʌnˈiːzɪ| adj intranquilo, preocupado; (*feeling*) desagradable; (*peace*) inseguro

uneducated |ʌnˈedjʊkeɪtɪd| adj ignorante, inculto

unemployed |ʌnɪmˈplɔɪd| adj parado, sin trabajo ♦ npl: **the ~** los parados

unemployment |ʌnɪmˈplɔɪmənt| n paro, desempleo

unending |ʌnˈendɪŋ| adj interminable

unerring |ʌnˈɜːrɪŋ| adj infalible

uneven |ʌnˈiːvn| adj desigual; (*road etc*) lleno de baches

unexpected |ʌnɪkˈspektɪd| adj inesperado; **~ly** adv inesperadamente

unfailing |ʌnˈfeɪlɪŋ| adj (*support*)

indefectible; (*energy*) inagotable

unfair |ʌnˈfeə| adj: **~ (to sb)** injusto (con uno)

unfaithful |ʌnˈfeɪθfʊl| adj infiel

unfamiliar |ʌnfəˈmɪlɪə| adj extraño, desconocido; **to be ~ with** desconocer

unfashionable |ʌnˈfæʃnəbl| adj pasado or fuera de moda

unfasten |ʌnˈfɑːsn| vt (*knot*) desatar; (*dress*) desabrochar; (*open*) abrir

unfavourable |ʌnˈfeɪvərəbl| (US **unfavorable**) adj desfavorable

unfeeling |ʌnˈfiːlɪŋ| adj insensible

unfinished |ʌnˈfɪnɪʃt| adj inacabado, sin terminar

unfit |ʌnˈfɪt| adj bajo de forma; (*incompetent*): **~ (for)** incapaz (de); **~ for work** no apto para trabajar

unfold |ʌnˈfəʊld| vt desdoblar ♦ vi abrirse

unforeseen |ʌnfɔːˈsiːn| adj imprevisto

unforgettable |ʌnfəˈɡetəbl| adj inolvidable

unfortunate |ʌnˈfɔːtʃnət| adj desgraciado; (*event, remark*) inoportuno; **~ly** adv desgraciadamente

unfounded |ʌnˈfaʊndɪd| adj infundado

unfriendly |ʌnˈfrendlɪ| adj antipático; (*behaviour, remark*) hostil, poco amigable

ungainly |ʌnˈɡeɪnlɪ| adj desgarbado

ungodly |ʌnˈɡɒdlɪ| adj: **at an ~ hour** a una hora inverosímil

ungrateful |ʌnˈɡreɪtfʊl| adj ingrato

unhappiness |ʌnˈhæpɪnɪs| n tristeza, desdicha

unhappy |ʌnˈhæpɪ| adj (*sad*) triste; (*unfortunate*) desgraciado; (*childhood*) infeliz; **~ about/with** (*arrangements etc*) poco contento con, descontento de

unharmed |ʌnˈhɑːmd| adj ileso

unhealthy |ʌnˈhelθɪ| adj (*place*) malsano; (*person*) enfermizo; (*fig: interest*) morboso

unheard-of adj inaudito, sin precedente

unhurt [ʌn'həːt] adj ileso

unidentified [ʌnaɪ'dɛntɪfaɪd] adj no identificado, sin identificar; *see also* **UFO**

uniform ['juːnɪfɔːm] n uniforme m ♦ adj uniforme

unify ['juːnɪfaɪ] vt unificar, unir

uninhabited [ʌnɪn'hæbɪtɪd] adj desierto

unintentional [ʌnɪn'tɛnʃənəl] adj involuntario

union ['juːnjən] n unión f; (*also*: **trade** ~) sindicato ♦ cpd sindical; **U~ Jack** n bandera del Reino Unido

unique [juː'niːk] adj único

unison ['juːnɪsn] n: **in** ~ (*speak, reply, sing*) al unísono

unit ['juːnɪt] n unidad f; (*section: of furniture etc*) elemento; (*team*) grupo; **kitchen** ~ módulo de cocina

unite [juː'naɪt] vt unir ♦ vi unirse; **~d** adj unido; (*effort*) conjunto; **U~d Kingdom** n Reino Unido; **U~d Nations (Organization)** n Naciones fpl Unidas; **U~d States (of America)** n Estados mpl Unidos

unit trust (*BRIT*) n bono fiduciario

unity ['juːnɪtɪ] n unidad f

universe ['juːnɪvəːs] n universo

university [juːnɪ'vəːsɪtɪ] n universidad f

unjust [ʌn'dʒʌst] adj injusto

unkempt [ʌn'kɛmpt] adj (*appearance*) descuidado; (*hair*) despeinado

unkind [ʌn'kaɪnd] adj poco amable; (*behaviour, comment*) cruel

unknown [ʌn'nəʊn] adj desconocido

unlawful [ʌn'lɔːful] adj ilegal, ilícito

unleaded [ʌn'lɛdɪd] adj (*petrol, fuel*) sin plombo

unless [ʌn'lɛs] conj a menos que; ~ **he comes** a menos que venga; ~ **otherwise stated** salvo indicación contraria

unlike [ʌn'laɪk] adj (*not alike*) distinto

de o a; (*not like*) poco propio de ♦ prep a diferencia de

unlikely [ʌn'laɪklɪ] adj improbable; (*unexpected*) inverosímil

unlimited [ʌn'lɪmɪtɪd] adj ilimitado

unload [ʌn'ləʊd] vt descargar

unlock [ʌn'lɔk] vt abrir (con llave)

unlucky [ʌn'lʌkɪ] adj desgraciado; (*object, number*) que da mala suerte; **to be** ~ tener mala suerte

unmarried [ʌn'mærɪd] adj soltero

unmistak(e)able [ʌnmɪs'teɪkəbl] adj inconfundible

unnatural [ʌn'nætʃrəl] adj (*gen*) antinatural; (*manner*) afectado; (*habit*) perverso

unnecessary [ʌn'nɛsəsrɪ] adj innecesario, inútil

unnoticed [ʌn'nəʊtɪst] adj: **to go** o **pass** ~ pasar desapercibido

UNO ['juːnəʊ] n abbr (= United Nations Organization) ONU f

unobtainable [ʌnəb'teɪnəbl] adj inconseguible; (*TEL*) inexistente

unobtrusive [ʌnəb'truːsɪv] adj discreto

unofficial [ʌnə'fɪʃl] adj no oficial; (*news*) sin confirmar

unorthodox [ʌn'ɔːθədɔks] adj poco ortodoxo; (*REL*) heterodoxo

unpack [ʌn'pæk] vi deshacer las maletas ♦ vt deshacer

unpalatable [ʌn'pælatabl] adj incomible; (*truth*) desagradable

unparalleled [ʌn'pærəleld] adj (*unequalled*) incomparable

unpleasant [ʌn'plɛznt] adj (*disagreeable*) desagradable; (*person, manner*) antipático

unplug [ʌn'plʌg] vt desenchufar, desconectar

unpopular [ʌn'pɔpjulə*] adj impopular, poco popular

unprecedented [ʌn'prɛsɪdəntɪd] adj sin precedentes

unpredictable [ʌnprɪ'dɪktəbl] *adj* imprevisible

unprofessional [ʌnprə'feʃənl] *adj* (*attitude, conduct*) poco ético

unqualified [ʌn'kwɔlɪfaɪd] *adj* sin título, no cualificado; (*success*) total

unquestionably [ʌn'kwestʃənəblɪ] *adv* indiscutiblemente

unreal [ʌn'rɪəl] *adj* irreal; (*extraordinary*) increíble

unrealistic [ʌnrɪə'lɪstɪk] *adj* poco realista

unreasonable [ʌn'riːznəbl] *adj* irrazonable; (*demand*) excesivo

unrelated [ʌnrɪ'leɪtɪd] *adj* sin relación; (*family*) no emparentado

unreliable [ʌnrɪ'laɪəbl] *adj* (*person*) informal; (*machine*) poco fiable

unremitting [ʌnrɪ'mɪtɪŋ] *adj* constante

unreservedly [ʌnrɪ'zɜːvɪdlɪ] *adv* sin reserva

unrest [ʌn'rest] *n* inquietud *f*, malestar *m*; (POL) disturbios *mpl*

unroll [ʌn'rəul] *vt* desenrollar

unruly [ʌn'ruːlɪ] *adj* indisciplinado

unsafe [ʌn'seɪf] *adj* peligroso

unsaid [ʌn'sed] *adj*: **to leave sth ~** dejar algo sin decir

unsatisfactory ['ʌnsætɪs'fæktərɪ] *adj* poco satisfactorio

unsavoury [ʌn'seɪvərɪ] (*US* **unsavory**) *adj* (*fig*) repugnante

unscrew [ʌn'skruː] *vt* destornillar

unscrupulous [ʌn'skruːpjuləs] *adj* sin escrúpulos

unsettled [ʌn'setld] *adj* inquieto, intranquilo; (*weather*) variable

unshaven [ʌn'ʃeɪvn] *adj* sin afeitar

unsightly [ʌn'saɪtlɪ] *adj* feo

unskilled [ʌn'skɪld] *adj* (*work*) no especializado; (*worker*) no cualificado

unspeakable [ʌn'spiːkəbl] *adj* indecible; (*awful*) incalificable

unstable [ʌn'steɪbl] *adj* inestable

unsteady [ʌn'stedɪ] *adj* inestable

unstuck [ʌn'stʌk] *adj*: **to come ~**

despegarse; (*fig*) fracasar

unsuccessful [ʌnsək'sesful] *adj* (*attempt*) infructuoso; (*writer, proposal*) sin éxito; **to be ~** (*in attempting sth*) no tener éxito, fracasar; **~ly** *adv* en vano, sin éxito

unsuitable [ʌn'suːtəbl] *adj* inapropiado; (*time*) inoportuno

unsure [ʌn'ʃuə*] *adj* inseguro, poco seguro

unsuspecting [ʌnsəs'pektɪŋ] *adj* desprevenido

unsympathetic [ʌnsɪmpə'θetɪk] *adj* poco comprensivo; (*unlikeable*) antipático

unthinkable [ʌn'θɪŋkəbl] *adj* inconcebible, impensable

untidy [ʌn'taɪdɪ] *adj* (*room*) desordenado; (*appearance*) desaliñado

untie [ʌn'taɪ] *vt* desatar

until [ʌn'tɪl] *prep* hasta ♦ *conj* hasta que; **~ he comes** hasta que venga; **~ now** hasta ahora; **~ then** hasta entonces

untimely [ʌn'taɪmlɪ] *adj* inoportuno; (*death*) prematuro

untold [ʌn'təuld] *adj* (*story*) nunca contado; (*suffering*) indecible; (*wealth*) incalculable

untoward [ʌntə'wɔːd] *adj* adverso

unused [ʌn'juːzd] *adj* sin usar

unusual [ʌn'juːʒuəl] *adj* insólito, poco común; (*exceptional*) inusitado

unveil [ʌn'veɪl] *vt* (*statue*) descubrir

unwanted [ʌn'wɔntɪd] *adj* (*clothing*) viejo; (*pregnancy*) no deseado

unwelcome [ʌn'welkəm] *adj* inoportuno; (*news*) desagradable

unwell [ʌn'wel] *adj*: **to be/feel ~** estar indispuesto/sentirse mal

unwieldy [ʌn'wiːldɪ] *adj* difícil de manejar

unwilling [ʌn'wɪlɪŋ] *adj*: **to be ~ to do sth** estar poco dispuesto a hacer algo; **~ly** *adv* de mala gana

unwind [ʌn'waɪnd] (*irreg: like* **wind²**) *vt* desenvolver ♦ *vi* (*relax*) relajarse

unwise [ʌn'waɪz] *adj* imprudente

unwitting [ʌn'wɪtɪŋ] *adj* inconsciente

unworthy [ʌn'wɜːðɪ] *adj* indigno

unwrap [ʌn'ræp] *vt* desenvolver

unwritten [ʌn'rɪtn] *adj* (*agreement*) tácito; (*rules*, *law*) no escrito

---

KEYWORD

---

up [ʌp] *prep*: **to go/be ~ sth** subir/ estar subido en algo; **he went ~ the stairs/the hill** subió las escaleras/la colina; **we walked/climbed ~ the hill** subimos la colina; **they live further ~ the street** viven más arriba en la calle; **go ~ that road and turn left** sigue por esa calle y gira a la izquierda

♦ *adv* 1 (*upwards*, *higher*) más arriba; **~ in the mountains** en lo alto (de la montaña); **put it a bit higher ~** ponlo un poco más arriba o alto; **~ there** ahí o allí arriba; **~ above** en lo alto, por encima, arriba

2: **to be ~** (*out of bed*) estar levantado; (*prices*, *level*) haber subido

3: **~ to** (*as far as*) hasta; **~ to now** hasta ahora o a la fecha

4: **to be ~ to** (*depending on*): **it's ~ to you** depende de ti; **he's not ~ to it** (*job*, *task etc*) no es capaz de hacerlo; **his work is not ~ to the required standard** su trabajo no da la talla; (*inf: be doing*): **what is he ~ to?** ¿que estará tramando?

♦ *n*: **~s and downs** altibajos *mpl*

upbringing [ʌp'brɪŋɪŋ] *n* educación *f*

update [ʌp'deɪt] *vt* poner al día

upgrade [ʌp'greɪd] *vt* (*house*) modernizar; (*employee*) ascender

upheaval [ʌp'hiːvl] *n* trastornos *mpl*; (*POL*) agitación *f*

uphill [ʌp'hɪl] *adj* cuesta arriba; (*fig: task*) penoso, difícil ♦ *adv*: **to go ~** ir cuesta arriba

uphold [ʌp'həʊld] (*irreg*) *vt* defender

upholstery [ʌp'həʊlstərɪ] *n* tapicería

upkeep [ʌp'kiːp] *n* mantenimiento

upon [ə'pɒn] *prep* sobre

upper ['ʌpə*] *adj* superior, de arriba ♦ *n* (*of shoe: also*: **~s**) empeine *m*; **~ class** *adj* de clase alta; **~ hand** *n*: **to have the ~ hand** tener la sartén por el mango; **~most** *adj* el más alto; **what was ~most in my mind** lo que me preocupaba más

upright ['ʌpraɪt] *adj* derecho; (*vertical*) vertical; (*fig*) honrado

uprising ['ʌpraɪzɪŋ] *n* sublevación *f*

uproar ['ʌprɔː*] *n* escándalo

uproot [ʌp'ruːt] *vt* (*also fig*) desarraigar

upset [*n* 'ʌpset, *vb*, *adj* ʌp'set] *n* (*to plan etc*) revés *m*, contratiempo; (*MED*) trastorno ♦ (*irreg*) *vt* (*glass etc*) volcar; (*plan*) alterar; (*person*) molestar, disgustar ♦ *adj* molesto, disgustado; (*stomach*) revuelto

upshot ['ʌpʃɒt] *n* resultado

upside-down *adv* al revés; **to turn a place ~** (*fig*) revolverlo todo

upstairs [ʌp'steəz] *adv* arriba ♦ *adj* (*room*) de arriba ♦ *n* el piso superior

upstart ['ʌpstɑːt] *n* advenedizo/a

upstream [ʌp'striːm] *adv* río arriba

uptake ['ʌpteɪk] *n*: **to be quick/slow on the ~** ser muy listo/torpe

uptight [ʌp'taɪt] *adj* tenso, nervioso

up-to-date *adj* al día

upturn ['ʌptɜːn] *n* (*in luck*) mejora; (*COMM: in market*) resurgimiento económico

upward ['ʌpwəd] *adj* ascendente; **~(s)** *adv* hacia arriba; (*more than*): **~(s) of** más de

urban ['ɜːbən] *adj* urbano

urchin ['ɜːtʃɪn] *n* pilluelo, golfillo

urge [ɜːdʒ] *n* (*desire*) deseo ♦ *vt*: **to ~ sb to do sth** animar a uno a hacer algo

urgent ['ɜːdʒənt] *adj* urgente; (*voice*) perentorio

urinate ['jʊərɪneɪt] *vi* orinar

urine ['jʊərɪn] *n* orina, orines *mpl*

urn [ɜːn] *n* urna; (*also: tea ~*) cacharro

metálico grande para hacer té

Uruguay ['juərəgwaɪ] n (el) Uruguay; **~an** [-'gwaɪən] adj, n uruguayo/a m/f

US n abbr (= United States) EE. UU.

us [ʌs] pron nos; (after prep) nosotros/as; see also **me**

USA n abbr (= United States of America) EE. UU.

usage ['ju:zɪdʒ] n (LING) uso

use [n ju:s, vb ju:z] n uso, empleo; (usefulness) utilidad f ♦ vt usar, emplear; **she ~d to do it** (ella) solía or acostumbraba hacerlo; **in ~** en uso; **out of ~** en desuso; **to be of ~** servir; **it's no ~** (pointless) es inútil; (not useful) no sirve; **to be ~d to** estar acostumbrado a, acostumbrar; **~ up** vt (food) consumir; (money) gastar; **~d** adj (car) usado; **~ful** adj útil; **~fulness** n utilidad f; **~less** adj (unusable) inservible; (pointless) inútil; (person) inepto; **~r** n usuario/a; **~r-friendly** adj (computer) amistoso

usher ['ʌʃə*] n (at wedding) ujier m; **~ette** [-'rɛt] n (in cinema) acomodadora

USSR n (HIST): **the ~** la URSS

usual ['ju:ʒuəl] adj normal, corriente; **as ~** como de costumbre; **~ly** adv normalmente

utensil [ju:'tɛnsl] n utensilio; **kitchen ~s** batería de cocina

uterus ['ju:tərəs] n útero

utility [ju:'tɪlɪtɪ] n utilidad f; (public ~) (empresa de) servicio público; **~ room** n ofis m

utilize ['ju:tɪlaɪz] vt utilizar

utmost ['ʌtməust] adj mayor ♦ n: **to do one's ~** hacer todo lo posible

utter ['ʌtə*] adj total, completo ♦ vt pronunciar, proferir; **~ly** adv completamente, totalmente

U-turn ['ju:'tɜ:n] n viraje m en redondo

V, v

v. abbr = **verse**; **versus**; (= volt) v; (= vide) véase

vacancy ['veɪkənsɪ] n (BRIT: job) vacante f; (room) habitación f libre; **"no vacancies"** "completo"

vacant ['veɪkənt] adj desocupado, libre; (expression) distraído

vacate [və'keɪt] vt (house, room) desocupar; (job) dejar (vacante)

vacation [və'keɪʃən] n vacaciones fpl

vaccinate ['væksɪneɪt] vt vacunar

vaccine ['væksi:n] n vacuna

vacuum ['vækjum] n vacío; **~ cleaner** n aspiradora; **~flask** (BRIT) n termo; **~-packed** adj empaquetado al vacío

vagina [və'dʒaɪnə] n vagina

vagrant ['veɪgrnt] n vagabundo/a

vague [veɪg] adj vago; (memory) borroso; (ambiguous) impreciso; (person: absent-minded) distraído; (: evasive): **to be ~** no decir las cosas claramente; **~ly** adv vagamente; distraídamente; con evasivas

vain [veɪn] adj (conceited) presumido; (useless) vano, inútil; **in ~** en vano

valentine ['væləntaɪn] n (also: ~ card) tarjeta del Día de los Enamorados

valet ['væleɪ] n ayuda m de cámara

valid ['vælɪd] adj válido; (ticket) valedero; (law) vigente

valley ['vælɪ] n valle m

valuable ['væljuəbl] adj (jewel) de valor; (time) valioso; **~s** npl objetos mpl de valor

valuation [vælju'eɪʃən] n tasación f, valuación f; (judgement of quality) valoración f

value ['vælju:] n valor m; (importance) importancia ♦ vt (fix price of) tasar, valorar; (esteem) apreciar; **~s** npl (principles) principios mpl; **~ added tax** (BRIT) n impuesto sobre el valor añadido; **~d** adj (appreciated) apreciado

valve [vælv] n válvula

van [væn] n (AUT) furgoneta (SP), camioneta (AM)

vandal ['vændl] n vándalo/a; **~ism** n vandalismo; **~ize** vt dañar, destruir

vanilla [və'nɪlə] n vainilla f

vanish ['vænɪʃ] vi desaparecer

vanity ['vænɪtɪ] n vanidad f

vantage point ['vɑːntɪdʒ-] n (for views) punto panorámico

vapour ['veɪpə*] (US **vapor**) n vapor m; (on breath, window) vaho m

variable ['veərɪəbl] adj variable

variation [veərɪ'eɪʃən] n variación f

varicose ['værɪkəʊs] adj: **~ veins** varices fpl

varied ['veərɪd] adj variado

variety [və'raɪətɪ] n (diversity) diversidad f; (type) variedad f; **~ show** n espectáculo de variedades

various ['veərɪəs] adj (several: people) varios/as; (reasons) diversos/as

varnish ['vɑːnɪʃ] n barniz m; (nail ~) esmalte m ♦ vt barnizar; (nails) pintar (con esmalte)

vary ['veərɪ] vt variar; (change) cambiar ♦ vi variar

vase [vɑːz] n florero

Vaseline ® ['væsɪliːn] n vaselina ®

vast [vɑːst] adj enorme

VAT [væt] (BRIT) n abbr (= value added tax) IVA m

vat [væt] n tina, tinaja

Vatican ['vætɪkən] n: **the ~** el Vaticano

vault [vɔːlt] n (of roof) bóveda; (tomb) panteón m; (in bank) cámara acorazada ♦ vt (also: ~ over) saltar (por encima de)

vaunted ['vɔːntɪd] adj: **much ~** cacareado, alardeado

VCR n abbr = **video cassette recorder**

VD n abbr = **venereal disease**

VDU n abbr (= visual display unit) UPV f

veal [viːl] n ternera

veer [vɪə*] vi (vehicle) virar; (wind) girar

vegan ['viːgæn] n vegetariano/a estricto/a, vegetaliano/a

vegeburger ['vedʒɪbɜːgə*] n hamburguesa vegetal

vegetable ['vedʒtəbl] n (BOT) vegetal m; (edible plant) legumbre f, hortaliza ♦ adj vegetal; **~s** npl (cooked) verduras fpl

vegetarian [vedʒɪ'teərɪən] adj, n vegetariano/a m/f

vehement ['viːmənt] adj vehemente, apasionado

vehicle ['viːɪkl] n vehículo; (fig) medio

veil [veɪl] n velo ♦ vt velar; **~ed** adj (fig) velado

vein [veɪn] n vena; (of ore etc) veta

velocity [vɪ'lɒsɪtɪ] n velocidad f

velvet ['velvɪt] n terciopelo

vending machine ['vendɪŋ-] n distribuidor m automático

veneer [və'nɪə*] n chapa, enchapado; (fig) barniz m

venereal disease [vɪ'nɪərɪəl-] n enfermedad f venérea

Venetian blind [vɪ'niːʃən-] n persiana

Venezuela [venɪ'zweɪlə] n Venezuela; **~n** adj, n venezolano/a m/f

vengeance ['vendʒəns] n venganza; **with a ~** (fig) con creces

venison ['venɪsn] n carne f de venado

venom ['venəm] n (bitterness) odio; **~ous** adj venenoso, lleno de odio

vent [vent] n (in jacket) respiradero; (in wall) rejilla (de ventilación) ♦ vt (fig: feelings) desahogar

ventilator ['ventɪleɪtə*] n ventilador m

venture ['ventʃə*] n empresa ♦ vt (opinion) ofrecer ♦ vi arriesgarse, lanzarse; **business ~** empresa comercial

venue ['venjuː] n lugar m

veranda(h) [və'rændə] n terraza

verb [vɜːb] n verbo; **~al** adj verbal

verbatim [vɜː'beɪtɪm] adj, adv palabra por palabra

verdict   595   vindicate

verdict ['vɜːdɪkt] *n* veredicto, fallo; *(fig)* opinión *f*, juicio

verge [vɜːdʒ] *(BRIT)* borde *m*; "**soft ~s**" *(AUT)* "arcén *m* no asfaltado"; **to be on the ~ of doing sth** estar a punto de hacer algo; **~ on** *vt fus* rayar en

verify ['vɛrɪfaɪ] *vt* comprobar, verificar

vermin ['vɜːmɪn] *npl (animals)* alimañas *fpl; (insects, fig)* parásitos *mpl*

vermouth ['vɜːməθ] *n* vermut *m*

versatile ['vɜːsətaɪl] *adj (person)* polifacético; *(machine, tool etc)* versátil

verse [vɜːs] *n* poesía; *(stanza)* estrofa; *(in bible)* versículo

version ['vɜːʃən] *n* versión *f*

versus ['vɜːsəs] *prep* contra

vertebra ['vɜːtɪbrə] *(pl ~e)* *n* vértebra

vertical ['vɜːtɪkl] *adj* vertical

verve [vɜːv] *n* brío

very ['vɛrɪ] *adv* muy ♦ *adj:* **the ~ book which** el mismo libro que; **the ~ last** el último de todos; **at the ~ least** al menos; **~ much** muchísimo

vessel ['vɛsl] *n (ship)* barco; *(container)* vasija; *see* **blood**

vest [vɛst] *n (BRIT)* camiseta; *(US: waistcoat)* chaleco; **~ed interests** *npl (COMM)* intereses *mpl* creados

vet [vɛt] *n (candidate)* investigar ♦ *n abbr (BRIT)* = **veterinary surgeon**

veteran ['vɛtərn] *n* veterano

veterinary surgeon *n (BRIT)* (US **veterinarian**) *n* veterinario/a *m/f*

veto ['viːtəu] *(pl ~es)* *n* veto ♦ *vt* prohibir, poner el veto a

vex [vɛks] *vt* fastidiar; **~ed** *adj (question)* controvertido

VHF *abbr* (= *very high frequency*) muy alta frecuencia

via ['vaɪə] *prep* por, por medio de

vibrant ['vaɪbrənt] *adj (lively)* animado; *(bright)* vivo; *(voice)* vibrante

vibrate [vaɪ'breɪt] *vi* vibrar

vicar ['vɪkə*] *n* párroco (de la Iglesia Anglicana); **~age** *n* parroquia

vice [vaɪs] *n (evil)* vicio; *(TECH)* torno de

banco

vice- [vaɪs] *prefix* vice-; **~-chairman** *n* vicepresidente *m*

vice squad *n* brigada antivicio

vice versa ['vaɪsɪ'vɜːsə] *adv* viceversa

vicinity [vɪ'sɪnɪtɪ] *n:* **in the ~ (of)** cercano (a)

vicious ['vɪʃəs] *adj (attack)* violento; *(words)* cruel; *(horse, dog)* resabiado; **~ circle** *n* círculo vicioso

victim ['vɪktɪm] *n* víctima

victor ['vɪktə*] *n* vencedor(a) *m/f*

victory ['vɪktərɪ] *n* victoria

video ['vɪdɪəu] *cpd* vídeo ♦ *n (~ film)* videofilm *m; (also: ~ cassette)* videocassette *f; (also: ~ cassette recorder)* magnetoscopio; **~ game** *n* videojuego; **~ tape** *n* cinta de vídeo

vie [vaɪ] *vi:* **to ~ (with sb for sth)** competir (con uno por algo)

Vienna [vɪ'ɛnə] *n* Viena

Vietnam [vjɛt'næm] *n* Vietnam *m; ~ese* [-nə'miːz] *n inv, adj* vietnamita *m/f*

view [vjuː] *n* vista; *(outlook)* perspectiva; *(opinion)* opinión *f*, criterio ♦ *vt (look at)* mirar; *(fig)* considerar; **on ~** *(in museum etc)* expuesto; **in full ~ (of)** en plena vista de; **in ~ of the weather/the fact that** en vista del tiempo/del hecho de que; **in my ~** en mi opinión; **~er** *n* espectador(a) *m/f; (TV)* telespectador(a) *m/f; ~finder* *n* visor *m* de imagen; **~point** *n (attitude)* punto de vista; *(place)* mirador *m*

vigour ['vɪgə*] *(US* **vigor**) *n* energía, vigor *m*

vile [vaɪl] *adj* vil, infame; *(smell)* asqueroso; *(temper)* endemoniado

villa ['vɪlə] *n (country house)* casa de campo; *(suburban house)* chalet *m*

village ['vɪlɪdʒ] *n* aldea; **~r** *n* aldeano/a *m/f*

villain ['vɪlən] *n (scoundrel)* malvado/a; *(in novel)* malo; *(BRIT: criminal)* maleante *m*

vindicate ['vɪndɪkeɪt] *vt* vindicar, justificar

vindictive [vɪn'dɪktɪv] adj vengativo

vine [vaɪn] n vid f

vinegar ['vɪnɪgə*] n vinagre m

vineyard ['vɪnjɑːd] n viña, viñedo

vintage ['vɪntɪdʒ] n (year) vendimia, cosecha ♦ cpd de época; **~ wine** n vino añejo

vinyl ['vaɪnl] n vinilo

viola [vɪ'əʊlə] n (MUS) viola

violate ['vaɪəleɪt] vt violar

violence ['vaɪələns] n violencia

violent ['vaɪələnt] adj violento; (intense) intenso

violet ['vaɪələt] adj violado, violeta ♦ n (plant) violeta f

violin [vaɪə'lɪn] n violín m; **~ist** n violinista m/f

VIP n abbr (= very important person) VIP m

virgin ['vɜːdʒɪn] n virgen f

Virgo ['vɜːgəʊ] n Virgo

virtually ['vɜːtjuəlɪ] adv prácticamente

virtual reality ['vɜːtjuəl-] n (COMPUT) mundo or realidad f virtual

virtue ['vɜːtjuː] n virtud f; (advantage) ventaja; **by ~ of** en virtud de

virtuous ['vɜːtjuəs] adj virtuoso

virus ['vaɪərəs] n (also: COMPUT) virus m

visa ['viːzə] n visado (SP), visa (AM)

visible ['vɪzəbl] adj visible

vision ['vɪʒən] n (sight) vista; (foresight, in dream) visión f

visit ['vɪzɪt] n visita ♦ vt (person: US: also: ~ with) visitar, hacer una visita a; (place) ir a, ir a conocer; **~ing hours** npl (in hospital etc) horas fpl de visita; **~or** n (in museum) visitante m/f; (invited to house) visita; (tourist) turista m/f

visor ['vaɪzə*] n visera

visual ['vɪzjuəl] adj visual; **~ aid** n medio visual; **~ display unit** n unidad f de presentación visual; **~ize** vt imaginar

vital ['vaɪtl] adj (essential) esencial, imprescindible; (dynamic) dinámico; (organ) vital; **~ly** adv: **~ly important**

de primera importancia; **~ statistics** npl (fig) medidas fpl vitales

vitamin ['vɪtəmɪn] n vitamina

vivacious [vɪ'veɪʃəs] adj vivaz, alegre

vivid ['vɪvɪd] adj (account) gráfico; (light) intenso; (imagination, memory) vivo; **~ly** adv gráficamente; (remember) como si fuera hoy

V-neck ['viːnɛk] n cuello de pico

vocabulary [vəu'kæbjuləri] n vocabulario

vocal ['vəukl] adj vocal; (articulate) elocuente; **~ cords** npl cuerdas fpl vocales

vocation [vəu'keɪʃən] n vocación f; **~al** adj profesional

vodka ['vɔdkə] n vodka m

vogue [vəug] n: **in ~** en boga

voice [vɔɪs] n voz f ♦ vt expresar; **~ mail** n fonobuzón m

void [vɔɪd] n vacío; (hole) hueco ♦ adj (invalid) nulo, inválido; (empty): **~ of** carente or desprovisto de

volatile ['vɔlətaɪl] adj (situation) inestable; (person) voluble; (liquid) volátil

volcano [vɔl'keɪnəu] (pl **~es**) n volcán m

volition [və'lɪʃən] n: **of one's own ~** de su propia voluntad

volley ['vɔlɪ] n (of gunfire) descarga; (of stones etc) lluvia; (fig) torrente m; (TENNIS etc) volea; **~ball** n vo(l)eibol m

volt [vəult] n voltio; **~age** n voltaje m

volume ['vɔljuːm] n (gen) volumen m; (book) tomo

voluntary ['vɔləntərɪ] adj voluntario

volunteer [vɔlən'tɪə*] n voluntario/a ♦ vt (information) ofrecer ♦ vi ofrecerse (de voluntario); **to ~ to do** ofrecerse a hacer

vomit ['vɔmɪt] n vómito ♦ vt, vi vomitar

vote [vəut] n voto; (votes cast) votación f; (right to ~) derecho de votar; (franchise) sufragio ♦ vt (chairman) elegir; (propose): **to ~ that** proponer

que ♦ *vi* votar, ir a votar; **~ of thanks**
voto de gracias; **~r** *n* votante *m/f*;
voting *n* votación *f*

vouch [vautʃ]: **to ~ for** *vt fus*
garantizar, responder de

voucher ['vautʃə*] *n* (for meal, petrol)
vale *m*

vow [vau] *n* voto ♦ *vt*: **to ~ to do/
that** jurar hacer/que

vowel ['vauəl] *n* vocal *f*

voyage ['vɔɪdʒ] *n* viaje *m*

vulgar ['vʌlɡə*] *adj* (rude) ordinario,
grosero; (in bad taste) de mal gusto;
~ity [-'ɡærɪt] *n* grosería; mal gusto

vulnerable ['vʌlnərəbl] *adj* vulnerable

vulture ['vʌltʃə*] *n* buitre *m*

W, w

wad [wɔd] *n* bolita; (of banknotes etc) *n*
fajo

waddle ['wɔdl] *vi* anadear

wade [weid] *vi*: **to ~ through** (water)
vadear; (fig: book) leer con dificultad;
wading pool (US) *n* piscina para niños

wafer ['weifə*] *n* galleta, barquillo

waffle ['wɔfl] *n* (CULIN) gofre *m* ♦ *vi*
dar el rollo

waft [wɔft] *vt* llevar por el aire ♦ *vi*
flotar

wag [wæɡ] *vt* menear, agitar ♦ *vi*
moverse, menearse

wage [weidʒ] *n* (also: **~s**) sueldo,
salario ♦ *vt*: **to ~ war** hacer la guerra;
~ earner *n* asalariado/a; **~ packet** *n*
sobre *m* de paga

wager ['weidʒə*] *n* apuesta

wag(g)on ['wæɡən] *n* (horse-drawn)
carro; (BRIT: RAIL) vagón *m*

wail [weil] *n* gemido ♦ *vi* gemir

waist [weist] *n* cintura, talle *m*; **~coat**
(BRIT) *n* chaleco; **~line** *n* talle *m*

wait [weit] *n* (interval) pausa ♦ *vi*
esperar; **to lie in ~** acechar a; **I
can't ~ to** (fig) estoy deseando; **to
~ for** esperar (a); **~ behind** *vi*

quedarse; **~ on** *vt fus* servir a; **~er** *n*
camarero; **~ing** *n*: **"no ~ing"** (BRIT:
AUT) "prohibido estacionarse"; **~ing
list** *n* lista de espera; **~ing room** *n*
sala de espera; **~ress** *n* camarera

waive [weiv] *vt* suspender

wake [weik] (pt **woke** or **waked**, pp
woken or **waked**) *vt* (also: **~ up**)
despertar ♦ *vi* (also: **~ up**) despertarse
♦ *n* (for dead person) vela, velatorio;
(NAUT) estela; **waken** *vt*, *vi* = **wake**

Wales [weilz] *n* País *m* de Gales; **the
Prince of ~** el príncipe de Gales

walk [wɔːk] *n* (stroll) paseo; (hike)
excursión *f* a pie, caminata; (gait) paso,
andar *m*; (in park etc) paseo, alameda
♦ *vi* andar, caminar; (for pleasure,
exercise) pasear ♦ *vt* (distance) recorrer
a pie, andar; (dog) pasear; **10
minutes' ~ from here** a 10 minutos
de aquí andando; **people from all ~s
of life** gente de todas las esferas;
~ out *vi* (audience) salir; (workers)
declararse en huelga; **~ out on** (inf) *vt
fus* abandonar; **~er** *n* (person) paseante
m/f, caminante *m/f*; **~ie-talkie**
['wɔːkɪ'tɔːkɪ] *n* walkie-talkie *m*; **~ing** *n*
el andar; **~ing shoes** *npl* zapatos *mpl*
para andar; **~ing stick** *n* bastón *m*;
W~man ® ['wɔːkmən] *n* Walkman ®
m; **~out** *n* huelga; **~over** (inf) *n*: **it
was a ~over** fue pan comido; **~way**
n paseo

wall [wɔːl] *n* pared *f*; (exterior) muro;
(city ~ etc) muralla; **~ed** *adj*
amurallado; (garden) con tapia

wallet ['wɔlɪt] *n* cartera (SP), billetera
(AM)

wallflower ['wɔːlflauə*] *n* alhelí *m*; **to
be a ~** (fig) comer pavo

wallow ['wɔləu] *vi* revolcarse

wallpaper ['wɔːlpeipə*] *n* papel *m*
pintado ♦ *vt* empapelar

walnut ['wɔːlnʌt] *n* nuez *f*; (tree) nogal
m

walrus ['wɔːlrəs] (pl **~** or **~es**) *n* morsa

waltz [wɔːlts] *n* vals *m* ♦ *vi* bailar el

vals

wand |wɒnd| n (also: magic ~) varita (mágica)

wander |ˈwɒndə*| vi (person) vagar; deambular; (thoughts) divagar ♦ vt recorrer, vagar por

wane |weɪn| vi menguar

wangle |ˈwæŋgl| (BRIT: inf) vt agenciarse

want |wɒnt| vt querer, desear; (need) necesitar ♦ n: for ~ of por falta de; ~s npl (needs) necesidades fpl; to ~ to do querer hacer; to ~ sb to do sth querer que uno haga algo; ~ed adj (criminal) buscado; "~ed" (in advertisements) "se busca"; ~ing adj: to be found ~ing no estar a la altura de las circunstancias

war |wɔː*| n guerra; to make ~ (on) (also fig) declarar la guerra (a)

ward |wɔːd| n (in hospital) sala; n (POL) distrito electoral; (LAW: child: also: ~ of court) pupilo/a; ~ off vt (blow) desviar, parar; (attack) rechazar

warden |ˈwɔːdn| n (BRIT: of institution) director(a) m/f; (of park, game reserve) guardián/ana m/f; (BRIT: also: traffic ~) guardia m/f

warder |ˈwɔːdə*| (BRIT) n guardián/ana m/f, carcelero/a

wardrobe |ˈwɔːdrəʊb| n armario, guardarropa, ropero (esp AM)

warehouse |ˈwɛəhaʊs| n almacén m, depósito

wares |wɛəz| npl mercancías fpl

warfare |ˈwɔːfɛə*| n guerra

warhead |ˈwɔːhed| n cabeza armada

warily |ˈwɛərɪlɪ| adv con cautela, cautelosamente

warm |wɔːm| adj caliente; (thanks) efusivo; (clothes etc) abrigado; (welcome, day) caluroso; it's ~ hace calor; I'm ~ tengo calor; ~ up vi (room) calentarse; (person) entrar en calor; (athlete) hacer ejercicios de calentamiento ♦ vt calentar; ~-hearted adj afectuoso; ~ly adv

afectuosamente; ~th n calor m

warn |wɔːn| vt avisar, advertir; ~ing n aviso, advertencia; ~ing light n luz f de advertencia; ~ing triangle n (AUT) triángulo señalizador

warp |wɔːp| vi (wood) combarse ♦ vt combar; (mind) pervertir

warrant |ˈwɒrənt| n autorización f; (LAW: to arrest) orden f de detención; (: to search) mandamiento de registro

warranty |ˈwɒrəntɪ| n garantía

warren |ˈwɒrən| n (of rabbits) madriguera; (fig) laberinto

warrior |ˈwɒrɪə*| n guerrero/a

Warsaw |ˈwɔːsɔː| n Varsovia

warship |ˈwɔːʃɪp| n buque m o barco de guerra

wart |wɔːt| n verruga

wartime |ˈwɔːtaɪm| n: in ~ en tiempos de guerra, en la guerra

wary |ˈwɛərɪ| adj cauteloso

was |wɒz| pt of be

wash |wɒʃ| vt lavar ♦ vi lavarse; (sea etc): to ~ against/over sth llegar hasta/cubrir algo ♦ n (clothes etc) lavado; (of ship) estela; to have a ~ lavarse; ~ away vt (stain) quitar lavando; (subj: river etc) llevarse; ~ off vi quitarse al lavar); ~ up vi (BRIT) fregar los platos; (US) lavarse; ~able adj lavable; ~basin (US ~bowl) n lavabo; ~ cloth (US) n manopla; ~er n (TECH) arandela; ~ing n (dirty) ropa sucia; (clean) colada; ~ing machine n lavadora; ~ing powder (BRIT) n detergente m (en polvo)

Washington |ˈwɒʃɪŋtən| n Washington m

wash: ~ing-up (BRIT) n fregado, platos mpl (para fregar); ~ing-up liquid (BRIT) n líquido lavavajillas; ~-out (inf) n fracaso; ~room (US) n servicios mpl

wasn't |ˈwɒznt| = was not

wasp |wɒsp| n avispa

wastage |ˈweɪstɪdʒ| n desgaste m; (loss) pérdida

waste |weɪst| n derroche m,

despilfarro; (of time) pérdida; (food)
sobras fpl; (rubbish) basura,
desperdicios mpl ♦ adj (material) de
desecho; (left over) sobrante; (land)
baldío, descampado ♦ vt malgastar,
derrochar; (time) perder; (opportunity)
desperdiciar; ~s npl (area of land)
tierras fpl baldías; ~ **away** vi
consumirse; **~ disposal unit** (BRIT) n
triturador m de basura; **~ful** adj
derrochador(a); (process)
antieconómico; **~ ground** (BRIT) n
terreno baldío; **~paper basket** n
papelera; **~ pipe** n tubo de desagüe

watch [wɔtʃ] n (also: wrist~) reloj m;
(MIL: group of guards) centinela m; (act)
vigilancia; (NAUT: spell of duty) guardia
♦ vt (look at) mirar, observar; (: match,
programme) ver; (spy on, guard) vigilar;
(be careful of) cuidarse de, tener
cuidado de ♦ vi ver, mirar; (keep guard)
montar guardia; **~ out** vi cuidarse,
tener cuidado; **~dog** n perro guardián;
(fig) persona u organismo encargado de
asegurarse de que las empresas actúan
dentro de la legalidad); **~ful** adj
vigilante, sobre aviso; **~maker** n
relojero/a; **~man** (irreg) n see **night**;
~ strap n pulsera (de reloj)

water ['wɔːtə*] n agua ♦ vt (plant)
regar ♦ vi (eyes) llorar; (mouth) hacerse
la boca agua; **~ down** vt (milk etc)
aguar; (fig: story) dulcificar, diluir;
~ closet n wáter m; **~colour** (US
~color) n acuarela; **~cress** n berro;
~fall n cascada, salto de agua;
~ heater n calentador m de agua;
~ing can n regadera; **~ lily** n nenúfar m;
~line n (NAUT) línea de flotación;
~logged adj (ground) inundado;
~ main n cañería del agua; **~melon** n
sandía; **~proof** adj impermeable;
~shed n (GEO) cuenca; (fig) momento
crítico; **~skiing** n esquí m acuático;
~tight adj hermético; **~way** n vía
fluvial o navegable; **~works** n central f
depuradora; **~y** adj (coffee etc) aguado;

(eyes) lloroso

watt [wɔt] n vatio

wave [weɪv] n (of hand) señal f con la
mano; (on water) ola; (RADIO, in hair)
onda; (fig) oleada ♦ vi agitar la mano;
(flag etc) ondear ♦ vt (handkerchief,
gun) agitar; **~length** n longitud f de
onda

waver ['weɪvə*] vi (voice, love etc)
flaquear; (person) vacilar

wavy ['weɪvɪ] adj ondulado

wax [wæks] n cera ♦ vt encerar ♦ vi
(moon) crecer; **~ paper** n (US) papel m
apergaminado; **~works** n museo de
cera ♦ npl figuras fpl de cera

way [weɪ] n camino; (distance)
trayecto, recorrido; (direction) dirección
f, sentido; (manner) modo, manera;
(habit) costumbre f; **which ~?** — this
~ ¿por dónde?, ¿en qué dirección? —
por aquí; **on the ~** (en route) en (el)
camino; **to be on one's ~** estar en
camino; **to be in the ~** bloquear el
camino; (fig) estorbar; **to go out of
one's ~ to do sth** desvivirse por
hacer algo; **under ~** en marcha; **to
lose one's ~** extraviarse; **in a ~** en
cierto modo o sentido; **no ~!** (inf) ¡de
eso nada!; **by the ~** ... a propósito ...;
"~ in" (BRIT) "entrada"; **"~ out"**
(BRIT) "salida"; **the ~ back** el camino
de vuelta; **"give ~"** (BRIT: AUT) "ceda
el paso"

waylay [weɪ'leɪ] (irreg) vt salir al paso a
wayward ['weɪwəd] adj díscolo
W.C. n (BRIT) wáter m
we [wiː] pl pron nosotros/as
weak [wiːk] adj débil, flojo; (tea etc)
claro; **~en** vi debilitarse; (give way)
ceder ♦ vt debilitar; **~ling** n
debilucho/a; (morally) persona de poco
carácter; **~ness** n debilidad f; (fault)
punto débil; **to have a ~ness for**
tener debilidad por

wealth [wɛlθ] n riqueza; (of details)
abundancia; **~y** adj rico

wean [wiːn] vt destetar

weapon ['wepən] n arma
wear [weə*] n (pt **wore**, pp **worn**) n (use) uso; (deterioration through use) desgaste m; (clothing): **sports/baby-** ropa de deportes/de niños ♦ vt (clothes) llevar; (shoes) calzar; (damage: through use) gastar, usar ♦ vi (last) durar; (rub through etc) desgastarse; **evening ~** ropa de etiqueta; **~ away** vt gastar ♦ vi gastarse; **~ down** vt gastar; (strength) agotar; **~ off** vi (pain etc) pasar, desaparecer; **~ out** vt desgastar; (person, strength) agotar; **~ and tear** n desgaste m
weary ['wɪərɪ] adj cansado; (dispirited) abatido ♦ vi: **to ~ of** cansarse de
weasel ['wiːzl] n (ZOOL) comadreja
weather ['weðə*] n tiempo ♦ vt (storm, crisis) hacer frente a; **under the ~** (fig: ill) indispuesto, pachucho; **~-beaten** adj (skin) curtido; (building) deteriorado por la intemperie; **~cock** n veleta; **~ forecast** n boletín m meteorológico; **~man** (irreg: inf) n hombre m del tiempo; **~ vane** n = **~cock**
weave [wiːv] (pt **wove**, pp **woven**) vt (cloth) tejer; (fig) entretejer; **~r** n tejedor(a) m/f; **weaving** n tejeduría
web [web] n (of spider) telaraña; (on duck's foot) membrana; (network) red f; **the (World Wide) W~** el o la Web
website ['websaɪt] n espacio Web
wed [wed] (pt, pp **wedded**) vt casar ♦ vi casarse
we'd [wiːd] = **we had**; **we would**
wedding ['wedɪŋ] n boda, casamiento; **silver/golden ~ (anniversary)** bodas fpl de plata/de oro; **~ day** n día m de la boda; **~ dress** n traje m de novia; **~ present** n regalo de boda; **~ ring** n alianza
wedge [wedʒ] n (of wood etc) cuña; (of cake) trozo ♦ vt acuñar; (push) apretar
Wednesday ['wednzdɪ] n miércoles m inv
wee [wiː] (Scottish) adj pequeñito
weed [wiːd] n mala hierba, maleza ♦ vt

escardar, desherbar; **~killer** n herbicida m; **~y** adj (person) mequetréfico
week [wiːk] n semana; **a ~ today/on Friday** de hoy/del viernes en ocho días; **~day** n día m laborable; **~end** n fin m de semana; **~ly** adv semanalmente, cada semana ♦ adj semanal ♦ n semanario
weep [wiːp] (pt, pp **wept**) vi, vt llorar; **~ing willow** n sauce m llorón
weigh [weɪ] vt, vi pesar; **to ~ anchor** levar anclas; **~ down** vt sobrecargar; (fig) agobiar; **~ up** vt sopesar
weight [weɪt] n peso; (metal ~) pesa; **to lose/put on ~** adelgazar/engordar; **~ing** n (allowance): **(London) ~ing** dietas (por residir en Londres); **~lifter** n levantador m de pesas; **~y** adj pesado; (matters) de relevancia o peso
weir [wɪə*] n presa
weird [wɪəd] adj raro, extraño
welcome ['welkəm] adj bienvenido ♦ n bienvenida ♦ vt dar la bienvenida a; (be glad of) alegrarse de; **thank you — you're ~** gracias — de nada
weld [weld] n soldadura ♦ vt soldar
welfare ['welfeə*] n bienestar m; (social aid) asistencia social; **~ state** n estado del bienestar
well [wel] n fuente f, pozo ♦ adv bien ♦ adj: **to be ~** estar bien (de salud) ♦ excl ¡vaya!, ¡bueno!; **as ~** también; **as ~ as** además de; **~ done!** ¡bien hecho!; **get ~ soon!** ¡que te mejores pronto!; **to do ~** (of business) ir bien; (person) tener éxito; **~ up** vi (tears) saltar
we'll [wiːl] = **we will**; **we shall**
well: ~-behaved adj bueno; **~-being** n bienestar m; **~-built** adj (person) fornido; **~-deserved** adj merecido; **~-dressed** adj bien vestido; **~-groomed** adj de buena presencia; **~-heeled** adj (wealthy) rico
wellingtons ['welɪŋtənz] npl (also: **wellington boots**) botas fpl de goma
well: ~-known adj (person) conocido;

~-mannered adj educado; **~-meaning** adj bienintencionado; **~-off** adj acomodado; **~-read** adj leído; **~-to-do** adj acomodado; **~-wisher** n admirador(a) m/f

Welsh [welʃ] adj galés/esa ♦ n (LING) galés m; **the ~** npl los galeses; **the ~ Assembly** el Parlamento galés; **~man** (irreg) n galés m; **~ rarebit** n pan m con queso tostado; **~woman** (irreg) n galesa

went [went] pt of **go**

wept [wept] pt, pp of **weep**

were [wə:*] pt of **be**

we're [wɪə*] = **we are**

weren't [wə:nt] = **were not**

west [west] n oeste m ♦ adj occidental, del oeste ♦ adv al or hacia el oeste; **the W~** el Oeste, el Occidente; **W~ Country** (BRIT) n: **the W~ Country** el suroeste de Inglaterra; **~erly** adj occidental; (wind) del oeste; **~ern** adj occidental ♦ n (CINEMA) película del oeste; **W~ Germany** n Alemania Occidental; **W~ Indian** adj, n antillano/a m/f; **W~ Indies** npl Antillas fpl; **~ward(s)** adv hacia el oeste

wet [wet] adj (damp) húmedo; (~ through) mojado; (rainy) lluvioso ♦ (BRIT) n (POL) conservador(a) m/f moderado/a; **to ~** mojarse; **"~ paint"** "recién pintado"; **~suit** n traje m térmico

we've [wi:v] = **we have**

whack [wæk] vt dar un buen golpe a

whale [weɪl] n (ZOOL) ballena

wharf [wɔ:f] (pl **wharves**) n muelle m

KEYWORD

what [wɔt] adj 1 (in direct/indirect questions) qué; **~ size is he?** ¿qué talla usa?; **~ colour/shape is it?** ¿de qué color/forma es?
2 (in exclamations): **~ a mess!** ¡qué desastre!; **~ a fool I am!** ¡qué tonto soy!
♦ pron 1 (interrogative) qué; **~ are you**

doing? ¿qué haces or estás haciendo?;
~ is happening? ¿qué pasa or está pasando?; **~ is it called?** ¿cómo se llama?; **~ about me?** ¿y yo qué?; **~ about doing ...?** ¿qué tal si hacemos ...?
2 (relative) lo que; **I saw ~ you did/ was on the table** lo que hiciste/ había en la mesa
♦ excl (disbelieving) ¡cómo!; **~, no coffee!** ¡que no hay café!

whatever [wɔt'evə*] adj: **~ book you choose** cualquier libro que elijas
♦ pron: **do ~ is necessary** haga lo que sea necesario; **~ happens** pase lo que pase; **no reason ~ or whatsoever** ninguna razón sea la que sea; **nothing ~** nada en absoluto

whatsoever [wɔtsəu'evə*] adj see **whatever**

wheat [wi:t] n trigo

wheedle ['wi:dl] vt: **to ~ sb into doing sth** engatusar a uno para que haga algo; **to ~ sth out of sb** sonsacar algo a uno

wheel [wi:l] n rueda; (AUT: also: steering ~) volante m; (NAUT) timón m ♦ vt (pram etc) empujar ♦ vi (also: ~ round) dar la vuelta, girar; **~barrow** n carretilla; **~chair** n silla de ruedas; **~ clamp** n (AUT) cepo

wheeze [wi:z] vi resollar

KEYWORD

when [wen]

adv cuando; **~ did it happen?** ¿cuándo ocurrió?; **I know ~ it happened** sé cuándo ocurrió
♦ conj 1 (at, during, after the time that) cuando; **be careful ~ you cross the road** ten cuidado al cruzar la calle; **that was ~ I needed you** fue entonces que te necesité
2 (on, at which): **on the day ~ I met him** el día en que le conocí
3 (whereas) cuando

whenever |wɛn'ɛvə*| *conj* cuando;
(*every time that*) cada vez que ♦ *adv*
cuando sea

where |wɛə*| *adv* dónde ♦ *conj*
donde; **this is ~** aquí es donde;
~abouts *adv* dónde ♦ *n*: **nobody
knows his ~abouts** nadie conoce su
paradero; **~as** *conj* visto que, mientras;
~by por lo cual; **wherever**
[-'ɛvə*] *conj* dondequiera que;
(*interrogative*) dónde*; **~withal** *n*
recursos *mpl*

whether |'wɛðə*| *conj* si; **I don't
know ~ to accept or not** no sé si
aceptar o no; **~ you go or not** vayas
o no vayas

KEYWORD

which |wɪtʃ| *adj* **1** (*interrogative: direct,
indirect*) qué; **~ picture(s) do you
want?** ¿qué cuadro(s) quieres?;
~ one? ¿cuál?

2: **in ~ case** en cuyo caso; **we got
there at 8 pm, by ~ time the
cinema was full** llegamos allí a las 8,
cuando el cine estaba lleno
♦ *pron* **1** (*interrogative*) cual; **I don't
mind ~** el/la que sea

2 (*relative: replacing noun*) que;
(: *replacing clause*) lo que; (: *after
preposition*) (el/la) que *etc*, el/la cual
etc; **the apple ~ you ate/~ is on the
table** la manzana que comiste/que
está en la mesa; **the chair on ~ you
are sitting** la silla en la que estás
sentado; **he said he knew, ~ is
true/I feared** dijo que lo sabía, lo cual
or lo que es cierto/me temía

---

whichever |wɪtʃ'ɛvə*| *adj*: **take
~ book you prefer** coja (*SP*) el libro
que prefiera; **~ book you take**
cualquier libro que coja

while |waɪl| *n* rato, momento ♦ *conj*
mientras; (*although*) aunque; **for a ~**
durante algún tiempo; **~ away** *vt*
pasar

whim |wɪm| *n* capricho

whimper |'wɪmpə*| *n* sollozo ♦ *vi*
lloriquear

whimsical |'wɪmzɪkl| *adj* (*person*)
caprichoso; (*look*) juguetón/ona

whine |waɪn| *n* (*of pain*) gemido; (*of
engine*) zumbido; (*of siren*) aullido ♦ *vi*
gemir; zumbar; (*fig: complain*)
gimotear

whip |wɪp| *n* látigo; (*POL: person*)
encargado de la disciplina partidaria en
el parlamento ♦ *vt* azotar; (*CULIN*) batir;
(*move quickly*): **to ~ sth out/off**
sacar/quitar algo de un tirón; **~ped
cream** *n* nata or crema montada; **~-
round** (*BRIT*) *n* colecta

whirl |wə:l| *vt* hacer girar, dar vueltas a
♦ *vi* girar, dar vueltas; (*leaves etc*)
arremolinarse; **~pool** *n* remolino;
~wind *n* torbellino

whirr |wə:*| *vi* zumbar

whisk |wɪsk| *n* (*CULIN*) batidor *m* ♦ *vt*
(*CULIN*) batir; **to ~ sb away** or **off**
llevar volando a uno

whiskers |'wɪskəz| *npl* (*of animal*)
bigotes *mpl*; (*of man*) patillas *fpl*

whiskey |'wɪskɪ| (*US, Ireland*) *n* =
whisky

whisky |'wɪskɪ| *n* whisky *m*

whisper |'wɪspə*| *n* susurro ♦ *vi, vt*
susurrar

whistle |'wɪsl| *n* (*sound*) silbido; (*object*) silbato ♦ *vi* silbar

white |waɪt| *adj* blanco; (*pale*) pálido
♦ *n* blanco; (*of egg*) clara; **~ coffee**
(*BRIT*) *n* café m con leche; **~-collar
worker** *n* oficinista *m/f*; **~ elephant** *n*
(*fig*) maula; **~ lie** *n* mentirilla; **~ness** *n*
blancura; **~ noise** *n* sonido blanco;
~ paper *n* (*POL*) libro rojo; **~wash**
(*paint*) jalbegue *m*, cal *f* ♦ *vt* (*also fig*)
blanquear

whiting |'waɪtɪŋ| *n inv* (*fish*) pescadilla

Whitsun |'wɪtsn| *n* pentecostés *m*

whizz |wɪz| *vi*: **to ~ past** or **by**
pasar a toda velocidad; **~ kid** (*inf*) *n*
prodigio

KEYWORD

who [hu:] *pron* 1 (*interrogative*) quién; **~ is it?**, **~'s there?** ¿quién es?; **~ are you looking for?** ¿a quién buscas?; **I told her ~ I was** le dije quién era yo 2 (*relative*) que; **the man/woman ~ spoke to me** el hombre/la mujer que habló conmigo; **those ~ can swim** los que saben *or* sepan nadar

whodun(n)it [hu:'dʌnɪt] (*inf*) *n* novela policíaca

whoever [hu:'evə*] *pron*: **~ finds it** cualquiera *or* quienquiera que lo encuentre; **ask ~ you like** pregunta a quien quieras; **~ he marries** no importa con quién se case

whole [həul] *adj* (*entire*) todo, entero; (*not broken*) intacto ♦ *n* todo; (*all*): **the ~ of the town** toda la ciudad, la ciudad entera ♦ *n* (*total*) total *m*; (*sum*) conjunto; **on the ~, as a ~** en general; **~food(s)** *n(pl)* alimento(s) *m(pl)* integral(es); **~hearted** *adj* sincero, cordial; **~meal** *adj* integral; **~sale** *n* venta al por mayor ♦ *adj* al por mayor; (*fig: destruction*) sistemático; **~saler** *n* mayorista *m/f*; **~some** *adj* sano; **~wheat** *adj* = **~meal; wholly** *adv* totalmente, enteramente

KEYWORD

whom [hu:m] *pron* 1 (*interrogative*): **~ did you see?** ¿a quién viste?; **to ~ did you give it?** ¿a quién se lo diste?; **tell me from ~ you received it** dígame de quién lo recibió 2 (*relative*): **to ~ a** quien(es); **of ~** de quien(es), del/de la que *etc*; **the man ~ I saw/to ~ I wrote** el hombre que vi/a quien escribí; **the lady about/with ~ I was talking** la señora de (la) que/con quien o (la) que hablaba

whore [hɔ:*] (*inf: pej*) *n* puta

KEYWORD

whose [hu:z] *adj* 1 (*possessive: interrogative*): **~ book is this?**, **~ is this book?** ¿de quién es este libro?; **~ pencil have you taken?** ¿de quién es el lápiz que has cogido?; **~ daughter are you?** ¿de quién eres hija?
2 (*possessive: relative*) cuyo/a, *pl* cuyos/as; **the man ~ son you rescued** el hombre cuyo hijo rescataste; **those ~ passports I have** aquellas personas cuyos pasaportes tengo; **the woman ~ car was stolen** la mujer a quien le robaron el coche
♦ *pron de quién*: **~ is this?** ¿de quién es esto?; **I know ~ it is** sé de quién es

KEYWORD

why [waɪ] *adv* por qué; **~ not?** ¿por qué no?; **~ not do it now?** ¿por qué no lo haces (or hacemos *etc*) ahora?
♦ *conj*: **I wonder ~ he said that** me pregunto por qué dijo eso; **that's not ~ I'm here** no es por eso (por lo) que estoy aquí; **the reason ~** la razón por la que
♦ *excl* (*expressing surprise, shock, annoyance*) ¡hombre!, ¡vaya! (*explaining*): **~, it's you!** ¡hombre, eres tú!; **~, that's impossible** ¡pero sí eso es imposible!

wicked ['wɪkɪd] *adj* malvado, cruel
wicket ['wɪkɪt] *n* (CRICKET: *stumps*) palos *mpl*; (: *grass area*) terreno de juego
wide [waɪd] *adj* ancho; (*area, knowledge*) vasto, grande; (*choice*) amplio ♦ *adv*: **to open ~** abrir de par en par; **to shoot ~** errar el tiro; **~-**

angle lens n objetivo de gran angular; **~-awake** adj bien despierto; **~ly** adv (travelled) mucho; (spaced) muy; **it is ~ly believed/known that** ... mucha gente piensa/sabe que ...; **~n** vt ensanchar; (experience) ampliar ♦ vi ensancharse; **~ open** adj abierto de par en par; **~spread** adj extendido, general

widow ['wɪdəu] n viuda; **~ed** adj viudo; **~er** n viudo

width [wɪdθ] n anchura; (of cloth) ancho

wield [wiːld] vt (sword) blandir; (power) ejercer

wife [waɪf] (pl **wives**) n mujer f, esposa

wig [wɪg] n peluca

wiggle ['wɪgl] vt menear

wild [waɪld] adj (animal) salvaje; (plant) silvestre; (person) furioso, violento; (idea) descabellado; (rough: sea) bravo; (: land) agreste; (: weather) muy revuelto; **~s** npl regiones fpl salvajes, tierras fpl vírgenes; **~erness** ['wɪldənɪs] n desierto; **~life** n fauna; **~ly** adv (behave) locamente; (lash out) a diestro y siniestro; (guess) a lo loco; (happy) a más no poder

wilful ['wɪlful] (US **willful**) adj (action) deliberado; (obstinate) testarudo

---

KEYWORD

will [wɪl] aux vb **1** (forming future tense): **I ~ finish it tomorrow** lo terminaré o voy a terminar mañana; **I ~ have finished it by tomorrow** ya lo habré terminado para mañana; **~ you do it? — yes I ~/no I won't** ¿lo harás? — sí/no

2 (in conjectures, predictions): **he ~ or he'll be there by now** ya habrá or debe (de) haber llegado; **that ~ be the postman** será or debe ser el cartero

3 (in commands, requests, offers): **~ you be quiet!** ¡quieres callarte?;

~ you help me? ¿quieres ayudarme?; **~ you have a cup of tea?** ¿te apetece un té?; **I won't put up with it!** ¡no lo soporto!

♦ vt (pt, pp **willed**): **to ~ sb to do sth** desear que alguien haga algo; **he ~ed himself to go on** con gran fuerza de voluntad, continuó

♦ n voluntad f; (testament) testamento

---

willing ['wɪlɪŋ] adj (with goodwill) de buena voluntad; (enthusiastic) entusiasta; **he's ~ to do it** está dispuesto a hacerlo; **~ly** adv con mucho gusto; **~ness** n buena voluntad

willow ['wɪləu] n sauce m

willpower ['wɪlpauə*] n fuerza de voluntad

willy-nilly [wɪlɪ'nɪlɪ] adv quiérase o no

wilt [wɪlt] vi marchitarse

win [wɪn] (pt, pp **won**) n victoria, triunfo ♦ vt ganar; (obtain) conseguir, lograr ♦ vi ganar; **~ over** vt convencer a; **~ round** (BRIT) vt = **~ over**

wince [wɪns] vi encogerse

winch [wɪntʃ] n torno

wind¹ [wɪnd] n viento; (MED) gases mpl ♦ vt (take breath away from) dejar sin aliento a

wind² [waɪnd] (pt, pp **wound**) vt enrollar; (wrap) envolver; (clock, toy) dar cuerda a ♦ vi (road, river) serpentear; **~ up** vt (clock) dar cuerda a; (debate, meeting) concluir, terminar

windfall ['wɪndfɔːl] n golpe m de suerte

winding ['waɪndɪŋ] adj (road) tortuoso; (staircase) de caracol

wind instrument [wɪnd-] n (MUS) instrumento de viento

windmill ['wɪndmɪl] n molino de viento

window ['wɪndəu] n ventana; (in car, train) ventanilla; (in shop etc) escaparate m (SP), vitrina (AM); **~ box** n jardinera de ventana; **~ cleaner** n

(person) limpiador m de cristales;
~ ledge n alféizar m, repisa; **~ pane** n
cristal m; **~ seat** n asiento junto a la
ventana; **~-shopping** n: to go **~-
shopping** ir de escaparates; **~sill** n
alféizar m, repisa

windpipe ['wɪndpaɪp] n tráquea

wind power n energía eólica

windscreen ['wɪndskriːn] n (US
windshield) n parabrisas m inv;
~ washer n lavaparabrisas m inv;
~ wiper n limpiaparabrisas m inv

windswept ['wɪndswept] adj azotado
por el viento

windy ['wɪndɪ] adj de mucho viento;
it's ~ hace viento

wine [waɪn] n vino; **~ bar** n enoteca;
~ cellar n bodega; **~ glass** n copa
(para vino); **~ list** n lista de vinos;
~ waiter n escanciador m

wing [wɪŋ] n ala; (AUT) aleta; **~s** npl
(THEATRE) bastidores mpl; **~er** n (SPORT)
extremo

wink [wɪŋk] n guiño, pestañeo ♦ vi
guiñar, pestañear

winner ['wɪnə*] n ganador(a) m/f

winning ['wɪnɪŋ] adj (team)
ganador(a); (goal) decisivo; (smile)
encantador(a); **~s** npl ganancias fpl

winter ['wɪntə*] n invierno ♦ vi
invernar; **wintry** ['wɪntrɪ] adj invernal

wipe [waɪp] n: to give sth a **~** pasar
un trapo sobre algo ♦ vt limpiar; (tape)
borrar; **~ off** vt limpiar con un trapo;
(remove) quitar; **~ out** vt (debt)
liquidar; (memory) borrar; (destroy)
destruir; **~ up** vt limpiar

wire ['waɪə*] n alambre m; (ELEC) cable
m (eléctrico); (TEL) telegrama m ♦ vt
(house) poner la instalación eléctrica
en; (also: **~ up**) conectar; (person:
telegram) telegrafiar

wiring ['waɪərɪŋ] n instalación f
eléctrica

wiry ['waɪərɪ] adj (person) enjuto y
fuerte; (hair) crespo

wisdom ['wɪzdəm] n sabiduría, saber

m; (good sense) cordura; **~ tooth** n
muela del juicio

wise [waɪz] adj sabio; (sensible) juicioso

...wise [waɪz] suffix: time**~** en cuanto a
o respecto al tiempo

wish [wɪʃ] n deseo ♦ vt querer; best
~es (on birthday etc) felicidades fpl;
with best ~es (in letter) saludos mpl,
recuerdos mpl; **to ~ sb goodbye**
despedirse de uno; **he ~ed me well**
me deseó mucha suerte; **to ~ to do/
sb to do sth** querer hacer/que
alguien haga algo; **to ~ for** desear;
~ful adj: it's **~ful thinking** eso sería
soñar

wisp [wɪsp] n mechón m; (of smoke)
voluta

wistful ['wɪstfʊl] adj pensativo

wit [wɪt] n ingenio, gracia; (also: **~s**)
inteligencia; (person) chistoso/a

witch [wɪtʃ] n bruja; **~craft** n brujería;
~-hunt n (fig) caza de brujas

--- KEYWORD ---

with [wɪð, wɪθ] prep **1** (accompanying,
in the company of) con (con+ mi, ti, sí
= conmigo, contigo, consigo); **I was
~ him** estaba con él; **we stayed
~ friends** nos quedamos en casa de
unos amigos; **I'm (not) ~ you**
(understand) (no) te entiendo; **to be
~ it** (inf: person: up-to-date) estar al
tanto; (: alert) ser despabilado
2 (descriptive, indicating manner etc)
con; de; **a room ~ a view** una
habitación con vistas; **the man ♦ the
grey hat/blue eyes** el hombre del
sombrero gris/de los ojos azules; **red
~ anger** rojo de ira; **to shake ~ fear**
temblar de miedo; **to fill sth ~ water**
llenar algo de agua

---

withdraw [wɪθ'drɔː] (irreg) vt retirar,
sacar ♦ vi retirarse; **to ~ money (from
the bank)** retirar fondos (del banco);
~al n retirada; (of money) reintegro;
~al symptoms npl (MED) síndrome m

de abstinencia; **~n** adj (person)
reservado, introvertido
wither ['wɪðə*] vi marchitarse
withhold [wɪθ'həuld] (irreg) vt
(money) retener; (decision) aplazar;
(permission) negar; (information) ocultar
within [wɪð'ɪn] prep dentro de ♦ adv
dentro; **~ reach (of)** al alcance (de);
~ sight (of) a la vista (de); **~ the
week** antes de acabar la semana; **~ a
mile (of)** a menos de una milla (de)
without [wɪð'aut] prep sin; **to go
~ sth** pasar sin algo
withstand [wɪθ'stænd] (irreg) vt
resistir a
witness ['wɪtnɪs] n testigo m/f ♦ vt
(event) presenciar; (document)
atestiguar la veracidad de; **to bear
~ to** (fig) ser testimonio de; **~ box** n
tribuna de los testigos; **~ stand** (US) n
= **~ box**
witty ['wɪtɪ] adj ingenioso
wives [waɪvz] npl of **wife**
wk abbr = **week**
wobble ['wɒbl] vi temblar; (chair)
cojear
woe [wəu] n desgracia
woke [wəuk] pt of **wake**
woken ['wəukən] pp of **wake**
wolf [wulf] n lobo; **wolves** [wulvz]
npl of **wolf**
woman ['wumən] (pl **women**) n
mujer f; **~ doctor** n médica;
women's lib (inf: pej) n liberación f
de la mujer; **~ly** adj femenino
womb [wu:m] n matriz f, útero
women ['wɪmɪn] npl of **woman**
won [wʌn] pt, pp of **win**
wonder ['wʌndə*] n maravilla,
prodigio; (feeling) asombro ♦ vi: **to
~ whether/why** preguntarse si/por
qué; **to ~ at** asombrarse de;
to ~ about pensar sobre or en; **it's no
~ (that)** no es de extrañarse (que
+ subjun); **~ful** adj maravilloso
won't [wəunt] = **will not**
wood [wud] n (timber) madera; (forest)

bosque m; **~ carving** n (act) tallado
en madera; (object) talla en madera;
~ed adj arbolado; **~en** adj de madera;
(fig) inexpresivo; **~pecker** n pájaro
carpintero; **~wind** n (MUS)
instrumentos mpl de viento de madera;
~work n carpintería; **~worm** n
carcoma
wool [wul] n lana; **to pull the ~ over
sb's eyes** (fig) engatusar a uno; **~en**
(US) adj = **~len**; **~len** adj de lana;
~lens npl géneros mpl de lana; **~ly** adj
lanudo, de lana; (fig: ideas) confuso;
~y (US) adj = **~ly**
word [wə:d] n palabra; (news) noticia;
(promise) palabra (de honor) ♦ vt
redactar; **in other ~s** en otras
palabras; **to break/keep one's ~**
faltar a la palabra/cumplir la promesa;
to have ~s with sb reñir con uno;
~ing n redacción f; **~ processing** n
proceso de textos; **~ processor** n
procesador m de textos
wore [wɔ:*] pt of **wear**
work [wə:k] n trabajo; (job) empleo,
trabajo; (ART, LITERATURE) obra ♦ vi
trabajar; (mechanism) funcionar,
marchar; (medicine) ser eficaz, surtir
efecto ♦ vt (shape) trabajar; (stone etc)
tallar; (mine etc) explotar; (machine)
manejar, hacer funcionar; **~s** n (BRIT:
factory) fábrica ♦ npl (of clock, machine)
mecanismo; **to be out of ~** estar
parado, no tener trabajo; **~ loose**
(part) desprenderse; (knot) aflojarse;
~ on vt fus trabajar en, dedicarse a;
(principle) basarse en; **~ out** vi (plans
etc) salir bien, funcionar ♦ vt (problem)
resolver; (plan) elaborar; **it ~s out at
£100** suma 100 libras; **~ up** vt: **to get
~ed up** excitarse; **~able** adj (solution)
práctico, factible; **~aholic**
[wə:kə'hɒlɪk] n trabajador(a) obsesivo
a m/f; **~er** n trabajador(a) m/f, obrero/
a; **~force** n mano f de obra; **~ing
class** n clase f obrera; **~ing-class** adj
obrero; **~ing order** n: **in ~ing order**

en funcionamiento; **~man** (irreg) n obrero; **~manship** n habilidad f, trabajo; **~sheet** n hoja de trabajo; **~shop** n taller m; **~ station** n puesto or estación f de trabajo; **~-to-rule** (BRIT) n huelga de celo

world [wəːld] n mundo ♦ cpd (champion) del mundo; (power, war) mundial; **to think the ~ of sb** (fig) tener un concepto muy alto de uno; **~ly** adj mundano; **~-wide** adj mundial, universal; **W~-Wide Web** n: **the W~-Wide Web** el World Wide Web

worm [wəːm] n (also: earth~) lombriz f

worn [wɔːn] pp of **wear** ♦ adj usado; **~-out** (object) gastado; (person) rendido, agotado

worried [ˈwʌrɪd] adj preocupado

worry [ˈwʌrɪ] n preocupación f ♦ vt preocupar, inquietar ♦ vi preocuparse; **~ing** adj inquietante

worse [wəːs] adj, adv peor ♦ n lo peor; **a change for the ~** un empeoramiento; **~n** vt, vi empeorar; **~ off** adj (financially): **to be ~ off** tener menos dinero; (fig): **you'll be ~ off this way** de esta forma estarás peor que nunca

worship [ˈwəːʃɪp] n adoración f ♦ vt adorar; **Your W~** (BRIT: to mayor) señor alcalde; (: to judge) señor juez

worst [wəːst] adj, adv peor ♦ n lo peor; **at ~** en lo peor de los casos

worth [wəːθ] n valor m ♦ adj: **to be ~** valer; **it's ~ it** vale or merece la pena; **to be ~ one's while (to do)** merecer la pena (hacer); **~less** adj sin valor; (useless) inútil; **~while** adj (activity) que merece la pena; (cause) loable

worthy [ˈwəːðɪ] adj respetable; (motive) honesto; **~ of** digno de

KEYWORD

would [wʊd] aux vb **1** (conditional tense): **if you asked him he ~ do it** si se lo pidieras, lo haría; **if you had**

asked him he ~ have done it si se lo hubieras pedido, lo habría or hubiera hecho

2 (in offers, invitations, requests): **~ you like a biscuit?** ¿quieres una galleta?; (formal) ¿querría una galleta?; **you ask him to come in?** ¿quiere hacerle pasar?; **~ you open the window please?** ¿quiere or podría abrir la ventana, por favor?

3 (in indirect speech): **I said I ~ do it** dije que lo haría

4 (emphatic): **it WOULD have to snow today!** ¡tenía que nevar precisamente hoy!

5 (insistence): **she ~n't behave** no quiso comportarse bien

6 (conjecture): **it ~ have been midnight** sería medianoche; **it ~ seem so** así parece que sí

7 (indicating habit): **he ~ go there on Mondays** iba allí los lunes

would-be (pej) adj presunto

wouldn't [ˈwʊdnt] = **would not**

wound¹ [wuːnd] n herida ♦ vt herir

wound² [waʊnd] pt, pp of **wind**

wove [wəʊv] pt of **weave**

woven [ˈwəʊvən] pp of **weave**

wrap [ræp] vt (also: ~ up) envolver; **~per n** (on chocolate) papel m; (BRIT: of book) sobrecubierta; **~ping paper** n papel m de envolver; (fancy) papel m de regalo

wreak [riːk] vt: **to ~ havoc (on)** hacer estragos (en); **to ~ vengeance (on)** vengarse (de)

wreath [riːθ, pl riːðz] n (funeral ~) corona

wreck [rek] n (ship: destruction) naufragio; (: remains) restos mpl del barco; (pej: person) ruina ♦ vt (car etc) destrozar; (chances) arruinar; **~age** n restos mpl; (of building) escombros mpl

wren [ren] n (ZOOL) reyezuelo

wrench [rentʃ] n (TECH) llave f inglesa; (tug) tirón m; (fig) dolor m ♦ vt arrancar; **to ~ sth from sb** arrebatar algo violentamente a uno

wrestle ['resl] *vi:* **to ~ (with sb)** luchar (con o contra uno); **~r** *n* luchador(a) *m/f* (de lucha libre); **wrestling** *n* lucha libre

wretched ['retʃɪd] *adj* miserable

wriggle ['rɪgl] *vi* (*also:* **~ about**) menearse, retorcerse

wring [rɪŋ] (*pt, pp* **wrung**) *vt* retorcer; (*wet clothes*) escurrir; (*fig*): **to ~ sth out of sb** sacar algo por la fuerza a uno

wrinkle ['rɪŋkl] *n* arruga ♦ *vt* arrugar ♦ *vi* arrugarse

wrist [rɪst] *n* muñeca; **~watch** *n* reloj *m* de pulsera

writ [rɪt] *n* mandato judicial

write [raɪt] (*pt* **wrote**, *pp* **written**) *vt* escribir; (*cheque*) extender ♦ *vi* escribir; **~ down** *vt* escribir; (*note*) apuntar; **~ off** *vt* (*debt*) borrar (como incobrable); (*fig*) desechar por inútil; **~ out** *vt* escribir; **~ up** *vt* redactar; **~-off** *n* siniestro total; **~r** *n* escritor(a) *m/f*

writhe [raɪð] *vi* retorcerse

writing ['raɪtɪŋ] *n* escritura; (*hand-*) letra; (*of author*) obras *fpl;* **in ~** por escrito; **~ paper** *n* papel *m* de escribir

written ['rɪtn] *pp de* **write**

wrong [rɒŋ] *adj* (*wicked*) malo; (*unfair*) injusto; (*incorrect*) equivocado, incorrecto; (*not suitable*) inoportuno, inconveniente; (*reverse*) del revés ♦ *adv* equivocadamente ♦ *n* injusticia ♦ *vt* ser injusto con; **you are ~ to do it** haces mal en hacerlo; **you are ~ about that, you've got it ~** en eso estás equivocado; **to be in the ~** no tener razón, tener la culpa; **what's ~?** ¿qué pasa?; **to go ~** (*person*) equivocarse; (*plan*) salir mal; (*machine*) estropearse; **~ful** *adj* injusto; **~ly** *adv* mal, incorrectamente; (*by mistake*) por error; **~ number** *n* (*TEL*): **you've got the ~ number** se ha equivocado de

número

wrote [rəut] *pt de* **write**

wrought iron [rɔːt-] *n* hierro forjado

wrung [rʌŋ] *pt, pp de* **wring**

wt. *abbr = weight*

WWW *n abbr (= World Wide Web)* WWW *m*

X, x

Xmas ['eksməs] *n abbr = Christmas*

X-ray ['eksreɪ] *n* radiografía ♦ *vt* radiografiar, sacar radiografías de

xylophone ['zaɪləfəun] *n* xilófono

Y, y

yacht [jɒt] *n* yate *m*; **~ing** *n* (*sport*) balandrismo; **~sman/woman** (*irreg*) *n* balandrista *m/f*

Yank [jæŋk] (*pej*) *n* yanqui *m/f*

Yankee ['jæŋkɪ] (*pej*) *n* = **Yank**

yap [jæp] *vi* (*dog*) aullar

yard [jɑːd] *n* patio; (*measure*) yarda; **~stick** *n* (*fig*) criterio, norma

yarn [jɑːn] *n* hilo; (*tale*) cuento, historia

yawn [jɔːn] *n* bostezo ♦ *vi* bostezar; **~ing** *adj* (*gap*) muy abierto

yd(s). *abbr = yard(s)*

yeah [jeə] (*inf*) *adv* sí

year [jɪə] *n* año; **to be 8 ~s old** tener 8 años; **an eight-~-old child** un niño de ocho años (de edad); **~ly** *adj* anual ♦ *adv* anualmente, cada año

yearn [jɜːn] *vi:* **to ~ for sth** añorar algo, suspirar por algo

yeast [jiːst] *n* levadura

yell [jel] *n* grito, alarido ♦ *vi* gritar

yellow ['jeləu] *adj* amarillo

yelp [jelp] *n* aullido ♦ *vi* aullar

yes [jes] *adv* sí ♦ *n* sí *m*; **to say/ answer ~** decir/contestar que sí

yesterday ['jestədɪ] *adv* ayer ♦ *n* ayer *m*; **~ morning/evening** ayer por la mañana/tarde; **~ all day** todo el día de ayer

yet [jet] *adv* ya; *(negative)* todavía
♦ *conj* sin embargo, a pesar de todo; **it
is not finished ~** todavía no está
acabado; **the best ~** el/la mejor hasta
ahora; **as ~** hasta ahora, todavía

yew [ju:] *n* tejo

yield [ji:ld] *n* (AGR) cosecha; (COMM)
rendimiento ♦ *vt* ceder; *(results)*
producir, dar; *(profit)* rendir ♦ *vi*
rendirse, ceder; (US: AUT) ceder el paso

YMCA *n abbr* (= *Young Men's Christian
Association*) Asociación f de Jóvenes
Cristianos

yog(h)ourt ['jəʊgət] *n* yogur *m*

yog(h)urt ['jəʊgət] *n* = **yog(h)ourt**

yoke [jəʊk] *n* yugo

yolk [jəʊk] *n* yema (de huevo)

─────────────
KEYWORD
─────────────

you [ju:] *pron* **1** *(subject: familiar)* tú, *pl*
vosotros/as (SP), ustedes (AM); *(polite)*
usted, *pl* ustedes; **~ are very kind**
eres/es muy amable; **~ Spanish
enjoy your food** a vosotros (or ustedes) los españoles os (or les) gusta la
comida; **~ and I will go** iremos tú y yo
2 *(object: direct: familiar)* te, *pl* os (SP),
les (AM); *(polite)* le, *pl* les, f la, *pl* las; **I
know ~** te/le etc conozco
3 *(object: indirect: familiar)* te, *pl* os (SP),
les (AM); *(polite)* le, *pl* les; **I gave the
letter to ~ yesterday** te/os etc di la
carta ayer
4 *(stressed)*: **I told YOU to do it** te lo
dije a ti que lo hicieras, a ti a quien dije
que lo hicieras; *see also* **3**, **5**
5 *(after prep: NB: con+ ti = contigo:
familiar)* ti, *pl* vosotros/as (SP), ustedes
(AM); *(: polite)* usted, *pl* ustedes; **it's
for ~** es para ti/vosotros etc
6 *(comparisons: familiar)* tú, *pl*
vosotros/as (SP), ustedes (AM); *(: polite)*
usted, *pl* ustedes; **she's younger
than ~** es más joven que tú/vosotros
etc
7 *(impersonal: one)*: **fresh air does**

~ good el aire puro (te) hace bien; **~
never know** nunca se sabe; **~ can't
do that!** ¡eso no se hace!

you'd [ju:d] = **you had**; **you would**

you'll [ju:l] = **you will**; **you shall**

young [jʌŋ] *adj* joven ♦ *npl (of animal)*
cría; *(people)*: **the ~** los jóvenes, la
juventud; **~er** *adj (brother etc)* menor;
~ster *n* joven *m/f*

your [jɔ:*] *adj* tu; *(pl)* vuestro; *(formal)*
su; *see also* **my**

you're [juə*] = **you are**

yours [jɔ:z] *pron* tuyo; *(pl)* vuestro;
(formal) suyo; *see also* **faithfully**;
mine[1]; **sincerely**

yourself [jɔ:'self] *pron* tú mismo;
(complement) te; *(after prep)* ti
(mismo); *(formal)* usted mismo;
(: complement) se; *(: after prep)* sí
(mismo); **yourselves** *pl pron* vosotros
mismos; *(after prep)* vosotros (mismos);
(formal) ustedes (mismos);
(: complement) se; *(: after prep)* sí
mismos; *see also* **oneself**

youth [ju:θ, *pl* ju:ðz] *n* juventud *f*;
(young man) joven *m*; **~ club** *n* club *m*
juvenil; **~ful** *adj* juvenil; **~ hostel** *n*
albergue *m* de juventud

you've [ju:v] = **you have**

Yugoslav ['ju:gəʊsla:v] *adj, n*
yugo(e)slavo/a *m/f*

Yugoslavia [ju:gəʊ'sla:vɪə] *n*
Yugoslavia

yuppie ['jʌpɪ] *(inf) adj, n* yupi *m/f*,
yupy *m/f*

YWCA *n abbr* (= *Young Women's
Christian Association*) Asociación f de
Jóvenes Cristianas

Z, z

zany ['zeɪnɪ] *adj* estrafalario

zap [zæp] *vt* (COMPUT) borrar

zeal [zi:l] *n* celo, entusiasmo; **~ous**
['zeləs] *adj* celoso, entusiasta

zebra ['ziːbrə] n cebra; ~ **crossing** (BRIT) n paso de peatones

zero ['zɪərəu] n cero

zest [zɛst] n ánimo, vivacidad f; (of orange) piel f

zigzag ['zɪgzæg] n zigzag m ♦ vi zigzaguear, hacer eses

zinc [zɪŋk] n cinc m, zinc m

zip [zɪp] n (also: ~ fastener, (US) ~per) cremallera (SP), cierre m (AM) ♦ vt (also:

~ up) cerrar la cremallera de; ~ **code** (US) n código postal

zodiac ['zəudɪæk] n zodíaco

zone [zəun] n zona

zoo [zuː] n (jardín m) zoo m

zoology [zuːˈɔlədʒɪ] n zoología

zoom [zuːm] vi: **to ~ past** pasar zumbando; ~ **lens** n zoom m

zucchini [zuːˈkiːnɪ] (US) n(pl) calabacín(ines) m(pl)

SPANISH VERB TABLES

1 Gerund. **2** Imperative. **3** Present. **4** Preterite. **5** Future. **6** Present subjunctive. **7** Imperfect subjunctive. **8** Past participle. **9** Imperfect. *Etc* indicates that the irregular root is used for all persons of the tense, *e.g.* **oír: 6** oiga, oigas, oigamos, oigáis, oigan.

agradecer 3 agradezco **6** agradezca *etc*

aprobar 2 aprueba **3** apruebo, apruebas, aprueba, aprueban **6** apruebe, apruebes, apruebe, aprueben

atravesar 2 atraviesa **3** atravieso, atraviesas, atraviesa, atraviesan **6** atraviese, atravieses, atraviese, atraviesen

caber 3 quepo **4** cupe, cupiste, cupo, cupimos, cupisteis, cupieron **5** cabré *etc* **6** quepa *etc* **7** cupiera *etc*

caer 1 cayendo **3** caigo **4** cayó, cayeron **6** caiga *etc* **7** cayera *etc*

cerrar 2 cierra **3** cierro, cierras, cierra, cierran **6** cierre, cierres, cierre, cierren

COMER 1 comiendo **2** come, comed **3** como, comes, come comemos, coméis, comen **4** comí, comiste, comió, comimos, comisteis, comieron **5** comeré, comerás, comerá, comeremos, comeréis, comerán **6** coma, comas, coma, comamos, comáis, coman **7** comiera, comieras, comiera, comiéramos, comierais, comieran **8** comido **9** comía, comías, comía, comíamos comíais, comían

conocer 3 conozco **6** conozca *etc*

contar 2 cuenta **3** cuento, cuentas, cuenta, cuentan **6** cuente, cuentes, cuente, cuenten

dar 3 doy **4** di, diste, dio, dimos, disteis, dieron **7** diera *etc*

decir 2 di **3** digo **4** dije, dijiste, dijo, dijimos, dijisteis, dijeron **5** diré *etc* **6** diga *etc* **7** dijera *etc* **8** dicho

despertar 2 despierta **3** despierto, despiertas, despierta, despiertan **6** despierte, despiertes, despierte, despierten

divertir 1 divirtiendo **2** divierte **3** divierto, diviertes, divierte, divierten **4** divirtió, divirtieron **6** divierta, diviertas, divierta, divirtamos, divirtáis, diviertan **7** divirtiera *etc*

dormir 1 durmiendo **2** duerme **3** duermo, duermes, duerme, duermen **4** durmió, durmieron **6** duerma, duermas, duerma, durmamos, durmáis, duerman **7** durmiera *etc*

empezar 2 empieza **3** empiezo, empiezas, empieza, empiezan **4** empecé **6** empiece, empieces, empiece, empecemos, empecéis, empiecen

entender 2 entiende **3** entiendo, entiendes, entiende, entienden **6** entienda, entiendas, entienda, entiendan

ESTAR 2 está **3** estoy, estás, está, están **4** estuve, estuviste, estuvo, estuvimos, estuvisteis, estuvieron **6** esté, estés, esté, estén **7** estuviera *etc*

HABER 3 he, has, ha, hemos, han **4** hube, hubiste, hubo, hubimos, hubisteis, hubieron **5** habré *etc* **6** haya *etc* **7** hubiera *etc*

HABLAR 1 hablando **2** habla,

hablad 3 hablo, hablas, habla, hablamos, habláis, hablan 4 hablé, hablaste, habló, hablamos, hablasteis, hablaron 5 hablaré, hablarás, hablará, hablaremos, hablaréis, hablarán 6 hable, hables, hable, hablemos, habléis, hablen 7 hablara, hablaras, hablara, habláramos, hablarais, hablaran 8 hablado 9 hablaba, hablabas, hablaba, hablábamos, hablabais, hablaban

hacer 2 haz 3 hago 4 hice, hiciste, hizo, hicimos, hicisteis, hicieron 5 haré etc 6 haga etc 7 hiciera etc 8 hecho

instruir 1 instruyendo 2 instruye 3 instruyo, instruyes, instruye, instruimos 4 instruyó, instruyeron 6 instruya etc 7 instruyera etc

ir 1 yendo 2 ve 3 voy, vas, va, vamos, vais, van 4 fui, fuiste, fue, fuimos, fuisteis, fueron 6 vaya, vayas, vaya, vayamos, vayáis, vayan 7 fuera etc 9 iba, ibas, iba, íbamos, ibais, iban

jugar 2 juega 3 juego, juegas, juega, jugamos, jugáis, juegan 4 jugué 6 juegue etc

leer 1 leyendo 2 leyó, leyeron 7 leyera etc

morir 1 muriendo 2 muere 3 muero, mueres, muere, mueren 4 murió, murieron 6 muera, mueras, muera, muramos, muráis, mueran 7 muriera etc 8 muerto

mover 2 mueve 3 muevo, mueves, mueve, mueven 6 mueva, muevas, mueva, muevan

negar 2 niega 3 niego, niegas, niega, niegan 4 negué 6 niegue, niegues, niegue, neguemos, neguéis, nieguen

ofrecer 3 ofrezco 6 ofrezca etc

oír 1 oyendo 2 oye 3 oigo, oyes, oye, oímos, oyen 4 oyó, oyeron 6 oiga etc 7 oyera etc

oler 2 huele 3 huelo, hueles, huele, huelen 6 huela, huelas, huela, huelan

parecer 3 parezco 6 parezca etc

pedir 1 pidiendo 2 pide 3 pido, pides, pide, piden 4 pidió, pidieron 6 pida etc 7 pidiera etc

pensar 2 piensa 3 pienso, piensas, piensa, piensan 6 piense, pienses, piense, piensen

perder 2 pierde 3 pierdo, pierdes, pierde, pierden 6 pierda, pierdas, pierda, pierdan

poder 1 pudiendo 2 puede 3 puedo, puedes, puede, pueden 4 pude, pudiste, pudo, pudimos, pudisteis, pudieron 5 podré etc 6 pueda, puedas, pueda, puedan 7 pudiera etc

poner 2 pon 3 pongo 4 puse, pusiste, puso, pusimos, pusisteis, pusieron 5 pondré etc 6 ponga etc 7 pusiera etc 8 puesto

preferir 1 prefiriendo 2 prefiere 3 prefiero, prefieres, prefiere, prefieren 4 prefirió, prefirieron 6 prefiera, prefieras, prefiera, prefiramos, prefiráis, prefieran 7 prefiriera etc

querer 2 quiere 3 quiero, quieres, quiere, quieren 4 quise, quisiste, quiso, quisimos, quisisteis, quisieron 5 querré etc 6 quiera, quieras, quiera, quieran 7 quisiera etc

reír 2 ríe 3 río, ríes, ríe, ríen 4 rio, rieron 6 ría, rías, ría, riamos, riáis, rían 7 riera etc

repetir 1 repitiendo 2 repite 3 repito, repites, repite, repiten 4 repitió, repitieron 6 repita etc 7 repitiera etc

rogar 2 ruega 3 ruego, ruegas, ruega, ruegan 4 rogué 6 ruegue, ruegues, ruegue, roguemos, roguéis, rueguen

saber 3 sé 4 supe, supiste, supo, supimos, supisteis, supieron 5 sabré *etc* 6 sepa *etc* 7 supiera *etc*

salir 2 sal 3 salgo 5 saldré *etc* 6 salga *etc*

seguir 1 siguiendo 2 sigue 3 sigo, sigues, sigue, siguen 4 siguió, siguieron 6 siga *etc* 7 siguiera *etc*

sentar 2 sienta 3 siento, sientas, sienta, sientan 6 siente, sientes, siente, sienten

sentir 1 sintiendo 2 siente 3 siento, sientes, siente, sienten 4 sintió, sintieron 6 sienta, sientas, sienta, sintamos, sintáis, sientan 7 sintiera *etc*

SER 2 sé 3 soy, eres, es, somos, sois, son 4 fui, fuiste, fue, fuimos, fuisteis, fueron 6 sea *etc* 7 fuera *etc* 9 era, eras, era, éramos, erais, eran

servir 1 sirviendo 2 sirve 3 sirvo, sirves, sirve, sirven 4 sirvió, sirvieron 6 sirva *etc* 7 sirviera *etc*

soñar 2 sueña 3 sueño, sueñas, sueña, sueñan 6 sueñe, sueñes, sueñe, sueñen

tener 2 ten 3 tengo, tienes, tiene,

tienen 4 tuve, tuviste, tuvo, tuvimos, tuvisteis, tuvieron 5 tendré *etc* 6 tenga *etc* 7 tuviera *etc*

traer 1 trayendo 3 traigo 4 traje, trajiste, trajo, trajimos, trajisteis, trajeron 6 traiga *etc* 7 trajera *etc*

valer 2 val 3 valgo 5 valdré *etc* 6 valga *etc*

venir 2 ven 3 vengo, vienes, viene, vienen 4 vine, viniste, vino, vinimos, vinisteis, vinieron 5 vendré *etc* 6 venga *etc* 7 viniera *etc*

ver 3 veo 6 vea *etc* 8 visto 9 veía *etc*

vestir 1 vistiendo 2 viste 3 visto, vistes, visten 4 vistió, vistieron 6 vista *etc* 7 vistiera *etc*

VIVIR 1 viviendo 2 vive, vivid 3 vivo, vives, vive, vivimos, vivís, viven 4 viví, viviste, vivió, vivimos, vivisteis, vivieron 5 viviré, vivirás, vivirá, viviremos, viviréis, vivirán 6 viva, vivas, viva, vivamos, viváis, vivan 7 viviera, vivieras, viviera, viviéramos, vivierais, vivieran 8 vivido 9 vivía, vivías, vivía, vivíamos, vivíais, vivían

volver 2 vuelve 3 vuelvo, vuelves, vuelve, vuelven 6 vuelva, vuelvas, vuelva, vuelvan 8 vuelto

VERBOS IRREGULARES EN INGLÉS

present	pt	pp	present	pt	pp
arise	arose	arisen	dig	dug	dug
awake	awoke	awaked	do (3rd	did	done
be (am, is,	was,	been	person;		
are;	were		he/she;		
being)			it/does)		
bear	bore	born(e)	draw	drew	drawn
beat	beat	beaten	dream	dreamed,	dreamed,
become	became	become		dreamt	dreamt
begin	began	begun	drink	drank	drunk
behold	beheld	beheld	drive	drove	driven
bend	bent	bent	dwell	dwelt	dwelt
beset	beset	beset	eat	ate	eaten
bet	bet, betted	bet, betted	fall	fell	fallen
bid	bid,	bid,	feed	fed	fed
	bade	bidden	feel	felt	felt
bind	bound	bound	fight	fought	fought
bite	bit	bitten	find	found	found
bleed	bled	bled	flee	fled	fled
blow	blew	blown	fling	flung	flung
break	broke	broken	fly (flies)	flew	flown
breed	bred	bred	forbid	forbade	forbidden
bring	brought	brought	forecast	forecast	forecast
build	built	built	forget	forgot	forgotten
burn	burnt,	burnt,	forgive	forgave	forgiven
	burned	burned	forsake	forsook	forsaken
burst	burst	burst	freeze	froze	frozen
buy	bought	bought	get	got	got, (US)
can	could	(been			gotten
		able)	give	gave	given
			go (goes)	went	gone
cast	cast	cast	grind	ground	ground
catch	caught	caught	grow	grew	grown
choose	chose	chosen	hang	hung,	hung,
cling	clung	clung		hanged	hanged
come	came	come	have (has;	had	had
cost	cost	cost	having)		
creep	crept	crept	hear	heard	heard
cut	cut	cut	hide	hid	hidden
deal	dealt	dealt			

present	pt	pp	present	pt	pp
hit	hit	hit	**seek**	sought	sought
hold	held	held	**sell**	sold	sold
hurt	hurt	hurt	**send**	sent	sent
keep	kept	kept	**set**	set	set
kneel	knelt,	knelt,	**shake**	shook	shaken
	kneeled	kneeled	**shall**	should	—
know	knew	known	**shear**	sheared	shorn,
lay	laid	laid			sheared
lead	led	led	**shed**	shed	shed
lean	leant,	leant,	**shine**	shone	shone
	leaned	leaned	**shoot**	shot	shot
leap	leapt,	leapt,	**show**	showed	shown
	leaped	leaped	**shrink**	shrank	shrunk
learn	learnt,	learnt,	**shut**	shut	shut
	learned	learned	**sing**	sang	sung
leave	left	left	**sink**	sank	sunk
lend	lent	lent	**sit**	sat	sat
let	let	let	**slay**	slew	slain
lie (lying)	lay	lain	**sleep**	slept	slept
light	lit, lighted	lit, lighted	**slide**	slid	slid
lose	lost	lost	**sling**	slung	slung
make	made	made	**slit**	slit	slit
may	might	—	**smell**	smelt,	smelt,
mean	meant	meant		smelled	smelled
meet	met	met	**sow**	sowed	sown,
mistake	mistook	mistaken			sowed
mow	mowed	mown,	**speak**	spoke	spoken
		mowed	**speed**	sped,	sped,
must	(had to)	(had to)		speeded	speeded
pay	paid	paid	**spell**	spelt,	spelt,
put	put	put		spelled	spelled
quit	quit,	quit,	**spend**	spent	spent
	quitted	quitted	**spill**	spilt,	spilt,
read	read	read		spilled	spilled
rid	rid	rid	**spin**	spun	spun
ride	rode	ridden	**spit**	spat	spat
ring	rang	rung	**split**	split	split
rise	rose	risen	**spoil**	spoiled,	spoiled,
run	ran	run		spoilt	spoilt
saw	sawed	sawn	**spread**	spread	spread
say	said	said	**spring**	sprang	sprung
see	saw	seen	**stand**	stood	stood

615

present	pt	pp	present	pt	pp
steal	stole	stolen	**tell**	told	told
stick	stuck	stuck	**think**	thought	thought
sting	stung	stung	**throw**	threw	thrown
stink	stank	stunk	**thrust**	thrust	thrust
stride	strode	stridden	**tread**	trod	trodden
strike	struck	struck, stricken	**wake**	woke, waked	woken, waked
strive	strove	striven	**wear**	wore	worn
swear	swore	sworn	**weave**	wove, weaved	woven, weaved
sweep	swept	swept			
swell	swelled	swollen, swelled	**wed**	wedded, wed	wedded, wed
swim	swam	swum	**weep**	wept	wept
swing	swung	swung	**win**	won	won
take	took	taken	**wind**	wound	wound
teach	taught	taught	**wring**	wrung	wrung
tear	tore	torn	**write**	wrote	written

LOS NÚMEROS

NUMBERS

un, uno(a)	1	one
dos	2	two
tres	3	three
cuatro	4	four
cinco	5	five
seis	6	six
siete	7	seven
ocho	8	eight
nueve	9	nine
diez	10	ten
once	11	eleven
doce	12	twelve
trece	13	thirteen
catorce	14	fourteen
quince	15	fifteen
dieciséis	16	sixteen
diecisiete	17	seventeen
dieciocho	18	eighteen
diecinueve	19	nineteen
veinte	20	twenty
veintiuno	21	twenty-one
veintidós	22	twenty-two
treinta	30	thirty
treinta y uno(a)	31	thirty-one
treinta y dos	32	thirty-two
cuarenta	40	forty
cincuenta	50	fifty
sesenta	60	sixty
setenta	70	seventy
ochenta	80	eighty
noventa	90	ninety
cien, ciento	100	a hundred, one hundred
ciento uno(a)	101	a hundred and one
doscientos(as)	200	two hundred
doscientos(as) uno(a)	201	two hundred and one
trescientos(as)	300	three hundred
cuatrocientos(as)	400	four hundred
quinientos(as)	500	five hundred
seiscientos(as)	600	six hundred
setecientos(as)	700	seven hundred
ochocientos(as)	800	eight hundred
novecientos(as)	900	nine hundred
mil	1 000	a thousand
mil dos	1 002	a thousand and two
cinco mil	5 000	five thousand
un millón	1 000 000	a million

LOS NÚMEROS

NUMBERS

primer, primero(a), 1º, 1er (1ª, 1era)	first, 1st
segundo(a) 2º (2ª)	second, 2nd
tercer, tercero(a), 3º (3ª)	third, 3rd
cuarto(a), 4º (4ª)	fourth, 4th
quinto(a), 5º (5ª)	fifth, 5th
sexto(a), 6º (6ª)	sixth, 6th
séptimo(a)	seventh
octavo(a)	eighth
noveno(a)	ninth
décimo(a)	tenth
undécimo(a)	eleventh
duodécimo(a)	twelfth
decimotercio(a)	thirteenth
decimocuarto(a)	fourteenth
decimoquinto(a)	fifteenth
decimosexto(a)	sixteenth
vigésimo(a)	twentieth
vigésimo(a) primero(a)	twenty-first
trigésimo(a)	thirtieth
centésimo(a)	hundredth
centésimo(a) primero(a)	hundred-and-first
milésimo(a)	thousandth

Números Quebrados etc

Fractions etc

un medio	a half
un tercio	a third
un cuarto	a quarter
un quinto	a fifth
cero coma cinco, 0,5	(nought) point five, 0.5
diez por cien(to)	ten per cent

N.B. In Spanish the ordinal numbers from 1 to 10 are commonly used; from 11 to 20 rather less; above 21 they are rarely written and almost never heard in speech. The custom is to replace the forms for 21 and above by the cardinal number.

LA HORA

THE TIME

¿qué hora es?

what time is it?

es/son
medianoche, las doce (de la
noche)
la una (de la madrugada)

it's o *it is*
midnight, twelve p.m.

one o'clock (in the morning),
one (a.m.)

la una y cinco
la una y diez
la una y cuarto *or* quince
la una y veinticinco

five past one
ten past one
a quarter past one, one fifteen
twenty-five past one, one
twenty-five

la una y media *or* treinta
las dos menos veinticinco, la una
treinta y cinco
las dos menos veinte, la una
cuarenta
las dos menos cuarto, la una
cuarenta y cinco
las dos menos diez, la una
cincuenta
mediodía, las doce (de la tarde)
la una (de la tarde)

half-past one, one thirty
twenty-five to two, one thirty-
five
twenty to two, one forty

a quarter to two, one forty-five

ten to two, one fifty

twelve o'clock, midday, noon
one o'clock (in the afternoon),
one (p.m.)

las siete (de la tarde)
seven o'clock (in the evening),
seven (p.m.)

a qué hora?
medianoche
las siete

(at) what time?
at midnight
at seven o'clock

en veinte minutos
hace quince minutos

in twenty minutes
fifteen minutes ago

619

LA FECHA

DATES

hoy	today
todos los días	every day
ayer	yesterday
esta mañana	this morning
mañana por la noche	tomorrow night
anteanoche; antes de ayer por la noche	the night before last
antes de ayer; anteayer	the day before yesterday
anoche	last night
hace dos días/seis años	2 days/six years ago
mañana por la tarde	tomorrow afternoon
pasado mañana	the day after tomorrow
todos los jueves, el jueves	every Thursday, on Thursday
va los viernes	he goes on Fridays
"miércoles cerrado"	"closed on Wednesdays"
de lunes a viernes	from Monday to Friday
para el jueves	by Thursday
un sábado de marzo	one Saturday in March
dentro de una semana	in a week's time
dentro de dos martes	a week next/on Tuesday/Tuesday week
el domingo que viene	next Sunday
esta semana/la semana que viene/la semana pasada	this/next/last week
dentro de dos semanas	in 2 weeks or a fortnight
dentro de tres lunes	two weeks on Monday
el primer/último viernes del mes	the first/last Friday of the month
el mes que viene	next month
el año pasado	last year
el uno de junio, el primero de junio (LAM)	the 1st of June, June first
el dos de octubre	the 2nd of October, October 2nd
nací en 1987	I was born in 1987
su cumpleaños es el 5 de junio	his birthday is on June 5th (BRIT) or 5th June (US)
el 18 de agosto	on 18th August (BRIT) or August 18th (US)
en el 96	in '96
en la primavera del 94	in the Spring of '94
del 19 al 3	from the 19th to the 3rd
¿qué fecha es hoy?, ¿a cuanto estamos?	what's the date?, what date is it today?

LA FECHA

hoy es 15, estamos a quince	today's date is the 15th, today is the 15th
mil novecientos ochenta y ocho	1988 - nineteen (hundred and) eighty-eight
hoy hace 10 años	10 years to the day
a final de mes	at the end of the month
a final de mes	at the month end (*ACCOUNTS*)
diariamente/semanalmente/ mensualmente	daily/weekly/monthly
anualmente	annually
dos veces a la semana/dos veces al mes/dos veces al año	twice a week/month/year
dos veces al mes	bi-monthly
en el año 2006 (dos mil seis)	in the year 2006
4 a. de C.	4 B.C., B.C. 4
79 d. de C.	79 A.D., A.D. 79
en el siglo XIII	in the 13th century
en o durante los (años) 80	in *or* during the 1980s
a mediados de la década de los 70	in the mid seventies
en mil novecientos noventa y tantos	in 1990 something

DATES

HEADINGS OF LETTERS

9 de octubre de 1995	9th October 1995 *or* 9 October 1995

PESOS Y MEDIDAS
CONVERSION CHARTS

In the weight and length charts the middle figure can be either metric or imperial. Thus 3.3 feet = 1 metre, 1 foot = 0.3 metres, and so on.

feet		metres	inches		cm	lbs		kg
3.3	1	0.3	0.39	1	2.54	2.2	1	0.4!
6.6	2	0.61	0.79	2	5.08	4.4	2	0.9
9.9	3	0.91	1.18	3	7.62	6.6	3	1.4
13.1	4	1.22	1.57	4	10.6	8.8	4	1.8
16.4	5	1.52	1.97	5	12.7	11.0	5	2.2
19.7	6	1.83	2.36	6	15.2	13.2	6	2.7
23.0	7	2.13	2.76	7	17.8	15.4	7	3.2
26.2	8	2.44	3.15	8	20.3	17.6	8	3.6
29.5	9	2.74	3.54	9	22.9	19.8	9	4.1
32.9	10	3.05	3.9	10	25.4	22.0	10	4.5
			4.3	11	27.9			
			4.7	12	30.1			

°C	0	5	10	15	17	20	22	24	26	28	30	35	37	38	40	50	10
°F	32	41	50	59	63	68	72	75	79	82	86	95	98.4	100	104	122	21

Km	10	20	30	40	50	60	70	80	90	100	110	120
Miles	6.2	12.4	18.6	24.9	31.0	37.3	43.5	49.7	56.0	62.0	68.3	74.

Liquids

gallons	1.1	2.2	3.3	4.4	5.5	pints	0.44	0.88	1.7
litres	5	10	15	20	25	litres	0.25	0.5	1